THE KENTUCKY CONSTITUTION

We,

the people

of the Commonwealth of Kentucky,

grateful to Almighty God for

the civil, political and religious liberties we enjoy,

and invoking the continuance

of these blessings,

do ordain and establish

this Constitution.

The Kentucky Constitution

Text and History

Aaron J. Silletto

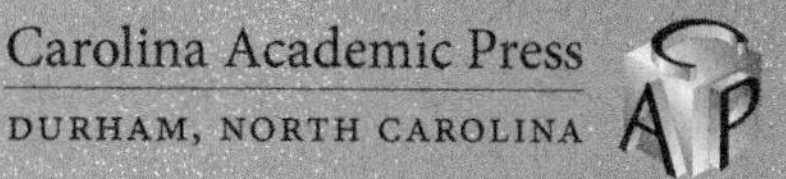
Carolina Academic Press
DURHAM, NORTH CAROLINA

Library of Congress cataloging-in-publication data is available at catalog.loc.gov

LCCN 2022048998
ISBN 978-1-5310-2554-0
eISBN 978-1-5310-2555-7

Carolina Academic Press
700 Kent Street
Durham, North Carolina 27701
(919) 489-7486
www.cap-press.com

Printed in the United States of America

To Sara and Daniel, with love.

—AJS

Contents

Preface

The Reasons for This Casebook

In January 1977, U.S. Supreme Court Justice William Brennan wrote a famous law review article,[1] in which he encouraged litigants and state courts to consider anew their state constitutions as potentially providing broader protections for individual rights than are available under the U.S. Constitution. Justice Brennan wrote his article after the end of the Warren Court (1953–69), which was noted for its expansive reading of the U.S. Constitution. During the Warren years, there was very little reason for a litigant or state court judge to consider his or her own state constitution when arguing or deciding constitutional issues because the liberal U.S. Supreme Court was seemingly in the business of maximizing the reach and scope of the U.S. Constitution. Over time, state constitutions took a backseat to the federal constitution in usage and utility.

But Justice Brennan foresaw the decisions of the more conservative Burger Court (1969–86) as limiting, or even clawing back, some of the expansive interpretations of the Constitution begun under the Warren Court. For him, this was reason enough for litigants and state court judges to reassess that strategy. He therefore encouraged state courts, in a project later referred to as a "New Federalism," to expand the scope of the civil rights and liberties safeguarded for their citizens under state constitutions.[2] Once again, litigants and state court judges began looking to and interpreting the unique features of their own state constitutions, which they rediscovered as founts of enhanced individual rights and protections against government overreach.

This rising tide of state constitutionalism continues today. And lest one think it an emphasis point for only the likes of liberal Justice Brennan, conservative jurists also have been giving state constitutions a larger role in the judicial dialogue between the state and federal courts. Notable conservative jurists like Sixth Circuit Judge Jeffrey Sutton have emphasized the role state constitutions play in American Constitutional Law, encouraging litigants and state court judges to seek answers first under their state charters.[3]

---

1. William J. Brennan, Jr., *State Constitutions and the Protection of Individual Rights*, 90 Harv. L. Rev. 489 (1977).

2. For an interesting discussion of the "New Judicial Federalism Movement" and how it developed in Kentucky, *see* Jennifer DiGiovanni, *Justice Charles M. Leibson and the Revival of State Constitutional Law: A Microcosm of a Movement*, 86 Ky. L.J. 1009 (1998).

3. *See* Jeffrey S. Sutton, 51 Imperfect Solutions: States and the Making of American Constitutional Law (2018).

For its part, the Supreme Court of Kentucky has stated that it is "often receptive and interested" in arguments of counsel based on the Kentucky Constitution.[4] In addition, the Conference of Chief Justices adopted a resolution in 2010 stating in part:

> WHEREAS, state constitutions contain different structures of government, unique provisions, and substantive provisions or declarations of rights that are often greater than federally guaranteed individual rights and liberties; and
>
> WHEREAS, being a competent and effective lawyer requires an understanding of both the federal Constitution and state constitutional law; NOW, THEREFORE, BE IT RESOLVED that the Conference of Chief Justices encourages all law schools to offer a course on state constitutional law.

The Kentucky Supreme Court's encouragement to offer state constitutional arguments, of course, presupposes a familiarity with, and knowledge of, its text. Yet, for many years, none of Kentucky's three law schools offered a course in Kentucky constitutional law. As a result, Kentucky lawyers have had to learn about the Kentucky Constitution as they go about their practice, usually in a piecemeal fashion, and usually for the first time in response to a motion or argument by opposing counsel. But for the most part, unless and until confronted with such a motion or argument, most Kentucky lawyers have labored under the apparent misperception that our state charter says no more than its federal counterpart. For the litigator, as Judge Sutton has observed, making only a federal constitutional argument when there also is an available state constitutional argument is the equivalent of a basketball player attempting only one of two available free throws with the game on the line.[5]

To help fill this gap in the legal education offered in the Commonwealth, the author (and others) proposed a course in Kentucky constitutional law at the Brandeis School of Law at the University of Louisville. The administration agreed and invited the author to teach the course in the spring of 2019. That act indirectly set the publication of this book in motion.

It did not take long for the author to realize that there was not a casebook or other text on the market suitable for use in a law school course on Kentucky constitutional law. This book was therefore born of necessity. Its principal aim is to present in a systematic way the most important cases that have interpreted the Kentucky Constitution.

Many lawyers avoid state constitutional issues because finding the relevant language in a document as long and complex as the Kentucky Constitution may be a chore. Because so few lawyers have been trained to deal with constitutions that give the text a status at least equal to that of the interpretive case law, many lawyers find that the analytic method for dealing with state constitutions is counterintuitive. Because of the relative scarcity of knowledge about the Commonwealth's Constitution among the practicing bar, at least when compared to knowledge the average law school graduate has about the U.S. Constitution, the author hopes this book may be of equal value as a

4. *Crutcher v. Commonwealth*, 500 S.W.3d 811, 815 (Ky. 2016).
5. Sutton, *supra* note 3, at 7.

reference for the practitioner as it may be as a casebook for a law student. More broadly, the author hopes this book also will have value for the non-lawyers of the Commonwealth who are interested in learning more about our state constitution, the structure of our government, and our individual rights and liberties.

This Casebook's Method

Five principles underlie this book's methodology. First and foremost is that the text of the Kentucky Constitution is the primary aid for its proper interpretation. Unlike most constitutional law textbooks that law schools have utilized over the years, in which the focus is primarily upon U.S. Supreme Court decisions to explain constitutional principles and design, this book instead uses the text of the Kentucky Constitution itself as its point of departure. If, as The Great Chief Justice, John Marshall, once famously said in another context, "we must never forget, that it is a constitution we are expounding,"[6] it is imperative that a student of the Constitution must first be familiar with the text to be explained. Because of the primacy of the text, the Kentucky Constitution is presented at the front of this book.

The second principle is that the reader can understand the Kentucky Constitution better by comparing it with the U.S. Constitution. In some instances, the Supreme Court of Kentucky has interpreted sections of the Kentucky Constitution to be coterminous with the interpretation the Supreme Court of the United States has afforded comparable provisions in the U.S. Constitution. In other instances, the Supreme Court of Kentucky has interpreted Kentucky's charter to afford greater protections for individual liberty—or to place greater restrictions on governmental action—than is the case under the federal charter. Understanding the similarities, but also the philosophical and interpretive differences, between the documents is helpful for shedding light on the Kentucky Constitution's meaning. The notes following the cases in this book therefore will often use a compare-and-contrast approach, with federal constitutional doctrines generally understood by lawyers and upper-level law students alike as a point of departure.

Third, some basic knowledge of Kentucky constitutional law is a benefit to every practitioner in the Commonwealth. The Kentucky Constitution reads like a legislative code, especially when compared to our Nation's charter. This means that the Constitution touches almost every area of legal practice. Whether a lawyer's practice involves real estate or commercial transactions, criminal law, municipal law, or even personal injury and tort law, the Kentucky Constitution has something to say about it. It is hoped, therefore, that the reader will find this book to be a helpful resource, regardless of his or her area of practice.[7]

---

6. *McCulloch v. Maryland*, 17 U.S. (4 Wheat.) 316, 407 (1819).

7. That said, there is not enough space available in a book of this type to provide a detailed analysis of every part of the Kentucky Constitution. No effort is made in these pages to provide a comprehensive study of the Constitution's treatment of such areas as local (county and city) government, taxation, or corporations. Each of these subjects could provide a basis for a stand-alone book or law school course.

The fourth principle is that a thorough understanding of the separation of powers is an essential key to understanding the Kentucky Constitution's meaning. In fact, some of the best known—and most important—cases in Kentucky constitutional law involve either interbranch conflicts or disputes between officials in the same branch of the government. And as will be fleshed out in further detail, most of the provisions in the Kentucky Constitution involve the separation of powers in some form or fashion—*e.g.*, by separating powers between the branches, by creating exceptions to default separation of powers rules, or by cabining a branch's discretion in the use of its powers. For these reasons, about half of the book is focused on some aspect of the separation of powers and those powers vested in each branch of government.

Finally, as of the date of this writing, notwithstanding the author's contention above that an understanding of Kentucky constitutional law is important to any area of legal practice in the Commonwealth, it is no longer specifically tested on the Kentucky bar examination.[8] Because it is not a "bar course," it is not necessary that Kentucky constitutional law be taught (as U.S. constitutional law is often taught in the law schools) as a set of black-letter rules to be memorized for later recounting on the bar exam. Rather, due both to the number of formal amendments to the document and to the shifting meanings afforded the document over time by the Commonwealth's high court, the current answer to any question of Kentucky constitutional law may not be the "right" answer for long. It is therefore important to ask the question often, "Did the Court get it right?" Many of the questions following the cases in this book will consider this question, highlighting tensions between various lines of cases and between the cases and the Constitution's text.

This book admittedly rides the wave of a recent resurgence in interest among lawyers around the country in state constitutional law. But unlike most books on state constitutional law, it does not attempt to present a 50-state survey of the field. Its focus is exclusively on the Kentucky Constitution, and therefore is intended for use by the law students and lawyers of Kentucky. Our Commonwealth's charter is exceptional in many respects. If this book better familiarizes the reader with the text and structure of the glorious Kentucky Constitution, it will have been a success.

Aaron J. Silletto
Louisville, Kentucky
November 2022

8. *See* SCR 2.080 (adopting the Uniform Bar Examination for admission to the Kentucky bar).

A Note on Editing

The cases in this book have been edited for length and content. In the text of the cases, an ellipsis shown as three points (...) represents an omission made by the court in its original opinion. An ellipsis shown as three asterisks (* * *) delineates an omission from the opinion made by this book's author.

To provide the full context in which the cases were decided, this book's author has left most of the opinions' discussion of the facts and background of the cases intact. In editing the opinions, most of the omissions from the text have been made in the discussion of any legal issues not relevant to the constitutional issues involved.

For the sake of clarity and readability, when a footnote has been omitted from the text of an opinion, the remaining footnotes in that opinion have been renumbered to eliminate any gaps in numbering.

Finally, to keep the formatting of the opinions consistent in this text, case citations within the opinions have been italicized, even if the citations were underlined in the original opinions.

Acknowledgments

This book would not have been possible without the encouragement and assistance of several people, for whom a word of thanks hardly seems sufficient.

The Kentucky constitutional law course I have taught at the Brandeis School of Law, and therefore this book, would not have happened without J. David Niehaus. We first met as colleagues at the Louisville Metro Public Defender's office. When, at first, I was apprehensive about teaching a law school course in 2019, David (who previously had taught criminal procedure at Brandeis Law) offered to co-teach it with me and show me the ropes. His input into case selection for, and his thoughts about the essential topics to be covered in, the course were instrumental in providing the bedrock on which the course, and thus this book, is built. David also donated a lot of time reading and providing invaluable feedback on several early drafts of this book, for which I am ever grateful. The Kentucky bar will long remember David as counsel for the petitioner in *Batson v. Kentucky*, 476 U.S. 79 (1986), but I am happy to call him a mentor and friend.

Also instrumental in bringing this book to fruition was Brett R. Nolan. Brett and I worked together at the Office of the Kentucky Attorney General—I in the Office of Civil and Environmental Law and he in the Solicitor General's Office. Brett has a wealth of knowledge about the Kentucky Constitution, and our discussions about it have been incredibly helpful to me, proving I am never too old to learn more about the subject. He was kind enough to review this book in draft form and provide helpful feedback. I am a better lawyer for our discussions about the subject of this book, and this book is all the better for Brett's input.

My former Brandeis Law student, Robert E. Ranney, provided helpful research assistance for the essay on Kentucky equal protection standards, when he probably should have been studying for the bar exam instead. Robert, you have my thanks and appreciation.

Thanks also to Professor Luke Milligan at Brandeis Law for his support of the law school's Ordered Liberty Program generally and my teaching Kentucky constitutional law in particular.

Though not a lawyer, this book might not have happened—or, at least, not *when* it happened—without Brandon Tosti. Brandon and I are old college friends, and he definitely is the encourager and optimist in our group. Just when this book started to feel like the proverbial boulder I was pushing uphill, Brandon succeeded in publishing his own book in 2021. Brandon led by example, showed me it could be done even while juggling the responsibilities of work and family, and provided endless encouragement to me as I completed this project. Thank you, brother!

I would like to thank Kelly Stephens, the Clerk of the Supreme Court of Kentucky, for assisting me in obtaining permission to use the photographs of the several Justices' portraits that appear in this book, from the Court, which owns the portraits, and the artists who created them. Thank you to Justices Scott and Venters for permission to use their likenesses, and to artists John Michael Carter and Stephen Sawyer for permission to reproduce their impressive artwork. And I also would like to thank Greg Woosley, general counsel for the Legislative Research Commission, who facilitated me obtaining the LRC's permission to include a photograph of the Kenton plaque in this book.

I would be remiss if I did not also acknowledge the confidence placed in me by the team at Carolina Academic Press. Everyone at CAP has been wonderful to work with, and this book is a reality thanks to them.

Finally, and most importantly, I owe a huge debt of thanks to my beloved wife, Sara. You are a supporter and encourager extraordinaire. Thank you for never complaining about becoming an "author's widow" as I worked long hours on this project, and for uplifting and cheering me on throughout the process. You believed in me and never doubted; you leaven me. I love you more than words can say.

About the Author

AARON J. SILLETTO is an Assistant Attorney General in the Office of the Kentucky Attorney General and an Adjunct Professor at the University of Louisville Brandeis School of Law, where he has taught a course in Kentucky constitutional law since 2019. In two decades of practicing law as a member of the Kentucky bar, Aaron has litigated both civil and criminal cases in the state and federal trial and appellate courts, often involving issues of state constitutional law. He has presented on trial practice and the Kentucky Constitution at seminars and continuing legal education courses, and he is the recipient of numerous accolades from his peers including selection to *Kentucky Super Lawyers*, a "Top Lawyer" rating from *Louisville Magazine*, inclusion in *The Best Lawyers in America*, and an AV Preeminent rating from Martindale Hubbell. Aaron lives in Louisville, Kentucky, with his wife and son.

The Constitution of the Commonwealth of Kentucky (1891)

Note: What follows is the complete text of the Kentucky Constitution in its current form, as it has been amended over the years, most recently in 2020. While the Constitution of the United States has been amended only 27 times since its ratification in 1788, each time by the addition of a new article at its end, the Kentucky Constitution has been amended much more frequently, each time by either adding new sections or repealing or revising the text of existing sections. Following each section's text are references to the effective date of the current version and the section's ratification and amendment history.

In addition, for certain sections that are comparable to, or deal with similar subject matter as, a provision of the U.S. Constitution, an additional reference is provided for the applicable federal constitutional provision. These additional references may be used as cross-references to perhaps more familiar constitutional provisions, as comparing them with the U.S. Constitutional analogues will aid in understanding the meaning of this document.

Preamble

We, the people of the Commonwealth of Kentucky, grateful to Almighty God for the civil, political and religious liberties we enjoy, and invoking the continuance of these blessings, do ordain and establish this Constitution.

Text as Ratified on: August 3, 1891, and revised September 28, 1891.

History: Not yet amended.

Federal Reference: U.S. Const. pmbl.

Bill of Rights

That the great and essential principles of liberty and free government may be recognized and established, we declare that:

Text as Ratified on: August 3, 1891, and revised September 28, 1891.

History: Not yet amended.

Section 1 Rights of life, liberty, worship, pursuit of safety and happiness, free speech, acquiring and protecting property, peaceable assembly, redress of grievances, bearing arms.

All men are, by nature, free and equal, and have certain inherent and inalienable rights, among which may be reckoned:

First: The right of enjoying and defending their lives and liberties.

Second: The right of worshipping Almighty God according to the dictates of their consciences.

Third: The right of seeking and pursuing their safety and happiness.

Fourth: The right of freely communicating their thoughts and opinions.

Fifth: The right of acquiring and protecting property.

Sixth: The right of assembling together in a peaceable manner for their common good, and of applying to those invested with the power of government for redress of grievances or other proper purposes, by petition, address or remonstrance.

Seventh: The right to bear arms in defense of themselves and of the State, subject to the power of the General Assembly to enact laws to prevent persons from carrying concealed weapons.

Text as Ratified on: August 3, 1891, and revised September 28, 1891.

History: Not yet amended.

Federal Reference: U.S. Const. amends. I; II; IV; V; XIV, §1; *see also* Decl. of Indep.

Section 2 Absolute and arbitrary power denied.

Absolute and arbitrary power over the lives, liberty and property of freemen exists nowhere in a republic, not even in the largest majority.

Text as Ratified on: August 3, 1891, and revised September 28, 1891.

History: Not yet amended.

Federal Reference: U.S. Const. amends. V; XIV, §1.

Section 3 Men are equal—No exclusive grant except for public services—Property not to be exempted from taxation—Grants revocable.

All men, when they form a social compact, are equal; and no grant of exclusive, separate public emoluments or privileges shall be made to any man or set of men, except in consideration of public services; but no property shall be exempt from taxation except as provided in this Constitution, and every grant of a franchise, privilege or exemption, shall remain subject to revocation, alteration or amendment.

Text as Ratified on: August 3, 1891, and revised September 28, 1891.

History: Not yet amended.

Federal Reference: U.S. Const. art. I, §9; amend. V; XIV, §1.

Section 4 Power inherent in the people—Right to alter, reform, or abolish government.

All power is inherent in the people, and all free governments are founded on their authority and instituted for their peace, safety, happiness and the protection of property. For the advancement of these ends, they have at all times an inalienable and indefeasible right to alter, reform or abolish their government in such manner as they may deem proper.

Text as Ratified on: August 3, 1891, and revised September 28, 1891.

History: Not yet amended.

Section 5 Right of religious freedom.

No preference shall ever be given by law to any religious sect, society or denomination; nor to any particular creed, mode of worship or system of ecclesiastical polity; nor shall any person be compelled to attend any place of worship, to contribute to the erection or maintenance of any such place, or to the salary or support of any minister of religion; nor shall any man be compelled to send his child to any school to which he may be conscientiously opposed; and the civil rights, privileges or capacities of no person shall be taken away, or in anywise diminished or enlarged, on account of his belief or disbelief of any religious tenet, dogma or teaching. No human authority shall, in any case whatever, control or interfere with the rights of conscience.

Text as Ratified on: August 3, 1891, and revised September 28, 1891.

History: Not yet amended.

Federal Reference: U.S. Const. art. VI; amend. I.

Section 6 Elections to be free and equal.

All elections shall be free and equal.

Text as Ratified on: August 3, 1891, and revised September 28, 1891.

History: Not yet amended.

Federal Reference: U.S. Const. amends. XV; XIX; XXIV; XXVI.

Section 7 Right of trial by jury.

The ancient mode of trial by jury shall be held sacred, and the right thereof remain inviolate, subject to such modifications as may be authorized by this Constitution.

Text as Ratified on: August 3, 1891, and revised September 28, 1891.

History: Not yet amended.

Federal Reference: U.S. Const. art. III, §2; amend. VII.

Section 8 Freedom of speech and of the press.

Printing presses shall be free to every person who undertakes to examine the proceedings of the General Assembly or any branch of government, and no law shall ever be made to restrain the right thereof. Every person may freely and fully speak, write and print on any subject, being responsible for the abuse of that liberty.

Text as Ratified on: August 3, 1891, and revised September 28, 1891.

History: Not yet amended.

Federal Reference: U.S. Const. amend. I.

Section 9 Truth may be given in evidence in prosecution for publishing matters proper for public information—Jury to try law and facts in libel prosecutions.

In prosecutions for the publication of papers investigating the official conduct of officers or men in a public capacity, or where the matter published is proper for public information, the truth thereof may be given in evidence; and in all indictments for libel the jury shall have the right to determine the law and the facts, under the direction of the court, as in other cases.

Text as Ratified on: August 3, 1891, and revised September 28, 1891.

History: Not yet amended.

Section 10 Security from search and seizure—Conditions of issuance of warrant.

The people shall be secure in their persons, houses, papers and possessions, from unreasonable search and seizure; and no warrant shall issue to search any place, or seize any person or thing, without describing them as nearly as may be, nor without probable cause supported by oath or affirmation.

Text as Ratified on: August 3, 1891, and revised September 28, 1891.

History: Not yet amended.

Federal Reference: U.S. Const. amend. IV.

Section 11 Rights of accused in criminal prosecution—Change of venue.

In all criminal prosecutions the accused has the right to be heard by himself and counsel; to demand the nature and cause of the accusation against him; to meet the witnesses face to face, and to have compulsory process for obtaining witnesses in his favor. He cannot be compelled to give evidence against himself, nor can he be deprived of his life, liberty or property, unless by the judgment of his peers or the law of the land; and in prosecutions by indictment or information, he shall have a speedy public trial by an impartial jury of the vicinage; but the General Assembly may provide by a general law for a change of venue in such prosecutions for both the defendant and the Commonwealth, the change to be made to the most convenient county in which a fair trial can be obtained.

Text as Ratified on: August 3, 1891, and revised September 28, 1891.

History: Not yet amended.

Federal Reference: U.S. Const. art. III, §2; amends. V; VI; XIV, §1.

Section 12 Indictable offense not to be prosecuted by information—Exceptions.

No person, for an indictable offense, shall be proceeded against criminally by information, except in cases arising in the land or naval forces, or in the militia, when in actual service, in time of war or public danger, or by leave of court for oppression or misdemeanor in office.

Text as Ratified on: August 3, 1891, and revised September 28, 1891.

History: Not yet amended.

Federal Reference: U.S. Const. amend. V.

Section 13 Double jeopardy—Property not to be taken for public use without compensation.

No person shall, for the same offense, be twice put in jeopardy of his life or limb, nor shall any man's property be taken or applied to public use without the consent of his representatives, and without just compensation being previously made to him.

Text as Ratified on: August 3, 1891, and revised September 28, 1891.

History: Not yet amended.

Federal Reference: U.S. Const. amend. V.

Section 14 Right of judicial remedy for injury—Speedy trial.

All courts shall be open, and every person for an injury done him in his lands, goods, person or reputation, shall have remedy by due course of law, and right and justice administered without sale, denial or delay.

Text as Ratified on: August 3, 1891, and revised September 28, 1891.

History: Not yet amended.

Federal Reference: U.S. Const. amend. VI.

Section 15 Laws to be suspended only by General Assembly.

No power to suspend laws shall be exercised unless by the General Assembly or its authority.

Text as Ratified on: August 3, 1891, and revised September 28, 1891.

History: Not yet amended.

Section 16 Right to bail—Habeas corpus.

All prisoners shall be bailable by sufficient securities, unless for capital offenses when the proof is evident or the presumption great; and the privilege of the writ of habeas corpus shall not be suspended unless when, in case of rebellion or invasion, the public safety may require it.

Text as Ratified on: August 3, 1891, and revised September 28, 1891.

History: Not yet amended.

Federal Reference: U.S. Const. art. I, §9.

Section 17 Excessive bail or fine, or cruel punishment, prohibited.

Excessive bail shall not be required, nor excessive fines imposed, nor cruel punishment inflicted.

Text as Ratified on: August 3, 1891, and revised September 28, 1891.

History: Not yet amended.

Federal Reference: U.S. Const. amend. VIII.

Section 18 Imprisonment for debt restricted.

The person of a debtor, where there is not strong presumption of fraud, shall not be continued in prison after delivering up his estate for the benefit of his creditors in such manner as shall be prescribed by law.

Text as Ratified on: August 3, 1891, and revised September 28, 1891.

History: Not yet amended.

Section 19 Ex post facto law or law impairing contract forbidden— Rules of construction for mineral deeds relating to coal extraction.

(1) No ex post facto law, nor any law impairing the obligation of contracts, shall be enacted.

(2) In any instrument heretofore or hereafter executed purporting to sever the surface and mineral estates or to grant a mineral estate or to grant a right to extract minerals, which fails to state or describe in express and specific terms the method of coal extraction to be employed, or where said instrument contains language subordinating the surface estate to the mineral estate, it shall be held, in the absence of clear and convincing evidence to the contrary, that the intention of the parties to the instrument was that the coal be extracted only by the method or methods of commercial coal extraction commonly known to be in use in Kentucky in the area affected at the time the instrument was executed, and that the mineral estate be dominant to the surface estate for the purposes of coal extraction by only the method or methods of commercial coal extraction commonly known to be in use in Kentucky in the area affected at the time the instrument was executed.

Text as Ratified on: November 8, 1988.

History: 1988 amendment was proposed by 1988 Ky. Acts ch. 117, §1; original version ratified August 3, 1891, and revised September 28, 1891.

Federal Reference: U.S. Const. art. I, §§9, 10.

Section 20 Attainder, operation of restricted.

No person shall be attainted of treason or felony by the General Assembly, and no attainder shall work corruption of blood, nor, except during the life of the offender, forfeiture of estate to the Commonwealth.

Text as Ratified on: August 3, 1891, and revised September 28, 1891.

History: Not yet amended.

Federal Reference: U.S. Const. art. I, §§9, 10.

Section 21 Descent in case of suicide or casualty.

The estate of such persons as shall destroy their own lives shall descend or vest as in cases of natural death; and if any person shall be killed by casualty, there shall be no forfeiture by reason thereof.

Text as Ratified on: August 3, 1891, and revised September 28, 1891.

History: Not yet amended.

Section 22 Standing armies restricted—Military subordinate to civil—Quartering soldiers restricted.

No standing army shall, in time of peace, be maintained without the consent of the General Assembly; and the military shall, in all cases and at all times, be in strict subordination to the civil power; nor shall any soldier, in time of peace, be quartered in any house without the consent of the owner, nor in time of war, except in a manner prescribed by law.

Text as Ratified on: August 3, 1891, and revised September 28, 1891.

History: Not yet amended.

Federal Reference: U.S. Const. amend. III.

Section 23 No office of nobility or hereditary distinction, or for longer than a term of years.

The General Assembly shall not grant any title of nobility or hereditary distinction, nor create any office the appointment of which shall be for a longer time than a term of years.

Text as Ratified on: August 3, 1891, and revised September 28, 1891.

History: Not yet amended.

Federal Reference: U.S. Const. art. I, §§9, 10.

Section 24 Emigration to be free.

Emigration from the State shall not be prohibited.

Text as Ratified on: August 3, 1891, and revised September 28, 1891.

History: Not yet amended.

Section 25 Slavery and involuntary servitude forbidden.

Slavery and involuntary servitude in this State are forbidden, except as a punishment for crime, whereof the party shall have been duly convicted.

Text as Ratified on: August 3, 1891, and revised September 28, 1891.

History: Not yet amended.

Federal Reference: U.S. Const. amend. XIII.

Section 26 General powers subordinate to Bill of Rights—Laws contrary thereto are void.

To guard against transgression of the high powers which we have delegated, We Declare that every thing in this Bill of Rights is excepted out of the general powers of government, and shall forever remain inviolate; and all laws contrary thereto, or contrary to this Constitution, shall be void.

Text as Ratified on: August 3, 1891, and revised September 28, 1891.

History: Not yet amended.

Rights of Victims of Crime

Section 26A Rights of victims of crime.

To secure for victims of criminal acts or public offenses justice and due process and to ensure crime victims a meaningful role throughout the criminal and juvenile justice systems, a victim, as defined by law which takes effect upon the enactment of this section and which may be expanded by the General Assembly, shall have the following rights, which shall be respected and protected by law in a manner no less vigorous than the protections afforded to the accused in the criminal and juvenile justice systems: victims shall have the reasonable right, upon request, to timely notice of all proceedings and to be heard in any proceeding involving a release, plea, sentencing, or in the consideration of any pardon, commutation of sentence, granting of a reprieve, or other matter involving the right of a victim other than grand jury proceedings; the right to be present at the trial and all other proceedings, other than grand jury proceedings, on the same basis as the accused; the right to proceedings free from unreasonable delay; the right to consult with the attorney for the Commonwealth or the attorney's designee; the right to reasonable protection from the accused and those acting on behalf of the accused throughout the criminal and juvenile justice process; the right to timely notice, upon request, of release or escape of the accused; the right to have the safety of the victim and the victim's family considered in setting bail, determining whether to release the defendant, and setting conditions of release after arrest and conviction; the right to full restitution to be paid by the convicted or adjudicated party in a manner to be determined by the court, except that in the case of a juvenile offender the court shall determine the amount and manner of paying the restitution taking into consideration the best interests of the juvenile offender and the victim; the right to fairness and due consideration of the crime victim's safety, dignity, and privacy; and the right to be informed of these enumerated rights, and shall have standing to assert these rights. The victim, the victim's attorney or other lawful representative, or the attorney for the Commonwealth upon request of the victim may seek enforcement of the rights enumerated in this section and any other right afforded to the victim by law in any trial or appellate court with jurisdiction over the case. The court shall act promptly on such a request and afford a remedy for the violation of any right. Nothing in this section shall afford the victim party status, or be construed as altering the presumption of innocence in the criminal justice system. The accused shall not have standing to assert the rights of a victim. Nothing in this section shall be construed to alter the powers, duties, and responsibilities of the prosecuting attorney. Nothing in this section or any law enacted under this section creates a cause of action for compensation, attorney's fees, or damages against the Commonwealth, a county, city, municipal corporation, or other political subdivision of the Commonwealth, an officer, employee, or agent of the Commonwealth, a county, city, municipal corporation, or any political subdivision of the Commonwealth, or an officer or employee of the court. Nothing in this section or any law enacted under this section shall be construed as creating:

(1) A basis for vacating a conviction; or

(2) A ground for any relief requested by the defendant.

Text as Ratified on: November 3, 2020.

History: Creation proposed by 2020 Ky. Acts ch. 85, §2.

Distribution of the Powers of Government

Section 27 Powers of government divided among legislative, executive, and judicial departments.

The powers of the government of the Commonwealth of Kentucky shall be divided into three distinct departments, and each of them be confined to a separate body of magistracy, to wit: Those which are legislative, to one; those which are executive, to another; and those which are judicial, to another.

Text as Ratified on: August 3, 1891, and revised September 28, 1891.

History: Not yet amended.

Section 28 One department not to exercise power belonging to another.

No person or collection of persons, being of one of those departments, shall exercise any power properly belonging to either of the others, except in the instances hereinafter expressly directed or permitted.

Text as Ratified on: August 3, 1891, and revised September 28, 1891.

History: Not yet amended.

The Legislative Department

Section 29 Legislative power vested in General Assembly.

The legislative power shall be vested in a House of Representatives and a Senate, which, together, shall be styled the "General Assembly of the Commonwealth of Kentucky."

Text as Ratified on: August 3, 1891, and revised September 28, 1891.

History: Not yet amended.

Federal Reference: U.S. Const. art. I, §1.

Section 30 Term of office of Senators and Representatives.

Members of the House of Representatives and Senators shall be elected at the general election in even-numbered years for terms of four years for Senators and two years for members of the House of Representatives. The term of office of Representatives and Senators shall begin upon the first day of January of the year succeeding their election.

Text as Ratified on: November 6, 1979.

History: 1979 amendment was proposed by 1978 Ky. Acts ch. 440, §1; original version ratified August 3, 1891, and revised September 28, 1891.

Federal Reference: U.S. Const. art. I, §§2, 3; amend. XVII; XX, §1.g

Section 31 Time of election and term of office of Senators and Representatives.

At the general election to be held in November, 1984, and every two years thereafter, there shall be elected for four years one Senator in each Senatorial District in which the term of his predecessor in office will then expire and in every Representative District one Representative for two years.

Text as Ratified on: November 6, 1979.

History: 1979 amendment was proposed by 1978 Ky. Acts ch. 440, §1; original version ratified August 3, 1891, and revised September 28, 1891.

Federal Reference: U.S. Const. art. I, §§2, 3; amend. XVII.

Section 32 Qualifications of Senators and Representatives.

No person shall be a Representative who, at the time of his election, is not a citizen of Kentucky, has not attained the age of twenty-four years, and who has not resided in this State two years next preceding his election, and the last year thereof in the county, town or city for which he may be chosen. No person shall be a Senator who, at the time of his election, is not a citizen of Kentucky, has not attained the age of thirty years, and has not resided in this State six years next preceding his election, and the last year thereof in the district for which he may be chosen.

Text as Ratified on: August 3, 1891, and revised September 28, 1891.

History: Not yet amended.

Federal Reference: U.S. Const. art. I, §§2, 3.

Section 33 Senatorial and Representative districts.

The first General Assembly after the adoption of this Constitution shall divide the State into thirty-eight Senatorial Districts, and one hundred Representative Districts, as nearly equal in population as may be without dividing any county, except where a county may include more than one district, which districts shall constitute the Senatorial and Representative Districts for ten years. Not more than two counties shall be joined together to form a Representative District: Provided, In doing so the principle requiring every district to be as nearly equal in population as may be shall not be violated. At the expiration of that time, the General Assembly shall then, and every ten years thereafter, redistrict the State according to this rule, and for the purposes expressed in this section. If, in making said districts, inequality of population should be unavoidable, any advantage resulting therefrom shall be given to districts having the largest territory. No part of a county shall be added to another county to make a district, and the counties forming a district shall be contiguous.

Text as Ratified on: August 3, 1891, and revised September 28, 1891.

History: Not yet amended.

Federal Reference: U.S. Const. art. I, §2.

Section 34 Officers of Houses of General Assembly.

The House of Representatives shall choose its Speaker and other officers, and the Senate shall have power to choose its officers biennially.

Text as Ratified on: August 3, 1891, and revised September 28, 1891.

History: Not yet amended.

Federal Reference: U.S. Const. art. I, §§2, 3.

Section 35 Number of Senators and Representatives.

The number of Representatives shall be one hundred, and the number of Senators thirty-eight.

Text as Ratified on: August 3, 1891, and revised September 28, 1891.

History: Not yet amended.

Section 36 Time and place of meetings of General Assembly.

(1) The General Assembly, in odd-numbered years, shall meet in regular session for a period not to exceed a total of thirty (30) legislative days divided as follows: The General Assembly shall convene for the first part of the session on the first Tuesday after the first Monday in January in odd-numbered years for the purposes of electing legislative leaders, adopting rules of procedure, organizing committees, and introducing and considering legislation. The General Assembly shall then adjourn. The General Assembly shall convene for the second part of the session on the first Tuesday in February of that year. Any legislation introduced but not enacted in the first part of the session shall be carried over into the second part of the session. In any part of the session in an odd-numbered year, no bill raising revenue or appropriating funds shall become a law unless it shall be agreed to by three-fifths of all the members elected to each House.

(2) The General Assembly shall then adjourn until the first Tuesday after the first Monday in January of the following even-numbered years, at which time the General Assembly shall convene in regular session.

(3) All sessions shall be held at the seat of government, except in case of war, insurrection or pestilence, when it may, by proclamation of the Governor, assemble, for the time being, elsewhere.

Text as Ratified on: November 7, 2000.

History: 2000 amendment was proposed by 2000 Ky. Acts ch. 407, §1; 1979 amendment was proposed by 1978 Ky. Acts ch. 440, §2, and ratified November 6, 1979; original version ratified August 3, 1891, and revised September 28, 1891.

Federal Reference: U.S. Const. art. I, §4; amend. XX, §2.

Section 37 Majority constitutes quorum—Powers of less than a quorum.

Not less than a majority of the members of each House of the General Assembly shall constitute a quorum to do business, but a smaller number may adjourn from day to day, and shall be authorized by law to compel the attendance of absent members in such manner and under such penalties as may be prescribed by law.

Text as Ratified on: August 3, 1891, and revised September 28, 1891.

History: Not yet amended.

Federal Reference: U.S. Const. art. I, §5.

Section 38 Each House to judge qualifications, elections, and returns of its members—Contests.

Each House of the General Assembly shall judge of the qualifications, elections and returns of its members, but a contested election shall be determined in such manner as shall be directed by law.

Text as Ratified on: August 3, 1891, and revised September 28, 1891.

History: Not yet amended.

Federal Reference: U.S. Const. art. I, §5.

Section 39 Powers of each House as to rules and conduct of members—Contempt—Bribery.

Each House of the General Assembly may determine the rules of its proceedings, punish a member for disorderly behavior, and, with the concurrence of two-thirds, expel a member, but not a second time for the same cause, and may punish for contempt any person who refuses to attend as a witness, or to bring any paper proper to be used as evidence before the General Assembly, or either House thereof, or a Committee of either, or to testify concerning any matter which may be a proper subject of inquiry by the General Assembly, or offers or gives a bribe to a member of the General Assembly, or attempts by other corrupt means or device to control or influence a member to cast his vote or withhold the same. The punishment and mode of proceeding for contempt in such cases shall be prescribed by law, but the term of imprisonment in any such case shall not extend beyond the session of the General Assembly.

Text as Ratified on: August 3, 1891, and revised September 28, 1891.

History: Not yet amended.

Federal Reference: U.S. Const. art. I, §5.

Section 40 Journals—When vote to be entered.

Each House of the General Assembly shall keep and publish daily a journal of its proceedings; and the yeas and nays of the members on any question shall, at the desire of any two of the members elected, be entered on the journal.

Text as Ratified on: August 3, 1891, and revised September 28, 1891.

History: Not yet amended.

Federal Reference: U.S. Const. art. I, §5.

Section 41 Adjournment during session.

Neither House, during the session of the General Assembly, shall, without the consent of the other, adjourn for more than three days, nor to any other place than that in which it may be sitting.

Text as Ratified on: August 3, 1891, and revised September 28, 1891.

History: Not yet amended.

Federal Reference: U.S. Const. art. I, §5.

Section 42 Compensation of members—Length of sessions—Legislative day.

The members of the General Assembly shall severally receive from the State Treasury compensation for their services: Provided, No change shall take effect during the session at which it is made; nor shall a session occurring in odd-numbered years extend beyond March 30; nor shall a session of the General Assembly occurring in even-numbered years continue beyond sixty legislative days, nor shall it extend beyond April 15; these limitations as to length of sessions shall not apply to the Senate when sitting as a court of impeachment. A legislative day shall be construed to mean a calendar day, exclusive of Sundays, legal holidays, or any day on which neither House meets.

Text as Ratified on: November 7, 2000.

History: 2000 amendment was proposed by 2000 Ky. Acts ch. 407, §2; 1979 amendment was proposed by 1978 Ky. Acts ch. 440, §3, and ratified November 6, 1979; original version ratified August 3, 1891, and revised September 28, 1891.

Federal Reference: U.S. Const. art. I, §6; amend. XXVII.

Section 43 Privileges from arrest and from questioning as to speech or debate.

The members of the General Assembly shall, in all cases except treason, felony, breach or surety of the peace, be privileged from arrest during their attendance on the sessions of their respective Houses, and in going to and returning from the same; and for any speech or debate in either House they shall not be questioned in any other place.

Text as Ratified on: August 3, 1891, and revised September 28, 1891.

History: Not yet amended.

Federal Reference: U.S. Const. art. I, §6.

Section 44 Ineligibility of members to civil office created or given increased compensation during term.

No Senator or Representative shall, during the term for which he was elected, nor for one year thereafter, be appointed or elected to any civil office of profit in this Commonwealth, which shall have been created, or the emoluments of which shall have been increased, during the said term, except to such offices as may be filled by the election of the people.

Text as Ratified on: August 3, 1891, and revised September 28, 1891.

History: Not yet amended.

Federal Reference: U.S. Const. art. I, §6.

Section 45 Collector of public money ineligible unless he has quietus.

No person who may have been a collector of taxes or public moneys for the Commonwealth, or for any county, city, town or district, or the assistant or deputy of such collector, shall be eligible to the General Assembly, unless he shall have obtained a quietus six months before the election for the amount of such collection, and for all public moneys for which he may have been responsible.

Text as Ratified on: August 3, 1891, and revised September 28, 1891.

History: Not yet amended.

Section 46 Bills must be reported by committee, printed, and read—How bill called from committee—Votes required for passage.

No bill shall be considered for final passage unless the same has been reported by a committee and printed for the use of the members. Every bill shall be read at length on three different days in each House, but the second and third readings may be dispensed with by a majority of all the members elected to the House in which the bill is pending. But whenever a committee refuses or fails to report a bill submitted to it in a reasonable time, the same may be called up by any member, and be considered in the same manner it would have been considered if it had been reported. No bill shall become a law unless, on its final passage, it receives the votes of at least two-fifths of the members elected to each House, and a majority of the members voting, the vote to be taken by yeas and nays and entered in the journal: Provided, Any act or resolution for the appropriation of money or the creation of debt shall, on its final passage, receive the votes of a majority of all the members elected to each House.

Text as Ratified on: August 3, 1891, and revised September 28, 1891.

History: Not yet amended.

Federal Reference: U.S. Const. art. I, §7.

Section 47 Bills to raise revenue must originate in House of Representatives.

All bills for raising revenue shall originate in the House of Representatives, but the Senate may propose amendments thereto: Provided, No new matter shall be introduced, under color of amendment, which does not relate to raising revenue.

Text as Ratified on: August 3, 1891, and revised September 28, 1891.

History: Not yet amended.

Federal Reference: U.S. Const. art. I, §7.

Section 48 Resources of Sinking Fund not to be diminished—Preservation of fund.

The General Assembly shall have no power to enact laws to diminish the resources of the Sinking Fund as now established by law until the debt of the Commonwealth be paid, but may enact laws to increase them; and the whole resources of said fund, from year to year, shall be sacredly set apart and applied to the payment of the interest and principal of the State debt, and to no other use or purpose, until the whole debt of the State is fully satisfied.

Text as Ratified on: August 3, 1891, and revised September 28, 1891.

History: Not yet amended.

Section 49 Power to contract debts—Limit.

The General Assembly may contract debts to meet casual deficits or failures in the revenue; but such debts, direct or contingent, singly or in the aggregate, shall not at any time exceed five hundred thousand dollars, and the moneys arising from loans creating such debts shall be applied only to the purpose or purposes for which they were obtained, or to repay such debts: Provided, The General Assembly may contract debts to repel invasion, suppress insurrection, or, if hostilities are threatened, provide for the public defense.

Text as Ratified on: August 3, 1891, and revised September 28, 1891.

History: Not yet amended.

Federal Reference: U.S. Const. art. I, §8.

Section 50 Purposes for which debt may be contracted—Tax to discharge—Public vote.

No act of the General Assembly shall authorize any debt to be contracted on behalf of the Commonwealth except for the purposes mentioned in Section 49, unless provision be made therein to levy and collect an annual tax sufficient to pay the interest stipulated, and to discharge the debt within thirty years; nor shall such act take effect until it shall have been submitted to the people at a general election, and shall have received a majority of all the votes cast for and against it: Provided, The General Assembly may contract debts by borrowing money to pay any part of the debt of the State, without submission to the people, and without making provision in the act authorizing the same for a tax to discharge the debt so contracted, or the interest thereon.

Text as Ratified on: August 3, 1891, and revised September 28, 1891.

History: Not yet amended.

Section 51 Law may not relate to more than one subject, to be expressed in title—Amendments must be at length.

No law enacted by the General Assembly shall relate to more than one subject, and that shall be expressed in the title, and no law shall be revised, amended, or the provisions thereof extended or conferred by reference to its title only, but so much thereof as is revised, amended, extended or conferred, shall be reenacted and published at length.

Text as Ratified on: August 3, 1891, and revised September 28, 1891.

History: Not yet amended.

Section 52 General Assembly may not release debt to State or to county or city.

The General Assembly shall have no power to release, extinguish or authorize the releasing or extinguishing, in whole or in part, the indebtedness or liability of any corporation or individual to this Commonwealth, or to any county or municipality thereof.

Text as Ratified on: August 3, 1891, and revised September 28, 1891.

History: Not yet amended.

Section 53 Investigation of accounts of Treasurer and Auditor—Report, publication, submission to Governor and General Assembly.

The General Assembly shall provide by law for monthly investigations into the accounts of the Treasurer and Auditor of Public Accounts, and the result of these investigations shall be reported to the Governor, and these reports shall be semiannually published in two newspapers of general circulation in the State. The reports received by the Governor shall, at the beginning of each session, be transmitted by him to the General Assembly for scrutiny and appropriate action.

Text as Ratified on: August 3, 1891, and revised September 28, 1891.

History: Not yet amended.

Section 54 No restriction on recovery for injury or death.

The General Assembly shall have no power to limit the amount to be recovered for injuries resulting in death, or for injuries to person or property.

Text as Ratified on: August 3, 1891, and revised September 28, 1891.

History: Not yet amended.

Section 55 When laws to take effect—Emergency legislation.

No act, except general appropriation bills, shall become a law until ninety days after the adjournment of the session at which it was passed, except in cases of emergency, when, by the concurrence of a majority of the members elected to each House of the General Assembly, by a yea and nay vote entered upon their journals, an act may become a law when approved by the Governor; but the reasons for the emergency that justifies this action must be set out at length in the journal of each House.

Text as Ratified on: August 3, 1891, and revised September 28, 1891.

History: Not yet amended.

Section 56 Signing of bills—Enrollment—Presentation to Governor.

No bill shall become a law until the same shall have been signed by the presiding officer of each of the two Houses in open session; and before such officer shall have affixed his signature to any bill, he shall suspend all other business, declare that such bill will now be read, and that he will sign the same to the end that it may become a law. The bill shall then be read at length and compared; and, if correctly enrolled, he shall, in the presence of the House in open session, and before any other business is entertained, affix his signature, which fact shall be noted in the journal, and the bill immediately sent to the other House. When it reaches the other House, the presiding officer thereof shall immediately suspend all other business, announce the reception of the bill, and the same proceeding shall thereupon be observed in every respect as in the House in which it was first signed. And thereupon the Clerk of the latter House shall immediately present the same to the Governor for his signature and approval.

Text as Ratified on: August 3, 1891, and revised September 28, 1891.

History: Not yet amended.

Federal Reference: U.S. Const. art. I, §7.

Section 57 Member having personal interest to make disclosure and not vote.

A member who has a personal or private interest in any measure or bill proposed or pending before the General Assembly, shall disclose the fact to the House of which he is a member, and shall not vote thereon upon pain of expulsion.

Text as Ratified on: August 3, 1891, and revised September 28, 1891.

History: Not yet amended.

Section 58 General Assembly not to audit nor allow private claim—Exception—Appropriations.

The General Assembly shall neither audit nor allow any private claim against the Commonwealth, except for expenses incurred during the session at which the same was allowed; but may appropriate money to pay such claim as shall have been audited and allowed according to law.

Text as Ratified on: August 3, 1891, and revised September 28, 1891.

History: Not yet amended.

Section 59 Local and special legislation.

The General Assembly shall not pass local or special acts concerning any of the following subjects, or for any of the following purposes, namely:

First: To regulate the jurisdiction, or the practice, or the circuits of the courts of justice, or the rights, powers, duties or compensation of the officers thereof; but the practice in circuit courts in continuous session may, by a general law, be made different from the practice of circuit courts held in terms.

Second: To regulate the summoning, impaneling or compensation of grand or petit jurors.

Third: To provide for changes of venue in civil or criminal causes.

Fourth: To regulate the punishment of crimes and misdemeanors, or to remit fines, penalties or forfeitures.

Fifth: To regulate the limitation of civil or criminal causes.

Sixth: To affect the estate of cestuis que trust, decedents, infants or other persons under disabilities, or to authorize any such persons to sell, lease, encumber or dispose of their property.

Seventh: To declare any person of age, or to relieve an infant or feme covert of disability, or to enable him to do acts allowed only to adults not under disabilities.

Eighth: To change the law of descent, distribution or succession.

Ninth: To authorize the adoption or legitimation of children.

Tenth: To grant divorces.

Eleventh: To change the names of persons.

Twelfth: To give effect to invalid deeds, wills or other instruments.

Thirteenth: To legalize, except as against the Commonwealth, the unauthorized or invalid act of any officer or public agent of the Commonwealth, or of any city, county or municipality thereof.

Fourteenth: To refund money legally paid into the State Treasury.

Fifteenth: To authorize or to regulate the levy, the assessment or the collection of taxes, or to give any indulgence or discharge to any assessor or collector of taxes, or to his sureties.

Sixteenth: To authorize the opening, altering, maintaining or vacating of roads, highways, streets, alleys, town plats, cemeteries, graveyards, or public grounds not owned by the Commonwealth.

Seventeenth: To grant a charter to any corporation, or to amend the charter of any existing corporation; to license companies or persons to own or operate ferries, bridges, roads or turnpikes; to declare streams navigable, or to authorize the construction of booms or dams therein, or to remove obstructions therefrom; to affect toll gates or to regulate tolls; to regulate fencing or the running at large of stock.

Eighteenth: To create, increase or decrease fees, percentages or allowances to public officers, or to extend the time for the collection thereof, or to authorize officers to appoint deputies.

Nineteenth: To give any person or corporation the right to lay a railroad track or tramway, or to amend existing charters for such purposes.

Twentieth: To provide for conducting elections, or for designating the places of voting, or changing the boundaries of wards, precincts or districts, except when new counties may be created.

Twenty-first: To regulate the rate of interest.

Twenty-second: To authorize the creation, extension, enforcement, impairment or release of liens.

Twenty-third: To provide for the protection of game and fish.

Twenty-fourth: To regulate labor, trade, mining or manufacturing.

Twenty-fifth: To provide for the management of common schools.

Twenty-sixth: To locate or change a county seat.

Twenty-seventh: To provide a means of taking the sense of the people of any city, town, district, precinct or county, whether they wish to authorize, regulate or prohibit therein the sale of vinous, spirituous or malt liquors, or alter the liquor laws.

Twenty-eighth: Restoring to citizenship persons convicted of infamous crimes.

Twenty-ninth: In all other cases where a general law can be made applicable, no special law shall be enacted.

Text as Ratified on: August 3, 1891, and revised September 28, 1891.

History: Not yet amended.

Section 60 General law not to be made special or local by amendment—No special powers or privileges—Law not to take effect on approval of other authority than General Assembly—Exceptions.

The General Assembly shall not indirectly enact any special or local act by the repeal in part of a general act, or by exempting from the operation of a general act any city, town, district or county; but laws repealing local or special acts may be enacted. No law shall be enacted granting powers or privileges in any case where the granting of such powers or privileges shall have been provided for by a general law, nor where the courts have jurisdiction to grant the same or to give the relief asked for. No law, except such as relates to the sale, loan or gift of vinous, spirituous or malt liquors, bridges, turnpikes or other public roads, public buildings or improvements, fencing, running at large of stock, matters pertaining to common schools, paupers, and the regulation by counties, cities, towns or other municipalities of their local affairs, shall be enacted to take effect upon the approval of any other authority than the General Assembly, unless otherwise expressly provided in this Constitution.

Text as Ratified on: August 3, 1891, and revised September 28, 1891.

History: Not yet amended.

Section 61 Provision to be made for local option on sale of liquor—Time of elections.

The General Assembly shall, by general law, provide a means whereby the sense of the people of any county, city, town, district or precinct may be taken, as to whether or not spirituous, vinous or malt liquors shall be sold, bartered or loaned therein, or the sale thereof regulated. But nothing herein shall be construed to interfere with or to repeal any law in force relating to the sale or gift of such liquors. All elections on this question may be held on a day other than the regular election days.

Text as Ratified on: November 5, 1935.

History: 1935 reenactment was proposed by 1934 Ky. Acts ch. 58, §1; repeal (by implication) was proposed by 1918 Ky. Acts ch. 63, §1, and ratified on November 4, 1919, effective July 1, 1920; original version ratified August 3, 1891, and revised September 28, 1891.

Federal Reference: U.S. Const. amend. XXI.

Section 62 Style of laws.

The style of the laws of this Commonwealth shall be as follows: "Be it enacted by the General Assembly of the Commonwealth of Kentucky."

Text as Ratified on: August 3, 1891, and revised September 28, 1891.

History: Not yet amended.

Counties and County Seats

Section 63 Area of counties—Boundaries—Creation and abolishment of counties.

No new county shall be created by the General Assembly which will reduce the county or counties, or either of them, from which it shall be taken, to less area than four hundred square miles; nor shall any county be formed of less area; nor shall any boundary line thereof pass within less than ten miles of any county seat of the county or counties proposed to be divided. Nothing contained herein shall prevent the General Assembly from abolishing any county.

Text as Ratified on: August 3, 1891, and revised September 28, 1891.

History: Not yet amended.

Section 64 Division of county or removal of county seat, election required—Minimum population of county.

No county shall be divided, or have any part stricken therefrom, except in the formation of new counties, without submitting the question to a vote of the people of the county, nor unless the majority of all the legal voters of the county voting on the question shall vote for the same. The county seat of no county as now located, or as may hereafter be located, shall be moved, except upon a vote of two-thirds of those voting; nor shall any new county be established which will reduce any county to less than twelve thousand inhabitants, nor shall any county be created containing a less population.

Text as Ratified on: August 3, 1891, and revised September 28, 1891.

History: Not yet amended.

Federal Reference: U.S. Const. art. IV, §3.

Section 65 Striking territory from county—Liability for indebtedness.

There shall be no territory stricken from any county unless a majority of the voters living in such territory shall petition for such division. But the portion so stricken off and added to another county, or formed in whole or in part into a new county, shall be bound for its proportion of the indebtedness of the county from which it has been taken.

Text as Ratified on: August 3, 1891, and revised September 28, 1891.

History: Not yet amended.

Impeachments

Section 66 Power of impeachment vested in House.

The House of Representatives shall have the sole power of impeachment.

Text as Ratified on: August 3, 1891, and revised September 28, 1891.

History: Not yet amended.

Federal Reference: U.S. Const. art. I, §2.

Section 67 Trial of impeachments by Senate.

All impeachments shall be tried by the Senate. When sitting for that purpose, the Senators shall be upon oath or affirmation. No person shall be convicted without the concurrence of two-thirds of the Senators present.

Text as Ratified on: August 3, 1891, and revised September 28, 1891.

History: Not yet amended.

Federal Reference: U.S. Const. art. I, §3; art. II, §4.

Section 68 Civil officers liable to impeachment—Judgment—Criminal liability.

The Governor and all civil officers shall be liable to impeachment for any misdemeanors in office; but judgment in such cases shall not extend further than removal from office, and disqualification to hold any office of honor, trust or profit under this Commonwealth; but the party convicted shall, nevertheless, be subject and liable to indictment, trial and punishment by law.

Text as Ratified on: August 3, 1891, and revised September 28, 1891.

History: Not yet amended.

Federal Reference: U.S. Const. art. I, §3.

The Executive Department

Officers for the State at Large

Section 69 Executive power vested in Governor.

The supreme executive power of the Commonwealth shall be vested in a Chief Magistrate, who shall be styled the "Governor of the Commonwealth of Kentucky."

Text as Ratified on: August 3, 1891, and revised September 28, 1891.

History: Not yet amended.

Federal Reference: U.S. Const. art. II, §1.

Section 70 Election of Governor and Lieutenant Governor—Term—Tie vote.

The Governor and Lieutenant Governor shall be elected for the term of four years by the qualified voters of the State. They shall be elected jointly by the casting by each voter of a single vote applicable to both offices, as shall be provided by law. The slate of candidates having the highest number of votes cast jointly for them for Governor and Lieutenant Governor shall be elected; but if two or more slates of candidates shall be equal and highest in votes, the election shall be determined by lot in such manner as the General Assembly may direct.

Text as Ratified on: November 3, 1992.

History: 1992 amendment was proposed by 1992 Ky. Acts ch. 168, §1; original version ratified August 3, 1891, and revised September 28, 1891.

Federal Reference: U.S. Const. art. II, §1; amend. XII.

Section 71 Gubernatorial succession.

The Governor shall be ineligible for the succeeding four years after the expiration of any second consecutive term for which he shall have been elected.

Text as Ratified on: November 3, 1992.

History: 1992 amendment was proposed by 1992 Ky. Acts ch. 168, §2; original version ratified August 3, 1891, and revised September 28, 1891.

Federal Reference: U.S. Const. amend. XXII.

Section 72 Qualifications of Governor and Lieutenant Governor—Duties of Lieutenant Governor.

The Governor and the Lieutenant Governor shall be at least thirty years of age, and have been citizens and residents of Kentucky for at least six years next preceding their election. The duties of the Lieutenant Governor shall be prescribed by law, and he shall have such other duties as delegated by the Governor.

Text as Ratified on: November 3, 1992.

History: 1992 amendment was proposed by 1992 Ky. Acts ch. 168, §3; original version ratified August 3, 1891, and revised September 28, 1891.

Federal Reference: U.S. Const. art. II, §1.

Section 73 When terms of Governor and Lieutenant Governor begin.

The Governor and the Lieutenant Governor shall commence the execution of the duties of their offices on the fifth Tuesday succeeding their election, and shall continue in the execution thereof until a successor shall have qualified.

Text as Ratified on: November 3, 1992.

History: 1992 amendment was proposed by 1992 Ky. Acts ch. 168, §4; original version ratified August 3, 1891, and revised September 28, 1891.

Federal Reference: U.S. Const. amend. XX, §1.

Section 74 Compensation of Governor and Lieutenant Governor.

The Governor and Lieutenant Governor shall at stated times receive for the performance of the duties of their respective offices compensation to be fixed by law.

Text as Ratified on: November 3, 1992.

History: 1992 amendment was proposed by 1992 Ky. Acts ch. 168, §5; original version ratified August 3, 1891, and revised September 28, 1891.

Federal Reference: U.S. Const. art. II, §1.

Section 75 Governor is Commander-in-Chief of army, navy and militia.

He shall be Commander-in-Chief of the army and navy of this Commonwealth, and of the militia thereof, except when they shall be called into the service of the United States; but he shall not command personally in the field, unless advised so to do by a resolution of the General Assembly.

Text as Ratified on: August 3, 1891, and revised September 28, 1891.

History: Not yet amended.

Federal Reference: U.S. Const. art. II, §2.

Section 76 Power of Governor to fill vacancies.

He shall have the power, except as otherwise provided in this Constitution, to fill vacancies by granting commissions, which shall expire when such vacancies shall have been filled according to the provisions of this Constitution.

Text as Ratified on: August 3, 1891, and revised September 28, 1891.

History: Not yet amended.

Federal Reference: U.S. Const. art. II, §2.

Section 77 Power of Governor to remit fines and forfeitures, grant reprieves and pardons—No power to remit fees.

He shall have power to remit fines and forfeitures, commute sentences, grant reprieves and pardons, except in case of impeachment, and he shall file with each application therefor a statement of the reasons for his decision thereon, which application and statement shall always be open to public inspection. In cases of treason, he shall have power to grant reprieves until the end of the next session of the General Assembly, in which the power of pardoning shall be vested; but he shall have no power to remit the fees of the Clerk, Sheriff or Commonwealth's Attorney in penal or criminal cases.

Text as Ratified on: August 3, 1891, and revised September 28, 1891.

History: Not yet amended.

Federal Reference: U.S. Const. art. II, §2.

Section 78 Governor may require information from state officers.

He may require information in writing from the officers of the Executive Department upon any subject relating to the duties of their respective offices.

Text as Ratified on: August 3, 1891, and revised September 28, 1891.

History: Not yet amended.

Federal Reference: U.S. Const. art. II, §2.

Section 79 Reports and recommendations to General Assembly.

He shall, from time to time, give to the General Assembly information of the state of the Commonwealth, and recommend to their consideration such measures as he may deem expedient.

Text as Ratified on: August 3, 1891, and revised September 28, 1891.

History: Not yet amended.

Federal Reference: U.S. Const. art. II, §3.

Section 80 Governor may call extraordinary session of General Assembly, adjourn General Assembly.

He may, on extraordinary occasions, convene the General Assembly at the seat of government, or at a different place, if that should have become dangerous from an enemy or from contagious diseases. In case of disagreement between the two Houses with respect to the time of adjournment, he may adjourn them to such time as he shall think proper, not exceeding four months. When he shall convene the General Assembly it shall be by proclamation, stating the subjects to be considered, and no other shall be considered.

Text as Ratified on: August 3, 1891, and revised September 28, 1891.

History: Not yet amended.

Federal Reference: U.S. Const. art. II, §3.

Section 81 Governor to enforce laws.

He shall take care that the laws be faithfully executed.

Text as Ratified on: August 3, 1891, and revised September 28, 1891.

History: Not yet amended.

Federal Reference: U.S. Const. art. II, §3.

Section 82 Succession of Lieutenant Governor.

The Lieutenant Governor shall be ineligible to the office of Lieutenant Governor for the succeeding four (4) years after the expiration of any second consecutive term for which he shall have been elected.

Text as Ratified on: November 3, 1992.

History: 1992 amendment was proposed by 1992 Ky. Acts ch. 168, §6; original version ratified August 3, 1891, and revised September 28, 1891.

Section 83 (Repealed 1992)

Catchline at time of repeal: "Lieutenant Governor is President of Senate—Right to vote."

Repeal Ratified on: November 3, 1992.

History: Repeal was proposed by 1992 Ky. Acts ch. 168, §18; original version ratified August 3, 1891, and revised September 28, 1891.

Section 84 When Lieutenant Governor to act as Governor—President of the Senate not to preside at impeachment of Governor—Certification of disability of Governor.

Should the Governor be impeached and removed from office, die, refuse to qualify, resign, certify by entry on his Journal that he is unable to discharge the duties of his office, or be, from any cause, unable to discharge the duties of his office, the Lieutenant Governor shall exercise all the power and authority appertaining to the office of Governor until another be duly elected and qualified, or the Governor shall be able to discharge the duties of his office. On the trial of the Governor, the President of the Senate shall not preside over the proceedings, but the Chief Justice of the Supreme Court shall preside during the trial.

If the Governor, due to physical or mental incapacitation, is unable to discharge the duties of his office, the Attorney General may petition the Supreme Court to have the Governor declared disabled. If the Supreme Court determines in a unanimous decision that the Governor is unable to discharge the duties of his office, the Chief Justice shall certify such disability to the Secretary of State who shall enter same on the Journal of the Acts of the Governor, and the Lieutenant Governor shall assume the duties of the Governor, and shall act as Governor until the Supreme Court determines that the disability of the Governor has ceased to exist. Before the Governor resumes his duties, the finding of the Court that the disability has ceased shall be certified by the Chief Justice to the Secretary of State who shall enter such finding on the Journal of the Acts of the Governor.

Text as Ratified on: November 3, 1992.

History: 1992 amendment was proposed by 1992 Ky. Acts ch. 168, §7; original version ratified August 3, 1891, and revised September 28, 1891.

Federal Reference: U.S. Const. art. I, §3; amends. XX, §§3, 4; XXV.

Section 85 President of Senate—Election—Powers.

A President of the Senate shall be elected by each Senate as soon after its organization as possible and as often as there is a vacancy in the office of President, another President of the Senate shall be elected by the Senate, if in session. And if, during the vacancy of the office of Governor, the Lieutenant Governor shall be impeached and removed from office, refuse to qualify, resign, or die, the President of the Senate shall in like manner administer the government.

Text as Ratified on: November 3, 1992.

History: 1992 amendment was proposed by 1992 Ky. Acts ch. 168, §8; original version ratified August 3, 1891, and revised September 28, 1891.

Federal Reference: U.S. Const. art. I, §3; amends. XX, §§3, 4; XXV.

Section 86 Compensation of President of the Senate.

The President of the Senate shall receive for his services the same compensation which shall, for the same period, be allowed to the Speaker of the House of Representatives, and during the time he administers the government as Governor, he shall receive the same compensation which the Governor would have received had he been employed in the duties of his office.

Text as Ratified on: November 3, 1992.

History: 1992 amendment was proposed by 1992 Ky. Acts ch. 168, §9; original version ratified August 3, 1891, and revised September 28, 1891.

Section 87 Who to act as Governor in absence of Lieutenant Governor and President of the Senate.

If the Lieutenant Governor shall be called upon to administer the government in place of the Governor, and shall, while in such administration, resign, or die during the recess of the General Assembly, if there be no President of the Senate, it shall be the duty of the Attorney General, for the time being, to convene the Senate for the purpose of choosing a President; and until a President is chosen, the Attorney General shall administer the government. If there be no Attorney General to perform the duties devolved upon him by this section, then the Auditor, for the time being, shall convene the Senate for the purpose of choosing a President, and shall administer the government until a President is chosen.

Text as Ratified on: November 3, 1992.

History: 1992 amendment was proposed by 1992 Ky. Acts ch. 168, §10; original version ratified August 3, 1891, and revised September 28, 1891.

Federal Reference: U.S. Const. amend. XX, §§3, 4; XXV.

Section 88 Signature of bills by Governor—Veto—Passage over veto—Partial veto.

Every bill which shall have passed the two Houses shall be presented to the Governor. If he approve, he shall sign it; but if not, he shall return it, with his objections, to the House in which it originated, which shall enter the objections in full upon its journal, and proceed to reconsider it. If, after such reconsideration, a majority of all the members elected to that House shall agree to pass the bill, it shall be sent, with the objections, to the other House, by which it shall likewise be considered, and if approved by a majority of all the members elected to that House, it shall be a law; but in such case the votes of both Houses shall be determined by yeas and nays, and the names of the members voting for and against the bill shall be entered upon the journal of each House respectively. If any bill shall not be returned by the Governor within ten days (Sundays excepted) after it shall have been presented to him, it shall be a law in like manner as if he had signed it, unless the General Assembly, by their adjournment, prevent its return, in which case it shall be a law, unless disapproved by him within ten days after the adjournment, in which case his veto message shall be spread upon the register kept by the Secretary of State. The Governor shall have the power to disapprove any part or parts of appropriation bills embracing distinct items, and the part or parts disapproved shall not become a law unless reconsidered and passed, as in case of a bill.

Text as Ratified on: August 3, 1891, and revised September 28, 1891.

History: Not yet amended.

Federal Reference: U.S. Const. art. I, §7.

Section 89 Concurrent orders and resolutions on same footing as bill.

Every order, resolution or vote, in which the concurrence of both Houses may be necessary, except on a question of adjournment, or as otherwise provided in this Constitution, shall be presented to the Governor, and, before it shall take effect, be approved by him; or, being disapproved, shall be repassed by a majority of the members elected to both Houses, according to the rules and limitations prescribed in case of a bill.

Text as Ratified on: August 3, 1891, and revised September 28, 1891.
History: Not yet amended.

Federal Reference: U.S. Const. art. I, §7.

Section 90 Contest of election for Governor or Lieutenant Governor.

Contested elections for Governor and Lieutenant Governor shall be determined by both Houses of the General Assembly, according to such regulations as may be established by law.

Text as Ratified on: August 3, 1891, and revised September 28, 1891.

History: Not yet amended.

Federal Reference: U.S. Const. amend. XII.

Section 91 Constitutional State officers—Election—Qualifications—Term of office—Duties—Secretary of State to record acts of Governor and report them to General Assembly.

A Treasurer, Auditor of Public Accounts, Commissioner of Agriculture, Labor and Statistics, Secretary of State, and Attorney-General, shall be elected by the qualified voters of the State at the same time the Governor and Lieutenant Governor are elected, for the term of four years, each of whom shall be at least thirty years of age at the time of his election, and shall have been a resident citizen of the State at least two years next before his election. The duties of all these officers shall be such as may be prescribed by law, and the Secretary of State shall keep a fair register of and attest all the official acts of the Governor, and shall, when required, lay the same and all papers, minutes and vouchers relative thereto before either House of the General Assembly. The officers named in this section shall enter upon the discharge of their duties the first Monday in January after their election, and shall hold their offices until their successors are elected and qualified.

Text as Ratified on: November 3, 1992

History: 1992 amendment was proposed by 1992 Ky. Acts ch. 168, §11; original version ratified August 3, 1891, and revised September 28, 1891.

Section 92 Qualifications of Attorney General.

The Attorney General shall have been a practicing lawyer eight years before his election.

Text as Ratified on: August 3, 1891, and revised September 28, 1891.

History: Not yet amended.

Section 93 Succession of elected Constitutional State Officers—Duties—Inferior officers and members of boards and commissions.

The Treasurer, Auditor of Public Accounts, Secretary of State, Commissioner of Agriculture, Labor and Statistics, and Attorney General shall be ineligible to reelection for the succeeding four years after the expiration of any second consecutive term for which they shall have been elected. The duties and responsibilities of these officers shall be prescribed by law, and all fees collected by any of said officers shall be covered into the treasury. Inferior State officers and members of boards and commissions, not specifically provided for in this Constitution, may be appointed or elected, in such manner as may be prescribed by law, which may include a requirement of consent by the Senate, for a term not exceeding four years, and until their successors are appointed or elected and qualified.

Text as Ratified on: November 3, 1992.

History: 1992 amendment was proposed by 1992 Ky. Acts ch. 168, §12; original version ratified August 3, 1891, and revised September 28, 1891.

Section 94 (Repealed 1992)

Catchline at time of repeal: "Register of Land Office may be abolished."

Repeal Ratified on: November 3, 1992.

History: Repeal was proposed by 1992 Ky. Acts ch. 168, §18; original version ratified August 3, 1891, and revised September 28, 1891.

Section 95 Time of election of elected Constitutional State officers.

The election under this Constitution for Governor, Lieutenant Governor, Treasurer, Auditor of Public Accounts, Attorney General, Secretary of State, and Commissioner of Agriculture, Labor and Statistics, shall be held on the first Tuesday after the first Monday in November, eighteen hundred and ninety-five, and the same day every four years thereafter.

Text as Ratified on: November 3, 1992.

History: 1992 amendment was proposed by 1992 Ky. Acts ch. 168, §13; original version ratified August 3, 1891, and revised September 28, 1891.

Federal Reference: U.S. Const. art. II, §1.

Section 96 Compensation of Constitutional State officers.

All officers mentioned in Section 95 shall be paid for their services by salary, and not otherwise.

Text as Ratified on: August 3, 1891, and revised September 28, 1891.

History: Not yet amended.

Federal Reference: U.S. Const. art. II, §1.

Officers for Districts and Counties

Section 97 Commonwealth's Attorney and Circuit Court Clerk—Election—Term.

In the year two thousand, and every six years thereafter, there shall be an election in each county for a Circuit Court Clerk, and for a Commonwealth's Attorney, in each circuit court district, unless that office be abolished, who shall hold their respective offices for six years from the first Monday in January after their election, and until the election and qualification of their successors.

Text as Ratified on: November 3, 1992.

History: 1992 amendment was proposed by 1992 Ky. Acts ch. 168, §14; original version ratified August 3, 1891, and revised September 28, 1891.

Section 98 Compensation of Commonwealth's Attorney.

The compensation of the Commonwealth's Attorney shall be by salary and such percentage of fines and forfeitures as may be fixed by law, and such salary shall be uniform in so far as the same shall be paid out of the State Treasury, and not to exceed the sum of five hundred dollars per annum; but any county may make additional compensation, to be paid by said county. Should any percentage of fines and forfeitures be allowed by law, it shall not be paid except upon such proportion of fines and forfeitures as have been collected and paid into the State Treasury, and not until so collected and paid.

Text as Ratified on: August 3, 1891, and revised September 28, 1891.

History: Not yet amended.

Section 99 County officers, justices of the peace, and constables—Election—Term.

At the regular election in nineteen hundred and ninety-eight and every four years thereafter, there shall be elected in each county a Judge of the County Court, a County Court Clerk, a County Attorney, Sheriff, Jailer, Coroner, Surveyor and Assessor, and in each Justice's District one Justice of the Peace and one Constable, who shall enter upon the discharge of the duties of their offices on the first Monday in January after their election, and who shall hold their offices four years until the election and qualification of their successors.

Text as Ratified on: November 3, 1992.

History: 1992 amendment was proposed by 1992 Ky. Acts ch. 168, §15; 1984 amendment was proposed by 1984 Ky. Acts ch. 35, §1, and ratified November 6, 1984; original version ratified August 3, 1891, and revised September 28, 1891.

Section 100 Qualifications of officers for counties and districts.

No person shall be eligible to the offices mentioned in Sections 97 and 99 who is not at the time of his election twenty-four years of age (except Clerks of County and Circuit Courts, who shall be twenty-one years of age), a citizen of Kentucky, and who has not resided in the State two years, and one year next preceding his election in the county and district in which he is a candidate. No person shall be eligible to the office of Commonwealth's Attorney unless he shall have been a licensed practicing lawyer four years. No person shall be eligible to the office of County Attorney unless he shall have been a licensed practicing lawyer two years. No person shall be eligible to the office of Clerk unless he shall have procured from a Judge of the Court of Appeals, or a Judge of a Circuit Court, a certificate that he has been examined by the Clerk of his Court under his supervision, and that he is qualified for the office for which he is a candidate.

Text as Ratified on: August 3, 1891, and revised September 28, 1891.

History: Not yet amended.

Section 101 Qualifications and jurisdiction of constables.

Constables shall possess the same qualifications as Sheriffs, and their jurisdictions shall be coextensive with the counties in which they reside. Constables now in office shall continue in office until their successors are elected and qualified.

Text as Ratified on: August 3, 1891, and revised September 28, 1891.

History: Not yet amended.

Section 102 Officers for new counties.

When a new county shall be created, officers for the same, to serve until the next regular election, shall be elected or appointed in such way and at such times as the General Assembly may prescribe.

Text as Ratified on: August 3, 1891, and revised September 28, 1891.

History: Not yet amended.

Section 103 Bonds of county officers and other officers.

The Judges of County Courts, Clerks, Sheriffs, Surveyors, Coroners, Jailers, Constables, and such other officers as the General Assembly may, from time to time, require, shall before they enter upon the duties of their respective offices, and as often thereafter as may be deemed proper, give such bond and security as may be prescribed by law.

Text as Ratified on: August 3, 1891, and revised September 28, 1891.

History: Not yet amended.

Section 104 Abolishment of office of assessor—Assessor may not succeed himself.

The General Assembly may abolish the office of Assessor and provide that the assessment of property shall be made by other officers; but it shall have power to reestablish the office of Assessor and prescribe his duties. No person shall be eligible to the office of Assessor two consecutive terms.

Text as Ratified on: August 3, 1891, and revised September 28, 1891.

History: Not yet amended.

Section 105 Consolidation of offices of sheriff and jailer.

The General Assembly may, at any time, consolidate the offices of Jailer and Sheriff in any county or counties, as it shall deem most expedient; but in the event such consolidation be made, the office of Sheriff shall be retained, and the Sheriff shall be required to perform the duties of Jailer.

Text as Ratified on: August 3, 1891, and revised September 28, 1891.

History: Not yet amended.

Section 106 Fees of county officers—Fees in counties having seventy-five thousand population or more.

The fees of county officers shall be regulated by law. In counties or cities having a population of seventy-five thousand or more, the Clerks of the respective Courts thereof (except the Clerk of the City Court), the Marshals, the Sheriffs and the Jailers, shall be paid out of the State Treasury, by salary to be fixed by law, the salaries of said officers and of their deputies and necessary office expenses not to exceed seventy-five per centum of the fees collected by said officers, respectively, and paid into the Treasury.

Text as Ratified on: August 3, 1891, and revised September 28, 1891.

History: Not yet amended.

Section 107 Additional county or district offices may be created.

The General Assembly may provide for the election or appointment, for a term not exceeding four years, of such other county or district ministerial and executive officers as may, from time to time, be necessary.

Text as Ratified on: August 3, 1891, and revised September 28, 1891.

History: Not yet amended.

Section 108 Abolishment of office of Commonwealth's Attorney.

The General Assembly may, at any time after the expiration of six years from the adoption of this Constitution, abolish the office of Commonwealth's Attorney, to take effect upon the expiration of the term of the incumbents, in which event the duties of said office shall be discharged by the County Attorneys.

Text as Ratified on: August 3, 1891, and revised September 28, 1891.

History: Not yet amended.

The Judicial Department

Section 109 The judicial power—Unified system—Impeachment.

The judicial power of the Commonwealth shall be vested exclusively in one Court of Justice which shall be divided into a Supreme Court, a Court of Appeals, a trial court of general jurisdiction known as the Circuit Court and a trial court of limited jurisdiction known as the District Court. The court shall constitute a unified judicial system for operation and administration. The impeachment powers of the General Assembly shall remain inviolate.

Text as Ratified on: November 4, 1975, effective January 1, 1976.

History: Repeal and reenactment proposed by 1974 Ky. Acts ch. 84, §1; original version ratified August 3, 1891, and revised September 28, 1891.

Federal Reference: U.S. Const. art. III, §1.

The Supreme Court

Section 110 Composition—Jurisdiction—Quorum—Special justices—Districts—Chief Justice.

(1) The Supreme Court shall consist of the Chief Justice of the Commonwealth and six associate Justices.

(2) (a) The Supreme Court shall have appellate jurisdiction only, except it shall have the power to issue all writs necessary in aid of its appellate jurisdiction, or the complete determination of any cause, or as may be required to exercise control of the Court of Justice.

(b) Appeals from a judgment of the Circuit Court imposing a sentence of death or life imprisonment or imprisonment for twenty years or more shall be taken directly to the Supreme Court. In all other cases, criminal and civil, the Supreme Court shall exercise appellate jurisdiction as provided by its rules.

(3) A majority of the Justices of the Supreme Court shall constitute a quorum for the transaction of business. If as many as two Justices decline or are unable to sit in the trial of any cause, the Chief Justice shall certify that fact to the Governor, who shall appoint to try the particular cause a sufficient number of Justices to constitute a full court for the trial of the cause.

(4) The Court of Appeals districts existing on the effective date of this amendment to the Constitution shall constitute the initial Supreme Court districts. The General Assembly thereafter may redistrict the Commonwealth, by counties, into seven Supreme Court districts as nearly equal in population and as compact in form as possible. There shall be one Justice from each Supreme Court district.

(5) (a) The Justices of the Supreme Court shall elect one of their number to serve as Chief Justice for a term of four years.

(b) The Chief Justice of the Commonwealth shall be the executive head of the Court of Justice and he shall appoint such administrative assistants as he deems necessary. He shall assign temporarily any justice or judge of the Commonwealth, active or retired, to sit in any court other than the Supreme Court when he deems such assignment necessary for the prompt disposition of causes. The Chief Justice shall submit the budget for the Court of Justice and perform all other necessary administrative functions relating to the court.

Text as Ratified on: November 4, 1975, effective January 1, 1976.

History: Repeal and reenactment proposed by 1974 Ky. Acts ch. 84, §1; original version ratified August 3, 1891, and revised September 28, 1891.

Federal Reference: U.S. Const. art. III, §§1, 2.

The Court of Appeals

Section 111 Composition—Jurisdiction—Administration—Panels.

(1) The Court of Appeals shall consist initially of fourteen judges, an equal number to be selected from each Supreme Court district. The number of judges thereafter shall be

determined from time to time by the General Assembly upon certification of necessity by the Supreme Court.

(2) The Court of Appeals shall have appellate jurisdiction only, except that it may be authorized by rules of the Supreme Court to review directly decisions of administrative agencies of the Commonwealth, and it may issue all writs necessary in aid of its appellate jurisdiction, or the complete determination of any cause within its appellate jurisdiction. In all other cases, it shall exercise appellate jurisdiction as provided by law.

(3) The judges of the Court of Appeals shall elect one of their number to serve as Chief Judge for a term of four years. The Chief Judge shall exercise such authority and perform such duties in the administration of the Court of Appeals as are prescribed in this section or as may be prescribed by the Supreme Court.

(4) The Court of Appeals shall divide itself into panels of not less than three judges. A panel may decide a cause by the concurring vote of a majority of its judges. The Chief Judge shall make assignments of judges to panels. The Court of Appeals shall prescribe the times and places in the Commonwealth at which each panel shall sit.

Text as Ratified on: November 4, 1975, effective January 1, 1976.

History: Repeal and reenactment proposed by 1974 Ky. Acts ch. 84, §1; original version ratified August 3, 1891, and revised September 28, 1891.

Federal Reference: U.S. Const. art. III, §§1, 2.

The Circuit Court

Section 112 Location—Circuits—Composition—Administration—Jurisdiction.

(1) Circuit Court shall be held in each county.

(2) The Circuit Court districts existing on the effective date of this amendment to the Constitution shall continue under the name "Judicial Circuits," the General Assembly having power upon certification of the necessity therefor by the Supreme Court to reduce, increase or rearrange the judicial districts. A judicial circuit composed of more than one county shall be as compact in form as possible and of contiguous counties. No county shall be divided in creating a judicial circuit.

(3) The number of circuit judges in each district existing on the effective date of this amendment shall continue, the General Assembly having power upon certification of the necessity therefor by the Supreme Court, to change the number of circuit judges in any judicial circuit.

(4) In a judicial circuit having only one judge, he shall be the chief judge. In judicial circuits having two or more judges, they shall select biennially a chief judge, and if they fail to do so within a reasonable time, the Supreme Court shall designate the chief judge. The chief judge shall exercise such authority and perform such duties in the administration of his judicial circuit as may be prescribed by the Supreme Court. The Supreme Court may provide by rules for administration of judicial circuits by regions designated by it.

(5) The Circuit Court shall have original jurisdiction of all justiciable causes not vested in some other court. It shall have such appellate jurisdiction as may be provided by law.

(6) The Supreme Court may designate one or more divisions of Circuit Court within a judicial circuit as a family court division. A Circuit Court division so designated shall retain the general jurisdiction of the Circuit Court and shall have additional jurisdiction as may be provided by the General Assembly.

Text as Ratified on: November 5, 2002

History: 2002 amendment was proposed by 2001 Ky. Acts ch. 163, §1; 1974 repeal and reenactment was proposed by 1974 Ky. Acts ch. 84, § 1, and ratified November 4, 1975, effective January 1, 1976; original version ratified August 3, 1891, and revised September 28, 1891.

Federal Reference: U.S. Const. art. III, §§1, 2.

The District Court

Section 113 Location—Districts—Composition—Administration—Trial commissioners—Jurisdiction.

(1) District Court shall be held in each county.

(2) The Circuit Court districts existing on the effective date of this amendment shall continue for District Court purposes under the name "Judicial Districts," the General Assembly having power upon certification of the necessity therefor by the Supreme Court to reduce, increase or rearrange the districts. A judicial district composed of more than one county shall be as compact in form as possible and of contiguous counties. No county shall be divided in creating a judicial district.

(3) Each judicial district created by this amendment initially shall have at least one district judge who shall serve as chief judge and there shall be such other district judges as the General Assembly shall determine. The number of district judges in each judicial district thereafter shall be determined by the General Assembly upon certification of necessity therefor by the Supreme Court.

(4) In a judicial district having only one judge he shall be the chief judge. In those districts having two or more judges they shall select biennially a chief judge and if they fail to do so within a reasonable time, the Supreme Court shall designate the chief judge. The chief judge shall exercise such authority and perform such duties in the administration of his district as may be prescribed by the Supreme Court.

(5) In any county in which no district judge resides the chief judge of the district shall appoint a trial commissioner who shall be a resident of such county and who shall be an attorney if one is qualified and available. Other trial commissioners with like qualifications may be appointed by the chief judge in any judicial district upon certification of the necessity therefor by the Supreme Court. All trial commissioners shall have power to perform such duties of the district court as may be prescribed by the Supreme Court.

(6) The district court shall be a court of limited jurisdiction and shall exercise original jurisdiction as may be provided by the General Assembly.

Text as Ratified on: November 4, 1975, effective January 1, 1976.

History: Repeal and reenactment proposed by 1974 Ky. Acts ch. 84, §1; original version ratified August 3, 1891, and revised September 28, 1891.

Federal Reference: U.S. Const. art. III, §§1, 2.

Clerks of Courts

Section 114 Selection—Removal.

(1) The Supreme Court shall appoint a clerk to serve as it shall determine.

(2) The Court of Appeals shall appoint a clerk to serve as it shall determine.

(3) The clerks of the Circuit Court shall be elected in the manner provided elsewhere in this Constitution. The clerks of the Circuit Court shall serve as the clerks of the District Court. The clerks of the Circuit Court shall be removable from office by the Supreme Court upon good cause shown.

Text as Ratified on: November 4, 1975, effective January 1, 1976.

History: Repeal and reenactment proposed by 1974 Ky. Acts ch. 84, §1; original version ratified August 3, 1891, and revised September 28, 1891.

Appellate Policy—Rule-Making Power

Section 115 Right of appeal—Procedure.

In all cases, civil and criminal, there shall be allowed as a matter of right at least one appeal to another court, except that the Commonwealth may not appeal from a judgment of acquittal in a criminal case, other than for the purpose of securing a certification of law, and the General Assembly may prescribe that there shall be no appeal from that portion of a judgment dissolving a marriage. Procedural rules shall provide for expeditious and inexpensive appeals. Appeals shall be upon the record and not by trial de novo.

Text as Ratified on: November 4, 1975, effective January 1, 1976.

History: Repeal and reenactment proposed by 1974 Ky. Acts ch. 84, §1; original version ratified August 3, 1891, and revised September 28, 1891.

Section 116 Rules governing jurisdiction, personnel, procedure, bar membership.

The Supreme Court shall have the power to prescribe rules governing its appellate jurisdiction, rules for the appointment of commissioners and other court personnel, and rules of practice and procedure for the Court of Justice. The Supreme Court shall, by rule, govern admission to the bar and the discipline of members of the bar.

Text as Ratified on: November 4, 1975, effective January 1, 1976.

History: Repeal and reenactment proposed by 1974 Ky. Acts ch. 84, §1; original version ratified August 3, 1891, and revised September 28, 1891.

Federal Reference: U.S. Const. art. III, §2.

Offices of Justices and Judges

Section 117 Election.

Justices of the Supreme Court and judges of the Court of Appeals, Circuit and District Court shall be elected from their respective districts or circuits on a nonpartisan basis as provided by law.

Text as Ratified on: November 4, 1975, effective January 1, 1976.

History: Repeal and reenactment proposed by 1974 Ky. Acts ch. 84, §1; original version ratified August 3, 1891, and revised September 28, 1891.

Federal Reference: U.S. Const. art. II, §2.

Section 118 Vacancies.

(1) A vacancy in the office of a justice of the Supreme Court, or of a judge of the Court of Appeals, circuit or district court which under Section 152 of this Constitution is to be filled by appointment by the Governor shall be filled by the Governor from a list of three names presented to him by the appropriate judicial nominating commission. If the Governor fails to make an appointment from the list within sixty days from the date it is presented to him, the appointment shall be made from the same list by the chief justice of the Supreme Court.

(2) There shall be one judicial nominating commission for the Supreme Court and the Court of Appeals, one for each judicial circuit, and one for each judicial district, except that a circuit and district having the same boundary shall have but one judicial nominating commission. Each commission shall consist of seven members, one of whom shall be the chief justice of the Supreme Court, who shall be chairman. Two members of each commission shall be members of the bar, who shall be elected by their fellow members. The other four members shall be appointed by the Governor from among persons not members of the bar, and these four shall include at least two members of each of the two political parties of the Commonwealth having the largest number of voters. Members of a judicial circuit or judicial district nominating commission must be residents of the circuit or district, respectively, and the lawyer members of the commission shall be elected by the members of the bar residing in the circuit or district, respectively. The terms of office of members of judicial nominating commissions shall be fixed by the General Assembly. No person shall be elected or appointed a member of a judicial nominating commission who holds any other public office or any office in a political party or organization.

Text as Ratified on: November 4, 1975, effective January 1, 1976.

History: Repeal and reenactment proposed by 1974 Ky. Acts ch. 84, §1; original version ratified August 3, 1891, and revised September 28, 1891.

Federal Reference: U.S. Const. art. II, §2.

Section 119 Terms of office.

Justices of the Supreme Court and judges of the Court of Appeals and circuit court shall severally hold their offices for terms of eight years, and judges of the district court for terms of four years. All terms commence on the first Monday in January next succeeding the regular election for the office. No justice or judge may be deprived of his term of office by redistricting, or by a reduction in the number of justices or judges.

Text as Ratified on: November 4, 1975, effective January 1, 1976.

History: Repeal and reenactment proposed by 1974 Ky. Acts ch. 84, §1; original version ratified August 3, 1891, and revised September 28, 1891.

Federal Reference: U.S. Const. art. III, §1.

Section 120 Compensation—Expenses.

All justices and judges shall be paid adequate compensation which shall be fixed by the General Assembly. All compensation and necessary expenses of the Court of Justice shall be paid out of the State Treasury. The compensation of a justice or judge shall not be reduced during his term.

Text as Ratified on: November 4, 1975, effective January 1, 1976.

History: Repeal and reenactment proposed by 1974 Ky. Acts ch. 84, §1; original version ratified August 3, 1891, and revised September 28, 1891.

Federal Reference: U.S. Const. art. III, §1.

Section 121 Retirement and removal.

Subject to rules of procedure to be established by the Supreme Court, and after notice and hearing, any justice of the Supreme Court or judge of the Court of Appeals, Circuit Court or District Court may be retired for disability or suspended without pay or removed for good cause by a commission composed of one judge of the Court of Appeals, selected by that court, one circuit judge and one district judge selected by a majority vote of the circuit judges and district judges, respectively, one member of the bar appointed by its governing body, and two persons, not members of the bench or bar, appointed by the Governor. The commission shall be a state body whose members shall hold office for four-year terms. Its actions shall be subject to judicial review by the Supreme Court.

Text as Ratified on: November 4, 1975, effective January 1, 1976.

History: Repeal and reenactment proposed by 1974 Ky. Acts ch. 84, §1; original version ratified August 3, 1891, and revised September 28, 1891.

Federal Reference: U.S. Const. art. III, §1.

Section 122 Eligibility.

To be eligible to serve as a justice of the Supreme Court or a judge of the Court of Appeals, Circuit Court or District Court a person must be a citizen of the United

States, licensed to practice law in the courts of this Commonwealth, and have been a resident of this Commonwealth and of the district from which he is elected for two years next preceding his taking office. In addition, to be eligible to serve as a justice of the Supreme Court or judge of the Court of Appeals or Circuit Court a person must have been a licensed attorney for at least eight years. No district judge shall serve who has not been a licensed attorney for at least two years.

Text as Ratified on: November 4, 1975, effective January 1, 1976.

History: Repeal and reenactment proposed by 1974 Ky. Acts ch. 84, § 1; original version ratified August 3, 1891, and revised September 28, 1891.

Section 123 Prohibited activities.

During his term of office, no justice of the Supreme Court or judge of the Court of Appeals, Circuit Court or District Court shall engage in the practice of law, or run for elective office other than judicial office, or hold any office in a political party or organization.

Text as Ratified on: November 4, 1975, effective January 1, 1976.

History: Repeal and reenactment proposed by 1974 Ky. Acts ch. 84, § 1; original version ratified August 3, 1891, and revised September 28, 1891.

Section 124 Conflicting provisions.

Any remaining sections of the Constitution of Kentucky as it existed prior to the effective date of this amendment which are in conflict with the provisions of amended Sections 110 through 125 are repealed to the extent of the conflict, but such amended sections are not intended to repeal those parts of Sections 140 and 142 conferring nonjudicial powers and duties upon county judges and justices of the peace. Nothing in such amended sections shall be construed to limit the powers otherwise granted by this Constitution to the county judge as the chief executive, administrative and fiscal officer of the county, or to limit the powers otherwise granted by the Constitution to the justices of the peace or county commissioners as executive, administrative and fiscal officers of a county, or of the fiscal court as a governing body of a county.

Text as Ratified on: November 4, 1975, effective January 1, 1976.

History: Repeal and reenactment proposed by 1974 Ky. Acts ch. 84, § 1; original version ratified August 3, 1891, and revised September 28, 1891.

Section 125 (Repealed 1975)

Catchline read at time of repeal: "Circuit Court for each county."

Repeal Ratified on: November 4, 1975, effective January 1, 1976.

History: Repeal was proposed by 1974 Ky. Acts ch. 84, § 1; original version ratified August 3, 1891, and revised September 28, 1891.

Section 126 (Repealed 1975)

Catchline read at time of repeal: "Jurisdiction of Circuit Courts."

Repeal Ratified on: November 4, 1975, effective January 1, 1976.

History: Repeal was proposed by 1974 Ky. Acts ch. 84, § 1; original version ratified August 3, 1891, and revised September 28, 1891.

Section 127 (Repealed 1975)

Catchline read at time of repeal: "Appeal from Circuit Court."

Repeal Ratified on: November 4, 1975, effective January 1, 1976.

History: Repeal was proposed by 1974 Ky. Acts ch. 84, § 1; original version ratified August 3, 1891, and revised September 28, 1891.

Section 128 (Repealed 1975)

Catchline read at time of repeal: "Circuit Court districts."

Repeal Ratified on: November 4, 1975, effective January 1, 1976.

History: Repeal was proposed by 1974 Ky. Acts ch. 84, § 1; original version ratified August 3, 1891, and revised September 28, 1891.

Section 129 (Repealed 1975)

Catchline read at time of repeal: "Election of Circuit Judges—Term—Commissions—Removal."

Repeal Ratified on: November 4, 1975, effective January 1, 1976.

History: Repeal was proposed by 1974 Ky. Acts ch. 84, § 1; original version ratified August 3, 1891, and revised September 28, 1891.

Section 130 (Repealed 1975)

Catchline read at time of repeal: "Qualifications of Circuit Judges."

Repeal Ratified on: November 4, 1975, effective January 1, 1976.

History: Repeal was proposed by 1974 Ky. Acts ch. 84, § 1; original version ratified August 3, 1891, and revised September 28, 1891.

Section 131 (Repealed 1975)

Catchline read at time of repeal: "Terms of Circuit Courts."

Repeal Ratified on: November 4, 1975, effective January 1, 1976.

History: Repeal was proposed by 1974 Ky. Acts ch. 84, § 1; original version ratified August 3, 1891, and revised September 28, 1891.

Section 132 (Repealed 1975)

Catchline read at time of repeal: "Additional Circuit Court districts—Population limits."

Repeal Ratified on: November 4, 1975, effective January 1, 1976.

History: Repeal was proposed by 1974 Ky. Acts ch. 84, § 1; original version ratified August 3, 1891, and revised September 28, 1891.

Section 133 (Repealed 1975)

Catchline read at time of repeal: "Compensation of Circuit Judges."

Repeal Ratified on: November 4, 1975, effective January 1, 1976.

History: Repeal was proposed by 1974 Ky. Acts ch. 84, §1; original version ratified August 3, 1891, and revised September 28, 1891.

Section 134 (Repealed 1975)

Catchline read at time of repeal: "When districts may be changed."

Repeal Ratified on: November 4, 1975, effective January 1, 1976.

History: Repeal was proposed by 1974 Ky. Acts ch. 84, §1; original version ratified August 3, 1891, and revised September 28, 1891.

Section 135 (Repealed 1975)

Catchline read at time of repeal: "Only Constitutional Courts permitted."

Repeal Ratified on: November 4, 1975, effective January 1, 1976.

History: Repeal was proposed by 1974 Ky. Acts ch. 84, §1; original version ratified August 3, 1891, and revised September 28, 1891.

Section 136 (Repealed 1975)

Catchline read at time of repeal: "Special Judges of Circuit Courts."

Repeal Ratified on: November 4, 1975, effective January 1, 1976.

History: Repeal was proposed by 1974 Ky. Acts ch. 84, §1; original version ratified August 3, 1891, and revised September 28, 1891.

Section 137 (Repealed 1975)

Catchline read at time of repeal: "Circuit Court in county having population of 150,000 or more—Separate district—Additional judges—Branches—General Term—Clerk—Criminal cases."

Repeal Ratified on: November 4, 1975, effective January 1, 1976.

History: Repeal was proposed by 1974 Ky. Acts ch. 84, §1; original version ratified August 3, 1891, and revised September 28, 1891.

Section 138 (Repealed 1975)

Catchline read at time of repeal: "Certain counties may constitute separate district—Additional judges—Practice."

Repeal Ratified on: November 4, 1975, effective January 1, 1976.

History: Repeal was proposed by 1974 Ky. Acts ch. 84, §1; original version ratified August 3, 1891, and revised September 28, 1891.

Section 139 (Repealed 1975)

Catchline read at time of repeal: "Quarterly Court for each county—Jurisdiction—County Judge to preside."

Repeal Ratified on: November 4, 1975, effective January 1, 1976.

History: Repeal was proposed by 1974 Ky. Acts ch. 84, §1; original version ratified August 3, 1891, and revised September 28, 1891.

County Courts

Section 140 County Court for each county—Judge—Compensation—Commission—Removal.

There shall be established in each county now existing, or which may be hereafter created, in this State, a Court, to be styled the County Court, to consist of a Judge, who shall be a conservator of the peace, and shall receive such compensation for his services as may be prescribed by law. He shall be commissioned by the Governor, and shall vacate his office by removal from the county in which he may have been elected.

Text as Ratified on: August 3, 1891, and revised September 28, 1891.

History: Not yet amended.

Section 141 (Repealed 1975)

Catchline read at time of repeal: "Jurisdiction of County Courts."

Repeal Ratified on: November 4, 1975, effective January 1, 1976.

History: Repeal was proposed by 1974 Ky. Acts ch. 84, §1; original version ratified August 3, 1891, and revised September 28, 1891.

Justices of the Peace

Section 142 Justices' districts—One Justice for each district—Jurisdiction and powers of Justices—Commissions—Removal.

Each county now existing, or which may hereafter be created, in this State, shall be laid off into districts in such manner as the General Assembly may direct; but no county shall have less than three nor more than eight districts, in each of which districts one Justice of the Peace shall be elected as provided in Section 99. The General Assembly shall make provisions for regulating the number of said districts from time to time within the limits herein prescribed, and for fixing the boundaries thereof. The jurisdiction of Justices of the Peace shall be coextensive with the county, and shall be equal and uniform throughout the State. Justices of the Peace shall be conservators of the peace. They shall be commissioned by the Governor, and shall vacate their offices by removal from the districts, respectively, in which they may have been elected.

Text as Ratified on: August 3, 1891, and revised September 28, 1891.

History: Not yet amended.

Section 143 (Repealed 1975)

Catchline read at time of repeal: "Police Court may be established in each city—Jurisdiction."

Repeal Ratified on: November 4, 1975, effective January 1, 1976.

History: Repeal was proposed by 1974 Ky. Acts ch. 84, §1; original version ratified August 3, 1891, and revised September 28, 1891.

Fiscal Courts

Section 144 Fiscal Court for each county—To consist of Justices of the Peace or Commissioners, and County Judge—Quorum.

Counties shall have a Fiscal Court, which may consist of the Judge of the County Court and the Justices of the Peace, in which Court the Judge of the County Court shall preside, if present; or a county may have three Commissioners, to be elected from the county at large, who, together with the Judge of the County Court, shall constitute the Fiscal Court. A majority of the members of said Court shall constitute a Court for the transaction of business. But where, for county governmental purposes, a city is by law separated from the remainder of the county, such Commissioners may be elected from the part of the county outside of such city.

Text as Ratified on: August 3, 1891, and revised September 28, 1891.

History: Not yet amended.

Suffrage and Elections

Section 145 Persons entitled to vote.

Every citizen of the United States of the age of eighteen years who has resided in the state one year, and in the county six months, and the precinct in which he offers to vote sixty days next preceding the election, shall be a voter in said precinct and not elsewhere but the following persons are excepted and shall not have the right to vote.

(1) Persons convicted in any court of competent jurisdiction of treason, or felony, or bribery in an election, or of such high misdemeanor as the General Assembly may declare shall operate as an exclusion from the right of suffrage, but persons hereby excluded may be restored to their civil rights by executive pardon.

(2) Persons who, at the time of the election, are in confinement under the judgment of a court for some penal offense.

(3) Idiots and insane persons.

Text as Ratified on: November 8, 1955.

History: 1955 amendment was proposed by 1954 Ky. Acts ch. 2, §1; original version ratified August 3, 1891, and revised September 28, 1891.

Federal Reference: U.S. Const. art. I, §2; amends. XIV, §2; XV; XVII; XIX; XXIV; XXVI.

Section 146 Soldiers or sailors stationed in State are not residents.

No person in the military, naval or marine service of the United States shall be deemed a resident of this State by reason of being stationed within the same.

Text as Ratified on: August 3, 1891, and revised September 28, 1891.

History: Not yet amended.

Section 147 Registration of voters—Manner of voting—Absent voting—Voting machines—"Election" defined—Election laws—Illiterate and disabled voters.

The General Assembly shall provide by law for the registration of all persons entitled to vote in cities and towns having a population of five thousand or more; and may provide by general law for the registration of other voters in the state. Where registration is required, only persons registered shall have the right to vote. The mode of registration shall be prescribed by the General Assembly. In all elections by persons in a representative capacity, the voting shall be viva voce and made a matter of record; but all elections by the people shall be by secret official ballot, furnished by public authority to the voters at the polls, and marked by each voter in private at the polls, and then and there deposited, or any person absent from the county of his legal residence, or from the state, may be permitted to vote in a manner provided by law. Counties so desiring may use voting machines, these machines to be installed at the expense of such counties. The word "elections" in this section includes the decision of questions submitted to the voters, as well as the choice of officers by them. The General Assembly shall pass all necessary laws to enforce this section, and shall provide that persons illiterate, blind, or in any way disabled may have their ballots marked or voted as herein required.

Text as Ratified on: November 6, 1945.

History: 1945 amendment was proposed by 1944 Ky. Acts ch. 5, §1; 1941 amendment was proposed by 1940 Ky. Acts ch. 74, §1, and ratified on November 4, 1941; original version ratified August 3, 1891, and revised September 28, 1891.

Section 148 Number of elections—Day and hours of election—Qualifications of officers—Employees to be given time to vote.

Not more than one election each year shall be held in this State or in any city, town, district, urban-county or county thereof, except as otherwise provided in this Constitution. All regular elections of State, county, city, town, urban-county, or district officers shall be held on the first Tuesday after the first Monday in November. All elections by the people shall be between the hours of six o'clock a.m. and seven o'clock p.m., but the General Assembly may change said hours, and all officers of any election shall be residents and voters in the precinct in which they act. The General Assembly shall provide by law that all employers shall allow employees, under reasonable regulations, at least four hours on election days, in which to cast their votes.

Text as Ratified on: November 3, 1992.

History: 1992 amendment was proposed by 1992 Ky. Acts ch. 168, §16; original version ratified August 3, 1891, and revised September 28, 1891.

Section 149 Privilege from arrest during voting.

Voters, in all cases except treason, felony, breach of surety of the peace, or violation of the election laws, shall be privileged from arrest during their attendance at elections, and while they are going to and returning therefrom.

Text as Ratified on: August 3, 1891, and revised September 28, 1891.

History: Not yet amended.

Section 150 Disqualification from office for using money or property to secure or influence election—Corporation not to use money or other thing of value to influence election—Exclusion from office for conviction of felony or high misdemeanor—Laws to regulate elections.

Every person shall be disqualified from holding any office of trust or profit for the term for which he shall have been elected who shall be convicted of having given, or consented to the giving, offer or promise of any money or other thing of value, to procure his election, or to influence the vote of any voter at such election; and if any corporation shall, directly or indirectly, offer, promise or give, or shall authorize, directly or indirectly, any person to offer, promise or give any money or any thing of value to influence the result of any election in this State, or the vote of any voter authorized to vote therein, or who shall afterward reimburse or compensate, in any manner whatever, any person who shall have offered, promised or given any money or other thing of value to influence the result of any election or the vote of any such voter, such corporation, if organized under the laws of this Commonwealth, shall, on conviction thereof, forfeit its charter and all rights, privileges and immunities thereunder; and if chartered by another State and doing business in this State, whether by license, or upon mere sufferance, such corporation, upon conviction of either of the offenses aforesaid, shall forfeit all right to carry on any business in this State; and it shall be the duty of the General Assembly to provide for the enforcement of the provisions of this section. All persons shall be excluded from office who have been, or shall hereafter be, convicted of a felony, or of such high misdemeanor as may be prescribed by law, but such disability may be removed by pardon of the Governor. The privilege of free suffrage shall be supported by laws regulating elections, and prohibiting, under adequate penalties, all undue influence thereon, from power, bribery, tumult or other improper practices.

Text as Ratified on: August 3, 1891, and revised September 28, 1891.

History: Not yet amended.

Section 151 Person guilty of fraud, intimidation, bribery, or corrupt practice to be deprived of office by suitable statutory means.

The General Assembly shall provide suitable means for depriving of office any person who, to procure his nomination or election, has, in his canvass or election, been guilty of any unlawful use of money, or other thing of value, or has been guilty of fraud, intimidation, bribery, or any other corrupt practice, and he shall be held responsible for acts done by others with his authority, or ratified by him.

Text as Ratified on: August 3, 1891, and revised September 28, 1891.

History: Not yet amended.

Section 152 Vacancies—When filled by appointment, when by election—Who to fill.

Except as otherwise provided in this Constitution, vacancies in all elective offices shall be filled by election or appointment, as follows: If the unexpired term will end at the next succeeding annual election at which either city, town, county, district or State officers are to be elected, the office shall be filled by appointment for the remainder of the term. If the unexpired term will not end at the next succeeding annual election at which either city, town, county, district or State officers are to be elected, and if three months intervene before said succeeding annual election at which either city, town, county, district or State officers are to be elected, the office shall be filled by appointment until said election, and then said vacancy shall be filled by election for the remainder of the term. If three months do not intervene between the happening of said vacancy and the next succeeding election at which city, town, county, district or State officers are to be elected, the office shall be filled by appointment until the second succeeding annual election at which city, town, county, district or State officers are to be elected; and then, if any part of the term remains unexpired, the office shall be filled by election until the regular time for the election of officers to fill said offices. Vacancies in all offices for the State at large, or for districts larger than a county, shall be filled by appointment of the Governor; all other appointments shall be made as may be prescribed by law. No person shall ever be appointed a member of the General Assembly, but vacancies therein may be filled at a special election, in such manner as may be provided by law.

Text as Ratified on: August 3, 1891, and revised September 28, 1891.

History: Not yet amended.

Federal Reference: U.S. Const. art. II, §2.

Section 153 Power of General Assembly as to elections.

Except as otherwise herein expressly provided, the General Assembly shall have power to provide by general law for the manner of voting, for ascertaining the result of elections and making due returns thereof, for issuing certificates or commissions to all persons entitled thereto, and for the trial of contested elections.

Text as Ratified on: August 3, 1891, and revised September 28, 1891.

History: Not yet amended.

Section 154 Laws as to sale or gift of liquor on election days.

The General Assembly shall prescribe such laws as may be necessary for the restriction or prohibition of the sale or gift of spiritous, vinous or malt liquors on election days.

Text as Ratified on: August 3, 1891, and revised September 28, 1891.

History: Not yet amended.

Section 155 School elections not governed by Constitution.

The provisions of Sections 145 to 154, inclusive, shall not apply to the election of school trustees and other common school district elections. Said elections shall be regulated by the General Assembly, except as otherwise provided in this Constitution.

Text as Ratified on: August 3, 1891, and revised September 28, 1891.
History: Not yet amended.

Municipalities

Section 156 (Repealed 1994)

Catchline at time of repeal: "Cities divided into six classes—General laws to be made for each class—Population limits for classes—Assignment to classes—Organization of cities."

Repeal Ratified on: November 8, 1994.

History: Repeal was proposed by 1994 Ky. Acts ch. 168, §§1, 6; original version ratified August 3, 1891, and revised September 28, 1891.

Section 156a General Assembly authorized to provide for creation, governmental structure, and classification of cities.

The General Assembly may provide for the creation, alteration of boundaries, consolidation, merger, dissolution, government, functions, and officers of cities. The General Assembly shall create such classifications of cities as it deems necessary based on population, tax base, form of government, geography, or any other reasonable basis and enact legislation relating to the classifications. All legislation relating to cities of a certain classification shall apply equally to all cities within the same classification. The classification of all cities and the law pertaining to the classifications in effect at the time of adoption of this section shall remain in effect until otherwise provided by law.

Text as Ratified on: November 8, 1994

History: Creation proposed by 1994 Ky. Acts ch. 168, §1.

Section 156b General Assembly authorized to permit municipal home rule for cities.

The General Assembly may provide by general law that cities may exercise any power and perform any function within their boundaries that is in furtherance of a public purpose of a city and not in conflict with a constitutional provision or statute.

Text as Ratified on: November 8, 1994
History: Creation proposed by 1994 Ky. Acts ch. 168, §1.

Section 157 Maximum tax rate for cities, counties, and taxing districts.

The tax rate of cities, counties, and taxing districts, for other than school purposes, shall not, at any time, exceed the following rates upon the value of the taxable property therein: For all cities having a population of fifteen thousand or more, one dollar and fifty cents on the hundred dollars; for all cities having less than fifteen thousand and not less than ten thousand, one dollar on the hundred dollars; for all cities having less than ten thousand, seventy-five cents on the hundred dollars; and for counties and taxing districts, fifty cents on the hundred dollars.

Text as Ratified on: November 8, 1994.

History: 1994 amendment was proposed by 1994 Ky. Acts ch. 168, §2; original version ratified August 3, 1891, and revised September 28, 1891.

Section 157a Credit of Commonwealth may be loaned or given to county for roads—County may vote to incur indebtedness and levy additional tax for roads.

The credit of the Commonwealth may be given, pledged or loaned to any county of the Commonwealth for public road purposes, and any county may be permitted to incur an indebtedness in any amount fixed by the county, not in excess of five per centum of the value of the taxable property therein, for public road purposes in said county, provided said additional indebtedness is submitted to the voters of the county for their ratification or rejection at a special election held for said purpose, in such manner as may be provided by law and when any such indebtedness is incurred by any county said county may levy, in addition to the tax rate allowed under Section 157 of the Constitution of Kentucky, an amount not exceeding twenty cents on the one hundred dollars of the assessed valuation of said county for the purpose of paying the interest on said indebtedness and providing a sinking fund for the payment of said indebtedness.

Text as Ratified on: November 2, 1909.

History: Creation proposed by 1908 Ky. Acts ch. 36, §1.

Section 157b Adoption of budget required for cities, counties, and taxing districts—Expenditures not to exceed revenues for fiscal year.

Prior to each fiscal year, the legislative body of each city, county, and taxing district shall adopt a budget showing total expected revenues and expenditures for the fiscal year. No city, county, or taxing district shall expend any funds in any fiscal year in excess of the revenues for that fiscal year. A city, county, or taxing district may amend its budget for a fiscal year, but the revised expenditures may not exceed the revised revenues. As used in this section, "revenues" shall mean all income from every source, including unencumbered reserves carried over from the previous fiscal year, and "expenditures" shall mean all funds to be paid out for expenses of the city, county, or taxing district during the fiscal year, including amounts necessary to pay the principal and interest due during the fiscal year on any debt.

Text as Ratified on: November 8, 1994.

History: Creation proposed by 1994 Ky. Acts ch. 168, §3.

Section 158 Maximum indebtedness of cities, counties, and taxing districts—General Assembly authorized to set additional limits and conditions.

Cities, towns, counties, and taxing districts shall not incur indebtedness to an amount exceeding the following maximum percentages on the value of the taxable property therein, to be estimated by the last assessment previous to the incurring of the indebtedness: Cities having a population of fifteen thousand or more, ten percent (10%); cities having a population of less than fifteen thousand but not less than three thousand, five percent (5%); cities having a population of less than three thousand, three percent (3%); and counties and taxing districts, two percent (2%), unless in case of emergency, the public health or safety should so require. Nothing shall prevent the issue of renewal bonds, or bonds to fund the floating indebtedness of any city, county, or taxing district. Subject to the limits and conditions set forth in this section and elsewhere in this Constitution, the General Assembly shall have the power to establish additional limits on indebtedness and conditions under which debt may be incurred by cities, counties, and taxing districts.

Text as Ratified on: November 8, 1994.

History: 1994 amendment was proposed by 1994 Ky. Acts ch. 168, §4; original version ratified August 3, 1891, and revised September 28, 1891.

Section 159 Tax to pay indebtedness in not more than forty years must be levied.

Whenever any city, town, county, taxing district or other municipality is authorized to contract an indebtedness, it shall be required, at the same time, to provide for the collection of an annual tax sufficient to pay the interest on said indebtedness, and to create a sinking fund for the payment of the principal thereof, within not more than forty years from the time of contracting the same.

Text as Ratified on: August 3, 1891, and revised September 28, 1891.

History: Not yet amended.

Section 160 Municipal officers—Election and term of office—Officers ineligible—Fiscal officers.

The Mayor or Chief Executive, Police Judges, members of legislative boards or councils of towns and cities shall be elected by the qualified voters thereof: Provided, The Mayor or Chief Executive and Police Judges of the towns of the fourth, fifth and sixth classes may be appointed or elected as provided by law. The terms of office of Mayors or Chief Executives and Police Judges shall be four years, and until their successors shall be qualified, and of members of legislative boards, two years. When any city of the first or second class is divided into wards or districts, members of legislative boards shall be elected at large by the qualified voters of said city, but so selected that an equal proportion thereof shall reside in each of the said wards or districts; but when in any city of the first, second or third class, there are two legislative boards, the less numerous shall be selected from and elected by the voters at large of said city; but other officers of towns or cities shall be elected by the qualified voters therein, or appointed by the local authorities thereof, as the General Assembly may, by a general law, provide; but when elected by the voters of a town or city, their terms of office shall be four years, and until their successors shall be qualified. No Mayor or Chief Executive of any city of the first or second class, after the expiration of three successive terms of office to which he has been elected under this Constitution shall be eligible for the succeeding term. No fiscal officer of any city of the first or second class, after the expiration of the term of office to which he has been elected under this Constitution, shall be eligible for the succeeding term. "Fiscal officer" shall not include an Auditor or Assessor, or any other officer whose chief duty is not the collection or holding of public moneys. The General Assembly shall prescribe the qualifications of all officers of towns and cities, the manner in and causes for which they may be removed from office, and how vacancies in such offices may be filled.

Text as Ratified on: November 6, 1986.

History: 1986 amendment was proposed by 1986 Ky. Acts ch. 140, § 1; original version ratified August 3, 1891, and revised September 28, 1891.

Section 161 Compensation of city, county, or municipal officer not to be changed after election or appointment or during term, nor term extended.

The compensation of any city, county, town or municipal officer shall not be changed after his election or appointment, or during his term of office; nor shall the term of any such officer be extended beyond the period for which he may have been elected or appointed.

Text as Ratified on: August 3, 1891, and revised September 28, 1891.

History: Not yet amended.

Section 162 Unauthorized contracts of cities, counties, and municipalities are void.

No county, city, town or other municipality shall ever be authorized or permitted to pay any claim created against it, under any agreement or contract made without express authority of law, and all such unauthorized agreements or contracts shall be null and void.

Text as Ratified on: August 3, 1891, and revised September 28, 1891.

History: Not yet amended.

Section 163 Public utilities must obtain franchise to use streets.

No street railway, gas, water, steam heating, telephone, or electric light company, within a city or town, shall be permitted or authorized to construct its tracks, lay its pipes or mains, or erect its poles, posts or other apparatus along, over, under or across the streets, alleys or public grounds of a city or town, without the consent of the proper legislative bodies or boards of such city or town being first obtained; but when charters have been heretofore granted conferring such rights, and work has in good faith been begun thereunder, the provisions of this section shall not apply.

Text as Ratified on: August 3, 1891, and revised September 28, 1891.

History: Not yet amended.

Section 164 Term of franchises limited—Advertisement and bids.

No county, city, town, taxing district or other municipality shall be authorized or permitted to grant any franchise or privilege, or make any contract in reference thereto, for a term exceeding twenty years. Before granting such franchise or privilege for a term of years, such municipality shall first, after due advertisement, receive bids therefor publicly, and award the same to the highest and best bidder; but it shall have the right to reject any or all bids. This section shall not apply to a trunk railway.

Text as Ratified on: August 3, 1891, and revised September 28, 1891.

History: Not yet amended.

Section 165 Incompatible offices and employments.

No person shall, at the same time, be a State officer or a deputy officer or member of the General Assembly, and an officer of any county, city, town, or other municipality, or an employee thereof; and no person shall, at the same time, fill two municipal offices, either in the same or different municipalities, except as may be otherwise provided in this Constitution; but a Notary Public, or an officer of the militia, shall not be ineligible to hold any other office mentioned in this section.

Text as Ratified on: August 3, 1891, and revised September 28, 1891.

History: Not yet amended.

Federal Reference: U.S. Const. art. I, §6.

Section 166 Expiration of city charters granted prior to Constitution.

All acts of incorporation of cities and towns heretofore granted, and all amendments thereto, except as provided in Section 167, shall continue in force under this Constitution, and all City and Police Courts established in any city or town shall remain, with their present powers and jurisdictions, until such time as the General Assembly shall provide by general laws for the government of towns and cities, and the officers and courts thereof; but not longer than four years from and after the first day of January, one thousand eight hundred and ninety-one, within which time the General Assembly shall provide by general laws for the government of towns and cities, and the officers and courts thereof, as provided in this Constitution.

Text as Ratified on: August 3, 1891, and revised September 28, 1891.

History: Not yet amended.

Section 167 Time of election of city, urban-county, and town officers.

All officers required to be elected in cities, urban-counties, and towns by this Constitution, or by general laws enacted in conformity to its provisions, shall be elected at the general elections in November in even-numbered years.

Text as Ratified on: November 3, 1992.

History: 1992 amendment was proposed by 1992 Ky. Acts ch. 168, §17; original version ratified August 3, 1891, and revised September 28, 1891.

Section 168 Ordinance not to fix less penalty than statute for same offense—Prosecution under one a bar.

No municipal ordinance shall fix a penalty for a violation thereof at less than that imposed by statute for the same offense. A conviction or acquittal under either shall constitute a bar to another prosecution for the same offense.

Text as Ratified on: August 3, 1891, and revised September 28, 1891.

History: Not yet amended.

Revenue and Taxation

Section 169 Fiscal year.

The fiscal year shall commence on the first day of July in each year, unless otherwise provided by law.

Text as Ratified on: August 3, 1891, and revised September 28, 1891.

History: Not yet amended.

Section 170 Property exempt from taxation—Cities may exempt factories for five years.

There shall be exempt from taxation public property used for public purposes; places of burial not held for private or corporate profit; real property owned and occupied by, and personal property both tangible and intangible owned by, institutions of religion; institutions of purely public charity, and institutions of education not used or employed for gain by any person or corporation, and the income of which is devoted solely to the cause of education, public libraries, their endowments, and the income of such property as is used exclusively for their maintenance; household goods of a person used in his home; crops grown in the year in which the assessment is made, and in the hands of the producer; and real property maintained as the permanent residence of the owner, who is sixty-five years of age or older, or is classified as totally disabled under a program authorized or administered by an agency of the United States government or by any retirement system either within or without the Commonwealth of Kentucky, provided the property owner received disability payments pursuant to such disability classification, has maintained such disability classification for the entirety of the particular taxation period, and has filed with the appropriate local assessor by December 31 of the taxation period, on forms provided therefor, a signed statement indicating continuing disability as provided herein made under penalty of perjury, up to the assessed valuation of sixty-five hundred dollars on said residence and contiguous real property, except for assessment for special benefits. The real property may be held by legal or equitable title, by the entireties, jointly, in common, as a condominium, or indirectly by the stock ownership or membership representing the owner's or member's proprietary interest in a corporation owning a fee or a leasehold initially in excess of ninety-eight years. The exemptions shall apply only to the value of the real property assessable to the owner or, in case of ownership through stock or membership in a corporation, the value of the proportion which his interest in the corporation bears to the assessed value of the property. The General Assembly may authorize any incorporated city or town to exempt manufacturing establishments from municipal taxation, for a period not exceeding five years, as an inducement to their location. Notwithstanding the provisions of Sections 3, 172, and 174 of this Constitution to the contrary, the General Assembly may provide by law an exemption for all or any portion of the property tax for any class of personal property.

Text as Ratified on: November 3, 1998.

History: 1998 amendment was proposed by 1998 Ky. Acts ch. 227, §1; 1990 amendment was proposed by 1990 Ky. Acts ch. 151, §1, and ratified on November 6, 1990; 1981 amendment was proposed by 1980 Ky. Acts ch. 113, §1, and ratified on November 3, 1981; 1975 amendment was proposed by 1974 Ky. Acts ch. 105, §1, and ratified on November 4, 1975; 1971 amendment was proposed by 1970 Ky. Acts ch. 186, §1, and ratified on November 2, 1971; 1955 amendment was proposed by 1954 Ky. Acts ch. 111, §1, and ratified on November 8, 1955; original version was ratified on August 3, 1891, and revised on September 28, 1891.

Section 171 State tax to be levied—Taxes to be levied and collected for public purposes only and by general laws, and to be uniform within classes—Classification of property for taxation—Bonds exempt—Referendum on act classifying property.

The General Assembly shall provide by law an annual tax, which, with other resources, shall be sufficient to defray the estimated expenses of the Commonwealth for each fiscal year. Taxes shall be levied and collected for public purposes only and shall be uniform upon all property of the same class subject to taxation within the territorial limits of the authority levying the tax; and all taxes shall be levied and collected by general laws.

The General Assembly shall have power to divide property into classes and to determine what class or classes of property shall be subject to local taxation. Bonds of the state and of counties, municipalities, taxing and school districts shall not be subject to taxation.

Any law passed or enacted by the General Assembly pursuant to the provisions of or under this amendment, or amended section of the Constitution, classifying property and providing a lower rate of taxation on personal property, tangible or intangible, than upon real estate shall be subject to the referendum power of the people, which is hereby declared to exist to apply only to this section, or amended section. The referendum may be demanded by the people against one or more items, sections, or parts of any act enacted pursuant to or under the power granted by this amendment, or amended section. The referendum petition shall be filed with the Secretary of State not more than four months after the final adjournment of the Legislative Assembly which passed the bill on which the referendum is demanded. The veto power of the Governor shall not extend to measures referred to the people under this section. All elections on measures referred to the people under this act shall be at the regular general election, except when the Legislative Assembly shall order a special election. Any measure referred to the people shall take effect and become a law when approved by the majority of the votes cast thereon, and not otherwise. The whole number of votes cast for the candidates for Governor at the regular election, last preceding the filing of any petition, shall be the basis upon which the legal voters necessary to sign such petition shall be counted. The power of the referendum shall be ordered by the Legislative Assembly at any time any acts or bills are enacted, pursuant to the power granted under this section or amended section, prior to the year of one thousand nine hundred and seventeen. After that time the power of the referendum may be ordered either by the petition signed by five percent of the legal voters or by the Legislative Assembly at the time said acts or bills are enacted. The General Assembly enacting the bill shall provide a way by which the act shall be submitted to the people. The filing of a referendum petition against one or more items, sections or parts of an act, shall not delay the remainder of that act from becoming operative.

Text as Ratified on: November 2, 1915.

History: 1915 amendment was proposed by 1914 Ky. Acts ch. 94, §1; original version ratified August 3, 1891, and revised September 28, 1891.

Section 172 Property to be assessed at fair cash value—Punishment of assessor for willful error.

All property, not exempted from taxation by this Constitution, shall be assessed for taxation at its fair cash value, estimated at the price it would bring at a fair voluntary sale; and any officer, or other person authorized to assess values for taxation, who shall commit any willful error in the performance of his duty, shall be deemed guilty of misfeasance, and upon conviction thereof shall forfeit his office, and be otherwise punished as may be provided by law.

Text as Ratified on: August 3, 1891, and revised September 28, 1891.

History: Not yet amended.

Section 172A Assessment for ad valorem tax purposes of agricultural and horticultural land.

Notwithstanding contrary provisions of Sections 171, 172, or 174 of this Constitution—

The General Assembly shall provide by general law for the assessment for ad valorem tax purposes of agricultural and horticultural land according to the land's value for agricultural or horticultural use. The General Assembly may provide that any change in land use from agricultural or horticultural to another use shall require the levy of an additional tax not to exceed the additional amount that would have been owing had the land been assessed under Section 172 of this Constitution for the current year and the two next preceding years.

The General Assembly may provide for reasonable differences in the rate of ad valorem taxation within different areas of the same taxing districts on that class of property which includes the surface of the land. Those differences shall relate directly to differences between nonrevenue-producing governmental services and benefits giving land urban character which are furnished in one or several areas in contrast to other areas of the taxing district.

Text as Ratified on: November 4, 1969.

History: Creation proposed by 1968 Ky. Acts. ch. 103, §1.

Section 172B Property assessment or reassessment moratoriums.

Notwithstanding contrary provisions of Sections 170, 171, 172, or 174 of this Constitution, the General Assembly may provide by general law that the governing bodies of county, municipal, and urban-county governments may declare property assessment or reassessment moratoriums for qualifying units of real property for the purpose of encouraging the repair, rehabilitation, or restoration of existing improvements thereon. Prior to the enactment of any property assessment or reassessment moratorium program, the General Assembly shall provide or direct the local governing authority to provide property qualification standards for participation in the program and a limitation on the duration of any assessment or reassessment moratorium. In no instance shall any such moratorium extend beyond five years for any particular unit of real property and improvements thereon.

Text as Ratified on: November 3, 1981.

History: Creation proposed by 1980 Ky. Acts ch. 113, §2.

Section 173 Officer receiving profit on public funds guilty of felony.

The receiving, directly or indirectly, by any officer of the Commonwealth, or of any county, city or town, or member or officer of the General Assembly, of any interest, profit or perquisites arising from the use or loan of public funds in his hands, or moneys to be raised through his agency for State, city, town, district, or county purposes shall be deemed a felony. Said offense shall be punished as may be prescribed by law, a part of which punishment shall be disqualification to hold office.

Text as Ratified on: August 3, 1891, and revised September 28, 1891.

History: Not yet amended.

Section 174 Property to be taxed according to value, whether corporate or individual—Income, license, and franchise taxes.

All property, whether owned by natural persons or corporations, shall be taxed in proportion to its value, unless exempted by this Constitution; and all corporate property shall pay the same rate of taxation paid by individual property. Nothing in this Constitution shall be construed to prevent the General Assembly from providing for taxation based on income, licenses or franchises.

Text as Ratified on: August 3, 1891, and revised September 28, 1891.

History: Not yet amended.

Federal Reference: U.S. Const. art. I, §§8, 9; amend. XVI.

Section 175 Power to tax property not to be surrendered.

The power to tax property shall not be surrendered or suspended by any contract or grant to which the Commonwealth shall be a party.

Text as Ratified on: August 3, 1891, and revised September 28, 1891.

History: Not yet amended.

Section 176 Commonwealth not to assume debt of county or city—Exception.

The Commonwealth shall not assume the debt of any county, municipal corporation or political subdivision of the State, unless such debt shall have been contracted to defend itself in time of war, to repel invasion or to suppress insurrection.

Text as Ratified on: August 3, 1891, and revised September 28, 1891.

History: Not yet amended.

Section 177 Commonwealth not to lend credit, nor become stockholder in corporation, nor build railroad or highway.

The credit of the Commonwealth shall not be given, pledged or loaned to any individual, company, corporation or association, municipality, or political subdivision of the State; nor shall the Commonwealth become an owner or stockholder in, nor make donation to, any company, association or corporation; nor shall the Commonwealth construct a railroad or other highway.

Text as Ratified on: August 3, 1891, and revised September 28, 1891.

History: Not yet amended.

Section 178 Law for borrowing money to specify purpose, for which alone money may be used.

All laws authorizing the borrowing of money by and on behalf of the Commonwealth, county or other political subdivision of the State, shall specify the purpose for which the money is to be used, and the money so borrowed shall be used for no other purpose.

Text as Ratified on: August 3, 1891, and revised September 28, 1891.

History: Not yet amended.

Section 179 Political subdivision not to become stockholder in corporation, or appropriate money or lend credit to any person, except for roads or State Capitol.

The General Assembly shall not authorize any county or subdivision thereof, city, town or incorporated district, to become a stockholder in any company, association or corporation, or to obtain or appropriate money for, or to loan its credit to, any corporation, association or individual, except for the purpose of constructing or maintaining bridges, turnpike roads, or gravel roads: Provided, If any municipal corporation shall offer to the Commonwealth any property or money for locating or building a Capitol, and the Commonwealth accepts such offer, the corporation may comply with the offer.

Text as Ratified on: August 3, 1891, and revised September 28, 1891.

History: Not yet amended.

Section 180 Act or ordinance levying any tax must specify purpose, for which alone money may be used.

Every act enacted by the General Assembly, and every ordinance and resolution passed by any county, city, town or municipal board or local legislative body, levying a tax, shall specify distinctly the purpose for which said tax is levied, and no tax levied and collected for one purpose shall ever be devoted to another purpose.

Text as Ratified on: November 5, 1996.

History: 1996 amendment was proposed by 1996 Ky. Acts ch. 98, §1; original version ratified August 3, 1891, and revised September 28, 1891.

Section 181 General Assembly may not levy tax for political subdivision, but may confer power—License and excise taxes—City taxes in lieu of ad valorem taxes.

The General Assembly shall not impose taxes for the purposes of any county, city, town or other municipal corporation, but may, by general laws, confer on the proper authorities thereof, respectively, the power to assess and collect such taxes. The General Assembly may, by general laws only, provide for the payment of license fees on franchises, stock used for breeding purposes, the various trades, occupations and professions, or a special or excise tax; and may, by general laws, delegate the power to counties, towns, cities and other municipal corporations, to impose and collect license fees on stock used for breeding purposes, on franchises, trades, occupations and professions. And the General Assembly may, by general laws only, authorize cities or towns of any class to provide for taxation for municipal purposes on personal property, tangible and intangible, based on income, licenses or franchises, in lieu of an ad valorem tax thereon: Provided, Cities of the first class shall not be authorized to omit the imposition of an ad valorem tax on such property of any steam railroad, street railway, ferry, bridge, gas, water, heating, telephone, telegraph, electric light or electric power company.

Text as Ratified on: November 3, 1903.

History: 1903 amendment was proposed by 1902 Ky. Acts ch. 50, §1; original version ratified August 3, 1891, and revised September 28, 1891.

Section 182 Railroad taxes—How assessed and collected.

Nothing in this Constitution shall be construed to prevent the General Assembly from providing by law how railroads and railroad property shall be assessed and how taxes thereon shall be collected. And until otherwise provided, the present law on said subject shall remain in force.

Text as Ratified on: August 3, 1891, and revised September 28, 1891.

History: Not yet amended.

Education

Section 183 General Assembly to provide for school system.

The General Assembly shall, by appropriate legislation, provide for an efficient system of common schools throughout the State.

Text as Ratified on: August 3, 1891, and revised September 28, 1891.

History: Not yet amended.

Section 184 Common school fund—What constitutes—Use—Vote on tax for education other than in common schools.

The bond of the Commonwealth issued in favor of the Board of Education for the sum of one million three hundred and twenty-seven thousand dollars shall constitute one bond of the Commonwealth in favor of the Board of Education, and this bond and the seventy-three thousand five hundred dollars of the stock in the Bank of Kentucky, held by the Board of Education, and its proceeds, shall be held inviolate for the purpose of sustaining the system of common schools. The interest and dividends of said fund, together with any sum which may be produced by taxation or otherwise for purposes of common school education, shall be appropriated to the common schools, and to no other purpose. No sum shall be raised or collected for education other than in common schools until the question of taxation is submitted to the legal voters, and the majority of the votes cast at said election shall be in favor of such taxation: Provided, The tax now imposed for educational purposes, and for the endowment and maintenance of the Agricultural and Mechanical College, shall remain until changed by law.

Text as Ratified on: August 3, 1891, and revised September 28, 1891.

History: Not yet amended.

Section 185 Interest on school fund—Investment.

The General Assembly shall make provision, by law, for the payment of the interest of said school fund, and may provide for the sale of the stock in the Bank of Kentucky; and in case of a sale of all or any part of said stock, the proceeds of sale shall be invested by the Sinking Fund Commissioners in other good interest-bearing stocks or bonds, which shall be subject to sale and reinvestment, from time to time, in like manner, and with the same restrictions, as provided with reference to the sale of the said stock in the Bank of Kentucky.

Text as Ratified on: August 3, 1891, and revised September 28, 1891.

History: Not yet amended.

Section 186 Distribution and use of school fund.

All funds accruing to the school fund shall be used for the maintenance of the public schools of the Commonwealth, and for no other purpose, and the General Assembly shall by general law prescribe the manner of the distribution of the public school fund among the school districts and its use for public school purposes.

Text as Ratified on: November 3, 1953.

History: 1953 amendment was proposed by 1952 Ky. Acts ch. 89, §1; 1949 amendment was proposed by 1948 Ky. Acts ch. 163, §1, and ratified on November 8, 1949; 1941 amendment was proposed by 1940 Ky. Acts ch. 64, §1, and ratified on November 4, 1941; original version ratified August 3, 1891, and revised September 28, 1891.

Section 187 Race or color not to affect distribution of school fund.

In distributing the school fund no distinction shall be made on account of race or color.

Text as Ratified on: November 5, 1996.

History: 1996 amendment was proposed by 1996 Ky. Acts ch. 98, §2; original version ratified August 3, 1891, and revised September 28, 1891.

Federal Reference: U.S. Const. amend. XIV.

Section 188 Refund of Federal direct tax part of school fund—Irredeemable bond.

So much of any moneys as may be received by the Commonwealth from the United States under the recent act of Congress refunding the direct tax shall become a part of the school fund, and be held as provided in Section 184; but the General Assembly may authorize the use, by the Commonwealth, of moneys so received or any part thereof, in which event a bond shall be executed to the Board of Education for the amount so used, which bond shall be held on the same terms and conditions, and subject to the provisions of Section 184, concerning the bond therein referred to.

Text as Ratified on: August 3, 1891, and revised September 28, 1891.

History: Not yet amended.

Section 189 School money not to be used for church, sectarian, or denominational school.

No portion of any fund or tax now existing, or that may hereafter be raised or levied for educational purposes, shall be appropriated to, or used by, or in aid of, any church, sectarian or denominational school.

Text as Ratified on: August 3, 1891, and revised September 28, 1891.

History: Not yet amended.

Federal Reference: U.S. Const. amend. I.

Corporations

Section 190 Regulation of corporations by General Assembly.

Except as otherwise provided by the Constitution of Kentucky, the General Assembly shall, by general laws only, provide for the formation, organization, and regulation of corporations. Except as otherwise provided by the Constitution of Kentucky, the General Assembly shall also, by general laws only, prescribe the powers, rights, duties, and liabilities of corporations and the powers, rights, duties, and liabilities of their officers and stockholders or members.

Text as Ratified on: November 5, 2002.

History: 2002 amendment was proposed by 2002 Ky. Acts ch. 341, §1; original version ratified August 3, 1891, and revised September 28, 1891.

Section 191 (Repealed 2002)

Catchline at time of repeal: "Unexercised charters granted prior to Constitution revoked."

Repeal Ratified on: November 5, 2002.

History: Repeal was proposed by 2002 Ky. Acts ch. 341, §2; original version ratified August 3, 1891, and revised September 28, 1891.

Section 192 (Repealed 2002)

Catchline at time of repeal: "Corporations restricted to charter authority—Holding of real estate limited."

Repeal Ratified on: November 5, 2002.

History: Repeal was proposed by 2002 Ky. Acts ch. 341, §2; original version ratified August 3, 1891, and revised September 28, 1891.

Section 193 (Repealed 2002)

Catchline at time of repeal: "Stock or bonds to be issued only for money or for property or labor at market value—Watered stock void."

Repeal Ratified on: November 5, 2002.

History: Repeal was proposed by 2002 Ky. Acts ch. 341, §2; original version ratified August 3, 1891, and revised September 28, 1891.

Section 194 (Repealed 2002)

Catchline at time of repeal: "Corporations to have place of business and process agent in State."

Repeal Ratified on: November 5, 2002.

History: Repeal was proposed by 2002 Ky. Acts ch. 341, §2; original version ratified August 3, 1891, and revised September 28, 1891.

Section 195 Corporation property subject to eminent domain; corporations not to infringe upon individuals.

The Commonwealth, in the exercise of the right of eminent domain, shall have and retain the same powers to take the property and franchises of incorporated companies for public use which it has and retains to take the property of individuals, and the exercise of the police powers of this Commonwealth shall never be abridged nor so construed as to permit corporations to conduct their business in such manner as to infringe upon the equal rights of individuals.

Text as Ratified on: August 3, 1891, and revised September 28, 1891.

History: Not yet amended.

Section 196 Regulation of common carriers—No relief from common-law liability.

Transportation of freight and passengers by railroad, steamboat or other common carrier, shall be so regulated, by general law, as to prevent unjust discrimination. No common carrier shall be permitted to contract for relief from its common law liability.

Text as Ratified on: August 3, 1891, and revised September 28, 1891.

History: Not yet amended.

Section 197 Free passes or reduced rates to officers forbidden.

No railroad, steamboat or other common carrier, under heavy penalty to be fixed by the General Assembly, shall give a free pass or passes, or shall, at reduced rates not common to the public, sell tickets for transportation to any State, district, city, town or county officer, or member of the General Assembly, or Judge; and any State, district, city, town or county officer, or member of the General Assembly, or Judge, who shall accept or use a free pass or passes, or shall receive or use tickets or transportation at reduced rates not common to the public, shall forfeit his office. It shall be the duty of the General Assembly to enact laws to enforce the provisions of this section.

Text as Ratified on: August 3, 1891, and revised September 28, 1891.

History: Not yet amended.

Section 198 (Repealed 2002)

Catchline at time of repeal: "Trusts and combinations in restraint of trade to be prevented."

Repeal Ratified on: November 5, 2002.

History: Repeal was proposed by 2002 Ky. Acts ch. 341, §2; original version ratified August 3, 1891, and revised September 28, 1891.

Section 199 Telegraph and telephone companies—Right to construct lines—Exchange of messages.

Any association or corporation, or the lessees or managers thereof, organized for the purpose, or any individual, shall have the right to construct and maintain lines of telegraph within this State, and to connect the same with other lines, and said companies shall receive and transmit each other's messages without unreasonable delay or discrimination, and all such companies are hereby declared to be common carriers and subject to legislative control. Telephone companies operating exchanges in different towns or cities, or other public stations, shall receive and transmit each other's messages without unreasonable delay or discrimination. The General Assembly shall, by general laws of uniform operation, provide reasonable regulations to give full effect to this section. Nothing herein shall be construed to interfere with the rights of cities or towns to arrange and control their streets and alleys, and to designate the places at which, and the manner in which, the wires of such companies shall be erected or laid within the limits of such city or town.

Text as Ratified on: August 3, 1891, and revised September 28, 1891.

History: Not yet amended.

Section 200 (Repealed 2002)

Catchline at time of repeal: "Domestic corporation consolidating with foreign does not become foreign."

Repeal Ratified on: November 5, 2002.

History: Repeal was proposed by 2002 Ky. Acts ch. 341, §2; original version ratified August 3, 1891, and revised September 28, 1891.

Section 201 Public utility company not to consolidate with, acquire or operate competing or parallel system—Common carriers not to share earnings with one not carrying—Telephone companies excepted under certain conditions.

No railroad, telegraph, telephone, bridge or common carrier company shall consolidate its capital stock, franchises or property, or pool its earnings, in whole or in part, with any other railroad, telegraph, telephone, bridge or common carrier company owning a parallel or competing line or structure, or acquire by purchase, lease or otherwise, any parallel or competing line or structure, or operate the same; nor shall any railroad company or other common carrier combine or make any contract with the owners of any vessel that leaves or makes port in this State, or with any common carrier, by which combination or contract the earnings of one doing the carrying are to be shared by the other not doing the carrying: Provided, however, That telephone companies may acquire by purchase or lease, or otherwise, and operate, parallel or competing exchanges, lines and structures, and the property of other telephone companies, if the state agency as may have jurisdiction over such matters shall first consent thereto, and if, further, each municipality wherein such property or any part thereof is located shall also first consent thereto as to the property within its limits, but under any such acquisition and operation toll line connections with the property so acquired shall be continued and maintained under an agreement between the purchasing company and the toll line companies then furnishing such service, and in the event they are unable to agree as to the terms of such an agreement the state agency as may have jurisdiction over such matters, shall fix the term of such agreement.

Text as Ratified on: November 7, 2000.

History: 2000 amendment was proposed by 2000 Ky. Acts ch. 399, §1; 1917 amendment was proposed by 1916 Ky. Acts ch. 125, §1, and ratified November 6, 1917; original version ratified August 3, 1891, and revised September 28, 1891.

Section 202 (Repealed 2002)

Catchline at time of repeal: "Foreign corporations not to be given privileges over domestic."

Repeal Ratified on: November 5, 2002.

History: Repeal was proposed by 2002 Ky. Acts ch. 341, §2; original version ratified August 3, 1891, and revised September 28, 1891.

Section 203 (Repealed 2002)

Catchline at time of repeal: "Liabilities under corporate franchise not released by lease or alienation."

Repeal Ratified on: November 5, 2002.

History: Repeal was proposed by 2002 Ky. Acts ch. 341, §2; original version ratified August 3, 1891, and revised September 28, 1891.

Section 204 Bank officer liable for receiving deposit for insolvent bank.

Any President, Director, Manager, Cashier or other officer of any banking institution or association for the deposit or loan of money, or any individual banker, who shall receive or assent to the receiving of deposits after he shall have knowledge of the fact that such banking institution or association or individual banker is insolvent, shall be individually responsible for such deposits so received, and shall be guilty of felony and subject to such punishment as shall be prescribed by law.

Text as Ratified on: August 3, 1891, and revised September 28, 1891.

History: Not yet amended.

Section 205 Forfeiture of corporate charters in case of abuse or detrimental use.

The General Assembly shall, by general laws, provide for the revocation or forfeiture of the charters of all corporations guilty of abuse or misuse of their corporate powers, privileges or franchises, or whenever said corporations become detrimental to the interest and welfare of the Commonwealth or its citizens.

Text as Ratified on: August 3, 1891, and revised September 28, 1891.

History: Not yet amended.

Section 206 Warehouses subject to legislative control—Inspection—Protection of patrons.

All elevators or storehouses, where grain or other property is stored for a compensation, whether the property stored be kept separate or not, are declared to be public warehouses, subject to legislative control, and the General Assembly shall enact laws for the inspection of grain, tobacco and other produce, and for the protection of producers, shippers and receivers of grain, tobacco and other produce.

Text as Ratified on: August 3, 1891, and revised September 28, 1891.

History: Not yet amended.

Section 207 (Repealed 2002)

Catchline at time of repeal: "Cumulative voting for directors of corporations—Proxies."

Repeal Ratified on: November 5, 2002.

History: Repeal was proposed by 2002 Ky. Acts ch. 341, §2; original version ratified August 3, 1891, and revised September 28, 1891.

Section 208 (Repealed 2002)

Catchline at time of repeal: "Corporation includes joint stock company or association."

Repeal Ratified on: November 5, 2002.

History: Repeal was proposed by 2002 Ky. Acts ch. 341, §2; original version ratified August 3, 1891, and revised September 28, 1891.

Railroads and Commerce

Section 209 (Repealed 2000)

Catchline at time of repeal: "Railroad Commission—Election, term, and qualifications of Commissioners—Commissioners' districts—Powers and duties—Removal—Vacancies."

Repeal Ratified on: November 7, 2000.

History: Repealed was proposed by 2000 Ky. Acts ch. 399, §3; original version ratified August 3, 1891, and revised September 28, 1891.

Section 210 Common carrier corporation not to be interested in other business.

No corporation engaged in the business of common carrier shall, directly or indirectly, own, manage, operate, or engage in any other business than that of a common carrier, or hold, own, lease or acquire, directly or indirectly, mines, factories or timber, except such as shall be necessary to carry on its business, and the General Assembly shall enact laws to give effect to the provisions of this section.

Text as Ratified on: August 3, 1891, and revised September 28, 1891.

History: Not yet amended.

Section 211 Foreign railroad corporation may not condemn or acquire real estate.

No railroad corporation organized under the laws of any other State, or of the United States, and doing business, or proposing to do business, in this State, shall be entitled to the benefit of the right of eminent domain or have power to acquire the right of way or real estate for depot or other uses, until it shall have become a body corporate pursuant to and in accordance with the laws of this Commonwealth.

Text as Ratified on: August 3, 1891, and revised September 28, 1891.

History: Not yet amended.

Section 212 Rolling stock, earnings, and personal property of railroads subject to execution or attachment.

The rolling stock and other movable property belonging to any railroad corporation or company in this State shall be considered personal property, and shall be liable to execution and sale in the same manner as the personal property of individuals. The earnings of any railroad company or corporation, and choses in action, money and personal property of all kinds belonging to it, in the hands, or under the control, of any officer, agent or employee of such corporation or company, shall be subject to process of attachment to the same extent and in the same manner, as like property of individuals when in the hands or under the control of other persons. Any such earnings, choses in action, money or other personal property may be subjected to the payment of any judgment against such corporation or company, in the same manner and to the same extent as such property of individuals in the hands of third persons.

Text as Ratified on: August 3, 1891, and revised September 28, 1891.

History: Not yet amended.

Section 213 Railroad companies to handle traffic with connecting carriers without discrimination.

All railroad, transfer, belt lines and railway bridge companies organized under the laws of Kentucky, or operating, maintaining or controlling any railroad, transfer, belt lines or bridges, or doing a railway business in this State, shall receive, transfer, deliver and switch empty or loaded cars, and shall move, transport, receive, load or unload all the freight in car loads or less quantities, coming to or going from any railroad, transfer, belt line, bridge or siding thereon, with equal promptness and dispatch, and without any discrimination as to charges, preference, drawback or rebate in favor of any person, corporation, consignee or consignor, in any matter as to payment, transportation, handling or delivery; and shall so receive, deliver, transfer and transport all freight as above set forth, from and to any point where there is a physical connection between the tracks of said companies. But this section shall not be construed as requiring any such common carrier to allow the use of its tracks for the trains of another engaged in like business.

Text as Ratified on: August 3, 1891, and revised September 28, 1891.

History: Not yet amended.

Section 214 Railroad not to make exclusive or preferential contract.

No railway, transfer, belt line or railway bridge company shall make any exclusive or preferential contract or arrangement with any individual, association or corporation, for the receipt, transfer, delivery, transportation, handling, care or custody of any freight, or for the conduct of any business as a common carrier.

Text as Ratified on: August 3, 1891, and revised September 28, 1891.

History: Not yet amended.

Section 215 Freight to be handled without discrimination.

All railway, transfer, belt lines or railway bridge companies shall receive, load, unload, transport, haul, deliver and handle freight of the same class for all persons, associations or corporations from and to the same points and upon the same conditions, in the same manner and for the same charges, and for the same method of payment.

Text as Ratified on: August 3, 1891, and revised September 28, 1891.

History: Not yet amended.

Section 216 Railroad must allow tracks of others to cross or unite.

All railway, transfer, belt lines and railway bridge companies shall allow the tracks of each other to unite, intersect and cross at any point where such union, intersection and crossing is reasonable or feasible.

Text as Ratified on: August 3, 1891, and revised September 28, 1891.

History: Not yet amended.

Section 217 Penalties for violating Sections 213, 214, 215, or 216—Attorney General to enforce.

Any person, association or corporation, willfully or knowingly violating any of the provisions of Sections 213, 214, 215, or 216, shall, upon conviction by a court of competent jurisdiction, for the first offense be fined two thousand dollars; for the second offense, five thousand dollars; and for the third offense, shall thereupon, ipso facto, forfeit its franchises, privileges or charter rights; and if such delinquent be a foreign corporation, it shall, ipso facto, forfeit its right to do business in this State; and the Attorney-General of the Commonwealth shall forthwith, upon notice of the violation of any of said provisions, institute proceedings to enforce the provisions of the aforesaid sections.

Text as Ratified on: August 3, 1891, and revised September 28, 1891.

History: Not yet amended.

Section 218 Long and short hauls.

It shall be unlawful for any person or corporation, owning or operating a railroad in this State, or any common carrier, to charge or receive any greater compensation in the aggregate for the transportation of passengers, or of property of like kind, under substantially similar circumstances and conditions, for a shorter than for a longer distance over the same line, in the same direction, the shorter being included within the longer distance; but this shall not be construed as authorizing any common carrier, or person or corporation, owning or operating a railroad in this State, to receive as great compensation for a shorter as for a longer distance: Provided, That upon application to the state agency as may have jurisdiction over such matters, such common carrier, or person or corporation owning or operating a railroad in this State, may in special cases, after investigation by the appropriate state agency, be authorized to charge less for longer than for shorter distances for the transportation of passengers, or property; and the appropriate state agency may, from time to time, prescribe the extent to which such common carrier, or person or corporation, owning or operating a railroad in this State, may be relieved from the operation of this section.

Text as Ratified on: November 7, 2000.

History: 2000 amendment was proposed by 2000 Ky. Acts ch. 399, §2; original ratified August 3, 1891, and revised September 28, 1891.

The Militia

Section 219 Militia, what to consist of.

The militia of the Commonwealth of Kentucky shall consist of all able-bodied male residents of the State between the ages of eighteen and forty-five years, except such persons as may be exempted by the laws of the State or of the United States.

Text as Ratified on: August 3, 1891, and revised September 28, 1891.

History: Not yet amended.

Section 220 General Assembly to provide for militia—Exemptions from service.

The General Assembly shall provide for maintaining an organized militia, and may exempt from military service persons having conscientious scruples against bearing arms; but such persons shall pay an equivalent for such exemption.

Text as Ratified on: August 3, 1891, and revised September 28, 1891.

History: Not yet amended.

Federal Reference: U.S. Const. art. I, §8.

Section 221 Government of militia to conform to Army regulations.

The organization, equipment and discipline of the militia shall conform as nearly as practicable to the regulations for the government of the armies of the United States.

Text as Ratified on: August 3, 1891, and revised September 28, 1891.

History: Not yet amended.

Federal Reference: U.S. Const. art. I, §8.

Section 222 Officers of militia—Adjutant General.

All militia officers whose appointment is not herein otherwise provided for, shall be elected by persons subject to military duty within their respective companies, battalions, regiments or other commands, under such rules and regulations and for such terms, not exceeding four years, as the General Assembly may, from time to time, direct and establish. The Governor shall appoint an Adjutant-General and his other staff officers; the generals and commandants of regiments and battalions shall respectively appoint their staff officers, and the commandants of companies shall, subject to the approval of their regimental or battalion commanders, appoint their noncommissioned officers. The Governor shall have power to fill vacancies that may occur in elective offices by granting commissions which shall expire when such vacancies have been filled according to the provisions of this Constitution.

Text as Ratified on: August 3, 1891, and revised September 28, 1891.

History: Not yet amended.

Section 223 Safekeeping of public arms, military records, relics, and banners.

The General Assembly shall provide for the safekeeping of the public arms, military records, relics and banners of the Commonwealth of Kentucky.

Text as Ratified on: August 3, 1891, and revised September 28, 1891.

History: Not yet amended.

General Provisions

Section 224 Bond—What officers to give—Liability on.

The General Assembly shall provide by a general law what officers shall execute bond for the faithful discharge of their duties, and fix the liability therein.

Text as Ratified on: August 3, 1891, and revised September 28, 1891.

History: Not yet amended.

Section 225 Armed men not to be brought into State—Exception.

No armed person or bodies of men shall be brought into this State for the preservation of the peace or the suppression of domestic violence, except upon the application of the General Assembly, or of the Governor when the General Assembly may not be in session.

Text as Ratified on: August 3, 1891, and revised September 28, 1891.

History: Not yet amended.

Federal Reference: U.S. Const. art. IV, §4.

Section 226 State lottery—Charitable lotteries and charitable gift enterprises—Other lotteries and gift enterprises forbidden.

(1) The General Assembly may establish a Kentucky state lottery and may establish a state lottery to be conducted in cooperation with other states. Any lottery so established shall be operated by or on behalf of the Commonwealth of Kentucky.

(2) The General Assembly may by general law permit charitable lotteries and charitable gift enterprises and, if it does so, it shall:

(a) Define what constitutes a charity or charitable organization;

(b) Define the types of charitable lotteries and charitable gift enterprises which may be engaged in;

(c) Set standards for the conduct of charitable lotteries and charitable gift enterprises by charitable organizations;

(d) Provide for means of accounting for the amount of money raised by lotteries and gift enterprises and for assuring its expenditure only for charitable purposes;

(e) Provide suitable penalties for violation of statutes relating to charitable lotteries and charitable gift enterprises; and

(f) Pass whatever other general laws the General Assembly deems necessary to assure the proper functioning, honesty, and integrity of charitable lotteries and charitable gift enterprises, and the charitable purposes for which the funds are expended.

(3) Except as provided in this section, lotteries and gift enterprises are forbidden, and no privileges shall be granted for such purposes, and none shall be exercised, and no schemes for similar purposes shall be allowed. The General Assembly shall enforce this section by proper penalties. All lottery privileges or charters heretofore granted are revoked.

Text as Ratified on: November 3, 1992.

History: 1992 amendment was proposed by 1992 Ky. Acts ch. 113, §1; 1988 amendment was proposed by 1988 Ky. Acts ch. 116, §1, and ratified on November 8, 1988; original version ratified August 3, 1891, and revised September 28, 1891.

Section 226a (Repealed 1935)

Catchline read at time of repeal: "Manufacture, sale or transportation of intoxicating liquors prohibited—Exception—Legislature to enforce."

Repeal Ratified on: November 5, 1935.

History: Repeal was proposed by 1934 Ky. Acts ch. 58, §1; creation proposed by 1918 Ky. Acts ch. 63, §1, and ratified on November 4, 1919.

Federal Reference: U.S. Const. amend. XVIII.

Section 227 Prosecution and removal of local officers for misfeasance, malfeasance, or neglect.

Judges of the County Court, Justices of the Peace, Sheriffs, Coroners, Surveyors, Jailers, Assessors, County Attorneys and Constables shall be subject to indictment or prosecution for misfeasance or malfeasance in office, or willful neglect in discharge of official duties, in such mode as may be prescribed by law, and upon conviction his office shall become vacant, but such officer shall have the right to appeal to the Court of Appeals. Provided, also, that the General Assembly may, in addition to the indictment or prosecution above provided, by general law, provide other manner, method or mode for the vacation of office, or the removal from office of any sheriff, jailer, constable or peace officer for neglect of duty, and may provide the method, manner or mode of reinstatement of such officers.

Text as Ratified on: November 4, 1919.

History: 1919 amendment was proposed by 1918 Ky. Acts ch. 62, §1; original version ratified August 3, 1891, and revised September 28, 1891.

Federal Reference: U.S. Const. art. I, §§2, 3.

Section 228 Oath of officers and attorneys.

Members of the General Assembly and all officers, before they enter upon the execution of the duties of their respective offices, and all members of the bar, before they enter upon the practice of their profession, shall take the following oath or affirmation: I do solemnly swear (or affirm, as the case may be) that I will support the Constitution of the United States and the Constitution of this Commonwealth, and be faithful and true to the Commonwealth of Kentucky so long as I continue a citizen thereof, and that I will faithfully execute, to the best of my ability, the office of... according to law; and I do further solemnly swear (or affirm) that since the adoption of the present Constitution, I, being a citizen of this State, have not fought a duel with deadly weapons within this State nor out of it, nor have I sent or accepted a challenge to fight a duel with deadly weapons, nor have I acted as second in carrying a challenge, nor aided or assisted any person thus offending, so help me God.

Text as Ratified on: August 3, 1891, and revised September 28, 1891.

History: Not yet amended.

Federal Reference: U.S. Const. art. II, §1; VI.

Section 229 "Treason" defined—Evidence necessary to convict.

Treason against the Commonwealth shall consist only in levying war against it, or in adhering to its enemies, giving them aid and comfort. No person shall be convicted of treason except on the testimony of two witnesses to the same overt act, or his own confession in open court.

Text as Ratified on: August 3, 1891, and revised September 28, 1891.

History: Not yet amended.

Federal Reference: U.S. Const. art. III, §3.

Section 230 Money not to be drawn from Treasury unless appropriated—Annual publication of accounts—Certain revenues usable only for highway purposes.

No money shall be drawn from the State Treasury, except in pursuance of appropriations made by law; and a regular statement and account of the receipts and expenditures of all public money shall be published annually. No money derived from excise or license taxation relating to gasoline and other motor fuels, and no moneys derived from fees, excise or license taxation relating to registration, operation, or use of vehicles on public highways shall be expended for other than the cost of administration, statutory refunds and adjustments, payment of highway obligations, costs for construction, reconstruction, rights-of-way, maintenance and repair of public highways and bridges, and expense of enforcing state traffic and motor vehicle laws.

Text as Ratified on: November 6, 1945.

History: 1945 amendment was proposed by 1944 Ky. Acts ch. 9, §1; original version ratified August 3, 1891, and revised September 28, 1891.

Federal Reference: U.S. Const. art. I, §9.

Section 231 Suits against the Commonwealth.

The General Assembly may, by law, direct in what manner and in what courts suits may be brought against the Commonwealth.

Text as Ratified on: August 3, 1891, and revised September 28, 1891.

History: Not yet amended.

Federal Reference: U.S. Const. amend. XI.

Section 232 Manner of administering oath.

The manner of administering an oath or affirmation shall be such as is most consistent with the conscience of the deponent, and shall be esteemed by the General Assembly the most solemn appeal to God.

Text as Ratified on: August 3, 1891, and revised September 28, 1891.

History: Not yet amended.

Section 233 General laws of Virginia in force in this State until repealed.

All laws which, on the first day of June, one thousand seven hundred and ninety-two, were in force in the State of Virginia, and which are of a general nature and not local to that State, and not repugnant to this Constitution, nor to the laws which have been enacted by the General Assembly of this Commonwealth, shall be in force within this State until they shall be altered or repealed by the General Assembly.

Text as Ratified on: August 3, 1891, and revised September 28, 1891.

History: Not yet amended.

Section 233A Valid or recognized marriage—legal status of unmarried individuals.

Only a marriage between one man and one woman shall be valid or recognized as a marriage in Kentucky. A legal status identical or substantially similar to that of marriage for unmarried individuals shall not be valid or recognized.

Text as Ratified on: November 2, 2004.

History: Creation proposed by 2004 Ky. Acts ch. 128, §1.

Section 234 Residence and place of office of public officers.

All civil officers for the State at large shall reside within the State, and all district, county, city or town officers shall reside within their respective districts, counties, cities or towns, and shall keep their offices at such places therein as may be required by law.

Text as Ratified on: August 3, 1891, and revised September 28, 1891.

History: Not yet amended.

Section 235 Salaries of public officers not to be changed during term—Deductions for neglect.

The salaries of public officers shall not be changed during the terms for which they were elected; but it shall be the duty of the General Assembly to regulate, by a general law, in what cases and what deductions shall be made for neglect of official duties. This section shall apply to members of the General Assembly also.

Text as Ratified on: August 3, 1891, and revised September 28, 1891.

History: Not yet amended.

Federal Reference: U.S. Const. art. I, §6; II, §1; III, §1.

Section 236 When officers to enter upon duties.

The General Assembly shall, by law, prescribe the time when the several officers authorized or directed by this Constitution to be elected or appointed, shall enter upon the duties of their respective offices, except where the time is fixed by this Constitution.

Text as Ratified on: August 3, 1891, and revised September 28, 1891.

History: Not yet amended.

Section 237 Federal office incompatible with State office.

No member of Congress, or person holding or exercising an office of trust or profit under the United States, or any of them, or under any foreign power, shall be eligible to hold or exercise any office of trust or profit under this Constitution, or the laws made in pursuance thereof.

Text as Ratified on: August 3, 1891, and revised September 28, 1891.

History: Not yet amended.

Section 238 Discharge of sureties on officers' bonds.

The General Assembly shall direct by law how persons who now are, or may hereafter become, sureties for public officers, may be relieved of or discharged from suretyship.

Text as Ratified on: August 3, 1891, and revised September 28, 1891.

History: Not yet amended.

Section 239 Disqualification from office for presenting or accepting challenge to duel—Further punishment.

Any person who shall, after the adoption of this Constitution, either directly or indirectly, give, accept or knowingly carry a challenge to any person or persons to fight in single combat, with a citizen of this State, with a deadly weapon, either in or out of the State, shall be deprived of the right to hold any office of honor or profit in this Commonwealth; and if said acts, or any of them, be committed within this State, the person or persons so committing them shall be further punished in such manner as the General Assembly may prescribe by law.

Text as Ratified on: August 3, 1891, and revised September 28, 1891.

History: Not yet amended.

Section 240 Pardon of person convicted of dueling.

The Governor shall have power, after five years from the time of the offense, to pardon any person who shall have participated in a duel as principal, second or otherwise, and to restore him to all the rights, privileges and immunities to which he was entitled before such participation. Upon presentation of such pardon the oath prescribed in Section 228 shall be varied to suit the case.

Text as Ratified on: August 3, 1891, and revised September 28, 1891.

History: Not yet amended.

Section 241 Recovery for wrongful death.

Whenever the death of a person shall result from an injury inflicted by negligence or wrongful act, then, in every such case, damages may be recovered for such death, from the corporations and persons so causing the same. Until otherwise provided by law, the action to recover such damages shall in all cases be prosecuted by the personal representative of the deceased person. The General Assembly may provide how the recovery shall go and to whom belong; and until such provision is made, the same shall form part of the personal estate of the deceased person.

Text as Ratified on: August 3, 1891, and revised September 28, 1891.

History: Not yet amended.

Section 242 Just compensation to be made in condemning private property—Right of appeal—Jury trial.

Municipal and other corporations, and individuals invested with the privilege of taking private property for public use, shall make just compensation for property taken, injured or destroyed by them; which compensation shall be paid before such taking, or paid or secured, at the election of such corporation or individual, before such injury or destruction. The General Assembly shall not deprive any person of an appeal from any preliminary assessment of damages against any such corporation or individual made by Commissioners or otherwise; and upon appeal from such preliminary assessment, the amount of such damages shall, in all cases, be determined by a jury, according to the course of the common law.

Text as Ratified on: August 3, 1891, and revised September 28, 1891.

History: Not yet amended.

Federal Reference: U.S. Const. amend. V.

Section 243 Child labor.

The General Assembly shall, by law, fix the minimum ages at which children may be employed in places dangerous to life or health, or injurious to morals; and shall provide adequate penalties for violations of such law.

Text as Ratified on: August 3, 1891, and revised September 28, 1891.

History: Not yet amended.

Section 244 Wage-earners in industry or of corporations to be paid in money.

All wage-earners in this State employed in factories, mines, workshops, or by corporations, shall be paid for their labor in lawful money. The General Assembly shall prescribe adequate penalties for violations of this section.

Text as Ratified on: August 3, 1891, and revised September 28, 1891.

History: Not yet amended.

Section 244a Old age assistance.

The General Assembly shall prescribe such laws as may be necessary for the granting and paying of old persons an annuity or pension.

Text as Ratified on: November 5, 1935.

History: Creation proposed by 1934 Ky. Acts ch. 59, §1.

Section 245 Revision of statutes to conform to Constitution.

Upon the promulgation of this Constitution, the Governor shall appoint three persons, learned in the law, who shall be Commissioners to revise the statute laws of this Commonwealth, and prepare amendments thereto, to the end that the statute laws shall conform to and effectuate this Constitution. Such revision and amendments shall be laid before the next General Assembly for adoption or rejection, in whole or in part. The said Commissioners shall be allowed ten dollars each per day for their services, and also necessary stationery for the time during which they are actually employed; and upon their certificate the Auditor shall draw his warrant upon the Treasurer. They shall have the power to employ clerical assistants, at a compensation not exceeding ten dollars per day in the aggregate. If the Commissioners, or any of them, shall refuse to act, or a vacancy shall occur, the Governor shall appoint another or others in his or their place.

Text as Ratified on: August 3, 1891, and revised September 28, 1891.

History: Not yet amended.

Section 246 Maximum limit on compensation of public officers.

No public officer or employee except the Governor, shall receive as compensation per annum for official services, exclusive of the compensation of legally authorized deputies and assistants which shall be fixed and provided for by law, but inclusive of allowance for living expenses, if any, as may be fixed and provided for by law, any amount in excess of the following sums: Officers whose jurisdiction or duties are coextensive with the Commonwealth, the mayor of any city of the first class, and Judges and Commissioners of the Court of Appeals, Twelve Thousand Dollars ($12,000); Circuit Judges, Eight Thousand Four Hundred Dollars ($8,400); all other public officers, Seven Thousand Two Hundred Dollars ($7,200). Compensation within the limits of this amendment may be authorized by the General Assembly to be paid, but not retroactively, to public officers in office at the time of its adoption, or who are elected at the election at which this amendment is adopted. Nothing in this amendment shall permit any officer to receive, for the year 1949, any compensation in excess of the limit in force prior to the adoption of this amendment.

Text as Ratified on: November 8, 1949.

History: 1949 amendment was proposed by 1948 Ky. Acts ch. 172, §1; original version ratified August 3, 1891, and revised September 28, 1891.

Section 247 Public printing—Contract for—Officers not to have interest in—Governor to approve.

The printing and binding of the laws, journals, department reports, and all other public printing and binding, shall be performed under contract, to be given to the lowest responsible bidder, below such maximum and under such regulations as may be prescribed by law. No member of the General Assembly, or officer of the Commonwealth, shall be in any way interested in any such contract; and all such contracts shall be subject to the approval of the Governor.

Text as Ratified on: August 3, 1891, and revised September 28, 1891.

History: Not yet amended.

Section 248 Juries—Number of jurors—Three-fourths may indict or give verdict.

A grand jury shall consist of twelve persons, nine of whom concurring, may find an indictment. In civil and misdemeanor cases, in courts inferior to the Circuit Courts, a jury shall consist of six persons. The General Assembly may provide that in any or all trials of civil actions in the Circuit Courts, three-fourths or more of the jurors concurring may return a verdict, which shall have the same force and effect as if rendered by the entire panel. But where a verdict is rendered by a less number than the whole jury, it shall be signed by all the jurors who agree to it.

Text as Ratified on: August 3, 1891, and revised September 28, 1891.

History: Not yet amended.

Section 249 Employees of General Assembly—Number and compensation.

The House of Representatives of the General Assembly shall not elect, appoint, employ or pay for, exceeding one Chief Clerk, one Assistant Clerk, one Enrolling Clerk, one Sergeant at Arms, one Doorkeeper, one Janitor, two Cloakroom Keepers and four Pages; and the Senate shall not elect, appoint, employ or pay for, exceeding one Chief Clerk, one Assistant Clerk, one Enrolling Clerk, one Sergeant at Arms, one Doorkeeper, one Janitor, one Cloakroom Keeper and three Pages; and the General Assembly shall provide, by general law, for fixing the per diem or salary of all of said employees.

Text as Ratified on: August 3, 1891, and revised September 28, 1891.

History: Not yet amended.

Federal Reference: U.S. Const. art. I, §§2, 3.

Section 250 Arbitration, method for to be provided.

It shall be the duty of the General Assembly to enact such laws as shall be necessary and proper to decide differences by arbitrators, the arbitrators to be appointed by the parties who may choose that summary mode of adjustment.

Text as Ratified on: August 3, 1891, and revised September 28, 1891.

History: Not yet amended.

Section 251 Limitation of actions to recover possession of land based on early patents.

No action shall be maintained for possession of any lands lying within this State, where it is necessary for the claimant to rely for his recovery on any grant or patent issued by the Commonwealth of Virginia, or by the Commonwealth of Kentucky prior to the year one thousand eight hundred and twenty, against any person claiming such lands by possession to a well-defined boundary, under a title of record, unless such action shall be instituted within five years after this Constitution shall go into effect, or within five years after the occupant may take possession; but nothing herein shall be construed to affect any right, title or interest in lands acquired by virtue of adverse possession under the laws of this Commonwealth.

Text as Ratified on: August 3, 1891, and revised September 28, 1891.

History: Not yet amended.

Section 252 Houses of reform to be established and maintained.

It shall be the duty of the General Assembly to provide by law, as soon as practicable, for the establishment and maintenance of an institution or institutions for the detention, correction, instruction and reformation of all persons under the age of eighteen years, convicted of such felonies and such misdemeanors as may be designated by law. Said institution shall be known as the "House of Reform."

Text as Ratified on: August 3, 1891, and revised September 28, 1891.

History: Not yet amended.

Section 253 Working of penitentiary prisoners—When and where permitted.

Persons convicted of felony and sentenced to confinement in the penitentiary shall be confined at labor within the walls of the penitentiary; and the General Assembly shall not have the power to authorize employment of convicts elsewhere, except upon the public works of the Commonwealth of Kentucky, or when, during pestilence or in case of the destruction of the prison buildings, they cannot be confined in the penitentiary.

That Section 253 of the Constitution be amended so that the Commonwealth of Kentucky may use and employ outside of the walls of the penitentiaries in such manner and means as may be provided by law, persons convicted of felony and sentenced to confinement in the penitentiary for the purpose of constructing or reconstructing and maintaining public roads and public bridges or for the purpose of making and preparing material for public roads and bridges, and that the Commonwealth of Kentucky may, by the use and employment of convict labor outside of the walls of the penitentiary by other ways or means, as may be provided by law, aid the counties for road and bridge purposes, work on the State farm or farms.

Text as Ratified on: November 2, 1915.

History: 1915 amendment was proposed by 1914 Ky. Acts ch. 93, §1; original version ratified August 3, 1891, and revised September 28, 1891.

Section 254 Control and support of convicts—Leasing of labor.

The Commonwealth shall maintain control of the discipline, and provide for all supplies, and for the sanitary condition of the convicts, and the labor only of convicts may be leased.

Text as Ratified on: August 3, 1891, and revised September 28, 1891.

History: Not yet amended.

Section 255 Frankfort is state capital.

The seat of government shall continue in the city of Frankfort, unless removed by a vote of two-thirds of each House of the first General Assembly which convenes after the adoption of this Constitution.

Text as Ratified on: August 3, 1891, and revised September 28, 1891.

History: Not yet amended.

Section 255A Personal right to hunt, fish, and harvest wildlife—Limitations.

The citizens of Kentucky have the personal right to hunt, fish, and harvest wildlife, using traditional methods, subject only to statutes enacted by the Legislature, and to administrative regulations adopted by the designated state agency to promote wildlife conservation and management and to preserve the future of hunting and fishing. Public hunting and fishing shall be a preferred means of managing and controlling wildlife. This section shall not be construed to modify any provision of law relating to trespass, property rights, or the regulation of commercial activities.

Text as ratified on: November 6, 2012.

History: Creation proposed by 2011 Ky. Acts ch. 4, §1.

Mode of Revision

Section 256 Amendments to Constitution—How proposed and voted upon.

Amendments to this Constitution may be proposed in either House of the General Assembly at a regular session, and if such amendment or amendments shall be agreed to by three-fifths of all the members elected to each House, such proposed amendment or amendments, with the yeas and nays of the members of each House taken thereon, shall be entered in full in their respective journals. Then such proposed amendment or amendments shall be submitted to the voters of the State for their ratification or rejection at the next general election for members of the House of Representatives, the vote to be taken thereon in such manner as the General Assembly may provide, and to be certified by the officers of election to the Secretary of State in such manner as shall be provided by law, which vote shall be compared and certified by the same board authorized by law to compare the polls and give certificates of election to officers for the State at large. If it shall appear that a majority of the votes cast for and against an amendment at said election was for the amendment, then the same shall become a part of the

Constitution of this Commonwealth, and shall be so proclaimed by the Governor, and published in such manner as the General Assembly may direct. Said amendments shall not be submitted at an election which occurs less than ninety days from the final passage of such proposed amendment or amendments. Not more than four amendments shall be voted upon at any one time. If two or more amendments shall be submitted at the same time, they shall be submitted in such manner that the electors shall vote for or against each of such amendments separately, but an amendment may relate to a single subject or to related subject matters and may amend or modify as many articles and as many sections of the Constitution as may be necessary and appropriate in order to accomplish the objectives of the amendment. The approval of the Governor shall not be necessary to any bill, order, resolution or vote of the General Assembly, proposing an amendment or amendments to this Constitution.

Text as Ratified on: November 6, 1979.

History: 1979 amendment was proposed by 1978 Ky. Acts ch. 433, § 1; original version ratified August 3, 1891, and revised September 28, 1891.

Federal Reference: U.S. Const. art. V.

Section 257 Publication of proposed amendments.

Before an amendment shall be submitted to a vote, the Secretary of State shall cause such proposed amendment, and the time that the same is to be voted upon, to be published at least ninety days before the vote is to be taken thereon in such manner as may be prescribed by law.

Text as Ratified on: August 3, 1891, and revised September 28, 1891.

History: Not yet amended.

Section 258 Constitutional Convention—How proposed, voted upon, and called.

When a majority of all the members elected to each House of the General Assembly shall concur, by a yea and nay vote, to be entered upon their respective journals, in enacting a law to take the sense of the people of the State as to the necessity and expediency of calling a Convention for the purpose of revising or amending this Constitution, and such amendments as may have been made to the same, such law shall be spread upon their respective journals. If the next General Assembly shall, in like manner, concur in such law, it shall provide for having a poll opened in each voting precinct in this state by the officers provided by law for holding general elections at the next ensuing regular election to be held for State officers or members of the House of Representatives, which does not occur within ninety days from the final passage of such law, at which time and places the votes of the qualified voters shall be taken for and against calling the Convention, in the same manner provided by law for taking votes in other State elections. The vote for and against said proposition shall be certified to the Secretary of State by the same officers and in the same manner as in State elections. If it shall appear that a majority voting on the proposition was for calling a Convention, and if the total number of votes cast for the calling of the Convention is equal to one-fourth of the number of qualified voters who voted at the last preceding general election in this State, the Secretary of State shall certify the same to the General Assembly at its next regular session, at which session a law shall be enacted calling a Convention to readopt, revise or amend this Constitution, and such amendments as may have been made thereto.

Text as Ratified on: August 3, 1891, and revised September 28, 1891.

History: Not yet amended.

Federal Reference: U.S. Const. art. V.

Section 259 Number and qualifications of delegates.

The Convention shall consist of as many delegates as there are members of the House of Representatives; and the delegates shall have the same qualifications and be elected from the same districts as said Representatives.

Text as Ratified on: August 3, 1891, and revised September 28, 1891.

History: Not yet amended.

Section 260 Election of delegates—meeting.

Delegates to such Convention shall be elected at the next general State election after the passage of the act calling the Convention, which does not occur within less than ninety days; and they shall meet within ninety days after their election at the Capital of the State, and continue in session until their work is completed.

Text as Ratified on: August 3, 1891, and revised September 28, 1891.

History: Not yet amended.

Section 261 Certification of election and compensation of delegates.

The General Assembly, in the act calling the Convention, shall provide for comparing the polls and giving certificates of election to the delegates elected, and provide for their compensation.

Text as Ratified on: August 3, 1891, and revised September 28, 1891.

History: Not yet amended.

Section 262 Determination of election and qualifications of delegates—Contests.

The Convention, when assembled, shall be the judge of the election and qualification of its members, and shall determine contested elections. But the General Assembly shall, in the act calling the Convention, provide for taking testimony in such cases, and for issuing a writ of election in case of a tie.

Text as Ratified on: August 3, 1891, and revised September 28, 1891.

History: Not yet amended.

Section 263 Notice of election on question of calling convention.

Before a vote is taken upon the question of calling a Convention, the Secretary of State shall cause notice of the election to be published in such manner as may be provided by the act directing said vote to be taken.

Text as Ratified on: August 3, 1891, and revised September 28, 1891.

History: Not yet amended.

Schedule

That no inconvenience may arise from the alterations and amendments made in this Constitution, and in order to carry the same into complete operation, it is hereby declared and ordained:

First: That all laws of this Commonwealth in force at the time of the adoption of this Constitution, not inconsistent therewith, shall remain in full force until altered or repealed by the General Assembly; and all rights, actions, prosecutions, claims and contracts of the State, counties, individuals or bodies corporate, not inconsistent therewith, shall continue as valid as if this Constitution had not been adopted. The provisions of all laws which are inconsistent with this Constitution shall cease upon its adoption, except that all laws which are inconsistent with such provisions as require legislation to enforce them shall remain in force until such legislation is had, but not longer than six years after the adoption of this Constitution, unless sooner amended or repealed by the General Assembly.

Second: That all recognizances, obligations and all other instruments entered into or executed before the adoption of this Constitution, to the State, or to any city, town, county or subdivision thereof, and all fines, taxes, penalties and forfeitures due or owing to this State, or to any city, town, county or subdivision thereof; and all writs, prosecutions, actions and causes of action, except as otherwise herein provided, shall continue and remain unaffected by the adoption of this Constitution. And all indictments which shall have been found, or may hereafter be found, for any crime or offense committed before this Constitution takes effect, may be prosecuted as if no change had taken place, except as otherwise provided in this Constitution.

Third: All Circuit, Chancery, Criminal, Law and Equity, Law, and Common Pleas Courts, as now constituted and organized by law, shall continue with their respective jurisdictions until the Judges of the Circuit Courts provided for in this Constitution shall have been elected and qualified, and shall then cease and determine; and the causes, actions and proceedings then pending in said first named courts, which are discontinued by this Constitution, shall be transferred to, and tried by, the Circuit Courts in the counties, respectively, in which said causes, actions and proceedings are pending.

Fourth: The Treasurer, Attorney-General, Auditor of Public Accounts, Superintendent of Public Instruction, and Register of the Land Office, elected in eighteen hundred and ninety-one, shall hold their offices until the first Monday in January, eighteen hundred and ninety-six, and until the election and qualification of their successors. The Governor and Lieutenant Governor elected in eighteen hundred and ninety-one shall hold their offices until the sixth Tuesday after the first Monday in November, eighteen hundred and ninety-five, and until their successors are elected and qualified. The Governor and Treasurer elected in eighteen hundred and ninety-one shall be ineligible to the succeeding term. The Governor elected in eighteen hundred and ninety-one may appoint a Secretary of State and a Commissioner of Agriculture, Labor and Statistics, as now provided, who shall hold their offices until their successors are elected and qualified, unless sooner removed by the Governor. The official bond of the present Treasurer shall be renewed at the expiration of two years from the time of his qualification.

Fifth: All officers who may be in office at the adoption of this Constitution, or who may be elected before the election of their successors, as provided in this Constitution, shall hold their respective offices until their successors are elected or appointed and qualified as provided in this Constitution.

Sixth: The Quarterly Courts created by this Constitution shall be the successors of the present statutory Quarterly Courts in the several counties of this State; and all suits, proceedings, prosecutions, records and judgments now pending or being in said last named courts shall, after the adoption of this Constitution, be transferred to the Quarterly Courts created by this Constitution, and shall proceed as though the same had been therein instituted.

Text as Ratified on: August 3, 1891, and revised September 28, 1891.

History: Not yet amended.

Ordinance

We, the representatives of the people of Kentucky, in Convention assembled, in their name and by their authority and in virtue of the power vested in us as Delegates from the counties and districts respectively affixed to our names, do ordain and proclaim the foregoing to be the Constitution of the Commonwealth of Kentucky from and after this date.

Done at Frankfort this twenty-eighth day of September, in the year of our Lord one thousand eight hundred and ninety-one, and in the one hundredth year of the Commonwealth.

Text as Ratified on: August 3, 1891, and revised September 28, 1891.

History: Not yet amended.

Appendix A: Constitutional Amendments Adopted Since 1891

Year Adopted	Section(s) Affected	Purpose
1903	181	Authorize the General Assembly to provide by general law for levying by cities and counties of license fees and franchise taxes based on income derived from property or other sources.
1909	157a	Permit state to give, pledge, or lend credit to counties for road purposes and permit counties to levy a tax of 20 cents per $100 of assessed property value to pay principal and interest on voted road and bridge bonds.
1915	171	Permit classification of property for tax purposes.
1915	253	Permit use of prisoners for road work.
1917	201	Permit telephone companies, under certain conditions, to buy or lease competing companies.
1919	227	Permit removal of local law enforcement officers for neglect of duty.
1919	226A	Prohibit manufacture, sale, or transportation of alcoholic beverages.
1935	226A	Repeal prohibition.
1935	244A	Permit old age pensions.
1941	186	Permit 10% of money appropriated by legislature for school purposes to be used in equalization fund, instead of being divided on a per capita basis.
1941	147	Permit the use of voting machines.
1945	147	Authorize the General Assembly to provide for absentee voting.
1945	230	Guarantee the receipts from certain tax sources shall be placed in the highway fund.
1949	246	Repeal the $5,000 salary limit and substitute limits of $12,000 per year for officials with statewide jurisdiction and mayors of first class cities, $8,400 for circuit judges, and $7,200 for all other officials.
1949	186	Changes from 90% to 75% the percentage of state appropriated school funds to be divided on a per capita basis.

1953	186	Repeal provisions of Section 186 which required school funds to be distributed on a per capita basis.
1955	145	Permit persons 18 years of age or older to vote, provided they meet other qualifications, and remove the word "male" from the constitutional description of voters.
1955	170	Exempt all household goods from taxation.
1969	172A	Permit agricultural land in urban areas to be assessed for taxation at its value for agricultural purposes and permit a unit of local government to tax property at different rates, in different areas, based upon services.
1971	170	Exempt from taxation up to $6,500 of the assessed value of a single family residence owned and occupied by a person age 65 or older.
1975	109–139, 141, 143	Restructure the state court system.
1975	170	Extend "homestead exemption" to residences other than single family dwellings.
1979	256	Increase from 2 to 4 the maximum number of amendments that may be submitted to the voters at any one election.
1979	30, 31, 36, 42	Change from odd-year to even-year election for members of the General Assembly.
1981	170, 172B	Provides certain property tax exemptions for residents age 65 and older and for the disabled. Permits property tax moratoriums under certain circumstances to encourage repair and renovation of properties.
1984	99	Permit sheriffs to succeed themselves.
1986	160	Permit mayors of cities of the first and second classes to run for election for three successive terms.
1988	19	Limit the mining of coal conveyed by any broadform deed to methods of coal extraction utilized in the area at the time the deed was signed.
1988	226	Permit the General Assembly to establish a Kentucky state lottery, alone or in conjunction with other states.
1990	170	Exempt from property taxation all real property owned and occupied by, and all personal property owned by, institutions of religion.
1992	226	Permits the General Assembly to establish and regulate charitable gaming.

1992	70–74, 82–87, 91, 93, 94, 95, 97, 99, 148, 167	Omnibus reform of Executive Branch and election schedule, including: succession for state officers; joint election of Governor and Lieutenant Governor; gubernatorial disability and absence from the state; abolition of elected Superintendent of Public Instruction; duties of Lieutenant Governor; and even-year elections for all but statewide officers.
1994	156, 156a, 156b, 157, 157b, 158	Changes method of classifying cities, grants "home rule" to cities, relaxes limitations on local government debt capacity, and requires balanced budgets by local governments.
1996	180, 187	Removed the requirement that public schools be racially segregated and the authority for local governments to levy a poll tax.
1998	170	Permit the General Assembly to exempt motor vehicles and other personal property from property tax and extend the homestead exemption to persons classified as totally disabled by any public or private retirement system.
2000	36, 42	Provide that the General Assembly shall meet in annual session in odd-numbered years for 30 days, provide that bills raising revenue or appropriating funds in an odd-numbered year session shall be agreed to by three-fifths of all members elected to each House, adjourn each odd-numbered year session by March 30.
2000	201, 209, 218	Abolish the Railroad Commission.
2002	112	Allow the creation of Family Court divisions of the Circuit Court.
2002	190–194, 198, 200, 202, 203, 207, 208	Permit the General Assembly to provide by general law for the regulation of corporations.
2004	233A	Recognizing only a marriage between one man and one woman as valid in Kentucky.[1]
2012	255A	Provide a constitutional right to hunt, fish, and harvest wildlife.
2020	26A	Provide constitutional rights for crime victims.

1. The U.S. Supreme Court found the amendment to be unconstitutional in *Obergefell v. Hodges*, 576 U.S. 644 (2015).

Appendix B: Constitutional Amendments Proposed by the General Assembly Since 1891 But Not Adopted

Year Submitted	Section(s) Affected	Purpose
1897	181	Would have permitted municipalities to tax property on the basis of income.
1905	147	Would have required voice voting instead of secret ballot.
1907	145	Would have made payment of taxes a prerequisite to voting.
1913	171	Would have permitted the General Assembly to classify property for tax purposes and determine which classes would be subject to local taxation.[2]
1921	186	Would have provided that 10% of the common school fund could be distributed on other than a per capita basis.
1921	91	Would have removed the Superintendent of Public Instruction from the list of elective officials.
1923	145	Would have permitted women to vote and hold office.
1925	246	Would have raised the $5,000 salary limit for certain elected officials.
1927	147	Would have permitted absentee voting.
1927	246	Would have abolished the $5,000 salary limit and substituted a provision that the General Assembly should fix reasonable compensation.
1929	256	Would have removed the two amendment restriction.
1929	246	Would have removed the salary limit on Judges of the Court of Appeals.
1931	158	Would have raised the debt limits of cities and counties in certain cases.
1933	172	Would have permitted the General Assembly to exempt real and personal property from taxation by the state.
1937	New	Would have permitted the General Assembly to reorganize local government and would have permitted consolidation of cities and counties.

2. Through error, the amendment was not publicized as required by Section 257 of the Constitution. Although the amendment was placed on the ballot, voted upon, and passed, the amendment was invalidated by *McCreary v. Speer*, 156 Ky. 783, 162 S.W. 99 (1914).

1937	256	Would have removed the limit on the number of constitutional amendments to be submitted at one time.
1939	145	Would have made women eligible to hold public office.
1939		Would have authorized and directed the General Assembly to provide aid to dependent children and needy blind.[3]
1943	54	Would have permitted the General Assembly to pass a compulsory workers' compensation law.
1943	246	Would have removed the $5,000 salary limit.
1951	256	Would have permitted an unlimited number of amendments to be submitted at one time and changed the time and manner of voting on amendments.
1953	91, 93	Would have removed the Secretary of State, Treasurer, Commissioner of Agriculture, Labor and Statistics, and the Superintendent of Public Instruction from the list of elective state officers.
1957	91, 93, 95, 96	Would have abolished the elective Superintendent of Public Instruction and established in his place a Commissioner of Education appointed by a 9-member Board of Education.
1959	New	Would have established a sales tax to provide a veterans' bonus.[4]
1959	99	Would have made sheriffs eligible to succeed themselves.
1963	246	Would have abolished the salary limit.
1963	256	Would have permitted the submission of 5 amendments to be voted on at one time.
1969	42	Would have authorized the General Assembly to meet annually for 60 legislative days and defined a legislative day as one on which at least one house was in session.
1973	91, 93, 95, 99, 183, 209	Would have deleted the requirement that the Superintendent of Public Instruction be elected; allowed sheriffs to succeed themselves; established a 7-member Board of Education; abolished the Railroad Commission.
1973	32, 36, 42	Would have required the General Assembly to meet annually for not longer than 45 legislative days, which need not be consecutive, nor longer than 4 months (6 months if

3. Through error was not publicized as required by Section 257 of the Constitution and thus could not be placed on the ballot. *See Arnett v. Sullivan*, 279 Ky. 720, 132 S.W.2d 76 (1939).

4. Although ratified by the voters, this amendment was declared invalid by the Court of Appeals. But the Court held its provisions to be valid, in part, when construed as a general statute rather than as an attempted constitutional amendment. *See Stovall v. Gartrell*, 332 S.W.2d 256 (Ky. 1960).

		approved by two-thirds of the members of both Houses); required legislators to have resided in their districts for 2 years rather than 1 year prior to election.
1981	71, 82, 93, 99	Would have permitted statewide constitutional officers to serve two successive terms and would have permitted sheriffs to succeed themselves.
1986	91, 93, 95, 183	Would have constitutionally established an appointed State Board of Education, which would have hired a state Superintendent of Public Instruction; would have abolished the constitutional office of elected Superintendent of Public Instruction.
1990	36	Would have allowed the General Assembly to call itself into extraordinary session.
1990	28	Would have allowed the General Assembly to create a system whereby it or a body it designated could reject administrative regulations promulgated by an agency of the Executive Branch.
1990	156, 157, 157a, 158, 159, 160, 166, 167, 170, 180, 181[5]	Would have altered the structure and powers of local government.
1992	91, 93, 94, 95, 201, 209, 218	Would have deleted the election of the Secretary of State, Treasurer, Commissioner of Agriculture, Superintendent of Public Instruction, and Railroad Commission.
1998	36, 42	Would have required the General Assembly to meet annually in odd-numbered years for 25 days, would have reduced the organizational session by 5 days.
2018	26A	Would have provided constitutional rights for crime victims.[6]
2020	97, 119, 122	Would have changed the terms of office for Commonwealth's Attorneys from 6 to 8 years, changed the terms of office for District Judges from 4 to 8 years, and required District Judges to be licensed attorneys for 8 years preceding their election, not 2 years.

5. In addition to repealing 9 sections and amending 2 others, listed above, the proposed amendment also would have created new Sections 156a, 156b, 156c, 157b, 157c, 157d, and 158a.

6. Although ratified by the voters, the amendment was declared invalid by the Supreme Court in *Westerfield v. Ward*, 599 S.W.3d 738 (Ky. 2019), because it was not presented to the voters and publicized in the manner required by Sections 256 and 257 of the Constitution.

2022	36, 42, 55, New	Would have repealed sections 36, 42, and 55; provided that General Assembly may meet for 30 legislative days in odd-numbered years and 60 legislative days in even-numbered years, plus no more than 12 additional legislative days in any year if convened by joint proclamation of the President of the Senate and Speaker of the House of Representatives; modified effective date of Acts of the General Assembly.
2022	26A	Would have clarified that nothing in the Constitution shall be construed to secure or protect a right to abortion or require funding for abortion.

THE KENTUCKY CONSTITUTION

One

Formation of a Commonwealth

A. Historical Background of the Kentucky Constitution of 1891

Introduction

In its history, Kentucky has had four state constitutions. The first Kentucky constitution took effect in 1792, when Kentucky was admitted as the fifteenth State in the Union. By design, the first constitution was intended to be in place only temporarily, providing for a constitutional convention to occur in seven years, and so Kentucky adopted its second constitution in 1799.

Abolitionist reformers believed slavery was the great evil that Kentuckians wanted to address in a third constitutional convention in 1849. They were badly mistaken. The truth was that other issues were far more important to most Kentuckians at the time, such as reforming the courts, promoting education, curbing the Governor's power of appointment, and restructuring the General Assembly. When the constitutional convention met in October 1849, only two of the one hundred delegates were emancipationists.

The result was that the 1850 Constitution was a thoroughly pro-slavery document. Voting rights were limited to "free white male citizen[s], of the age of twenty-one years."[1] Because the delegates believed Christian clergy to be the leaders of anti-slavery sentiment in Kentucky, the constitution precluded clergy and religious teachers from serving in the General Assembly[2] or as Governor.[3] The constitution also expressly excluded "negroes, mulattoes, and Indians" from service in the militia.[4] To further entrench slavery in the Commonwealth, Article X of the 1850 Constitution precluded the General Assembly from passing any laws to emancipate slaves without obtaining the permission of, and paying compensation to, the owners of any slaves so emancipated.[5] It also required the General Assembly to enact laws requiring all free black persons and emancipated slaves to leave Kentucky, and punishing their refusal to leave as a

1. Ky. Const. (1850) art. II, §8.
2. Ky. Const. (1850) art. II, §27.
3. Ky. Const. (1850) art. III, §6.
4. Ky. Const. (1850) art. VII, §1.
5. Ky. Const. (1850) art. X, §1.

felony.[6] And included in the Bill of Rights to the 1850 Constitution was a provision constitutionalizing the right to property in persons: "The right of property is before and higher than any constitutional sanction; and the right of the owner of a slave to such slave, and its increase, is the same, and inviolable as the right of the owner of any property whatever."[7] Because the delegates were overwhelmingly pro-slavery, there was very little debate or opposition in the convention to any of these provisions.

It is worth noting that Kentucky's history—before, during, and after the Civil War—is complicated. As evidenced by the content of Kentucky's third constitution, an overwhelmingly pro-slavery sentiment existed in the state before the war. Yet, despite being represented by a star in the Confederate flag, Kentucky remained a part of the Union. Kentuckians died fighting on both sides of the conflict. Even after a hard-fought war over slavery and a Union victory, most Kentucky citizens held pro-slavery views. Popular opinion in the Commonwealth after the war turned in favor of the South and against Reconstruction.

By the time the Thirteenth Amendment to the U.S. Constitution took effect in December 1865, outlawing slavery nationwide, Kentucky had been one of only two States (Delaware being the other) in which slavery still existed legally. The Fourteenth Amendment, which granted U.S. citizenship to the freed slaves and promised them the equal protection of the laws, took effect in late July 1868. Then the Fifteenth Amendment took effect in March 1870, prohibiting the states and the federal government from denying citizens the right to vote based on their race, color, or previous servitude. The Kentucky General Assembly voted against each of the Civil War Amendments when Congress submitted them to the states for ratification.[8] But after the amendments were ratified by the requisite three-fourths of the States, Kentucky's 1850 Constitution, with its focus on preserving the institution of slavery, was hopelessly out of date.

After the Civil War, in addition to the slavery issue, reformers identified other problems that warranted constitutional reform. The General Assembly approved referenda to call a constitutional convention in 1875, 1879, 1881, 1883, and 1885, all of which were rejected by voters. The rejection of the referenda was primarily attributable to the method devised by the legislature to determine the number of citizens eligible to vote for members of the House of Representatives, a majority of which were needed to approve the call. At the time of each of the five failed referenda, Kentucky law defined eligible voters as taxpayers—a number much larger than the number of actual voters.

After the 1885 referendum failed, the General Assembly established the first statewide voter registration law and defined eligible voters to mean registered voters. The voter registration law reduced the number of eligible voters, a majority of whom voted

---

6. Ky. Const. (1850) art. X, §2.

7. Ky. Const. (1850) art. XIII, §3.

8. The Kentucky General Assembly ratified the Thirteenth, Fourteenth, and Fifteenth Amendments in 1976. *See* 1976 Ky. Acts ch. 269. It had earlier rejected the amendments in February 1865, January 1867, and March 1869, respectively.

to approve a constitutional convention in 1887 and 1889.[9] In August 1890, the voters elected 100 delegates to the constitutional convention that met the following month in Frankfort. A majority of the delegates were members of the Democratic Party, with the balance being Republicans or Populists.

Before it adjourned in April 1891, the constitutional convention addressed many of the problems reformers had identified in the third constitution over the prior 25 years. In the process, the convention placed new restraints on the government, both at the state and local levels, which affected both the legislative and executive branches.

Changes Required by the Civil War Amendments

The 1890 convention addressed each of the third constitution's pro-slavery provisions. Gone was the constitutional right to property in persons. In its place, the new Constitution expressly outlawed slavery.[10] The convention also deleted the third constitution's prohibitions on ministers serving in the General Assembly or as Governor. The new Constitution allowed every male citizen of the United States over 21 years old to vote,[11] and recognized the "inherent and inalienable" right of "[a]ll men," including former slaves, to bear arms in defense of themselves and the state.[12] Finally, it opened membership in the state militia to every able-bodied male resident of the Commonwealth between the ages of 18 and 45, without regard to race.[13] Thus, in each of the areas where the Civil War Amendments had rendered the third constitution obsolete, the convention adopted changes to the constitutional text to bring the document current.[14]

However, the 1890 convention was not entirely progressive on all issues concerning race and sex. The new Constitution allowed local governments to levy poll taxes, which had the effect of discriminating against the poor and racial minorities in the exercise of their right to vote.[15] Further, the Constitution required separate public schools to

---

9. Under the 1850 Constitution, a convention was the only means of amending the constitution. If the General Assembly approved submitting the issue to the voters, the voters had to approve the calling of a convention at two consecutive elections. Ky. Const. (1850) art. XII, §1. Once the calling of a convention was approved by the voters, it became the duty of the General Assembly to enact a law calling the convention and providing for the election of 100 convention delegates, one from each Representative district. *Id.*

10. Ky. Const. §25.

11. Ky. Const. §145.

12. Ky. Const. §1(7).

13. Ky. Const. §219.

14. What is now Section 2 of the 1891 Constitution was formerly part of the Bill of Rights of the 1850 Constitution. Ky. Const. (1850) art. XIII, §2. "Section 2 . . . had its genesis in pre-Civil War efforts to use the Kentucky Constitution to protect slavery." John David Dyche, *Section 2 of the Kentucky Constitution—Where Did It Come From and What Does It Mean?*, 18 N. Ky. L. Rev. 503, 504 (1990). But the provision was kept in the Constitution by the 1890 convention as a substantive protection for private property rights in a post-slavery Kentucky. *Id.* at 511.

15. Ky. Const. §180.

be maintained for white and "colored" children.[16] As well, women still did not have a constitutional right to vote.

Powers of the Legislature

A primary complaint of the General Assembly's critics before the 1890 convention was that the legislature spent most of its time addressing the needs and wants of specific localities and individual citizens and businesses, rather than focusing on legislation that concerned the entire Commonwealth. Examples of such private legislation included bills to classify and charter cities (resulting in each city and town having its own legislative charter, with each charter including different powers and limitations), to charter corporations (because Kentucky had no general corporation laws), to provide relief to individual married women (because Kentucky lacked a married women's property act), and to allow different counties to punish similar criminal offenses differently. In 1887–88 alone, the General Assembly enacted 1,403 local and private statutes and only 168 general statutes. The resulting overlapping and contradictory laws made it difficult even for Kentucky lawyers to know what the applicable law was on many subjects.

Thus, the powers entrusted to the legislative branch, and the constitutional limits on that authority, were a central focus of the convention.[17] The Constitution the convention drafted prohibited most local and special legislation, requiring the General Assembly instead to legislate through general laws that applied statewide.[18] The new Constitution also enacted procedural reforms of the legislative process, such as requiring most bills to be reported by a committee and read three times each in the House and the Senate.[19] It limited each bill to one subject, which was required to be stated in its title, and it prohibited the General Assembly from amending laws by title only, requiring instead that amendments be published at length so legislators would know what they were amending.[20]

---

16. Ky. Const. §187.

17. The Supreme Court of Kentucky has noted multiple times that restraining the legislature, especially regarding local and special legislation, was a primary focus of the 1890 convention. *E.g.*, *Tabler v. Wallace*, 704 S.W.2d 179, 183 (Ky. 1985) ("Concern for limiting the powers of the legislature in general, and with cutting off special and local legislation in particular, was the primary motivating force behind enactment of the new Kentucky Constitution of 1891."); *see also Zuckerman v. Bevin*, 565 S.W.3d 580, 589 (Ky. 2018) ("Most scholars accept that Kentucky's 1890 Constitutional Convention was necessitated by excessive proliferation of special legislation for the benefit of individual persons and corporations, an unequal tax burden and mounting local public debts, a desire to exercise control over railroads and railroad rates, and the 1850 antebellum constitution's indefensible protections for slavery.").

18. *See* Ky. Const. §§59, 60.

19. Ky. Const. §46. Each chamber could vote to discharge a bill from committee if the committee failed to report it. *Id.* Also, either chamber could vote to waive a bill's second and third readings in that chamber. *Id.*

20. Ky. Const. §51.

The fourth Constitution also curbed the legislative power by retaining a provision from the 1850 Constitution that limited the General Assembly to biannual sessions, in even-numbered years, of no more than 60 days.[21] The 60-day limit on legislative sessions has been called "the most significant restriction placed on the General Assembly" by the new Constitution.[22]

The convention also gave the Governor more influence in the legislative process, by allowing him for the first time the power to exercise a line-item veto of appropriations bills[23] and to set the General Assembly's agenda for any special legislative sessions he might call.[24] And the new Constitution also precluded the General Assembly from interfering in the judicial process or catering to special interests by prohibiting it from capping damages to be awarded for injuries resulting in death, or for personal injuries or property damage.[25]

Restraints on Executive Branch Officials

A financial scandal had rocked the Commonwealth in the spring of 1888. And the story of "Honest Dick" Tate is one of the more colorful chapters in the history of Kentucky state government.

Gubernatorial candidate William O. Bradley, a Republican, had made a campaign issue in 1887 out of the need to audit the state treasury. Bradley lost the election, but the public favored his proposal, and at its next session, the General Assembly also called for an audit of the treasury.

State Treasurer James William "Honest Dick" Tate, a Democrat, had long been a fixture in Kentucky politics, having held office as Treasurer since 1867 and having held other offices before that. He was personally very popular and well regarded. Tate claimed to need more time to get his books in order, which delayed the establishment of the commission that was to audit them. But eventually the commission did audit the books.

In early 1888, Tate began depositing only checks into the state treasury and stopped making any cash deposits. On March 14, 1888, one of Tate's clerks, Henry Murray, noticed him filling two tobacco sacks with gold and silver coins. The coins were later valued around $100,000 (or almost $2.9 million in 2022 dollars), constituting most of the funds in the state treasury at the time. Tate left Frankfort for Louisville, leaving behind a note saying he would return in two days. Because of his record of trustworthiness, nobody questioned him. But after not being heard from for a week, suspicions arose.

---

21. Ky. Const. §42; *see also* Ky. Const. (1850) art. II, §24.

22. *Beshear v. Acree*, 615 S.W.3d 780, 807 (Ky. 2020) (quoting Sheryl G. Snyder & Robert M. Ireland, *The Separation of Governmental Powers under the Kentucky Constitution: A Legal and Historical Analysis of L.R.C. v. Brown*, 73 Ky. L.J. 165, 181 (1984)).

23. Ky. Const. §88.

24. Ky. Const. §80.

25. Ky. Const. §54.

Leaving his wife and daughter behind, Tate had boarded a train in Louisville headed to Cincinnati. He was never seen again. Tate's daughter later admitted to receiving at least four letters from her father between April and December 1888, postmarked from British Columbia, Japan, China, and San Francisco. Another witness testified to seeing an 1888 letter from Tate postmarked from Brazil, the last known communication from him. A *New York Times* article later claimed that Tate had died in China in 1890.

In the investigation of Tate, the state's ledger showed that Tate had made loans and advances to other Democratic state officials, which were often left unpaid, including an advance of several thousand dollars to Governor Preston Leslie in 1872. Tate also had used some of the state funds to make investments of his own. Governor Simon Bolivar Buckner announced that, due to Tate's poor bookkeeping, embezzlement, and theft, he had misappropriated $247,128.50 (or over $7.5 million in 2022 dollars) from the state treasury.

Because of his malfeasance, the Kentucky House of Representatives impeached Tate on six counts. The Senate tried him *in absentia*, convicting him on four counts[26] and removing him from office. A grand jury also indicted Tate.

Republicans and some Democrats blamed the state auditor, a Democrat, for failing to examine Tate's accounts more closely. It did not appear that the auditor was complicit in Tate's embezzlement and theft, but he certainly neglected to do his job. Reformers began agitating for constitutional changes to require monthly audits of the treasurer's accounts and to impose term limits on the treasurer, auditor, and other state officers.

In response to the Tate scandal, the convention included a new provision in the Constitution requiring the General Assembly to provide by law for monthly investigations into the accounts of both the Treasurer and the Auditor of Public Accounts.[27] In addition, the 1891 Constitution for the first time prohibited the Lieutenant Governor, Treasurer, Auditor of Public Accounts, Secretary of State, Commissioner of Agriculture, and Attorney General from serving two consecutive terms in office.[28] Earlier constitutions already had prohibited the Governor from serving consecutive terms,[29] and the 1891 Constitution included a similar prohibition.[30]

Though the line-item veto power conferred on the Governor for the first time in the 1891 Constitution enlarged the Governor's influence over the legislative process, the Constitution permitted the General Assembly to override a gubernatorial veto, or a line-item veto, by the vote of a majority of all the members elected to the House of Representatives and the Senate.[31] Thus, 51 votes are needed to override a veto in the House, and 20 in the Senate.

---

26. The Senate convicted Tate of the theft of more than $197,964.66 (or over $6 million in 2022 dollars) of the state's money.

27. Ky. Const. §53.

28. Ky. Const. §82 (Lieutenant Governor); *id.* §93 (other statewide constitutional officers).

29. Ky. Const. (1850) art. III, §3.

30. Ky. Const. §71.

31. Ky. Const. §88.

Kentucky's fourth Constitution also included a provision limiting the salaries of most state officials. Most public officers, other than the Governor, were limited to a salary of $5,000.[32]

Local Government

Before 1891, the constitution did not limit the General Assembly's power to determine the number of counties in the state. When Kentucky was admitted to the Union in 1792, it included nine counties. By the time the second constitution was approved in 1799, 43 more counties had been created. By the time of the 1850 Constitution, Kentucky had 100 counties. When the 1890 constitutional convention met, the General Assembly had carved the Commonwealth of Kentucky into 119 counties, more than 60% of which were unable to support themselves. The state government had to appropriate state funds to assist these counties in meeting their financial obligations.

In eastern Kentucky, the small size of some counties accentuated rivalries between families and political factions. These rivalries often boiled over into homicides and armed conflict. One example is the Rowan County War of 1884–87, which had at its root the Underwood-Holbrook feud, and featured vote buying, gambling, falsifying county records, business failures, and multiple deaths. Because the county government was unable to preserve the peace, the state militia was called upon three times to quell the violence in Rowan County. After his election in 1887, Governor Buckner appointed Samuel E. Hill to be the state's Adjutant General. A report to the Governor by Adjutant General Hill recommended that Rowan County be dissolved because of the violence and the county government's inability to preserve the peace.

At about the same time, a similar, and more famous, feud caused outbreaks of violence in Pike County. The Hatfield family were mostly residents of Logan County, West Virginia, and the McCoy family lived on the Kentucky side of the Tug Fork. Legend has it that the Hatfield-McCoy feud of 1863–91 began when Asa McCoy returned home after serving as a Union soldier in the Civil War. Asa McCoy was killed by the Logan Wildcats, a local militia working in association with the Confederate Army, and a member of the Hatfield family was widely believed to have committed the murder. Over time, the feud claimed dozens of lives between the two families. At one point, the Governors of Kentucky and West Virginia even threatened to have their militias invade each other's states.[33] Governor Buckner sent Adjutant General Hill to Pike County in January 1888 to investigate the Hatfield-McCoy feud, and once there, General Hill

32. Ky. Const. §246.

33. In December 1887 or January 1888, a band of armed men from Kentucky had entered West Virginia, kidnapped one Plyant Mahon, and jailed him in Pike County, Kentucky to await trial on a charge of willful murder. In the raid, a leader of the Hatfield clan had been killed. The governor of West Virginia requested that Governor Buckner return Mahon to West Virginia because the raid was illegal. Buckner refused, thus igniting a political and legal battle between the two governors. The federal court in Louisville later determined that Buckner was not personally involved in the raid or the Mahon kidnapping. In a case that eventually reached the U.S. Supreme Court, Mahon's petition for a writ of habeas corpus was denied, the Court holding that the illegal actions of private parties did not

organized a company of state militia to assist the civil authorities in maintaining the peace.

Thinking it would help maintain law and order and quell violence in the region, reformers urged constitutional limitations on the General Assembly's ability to create new counties.

To that end, the new Constitution made it nearly impossible for the General Assembly to form new counties. A new county could not contain, or reduce an existing county to, less than 400 square miles or 12,000 inhabitants.[34] Nor could a new county's boundary pass within ten miles of the county seat of any other county.[35] The new Constitution required voter approval to divide a county or move a county seat,[36] and also required any territory stricken off from one county to form another to bear its proportion of the indebtedness of the county from which it was stricken.[37]

Due to these restrictions on the General Assembly's power, only one new county has been created since the adoption of the 1891 Constitution. McCreary County was formed from parts of Wayne, Pulaski, and Whitley Counties in 1912, bringing to 120 the number of counties in the Commonwealth.[38]

The delegates to the 1890 convention, who predominantly came from the rural parts of the Commonwealth, distrusted cities, which they viewed as harboring more extravagance and fraud than any other part of government. The 1850 Constitution had been the first in the Commonwealth to contain provisions related to local government, but it left most of the particulars to the General Assembly. The result had been an ever-increasing number of special and local laws, piecemeal regulation of cities, and laws that benefited or harmed local governments based on favoritism and corruption by legislators.

Though the 1891 Constitution prohibited most special and local legislation,[39] it also required the General Assembly to group all cities into one of six classes based on pop-

---

preclude Mahon's detention by Kentucky officials and trial on the Pike County indictment. *Mahon v. Justice*, 127 U.S. 700 (1888).

34. Ky. Const. §§63, 64.

35. Ky. Const. §63.

36. Ky. Const. §64.

37. Ky. Const. §65.

38. The General Assembly's attempted creation of Beckham County in 1904 from parts of Carter, Elliott, and Lewis Counties was ruled unconstitutional under Sections 63 and 64. *Zimmerman v. Brooks*, 118 Ky. 85, 80 S.W. 443 (1904).

39. Ky. Const. §§59, 60. "Prof. Ireland noted the connection between county government and special and local legislation, stating 'while some argued that local legislation increased the power of the legislature over the counties, the reverse was often true,' since legislators were 'besieged' with demands for local and special bills. From this perspective, §59 is seen more as a limitation on county and municipal government. This view makes much sense when one considers that in the Kentucky session laws from 1865 to 1890, approximately 50% of all acts related to municipal or county matters: incorporating a town or amending its charter, changing court times, adjusting court jurisdiction, authorizing issuance of bonds, providing for school matters, declaring a stream navigable, regulating fishing on a given stream, and on and on." *Calloway Cnty. Sheriff's Dep't v. Woodall*, 607 S.W.3d 557,

ulation and to legislate equally within each class.[40] All charters granted prior to the new Constitution were expressly revoked.[41] The convention hoped that these structural reforms would curb the corruption they saw affecting local governments.

Railroads and Corporations

Between 1865 and 1880, Kentucky saw a dramatic increase in railroad track mileage in the state, including by the powerful Louisville and Nashville Railroad (L&N). Farmers and other shippers complained that the railroads charged discriminatory rates favoring larger shippers and those that shipped for longer distances, to the detriment of smaller shippers and those who shipped their goods for shorter distances. A legislative investigation revealed that the railroad lobby, on behalf of L&N and other railroads, showered gifts on legislators, such as free passes and whiskey. When rural reformers forced the legislature to create a Railroad Commission in 1880, the railroads ensured that it had no real regulatory authority. The railroads also were successful in obtaining special tax breaks for the industry and in defeating any broad reform measures.

To be fair, while railroads and other corporations were powerful, they did not completely control the General Assembly. The railroads unsuccessfully lobbied the General Assembly to repeal the law establishing the Railroad Commission at every legislative session from 1882 to 1890, and unsuccessfully resisted its increased taxation of railroad property.[42] The General Assembly enacted an early wrongful death statute in 1854, which remained in effect into the early 20th century.[43] After failing to achieve a legislative exemption from tort liability, the L&N unsuccessfully challenged the wrongful death statute in court.[44] Nevertheless, the popular sentiment was that the new Constitution should provide greater protections from railroads and other corporations to the public.

To that end, the 1891 Constitution required all property in the Commonwealth to be taxed,[45] thus precluding special tax treatment of the railroads, and further required corporate property to be taxed at the same rate as property owned by individuals.[46] The new Constitution codified the powers and duties of the Railroad Commission[47] and subjected corporations and railroads to stricter regulation by the state.[48] The new constitutional provisions directed at corporations and railroads were intended to ben-

---

570 n.13 (Ky. 2020) (cleaned up) (citing Robert M. Ireland, Little Kingdoms: The Counties of Kentucky, 1850–1891, 10 (1977)).

40. Ky. Const. §156.
41. Ky. Const. §166.
42. *Woodall*, 607 S.W.3d at 569.
43. *Id.* at 570.
44. *Id.* (citing *Schoolcraft's Adm'r v. Louisville & Nashville R.R.*, 92 Ky. 233, 17 S.W. 567 (1891)).
45. Ky. Const. §172.
46. Ky. Const. §174.
47. Ky. Const. §209.
48. *See* Ky. Const. §§190–208 (corporations); *id.* §§209–218 (railroads).

efit the public at large, and were a direct response to perceived abuses that had arisen over the years.[49]

Debt and Credit

Before the 1891 Constitution, many Kentucky cities and counties had borrowed extensively to fund transportation projects. Even though few of these ventures proved profitable, the local governments remained liable for the debts. This led to reformers seeking constitutional limitations on borrowing by local governments.

To address these concerns, the new Constitution included provisions imposing maximum property tax rates[50] and maximum levels of indebtedness[51] on cities, counties, and other local taxing districts.

The new Constitution also largely prohibited the General Assembly from authorizing new debt, unless approved by the voters.[52] As an additional measure to keep the Commonwealth from investing in turnpikes or other transportation projects, the 1891 Constitution also prohibited the Commonwealth from lending its credit to any individual, business, or corporation, or becoming an owner or stockholder in any business or corporation.[53] A similar constitutional provision was included to prevent cities and counties from investing in railroads or other projects, except for certain road projects, by prohibiting the General Assembly from authorizing them to become an owner or stockholder, or loan their credit to any business or corporation.[54]

Voting

Before the ratification of the current Constitution, Kentucky voters cast their votes by voice rather than by secret written ballot.[55] This led to the commonplace practice of buying and selling votes. Candidates for elective offices in Kentucky routinely set aside campaign funds for the purpose of buying votes.

To counter this blatant election fraud, the convention resisted efforts to delete the constitutional provision requiring all elections to be free and equal.[56] The new Constitution also included a provision, not found in Kentucky's prior constitutions, requiring all elections by the people to be by secret ballot and guaranteeing the right to vote in private at the polls.[57] It also expressly disqualified any person from holding office who gave or offered any money or other thing of value to influence his election or influ-

49. *See Zuckerman*, 565 S.W.3d at 592.
50. Ky. Const. §157.
51. Ky. Const. §158.
52. Ky. Const. §50.
53. Ky. Const. §177.
54. Ky. Const. §179.
55. Ky. Const. (1850) art. VIII, §15.
56. Ky. Const. §6; *see also* Ky. Const. (1850) art. XIII, §7.
57. Ky. Const. §147.

ence the vote of any voter,[58] revoked the charters of corporations that gave or offered anything of value to influence an election,[59] and required the General Assembly to enact laws for ousting any person from elective office who engages in election fraud, intimidation, bribery, or other corrupt practices.[60]

Women were not permitted to vote in most elections prior to 1891, though they were allowed to vote for school trustees. The convention rejected a proposal to allow women the right to vote in all elections. It also rejected another proposal to allow women greater voting rights in school elections and to permit women to be eligible for election to school office. The convention did include a provision in the new Constitution to exclude school district elections from the general constitutional requirements applicable to other elections,[61] which implicitly allowed the General Assembly, by statute, to continue to permit women to vote in school elections.

Labor

In the years before the 1890 convention, several reform measures favored by labor leaders had failed to achieve passage by the General Assembly. One such issue was the employment of children in dangerous occupations, like coal mining. Another was employers—especially in the coal mining industry—paying their workers in company scrip rather than in money.

The labor record of the constitutional convention was mixed. The 1891 Constitution addressed several labor issues, requiring the General Assembly to outlaw both child labor[62] and employers paying their employees in company scrip.[63] The new Constitution also limited the use of inmate labor to public works projects,[64] thus prohibiting private employers from replacing striking employees by leasing inmate labor.

But other reform proposals sought by labor organizations did not fare as well. For example, the convention rejected proposals limiting work hours on public projects, providing for arbitration of labor-management disputes, requiring designation of goods manufactured with inmate labor, governing the work conditions and minimum safety requirements in mines, and providing for equal property rights for married women.[65]

58. Ky. Const. §150.
59. *Id.*
60. Ky. Const. §151.
61. Ky. Const. §155.
62. Ky. Const. §243.
63. Ky. Const. §244.
64. Ky. Const. §253.
65. *See Zuckerman*, 565 S.W.3d at 591.

Lotteries

State sanctioned lotteries, especially the Louisiana State Lottery, were accused by reformers of corrupting state governments across the country, including the nascent State of North Dakota. Prior to the fourth Constitution, the General Assembly had chartered lotteries to raise money for public improvement projects. At the third constitutional convention, an effort to constitutionally prohibit lotteries had failed. The 1890 convention, however, approved a provision prohibiting all lotteries.[66]

Continued Constitutional Reform after the 1890 Convention

Though the current Constitution, like those before it, still allows for calling constitutional conventions,[67] Kentucky has not had a constitutional convention since it was adopted. The General Assembly approved referenda to call conventions in 1931,[68] 1947,[69] 1960,[70] and 1977.[71] Each time, the voters rejected the call at the polls.

In the mid-1960s, the General Assembly tried another avenue to amend the Constitution. It created a Constitution Revision Assembly in 1964,[72] which was tasked with studying the current constitution and proposing any amendments or revisions to it they felt were advisable. The Constitution Revision Assembly was composed of one delegate from each of the Commonwealth's 38 senatorial districts, five delegates chosen from the state at-large, and every elected former Governor of the Commonwealth. This distinguished group studied the Constitution for two years, after which it submitted a proposed new Constitution to the General Assembly for its consideration, which was much shorter in length than the current Constitution.

66. Ky. Const. §226.

67. Ky. Const. §§258–263.

68. 1930 Ky. Acts ch. 174.

69. 1946 Ky. Acts ch. 145.

70. 1960 Ky. Acts ch. 4. Unlike the General Assembly's three other convention proposals, which called for conventions that were unlimited as to subject matter, the 1960 proposal would have limited the convention to considering the following 12 subjects: "(1) The organization and powers of municipal, county and other local governments; (2) The judicial department and courts; (3) Compensation of public officers and employees; (4) The order of succession of persons entitled to act as Governor and the circumstances under which the Governor is disqualified to act; (5) Misfeasance, malfeasance and non-feasance of public officers; (6) Official oaths; (7) The Railroad Commission; (8) The legislative department; (9) The mode of revision or amendment of the Constitution; (10) Incompatibility of offices; (11) Terms and tenure of state officers other than Governor and Lieutenant Governor; [and] (12) Removal of limitations on the holding of real estate[.]" *Id.* §4. The proposed convention would have been permitted to make "no change ... in the Bill of Rights," and "any Constitution agreed upon by the convention [would] not become effective until submitted to the voters of the Commonwealth for their approval, by a majority of those voting." *Id.* The Court of Appeals upheld the validity of the proposed limited convention, holding that the sovereign people of the Commonwealth may limit the authority of the convention delegates, who serve as their agents. *Chenault v. Carter*, 332 S.W.2d 623, 626 (Ky. 1960).

71. 1976 Ky. Acts ch. 228.

72. 1964 Ky. Acts ch. 4.

The General Assembly then enacted a statute[73] in 1966 submitting the Constitution Revision Assembly's proposal to the voters for their ratification at the general election that November. The statute invoked "the inherent power of the people under Section 4 of the present Constitution" as its basis for submitting the proposed constitution directly to the people,[74] rather than the amendment or convention processes specifically provided for in the Constitution. Holding that "the people" always have the "right to alter, reform or abolish their government" under Section 4, the Court of Appeals upheld the proposed constitution from a constitutional challenge.[75] However, the voters overwhelmingly rejected the new constitution at the 1966 election.

Legislatively proposed individual amendments have proven to be the only successful means of amending the current Constitution. For the first time in the history of the Commonwealth, the 1891 Constitution allowed the General Assembly to propose individual constitutional amendments, subject to ratification by the voters.[76] The voters approved a constitutional amendment[77] in 1979 to increase from two to four the number of constitutional amendments the General Assembly may propose to the voters at any one election. This amendment specifically allowed amendments to relate not just to a single subject, but to "a single subject or to related subject matters." It also made clear that a single amendment may amend as many articles or sections of the Constitution "as may be necessary and appropriate in order to accomplish the objectives of the amendment." These changes liberalized the Constitution's stringent standard for the General Assembly to propose amendments to the voters, and expanded the potential reach of future amendments, accelerating the rate of constitutional change.

From 1891 to 2022, the General Assembly submitted 83 proposed amendments to the voters of the Commonwealth. Of those, the voters approved 42 and rejected 41.[78] By way of comparison, the U.S. Constitution has been amended 27 times. Congress proposed another six amendments that failed of ratification by the requisite three-fourths of the States. Thus, the Kentucky General Assembly has proposed two and a half times as many constitutional amendments to the voters of the Commonwealth in about 130 years as Congress has proposed to the States in 235 years.

Legislative Branch

Some of the more significant constitutional amendments ratified by the voters since the adoption of the current Constitution have eased its restraints on the power of the General Assembly.

---

73. 1966 Ky. Acts ch. 37.

74. *Id.* §7.

75. *See Gatewood v. Matthews*, 403 S.W.2d 716 (Ky. 1966).

76. Ky. Const. §§256–257.

77. 1978 Ky. Acts ch. 433 (amending Ky. Const. §256).

78. Following the text of the Constitution at the front of this volume, Appendix A describes each constitutional amendment adopted since 1891. Appendix B describes each constitutional amendment that the General Assembly proposed which the voters did not adopt.

Figure 1-1. Photo of commemorative plaque honoring William G. Kenton outside the chambers of the House of Representatives, Kentucky State Capitol. Reproduced with permission of the Legislative Research Commission.

In 1979, voters approved what became known as the Kenton Amendment,[79] so called because its primary sponsor was Rep. William G. Kenton, who was then Speaker of the House of Representatives. The amendment made several significant changes to the legislative branch, including: (1) moving elections for members of the House and Senate from odd-numbered years to even-numbered years; (2) allowing the General Assembly to meet for up to ten legislative days in odd-numbered years to elect legislative leaders, adopt rules of procedure, and organize committees; and (3) allowing the 60-day regular legislative sessions in even-numbered years to extend through April 15.

79. 1978 Ky. Acts ch. 440 (amending Ky. Const. §§30, 31, 36, 42).

After the ratification of the Kenton Amendment, a legislator would serve the first year of his or her term in interim activity, such as committee meetings and hearings on proposed legislation, before the start of the next regular legislative session. This allowed more time for legislators to familiarize themselves with the legislative process and the issues that would confront them in the next session. Also, by stretching regular sessions over three and a half months, the amendment allowed the General Assembly to take a ten-day veto recess before reconvening to consider overriding the Governor's vetoes.

Also in 1979, newly elected Governor John Y. Brown, Jr., announced he would not follow the longstanding practice of prior Governors influencing elections for legislative leaders. Previously, Governors had handpicked legislative leaders, which allowed the Executive Branch to dominate the legislative process. All subsequent Governors have followed Governor Brown's lead and not interfered in the Legislative Branch's internal matters. In conjunction, the Kenton Amendment and Governor Brown's hands-off approach to leadership elections helped make the General Assembly a more equal—and more independent—branch of state government.

Then, in 2000, voters ratified an amendment[80] that provided for annual legislative sessions. In addition to the 60-day regular sessions in even-numbered years, the 2000 amendment allowed the General Assembly to meet in regular session for 30 legislative days before March 30 in odd-numbered years.

The General Assembly proposed another constitutional amendment regarding legislative sessions, which the voters rejected in 2022.[81] That amendment would have eliminated the deadlines of March 30 in odd-numbered years and April 15 in even-numbered years to conclude regular legislative sessions, and it would have allowed the General Assembly to convene itself—for up to 12 legislative days annually—on the joint proclamation of the Speaker of the House of Representatives and the Senate President.

Though still a part-time legislature, the Kentucky General Assembly plays a much more active role in the government of the Commonwealth than was envisioned by the convention delegates in 1891.

Executive Branch

In 1992, the General Assembly proposed, and the voters ratified, a constitutional amendment[82] overhauling the Executive Branch. The amendment required the Governor and Lieutenant Governor to be elected jointly as a slate, permitted all statewide constitutional officers (Governor, Lieutenant Governor, Treasurer, Auditor of Public Accounts, Commissioner of Agriculture, Secretary of State, and Attorney General) to serve two consecutive terms in office, and provided for the succession in office in the event of the death or incapacity of the Governor and Lieutenant Governor. By

80. 2000 Ky. Acts ch. 407 (amending Ky. Const. §§36, 42).

81. 2021 Ky. Acts ch. 27.

82. 1992 Ky. Acts ch. 168 (amending Ky. Const. §§70, 71, 72, 73, 74, 82, 84, 85, 86, 87, 91, 93, 95, 97, 99, 148, 167; repealing Ky. Const. §§83, 94).

eliminating the one-term limit for all state constitutional officers, the 1992 amendment eased one of the principal restraints on the Executive Branch that the constitutional convention had implemented in response to the "Honest Dick" Tate scandal.

The 1992 amendment also permitted the Senate for the first time to elect the Senate President. Previously, the Constitution had provided that the Lieutenant Governor filled that role—much in the same way the U.S. Constitution provides for the Vice President also to serve as President of the Senate. Thus, the amendment eliminated the roles of the Lieutenant Governor—whose office is "primarily executive" in nature[83]—in legislative debates and in casting tie-breaking votes in the Senate.[84] By eliminating these legislative duties of an otherwise executive officer, the amendment created more separation between the Legislative and Executive branches, further emphasizing the separation of powers under the Kentucky Constitution.

Judicial Branch

The voters approved a constitutional amendment[85] at the November 1975 general election to reform and completely restructure the Judicial Branch. The "Judicial Article" approved by the voters made multiple changes to the Kentucky court system, including: (1) creating a "unified court system" called the Court of Justice; (2) converting the old Court of Appeals, which up to that point had been the Commonwealth's sole appellate court, into the present Supreme Court effective January 1976; (2) also beginning in January 1976, creating for the first time an intermediate appellate court, which was named the Court of Appeals, so that all appeals would not have to be heard by the high court; (3) consolidating the multiple trial courts of limited jurisdiction—*e.g.*, county courts, quarterly courts, police courts, and justice of the peace courts—into a single trial court called the District Court beginning in January 1978; (4) eliminating in January 1978 the judicial functions of county judges (now referred to in statute as county judge/executives) and justices of the peace (also sometimes referred to as magistrates), though retaining the legislative and executive functions of those offices; (5) guaranteeing for the first time a right to judicial appeal, rather than continuing General Assembly control over the appellate courts' jurisdiction; (6) requiring all judges and justices to first be members of the bar; and (7) clarifying that the Supreme Court has the power to prescribe procedural rules and govern admission to, and the discipline of, the bar.

The ratification of the Judicial Article consolidated judicial power in the new unified judicial system, rather than diffusing that power through a series of redundant courts with overlapping jurisdiction. The creation of an intermediate Court of Appeals gave the Supreme Court more control over its docket; vesting in the Supreme Court

83. *Rouse v. Johnson*, 234 Ky. 473, 28 S.W.2d 745, 748 (1930).

84. Section 83 of the Constitution, which was repealed by the 1992 amendment, had provided that "[the Lieutenant Governor] shall, by virtue of his office, be president of the senate, have a right, when in committee of the whole, to debate and vote on all subjects, and when the senate is equally divided, to give the casting vote."

85. 1974 Ky. Acts ch. 84 (repealing and reenacting Ky. Const. §§109–124; repealing Ky. Const. §§125–139, 141, 143).

power to prescribe rules of practice and procedure further insulated the courts from legislative control. The Judicial Article has had the effect of further insulating the judicial branch from incursions by the other branches, thereby making it a "more equal" branch in Kentucky's system of separated powers.

In 2002, the voters approved an amendment[86] to Section 112 that allows the Supreme Court to designate a specific division of a Circuit Court as a Family Court. A Family Court retains the general jurisdiction of the Circuit Court, but also has additional jurisdiction as provided by the General Assembly. This provision allows Family Courts to hear family law cases that would otherwise be heard in either the Circuit Courts or the District Courts, allowing for a "one family, one judge" model for handling cases.

Local Government

With some frequency, constitutional amendments proposed by the General Assembly have dealt with issues of concern to local governments. An amendment ratified in 1903 permitted cities to impose license or franchise taxes in lieu of ad valorem property taxes.[87] Voters also ratified an amendment[88] in 1984 to permit sheriffs to succeed themselves in office, and in 1986, approved another amendment[89] to permit mayors of larger cities to serve three consecutive terms in office.

In 1994, voters ratified an amendment[90] allowing the General Assembly more latitude to classify cities on a basis other than population and legislate with respect to each class,[91] and to grant cities more independence to govern themselves, known as "home rule."[92] The 1994 amendment also allowed cities and counties to incur long-term debt without voter approval,[93] thus giving them additional flexibility with respect to their finances.

Railroads and Corporations

The Commonwealth's economy has changed considerably from what it was in 1891. The railroads no longer wield the same political clout they once did. The rise of other business forms, such as limited liability companies, has made the corporation a less popular form for conducting business. The restrictions on railroads and corporations, which had been so important to the framers of the 1891 Constitution, now seem antiquated, and in any event, are much less important today. Changing times, and changing public attitudes about railroads and corporations, have resulted in a loosening of some of the Constitution's restrictions on such businesses.

---

86. 2001 Ky. Acts ch. 163 (amending Ky. Const. §112).
87. 1902 Ky. Acts ch. 50 (amending Ky. Const. §181).
88. 1984 Ky. Acts ch. 35 (amending Ky. Const. §99).
89. 1986 Ky. Acts ch. 140 (amending Ky. Const. §160).
90. 1994 Ky. Acts ch. 168 (repealing Ky. Const. §156; adopting Ky. Const. §§156a, 156b, 157b; amending Ky. Const. §158).
91. *See* Ky. Const. §156a.
92. *See* Ky. Const. §156b.
93. *See* Ky. Const. §158.

In 2000, voters approved a constitutional amendment[94] abolishing the Railroad Commission. Federal preemption had by then already made the Commission obsolete. Rather than having a separate Commission elected statewide to regulate the railroads, the amendment confers the power to regulate railroads on an "appropriate state agency" (currently, by statute, the Kentucky Transportation Cabinet). The 2000 amendment left other constitutional provisions specific to railroads in place.[95]

Two years later, the voters approved another amendment[96] permitting the General Assembly to regulate corporations by general laws. The amendment also repealed 10 sections of the Constitution that had prevented the General Assembly from modernizing corporate law to adapt to changing business practices. But the amendment left some other constitutional provisions in place that regulate corporations, common carriers, banks, and other businesses.[97]

Debt and Credit

Kentucky voters ratified an amendment[98] in 1909 to permit the credit of the Commonwealth to be given, pledged, or loaned to counties for public road purposes. This new constitutional provision therefore provides an exception to Section 177's otherwise total prohibition on lending the credit of the Commonwealth.

Voting and Civil Rights

Since the adoption of the 1891 Constitution, voters have ratified several amendments relating to voting and civil rights. A couple of these changes were precipitated by World War II, which had caused an absence of many voters from the state. A 1941 amendment[99] permitted the use of voting machines in Kentucky elections. In 1945, voters ratified an amendment[100] to allow for absentee voting.

In 1955, the voters ratified an amendment[101] to Section 145. This amendment lowered the voting age from 21 to 18. It also extended the right to vote in the Constitution to women, by deleting the Constitution's restriction of the right to vote to "male" citizens.[102]

---

94. 2000 Ky. Acts ch. 399 (amending Ky. Const. §§201, 218; repealing Ky. Const. §209).

95. *See* Ky. Const. §§210–218.

96. 2002 Ky. Acts ch. 341 (amending Ky. Const. §190; repealing Ky. Const. §§191, 192, 193, 194, 198, 200, 202, 203, 207, 208).

97. *See* Ky. Const. §§195, 196, 197, 199, 201, 204, 205, 206.

98. 1908 Ky. Acts ch. 36 (adopting Ky. Const. §157a).

99. 1940 Ky. Acts ch. 74 (amending Ky. Const. §147).

100. 1944 Ky. Acts ch. 5 (amending Ky. Const. §147).

101. 1954 Ky. Acts ch. 2 (amending Ky. Const. §145).

102. The Nineteenth Amendment to the U.S. Constitution had already extended the franchise to women nationwide in 1920.

Voters also approved a 1996 amendment[103] to delete the Constitution's provisions allowing for poll taxes and requiring separate schools for white and "colored" children to be maintained.[104]

Lotteries and Gambling

In 1987, Wallace Wilkinson campaigned for Governor on a platform that included amending the Kentucky Constitution to allow for the creation of a state lottery, so the cash-strapped state could raise revenue without raising taxes. Wilkinson was elected, and his election gave momentum to such an amendment. The General Assembly then proposed a constitutional amendment[105] in 1988 to allow for the creation of a state lottery to be "operated by or on behalf of the Commonwealth of Kentucky." Voters approved the amendment at the general election that year.

Kentucky's highest court in 1971 construed "lottery," as used in Section 226, to mean any "scheme for the distribution of prizes or things of value purely by lot or chance among persons who have paid or agreed to pay a consideration for the chance to share in the distribution."[106] This includes bingo games, even when such games are conducted on behalf of nonprofit entities. Notwithstanding the prohibition on charitable gaming, bingo games continued to be a popular means of nonprofit fundraising. In response, the General Assembly proposed, and the voters ratified, a constitutional amendment[107] in 1992 to allow the General Assembly to permit and regulate charitable gaming, such as raffles and bingo games.

Conclusion

Due to its length and complexity, the Kentucky Constitution of 1891 is certainly open to the criticism that it more closely resembles a complete legal code than it does a framework for government or a charter of individual liberties. It is a product of the legal and political issues that were prevalent in the Commonwealth at the end of the 19th century. For all its complexity, the Commonwealth's fourth charter is designed to shackle government power to a far greater extent than the U.S. Constitution or the constitutions of many other States.

---

103. 1996 Ky. Acts ch. 98 (amending Ky. Const. §§180, 187).

104. Poll taxes as a condition of voting were already prohibited in federal elections under the Twenty-fourth Amendment, which was ratified in 1964. The U.S. Supreme Court also held in *Harper v. Virginia State Board of Elections*, 383 U.S. 663 (1966), that poll taxes as a condition of voting in state elections violated the Equal Protection Clause of the Fourteenth Amendment. "Separate but equal" schools for white and black children also were found to violate the Equal Protection Clause in *Brown v. Board of Education of Topeka*, 347 U.S. 483 (1954).

105. 1988 Ky. Acts ch. 116 (amending Ky. Const. §226).

106. *Otto v. Kosofsky*, 476 S.W.2d 626, 629 (Ky. 1971). But note that the Court, applying the original public meaning of the term at the time the Constitution was ratified, previously had held that pari-mutuel wagering on horse races was not a "lottery" prohibited by Section 226. *Commonwealth v. Ky. Jockey Club*, 238 Ky. 739, 38 S.W.2d 987, 994 (1931).

107. 1992 Ky. Acts ch. 113 (amending Ky. Const. §226).

Some of these shackles place structural limits on the government, such as those separating the legislative, executive, and judicial powers and those dividing the executive power among several statewide elective offices. Other shackles are temporal in nature, such as those limiting the terms of Executive Branch officers or the number of days the General Assembly can meet each year. Others remove certain subjects from government control at all, such as limits on damages recoverable in tort actions. Still others place fiscal restraints on both state and local governments, such as those prohibiting debt without voter approval, constraining the taxing power, and limiting the salaries of state officials. Each of these restraints on state or local government power serve to erect additional hedges around individual liberty and to protect citizens' pockets.

The delegates to the 1890 convention also believed that unchecked power or influence of corporations and special interests were potentially as corrosive of individual liberty as government power. For this reason, the Kentucky Constitution also limits their power and influence in several ways, such as prohibiting their influencing of elections and allowing greater regulation of them by the General Assembly. By reducing corporate influence, the delegates believed that individual citizens could exert more influence over their government.

The Kentucky Constitution as it was initially written also can be criticized on the grounds that it permitted discrimination on the basis of race and sex with regard to voting rights and education. To our 21st century eyes, these are grave shortcomings. And yet, the same convention delegates who allowed poll taxes, required segregated schools, and denied women the vote, also made it easier to amend the Constitution to reflect evolving popular sentiment and a growing understanding of political equality. The present Constitution is therefore adaptable to modern circumstances in a way that Kentucky's previous constitutions and the U.S. Constitution are not.

Though certainly not perfect, and though equally likely to be amended further, the Kentucky Constitution stands as a bulwark of individual liberty. It has stood the test of time, and yet is adaptable to an uncertain future. By understanding the history and background of its text, Kentucky lawyers and citizens may better seek to preserve the blessings of civil, political, and religious liberty the Constitution secures.

Bibliography

Clark, Thomas D., A History of Kentucky (Ashland, KY: The Jesse Stuart Foundation 1992).

Ireland, Robert M., The Kentucky State Constitution (New York: Oxford University Press, 2nd ed. 2012).

Klotter, James C. and Craig Thompson Friend, A New History of Kentucky (Lexington, KY: University Press of Kentucky, 2nd ed. 2018).

Legislative Research Commission, Informational Bulletin No. 115: *County Government in Kentucky* (Frankfort, KY: Sept. 2021).

Legislative Research Commission, Informational Bulletin No. 145: *Kentucky Municipal Statutory Law* (Frankfort, KY: Sept. 2021).

Legislative Research Commission, Informational Bulletin No. 176: *Impeachment in Kentucky* (Frankfort, KY: Sept. 1991).

Metzmeier, Kurt X., et al., United at Last: The Judicial Article and the Struggle to Reform Kentucky's Courts (Frankfort, KY: Administrative Office of the Courts 2006).

B. Sovereignty and Formation of a Constitution

> "All power is inherent in the people, and all free governments are founded on their authority and instituted for their peace, safety, happiness and the protection of property. For the advancement of these ends, they have at all times an inalienable and indefeasible right to alter, reform or abolish their government in such manner as they may deem proper." (Ky. Const. §4.)
>
> "Amendments to this Constitution may be proposed in either House of the General Assembly at a regular session, and if such amendment or amendments shall be agreed to by three-fifths of all the members elected to each House, such proposed amendment or amendments ... shall be entered in full in their respective journals. Then such proposed amendment or amendments shall be submitted to the voters of the State for their ratification or rejection at the next general election for members of the House of Representatives...." (Ky. Const. §256.)

What is a constitution? What makes a constitution legitimate? Who has the authority to create a constitution, or to change it? What is its purpose? These questions are fundamental to understanding any constitution, whether of a State or the Federal government.

In Kentucky, Section 4 of our Constitution attempts to answer these questions. It declares, "All power is inherent in the people," and it therefore must follow that "the people" have the right and the power to create or change their foundational charter. The Constitution declares this right both "inalienable and indefeasible." Being "inalienable," the right cannot be taken away or given away. As an "indefeasible" right, it may not be lost, annulled, or overturned.

The Constitution's preamble states that the power ordaining and establishing the Constitution is "We, the people." Section 4 also addresses the purpose of the document: to form a government to provide for the "peace, safety, happiness and the protection of property" of "the people."

But answering these questions does not immediately reveal the mechanism available to the people for exercising their power to alter, reform, or abolish their government. The cases that follow will explore how a constitution is made and may be amended, and under what conditions.

Miller v. Johnson

Court of Appeals of Kentucky (1892)

92 Ky. 589, 18 S.W. 522

Opinion of the Court by Chief Justice Holt.

The question presented is a grave and exceedingly important one. It reaches to the very foundation of constitutional government. Little aid in arriving at a correct solution of it is furnished by precedent. Little, if indeed any, authority of direct bearing can be found.

Under the provisions of the Constitution of 1849, steps were taken to form a new one. We must assume, in view of what has taken place, that they were legal. As the result the Legislature passed the Act of May 3, 1890, providing for the calling of a convention for such purpose, and the election of delegates.

It provided that before any form of constitution made by them should become operative, it should be submitted to the voters of the State, and ratified by a majority of those voting. The Constitution then in force authorized the Legislature, the preliminary steps having been taken, to call a convention for "the purpose of re-adopting, amending or changing" it, but contains no provision giving the Legislature the power to require a submission of its work to a vote of the people.

The convention met in September, 1890, and having in April, 1891, completed a draft of a constitution, it, by ordinance, submitted it to a popular vote, and then adjourned until September following. During the recess the work was approved by a majority of nearly one hundred and forty thousand, the total vote cast being two hundred and eighty-eight thousand, three hundred and sixty. When the convention re-assembled, the delegates, moved no doubt by patriotic impulse, made numerous changes in the instrument, some of which are claimed to be material, while others were but a change of language or the correction of grammatical errors; and as thus amended it was promulgated by the convention on September 28, 1891, as the Constitution of the State.

The appellants, who are voters and taxpayers, suing for themselves and per an order of court for all others united with them in interest, as provided by our Code of Practice, shortly thereafter brought this action against the Public Printer and the Secretary of State, to enjoin the one from printing, at the public expense, the instrument so promulgated; and the other from preserving it in the State archives as the Constitution of the State; and also asking that it be adjudged not to be such, but spurious and invalid. This is asked upon the ground that the instrument promulgated by the convention is not the one adopted by the vote of the people, owing to the changes subsequently made in it.

* * *

It is conceded by all that the people are the source of all governmental power; and as the stream can not rise above its source, so there is no power above them. Sovereignty resides with them, and they are the supreme law-making power. Indeed, it has been declared in each of the several constitutions of this State, that "all power is inherent in the people," and this is true from the very nature of our government. It is contended by some, however, that inasmuch as the then existing constitution provided for the calling of a convention by the Legislature, without giving the latter the power to direct a submission to a vote of the people of the proposed new one, and gave the power to the convention to make one, that therefore it was not necessary, to its validity, to submit it to a popular vote, and that in attempting to require this, the Legislature exceeded its power. In other words, that the convention had plenary power in the matter, not because of ultimate sovereignty, but because the constitution gave it; that it submitted its work to the people merely to know if it pleased them; and that the Legislature could no more control them in this matter than it could in the framing of the instrument. Others contend that a ratification by a popular vote is necessary in all cases; that the attempted limitation upon the power of the convention by the Legislature was valid; and even if not, yet as delegates were elected under the statute, and with the understanding probably, upon the part of the people, that they were to pass upon the work; and as the convention actually submitted it to them, that the determination by the principal was final, and terminated the power of the agent. Each of these various views is supported by more or less authority, but we need not determine which of them is in our opinion correct, because another question properly in advance presents itself.

If a set of men, not selected by the people according to the forms of law, were to formulate an instrument and declare it the constitution, it would undoubtedly be the duty of the courts to declare its work a nullity. This would be revolution, and this the courts of the existing government must resist until they are overturned by power and a new government established.

The convention, however, was the offspring of law. The instrument which we are asked to declare invalid as a constitution, has been made and promulgated according to the forms of law. It is a matter of current history, that both the executive and legislative branches of the government have recognized its validity as a constitution, and are now daily doing so. Is this question, therefore one of a judicial character? Does its determination fall within the organic power of a court? It is our undoubted duty, if a statute be unconstitutional, to so declare it. Also, if a provision of the State Constitution be in conflict with the Federal Constitution, to hold the former invalid; but this is a very different case.

It may be said, however, that for every violation of, or non-compliance with, the law there should be a remedy in the courts. This is not, however, always the case. For instance, the power of a court as to the acts of other departments of the government is not an absolute one, but merely to determine whether they have kept within constitutional limits. It is a duty rather than a power. The judiciary can not compel a co-equal department to perform a duty. It is responsible to the people; but if it does act, then when the question is properly presented, it is the duty of the court to say whether it has conformed to the organic law. While the judiciary should protect the rights of the people with great care and jealousy, because this is its duty, and also because in times of great popular excitement, it is usually their last resort, yet it should at the same time be careful not to overstep the proper bounds of its power as being perhaps equally dangerous; and especially where such momentous results might follow, as would be likely in this instance, if the power of the judiciary permitted, and its duty required, the overthrow of the work of the convention.

After the American Revolution, the State of Rhode Island retained its colonial charter as its constitution, and no law existed providing for the making of a new one. In 1841 public meetings were held resulting in the election of a convention to form a new one, it to be submitted to a popular vote. The convention framed one, submitted it to a vote and declared it adopted. Elections were held for State officers, who proceeded to organize a new government. The charter government did not acquiesce in these proceedings, and finally declared the State under martial law. It called another convention, which, in 1843, formed a new constitution. Whether the charter government, or the one established by the voluntary convention, was the legitimate one, was uniformly held by the courts of the State not to be a judicial, but a political question; and the political department having recognized the one, it was held to be the duty of the judiciary to follow its decision.

* * *

Let us illustrate the difficulty of a court deciding the question. Suppose this court were to hold that the convention when it re-assembled had no power to make any material amendment, and that such as were made are void by reason of the people having theretofore approved the instrument. Then next this court must determine what amendments were material, and we find the court in effect making a constitution. This would be arrogating sovereignty to itself. Perhaps the members of the court might differ as to what amendments are material, and the result would be confusion and anarchy. One judge might say that all the amendments, material and immaterial, were void. Another that the convention had the implied power to correct palpable errors, and then the court might differ as to what amendments are material. If the instrument, as ratified by the people, could not be corrected or altered at all, or if the court must determine what changes were material, then the instrument as passed upon by the people, or as fixed by the court, would be lacking a promulgation by the convention, and if this be essential, then the question would arise: What constitution are we now living under, and what is the organic law of the State? A suggestion of these matters shows what endless confusion and harm to the State might, and likely would, arise.

If through error of opinion the convention exceeded its power, and the people are dissatisfied, they have ample remedy, without the judiciary being asked to overstep the proper limits of its power. The instrument provides for amendment and change. If a wrong has been done, it can and the proper way in which it should be remedied, is by the people acting as a body politic. It is not a question whether merely an amendment to a constitution, made without calling a convention, has been adopted as required by that constitution. If it provides how it is to be done then, unless the manner be followed, the judiciary, as the interpreter of that constitution, will declare the amendment invalid. (*Koehler v. Hill*, 60 Iowa 543, 14 N.W. 738; *State v. Tufly*, 19 Nev. 391, 12 P. 835.)

But it is a case where a new constitution has been formed and promulgated according to the forms of law. Great interests have already arisen under it; important rights exist by virtue of it; persons have been convicted of the highest crimes known to the law according to its provisions; the political power of the government has in many ways recognized it, and under such circumstances it is our duty to treat and regard it as a valid constitution and now the organic law of our Commonwealth.

We need not consider the validity of the amendments made after the convention re-assembled. If the making of them was in excess of its power, yet as the entire instrument has been recognized as valid in the manner suggested, it would be equally an abuse of power by the judiciary, and violation of the rights of the people, who can and properly should remedy the matter, if not to their liking, if it were to declare the instrument or a portion invalid, and bring confusion and anarchy upon the State.

The judgment of the lower court dismissing the action is affirmed.

* * *

Notes and Questions

1. The third Constitution of Kentucky (1850), in Article XII, Section 1, stated that, after the General Assembly proposed, and the voters of the Commonwealth approved, the calling of a constitutional convention, the convention shall "consist of as many members as there shall be in the House of Representatives, and no more, ... and to meet within three months after their election for the purpose of re-adopting, amending, or changing the Constitution...." As the *Miller* Court observed, the 1850 Constitution did not require that the constitutional convention first submit any proposed changes to the constitution to the voters for ratification before they took effect. The Court refused to graft a ratification requirement onto the process when the text of the Constitution did not call for it. Notice that the current Constitution also does not require a constitutional convention's work to be ratified by the voters. *See* Ky. Const. §§258–263.
2. Kentucky's first three constitutions did not include any mechanism for proposing or ratifying individual constitutional amendments. A constitutional convention was the only way to amend those constitutions. Kentucky's fourth, and current, constitution is the first to permit amendments without the necessity of a convention.
3. The 1850 Constitution also included a provision textually similar to Section 4 of the current Constitution. That provision read: "[A]ll power is inherent in the people, and all free governments are founded on their authority, and instituted for their peace, safety, happiness, security, and the protection of property. For the advancement of these ends, they have, at all times, an inalienable and indefeasible right to alter, reform, or abolish their government, in such manner as they might think proper." Ky. Const. (1850) art. XIII, §4.
4. How did the concept of the separation of powers affect the outcome of the case?
5. For purposes of the separation of powers, in which branch of government would a constitutional convention be?

Gatewood v. Matthews

Court of Appeals of Kentucky (1966)
403 S.W.2d 716

Opinion of the Court by Judge Williams.

W. C. Gatewood, individually and for all residents, voters and taxpayers of the Commonwealth of Kentucky, brought this suit in the Franklin Circuit Court demanding a declaration of rights and seeking to enjoin the Attorney General and the Secretary of State from certifying the question of adoption of a proposed Constitution. The Franklin Circuit Court delivered a well reasoned opinion defining the rights of the appellant and those he represents, and declined to issue an injunction. This appeal results.

By amendment to KRS 7.170, the 1964 General Assembly established the "Constitution Revision Assembly" to carry on a program of study, review, examination and exposition of the Constitution of Kentucky, to propose and publish drafts, amendments, or revisions thereof, and to report the result of its work to the General Assembly. Pursuant to that mandate, a Constitution Revision Assembly was appointed by majority vote of the Governor, Lieutenant Governor, Speaker of the House, and Chief Justice of the Court of Appeals. The Assembly was composed of all former living Governors, one delegate from each of the 38 Senatorial Districts, and five delegates from the State-at-large. The Assembly conducted detailed studies on each section of the Constitution. At the conclusion of its labors it recommended to the 1966 General Assembly a draft of a reformed Constitution.

In 1966, the General Assembly passed Senate Bill 161, which submits to the voters at the general election on November 8, 1966, adoption or rejection of the Constitution prepared by the Constitution Revision Assembly. S.B. 161 requires publication of the proposed Constitution in at least two newspapers of general circulation published in Kentucky, once not less than ninety days before and once not less than seven days before the date of the election. It further directs the Attorney General to cause "the proposed Constitution and schedule or summaries thereof to be further publicized by other communication media in order that the voters of the Commonwealth may have a reasonable opportunity to become informed on the issue to be decided by them."

The primary question to be considered is whether by the terms of Sections 256 and 258 of the Constitution the people have imposed upon themselves exclusive modes of amending or of revising their Constitution.

Section 258 authorizes the General Assembly to enact a law at two successive sessions providing for taking the sense of the people as to the necessity and expediency of calling a convention for the purpose of revising the Constitution. Section 256 provides for the proposal of amendments to the Constitution by the General Assembly.

It is the appellant's contention that those sections do represent exclusive modes of reforming the Constitution. He points out that in each of the former constitutions of this Commonwealth there has been a section which established procedure for revision. (Article XI, 1792 Const.; Article IX, 1799 Const.; Article XII, 1850 Const.; and sections

256–263, 1891 Const.) It is his argument that whatever power the Constitution has conferred upon the legislature in reference to proposing amendments or other modes of revision must be strictly pursued.

This is the first time this Court has had before it the question of whether sections 256 and 258 provide exclusive modes for changing the Constitution. In several cases we have considered efforts to amend or revise the Constitution in compliance with one of those sections. In each case this Court has held that such effort must follow precisely the procedure established in that particular section. *Harrod v. Hatcher*, 281 Ky. 712, 137 S.W.2d 405 (1940); *Arnett v. Sullivan*, 279 Ky. 720, 132 S.W.2d 76 (1939); *McCreary v. Speer*, 156 Ky. 783, 162 S.W. 99 (1914). In no case have we held that sections 256 and 258 are the exclusive modes of changing the constitution.

Here the proposed procedure does not follow the dictates of section 256 or 258 of the Constitution. In fact, there is no section specifically setting out the mode of revision prescribed in S.B. 161. If there be authority for such action it must be derived from the sovereign power of the people as delineated in section 4 of the Bill of Rights:

> "All power is inherent in the people, and all free governments are founded on their authority and instituted for their peace, safety, happiness and the protection of property. For the advancement of these ends, they have at all times an inalienable and indefeasible right to alter, reform or abolish their government in such manner as they may deem proper."

These words were supposedly penned by Thomas Jefferson as section 2, Article XII, of the 1792 Constitution. In any event they express the historical experience of the people in securing a government in which they have freedom of action not permitted by "the Divine Right of Kings." They simply and forcefully state the doctrine of popular sovereignty. The doctrine was recognized in *Miller v. Johnson*, 92 Ky. 589, 18 S.W. 522, 15 L.R.A. 524 (1892), where it was said:

> "It is conceded by all that the people are the source of all governmental power; and, as the stream cannot rise above its source, so there is no power above them. Sovereignty resides with them, and they are the supreme law-making power. Indeed, it has been declared in each of the several constitutions of this state that 'all power is inherent in the people;' and this is true, from the very nature of our government...."

The Bill of Rights has always been recognized as the supreme law of the Commonwealth. That fact is emphasized by section 26 of the Constitution, which is carried over from the past constitutions:

> "To guard against transgression of the high powers which we have delegated, We Declare that every thing in this Bill of Rights is excepted out of the general powers of government, and shall forever remain inviolate; and all laws contrary thereto, or contrary to this Constitution, shall be void."

It is inconceivable to assume the people might be divested of the power to reform their government by the procedures established in sections 256 and 258 of the Constitution.

Nowhere is that power limited either expressly or by necessary implication. In fact, one portion of a resolution offered at the 1890 Convention is as follows:

> "Resolved, That the Constitution shall not be altered, amended or changed in any way except as provided in this article."
>
> Vol. I, Debates, Constitutional Conventions, 1890, p. 144.

It was not adopted. The power of the people to change the Constitution is plenary, and the existence of one mode for exercising that power does not preclude all others.

History shows there were popular ratifications of both the 1850 and 1891 Constitutions despite the lack of provision therefor. *Miller v. Johnson, supra.* The legislative limitation that a constitution adopted by a convention should not become effective until ratified by a vote of the people was upheld in *Gaines v. O'Connell*, 305 Ky. 397, 204 S.W.2d 425 (1947), where we said:

> "The challenge of this limitation upon the Convention, if one should be held, is that the constitutional provisions with respect to this mode of revision deal with every phase of the calling, organization and duties of a convention, and contain no authority for the General Assembly to bind the members to submit their work to a vote of the people. Hence, it is argued, the framers of the present constitution did not intend to confer upon the Legislature the power to restrict or limit the action of the convention."
>
> …
>
> "Since the constitution of Kentucky … contains no inhibition or restriction upon the General Assembly in this matter of initiating a call for a Constitutional Convention, it was at liberty to exercise its plenary power in attaching the condition to the submission of the question of calling a convention. When they vote upon it, they will do so with the assurance that the result of the deliberations of the Convention, if called, will be submitted to them for ratification or rejection. By this course, the people keep a firm hold upon their liberties and may obtain a charter of government wanted by the majority." …

And in *Chenault v. Carter*, Ky., 332 S.W.2d 623 (1960), we held that the legislature was not prohibited from limiting a convention to consideration of only twelve subjects.

* * *

In the ultimate sense, the legislature does nothing unless and until the people ratify and choose to give the revised constitution life by their own direct action. In this respect the legislature merely performs the role of messenger or conduit. The process is no more than corollary to the right of petition and address reserved to the people in section 1 of the Constitution.

We cannot accept the proposition that section 4 has been preserved throughout all these years as a mere relic, a museum piece without meaning or substance as a viable principle of free government. To the contrary, it seems clear to the majority of this Court that in each of our four constitutions the Bill of Rights has been purposefully set aside as supreme and inviolate because it represents those things that are basic and eternal, all other matters being transitory and subject to change. It follows that nothing else in the Constitution can be construed as a limitation, restriction or modification of any of these fundamental rights.

Each of the four constitutions of this state has provided a method or methods of amendment and revision. Significantly, in none of them have such specified procedures been declared exclusive. The reason is obvious. The right of each generation to choose for itself is inalienable, as it was recognized and said from the very beginning. Being thus inalienable, that right cannot be cut down or subjected to conditions any more than it could be completely denied by one generation to another. So long as the people have due and proper notice and opportunity to acquaint themselves with any revision, and make their choice directly by a free and popular election, their will is supreme, and it is to be done.

As a practical matter, the intent of the framers of the Constitution is more than satisfied by this proposed action. Section 258 directs that two sessions of the legislature provide for a vote by the people on calling a convention. Two sessions were apparently thought necessary adequately to inform the public of the impending election. Further, the right to vote for delegates assured the people of a voice through their elected representatives. Here the procedure goes even further. News and information are disseminated faster and more efficiently today than was anticipated when the Constitution was drafted. But even more significant is the fact the people need not rely on a representative to speak for them. They participate directly and individually. Each person may cast his vote for or against the adoption of the proposed constitution knowing full well what it says. Another thing of significance is that until he casts his vote the document is as nothing. Only a majority vote of the people can give it force and effect.

The question to be submitted to the voters is set out in S.B. 161, as follows:

> "Are you in favor of reforming the Constitution of the Commonwealth to cause same to be in the same form and language as finally submitted to the Governor and the General Assembly of Kentucky by the Constitution Revision Assembly and set forth in Senate Bill No. 161 enacted at the Regular Session of the General Assembly of Kentucky held in the year 1966 and as heretofore scheduled and published as required by law?"

Suffice it to say the question conforms to the requirement of the statute, KRS 118.170(3), and affords an intelligible opportunity to the voters to express a clearly defined preference. *Turner v. Board of Education of Scottsville Independent School Dist.*, Ky., 266 S.W.2d 321 (1954); *Armstrong v. Fiscal Court of Carter County*, 162 Ky. 564, 172 S.W. 972 (1915); *Stone v. Gregory*, 110 Ky. 492, 61 S.W. 1002 (1901).

S.B. 161 provides that the complete text of the reformed Constitution shall be published in at least two newspapers of general circulation in the Commonwealth; once not less than ninety days before and again not less than seven days before the election. In addition, the Attorney General is directed to cause the proposed Constitution and schedule or summaries thereof to be publicized by other communication media. There is nothing vague or uncertain about the mandatory publication of the proposed Constitution, and the Attorney General's honorable and full compliance with the legislative direction must be expected and is to be presumed. To anticipate otherwise would constitute an unwarranted excursion outside the scope of judicial authority both as an intrusion upon the executive function and an invasion of that shadowy area where no justiciable controversy resides. *Combs v. Matthews*, Ky., 364 S.W.2d 647 (1963).

The action taken by the legislature does not violate the form or the spirit of the Constitution of Kentucky or the Constitution of the United States. When the people vote on the proposed Constitution it will be an expression of the inalienable right of the ultimate sovereign to reform the government. That right is guaranteed by Section 4 of the Bill of Rights, and is not preempted by the inclusion in the Constitution of alternate modes of revision.

The judgment is affirmed.

* * *

Judge Hill, dissenting.

I am not so much disturbed by the immediate result of this decision as I am by the establishment of a constitutional principle which is both contrary to logic and legal precedent and destructive to six sections (258–263) of the present Constitution of the Commonwealth of Kentucky.

The authors of our Constitution outlined in section 258 definite and specific steps for its revision. This is the one and only mode of revision contained therein. Had the authors intended any other mode of revision, they would have said so. Had they intended its revision in "any manner as they (the people) may deem proper," as is urged by appellees, section 258 would have been an indulgence in idle curiosity and speculation. I believe there is no reasonable-minded person in this Commonwealth who doubts that it was the intention of the authors of the Constitution to provide an exclusive plan for revision.

It appears to me that the only justification for the majority opinion is expediency. The net result of the opinion recognizes the right of the legislature to repeal the Constitution either in toto or by piecemeal. Nowhere in the Constitution is the legislature given the authority to formulate or submit to the people a new constitution. Here we are testing a legislative act and not a process of revision of the Constitution. The legislature either has or does not have the authority to legislate on this important question.

The only source of power which appellees are able to invoke is section 4 of the Constitution. This section provides as follows:

> "All power is inherent in the people, and all free governments are founded on their authority and instituted for their peace, safety, happiness and the protection of property. For the advancement of these ends, they have at all times an inalienable and indefeasible right to alter, reform or abolish their government in such manner as they may deem proper."

On its face, this section is an expression of political philosophy. It is a cocky boast of a sovereign people revelling in the enjoyment of new-won freedom and sovereignty. It is said this philosophy came from the pen of Jefferson. Appellant argues it only has historic value. I would not degrade it on that theory but would recognize that it may well leave in "the people" a residual power to accomplish ends not otherwise provided for in the Constitution. It should be recognized, however, that the practical application of this section is almost impossible. It provides no plan of implementation. Who are "the people?" Certainly, they are not the legislature. Under this section how do "they" (the people) act? I point out these difficulties in section 4 simply to emphasize the general, broad, and vague nature of the reservation of power contained therein and to further emphasize the utter dependence of section 4 upon section 258 for its implementation.

Without explaining just why section 4 empowers the legislature to pass the Act before us, the appellees rely upon section 26 of the Constitution. In doing so, they remove the trapdoor of their own scaffold. Section 26 is as follows:

> "To guard against transgressions of the high powers which we have delegated, We Declare that everything in this Bill of Rights is excepted out of the general powers of government, and shall forever remain inviolate; and all laws contrary thereto, or contrary to this Constitution shall be void."

Appellees cite this section to bolster their argument that section 4 of the Bill of Rights takes precedence over other sections. Ignoring the fact that this is contrary to settled principles of constitutional construction and contract law, the majority decision seems to overlook exactly what section 26 provides. Insofar as we are concerned in this case, it provides in effect that the power granted by section 4 "is excepted out of the general powers of government." In other words, the power exercisable by the people cannot be exercised by the government.

It cannot be successfully argued that the legislature in passing the Act before us was not exercising the general powers of government. The legislature has undertaken to preempt the right of the people which is reserved to them by section 4. This is exactly what section 26 says the government, acting through its legislature, cannot do. The case for appellees completely falls. Section 4 gives the legislature no authority to do anything. The argument might well stop here.

***

The truth is, "the people" spoke when they enacted and adopted the Constitution of the Commonwealth of Kentucky. Until "they" speak again, the legislature exercising the general powers of government must conform to the plain mandates of that document.

***

Perhaps the most celebrated and quoted case on the constitutional question involved here is *Miller v. Johnson*, 92 Ky. 589, 18 S.W. 522 (1892). I quote from *Miller*:

> "If a set of men, not selected by the people according to the forms of law, were to formulate an instrument and declare it the constitution, it would undoubt-

> edly be the duty of the courts to declare its work a nullity. This would be revolution, and this the courts of the existing government must resist until they are overturned by power, and a new government established."
>
> ...
>
> "If it provides how it is to be done, then, unless the manner be followed, the judiciary, as the interpreter of that constitution, will declare the amendment invalid."

* * *

The Constitutional rules of construction pertaining to this Act may not be understood by the layman. However, they are readily apparent to the trained legal mind. Those ardent supporters of a new constitution, and there is need for improvement, may become impatient and demand a short cut to a new constitution. But the Constitution of this Commonwealth should not be circumvented or a section or syllable masticated in the interest of expediency.

However unpopular my position, and irrespective of the loneliness of my dissent, I consider it my duty to speak out in support of the sacred and solemn Constitution of this Commonwealth and in support of the rights of "the people" who to this good hour have had no opportunity to be heard.

Notes and Questions

1. Why did the Court determine that it was not necessary for the General Assembly to follow Sections 256 or 258 when amending the Constitution?
2. The dissent describes Section 4 as "an expression of political philosophy ... a cocky boast of a sovereign people revelling in the enjoyment of new-won freedom and sovereignty," but practically impossible to apply because it does not include a "plan of implementation." Do you agree?
3. How did the *Gatewood* Court interpret Section 26 in this case, and how did that interpretation affect how it interpreted Section 4?
4. Following the Court's decision in the *Gatewood* case, the question that Senate Bill 161 required to be submitted to the voters was included on the ballot on November 8, 1967. The proposed new constitution was rejected by the voters, by a vote of 517,034 to 143,133. The new charter did not carry one of Kentucky's 120 counties.
5. The next push to amend the entire constitution—this time by calling a constitutional convention—also was ill-fated. After the General Assembly voted in both 1974 and 1976 to call for a referendum on a constitutional convention, the issue came before the voters once again in 1977. (*See* Ky. Const. §258.) The voters again rejected a constitutional overhaul, by a 165,311 to 254,934 vote. Since 1977, the General Assembly's efforts to amend the Constitution have exclusively been by specific amendment proposals, rather than by trying to adopt an altogether new charter.

Westerfield v. Ward

Supreme Court of Kentucky (2019)
599 S.W.3d 738

Opinion of the Court by Chief Justice Minton.

We accepted transfer of this appeal from the judgment of the Franklin Circuit Court that invalidated the submission of a proposed constitutional amendment to the voters of Kentucky in a single-sentence ballot question. We hold that the issue of whether the proposed amendment was properly submitted to and adopted by the voters is justiciable. We further hold that Sections 256 and 257 of the Kentucky Constitution require the entirety of a proposed constitutional amendment to be published and submitted to the voters irrespective of statutory requirements prescribed by the legislature. The proposed amendment as submitted to the voters in the form of the present ballot question is invalid. Accordingly, we affirm the judgment of the Franklin Circuit Court.

I. Facts and Background.

Under Sections 256 and 257 of the Kentucky Constitution, the General Assembly has the authority to propose a constitutional amendment to be published and submitted to the people for ratification. Section 256 governs the process for submitting a proposed amendment to the electorate and provides, in pertinent part:

> Amendments to this Constitution may be proposed in either House of the General Assembly at a regular session, and if such amendment or amendments shall be agreed to by three-fifths of all the members elected to each House, such proposed amendment or amendments, with the yeas and nays of the members of each House taken thereon, shall be entered in full in their respective journals. *Then such proposed amendment or amendments shall be submitted to the voters of the State for their ratification or rejection at the next general election for members of the House of Representatives, the vote to be taken thereon in such manner as the General Assembly may provide*, and to be certified by the officers of election to the Secretary of State in such manner as shall be provided by law, which vote shall be compared and certified by the same board authorized by law to compare the polls and give certificates of election to officers for the State at large.[1]

Section 257 governs publication of the amendment to the electorate. That section provides, in full:

> Before an amendment shall be submitted to a vote, the Secretary of State shall cause such proposed amendment, and the time that the same is to be voted upon, to be published at least ninety days before the vote is to be taken thereon in such manner as may be prescribed by law.[2]

1. Ky. Const. §256 (emphasis added).
2. Ky. Const. §257.

The General Assembly enacted Kentucky Revised Statute (KRS) 118.415 ostensibly to implement Sections 256 and 257. That statute provides generally that the amendment to be published and submitted to the electorate may be in the form of a ballot question. It also provides the process by which the ballot question must be published and submitted to the electorate. The statute states, in pertinent part, the following:

> (1) The General Assembly may state the substance of the amendment proposed to the Constitution of Kentucky in the form of a question in a manner calculated to inform the electorate of the substance of the amendment. When an amendment to the Constitution has been proposed by the General Assembly, the Secretary of State shall cause the question calculated to inform the electorate of the substance of the amendment which is prepared by the General Assembly or the Attorney General to be published at least one (1) time in a newspaper of general circulation published in this state, and shall also cause to be published at the same time and in the same manner the fact that the amendment will be submitted to the voters for their acceptance or rejection at the next regular election at which members of the General Assembly are to be voted for. The publication shall be made not later than the first Tuesday in August preceding the election at which the amendment is to be voted on.[3]

On January 2, 2018, Senator Whitney Westerfield introduced Senate Bill 3 ("SB 3"), entitled "AN ACT proposing to create a new section of the constitution of Kentucky relating to crime victim's rights." SB 3, colloquially known as "Marsy's Law," proposed an amendment to the Kentucky Constitution that would provide certain rights to crime victims. Section 1 of SB 3, which contains the text of the proposed amendment, provides the following:

> SECTION 1. IT IS PROPOSED THAT A NEW SECTION BE ADDED TO THE CONSTITUTION OF KENTUCKY TO READ AS FOLLOWS:
>
> To secure for victims of criminal acts or public offenses justice and due process and to ensure crime victims a meaningful role throughout the criminal and juvenile justice systems, a victim, as defined by law which takes effect upon the enactment of this section and which may be expanded by the General Assembly, shall have the following rights, which shall be respected and protected by law in a manner no less vigorous than the protections afforded to the accused in the criminal and juvenile justice systems: victims shall have the reasonable right, upon request, to timely notice of all proceedings and to be heard in any proceeding involving a release, plea, sentencing, or other matter involving the right of a victim other than grand jury proceedings; the right to be present at the trial and all other proceedings, other than grand jury proceedings, on the same basis as the accused; the right to proceedings free from unreasonable delay; the right to consult with the attorney for the Commonwealth or the attorney's designee; the right to reasonable protection from the accused and

3. KRS 118.415.

those acting on behalf of the accused throughout the criminal and juvenile justice process; the right to timely notice, upon request, of release or escape of the accused; the right to have the safety of the victim and the victim's family considered in setting bail, determining whether to release the defendant, and setting conditions of release after arrest and conviction; the right to full restitution to be paid by the convicted or adjudicated party in a manner to be determined by the court, except that in the case of a juvenile offender the court shall determine the amount and manner of paying the restitution taking into consideration the best interests of the juvenile offender and the victim; the right to fairness and due consideration of the crime victim's safety, dignity, and privacy; and the right to be informed of these enumerated rights, and shall have standing to assert these rights. The victim, the victim's attorney or other lawful representative, or the attorney for the Commonwealth upon request of the victim may seek enforcement of the rights enumerated in this section and any other right afforded to the victim by law in any trial or appellate court with jurisdiction over the case. The court shall act promptly on such a request and afford a remedy for the violation of any right. Nothing in this section shall afford the victim party status, or be construed as altering the presumption of innocence in the criminal justice system. The accused shall not have standing to assert the rights of a victim. Nothing in this section shall be construed to alter the powers, duties, and responsibilities of the prosecuting attorney. Nothing in this section or any law enacted under this section creates a cause of action for compensation, attorney's fees, or damages against the Commonwealth, a county, city, municipal corporation, or other political subdivision of the Commonwealth, an officer, employee, or agent of the Commonwealth, a county, city, municipal corporation, or any political subdivision of the Commonwealth, or an officer or employee of the court. Nothing in this section or any law enacted under this section shall be construed as creating:

(1) A basis for vacating a conviction; or

(2) A ground for any relief requested by the defendant.[4]

The General Assembly, under KRS 118.415, prepared a ballot question to be published and submitted to the voters for their ratification. That question is included in Section 2 of SB 3 and states the following:

Are you in favor of providing constitutional rights to victims of crime, including the right to be treated fairly, with dignity and respect, and the right to be informed and to have a voice in the judicial process?[5]

SB 3 passed the Kentucky House and Kentucky Senate on January 24, 2019 and was enrolled on January 25, 2018. That same day, SB 3 was delivered to the Secretary of State, Alison Lundergan Grimes ("Secretary Grimes") to be published and submitted

4. 2018 Ky. Acts, Ch. 1 (S.B. 3 §1).
5. 2018 Ky. Acts, Ch. 1 (S.B. 3 §2).

to the electorate at the November 6, 2018 election. On July 22, 2018, Secretary Grimes published the proposed question in the Louisville Courier-Journal and the Lexington Herald-Leader. On August 27, 2018, Secretary Grimes certified the question to the county clerks for placement on the November 6, 2018 ballot.

On August 7, 2018, Appellees, David M. Ward and Kentucky Association of Criminal Defense Lawyers, Inc. (together, "KACDL") filed a declaratory judgment action in Franklin Circuit Court against Secretary Grimes in her official capacity and the State Board of Elections, seeking a declaration that the ballot question in SB 3 failed to inform the voters adequately of the substance of the amendment in violation of Kentucky's statutory and constitutional requirements. The action also sought, in the alternative, injunctive relief that would prevent Secretary Grimes from certifying the ballot question to the county clerks or would direct her to rescind her certification if made.

On August 20, 2018, the Appellants, Senator Whitney Westerfield and Marsy's Law for Kentucky, LLC, (together, "Westerfield") filed an Intervening Answer.[6] KACDL filed a motion for summary judgment, Westerfield filed a cross-motion for summary judgment, and arguments were heard on October 9, 2018.

On October 15, 2018, the Franklin Circuit Court ruled that the ballot question did not adequately state the substance of the amendment and thereby violated the requirement in KRS 118.415 that the question be "in a manner calculated to inform the electorate of the substance of the amendment." Accordingly, the circuit court allowed the question to appear on the ballot at the November 6, 2018 election, but enjoined Secretary Grimes from certifying the ballots cast for or against the proposed amendment. On the same day as the circuit court's ruling, Westerfield filed a Notice of Appeal, and KACDL filed a Notice of Cross Appeal, to the Court of Appeals. And this Court accepted transfer of that appeal from the Court of Appeals.

The proposed amendment was approved by the voters at the November election with 63 percent of the vote.[7]

II. Analysis.

1. This Court has the authority to hear a constitutional challenge to a proposed constitutional amendment after it has been adopted by the voters.

Before addressing the merits of Westerfield's statutory and constitutional claims, we consider whether we have the authority to do so. Relying on the doctrine of separation of powers, Westerfield argues that the issue of whether the amendment was properly adopted—under either statutory or constitutionally mandated procedures—is a nonjusticiable political question because the ballot referendum has been conducted and the people have voted to adopt the amendment. In Westerfield's view, to assume jurisdiction to declare void a constitutional amendment adopted by the people would

6. Representative Joseph Fischer was later permitted to intervene as a party Defendant and is now an Appellant in this appeal.

7. The amendment was approved by the voters 62.81 percent to 37.19 percent. 868,932 voters voted for the amendment and 514,440 voted against it.

be an invasion of the legislative function of the people and would violate the "unusually forceful" separation of powers doctrine embedded in Kentucky's Constitution. Having rejected such an argument with respect to alleged constitutional violations on at least two occasions, we again find this issue to be justiciable.

Although we recognize that Kentucky's Constitution contains a uniquely stringent separation of powers provision,[8] we note that the doctrine does not "destroy the power of the courts to pronounce an act unconstitutional when its enactment is either expressly or by necessary implication inhibited and subversive of the purposes and intention of the makers of the [Kentucky] constitution...."[9] That sentiment is especially true when the act is an amendment to the Commonwealth's organic law and the challenge is based on a failure to comply with constitutional requirements for submission to the people.

In *Stovall v. Gartrell*, for example, this Court invalidated a legislatively proposed constitutional amendment that had been voted on and adopted by the people.[10] In rejecting the argument that "a court may not inquire into the manner in which a proposed amendment was passed in the legislature, since it was done within the constitutional framework and the people have finally voted on the question[,]" we explained the following:

> The Act proposed a constitutional amendment. It could be adopted as such only if the constitutional requirements with respect to adoption were strictly followed (which includes the statutory procedures authorized by and implementing the Constitution).... [N]either the legislature nor the people, or both, can short-circuit the Constitution. When the question is raised in the proper manner and at the proper time, as here, the validity [of] a proposed change in the Constitution is a judicial question.[11]

In *McCreary v. Speer*, this Court invalidated a proposed constitutional amendment after a vote was taken and the election had been certified claiming the Secretary of State failed to comply with the requirement of Section 257 that the proposed amendment be published at least 90 days before the election.[12] Similarly, the Court determined that it had authority to hear the challenge despite a favorable vote at the general election:

---

8. *See Legislative Research Comm'n ex rel. Prather v. Brown*, 664 S.W.2d 907, 912 (Ky. 1984) ("Unlike the federal constitution, the framers of Kentucky's constitution included an express separation of powers."); *Sibert v. Garrett*, 197 Ky. 17, 246 S.W. 455, 457 (Ky. 1922) ("Perhaps no state forming a part of the national government of the United States has a Constitution whose language more emphatically separates and perpetuates what might be termed the American tripod form of government than does our Constitution....").

9. *Sibert*, 246 S.W. at 458.

10. 332 S.W.2d 256, 263 (Ky. 1960).

11. *Id.* at 258 (citing *Miller v. Johnson*, 92 Ky. 589, 18 S.W. 522, 13 Ky. L. Rptr. 933 (Ky. 1892); *McCreary v. Speer*, 156 Ky. 783, 162 S.W. 99 (Ky. 1914)) (other citations omitted).

12. 162 S.W. at 101, 104 (action brought by a taxpayer to restrain the Governor from proclaiming that the amendment had been adopted as provided in Section 256).

> It is argued that this conclusion puts it in the power of an officer of the state to defeat the will of the people and prevent an amendment of the Constitution; but the Secretary of State is an officer created by the Constitution. The duty to publish the proposed amendment is a duty imposed by the Constitution, and, when the Constitution has provided that it may only be amended when certain things have been done by the agencies it selects for that purpose, to amend the Constitution in any other way is to ignore its provisions.
>
> The fact that a majority voted for the amendment, unless the vote was taken as provided by the Constitution, is not sufficient to make a change in that instrument. Whether a proposed amendment has been legally adopted is a judicial question, for the courts must uphold and enforce the Constitution as it is written until it is amended in the way which it provides for.[13]

Likewise, we find the constitutional challenges to the proposed amendment in this case to be justiciable, despite the voters having voted overwhelmingly in favor of the ballot question at the November 6, 2018 election. Like the challenges in both *Stovall* and *McCreary*, KACDL has challenged the proposed amendment in this case claiming it failed to comply with constitutional requirements with respect to the adoption of an amendment. And, like the mandatory constitutional prerequisite at issue in *McCreary*, we conclude below that Section 256 contains a similar constitutional requirement over which the General Assembly has no discretion.[14] It is precisely this type of challenge we have determined to be justiciable.

* * *

In sum, though the proposed amendment received 63 percent of the vote at the November election, the question of whether the amendment was properly adopted in accordance with mandatory constitutional requirements is a judicial one. * * * Accordingly, we proceed to the merits of KACDL's claim.

* * *

3. The proposed amendment violates Section 256 of the Kentucky Constitution.

We turn now to the merits of KACDL's constitutional challenge. KACDL argues that the proposed amendment is invalid because it failed to satisfy the requirement that it be published and submitted to the electorate. * * *

---

13. *Id.* at 104.

14. * * * Westerfield also cites to *Miller v. Johnson*, 92 Ky. 589, 18 S.W. 522, 13 Ky. L. Rptr. 933 (Ky. 1892); *Gatewood v. Matthews*, 403 S.W.2d 716 (Ky. 1966); and *Gaines v. O'Connell*, 305 Ky. 397, 204 S.W.2d 425 (Ky. 1947), for further support that a favorable vote taken by the people renders constitutional challenges to a proposed amendment nonjusticiable. While those cases stand for the proposition that "[s]overeignty resides with [the people], and they are the supreme lawmaking power," this does not require this Court to refrain from judicial review of a constitutional amendment simply because the people have voted favorably at the ballot. *McCreary* and *Stovall* make clear that mandatory constitutional requirements pertaining to such amendments must be strictly followed—particularly those that are designed to ensure that the amendment-adoption process is truly in the hands of the people.

To reiterate, Section 256 allows the General Assembly to propose an amendment to the Kentucky Constitution and requires that it be submitted to the electorate for a vote. That section provides, in pertinent part, the following:

> Amendments to this constitution may be proposed in either House of the General Assembly at a regular session, and if such amendment or amendments shall be agreed to by three-fifths of all the members elected to each House, such proposed amendment or amendments, with the yeas and nays of the members of each house taken thereon, shall be entered in full in their respective journals. Then *such proposed amendment or amendments shall be submitted to the voters of the State for their ratification or rejection at the next general election for members of the House of Representatives, the vote to be taken thereon in such manner as the General Assembly may provide....*[15]

When interpreting constitutional provisions, we look first and foremost to the express language of the provision, "and words must be given their plain and usual meaning."[16] This Court must not construe such plain and definite language "in such a manner as to thwart the deliberate purpose and intent of the framers of that instrument."[17] Further, "[i]t is to be presumed that in framing the constitution great care was exercised in the language used to convey its meaning and as little as possible left to implication[.]"[18]

We have previously interpreted Section 256 as granting to the General Assembly the exclusive authority to determine the procedure by which a proposed amendment must be submitted to the electorate. Although not central to the holding of the case, we first expressed this view in *Funk v. Fielder*, where we explained that the phrase "'the vote to be taken thereon in such manner as the General Assembly may provide' left it open for the legislature to prescribe the manner, and, in so doing, it enacted KRS 118.430."[19]

Now, however, we are unable to square such a statement with the plain text of Section 256. The provision expressly provides that "such proposed amendment or amendments shall be submitted to the voters[.]"[20] This statement is separate and apart from the phrase "the vote to be taken thereon in such manner as the General Assembly may provide." A plain reading of this text suggests that the Framers intended to impose a mandatory requirement that the amendment be submitted to the voters, and that they intended to leave only the way the vote was to be taken to the General Assembly's

---

15. Ky. Const. §257 (emphasis added).

16. *Fletcher v. Graham*, 192 S.W.3d 350, 357–58 (Ky. 2006) (citing *City of Louisville Mun. Hous. Comm'n v. Pub. Hous. Admin.*, 261 S.W.2d 286, 287 (Ky. 1953)).

17. *Harrod v. Hatcher*, 281 Ky. 712, 137 S.W.2d 405, 408 (Ky. 1940).

18. *City of Louisville v. German*, 286 Ky. 477, 150 S.W.2d 931, 935 (Ky. 1940).

19. 243 S.W.2d 474, 476 (Ky. 1951). *See also Hatcher v. Meredith*, 295 Ky. 194, 173 S.W.2d 665, 670 (Ky. 1943). KRS 118.430 was later amended to become KRS 118.415. For our purposes, the two statutes are substantially the same. In *Stovall*, we again accepted this interpretation as valid, explaining that KRS 118.430, "was enacted pursuant to the authority given the General Assembly by section 256 of the Constitution to provide by law the manner in which the vote shall be taken on an amendment." 332 S.W.2d at 263.

20. Ky. Const. §256.

discretion. To allow the phrase "in such manner as the General Assembly may provide" to modify both "the vote to be taken" and "shall be submitted to the voters," would go against ordinary rules of sentence structure.

We acknowledge that it is possible to interpret the phrase "the vote to be taken thereon" to encompass not only the logistical details of the voting process but also the form of the amendment to be submitted for a vote. But we find it unimaginable that the Framers intended to grant such broad authority over the process of modifying our organic document solely to the General Assembly. And a review of the Constitutional Debates shows the Framers' view that amending the Constitution should be more difficult than passing a statute and that it should be largely in the hands of the people.

For example, in rejecting the notion that allowing amendments to the Constitution would make the document nothing more than a statute to be changed by the legislature, Delegate Jonson[21] noted that Section 256 imposed both a heightened requirement for passage in the General Assembly and "then instead of its taking effect at the will of the Legislature *it must be remitted back to the people for whom this Constitution is being made, and for whom it will furnish the means of government*."[22] Similarly, Delegate Lassing[23] expressed his view that the people's ratification of such an amendment was imperative:

> It does seem to me that the organic law of the state should not be easily changed. It does seem to me that ample opportunity should be given to the people of the State to take a sober second-thoughted deliberative consideration of the matter before anything [*sic*] is inserted in the organic law different from what it is now.... An organic law, as I conceive it, should not be as easily, or nearly as easily, changed as a statute.[24]

In addition to its being contrary to the plain language, an interpretation that would give to the legislature absolute authority to choose the way an amendment is even submitted to the electorate would seem to undermine the Framers' concerns entirely and would yield an absurd result. For example, were this the case, the General Assembly could have just as easily provided in KRS 118.415 that only a ten-word summary of an amendment may be submitted to the electorate for a vote. Such a procedure would surely be at odds with the Framers' idea that it should not be entrusted to the legislature alone to amend our organic document.

With the Framers' intentions in mind, we also find it impossible to read Section 256 as saying anything other than the proposed amendment itself must be placed on the ballot. The meaning of the phrase "such proposed amendment or amendments shall be submitted to the voters" is plain and its direction is clear: *the amendment* is to be presented to the people for a vote.

---

21. Jep. C. Jonson was the Delegate from McLean County. Ky. Const. Ordinance.
22. 1890–91 Ky. Const. Debates 5246–47 (emphasis added).
23. L. W. Lassing was the Delegate from Boone County. Ky. Const. Ordinance.
24. 1890–91 Ky. Const. Debates 5252. * * *

Again, we acknowledge that it is possible to interpret the phrase "submit" as something other than presentation of the thing itself to the people. But such an interpretation would go against the word's ordinary meaning[25] and is contrary to the idea, repeated throughout the Constitutional Debates, that the modification of our organic document requires a meaningful, thoughtful opportunity for the voters to know what they are voting on—one that is separate and apart from the legislature's. We simply cannot read this section to allow anything less. * * *

Accordingly, we hold that Section 256 imposes a mandatory constitutional directive on the General Assembly to submit the amendment, in its entirety, to the electorate for a vote, and leaves to the discretion of the General Assembly only the way the vote must be taken. Strict compliance with such textual directives pertaining to constitutional amendments is required.[26] Because the form of the proposed amendment submitted to the electorate at the ballot was something less than the full text, the amendment violates Section 256 and is void.

4. The proposed amendment violates Section 257 of the Kentucky Constitution.

Having determined that Section 256 requires the entirety of a proposed constitutional amendment to be submitted to the people for a vote, we turn now to whether Section 257 also requires the entire amendment to be published. * * * We hold that it does. * * *

Again, Section 257 governs the publication of a proposed amendment before it is sent to the electorate for a vote. It provides the following:

> Before an amendment shall be submitted to a vote, the Secretary of State shall cause such proposed amendment, and the time that the same is to be voted upon, to be published at least ninety days before the vote is to be taken thereon in such manner as may be prescribed by law.

Bound by the same principles of construction, we find it impossible to construe this constitutional provision in a way that is different from Section 256. We note that both Section 256 and Section 257 require that "such proposed amendment" be submitted or published. And, like Section 256, the phrase "in such manner as may be prescribed by law" plainly modifies the word "published." Had the Framers intended for these provisions to be construed differently—i.e., for "such proposed amendment" to mean the entirety of the amendment in one provision but not the other—then it would almost certainly have used different language. But it did not, and, like Section 256, we

---

25. Merriam-Webster presently defines submit as "to present or propose to another for review, consideration, or decision." * * * A similar definition was in effect at the time Section 257 was drafted: "to leave or commit to the discretion or judgment of another or others; to refer[.]" * * *

26. *Stovall v. Gartrell*, 332 S.W.2d 256, 263 (Ky. 1960) (citation omitted). *See also Gatewood v. Matthews*, 403 S.W.2d 716, 718 (Ky. 1966) (noting that, with respect to challenges to constitutional amendments based on Sections 256 and 258, "this court has held that such efforts must follow precisely the procedure established in that particular section") (citing *Harrod v. Hatcher*, 281 Ky. 712, 137 S.W.2d 405 (1940); *Arnett v. Sullivan*, 279 Ky. 720, 132 S.W.2d 76 (1939); *McCreary v. Speer*, 156 Ky. 783, 162 S.W. 99 (1914)).

think the directive in this provision is clear: The Secretary of State must cause the amendment to be published at least ninety days before it is submitted to the people for a vote, but the General Assembly has discretion over the way that publication may take place.[27]

Recognizing that the two provisions must be construed in the same way, it becomes even more clear that the intent of the Framers was not to give to the General Assembly absolute authority to determine the form of the amendment that must be published and submitted. Were that the case, it would be entirely possible for a proposed constitutional amendment to be put to a vote of the people without them ever having an opportunity to read the full text of it—either at the ballot box or in their local newspaper.[28] Given the Framers' desire to place in the hands of the people the authority to amend our organic document, they could not possibly have intended this result. Our constitution is too important and valuable to be amended without the full amendment ever being put to the public.

Accordingly, we hold that Section 257 requires the Secretary of State to publish the entirety of the proposed amendment at least ninety days before the vote is to be taken thereon but leaves to the General Assembly the discretion to determine in what manner that publication may occur. Strict compliance with this constitutional procedural directive is required.[29] Because Secretary Grimes failed to cause the entirety of the proposed amendment to be published, the proposed amendment also violates Section 257 of the Kentucky Constitution and is void.

III. Conclusion.

In sum, we hold that Section 256 of the Kentucky Constitution requires the General Assembly to submit the full text of a proposed constitutional amendment to the electorate for a vote. Likewise, Section 257 requires the Secretary of State to publish the full text of the proposed amendment at least ninety days before the vote. Because the form of the amendment that was published and submitted to the electorate for a vote in this case was not the full text, and was instead a question, the proposed amendment is void.

Therefore, we affirm the judgment of the Franklin Circuit Court.

All sitting. All concur.

---

27. The General Assembly has exercised this discretion by requiring publication to occur "one (1) time in a newspaper of general circulation published in this state." KRS 118.415(1).

28. In fact, that is exactly what was done in this case. Only the 38-word ballot question drafted by the General Assembly, and not the 553-word amendment, was published and submitted to the electorate. * * *

29. See *Stovall v. Gartrell*, 332 S.W.2d 256, 263 (Ky. 1960) (citation omitted). *See also Gatewood v. Matthews*, 403 S.W.2d 716, 718 (Ky. 1966) (noting that, with respect to challenges to constitutional amendments based on Sections 256 and 258, "this court has held that such efforts must follow precisely the procedure established in that particular section") (citing *Harrod v. Hatcher*, 281 Ky. 712, 137 S.W.2d 405 (1940); *Arnett v. Sullivan*, 279 Ky. 720, 132 S.W.2d 76 (1939); *McCreary v. Speer*, 156 Ky. 783, 162 S.W. 99 (1914)).

Notes and Questions

1. Compare the text of the ballot question approved in *Gatewood* with the text of the ballot question disapproved in *Westerfield.* What differences in the underlying facts of the cases can explain the different outcomes in the two cases?

2. The Court held that SB 3 violated Sections 256 and 257 of the Constitution. However, the Court did not address whether the proposed amendment was still valid under Section 4. Do you think this effort to amend the Constitution could have been saved under Section 4, as construed by *Gatewood*? Do you think that *Gatewood* remains good law today after *Westerfield*?

3. After the Supreme Court struck down the Marsy's Law amendment in 2019 in *Westerfield*, the General Assembly again proposed the amendment to the voters in 2020. This time, to conform with the Supreme Court's interpretation of Sections 256 and 257, the entire text of the amendment was printed on the ballot. The voters ratified the amendment, by 1,156,883 (63.4%) to 668,866 (36.6%) votes, thereby adding Section 26A to the Kentucky Constitution. Once again, the same plaintiffs as in *Westerfield* sued to enjoin the certification of the election results, but the Supreme Court held they did not have standing to do so. *See Ward v. Westerfield*, 653 S.W.3d 48 (Ky. 2022).

4. The Marsy's Law amendment was first adopted in California in 2008 (*see* Cal. Const. art. I, §28). In addition to Kentucky, similar amendments to state constitutions have been adopted in Florida (Fla. Const. art. I, §16), Georgia (Ga. Const. art. I, §1 ¶XXX), Illinois (Ill. Const. art. I, §8.1), Nevada (Nev. Const. art. 1, §8A), North Carolina (N.C. Const. art. I, §37), North Dakota (N.D. Const. art. I, §25), Ohio (Ohio Const. art. I, §10a), Oklahoma (Okla. Const. art. II, §34), South Dakota (S.D. Const. art. VI, §29), and Wisconsin (Wisc. Const. art. I, §9m). Voters in Montana and Pennsylvania also voted to approve Marsy's Law constitutional amendments, but as in *Westerfield*, the courts in those states invalidated the amendments because they violated other provisions of those states' constitutions. *See League of Women Voters of Pa. v. DeGraffenreid*, 265 A.3d 207 (Pa. 2021); *Mont. Ass'n of Counties v. Mont. ex rel. Fox*, 404 P.3d 733 (Mont. 2017).

Two

The Government's Relationship to the Governed

A. Government Power, Reasonableness, and Equality

> "Absolute and arbitrary power over the lives, liberty and property of freemen exists nowhere in a republic, not even in the largest majority." (Ky. Const. §2.)
>
> "All men, when they form a social compact, are equal; and no grant of exclusive, separate public emoluments or privileges shall be made to any man or set of men, except in consideration of public services . . ." (Ky. Const. §3.)

In Sections 2 and 3, the Kentucky Constitution declares it to be among the "great and essential principles of liberty and free government" (Ky. Const. Bill of Rights pmbl.) that the government erected by the Constitution does not exercise any "absolute and arbitrary power" over the people, and that it must treat all citizens—*i.e.*, those who "form[ed] a social compact"—as "equal." But what is "absolute and arbitrary power"? And in a Commonwealth having citizens who are both rich and poor, both educated and uneducated, and of all races, ethnicities, and national origins, what does it mean to require the government to treat everyone as though they "are equal"? The following cases explore the breadth and depth of these foundational principles.

City of Louisville v. Kuhn

Court of Appeals of Kentucky (1940)
284 Ky. 684, 145 S.W.2d 851

Opinion of the Court by Judge Thomas.

The legislative department of the city of Louisville in April 1938 enacted "An ordinance pertaining to the regulation of sanitary conditions, public health, public safety, public welfare, public morals, business hours and conduct of barber shops." The enacting portion of the ordinance was preceded with eleven "whereases" employed, no doubt, to stabilize the confidence of the enacting board or boards in its authority to prescribe as is done in section III of the ordinance, which says: "That it shall be unlawful for any person, firm, association or corporation to keep open any barber shop or to conduct any barber business therein, within said city upon any of the hereinafter mentioned holidays or on any other day before the hour of eight o'clock A. M., or after the hour of six o'clock P. M., excepting Saturdays and the day preceding holidays or after the hour of eight o'clock P. M. on Saturdays and the day preceding holidays."

Section V penalizes violations of all prohibitory provisions of the ordinance, including section III, and subjects the violator to a fine of not less than $19 nor more than $100; or by imprisonment for a period not exceeding thirty days, or both fine and imprisonment, and makes each day during which the ordinance is violated a separate offense. Other provisions relate to prescribed sanitary precautions, inspection of the premises, licensing of members of the trade or occupation, and other requirements looking to the preservation of sanitary conditions, and the qualification of those engaged in the trade as a means of promoting sanitation and the safety of patrons.

This action was filed in the Jefferson circuit court by appellee as plaintiff below, against the appellant and defendant below, and in plaintiff's petition he averred that he was a barber by trade, had complied with regulatory laws affecting his qualification as such, and had obtained a license to operate a barber shop in the city of Louisville. He averred that section III, *supra*, of the ordinance was invalid as an improper exercise of the Police Power, in that it invaded fundamental rights guaranteed to him and others similarly situated, by both the Federal and our State Constitutions. The petition was amended the second time, and an answer and responsive pleadings were filed to an issue. The trial court upon submission to it of the demurrer to the petition and other interlocutory motions, overruled it and sustained the prayer of plaintiff's petition by adjudging the attacked section void, which was followed by granting a permanent injunction against defendant's prosecution as he had averred was threatened, thereby making permanent a temporary restraining order to the same effect granted upon the filing of the petition. From that judgment defendants prosecute this appeal.

It is at once apparent that we are again confronted with what we in the case of *Ashland Transfer Company v. State Tax Commission*, 247 Ky. 144, 56 S.W.2d 691, 87 A.L.R. 534, and other courts in their respective jurisdictions, describe as the "Police Power" possessed by the sovereignty and by its subordinate units when the power was properly delegated to them. We found that it was indefinable or, if definable, at all, it was a difficult task to do so. A reading of judicial opinions and authorized texts will reveal that to a degree and in a sense, practically every law enacted by the legislative departments in our form of government emanates from authority conferred by and springing from the exercise of the Police Power. Its fundamental purpose is the bettering of the conditions of living, and involves a multiplicity of objects looking to that end—chiefly the improvement of morals, health, education, co-operation, and all things else tending to make government ball bearing and smooth running. However, notwithstanding the scope so embraced by the power under consideration it possesses its limitations as is guaranteed to the citizen by Bills of Rights contained in both the Federal and our State Constitutions, each of which proclaim and declare as an inviolate right that the citizen's property and personal rights may not be taken away from him without due process of law. Hence, section 26 of our Constitution prescribes that "To guard against transgression of the high powers which we have delegated, we declare that everything in this Bill of Rights is excepted out of the general powers of government, and shall forever remain inviolate; and all laws contrary thereto, or contrary to this Constitution, shall be void."

The right of acquiring, possessing and protecting property, and of pursuing one's safety and happiness is guaranteed by section 1 of our Constitution (a part of our Bill of Rights) and its section 2—also a part of the Bill of Rights—prescribes that "absolute and arbitrary power over the lives, liberty and property of freemen exists nowhere in a republic, not even in the largest majority." In dealing with the scope and breadth of the authority of legislatures as founded on the doctrine now under consideration, the courts, without exception, not only hold that a law-making body may not transgress the inhibitions contained in Bills of Rights as incorporated in Constitutions, but also hold that when it is attempted it is within the power of courts to so declare and hold enactments in violation of the Bill of Rights illegal and therefore void. Up to this point there is and can be no dissent. Necessarily, from what we have said, the Police Power possessed by legislative bodies authorizes them in proper instances to enact laws relating to almost if not all professions, and a multiplicity of other subjects affecting the public weal and for its betterment. The authority conferred by the doctrine under consideration, if conditions demand it, would approve complete prohibitive legislation of some activities, or in certain areas if based upon sufficient reasons, which it is not necessary for us to refer to.

Likewise, activities and engagements that are permissible may be regulated or licensed, or otherwise dealt with so as to improve conditions calculated to contribute to the public welfare. Such regulations may relate to qualifications of those engaged in the particular activity, business or profession, and sometimes it may authorize the limitation of hours in which a particular calling may be prosecuted, and a prohibition of its prosecution within other periods of the day. But, whatever direction or phase that the legislation may take—whether of a prohibitory or regulatory character—it must not exceed or go beyond the limits of reasonability, or be rested upon assumed grounds for which there is no foundation in fact, nor may the legislation as enacted be more destructive of the interest of the public at large than beneficial.

The particular subject matter and occupational profession involved in this case, as we have seen, is that of the trade of a barber, the services of which is an admitted necessity. It is also admitted—but if not it should be—that the usual, proper, and ordinary method of conducting the business is not only a necessity but possesses no inherent vice resulting in possible detriment to the body politic, except as related to the sanitary condition of the premises, and the qualifications of those engaged in it. Therefore, in so far as the provisions of the attacked ordinance relate to such matters there can be no legal objections raised thereto. The right as emanating from the Police Power to so regulate such particular features of the barbering business is everywhere upheld and it was done by this court in the case of *Commonwealth v. Ward*, 136 Ky. 146, 123 S.W. 673. But the question of hours within which the prosecution of the business may be conducted and correspondingly prohibited during other hours of the day, was not involved in that case, and which makes our opinion rendered therein completely inapplicable to the question here involved. Manifestly, and clearly, there is a broad distinction between *qualifications* for engagement in and *conditions under which* a particular business may be conducted, and the hours during which it may be done. If it is a lawful one, and necessary for the comfort and convenience of members of the public—though operating under regulatory requirements for guaranteed qualifications of those engaged in it—the hours that may be devoted to its prosecution may not be unreasonably interfered with by the arbitrary *ipse dixit* of the legislative branch of the government, there being no plausible ground therefor. It is true that legislative bodies possess what the opinions designate as "the primary authority" to determine whether or not the particular enactment is justified under authority conferred by the Police Power. Therefore, when the law-making department has so determined the rule is, that the courts should hesitate to declare otherwise.

But the power of the courts to so declare is not thereby denied or taken away. In determining such questions judicial knowledge may be consulted and relied on, and if from that knowledge, or any other source, it appears that the grounds upon which the legislature based its action are arbitrary and unfounded in fact it is not only the right but the duty of courts to say so and declare the consequences. Through avenues to which resort may be had we know that the requirement that barber shops shall be closed at 6 o'clock P. M., and remain so until 8 o'clock A. M., the following day, results in the deprivation of possibly the most profitable hours for the prosecution of the business than would result from prohibiting its conduct during any other portion of the twenty-four hours of the day. Laborers, businessmen, traveling men, and most all others making up the sum total of patrons of such institutions apply for the services received between the hours of, say 6 and 9 o'clock P. M., and 5 and 9 o'clock A. M. It is not made to appear—and from the same sources we conclude it is untrue—that during such prohibited hours, or others approximating them, a barber shop conducted in the usual and ordinary way possesses no vice that could remotely threaten the standards of pure and upright living, or the public welfare. On the contrary, to deny the right of either the barber or of his patrons to render and receive such services within the reasonable time indicated would be followed by incalculable inconvenience and detriment to both the barber and his patrons. Besides, such inhibitive provisions in the circumstances limits *pro tanto* the right of all members of the profession to acquire property, which is guaranteed to them by our Constitution in that portion of it containing the Bill of Rights. They are also thereby deprived of such privilege without due process of law, provided such deprivation is unjustified under the authority conferred by the Police Power, which the city invokes in this case.

Turning now to the adjudged law applicable to the concrete question—i.e., the limiting of hours within which the business of one engaged in the profession of barbering may conduct his business—we find that the courts of every state in the Union before which the question was presented (except one and possibly two) hold that when the prohibited hours are such as to be unreasonable, followed by the difficulties and inconveniences supra, the prohibitive enactment is invalid and void. * * * On the general question of the extent of the Police Power and prescribing the guards thrown around it beyond which legislation is inhibited, we cite the domestic case of *Tolliver v. Blizzard*, 143 Ky. 773, 137 S.W. 509, 34 L.R.A., N.S., 890, and the case of *Lawton v. Steele*, 152 U.S. 133, 14 S.Ct. 499, 38 L.Ed. 385. In the *Tolliver* case it was declared, in substance, that if the enactment was referable to the Police Power, then the court must be able to say that it tends in some degree toward the prevention of offenses, or the preservation of the public health, morals, safety, or welfare of the people as based upon some reasonable grounds. Therefore, if it is apparent that there is no plausible or reasonable connection between the provisions of the statute and the supposed evils to be suppressed, there exists no authority for its enactment. That principle has been declared by every opinion rendered by this court dealing with the question, and we have been able to find none announcing a contrary doctrine, from all of which it may confidently be said that the legislature may not, under the guise of protecting the public interest, arbitrarily interfere with private business by imposing unusual, unreasonable and unnecessary restrictions upon *lawful occupations*. * * * This opinion might be extended by collating other authorities supporting the propositions advanced, but they would be but cumulative and, therefore, serve no useful or educational purpose in substantiating the conclusion that the trial court was correct when it determined that section III of the involved ordinance was invalid as a proper exercise of the Police Power, since the restrictions therein contained are unreasonable as applicable to the lawful and necessary business of the involved occupation of barbering.

* * *

Wherefore, for the reasons stated, the judgment is affirmed.

The Whole Court sitting, except Perry, J., who was absent.

Cammack, J., dissenting.

Notes and Questions

1. How might the *Kuhn* case have been decided differently if the occupation and location involved was something other than a barber and barber shop (*e.g.*, a bar or tavern)?

2. In *Lochner v. New York*, 198 U.S. 45 (1905), the U.S. Supreme Court declared unconstitutional a state law limiting the hours bakers could work to 60 hours per week. The *Lochner* Court found that law violated the "freedom of contract" in violation of "substantive due process" under the Fourteenth Amendment. The "*Lochner* era" ended when the Supreme Court abrogated that decision in *West Coast Hotel Co. v. Parrish*, 300 U.S. 379 (1937), which held that a state law prescribing working conditions for women and minors did not violate the Due Process Clause. Unlike *Lochner*, the *Kuhn* holding that the Commonwealth's "police power" under Section 2 does not permit the state or a local government to enact "unusual, unreasonable and unnecessary restrictions upon *lawful occupations*" has never been overruled. "Economic substantive due process" is alive and well in Kentucky as a matter of state constitutional law.

3. When the Supreme Court evaluated the Governor's emergency orders issued in 2020 to grapple with the public health emergency caused by the novel coronavirus (COVID-19), the Court distinguished *Kuhn* as follows: "In striking the barbershop ordinance, the Court concluded the restrictions were 'unreasonable.' In short, while health reasons justified licensing barbers and certain restrictions, the hours of operation were not reasonably related to any legitimate governmental purpose." *Beshear v. Acree*, 615 S.W.3d 780, 817 (Ky. 2020). As it related to the public health emergency, the Court stated that "insofar as public health is concerned, private property may become of public interest and the constitutional limitations upon the exercise of the power of regulation come down to a question of 'reasonability.'" *Id.* at 817–18 (quoting *Adams, Inc. v. Louisville & Jefferson Cnty. Bd. of Health*, 439 S.W.2d 586, 590 (Ky. 1969)).

Illinois Central Railroad Co. v. Commonwealth

Court of Appeals of Kentucky (1947)
305 Ky. 632, 204 S.W.2d 973

Opinion of the Court by Judge Siler.

Illinois Central Railroad Company, appellant, was convicted of the misdemeanor of deducting wages from its employee for time spent in voting, such wage deduction being an offense denounced by KRS 118.340. Following a judgment in favor of the Commonwealth, appellee, for a $100 fine for this offense, the appellant moved for this appeal.

Among others, appellant now makes the contention that the trial court committed reversible error in upholding, through the effect of its judgment, the constitutionality of that law upon which this conviction rests.

There is no dispute about the facts of this case. On November 7, 1944, election day, W. K. Wall was under an employment contract to work for appellant at an hourly wage of $1.04. His home was within 4 blocks of his voting place. His route from home to working place passed within 2 blocks of that same voting place. His 8 hour working day extended from 8:00 a.m. to 4:40 p.m. with a 40 minute interval for lunch. His voting place was open from 6:00 a.m. to 4:00 p.m. He went to work at his usual hour of 8:00 a.m. on that day, and he continued to work until 2:40 p.m., following his usual 40 minute lunch period. He ceased work at 2:40 p.m. and used some part of the 2 hour remainder of his working day in voting at his usual voting place. He claimed for the controversial day 8 hours of wages, representing a 6 hour working period for his employer and a 2 hour voting period for his country. The railroad refused to pay for the 2 hour voting period. This indictment, conviction and judgment followed.

Sec. 148, Ky. Constitution, says, in substance, that the legislative authority shall provide by law that employers must allow employees, under reasonable regulations, at least 4 hours to vote on election days. This section does not say that the 4 hours shall be allowed with pay, but the Commonwealth contends that any correct interpretation of it must add the pay feature.

KRS 118.340, enacted under the enabling power of Sec. 148, Ky. Constitution, says, in substance, that an employee entitled to vote at an election shall have the right to absent himself on election day for 4 hours between opening and closing time of the polls, provided such employee has made prior application for this privilege and subject to the employer's right to fix the time of its exercise.

KRS 118.990 says that any employer, who deducts from the usual wages of an employee absenting himself under the provisions of this law, shall thereby become guilty of a misdemeanor and subject to a fine ranging from $50 to $500.

Appellant says that it had 4,849 employees in Kentucky on the day in question, that a full payment to all of them within the terms of this statute would have cost appellant at least $11,591.63, that for such an expenditure there would have been to appellant no value received.

Voting is the privilege of a free people. One of its primary purposes is to keep people free. There is no such thing as a popular election in some countries of the old world. Dictatorships will have none of them. This glorious country belongs to the farmers, to the working people, to the little people whose name is legion, to the middlesized people who are the salt of the earth, to those of the big people who would yet remain little people because their God-fearing hearts make them humble. No group of people in America has a greater stake in its government, in its rocks and rills, in its woods and templed hills, than ordinary working men. No group in America can be more interested in voting for a clean, righteous, free, statesmanlike government than that group known as workers. The woman with the sun bonnet and the checkered apron who trudges off of the mountain side in Leslie County and walks down the creek a mile to cast her vote—she is an American queen in calico, but her only pay for voting is the satisfaction of knowing that Columbia, by God's help and hers, shall continue as the gem of the mighty ocean. Let no man cease to thank his God as he looks in at the open door of his voting place, as he realizes that here his quantity, though cast in overalls, is exactly the same as the quantity of the President of the United States. There is a satisfaction and privilege in voting in a free country that cannot be measured in dollars and cents.

We have no fault whatever to find in any statutory provision securing to workers the right to absent themselves 4 hours on election days to cast their votes. Such a provision could not and would not antagonize any part of either the Kentucky or the United States Constitution. Both of these instruments practically raise their own voices and shout their approval of a statute of that character.

But a statutory provision which has the effect of requiring an employer to pay an employee for 4 hours of unemployed time, whether or not he votes, whether or not he has opportunity to vote before he starts to work, whether or not he spends just 10 minutes in voting—this could not, we think, be constitutional. It does not seem to be in keeping with the American tradition.

Ky. Constitution, Sec. 2, contains these words: "Absolute and arbitrary power over the lives, liberty and property of freemen exists nowhere in a republic, not even in the largest majority."

If we interpret the above constitutional provision correctly, it inhibits the legislative power of this state from arbitrarily passing a law taking property away from one person and giving it to another person without value received or without any contractual basis. And this inhibition still stands, regardless of the merit or glory or value or need of the person on the receiving end of the transaction. Hardly a more worthy objective could be designed than that of building a great hospital for crippled children of all creeds and colors, a marvelous, public enterprise, and yet the constitution would not sanction a law saddling the burden of such an undertaking upon the farmers of Kentucky to the exclusion of its butchers, bakers and candlestick makers. Such a law would constitute an exercise of arbitrary power over the property of that group of freemen known as farmers. Its arbitrariness would lie in its unfairness and in its preferment. The law will not countenance a public maintenance of a private enterprise. Neither should the law demand a private maintenance of a public enterprise. Voting is a public enterprise. But if its maintenance is required by the employer group rather than by the entire, broad, general public, then that amounts to a requirement of private maintenance of a public enterprise.

* * *

The Commonwealth makes the contention that our legislative authority had a right, under the exercise of its police power, to adopt the law in question, since its adoption was in the interest of the general welfare of the public. A state's police power is truly a thing of vitality and reality, and it is a power which is both broad and useful. In a general way it extends to all the great, public needs. However, we have said that the legislative authority may not, under the guise of promoting public interest, arbitrarily interfere with private business. *City of Louisville v. Kuhn*, 284 Ky. 684, 145 S.W.2d 851. And it is always appropriate to remember that the police power is not without its limitations, since clearly it may not unreasonably invade and violate those private rights which are guaranteed under either federal or state constitution. 11 Am. Jur. 992.

Wherefore, the motion for an appeal is sustained and appellee's judgment, for the reasons herein indicated, is now reversed with directions for further proceedings consistent herewith.

Notes and Questions

1. The Court relies on Section 2 in declaring that the state government may not require private businesses to pay their employees for time spent voting, and not working. Though not at issue in this case as decided, could the state statutes at issue also violate Section 13?
2. Recalling the old nursery rhyme, the Court sets the interests of the "butchers, bakers and candlestick makers" against those of Kentucky's farmers. Idiomatically, however, the phrase "the butcher, the baker, and the candlestick maker" has also come to mean

people of all ethnicities, professions, and socioeconomic classes. How do the literal and idiomatic meanings of the phrase shed light on the Court's holding?

3. Though not a direct quote, the "butchers, bakers and candlestick makers" phrase perhaps also recalls the famous passage from Adam Smith's Wealth of Nations (1776): "It is not from the benevolence of the butcher, the brewer, or the baker that we expect our dinner, but from their regard to their own interest. We address ourselves, not to their humanity, but to their self-love, and never talk to them of our own necessities, but of their advantages." Smith, the godfather of modern economic theory, advocated for free market economic policies, and the quoted passage argues that a person's self-interest is the basis of all rational economic choices made in a free market. Can free market economic theory, such as that advocated by Smith, help explain why the Court in *Illinois Central* understood the statutes at issue to be arbitrary?

Bond Bros. v. Louisville & Jefferson County Metropolitan Sewer District

Court of Appeals of Kentucky (1948)
307 Ky. 689, 211 S.W.2d 867

Opinion of the Court by Commissioner Stanley.

The appeals of Louisville and Jefferson County Metropolitan Sewer District and the City of Louisville v. Bond Brothers and the B. F. Goodrich Company, seek to reverse judgments that no power was reposed in the appellant to establish a different rate of sewer service charges for property located outside the limits of Louisville than within. The judgments in that relation are reversed for the reasons given in the cases of the *Louisville & Jefferson County Metropolitan Sewer District v. Joseph A. Seagram & Sons, et al.*, and the *Louisville & Jefferson County Metropolitan Sewer District v. International Harvester Company*, 307 Ky. 413, 211 S.W.2d 122. These two suits sought to have it judicially declared that the plaintiffs are not liable for the payment of any sewer service charges. Both parties prosecute appeals from that part of the judgments in their cases denying such declaration and adjudging them to be liable. The question is whether the parties for a valuable consideration are relieved from the imposition of service charges for the use of a sewer serving both industries by virtue of a judgment in which was incorporated a contract between the Commissioners of Sewerage of Louisville and Producers Wood Preserving Company, predecessor in title and right of the appellants.

* * *

Prior to 1928 the Producers Wood Preserving Company owned a tract of 170 acres on the headwaters of a stream, called Paddy's Run, in Jefferson County. It used the creek for the disposal of a large volume of water utilized in the creosoting plant. In a major construction (for which purposes the Board of Sewerage Commissioners was created; see Acts of 1920, Chap. 86) it was deemed necessary to run an open drainage channel following the course of Paddy's Run through the property. In a condemnation proceeding a verdict for $49,500 was returned in favor of the company for 9.3 acres of land taken and incidental damages. The right of way was from 175 to 300 feet wide. The company was not satisfied, and on its appeal we reversed the judgment and held it to be entitled to additional compensation for having its manufacturing plant on the south side of the stream cut off from access to its property on the north side. It had pleaded $175,000 damages on this account. *Producers' Wood Preserving Company v. Commissioners of Sewerage*, 227 Ky. 159, 12 S.W.2d 292.

Upon the return of the case, the parties came to an agreement by which the company should retain the amount paid under the judgment for the property taken, and acquire certain further rights. The contract was later embodied in an agreed judgment. In the judgment the Commissioners of Sewerage were granted a perpetual easement over the land to construct, use and maintain a covered concrete sewer. The Commissioners were required to "cause the existing ditch to be filled even with or above the natural surface within three years." The company was granted the right at any time it should desire to fill the valley of Paddy's Run up to the level of the high ground, and in doing so to fill the right-of-way granted the Commissioners. It was also given the right to use the surface over the sewer. The agreed judgment further provided that the Commissioners would—

> "Construct suitable openings or connections into its main sewer on either side thereof, for defendant's use in connecting its sewerage and storm water or natural drainage from the defendant's existing property.
>
> "If the existing drainage ditch be changed so as to require the removal of, or other expense in connection with existing water mains or electric wires or bridges, the plaintiff will pay the cost thereof, it being the purpose and intent that plaintiff (Commissioners of Sewerage) shall maintain such connections and ways, or pay the cost of substituting others equally as good and serviceable."

Following the judgment, the company executed a consistent deed, embodying the above and other terms, to the Commissioners on June 11, 1929.

It is also expressly provided in the deed: "All grants herein by or to either party hereto shall be also to their successors and assigns, and all covenants entered into herein shall be for the benefit of and shall also obligate their successors and assigns, and all agreements, stipulations and covenants shall run with the land hereby granted and be for and to the successors and assigns of the parties hereto."

Bond Brothers is the corporate successor of the Producers Wood Preserving Company and the grantee in a deed (dated April 30, 1935) containing the rights given and reserved in its deed to the Board of Sewerage Commissioners. The City of Louisville, as successor to the rights and liabilities of its Board of Sewerage Commissioners, has performed the obligations of the judgment. Producers Wood Preserving Company and Bond Brothers have continuously used the facilities without charge. Goodrich acquired title by mesne conveyances from Producers Wood Preserving Company to about 54 acres of the tract on which it has operated two large manufacturing plants. It uses nearly one billion gallons of water a year and Bond Brothers also a very large quantity. Both companies get the water from their own wells and from the Louisville Water Company. This drains into the sewer referred to in the contract and judgment, which is now maintained and operated by the Metropolitan Sewer District, although it is still owned by the City of Louisville. Since it established its plants more than fifteen years ago, Goodrich has had the unrestricted use of the sewer without charge.

* * *

II. The Metropolitan District and City of Louisville claim the right and authority to abrogate the contract and judgment under the police power. The argument rests upon the proposition that the construction we have given the contract has the effect of bartering away the city's police power and it is undisputed that cannot be done. By contract and judgment of the court the appellees acquired a valuable property right, namely, the use of the sewer in consideration of the surrender of another adjudicated property right, i.e., to compensation for damages to the property suffered in behalf of the public. The appellees maintain that police power cannot be used as a means of taking property without compensation or to impair the obligations of a contract, except perhaps in a case of emergency.

As we have observed in the St. Matthews Sanitary Association opinion delivered today, *Louisville & Jefferson County Metropolitan Sewer District v. St. Matthews Sanitary Ass'n*, 307 Ky. 348, 208 S.W.2d 490, the construction of sewers and drains is a certain object of the police power. To accomplish that objective the full force of the power may be applied, and that may require that property rights be subordinated even though they are otherwise within the protection of the Constitution. In doing so we do not doubt that the cost may be met by special assessment upon property benefited or by requiring payment for the use of the facility. And, further, that such usage or service charge may be imposed for the operation and maintenance of the facility when it is contemporaneously implemented as an incident of the plan and program for the abatement or prevention of a nuisance. 17 Am. Jur., Drains and Sewers, Secs. 60, 66. If the menace has been removed, public necessity and general welfare have been met and served and the object has been accomplished. The question is whether the police power may be asserted years afterward to destroy property rights or to abrogate a contract made by the same unit of government in order to raise revenue to operate and maintain the facilities.

Whether the authority to "collect sewer rates, rentals, and other charges, for service rendered by the facilities of the district" (KRS 76.080(10)) in the ordinary case comes from the police power or from the right of the city to require payment for the use of its facilities is not a material question. In such a case there is no clash with rights protected from seizure or impairment by the Constitution. We are here dealing with supremacy in such a conflict. The touchstone is necessity and reasonable relationship. It is fundamental that such as extraordinary power is not without limitation, for it may not operate unreasonably beyond the occasion or necessity of the case. It may not unreasonably invade private rights and thus violate those rights guaranteed under either the Federal or the State Constitution. 11 Am. Jur., Constitutional Law, Sec. 259. The exercise of the power must have a substantial basis and cannot be made a mere pretext for actions that do not come within its scope. To state it another way, the action of the government may not arbitrarily invade liberty or property rights under the guise of police regulation. *Beacon Liquors v. Martin*, 279 Ky. 468, 131 S.W.2d 446; *City of Louisville v. Kuhn*, 284 Ky. 684, 145 S.W.2d 851.

It has been said that the law of nuisances ordinarily furnishes help in ascertaining the scope of the power. *Euclid v. Ambler Realty Co.*, 272 U.S. 365, 47 S. Ct. 114, 71 L. Ed. 303, 54 A. L. R., 1016. But a legislative body, or any other, attempting to exercise the power under delegation, cannot declare something a nuisance when in fact it is not, nor "under the guise of its police power may act arbitrarily and unreasonably without a rational relation to the protection of the common welfare." *City of Mt. Sterling v. Donaldson Baking Company*, 287 Ky. 781, 155 S.W.2d 237, 239.

If the representatives of the city made a bad bargain, as subsequent events have developed, we see no more authority for relieving the city and its agency of that bargain without compensation than there was for the taking of the right of way over the land in the first place without compensation because the public very much wants the relief now just as it wanted relief then. Our Bill of Rights recognizes as inalienable "the right of acquiring and protecting property" and declares that the property of no citizen shall be taken "or applied to public use without the consent of his representatives, and without just compensation being previously made to him." Kentucky Constitution, Secs. 1 and 13. * * *

We have an analogue in *City of Louisville v. Weible & Willinger*, 84 Ky. 290, 1 S.W. 605, 606, 8 Ky. L. Rep. 361. The city had made a contract with Wible & Willinger to remove from the streets and other public places the carcasses of animals free of cost. Before its expiration the city, in disregard of their rights, proposed to sell the same privilege to the highest bidder. To sustain its action the city claimed that as removal and disposal of dead animals "is one of the police powers of the city necessary to be exercised at all times to preserve the health, comfort, and cleanliness of the city, she has no legal power to limit or surrender its control, by contract, over that subject, or kindred ones, beyond her recall at pleasure."

After commenting upon the principle that the sovereign may not surrender its police power, the court stated that the city had not done so by the contract but had exercised it "in an efficient and prudent manner" for a sufficient consideration; that it had then "without just cause, or any cause, of complaint capriciously tired of its contract, and proposed to break it." The court observed that if the firm had breached its contract or it had become necessary for the city to establish new regulations or withdraw the contract altogether in order to prevent a nuisance arising it might do so under the police power. "But to allow the city to disregard or recall its contract with its contractors, or employees engaged to service by fixed terms, upon its mere caprice, or to gain a pecuniary advantage, would be the exercise of an arbitrary power that does not exist in the land."

In the present case there is not only a contract but a judgment. We perceive no authority in the city, a party to that case, or the Metropolitan District, its operating agency, to nullify the judgment and cancel a fixed and adjudicated right of a successful litigant. * * *

The police power cannot be used to raise revenue unless it be an incident in the accomplishment of a proper end of promoting order, safety, health, morals or general welfare, to which end the fees have a reasonable relation. The object must always be regulation. 16 C. J. S., Constitutional Law, sec. 174; *Great Atlantic & Pacific Tea Company v. Kentucky Tax Commission*, 278 Ky. 367, 128 S.W.2d 581; *Reeves v. Adam Hat Stores*, 303 Ky. 633, 198 S.W.2d 789.

* * *

Without extending the opinion further—perhaps now beyond due bounds—we hold that the appellants' contract cannot be abrogated or their vested rights destroyed by imposing the sewer service charges promulgated by the Metropolitan District without due compensation being made.

The judgments are, therefore, reversed for consistent proceedings.

Notes and Questions

1. The cited basis for the Court's decision was Sections 1 and 13. How would you decide the case under Section 2?
2. Could the City's efforts to abrogate the contract and judgment from the earlier litigation also implicate Section 19?
3. How does the Court's decision in *Bond Brothers* restrain or affect how the state government in Kentucky relates to its citizens?

Sanitation District No. 1 of Jefferson County v. City of Louisville

Court of Appeals of Kentucky (1948)
308 Ky. 368, 213 S.W.2d 995

Opinion of the Court by Commissioner Stanley.

This case is a sequel of *Sanitation District No. 1 v. Louisville & Jefferson County Metropolitan Sewer District*, 307 Ky. 422, 208 S. W. 2d 751 and of *Engle v. Bonnie*, 305 Ky. 850, 204 S. W. 2d 963. The latter related to an Act relative to the incorporation of cities. KRS 81.030 et seq. In the former case there was a declaration of powers and rights of the respective parties in relation to a proposed contract between the two sewer districts. The Sanitation District contemplated the construction of a sewer system and issuance of revenue bonds to cover the cost. The proposed contract provided that it should be connected with the sewer system of Louisville then and now being maintained by the Metropolitan Sewer District. The particular question in this court was whether either the City of Louisville or Metropolitan Sewer District would become responsible for the debts and liabilities of Sanitation District in the event of annexation of the territory by the City, and thereby relieve the users of the local system from the obligation of paying for its construction.

We held the Metropolitan Sewer District Act had impliedly repealed Ky. Rev. Sts. 220.530, which was a part of the Act of 1940 under which the Sanitation District was organized, and that the City upon annexation of the territory would not have to pay the bonds. We also held that Metropolitan District could not be required to assume such obligations although there appears to be no obstacle to its voluntarily doing so. Immediately afterward, a bill was introduced in the Legislature (H. B. 464) re-enacting KRS 220.530 with amendments making it more direct and specific. It was aimed directly at the St. Matthews situation, though general in characterization and specification. The bill was passed with an emergency provision which made it effective in ten days.

The City of Louisville instituted this suit challenging the constitutionality of the Act. The circuit court declared the Act unconstitutional and void "in its attempted application to the pending annexation proceedings by the City of Louisville to annex the territory comprised in Sanitation District No. 1 of Jefferson County because, (1) it attempts to delay and prohibit those proceedings and (2) it would impose the debts and liabilities of the district upon the City."

Section 1, paragraph (1) of the Act is as follows: "Where a city annexes an entire sanitation district organized under this Chapter, the city shall be liable from and after the date of such annexation for all of the debts and liabilities of such district, including, but not by way of limitation, all revenue bonds and all debts and liabilities secured by revenues of the district, and all other bonded and floating debt of the district, and such debts and liabilities shall be payable out of the general funds of the city, and such city shall be the owner of all the property and rights of the district, and the users of sewers in the district shall be relieved from any further rentals and obligations, except that if the territory in the district becomes part of the territory in a metropolitan sewer district formed under Chapter 76 of the Kentucky Revised Statutes, such users shall pay the regular charges of such metropolitan sewer district, and the sanitation district shall thereupon be automatically dissolved."

Paragraphs (2) and (3) provide that if only a portion of the territory embraced in a sanitation district should be annexed, the city would acquire proportionate rights and assume proportionate obligations.

Section 2 of the Act declares that it shall prevail over any existing law in conflict with it, and section 3 is a severance provision to the effect that if any part of the Act is held to be unconstitutional or invalid, no other part shall be affected by such decision.

* * *

The City of Louisville enacted an ordinance on May 28, 1947, annexing territory which is practically coextensive with that embraced by Sanitation District No. 1. A remonstrance against annexation was filed and the case was pending in the Jefferson Circuit Court (KRS 81.100 et seq.) at the time the Act under consideration was passed and is still pending.

The gist and explicit purpose of the Act of 1948 is to impose the payment of the cost of a community public improvement upon the general revenues of the City, if it should be annexed. While the probable intent was that all of it should not be paid in cash at the time of the annexation, the legal effect is the same, for there would be an assumption of the entire debt though actual payment might be made as the coupons and bonds severally mature.

It is stipulated in the record that Louisville does not now have general revenues over and above its necessary governmental expenses sufficient to enable it to assume in one year any part of the debts and liabilities of the Sanitary District in the event of annexation of all or any part of the territory. Nor is it presently contemplated that the City will at any time in the foreseeable future have general revenues sufficient to permit it to assume in any one year the amount of expenditures which would be required to construct and complete the sewerage system of the Sanitary District in accordance with the contracts which it has made. The assumption of any such debts or obligations would result in the City becoming indebted in an amount exceeding the income and revenue provided for the year within which annexation might take place. This, of course, can not be legally done. As said in *Sanitation District No. 1 v. Louisville and Jefferson County Metropolitan Sewer District, supra*, 307 Ky. 422, 208 S. W. 2d 751, 754, "the parties could not contract, or the statute provide, or the courts lawfully adjudge a liability upon the city which is prohibited by Section 157 of the Constitution." The financial condition of the City, as shown in the stipulation, would permit the valid issuance of voted tax-payable bonds within the limitations of Section 158 of the Constitution. But it is important to note that the 1948 Act does not authorize or contemplate the issuance of such bonds. It strictly confines the payment of the obligations out of the general funds.

The argument of the Sanitation District is, in brief, that the Act cannot be held constitutionally invalid or inapplicable because annexation is optional; that it is a "take it or leave it" proposition, for if the City is unable financially to pay the bill, it must not take in the territory or any part of it. All of that is true except for the inescapable fact that the City really has no choice if the conditions cannot be met in the foreseeable future.

Since the creation of municipalities and all matters in relation to annexation are political acts, whether they shall be done or not is within the power and discretion of the Legislature as the political department of the government; hence the assent or the will of the people particularly affected is not controlling, for they hold their property subject to the exercise of the legislative power. *Cheaney v. Hooser*, 9 B. Mon. 330, 48 Ky. 330; *Carrithers v. City of Shelbyville*, 126 Ky. 769, 104 S. W. 744, 17 L. R. A., N. S., 421; *Gernert v. City of Louisville*, 155 Ky. 589, 159 S. W. 1163, 51 L. R. A., N. S., 363; *Allen v. Hollingsworth*, 246 Ky. 812, 56 S. W. 2d 530. Of course, in these acts, as in all others, the Legislature is subject to all the curbs and restraints of the Constitution. There is no specific limitation with respect to annexation of territory by a city, but it seems to us that the present Act offends some of the general provisions. And a municipal corporation, though created by the Legislature, having authority to prosecute and defend suits in the courts, may invoke the protection afforded by the Constitution to prevent a violation of its rights. 2 Cooley, page 397, note.

Section 2 of our Bill of Rights is unique, only the Constitution of Wyoming having a like declaration. Article 1, Section 7, Constitution of Wyoming. Section 2, Kentucky Constitution, reads: "Absolute and arbitrary power over the lives, liberty and property of freemen exists nowhere in a republic, not even in the largest majority."

This is regarded by an eminent authority as a good definition of constitutional government, as distinguished from a pure democracy. Stimson, Federal and State Constitutions, page 192, section 182, note 2. It is the affirmance of fundamental principles recognized throughout the federal and state constitutions and sanctioned by the laws of all free people. Most of these principles are expressed in the various bills of right, but they are to be found also in the historical development of constitutional government from despotism. So it may be said that whatever is contrary to democratic ideals, customs and maxims is arbitrary. Likewise, whatever is essentially unjust and unequal or exceeds the reasonable and legitimate interests of the people is arbitrary. *City of Cambellsburg (Campbellsville) v. Odewalt*, Ky., 24 Ky. L. Rep. 1739, 72 S. W. 314; *City of Louisville v. Kuhn*, 284 Ky. 684, 145 S. W. 2d 851; *Kenton & Campbell Benevolent Burial Association v. Goodpaster*, 304 Ky. 233, 200 S. W. 2d 120; *Illinois Central R. Co. v. Commonwealth*, 305 Ky. 632, 204 S. W. 2d 973; *Weaver v. Public Service Commission*, 40 Wyo. 462, 278 P. 542. Section 2 of the Constitution is a curb on the legislative as well as on any other public body or public officer in the assertion or attempted exercise of political power. It seems to us that the present Act must be regarded as arbitrary within the contemplation of that section and that it also offends certain specific provisions.

By this Act the Legislature has recognized its own enactments authorizing the annexation of territory by cities of the first class, but has by the Act imposed such oppressive terms or conditions as to deny effectually the right of the City of Louisville to avail itself of that authorization. It would require the City to do an illegal thing by exceeding its current revenues or assuming an unconstitutional debt.

There is no conceivable reason for the imposition of this burden in case of annexation of the territory of a sanitary district by a city of the first class, except to make annexation so oppressive as to make it prohibitive.

* * *

The statutes provide that where a city of the first class annexes territory of a smaller city or town it shall be bound for its debts and liabilities, wholly or proportionally. KRS 81.130. And we recognize the law generally to be that even without specific statutes, where one municipality annexes another, or where two cities merge, the debts of each thereby become the debts of the annexing or the combined municipality, and recognize that the Legislature has power to shift tax burdens. But there would be no assumption of a public debt or a shifting of tax burdens in the application of this Act of 1948, except perhaps that incurred in anticipation of the preliminary tax authorized by KRS 220.370. The very law under which the Sanitation District functions and proposes to pay for its sewers declares that the bonds are not to be regarded as a public debt. The security of the bondholder will be the power and the duty of the District Board of Directors to collect charges from the users of the sewers for a sinking fund and his right to have the courts enforce the contract and his liens. By this Act in case of annexation those obligations are converted or made into a public debt, payable by general taxation. The Act transmutes into a public debt what would be private obligations but for the legislative sanction. The Act does not shift tax burdens from one section to the entire City, for there will be no tax burden to be shifted. A public debt is ipso facto created by annexation.

Appropriate to our present consideration is the following comment of a distinguished authority, 2 Cooley's Constitutional Limitations, page 1035, note, as follows: "The general idea of our tax system is, that those shall vote the burdens who are to pay them; and it would be intolerable that a central authority should have power, not only to tax localities, for local purposes of a public character, which they did not approve, but also, if it so pleased, to compel them to assume and discharge private claims not equitably chargeable upon them."

Section 3 of the Constitution reads: "No grant of exclusive, separate public emoluments or privileges shall be made to any man or set of men, except in consideration of public services."

This is the correlative of that part of Section 13 which declares that private property of no man shall be taken or applied to a public use without consent and compensation. It is never competent for the Legislature to dispense public funds to any individual or group of individuals without benefit to the public interest or welfare. Thus, it was held in *Barker v. Crum*, 177 Ky. 637, 198 S. W. 211, L. R. A. 1918F, 673, that public funds could not be used for the benefit of a few favored boys in each county, selected in accordance with the legislative act, for the payment of their tuition at the University of Kentucky. To sustain the present Act of 1948 would be to recognize constitutional sanction of an act which in effect would relieve private property or its owners from the payment of money for the satisfaction of their bonds issued to cover the cost of their community sewer system.

* * *

We are constrained to hold that the Act is unconstitutional. * * *

The judgment of the circuit court is accordingly affirmed.

Notes and Questions

1. The Court states that Section 2 is "a good definition of constitutional government, as distinguished from a pure democracy." How is a "constitutional government" distinguishable from "a pure democracy"? What does it mean that Kentucky's constitution establishes a "constitutional government" and not "a pure democracy"? Are constitutional government and pure democracy mutually exclusive? How does constitutional government in Kentucky relate to Section 2's prohibition against "absolute and arbitrary power"?
2. The Court defines what is "arbitrary" under Section 2 as: "whatever is contrary to democratic ideals, customs and maxims" or "whatever is essentially unjust and unequal or exceeds the reasonable and legitimate interests of the people." Note that, in this sense of the word, "arbitrary" does not necessarily mean something that is the product of random choice or personal whim; rather, the word is used in the sense of an unrestrained, autocratic use of authority or power.
3. Note also how the Court construes Section 3 to preclude "dispens[ing] public funds to any individual or group of individuals without benefit to the public interest or welfare." Thus, there must be some benefit to the Commonwealth before any funds may be appropriated from the state treasury. How might this provision affect legislative appropriations to private corporations or nonprofits?
4. Consider that Sections 3 and 13 serve correlative purposes. Section 3 prohibits granting special emoluments or privileges to any person, except in consideration for public service the person has provided to the Commonwealth. Section 13, on the other hand, prevents a person's property from being taken from him for public use, except in consideration for just compensation having been made to him. The person therefore cannot *receive* property from the Commonwealth if he does not also provide something of value, and the person's property cannot be *taken* from him if the Commonwealth does not pay its value to him. Viewed in this way, the two Sections shield the property of both the Commonwealth and any person from being misappropriated by the other.

Reid v. Cowan

Court of Appeals of Kentucky (1973)
502 S.W.2d 41

Opinion of the Court by Chief Justice Palmore.

On October 2, 1970, in the Clay Circuit Court the appellants, Lee Reid, Jr., John Reid, and Freddy Gilbert, were found guilty by a jury and convicted of forcible rape, KRS 435.090, upon a female over 12 years of age named Jean Hall. Lee Reid, Jr., was sentenced to 20 years and the other two appellants to 10 years in the penitentiary. The crimes were alleged to have been committed on or about June 28, 1970.

Several abortive attempts to secure post-conviction relief, which need not be detailed here, culminated in an RCr 11.42 hearing on September 16, 1971, and an order dated August 24, 1972 (evidently entered, however, on October 24, 1972), granting Lee Reid, Jr., 30 days in which to file a belated appeal pursuant to a finding to the effect that it was not clear from the record whether he had been advised of his right of appeal, cf. RCr 11.02(2), either by the trial court or by the retained counsel who had represented him during the trial.

Lee Reid, Jr., was represented in the RCr 11.42 hearing by court-appointed counsel. Though RCr 11.42(5) requires that counsel so appointed continue to represent the movant for purposes of appeal, for some undisclosed reason no notice of appeal was filed within the 30-day period allowed by the order for that purpose. Evidently, however, Reid was expecting counsel to prosecute an appeal, because on November 16, 1972, he wrote a letter asking counsel to withdraw and have new counsel appointed in view of a conversation in which counsel purportedly had told Reid's parents he was "not going to prosecute an appeal due to ill health."

On January 2, 1973, counsel for Lee Reid, Jr., moved the Clay Circuit Court for permission to withdraw, and on the same day an order was entered accordingly. It did not, however, designate a new counsel.

Meanwhile, on September 18, 1972, Lee Reid, Jr., had filed in this court, pro se, a petition for mandamus against the judge of the Clay Circuit Court stating that the court-appointed attorney had failed to perfect the appeal and demanding, in substance, that the judge see to it that it was done. A response filed by the judge stated merely that the belated appeal had been granted by an order entered on October 24, 1972 (the date of the response), a copy of which order was attached to the response. It is the same order hereinbefore mentioned as having been dated August 24, 1972, so it would seem that although the hearing had been held on September 16, 1971, the order granting a belated appeal was not signed until August 24, 1972, and then not entered officially until October 24, 1972. On January 23, 1973, this court entered an order denying relief "for the reasons stated in the response," upon the basis, of course, that when the response was filed the trial judge had done all he was required to do.

The proceeding now before this court is an appeal from an adverse judgment in a habeas corpus action filed by the three appellants on August 20, 1973, in the Lyon

Circuit Court. In addition to alleging ineffective counsel on Lee Reid, Jr.'s effort to secure and perfect a belated appeal, their petition discloses that on November 21, 1972, they filed in the Clay Circuit Court a motion for new trial based on newly discovered evidence in the form of an affidavit by Jean Hall, the original prosecuting witness, to the effect that in her testimony she had lied about her age at the time of the alleged offense, having been 17 rather than 15 years of age, and that she had not been raped but had freely and willingly consented to the acts of intercourse "while under the influence of intoxicating liquors." Filed in support of the petition for habeas corpus were a birth certificate showing that a person named Ima Jean Hall was born in Shelby County, Kentucky, on April 17, 1953 (17 years before the alleged rape) and the affidavits of 11 of the jurors who tried the case to the effect that if they had read Jean Hall's affidavit they would not have convicted the appellants. Evidently the Clay Circuit Court has never passed on this motion for new trial.

No one realizes any better than do the members of this court how burdensome and vexatious post-conviction proceedings are. Most of them are utterly devoid of merit, as indeed this one may prove to be. But this case illustrates how the burden proliferates when the duly-constituted officers of the Commonwealth at the trial level do not treat a post-conviction proceeding with enough care to see that it is promptly, thoroughly and properly handled in the first instance. It simply will not die on the vine or go away if ignored or summarily sloughed off.

These men have been bandied about in such a fashion that this court would be thoroughly justified in setting them free pursuant to their habeas corpus petition. Section 3 [*sic*] of our Constitution forbids the existence of arbitrary power, and sometimes in a criminal case the only way that protection can be enforced is by declaring that the rights of the state have been forfeited through the arbitrary actions of its officers. *Cf. Balsley v. Commonwealth*, Ky., 428 S.W.2d 614 (1968). Sometimes, as Holmes remarked, because the constable blundered the criminal must go free, that being the most effective method of helping the constable not to blunder the next time.

We have concluded, however, that since the appellants are now represented by the public defender they can obtain a prompt resolution of their claims in the Clay Circuit Court. Their troubles appear to have emanated not so much from any default or cavalier attitude on the part of the trial judge as from the lack of counsel and neglect on the part of counsel when they had one. The public defender may proceed in the trial court to obtain a determination of their motion for a new trial and a review of that disposition if it be unfavorable to them, and to secure another order on the question of a belated appeal.

We do not reach the question of whether the newly discovered evidence was timely presented or is sufficient to require a new trial. Nor do we find it necessary to consider under what circumstances habeas corpus would be a proper remedy by reason of the inadequacy of RCr 11.42.

The judgment is affirmed.

Palmore, C.J., and Jones, Milliken, Osborne, Reed, Steinfeld and Stephenson, JJ., sitting.

All concur.

Notes and Questions

1. What does the Court say about how Section 2's prohibition on arbitrary power applies in a criminal case? How might future court decisions apply *Reid* in other contexts?
2. The Supreme Court declined to grant relief under Section 2 and *Reid* in *Pettway v. Commonwealth*, 470 S.W.3d 706 (Ky. 2015), a criminal murder case. In that case, the prosecution had on two occasions made late discovery disclosures. The first time was after the trial had begun, and the trial court accordingly granted a mistrial. The second time was shortly before the second trial began, and the trial court suppressed the evidence. Notwithstanding the trial court's granting relief to the defendant both times, he urged the Supreme Court to order his murder indictment be dismissed as a sanction under Section 2. Acknowledging Chief Justice Palmore's statement in *Reid* that the criminal sometimes must go free because the constable blundered, the Court held, "There was no blunder that could not be appropriately addressed, as the trial court did here, under our rules of procedure. This claim has no merit." *Pettway*, 470 S.W.3d at 712. What does *Pettway* say about when relief under Section 2 may be available under *Reid*?
3. The reference in the Court's opinion to Justice Oliver Wendell Holmes, who served on the U.S. Supreme Court from 1902 to 1932, actually refers to an opinion by Judge Benjamin Cardozo adopting the exclusionary rule in *People v. Defore*, 242 N.Y. 13, 150 N.E. 585, 587 (1926): "The criminal is to go free because the constable has blundered." At the time, Cardozo was a judge of the New York Court of Appeals, that state's highest court; he would later serve as an Associate Justice of the U.S. Supreme Court from 1932 until his death in 1938. The first case in which a U.S. Supreme Court opinion quoted Carzozo's famous sentence was *Elkins v. United States*, 364 U.S. 206, 216 (1960).
4. Rule 11.42 of the Kentucky Rules of Criminal Procedure (RCr), cited in the opinion, is the state court rule governing motions to vacate, correct, or set aside a sentence imposed in a criminal case. It is the approved means in Kentucky of seeking collateral review of a criminal conviction for issues such as ineffective assistance of counsel. *See Richardson v. Howard*, 448 S.W.2d 49 (Ky. 1969).

Johnson v. Dixon

Court of Appeals of Kentucky (1973)
501 S.W.2d 256

Opinion of the Court by Commissioner Cullen.

For the 1971–72 school year, Howard Johnson and his wife Janet, both natives of Barren County, were employed by the Hart County Board of Education on one-year contracts to teach at the secondary level in the Hart County school system. In March 1972 they were told by the superintendent that they would not be reemployed at the secondary level, because there were two Hart County natives who were available for the jobs and the board's policy was to give preference to Hart County natives; however, the superintendent offered the Johnsons employment at the primary level if they chose to become qualified for those positions by attending summer school. In April 1972 the Johnsons received official notice from the board that they would not be reemployed at the secondary level "since there are no positions available for them" but that they would be employed at the primary level upon becoming qualified. The Johnsons chose not to qualify for and accept the positions at the primary level, but instead they brought suit against the superintendent, the board and the individual board members alleging that their denial of reemployment at the secondary level was arbitrary and discriminatory in violation of their rights under Sections 1 and 3 of the Kentucky Constitution and deprived them of the equal protection of the law guaranteed by the Fourteenth Amendment to the United States Constitution. They sought judgment directing that they be reemployed and they asked for both compensatory and punitive damages.

The action was commenced in June 1972, well before the start of school for the 1972–73 year, but judgment was not entered until January 1973, in the middle of the 1972–73 year. In the meantime Janet Johnson had obtained a teaching job at the secondary level in another county, but since no similar job was available there for Howard, he took employment in building construction work.

The judgment was a summary one, based on the pleadings, depositions, etc., dismissing the complaint. The Johnsons have appealed.

The first question for consideration is whether the Johnsons have a valid claim for relief if the fact be established that the sole reason the Johnsons were not reemployed was that the board had a policy of giving preference in employment to Hart County natives. In considering that question we recognize that under the statute, KRS 161.750, cause is not required for denial of reemployment to a teacher employed under a limited contract (as were the Johnsons). Nevertheless, it is clear that public employment cannot be denied solely on the basis of an unconstitutionally discriminatory classification. *See* 15 Am.Jur.2nd, Civil Rights, sec. 57, p. 443; *Wieman v. Updegraff*, 344 U.S. 183, 73 S. Ct. 215, 97 L. Ed. 216.

Classifications based on alienage, nationality, or duration of residence have been held to be inherently suspect and therefore unconstitutional unless the public body making the classification can demonstrate that the classification is necessary to promote a compelling governmental interest. *See Dunn v. Blumstein*, 405 U.S. 330, 92 S. Ct. 995, 31 L. Ed. 2d 274; *Graham v. Richardson*, 403 U.S. 365, 91 S. Ct. 1848, 29 L. Ed. 2d 534. We believe the same holding must apply to a classification based on place of birth, as is the one here claimed to exist.

It must be remembered that the local schools are state institutions operated and maintained by the state through the agency of local district boards. *See Louisville v. Board of Education*, 154 Ky. 316, 157 S.W. 379. There was evidence in the instant case that most of the funds of the Hart County School system come from state appropriations. Thus, the compelling governmental interest required to be shown to sustain the classification here in question would have to be a state interest.

The only basis suggested by the appellees of support for a policy of preference to Hart County natives is that natives have demonstrated a greater continuity in employment than nonnatives. In our opinion this does not show a compelling governmental interest.

Our conclusion is that such a policy would be unconstitutionally discriminatory and preferential, in violation of Sections 1, 2 and 3 of the Kentucky Constitution.

* * *

The judgment is reversed, with directions for further proceedings in conformity with this opinion.

All concur.

Notes and Questions

1. In addition to violating Section 2 (as "arbitrary" and "discriminating") and Section 3 (being unconstitutionally "preferential"), the Court also holds that the school board's hiring policy of preference in favor of Hart County natives also violated Section 1. What provision(s) of Section 1 do you believe the Court had in mind?
2. Note that *Johnson v. Dixon* had only to do with whether a state agency could discriminate based on county of birth, but not place of residence. Numerous state statutes require residence within the Commonwealth or within a specific county as a prerequisite for holding office. *See, e.g.*, Ky. Const. § 234. Why might such regulations be reasonable? Do you think they present constitutional issues?
3. Kentucky has 120 counties. Does this fact at all help explain why county of origin is a suspect class in this state?

Kentucky Milk Marketing and Antimonopoly Commission v. Kroger Co.

Supreme Court of Kentucky (1985)

691 S.W.2d 893

Opinion of the Court by Chief Justice Stephens.

The basic issue we resolve on this appeal is the constitutionality of the so-called Kentucky Milk Marketing Law, KRS 260.675 to KRS 260.760, (1960).[1]

Procedural History

On September 18, 1982, the Commission, following a hearing, entered an order which found Kroger in violation of KRS 260.705[2] and levied a $4,500 fine against it. This action was filed on October 4, 1982 in the Franklin Circuit Court and was initially an appeal of that order pursuant to KRS 260.745. On the same day, the trial court, *ex parte*, entered a restraining order which enjoined the Commission from enforcing its order; from conducting any further investigation or hearings for violations of the law; and from enforcing any rules, regulations or orders against Kroger. Shortly thereafter, Kroger filed an amended complaint which, through the vehicle of a declaratory judgment, KRS 418.040, challenged the constitutionality of the entire Kentucky Milk Marketing Act. The suit is therefore in the nature of an appeal and a declaratory judgment.

Following the voluntary recusal of the regular Franklin County circuit judges, we appointed Honorable George M. Barker as special judge. On a motion by the Commission to dissolve the restraining order, the trial judge heard proof relevant to the merits.[3] Although the court ruled that Kroger was not entitled to a temporary injunction and dissolved the restraining order, it ruled that Kroger was entitled to partial relief; viz., a stay of the Commission's order during the pendency of the action on the merits. This order was entered on January 5, 1983.

Ruling of the Trial Judge

Following submission of the case on the merits, the trial judge ruled, on August 26, 1983, as follows:

(1) KRS 260.675 to KRS 260.700, and all regulations and practices related thereto were invalid as being in violation of the Sherman Anti-Trust Act, 15 USC Sec 1 et seq.

(2) The statute, regulations and practices were also invalid and unconstitutional as being in violation of Sections 1 and 2 of the Kentucky Constitution.

1. The Appellants Ewing, Rickard, Cassity, Manley, and Rushing are the members of the Kentucky Milk Marketing and Antimonopoly Commission and Appellant Claycomb is the executive director thereof. For convenience, Appellants will hereinafter be referred to as Commission and Appellee will be referred to as Kroger.

2. This statute and the entire Milk Marketing Act will be analyzed at a later point in this opinion.

3. The trial court heard all proof at that hearing except a deposition covering a study of the Kentucky Milk Marketing and Antimonopoly Commission.

(3) The Commission and all its officers and employees were permanently restrained from enforcing the Kentucky Milk Marketing Law and any and all regulations and practices promulgated pursuant thereto.

The judgment found Kroger not guilty of the offense charged by the Commission.

An appeal was filed by the Commission and, upon appropriate motion and for obvious reasons, we transferred the case to this Court.

CONTENTIONS OF APPELLANTS

On appeal, the Commission alleges: (1) that the Kentucky Milk Marketing Law is not in violation of the Sherman Anti-Trust Act; (2) that the trial court erred in holding that Kroger met its burden of proof; (3) that the Kentucky Milk Marketing and Antimonopoly Commission does not violate Sections 1 and 2 of the Kentucky Constitution; (4) that the federal courts have exclusive jurisdiction of all matters involving the Sherman Anti-Trust Act; (5) that the judgment of the trial court should be reviewed with respect to the appellants, *as individuals*, and (6) that those specific provisions of the Kentucky Milk Marketing and Antimonopoly Commission which were declared unconstitutional are severable.

We disagree and affirm the judgment of the trial court. Because we decide this case on the basis of the Kentucky Constitution, we need not discuss contentions (1) and (4), which relate to the Sherman Anti-Trust Act.

THE REGULATION OF THE DAIRY INDUSTRY

In order to guarantee that the consuming public has an adequate supply of wholesome milk and milk products, government has long been regulating the dairy industry. Marketing conditions in the late 1930's led to federal and state legislation to bring purity and stability to milk products. Federal marketing orders[4] provide a minimum price which must be paid to farmers for the milk they sell. These orders do not guarantee a sale of milk, but do guarantee a minimum price in the event of sale. Under the federal program, milk which is not sold is purchased by the Federal Government and is generally made into butter or cheese, then stored and ultimately given away.[5]

The Kentucky Milk Marketing Law

As noted, KRS 260.675 to KRS 260.760 (1960) inclusive, is known as the "Milk Marketing Law."

In summary, this law prohibits any distributor, processor, bulk milk handler, store, or producer-handler from engaging in any marketing practice established as unreasonable by the Commission (or the Act), *for the purpose or with the effect of restraining, lessening or destroying competition* or injuring one or more competitors or injuring one

4. Promulgated under the authority of the Agriculture Marketing Administration Act of 1937.

5. We will not unduly lengthen this opinion to discuss the philosophical merits/demerits or the necessity or efficacy of this program, *or*, for that matter, of the Kentucky Milk Marketing Law. Our function, obviously, is to test the content of the Kentucky Milk Marketing Law, and its enforcement by the Commission, by the standards set up by our Constitution.

or more persons dealing in milk production or to impair or prevent fair competition in the sale of milk and milk products. KRS 260.705. Specifically, this section of the Act prohibits selling "*below cost*" for the purpose of injuring or destroying competition or with the effect of otherwise injuring a competitor, or destroying competition, or of creating a monopoly. KRS 260.705(a).

Farmers, as producers of milk, are not affected by the law. The place it first touches is at the level of so-called processor-distributors.[6] The processor-distributors are required to file with the Commission price schedules which can only be superseded, changed or withdrawn on forms prescribed. KRS 260.710. Regulations of the Commission require that price changes be filed at least twenty (20) days in advance of the proposed effective date. Although the Commission, under restrictions set out in KRS 260.710, may not set or establish a price for the regulation of milk products, *it does have the authority to review price schedules to insure that no processor-distributor is selling below cost.* Thus, KRS 260.705(1)(a) limits and forbids a practice which would:

> "advertise for sale any article or product *at less than the cost thereof to such vendor . . .*" (Emphasis added.)

In the case of processor-distributors, KRS 260.680(12) defines "cost" as follows:

> "Cost to the processor or distributor" means the price paid for raw materials, plus the cost of doing business, as evidenced by the standards and methods of accounting regularly employed by such processor or distributor. The cost of doing business means all costs of doing business incurred in the conduct of the business and shall include without limitation that following items of expense: labor (including salaries of executives and officers), rent, interest on borrowed capital, depreciation, power, supplies, maintenance of equipment, selling costs, transportation, delivery cost, credit losses, all overhead expense, and all types of licenses, taxes, insurance and advertising, ...

In the case of retailers, KRS 260.680(17) defines "Cost" as follows:

> "Cost to the store" means the invoice price paid by the retailer plus the retailer's cost of doing business, as evidenced by the standards and methods of accounting regularly employed by such store, including, but not limited to, all costs incurred in the conduct of said store such as labor (including salaries of executives and officers), rent, interest on borrowed capital, depreciation, power, supplies, maintenance of equipment, selling costs, advertising, transportation, delivery costs, credit losses, all overhead expenses, and all types of licenses, taxes, insurance and advertising;

KRS 260.715 sets forth the powers and duties of the Commission. The relevant provisions therein authorize an investigation and hearing in response to alleged violations of

---

6. The definition section of the Act, KRS 260.680, defines "producer" as "every person who produces milk or cream from cows and thereafter sells the same as milk, cream, or other dairy products." Subsection (10) defines a distributor as a person engaged in the business of distributing the milk products at *wholesale or retail to consumers, stores or other distributors.*

the Milk Marketing Law or the regulations enacted pursuant thereto. The Commission has the specific authority to *suspend or revoke* the licenses of processor-distributors and retailers. KRS 260.735. It also has the power to impose fines up to $500 for each violation, and to imprison violators for not less than 1 day nor more than 30 days. KRS 260.991.

In essence, the ostensible purpose of the Milk Marketing Law is to prevent any practices that would tend to eliminate competition or tend to create a monopoly. By legislative fiat, one proscribed practice the statute says tends to create a monopoly or unfair competition is the sale of milk products below cost. KRS 260.680(17); KRS 260.710.

In a well-reasoned opinion, the trial court found from the evidence presented that the Kentucky Milk Marketing Law, *as administered by the Commission*, is, in actuality, not an anti-monopoly law but rather, a minimum retail mark-up law. In so finding, the trial court in effect applied the old adage, "If it walks like a duck and quacks like a duck, it is a duck." We agree.

In prohibiting sales "below cost", the statutory definition of "cost to the store" includes the *invoice price paid by the retailer, plus* his cost of doing business, including (but not limited to): *all cost incurred in the conduct of said store* such as labor, salaries, rent, interest, depreciation, power, supplies, maintenance, selling cost, advertising, transportation, delivery cost, credit losses, *all* overhead expenses, and *all* types of licenses, taxes, insurance and advertising. The evidence is incontrovertible that many, if not all, of the costs incurred by grocery retailers have nothing to do with the actual cost of selling milk. According to the evidence, the procedure used by the Commission requires the seller to submit all costs incurred by the stores in terms of a percentage of gross sales, (less sales and excise taxes). Prior to this litigation the minimum legal price was determined by adding that percentage to the invoice price of the milk, to determine the "cost" that was proper, as not being "*below* cost." The method was changed to require that the proposed selling price be multiplied by the percentage, with the result being added to the invoice price of the milk. If the result was *less* than the proposed selling price, the price was legal. If, however, the result was *greater* than the proposed selling price, then the proposed price was illegal.

A review of the proceedings of the Commission for the previous thirteen (13) years reveals that it followed the statutory definition. However, in a directive to all retail stores, dated May 19, 1974, the appellant, Claycomb, as Executive Director of the Commission, declared that a figure of fifteen (15) percent over the invoice cost of milk would ... "be needed in order for the retailer to realize *a reasonable profit* on the sale of the product." Apparently recognizing that this directive revealed the real purpose of the Act, the Commission rescinded it on September 15, 1975. The trial court found, and we agree, that the "mark up" required does include an actual profit over and above the cost of selling milk products.

It is understandable that the *cost* of selling items in the grocery department (including milk) is lower than any other department of a grocery store. In the case of Kroger, it is 4% in the grocery department, 15% in the produce department, and 30% in the delicatessen. The evidence also shows that, in the case of Kroger, and most supermarkets, over 8,000 items are offered for sale to the public. Under the Kentucky Milk Marketing Law, only three of those items are singled out for special treatment as to price control.

That the Kentucky Milk Marketing Law mandates a minimum mark-up, including a profit, is even more clear by noting what happens as the result of an increase *in the invoice price of milk.* As an example, it was shown that if the invoice cost of a gallon of ice cream was increased from \$1.65 to \$1.75, the law as applied would require an increase in selling price from \$2.05 to \$2.19. As the trial court opined, "obviously, the cost of selling the ice cream could not have increased but the law requires the consumer to pay 14 cents more for the product because of a 10 cent increase in price."

Under these circumstances, we have no problem in concluding that the Kentucky Milk Marketing Law, while ostensibly and facially an anti-monopoly law, is in actuality and practice, a minimum mark-up law.

Factual Background of this Litigation

With our analysis of the Kentucky Milk Marketing Law, it is now appropriate to recite the facts which gave rise to the actions of the Commission against Kroger, and this resultant litigation.

On July 2, 1982, a letter was sent by a competitor of Kroger to the Commission complaining that Kroger was selling vanilla ice cream at \$1.99 per gallon. Following the complaint, the Commission notified Kroger that a formal hearing would be held and requested a factual justification for this price, viz., that the item was not being sold "below cost." At the hearing, Kroger established its dock cost was \$1.65 per gallon. Kroger further established that its total store expense was 16.61% of sales and its advertising, warehousing and transportation expense amounted to an additional 3.45% of sales, thus setting the total cost of doing business at 20.06% of sales. This percentage, when applied to the dock cost, made a total cost of \$1.99 per gallon. The Commission rejected this formula, requiring that the percentage of cost be multiplied by the *selling price* of \$1.99, which, when added to the dock cost of \$1.65, made the minimum legal price \$2.05 per gallon.

Kroger, in the course of business, acts as its own processor-distributor. As such, it is not required to file a price schedule, and thus technically has no *invoice cost* of its product. It has been the custom of the Commission in similar situations to accept the "certified cost"[7] in the product data submitted by the retailer. This was not done in this case.

Strangely enough, there are no rules or regulations published by the Commission which establish the proper procedures to set a minimum retail sales price. Appellant Claycomb testified that there were two methods of establishing certified cost used by the Commission, *one of which would have justified* Kroger's price. However at the hearing, appellant Ewing, who is interestingly enough a competitor of Kroger, ruled that the

7. In this case the cost, as stated, is \$1.65.

other method should be used.[8] Yet no reason was given, nor indeed is one apparent, as to why this other method was used.[9] Additionally, it is clear that the Commission has the legal authority to promulgate regulations on such matters. *Kentucky Milk Mktg. & Antimonopoly Commission v. Borden Co.*, Ky., 456 S.W.2d 831 (1970). It seems that fairness and objectivity would require that such be done.

Based on these facts, the trial court found that the Commission's finding that Kroger was guilty of selling "below cost" was arbitrary and capricious, and found Kroger not guilty.

Is the Kentucky Milk Marketing Law Violative of Kentucky Constitution, Section 2

Section 2 of our Constitution is simple, short and expresses a view of governmental and political philosophy that, in a very real sense, distinguishes this republic from all other forms of government which place little or no emphasis on the rights of individuals in a society. It is as follows:

> "§2. Absolute and arbitrary power denied. *Absolute and arbitrary power over the* lives, liberty and *property of free men exists nowhere in a republic, not even in the largest majority*." (Emphasis added.)

While there are numerous cases which have been decided on the basis of this bulwark of individual liberty, the number is relatively few, in view of its potential importance to our jurisprudence.

Section 2 is a curb on the legislature as well as on any other public body or public officer in the assertion or attempted exercise of political power. *Sanitation Dist. No. 1 v. City of Louisville*, 308 Ky. 368, 213 S.W.2d 995 (1948). Whatever is contrary to democratic ideals, customs and maxims is arbitrary. Likewise, whatever is essentially unjust and unequal or exceeds the reasonable and legitimate interests of the people is arbitrary, *Id.* No board or officer vested with governmental authority may exercise it arbitrarily. If the action taken rests upon reasons so unsubstantial or the consequences are so unjust as to work a hardship, judicial power may be interposed to protect the rights of persons adversely affected. *Wells v. Board of Education of Mercer County*, Ky., 289 S.W.2d 492, 494 (1956). Our function is to decide a test of regularity and legality of a board's action by statutory law and by the constitutional protection against the exercise of arbitrary official power. *Id.*

Section 2 is broad enough to embrace the traditional concepts of both due process of law and equal protection of the law. *Pritchett v. Marshall*, Ky., 375 S.W.2d 253, 258 (1963). Unequal enforcement of the law, if it rises to the level of conscious violation of the principle of uniformity, is prohibited by this Section. *City of Ashland v. Heck's, Inc.*,

---

8. Ewing was Vice-Chairman of the Commission and even though he was a competitor of Kroger he did not recuse himself at the hearing, though he had done so in other cases involving his company's competition.

9. The evidence also shows that the standard which would have justified Kroger's price had been generally used by the Commission.

Ky., 407 S.W.2d 421 (1966); *Standard Oil v. Boone County Bd. of Sup'rs*, Ky., 562 S.W.2d 83 (1978). The question of reasonableness is one of degree and must be based on the facts of a particular case. *Boyle Cty. Stockyards Co. v. Commonwealth, etc.*, Ky.App., 570 S.W.2d 650 (1978).

The majority of this Court believes that the Kentucky Milk Marketing Law, on its face, and in its enforcement by the Commission in this particular case, is violative of Section 2 of the Kentucky Constitution.

As we have previously said,[10] the statutory purpose of the law is to prevent monopolies and unfair practices in the sale of milk and milk products. As we have also said, the law is in reality and in practice not an anti-monopoly statute, but is rather a minimum mark-up law. We believe an enactment of such a nature is an arbitrary exercise of power by the General Assembly over the lives and property of free men.

Even though we decide this case on Kentucky Constitutional grounds, we are cognizant that minimum mark-up laws (unless authorized as state action) are violative of the Sherman Anti-Trust Act. *Alcoholic Beverage Control Board v. Taylor Drug Stores*, Ky., 635 S.W.2d 319 (1982). The effect of the Kentucky Milk Marketing Law is price fixing by requiring minimum mark-ups. This certainly, by any criteria, is arbitrary and is inimical to the public interest. It is an invasion of the right of merchants to sell competitively, and of the public to buy competitively in the open market.

In the case of *General Electric Co. v. American Buyers Cooperative*, Ky., 316 S.W.2d 354 (1958), we held sections of Kentucky's Fair Trade Act unconstitutional. The Act enforced price fixing not only against parties to a minimum resale agreement, but also against a nonsignee if he knowingly breaches a resale agreement which was made between the producer and a third person. In effect the statute approved agreements by which a producer could require purchaser-retailer to resell the property at a certain invoice mark-up. In language relevant to the present case, we said:

> Our Bill of Rights declares as one of "the great and essential principles of liberty and free government" and as "inherent and inalienable ... the right of acquiring and protecting property".... This is free enterprise. Our economic system is founded upon competition—"the life of trade." It is an established principle that the constitutional guaranty of the right of property protects it ... from any unjustifiable impairment or abridgement of this right, such as depriving the owner of any of its essential attributes or such as restricts or interrupts its common necessary or profitable use.... *The right of the owner to fix the price at which his property shall be sold is an inherent attribute of the property itself ...*"
>
> Supplemental to this property right provision is §2 of the Constitution which forbids the exercise of arbitrary power of government over the "property of free men." (Emphasis added.) *Id.* at page 360.

---

10. See discussion of the nature of Kentucky Milk Marketing Law, *supra*.

The Kentucky Milk Marketing Law, whether interpreted as a minimum mark-up law or interpreted as simply requiring that a retailer may not sell "below cost", is clearly an arbitrary interference with "the right of the owner to fix the price at which his property shall be sold." *Id.* It is an arbitrary interference with the free flow of commerce—the free enterprise system—and is not justified or to be justified by the police power of the state. It is clearly a violation of the letter and spirit of Section 2 of our Bill of Rights.

Was the Kentucky Milk Marketing Law Administered in an Arbitrary Manner so as to be Violative of Kentucky Constitution, Section 2

Appellants argue that Kroger did not meet its burden of proof in declaring the Kentucky Milk Marketing Law unconstitutional. We are well aware that the presumption of constitutionality of a statute is axiomatic. *Walters v. Binder*, Ky., 435 S.W.2d 464 (1968). It is sufficient to say that we believe the Milk Marketing Law is clearly in violation of Section 2 of the Kentucky Constitution and that the presumption of constitutionality has been overcome.

As we previously have said, the Kentucky Milk Marketing Law, in being administered by the Commission, has been treated as a minimum retail mark-up law. There have been no forms or standardized procedures provided by the Commission which would enable a respondent to justify his selling cost. The formula used by the Commission for many years was, without reason or explanation, changed by the Commission in this particular case. Vice-Chairman Ewing, even though he had regularly recused himself when competitors were involved in the past, failed to do so in this particular case. As we have also said, the Commission, without reason or explanation, refused to accept Kroger's "invoice cost" per gallon, even though it regularly had done so in similar situations in the past. Moreover, the order handed down by the Commission contained no findings of fact. Based on these facts, the trial court held, and we agree, that the Commission finding Kroger guilty of a statutory violation was "arbitrary and capricious, prejudicing the substantial rights of (Kroger)."

* * *

The entire Act, from its definition section to its penalty section, has the purpose of enforcing the provisions of KRS 260.705. We conclude, therefore, that all parts of the statute are essentially and inseparably connected, and not severable.

* * *

The judgment of the trial court is affirmed, but the case is remanded with directions to modify the judgment in a manner consistent with this opinion.

Stephens, C.J., Leibson, J., and William L. Shadoan and William P. McEvoy, Special Justices, concur.

Stephenson, J., concurs in a separate opinion in which Aker and Gant, JJ., join.

* * *

Notes and Questions

1. The *Kentucky Milk Marketing* case is generally considered the primary Kentucky case on due process and equal protection of the law. Unlike the Constitution of the United States, there is no Equal Protection Clause or Due Process Clause in the Kentucky Constitution. However, note that the Court here states that Section 2, and its prohibition on "[a]bsolute and arbitrary power," is broad enough to embrace both concepts.
2. How do Sections 1 and 2 of the Kentucky Constitution interrelate to protect the right to property?
3. What relationship does the free enterprise economic system have to the principle of due process of law?
4. In discussing the *Kentucky Milk Marketing* case, one Kentucky lawyer observed, "The Supreme Court of Kentucky apparently believes that section 2, unlike the United States Constitution, *does* embody a particular economic theory known as the 'free enterprise system.' Although this belief is not devoid of historical support, it is directly at odds with the prevailing federal Constitutional jurisprudence of this century." John David Dyche, *Section 2 of the Kentucky Constitution—Where Did It Come From and What Does It Mean?*, 18 N. Ky. L. Rev. 503, 523 (1990).

Remote Services, Inc. v. FDR Corporation

Supreme Court of Kentucky (1989)

764 S.W.2d 80

OPINION OF THE COURT BY CHIEF JUSTICE STEPHENS.

On this appeal we decide the constitutionality of one of Kentucky's so-called Unfair Trade Practices Acts, KRS 365.030.

On June 25, 1986, appellee filed a complaint in the Jefferson Circuit Court alleging that appellants had violated the provisions of KRS 365.030 by selling gasoline and gasoline products at less than cost for the purpose of injuring competitors and destroying competition. Appellants answered, claiming among other things, that the statute was in violation of Section 2 of the Kentucky Constitution, Appellants filed a motion for summary judgment to which appellee did not respond. The trial court entered the requested judgment. Thereafter, the trial court withdrew the judgment, and permitted appellee to respond to the motion. Following a response, the trial court reinstated the summary judgment.

The basis of the trial court's decision was that the statute violated Section 2 of the Kentucky Constitution, as well as the Sherman Anti-Trust Act[1] and the Commerce Clause of the United States Constitution.[2]

---

1. 15 U.S.C. §§1 et seq.
2. U.S. Const. Art. I, §8.

On appeal, the Kentucky Court of Appeals, in a 2–1 decision, reversed the trial court. The majority declared that KRS 365.030 is not a minimum mark-up law, and is not a method of "retail price maintenance." It categorized the statute as a "trade-practice measure." The majority further stated that the legislative purpose recognized that

> "... the monopolistic potential of price undercutting is, in the long run, more hostile to public interest than is the value of temporarily low prices. The benefits to be gained from transiently low prices are so Lilliputian as to be grossly outweighed by the potential for an economic leviathan to destroy all competition and thus to consume the consuming public."

Slip op. at 3.

The Court of Appeals distinguished the case of *Kentucky Milk Marketing v. Kroger Company*, Ky., 691 S.W.2d 893 (1985), by identifying the offending statute therein as a minimum retail mark-up law, as opposed to the statute *sub judice*, which, as stated, it described as a permissible "trade-practice measure."

We disagree, and reverse the Court of Appeals. The pertinent sections of the challenged statute are as follows:

> 365.030. Sale at less than cost or gift of commodity to destroy competition prohibited. (1) Except as provided in KRS 365.040, *no person engaged in business within this state shall sell, offer for sale or advertise for sale any article or product, or service or output of a service trade, at less than the cost thereof to such vendor*, or give, offer to give or advertise the intent to give away any article or product, or service or output of a service trade, *for the purpose of injuring competitors and destroying competition.*
>
> ....
>
> (3) As applied to production, "cost" includes the cost of raw materials, labor and all overhead expenses of the producer. *As applied to distribution, 'cost' means the invoice or replacement cost, whichever is lower, of the article or product to the distributor and vendor plus the cost of doing business by the distributor and vendor. The "cost of doing business" or "overhead expense" means all costs of doing business incurred in the conduct of the business and must include without limitation the following items of expense: Labor (including salaries of executives and officers), rent, interest on borrowed capital, depreciation, selling cost, maintenance of equipment, delivery cost, credit losses, all types of licenses, taxes, insurance and advertising.* "Vendor" includes any person who performs work upon, renovates, alters or improves any personal property belonging to another person. (Emphasis added.)

By the simple and unequivocal wording of this statute, the General Assembly has proscribed, as being an unfair trade practice, the selling of a product, a service, or the output of a service trade at a price which is less than cost for the purpose of injuring competitors or destroying competition. The General Assembly has defined "cost" as applied to distribution, as "the invoice or replacement cost, whichever is lower, of the article or product to the distributor and vendor plus the cost of doing business by the distributor and vendor."[3] Further the statute defines "cost of doing business" as expenses incurred for labor (including executive salaries), rent, interest, depreciation, selling cost, maintenance of equipment, delivery cost, etc. In a word, *cost* means all those items of actual expense which must be recovered before a profit can be realized.

Appellants, as defendants in the trial court, were accused by the appellee, as plaintiff, of violating the statute by selling below cost for the purpose of injuring plaintiff, a competitor. As this case was decided by summary judgment, we must, perforce, take all allegations thereof as being true. Moreover, appellants have conceded they were violating the statute for the purpose of injuring competitors.

The Court of Appeals upheld KRS 365.030 as maintaining a competitive sales environment. Analyzing the legislative policy of the General Assembly in enacting the statute, it concluded, in a quantum leap of logic and with a considerable amount of fact finding on its own, that temporary price cutting would lead to monopolies which would "consume the consuming public." There is no basis for such a conclusion in the record before us and no such conclusion can be justified by the wording of the statute. That statement, at best, represents a subjective view of the majority, and does not comport with either the facts or viable economic theory.

The statute presently in question is strikingly similar to that in the *Milk Marketing* case, *supra*, which we declared to be a minimum mark-up law and in violation of Section 2 of the Kentucky Constitution. For the reasons which follow we believe that case and the rationale for the decision therein is dispositive of the issue before us.

In *Milk Marketing*, we decided the constitutionality of KRS 260.675 et seq. The purpose of that statute was to prevent any practices that would tend to eliminate competition or tend to create a monopoly. One proscribed practice set out in that statute was the sale of milk products "below cost." The statute carefully defined "below cost;" cost was said to include the invoice price of milk, plus the cost of doing business, including labor, salaries, rent, interest, depreciation, power, supplies, maintenance, selling costs, transportation, delivery costs, lease, taxes, etc. It was the definition of "cost," which was not confined to cost of the product, but included other legitimate competitive advantage, that abrogated the constitutionality of the statute.

The prohibition of selling below cost and the definition of cost is nearly identical in KRS 260.675 et seq., and in KRS 365.030(1), (3). The statutes are a virtual image of each other. They both prohibit sales below cost for anti-competitive purposes; and they both require adherence to essentially the same cost determination formula. Therefore, they must withstand the same constitutional muster.

3. Use of the lower of invoice or replacement cost is subject to the provisions of subsection (2), which prohibits using an artificially low invoice cost except under specified conditions.

In *Milk Marketing*, as noted, we declared the statute to be a minimum mark-up law. Since the statutes are so similar, we must, *a fortiori* conclude that KRS 365.030 is also a minimum mark-up law. It clearly is. We further declared the statutes at issue in *Milk Marketing* violated Section 2 of the Kentucky Constitution. We held that they were *facially* unconstitutional and were unconstitutional in their enforcement. *Id.*, at 899.

We believe the reasoning in *Milk Marketing* is clearly applicable to this case. Section 2 of the Kentucky Constitution is that part of our constitution which guarantees due process of law to our citizens and extends equal protection of the law to all its citizens, corporate or otherwise. It protects "free men" from absolute and arbitrary power over their "lives, liberty and property." As we said in *Milk Marketing*, when testing a minimum mark-up law by the provisions of Section 2,

> "[t]his certainly by any criteria, is arbitrary and is inimical to the public interest. It is an invasion of the right of merchants to sell competitively, and of the public to buy competitively in the open market." *Id.*, at p. 900.

We therefore conclude that since KRS 365.030 is a minimum mark-up law, it is facially unconstitutional as being violative of Section 2 of the Kentucky Constitution.

The decision of the Court of Appeals is reversed, and the judgment of the trial court is affirmed.

Combs, Leibson and Wintersheimer, JJ., concur.

Vance, J., dissents in a separate dissenting opinion in which Gant and Lambert, JJ., join.

Justice Vance, dissenting.

Respectfully, I dissent. The majority condemns K.R.S. 365.030 on the basis that it is not a "trade-practice regulation" but is in fact a "minimum mark-up" law.

This case was decided on a summary judgment and therefore all of the allegations of the complaint must be taken as true. The appellee alleged that appellants were selling their product below cost as defined by statute and further alleged that such sales below cost were for the purpose of destroying competition. Appellants have, in fact, conceded they were violating the statute for the purpose of injuring competitors.

I concede that the statute is unconstitutional if it is, in fact, a minimum mark-up statute. I am astounded that the majority can find anything about the statute which requires any mark-up whatever above cost. The majority opinion does not specify in any particular where a mark-up of any kind occurs by reason of the statute.

As I read the statute it would permit the appellants to sell their product at exactly cost. It does not require them to make profit to comply with the law. What it does require is that appellants do not sell their product at a price below their cost for the purpose of destroying competition by the appellee. This is exactly what the appellants admit they have been doing.

I believe the Court of Appeals was exactly right when it noted that "the monopolistic potential of price undercutting is, in the long run, more hostile to the public interest than is the value of temporarily low prices. The benefits to be gained from transiently low prices are so Lilliputian as to be grossly outweighed by the potential for an economic leviathan to destroy all competition and thus to consume the consuming public."

The statute in question does not prohibit all sales below cost, but only those below cost sales *which are made for the purpose of injuring competitors and destroying competition*. Thus, sales in good faith in liquidating a business, sales where the goods have been damaged, sales made under a court order, or sales to meet in good faith the price of a competitor may be made below cost because such sales are not for the purpose of destroying competition.

In this country we have long recognized a legitimate state interest in regulating monopolistic practices. Thus, utilities, which are essentially monopolies, are regulated by the Public Service Commission to protect consumers. For competitive enterprises a statute such as K.R.S. 365.030 is an anti-monopoly statute, pure and simple, and it is well within the recognized police power of the state. It prevents a rich and powerful competitor from reducing its price below cost until it squeezes its competitor out of the market, after which, because it no longer has any competition, it can raise its prices as unreasonably high as it pleases.

This case was decided by summary judgment, and there is no evidence in the record, as yet, to show the extent that appellants were selling below their cost, but their admission that they were violating the statute with an intent to injure their competitors is, in itself, an admission of a cannibalistic practice designed to monopolize the market to some extent at least. Even though the procedure in this case has prevented the taking of evidence, as judges we are not required to blind ourselves to the history of monopoly in this country, and its dire consequences. The lessons learned from the robber barons of a past age are still there to see. The ability of a national dairy or bakery or oil company to sustain itself from the profits of a thousand subsidiaries across the country, while deliberately absorbing a substantial loss from below cash sales in one locality for the purpose of eliminating a local competitor in that locality is plain to see. The purpose of statutes prohibiting below cost sales is to prevent such monopolistic practices. The statute in question does not require or guarantee a mark-up, it simply prohibits sales below cost for the purpose of eliminating competition.

The majority places great reliance upon the similarity of the statute in question here to the statute which was held unconstitutional in *Kentucky Milk Marketing v. Kroger Co.*, Ky., 691 S.W.2d 893 (1985). In that case, however, there was a trial on the merits and evidence which showed that the statute as applied by the milk marketing commission resulted in a mark-up or profit. There is no marketing commission to regulate the enforcement of the statute in question, and there is no evidence in the record which shows that any mark-up results from compliance with the statute.

I would reverse the summary judgment and remand to the trial court for further proceedings.

Gant and Lambert, JJ., join in this dissenting opinion.

Notes and Questions

1. In what ways was the statute at issue here like the statute at issue in the *Milk Marketing* case? How were the statutes different?
2. The dissent mentions multiple times that the case was decided by the trial court on a summary judgment motion, rather than having a full trial. Is that a distinction between this case and the *Milk Marketing* case that makes a difference?
3. As the *Remote Services* case reads the *Milk Marketing* case, might any statute that invades "the right of merchants to sell competitively, and of the public to buy competitively in the open market" violate Section 2?

B. A Brief History of Equal Protection Analysis in Kentucky

Students of federal constitutional law are familiar with the "tiers of scrutiny" approach to analyzing equal protection issues under the Fourteenth Amendment. In constitutional challenges to statutes under the Equal Protection Clause,[1] the general rule is that legislative classifications that are rationally related to a legitimate state interest are valid.[2] Most economic and social legislation is subject to this "rational basis" scrutiny.[3]

However, when laws classify on the basis of race, alienage, or national origin, or when they impinge on personal rights guaranteed under the U.S. Constitution, the highest tier of scrutiny—"strict scrutiny"—applies.[4] Under strict scrutiny, such classifications are constitutional only if they are narrowly tailored and further compelling governmental interests.[5]

In between rational basis scrutiny and strict scrutiny lies "intermediate scrutiny," a form of heightened scrutiny that applies to classifications based on sex and illegitimacy.[6] Under intermediate scrutiny, such classifications survive only if they are substantially related to important governmental objectives.[7]

There is no Equal Protection Clause in the Kentucky Constitution. But the Kentucky courts have found a similar guarantee of equal protection of the laws in Sections 1, 2,

---

1. "No State shall ... deny to any person within its jurisdiction the equal protection of the laws." U.S. Const. amend. XIV, §1.
2. *City of Cleburne v. Cleburne Living Ctr.*, 473 U.S. 432, 439 (1985).
3. *Id.*
4. *Id.*
5. *Adarand Constructors, Inc. v. Pena*, 515 U.S. 200, 227 (1995).
6. *City of Cleburne*, 473 U.S. at 440–41.
7. *Mississippi Univ. for Women v. Hogan*, 458 U.S. 718, 724 (1982).

and 3 of the Kentucky Constitution.[8] The more recent Kentucky cases have analyzed classification and equal protection questions using the same tiers of scrutiny tests now used by the federal courts.[9] But as evidenced by the readings in this chapter, that has not always been the case.

The Traditional Test

For a long time, the Kentucky courts have applied the same "standards for classification" under the Kentucky Constitution as "those under the Fourteenth Amendment to the Federal Constitution."[10] Kentucky's highest court held, soon after the adoption of the present Constitution, that "[t]here is no provision of our Constitution that fixes a different standard from that prescribed by the equal protection clause of the Fourteenth Amendment to the Federal Constitution."[11]

Under the traditional *Ecklar* test, a "classification" does not violate equal protection guarantees if (1) the classification applies equally to all in a class; and (2) there are "distinctive and natural reasons inducing and supporting the classification."[12] The Supreme Court has noted more recently that "[o]ther cases decided contemporaneously with or prior to *Ecklar* use the same or similar language as *Ecklar* in interpreting Section 3 or Section 3's predecessor provision in the 1850 Constitution, Art. XIII, §1."[13] "In these earlier decisions," the Supreme Court observed, Kentucky courts "addressed claims of partial/class legislation under Kentucky's equal protection guarantee, *i.e.*, the state constitution's prohibition on 'exclusive, separate privilege.'"[14]

8. *See, e.g., Ky. Milk Mktg. & Antimonopoly Comm'n v. Kroger Co.*, 691 S.W.2d 893, 899 (Ky. 1985) ("Section 2 is broad enough to embrace the traditional concepts of both due process of law and equal protection of the law."); *Zuckerman v. Bevin*, 565 S.W.3d 580, 594 (Ky. 2018) ("Citizens of Kentucky enjoy equal protection of the law under the 14th Amendment of the United States Constitution and Sections 1, 2, and 3 of the Kentucky Constitution. Sections 1, 2, and 3 of the Kentucky Constitution provide that the legislature does not have arbitrary power and shall treat all persons equally." (citation omitted)); *Calloway Cnty. Sheriff's Dep't v. Woodall*, 607 S.W.3d 557, 573 (Ky. 2020) ("[S]tate constitutional challenges to legislation based on classification succeed or fail on the basis of equal protection analysis under Sections 1, 2, and 3 of the Kentucky Constitution.").

9. *See, e.g., Zuckerman*, 565 S.W.3d at 595; *Woodall*, 607 S.W.3d at 563–64.

10. *Reynolds Metal Co. v. Martin*, 269 Ky. 378, 107 S.W.2d 251, 260 (1937).

11. *Williams v. City of Bowling Green*, 254 Ky. 11, 70 S.W.2d 967, 968 (1934).

12. *Safety Bldg. & Loan Co. v. Ecklar*, 106 Ky. 115, 50 S.W. 50, 51 (1899), *overruled in part on other grounds by Linton v. Fulton Bldg. & Loan Ass'n*, 262 Ky. 198, 90 S.W.2d 22 (1936).

13. *Woodall*, 607 S.W.3d at 566 (citing *Commonwealth v. Remington Typewriter Co.*, 127 Ky. 177, 105 S.W. 399, 402–03 (1907); *Simpson v. Ky. Citizens' Bldg. & Loan Ass'n*, 101 Ky. 496, 41 S.W. 570 (1897), *overruled in part on other grounds by Linton*, 262 Ky. 198, 90 S.W.2d 22; *Schoolcraft's Adm'r v. Louisville & Nashville R.R.*, 92 Ky. 233, 17 S.W. 567, 568 (1891); *Ky. Tr. Co. v. Lewis*, 82 Ky. 579, 583–84 (1885); *Smith v. Warden*, 80 Ky. 608, 611 (1883); *Gordon v. Winchester Bldg. & Accumulating Fund Ass'n*, 75 Ky. 110, 113–14 (1876)).

14. *Woodall*, 607 S.W.3d at 566–67 (citing Ky. Const. §3; Ky. Const. (1850) art. XIII, §1).

Toward the middle of the 20th century, Kentucky courts began to view legislative classifications through the lens of arbitrariness and unreasonableness.[15] As one example, the old Court of Appeals applied the arbitrary and unreasonable test in *Elrod v. Willis*.[16] The *Elrod* Court held that "where legislation makes an improper discrimination by conferring particular privileges upon a class arbitrarily selected, and there can be no reasonable or substantial ground justifying the inclusion of one and the exclusion of the other, it is called class legislation. However, ... an Act will not be held invalid unless the classification is clearly unreasonable and arbitrary.... [T]he crucial test is the extent to which the law operates and the manner in which it applies, or the objectives sought to be attained by it.... What classification is reasonable rests in the discretion of the legislative body in the first instance, and in the second it is in the province of the courts to adjudicate when it should be classed as arbitrary or unreasonable."[17]

Another example can be found in *Louisville & Jefferson County Metropolitan Sewer District v. Joseph E. Seagram & Sons, Inc.*[18] The *Seagram* Court applied a similar test, observing that "a system of classification founded upon a natural and reasonable basis, with a logical relation to the purposes and objectives of the authority granted, does not offend the principle of equal rights under law."[19]

The "distinctive and natural reasons inducing and supporting [a] classification" under *Ecklar*,[20] the "reasonable or substantial ground justifying" a classification under *Elrod*,[21] and the "natural and reasonable basis" for a classification under *Seagram*[22] all

---

15. *See, e.g., Sanitation Dist. No. 1 of Jefferson Cnty. v. City of Louisville*, 308 Ky. 68, 213 S.W.2d 995, 999–1001 (1948) (holding statute unconstitutional as "arbitrary" under Section 2 and "at war with equality" under Section 3); *Goodwin v. City of Louisville*, 309 Ky. 11, 215 S.W.2d 557, 559 (1948) (noting "clearly arbitrary" standard); *Reeves v. Wright & Taylor*, 310 Ky. 470, 220 S.W.2d 1007, 1009–10 (1949) (characterizing the equal protection standard alternately as "unreasonable, arbitrary and capricious," "an unreasonable classification," and "capricious, arbitrary, or ... lacking in foundation"); *Rosenberg v. Queenan*, 261 S.W.2d 617, 618 (Ky. 1953) (holding "it is only where the classifications are arbitrary and unreasonable so as to exclude one or more of a class without a reasonable basis" that a statute violates Section 3); *Wooley v. Spalding*, 293 S.W.2d 563, 565 (Ky. 1956) (observing that uniformity under Section 3 "does not require equal classification but it does demand that there shall be a substantially uniform system ... without discrimination as between different sections of a district or county"); *City of Louisville v. Klusmeyer*, 324 S.W.2d 831, 834 (Ky. 1959) (noting that legislation that "arbitrarily or beyond reasonable justification discriminates against some persons or objects and favors others" violates Section 3); *Watkins v. State Prop. & Bldgs. Comm'n of Ky.*, 342 S.W.2d 511, 513 (Ky. 1960) ("Substantially all legislation involves classification of some sort, and the classification here is reasonably relevant to the purposes of the Act."); *Hallahan v. Mittlebeeler*, 373 S.W.2d 726, 728 (Ky. 1963) (holding standard for judging classifications is whether they are "unreasonable and arbitrary, *i.e.*, whether the classifications rest on natural and reasonable distinctions"); *Jefferson Cnty. v. King*, 479 S.W.2d 880, 882 (Ky. 1972) (holding legislative classifications valid if they "are directly related to the accomplishment of a valid public purpose and have a reasonable basis").

16. 305 Ky. 225, 203 S.W.2d 18 (1947).

17. *Id.*, 203 S.W.2d at 21.

18. 307 Ky. 413, 211 S.W.2d 122 (1948).

19. *Id.*, 211 S.W.2d at 125.

20. 50 S.W. at 51.

21. 203 S.W.2d at 21.

22. 211 S.W.2d at 125.

seem to be driving at the same standard, and reflect concerns about both arbitrariness under Section 2 of the Kentucky Constitution and equality under Section 3.

Advent of Tiers of Scrutiny in Kentucky

The U.S. Supreme Court first opened the door to viewing some classifications with heightened scrutiny in 1938, in *United States v. Carolene Products Co.*[23] The *Carolene Products* case applied what we now know as "rational basis" scrutiny—by assuming a statute "rests upon some rational basis within the knowledge and experience of the legislators"[24]—but its now-famous Footnote Four stated that statutes "may" be "subjected to more exacting judicial scrutiny" when the legislation: (1) "appears on its face to be within a specific prohibition of the Constitution, such as those of the first ten Amendments, which are deemed equally specific when held to be embraced within the Fourteenth"; (2) "restricts those political processes which can ordinarily be expected to bring about repeal of undesirable legislation"; or (3) discriminates against "discrete and insular minorities," whether by religion, nationality, or race.[25]

The Court first applied any form of heightened scrutiny in *Skinner v. Oklahoma ex rel. Williamson.*[26] In *Skinner*, the Court invalidated under the Equal Protection Clause an Oklahoma statute that required the sterilization of "habitual criminals." But the law required the sterilization of only certain felons and not others; white-collar criminals generally were excluded from its requirements. The Court described the statute as "legislation which involves one of the basic civil rights of man" because marriage and procreation "are fundamental to the very existence and survival of the race."[27] The Court stated its view that "*strict scrutiny* of the classification" made by the law was "essential, lest unwittingly or otherwise invidious discriminations are made against groups or types of individuals in violation of the constitutional guaranty of just and equal laws."[28] A short time later, the Court referred to its analysis of race-based classifications as "the most rigid scrutiny."[29]

The constitutional test for applying strict scrutiny to statutes took shape over time. In *Kramer*, the Court held the Equal Protection Clause required a classification affecting the fundamental right to vote must be "necessary to promote a *compelling state interest*."[30] Then in *Bakke*, the Court held, "When [classifications] touch upon an individual's race or ethnic background, he is entitled to a judicial determination that the burden he is asked to bear on that basis is *precisely tailored* to serve a *compelling*

23. 304 U.S. 144, 152 n.4 (1938).
24. *Id.* at 152.
25. *Id.* at 152 n.4.
26. 316 U.S. 535 (1942).
27. *Id.* at 541.
28. *Id.* (emphasis added).
29. *Korematsu v. United States*, 323 U.S. 214, 216 (1944).
30. *Kramer v. Union Free Sch. Dist. No. 15*, 395 U.S. 621, 627 (1969) (emphasis added).

governmental interest."[31] The Court solidified this line of cases in *Adarand Constructors*, when it held that "all racial classifications, imposed by whatever federal, state, or local governmental actor, must be analyzed by a reviewing court under strict scrutiny. In other words, such classifications are constitutional only if they are *narrowly tailored* measures that further *compelling governmental interests*."[32]

What is now known as intermediate scrutiny is of a more recent vintage. In *Reed v. Reed*,[33] the Supreme Court unanimously held an Idaho law that preferred men over women in probate court appointments of estate administrators to violate the Equal Protection Clause. The Court held, "To give a mandatory preference to members of either sex over members of the other, merely to accomplish the elimination of hearings on the merits, is to make the very kind of arbitrary legislative choice forbidden by the Equal Protection Clause of the Fourteenth Amendment; and whatever may be said as to the positive values of avoiding intrafamily controversy, the choice in this context may not lawfully be mandated solely on the basis of sex."[34] The Court in *Reed* did not explicitly hold that sex-based classifications, like those based on race, alienage, and national origin, are inherently suspect and therefore subject to heightened scrutiny. That came later.

In *Frontiero v. Richardson*,[35] a case concerning federal spousal benefits for members of the Armed Forces and thus not arising under the Fourteenth Amendment, four justices nevertheless concluded that "classifications based upon sex, like classifications based upon race, alienage, or national origin, are inherently suspect, and must therefore be subjected to strict judicial scrutiny."[36] Justice Stewart did not join the plurality opinion, but he agreed that "the statutes before us work an invidious discrimination in violation of the Constitution."[37]

In 1976, the Supreme Court decided *Craig v. Boren*.[38] That case concerned an Oklahoma law prohibiting the sale of 3.2% beer to males 18 to 20 years old but allowing its sale to females of the same age. Not satisfied that "sex represents a legitimate, accurate proxy for the regulation of drinking and driving," the Court held that, "under *Reed*, Oklahoma's 3.2% beer statute invidiously discriminates against males 18–20 years of age."[39] Most importantly for this discussion, the Court held that sex-based classifications were subject to a standard of review higher than the rational basis, though not quite strict scrutiny: "classifications by gender must serve *important governmental objectives* and must be *substantially related* to achievement of those objectives."[40] The Court has,

31. *Regents of Univ. of Cal. v. Bakke*, 438 U.S. 265, 299 (1978) (emphasis added).
32. *Adarand Constructors*, 515 U.S. at 227 (emphasis added).
33. 404 U.S. 71 (1971).
34. *Id.* at 76–77.
35. 411 U.S. 677 (1973).
36. *Id.* at 688.
37. *Id.* at 691 (Stewart, J., concurring in the judgment) (citing *Reed*, 404 U.S. 71).
38. 429 U.S. 190 (1976).
39. *Id.* at 204.
40. *Id.* at 197 (emphasis added).

at times, referred to this standard of review as requiring legislative classifications based on sex to be supported by an "exceedingly persuasive justification."[41]

By the early 1970s, the Kentucky courts began borrowing from the federal heightened scrutiny standard in equal protection cases. In *Commonwealth, Alcoholic Beverage Control Board v. Burke*,[42] the Court of Appeals considered Kentucky statutes that prohibited women from serving as bartenders or consuming whiskey at a bar. The unanimous Court first found "that this discrimination is invidious and arbitrary and that the statutes are unconstitutional in their application to women under the Equal Protection Clause of the Fourteenth Amendment of the United States Constitution."[43] The Court saw the U.S. Supreme Court's recent case of *Reed v. Reed* as supporting its conclusion.[44] The Court then held this same discrimination on the basis of sex also violated the Kentucky Constitution: "Such discrimination is not only solely based on sex but is compounded by a nonrational discrimination within the classification (females); the state does not attempt to demonstrate any compelling interest to be served by such compounded discrimination. Therefore, in these aspects the statutes are arbitrary and violate Section 2 of the Constitution of Kentucky."[45] By invoking the "compelling interest" standard, the Court of Appeals imported heightened scrutiny into equal protection analysis under the Kentucky Constitution.

Shortly thereafter, in *Johnson v. Dixon*,[46] the Court considered a county school board's hiring preference for teachers born in that county. Citing federal cases, the Court observed that "[c]lassifications based on alienage, nationality, or duration of residence have been held to be inherently suspect and therefore unconstitutional unless the public body making the classification can demonstrate that the classification is necessary to promote a compelling governmental interest."[47] The Court rejected the school board's proffered justification for the preference: that "natives have demonstrated a greater continuity in employment than nonnatives."[48] It held that the school board's justification "does not show a compelling governmental interest," and the discrimination on the basis of county of birth was therefore "unconstitutionally discriminatory and preferential, in violation of Sections 1, 2 and 3 of the Kentucky Constitution."[49] Federal "strict scrutiny" was now embedded in Kentucky equal protection analysis.

But even as Kentucky adopted federal heightened scrutiny of certain classifications, rational basis scrutiny still was the default measure of equal protection violations: "A classification by the legislature should be affirmed unless it is positively shown that

41. *E.g., United States v. Virginia*, 518 U.S. 515, 531 (1996).

42. 481 S.W.2d 52 (Ky. 1972).

43. *Id.* at 54.

44. *Id.*

45. *Id.*

46. 501 S.W.2d 256 (Ky. 1973).

47. *Id.* at 257 (citing *Dunn v. Blumstein*, 405 U.S. 330 (1972); *Graham v. Richardson*, 403 U.S. 365 (1971)).

48. *Id.* at 258.

49. *Id.*

the classification is so arbitrary and capricious as to be hostile, oppressive and utterly devoid of rational basis."[50]

More recent Kentucky cases have exclusively relied on federal precedent as providing the source for the three tiers of scrutiny used in equal protection cases under the state constitution. In *Steven Lee Enterprises v. Varney*,[51] the Supreme Court cited exclusively federal cases for the proposition that strict scrutiny applied to equal protection claims implicating fundamental rights or suspect classifications, such as race, alienage, or ancestry,[52] while rational basis scrutiny applies to a statute that "merely affects social or economic policy."[53] The Court also cited exclusively federal cases for the proposition that "a higher level of scrutiny than mere 'rational basis' analysis" applied to classifications based on illegitimacy and gender.[54]

Similarly, in *D.F. v. Codell*,[55] the Supreme Court acknowledged there are "three levels of review" for equal protection claims under Sections 1, 2, and 3 of the Kentucky Constitution.[56] The *Codell* Court reiterated the federal equal protection standards set forth in *Varney*, stating strict scrutiny applies "whenever a statute makes a classification on the basis of a 'suspect class,' such as race, or when a statute significantly interferes with the exercise of a fundamental right."[57] Under this highest level of review, "the challenged statute can survive only if it is suitably tailored to serve a 'compelling state interest.'"[58] On the other end of the spectrum, the lowest standard of review, rational basis scrutiny, applies "if the statute merely affects social or economic policy,"[59] and requires a legislative distinction between persons only to bear "a rational relationship to a legitimate state end."[60] The Supreme Court then described intermediate scrutiny as providing greater constitutional protection for "groups, like women, who are not 'suspect classes' but who 'have been historically victimized by intense and irrational discrimination.'"[61] Like *Varney*, the *Codell* opinion defined this "heightened scrutiny" as permitting "discriminatory laws [to] survive equal protection analysis only to the extent they are *substantially related* to a legitimate state interest."[62]

---

50. *Delta Air Lines, Inc. v. Commonwealth, Revenue Cabinet*, 689 S.W.2d 14, 19 (Ky. 1985).

51. 36 S.W.3d 391 (Ky. 2000).

52. *Id.* at 394 (citing *Mass. Bd. of Ret. v. Murgia*, 427 U.S. 307, 312 (1976)).

53. *Id.* (citing *City of Cleburne*, 473 U.S. at 440).

54. *Id.* (citing *Lalli v. Lalli*, 439 U.S. 259 (1978); *Weber v. Aetna Cas. & Sur. Co.*, 406 U.S. 164 (1972)).

55. 127 S.W.3d 571 (Ky. 2003).

56. *Id.* at 575 (citing *Varney*, 36 S.W.3d at 394–95).

57. *Id.* (citing *Grutter v. Bollinger*, 539 U.S. 306, 326 (2003); *Zablocki v. Redhail*, 434 U.S. 374, 387 (1978)) (cleaned up).

58. *Id.* (citing *Varney*, 36 S.W.3d at 394).

59. *Id.*

60. *Id.* (citing *Chapman v. Gorman*, 839 S.W.2d 232, 239 (Ky. 1992)).

61. *Id.* (citing *Montgomery v. Carr*, 101 F.3d 1117, 1121 (6th Cir. 1996); *Craig*, 429 U.S. 190).

62. *Id.* (citing *Varney*, 36 S.W.3d at 394 (emphasis in original)).

More recently, in *Vision Mining, Inc. v. Gardner*,[63] the Supreme Court cited to *Varney* and *Codell*, which import federal equal protection standards into Kentucky law, to summarize the three tiers of scrutiny:

> Currently, there are three levels of review applicable to an equal protection challenge. Strict or intermediate scrutiny applies whenever a statute makes a classification on the basis of a "suspect" or "quasi-suspect" class, respectively. Conversely, "if the statute merely affects social or economic policy, it is subject" to a less searching form of judicial scrutiny, *i.e.* the "rational basis" test.[64]

Citing exclusively federal cases, the Court defined "suspect class" to include "[r]ace, ethnicity, alienage, and national origin,"[65] and it defined "quasi-suspect class" to include "[g]ender and illegitimacy."[66]

Kentucky cases after 2011 tend to cite to *Varney*, *Codell*, or *Vision Mining* as setting forth the applicable standards for evaluating equal protection claims arising under Sections 1, 2, and 3 of the Kentucky Constitution. But, as will be discussed below, that is not always the case; at times, Kentucky courts will deviate from these familiar federal standards.

Does a Heightened Rational Basis Test Exist in Kentucky?

Justice Charles M. Leibson, who served on the Supreme Court of Kentucky from 1983 to 1995, was a part of the "New Judicial Federalism movement," which emphasized using an independent analysis of state constitutions to provide greater protections for individual liberty than are available under comparable provisions in the U.S. Constitution.[67] While on the Court, Justice Leibson pioneered a different method of analyzing equal protection claims under the Kentucky Constitution, which is less deferential to legislative enactments than federal rational basis scrutiny.

Tabler v. Wallace[68] concerned a statute of repose that barred construction defect claims after five years had elapsed from the date of substantial completion of an im-

---

63. 364 S.W.3d 455 (Ky. 2011).

64. *Id.* at 465–66 (citing *Varney*, 36 S.W.3d at 394–95; *Codell*, 127 S.W.3d at 575–576) (cleaned up).

65. *Id.* at 466 n.23 (citing *Bakke*, 438 U.S. at 291; *Graham*, 403 U.S. at 372; *Hirabayashi v. United States*, 320 U.S. 81, 100 (1943)).

66. *Id.* at 466 n.24 (citing *United States v. Virginia*, 518 U.S. at 531; *Clark v. Jeter*, 486 U.S. 456, 461 (1988)).

67. *See* Jennifer DiGiovanni, *Justice Charles M. Leibson and the Revival of State Constitutional Law: A Microcosm of a Movement*, 86 Ky. L.J. 1009, 1009–19 (1998). The "New Judicial Federalism movement" is usually seen as a reaction by state court judges to the U.S. Supreme Court's jurisprudence under Chief Justices Burger and Rehnquist, which tended to be more conservative than that of the Warren Court. *See, e.g.*, William J. Brennan, Jr., *State Constitutions and the Protection of Individual Rights*, 90 Harv. L. Rev. 489 (1977).

68. 704 S.W.2d 179 (Ky. 1986).

provement to real property.[69] The statute at issue benefitted only architects, engineers, and builders, and so it was challenged on equal protection grounds.[70]

Justice Leibson, writing for the majority in *Tabler*, melded Section 59 of the Kentucky Constitution, which prohibits special legislation, with Sections 1, 2, and 3: "Section 59 is more than simply another way of restating the generalized language of the equal protection clause of the Fourteenth Amendment to the United States Constitution. Indeed, Sections 1, 2 and 3 of the Kentucky Constitution[,] which provide that the General Assembly is denied arbitrary power and shall treat all persons equally, suffice to embrace the equal protection clause of the Fourteenth Amendment."[71] Putting the four constitutional provisions together, Justice Leibson stated, "[t]he fundamental question is whether the General Assembly had a *reasonable basis* for this legislation."[72] He eschewed the traditional test for deciding equal protection cases, finding that the question was no longer "whether the statute is arbitrary and discriminatory."[73] Rather, combining "equal protection and special legislation," the question was "whether the General Assembly had a *rational justification* for creating a special class and conferring special privileges and immunity on that class at the time the statute in question was enacted."[74]

And this was no deferential federal rational basis review, in which "any reason however imaginative that *could* have existed requires [the Court] to uphold otherwise discriminatory legislation."[75] Instead, the burden was on the proponents of the statute to demonstrate "a *substantial and justifiable reason*" for the legislative classification.[76] The Court found the proponents of the statute at issue in *Tabler* had failed to meet their burden because they "offered only ... possible reasons that could have existed, not ... reasons that did in fact exist."[77] Contrary to federal rational basis review, in which any conceivable rational reason for the legislation—even if not the actual reason for the legislation—would be enough to save it, under the Kentucky Constitution as Justice Leibson articulated it, "[t]he creative abilities of lawyers suggesting possible reasons after the fact does not suffice."[78] Justice Leibson wrote, "Where to draw the line as to what constitutes a 'reasonable basis' for otherwise discriminatory legislation is a difficult matter. We do not do so here beyond stating that imaginative reasons that *could* exist, without anything of a positive nature to suggest that they *did* exist, do not suffice."[79] The Court found the statute at issue unconstitutional.

---

69. *Id.* at 180.
70. *Id.* at 181–83.
71. *Id.* at 183.
72. *Id.* at 185 (emphasis added).
73. *Id.* at 187.
74. *Id.* (emphasis added).
75. *Id.* at 186 (emphasis in original).
76. *Id.* (emphasis added).
77. *Id.* at 185.
78. *Id.*
79. *Id.* at 187 (emphasis in original); *see also Gillis v. Yount*, 748 S.W.2d 357, 362 (Ky. 1988) (quoting *Tabler*, 704 S.W.2d at 187).

The burden placed on the legislation's proponent to prove a "substantial and justifiable reason" for it indicates a degree of scrutiny higher than rational basis, at least under the federal precedents. Though not expressly stating that Kentucky courts would hold legislation to a higher standard than the federal courts do in the face of an equal protection standard, it is hard to escape the conclusion that that is exactly what *Tabler* did.

Justice Leibson would again deploy this heightened form of rational basis scrutiny in *Wasson v. Commonwealth*.[80] At issue in that case was a state statute that criminalized "deviant sexual intercourse" between consenting adults of the same sex. The Court held the statute to be unconstitutional. The *Wasson* case is best known for its discussion of the right to privacy, which it held is more robustly protected under Sections 1 and 2 of the Kentucky Constitution than it is under the U.S. Constitution.[81] But Justice Leibson, writing for the Court, also evaluated the statute under an equal protection analysis.[82]

In introducing the equal protection analysis of the statute, Justice Leibson framed the issue "not [as] whether sexual activity traditionally viewed as immoral can be punished by society, but whether it can be punished solely on the basis of sexual preference."[83] The opinion then treated sexual orientation as a "suspect class," a status it does not have under federal law, finding homosexuals "are a separate and identifiable class for Kentucky constitutional law analysis because no class of persons can be discriminated against under the Kentucky Constitution. All are entitled to equal treatment, unless there is *a substantial governmental interest*, a rational basis, for different treatment."[84] The Court held the statute violated the equal protection guarantees of Sections 2 and 3 of the Kentucky Constitution: "We have concluded that it is 'arbitrary' for the majority to criminalize sexual activity solely on the basis of majoritarian sexual preference, and that it denied 'equal' treatment under the law when there is no rational basis, *as this term is used and applied in our Kentucky cases*."[85]

In holding in *Wasson* that the statute at issue denied homosexuals the equal protection of the laws, Justice Leibson relied on his earlier opinion for the Court in *Tabler*, stating that "[t]he fundamental question is whether the General Assembly has a reasonable basis for this legislation sufficient to justify creating a separate classification for certain persons."[86] Later, the *Wasson* opinion cites again to *Tabler* for the proposition that "possible reasons that could have existed" will not serve as "a reasonable basis for [the] legislation"; rather, there must be rational "reasons that did in fact exist" to justify the statute.[87] In conclusion, Leibson wrote for the Court that it "can attribute no legislative purpose to this statute except to single out homosexuals for different treatment

80. 842 S.W.2d 487 (Ky. 1992).
81. *See id.* at 492–99
82. *See id.* at 499–502.
83. *Id.* at 499.
84. *Id.* at 500 (emphasis added).
85. *Id.* (emphasis added).
86. *Id.* (quoting *Tabler*, 704 S.W.2d at 185).
87. *Id.* at 501 (quoting *Tabler*, 704 S.W.2d at 185).

for indulging their sexual preference by engaging in the same activity heterosexuals are now at liberty to perform.... Sexual preference, and not the act committed, determines criminality, and is being punished. Simply because the majority, speaking through the General Assembly, finds one type of extramarital intercourse more offensive than another, does not provide a rational basis for criminalizing the sexual preference of homosexuals."[88]

It is important to note that Justice Leibson went to the trouble in *Wasson* of analyzing whether homosexuals are to be considered a suspect class under Kentucky law, but then applied the same equal protection test he applied in *Tabler*. Under this form of heightened rational basis scrutiny, therefore, all legislation—whether involving a suspect class or not—receives the same treatment.[89] And all legislative classifications must be justified by a "substantial and justifiable reason," with the burden of proof on the party supporting the statute, not on the party challenging its constitutionality as in the case of federal rational basis scrutiny.

One commentator has surmised that, "if the speculation that Kentucky's *Tabler* equal protection test applies to all classifications is correct, the people of Kentucky would enjoy a test that not only offers a higher degree of protection to claimants across the board than the federal standards, but also would be easier to apply. There would be no need to inquire whether or not a given claimant was a member of a protected or suspect class, because all claimants would be entitled to a review using the equivalent of the most stringent federal tier of review, strict scrutiny."[90] This commentator's conclusion may be a bit hyperbolic, at least insofar as the *Tabler* test is less an adoption of across-the-board strict scrutiny, and more a return to the traditional "reasonable or substantial ground" standard for classifications under *Elrod*.[91] But by both placing the burden of proof on the legislation's proponent, rather than its opponent, and requiring proof of the "real" reason for the legislation, and not merely a *post-hoc*, hypothetical justification, the *Tabler* test certainly raises the bar for any legislative classification to be valid.

The *Tabler* equal protection test has been observed but rarely utilized by the Kentucky courts since Justice Leibson left the bench in 1995.

In 2005, the Supreme Court of Kentucky decided *Elk Horn Coal Corp. v. Cheyenne Resources, Inc.*,[92] a case involving the constitutionality of Kentucky's damages-for-delay statute,[93] which imposed a 10% penalty on any unsuccessful second or successive appeal from a monetary judgment. In finding the statute violated equal protection of the law under Sections 1, 2, and 3 of the Kentucky Constitution, the Court first summarized

---

88. *Id.* at 501–02.

89. *See* DiGiovanni, *supra* note 67, 86 Ky. L.J. at 1045 ("The end result seems to be that the *Tabler* equal protection test applies to all classifications.").

90. *Id.* at 1045–46.

91. 203 S.W.2d at 21.

92. 163 S.W.3d 408 (Ky. 2005).

93. KRS 26A.300.

the difference between the Kentucky equal protection standard and the rational basis standard applied by federal courts under the Fourteenth Amendment:

> Because of this additional protection [provided by Sections 1, 2, and 3 of the Constitution, in conjunction with Section 59], we have elected at times to apply a guarantee of individual rights in equal protection cases that is higher than the minimum guaranteed by the Federal Constitution. Instead of requiring a "rational basis," we have construed our Constitution as requiring a "reasonable basis" or a "substantial and justifiable reason" for discriminatory legislation in areas of social and economic policy. *Cases applying the heightened standard are limited to the particular facts of those cases.* We need not decide, however, whether the facts of this case require us to invoke Kentucky's heightened standard because we hold that KRS 26A.300 fails the rational basis test, which is sufficient to show a violation of the equal protection provisions of both Constitutions.[94]

Thus, the *Elk Horn Coal* Court acknowledged the heightened rational basis standard for Kentucky equal protection cases but opted not to use it. However, the Court's statement that cases using heightened scrutiny under *Tabler* are "limited to the particular facts of those cases" adds some confusion to the analysis, making it unclear when the heightened standard applies to a particular case.

In 2009, the Supreme Court cited *Elk Horn Coal* for the proposition that "Sections 1, 2, and 3 of the Kentucky Constitution provide that the legislature does not have arbitrary power and shall treat all persons equally. A statute complies with Kentucky equal protection requirements if a 'reasonable basis' or 'substantial and justifiable reason' supports the classifications that it creates."[95] But, rather than applying *Tabler* burden-shifting and requiring the proponent of the statute at issue to justify the classification it made, the Court stated, "Analysis begins with the presumption that legislative acts are constitutional."[96] Thus, the Court required the party challenging the constitutionality of the statute to bear the burden of proof.

Most recently, a sea change occurred in *Calloway County Sheriff's Department v. Woodall*,[97] a case involving a legislative classification in a worker's compensation stat-

---

94. *Elk Horn Coal*, 163 S.W.3d at 419–19 (footnotes omitted; emphasis added) (citing *Tabler*, 704 S.W.2d at 185–87).

95. *Cain v. Lodestar Energy, Inc.*, 302 S.W.3d 39, 43 (Ky. 2009) (citing *Elk Horn Coal*, 163 S.W.3d 408). Similarly, in dissent in *Lexington-Fayette Urban County Government v. Johnson*, Justice Abramson stated, "Citing *Elk Horn Coal Corp. v. Cheyenne Res., Inc.*, 163 S.W.3d 408, 419 (Ky. 2005), Appellees note that instead of applying the federal constitutional 'rational basis' standard for legislative classifications, this Court has 'construed our Constitution as requiring a "reasonable basis" or a "substantial and justifiable reason" for discriminatory legislation in areas of social and economic policy.' Indeed, *this is the controlling standard under Kentucky law*..." 280 S.W.3d 31, 37 (Ky. 2009) (Abramson, J., dissenting) (emphasis added). The majority in *Johnson* did not reach the constitutional issue, finding its interpretation of the local ordinances at issue mooted it. *Id.* at 32.

96. *Cain*, 302 S.W.3d at 43 (citations omitted).

97. 607 S.W.3d 557 (Ky. 2020).

ute. In *Woodall*, the Court decoupled Section 59 of the Kentucky Constitution from the equal protection analysis under Sections 1, 2, and 3. The Court "return[ed] to the original test for Section 59: local or special legislation, according to the well-known meaning of the words, applies exclusively to particular places or particular persons."[98] Further, the Court held that "state constitutional challenges to legislation based on classification succeed or fail on the basis of equal protection analysis under Sections 1, 2, and 3 of the Kentucky Constitution. As for analysis under Sections 59 and 60, the appropriate test is whether the statute applies to a particular individual, object or locale."[99]

The effect of *Woodall* was to overrule a raft of cases[100] holding that the test for assessing legislation *under Section 59* is whether the law applies equally to all in a class, and whether there are "distinctive and natural reasons inducing and supporting the classification."[101] But the Court did not overrule the equal protection analysis in any of those cases, even going so far as to state in a footnote that "we do not necessarily 'overrule' the results of any prior decision, except to the extent that those decisions have erroneously applied an inappropriate analysis. For example, in *Elk Horn Coal*, while the Court discussed *Tabler* ... and other cases, the Court ultimately applied equal protection provisions under §§1, 2 and 3 holding that no rational basis existed for KRS 26A.300's 10% penalty against unsuccessful appellants."[102] Further, in its separate equal protection analysis, the Court seemed to endorse the heightened *Tabler* standard, stating that, "to comply with federal equal protection requirements, the classification must be rationally related to a legitimate state interest, and to comply with Kentucky's equal protection requirements, the classification must be supported by a 'reasonable basis' or a 'substantial and justifiable reason.'"[103]

The *Woodall* Court noted *Elk Horn Coal*'s observation that the heightened Kentucky equal protection standard has only been applied "at times," and that the cases applying that standard "are limited to the[ir] particular facts."[104] It opined that "[n]o one knows or can possibly know when a given statute will strike any judge, or four justices of this court, as worthy of the heightened standard," and that "[t]his unfettered discretion is unworthy of any legal system."[105] Despite the Court's dissatisfaction with the current state of the law, in which no one can know for certain whether federal rational basis review or a heightened standard of review peculiar to Kentucky will apply, it did not overrule *Tabler*'s equal protection analysis.

---

98. *Id.* at 572.
99. *Id.* at 573.
100. These cases include but are not limited to *Elk Horn Coal*, *Wasson*, and *Tabler*.
101. *Woodall*, 607 S.W.3d at 566 (quoting *Ecklar*, 50 S.W. at 51).
102. *Id.* at 573 n.17 (citing *Elk Horn Coal*, 163 S.W.3d at 421).
103. *Id.* at 564 (citations omitted).
104. *Id.* at 568–69 (citing *Elk Horn Coal*, 163 S.W.3d at 418–19).
105. *Id.*

Conclusion

At present, Kentucky equal protection law operates on two tracks simultaneously. On the one hand, most of the time Kentucky courts apply the same three tiers of scrutiny that are used by the federal courts. Importing this federal case law into the Kentucky Constitution has the benefit of making the analysis more comfortable for practitioners by conforming Sections 1, 2, and 3 to the more familiar contours of the Equal Protection Clause of the Fourteenth Amendment. But this method ignores, or at least glosses over, the textual differences between Sections 1, 2, and 3 and the Fourteenth Amendment.

On the other hand, the Supreme Court of Kentucky continues to acknowledge the existence of a different equal protection standard, and therefore a slightly different analysis to be used, when evaluating legislative classifications under Kentucky law. Kentucky equal protection cases thus far have failed to explain fully: (1) how the "reasonable basis" or a "substantial and justifiable reason" standard under *Tabler* differs, if at all, from the federal rational basis standard; (2) whether "possible reasons that could have existed" for a legislative classification are sufficient to serve as a "reasonable basis" for a classification, or whether courts instead should only look at the "reasons that did in fact exist" to justify a challenged statute; and (3) whether the party challenging the constitutionality of a statute has the burden of proving to the court that the law is unconstitutional (as under federal rational basis review), or if the party seeking to apply the statute must shoulder the burden of proving the law is constitutional (as under federal strict or intermediate scrutiny). After *Woodall*, the Court has seemingly acknowledged these issues, but has left them to be decided another day.

Three

The Separation of Powers

A. Building Blocks: A Structural Reading of the Kentucky Constitution

After considering what a state constitution is and who has the right to make and amend it, and after seeing how the Kentucky Constitution requires the government to relate to its citizens, it will be helpful also to think about how the Constitution itself is structured.

When "We, the people" adopt a constitution, we implicitly acknowledge that "the people" are the irreducible minimum unit of governmental authority. According to the Preamble to the Kentucky Constitution, "We the people ... ordain and establish this Constitution." Section 4 then declares that "[a]ll power is inherent in the people, and all free governments are founded on their authority." Thus, "the people" are sovereign.

These individual sovereigns then, to protect their "peace, safety, happiness and ... property"[1] and to continue their "civil, political and religious liberties,"[2] form a government. But note that the Constitution does not set up a government by any mode, but by a social compact.[3] This social compact starts from the premise that "[a]ll men ... are equal."[4] It is therefore a mutual protection pact among equals.

At the same time the Kentucky Constitution erects a government to protect the rights, and secure the liberties, of the people, it also carves out a vast space that is excepted from any powers delegated to the government. The Bill of Rights, Sections 1 to 26 of the Constitution, sets forth "great and essential principles of liberty and free government,"[5] which are "excepted out of the general powers of government, and shall forever remain inviolate."[6] Thus, the rights enumerated in the Bill of Rights are not to be subject to governmental regulation at all, because not only have the people not delegated power to the government to regulate in these areas, but also no lawful, constitutional government may do so.

1. Ky. Const. §4.
2. Ky. Const. pmbl.
3. Ky. Const. §3.
4. *Id.*
5. Ky. Const. Bill of Rights pmbl.
6. Ky. Const. §26.

In those remaining areas of life, which the Bill of Rights does not except out of the power of government altogether, the state government may govern. However, the government's powers are "divided into three distinct departments"—legislative, executive, and judicial.[7] Any powers "which are legislative" are assigned to one department, any powers "which are executive" are assigned to a second, and any powers "which are judicial" are assigned to the third. The Kentucky Constitution then prohibits one of these departments from "exercis[ing] any power properly belonging to either of the others," except as the Constitution expressly provides.[8] Unlike at the federal level, where the separation of powers is implied from the structure of the Constitution of the United States, the separation of powers is an expressly stated feature of the Kentucky Constitution and is a key to understanding its meaning. Section 28 is textually like the separation of powers provision found in the constitution of another Commonwealth, Massachusetts, which declares that government powers are separated among the three departments "to the end it may be a government of laws and not of men."[9]

The first 28 Sections of the Kentucky Constitution represent the irreducible minimum of constitutional government. They define the areas of life that must remain off limits to the government altogether, divide the remaining governmental power among the three branches, and bar any of the three branches from invading the province of either of the others. What follows Section 28 provides additional rules for the operation of the government, further fleshing out what form the Commonwealth's constitutional government is to take.

The Kentucky Constitution provides, "The legislative power shall be vested in ... the 'General Assembly of the Commonwealth of Kentucky.'"[10] By vesting "[t]he legislative power," the Constitution vests *all* the legislative power to the General Assembly; in other words, if a matter is properly the subject of any public legislation *at all*, it is within the jurisdiction of the General Assembly. Compare Section 29 with the Legislative Vesting Clause of the U.S. Constitution, which grants to Congress only the "legislative powers *herein granted*" in the Constitution.[11] These textual differences reflect the way in which James Madison distinguished the respective scope of federal and state power in The Federalist No. 45: "The powers delegated by the proposed Constitution to the federal government, are few and defined. Those which are to remain in the State governments are numerous and indefinite."

Similarly, Section 69 states, "The supreme executive power of the Commonwealth shall be vested in ... the 'Governor of the Commonwealth of Kentucky.'" This provision is quite like the Executive Vesting Clause in Article I, Section 1 of the U.S. Constitution, which states, "The executive power shall be vested in a President of the United States of America." The chief difference between the federal and Kentucky constitutions con-

7. Ky. Const. §27.
8. Ky. Const. §28.
9. *See* Mass. Const. pt. I, art. XXX.
10. Ky. Const. §29.
11. U.S. Const. art. I, §1 (emphasis added).

cerning the executive power is the additional provision in Section 91 of the Kentucky Constitution for the creation of additional executive offices, thus ensuring the diffusion of at least some portion of the executive power rather than concentrating all executive power in one person.

Section 109 declares, "The judicial power of the Commonwealth shall be vested exclusively in one Court of Justice which shall be divided into a Supreme Court, a Court of Appeals, a trial court of general jurisdiction known as the Circuit Court and a trial court of limited jurisdiction known as the District Court." Under this Section, the Kentucky court system is "a unified judicial system for operation and administration." The U.S. Constitution is less exact in its description of the federal court system, leaving it to Congress to flesh out the details: "The judicial power of the United States, shall be vested in one Supreme Court, and in such inferior courts as the Congress may from time to time ordain and establish."[12]

Structurally, after dividing the government's powers between the legislative, executive, and judicial departments, a good many of the remaining provisions of the Kentucky Constitution are crafted to slightly alter the "default rule," creating exceptions or modifications to the strict separation of powers. Several sections require one department or another to act in a certain way, removing any discretion it otherwise may have in the area. Examples of this kind provision include Section 61, which requires the General Assembly to enact laws to provide for local option elections so localities may vote to be either "wet" or "dry," and Section 183, which requires it to enact laws creating a system of common schools. The legislature has no choice in either matter, and may no more declare the entire state "wet" than it may privatize all the schools.

Another type of modification to the default separation of powers rule includes those Sections that restrain or curb a department's use of its powers. For example, Sections 46 and 51 govern the General Assembly's process for enacting a bill into law. Unlike an Act of Congress, which may be passed the same day the bill is introduced or relate to many subjects, these Sections generally require an Act of the General Assembly to be referred to and reported from committees in both the House of Representatives and the Senate, read on three separate days in each chamber, and limited to one subject per bill. Sections 59 and 60 also curb the lawmaking process, by ensuring the Acts of the state legislature pertain to the entire Commonwealth, and not be of purely "local" or "special" concern.

Finally, the Constitution also provides for certain situations in which one department of the government will perform a function that otherwise would be assigned by Section 27 to another department. For example, Sections 66 and 67 confer upon the House of Representatives and the Senate, respectively, the powers to impeach and to try impeachments, which would otherwise be "judicial" powers. Section 88 allows the Governor to veto entire bills, or line items in appropriations bills; these functions otherwise would be part and parcel of the "legislative" power to enact laws and determine

12. U.S. Const. art. III, §1.

their content. And Section 110(5)(b) requires the Chief Justice of the Supreme Court to submit the budget of the Court of Justice to the General Assembly, an otherwise "executive" task.

The Constitution's structure is designed with one goal in mind—protecting the rights and liberties of the people. It does this by diffusing the power delegated by the people to the government among its three constituent departments, and then by providing specific instructions to each department or tweaking the scope of their respective powers.

Figure 3-1 depicts the structure of the Kentucky Constitution as described above.

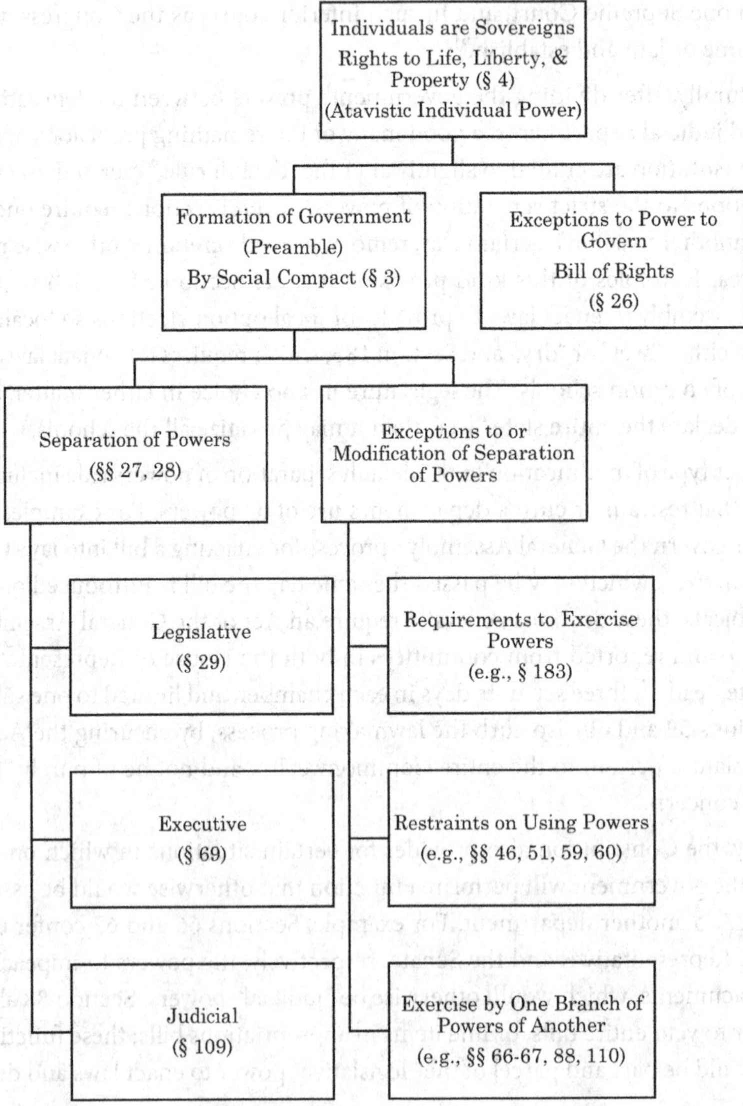

Figure 3-1. Flow Chart Showing Organization of the Kentucky Constitution.

B. Primary Rule of Construction: Delegated Powers Divided

> "The powers of the government of the Commonwealth of Kentucky shall be divided into three distinct departments, and each of them be confined to a separate body of magistracy, to wit: Those which are legislative, to one; those which are executive, to another; and those which are judicial, to another." (Ky. Const. §27.)

> "No person or collection of persons, being of one of those departments, shall exercise any power properly belonging to either of the others, except in the instances hereinafter expressly directed or permitted." (Ky. Const. §28.)

Sections 27 and 28 are the principal separation of powers provisions in the Kentucky Constitution, and they are central to understanding the structure of the Constitution and the government it creates. The positive-negative approach to the separation of powers embodied by these provisions reinforces the principle, which has led the Supreme Court of Kentucky to observe that the Commonwealth has the textually strongest constitutional separation of powers protections in the Nation.

As you read the following cases, keep in mind the several ways in which one branch of government can violate the separation of powers doctrine. The first type of separation of powers violation occurs when a member of one branch usurps the powers rightfully belonging to another branch, as when the Governor exceeds the scope of authority delegated to him or her by the General Assembly and writes laws out of whole cloth via executive order. This is an example of a "classic" separation of powers violation.

The second type of separation of powers violation presents the other side of the coin: one branch of government excessively delegating its power to another branch of government, such as when the General Assembly enacts a law providing that an executive branch agency may adopt any administrative regulation it wants, free of any guidance that cabins the agency's discretion. This is an example of a violation of the "nondelegation doctrine."

The following chapters will consider both types of separation of powers issues, and then look at some of the powers the Constitution assigns to each branch of government.

Commonwealth v. Associated Industries of Kentucky

Court of Appeals of Kentucky (1963)
370 S.W.2d 584

Opinion of the Court by Judge Moremen.

This is an agreed case testing the constitutionality of KRS 341.145 which relates to unemployment compensation. The trial court declared the Act unconstitutional as violative of Sections 180 and 28 of the Kentucky Constitution.

The Act in question (KRS 341.145) as amended in 1952, authorized the Commissioner of Economic Security to enter into reciprocal administrative arrangements with agencies of other states or the federal government for the purpose of broadening the coverage of unemployment compensation. This law was passed to permit the participation of Kentucky in an interstate unemployment plan originated by the federal government. Its basic purpose was to provide unemployment compensation benefits to those persons employed in more than one state. The plan authorizes adding together work periods in different states to determine a base period permitting an unemployed person to qualify for benefits which he otherwise might not do if his employment period was limited to employment in the state where the compensation claim is filed.

Under the plan the laws of the last state where a person was employed shall be applicable with respect to benefit years, base periods, qualifying wages, benefit rates and duration of benefits. The work and wage records of the employee in other states which are parties to the agreement shall be taken into account in the computation of benefits, and such other states are required to reimburse the state paying the claim for their fair share thereof.

KRS 341.145(3)(a) provides in part:

> 'Reimbursements to another state or the Federal Government, paid from the fund pursuant to this subsection, *shall be deemed to be benefits* for the purposes of this chapter ...' (Our emphasis.)

* * *

The more difficult question involves the delegation of power by the legislature to other states and the federal government to fix by their laws the various criteria for determining eligibility for, the amounts and the duration of compensation payments. While the judgment and appellee's brief refer to §28 of the Kentucky Constitution, perhaps §29 is more clearly involved.

The question seems to be whether or not the General Assembly may delegate to other states and the federal government the authority to fix by laws and regulations the conditions under which Kentucky taxes may be expended. The legislature has not adopted particular laws and regulations, and the plan obviously contemplates the future changes in such laws and regulations.

* * *

Through many of the opinions of this court and those of other states and the federal courts runs the theme that legislative power may not be delegated and, so far as we have been able to find, the opinions have devoted little time to determining the origin of this dogma or even the necessity for its existence.

We find nothing in our State Constitution that declares explicitly: 'Legislative power may not be delegated.' Here are the three sections of the Constitution usually quoted in support of that statement.

'§27. The powers of the government of the Commonwealth of Kentucky shall be divided into three distinct departments, and each of them be confined to a separate body of magistracy, to wit: Those which are legislative, to one; those which are executive, to another; and those which are judicial, to another.'

'§28. No person or collection of persons, being of one of those departments, shall exercise any power properly belonging to either of the others, except in the instances hereinafter expressly directed or permitted.'

'§29. The legislative power shall be vested in a House of Representatives and a Senate, which, together, shall be styled the 'General Assembly of the Commonwealth of Kentucky.''

We can read into §27 only an intent to divide the sovereign power, which at one time existed in one person under the divine right of a king, into three separate and distinct departments.

Section 28 seems merely to prohibit one department from grabbing power that properly belongs to another, and the simple wording of §29 sets up the mechanics for the exercise of legislative power in a bicameral assembly.

Section 29 uses the word 'vested' and though it is quite generally considered to be a word of art, still the word has no settled meaning which precludes the one in whom the title is vested from permitting others to use it or even divesting title entirely. When one is once vested with the title, say to real estate, he is not forever precluded from allowing others to use that real estate permissively or otherwise dispose of it.

Although we have found nothing in the Constitution that declares legislative power may not be delegated, we do find instances where the legislature is inferentially authorized to delegate its legislative power, such as §156 of the Constitution where it is said:

> '... The General Assembly, by a general law, shall provide how towns may be organized, *and enact laws for the government of such towns until the same are assigned to one or the other of the classes* above named; but such assignment shall be made at the first session of the General Assembly after the organization of said town or city.' (Our emphasis.)

The Supplement §166 of the Constitution reads in part:

> 'All acts of incorporation of cities and towns heretofore granted, and all amendments thereto, except as provided in section 167, shall continue in force under this Constitution, and all City and Police Courts established in any city or town shall remain, with their present powers and jurisdictions, until such time as the General Assembly *shall provide by general laws for the government of towns and cities, and the officers and courts thereof*; ...' (Our emphasis.)

It will be noted that neither section specifically affirms the right of the General Assembly to delegate a portion of its legislative power to the governmental body of a municipality. Inferentially it has the right to define the means of government and by statute set up law-making bodies for cities of the various classes and, thereby, delegate a portion of its power.

Even if we assign to the word 'vested,' as used in §29, its usual meaning descriptive of a right which is complete and one of which the person to whom it belongs cannot be divested without consent, we find no admonition—here the right is and here it will remain. If the word is one of absolute limitation (a vested right may never be divested, even with the permission of the owner) then what right has the General Assembly to divest itself of this vested legislative power?

So, we repeat, the genesis of the phrase 'legislative power may not be delegated' is not in the Constitution itself. That document indicates that it should be delegated in certain cases.

A research of many of the decided cases in this country discloses that this proposition is of rather obscure origin. Most often quoted, as authority, is Judge Cooley's statement that:

> 'One of the settled maxims in constitutional law is, that the power conferred upon the legislature to make laws cannot be delegated by that department to any other body or authority. Where the sovereign power of the State has located the authority, there it must remain; and by the constitutional agency alone the laws must be made until the constitution itself is changed.'

This passage was cited by this Court with approval as late as the year 1958. *See Dawson v. Hamilton*, Ky., 314 S.W.2d 532.

In turn, and as authority for his statement, Cooley relies upon this quotation from Locke on Civil Government:

> 'Fourthly. The legislative neither must nor can transfer the power of making laws to anybody else, or place it anywhere but where the people have.'

We suppose that all people who live in a democracy and enjoy its fruits must hold in high regard all pronouncements of John Locke, his contemporaries and those who followed him: Whose ideas in turn led to the American and the French Revolutions, and the practical application of his novel conception that 'all power is inherent in the people and all free government founded on authority.' But we must also remember that Locke's works on social and governmental policies were written at a time when the principles of democracy had begun their tremendous struggle with that of the divine right of kings. We must remember too that Locke himself believed that all matters pertaining to the divine or the secular should be examined carefully and that no 'innate principle' should be accepted or continued in practice merely because it was venerable.

'He believed that in attacking 'innate principles' he was pleading for universal reasonableness instead of blind reliance on authority and was thus, as he says, not 'pulling up the foundations of knowledge,' but 'laying those foundations surer.' When men heard that there were propositions that could not be doubted, it was a short and easy way to assume that what are only arbitrary prejudices are 'innate' certainties.' (Encyclopedia Britannica.)

But above all, Locke believed that all human ideas, even the most complex and abstract, ultimately depended upon 'experience' to dedicate their truth. It has been said of him that his 'Essay Concerning Human Understanding' (1690) 'represents the first major modern presentation of the empirical theory of knowledge. In developing an account of human knowledge in terms of how it is derived from experience, what its nature is, and how limited it is, Locke provided the basic pattern of future empirical philosophy.'

So, if Locke was the fountainhead of the thesis that power could not be delegated, we feel sure that the experience of the last several centuries would have caused him to repudiate this idea. Experience has demonstrated some of the power must be invested in other bodies so that the government may function in a world that progressively is becoming more complex. There is nothing wrong with this so long as the delegating authority retains the right to revoke the power. The wrong (and the hypocrisy) lies in affirming the truth of the catch phrase while at the same time denying its existence by a devolution of the power. The plain realities of recent cases show that rarely enactments involving this question are held defective.

In 1 Am.Jur.2nd 898, it is said:

> 'The rule precluding the delegation of power by the legislature does not embrace every power the legislature may properly exercise. Any power not legislative in character which the legislature may exercise it may delegate. What the rule precludes is the delegation of those powers which are strictly or inherently and exclusively legislative and the legislature's abdication of its own power and the conferring of such power upon an administrative agency to be exercised in its uncontrolled discretion.
>
> 'The Constitution does not demand the impossible or the impracticable and has never been regarded as denying to the legislature the necessary resources of flexibility and practicality to perform its function. In fact, the Supreme Court has held that a constitutional power implies a power of delegation of authority under it sufficient to effect its purposes. The delegation to administrative agencies of some legislative power is necessary particularly in modern regulatory enactments in which the legislature is incapable of defining the multitudinous details. Such delegation is not precluded by the basic concept of a 'government of laws, and not of men.' There is no doubt that the legislature may delegate to an administrative agency the exercise of a limited portion of its legislative power with respect to some specific subject matter.'

In *Field v. Clark*, 143 U.S. 649, 12 S.Ct. 495, 36 L.Ed. 294 (1892) it was said:

> 'That congress cannot delegate legislative power to the president is a principle universally recognized as vital to the integrity and maintenance of the system of government ordained by the constitution.'

As late as 1932 in *United States v. Shreveport Grain & Elevator Co.*, 287 U.S. 77, 85, 53 S.Ct. 42, 44, 77 L.Ed. 175 (1932) it was said:

'That the legislative power of Congress cannot be delegated is, of course, clear.'

Still Davis in his work 'Administrative Law Treatise' is able to make this statement:

> 'In only two cases (*Panama Refining Co. v. Ryan*, 293 U.S. 388, 55 S.Ct. 241, 79 L.Ed. 446 (1935); *A. L. A. Schechter Poultry Corp. vs. United States*, 295 U.S. 495, 55 S.Ct. 837, 79 L.Ed. 1570, 97 A.L.R. 947 (1935)) in all American history have congressional delegations to public authorities been held invalid. Neither delegation was to a regularly constituted administrative agency which followed an established procedure designed to afford the customary safeguards to affected parties. The *Panama* case was influenced by exceptional executive disorganization and in absence of such a special factor would not be followed today. The *Schechter* case involved excessive delegation of the kind that Congress is not likely again to make. The fact is that Congress avoided such delegation through the entire period of the Second World War.'

The pressures and the practicabilities of administration of modern government have led the courts to the continuous affirmation of the existence of this judge-made rule while at the same time denying its existence by the holding or decision in nearly all cases. This has sometimes been done by holding where 'standards' are set up—however vague or general they may be—that legislative power has not been delegated because only details of the policy were devolved. We will not, however, examine that pretense here.

We have decided we will meet this problem with full recognition that legislative power often has been delegated, with full court approval, and it is not necessary to disguise such action in form of expression or words which have no verity.

In the case under consideration the specific issue is presented by KRS 341.145(3) (a) which reads in part:

> 'Any provisions of this chapter to the contrary notwithstanding, the commissioner is hereby authorized to enter into reciprocal arrangements with duly authorized agencies of other states or of the Federal Government, or both, whereby workers with potential rights to benefits in this and another state or other states or the Federal Government may have such rights determined upon the basis of his combined potential rights in such jurisdictions. Benefits, based upon such combined potential rights, may be paid either under provisions of this chapter or under the provisions of the law of another state or the Federal Government, or under such combination of provisions of both laws as may be agreed upon as being fair and reasonable to all affected interests. No such an arrangement shall be entered into unless each agency entering into such arrangement shall agree to reimburse the fund of the other agency to the extent of the liability incurred under terms of the arrangement.'

By passing that act the General Assembly has expressed its opinion about the necessity and desirability of investing in another the power to carry out the terms of the policy embodied in the enactment. The ephemeral qualities of each session of the legislature are such the desirable and beneficial purpose of the act could not be fulfilled if complete detailed laws were required for each case presented. By delegation it will accomplish the goal desired which otherwise could not be attained. The fact that the laws of other states may change is additional reason why the commissioner should be granted flexible power.

We find the acceptance of the laws of other states or of the federal government to be a sufficient and effective safeguard to the exercise of power by the commissioner—so much more than if the commissioner were handed that power without limitation. Since the General Assembly has seen fit to accept the judgment of other legislative bodies as to scales of base period, qualifying wages, et cetera, now and in the future, and adopted them as their own in these special cases, we see no reason it should be denied this right.

It will be noted that under §28 of the Constitution, above quoted, no branch of the government shall exercise power properly belonging to another. This case demands judicial self-restraint and the accord of high respect to a policy determination which has been made by the General Assembly.

We believe the act to be constitutional in all aspects and the judgment is therefore reversed.

Montgomery, J., dissenting.

Notes and Questions

1. *Associated Industries* was the first Kentucky case to explicitly permit the General Assembly to delegate legislative authority to the Executive Branch. Previously, the rule had been that "the legislature may not in any degree abdicate its power. If it may not make the effectiveness of a specific act dependent upon the will of another, certainly it may not delegate to another the power to enact a law, whether in form or effect." *Bloemer v. Turner*, 281 Ky. 832, 137 S.W.2d 387, 390 (1939). Thus, "[t]he legislature cannot delegate its power to make a law; but it can make a law to delegate a power to determine some fact or state of things upon which the law makes, or intends to make, its own action depend." *Id.*, 137 S.W.2d at 391 (quotation omitted). Older cases such as *Bloemer* differentiated between legislative and administrative functions of government; it prohibited any delegation of the legislative function (*e.g.*, setting a speed limit on a public road at 45 m.p.h.), but allowed the General Assembly to delegate the administration of a statute to the Executive Branch (*e.g.*, the Department of Highways may determine whether a 55 m.p.h. speed limit on a public road is safe, and if it is not, the speed limit will be 45 m.p.h.). But after *Associated Industries*, the High Court shifted its focus away from the quality of the delegated authority—legislative vs. administrative—and now focuses instead on the quantity of delegated authority—*i.e.*, whether the legislature enacted sufficient standards to guide the agency. *See Ky. Comm'n on Human Rights v. Fraser*, 625 S.W.2d 852, 854 (Ky. 1981) ("The general test for delegation of powers to an administrative agency in Kentucky is that of safeguards, procedural and otherwise, which prevent an abuse of discretion by the agency" (citation omitted)).

2. For the Court, what justified the departure from the prior line of cases that precluded any delegation of legislative authority?
3. Is *Associated Industries* and its allowance for some delegations of authority consistent with the text of Sections 27 and 28 of the Kentucky Constitution?

Commonwealth ex rel. Beshear v. Bevin

Supreme Court of Kentucky (2019)
575 S.W.3d 673

OPINION OF THE COURT BY CHIEF JUSTICE MINTON.

When it enacted Kentucky Revised Statute ("KRS") 12.028, the General Assembly empowered the Governor "between sessions of the General Assembly, temporarily [to] effect a change in the state government organizational structure" of "any organizational unit or administrative body" in the Commonwealth.[1] And the Governor exercised that authority when he issued Executive Order ("EO") 2017-364, which made several changes to various state education boards. The Attorney General sued in circuit court to challenge the validity of the executive order, and that court upheld it. On discretionary review, we find no statutory or constitutional infirmity with the Governor's use of the executive order to affect a temporary government reorganization on the facts before us, so we affirm the circuit court's judgment.

I. Background.

Central to this dispute is KRS 12.028, Subsection 1 of which gives the Governor the ability to "propose to the General Assembly, for [the General Assembly's] approval, changes in the state government organizational structure which may include the creation, alteration or abolition of any organizational unit[2] or administrative body[3] and the transfer of functions, personnel, funds, equipment, facilities, and records from one (1) organizational unit or administrative body to another." And Subsection 2 states in relevant part: "Recognizing that changes in the state government organizational structure may need to be made as rapidly as possible to achieve greater economy, efficiency, and improved administration as the needs of government dictate, the Governor ... may, between sessions of the General Assembly, temporarily effect a change in the state government organizational structure as described in subsection (1)[.]" Subsection (5)

1. KRS 12.028(1) and (2).

2. KRS 12.010(1) defines "organizational unit" to mean "any unit of organization in the executive branch of the state government that is not an administrative body, including but not limited to any agency, program cabinet, department, bureau, division, section or office[.]"

3. KRS 12.010(8) defines "administrative body" to mean "any multi-member body in the executive branch of the state government, including but not limited to any board, council, commission, committee, authority or corporation, but does not include 'branch,' 'section,' 'unit' or 'office[.]'"

emphasizes the temporary nature of such a reorganization: "A temporary reorganization effected under subsection[ ] (2) ... shall be terminated ninety (90) days after sine die adjournment of the next regular session of the General Assembly unless otherwise specified by the General Assembly."

Exercising this legislatively-recognized power under KRS 12.028, the Governor issued EO 2017-364, the effect of which the circuit court aptly summarized:

> The Order creates the Charter Schools Advisory Council, to advise the Kentucky Department of Education on charter schools, and allow[ ] overlapping membership with other education boards; altered the Standards and Assessments Process Review Committee's membership to allow membership overlap with other boards; modified the Council on Postsecondary Education to guarantee that a citizen member is a non-voting, non-member advisor to the Kentucky Board of Education; and changed the Kentucky Board of Education to include four non-voting, non-member advisors who are on the Council on Postsecondary Education, the Education Professional Standards Board, the School Curriculum Assessment and Accountability Council, and the Charter Schools Advisory Council, or an individual with experience in education. The Order restructured the School Curriculum[ ] Assessment and Accountability Council with 15 members, rather than the previous 17 members, and altered membership requirements; reorganized the Reading, Diagnostic, and Intervention Grant Steering Committee with one less member at 15, and modified the membership requirements; reorganized the State Advisory Council for Gifted and Talented Education, reducing membership numbers from 19 to 11, and altering membership criteria; and abolished and re-created the State Advisory Panel for Exceptional Children as the State Advisory Council for Exceptional Children with 21 members, rather than 20 previous members, and additional[ly] represents individuals with disabilities. The Order finally abolished and re-created the Education Professional Standards Board with 13 members instead of the previous 15 members, and provided new membership criteria, and altered the appeal process for decisions—appeals now go to the Kentucky Board of Education for review before appeal to the Circuit Court rather than automatically going to the Circuit Court for review of the Board's final decision[.]

The circuit court upheld the validity of EO 2017-364 except for the portion restructuring the appeal process within the Education Professional Standards Board, which the circuit court ruled unconstitutional. And the Governor has not appealed that ruling. The Attorney General appealed the remainder of the trial court's ruling and sought immediate transfer of the case directly to this Court, which we granted.

II. Analysis.

KRS 12.028 authorizes the Governor to effectuate for the interim between legislative sessions a temporary reorganization of the state's "organizational units and administrative bodies." The Governor executed this authorization by promulgating EO 2017-364, temporarily reorganizing various state education boards. The Attorney General makes several constitutional and statutory arguments challenging the validity of the temporary reorganization mechanism itself and some of its inner workings. We address those challenges below.

* * *

The Attorney General makes three constitutional arguments. He asserts that the Governor's power to affect a temporary reorganization outside of legislative session to be a violation of: 1) the suspension provision of Section 15 of the Kentucky Constitution; 2) the education provision of Section 183 of the Kentucky Constitution; and 3) the separation of powers doctrine generally and the nondelegation doctrine specifically.

1. The temporary reorganization mechanism does not violate Section 15 of the Kentucky Constitution.

The Attorney General first argues that the temporary reorganization mechanism of KRS 12.028, as used in EO 2017-364, violates Section 15 of the Kentucky Constitution. Section 15 states, "No power to suspend laws shall be exercised unless by the General Assembly or its authority." The Attorney General posits that EO 2017-364 "suspend[ed] laws" by effecting changes to the various Kentucky education boards in conflict with the boards' governing statutes. For example, KRS 161.028(2)(a) provides that the Education Professional Standards Board "shall be composed of seventeen (17) members," yet EO 2017-364 reduces the number of members to fifteen. This, the Attorney General argues, is an unconstitutional suspension and rewriting by the Governor of duly enacted law.

But the Attorney General's argument fails to persuade us because even if we were to agree that the changes made by EO 2017-364 constitute a suspension of law, the Attorney General ignores the latter half of Section 15: "No power to suspend laws shall be exercised *unless by the General Assembly or its authority*."[4] In *Lovelace v. Commonwealth*, this Court recognized that when the General Assembly expressly grants to another branch the power to suspend a law, that branch constitutes the General Assembly's authority for purposes of Section 15 and that branch's execution of a suspension of the laws does not violate Section 15.[5]

At issue in *Lovelace* was the constitutionality of a statute allowing the judiciary to probate the sentence of a convicted criminal in certain situations.[6] In upholding the constitutionality of that statute, the Court said this:

> We need not here inquire into the extent to which the power to suspend the rendition and entry of a judgment inheres in the court as a judicial function or how far other statutes should be construed as requiring the rendition of judgment in a reasonable time after the verdict. Whatever the extent of those

---

4. (emphasis added).

5. 285 Ky. 326, 147 S.W.2d 1029, 1034–35 (1941); *see also Commonwealth, ex rel. Armstrong v. Collins*, 709 S.W.2d 437, 442–43 (Ky. 1986) (favorably discussing *Lovelace*).

6. 147 S.W.2d at 1034–35.

> directions and limitations may be, the power in the legislature to authorize the courts to suspend those laws is in the logically implied affirmation contained in Section 15 of the Constitution of Kentucky, declaring "No power to suspend laws shall be exercised, unless by the general assembly or its authority." By this act of 1936, the General Assembly has exercised that constitutional power and has authorized the courts to suspend the implications of the law which require entry and pronouncement of judgment without unreasonable delay.[7]

By enacting KRS 12.028, the General Assembly granted the Governor the authority in the interim between legislative session to reorganize temporarily state organizational units and administrative agencies. KRS 12.028 is the General Assembly's authority for purposes of Section 15. This is the difference between the present case and the cases the Attorney General relies on to support his position. In *Baker v. Fletcher*,[8] *Fletcher v. Commonwealth*,[9] and *Beshear v. Haydon Bridge*,[10] the General Assembly had not granted the Governor the authority to suspend the law. Here, the temporary reorganization mechanism established by KRS 12.028, in conjunction with the Governor's exercise of that temporary reorganization mechanism by his issuance of EO 2017-364, not only does not violate Section 15 but directly conforms to it because the General Assembly has explicitly designated the Governor under its authority to suspend the law.

Simply put, the temporary reorganization mechanism laid out by KRS 12.028 and executed by EO 2017-364 does not violate Section 15 of the Kentucky Constitution because the Governor possesses the General Assembly's authority to do so under that constitutional provision by virtue of the General Assembly having so stated.

* * *

3. *The temporary reorganization mechanism does not violate the separation of powers or nondelegation doctrines.*

Finally, the Attorney General argues that the temporary reorganization mechanism violates the separation of powers doctrine. "It is well settled law in the state of Kentucky that one branch of Kentucky's tripartite government may not encroach upon the inherent powers granted to any other branch."[11] The Attorney General adds that the temporary reorganization mechanism violates the nondelegation doctrine, a principle deriving from the separation of powers doctrine. "The nondelegation doctrine recognizes that the Constitution vests the powers of government in three separate branches and, under the doctrine of separation of powers, each branch must exercise its own power rather than delegating it to another branch."[12] The Attorney General argues that

---

7. *Id.* (internal citations omitted).

8. 204 S.W.3d 589 (Ky. 2006).

9. 163 S.W.3d 852 (Ky. 2005).

10. 304 S.W.3d 682 (Ky. 2010).

11. *Elk Horn Coal Corp. v. Cheyenne Res., Inc.*, 163 S.W.3d 408, 422 (Ky. 2005) (quoting *Smothers v. Lewis*, 672 S.W.2d 62, 64 (Ky. 1984)).

12. *TECO Mech. Contractor, Inc. v. Commonwealth*, 366 S.W.3d 386, 397 (Ky. 2012) (citing *Bd. of Trs. of Jud. Form Ret. Sys. v. Atty. Gen.*, 132 S.W.3d 770, 781 (Ky. 2003)).

only the General Assembly—the legislative department—has the power to reorganize the Commonwealth's education boards and that the delegation of this power to the Governor—the executive department—violates the principle of the separation of powers.

Our precedent ostensibly disposes of this issue. As we stated in *Brown v. Barkley*: "[W]e are satisfied that the transfer of an existing, legislatively-created function from one executive agency or department to another *is essentially an executive action ... and is not an exercise of legislative power by the chief executive*[.]"[13] And we reaffirmed this principle in *Legislative Research Comm'n ex rel. Prather v. Brown*: "[O]nce the General Assembly has made a determination that the power to reorganize state government in the interim between legislative sessions does exist, and determines that that power is in the hands of the Governor, such interim action is purely an executive function."[14] So *Legislative Research Comm'n* and *Barkley* stand for the rule that the power temporarily to reorganize organizational units and administrative agencies of state government during the interim between sessions is a legislatively recognized and sanctioned executive power that does not encroach on the legislative power of the General Assembly.

Leaving aside the unassailability of that rule as it applied to the facts in both of those cases, it simply does not apply to the facts in the present case. "It would be difficult, perhaps impossible, to define the extent of the legislative power of the state, unless by saying that so far as it is not restricted by the higher law of the state and federal constitutions, it may do everything which can be effected by means of a law."[15] "The legislative power we understand to be the authority under the constitution to make the laws, and to alter and repeal them[.] The difference between the departments undoubtedly is that the legislat[ure] makes, the executive executes, and the judiciary construes, the law."[16]

In the present case, the General Assembly created, by statute, the various education boards at issue. The General Assembly, by statute, outlined various aspects of those boards, ranging from the number of members populating them to the duties and responsibilities of those boards. Simply put, KRS 12.028, which allows the Governor to change the makeup and functions of those boards—even going so far as abolishing existing boards and creating new ones—is a grant of legislative authority to the executive department. KRS 12.028 allows the executive department to engage in lawmaking by allowing the Governor to alter the General Assembly's duly enacted statutes outlining the various aspects of the state's education boards.

Simply because this lawmaking occurs in the interim—the period when the legislature is not in session—does not alter the fact that the power being exercised by the Governor is lawmaking. The making and changing of laws is the hallmark of the legislative power no matter if it occurs during the legislative session or in the interim. And lawmaking in the interim is still lawmaking. KRS 12.028 allows the Governor to

13. 628 S.W.2d 616, 622 (Ky. 1982) (emphasis added).

14. 664 S.W.2d 907 (Ky. 1984).

15. *Slack v. Maysville & Lexington R.R.*, 52 Ky. 1, 12 (Ky. 1852).

16. *Purnell v. Mann*, 105 Ky. 87, 50 S.W. 264, 266 (1899) (citations omitted).

"between sessions of the General Assembly, temporarily effect a change in the state government organization structure" that "include[s] the creation, alteration or abolition of any organizational unit or administrative body and the transfer of functions, personnel, funds, equipment, facilities, and records from one (1) organizational unit or administrative body to another." Simply put, KRS 12.028 allows the Governor to change the law. That is an exercise of legislative power. The time within which an action occurs does not change the nature of the action—simply because the changing of statutes occurs outside of session does not change the fact that statutes are being changed—lawmaking is occurring.

Moreover, we cannot say as our precedent may suggest that because the General Assembly has prescribed a statute that allows the Governor to change statutes, the Governor is simply executing the laws by acting under a grant of legislative authority. Taking this notion to its logical conclusion, the General Assembly could pass a law stating, "The Governor shall have the power to change all laws of this Commonwealth between sessions of the General Assembly," and, under the "executing the laws" rule, there would be no separation of powers violation because the Governor, if he or she changes all laws in the Commonwealth, would simply be executing the statute. But at its core, the execution of the statute at issue in the present case allows the Governor to engage in lawmaking—exercise legislative authority.

All this being true, the delegation of legislative power by the General Assembly to the executive department is not totally prohibited: "[T]he nondelegation doctrine recognizes that ... given the realities of modern rule-making, [the legislature] neither has the time nor the expertise to do it all; it must have help."[17] "As a result of this reality, we have acknowledged that [other branches] may exercise legislative ... authority if certain protections are in place."[18] "The General Assembly may validly vest legislative ... authority in [another branch] if the law delegating that authority provides 'safeguards, procedural and otherwise, which prevent an abuse of discretion by the agency.'"[19] "The doctrine of the separation of powers was adopted ... to preclude the exercise of arbitrary power. The purpose was ... to save the people from autocracy."[20] "The purpose of the nondelegation doctrine should no[ ] longer be either to prevent delegation or to require statutory standards; the purpose should be the much deeper one of protecting against unnecessary and uncontrolled discretionary power."[21]

---

17. *Bd. of Trs. of Jud. Form Ret. Sys.*, 132 S.W.3d at 781 (citing *Mistretta v. U.S.*, 488 U.S. 361, 372, 109 S.Ct. 647, 102 L.Ed.2d 714 (1989)).

18. *TECO Mechanical Contractor, Inc. v. Com.*, 366 S.W.3d 386, 397 (Ky. 2012).

19. *TECO*, 366 S.W.3d at 397–98 (quoting *Kentucky Commission on Human Rights v. Fraser*, 625 S.W.2d 852, 854 (Ky. 1981)) (citing *Butler v. United Cerebral Palsy of Northern Ky., Inc.*, 352 S.W.2d 203, 208 (Ky. 1961)).

20. *Fletcher v. Commonwealth*, 163 S.W.3d 852, 863 (Ky. 2005) (quoting *Myers v. U.S.*, 272 U.S. 52, 293, 47 S.Ct. 21, 71 L.Ed. 160 (1926)).

21. *Miller v. Covington Development Authority*, 539 S.W.2d 1, 5 n.9 (Ky. 1976) (quoting Davis, *Administrative Law Text*, §2.08 (3d ed. 1972)).

Every reorganization plan the Governor effectuates between sessions is reviewed by members of the General Assembly both at the front and back ends.[22] Even though the Governor can implement the temporary plan in the interim, changes made by the temporary reorganization only survive until the General Assembly's next regular session.[23] Not only can the General Assembly affirmatively reject the Governor's reorganization plan and restore the status quo ante—the Governor's temporary reorganization automatically reverts to the status existing before the Governor instituted it, even by the General Assembly's inaction. The fate of the entire temporary executive reorganization-outside-of-session mechanism rests wholly in the hands of the General Assembly. The General Assembly is instrumentally involved in the temporary reorganization process and has erected its own checks against the executive's permanent use of executive power to organize state government.

The Attorney General aptly observes that broad reorganization authority that the Governor can effectuate temporarily can, and often does, transmute into a de facto permanent reorganization of state government by executive order. This is so, the Attorney General argues, because the temporary reorganization mechanism of KRS 12.028 does not prohibit the Governor from effectuating temporary reorganization plans in a continuous loop, uninterrupted by affirmative action of the General Assembly. There may be a point at which this continuous reorganization loop by executive order unconstitutionally encroaches upon the legislative power of our General Assembly as the Governor effectuates what amounts to a permanent change in the laws that govern organizational units and administrative bodies. But such is not the case before us today. And even if it were, some may view as legislative approval the General Assembly's repeated acquiescence in the continuous loop of executive orders that effectively institute the same reorganizational changes year after year. In any event, the Attorney General has only placed one executive order in issue before us in this case, framing this case as a challenge to the constitutionality of EO 2017-364 and this application of KRS 12.028 under the facts presented here, not as a facial challenge to that statute.

---

22. KRS 12.028(3) ("Any reorganization proposed under subsection ... (2) ... shall be set forth in a reorganization plan which shall be filed with the Legislative Research Commission."); KRS 12.028(4) ("When a proposed reorganization plan is submitted for review under subsection (2) ... the presiding co-chairman of the Legislative Research Commission shall determine which interim joint legislative committee has appropriate jurisdiction and shall refer the plan to such committee[.] ... The interim joint legislative committee ... shall review the plan to determine whether the plan can reasonably be expected to achieve greater economy, efficiency or improved administration in state government."); KRS 12.028(5) ("The Governor ... shall recommend legislation to the General Assembly [during the session immediately following the interim period in which the reorganization change was effectuated] to confirm the temporary reorganization plan. The subject matter of each executive order relating to reorganization shall be presented to the General Assembly in a separate bill.").

23. KRS 12.028(5) ("A temporary reorganization effected under subsections (2) to (4) of this section shall be terminated ninety (90) days after sine die adjournment of the next regular session of the General Assembly unless otherwise specified by the General Assembly.... If the General Assembly fails to enact a temporary reorganization plan, the Governor ... shall not effect the plan prior to the next succeeding session of the General Assembly.").

Ultimately, the General Assembly continues to maintain control of the temporary-reorganization-outside-of-legislative-session mechanism. The General Assembly can put an end to the mechanism. Not only that, but the General Assembly could choose explicitly to exempt certain boards from the executive's reorganization power or limit the executive's reorganization power in any way it chooses. And the fact that the executive's interim change only lasts for a period of time between regular sessions and that it can only be effectuated again by another executive order further evidences the temporary nature of the executive's change. The General Assembly's continued extensive control over this temporary mechanism precludes this Court at this time from determining that the General Assembly has abdicated the lawmaking power of the legislative department and delivered it into the hands of the executive department.

In sum, on the facts before us, neither KRS 12.028 nor EO 2017-364 constitutes an unconstitutional delegation of legislative power. Nor did the Governor's reorganization of the Education Professional Standards Board, besides the Governor's restructuring of its appeal process, constitute an unconstitutional infringement on the judiciary's power because the temporary reorganization of this board does not impute the judicial power in any way.[24]

III. Conclusion.

We affirm the judgment of the Franklin Circuit Court.

All sitting. Minton, C.J.; Hughes, Kller, Lambert, and Wright JJ., concur. VanMeter, J. concurs in result only by separate opinion, which Buckingham, J., joins.

Justice VanMeter, concurring in result only:

While I agree with the result of the majority opinion, I disagree with that portion that states that the Governor is exercising "legislative power." In my view he is exercising his "executive power" as authorized by the legislature and the Kentucky Constitution.

Buckingham, J., joins.

Notes and Questions

1. How persuasive is the Supreme Court's analysis and conclusion that, by reorganizing the executive branch boards, the Governor was exercising legislative, as opposed to executive, power?

2. How does the Court's holding in *Beshear v. Bevin* square with Section 28 of the Constitution?

3. The nondelegation doctrine under the Kentucky Constitution is more restrictive than it is under the U.S. Constitution, even when a state statute incorporates the

24. *See Am. Beauty Homes Corp. v. Louisville & Jefferson Cty. Planning & Zoning Comm'n*, 379 S.W.2d 450, 458 n.20 (Ky. 1964) ("It is very doubtful that characterizing the function of an administrative agency as *quasi-judicial* serves any purpose but to confuse. Though such an agency may adjudicate, it does not exercise judicial power and the term, instead of correlating the agency with the judiciary, may mean exactly the opposite.") (citations omitted).

standards in a federal statute. *Diemer v. Commonwealth, Transp. Cabinet, Dept. of Highways*, 786 S.W.2d 861, 864–66 (Ky. 1990).

4. The statute at issue in *Beshear v. Bevin*, KRS 12.028, was amended in 2021 to remove from the Governor the authority to unilaterally reorganize the structure of state government between legislative sessions. *See* 2021 Ky. Acts ch. 5 §1. Now, the Governor may propose a reorganization plan to the General Assembly, but the plan does not take effect unless it is approved by the General Assembly at its next session. The stated reason the General Assembly gave for amending the law was that "ensuring checks and balances on the executive branch of government help[s] ensure a balance of power within the three branches of government." *Id.* §3.

Four

The Legislative Branch

A. The Legislative Power

> "The legislative power shall be vested in a House of Representatives and a Senate, which, together, shall be styled the 'General Assembly of the Commonwealth of Kentucky.'" (Ky. Const. §29.)

What is "the legislative power"? The opinions of Kentucky's appellate courts are replete with statements to the effect that it is the power of the legislative branch to set policy: "It is elementary that the legislative branch of government has the prerogative of declaring public policy and that the mere wisdom of its choice in that respect is not subject to the judgment of a court." *Fann v. McGuffey*, 534 S.W.2d 770, 779 (Ky. 1975). But that alone does not define what legislative power is or is not. By creating and modifying the common law, for example, the courts can also be said to establish policy of a sort.

Other cases describe the legislative power by reference to the person or persons exercising it: "If there is one essential characteristic inherent in legislative power, it is that such power must be exercised by an elected representative or representatives of the people, and not by a person, persons or agency created or designated by those representatives." *Miller v. Covington Dev. Auth.*, 539 S.W.2d 1, 4 (Ky. 1976). But this explanation does not define what those elected representatives may do, or not, when they act in concert.

Perhaps the most comprehensive definition of the legislative power is "discretion as to what the law shall be." *Johnson v. Commonwealth ex rel. Meredith*, 291 Ky. 829, 165 S.W.2d 820, 825 (1942). At its most elemental level, it is the power to coerce or prohibit action by others, and to make generally applicable rules of private conduct. The government may invade private rights pursuant to its "police power," but "only if the legislation bears a real and substantial relation to the public health, safety, morality or some other phase of the general welfare." *Dep't for Nat. Res. & Envtl. Prot. v. No. 8 Ltd. of Va.*, 528 S.W.2d 684, 686 (Ky. 1975). By conferring *the* (singular) legislative power upon the General Assembly, Section 29 of the Constitution denies the power to legislate to any other person or collection of persons.

Unlike the United States Congress, which under the U.S. Constitution is limited to the "legislative Powers herein granted," U.S. Const. art. I, §1, the General Assembly is not limited to a defined list of limited legislative powers. The default rule is not (as it is in the case of Congress) that the legislature cannot act in the absence of an express constitutional fount of authority. Rather, the default rule is that the General Assembly has the power to act unless there is an express constitutional curb on its authority. "[S]tate Constitutions do not delegate power to the Legislature of the state, which body has all power unless prohibited or limited by the Constitution. In other words, state Constitutions unlike the federal one only prescribe inhibitions and limitations upon legislative power and that unless the legislative body is so prescribed and limited by the Constitution its authority is unlimited and it may enact upon any subject in the mode and manner it sees proper." *Rouse v. Johnson*, 234 Ky. 473, 28 S.W.2d 745, 747 (1930).

Following Section 29, which vests "the legislative power" in the General Assembly, the Kentucky Constitution includes a number of sections that shape the manner in which the General Assembly may use its constitutionally delegated power to legislate. Sections 30 through 44 and 47 are structural provisions, analogous to provisions applicable to Congress in the U.S. Constitution. Sections 45, 46, and 48 to 62 are procedural requirements or limitations on the legislative power without parallel in the U.S. Constitution. In addition, there are several provisions scattered throughout the Kentucky Constitution (*e.g.*, Section 183) that impose other obligations and limits on the legislative power.

In this chapter, we will consider those constitutional curbs on the legislative power, which constrain the General Assembly's discretion not to act, prohibit the exercise of the legislative power in certain ways, or prohibit the exercise of legislative power altogether.

Legislative Research Commission ex rel. Prather v. Brown

Supreme Court of Kentucky (1984)

664 S.W.2d 907

OPINION OF THE COURT BY CHIEF JUSTICE STEPHENS.

On this appeal, we address the constitutionality of several acts of the Kentucky General Assembly passed by that body's 1982 regular session. This case has been trumpeted abroad as a test of the relative constitutional powers of the Governor of the Commonwealth as opposed to those of the General Assembly and has further been described as a power struggle between these two particular branches of our state government.

It is more accurately a case which deals with legislative enactments that confer certain powers on the Legislative Research Commission,[1] most of which are designed to be exercised by that body when the General Assembly is adjourned. The basic legal issues involved deal with the delegation of powers by the General Assembly to the LRC and the application of the historical doctrine of the separation of powers to the particular statutes in question. An answer to the questions posed by this litigation necessarily requires consideration of the nature and limitations of the LRC.

1. For brevity, we will hereinafter describe the Legislative Research Commission as "LRC".

I. Procedural History

The LRC, acting by and through appellants Prather, President Pro Tem of the Senate, and Richardson, Speaker of the House of Representatives, Co-Chairmen of the LRC, filed this action in Franklin Circuit Court. The complaint sought a declaration of rights as to the validity of several statutes, following a challenge thereto by the Governor. The appellees, by counterclaim, impleaded certain additional statutes[2] in order to insure that all issues were litigated. Following an evidentiary hearing, the trial court rendered a written opinion and a judgment.

Based on agreements and stipulations of the parties, not all of the statutes in question were submitted to the trial court for judgment, and we will not, perforce, decide those issues. The general subject matters of the controverted statutes are as follows: the power of the LRC to act in the stead of the General Assembly while it is adjourned; the power of the Speaker of the House and the President Pro Tem of the Senate to make appointments to and to serve as members of certain boards and commissions; the power of the LRC to determine or to approve budget reductions when the General Assembly is adjourned; the power of the LRC to approve the action of the executive in applying for so-called Federal "Block Grants;" the power of the LRC to grant or withhold legal effect from any executive order promulgated by the Governor which reorganizes the administrative structure of the executive branch of government; and the power of the LRC to delay the legal effect of administrative regulations adopted by the Governor.

II. Judgment of the Trial Court

The trial court ruled that each and every questioned statute was constitutionally defective; in effect, ruling in favor of the appellees.

In summary, the court declared that the powers of the LRC were limited to "oversight" and that a statutory attempt to authorize the LRC to conduct the business of the General Assembly was a violation of Kentucky's separation of powers doctrine. The right of the appellants to make certain appointments to boards and commissions was declared invalid for the reason that the power of appointment was an executive function. The right of the LRC to veto executive decisions concerning the administration of the budget was held to be executive in nature and not the subject of proper delegation by the General Assembly. The legislative power of the LRC to approve an executive request for a Federal Block Grant was held to be void because such action constitutes "lawmaking after adjournment of the full General Assembly." The power of the LRC to, in effect, veto a Governor's reorganization plan was similarly held invalid as being the unconstitutional exercise of lawmaking authority following the adjournment of the General Assembly. Finally, the power given to the LRC to delay the effect of executive administrative regulations was declared to be a violation of the separation of powers doctrine.

* * *

---

2. The statutes, grouped by subject matter, will be discussed in detail at a later point in this opinion.

III. Contentions of the Parties

In essence, the appellants, representing the LRC, argue that the LRC is a "legitimate arm" of the General Assembly, and that it may carry out any and all necessary functions of the General Assembly, following the adjournment of the General Assembly. In furtherance of this argument Appellants claim that even though some of the authority given to the LRC under the questioned statutes may be technically executive in nature, such incursion by the legislative branch into the powers of the executive is constitutionally permissible under a so-called "liberal" construction of the Kentucky constitutional provisions creating the separation of powers doctrine.

Predictably, appellees urge that the powers given to the LRC by the statutes constitute far more than mere "oversight" and actually constitute the power to *legislate*. Moreover, appellees argue that this Court has consistently ruled that the doctrine of the separation of powers in this Commonwealth must be strictly construed and that all such incursions by one branch of government into the sphere of influence of another branch are constitutionally prohibited.

IV. A History of the LRC

Because the statutes in question grant the LRC much power, authority and responsibility, it will be helpful to discuss the nature of this organization, and to identify its role in the constitutional scheme of the organization of state government.

The parent of the present LRC, The Legislative Council, was given birth by the 1936 session of the General Assembly.[3] It was composed of fifteen members: five Senators appointed by the Lieutenant Governor, five Representatives appointed by the Speaker of the House, and five state officials appointed by the Governor. It was empowered solely to engage in fact-finding. In 1944, the Legislative Council's membership was enlarged to sixteen members, none of whom were appointed by the Governor.[4] The eight Senators and eight Representatives serving were appointed by the Lieutenant Governor and the Speaker of the House, respectively. The Council's powers were expanded to include organizational functions prior to each regular session of the General Assembly. In 1948, the Council was renamed the Legislative Research Commission, and its membership was reduced to seven: the Governor as Chairman, the President Pro Tem of the Senate, the Speaker of the House, and the majority and minority floor leaders of the Senate and the House.[5] Its powers were essentially unchanged. Subsequently, the Lieutenant Governor replaced the Governor as Chairman.[6] In 1974, the Lieutenant Governor was removed as a member and under the present statute all members of the LRC are members of the legislative branch of government.[7]

3. §§4618-138 through 4618-142, Carroll's Kentucky Code (1936).

4. 1944 Kentucky Acts, Chapter 149.

5. 1948 Kentucky Acts, Chapter 15.

6. 1956 Acts, First Extraordinary Session, Ch. 7, Art. XII, §1.

7. 1974 Kentucky Acts, Chapter 353.

It is patently clear that the LRC as it currently exists, and as it has existed since 1974, is as appellants concede, an "arm" of the General Assembly. It is beyond cavil that the primary role, if not the exclusive role, of the LRC has been historically that of a research, fact-finding, secretariat and general support agency for the General Assembly. Since the LRC's membership consists of a small percentage of the total membership of the two houses of the General Assembly, no one could argue that it has any powers not given to it by its parent, the General Assembly, and no one could argue that it can legislate. The legislative power lies solely within the province of the General Assembly *and its entire, publicly elected membership*. Our constitution makes that clear. Ky. Const. Sec. 29 states, "[T]he legislative power shall be vested in a House of Representatives and a Senate, which, together shall be styled the 'General Assembly of the Commonwealth of Kentucky.'" Whatever else the LRC may constitutionally do, it may not legislate.[8]

V. The Separation of Powers Doctrine

President George Washington, in his farewell address, described the problem which is addressed by the separation of powers doctrine when he said:

> The spirit of encroachment [of one branch of government into the functions of another] tends to consolidate the powers of all the departments in one, and thus to create, whatever the form of government, a real despotism. XIII, *Writings of George Washington*, 277, 306 (Ford ed., N.Y., 1892).

Montesquieu, the father of the doctrine of separation of powers, articulated the concept by writing:

> Here then is the fundamental constitution of the government we are treating of. The legislative body being composed of two parts, they check one another by the mutual privilege of rejecting. They are both restrained by the executive power, as the executive is by the legislative. 1 Montesquieu, *The Spirit of Laws*, Book XI, Chapter VI, 159 (1823).

The extent to which a country can successfully resolve the conflict among the three branches of government is, to a very great extent, the measure of that nation's capacity to self-govern.

The framers of Kentucky's four constitutions obviously were cognizant of the need for the separation of powers. Unlike the federal constitution, the framers of Kentucky's constitution included an express separation of powers provision. They were undoubtedly familiar with the potential damage to the interests of the citizenry if the powers of government were usurped by one or more branches of that government. Our present constitution contains explicit provisions which, on the one hand, mandate separation among the three branches of government, and on the other hand, specifically prohibit incursion of one branch of government into the powers and functions of the others. Thus, our constitution has a double-barreled, positive-negative approach:

---

8. For an extensive discussion of the governmental scheme set up by the framers of the Constitution see *Brown v. Barkley*, Ky., 628 S.W.2d 616 (1982).

> Section 27 *The powers of the government of the Commonwealth of Kentucky shall be divided into three distinct departments, and each of them be confined to a separate body of magistracy*, to wit: Those which are legislative, to one; those which are executive, to another; and those which are judicial, to another.

(Emphasis added.)

> Section 28 No person or collection of persons, being of one of those departments, shall exercise any power properly belonging to either of the others, except in the instances hereinafter expressly directed or permitted.

Subsequent provisions of the Constitution proceed logically and consistently with the policy established in Sections 27 and 28 that grant powers to the three branches of government. Section 29 vests the legislative power in the General Assembly, Section 69 vests the executive power in the Governor and finally, Section 109, as amended by the people in 1975, establishes the judicial power in the Court of Justice.[9]

A motivating factor that led to the drafting and eventual adoption of our present constitution was a strong desire on the part of the people to curb the power of the General Assembly. Convention delegate John D. Carroll from Henry County exemplified that spirit when he stated,

> "It is a well known fact that one of the prime causes for the calling of this convention was the abuses practiced by the legislative department of this state...." 1 Debates of Constitutional Convention of 1890, p. 1482.

According to delegate J.F. Askew, there was a great necessity to "reform the legislative department...." *Id.* at 3821. A noted Kentucky constitutional historian, Dr. Robert Ireland, clearly established in his testimony before the trial court that the desire to curb the power of the General Assembly was the primary motivation for calling the 1891 Constitutional Convention.

Even a cursory reading of Kentucky history reveals the factual basis for the conclusions of delegates Carroll and Askew and the opinion of Dr. Ireland. The then General Assembly was dominated by a few, powerful special interests who wielded that power for their own benefit. This situation obviously does not exist today; however, constitutions are operative until and unless changed by the people.

A case which was contemporaneously decided with the adoption of our present constitution, *Pratt v. Breckinridge*, 23 Ky.Law Rep. 1858, 112 Ky. 1, 65 S.W. 136 (1901) stated:

> From this it seems clear that the makers of the constitution intended the legislature to discuss and enact laws, and *to do nothing else*. 65 S.W. at 140. (Emphasis added.)

---

9. A reading of these sections of the constitution shows that certain normal functions of one branch were specifically granted to another branch, e.g. the veto power of the Governor over Acts of the General Assembly, Ky. Const. Sec. 88 and 89, the power of the General Assembly to remove its own member, Ky. Const. Sec. 39.

Moreover, it has been our view, in interpreting Sections 27 and 28, that the separation of powers doctrine is fundamental to Kentucky's tripartite system of government and must be "strictly construed." *Arnett v. Meredith*, Ky., 275 Ky. 223, 121 S.W.2d 36, 38 (1938). In *Sibert v. Garrett*, 197 Ky. 17, 246 S.W. 455 (1922), we expounded at some length on the history and the purposes of Sections 27 and 28:

> "Perhaps no state forming a part of the national government of the United States has a Constitution whose language more emphatically separates and perpetuates what might be termed the American tripod form of government than does our Constitution, which history tells us came from the pen of the great declaimer of American independence, Thomas Jefferson.... 246 S.W. at 457.
>
> ... *We conceive it to be the duty of the courts to adopt the construction most conducive ... [to prevent] ... the destruction of the edifice as contemplated*." 246 S.W. at 458. (Emphasis added.)

Appellants urge this court to adopt a so-called liberal construction of the separation of powers doctrine and argue that the General Assembly is the "dominant" branch of government. In support of this argument, they claim that in *Brown v. Barkley*, Ky., 628 S.W.2d 616 (1982), we denigrated the power of the Governor and gave the General Assembly a dominant role in the tripod, by allegedly giving to the General Assembly all "residual" powers. We do not agree and we do not so interpret *Barkley*.

In *Barkley*, following a lengthy discussion of the inherent or implied powers of the Governor, we said:

> The extent that the Governor has any implied or inherent powers in addition to those the Constitution expressly gives him, it seems clear that such unexpressed executive power is subservient to the overriding authority of the legislature.... 628 S.W.2d at 621.
>
> Practically speaking, except for those conferred upon him specifically by the Constitution, his powers like those of the executive officers created by Const. Sec. 91, are only what the General Assembly chooses to give him. 628 S.W.2d at 623.

These words, plus the following, are seized upon by appellants in their argument as proof that somehow, this Court has sawed off one of the legs of the tripod, viz., that of the executive, and that we have made that branch of government less than equal to the other two branches. Appellants remind us that we also said in *Barkley*:

> It is axiomatic that under our Constitution *the General Assembly has all powers not denied to it or vested elsewhere by the Constitution.* (Emphasis added.)

and:

> Whereas the judicial branch must be and is largely independent of intrusion by the legislative branch, the executive branch exists principally to do its [the legislature's] bidding. 628 S.W.2d at 623.

The inference appellants draw from this language is that the General Assembly possesses all powers and authority to act which are not specifically denied it by the Constitution and has the authority to act in exercising those powers. It is argued that *all powers*, residual in nature, belong to the legislative branch. We do not agree.

To place this interpretation on that language would be tantamount to saying that we were repealing Sections 27 and 28 of the Kentucky Constitution. We would in effect be eliminating the separation of powers doctrine. We would reach a result which would fly in the face of history and the legal precedents of this Commonwealth. Our review of that doctrine's history and our description of its language most assuredly confirm this. Nothing in *Barkley* can be construed to deny the existence of the doctrine of separation of powers and the equality of the three coparceners in government. Implicit in *Barkley* is that the General Assembly as the legislative branch, has all powers *which are solely and exclusively legislative in nature.* To argue that any other power is given to the General Assembly simply won't wash. The power referred to in *Barkley* is *legislative power and legislative power only.* In summation, our view is best expressed in *Sibert v. Garrett*, 197 Ky. 17, 246 S.W. 455 (1922), which we reaffirm. There we stated:

> But a deeper probing into and investigation of the subject will reveal the truth that the rule so generally stated means, not that the Legislature has "all powers" not withheld by the Constitution, but that it "may pass any acts that are not expressly or by necessary implication inhibited by their own Constitutions or by the Federal Constitution." *In other words, the Legislature may perform all legislative acts not expressly or by necessary implication withheld from it, but it may not perform or undertake to perform executive or judicial acts*, except in such instances as may be expressly or by necessary implication directed or permitted by the constitution of the particular state. *To adopt the latitudinous construction that the Legislature may do anything not expressly or impliedly prohibited by the Constitution would, to our minds, at once destroy the separation of the powers of government into the three great departments.* 246 S.W. at 457. (Emphasis added.)

Nearly every one of our sister state courts have similarly resisted any weakening of the doctrine of the separation of powers. See, e.g., *In re Opinion of the Justices*, N.C.App., 295 S.E.2d 589 (1982), and *State ex rel. McLeod v. McInnis*, 278 S.C. 307, 295 S.E.2d 633 (1982). In like manner, the United States Supreme Court, in striking down a federal statute, has spoken to the issue. The Court ruled that an attempt by Congress to vest veto authority in itself over executive action violated the separation of powers doctrine of the United States Constitution. *Immigration and Naturalization Service v. Chadha, Et al.*, 462 U.S. 919, 103 S.Ct. 2764, 77 L.Ed.2d 317 (1983). There the court said:

> "The hydraulic pressure inherent within each of the separate Branches to exceed the outer limits of its power, even to accomplish desirable objectives, must be resisted." 103 S.Ct. at 2784.

We should not abandon the philosophical principles that were incorporated by the framers of our present constitution. The purpose of the separation of powers doctrine is uncontroverted. The precedents established by this court have been uniform in retaining the goals set out by the framers. The separation of powers doctrine is set in the concrete of history and legal precedent. We will not overrule those cases and we will not, by the fiat of judicial legislation, change the clear and imperative meaning of our constitution. Such action is within the sole province of the voters of this Commonwealth.

We conclude that any statute subject to the scrutiny of Sections 27–28 of the Kentucky Constitution should be judged by a strict construction of those time-tested provisions.

VI. Post-Adjournment Powers of the General Assembly and the LRC

Two major legal questions dominate this area: (1) can the General Assembly delegate its authority to legislate to the LRC and (2) can the General Assembly legislate through its agent, the LRC, while the General Assembly is in adjournment? The answers to these legal questions are inextricably intertwined and relate to the nature and role of the LRC.

We premise this discussion on our previous conclusion that the LRC is part and parcel of the General Assembly and is under its control. It must also be remembered that the LRC is a service agency of the General Assembly. Its functions are limited. Its nature, role and authority do not change our form of government from a tripod into a quadrapod.

(1) Can the General Assembly Delegate its Authority to Legislate to the LRC?

Ky. Const. Sec. 29 reads:

> "The legislative power shall be vested in a House of Representatives and a Senate, which, together, shall be styled the 'General Assembly of the Commonwealth of Kentucky.'"

Ky. Const. Sec. 60 provides: "No law ... shall be enacted to take effect upon the approval of any other authority than the general assembly." While this is not a precise, written constitutional prohibition preventing the General Assembly from delegating its legislative powers to another entity, we have spoken many times on the subject. In *Bloemer v. Turner*, Ky., 281 Ky. 832, 137 S.W.2d 387, 390 (1940), we declared that the Kentucky Constitution "... made sure that the legislature may not in any degree abdicate its power." Further firming up its position, the Court in *Bloemer* said: *It is an accepted principle that "the legislative department has no right to deputize to others the power to perform its governing functions."* 137 S.W.2d at 391. (Emphasis added.) Recognizing there are practical limitations to the hard and fast rule announced, particularly when it involves the implementation of legislative will, we stated:

> But, obviously the legislature cannot deal with subordinate rules or cover the details of administration and execution in its regulatory enactments. Perforce, these must be left to those upon whom the duty of carrying out the legislative will devolves. However, the legislature must lay down policies and establish standards. *Ibid.*

Under *Bloemer*, the General Assembly cannot delegate its *power to make a law*. It can, however, establish standards for administration and delegate authority to implement a law. As in so many instances, the principle is easy to state. Its application is difficult.[10]

The practical modification or exception developed in *Bloemer* was further explained and expanded in *Commonwealth v. Associated Industries of Kentucky*, Ky., 370 S.W.2d 584 (1963). The rule of that case is that Ky. Const. Sec. 29 does not absolutely prohibit the General Assembly's delegation of legislative power.

A more recent statement of the applicable principles is found in *Holsclaw v. Stephens*, Ky., 507 S.W.2d 462 (1974). In that case we stated:

> ... when we say that the legislature may not delegate its powers, we mean that *it may not delegate the exercise of its discretion as to what the law shall be, but not that it may not confer discretion in the administration of the law itself* ... Generally speaking *a delegation of discretion* is not unlawful if sufficient standards controlling the exercise of that discretion are found in the act ... such as procedural safeguards *and* the right of the delegating authority to withdraw the delegation. 507 S.W.2d at 471. (Emphasis added.)

It is clear from the aforementioned cases that delegation, of legislative power, to be lawful, must not include the exercise of discretion as to what the law shall be. In addition, such delegation must have standards controlling the exercise of administrative discretion. Finally, the delegating authority must have the right to withdraw the delegation.

Therefore, we conclude that the General Assembly, which constitutionally holds legislative power, cannot delegate that power to the LRC.

(2) While in Adjournment Can the General Assembly Legislate Through its Agent, the LRC?

We begin by reiterating that under Ky. Const. Sec. 29 the General Assembly is the sole legislative branch of government and that its powers, procedures and limitations are set forth in Sections 29 through 68 of that Constitution.

The Kentucky General Assembly is not one of continuous session and a necessary corollary thereto is that it cannot legislate after it has adjourned *sine die*. A legislative body ceases to exist at the moment of its adjournment. *Anderson v. Dunn*, 19 U.S. (6 Wheaton) 204, 5 L.Ed. 242 (1821).

As we have concluded above, the General Assembly may not delegate its authority to legislate. It follows, therefore, that given the inability to delegate said authority, the General Assembly may not bestow upon its agent, the LRC, nor can the LRC seize for itself, the power to legislate.[11]

---

10. The basic rule prohibiting delegation was forcefully reiterated in *Dawson v. Hamilton*, Ky., 314 S.W.2d 532 (1958).

11. *See, State ex rel. McLeod v. McInnis*, 278 S.C. 307, 295 S.E.2d 633 (1982); *In re Opinion of the Justices*, 305 N.C. 767, 295 S.E.2d 589 (1982); *General Assembly v. Byrne*, 90 N.J. 376, 448 A.2d 438 (1982); *State ex rel. Judge v. Legislative Finance Committee*, 168 Mont. 470, 543 P.2d 1317 (1975); *Jewett v. Williams*, 84 Idaho 93, 369 P.2d 590 (1962); *State ex rel. Jones v. Atterbury*, 300 S.W.2d 806

With the preceding background we move on to analyze the challenged statutes. In each instance, one or more legal questions have been raised. We shall apply the law stated above, to each statute and determine its validity. Since certain additional legal issues have been raised, we shall discuss those where appropriate.

* * *

VIII. LRC Review of Administrative Regulations

The General Assembly has in its recent history exercised "oversight" and review of administrative regulations promulgated by the various executive agencies, boards and commissions. KRS 13.080–13.125. This "oversight" and review has been achieved through a subcommittee of the LRC known as the Administrative Regulation Review Subcommittee. KRS 13.087. The effect of this LRC subcommittee's actions was *recommendatory* in nature. KRS 13.087.

However, the 1982 General Assembly made several major changes in the nature of this subcommittee's actions which are the subject of this law suit. KRS 13.085(1)(d) and (e) (effective 7-15-82) provide that no regulation made by any administrative body shall become effective until it has been forwarded to the LRC *and* until it has been *reviewed and accepted* by the LRC, *or* it has been placed before and not disapproved by the General Assembly. KRS 13.087(4) requires that the LRC shall submit all regulations to one of its subcommittees to determine "… *if the regulation conforms to the statutory authority under which it was promulgated and if it carries out the legislative intent of the statutory authority* under which it was promulgated." (Emphasis added.) The subcommittees' findings are reported to the LRC which then either finds that the regulation conforms to the legislative intent of the statutory authority and accepts the regulation, or attaches a notation of its objection to the regulation and returns it to the promulgating administrative body. KRS 13.087(5) provides that the administrative body may then revise the regulation so as to make it comply with the LRC's determination of the legislative intent or that body may return it unchanged to the LRC. KRS 13.087(6) provides that if the General Assembly is in session when an administrative body returns a regulation, that is objected to by the LRC, then the regulation shall be put before the General Assembly. KRS 13.087(7) requires a monthly reporting to the LRC of all subcommittee actions regarding administrative regulations. KRS 13.087(8) requires that all regulations not accepted by the LRC *or* one of its subcommittees shall be placed before the General Assembly. KRS 13.087(9) provides that the *General Assembly* may, during its regular sessions, and by joint resolution, or bill, require regulations submitted to the LRC to be laid before the General Assembly and may void any regulation already in effect. KRS 13.088(1) provides a procedure for the Governor to issue an executive order, in the event of an emergency, to permit applicable regulations to become effective immediately, provided that the emergency regulations are submit-

(Mo. 1957); *State ex rel. Robinson v. Fluent*, 30 Wash.2d 194, 191 P.2d 241 (1948), *cert. denied sub nom. Washington Pension Union v. Washington*, 335 U.S. 844, 69 S.Ct. 66, 93 L.Ed. 394 (1948); *State ex rel. Hamblen v. Yelle*, 29 Wash.2d 68, 185 P.2d 723 (1947); *In re Opinion of the Justices*, 248 Ala. 590, 29 So.2d 10 (1947).

ted to the LRC for review. KRS 13.088(2) provides that an emergency regulation shall expire when final review action is taken as provided by KRS 13.080 and 13.085. KRS 13.088(3) provides that when the LRC or a subcommittee thereof has an objection to a regulation, such regulation cannot be filed as an emergency regulation. KRS 13.092(1) provides that when the General Assembly is not in session, no administrative regulation, excepting an emergency regulation, shall become effective until accepted by the LRC. KRS 13.092(2) provides that until an administrative regulation is accepted by the LRC, it shall be of no force or effect. KRS 13.092(3) states that if any of the provisions of KRS 13.092 are held to be unconstitutional, no administrative body shall have authority to promulgate any regulations, notwithstanding any other provision of the law.

It is clear that if the LRC subcommittee or the LRC itself disapproved of a proposed regulation, the regulation's implementation would be delayed until the next session of the General Assembly. Therefore, KRS 13.085 and KRS 13.087 provide a device whereby the LRC or a subcommittee thereof could block, for a period of nearly twenty-one months, the administrative policy of the executive branch of government. KRS 13.085 and KRS 13.087 have the effect of creating a legislative veto of the administrative policy of the executive branch of government. One of appellants' witnesses testified to this effect when he said:

Q. 43. Well, in practical effect it is a legislative veto?

A. *It's a legislative veto*; right.

Q. 44. It's a legislative veto...

A. Yes, sir.

Q. 45. ... of proposed regulations by departments of government?

A. Yes, sir.

Under pre-existing law, LRC objections to prepared regulations were precatory. The objections did not have the force of law. The changes in KRS 13.085, 13.087 and 13.092 which require LRC approval or LRC subcommittee approval of regulations have the effect of preventing the executive from dealing with emergencies. The power to suspend a regulation's effective date for up to twenty-one months is the power to effectively prevent a regulation from having the force of law. In addition, the legislature has statutorily attempted to deliver this power into the hands of seven members of the General Assembly or into the control of a subcommittee thereof.[12]

The trial court held that such constituted a violation of the separation of powers doctrine. The judgment stated that delegation of legislative powers to the LRC when the General Assembly was in adjournment was improper and declared that neither the General Assembly nor its designee could *legislate* when the General Assembly was not in session.

The adoption of administrative regulations necessary to implement and carry out the purpose of legislative enactments is executive in nature and is ordinarily within

12. In essence, as we have said, a "quadrapod", instead of a tripod.

the constitutional purview of the executive branch of government. Ky. Const. Secs. 27–28, 42, 88 and 89. *Brown v. Barkley*, Ky., 628 S.W.2d 616 (1982). We conclude that KRS 13.085(1)(d) and (e); KRS 13.087(4), (5), (6), (7), (8), (9); KRS 13.088(2)(3); and KRS 13.092(1) and (2) which set out the plan and the rules for providing legislative or LRC review of proposed regulations as those statutes are presently written are violative of Ky. Const. Secs. 27–28 and are a legislative encroachment into the power of the executive branch.[13]

It will also be recalled that the review of the regulations was for the stated legislative purpose of determining if they comported with statutory authority and if they carried out the legislative intent. It requires no citation of authority to state unequivocally that such a determination is a judicial matter and is within the purview of the judiciary, the Court of Justice.[14] For this reason, we also conclude that the statutory scheme discussed above violates the separation of powers doctrine. *See, Butler v. United Cerebral Palsy of Northern Kentucky, Inc.*, Ky., 352 S.W.2d 203 (1961).

One further question remains. Appellants argue that KRS 13.092(3), a non-severability clause, is applicable. The statute, in essence, provides that if the LRC or its subcommittee cannot constitutionally veto proposed regulations, then the executive department cannot issue any more regulations.

The trial court declared KRS 13.092(3) to be void as being in contravention of the Governor's constitutional duty to faithfully execute the laws of the Commonwealth under Sections 69 and 81 of the Kentucky Constitution.

Under Kentucky's Constitution, the executive powers and responsibilities of the Commonwealth lie within the province of the Governor. Ky. Const. Sec. 69. Under Section 81 the Governor has the positive duty to go forward and "take care that the laws be faithfully executed". Ky. Const. Sec. 81. In *Brown v. Barkley*, Ky., 628 S.W.2d 616 (1982), we reaffirmed this executive duty when we said:

> We do not doubt that if the General Assembly should pass a law that requires implementation, and appropriate funds for that purpose but omit specifying the manner in which it is to be carried out, *the chief executive would be required to carry it out and have the right to choose the means by which to do it.* 628 S.W.2d at 623. (Emphasis added.)

This right, this duty, exists because of the specific constitutional duties conferred on the Governor.

The non-severability clause that appears in KRS 13.092(3) has the effect of throwing the baby out with the bath water. The adoption and use of administrative regulations are important tools in the operation of modern government, at all levels. The purpose

---

13. Under *Chadha, supra*, we conclude that the legislative veto of the action of the executive is also a violation of the separation of powers.

14. This is not to say that any person, or organization including the LRC, does not have the unrestricted right to form an opinion as to whether a proposed action is legal or not. What we do say is that the determination of such as far as it causes the veto of executive action, is invalid.

is to enable the Governor to successfully carry out the constitutionally mandated executive and administrative duties bestowed upon that office: *General Assembly v. Byrne*, 90 N.J. 376, 448 A.2d 438 (1982); *Burton v. Mayer*, 274 Ky. 245, 118 S.W.2d 161 (1938). There is no constitutional authority, however, whereby the governor can add, directly or indirectly, to the content of a statute by means of an administrative regulation and, a fortiori, no administrative regulation can be adopted unless it is necessary and is related to the content of the legislative act and to its effective administration.

The statute in question not only impliedly reorganizes the executive duties of the Governor, but also attempts to usurp these powers. Having failed at the first part, it further attempts to restrict the ability of the Governor to carry out his sworn duties. The General Assembly, by enacting the clause, has restricted the power of the Governor to carry out his duties. In *Kenton Water Company v. City of Covington*, 156 Ky. 569, 161 S.W. 988 (1913), we said:

> [W]here the Constitution has by express provision denied the Legislature the right to require a particular thing to be done, or to legislate upon a particular subject or in a particular way, then the Legislature cannot by indirection require it to be done by attaching it as a condition to the exercise of some power which it has granted and which is essential to the public welfare that it be exercised. To do this would be to permit the constitutional provision to be indirectly violated and render it a nullity.... 161 S.W. at 992.

The restriction placed on the executive by KRS 13.092(3) effectively and unconstitutionally limits and interferes with the governor's mandated duties. It should also be noted that the General Assembly, through its enactment of KRS 446.090 clearly established the necessity of being able to sever a constitutionally infirm section of any statute from the sound portion thereof.

We, therefore, conclude that Section 3 of KRS 13.092 is void and we affirm the trial court.

* * *

In accordance with the above, the judgment of the Franklin Circuit Court is affirmed in part, and reversed in part with directions that it be modified in accordance with this opinion.

All concur.

Notes and Questions

1. What kind of separation of powers violations (classic usurpation vs. nondelegation) were at issue in this case?

2. The Supreme Court declined to "adopt a so-called liberal construction of the separation of powers" in *LRC v. Brown*. What kind of construction did the Court adopt? What does this say about the importance of the separation of powers under the Kentucky Constitution?

3. A well-known and oft-cited law review article has said that "[t]he decision of the Kentucky Supreme Court in *Legislative Research Commission v. Brown* ... has been called Kentucky's *Marbury v. Madison* because of the number of fundamental constitutional issues which were resolved by the Court in that case." Sheryl G. Snyder & Robert M. Ireland, *The Separation of Governmental Powers Under the Constitution of Kentucky: A Legal and Historical Analysis of L.R.C. v. Brown*, 73 Ky. L.J. 165, 167 (1984). Mr. Snyder was one of the Governor's attorneys in *LRC v. Brown*, and Dr. Ireland, a history professor at the University of Kentucky, testified on behalf of the Governor in the case as an expert regarding the 1890 constitutional convention. Though the article is written from the winner's perspective, it provides an interesting historical background on the case and the separation of powers between the executive and legislative branches of the Kentucky state government.

B. Special and Local Legislation

> "The General Assembly shall not pass local or special acts...." (Ky. Const. §59.)
>
> "The General Assembly shall not indirectly enact any special or local act by the repeal in part of a general act, or by exempting from the operation of a general act any city, town, district or county; but laws repealing local or special acts may be enacted...." (Ky. Const. §60.)

Sections 59 and 60 of the Constitution, together, prohibit "local" or "special" legislation. At times, the Supreme Court and its predecessor have struggled to define what the Constitution means by "special" acts. An early case defines both terms as follows: "Special legislation is such as relates either to particular persons, places, or things, or to persons, places, or things, which though not particularized, are separated by any method of selection from the whole class to which the law might, but for such legislation, be applied, while a local law is one whose operation is confined within territorial limits, other than those of the whole state or any properly constituted class or locality therein." *King v. Commonwealth*, 194 Ky. 143, 238 S.W. 373, 376 (1922).

Take note that Section 59 does not prevent the General Assembly from legislating *at all* regarding the 29 itemized subjects. The legislature may do so, but not in a "local" or "special" way. For example, the General Assembly can enact statutes of limitations for tort claims, but not a law that provides for a different limitations period in Jefferson County than the period applicable to the same tort in the rest of the Commonwealth (a local act). *See* Section 59(5). Similarly, the General Assembly may enact a general law regulating adoptions but not a law allowing one specific person, A.B., to adopt another person, C.D. (a special act). *See* Section 59(9).

Zuckerman v. Bevin

Supreme Court of Kentucky (2018)
565 S.W.3d 580

Opinion of the Court by Justice VanMeter.

Under Section 14(b) of the Taft-Hartley Act, 29 U.S.C.[1] §164(b), Congress authorized states to enact right-to-work laws, *i.e.*, laws that prohibit union shop agreements and agency shop agreements. In 2017, Kentucky's legislature passed, and the Governor signed, 2017 HB[2] 1, commonly referred to as the Kentucky Right to Work Act, 2017 Ky. Acts ch. 1, §15 (the "Act"). Significantly, this Act amended KRS[3] 336.130(3) to provide that no employee is required to become, or remain, a member of a labor organization, or to pay dues, fees, or assessments to a labor organization. The Act's stated goal was "to attract new business and investment into the Commonwealth as soon as possible." 2017 Ky. Acts ch. 1, §14. The issue we must decide in this case is whether the Franklin Circuit Court erred in dismissing constitutional challenges to the validity of the Act, specifically that it violated the Kentucky Constitution's provisions requiring equal protection of the laws, prohibiting special legislation, prohibiting takings without compensation, and that it was improperly designated as emergency legislation. We hold that the trial court did not err and therefore affirm the Franklin Circuit Court's Order dismissing the challenges to the Act.

I. Factual Background.

Bills virtually identical to 2017 HB 1 were introduced in almost every session of the legislature beginning in 2000[4] but never passed. Governor Bevin, as a candidate in 2015, actively campaigned on a platform of "right to work." * * * Following his election, he encouraged the electorate in 2016 to support legislative candidates who similarly favored "right to work." When the membership and leadership of the House changed with the 2016 election, the new majority's top priorities were the passage of a number of bills, including 2017 HB 1.

The House Economic Development and Workforce Investment Committee convened a hearing on HB 1 on January 4, 2017. At the hearing, proponents of the Bill testified in support of the Bill. * * * Their testimony included statistics that right-to-work states experience superior economic development and superior employment growth in both union and non-union jobs, specifically referring to Michigan, Indiana, and Tennessee. They cited Kentucky's disadvantage in attracting certain new employers to locate in the state due to the Commonwealth's status as a non-right-to-work state. In addition, Speaker Jeff Hoover referred to a study by Dr. Jeffrey Eisenach that concluded right-to-work greatly benefited job creation, specifically "[p]rivate sector employment

1. United States Code.
2. House Bill.
3. Kentucky Revised Statutes.
4. 2000 HB 12; 2003 Senate Bill ("SB") 77; 2004 HB 173; 2005 SB 205; 2006 HB 38; 2007 HB 328; 2009 SB 165; 2011 HB 345; 2013 HB 308; 2014 HB 496; 2015 SB 1; 2016 SB 3. * * *

grew by 17.4 percent in right-to-work states between 2001 and 2013." * * * Mr. David Adkisson referred to an LSU[5] study which reported that one-third of businesses looking to expand or relocate indicated that right-to-work was important. Mr. Kevin Grove spoke to his experience in attracting industrial development to the Louisville metropolitan area, and the advantage accruing to across-the-river Indiana due to that state's enactment of right-to-work legislation in 2012. The witnesses opposing the Bill, Ms. Anna Baumann and Mr. Bill Londrigan, provided testimony to refute the statistics and claims of the proponents. Much of this testimony is contained in Appellants' brief in this Court and accompanying attachments. 2017 HB 1 was quickly passed, largely on a partisan basis, and signed into law on an emergency basis.[6]

In May 2017, Fred Zuckerman, et al.,[7] filed an action in Franklin Circuit Court against the Commonwealth[8] challenging the Act on several Kentucky constitutional grounds. Thereafter, Barry Bright, Jacob Purvis and William Purvis filed a motion, which the trial court granted, to intervene as defendants on the side of the Commonwealth.

In June 2017, the Commonwealth filed a motion to dismiss. The Unions subsequently filed a motion for partial summary judgment. After a September 2017 hearing, the trial court issued its Order denying the Unions' motion and granting the Commonwealth's motion. The Unions appealed. Because this case involves significant and important constitutional issues of great and immediate public importance, we granted transfer of the case from the Court of Appeals. CR[9] 74.02.

* * *

III. Labor-Management Background.

A detailed history of Labor-Management relations would unduly prolong this opinion, but an overview is helpful to the analysis of the issues before us, particularly because 1) the Unions base their challenges under the Kentucky Constitution, in part, on "the letter and the spirit of the document,"[10] and 2) right-to-work laws are explicitly authorized under federal law. 29 U.S.C. §164(b).

---

5. Louisiana State University.

6. Except for the Act's designation as emergency legislation, purportedly in violation of Ky. Const. §55, no claim is made that the Act's passage and enactment did not comport with the requirements of the Constitution for a valid law.

7. The plaintiffs/appellants are Fred Zuckerman and William Londrigan, as representatives respectively of the General Drivers, Warehousemen and Helpers Local Union No. 89 and the Kentucky State AFL-CIO, Affiliated Unions and their Members (collectively "the Unions").

8. The defendants/appellees are Office of the Governor, *ex. rel.* Matthew G. Bevin, in his official capacity as Governor, and the Commonwealth of Kentucky, Kentucky Labor Cabinet, *ex rel.* Derrick K. Ramsey, in his official capacity as Secretary of the Kentucky Labor Cabinet (collectively "the Commonwealth").

9. Kentucky Rules of Civil Procedure.

10. *E.g.*, Appellants' Brief at 11, Union *Amicae*'s Brief at 1–5, 7. We recognize the importance of labor unions in United States' history and that of Kentucky. We acknowledge that unions have played a significant role in providing a path for many working families to the middle class, for improving work-

A. Kentucky Labor Law History to 1890.

Trade or labor unions in Kentucky were initially formed in the more urbanized areas of Louisville, Northern Kentucky, *i.e.*, Covington and Newport, and in the coal fields of Eastern Kentucky. *See generally* John Hennan, *Toil, Trouble, Transformation: Workers and Unions in Modem Kentucky*, 113 REG. OF THE KY. HIST. SOC'Y 233, 236–37 (2015) (attributing this formation to the post-Civil War period, although some scholars believe union activity existed in antebellum Kentucky). The first reported Kentucky case we have found involving a trade organization was *Sayre v. Louisville Union Benevolent Ass'n*, 62 Ky. (1 Duv.) 143, 145–46 (1863), in which the court generally recognized the right of workingmen to combine for their own protection and to obtain such wages as they choose to demand, but also noted combinations that prejudice the public by unduly elevating or depressing wages, tolls, or prices of any merchantable commodity are indictable as conspiracies. Four years later, the court decided *Lee v. Louisville Pilot Benevolent & Relief Ass'n*, 65 Ky. (2 Bush) 254 (1867). In *Lee*, the court affirmed the right of the organization to charge and collect dues, since "[t]he presumed object of the tariff was uniformity of charges, harmony, efficiency, and fidelity, and not unjust monopoly, or the extortion of exorbitant fees." *Id.* at 255.

Surprisingly, in the period pre-dating the 1890–91 Kentucky Constitutional Convention, that is it. In that era, and although courts recognized workingmen's right to organize, they also recognized employers' rights to conduct business as they saw fit and, absent a contract, to hire and fire employees generally at will. Furthermore, statutory laws regulating labor contracts, maximum hours, minimum pay, and the like, were generally held unconstitutional as an infringement of the employer's and individual employee's right of contract. *See generally* F. J. Stimson, HANDBOOK TO THE LABOR LAW OF THE UNITED STATES (New York: Charles Scribner's Sons, 1896), 1–19. Perhaps the most famous, or infamous, case of this era is *Lochner v. New York*, 198 U.S. 45, 25 S.Ct. 539, 49 L.Ed. 937 (1905), *abrogated by West Coast Hotel Co. v. Parrish*, 300 U.S. 379, 57 S.Ct. 578, 81 L.Ed. 703 (1937), which held that New York's law prohibiting bakery employees from working more than sixty hours in a week was unconstitutional.

---

ing conditions and pay, for general acceptance of the forty-hour work week, and for other benefits. In 1933, our predecessor court had recognized the important function of labor unions:

> the rights of economic self-preservation; of improving economic and social conditions; of agreement among men; of free speech and action; of pursuing one's safety and happiness; of striving to achieve legitimate ends and benefits by concert of action or collective bargaining; and the privilege of assembling together in a peaceable manner for the common good. Upon this side may be placed also the unconscionable sweatshops and lamentable conditions under which employees are all but compelled to work—those things which challenge an enlightened, humane society to opposition.

Music Hall Theatre v. Moving Picture Mach. Operators Local No. 165, 249 Ky. 639, 642, 61 S.W.2d 283, 284–85 (1933).

The issues in this case, however, are not whether unions are beneficial organizations, but whether the legislature's passing of the Act violated any provision of the Kentucky Constitution as argued by the Unions and the Union *Amicae*.

Two cases which post-date the 1890 Constitutional Convention, but which indicate the state of Kentucky labor law in this era are *Hetterman v. Powers*, 102 Ky. 133, 143, 43 S.W. 180, 182 (1897) (holding that a Union was entitled to equitable protection in the use of label or mark designating product of labor of the members), and *Underhill v. Murphy*, 117 Ky. 640, 643–45, 78 S.W. 482, 482–83 (1904) (upholding use of strike injunction to protect owner's business and to prevent violence toward and intimidation of his employees).

B. 1890 Constitutional Convention.

Following the Civil War, special legislation was used as a means to encourage Kentucky's economic development. To say that these enactments got out-of-hand would be an understatement. Most scholars accept that Kentucky's 1890 Constitutional Convention was necessitated by excessive proliferation of special legislation for the benefit of individual persons and corporations, an unequal tax burden and mounting local public debts, a desire to exercise control over railroads and railroad rates, and the 1850 antebellum constitution's indefensible protections for slavery. *See generally* Thomas D. Clark, A History of Kentucky (Ashland, Ky.: The Jesse Stuart Found., 1988), 419–28. This Court has on many occasions recognized the need to curtail special legislation as the primary reason for the 1891 Constitution. *See, e.g., Yeoman v. Commonwealth, Health Policy Bd.*, 983 S.W.2d 459, 466 (Ky. 1998) (citing Sheryl G. Snyder & Robert M. Ireland, *The Separation of Governmental Powers Under the Constitution of Kentucky: A Legal and Historical Analysis of L.R.C. v. Brown*, 73 Ky. L. J. 165 (1984–85)); *Tabler v. Wallace*, 704 S.W.2d 179, 183 (Ky. 1985) (stating "[c]oncern for limiting the powers of the legislature in general, and with cutting off special and local legislation in particular, was the primary motivating force behind enactment of the new Kentucky Constitution of 1891[ ]").

To illustrate the problem of special legislation, in its 1888 session, the legislature passed 1,403 local and private acts, which took up 3,146 pages in a three-volume set. 1888 Acts of the General Assembly of the Commonwealth of Kentucky (Frankfort, KY: John D. Woods, 1888).[11] By contrast, it passed 128 public acts, comprising 217 pages. *Id.* In 1890, the legislative record was similarly skewed in favor of special or local legislation: 1,726 local or private acts, in 4,703 pages, as opposed to 174 public acts, comprising 174 pages. 1890 Acts of the General Assembly of the Commonwealth of Kentucky (Frankfort, KY: E. Polk Johnson, 1890). In each of these sessions, local or special acts accounted for over 90% of the total legislation passed.

---

11. These numbers come from the table of contents of the Kentucky Acts' volumes. Interestingly, a number of the Public Acts had a decidedly local or restricted impact. *See, e.g.*, 1888 Ky. Acts ch. 632 (amending Ky. Gen. Stat. ch. 70, §6 to increase from sixty days to six months the time period in which to file a mechanics' lien, but such amendment applied only to Madison County); 1888 Ky. Acts ch. 650 (exempting the Nicholasville, Danville and Lancaster Turnpike Company from the provisions of 1886 Ky. Acts ch. 1127 (requiring State's Sinking Fund Commissioners to approve the directors of a turnpike company in which the State of Kentucky owned stock)); 1888 Ky. Acts ch. 1347 (amending Ky. Gen. Stat. ch. 106, art. 2, §3 (relating to taverns, tippling-houses, etc.), but such amendment applied only to Madison County).

Some of the special legislation exempted railroads and other corporations from taxation and created monopolies, which were decried by a number of the delegates. *E.g.*, I 1890 Ky. Const. Debates (Frankfort, Ky.: E. Polk Johnson, 1890), 466 (Del. Knott comments). Another point of view was that this legislation had encouraged economic development, expansion of railroads, and development of the state's natural resources. *See* Clark, A History of Kentucky, 419–20 (describing editor Henry Watterson and his efforts to promote industrial development).[12] This pro-development point of view was also reflected in the 1890 debates. *See* IV 1890 Ky. Const. Debates, 5014 (Del. Burham comments).[13]

We include these comments not to re-debate the issues of the late nineteenth century, but merely to point out that the framers of the 1891 Constitution were a varied assortment of men, representing different parts of the Commonwealth and economic interests. *See* Clark, 431 (stating "[t]his fourth convention was composed of as motley a delegation of constitutionalists as had ever been seen in a convention hall.... Farmer members opposed the sinister influence of corporations; and corporation lawyers, lobbyists and self-styled constitutionalists opposed [Farmers'] Alliance leadership[ ]"). Thus, selective quotations from a four-volume set of over 6,000 pages is not a useful exercise in "divining the intent of the framers." Our task, in the interpretation of Kentucky's Constitution,

> rests on the express language of the provision, and words must be given their plain and usual meaning. *City of Louisville Mun. Hous. Comm'n v. Pub. Hous. Admin.*, 261 S.W.2d 286, 287 (Ky. 1953). This Court is "not at liberty to construe ... plain and definite language of the Constitution in such a manner as to thwart the deliberate purpose and intent of the framers of that instrument."

---

12. To quote Dr. Clark:

> Henry Watterson and his "new departure" Democrats were diligent on the behalf of new industry. In Louisville, Watterson took the lead in pointing out new and profitable industrial opportunities. Boards of commerce distributed thousands of circulars at home and abroad describing Kentucky's resources and proclaiming Kentucky a land of unlimited business promise. Using the state's credit to encourage corporations was too unusual, however, for conservative agrarian legislators, and enthusiastic "new departure" partisans had to content themselves with granting generous tax exemption and special privileges. This encouragement to capital was soon noticeable, for railway mileage increased from 567 miles built and projected in 1860, to more than 1,500 miles in operation, in 1880. These roads represented a stated capital investment of $100,000,000. Along with the expansion of the Kentucky railway system, eastern capital poured into the state to develop timber and coal resources, and to build distilleries and tobacco warehouses.

Clark, A History of Kentucky, at 420.

13. Burnam stated:

> I would hold these corporations to their just responsibility for every infraction of private right or public law, but I shall never consent by my vote, in obedience to popular clamor, to strike down those great benefactors of the Commonwealth ... which are daily and hourly giving employment and to thousands of laborers, who have linked with bands of iron the different portions of the country, and strengthened and consolidated the power, the civilizations and true greatness of the human race.

> *Harrod v. Hatcher*, 281 Ky. 712, 137 S.W.2d 405, 408 (1940). In fact, our predecessor Court recognized as a "cardinal rule" of constitutional interpretation the principle that rules of construction may not be employed where the language of the provision is clear and unambiguous. *Grantz v. Grauman*, 302 S.W.2d 364, 366 (Ky. 1957). "It is to be presumed that in framing the constitution great care was exercised in the language used to convey its meaning and as little as possible left to implication[.]" *City of Louisville v. German*, 286 Ky. 477, 150 S.W.2d 931, 935 (1940).

Fletcher v. Graham, 192 S.W.3d 350, 358 (Ky. 2006).

To demonstrate the point that the 1891 Constitution does not reflect a "pro-labor, populist, progressive" point of view, as argued by the Unions and the Union *Amicae*, the Convention adopted only three explicitly pro-labor provisions. These sections were Section 243 relating to the minimum age of child labor, Section 244 requiring all wage earners to be paid in lawful money, and Section 253 restricting the labor of penitentiary labor to public works.[14] Other explicitly pro-labor proposals, such as those advocated by the Louisville Trades and Labor Assembly, Unions and Lodges, were not adopted—rejected either in committee or by the Convention: designation of the number of hours that constitute a day's work on public projects; establishment of a Board of Arbitration "with full power to settle all industrial difficulties between employer and employee[;]" and designation of goods and wares manufactured by convict labor. I 1890 Ky. Const. Debates, 240 (Trades and Labor Assembly, Unions and Lodges, in the City of Louisville Petition). In addition, the Convention rejected an amendment to Section 243 which would have authorized the legislature to "provide by law for the proper ventilation of mines, the construction of escapements, shafts and such other appliances as may be necessary to protect the health and secure the safety of the workmen therein." I 1890 Ky. Const. Debates, 265 (Del. Ramsey Resolution). Equal rights for women, another progressive reform which had been advocated by the Knights of Labor, then a national labor organization with a number of Kentucky locals, were similarly not espoused by the Convention. *See* II 1890 Ky. Const. Debates, 2371–72 (vote tabling provision to grant married women equal property rights). A provision to authorize women's suffrage, likewise, was not adopted in the final document.[15]

---

14. Prior to 1891, neither the constitution nor statutes limited where convict labor could be employed. Employers therefore could lease convict labor to lower wages or to take the place of free, striking workers. *See* Henry C. Mayer, *Glimpses of Union Activity among Coal Miners in Nineteenth-Century Eastern Kentucky*, 86 Reg. of the Ky. Hist. Soc'y 216, 220 (1988).

15. Laura Clay, leader of the women's suffrage in Kentucky and daughter of Cassius Marcellus Clay, the "Lion of White Hall," was permitted to address the Convention. Her plea was not for recognition of women's suffrage as a constitutional right, but merely for a provision authorizing the legislature to enact women's suffrage "when the time shall come." II 1890 Ky. Const. Debates 2090–93. This limited provision was not included in the drafted Constitution; Section 145 limited suffrage to "[e]very male citizen ... of the age of twenty-one." In 1912, the legislature authorized women to vote in elections for county school superintendents, as authorized by Ky. Const. §155. *Crook v. Bartlett*, 155 Ky. 305, 159 S.W. 826 (1913).

The Convention adopted specific sections directed at corporations and railroads. Ky. Const. §§190–218. These provisions, however, ran to the benefit of the public at large, and were designed to correct the abuses which had occurred as a result of special legislation. *See, e.g.*, §194 (requiring all corporations organized or carrying on business in the state to have a place of business and a registered agent); §197 (prohibiting common carriers from issuing free passes to public officials); §212 (subjecting railroad rolling stock and personal property to execution and attachment); §§213–15, 217–18 (requiring railroads not to discriminate or to give preferential treatment or rates). Similarly, and as to taxation, several provisions addressed special legislation abuses. *E.g.*, §174 (subjecting corporate and individually owned property to uniform tax rates); §§177, 179 (prohibiting Commonwealth, counties or municipalities from becoming shareholders in corporations).

After the publication of the proposed Constitution in April 1891, the reaction of labor groups was mixed. Herbert Finch, Organized Labor in Louisville, Kentucky, 1880–1914 (1965) (unpublished Ph.D. dissertation, Univ. of Kentucky) (on file with the William T. Young Library, Univ. of Kentucky), 206–07. The Trades and Labor Assembly in Louisville "decided almost unanimously to vote against" the new Constitution. *Against the New*, The Courier-Journal (Louisville), Mon., Jun. 15, 1891, p. 5, col. 4 * * *. Conversely, the Knights of Labor did endorse it at its annual state convention in July 1891, "by a close vote." *Knights' Labor*, The Courier-Journal (Louisville), Wed., Jul. 29, 1891, p. 8, col. 2 * * *.

In the final analysis, Dr. Clark has been quoted,

> *[T]he 1890 convention created a static document to protect [Kentucky's] agrarian society from an emerging industrial order*: "One gets the impression ... that many of the delegates were, in fact, little Red Riding Hoods trudging alone and frightened through the perplexing forest of constitutional law, hoping that the big bad wolves of industrial and progressive changes were mere figments of their badly agitated imagination, and that a rigid constitution with static provisions would serve to dispel these threatening wraiths."

William Green, *Constitutions*, The Kentucky Encyclopedia (Lexington: The Univ. Press of Kentucky, 1992), 225 (emphasis added). No doubt exists but that the 1890 Convention sought to rein in the reign of special legislation, *i.e*, elimination of special tax breaks for railroads, equalization of tax burden, elimination of implied powers. The resulting document was "[n]ot so much a fundamental rule of government as a piece of omnibus legislation." Clark, 432.

* * *

With that background, we turn to the claims in this case.

IV. Analysis.

As previously noted, the Unions raise four constitutional challenges to the Act: (a) violation of Kentucky's equal protection of the laws provisions; (b) violation of Kentucky's prohibition on special legislation; (c) violation of Kentucky's prohibition of takings without compensation; and (d) improper designation as emergency legislation. We address each claim in turn.

A. Equal Protection.

Citizens of Kentucky enjoy equal protection of the law under the 14th Amendment of the United States Constitution and Sections 1, 2, and 3 of the Kentucky Constitution. *D.F. v. Codell*, 127 S.W.3d 571, 575 (Ky. 2003) (citation omitted).[16] Sections 1, 2, and 3 of the Kentucky Constitution provide that the legislature does not have arbitrary power and shall treat all persons equally. "[U]nless a statutory classification is arbitrary, or not founded on any substantial distinction suggesting the necessity or propriety of such legislation, the courts have no right to interfere with the exercise of legislative discretion." *Ky. Ass'n of Chiropractors, Inc. v. Jefferson Cnty. Med. Soc'y*, 549 S.W.2d 817, 822 (Ky. 1977). As noted earlier, our analysis begins with the presumption that legislative acts are constitutional. *United Dry Forces v. Lewis*, 619 S.W.2d 489, 493 (Ky. 1981); *Sims v. Bd. of Educ.*, 290 S.W.2d 491, 493 (Ky. 1956); *Brooks v. Island Creek Coal Co.*, 678 S.W.2d 791, 792 (Ky. App. 1984). The goal of equal protection provisions is to "keep[] governmental decisionmakers from treating differently persons who are in all relevant respects alike." *Nordlinger v. Hahn*, 505 U.S. 1, 10, 112 S.Ct. 2326, 2331, 120 L.Ed.2d 1 (1992). However, because nearly all legislation differentiates in some manner between different classes of persons, neither the federal nor state constitutions forbid such classification per se. *Romer v. Evans*, 517 U.S. 620, 631, 116 S.Ct. 1620, 1627, 134 L.Ed.2d 855 (1996). Accordingly, the level of judicial scrutiny applied to an equal protection challenge depends on the classification made in the statute and the interest affected by it. *See Mem'l Hosp. v. Maricopa Cnty.*, 415 U.S. 250, 253, 94 S.Ct. 1076, 1080, 39 L.Ed.2d 306 (1974).

Currently, three levels of review may apply to an equal protection challenge. *See, e.g., Steven Lee Enters. v. Varney*, 36 S.W.3d 391, 394–95 (Ky. 2000). Strict scrutiny applies whenever a statute makes a classification based on a "suspect" class. *See Codell*, 127 S.W.3d at 575–76 (discussing strict scrutiny). In *Varney*, for example, we noted race, alienage, and ancestry as suspect classes. 36 S.W.3d at 394. In such cases, or when a statute affects a fundamental right, a statute is "sustainable only if [it] is suitably tailored to serve a 'compelling state interest.'" *Id.* (citation omitted). The next level of analysis, heightened rational basis scrutiny, applies to quasi-suspect classes, such as gender or illegitimacy. *Id.* Under this standard, "discriminatory laws survive equal protection analysis only 'to the extent they are substantially related to a legitimate state interest.'" *Id.* (quoting *City of Cleburne v. Cleburne Living Ctr., Inc.*, 473 U.S. 432, 441, 105 S.Ct. 3249, 3255, 87 L.Ed.2d 313 (1985)). On the other hand, a statute that "merely affects social or economic policy . . . is subject" to a less searching form of judicial scrutiny, *i.e.* the "rational basis" test. *Codell*, 127 S.W.3d at 575 (citation omitted).

16. The Unions make no claim under the 14th Amendment. That provision requires persons who are similarly situated to be treated alike. Federal courts have held that right-to-work laws do not violate any provision of the United States Constitution. * * *

Rational basis review is appropriate for evaluating the Act since the Act is expressly permitted by the Taft-Hartley Act §14(b). The Supreme Court long ago held that, under federal law, union membership is not a suspect classification triggering strict scrutiny. *City of Charlotte v. Local 660, Int'l Ass'n of Firefighters*, 426 U.S. 283, 286, 96 S.Ct. 2036, 2038, 48 L.Ed.2d 636 (1976). The result is the same under Kentucky case law, which recognizes that statutes relating to labor and labor organizations are proper objectives for exercise of the Commonwealth's police power. *Hamilton v. Int'l Union of Operating Eng'rs*, 262 S.W.2d 695, 700 (Ky. 1953); *see also Ky. Harlan Coal Co. v. Holmes*, 872 S.W.2d 446, 451 (Ky. 1994), *abrogated on other grounds by Vision Mining, Inc. v. Gardner*, 364 S.W.3d 455 (Ky. 2011) (stating "the Commonwealth's power to legislate public policy in the area of employer/employee relations derives from its police power[ ]"); *Commonwealth v. Reinecke Coal Min. Co.*, 117 Ky. 885, 894, 79 S.W. 287, 289–90 (1904) (statute relating to timely payment of coal miners and forbidding blacklisting of employees was valid exercise of police power). Furthermore, "[t]he essential predicate of the police power is the health, morals, safety, and general welfare of the people." *Jones v. Russell*, 224 Ky. 390, 392, 6 S.W.2d 460, 461 (1928). The legislature "in making police regulations has the right to make classifications based upon natural and reasonable distinctions, but is without right to exercise the power to classify arbitrarily and without any reasonable basis inherent in the objects of the classification." *Id.* at 393, 6 S.W.2d at 461. A statute complies with Kentucky equal protection requirements if a "rational basis" supports the classifications that it creates. *Elk Horn Coal Corp. v. Cheyenne Res., Inc.*, 163 S.W.3d 408, 418–19 (Ky. 2005) (citation omitted); *Waggoner v. Waggoner*, 846 S.W.2d 704, 707 (Ky. 1992) (citation omitted).

In *Varney*, we quoted at length from *Heller v. Doe by Doe*, 509 U.S. 312, 319–21, 113 S.Ct. 2637, 2642–43, 125 L.Ed.2d 257 (1993), as "[t]he best summary of what rational basis analysis entails and what it does not entail[:]"

> We many times have said, and but weeks ago repeated, that rational-basis review in equal protection analysis is not a license for courts to judge the wisdom, fairness, or logic of legislative choices. Nor does it authorize the judiciary to sit as a superlegislature to judge the wisdom or desirability of legislative policy determinations made in areas that neither affect fundamental rights nor proceed along suspect lines. For these reasons, a classification neither involving fundamental rights nor proceeding along suspect lines is accorded a strong presumption of validity. Such a classification cannot run afoul of the Equal Protection Clause if there is a rational relationship between the disparity of treatment and some legitimate governmental purpose. Further, a legislature that creates these categories need not actually articulate at any time the purpose or rationale supporting its classification. Instead, a classification must be upheld against equal protection challenge if there is any reasonably conceivable state of facts that could provide a rational basis for the classification.
>
> A State, moreover, has no obligation to produce evidence to sustain the rationality of a statutory classification. A legislative choice is not subject to court-

> room factfinding and may be based on rational speculation unsupported by evidence or empirical data. A statute is presumed constitutional, and the burden is on the one attacking the legislative arrangement to negative every conceivable basis which might support it, whether or not the basis has a foundation in the record. Finally, courts are compelled under rational-basis review to accept a legislature's generalizations even when there is an imperfect fit between means and ends. A classification does not fail rational-basis review because it is not made with mathematical nicety or because in practice it results in some inequality. The problems of government are practical ones and may justify, if they do not require, rough accommodations—illogical, it may be, and unscientific.

Varney, 36 S.W.3d at 395 (internal quotations and ellipses omitted).

In *Elk Horn Coal*, we explained that the statute under consideration, KRS 26A.300, did not treat all unsuccessful appellants the same, and thus was "discriminatory. But the state may discriminate in certain matters if there is a rational basis for such discrimination." 163 S.W.3d at 413. As previously noted, "[i]n areas of social and economic policy, a statutory classification that neither proceeds along suspect lines nor infringes fundamental constitutional rights must be upheld against an equal protection challenge if ... any reasonably conceivable state of facts ... could provide a rational basis for the classification." *Id.* (quotation and footnote omitted);[17] *see also Popplewell's Alligator Dock No. 1, Inc. v. Revenue Cabinet*, 133 S.W.3d 456, 466–67 (Ky. 2004) (upholding sales and use tax exemption for gasoline sales for industrial-type commercial vessels); *Commonwealth v. Howard*, 969 S.W.2d 700, 703–04 (Ky. 1998) (upholding juvenile DUI statute which imposes lower blood alcohol level for drivers under 21 years of age).

In *Delta Air Lines, Inc. v. Commonwealth, Revenue Cabinet*, in upholding a sales and use tax classification, we held:

> The standards for classifications under the Kentucky constitution are the same as those under the Fourteenth Amendment to the Federal constitution. A single standard can be applied to both the State and Federal constitutions in regard to classification for sales tax exemptions. This Court has determined that economic factors are valid considerations which the legislature may take into account in developing a legitimate tax classification. The legislature has a great freedom of classification and the presumption of validity can be overcome

17. In *Elk Horn Coal*, we acknowledged that, on occasion based on particular facts, we had elected to apply a higher level of scrutiny to equal protection analysis in cases involving social and economic legislation. 163 S.W.3d at 418 nn. 43–44 (citing *Tabler*, 704 S.W.2d at 186–87 as requiring substantial and justifiable reason for discriminatory legislation). A cursory reading of *Tabler*, however, discloses that the decision addressed the prohibition of special legislation in sections 59 and 60 of the Kentucky Constitution, specifically section 59(5) regulating limitation of civil causes. In *Elk Horn Coal*, we declined to address this "heightened" standard because of our view that the legislation in question failed even the rational basis test as "arbitrary and irrational." 163 S.W.3d at 421.

> only by the most explicit demonstration that it is hostile and oppressive against particular persons and classes.

689 S.W.2d 14, 18 (Ky. 1985) (citations omitted). "A classification by the legislature should be affirmed unless it is positively shown that the classification is so arbitrary and capricious as to be hostile, oppressive and utterly devoid of rational basis." *Id.* at 19.

The Unions and the Union *Amicae* strenuously argue that the Act creates a classification which has no substantial or justifiable basis. They claim right-to-work policies reduce wages for union and non-unions employees, have mixed impact on employment outcomes, and have no statistically significant impact on overall state employment. They argue the true motivation is "to starve labor organizations and their members based on perceived political bent." The Commonwealth, conversely, argues that the legislature reasonably could conclude that the Act would, as testified by the proponents of 2017 HB 1, benefit Kentucky and its citizens by joining other right-to-work states with superior economic development, employment growth in both union and non-union jobs, and eliminate Kentucky's disadvantage with respect to its neighboring right-to-work states in competing to attract new businesses. The Commonwealth further argues that the legislature might have sought to provide economic freedom for workers who desired not to support any union activities.

The legislature is permitted to set the economic policy for the Commonwealth. Even assuming that the Act creates a classification that discriminates between labor unions and all other organizations operating in the state,[18] or any sort of classification among union and non-union workers, we are unable to say that the legislature did not have a reasonable basis for so doing. As stated in *Varney*, "[a] legislative choice is not subject to courtroom factfinding and may be based on rational speculation unsupported by evidence or empirical data." 36 S.W.3d at 395. The legislature clearly established a rational basis for the Act: to promote economic development, to promote job growth,

---

18. We reject the Unions' analogy that labor unions are akin to the Kentucky Bar Association ("KBA") for purposes of the Act. Historically, labor unions, as opposed to trade or craft unions, arose as associations of workers/employees to improve pay and working conditions and to provide a unified group to assert rights against their employer. *See Music Hall Theatre*, 249 Ky. at 642, 61 S.W.2d at 284–85. These same functions are largely served today through an overlay of federal law and collective bargaining agreements. Unions are voluntary organizations, even in non-right-to-work states. The KBA, by contrast, exists by virtue of the state constitution. *See* Ky. Const. §116 (requiring the Kentucky Supreme Court to "by rule, govern admission to the bar and the discipline of members of the bar[ ]"). The KBA's purpose is

> to maintain a proper discipline of the members of the bar in accordance with these rules and with the principles of the legal profession as a public calling, to initiate and supervise, with the approval of the court, appropriate means to insure a continuing high standard of professional competence on the part of the members of the bar, and to bear a substantial and continuing responsibility for promoting the efficiency and improvement of the judicial system.

Kentucky Rules of the Supreme Court ("SCR") 3.025. The KBA is not a voluntary association, SCR 3.030(1), except in the sense that no one is required to practice law in Kentucky. The essential tenor of SCR 3.025 is that the KBA exists for the protection of the public: "proper discipline … of the bar," "high standard of professional competence" and "efficiency and improvement of the judicial system[.]"

and to remove Kentucky's economic disadvantages in competing with neighboring states. Additionally, and even though not required, the proponents of the Act tendered empirical evidence to support the claimed benefits.

One does not need an advanced degree in labor economics to recognize that employers might be attracted to locate in a state where wages are lower as opposed to a state where wages are higher. To the extent this conclusion might be characterized as speculative, it is undoubtedly rational. The legislature can clearly make a policy decision that the Act might result in more jobs, albeit at lower wages, and that this result, in turn, might benefit the overall economic climate of Kentucky. In fact, this result is supported by some of the economic studies noted by the Unions. *See* Robert Bruno, Affidavit at 5 (stating that some studies suggest right to work laws increase manufacturing employment, while other studies find no effect). All the while, of course, for any given workplace, the majority of workers retain the federally-protected right to organize.

The Act does not violate the equal protection provisions of the Kentucky Constitution. We are unable to say the legislature's "classification is so arbitrary and capricious as to be hostile, oppressive and utterly devoid of rational basis." *Delta Air Lines*, 689 S.W.2d at 19. To the extent the Unions claim they will be prohibited from collecting a fee for legally-protected, legally authorized services, that claim is addressed, *infra*, in our discussion on *Taking for Public Purpose without Just Compensation.*

As to the Unions' claim that the Act impairs their freedom to contract, Kentucky law has long recognized that the police power, based on "the general welfare of the community," may validly infringe on the right to contract. *City of Covington v. Sanitation Dist. No. 1*, 301 S.W.2d 885, 888 (Ky. 1957). "The exercise of such a power must be reasonable and in conformity with the necessity of the case and have a substantial basis for the action." *Id.* at 889. Based on our previous discussion concerning the legislature's stated reasons for enacting the Act, we hold that its enactment satisfies this test.

B. Special Legislation.

The Unions claim the Act constitutes special legislation in violation of Sections 59 and 60 of the Kentucky Constitution. Specifically, Section 59 states: "[t]he General Assembly shall not pass local or special acts concerning any of the following subjects, or for any of the following purposes, namely: ... Twenty-fourth: To regulate labor, trade, mining or manufacturing." The purpose of this section is not to prevent the legislature from enacting any laws concerning labor, trade, mining or manufacturing. That would be absurd.[19] Rather, the intent is for any acts touching these subjects be general acts. *See, e.g., Waggoner*, 846 S.W.2d at 706–07 (stating "[t]he fact that the [legislature] deals with

19. If the meaning were to prohibit all laws addressing these subjects, then entire Titles of the Kentucky Revised Statutes would be void. *E.g.*, KRS Title XXVII: Labor and Human Rights; KRS Title XXVII: Mines and Minerals; KRS Title XXIX: Commerce and Trade. Examples of Chapters within these titles are KRS Chapter 341, Unemployment Compensation; KRS Chapter 350, Surface Coal Mining; and KRS Chapter 355, Uniform Commercial Code.

a special subject does not *per se* make it special legislation[ ]"); *D.E. Hewitt Lumber Co. v. Brumfield*, 196 Ky. 723, 727, 245 S.W. 858, 860 (1922) (holding that §59 "inhibitions apply only to local and special legislation, and therefore do not apply here unless the [Workers'] Compensation Act is either a local or a special act[ ]"). Furthermore, we note the purpose of these sections is to "prevent special privileges, favoritism, and discrimination, and to ensure equality under the law ... [and to] prevent the enactment of laws that do not operate alike on all individuals and corporations." *Louisville/Jefferson Cnty. Metro Gov't v. O'Shea-Baxter, LLC*, 438 S.W.3d 379, 383 (Ky. 2014) (quotations and citations omitted).

Special legislation is defined as arbitrary and irrational legislation that favors the economic self-interest of the one or the few over that of the many. *Yeoman*, 983 S.W.2d at 468. "Local" or "special" legislation applies exclusively to special or particular places, or special and particular persons, and is distinguished from a statute intended to be general in its operation, and that relates to classes of persons or subjects. More specifically, "[a] 'local law' is one whose operation is confined within territorial limits other than those of the whole state, or any properly constituted class or locality therein." *Ravitz v. Steurele*, 257 Ky. 108, 115, 77 S.W.2d 360, 364 (1934). Here, the Act is clearly not a local act because its application is statewide.

In *Johnson v. Commonwealth ex rel. Meredith*, our predecessor court noted a clear distinction between a general and a special law, stating "'[a] statute which relates to persons or things as a class is a general law, while a statute which relates to particular persons or things *of a class* is special.'" 291 Ky. at 837, 165 S.W.2d at 825 (quoting *State ex rel v. Tolle*, 71 Mo. 645, 650 (1880)); *see also Ravitz*, 257 Ky. 108, 77 S.W.2d 360; *Stevenson v. Hardin*, 238 Ky. 600, 603, 38 S.W.2d 462, 463–64 (1931) (law excepting party nominations from mandatory primary held to be general law as applying to all statewide officers—"general in its application and applies in an equal manner to all persons similarly situated"). In *Johnson*, the issue concerned the authorization of all executive departments of the state to employ a certain class of professional assistants. The court opined that it "can conceive nothing more foreign to special legislation" than this statute. 291 Ky. at 837, 165 S.W.2d at 825.

Our case law has long recognized a simple, two-part test for determining whether a law constitutes general legislation in its constitutional sense: (1) equal application to all in a class, and (2) distinctive and natural reasons inducing and supporting the classification. *Yeoman*, 983 S.W.2d at 466; *Waggoner*, 846 S.W.2d at 707; *Schoo v. Rose*, 270 S.W.2d 940 (Ky. 1954); *Droege v. McInerney*, 120 Ky. 796, 87 S.W. 1085 (1905); *Safety Bldg. & Loan Co. v. Ecklar*, 106 Ky. 115, 50 S.W. 50 (1899); *see also Burrow v. Kapfhammer*, 284 Ky. 753, 761–62, 145 S.W.2d 1067, 1072 (1940) (holding unconstitutional hour and wages law which applied to restaurants employing waiters, but not to hotel dining room waiters).

Frankly, the Act applies to all collective bargaining agreements entered into on or after January 9, 2017, with the exception of certain employees covered or exempted by federal law. KRS 336.132. With the exceptions required by federal law, it applies to all employers and all employees, both public and private. It does not single out any particular union, industry or employer. It applies statewide. We have previously rejected constitutional challenges to legislation that purportedly promoted or harmed organized labor as claimed special legislation, so long as a rational basis existed for the statute. *See Hamilton*, 262 S.W.2d at 700. And in *Waggoner*, we stated "[t]he responsibility of this Court is to draw all reasonable inferences and implications from the act as a whole and thereby sustain its validity." 846 S.W.2d at 707 (citing *Graham v. Mills*, 694 S.W.2d 698 (Ky. 1985)). In *Tabler*, we required that "a substantial and justifiable reason [must appear] from legislative history, from the statute's title, preamble or subject matter, or from some other authoritative source." 704 S.W.2d at 186. The legislature clearly established a rational basis for the Act: to promote economic development, to promote job growth, and to remove Kentucky's economic disadvantages in competing with neighboring states. As noted above, testimony supporting the legislation was presented at House committee hearings in January 2017. The Unions and Union *Amicae*, as noted, disagree, but we are unable to say that the legislature's rationale is unreasonable.[20]

* * *

V. Conclusion.

Based on the foregoing reasons, we hold that the Unions' constitutional challenges to the Act are without merit. In this area of economic legislation, the legislature and the executive branch make the policy, not the courts. Long ago, in an opinion upholding a provision of the Railway Labor Act that authorized a union shop agreement notwithstanding a state's right-to-work law, Justice William O. Douglas aptly wrote, "[m]uch might be said pro and con if the policy issue were before us." *Ry. Emps. Dep't v. Hanson*, 351 U.S. 225, 233, 76 S.Ct. 714, 719, 100 L.Ed. 1112 (1956). But, he continued,

> the question is one of policy with which the judiciary has no concern.... [The legislature], acting within its constitutional powers, has the final say on policy issues. If it acts unwisely, the electorate can make a change. The task of the judiciary ends once it appears that the legislative measure adopted is relevant or appropriate to the constitutional power which [the legislature] exercises.

Id. at 234, 76 S.Ct. at 719 (emphasis added). * * * We therefore AFFIRM the Franklin Circuit Court's Order dismissing the complaint.

* * *

20. The concurring in part/dissenting in part opinion seems to suggest that any time the legislature seeks to alter any policy yet grandfather pre-existing rights, duties or obligations, then the resulting legislation is constitutionally infirm under Sections 59 and 60. Such analysis ignores the longstanding case law cited in this opinion that establishes the two-part test for analyzing legislation under a special legislation challenge, and would severely hinder any legislative effort to effect change in socio-economic policy.

Notes and Questions

1. The Court in *Zuckerman* analyzed the equal protection issue under Sections 1, 2, and 3 of the Kentucky Constitution because the Plaintiffs had not asserted any claims under the Fourteenth Amendment. How does the equal protection analysis differ, if at all, under the Federal and State Constitutions?
2. Is there a basis in the text of Sections 1, 2, and 3 for application of the three tiers of scrutiny for equal protection claims?
3. Congress often passes laws that apply only to particular states or persons, or to particular industries. What problems can arise when such "local or special acts" are enacted? Why did the framers of the Kentucky Constitution seek to prevent such laws?
4. In "special legislation" cases, the outcome often may hinge upon how the "classification" is defined. In *Zuckerman*, the majority defined the classification as "all collective bargaining agreements." Could the classification have been drawn differently? How might the outcome of the case have changed if the classification was different?

Calloway County Sheriff's Department v. Woodall

Supreme Court of Kentucky (2020)

607 S.W.3d 557

Opinion of the Court by Justice VanMeter.

KRS[1] Chapter 342.750 provides certain income benefits to an employee's family when an employee dies as a result of a workplace accident. In addition, if the death occurs within four years of the injury, the employee's estate is entitled to a $50,000 lump-sum payment. In this case, ten years after a workplace injury, Steven Spillman died as a result of surgery necessitated by that injury. The issues we address in this opinion are whether Karen Woodall, Spillman's surviving spouse, is entitled to a statutory income benefit and whether the time limitation as to the lump-sum benefit violates the federal and Kentucky constitutional guarantees of equal protection and Kentucky's prohibition against special legislation. We hold that Woodall is entitled to the income benefit and that the time limitation does not violate the constitutional provisions. We therefore affirm the Court of Appeals' opinion affirming the Workers' Compensation Board ("Board").

I. Factual and Procedural Background.

Spillman was working for the Calloway County Sheriff's Department ("the Department") on March 4, 2007, when he was involved in a serious motor vehicle accident.

1. Kentucky Revised Statutes.

In 2010, Spillman was awarded permanent partial disability ("PPD") benefits dating to June 2007. The case was re-opened in 2013, and in October of that year, he was awarded increased PPD benefits for the remainder of the 425 weeks that he was entitled to those benefits. In January 2017, Spillman underwent surgery for his work-related injury. Unfortunately, he developed a pulmonary embolism following surgery and died on January 17, 2017.

At all times relevant to this matter, Spillman and Woodall were married. Following Spillman's death, Woodall and Jennifer Nelson, Spillman's daughter, were named co-administrators of Spillman's estate.[2] Woodall, in her individual capacity as Spillman's spouse, and the Estate filed a motion to re-open Spillman's workers' compensation claim. Woodall sought income benefits under KRS 342.750(1)(a) while the Estate sought a lump-sum benefit under KRS 342.750(6).

The ALJ denied all benefits, finding that they were time barred, and dismissed the claims. The Board found that Woodall was eligible for the surviving spouse income benefits under KRS 342.750(1)(a), but that the Estate was not entitled to the lump-sum death benefit. The Court of Appeals affirmed the Board on both issues. Both parties have appealed to this Court.

II. Standard of Review.

When reviewing workers' compensation cases, we review questions of law de novo. *Saint Joseph Hosp. v. Frye*, 415 S.W.3d 631, 632 (Ky. 2013). In this case, the facts are undisputed and all issues under review are legal issues. Therefore, we engage in a de novo review.

III. Analysis.

* * *

B. KRS 342.750(6) Lump-Sum Death Benefit.

The final issue we must address is whether the four-year limitation on lump-sum benefits under KRS 342.750(6) is constitutional. That statute provides, in pertinent part,

> [I]f death occurs within four (4) years of the date of injury as a direct result of a work-related injury, a lump-sum payment of fifty thousand dollars ($50,000) shall be made to the deceased's estate, from which the cost of burial and cost of transportation of the body to the employee's place of residence shall be paid.

The Estate argues that this time limitation violates the 14th Amendment to the United States Constitution and sections 1, 2, 3, 59, and 60 of the Kentucky Constitution. Specifically, it argues that the time limitation violates the constitutions' guarantee of equal protection of the law and the Kentucky Constitution's prohibition against special legislation.

---

2. We refer to Woodall and Nelson in their capacities as co-administrators of the Estate of Steven Spillman collectively as the "Estate."

1. Equal Protection.

Our equal protection guarantees, both under the federal and state constitutions, seek to "keep[ ] governmental decision makers from treating differently persons who are in all relevant respects alike." *Vision Mining, Inc. v. Gardner*, 364 S.W.3d 455, 465 (Ky. 2011) (quoting *Nordlinger v. Hahn*, 505 U.S. 1, 10, 112 S.Ct. 2326, 120 L.Ed.2d 1 (1992)) (internal quotation marks omitted). Classifications are not per se unconstitutional, however. *Vision Mining*, 364 S.W.3d at 465. Rather, classifications are subject to different levels of judicial review based on their content. *Id.* The highest level of review, "strict scrutiny," applies when a classification affects a fundamental right or suspect classification, such as race, alienage or ancestry. *Steven Lee Enters. v. Varney*, 36 S.W.3d 391, 394 (Ky. 2000). An intermediate level of review, "heightened scrutiny," applies to classifications such as gender or illegitimacy. *Id.* The lowest level of review, "rational basis," applies to statutes that merely affect only social or economic policy. *Teco/Perry Cty. Coal v. Feltner*, 582 S.W.3d 42, 46 (Ky. 2019); *Zuckerman v. Bevin*, 565 S.W.3d 580, 595 (Ky. 2018); *Varney*, 36 S.W.3d at 394–95.

Kentucky courts have long held that "[w]orkers' compensation statutes concern matters of social and economic policy." *Feltner*, 582 S.W.3d at 46 (citing *Cain v. Lodestar Energy, Inc.*, 302 S.W.3d 39, 42 (Ky. 2009)). As a result, most classifications created within our workers' compensation statutes only need satisfy rational basis review.[3] Thus, to comply with federal equal protection requirements, the classification must be rationally related to a legitimate state interest, and to comply with Kentucky's equal protection requirements, the classification must be supported by a "reasonable basis" or a "substantial and justifiable reason." *Id.* (citing *Cain*, 302 S.W.3d at 42–43). In fact, "[a] person challenging a law upon equal protection grounds under the rational basis test has a very difficult task because a law must be upheld if ... any reasonably conceivable state of facts ... could provide a rational basis for the classification." *Commonwealth ex rel. Stumbo v. Crutchfield*, 157 S.W.3d 621, 624 (Ky. 2005) (citing *United States R.R. Ret. Bd. v. Fritz*, 449 U.S. 166, 178–79, 101 S. Ct. 453, 461, 66 L.Ed.2d 368 (1980)). Furthermore, "the General Assembly need not articulate its reasons for enacting the statute, and this is particularly true where the legislature must necessarily engage in a process of line drawing." *Id.* (citing *Fritz*, 449 U.S. at 179, 101 S. Ct. at 461). Accordingly, "[o]ur General Assembly, under the Equal Protection Clause, has great latitude to enact legislation that may appear to affect similarly situated people differently." *Id.* (citation omitted).

In the present case, Woodall argues that the time restriction in KRS 342.750(6) treats the estates of injured workers who die more than four years after their injuries differently than it treats the estates of workers who die within four years after their injuries, without a rational basis for doing so. The Court of Appeals rejected this argument. It held instead that the time limitation "serves to bar stale claims, which provides stability and foreseeability to claimants and employers alike, thereby promoting the overall

3. Obviously, if a classification within these statutes were to be based on a protected class, then a higher level of review would apply. That is not the case here.

viability of the workers' compensation system." * * * With these arguments in mind, we now consider whether the time limitation contained within KRS 342.750(6) denies equal protection of the laws to those workers who die from a work-related injury more than four years after the date of the injury.

* * *

That noted, this Court has held on multiple occasions that "no constitutional impediment [exists] to repose provisions in the workers' compensation scheme." *Wright v. Oberle-Jordre Co.*, 910 S.W.2d 241, 245 (Ky. 1995); *see also Nygaard v. Goodin Bros., Inc.*, 107 S.W.3d 190, 192 (Ky. 2003) (holding legislature is not constrained in including statutes of repose in statutory causes of action such as workers' compensation); *William A. Pope Co. v. Howard*, 851 S.W.2d 460, 463 (Ky. 1993) (stating "[w]e have not been persuaded that there is any constitutional prohibition against the enactment of repose provisions within the Workers' Compensation Act[ ]").[4]

The Estate cites this Court's decisions in *Vision Mining, Inc. v. Gardner* and *Parker v. Webster Cty. Coal, LLC*, 529 S.W.3d 759, 770 (Ky. 2017), both of which invalidated statutory classifications within KRS Chapter 342 on equal protection grounds. Neither case, however, involved time limitations contained within the statutory scheme and do not, therefore, compel the Estate's argued result. In this case, the four-year limit applies equally to all injured workers. Substantial and justifiable reasons support this classification and the classification is rationally related to a legitimate government purpose.

Employers are entitled to rely on repose provisions, "freeing them from any liability for compensation after the passage of" the repose period. *Wright*, 910 S.W.2d at 245. Here, we are similarly persuaded that employers are entitled to rely on the repose provision of KRS 342.750(6). We agree that doing so bars stale claims, permits assessment of risk, and spreads costs within the workers' compensation system.

We therefore hold that the time limitation in KRS 342.750(6) satisfies both state and federal equal protection guarantees.

2. Special Legislation.

Finally, but no less importantly, we turn to the Kentucky Constitution's prohibition on special legislation. For too long this Court has misconstrued the proper analysis for the special legislation prohibition contained within Kentucky Constitution Section 59, and conflated its meaning with Kentucky Constitution Section 3's prohibition on "exclusive, separate public emoluments or privileges[,]" the basis of Kentucky's guarantee of equal protection. Such interpretation does not comport with a proper interpretation of these sections as understood in 1891.

In analyzing claims under Section 59, this Court for over 65 years has seen fit to apply the test set out in *Schoo v. Rose*, 270 S.W.2d 940 (Ky. 1954),[5] which stated "in

---

4. By contrast, constitutional rights may be implicated in the abolition of common law rights of action. *See, e.g.*, *Saylor v. Hall*, 497 S.W.2d 218, 225 (Ky. 1973) (holding that statute of repose in KRS 413.135 violates Sections 14, 54, and 214 of the Kentucky Constitution).

5. Or a case which cited to *Schoo* as authority.

order for a law to be general in its constitutional sense it must meet the following requirements: (1) [i]t must apply equally to all in a class, and (2) there must be distinctive and natural reasons inducing and supporting the classification." *Id.* at 941. However, *Schoo*'s foundation is based on cases interpreting the federal Equal Protection clause or Section 3, *not* Section 59's prohibition on special legislation.[6] *See Safety Bldg. & Loan Co. v. Ecklar*, 106 Ky. 115, 50 S.W. 50 (1899), *overruled in part by Linton v. Fulton Bldg. & Loan Ass'n*, 262 Ky. 198, 90 S.W.2d 22 (1936). In fact, the *Schoo* test comes straight from *Ecklar*: "the true test whether a law is a general one, in the constitutional sense, is not alone that **it applies equally to all in a class**—though that is also necessary—but, in addition, **there must be distinctive and natural reasons inducing and supporting the classification**." 106 Ky. at 121–22, 50 S.W. at 51 (emphasis added). Other cases decided contemporaneously with or prior to *Ecklar* use the same or similar language as *Ecklar* in interpreting Section 3 or Section 3's predecessor provision in the 1850 Constitution, Art. XIII, §1. *See, e.g., Commonwealth v. Remington Typewriter Co.*, 127 Ky. 177, 105 S.W. 399, 402–03 (1907); *Simpson v. Kentucky Citizens' Bldg. & Loan Ass'n*, 101 Ky. 496, 41 S.W. 570 (1897), *overruled in part by Linton*, 262 Ky. 198, 90 S.W.2d 22; *Schoolcraft's Adm'r v. Louisville & Nashville R.R.*, 92 Ky. 233, 238, 17 S.W. 567, 568 (1891); *Kentucky Trust Co. v. Lewis*, 82 Ky. 579, 583–84 (1885); *Smith v. Warden*, 80 Ky. 608, 611 (1883); *Gordon v. Winchester Bldg. & Accumulating Fund Ass'n*, 75 Ky. 110, 113–14 1876. In these earlier decisions, our predecessor court addressed claims of partial/class legislation under Kentucky's equal protection guarantee, *i.e.*, the state constitution's prohibition on "exclusive, separate privilege." Ky. Const. §3; Ky. Const. of 1850, Art. XIII, §1.

The original test for a violation of Section 59's prohibition on special and local legislation was simply "special legislation applies to particular places or persons as distinguished from classes of places or persons." *Greene v. Caldwell*, 170 Ky. 571, 587,

---

6. The court in *Schoo* included a citation to *Droege v. McInerney*, 120 Ky. 796, 87 S.W. 1085, 1085 (1905). *Droege* involved a local statute concerning county election boards in counties containing second class cities. With respect to local acts, the 1891 Constitution permitted the legislature to classify cities. Ky. Const. §156. Such a classification, however, had to relate to "the purpose of organization and government[;]" otherwise, it was an unconstitutional local law. *See Richardson v. Mehler*, 111 Ky. 408, 63 S.W. 957, 962 (1901) (noting that §156, with regard to municipalities, is an exception to §59, and that "the classification of cities authorized by the constitution ... is confined to legislation for purposes of municipal government only, and that legislation relating to matters not under municipal control, or affecting the municipal government, is unconstitutional[ ]"); *see also City of Louisville v. Kuntz*, 104 Ky. 584, 47 S.W. 592, 593 (1898). *Droege*, *Richardson*, *Kuntz*, and similar cases involving local laws are thus properly viewed as interpretations of §156. We note, of course, that §156 has been amended and replaced with §156a and §156b. We refrain from any interpretation of these amended sections since this case does not involve a local law. We do, however, note that, like its predecessor, §156a permits classification of cities.

Klein v. City of Louisville, 224 Ky. 624, 6 S.W.2d 1104 (1928), cited by the concurring opinion, involved numerous state constitutional challenges to authorizing cities of the first class to construct and operate bridges across navigable streams constituting a state boundary. As concerns §§59 and 156, the act in question related to the classification of cities as permitted by Ky. Const. §156. In rejecting this challenge, the court noted that "if the act is within the purview of [§156] the provisions of section 59 do not apply to it." 224 Ky. at 629, 6 S.W.2d at 1106. *Klein*, thus, supports the foregoing analysis of the interplay of §§59 and 156.

186 S.W. 648, 654 (1916); *see also Singleton v. Commonwealth*, 164 Ky. 243, 175 S.W. 372, 373 (1915) (holding "[l]ocal or special legislation, according to the well-known meaning of the words, applies exclusively to special or particular places, or special and particular persons, and is distinguished from a statute intended to be general in its operation and that relating to classes of persons or subjects[ ]") (quoting *Stone v. Wilson*, 19 Ky. L. Rptr. 126, 39 S.W. 49, 50 (1897), *overruled on other grounds by Vaughn v. Knopf*, 895 S.W.2d 566 (Ky. 1995));[7] *Commonwealth v. E. H. Taylor, Jr. Co.*, 101 Ky. 325, 41 S.W. 11, 15 (1897) (holding that a whiskey tax did not constitute special legislation because "[i]t cannot be contended that this law applies alone to the [distiller], or to Franklin County, or to the Seventh congressional district. It operates upon a multitude of property of like character, owned by persons all over the state, and ... is neither local nor special, but general[ ]").[8]

After the decision in *Greene*, however, and with the passage of time, the clear distinction between special/local laws and partial/class laws became muddled. The reason for the muddling would seem to be that partial/class legislation was short-handedly referred to as "special legislation." Presumably, as lawyers and judges looked to apply the constitution and case law to various statutes and situations, they quite obviously saw a constitutional section, Section 59, which addressed "local and special" legislation and read case law that applied, erroneously, a classification test to it. In a few cases addressing claims of Section 59 violations, the court might include citation to *Singleton* or *Stone*, but invariably, in the same paragraph, cite *Ecklar* and *Remington Typewriter* originally decided under Section 3. *E.g.*, *Markendorf v. Friedman*, 280 Ky. 484, 133 S.W.2d 516 (1939); *Lakes v. Goodloe*, 195 Ky. 240, 242 S.W. 632 (1922). The effect was to equate special/local legislation with class legislation.

The result has been that our analysis of two constitutional sections, that proceed from different constitutional eras with different purposes,[9] essentially apply the same

---

7. Significantly, Judge John Carroll—who authored *Greene*, *Singleton* and *Remington Typewriter*—was a delegate to the 1890–91 Constitutional Convention. His analysis of §§3's and 59's meanings and purposes is more reflective of the delegates' original understanding than one developed decades after the fact.

8. In *Zuckerman*, we purported to apply the *Schoo* test, but we noted "[f]rankly, the Act applies to all collective bargaining agreements entered into on or after January 9, 2017.... With the exceptions required by federal law, it applies to all employers and all employees, both public and private. It does not single out any particular union, industry or employer. It applies statewide." 565 S.W.3d at 600. This conclusion is consistent with the original §59 analysis.

9. The constitutional prohibition against "exclusive, separate" privilege has been included in all four Kentucky Constitutions, beginning with the Commonwealth's 1792 founding. Ky. Const. of 1792, Art. XII, §1; *see also* Ky. Const. of 1799, Art. X, §1. The section, however, has an even earlier origin, the 1776 Virginia Declaration of Rights, section 4, providing "[t]hat no man, or set of men, are entitled to exclusive or separate emoluments or privileges from the community, but in consideration of public services; which, not being descendible, neither ought the offices of magistrate, legislator, or judge to be hereditary." Drafted by George Mason, this provision asserted the equality of all citizens and rejected ideas of privileged political classes or hereditary offices. Before the Civil War, most state courts ascribed equal protection to their state constitutions' "exclusive, separate" privilege clause to prohibit partial or special laws. *See* Melissa L. Saunders, *Equal Protection, Class Legislation, and Colorblindness*,

analysis. For example, in *Waggoner v. Waggoner*, 846 S.W.2d 704 (Ky. 1992), this Court stated that a statute passes muster under Section 59 if the classification is "based upon reasonable and natural distinctions that relate logically to the purpose of the Act." *Id.* at 707. Similarly, it will be upheld under the federal and state equal protection clauses "if its classification is not arbitrary, or if it is founded upon any substantial distinction suggesting the necessity, or propriety, of such legislation." *Id.* at 708. Thus, the tests seem to be a difference without a distinction. This makes little sense. The reason is that the currently applied test for Section 59, the *Schoo* test, originated with equal protection cases interpreting a different constitutional section, namely Section 3's prohibition on "exclusive, separate" privileges.

We are mindful of the doctrine of stare decisis "which simply suggests that we stand by precedents and not disturb settled points of law. Yet, this rule is not inflexible, nor is it of such a nature as to require perpetuation of error or illogic." *D & W Auto Supply v. Dep't of Revenue*, 602 S.W.2d 420, 424 (Ky. 1980).

The problem with applying an equal protection analysis to the special legislation prohibition is that over the last 30 years, it has been cited to enhance Kentucky's equal protection provisions. *See, e.g., Elk Horn Coal Corp. v. Cheyenne Res., Inc.*, 163 S.W.3d 408, 418 (Ky. 2005); *Commonwealth v. Wasson*, 842 S.W.2d 487 (Ky. 1992); *Perkins v. N.E. Log Homes*, 808 S.W.2d 809 (Ky. 1991); *Tabler v. Wallace*, 704 S.W.2d 179 (Ky. 1986). In *Elk Horn Coal*, this Court stated:

> [T]he equal protection provisions of the Kentucky Constitution are enhanced by Section [*sic*] 59 and 60....
>
> Because of this additional protection, **we have elected at times** to apply a guarantee of individual rights in equal protection cases that is higher than the minimum guaranteed by the Federal Constitution. Instead of requiring a "rational basis," we have construed our Constitution as requiring a "reasonable basis" or a "substantial and justifiable reason" for discriminatory legislation in areas of social and economic policy. **Cases applying the heightened standard are limited to the particular facts of those cases.**

163 S.W.3d at 418–19 (emphasis added) (citations and footnotes omitted). The highlighted portions of this quotation point out the problem. No one knows or can possibly know when a given statute will strike any judge, or four justices of this court,

96 Mich. L. Rev. 245, 251–68 (1997) (discussing antebellum court decisions striking down partial or special laws that singled out individuals for special benefits or burdens). Our predecessor court's 1876 decision in *Gordon*, however, was the first Kentucky case to apply the prohibition directly and hold an act unconstitutional. *See Barbour v. Louisville Bd. of Trade*, 82 Ky. 645, 650 (1885) (noting *Gordon* as the "first case in which the meaning of this provision arose and was decided, without division[ ]"). Professor Saunders also connected the antebellum prohibition of "exclusive, separate" privilege with the adoption of 14th Amendment's equal protection clause. Saunders, *supra*, at 285–93. The similar treatment of claims under the 14th Amendment's equal protection clause and Kentucky's Section 3 are, thus, unsurprising.

By contrast, §§59 and 60 first appear in the 1891 Constitution, and, as discussed *infra*, were designed to rectify the inefficiency that characterized postbellum legislative sessions.

as worthy of the heightened standard. This unfettered discretion is unworthy of any legal system.

This Court's decision in *Tabler* is the genesis of the heightened standard analysis of Section 59. To be clear, the *Tabler* court did not create the muddle of conflating Sections 3 and 59's analysis. That process had begun long before. The *Tabler* court did, however, imbue Section 59 with an inappropriate purpose by relating a historical narrative of the 1880's and the 1890–91 Constitutional Convention that is overly simplistic and misleading. According to *Tabler*, this era was one dominated by corporations and railroads and their lobbyists running roughshod over an especially malleable and corrupt legislature. *See Tabler*, 704 S.W.2d at 183 (stating "[u]nbridled legislative power had become the captive of special interest groups. Concern for limiting the powers of the legislature in general, and with cutting off special and local legislation in particular, was the primary motivating force behind enactment of the new Kentucky Constitution of 1891[.]") And the call for the Constitutional Convention only passed because the people "rose up" in reaction. *See id.* at 186 (noting that due to a growing number of lawsuits "railroads and others had sought and obtained special privileges from the General Assembly during the 1880's and thus precipitated a constitutional convention[ ]").

This narrative ignores a number of salient facts. First, the idea that the legislature was controlled by the railroads or other corporations is demonstrably false. Although the legislature had chartered nearly 300 railroads, most never came into operation. In 1885, three railroads owned or controlled 80% of statewide trackage: the Louisville & Nashville, the Chesapeake & Ohio, and the Cincinnati Southern. 6th Ann'l Rep't of the Railroad Commissioners of Kentucky 5–6 (1886). While the L&N in particular was, no doubt, a ruthless competitor and a source of ire to many Kentuckians, neither it nor the other two railroads controlled the legislature. These three fought the Railroad Commission relentlessly after its establishment in 1880, unsuccessfully lobbied for its repeal in every legislative session from 1882 to 1890, 12th Ann'l Rep't of the Railroad Commissioners of Kentucky 6 (1891), and unsuccessfully fought its increased taxation of railroad property. *Cincinnati, New Orleans & Tex. Pac. R.R. v. Commonwealth*, 81 Ky. 492 (1883), *aff'd* 115 U.S. 321, 6 S.Ct. 57, 29 L.Ed. 414 (1885).[10]

---

10. Other instances of the legislature not responding to corporate/railroad interest exist. In 1876, it elected James Beck to the United States Senate over Preston Leslie, the L&N's preferred candidate. Thomas D. Clark, *A History of Kentucky* 422 (6th ed., 1988). Over two legislative sessions, 1876 and 1878, it reduced the permitted rate of interest from ten percent to six percent, notwithstanding opposition by commercial and financial interests. Edward F. Pritchard, Jr., "Popular Political Movements in Kentucky 1875–1900," 41–43 (1935). And, in 1886, the legislature enacted the Hewitt Tax Law eliminating many tax exemptions and increasing by $90,000,000 the assessed value of all Kentucky property. *Id.* at 96–97.

One act sometimes cited to prove railroad domination of the legislature was the 1884 law to exempt new railroad facilities from taxation for period of five years from the start of construction. Act of May ___, 1884, ch. 1632, 1883 Ky. Acts 1:135. That argument certainly exists, but countervailing arguments can be made. The originally proposed bill contained a ten-year exemption, which was amended to five years. S.J. 1036 (Ky. 1883). Would not a controlling railroad lobby have gotten the ten-year exemption? And a better law for the railroads would have been exemption from taxation for five years "after completion," as opposed to "from the start of construction." Additionally, the exemption would encourage

Second, the legislature did not exempt railroads from tort liability. The opposite is true. In 1854, it enacted an early wrongful death statute, providing a cause of action for death due to a railroad's negligence, and also providing for loss or damage to property. Stanton, 2 Rev. Stat. 510 §1 (Ky. 1860). This statute was in effect throughout the postbellum period and into the 20th century. The L&N's challenge under the 1850 Constitution, alleging a violation of Article XIII, Section 1's prohibition on exclusive, separate privilege, was rejected by our predecessor court in 1891. *Schoolcraft's Adm'r*, 92 Ky. 233, 17 S.W. 567.

Third, legislative dysfunction in enacting so much special legislation was a result more of constituent demand, than of corporate or railroad lobbying. Gubernatorial addresses and contemporary newspapers articles so confirm. *See, e.g.*, H.J. 44, 72 (Ky. 1875) (address of Gov. James B. McCreary, noting time spent during legislative sessions on local and private bills); H.J. 8, 28 (Ky. 1869) (address of Gov. John W. Stevenson "call[ing] attention to the increasing legislation on local and individual interests[ ]"); "Stop Local Legislation," *Hickman Courier*, Oct. 2, 1885, at 5) (quoting *Louisville Commercial*) (noting "[t]he members excused their neglect of general legislation with the plea that their constituents demanded attention to their local bills[ ]"); *Owensboro Messenger*, Mar. 14, 1882, at 2 (stating "[t]he complaint that the Legislature occupies its time with local bills is general ...; but we dare say the members act in accordance with the wishes of their constituents in giving local measures precedence[ ]"); "Local Legislation," *Courier-Journal* (Louisville), May 26, 1873, at 2 (opining that "the people of the State are themselves, in great measure, responsible for the vast number of local and private measures that have been the curse of Kentucky legislation[ ]"); *see also* Robert M. Ireland, *Little Kingdoms: The Counties of Kentucky*, 1850–1891, 8–17 (1977) (detailing many local acts and the inefficiency caused by their proliferation).[11] Professor J. Willard Hurst, the preeminent American legal historian,[12] opined that the case against special legislation "came to be [the] undue drain on the time of legislatures." James Willard Hurst, *Law and the Conditions of Freedom in the Nineteenth Century United States* 17 (1984). In other words, contemporary sources and legal historians demonstrate that the main problem with local and special legislation was the resulting

---

construction of new railroads to underserved areas. *See* Carl B. Boyd, Jr., *Local Aid to Railroads in Central Kentucky: 1850–1891*, 62 Reg. Ky. St. Hist. Soc'y 4, 10–13 (1964) (noting demand for railroad construction came from local communities).

11. Prof. Ireland noted the connection between county government and special and local legislation, stating "[w]hile some argued that local legislation increased the power of the legislature over the counties, the reverse was often true[,]" since legislators were "besieged" with demands for local and special bills. Ireland, *Little Kingdoms* at 10. From this perspective, §59 is seen more as a limitation on county and municipal government. This view makes much sense when one considers that in the Kentucky session laws from 1865 to 1890, approximately 50% of all acts related to municipal or county matters: incorporating a town or amending its charter, changing court times, adjusting court jurisdiction, authorizing issuance of bonds, providing for school matters, declaring a stream navigable, regulating fishing on a given stream, and on and on.

12. Kermit L. Hall, *American Legal History as Science and Applied Politics*, 4 Benchmark 229, 232 (1990) (describing Prof. Hurst as the dean of American legal historians").

legislative inefficiency and wasted time, as opposed to the corrupt, rent-seeking motive ascribed by the *Tabler* court. The simple test set forth by our predecessor court evinces a purpose to the special legislation prohibition that is rooted in legislative efficiency, i.e., to put an end to the interminable legislative sessions of the 1870s and 1880s and the proliferation of special and local laws that predominated the Kentucky session laws before 1891. The vast majority of these laws addressed exceedingly mundane and trivial matters unworthy of state legislative consideration.

As to why the people finally voted for the call of the 1890–91 Constitutional Convention, additional facts need mentioning.[13] The Third Constitution contained barriers to its alteration. Individual amendments were not permitted, and change could only be made by a constitutional convention called by the affirmative vote by a majority of all citizens entitled to vote at two successive biennial elections. Ky. Const. of 1850, Art. XII, §1. This electoral procedure was especially onerous to satisfy, and calls failed in 1875, 1879, 1883, and 1885. The requisite majority was only obtained when the legislature provided "those who came to vote could be considered as the total entitled to vote for representatives." Hambleton Tapp & James C. Klotter, *Kentucky: Decades of Discord* 1865–1890, 259 (1977). The legislature had, thus, been trying to call a convention for 15 years, and only with legislative sleight of hand was the call able to succeed.

Next, special legislation was not the only pressing need requiring redress in the 1890–91 Constitutional Convention. Contemporary newspapers advocating an affirmative vote for the call gave several reasons: rid the 1850 constitution's references to slavery, provide a means of amendment, replace voice voting with vote by ballot, restrict municipalities and counties as to indebtedness and taxation, reform the jury system, provide term limits for officers, reform the court system, as well as limiting special and local legislation. *E.g.*, "The Constitutional Convention," *Evening Bulletin* (Maysville), July 12, 1889, at 2; "A Constitutional Convention, *Twice-A-week Messenger* (Owensboro), July 25, 1889, at 4. Contrary to the *Tabler* court's assertion as to the cause of the Convention,[14] the delegates themselves also gave varied reasons as to the primary cause: enforcement of criminal laws, Del. Thomas S. Pettit, 1890–91 Const. Debates at 4680–81, Del. J. F. Montgomery, *id.* at 4041, and Del. Laban T. Moore, *id.* at 4170; judicial reform, Del. Francis A. Hopkins, *id.* at 1684; suppression of pools, trusts and combinations, Del. L. W. Lassing, *id.* at 3784; adoption of ballot voting and aid to common schools, Del. William Beckner, *Courier-Journal* (Louisville), June 15, 1890, at 13.

13. As an aside, pontificating on the electoral motives of large number of voters would appear to be the height of judicial hubris. Over 160,000 voters in 1887 and over 180,000 voters in 1889 approved the convention call. *See* "23,403 Majority: The Official Report of the Vote of the State for Calling a Constitutional Convention," *Courier-Journal* (Louisville), Aug. 22, 1887, at 5; "For the Constitution: The Results of the Election Held Last August Finally Made Known," *Courier-Journal* (Louisville), Sept. 26, 1889, at 5.

14. In *Tabler*, Justice Leibson, writing for the majority, includes four quotations to support the narrative as to the purpose motivating the call. 704 S.W.2d at 183–84. While arguments exist that those quotations are taken out of context, suffice to note that contemporary newspaper editors and convention delegates believed the call was due to other issues.

This historical digression has been necessary to demonstrate that reasons the *Tabler* court gave for "super-charging" *Schoo*'s flawed analysis were erroneous and ultimately misleading. Seven years after *Tabler*, the Court, in *Perkins*, essentially doubled down on its analysis, comparing other states' constitutions to Kentucky's and stating "[b]ut few have additional protection against local and special legislation as we have in Kentucky Constitution §59." 808 S.W.2d at 818. Incredibly, this statement blatantly ignored widespread prohibition of special legislation. 1) Kentucky convention delegates freely acknowledged copying Section 59's provisions from other state's constitutions: Illinois, Missouri, New Jersey, New York, Pennsylvania, Texas, West Virginia, and Wisconsin. 1890–91 Ky. Const. Debates at 3992. 2) In 1890, thirty-five states' constitutions prohibited local and special legislation. Charles C. Binney, *Restrictions upon Local and Special Legislation in State Constitutions*, 130–31 (1894). 3) The federal government, in 1886, had imposed similar restrictions on territorial governments. U.S. Stats. at Large, ch. 818, 24 Stat. 170 (1886). And 4) currently, no less than forty-six states have prohibitions on local and special legislation! Justin R. Long, "State Constitution Prohibitions on Special Laws," 60 Cleve. St. L. Rev. 719, 721 n.6 (2012).

To conclude, our obligation as judges is to uphold Kentucky's constitution. We have done so in several opinions over the last few years, even when doing so overturned established precedent. *E.g., Westerfield v. Ward*, 599 S.W.3d 738 (Ky. 2019), *reh'g denied* (Oct. 31, 2019) (rejecting proposed constitutional amendment as noncompliant with Ky. Const. §§256–57, implicitly overruling *Funk v Fielder*, 243 S.W.2d 474 (Ky. 1951)); *Commonwealth v. Claycomb ex rel. Claycomb*, 566 S.W.3d 202 (Ky. 2018) (holding medical review panel act violated Ky. Const. §14); *Bevin v. Commonwealth ex rel. Beshear*, 563 S.W.3d 74 (Ky. 2018) (overturning pension bill enacted in violation of constitutional provisions); *Maupin v. Commonwealth*, 542 S.W.3d 926 (Ky. 2018) (holding Ky. Const. §115 bars the Commonwealth from appealing a judgment of acquittal, overruling *Brindley v. Commonwealth*, 724 S.W.2d 214 (Ky. 1986)); *D & W Auto Supply*, 602 S.W.2d at 425 (overruling enrolled bill doctrine set forth in *Lafferty v. Huffman*, 99 Ky. 80, 35 S.W. 123, 126 (1896) and fifteen cases which had followed *Lafferty*). In nonconstitutional cases, we have reasserted the correctness of decisions rendered decades ago, overruling more recent cases. *See Ellington v. Becraft*, 534 S.W.3d 785, 793–94 (Ky. 2017) (citing *Riley v. Buchanan*, 116 Ky. 625, 76 S.W. 527 (1903) to overturn more recent, albeit unnamed, cases concerning the establishment of public roads).

In this same vein, we hold that the test for claimed violations of Section 3, Kentucky's equal protection clause, is inappropriate for Section 59.[15] We therefore return to the original test for Section 59: local or special legislation, according to the well-known meaning of the words, applies exclusively to particular places or particular persons.

---

15. We importantly note that while we return to §59's proper analysis, we do not necessarily "overrule" the results of any prior decision, except to the extent that those decisions have erroneously applied an inappropriate analysis. For example, in *Elk Horn Coal*, while the Court discussed *Tabler*, *Perkins* and other cases, the Court ultimately applied equal protection provisions under §§1, 2 and 3 holding that no rational basis existed for KRS 26A.300's 10% penalty against unsuccessful appellants. 163 S.W.3d at 421.

Singleton, 175 S.W. at 373. In departing from more recent analysis of special legislation, we note that "cases decided contemporaneously or close in time [to the constitutional convention] would appear to be persuasive of Delegates' intent[ ]"). *Williams v. Wilson*, 972 S.W.2d 260, 267 (Ky. 1998). Furthermore, as to constitutional interpretation, "the meaning, purpose, and reach of the words used must be deduced from the intention they express considered in the light of the history that pertains to the subject. The terms used are to be construed according to their meaning at the time of the adoption of the Constitution." *Commonwealth v. Ky. Jockey Club*, 238 Ky. 739, 751, 38 S.W.2d 987, 992 (1931) (internal quotation and citation omitted).[16]

Some may say that with this simple test legislators will be able to draft around the Section 59 prohibition by avoiding express reference to a specific person, entity or locale but articulating criteria for a statute's application that as a practical matter only a specific person, entity or locale can satisfy, essentially reverting to the ways of the 1870s and 1880s.[17] The answer to this objection is that Kentucky's courts, in that pre-1891 Constitution period, had only just begun to apply the "exclusive, separate" privilege prohibition of the Bill of Rights to evaluate class or partial legislation, and to equate that section with equal protection. Over the last 130 years, courts have had experience with the analysis and have shown little hesitancy in engaging a more rigorous analysis with respect to classification legislation.

To summarize, and for the sake of clarity going forward, state constitutional challenges to legislation based on classification succeed or fail on the basis of equal protection analysis under Sections 1, 2, and 3 of the Kentucky Constitution. As for analysis under Sections 59 and 60, the appropriate test is whether the statute applies to a particular individual, object or locale.

Applying the correct test, we hold that KRS 342.750(6) does not violate Sections 59 and 60 for the simple reason that the statute does not apply to a particular individual, object or locale. It applies statewide to all employers and employees.

---

16. The concurring opinion concludes, quoting from *Daniel's Adm'r v. Hoofnel*, 287 Ky. 834, 839, 155 S.W.2d 469, 472 (1941), by criticizing that we are departing from an interpretation consistently adhered to. Far from being consistent, as shown herein, this Court has inconsistently analyzed the prohibition of §59 and conflated that analysis with that of §3. No good reason exists for perpetuating this error, especially in this case wherein this Court unanimously agrees on the result.

17. While the legislature has generally adhered to the prohibition as originally understood, on occasion it has enacted special legislation, which the Court held to violate §59. *See Univ. of Cumberlands v. Pennybacker*, 308 S.W.3d 668 (Ky. 2010) (act to create a scholarship program which had clearly been drafted to provide scholarships to an equally unconstitutionally funded pharmacy school at a private, religious university; the Court applied the *Schoo* test but reached correct result since the statute applied to particular object); *Commonwealth, Dep't of Highways v. McCoun*, 313 S.W.2d 585 (Ky. 1958) (joint resolution authorizing two named individuals to pursue claims against the Department of Highways); *Dep't of Conservation v. Sowders*, 244 S.W.2d 464 (1951) (resolution authorizing designated family to file for and receive workers' compensation benefits); *Bentley v. Commonwealth*, 239 S.W.2d 991 (Ky. 1951) (resolution authorizing individual to engage in the practice of dentistry); *Reid v. Robertson*, 304 Ky. 509, 510, 200 S.W.2d 900, 901 (1947) (act to provide individual a veterinary medicine license).

IV. Conclusion.

For the reasons set forth above, the decision of the Court of Appeals is hereby affirmed, and this matter is therefore remanded to the ALJ for a determination of whether Woodall is eligible for an award of benefits pursuant to KRS 342.750(1)(a).

All sitting. Minton, C.J.; Hughes, Lambert and Nickell, JJ., concur. Keller, J., concurs in part and concurs in result only by separate opinion in which Wright, J., joins.

* * *

Notes and Questions

1. As the *Woodall* Court explained, the standard for equal protection challenges under Sections 1, 2, and 3 and the standard for special legislation challenges under Sections 59 and 60 had merged under the *Schoo* test. But *Woodall* makes clear that Sections 59 and 60 are properly interpreted, not merely as a redundant protection of the same interests served by the Equal Protection Clause and Sections 1, 2, and 3, but as a separate protection of a different constitutional interest.
2. *Woodall* included a lengthy discussion of the historical background of the 1890 constitutional convention. Before he wrote the opinion of the Court in *Woodall*, Justice VanMeter wrote a law review article discussing the history relevant to Sections 59 and 60 and the cases construing those constitutional provisions. *See* Laurance B. VanMeter, *Reconsideration of Kentucky's Prohibition of Special and Local Legislation*, 109 Ky. L.J. 523 (2021). The historical discussion in *Woodall* reads like an abbreviated version of Justice VanMeter's law review article, making the law review article a valuable bit of explanatory material for understanding the *Woodall* decision.
3. How does *Woodall*'s historical discussion aid in understanding the meaning of the Kentucky Constitution?
4. Section 156 of the Constitution (repealed in 1994) required the General Assembly to separate all cities in the Commonwealth into six classes based on population, and permitted it to legislate differently with respect to each class of cities regarding "the existence and regulation of municipal powers and to matters of local government." *Mannini v. McFarland*, 294 Ky. 837, 172 S.W.2d 631, 632 (1943). Thus, Section 156 provided an exception to the prohibition on local or special laws in Sections 59 and 60. *Id.* When the voters repealed Section 156 in 1994, they approved a replacement provision, Section 156a, which does not require six classes based on population, but rather, "such classifications of cities as it deems necessary based on population, tax base, form of government, geography, or any other reasonable basis." The Supreme Court has held that Section 156a, like Section 156 before it, is an exception to the prohibition of local or special laws in Sections 59 and 60. *See Louisville/Jefferson Cnty. Metro Gov't Waste Mgmt. Dist. v. Jefferson Cnty. League of Cities, Inc.*, 626 S.W.3d 623, 628 (Ky. 2021) ("If legislation relating to local government is permitted by Section 156a, then it is obviously constitutional. Conversely, if not permitted under this section, reference to other sections of the constitution is superfluous."). Under Section

156a, the General Assembly has separated all Kentucky cities into two classes: cities of the first class and home rule class cities. KRS 81.005.

5. Upon the ratification of the Judicial Article, which reformed the Judicial Branch of Kentucky government starting in 1976, the General Assembly, upon the Supreme Court issuing a "certification of necessity," may "reduce, increase or rearrange" the judicial circuits or judicial districts in the Commonwealth, Ky. Const. §§112(2) and 113(2), or change the number of judges in any judicial circuit or judicial district, Ky. Const. §§112(3) and 113(3). Thus, if the Supreme Court certifies the necessity of changing the composition of only one judicial circuit or the number of District Court judges in only one judicial district, the General Assembly may do so. These more recently adopted judicial redistricting provisions therefore also serve as exceptions to the prohibition on local or special legislation regarding "the circuits of the courts of justice" in Section 59(1).

C. Legislative Innovation and Access to the Courts

> "All courts shall be open, and every person for an injury done him in his lands, goods, person or reputation, shall have remedy by due course of law, and right and justice administered without sale, denial or delay." (Ky. Const. §14.)

Section 14 is short in length but has been responsible for a large swath of the cases concerning Kentucky constitutional law. The roots of Section 14 may be traced back as far as *Magna Carta*. Clause 40 of the Great Charter that King John signed at Runnymede in 1215 provided, "To no one will we sell, to no one deny or delay right or justice." (Note the use of the royal "we" in the *Magna Carta*.) But other than general agreement that the text of "open courts" provisions in state constitutions throughout the United States, such as Section 14 of the Kentucky Constitution, can be traced back to *Magna Carta*, there is not much agreement from state to state on what these words mean in practice.

Section 14 includes three separate clauses, each protecting slightly different rights: (1) the right to have access to "open" courts; (2) the right of a person suffering an "injury" to have a "remedy by due course of law"; and (3) the right to have justice administered "without sale, denial or delay." The open courts provision of Section 14 protects against "unreasonable or arbitrary" actions by a judge that "would so unduly delay a trial or such preparation for trial, as to amount to a denial of justice." *J.B.B. Coal Co. v. Halbert*, 169 Ky. 687, 184 S.W. 1116, 1121 (1916). The right to a remedy for injury will be discussed later in Chapter 7's discussion of the jural rights doctrine. The following case considers the right to have "justice administered without ... delay."

Commonwealth, Cabinet for Health and Family Services ex rel. Meier v. Claycomb ex rel. Claycomb

Supreme Court of Kentucky (2018)
566 S.W.3d 202

Opinion of the Court by Chief Justice Minton.

Of all the rights guaranteed by state constitutions but absent from the federal Bill of Rights, the guarantee of a right of access to the courts to obtain a remedy for injury is possibly the most important.[1] Kentucky's version of this guarantee, referred to in our jurisprudence as the open-courts provision, appears in the Bill of Rights, Section 14, of the Kentucky Constitution, which states: "All courts shall be open, and every person for an injury done him in his lands, goods, person or reputation, shall have remedy by due course of law, and right and justice administered without sale, denial or delay."

The Kentucky General Assembly in its 2017 regular session enacted Kentucky Revised Statutes ("KRS") Chapter 216C, the Medical Review Panel Act, establishing a mandatory process to delay certain medical-malpractice claimants' ability to access immediately the courts of the Commonwealth by creating medical-review panels and requiring a panel's opinion about the merits of the claimant's proposed complaint against health-care providers before the claimant may file suit. This case presents to us on discretionary review a legal challenge to KRS Chapter 216C in which the trial court declared the Act unconstitutional on several grounds. We hold that because the Act delays access to the courts of the Commonwealth for the adjudication of common-law claims, Chapter 216C violates Section 14 of the Kentucky Constitution.

I. Background.

A. The General Assembly enacts the Medical Review Panels Act.

KRS Chapter 216C "provides for the establishment of medical review panels to review proposed malpractice complaints against health care providers...."[2] KRS 216C.020(1) makes clear:

> All malpractice and malpractice-related claims against a health care provider, other than claims validly agreed for submission to a binding arbitration procedure, shall be reviewed by a medical review panel. Such an action may not be commenced in a court in Kentucky before:
>
> (a) The claimant's proposed complaint has been presented to a medical review panel established under this chapter; and
>
> (b) An opinion is given by the panel. If the panel has not given its opinion within nine (9) months after the filing of the proposed complaint, the plaintiff may commence the action in court.

1. Thomas R. Phillips, *The Constitutional Right to a Remedy*, 78 N.Y.U.L. Rev. 1309, 1310 (2003).
2. KRS 216C.005.

KRS 216C.010(4) defines *health care provider* to mean:

> [A]ny health facility as defined in KRS 216B.015, or a provider, including natural persons, of health care or health services, including, but not limited to those licensed, certified, registered under, or subject to KRS 194A.700 to 194A.729 or KRS Chapter 310, 311, 311A, 31 IB, 312, 313, 314, 314A, 315, 319, 319A, 320, 327, 333, 334A, or 335 and the current and former officers, directors, administrators, agents, or employees of any such persons or entities acting within the course and scope of their office, employment, or agency.

In other words, as the trial court noted, the medical review panel must first review any malpractice or malpractice-related claim filed on or after June 29, 2017, against any individual or entity bearing some sort of relationship to the health care profession and industry, "other than claims validly agreed for submission to a binding arbitration procedure,"[3] before that claim is subject to adjudication:

> Any action involving a dependent claim accruing after June 29, 2017, shall be immediately and automatically stayed until:
>
> (a) The claimant's proposed complaint against the health care provider has been presented to a medical review panel established under this chapter and an opinion is given by the panel; or
>
> (b) Nine (9) months after the filing of the proposed complaint if the panel has not given its opinion.[4]

The panel does not engage in any adjudication of a claimant's claim.[5] Rather, the entire purpose and function of the panel is to generate an opinion about the merits of the claim, an opinion that may or may not have any evidentiary usefulness in a court of law.[6] Finally, Chapter 216C does allow the parties to bypass medical review panel review, but only if *all* parties involved in the action agree.[7]

B. The trial court declares the Medical Review Panels Act unconstitutional.

Ezra Claycomb, a minor, by and through his next friend, natural guardian, and parent, Tonya Claycomb, individually and on behalf of all others similarly situated, sued the Commonwealth in the trial court, challenging the constitutionality of Chapter 216C. Ezra suffers from severe brain damage and cerebral palsy allegedly caused by medical malpractice. But for Chapter 216C, Claycomb could immediately file a medical-malpractice suit in circuit court.

---

3. KRS 216C.020(1).

4. KRS 216C.020(2).

5. A party to the action or a panel member may invoke the jurisdiction of a court of the Commonwealth that would otherwise have subject-matter jurisdiction over the case but only for the limited purpose of ruling on certain motions allowed by Chapter 216C, none of which allow adjudication of a claimant's case. *See* KRS 216C.240; KRS 216C.250.

6. *See* KRS 216C.180.

7. *See* KRS 216C.030(1).

Claycomb specifically argued in the trial court that Chapter 216C violates: (1) the equal protection and due process guarantees under Sections 1, 2, and 3 of the Kentucky Constitution; (2) the open-courts and jural rights guarantees under Sections 7, 14, 54, and 241; (3) the separation of powers doctrine under Sections 27, 28, 109, and 116; (4) the prohibition against special legislation under Sections 59 and 60; and (5) the subject and title requirements of Section 51. The trial court found violations of the equal protection guarantee, the prohibition against special legislation (although did not provide an analysis of that issue), the separation of powers doctrine, and the open-courts and jural rights guarantees but found that Chapter 216C did not violate the subject and title requirements of Section 51.[8] The trial court found the entirety of Chapter 216C unconstitutional and permanently enjoined the Commonwealth from enforcing any of its provisions.

The Commonwealth then requested in the Court of Appeals emergency relief from the trial court's order under Kentucky Rule of Civil Procedure ("CR") 65.08(7) and suspension of the enforcement of the permanent injunction under CR 65.08(2), which the Court of Appeals granted. This Court then accepted transfer to decide the merits of the case.

II. Analysis.

At the outset, we note that our analysis focuses solely on Section 14 of the Kentucky Constitution because we find Chapter 216C violates that constitutional provision.[9]

A. Section 14 acts as a limitation against all departments of government interfering with its guarantees.

For more than two and a quarter centuries, the language of Section 14 has appeared verbatim in all four of Kentucky's constitutions, first as Article XII, §13 of the original one in 1792. But as the former Dean of the University of Kentucky College of Law, the late Thomas R. Lewis, notes in his scholarly analysis, the remedy guarantee provided for in Section 14 is an ancient right dating from Magna Carta in 1215.[10]

Tracing the pedigree of Section 14 to Magna Carta brings up a fundamental question with which Kentucky's highest court has famously struggled since the antebellum years of the Commonwealth: Is Section 14 a limitation on *all* departments of state government interfering with its guarantees, or *just the judiciary*?

Dean Lewis's ultimate conclusion about the reach of Section 14, as confirmed by his study of the historic explication of the right by Sir William Blackstone, is: "[T]hat common law courts resolve disputes, creating precedents, and thus law, in the absence of governing legislation *but subject to modification by the people through their elected*

---

8. It appears that Claycomb has abandoned his Section 51 challenge in this appeal.

9. Because we find a violation of Section 14, which results in the striking down of Chapter 216C in its entirety, we need not reach Claycomb's other constitutional challenges.

10. Thomas Lewis, *Jural Rights under Kentucky's Constitution: Realities Grounded in Myth*, 80 Ky. L.J. 953, 964–65 (1991–92).

representatives."[11] In other words, Blackstone and Dean Lewis would likely argue, as has the Commonwealth in this case, that the constraints on government reflected in Section 14 do not apply to the popularly elected legislature.

Almost 200 years ago, this Commonwealth's highest court "found that access to courts was 'clearly indicative of the duty which the functionaries of the government owe to the citizens' and that if 'it shall occur that the right of the citizen has been invaded contrary to the constitution, it is the duty of the judiciary to shield him from oppression.'"[12] In *Commonwealth ex rel. Tinder v. Werner*, the court identified the history of its decisions related to striking down acts of the legislature that sought to restrict plaintiffs' rights to the redress of civil wrongs.[13] In "*Blair v. Williams*[14] and *Lapsley v. Brashears*,[15] [Kentucky's highest court] held unconstitutional an act of the legislature permitting a stay of two years on the debtor giving bond and security unless the creditor endorsed on his execution a willingness to accept notes on the Bank of Kentucky or the Bank of the Commonwealth of Kentucky...."[16] Those decisions "nearly destroyed this court:"

> As was foreseen, those decisions produced very great exasperation and consequent denunciation of the court. The Judges were charged with arrogating supremacy over the popular will—their authority to declare void any act of the Legislature was denied, and they were denounced by the organs and stump orators of the dominant relief party as usurpers and self-made kings. No popular controversy, waged without bloodshed, was ever more absorbing or acrimonious than that which raged, like a hurricane, over Kentucky for about three years succeeding the promulgation of those judicial decisions.[17]

Some years later, after the "hard money" fight had subsided, the court in *Johnson v. Higgins*[18] and *Barkley v. Glover*[19] "held that Section 14 of the [Kentucky] Constitution was a limitation on the judicial branch of the government and not a limitation on the legislative branch, and that it prohibited the courts from arbitrarily delaying or denying to its citizens the administration of justice, but constituted no limitation upon the legislature in formulating procedural methods to be used by the courts."[20]

This rule changed with the decision in *Ludwig v. Johnson*, the seminal case establishing the open-courts and jural rights doctrines in Kentucky jurisprudence, which stated:

---

11. *Id.* (emphasis added).

12. Michael L. Buenger and Paul J. De Muniz, *American Judicial Power: The State Court Perspective*, 200–01 (2015) (quoting *Davis v. Ballard*, 1 J.J. Marsh. 563, 568, 24 Ky. 563 (1829)).

13. 280 S.W.2d 214 (Ky. 1955).

14. 14 Ky. 34 (Ky. 1823).

15. 14 Ky. 47 (Ky. 1823).

16. *Werner*, 280 S.W.2d at 215.

17. *Id.* (citing Arndt Mathias Stickles, *The Critical Court Struggle in Kentucky*, 1819–1829 (1929)) (quoting George Robertson, *Scrap Book of Law and Politics, Men and Times* (1855)).

18. 60 Ky. 566 (Ky. 1861).

19. 61 Ky. 44 (Ky. 1862).

20. *Werner*, 280 S.W.2d at 215 (internal citations omitted).

> [I]t is said in effect that section 14 of our Constitution is a restriction on the judicial, and not on the legislative, branch of government, but this observation was unnecessary in the decision of those cases, and is clearly unsound in view of section 26 of our Constitution, which is the concluding section of the Bill of Rights, and which reads: "To guard against transgression of the high powers which we have delegated, We Declare that everything in this Bill of Rights is excepted out of the general powers of government, and shall forever remain inviolate; and all laws contrary thereto, or contrary to this constitution, shall be void."[21]

So our predecessors on the Commonwealth's highest court recognized in *Ludwig* that when Section 14 is read in conjunction with Section 26, the Bill of Rights of the Kentucky Constitution establishes "a limitation on the power of the legislature to enact laws which are in contravention of the plain provisions of Section 14."[22] This conclusion led our predecessors in *Werner* to the ultimate conclusion "that section 14, when construed in the light of section 26, prohibits the legislature from invading the province of the judiciary and that the prohibition of section 14 applies to the legislative branch of the government as well as to the judicial."[23]

This Court has never retreated from that position, and we find no reason to do so today.

Sir Edward Coke and Blackstone, two of England's most preeminent legal scholars, undeniably viewed the ancient guarantees now reflected in the language of Section 14 of Kentucky's Constitution as checks on royal abuse, not on parliamentary excesses. With all due respect to the conclusion reached by Dean Lewis, who would exempt the modern legislative branch from the constraints of Section 14, that conclusion overlooks a fundamental difference between English and American jurisprudence:

> Unlike Coke and Blackstone, the rebellious American colonists saw both the Crown *and Parliament* as oppressors.[24] Parliamentary initiatives during the 1760s and 1770s convinced the colonists that the informal constitution securing English rights against royal infringement *was inadequate* to protect against *all forms of government oppression*. When independence was declared, some of the new American states began adopting formal written constitutions to structure their new governments and to help secure their most fundamental rights. As Gordon Wood notes, they recognized that laws protecting their ba-

---

21. 243 Ky. 533, 49 S.W.2d 347, 351 (1932).

22. *Werner*, 280 S.W.2d at 216.

23. *Id.* at 216.

24. Jonathan M. Hoffman, *By the Courts of the Law: The Origins of the Open Courts Clause of State Constitutions*, 74 Or. L. Rev. 1279, 1301 (1995) (discussing Britain's perceived interference with American colonial courts leading up to the American Revolution and comparing colonial grievances over royal abuses with conflict between Coke and Crown 150 years earlier). "Lord Coke was a fervent advocate of parliamentary supremacy, whereas the colonists ended up resisting parliamentary as well as royal authority." *Id.*

> sic freedoms must be of "a nature more sacred than those which established a turnpike road."[25, 26]

Furthermore, "[i]n contrast to England ... early state constitutions transformed the right from a restriction on monarchical power to a positive obligation to provide access to an independent judiciary for vindication of rights, *particularly against overreaching legislatures*."[27]

As the Tennessee Supreme Court has explained:

> This declaration, copied from the great charter [Magna Carta], is not a collection of unmeaning epithets. In England, the reason of riveting this barrier around the rights of the subject was well understood. Their sovereign was wont to interfere in the administration of justice; "a remedy by due course of law" was often refused, under the mandate of men in power, and the injured man denied justice; *they were ordered sometimes not to proceed with particular causes, and justice was delayed*; and the obtainment of their rights was often burdened with improper conditions and sacrifices, and justice was sold. So anxious were they to stop this enormous evil, that a part of the official oath of a judge was that he would proceed to do right and justice, notwithstanding any letter or order to him to the contrary.
>
> This clause of *Magna Carta*, why is it inserted in our Bill of Rights? Was it from apprehensions of our executive? We had left him no power. Whatever power is considered as properly belonging to the executive department elsewhere is, by our institutions, conferred upon the legislature. It is the more important, therefore, and so the framers of our constitution decreed, that the judicial department should be independent and coordinate, and that the legislature should have no judicial power. Danger might justly be apprehended from this quarter. If the legislature, possessing a large share of executive power, be permitted to exercise judicial power also, or control the action of the judges within their peculiar sphere, the liberty of the citizens, under the government of good legislators, would be in imminent peril, and under bad ones would be entirely destroyed.[28]

Although much of our law is rooted in English law, we cannot ignore the fundamental distinctions that developed in America. The framers of written constitutions for the new American states were clearly wary of the power of *all* branches of government. "Many framers of the original state constitutions in colonial America adopted [Sec-

25. Gordon S. Wood, *Foreword: State Constitution-Making in the American Revolution*, 24 Rutgers L.J. 911, 920 (1993) (citing *The Crisis, No. XI*, 81–87 (New York 1775)).

26. Phillips, *supra* note 1 at 1323; *see also*, William C. Koch, Jr., *Reopening Tennessee's Open Courts Clause: A Historical Reconsideration of Article I, Section 17 of the Tennessee Constitution*, U. Mem. L. Rev. (1997) ("Few courts continue to insist that the open courts provision has no application to legislative actions.").

27. Buenger and De Muniz, *supra* note 12 at 200 (emphasis added).

28. *Id.* (quoting *Fisher's Negroes v. Dabbs*, 14 Tenn. 119, 137–38 (Tenn. 1834)) (emphasis added).

tion 14's guarantees] as their own, recognizing it as a constraint on both judicial and legislative power."[29]

To characterize, as the Commonwealth insisted at oral argument, certain sections of the Kentucky Bill of Rights as applying only to the judicial department of the Commonwealth is to ignore the common understanding of the original framers and the original meaning of the words they employed—*all* branches of government can oppress the people and such oppression must be guarded against. So the framers of Kentucky's First Constitution included Section 28 in the Kentucky Bill of Rights: "To guard against transgressions of the high powers which we have delegated, WE DECLARE, that everything in this article is excepted out of the general powers of government, and shall forever remain inviolate; and that all laws contrary thereto, or contrary to this Constitution, shall be void."[30] This is the same provision, now Section 26, that this Court in *Ludwig* identified as making clear that Section 14 applies to *all* branches of government.

Based upon the plain text of Section 14, its history, and our long-standing precedent interpreting its reach, we hold that Section 14 acts as a restraint on the power of all departments of state government. As Justice Hughes observed at oral argument of this case, Section 14 is a right "of the people," and the people deserve to be protected against all departments of government infringing on their right to seek immediate redress for common-law personal-injury claims.

B. The plain words of Section 14, coupled with a historical understanding of the remedies guarantee offered by it, mandate that Chapter 216C be declared unconstitutional.

Now that we have clarified that Section 14 does apply to all departments of government, we turn to evaluating its implications for the case at hand. In our review, we must remember our duty to presume that the statutes we address are constitutional.[31] Additionally, "[i]t is a well-established principle that '[a] facial challenge to a legislative Act is ... the most difficult challenge to mount successfully, since the challenger must establish that no set of circumstances exists under which the Act would be valid.'"[32] "The violation of the Constitution must be clear, complete and unmistakable in order to find the law unconstitutional."[33]

We have held that Section 14 protects "[t]he right of every individual in society to access a system of justice to redress wrongs," and such protection "is basic and fundamental to our common law heritage."[34] The right to a remedy protected in Section 14

29. Phillips, *supra* note 1 at 1304.

30. Ky Const. Art. XII, §28 (1792).

31. *Utility Mgmt. Grp., LLC v. Pike Cnty. Fiscal Court*, 531 S.W.3d 3, 12 (Ky. 2017) (citing *Curd v. Ky. State Bd. of Licensure*, 433 S.W.3d 291, 305 (Ky. 2014)).

32. *Harris v. Commonwealth*, 338 S.W.3d 222, 229 (Ky. 2011) (quoting *Rust v. Sullivan*, 500 U.S. 173, 183, 111 S.Ct. 1759, 114 L.Ed.2d 233 (1991)).

33. *Kentucky Indus. Util. Customers, Inc. v. Kentucky Utils. Co.*, 983 S.W.2d 493, 499 (Ky. 1998).

34. *O'Bryan v. Hedgespeth*, 892 S.W.2d 571, 578 (Ky. 1995).

applies to actions for death and personal injuries, among other types of actions.[35] And medical-malpractice claims fall under this category of claims.

"The most widespread and important ... provision [of states' bills of rights] is probably the guarantee of a right of access to the courts to obtain a remedy for injury."[36] "It is one of the oldest of Anglo-American rights, rooted in Magna Carta and nourished in the English struggle for individual liberty and conscience rights."[37] Former Chief Justice of the Texas Supreme Court Thomas Phillips sheds light on the origin of the rights secured by Section 14:

> The motivations for the original guarantee are actually easier to discern than those of our own states' framers. The barons had little interest in abstract pronouncements of ideal governance; they were after specific language to compel particular action.[38] The barons were displeased because the royal courts, which fast were displacing local feudal courts as the preferred forum for dispute resolution, operated on a fee scale, with different charges for particular writs. "The system invited abuse; more expensive writs worked faster than cheaper ones, were more potent, and could achieve access to a more favorable forum."[39]

The rights guaranteed by Section 14 arose to prevent royal abuse through the courts: "These provisions were intended to address two abuses in England's medieval justice system: (1) the random exploitation of judicial power without lawful judgment, and (2) the practice of the selling of writs to gain access to the King's courts."[40] The framers of our own Constitution recognized this, as well:

> We have all read that King John had the habit of gathering gear by every wile that was justified by honor, and a good many that were not.... When he went hunting or junketing about the kingdom his justiciary was at his heels, under the idea that the King, as the fountain of justice, must be present in person as in theory when an appeal for justice should be made by one of his subjects. But in consequence the nomadic nature of the court—here to-day and gone to-morrow—there were the most intolerable delays in the administration of justice.... So, when he was confronted by the old barons who had assembled on the plain of Running Mead (sic) to persuade him to accede to the demands

---

35. *Fireman's Fund Ins. Co. v. Government Emps. Ins. Co.*, 635 S.W.2d 475, 477 (Ky. 1982) (internal citations omitted) (overruled on other grounds by *Perkins v. Northeastern Log Homes*, 808 S.W.2d 809 (Ky. 1991)).

36. Phillips, *supra* note 1 at 1310.

37. *Id.* (citing A.E. Dick Howard, *The Road from Runnymeade: Magna Carta and Constitutionalism in America*, 6–8 (1968)).

38. *See* William Sharp McKechnie, *Magna Carta: A Commentary on the Great Charter of King John* 51–52, 120 (2d ed. 1914).

39. Phillips, *supra* note 1 at 1320 n.35. (quoting David Schuman, *Oregon's Remedy Guarantee: Article I, Section 10 of the Oregon Constitution*, 65 Or. L. Rev. 35, 37 (1986)).

40. Buenger and De Muniz, *supra* note 12 at 200.

suggested by Langdon, he graciously promised that he would "... delay justice to no man...."[41]

Sir Edward Coke, in his Second Part of the Institutes of the Laws of England,[42] described the rights guaranteed by Section 14 as a "'roote' from which 'many fruitful branches of the law of England have sprung.'"[43] "One such branch was the protection of individuals' rights from official acts of oppression...."[44] "Another was 'the rights of subjects in their private relations with one another....'"[45] Coke further stated about the rights as guaranteed in Section 14:

> [E]very subject of this realm, for injury done to him in goods, lands, or person, by any other subject... may take his remedy by the course of the law, and have justice, and right for the injury done to him, freely without sale, fully without any denial, and speedily without delay.... [J]ustice must have three qualities; it must be... free; for nothing is more odious than Justice let to sale; full, for justice ought not to limp, or be granted piece-meal; and speedily, for delay is a kind of denial; and then it is both justice and right.[46]

During the next century, Sir William Blackstone described the right to a remedy as one of the critical means through which a civilized society served its principal aim—the preservation of an individual's absolute rights to life, liberty, and property.[47] Blackstone identified three absolute rights: "personal security, personal liberty, and private property."[48] "Personal security include[s] the right to life and limb, and... to body (freedom from assault), health, and reputation."[49]

Blackstone described the right to a remedy as "one of the five subordinate rights through which people vindicated their absolute rights, and it encompassed both the substance of the law and the procedures through which courts applied that law."[50] Once a person was injured, the right to an "adequate remedy" immediately attached, though judicial process might be necessary to ascertain the exact parameters of that right.[51] "The right to a remedy dictated that common-law courts exercise general jurisdiction, being open for all cases involving injury to individual rights, '[f]or it is a settled and

41. 1 *Debates of the Constitutional Convention of 1890*, 732, (1890) (J. Proctor Knott, Madison County).

42. Phillips, *supra* note 1 at 1320 (citing Hastings Lyon & Herman Block, *Edward Coke: Oracle of the Law*, 348 (1929)).

43. Phillips, *supra* note 1 at 1320 (quoting Edward Coke, *The Second Part of the Institutes of the Laws of England*, 45 (photo reprint 1986) (London, W. Clarke & Sons 1817) (1641)).

44. Phillips, *supra* note 1 at 1320 (quoting Coke, *supra* note 38).

45. Phillips, *supra* note 1 at 1320.

46. Phillips, *supra* note 1 at 1320 (quoting Coke, supra note 38).

47. Phillips, *supra* note 1 at 1321 (citing William Blackstone, *Commentaries on the Law of England*, 124 (1765)).

48. Phillips, *supra* note 1 at 1321 (citing Blackstone, *supra* note 42 at 125 and 129).

49. Phillips, *supra* note 1 at 1321.

50. Phillips, *supra* note 1 at 1321 (citing Blackstone, *supra* note 42 at 141–44).

51. Phillips, *supra* note 1 at 1322 (citing Blackstone, *supra* note 42 at 116).

invariable principle ... that every right when withheld must have a remedy, and every injury its proper redress.'"[52]

So Blackstone was "concerned [with both] the physical availability of judicial process [and] with the substantive opportunity to assert claims to protect absolute rights."[53] As Blackstone stated, "'Since the law is ... the supreme arbiter of every man's life, liberty, and property, courts of justice must at all times be open to the subject, and the law be duly administered therein' to satisfy the subordinate right of 'applying to the courts of justice for redress of injuries.'"[54]

Coke and Blackstone observed that included among the rights protected by the remedies guarantee are "the rights of subjects in their private relations with one another,"[55] which includes the "absolute right[ ] of personal security."[56] "Personal security include[s] the right to life and limb, and ... to body (freedom from assault), health, and reputation."[57] In order to protect against violations of such rights, Coke and Blackstone identified the necessary remedy that immediately attaches upon injury done to a person: "[E]very subject of this realm, for injury done to him in goods, lands, or person, by any other subject ... may take his remedy by the course of the law, and have justice, and right for the injury done to him ... *speedily without delay*." Indeed, "[t]he placement of access to [courts] provisions in states' bills of rights suggests that the drafters of state constitutions did not view the right as merely an operational detail of the courts but rather as an individualized, particularized and positive right...."[58]

The General Assembly, through Chapter 216C, has created a mandatory delay affecting the ability of all medical-malpractice claimants to seek any redress, unless all parties either "validly agree[ ] ... to a binding arbitration procedure"[59] or agree to bypass the medical review panel process.[60] Chapter 216C takes away the ability of medical-malpractice claimants to seek immediate redress in the forum of the claimant's choosing. Chapter 216C contravenes one of the main purposes of Section 14—to prohibit legislatively created delays in the ability of a claimant to seek immediate redress in the courts of the Commonwealth for common-law personal injury, i.e., to prevent the people from being "ordered ... not to proceed with particular causes[ ] and [from] justice [being] delayed."[61]

Section 14 provides for courts to be "open." Section 14 affords "every person for an injury done him in his ... person ... remedy by due course of law, and right and justice administered without ... delay." Forcing a medical-malpractice claimant seeking

52. Phillips, *supra* note 1 at 1322 (quoting Blackstone, *supra* note 42 at 109).
53. Phillips, *supra* note 1 at 1322 (citing Blackstone, *supra* note 42 at 141).
54. *Id.*
55. Phillips, *supra* note 1 at 1320.
56. Phillips, *supra* note 1 at 1321 (citing Blackstone, *supra* note 42 at 125 and 129).
57. Phillips, *supra* note 1 at 1321 n. 44
58. Buenger and De Muniz, *supra* note 12 at 202.
59. KRS 216C.020(1).
60. KRS 216C.030(1).
61. Buenger and De Muniz, *supra* note 12 at 200–01 (quoting *Dabbs*, 14 Tenn. at 137–38).

immediate redress for an alleged common-law personal-injury to be at the mercy of the other parties involved when attempting to bypass the panel process cannot satisfy Section 14's mandate that "[a]ll courts ... be open" and every Kentuckian "shall have remedy by due course of law, and right and justice administered without ... delay."

Admittedly, delays are inherent in every adjudicatory proceeding. What makes the delay imposed by Chapter 216C unconstitutional is the General Assembly's *usurpation* of a claimant's freedom to access the adjudicatory method of his or her choosing at the time of his or her choosing. Chapter 216C is in contravention of Section 14 because no *adjudication whatsoever* takes place of a medical-malpractice claimant's claim unless a valid agreement has been made to arbitrate or bypass the panel process. Claimants may only seek immediate redress for their common-law personal-injury claims through arbitration or the courts if, and only if, the adverse parties agree to proceed through arbitration or the courts. This is an untenable restriction on the exercise of the individual's right to receive "remedy by due course of law, and right and justice administered without ... delay" from an "open" court system.[62]

The mandatory imposition of a delay in seeking immediate redress for a common-law personal-injury claim in the adjudicatory forum of the claimant's choosing cannot amount to "due course of law," because it is as though *no* "course of law" is taking place whatsoever. No "right and justice" is being "administered" at all. And, not only have the courts become closed, in contravention of the mandate that they "shall be open," but seemingly every dispute-resolution process for malpractice claims has been closed, unless all parties agree to arbitrate or bypass the panel process.

Justice Keller suggests that we have failed to consider what the phrase "due course of law" was intended to entail, seemingly glancing over the wise words of the Kansas Supreme Court that we borrow:

> It is not an easy task to deduce either from reason or the authorities a satisfactory definition of ... "due course of law." We feel safe, however, ... in saying these terms do not mean any act that the Legislature may have passed if such act does not give to one opportunity to be heard before being deprived or property, liberty, or reputation, or having been deprived of either does not afford a like opportunity of showing the extent of his injury and give an adequate remedy to recover therefor. Whatever these terms may mean more than this, *they do mean due and orderly procedure of courts* in the ascertainment of damages for injury, to the end that the injured one "shall have remedy"—that is, proper and adequate remedy—thus to be ascertained. *To refuse hearing and remedy for injury after its infliction is small remove from infliction of penalty before and without hearing.*[63]

62. Ky. Const. §14.
63. *Hanson v. Krehbiel*, 68 Kan. 670, 75 P. 1041, 1043 (1904).

Chapter 216C "refuse[s] hearing and remedy for injury after its infliction"[64] by forcing alleged wronged claimants to wait before they can begin the process of seeking redress. "Those terms ... 'due course of law' ... do not mean merely an act of the General Assembly. If they did, every restriction upon legislative authority would be at once abrogated."[65]

Chapter 216C is an unacceptable deviation from the "[t]he right of every individual in society to access a system of justice to redress wrongs."[66] Instead of affording claimants the ability to choose the process of redress they wish at the time they wish to exercise it, Chapter 216C forecloses all immediate access to any system of justice unless the other side agrees. Access to the adjudicatory method of their choice for *immediate* redress of common-law personal-injury claims is a constitutional right that all claimants have, unless they choose to give it up; the government cannot take away that right.

We do note, however, that proceeding through an alternative means of adjudication of a claim is not per se unconstitutional under Section 14. Whether through arbitration, mediation, administrative proceedings, or some other form of dispute-resolution process, if a claimant (1) has voluntarily agreed to seek redress of their common-law claims through that process and (2) has meaningfully waived access to the courts, then proceeding through a dispute-resolution process outside the court system that resulted in a delayed adjudication of a claim would, nevertheless, seem to pass constitutional muster under Section 14. But under Chapter 216C, common-law personal-injury claimants have no ability to seek any *immediate redress from the adjudicatory forum of their choosing* unless all parties agree to bypass the panel process. Under these circumstances, with their backs against the wall, claimants choosing to arbitrate cannot be said to have meaningfully waived their right to immediate access to the courts.

We must also point out that the remedy guarantee of Section 14 applies only to claims, "for an injury done [to a claimant] in his lands, goods, person or reputation."[67] And the protections of Section 14 apply only to *claims originating out of the common law*.[68] If the legislature affords a right to claimants outside the common law, then a delay in adjudication of that claim is not per se unconstitutional under Section 14. Section 14 only prevents the legislature from encroaching upon the realm of the judiciary, the creator of the common law, by imposing mandatory delays in the adjudication

64. *Id.*

65. *Hoke v. Henderson*, 15 N.C. 1, 15 (N.C. 1833).

66. *O'Bryan*, 892 S.W.2d at 578.

67. Ky. Const. §14; *see Mullins v. Manning Coal Corp*, 938 S.W.2d 260, 263 (Ky. 1997) ("An employee's right to occupational disease benefits is purely statutory in nature and does not fall under the ambit of §14 of the Kentucky Constitution."); *see also Adkins v. R & S Body Co.*, 58 S.W.3d 428 (Ky. 2001); *Shamrock Coal Co. v. Maricle*, 5 S.W.3d 130 (Ky. 1999).

68. *See Adkins*, 58 S.W.3d at 430 ("Unlike the common law remedy for personal injury, the statutory remedy for injured workers is not predicated on redressing a tortious act.... Any rights that a worker acquires to a remedy under Chapter 342 are purely statutory and, therefore, do not come within the ambit of Section 14 of the Kentucky Constitution...."); *Shamrock Coal*, 5 S.W.3d at 134 ("There was no common law cause of action for non-disabling category one pneumoconiosis in existence at the time of the adoption of the present Constitution; therefore, the jural rights doctrine is inapplicable.").

of common-law claims grounded in claims "for an injury done [to the claimant] in his lands, goods, person or reputation."[69] Here, medical-malpractice claims, a subset of personal-injury and wrongful-death claims, have been a recognized part of the common law for centuries,[70] and as such, the legislature cannot delay claimants from seeking immediate redress of such claims through the courts.

Lastly, there is no support, either from the text of Section 14, or from case law interpreting that provision, to interpose a "reasonableness" evaluation of the delay to determine if a delay can, in some circumstances, be constitutionally tolerable. "Where a constitutional provision is free from all ambiguity there is no room for interpretation or addition. It must be accepted by the courts as it reads."[71] "The basic rule ... is to interpret a constitutional provision according to what was said and not what might have been said; according to what was included and not what might have been included."[72] "Neither legislatures nor courts have the right to add to or take from the simple words and meaning of the constitution."[73] Finally, "It is hornbook law that in interpreting Constitutions the words employed therein should be given the meaning and significance that they possessed at the time they were employed, and the one that the delegates of the convention that framed the instrument, and the people who voted their approval of it, intended to express and impart."[74] Section 14, originally written and adopted in 1792, does not proscribe the creation of "undue" or "unreasonable" delay on a Kentuckian's access to due course of law; Section 14 plainly proscribes delay.

The Commonwealth argued at oral argument that this Court has never interpreted Section 14 in such an absolutist way. But our research fails to uncover a single case where the General Assembly attempted to foreclose a common-law personal-injury claimant's right to immediate adjudicatory redress. This Court has never interpreted Section 14 in such an absolutist way because this Court has never been called upon to interpret Section 14 against a statutory framework like Chapter 216C.

* * *

The entirety of Chapter 216C violates Section 14, and there is "no set of circumstances ... under which the Act would be valid." * * * Therefore, we must declare the entire Act void as unconstitutional.

---

69. Ky. Const. §14; *see Mullins*, 938 S.W.2d 260 at 263 ("An employee's right to occupational disease benefits is purely statutory in nature and does not fall under the ambit of §14 of the Kentucky Constitution."); *Adkins v. R & S Body Co.*, 58 S.W.3d 428 (Ky. 2001); *see also Shamrock Coal Co. v. Maricle*, 5 S.W.3d 130 (Ky. 1999).

70. Kathy Kendall, *Latent Medical Errors and Maine's Statute of Limitations for Medical Malpractice: A Discussion of the Issues*, 53 Me. L. Rev. 589 (2001) (tracing the origin of medical malpractice claims to 4050 B.C. Sumer, which required negligent healers to pay their victims an amount of money proportional to the degree of disability incurred).

71. *Talbott v. Public Serv. Commn.*, 291 Ky. 109, 163 S.W.2d 33, 38 (1942).

72. *Pardue v. Miller*, 306 Ky. 110, 206 S.W.2d 75, 78 (1947).

73. *Jefferson Cnty. ex rel. Grauman v. Jefferson Cnty. Fiscal Court*, 273 Ky. 674, 117 S.W.2d 918, 924 (1938).

74. *City of Lexington v. Thompson*, 250 Ky. 96, 61 S.W.2d 1092, 1096 (1933).

III. Conclusion.

Because Chapter 216C violates Section 14 of the Kentucky Constitution, the Act is void in its entirety. Accordingly, we affirm, for the reasons stated in this opinion, the judgment of the trial court.

All sitting. Hughes, VanMeter, and Venters, JJ., concur. Cunningham, J., concurs in result only by separate opinion. Keller, J., concurs in result only by separate opinion, in which Cunningham and Wright, JJ., join.

* * *

Justice Keller, concurring in result only:

The majority opinion holds that, pursuant to Ky. Const. §14, any delay to bringing a personal injury or wrongful death action is unconstitutional. I cannot wholly concur in such a holding because I believe the ramifications of such a broad holding are, at this time, unknown and unforeseeable. Kentucky Constitution §14 states, *in toto*:

> All courts shall be open, and every person for an injury done him in his lands, goods, person or reputation, shall have remedy by due course of law, and right and justice administered without sale, denial or delay.

We can clearly see a constitutionally-mandated reverence for Kentuckians' rights to access the courts within these provisions. I agree with the majority's respectful stance of our Constitution's guarantee of every citizen's right to open courts.

In recognizing this fundamental right to open courts through §14, however, the majority has decided that this constitutional provision guarantees that right without any delay. The majority has held that there is no "reasonableness" standard within §14 and the provision "plainly proscribes delay" of any kind. I cannot fully concur in this holding. The provision states that there can be no delay and every person "shall have remedy by due course of law." But what is "due course of law"? I would posit that such a phrase could possibly embrace procedural requirements that the legislature creates. Such requirements must, of course, comport with the remaining constitutional provisions. But I am not so convinced that the framers intended the General Assembly to be so restricted from placing otherwise constitutionally sound processes for litigants to gain access to the courts.

* * *

I concur in the result, here, because the MRPA clearly interferes with a fundamental right to access the courts in an unreasonably broad way. However, I cannot say that any *measure* the legislature may create to impose procedural steps *prior* to the bringing of an action under §14 would *always* be unconstitutional. By thus holding, we begin to invade the role of the legislature and tie the General Assembly's hands. The MRPA overstepped constitutional bounds. But I do not agree that any similar measure will, *ipso facto*, violate §14 because it creates any delay before bringing an action. Therefore, I concur in the majority's result only.

Cunningham and Wright, JJ., join.

Notes and Questions

1. Recognizing a split of authority, the *Claycomb* Court nevertheless held that Section 14 applied not only to the judicial branch, but also to the legislative branch. The rights preserved by Section 14 belong to "the people," *i.e.*, they are personal rights of the individual against the government. Keep this point in mind when reading Chapter 7 on the jural rights doctrine.
2. In her concurrence, Justice Keller, joined by two other justices, would keep the door open to the possibility that some amount of delay mandated by the General Assembly before a claimant may file a civil action might be permissible. Chief Justice Minton and the majority state that Section 14 proscribes "delay," and not merely "undue" or "unreasonable" delay, apparently holding that no amount of delay would ever be permissible. What are the ramifications of such a broad holding? How might the *Claycomb* holding apply in other contexts, *e.g.*, court-ordered mediation before trial?
3. Near the end of the opinion, citing *City of Lexington v. Thompson*, 250 Ky. 96, 61 S.W.2d 1092, 1096 (1933), the Court hewed to an originalist (or textualist) interpretive philosophy regarding the Kentucky Constitution: "[I]n interpreting Constitutions the words employed therein should be given the meaning and significance that they possessed at the time they were employed, and the one that the delegates of the convention that framed the instrument, and the people who voted their approval of it, intended to express and impart." This is an example of "public meaning originalism" in constitutional interpretation, which emphasizes that the words of the text mean what a reasonably informed observer would have understood the words to mean at the time they were adopted (in contradistinction to its cousin, "original intent originalism," which involves the primacy of the subjective intent of the framers).

D. Constitutional Restraints on the Lawmaking Process

"No bill shall be considered for final passage unless the same has been reported by a committee and printed for the use of the members. Every bill shall be read at length on three different days in each House, but the second and third readings may be dispensed with by a majority of all the members elected to the House in which the bill is pending. But whenever a committee refuses or fails to report a bill submitted to it in a reasonable time, the same may be called up by any member, and be considered in the same manner it would have been considered if it had been reported...." (Ky. Const. §46.)

"No law enacted by the General Assembly shall relate to more than one subject, and that shall be expressed in the title, and no law shall be revised, amended, or the provisions thereof extended or conferred by reference to its title only, but so much thereof as is revised, amended, extended or conferred, shall be reenacted and published at length." (Ky. Const. §51.)

The U.S. Constitution delegates legislative power to the Congress regarding only specific subjects, U.S. Const. art. I, §8, whereas, as discussed previously, the Kentucky Constitution grants the entirety of the legislative power to the General Assembly, Ky. Const. §29. Both constitutions require bicameral passage and presentment to the chief executive as a precondition to a law becoming effective, U.S. Const. art. I, §7; Ky. Const. §§56, 88, but otherwise, the U.S. Constitution does not contain any specific procedural restraints on how the Congress does its job of enacting legislation.

The Kentucky Constitution, however, contains multiple restraints on the lawmaking process, for which there is no analogue in our national charter. For example, Section 46 generally requires bills to be reported to the floor of each legislative chamber by a committee, and to be read at length on three different days in each chamber. Effectively, this means that a bill needs at least five legislative days in the General Assembly to become a law—assuming that the bill is read for the first time in the second chamber on the same day it was passed by the first chamber. In Congress, it will often occur that a bill is passed by one chamber, and then passed by the other chamber without being referred to a committee or being read more than once.

A similar procedural restraint on the General Assembly is found in Section 51, which requires that a bill may relate to only one subject, and that the subject must be expressed in the title of the bill. That is why the titles of bills pending before the General Assembly are short and relatively non-specific, *e.g.*, "An Act relating to insurance." On the other hand, bills enacted into law by Congress often relate to more than one subject, as it facilitates the sort of "logrolling" needed to pass some more controversial laws. Further, bills enacted by Congress often have a paragraph-long title, with "and for other purposes" tacked on at the end. The practical effect of Section 51 is to make it more difficult to sneak a surprise, unrelated provision into a bill as it makes its way through the legislative process.

Bevin v. Commonwealth ex rel. Beshear

Supreme Court of Kentucky (2018)
563 S.W.3d 74

OPINION OF THE COURT BY JUSTICE VENTERS:

Appellant, Governor Matthew G. Bevin, appeals from an opinion and order of the Franklin Circuit Court granting summary judgment to the Kentucky Education Association, the Kentucky State Lodge Fraternal Order of Police, the Board of Trustees of the Teachers' Retirement System of the State of Kentucky, the Board of Trustees of the Kentucky Retirement Systems, and Kentucky Attorney General Andy Beshear, which together we refer to as "Appellees." Appellants are supported in this appeal by an Amicus Curiae brief filed by Senate President, Bertram Robert Stivers, II, and Speaker

Pro Tempore of the Kentucky House of Representatives, David W. Osborne, together referred to herein as Amicus.

As Plaintiffs in the circuit court, Appellees filed suit challenging the validity of Senate Bill 151 (SB 151), based upon what they contend to be its flawed enactment. SB 151 was passed during the 2018 session of the Kentucky General Assembly and it ostensibly makes several modifications to the various state government employee pension plans, including the pension plans for teachers, state police, and county employees.

The circuit court held that in passing SB 151 the legislature violated §46 of the Kentucky Constitution by failing to give the bill a reading on three different days in each legislative chamber (the "three-readings" requirement), and by failing to obtain 51 votes in the House of Representatives as required for a bill which appropriates money or creates a debt. Upon its conclusion that SB 151 was not passed in compliance with the Kentucky Constitution, the circuit court voided the bill without addressing the substantive issues of whether the legislation violated the inviolable contract status afforded to state pensions under KRS 161.714[1] and whether the legislation violated the prohibition against impairment of contracts contained in §19 of the Kentucky Constitution.[2]

On appeal, Appellants first assert that a judicial interpretation of the three-readings requirement of §46 is a non-justiciable matter, related exclusively to the legislative branch of government under principles connected with separation of powers and the political question doctrine, and thus, the circuit court erred by adjudicating it. Consistent with that argument, Appellants further assert that this Court is without authority to declare the meaning of §46.

For the reasons set forth below, we disagree. Upon review, we conclude that the passage of SB 151 did not comply with the three-readings requirement of §46 and that the legislation is, therefore, constitutionally invalid and declared void. Based upon this disposition, we do not address the arguments challenging the substantive provisions of SB 151. Our disposition renders moot the question of whether SB 151 constitutes an appropriation or created a debt subjecting it to the 51-vote majority provision of §46. To address issues that may or may not recur in subsequent legislation would be an advisory opinion. The "courts do not function to give advisory opinions, even on important public issues, unless there is an actual case in controversy." *Newkirk v. Commonwealth*, 505 S.W.3d 770, 774 (Ky. 2016) (quoting *Philpot v. Patton*, 837 S.W.2d 491,

---

1. "It is hereby declared that in consideration of the contributions by members and in further consideration of benefits received by the state from the member's employment, KRS 161.220 to 161.710 shall constitute, except as provided in KRS 6.696, an inviolable contract of the Commonwealth, and the benefits provided herein shall, except as provided in KRS 6.696, not be subject to reduction or impairment by alteration, amendment, or repeal." Other statutory provisions provide the same protection to the various other state government pension plans.

2. The trial court also granted motions to dismiss filed by named defendants, Bertram Robert Stivers, II, as President of the Kentucky Senate, and David W. Osborne, as Speaker Pro Tempore of the Kentucky House of Representatives based upon the doctrine of legislative immunity. President Stivers and Speaker Osborne have filed a joint Amicus Curiae brief supporting the positions of the Governor.

493 (Ky. 1992)). The substantive merits of any future legislation on the subject matter before us should proceed without being influenced by this Court's opinion on the present legislation.

I. Factual and Procedural Background

In response to the inadequate funding of Kentucky's public employee pension systems and a rising concern about the ability of those systems to meet future obligations, the Kentucky General Assembly opened its 2018 session with ambitious plans to address the looming financial threat by reforming the public pension systems. As an initial step toward that goal, Senate Bill 1 (SB 1) was introduced in the Senate on February 20, 2018. With the title, "AN ACT relating to retirement," SB 1 would make several changes to the Kentucky Employees Retirement System, County Employees Retirement System, State Police Retirement System, and Kentucky Teachers' Retirement System. The title of the bill is important because Section 51 of the Kentucky Constitution requires:

> No law enacted by the General Assembly shall relate to more than one subject, and that shall be expressed in the title, and no law shall be revised, amended, or the provisions thereof extended or conferred by reference to its title only, but so much thereof as is revised, amended, extended or conferred, shall be reenacted and published at length.

Vocal opponents of SB 1 complained that it reduced annual cost-of-living-adjustments for retired public employees, put newly-hired employees into a hybrid-cash balance plan rather than the defined-benefits plans enjoyed by current employees, and limited the extent to which unused sick-leave credit could be used to enhance the retirement benefits for current and future public employees. Resistance to SB 1 led to protests at the Capitol and in other forums around Kentucky. Legislative action on the bill stalled. Senate leadership referred SB 1 back to committee for additional study. No further action was taken on the bill, but the concern for the solvency of the pension systems did not subside.

On the fifty-seventh day of the sixty-day legislative session, the House Committee on State Government met to address pension-reform alternatives. Consensus on a plan for reform was reached. With time waning for legislative action, the Committee was confronted with §46's requirement for the bill to be read at length on three different days. Section 46 states in pertinent part:

> No bill shall be considered for final passage unless the same has been reported by a committee and printed for the use of the members. *Every bill shall be read at length on three different days in each House,* but the second and third readings may be dispensed with by a majority of all the members elected to the House in which the bill is pending.

(Emphasis added.)

To pass the newly agreed-upon reform, the Committee invoked the following previously-used legislative maneuver: a different bill which had already been given one or more readings in each chamber would be "amended" by inserting the newly agreed-upon pension-reform text, with the expectation that the previous readings of the bill would count toward the three-reading requirement. To this end, SB 151 was selected.[3]

SB 151 had originated in the Senate with the title, "AN ACT relating to the local provision of wastewater services." In its original form, SB 151 consisted of eleven pages of text concerning contracts for the acquisition of local wastewater facilities.

When SB 151 was called in the House, it was amended by a Committee Substitute containing the pension reform language. The Committee Substitute removed every word of the bill pertaining to wastewater facilities and replaced those words with 291 pages of text addressing pension reform, much of which had been part of SB 1 but modified to remove the language that drew the most aggressive opposition.

When the Committee Substitute was introduced, SB 151 had already received three readings on different days in the Senate and two readings in the House. All the readings of the bill, however, in both substance and title, were in its form as a bill pertaining to local wastewater services. The principal issue before us is whether any of the prior readings of SB 151 in its original form can be counted toward satisfaction of the three-readings requirement of the bill after its transformation from a wastewater bill to a pension reform bill. Appellants and Amicus assert that the prior readings should count toward the three-reading requirement, while Appellees contend that none count.

Our review of SB 151 in its final 291-page version discloses th at the great majority of its text mirrors the language previously seen in SB 1. SB 1 and SB 151 were identical in many substantive respects, but the most significant difference is that the more serious reforms of the substituted version of SB 151 applied only to future public employees. Current employees remained largely unaffected.

Although several legislators opposing the pension reform embodied in SB 151 raised questions about the procedure by which it was being considered, none specifically objected to the practice of stripping out the wastewater services provisions and replacing them with pension-reform language. Silence on that aspect of the controversy lends credence to Appellants' claim that this legislative maneuver has long been regarded as an acceptable practice in the General Assembly. * * *

With newly-inserted language transforming the act from a wastewater bill to a pension reform bill, SB 151 was voted out of Committee and reported favorably to the

3. It is suggested that this procedure conflicts with House Rule 60, which provides in relevant part: "No amendment [of a bill] shall be in order that is not germane to the matter under consideration and unless it shall have been printed and previously distributed by the Clerk at least one legislative day prior to consideration of the bill or resolution." However, because pursuant to Section 39 "[e]ach House of the General Assembly may determine the rules of its proceedings," we necessarily abstain from considering whether Rule 60 was violated. The General Assembly itself is the final arbiter of its own rules. "'Proper respect for a coordinate branch of the government' requires that we strike down an Act of Congress only if 'the lack of constitutional authority to pass [the] act in question is clearly demonstrated.'" *National Federation of Independent Business v. Sebelius*, 567 U.S. 519, 538, 132 S.Ct. 2566, 183 L.Ed.2d 450 (2012).

House floor, where it was immediately called up for final passage. Bearing only the title "AN ACT relating to the local provision of wastewater services," SB 1 was read in the full House "by title only" and then voted on as a pension reform bill.

To summarize, SB 151 with its original wastewater services title and text was "read" twice in the House before the introduction of the Committee Substitute that removed and replaced all its text but left the title intact. Thereafter, the House again "read" SB 151 by its title as a wastewater services bill but with the substantive text of a pension reform bill. Appellants assert that this final reading of the bill by its title provided the third-reading required by §46. The House voted to pass SB 151 by a vote of 49 to 46 with five members abstaining. After the voting was completed, the title of SB 151 was then amended to identify it as a measure relating to retirement and public pensions, thus, complying with the subject-title match requirement of Section 51 of the Kentucky Constitution.

During its course through the legislative process, SB 151 received three readings in the Senate as a bill, in substance and title, pertaining to local wastewater services. In the House, it received two readings as a bill, in substance and title, pertaining to local wastewater services, and then it received a final "reading" in the House, still designated by title as a bill pertaining to local wastewater service but with the its textual content relating exclusively to public pension reform. Consequently, SB 151 was never "read" in either chamber by its title as an act relating to retirement and public pensions.

After the final vote and in due course, the Speaker Pro Tempore of the House signed the bill[4] and referred it back to the Senate the same day, where, with no additional reading by text or title in its newly-amended form, SB 151 passed by a vote of 22–15. SB 151 was then signed by Senate President Stivers and sent to the Governor for his signature, which occurred on April 10, 2018.

The Kentucky Attorney General and various associations representing public employees and retirees promptly brought an action in Franklin Circuit Court challenging the enactment and validity of SB 151. With no dispute about the material facts, the circuit court granted summary judgment to Appellees. As relevant to this appeal, the circuit court held that SB 151 was passed in violation of §46. The circuit court also determined that the bill constituted an appropriation and/or the creation of a debt and was thus in violation of the 51-vote majority requirement of §46. Because of the trial court's disposition of the case, it did not reach the merits of the inviolable contract issue. Appellants promptly appealed to the Court of Appeals. This Court accepted immediate transfer of the proceedings pursuant to CR 74.02.

* * *

---

4. Section 56 requires that a bill be signed by the Speaker of the House. Because the Speaker position was vacant for most of the 2018 Legislative Session, the Speaker Pro Tempore fulfilled this function. While the Attorney General originally argued the enactment was invalid because it was not signed by the Speaker of the House, that issue has now been abandoned.

III. Legislative Compliance with Section 46 is a Justiciable Issue

We first consider the threshold issue raised by Appellants and Amicus asserting that the judicial branch should abstain from adjudicating legislative compliance with §46's three-reading requirement because doing so would violate the well-established doctrine of the non-justiciability of political questions.

The "political question" doctrine is natural corollary to the more familiar concept of separation of powers. *Baker v. Carr*, 369 U.S. 186, 210, 82 S.Ct. 691, 7 L.Ed.2d 663 (1962). The doctrine holds that the judicial branch "should not interfere in the exercise by another department of a discretion that is committed by a textually demonstrable provision of the Constitution to the other department," *Fletcher v. Commonwealth*, 163 S.W.3d 852, 860 (Ky. 2005); or seek to resolve an issue for which it lacks judicially discoverable and manageable standards, *Vieth v. Jubelirer*, 541 U.S. 267, 276, 124 S.Ct. 1769, 158 L.Ed.2d 546 (2004).

Appellants argue that the processes and procedures by which a bill becomes a law are exclusively assigned to the legislative branch and that the legislature has exclusive authority to determine what is required by §46. They argue that judicial intrusion into that question would violate the stringent separation of powers doctrine embedded in Kentucky's constitution. Amicus further contends that, regardless of the justiciability of the three-readings requirement, the provision is not mandatory but is instead merely directory to the legislative branch.

We recognize the wisdom and viability of the political question doctrine, and we acknowledge our obligation to refrain from interfering with the internal processes and internal rules by which the other branches perform their constitutional functions. However, in this instance we are not addressing whether the passage of SB 151 conformed to the internal rules and processes of the General Assembly. We are confronted, instead, with the question of what §46 of the Kentucky Constitution means when it says that "[e]very bill shall be read at length on three different days in each House"; and whether the enactment of SB 151 comports with that constitutional provision.

We must reject the argument that this Court has no voice in that determination. The foundational principle described in *Marbury v. Madison*, 5 U.S. 137, 177–78, 1 Cranch 137, 2 L.Ed. 60 (1803), has been a cornerstone of the American republic for as long as the republic has endured: "It is emphatically the province and duty of the judicial department to say what the law is. Those who apply the rule to particular cases, must of necessity expound and interpret that rule.... This is of the very essence of judicial duty."

Kentucky has not wavered in its allegiance to that principle. *See Stephenson v. Woodward*, 182 S.W.3d 162, 174 (Ky. 2005) ("[J]ust as this court will not infringe upon the independence of the legislature, we will not cast a blind eye to our own duty to interpret the Constitution and declare the law."). Section 46 is not a procedural rule or policy written and adopted by the legislature to perform its constitutional function; it is an explicit provision of the Kentucky Constitution.

A. The issue before this Court is not a political question.

In support of the argument that the three-readings requirement of §46 is a non-justiciable political question, Appellants cite §39 of the Kentucky Constitution, which provides: "Each House of the General Assembly may determine the rules of its proceedings." From this provision, Appellants reason that the three-reading requirement is a "procedural requirement" imposed by the Constitution, "leav[ing] it to the General Assembly to determine how this requirement must be met."

Appellants also cite *Sibert v. Garrett*, 197 Ky. 17, 246 S.W. 455, 457 (1922), for the frequently-repeated observation that "[p]erhaps no state forming a part of the national government of the United States has a Constitution whose language more emphatically separates and perpetuates what might be termed the American tripod form of government than does our Constitution...." We note that *Sibert* also reminds us the separation of powers doctrine "does not destroy the power of the courts to pronounce an act unconstitutional when its enactment is either expressly or by necessary implication inhibited and subversive of the purposes and intention of the makers of the [Kentucky] constitution...." *Id.* at 457.

Sibert emphasizes that under Kentucky's strong separation of powers doctrine, the power to declare a legislative enactment unconstitutional when its enactment violates constitutional principles is solidly within the Court's constitutional authority. We reiterated this point in *Rose v. Council for Better Education, Inc.*:

> To avoid deciding the case because of "legislative discretion," "legislative function," etc., would be a denigration of our own constitutional duty. To allow the General Assembly (or, in point of fact, the Executive) to decide whether its actions are constitutional is literally unthinkable.

790 S.W.2d 186, 209 (Ky. 1989).

The Court's power to determine the constitutional validity of a statute "does not infringe upon the independence of the legislature." *Stephenson*, 182 S.W.3d at 174 ("[W]e will not cast a blind eye to our own duty to interpret the Constitution and declare the law."). Far from being an intrusion into the arena constitutionally assigned to the legislature, the Kentucky Constitution and the constitutions of the United States and virtually all states vest the ultimate authority for discerning the meaning of constitutional provisions in the judicial branch. Interpreting the Constitution is, after all, "the very essence of judicial duty." *Marbury*, 5 U.S. at 177.

The Court's power, indeed, its duty, to declare the meaning of constitutional provisions is a primary function of the judicial branch in the scheme of checks and balances that has protected freedom and liberty in this country and in this Commonwealth for more than two centuries. The power of judicial review is an integral and indispensable piece of the separation of powers doctrine. To desist from declaring the meaning of constitutional language would be an abdication of our constitutional duty. *Philpot v. Haviland*, 880 S.W.2d 550, 553 (Ky. 1994).

Quoting *Baker v. Carr*, we recognized in *Philpot* six standards for determining when the Courts should defer the resolution of an issue based upon the political question doctrine. Those standards are:

1. a textually demonstrable constitutional commitment of the issue to a coordinate political department; or

2. a lack of judicially discoverable and manageable standard for resolving it; or

3. the impossibility of deciding without an initial policy determination of a kind clearly for nonjudicial discretion; or

4. the impossibility of a court's undertaking independent resolution without expressing lack of respect due coordinate branches of government; or

5. an unusual need for unquestioning adherence to a political decision already made; or

6. the potentiality of embarrassment from multifarious pronouncements by various departments on one question.

880 S.W.2d at 553.

Applying these standards to the present case, we first note that there is no "textually demonstrable constitutional commitment" assigning to the General Assembly the sole authority to define the meaning of §46's three-readings requirement. We acknowledge without reservation the General Assembly's explicit power under Section 39 to make its own rules for its own proceedings, but as noted above, we are not tasked with deciding the meaning of the legislature's own rules. We take no issue with those rules. Section 46 is not a rule of the General Assembly to be defined, interpreted, and applied exclusively by the General Assembly.

Second, under the circumstances presented here, we do not lack judicially discoverable and manageable standards for resolving the meaning of §46. What constitutes or does not constitute a "reading" of a bill on different days is, under the most deferential of standards, something to be resolved under ordinary rules of constitutional interpretation.

Third, the determination of the three-reading requirement is not dependent upon an "initial policy determination of a kind clearly for nonjudicial discretion." We leave the policy implications to the General Assembly. Our determination of the meaning of §46 does not involve policy. Furthermore, this Court can undertake an independent resolution of the three-readings issue with no lack of respect for the legislature. Our review of §46 simply follows our normal rules of constitutional construction. As further explained below, we indeed agree with Appellants' assertion that a reading by title only conforms to the constitutional demand for the bill to be "read at length," and we respectfully agree that a bill need not be reread in its entirety following each amendment.

Concerning the fifth *Baker* factor, the question before us presents no "unusual need" to adhere to political decisions already made. Finally, there is no potential for "embarrassment from multifarious pronouncements by various departments on one question" that would weigh against a judicial interpretation of whether SB 151 was passed in compliance with §46.

Appellants rely heavily upon *Philpot*, 880 S.W.2d 550, and we agree that *Philpot* presents an excellent example of the political question doctrine's application. *Philpot* examined the following provision of §46:

> No bill shall be considered for final passage unless the same has been reported by a Committee and printed for the use of the members.... But whenever a committee refuses or fails to report a bill submitted to it in a reasonable time, the same may be called up by any member, and be considered in the same manner it would have been considered if it had been reported.

The Senate incorporated this provision in its own Senate Rule 48, which permitted any member to call up the bill he or she thought had been held too long in committee, but which also provided that the ascertainment of whether the bill had been held an unreasonable time was to be determined by a majority vote of the elected members. A group of senators challenged Senate Rule 48 as being in violation of §46. Applying the political question doctrine, we held:

> Had the Senate simply failed to adopt a rule implementing the Constitutional mandate whereby "any member" could set in motion a procedure guaranteed to address a committee's failure or refusal to report a bill, this Court could then take note of such default. However, once the Senate adopted a procedure such as Rule 48 provides, this Court has no authority to edit or rewrite it on the grounds that it could be improved upon.
>
> ....
>
> We are of the opinion ... that the determination of what is a "reasonable time" in this context, is a matter for the legislature to determine, under Section 39 of the Kentucky Constitution. For us to presume to define a "reasonable time" would result in the judiciary usurping the power of the Senate to determine for itself through its own rules when a committee has failed to report a bill within a reasonable time.
>
> ....
>
> [T]his Court is of the opinion that it is most appropriate for the Kentucky State Senate to determine what constitutes a "reasonable time" for a committee to retain proposed legislation. Such a determination is a political question, which traditionally courts have declined to address in the exercise of proper restraint, and have left to the appropriate branch of government. The Kentucky Senate has the "full knowledge and appreciation ascribed to the ... legislature of the political, social and economic conditions which have prevailed" since the legislation was introduced, and thus, the Senate is best able to determine when a committee has held a bill an unreasonable period of time.

Philpot, 880 S.W.2d at 552–54.

Appellants argue that *Philpot* is directly on point because, just as we found the definition of "reasonable time" to be a political question, we must similarly agree that the determination of what "read at length on three different days in each House" is also a political question. We are persuaded that *Philpot* is distinguishable from the present case.

First, *Philpot* involved an action to have this Court preemptively define the meaning of a "reasonable time." There was no constitutional challenge to enacted legislation. Second, unlike the inherently variable and necessarily imprecise term, "reasonable time," which implicates "a lack of judicially discoverable and manageable standard for resolving it," *Baker*, 369 U.S. at 217, 82 S.Ct. 691, whether a bill has been "read at length on three different days" is a straight-forward matter clearly susceptible to judicial review.

Appellants also cite *Gunn v. Hughes*, 210 So.3d 969 (Miss. 2017). In *Gunn*, the Mississippi Supreme Court addressed a provision in the Mississippi Constitution which provides that "every bill shall be read in full *immediately* before the vote on its final passage upon the demand of any member." *See* Article 4, Section 59 of the Mississippi Constitution. Representative Hughes brought a lawsuit alleging that upon his request to have certain bills fully read aloud as required by that article, House Speaker Gunn had the bills electronically read aloud by a machine at such a fast pace as to be incomprehensible, and could not, therefore, qualify as an actual "reading" of the bill. The Mississippi Supreme Court rejected that argument, stating:

> By requesting the courts to force Speaker Gunn to read bills in a particular manner, Rep. Hughes seeks to involve the judiciary in legislative procedural matters. The text of our state Constitution that imposes upon the Legislature the obligation to read bills upon a member's request, necessarily commits upon the Legislature the obligation to determine how that requirement will be carried out. So this case must be dismissed, not as a matter of judicial discretion, but because we are without constitutional authority to adjudicate it. The constitutional authority, and duty, to decide the matter lies squarely within the legislative branch of our government.

210 So.3d at 974.

We do not disagree with the Mississippi Court's resolution in *Gunn*; but *Gunn* is also readily distinguishable. However preposterous it was to physically read aloud a bill at an incomprehensible pace, it cannot be disputed that the bill was literally read aloud in its entirety. The Court declined to engage in the minutia of directing the legislature how fast or slow it must read the bill. In the case before us, *nothing* happened that can even plausibly comport with any conception of the phrase "read at length on three different days." Under any plausible meaning of those words that remains faithful to the English language, we can say with certainty that no part of SB 151 that eventually was sent to the Governor, including its title, was ever "read" in either chamber. The rationale of *Gunn* remains unpersuasive.

Appellees direct our attention to *D & W Auto Supply v. Department of Revenue*, 602 S.W.2d 420 (Ky. 1980). In *D & W Auto Supply*, we addressed the provision contained in §46 which requires that an appropriation bill receive a majority vote of all members sitting, which in the House of Representatives is 51 votes. The anti-littering appropriation bill in *D & W Auto Supply* received only 48 votes.

To determine whether a constitutional violation had occurred under these circumstances, we revisited and overruled the "enrolled bill doctrine"[5] that had been the controlling rule in Kentucky since 1896 pursuant to *Lafferty v. Huffman*, 99 Ky. 80, 35 S.W. 123 (1896). Under the enrolled bill doctrine, when attested by the presiding officers as the law required, an enrolled bill, "must be accepted by the courts as the very bill adopted by the legislature, and that its mode of enactment was in conformity to all constitutional requirements. When so authenticated, it imports absolute verity, and is unimpeached by the [legislative] journals." *Id.* at 126. The doctrine "conclusively presumes the validity of a bill passed by the legislature and signed by the legislative officers." *D & W Auto Supply*, 602 S.W.2d at 423. *D & W Auto Supply* overruled *Lafferty* and, citing §26,[6] replaced it with this rule:

> Section 26 of the Kentucky Constitution provides that any law contrary to the constitution is "void." The proper exercise of judicial authority requires us to recognize any law which is unconstitutional and to declare it void. Without belaboring the point, we believe that under section 228 of the Kentucky Constitution it is our obligation to "support... the Constitution of this Commonwealth." We are sworn to see that violations of the constitution by any person, corporation, state agency or branch of government are brought to light and corrected. To countenance an artificial rule of law that silences our voices when confronted with violations of our constitution is not acceptable to this court.
>
> We believe that a more reasonable rule is ... the "extrinsic evidence" rule.... Under this approach there is a prima facie presumption that an enrolled bill is valid, but such presumption may be overcome by clear, satisfactory and convincing evidence establishing that constitutional requirements have not been met.

D & W Auto Supply, 602 S.W.2d at 424–25 (citations omitted).

By abolishing the enrolled bill doctrine, *D & W Auto Supply* adopted the extrinsic evidence rule, rejecting the exclusion of the judiciary from examining whether an enactment was passed in violation of the constitution and fatally undercutting Appellants' assertion that the meaning of the three-readings requirement is not within judicial purview. Further undercutting Appellants' argument is the fact that *D & W*

5. An enrolled bill means "The final copy of a bill or joint resolution which has passed both chambers in identical form." * * *

6. "To guard against transgression of the high powers which we have delegated, We Declare that everything in this Bill of Rights is excepted out of the general powers of government, and shall forever remain inviolate; and all laws contrary thereto, or contrary to this Constitution, shall be void." Ky. Const. Sec. 26.

Auto Supply specifically held that a bill passed in violation of the majority-vote clause of §46 was unconstitutional, and therefore, void.

Based upon the foregoing analysis, we reject Appellants' position that this Court must abstain from hearing Appellees' challenge to SB 151. We are satisfied that judicial review of the meaning of any provision of the Kentucky Constitution is well within the separate powers assigned the judicial branch and that the question before us is not a non-justiciable political question.

B. The three-readings clause of §46 is a mandatory, rather than directory constitutional provision.

Amicus raises another important point implicating the justiciability of this matter. Although not raised or addressed in the trial court, we find it worthy of consideration and essential to a clear interpretation of §46. Amicus asserts that the bill "shall be read at length on three different days in each House" clause of §46 is not a mandatory prerequisite for the valid enactment of a bill, but rather is a mere directive, an instructional guide to be interpreted or even waived at the discretion of the General Assembly. We find no preservation of the issue as required by CR 76. Nevertheless, because of the importance of the issue and its close connection to the issue of justiciability, we address it.

If the word "shall" as used in the three-reading clause of §46 is mandatory, the issue of the clause is justiciable. If the word "shall" as used there is merely directory, the legislature's failure to comply may not affect the ultimate validity of the bill. As explained by our predecessor court in *Skaggs v. Fyffe*, 266 Ky. 337, 98 S.W.2d 884, 886 (1936), "[a] proceeding not following a mandatory provision of a statute is rendered illegal and void, while an omission to observe or failure to conform to a directory provision is not."

"In determining the nature of the statutory provision, the use of the word 'shall' with reference to some requirements ... is usually indicative that it is mandatory, but it will not be so regarded if the legislative intention appears otherwise." *Id. Skaggs* further explained that "directory" refers to the use of the word "shall" to give "directions which ought to be followed" to "accomplish a given end." *Skaggs* holds that "[I]f the directions given by the statute are violated, but the given end is in fact accomplished without affecting the real merits of the case, then the statute is to be regarded as directory merely." *Id.* (quoting *Varney v. Justice*, 86 Ky. 596, 6 S.W. 457, 459 (1888)).

In support of the argument that §46's use of "shall" is merely directory, Amicus directs our attention to *Hamlett v. McCreary*, 153 Ky. 755, 156 S.W. 410 (1913). *Hamlett* addressed the "[n]o bill shall become law" language contained in the first clause of §56 of the Kentucky Constitution:

> *No bill shall become a law* until the same shall have been signed by the presiding officer of each of the two Houses in open session; and before such officer shall have affixed his signature to any bill, he shall suspend all other business, declare that such bill will now be read, and that he will sign the same to the end that it may become a law. The bill shall then be read at length and compared;

> and, if correctly enrolled, he shall, in the presence of the House in open session, and before any other business is entertained, affix his signature, which fact shall be noted in the journal, and the bill immediately sent to the other House. When it reaches the other House, the presiding officer thereof shall immediately suspend all other business, announce the reception of the bill, and the same proceeding shall thereupon be observed in every respect as in the House in which it was first signed. And thereupon the Clerk of the latter House shall immediately present the same to the Governor for his signature and approval.

Ky. Const. Sec. 56 (emphasis added).

In *Hamlett*, the General Assembly passed a bill relating to bond payment premiums, but the bill was not signed by the President of the Senate. The Governor declined to sign the bill, and he did not veto it; he simply ignored it. Hamlett later sought payment upon the terms contained in the bill. When payment was refused, he brought a mandamus action to compel payment in compliance with the bill.

The *Hamlett* Court, noting the prefatory "no bill shall become law" language of §56, held that "Section 56 of the Kentucky Constitution … is mandatory in its provisions and not merely declaratory, since it prohibits a bill from becoming a law until it shall have been signed by the presiding officer of each house." *Hamlett*, 156 S.W. at 412. In its analysis, the Court quoted from the Missouri case *State v. Mead*, 71 Mo. 266 (Mo. 1879), as follows:

> We are convinced that the initial clause of the section that 'no bill shall become a law until the same shall have been signed by the presiding officer of each of the two houses in open session' is mandatory, though it is quite evident that the mandate of the Constitution would be obeyed, so far as concerns proper authentication of the bill, when it receives the signature of the respective presiding officers in open session. *But we do not regard the other clauses of the section under review as mandatory; for it is to be observed that those clauses do not declare that 'no bill shall become a law,' if the presiding officers or the members fail to perform the duties which the residue of the section imposes, but the only penalty directly expressed is that contained in the initial clause just noted.*

Id. at 412–13 (emphasis added).

Amicus argues from the *Mead* rationale that because the three-readings requirement of §46 is not prefaced with the phrase, "no bill shall become law until" or similar language, it too should be construed as directory rather than mandatory. *Mead*, an 1879 Missouri case, is not a controlling authority upon our review, but we appreciate its instructive value.

In its entirety, §46 states:

> *No bill shall be considered for final passage unless* the same has been reported by a committee and printed for the use of the members. Every bill shall be read at length on three different days in each House, but the second and third read-

> ings may be dispensed with by a majority of all the members elected to the House in which the bill is pending. But whenever a committee refuses or fails to report a bill submitted to it in a reasonable time, the same may be called up by any member, and be considered in the same manner it would have been considered if it had been reported. *No bill shall become a law unless*, on its final passage, it receives the votes of at least two-fifths of the members elected to each House, and a majority of the members voting, the vote to be taken by yeas and nays and entered in the journal: Provided, Any act or resolution for the appropriation of money or the creation of debt shall, on its final passage, receive the votes of a majority of all the members elected to each House.

Ky. Const. Sec. 46 (emphasis added).

In the context of statutory interpretation, *Skaggs* further explained:

> Whether a statute is to be deemed directory or mandatory depends, not on form, but on the legislative intent, which is to be ascertained by interpretation from consideration of the entire act, its nature and object, and the consequence of construction one way or the other. If the provision relates to some immaterial matter, not reaching the substance, or not of the essence of the thing to be done, and by an omission to observe it the rights of those interested will not be prejudiced—as where compliance is a matter of convenience or the directions are given merely with a view to securing proper, orderly, or prompt procedure—it is generally regarded as but directory. Of course, the term "mandatory" embraces the converse character of provisions, which are conditions precedent.

98 S.W.2d at 886 (citations omitted).

More recently, in *Vandertoll v. Commonwealth*, we explained the meaning of "shall" as follows:

> KRS 446.080(4) states that "[a]ll words and phrases shall be construed according to the common and approved usage of language...." "In common or ordinary parlance, and in its ordinary signification, the term 'shall' is a word of command and ... must be given a compulsory meaning." "If the words of the statute are plain and unambiguous, the statute must be applied to those terms without resort to any construction or interpretation." Shall means shall.

110 S.W.3d 789, 795–96 (Ky. 2003).

While Amicus correctly observes that the three-readings clause of §46 is not prefaced with the phrase, "no bill shall become law," we are unable to discern any indication that the framers of our Constitution intended to simply offer a mere helpful suggestion on how pending legislation might be presented in each chamber.[7] Regardless of what it means for a bill to be "read at length," there is no doubt from the language employed that the drafters predicated the validity of the legislation upon compliance with the

7. See the discussion of same in the following section of this opinion.

mandate to read at length, "every bill." Moreover, we remain mindful of the special consideration that must be accorded to constitutional provisions:

> In *Arnett v. Sullivan*, [279 Ky. 720, 132 S.W.2d 76 (Ky. 1939)] an exhaustive review of the authorities was entered into as to the correct theory of constitutional construction, that is, as to whether or not constitutional provisions are mandatory or directory, and it was there said: "with few exceptions, and only where the provision under consideration was of such a nature as to scarcely present the question, *the rule is declared that constitutional provisions are mandatory and never directory*."

Harrod v. Hatcher, 281 Ky. 712, 137 S.W.2d 405, 406 (1940) (emphasis added). For the foregoing reasons, we are compelled to regard the three-readings requirement of §46 as mandatory, rather than directory as urged by Amicus.

In summary, we conclude that the question of what §46 requires, and whether the enactment of SB 151 conformed with those requirements, is a justiciable cause.

IV. The Enactment of SB 151 Fails to Comply with the Three-Readings Requirement of §46 of the Kentucky Constitution.

Having crossed the threshold issue of justiciability, we proceed to examine the meaning of the three-readings provision of §46 and whether SB 151 was passed in compliance with that Constitutional provision.

As with the words we find in contracts and statutes, "words used in the Constitution must be given their plain and ordinary meaning." *City of Louisville Municipal Housing Commission v. Public Housing Administration*, 261 S.W.2d 286, 287 (Ky. 1953); *Court of Justice ex rel. Administrative Office of the Courts v. Oney*, 34 S.W.3d 814, 816 (Ky. App. 2000). Of similar import, "where the language of the Constitution leaves no doubt of the intended meaning of the section under consideration, courts may not employ rules of construction." *Grantz v. Grauman*, 302 S.W.2d 364, 366 (Ky. 1957) (citations omitted). "[I]n construing one section of a Constitution a court should not isolate it from other sections, but all the sections bearing on any particular subject should be brought into consideration and be so interpreted as to effectuate the whole purpose of the Constitution." *Id.*

One of the cardinal rules for the interpretation of statutes is that the courts should avoid adopting a construction which would be unreasonable and absurd in preference to one that is "reasonable, rational, sensible and intelligent." *Johnson v. Frankfort & C. R. R.*, 303 Ky. 256, 197 S.W.2d 432, 434 (1946). The same rule also applies in our efforts to construe the meaning of constitutional provisions.

We apply these long-established principles in our review of §46. At first glance, the phrase, "Every bill shall be read at length on three different days in each House" seems simple and clear. In its plain ordinary sense, "to read" simply means to look at and comprehend or to speak aloud written words. At first glance, one might reasonably surmise that to be "read at length" in each House of the General Assembly, the words of each bill must be collectively looked at and spoken aloud in its entirety.

We agree with Appellants and Amicus that such a literal interpretation of the words produces an unreasonable and absurd result. To recognize the absurdity of reading aloud every word of every bill in each house, one need only imagine reading the 291-page bill now under review and extending that consumption of legislative time and attention to every bill considered by the General Assembly in each session and doing so three times on different days. The framers of our Constitution were not intent upon burdening the legislature with such an absurd waste of time.

We do not purport to state within the pages of this opinion all the ways by which a bill may be "read" in compliance with §46, nor do we conclude that there is only one way that a bill can be "read" in compliance with §46. We are satisfied that the common legislative practice of reading only the title of the bill and electronically publishing simultaneously the full text of the bill to the electronic legislative journal available on every legislator's desk satisfies the constitutional mandate of §46. *See Richards Furniture Corp. v. Board of County Comm'rs of Anne Arundel County*, 233 Md. 249, 196 A.2d 621, 627 (1964) ("[A] reading of a bill by a reading of its title only is a sufficient 'reading' thereof to satisfy the constitutional provision relating to three readings."); *cf. McClellan v. Stein*, 229 Mich. 203, 201 N.W. 209, 211 (1924) ("While the method of first and second reading by title has been criticized as not in strict conformance with the constitutional provision upon the subject, in view of the customary legislative rule and practice of supplying each member with a printed copy at least five days before passage of any bill, this court has declined to hold invalid laws so passed where the journal showed the third reading was in full.").

Nevertheless, while we agree that the mode chosen by the General Assembly to "read" a bill passes constitutional muster, we are constrained to the conclusion that SB 151, as finally enacted, never received such readings in either legislative chamber.

The words "SB 151" were, indeed, "read" three times but the title read along with that designation each time was "AN ACT relating to the local provision of wastewater services." Although read only by title, the title by which SB 151 was read never had any connection with the subject matter of the measure enacted: "AN ACT relating to retirement," nor did it connote any information to signify that the act related to public pensions or the retirement benefits of public employees. Nothing in the utterance of the bill's numerical designation, SB 151, conveyed any information that the reading was related to a pension reform bill. The title as read in each chamber pertained to the local wastewater services measure that was discarded.

In deference to the General Assembly, we necessarily stop short of providing a complete and precise definition of what must occur to qualify as a reading of the bill, but we are well-settled in the conviction that what occurred here falls far short of the requirements of §46.

As noted above, §51 of the Kentucky Constitution requires that every law enacted by the General Assembly shall relate to only one subject and that subject "shall be expressed in the title." A fundamental premise underlying our holding that reading a bill "by title only" is an appropriate mode of compliance with §46's mandate to read a bill "at length" is the assumption that the title so read is germane to the law being enacted.

As we have noted, requiring every bill to be read aloud in its entirety in each legislative chamber would be an absurd construction of §46; reading the bill by title only is sufficient. But, it is equally absurd to suggest that §46 is satisfied by reading the title of a bill that has absolutely nothing to do with the subject matter of the bill.

Appellants maintain that the artifice used to enact SB 151 has been employed in the past on numerous occasions to enact numerous bills, and so a ruling affirming the trial court threatens the validity of many current laws. We are not persuaded. Any infirmities that might have been raised in timely fashion to challenge the enactment of now well-established laws are beyond the purview of this opinion. Moreover, we are not persuaded from the record here that such a potential parade of horrors awaits.

Appellants make much of the fact the Kentucky Education Reform Act (KERA) was passed using the same stratagem used to enact SB 151 as a pension reform measure. An examination of that argument discloses that KERA was indeed passed after last-minute amendments were substituted. But, the amendments made to the KERA bill did not gut the contents of the bill and replace it with legislation relating to an entirely different subject matter, while retaining the original title, thus misdescribing the tenor of the legislation embodied by the bill.

We emphasize now that this opinion does not challenge the legislative process used here. We have no quarrel with the use of a committee substitute to change the language of legislation as it navigates the legislative process. The procedure itself is a matter beyond our sphere of authority. Our opinion is directed to the question of whether the reading of a bill "by title only" can satisfy the constitutional requirement of §46 when the title so read has absolutely nothing to do with the substance of the bill. We can accept the argument of practicality that the reading of a bill "by title only" would achieve the framers' purpose for §46. But, essential to the validity of that argument is the premise that the title of the bill is germane to the subject of the bill so that the reading by title only triggers some recognition of the bill's contents.

Of course, legislators may amend the text of a bill between its readings without running afoul of §46. Ordinarily, the revised text is some variation of the original text and remains consistent with the theme reflected in the title of the bill. The complete elimination of all the words of the prior readings and their total replacement with words bearing no relationship to the title of the bill is a far different matter with respect to §46 compliance. *Hoover v. Board of County Comm'rs, Franklin County*, 19 Ohio St.3d 1, 482 N.E.2d 575, 579 (1985) ("[A]mendments which do not vitally alter the substance of a bill do not trigger a requirement for three considerations anew of such amended bill. But, when the subject or proposition of the bill is thereby wholly changed, it would seem to be proper to read the amended bill three times, and on different days....") (quotation marks and citations omitted); *Magee v. Boyd*, 175 So.3d 79, 114 (Ala. 2015) ("[I]t is clear that the substitute version of HB 84 was not read 'on three different days' in each house. However, we hold that an amended bill or a substitute bill, if germane to and not inconsistent with the general purpose of the original bill, does not have to be read three times on three different days to comply with §63 [Alabama's the three readings requirement.]); *State v. Ryan*, 92 Neb. 636, 139 N.W. 235, 238 (1912) (allowing amendments to be introduced after the legislative session ends so long as "the amendment is germane to the subject of the original bill and not an evident attempt to evade the Constitution"); *State v. Hocker*, 36 Fla. 358, 18 So. 767, 770 (1895) (explaining that three re-readings are unnecessary when the amendments in question are "made germane to [the bill's] general subject, either to the body of the bill or to its title").

We are fully satisfied that compliance with §46 as we have herein construed it will not create the legislative impediment Appellants portend. As plainly stated within the section itself, the second and third readings may be dispensed with by a majority vote. A bill with majority support can be passed with only *one reading*. Our construction of §46 does not portend legislative gridlock.

Our interpretation of §46 is based in part upon our consideration of the Constitutional Debates of 1891 that preceded the adoption of the present Kentucky Constitution. We find ample support for the position that the purpose of §46 is to ensure that every legislator has a fair opportunity to fully consider a bill before it is called for a vote. For example, Delegate Strauss, explaining the purpose of §46, stated:

> [T]he effort of the Committee [drafting §46] was to prevent hasty and inconsiderate, and sometimes corrupt legislation....
>
> Sometimes it has happened in the history of our State, as of other States, that very important measures, affecting the interest of the whole people, especially revenue matters, have been introduced, without referring them to any Committee, frequently at the end of a session, without printing, and pushed through, to the great loss and detriment of the State.... [The Legislature] ought to give each general measure that degree of consideration which would secure accuracy, and we put this in to secure that consideration.... [U]nder our old constitution the reading of a bill for three consecutive days was evaded. It was waived, by unanimous consent, and bills of every character were put through without any sort of consideration.... To correct that evil, this section was drawn[.][8]

This emphasis upon "consideration" of each bill connotes more than simply a legislator's awareness of what a bill was about, although that result would undoubtedly be achieved by satisfying the first purpose.

This is further evidenced by the fact that §46 requires not only that the bill be printed, "so that every member shall have an opportunity at least of knowing what he has voted on,"[9] but also that it be read. In discussing the reading requirement, Delegate Clay

8. 3 Kentucky Constitutional Debates 3858 (1891).

9. In discussing Section 46, Delegate Buckner stated the following: "[B]efore consideration by the House before which the bill comes, *it shall be printed, so that every member shall have an opportunity at least of knowing what he has voted on*. Then it shall be read." *Id.* at 3869.

explained that, because the "Orders of the Day" must be completely gone through after each reading of a bill, and because that process would take at least a week, "a bill [that] is not opposed at all, [would take] twenty or more days to pass [and] ... the [legislative] session shall not extend beyond sixty days."[10]

In response to this concern, the framers adopted an amendment that allowed the second and third reading to be dispensed with by a majority of all members.[11] This is important because it shows that the framers intended for the process to allow enough time for all legislators to consider a bill to their satisfaction before it is called for a vote, even after the bill has been printed so that each member could see what they were voting on. Had the framers been solely concerned with members simply knowing what it was they were voting on, as the Appellants argue, there would have been no need to require three readings.

In addition, an excerpt from Delegate Beckham provides perhaps the clearest evidence that the purpose of the reading requirement was to give members a fair opportunity to consider each bill, and not simply to ensure each member knew what they were voting on. Beckham stated the following:

> It seems to me that the fact of the printing having been done, every member having fair opportunity to fully consider the bill, with it in his own hands, dispenses with the necessity of reading it on three different days; but, I think, it ought to be read once, and then the body considering it, if it sees proper, can dispense with the second and third readings.[12]

Here, Beckham states the purpose of the three-readings requirement—to give every member fair opportunity to fully *consider* the bill—but believes it is satisfied with the printing requirement. Nonetheless, Beckham agrees that the readings are still important, and a version of the bill requiring both printing and three readings, with the second and third capable of being dispensed with, is ultimately adopted.[13]

In sum, we are convinced that the purpose of §46 was not simply to ensure that legislators knew what they were voting on. Rather, the purpose was to ensure that every legislator had a fair opportunity to fully consider each piece of legislation that would be brought to a vote. That purpose cannot be achieved by reading a bill only by its title which has no rational relationship to the subject of the law being enacted. The "reading" of SB 151 failed to comply even with this minimal requirement of §46 of the

---

10. *Id.* at 3866.

11. In response to Clay's concern, Delegate Carroll stated the following: "[T]he Committee have agreed to accept the amendment of the Delegate from Shelby to the first part of this section, and that dispenses with the necessity of reading the bill on three different days and obviates to a very great extent the objection urged by [Delegate Clay]." *Id.* The amendment in question inserted a provision that allowed the second and third reading to be dispensed with upon a vote of a majority of all members elected in the House in which the bill is pending. *Id.* at 3862 (amendment offered by Delegate from Shelby, J. C. Beckham).

12. *Id.* at 3866.

13. *Id.* at 3870.

Kentucky Constitution. Consequently, we declare the enactment of SB 151 was contradictory to the Kentucky Constitution and is hereby declared void and of no effect.

* * *

VII. Conclusion

For the foregoing reasons, the Opinion and Order of the Franklin Circuit Court is affirmed.

All sitting. All concur. VanMeter, J., also concurs by separate opinion in which Cunningham and Wright JJ., join.

* * *

Notes and Questions

1. The use of a "committee substitute" to replace the entire text of a pending bill is common in both Congress and state legislatures throughout the country. It is also common for a legislative chamber to amend the title of a bill after passage. What would the General Assembly have to do when employing these procedures to ensure the laws it enacts would pass constitutional muster?
2. There is no provision in the U.S. Constitution comparable to Section 46 of the Kentucky Constitution. Though the Congress uses a system of committees, there is no constitutional requirement that a bill be reported by a committee or read a certain number of times before Congress may enact it.
3. What, if anything, do the legislative restraints in Section 46 say about the issues motivating the adoption of a new Constitution in 1890–91?

Commonwealth ex rel. Armstrong v. Collins

Supreme Court of Kentucky (1986)

709 S.W.2d 437

Opinion of the Court by Chief Justice Stephens.

The basic issue we address is to what extent, if any, the General Assembly of the Commonwealth may, in adopting a budget bill and based on the financial condition of the Commonwealth provide therein for the reduction, elimination and transfer of appropriated funds, and for all practical purposes, provide as a result thereof, that the effectiveness of certain existing statutes is temporarily modified.

Background

At its regular session in 1984, the General Assembly passed a biennial budget.[1] This document appropriated the revenue for the Commonwealth and determined how that

1. House Bill 474, Chapter 418 of the 1984 Acts hereinafter referred to as HB 474, or the budget bill.

revenue would be expended for the operation, maintenance and support of the three branches of state government and the myriad of ancillary state agencies and programs.[2] This document, included a reduction in appropriations for various salary increases and transfers of funds from various trust and agency accounts to the General Fund to cover central administrative expenses.

In addition, at the same session the General Assembly passed corollary legislation[3] which conferred upon the General Assembly the authority to provide, in a budget bill, for the suspension or modification of the operation of an existing statute if the General Assembly found that such action is required by the financial condition of state government.

Procedural History

The appellant, Attorney General of the Commonwealth, on June 6, 1984 filed a petition for declaratory judgment in the Franklin Circuit Court challenging the constitutional validity of those legislative acts.[4] Basically, the petition claimed that the legislative enactments violated the prescriptions of Section 51 of the Kentucky Constitution, both as to the germaneness of the titles of the acts and as to the failure to follow the procedural requirement of Section 51 for the enactment and publication of amendments to existing law. A temporary restraining order was entered by the trial judge which prevented various officials in the Executive branch of government from transferring funds from certain designated trust and agency funds[5] and other special accounts to the general operating fund of the Commonwealth. Following normal briefing and arguments, the trial court entered its findings of fact, conclusions of law and declaratory judgment. A notice of appeal was timely filed by the Attorney General and upon appropriate motion, and for obvious reasons, we transferred the appeal directly to this Court.

Decision of the Trial Court

In rejecting the contentions of the Attorney General in the main, the trial court declared that the General Assembly has, under Ky. Const. Secs. 15 and 51, the authority to "suspend existing laws in a budget bill if the provision is germane to the broad subject of appropriations." It further declared that the procedural requirements of Ky. Const. Sec. 51 were not applicable to the challenged statutes because they only effected a "suspension" of existing statutes and were not an "express or implied repeal" of existing statutes.

2. The specific provisions of the statutes under attack will be more fully described in the appropriate parts of this opinion.

3. Senate Bill 294, Chapter 410 of the 1984 Acts hereinafter referred to as SB 294 or KRS 446.085.

4. Mr. Thompson was sued in his official capacity. He resigned the position of Secretary of the Finance and Administration Cabinet, and the Governor of Kentucky has appointed Gordon C. Duke to that office.

5. For a description of trust and agency funds, see *infra.*, p. 18, *et seq.*

The trial court also upheld the General Assembly's authority to suspend previously authorized salaries, trust and agency funds.[6] It declared certain transfers of funds invalid because they accomplished more than "the mere suspension of existing statutory provisions" and because they were not "germane" to appropriations within the aegis of Kentucky Constitution Section 51.[7] The former ruling is before us on appeal, the latter is not.

Contentions of the Parties

The appellant urges us to reverse the trial court because of what he maintains is an erroneous and "cryptic analysis" by the trial court of Sections 51 and 15 of the Kentucky Constitution. In essence, appellant argues that the titles to the two acts in question do not pass Section 51's constitutional requirement that the content of the act be germane to the title thereof. The Attorney General also urges us to declare as error the ruling that the procedural requirement of Section 51 does not apply to a "suspension" of existing statutes. Further, appellant argues the trial court erroneously concluded that Section 15 of the Kentucky Constitution permitted the statutory suspension and modification contained in HB 474. Finally, it is argued that the trial court erroneously applied the "germaneness" test of Section 51 to the various provisions of the acts in question.

The Challenged Statutes

SB 294 provides as follows:

> "(1) *Nothing in a budget bill adopted by the general assembly shall be construed to effect a repeal or amendment in the Kentucky Revised Statutes*, and if any repeal or amendment appears to be effected in any of the Kentucky Revised Statutes, it shall be disregarded, shall be null and void, and the law as it existed prior to the effective date of the budget bill shall be given full force and effect.
>
> "(2) Notwithstanding the provisions of subsection (1) of this section *the general assembly may provide in a budget bill for the suspension or modification of the operation of a statute* if the general assembly finds that the financial condition of state government requires such suspension or modification. Such suspension or modification shall not extend beyond the duration of the budget bill." (Emphasis added.)

It is clear from the plain language of the statute that in Section (1) the General Assembly deprives itself of the legal authority to *repeal or amend*, through the device

---

6. Specifically the trial court approved the transfer of funds in the following areas: Board of Elections; Kentucky Development Finance Authority; University of Kentucky; Banking and Securities; Fish and Wildlife Resources; Road Fund; Capital Construction of Road Fund; Education and Humanities; Local Jail Support (medical contracts).

7. Those declared invalid were: Unified prosecutorial system, only insofar as it provides that a county or a circuit will receive funds proportional to the state's total criminal case load; Auditor of Public Accounts, only insofar as it imposes additional duties on the Auditor; Corrections, only insofar as it creates a scheme for investigating and reporting on community and private corporate availability of correctional services; Department of Social Services, only insofar as it exempts certain personnel from salary ceilings and imposes a limit on administrative costs; Transportation Cabinet, only insofar as it places a ceiling on the number of full time positions in the Transportation Cabinet.

of a budget bill, any other existing law appearing in the Kentucky Revised Statutes. However, in Section (2), the General Assembly gives itself the power to *suspend or modify the operation* of any statute, but only if the financial condition of state government so requires. The duration of such suspension is limited to the duration of the budget.

The General Assembly has, by this statute, drawn a line between its power in the budget bill to suspend or modify existing statutes, as opposed to repealing or amending existing statutes. It cannot repeal or amend, but it can suspend or modify existing statutes through the provisions of a budget bill.

Armed with this legislation, the General Assembly, in its biennial budget bill for the years 1984–1986, exercised this authority by drafting items relating to the reduction of increases in state officials' salaries, items providing for the transfer of monies from agencies and special funds to the states' general fund and items qualifying funds for resource recovery road projects, school books, and local jail support.

It is our role to determine * * * if both SB 294 and the budget bill comply with the requirements of the title section of Kentucky Constitution Section 51. If the answer to the second inquiry is in the affirmative we must, finally, examine each contested "modification or suspension" contained in the budget bill to determine if such actually constitutes a repeal or amendment, or if each is only a modification or suspension within the purview of SB 294(2) and of the re-enactment and publication section of Kentucky Constitution Section 51.

* * *

Do the Titles of SB 294 and HB 474 Comport with the Mandate of Kentucky Constitution, Section 51?

Kentucky Constitution Section 51 is as follows:

> "No law enacted by the General Assembly shall relate to more than one subject, and that shall be expressed in the title, and no law shall be revised, amended, or the provisions thereof extended or conferred by reference to its title only, but so much thereof as is revised, amended, extended or conferred, shall be re-enacted and published at length".

There are two proscriptions contained in this oft-litigated section. One directs that an act of the General Assembly shall only relate to one subject and requires that the subject shall be expressed in the title of the act. The other directs that no existing law shall be revised, amended, or its provisions conferred or extended by referring to its title only, but rather when such action is intended, the law is required to be re-enacted at length. Appellant attacks HB 474 and SB 294 with respect to the first proscription of Section 51 and HB 474 with respect to the second.

(A) Do the Titles to SB 294 and HB 474 Properly Describe the Subject of Those Acts.

Ky. Const. Sec. 51 has always been liberally construed, with all doubts being resolved in favor of the validity of the legislative action. The purpose of the section is said to be to prevent the enactment of "surreptitious" legislation. *Bowman v. Hamlett*, 159 Ky. 184, 166 S.W. 1008 (1914); *Dawson v. Commonwealth, Department of Transportation*, Ky., 622 S.W.2d 212 (1981). The framers of the Constitution intended to prevent surprise and fraud upon the members of the General Assembly and other interested parties, thus preventing the practice of "log rolling". *Commonwealth ex rel. Meredith v. Johnson*, 292 Ky. 288, 166 S.W.2d 409, 411 (1942).

The title need only furnish general notification of the general subject in the act. If the title furnishes a "clue" to the act's contents, it passes constitutional muster. *Talbott v. Laffoon*, 257 Ky. 773, 79 S.W.2d 244 (1935).

> "Section 51 of our Constitution ... was to prevent the evil that had grown up of legislating in one act upon as many distinct and wholly disconnected subjects as the legislative body saw fit, without any indication in the title of the act as to what its contents might be.... [Prior to its adoption] [i]t was then competent for the Legislature to legislate upon a multiplicity of unrelated subjects which were neither remotely germane to, or in any wise connected with, the one or ones named in the title ... *[t]o circumvent such deceptive practices resulting in deceitful, selfish, and other baleful consequences, the provision was inserted in the Constitution.*" *Id.* at 246. (Emphasis added.)

Do the challenged titles provide the reader a clue as to the contents of the act? Do the acts perpetrate a fraud? Did the General Assembly in providing a title to the acts and placing it in juxtaposition with the content of the acts effect something deceitful, selfish or baleful? We think not.

The challenged SB 294 title is as follows:

> "AN ACT relating to the relationship of the budget bill to the Kentucky Revised Statutes, and declaring an emergency."

The challenged two paragraphs of SB 294 limit the General Assembly's right to *repeal or amend* in a budget bill but permit the *suspension or modification* of such existing statutes, but only in the event that the financial conditions of the state mandate emergency action. The substance of the act thus permits suspension or modification of Kentucky Revised Statutes by a budget bill. The act expresses the relationship of a budget bill to all existing statutory law—which is primarily what the title says it does. The "germaneness" argument here is little short of specious.

The title of HB 474, the biennial budget bill, is as follows:

> "AN ACT relating to appropriations for the operation, maintenance, support, and functioning of the government of the Commonwealth of Kentucky and its various officers, cabinets, departments, boards, commissions, institutions, subdivisions, agencies, and other state supported activities."

The various contested provisions of HB 474, provide for the transfer of funds from various trust and agency accounts to the general fund of the Commonwealth, and also provide for the reduction of raises made in various officers' salaries. The title to the act refers to "appropriation" for the operation, etc., of state government. Certainly, the title does not tell the reader that—in the voluminous act—the General Assembly has authorized the reduction of salary increases and the transfer of trust and agency funds. However, under the case law cited above all that is necessary is that the act give a "clue" as to its content and that the act be not deceitful, selfish or result in "baleful" consequences.

HB 474 is a budget—a biennial budget—directing the expenditure of literally billions of dollars to be used in the operation of state government. The provisions thereof that suspend or modify the expenditure of monies in the event of a financial problem are clearly appropriations, in the broad sense. Appropriation of the people's money is the exclusive responsibility of the General Assembly, including the power to suspend or modify such appropriation under emergency financial circumstances. Moreover, such modification or suspension is obviously part of the whole framework of the budget, and no one could possibly be deceived by the inclusion of such provisions. The fact that the title tells the reader that the act is an appropriation for the funding of state government clearly alerts one to the fact that the act deals with "appropriations" including possible changes. No person could claim to have been misled by the title of HB 474 because the content of the act sets a course of action when the financial condition of the Commonwealth deteriorates. We believe that the title of HB 474 clearly complies with Ky. Const. Sec. 51.

(B) Do the Challenged Portions of HB 474 Comport with the Provision of Kentucky Constitution, Section 51 that Requires Amendment of Statutes to be Done at Length?

This second part of Section 51 is not nearly so often litigated as the so-called "title" section. The purpose of this section is perhaps best explained by one of the framers:

> "The members of the General Assembly did not know what they were voting for half the time, and this section ... provides when an act is amended ... shall be set out in full, so every man will understand what it is when voting on it, and the people will know what change has been made when they see it." *Spalding, Chairman of the Legislative Committee, Volume 3, p. 3792, Debates of the Constitutional Convention.*

As the court said, in *Board of Penitentiary Commissioners v. Spencer*, 159 Ky. 255, 166 S.W. 1017 (1914):

> "When any person, lawyer or layman, takes up an act of the Legislature, to read and understand what changes have been made in an old law, he ought to have before him in the act that he is reading the whole of the law as it appears when amended or revised by the new act..." *Id.* at 1024.

This part of Section 51 may be described as the re-enactment and publication requirement of that section. As stated, its application is limited by its own wording to amendment, revision, extension or conferring of existing statutes. Its purpose is to prevent deceitful practices and to provide full and easily accessible information to legislators and to the public when the General Assembly is so effecting existing law.

If a challenged statutory enactment falls within the proscribed activities, as opposed to merely being suspensory in nature, it is violative of this second part of Section 51. If it is, however, merely a suspension or modification, it is not violative thereof. The same restriction appears in SB 294(2), wherein the General Assembly restricted itself to the same limitation of Ky. Const. Sec. 51.

* * *

We repeat ourselves when we say that the General Assembly has, constitutionally speaking, the power in a budget bill to repeal or amend the manner in which public funds are used. Ky. Const. Sec. 51, the "title" section, has not been violated by the matters clearly relating to appropriations. What we decide is simply that the transfers of funds which are merely temporary, determinable suspensions of the operation of the statutes relating to appropriations of public funds are within the legislative authority as set out in SB 294 and Ky. Const. Sec. 51, the amendment section.

* * *

There is no need to "wrap up" this opinion with a lengthy summary. The General Assembly has the basic constitutional power and responsibility to tax and to spend the public's money. This power, as we have seen in prior decisions, is exclusive to the General Assembly and includes the power to use a budget bill to repeal, amend, modify and suspend existing statutes. Such power must be exercised within all constitutional proscriptions, including those of Section 51. The General Assembly, in the questioned statute hereinbefore described and relying on its own specific statutory authority, did precisely that.

The judgment of the trial court is affirmed.

Stephens, C.J., and Gant, Leibson, Stephenson, White and Wintersheimer, JJ., concur.

Vance, J., dissents, and files a dissenting opinion.

* * *

Notes and Questions

1. Like Section 46, there is no provision in the U.S. Constitution comparable to Section 51. Bills enacted by the Congress often relate to more than one subject—part of the "logrolling" process—and often have long titles that do not reveal the full content of the bill (*e.g.*, titles that end with "and for other purposes").
2. Other than Sections 46 and 51, what other procedural restraints are there on the General Assembly that have no analogue applicable to the Congress in the U.S. Constitution?

E. Legislative Control of Public Education: Power and Duty

"The General Assembly shall, by appropriate legislation, provide for an efficient system of common schools throughout the State." (Ky. Const. §183.)

In 1973, the Supreme Court of the United States decided *San Antonio Independent School District v. Rodriguez*, 411 U.S. 1 (1973). In *Rodriguez*, the plaintiffs had challenged the constitutionality of the funding of the Texas public school system. Because the funding was tied to local property taxes, there were disparities in education spending from school district to school district, which adversely affected the less affluent school districts. The federal District Court found that the funding of the Texas school system discriminated based on wealth, and that wealth was a "suspect" classification that warranted strict scrutiny under the Equal Protection Clause. However, the Supreme Court held that wealth was not a suspect class, declined to find that education was a fundamental right under the U.S. Constitution, and upheld the funding of the Texas school system under rational basis review.

The *Rodriguez* decision accelerated a wave of litigation in the state courts that had begun a couple years earlier. With the availability of federal claims foreclosed, claimants attacked funding disparities between rich and poor school districts under state constitutional Due Process Clause equivalents. Most of these claims also were unsuccessful.

Lawyers then turned to state constitutional education guarantees of "an efficient system of common schools" as grounds for closing the wealth gap between school districts, launching a second wave of state court litigation. All state constitutions have some form of education clause—Kentucky's is Section 183. Since the late 1980s, plaintiffs have won about two-thirds of the cases challenging school funding based upon these education clauses. Such a case found its way to the Supreme Court of Kentucky in 1989.

Rose v. Council for Better Education, Inc.

Supreme Court of Kentucky (1989)
790 S.W.2d 186

Opinion of the Court by Chief Justice Stephens.

The issue we decide on this appeal is whether the Kentucky General Assembly has complied with its constitutional mandate to "provide an efficient system of common schools throughout the state."[1]

In deciding that it has not, we intend no criticism of the substantial efforts made by the present General Assembly and by its predecessors, nor do we intend to substitute our judicial authority for the authority and discretion of the General Assembly. We are, rather, exercising our constitutional duty in declaring that, when we consider the

1. Ky. Const. Sec. 183.

evidence in the record, and when we apply the constitutional requirement of Section 183 to that evidence, it is crystal clear that the General Assembly has fallen short of its duty to enact legislation to provide for an efficient system of common schools throughout the state. In a word, the present system of common schools in Kentucky is not an "efficient" one in our view of the clear mandate of Section 183. The common school system in Kentucky is constitutionally deficient.

In reaching this decision, we are ever mindful of the immeasurable worth of education to our state and its citizens, especially to its young people. The framers of our constitution intended that each and every child in this state should receive a proper and an adequate education, *to be provided for by the General Assembly*. This opinion dutifully applies the constitutional test of Section 183 to the existing system of common schools. We do no more, nor may we do any less.

The goal of the framers of our constitution, and the polestar of this opinion, is eloquently and movingly stated in the landmark case of *Brown v. Board of Education*:

> "*education is perhaps the most important function of state and local governments.* Compulsory school attendance laws and the great expenditures for education both demonstrate our recognition of the importance of education to our democratic society. It is required in the performance of our most basic public responsibilities, even service in the armed forces. It is the very foundation of good citizenship. Today it is a principal instrument in awakening the child to cultural values, in preparing him for later professional training, and in helping him to adjust normally to his environment. In these days, it is doubtful that any child may reasonably be expected to succeed in life if he is denied the opportunity of an education. *Such an opportunity, where the state has undertaken to provide it, is a right which must be made available to all on equal terms.*" *Id.*, 347 U.S. 483, 493, 74 S.Ct. 686, 691, 98 L.Ed. 873 (1954). (Emphasis added.)

These thoughts were as applicable in 1891 when Section 183 was adopted as they are today and the goals they express reflect the goals set out by the framers of our Kentucky Constitution.

I. Procedural History

This declaratory judgment action was filed in the Franklin Circuit Court by multiple plaintiffs, including the Council for Better Education, Inc. a non-profit Kentucky corporation whose membership consists of sixty-six local school districts in the state. Also joining as plaintiffs were the Boards of Education of the Dayton and Harlan Independent School Districts and the school districts of Elliott, Knox, McCreary, Morgan and Wolfe Counties. Twenty-two public school students from McCreary, Wolfe, Morgan and Elliott Counties and Harlan and Dayton Independent School districts were also named, suing, respectively, by and through their parents as next friends.

* * *

The defendants named in the complaint were the Governor, the Superintendent of Public Instruction, the State Treasurer, the President *Pro Tempore* of the Senate, the Speaker of the House of Representatives and the State Board of Education and its individual members.

The complaint included allegations that the system of school financing provided for by the General Assembly is inadequate; places too much emphasis on local school board resources; and results in inadequacies, inequities and inequalities throughout the state so as to result in an inefficient system of common school education in violation of Kentucky Constitution, Sections 1, 3 and 183 and the equal protection clause and the due process of law clause of the 14th Amendment to the United States Constitution. Additionally the complaint maintains the entire system is not efficient under the mandate of Section 183.

The relief sought by the plaintiffs was a declaration of rights to the effect that the system be declared unconstitutional; that the funding of schools also be determined to be unconstitutional and inadequate; that the defendant, Superintendent of Public Instruction be enjoined from further implementing said school statutes; that a mandamus be issued, directing the Governor to recommend to the General Assembly the enactment of appropriate legislation which would be in compliance with the aforementioned constitutional provisions; that a mandamus be issued, directing the President *Pro Tempore* of the Senate and the Speaker of the House of Representatives to place before the General Assembly appropriate legislation which is constitutionally valid; and that a mandamus be issued, directing the General Assembly to provide for an "equitable and adequate funding program for all school children so as to establish an 'efficient system of common schools.'"

The answers filed by the various defendants were basically identical. It was pled that the complaint failed to state a claim against any of the defendants; that the court had no jurisdiction because the subject matter is purely a "political" one; that all school boards should have been joined as parties defendants; that all members of the General Assembly (1986) should also have been joined as parties defendant; that all the plaintiffs lacked standing to bring the action; that, specifically, the plaintiff Council for Better Education, Inc., had no legal authority to sue; that the plaintiff school boards similarly had no legal authority to sue; that the class action was improper; and as would be expected, the defendants denied all of the alleged constitutional violations and the facts underlying such alleged violations.

The defendants also filed a self-styled "affirmative defense" claiming that education reform laws passed by the General Assembly at a special session in 1985 and various budget changes and other educational laws passed by the General Assembly at its 1986 regular session inferentially corrected the situation alleged in the complaint. Reference was also made to past legislative efforts of the General Assembly in the education field, presumably to further demonstrate the General Assembly's compliance with its constitutional mandate.

In the trial court, the defendants moved for a summary judgment, based primarily on the claim that no relief could be granted against the General Assembly because of lack of service on all 138 members thereof and that the parties lacked standing or legal capacity to sue. The trial court overruled this motion in its entirety.

The case was tried by the court without the intervention of a jury. Evidence was presented by deposition, along with oral testimony and much documentary evidence. The trial court entered the first of several orders, findings of fact and judgments on May 31, 1988.[2] Generally, that order found Kentucky's common school finance system to be unconstitutional and discriminatory and held that the General Assembly had not produced an efficient system of common schools throughout the state. On October 14, 1988 a final, appealable judgment was entered.

A notice of appeal was timely filed by the present appellants, John A. Rose, President *Pro Tempore* of the Senate of Kentucky and Donald J. Blandford, Speaker of the House of Representatives of Kentucky.

Upon a motion properly made, we transferred the appeal to this Court.

II. Analysis of Trial Court's Findings of Fact

Conclusions of Law and Judgment

Following the trial of this case, the circuit judge, in three separate documents, prepared extensive findings of fact, conclusions of law and judgment(s). Because of the length of these documents, we feel it important to analyze them in some detail.

Document Number I

Following the bench trial, and upon proper submission, the judge on May 31, 1988 entered a document that is styled, "Findings of Fact, Conclusions of Law and Judgment."

The trial judge identified four issues before him: (1) The necessity for defining the phrase "an efficient system of common schools" as contained in Section 183 of the Kentucky Constitution; (2) Whether education is a "fundamental right" under our Constitution; (3) Whether Kentucky's current method of financing its common schools violates Section 183, and (4) Whether students in the so-called "poor" school districts are denied equal protection of the laws.

"Efficient," in the Kentucky constitutional sense was defined as a system which required "substantial uniformity, substantial equality of financial resources and substantial equal educational opportunity for all students." Efficient was also interpreted to require that the educational system must be adequate, uniform and unitary.

Because of the language of Section 183, the trial court ruled that education, indeed, is a fundamental right in Kentucky.

In ruling on the issue of whether Kentucky's method of school financing violates Section 183 and underpinning the point with extensive findings of fact, the trial court declared that students in property poor school districts are offered a minimal level of educational opportunities, which is inferior to those offered to students in more affluent districts. Such "invidious" discrimination, based on the place of a student's

2. An analysis of these documents follows.

residence, was determined to be unconstitutional. The trial court ruled that the school finance system violates the equal protection guarantees of Section 1 and 3 of the Kentucky Constitution.

In its judgment, the trial court ruled: (1) The Kentucky finance "system" of its common schools is unconstitutional and discriminatory; and (2) The system of common schools is not efficient within the purview of Section 183 of the Kentucky Constitution. The Court indicated it would appoint a "small select committee," the purpose of which was to review all relevant data, provide additional analysis, consult with financial experts and propose remedies to "correct the deficiencies in the present common school financing system." The Court clearly stated that the Committee's plan, "when adopted by this Court," would not "intrude" on the prerogatives of the Executive and Legislative branches of government. Indeed, the report would only be an aid to serve as a guide in establishing "the parameters of the Constitutional requirements of Sections 1, 3 and 183."

In this open ended document, the Court ruled the school finance system unconstitutional, but gave few guidelines, or criteria, to guide the General Assembly in any action it might take to rectify the constitutional failure. The work of the Committee, if adopted by the Court, was to serve as a guidepost in this murky area.

Document Number II

On June 7, 1988, the trial court, in this document, appointed the members of the "select committee." Apparently fearing he would improperly delegate some of his judicial authority by the creation of this committee, the trial judge emphasized that its role would be "advisory only" to him. But he noted that the report would be of "immense benefit" to him in preparing his final judgment. The Committee was ordered to complete its work by September 15, 1988.

Modifying or explaining part of document # I, the court emphatically stated that there is "no judicial intent to merely redivide the funds now available to the common school districts." Moreover, he emphasized that funds should not be taken away (presumably by the General Assembly) from any school district to increase the funding level of more impoverished districts. It is a fair inference from this statement that the trial court was strongly suggesting that additional revenues were needed to make the system "efficient."

The defendant State Board of Education was ordered to pay, out of its funds, all expenses of the Committee.

Document Number III

This final order entered on October 14, 1988, and, cumulated with the first two documents, constitutes the subject matter of this appeal.

Addressing the committee report, but steadfastly maintaining that the report adopted was only part of his decision, the court agreed that the goals set out by the committee for the establishment of an "efficient" school system were "salutary" ones. While not technically adopting the report as part of this final Findings of Fact, Conclusions of

Law and Judgment, it is clear that the trial court did, indeed, adopt certain principles from the Committee's report.

In his additional Findings of Fact, the judge modified his previous definition of an "efficient" system of schools. It is a "... tax supported, coordinated organization, which provides a free, adequate education to all students throughout the state, regardless of geographical location or local fiscal resources." He opined that an efficient system (of schools) must have "substantial" uniformity.

Ever broadening the definition and setting non-instructional standards, the trial court required an efficient school system to provide sufficient physical facilities, teachers, support personnel, and instructional materials to enhance the educational process. An adequate school system must also include careful and comprehensive supervision at all levels to monitor personnel performance and minimize waste. If and where waste and mismanagement exist, including but not limited to improper nepotism, favoritism, and misallocation of school monies, they must be eliminated, through state intervention if necessary. The General Assembly has all the power necessary to guarantee that the resources provided by Kentucky taxpayers for schools are spent wisely.

The trial court thus, with a very broad brush, included in its constitutional definition of "efficient" goals to be met by an education and requirements as to school financing, curriculum, personnel, accessibility to all children, physical facilities, instructional materials and management of the schools.

Moreover, the trial court made it clear that the duty—the absolute, unequivocal duty—to provide this system is *solely* the responsibility of the General Assembly. The court reiterated that its judicial power did not extend to specifying to the General Assembly the methods by which to implement and maintain this efficient system of education.

Addressing again the question of financing this massive task, the trial court stated directly what had been implied previously, that "substantial additional monies" will have to be raised to provide this constitutional school system. The court suggested three possible ways of financing: 1) increasing existing taxes, 2) levying new taxes, or 3) reallocating existing funds. Since a major reallocation of funds would "cripple" other government functions, the trial court postulated that the imposition of new taxes appeared to be the only viable alternative.

The trial judge agreed that the separation of powers doctrine would prohibit courts from directing the General Assembly as to how the school system should be financed. But, he reiterated that the General Assembly must provide an efficient system.

Finally, although the trial court encouraged the protection of local school boards, he re-emphasized the General Assembly's authority and responsibility for the establishment and maintenance of the school system.

In the "judgment," the trial judge retained continuing jurisdiction over the subject matter for the purpose of enforcing the judgment. To that effect, he ordered a progress report be made to him on a day certain.

With this lengthy and dramatic series of documents, the Franklin Circuit Court brought into sharp focus a problem that many dedicated citizens of the Commonwealth have "wrestled" with for many years. It placed the sole responsibility for the establishment and maintenance of an efficient system on the General Assembly. It defined "efficient" in an multi-faceted manner, and directed that all these criteria are not only relevant, but are essential, if the development of a constitutionally valid system of common schools is to be had.

The trial court examined the evidence and declared that the present school system was unconstitutional.

On appeal, this Court must now review the basis for the trial court's ruling.

III. Contentions of the Parties

The two remaining defendants, now appellants before this Court, raise numerous issues on appeal. They allege that the Council for Better Education, Inc., does not have either the legal authority or the standing to maintain this action; that the purported class action of the student plaintiffs is not proper; that only 5 of the 22 students are properly before the Court; that the complaint does not state a "cognizable claim" against the two named legislators; that the trial court erred in finding that the system of common schools provided by the General Assembly is not efficient; that the trial court erred in ruling that House Bill 1 and House Bill 44 are part of an unconstitutional system;[3] that the trial court's definition and standards set for an efficient school system are at variance with Section 183; that the trial court's strong reliance on foreign cases was inappropriate; that the trial court erred in declaring that the school system violates the 14th Amendment of the U.S. Constitution; that the trial court's judgment violates the separation of powers provisions of the Kentucky Constitution; and finally, it is claimed that the trial court erred in directing the expenses of the select committee to be paid by the Kentucky Department of Education.

Appellees, predictably, defend the trial court's action.

Prior to dealing with these contentions we believe it would be beneficial to give a brief history of school financing in Kentucky, and to review the evidence before us.

IV. School Financing in Kentucky—Past and Present

As originally enacted, Section 186 of our Constitution mandated that school funds appropriated by the General Assembly be apportioned to each individual local school district on the basis of a set amount for each child aged 5 through to 17 years. Thus, state money was given on the basis of a census of school age children—whether they attended school or not. Differences in populations of the districts were not perceived as affecting the quality of the education.

---

3. H.B. 1 is codified as KRS 160.470 and H.B. 44 is codified in KRS 68.245, 132.010, .020, .023, .027, .690, other sections of Ch. 32, and 160.470. Throughout this opinion, the legislation will be referred to as H.B. 1 and H.B. 44.

In 1930, the General Assembly adopted a law (an Act approved March 15, 1930, Ch. 36, 1930 Ky. Acts, codified at KS 4364, 4399a-8, 4434a-14a) which appropriated state money for an equalization fund designed to increase per-pupil expenditures in those districts where the standard of education was low. That legislative effort was invalidated in *Talbott v. Kentucky State Board of Education*, 244 Ky. 826, 52 S.W.2d 727 (1932). The basis of the decision was that the attempt to equalize expenditures violated the mandate of Section 186—viz., state funds are limited to a per capita appropriation.

In 1941, Section 186 was amended to permit 10% of state funds to be used for equalization purposes and in 1944 it was further amended to allow 25% of the funds to be so expended. In 1952, the constitutional provision requiring per capita expenditures was eliminated, thus strengthening the role of the General Assembly in its duty to provide for an efficient system of common schools, as provided in Section 183.

In an apparent response to that latest constitutional amendment, and in an attempt to equalize inequities in the educational efforts and abilities to encourage more financial input and effort by local school districts, the General Assembly enacted the so-called Minimum Foundation Program[4] [hereinafter MFP]. To qualify as a participant in this program, a district was required to levy a minimum real property tax of $1.10 per $100 of assessed value in the district. The maximum tax was set at $1.50 per $100.00 of assessed value (1½% of the total assessed value of the real property in the district). Most districts levied the maximum rates, because the assessed values were very low. The assessments ranged from 33⅓% of the fair cash value of the property to as low as 12½% of that value. The median statewide assessment rate was 27%.

As a result of this law and diverse local assessments of fair cash value, a lawsuit was filed directly attacking this legislation and the problem of built-in disparity in local school tax levies. Our Court's predecessor, the Court of Appeals, in the case of *Russman v. Luckett*, Ky., 391 S.W.2d 694 (1965), declared that Section 172 of the Kentucky Constitution requires property to be assessed at 100% of its fair cash value. The mandate of the Court directed the Revenue Cabinet to see that all property in the Commonwealth was so assessed.

The ink was barely dry on this opinion, when, pursuant to a call for a special session by the Governor, the General Assembly enacted H.B. 1, known pleasantly as the "rollback law." Its effect was to countermand and negate the effect of *Russman*. This law reduced the tax rates on property proportionately to offset the increase in assessment required by this Court. It is certainly arguable that, by enacting the "rollback law," the General Assembly continued, or even exacerbated, the inequities that *Russman* intended to correct. Specifically, H.B. 1 reduced the school, county and city property tax revenues to the 1965 level, except for "net assessment growth" resulting from new property.[5]

---

4. KRS 157.310–.440. Its stated legislative purpose was "… to assure substantially equal public school educational opportunities." KRS 157.310. A further description of the MFP appears, *infra*.

5. Examples include a vacant lot having a house built on it or a farm being developed into a subdivision.

In deference to the education problem, the bill permitted local school districts to take two (2) one-time only 10% increases in their tax levies, for their 1967 and 1968 revenues. The bill virtually froze the revenues available to local school districts and created the ominous spectacle of different maximum tax rates for the then 180 local school districts in Kentucky.

In an attempt to enable more local tax efforts the General Assembly at its regular session in 1966 enacted legislation[6] which enabled local school districts to levy one of three specialized permissive taxes: (1) an occupational tax on wages and profits; (2) a tax on gross utility receipts, and (3) an excise tax on income. All of these taxes were, however, specifically permitted to be recalled by the voters.[7]

The story continues. At its regular session in 1972, the General Assembly redefined the terms "net assessment growth" to include not only new property, but also the difference in the assessed valuation of all property subject to tax in the previous year, thus boosting total revenues by the tax on property value inflation.

In 1976, the handling of revenue took another turn. The General Assembly transferred the levy and collection of the required local tax effort to the State, to be included as part of the receipts of the General Fund.[8] To provide funds which would help equalize, to some extent, the disparities in local financial effort, the General Assembly, also in 1976 passed the so-called Power Equalization Program[9] [hereinafter PEP].

In 1979, the then Lieutenant Governor, in the Governor's absence from the state, called yet another special session of the General Assembly. At that session, H.B. 44 was enacted. This law required school districts to *reduce* their tax rates on real property each year so that current revenue could not exceed the previous year's revenue by more than 4%. However, in order to institute any increase in revenue, H.B. 44 required the elected school board members to hold a public hearing on the matter. If the proposed increase (through a *tax rate* increase) would generate more than the 4% increase, the voters could force a public referendum on the excess. In other words, an increase of up to 4% (over the previous year) would not be approved without a public hearing. If the increase proposed were more than 4%, the excess thereof was subject to a vote of the public.

The record in this case shows the property tax rate declined statewide nearly 33% from 1979 to 1981, directly as a result of H.B. 44. Although the tax base (total assessed value) has increased, there has been little or no increase in local revenues for schools.

---

6. KRS 160.597.

7. The effect of the permissive taxes has been to create further inequities across the state because, even if the voters did not veto them, those counties with a high population and high payrolls would produce many times more revenue than counties (districts) not so blessed.

8. As the trial judge stated, the appearance that this created additional monies was strictly an illusion; rather it altered the *method* of levy and collection. No new funds were provided to local schools by the state.

9. KRS 157.545 et seq. The relevant details of this program (PEP) will be discussed *infra*.

As can be seen, the state's contribution to the local school programs (the so-called common schools) arises primarily from the MFP and the PEP. It is essential to a decision in this case to give a brief summary of each of these legislative acts.

To qualify as a participant in the MFP, a local school district must operate and pay its teachers for 185 days per school year, and it must actually operate its school(s) the same number of days. The State Superintendent of Public Instruction allots the classroom units to each district, the number of which depends on the average daily attendance in each grade. Each district receives a grant of money from the MFP based on the number of classroom units assigned to it. The funds may be used for teachers' salaries, current expenses, capital outlay and transportation of students.

The state also provides financial resources to local school districts through the PEP. Each year, the Kentucky Department of Revenue determines the equalized fair cash value of all taxable property in each local school district. That data is certified to the Superintendent of Public Instruction. The Superintendent determines annually the maximum tax rate that the PEP fund will equalize and then applies an equal rate to all districts. In order for a local district to receive funds, each local school district must levy a minimum equivalent tax rate of 25 cents per $100 of valuation, or the maximum rate supported by the PEP, whichever is greater. The "minimum equivalent tax rate" is defined as the quotient derived from dividing the districts' previous year's income from tax levies by the total assessed property valuation plus the assessment for motor vehicles.

As pointed out by the trial court, the mandated underlying tax rate has been so low that the results have been that only a fraction of the 25 cents local tax is actually equalized through the PEP.[10]

If one were to summarize the history of school funding in Kentucky, one might well say that every forward step taken to provide funds to local districts and to equalize money spent for the poor districts has been countered by one backward step.

It is certainly true that the General Assembly, over the years, has made substantial efforts to infuse money into the system to improve and equalize the educational efforts in the common schools of Kentucky. What we must decide, based solely on the evidence in the record as tested by the Kentucky Constitution, Section 183, is whether the trial court was correct in declaring that those efforts have failed to create an efficient system of common schools in this Commonwealth.

V. The Evidence

As we proceed to summarize the evidence before us, the legal test we must apply is whether that evidence supports the conclusion of the trial court that the Kentucky system of common schools is not efficient.[11] It is textbook law that before an appellate

---

10. Nine cents per hundred in 1985–86, 10 cents per hundred in 1986–87, and 13 cents per hundred thereafter.

11. Obviously, we will consider (later in the opinion) as a legal proposition, whether the trial court's definition of "efficient" within the aegis of Kentucky Constitution, Section 183 is correct.

court may overturn the trial court's finding, such finding must be clearly erroneous. CR 52.01; *Yates v. Wilson*, Ky., 339 S.W.2d 458 (1960).

The evidence in this case consists of numerous depositions, volumes of oral evidence heard by the trial court, and a seemingly endless amount of statistical data, reports, etc. We will not unduly lengthen this opinion with an extensive discussion of that evidence. As a matter of fact, such is really not necessary. The overall effect of appellants' evidence is a virtual concession that Kentucky's system of common schools is underfunded and inadequate; is fraught with inequalities and inequities throughout the 177 local school districts; is ranked nationally in the lower 20–25% in virtually every category that is used to evaluate educational performance; and is not uniform among the districts in educational opportunities. When one considers the evidence presented by the appellants, there is little or no evidence to even begin to negate that of the appellees. The tidal wave of the appellees' evidence literally engulfs that of the appellants.

In spite of the Minimum Foundation Program and the Power Equalization Program, there are wide variations in financial resources and dispositions thereof which result in unequal educational opportunities throughout Kentucky. The local districts have large variances in taxable property per student. Even a total elimination of all mismanagement and waste in local school districts would not correct the situation as it now exists. A substantial difference in the curricula offered in the poorer districts contrasts with that of the richer districts, particularly in the areas of foreign language, science, mathematics, music and art.

The achievement test scores in the poorer districts are lower than those in the richer districts and expert opinion clearly established that there is a correlation between those scores and the wealth of the district. Student-teacher ratios are higher in the poorer districts. Moreover, although Kentucky's per capita income is low, it makes an even lower per capita effort to support the common schools.

Students in property poor districts receive inadequate and inferior educational opportunities as compared to those offered to those students in the more affluent districts.

That Kentucky's overall effort and resulting achievement in the area of primary and secondary education are comparatively low, nationally, is not in dispute. Thirty-five percent of our adult population are high school drop-outs. Eighty percent of Kentucky's local school districts are identified as being "poor," in terms of taxable property. The other twenty percent remain under the national average. Thirty percent of our local school districts are "functionally bankrupt."

* * *

Numerous well-qualified educators and school administrators testified before the trial court and all described Kentucky's educational effort as being inadequate and well below the national effort.

With this background of Kentucky's overall effort with regard to education and its comparison to other states in the area, and nationally, we proceed to examine the trial court's finding relative to inequity and lack of uniformity in the overabundance of local school districts. We will discuss the educational opportunities offered and then address the disparity in financial effort and support.

Educational Effort

The numerous witnesses that testified before the trial court are recognized experts in the field of primary and secondary education. They have advanced college degrees, they have taught school, they have been school administrators, they have been participants at a local or state level in Kentucky's education system, and they have performed in-depth studies of Kentucky's system. Without exception, they testified that there is great disparity in the poor and the more affluent school districts with regard to classroom teachers' pay; provision of basic educational materials; student-teacher ratio; curriculum; quality of basic management; size, adequacy and condition of school physical plants; and per year expenditure per student. Kentucky's children, simply because of their place of residence, are offered a virtual hodgepodge of educational opportunities. The quality of education in the poorer local school districts is substantially less in most, if not all, of the above categories.

Can anyone seriously argue that these disparities do not affect the basic educational opportunities of those children in the poorer districts? To ask the question is to answer it. Children in 80% of local school districts in this Commonwealth are not as well-educated as those in the other 20%.

Moreover, most of the witnesses before the trial court testified that not only were the state's educational opportunities unequal and lacking in uniformity, but that all were inadequate. Testimony indicated that not only do the so-called poorer districts provide inadequate education to fulfill the needs of the students but the more affluent districts' efforts are inadequate as well, as judged by accepted national standards.

As stated, when one reads the record, and when one considers the argument of counsel for the appellants, one can find no proof, no statement that contradicts the evidence about the existing inequalities and lack of uniformity in the overall performance of Kentucky's system of common schools.

Summarizing appellants' argument, and without intending to give it short shrift, it is contended that over the years the General Assembly has continually enacted such programs as the MFP, the PEP, and other progressive programs during recent sessions of the General Assembly. Moreover, uncontroverted evidence is adduced to show that the overall amount of money appropriated for local schools has increased by a substantial amount. The argument seems to be to the effect that "we have done our best." However, it is significant that all the experts were keenly aware of the legislative history, including substantive legislation and increased funding and yet, all of them stated that inequalities still exist, and indeed have been exacerbated by some of the legislation. Appellants conceded, the trial court found and we concur that in spite of legislative efforts, the total local and state effort in education in Kentucky's primary and secondary education is inadequate and is lacking in uniformity. It is discriminatory as to the children served in 80% of our local school districts.

Financial Effort

Uniform testimony of the expert witnesses at trial, corroborated by data, showed a definite correlation between the money spent per child on education and the quality of the education received. As we have previously stated in our discussion of the history of Kentucky's school finances, our system does not require a minimum local effort. The MFP, being based on average daily attendance, certainly infuses more money into each local district, but is not designed to correct problems of inequality and lack of uniformity between local school districts. The experts stated that the PEP, although a good idea, was and is underfunded.

The disparity in per pupil expenditure by the local school boards runs in the thousands of dollars per year. Moreover, between the extreme high allocation and the extreme low allocation lies a wide range of annual per pupil expenditures. In theory (and perhaps in actual practice) there could be 177 different per pupil expenditures, thus leading to 177 different educational efforts. The financing effort of local school districts is, figuratively speaking, a jigsaw puzzle.

It is argued by the appellants that the so-called permissive taxes,[12] are at least part of the solution to equalizing local financial efforts. There are two easy answers that dispose of this argument. First, the taxes are permissive. Responding to obvious voter resistance to the imposition of taxes, 89 districts have enacted the tax on gross utility receipts; 5 districts have enacted the occupational tax; 82 districts have also enacted a special building tax, normally for a specific project for one time only, and not affecting teacher pay, instructional equipment, or any of the specific needs of educational opportunity. As the nature of the taxes is permissive, in many districts they are not adopted and therefore do not produce one cent in additional local revenue.

Secondly, according to the testimony of the expert witnesses, even if all the permissive taxes were enacted, the financial effort would still be inadequate, and because the population of the districts is in direct proportion to the amount of money that could and is raised by these taxes, the overall problem of an unequal local effort would be exacerbated by such action. Clearly, the permissive taxes are not the solution to the problems. Rather, they contribute to the disparity of per pupil expenditures.

Additionally, because the assessable and taxable real and personal property in the 177 districts is so varied, and because of a lack of uniformity in tax rates, the local school boards' tax effort is not only lacking in uniformity but is also lacking in adequate effort. The history of school financing in Kentucky, certainly corroborates the trial court's finding as to the lack of uniformity and the lack of adequacy of local and state funding of education in the state. Based on the record before us, it is beyond cavil that the trial court's finding was correct.

Having discussed the procedure, the contentions of the parties, the history of school finance, and having briefly analyzed the facts, we now proceed to discuss the legal arguments raised before us by the parties.

---

12. See *supra* note 6 and accompanying text.

* * *

X. What is an "Efficient System of Common Schools"?

In a few simple, but direct words, the framers of our present Constitution, set forth the will of the people with regard to the importance of providing public education in the Commonwealth.

> "*General Assembly to provide for school system*—The General Assembly shall, by appropriate legislation, provide for an efficient system of common schools throughout the State." Ky. Const. Sec. 183.

Several conclusions readily appear from a reading of this section. First, it is the obligation, the sole obligation, of the General Assembly to provide for a system of common schools in Kentucky. The obligation to so provide is clear and unequivocal and is, in effect, a constitutional mandate. Next, the school system must be provided throughout the entire state, with no area (or its children) being omitted. The creation, implementation and maintenance of the school system must be achieved by appropriate legislation. Finally, the system must be an efficient one.

It is, of course, the last "conclusion" that gives us pause and requires study and analysis. What, indeed, is the meaning of the word "efficient" as used in Section 183?

The Constitutional Debates

A brief sojourn into the Constitutional debates will give some idea—a contemporaneous view—of the depth of the delegates' intention when Section 183 was drafted and eventually made its way into the organic law of this state. It will provide a background for our definition of "efficient."

Comments of Delegate Beckner on the report which led to the selection of the language in Section 183 reflect the framers' cognizance of the importance of education and, emphasized that the educational system in Kentucky must be improved. Referring to the education of our children, he admonished the delegates, "do not let us make a mistake in dealing with the most vital question that can come before us." III *Debates Constitutional Convention 1890* 4459 [hereinafter *Debates*].

After summarizing other achievements made in the proposed new Constitution he continued—

> "If, however, after accomplishing so much good on these lines—we forget the children, and, in the slightest degree, fail to appreciate the obligations of the State to provide sufficient facilities for training them to be good citizens, we will deserve and receive in the great hereafter anathema, and not ascription of praise." *Id.* at 4460.

Incorporating a report made to the Kentucky legislature in 1822, Beckner quoted (referring to a system of common schools):

> "'... It is a system of practical equality in which the children of the rich and poor meet upon a perfect level and the only superiority is that of the mind.'" *Id.* at 4460.

Beckner further declared, "Instruction of children under the auspices of the State has become the settled policy of our people." *Id.* at 4461.

Beckner set out four permanent justifications for and characteristics of state provided schools:

> 1) The education of young people is essential to the prosperity of a free people.
>
> 2) The education should be universal and should embrace all children.
>
> 3) Public education should be supervised by the State, to assure that students develop patriotism and understand our government.
>
> 4) Education should be given to all—rich and poor—so that our people will be homogeneous in their feelings and desires.

Id. at 4462–63.

One final passage merits quotation. Since education provided by the State is no longer an open question, the only thing that remains is how it shall be made "most valuable and effective." Let Mr. Beckner's answer be a guidepost for all Kentuckians today and in the future:

> "If public schools have come to stay, if they are a part and parcel of our free institutions, woven into the very web and woof of popular government; and if they are in the future to be the dependence of the people of Kentucky for the instruction of their youth, what is the logic of the situation? Manifestly to encourage and improve them, *to seize every opportunity to make them more efficient,* to treat them with no niggard or stinted hand, but just in so far as we love our children, to try to make their training-places fit nurseries of immortal spirits that have divine purposes to fulfill on earth, and cannot hope to succeed, unless their intellectual powers be properly developed." *Id.* at 4463. (Emphasis added.)

As if these powerful words were not sufficient to show the purpose of Section 183, consider those of delegate Moore—

> "Common schools make patriots and men who are willing to stand upon a common land. The boys of the humble mountain home stand equally high with those from the mansions of the city. There are no distinctions in the common schools, *but all stand upon one level.*" *Id.* at 4531. (Emphasis added.)

It serves no purpose to further lengthen this opinion with more verbiage from the Constitutional debates. Delegates Beckner and Moore told their fellow delegates and have told us, what this section means.

> — The providing of public education through a system of common schools by the General Assembly is the most "vital question" presented to them.
>
> — Education of children must not be minimized to the "slightest degree."
>
> — Education must be provided to the children of the rich and poor alike.
>
> — Education of children is essential to the prosperity of our state.

— Education of children should be supervised by the State.

— There must be a constant and continuing effort to make our schools more efficient.

— We must not finance our schools in a *de minimis* fashion.

— All schools and children stand upon one level in their entitlement to equal state support.

This Court, in defining efficiency must, at least in part, be guided by these clearly expressed purposes. The framers of Section 183 emphasized that education is essential to the welfare of the citizens of the Commonwealth. By this animus to Section 183, we recognize that education is a fundamental right in Kentucky.

Legal Precedents in Kentucky

Although the Court did not specifically comment on Section 183 in *Major v. Cayce*, 98 Ky. 357, 33 S.W. 93 (1895), it did state the essential requirements of a statute which the General Assembly enacted in compliance with that constitutional provision.

> "[U]nder the school law the pupils, all within the age and resident in the district, are entitled to attend these common schools, and to receive tuition in all the branches [of learning] prescribed by the state board of education to be taught therein, free of expenses..." 33 S.W. at 94.

This decision, very close in time to the adoption of the present Constitution, recognized a prohibition against any practice which "impairs the equal benefit of the common-school system" to all students. *Id.* at 95.

In *City of Louisville v. Commonwealth*, 134 Ky. 488, 121 S.W. 411 (1909), the Court held:

> "In this state the subject of public education has always been regarded and treated as a matter of state concern. In the last Constitution, as well as in the one preceding it, *the most explicit care was evinced to promote public education as a duty of the state....*
>
> In obedience to that requirement, the General Assembly has provided a system of public schools.... All [schools throughout the state] have the one main essential—that they are free schools, open to all the children of proper school age residing in the locality, *and affording equal opportunity for all* to acquire the learning taught in the various common school branches...." 121 S.W. at 412. (Emphasis added.)

The decision, specifically relying on Section 183, postulated: public education in the common schools is a duty of the state; that the General Assembly attempted to obey the mandate (as it certainly has attempted to do now); and although there are certain different provisions for different localities, all common schools must be free, open to all students, and provide equal opportunities for all students to acquire the same education. In other words, although by accident of birth and residence, a student lives in a poor, financially deprived area, he or she is still entitled to the same educational opportunities that those children in the wealthier districts obtain. What principle could be more fair, more just, and more importantly, what would be more consistent with the purpose of Section 183 and the common school system it spawned?

We further emphasized the mandate of Section 183 in *Board of Education of Boyle County v. McChesney*, 235 Ky. 692, 32 S.W.2d 26 (1930). Affirming the General Assembly's constitutional duty to provide for an efficient system, the Court idealistically observed the citizens' burden.

> "Onerous taxes are levied annually and paid willingly by the people for this essential governmental service." 32 S.W.2d at 28.

In the case of *Commonwealth ex rel. Baxter v. Burnett*, 237 Ky. 473, 35 S.W.2d 857 (1931), we again emphasized the constitutional mandate of Section 183, and the great importance of public education. In addition, the element of "efficiency" was highlighted. The Court also acknowledged and approved strong, centralized control (by the state) of the system of common schools.

> "In the progress towards the highest degree of efficiency the legislature more and more has centralized the control of schools and sought uniformity and equality of advantage for the school children of the state as a whole." 35 S.W.2d at 859.

Describing the growing centralization as "progress," we restated the overall goals of the system as "uniformity and equality" for the school children of the state "as a whole." What could be clearer? Since the Constitution acknowledges the importance of education to this Commonwealth and since the establishment and maintenance of a system of common schools is a mandated duty of the General Assembly, it is part and parcel of this overall goal that the system have the twin attributes of uniformity and equality.

In *Wooley v. Spalding*, Ky., 293 S.W.2d 563 (1956), a suit was filed by citizens and taxpayers to prohibit the defendant superintendent of Marion County schools from expending funds in alleged illegal ways, to prohibit sectarian instruction from being given in public schools and to seek the reopening and proper operation of a high school. The trial court denied the request, but our predecessor Court reversed and granted the requested injunction. In language which brings together and re-emphasizes earlier decisions, we said,

> "The fundamental mandate of the Constitution and Statutes of Kentucky is that there shall be equality and that all public schools shall be nonpartisan and nonsectarian.
>
> Uniformity does not require equal classification but it does demand that there shall be a substantially uniform system and equal school facilities without discrimination as between different sections of a district or a county." *Id.* at 565 (references omitted).

The lack of uniformity and the unequal educational opportunity existing in the county was said to constitute "a violation of both the spirit and intent of Section 183 of our State Constitution." *Id.* That reasoning therein applies, *a fortiori*, to the entire state system of common schools. Public schools must be efficient, equal and substantially uniform.

As can be seen, this Court, since the adoption of the present Constitution, has, in reflecting on Section 183, drawn several conclusions:

1) The General Assembly is mandated, is duty bound, to create and maintain a system of common schools—throughout the state.

2) The expressed purpose of providing such service is vital and critical to the well being of the state.

3) The system of common schools must be efficient.

4) The system of common schools must be free.

5) The system of common schools must provide equal educational opportunities for all students in the Commonwealth.

6) The state must control and administer the system.

7) The system must be, if not uniform, "substantially uniform," with respect to the state as a whole.

8) The system must be equal to and for all students.

* * *

Before proceeding, therefore, to a definition of "efficient" we must address a point made by the appellants with respect to our authority to enter this fray and to "stick our judicial noses" into what is argued to be strictly the General Assembly's business.

Appellants argue and cite several cases to support their position, that the General Assembly has sole and exclusive authority to determine whether the system of common schools is constitutionally "efficient" and that a Court may not substitute its judgment for that of the General Assembly.

* * *

The issue before us—the constitutionality of the system of statutes that created the common schools—is the only issue. To avoid deciding the case because of "legislative discretion," "legislative function," etc., would be a denigration of our own constitutional duty. To allow the General Assembly (or, in point of fact, the Executive) to decide whether its actions are constitutional is literally unthinkable.

* * *

The judiciary has the ultimate power, and the duty, to apply, interpret, define, construe all words, phrases, sentences and sections of the Kentucky Constitution as necessitated by the controversies before it. It is solely the function of the judiciary to so do. This duty must be exercised even when such action serves as a check on the activities of another branch of government or when the court's view of the constitution is contrary to that of other branches, or even that of the public.

* * *

Definition of "Efficient"

We now hone in on the heart of this litigation. In defining "efficient," we use all the tools that are made available to us. In spite of any protestations to the contrary, we do not engage in judicial legislating. We do not make policy. We do not substitute our judgment for that of the General Assembly. We simply take the plain directive of the Constitution, and, armed with its purpose, we decide what our General Assembly must achieve in complying with its solemn constitutional duty.

Any system of common schools must be created and maintained with the premise that education is absolutely vital to the present and to the future of our Commonwealth. As Herbert Spencer observed, "Education has for its object the formation of character." H. Spencer, *Social Studies* pt. 1, ch. 2, p. 17 (1851). No tax proceeds have a more important position or purpose than those for education in the grand scheme of our government. The importance of common schools and the education they provide Kentucky's children cannot be overemphasized or overstated.

The sole responsibility for providing the system of common schools is that of our General Assembly. It is a duty—it is a constitutional mandate placed by the people on the 138 members of that body who represent those selfsame people.

The General Assembly must not only establish the system, but it must monitor it on a continuing basis so that it will always be maintained in a constitutional manner. The General Assembly must carefully supervise it, so that there is no waste, no duplication, no mismanagement, at any level.

The system of common schools must be adequately funded to achieve its goals. The system of common schools must be substantially uniform throughout the state. Each child, *every child*, in this Commonwealth must be provided with an equal opportunity to have an adequate education. Equality is the key word here. The children of the poor and the children of the rich, the children who live in the poor districts and the children who live in the rich districts must be given the same opportunity and access to an adequate education. This obligation cannot be shifted to local counties and local school districts.

As we have indicated, Section 183 requires the General Assembly to establish a system of common schools that provides an equal opportunity for children to have an adequate education. In no way does this constitutional requirement act as a limitation on the General Assembly's power to create local school entities and to grant to those entities the authority to supplement the state system. Therefore, if the General Assembly decides to establish local school entities, it may also empower them to enact local revenue initiatives to supplement the uniform, equal educational effort that the General Assembly must provide. This includes not only revenue measures similar to the special taxes previously discussed, but also the power to assess local ad valorem taxes on real property and personal property at a rate over and above that set by the General Assembly to fund the statewide system of common schools. * * * Such local efforts may not be used by the General Assembly as a substitute for providing an adequate, equal and substantially uniform educational system throughout this state.

Having declared the system of common schools to be constitutionally deficient, we have directed the General Assembly to recreate and redesign a new system that will comply with the standards we have set out. Such system will guarantee to all children the opportunity for an adequate education, through a *state* system. To allow local citizens and taxpayers to make a supplementary effort in no way reduces or negates the minimum quality of education required in the statewide system.

We do not instruct the General Assembly to enact any specific legislation. We do not direct the members of the General Assembly to raise taxes. It is their decision how best to achieve efficiency. We only decide the nature of the constitutional mandate. We only determine the intent of the framers. Carrying-out that intent is the duty of the General Assembly.

A child's right to an adequate education is a fundamental one under our Constitution. The General Assembly must protect and advance that right. We concur with the trial court that an efficient system of education must have as its goal to provide each and every child with at least the seven following capacities: (i) sufficient oral and written communication skills to enable students to function in a complex and rapidly changing civilization; (ii) sufficient knowledge of economic, social, and political systems to enable the student to make informed choices; (iii) sufficient understanding of governmental processes to enable the student to understand the issues that affect his or her community, state, and nation; (iv) sufficient self-knowledge and knowledge of his or her mental and physical wellness; (v) sufficient grounding in the arts to enable each student to appreciate his or her cultural and historical heritage; (vi) sufficient training or preparation for advanced training in either academic or vocational fields so as to enable each child to choose and pursue life work intelligently; and (vii) sufficient levels of academic or vocational skills to enable public school students to compete favorably with their counterparts in surrounding states, in academics or in the job market.[13]

The essential, and minimal, characteristics of an "efficient" system of common schools, may be summarized as follows:

1) The establishment, maintenance and funding of common schools in Kentucky is the sole responsibility of the General Assembly.

2) Common schools shall be free to all.

3) Common schools shall be available to all Kentucky children.

13. In recreating and redesigning the Kentucky system of common schools, these seven characteristics should be considered as *minimum* goals in providing an adequate education. Certainly, there is no prohibition against higher goals—whether such are implemented statewide by the General Assembly or through the efforts of any local education entities that the General Assembly may establish—so long as the General Assembly meets the standards set out in this Opinion.

4) Common schools shall be substantially uniform throughout the state.

5) Common schools shall provide equal educational opportunities to all Kentucky children, regardless of place of residence or economic circumstances.

6) Common schools shall be monitored by the General Assembly to assure that they are operated with no waste, no duplication, no mismanagement, and with no political influence.

7) The premise for the existence of common schools is that all children in Kentucky have a constitutional right to an adequate education.

8) The General Assembly shall provide funding which is sufficient to provide each child in Kentucky an adequate education.

9) An adequate education is one which has as its goal the development of the seven capacities recited previously.

XI. Is the Present System "Efficient"?

We have described, *infra*, in some detail, the present system of common schools. We have noted the overall inadequacy of our system of education, when compared to national standards and to the standards of our adjacent states. We have recognized the great disparity that exists in educational opportunities throughout the state. We have noted the great disparity and inadequacy, of financial effort throughout the state.

In spite of the past and present efforts of the General Assembly, Kentucky's present system of common schools falls short of the mark of the constitutional mandate of "efficient." When one juxtaposes the standards of efficiency as derived from our Constitution, the cases decided thereunder, the persuasive authority from our sister states and the opinion of experts, with the virtually unchallenged evidence in the record, no other decision is possible.

XII. Did the Trial Court's Judgment Violate the Separation of Powers Provision of the Kentucky Constitution?

Appellants assert that the trial court's judgment violates the separation of powers doctrine in that it exceeded the authority of the court in "dictating" to the General Assembly, and it exceeded the authority of the court by creating a type of open-ended judgment which required legislator-defendants to report their progress to the trial court.

Our constitutional provisions which relate to separation of powers between the three separate and independent branches of government were authored by Thomas Jefferson. They are as follows:

> "Sec. 27. The powers of the government of the Commonwealth of Kentucky shall be divided into three distinct departments, and each of them be confined to a separate body of the magistracy, to-wit: Those which are legislative, to one; those which are executive, to another; and those which are judicial, to another."

> "Sec. 28. No person or collection of persons, being of one of those departments, shall exercise any power properly belonging to either of the others, except in the instances hereinafter expressly directed or permitted."

Section 29 vests the legislative power in the General Assembly, and Section 109 grants the judicial power to the Court of Justice.

Because of the specific wording of the Constitution, we have previously noted the strength of the separation of powers doctrine in this state:

> "Our present Constitution contains explicit provisions which, on one hand, *mandate* separation among the three branches of government, and on the other hand, specifically *prohibit* incursion of one branch of government into the powers and functions of the other. Thus, our constitution has a double-barreled, positive-negative approach...." *Legislative Research Commission v. Brown*, Ky., 664 S.W.2d 907, 912 (1984). (Emphasis added.)

Moreover, in *Brown*, we reiterated that the doctrine of separation of powers must be "strictly construed." *Id.*

Simply stated, we have declared that the power to legislate belongs to the General Assembly, and the power to adjudicate belongs to the judiciary. It is our goal to honor both the letter and spirit of that constitutional mandate.

> "Our functions are to determine the constitutional validity and to declare the meaning of what the legislative department has done. We have no other concern." *Johnson v. Commonwealth*, 291 Ky. 829, 165 S.W.2d 820, 825 (1942).

With these principles to guide us, we now address appellants' contentions.

It is argued that the trial court directed the General Assembly to enact specific legislation and to raise taxes and that such is a violation of the separation of powers. We do not agree that that is what the judgment of the trial court does. The trial judge did define "efficient," he did declare that a common school education is a fundamental constitutional right in this state, and he did say that any educational system to be "efficient," must have certain characteristics. He commented on the possible methods of financing the system of common schools in Kentucky and did, of course, opine that additional money would be required. This later conclusion was based on an abundance of virtually uncontested and unchallenged evidence in this record.

Moreover, the trial judge specifically denied that he was directing the General Assembly to enact any *specific legislation*, including raising taxes. His mandate to the General Assembly was to bring the system of common schools into compliance with Section 183 of our Constitution. He did as we have done, established certain criteria, standards and goals which must be met to so comply. It is clear that the specifics of the legislation will be left up to the wisdom of the General Assembly. Clearly, no "legislating" is present in the decision of the trial court, and more importantly, as we have previously said, there is none present in the decision of this Court. We do not agree with appellants.

However, we agree with appellants that the decision of the trial court to require the appellants to report to him on their progress is a clear incursion, by the judiciary, of the functions of the legislature.

The implications of such an open-ended judgment are very clear. The trial court retains jurisdiction and supervision of the General Assembly's effort to provide a constitutional system of common schools. Under such an order, the General Assembly, in theory if not in practice, would literally have to confer, report, and comply with the judge's view of the legislation proposed to comply with the order. The legislation would be that of the joint efforts of the General Assembly and the trial court, with the latter having the final word. This is, without doubt, the type of action that was eschewed when the framers of the four constitutions of this state placed the separation of powers doctrine in the organic law of this state.

Our job is to determine the constitutional validity of the system of common schools within the meaning of the Kentucky Constitution, Section 183. We have done so. We have declared the system of common schools to be unconstitutional. It is now up to the General Assembly to re-create, and re-establish a system of common schools within this state which will be in compliance with the Constitution. We have no doubt they will proceed with their duty.

The enactments of the General Assembly, in this subject area, or in any area, is always subject to the scrutiny of the Court of Justice, under the authority described in *Brown*, *supra*, and *Johnson*, *supra*.

* * *

Summary/Conclusion

We have decided this case solely on the basis of our Kentucky Constitution, Section 183. We find it unnecessary to inject any issues raised under the United States Constitution or the United States Bill of Rights in this matter. We decline to issue any injunctions, restraining orders, writs of prohibition or writs of mandamus.

We have decided one legal issue—and one legal issue only—viz., that the General Assembly of the Commonwealth has failed to establish an efficient system of common schools throughout the Commonwealth.

Lest there be any doubt, the result of our decision is that Kentucky's *entire system* of common schools is unconstitutional. There is no allegation that only part of the common school system is invalid, and we find no such circumstance. This decision applies to the entire sweep of the system—all its parts and parcels. This decision applies to the statutes creating, implementing and financing the *system* and to all regulations, etc., pertaining thereto. This decision covers the creation of local school districts, school boards, and the Kentucky Department of Education to the Minimum Foundation Program and Power Equalization Program. It covers school construction and maintenance, teacher certification—the whole gamut of the common school system in Kentucky.

While individual statutes are not herein addressed specifically or considered and declared to be facially unconstitutional, the statutory system as a whole and the interrelationship of the parts therein are hereby declared to be in violation of Section 183 of the Kentucky Constitution. Just as the bricks and mortar used in the construction of a schoolhouse, while contributing to the building's facade, do not ensure the overall structural adequacy of the schoolhouse, particular statutes drafted by the legislature in crafting and designing the current school system are not unconstitutional in and of themselves. Like the crumbling schoolhouse which must be redesigned and revitalized for more efficient use, with some component parts found to be adequate, some found to be less than adequate, statutes relating to education may be reenacted as components of a constitutional system if they combine with other component statutes to form an efficient and thereby constitutional system.

Since we have, by this decision, declared the system of common schools in Kentucky to be unconstitutional, Section 183 places an absolute duty on the General Assembly to re-create, re-establish a new system of common schools in the Commonwealth. As we have said, the premise of this opinion is that education is a basic, fundamental constitutional right that is available to all children within this Commonwealth. The General Assembly should begin with the same premise as it goes about its duty. The system, as we have said, must be efficient, and the criteria we have set out are binding on the General Assembly as it develops Kentucky's new system of common schools.

As we have previously emphasized, the *sole responsibility* for providing the system of common schools lies with the General Assembly. If they choose to delegate any of this duty to institutions such as the local boards of education, the General Assembly must provide a mechanism to assure that the ultimate control remains with the General Assembly, and assure that those local school districts also exercise the delegated duties in an efficient manner.

The General Assembly must provide adequate funding for the system. How they do this is their decision. However, if ad valorem taxes on real and personal property are used by the General Assembly as part of the financing of the redesigned state system of common schools, the General Assembly has the obligation to see that *all such property* is assessed at 100% of its fair market value. *Russman v. Luckett*, Ky., 391 S.W.2d 694 (1965). Moreover, because of the great disparity of local tax efforts in the present system of common schools, the General Assembly must establish a uniform *tax rate* for such property. In this way, all owners of real and personal property throughout the *state* will make a comparable effort in the financing of the state system of common schools.

This decision has not been reached without much thought and consideration. We do not take our responsibilities lightly, and we have decided this case based on our perception and interpretation of the Kentucky Constitution. We intend no criticism of any person, persons or institutions. We view this decision as an opportunity for the General Assembly to launch the Commonwealth into a new era of educational opportunity which will ensure a strong economic, cultural and political future.

Because of the enormity of the task before the General Assembly to recreate a new statutory system of common schools in the Commonwealth, and because we realize that the educational process must continue, we withhold the finality of this decision until 90 days after the adjournment of the General Assembly, *sine die*, at its regular session in 1990.

Combs, Gant, Lambert and Wintersheimer, JJ., concur.

Gant and Wintersheimer, JJ., file separate concurring opinions.

Leibson and Vance, JJ., file separate dissenting opinions.

* * *

JUSTICE VANCE, DISSENTING.

I respectfully dissent. I believe the majority opinion is inherently inconsistent in that it says that our system of common schools, to be constitutionally efficient, must provide substantially equal educational opportunity for children throughout the Commonwealth, yet it actually permits the continuation of a system which does not provide substantially equal educational opportunity.

I believe this is so because the opinion expressly holds that individual school districts may continue to levy taxes for school purposes to be used solely within the district.[1] Primarily, it is the levy of these taxes by local school districts, which produces greatly disparate revenues in richer counties than in poorer ones, that has caused the great disparity in school funding per child in the various districts throughout the Commonwealth.

Although there are factors other than the amount of money available per child that must be considered when determining the equality of educational opportunity, I submit that this whole case is predicated upon the proposition that children who reside in districts where the amount of funding available per child is disproportionately less than is available in other districts will be denied an educational opportunity which is equal to the educational opportunity afforded in districts with vastly greater resources.

Because the value of taxable property is so much greater in some districts than others, the continued levy of school taxes for use within individual districts, even if levied at a uniform rate throughout the state and property is assessed at 100 percent of its value, will continue to produce much more revenue in richer counties than in poorer ones. It follows that the continuation of such a tax policy will leave us exactly where we are now, and the school system will not provide substantially equal educational opportunity throughout the Commonwealth, but will in fact, result in better educational opportunity for those who reside in the wealthier sections of the state.

---

1. The taxes levied by local school districts are local in the sense that they are levied upon property within the district, but this court has held on many occasions that these taxes are in fact state taxes which have been authorized by the General Assembly to fulfill the requirements of §183 of the Kentucky Constitution. *Cullinan v. Jefferson County*, Ky., 418 S.W.2d 407 (1967); *Board of Education v. City of Louisville*, 288 Ky. 656, 157 S.W.2d 337 (1941); *Commonwealth v. Louisville National Bank*, 220 Ky. 89, 294 S.W. 815 (1927).

* * *

I do not concur with the majority that the present system of common schools has, on the basis of the record before us, been shown to be *constitutionally* under-funded or inadequate.

* * *

There is now imposed a requirement that the system be adequately funded, but no specific standards have been established to determine the adequacy of funding. Instead, it is held that the school system must be funded adequately so as to achieve seven goals, each of which is expressed in the most general terms. * * *

How will the General Assembly be able to know if the legislation it enacts will provide each and every student throughout the Commonwealth with a sufficient grounding in the arts to enable that student to appreciate his cultural or historical heritage? This goal, like the other seven, is so vague that regardless of what legislation is enacted by the General Assembly the door has been opened for another group or groups of students to sue the General Assembly *ad infinitum*, claiming that in some respects the General Assembly has failed to provide a system of common schools which achieves the seven goals of an efficient system. I fear it will be the courts rather than the General Assembly, which will end up monitoring the common school system.

I am willing to declare, on the basis of this record, that the system of common schools throughout the state does not meet the constitutional imperative of substantially equal educational opportunity for all children. I would go no further. * * *

Justice Leibson, dissenting.

Respectfully, I dissent.

I agree in principle with the majority's opinion that the General Assembly has failed thus far to, "by appropriate legislation, provide for an efficient system of common schools throughout the State."[1] Ky. Const., §183. Nevertheless, this case should be reversed and dismissed because it does not present an "actual" or "justiciable" controversy. *See* KRS 418.040; *Black's Law Dictionary*, 5th ed. 1979, p. 777.

An "actual controversy" for purposes of adjudication requires three things: (1) a justiciable issue (2) involving the legal rights (3) of adverse parties. *Revis v. Daugherty*, 215 Ky. 823, 287 S.W. 28 (1926); *Veith v. City of Louisville*, Ky., 355 S.W.2d 295 (1962).

An actual controversy is one admitting of specific relief through a decree conclusive in character. A judicial pronouncement in the present case where there are public questions of the utmost importance but no such justiciable controversy will cause more problems than it will solve. Worse yet, it opens the doors of the courthouse to a host of new lawsuits by litigants seeking a forum to argue questions of public policy which are incapable of specific judicial resolution. In line with the legal truism that "bad

1. By "throughout" I do not mean everywhere, but simply not in all school districts. For examples to the contrary: Woodford County has been praised as a "model" district; Jefferson County has been recently televised nationally as an example of a successful program.

cases make bad law," we can expect this case to be cited as precedent in a new wave of litigation involving issues that should be debated in the forum of public opinion, and then legislated rather than litigated.

To qualify as a judicial controversy the issues must touch legal relationships of parties having adverse legal interests, clearly definable, concrete, and admitting of specific resolution. The Declaratory Judgment Act, KRS 418.040, was never intended for advisory opinions. As the late great wordsmith, Judge Gus Thomas, so aptly said:

> "[C]ontroverted questions are justiciable ones, and … do [] not include abstract legal questions designed merely to furnish information to the inquirer and which, if jurisdiction was taken, would convert courts into a sort of law school for the instruction of the inquisitive mind." *Oldham County v. Arvin*, 244 Ky. 551, 51 S.W.2d 657, 658–59 (1932).

I. The Problems Related to the Issues

* * *

The case as presented to us neither asks for nor is amenable to specific relief through a decree conclusive in character. The appellees have made it painfully clear throughout that they do not want our Court to declare any particular statute or group of statutes unconstitutional, including the system of local school districts, local financing and local administration now in place. Yet, the Majority Opinion decides otherwise:

> "Lest there by any doubt, the result of our decision is that Kentucky's *entire system* of common schools is unconstitutional …—all its parts and parcels. This decision applies to the statutes creating, implementing and financing the *system* and to all regulations, etc., pertaining thereto. [Emphasis original.]

If this verbiage is taken literally, local school districts who are the members of the Council for Better Education, the moving force behind this lawsuit may be eaten up by the monster they created when they invited the courts into the dialogue about how to improve the public school system. The statutes that create them have now been declared unconstitutional. Unable to rationalize an opinion that declares *nothing* unconstitutional, we seem to have declared *everything* unconstitutional.

Elsewhere, the Opinion states that "individual statutes are not herein addressed specifically or considered and declared to be facially unconstitutional." But our "school system" is nothing more and nothing less than the statutes, individually and collectively, structuring its existence and providing for its financing. The system does not exist apart from the statutes, and cannot be declared unconstitutional without specifying which of its components, in whole or in part, make it so.

At oral argument appellees' counsel conceded that, in asking that we declare the system unconstitutional but not the statutes, they were presenting us with a "Gordian" knot. But ask they did, thus presenting us with an insolvable, nonjusticiable dilemma. And, we have responded with what could be expected when you open Pandora's box, an Opinion which at the same time declares everything unconstitutional and nothing unconstitutional. This is more than just a vain act or a bad precedent. This result may well create havoc in the educational process. It adds to the General Assembly's burden in seeking to improve our educational system rather than lightening the load.

The lawsuit filed in Franklin Circuit Court, carefully analyzed, does no more than ask the courts to demand that the Governor and the General Assembly proceed to improve the public school system, specifically by telling the executive and legislative branch to propose and enact new taxes. While for the most part the trial court's response, like ours, was limited to advice and comments rather than judicial decision-making, its decision went further by granting specific relief in two areas: (1) a mandate to the General Assembly to impose additional new taxes and (2) an order to the President Pro Tempore of the Senate and the Speaker of the House of Representatives to return to Franklin Circuit Court to report on the General Assembly's progress. Both of these, the only concrete or specific "relief" granted, are invalidated by our decision, and rightly so, recognizing they are orders that exceed the power of the judiciary.

As to funding, we state only that "[t]he General Assembly must provide adequate funding for the system. How they do this is their decision."

As to Judge Corns' Order to the leadership of the General Assembly to report to him on its progress, we declare this "a clear incursion, by the judiciary, of the functions of the legislature."

On the other hand, in our Opinion we ordered nothing specific, only that the General Assembly comply with the Constitution, which, of course, it is already duty bound to do.

I say this with one major reservation, because there is one portion of our Opinion that seems to do more than simply encourage the General Assembly to enact legislation to improve the school system. It states:

> "[B]ecause of the great disparity of local tax efforts in the present system of common schools, the General Assembly must establish a uniform *tax rate* for such property." [Emphasis original.]

If this sentence means what it says, we have done what we were not asked to do, declare unconstitutional the statutes permitting local school districts to set local tax rates within certain guidelines. Destroying the power presently assigned by statute to local school districts to set local school tax rates may or may not work an improvement. Either way, certainly, it is beyond the scope of the relief sought by the appellees. It is the last thing they would want done, as they have said in no uncertain terms. Yet it is the only thing of a judicial nature that we have decided in our Majority Opinion, and it is beyond the parameters of this lawsuit.[2]

---

2. The Response to the Petition for Rehearing filed by the appellee, Council for Better Education, requests us to add this clarification to the Majority Opinion:

> "The record in this case clearly shows that no school district in Kentucky is overfunded. No district is funded to the level of the National average. Therefore, to take money from one district and give it to another would be a step toward a mediocre system statewide. This would violate Section 183 of the constitution and would not be approved by this Court."

Perhaps, since we are prepared to enter the political arena, we should be prepared to go this extra mile.

We were only asked to decide one issue in this lawsuit: whether the General Assembly has responded adequately to its constitutional responsibility. This is a political question, pure and simple. We have undertaken to "enter upon policy determinations for which judicially manageable standards are lacking." *Baker v. Carr*, *supra*, 369 U.S. at 226, 82 S.Ct. at 715. Without such standards, a case is not justiciable. It is not enough to decide that Kentucky does not have an "efficient system of common schools throughout the State," as Section 183 of the Constitution requires, without specifying what statutes are unconstitutional, and why. Yet, the former is not asked, and the latter is not possible. I repeat, this case is not justiciable.

* * *

We have exceeded the judicial power vested in the Court of Justice by Section 109 of the Constitution and violated the doctrine of separation of powers constitutionalized in Sections 27 and 28 of the Kentucky Constitution.

* * *

Our Majority Opinion is fundamentally unsound, not because there is no problem but because the case does not present issues capable of judicial resolution. We have now become part of the problem when we intend to be part of the solution.

Notes and Questions

1. The opinion of the Court in *Rose* identifies five "elements," seven "capacities," and nine "essential, and minimal, characteristics of an 'efficient' system of common schools." Do these five elements and nine characteristics described by the Court bear any relation to the text of Section 183?
2. Quoting *Baker v. Carr*, Justice Leibson argued the case was non-justiciable because it involved "policy determinations for which judicially manageable standards are lacking." Do you agree?
3. Does *Rose* hold that, for every right in the Kentucky Constitution, there must be an available judicial remedy?
4. After *Rose*, the General Assembly enacted the Kentucky Education Reform Act of 1990, or "KERA." *See* 1990 Ky. Acts ch. 476. KERA completely overhauled the public school system in Kentucky, including their funding and governance, professional development for teachers, curriculum, raising the compulsory attendance age, and strengthening the system against political corruption.

Five

The Judicial Branch

A. The Judicial Power

"The judicial power of the Commonwealth shall be vested exclusively in one Court of Justice which shall be divided into a Supreme Court, a Court of Appeals, a trial court of general jurisdiction known as the Circuit Court and a trial court of limited jurisdiction known as the District Court. The court shall constitute a unified judicial system for operation and administration. The impeachment powers of the General Assembly shall remain inviolate." (Ky. Const. §109.)

"(2)(a) The Supreme Court shall have appellate jurisdiction only, except it shall have the power to issue all writs necessary in aid of its appellate jurisdiction, or the complete determination of any cause, or as may be required to exercise control of the Court of Justice....

"(5) ... (b) The Chief Justice of the Commonwealth shall be the executive head of the Court of Justice and he shall appoint such administrative assistants as he deems necessary. He shall assign temporarily any justice or judge of the Commonwealth, active or retired, to sit in any court other than the Supreme Court when he deems such assignment necessary for the prompt disposition of causes...." (Ky. Const. §110.)

"The Supreme Court shall have the power to prescribe rules governing its appellate jurisdiction, rules for the appointment of commissioners and other court personnel, and rules of practice and procedure for the Court of Justice. The Supreme Court shall, by rule, govern admission to the bar and the discipline of members of the bar." (Ky. Const. §116.)

The creation of courts is indispensable to constitutional government. "The institution called a court is a governmental machine, created by the people of the sovereignty for the accomplishment of an essential purpose in the preservation of civilized society. That purpose, briefly stated, is to investigate and adjudicate controversies between citizens when they are unable to amicably adjust them; and between citizens and the government, or some of its subdivisions. The principles upon which such adjustments are made are supposed to be rooted in the soil of unalloyed justice." *Commonwealth ex rel. Ward v. Harrington*, 266 Ky. 41, 98 S.W.2d 53, 55 (1936). "The judicial power," which Section 109 vests in the Court of Justice, may be defined as "the constitutional authority to make final and enforceable decisions of questions of law raised by a claim of legal right." *See American Beauty Homes Corp. v. Louisville & Jefferson Cnty. Planning & Zoning Comm'n*, 379 S.W.2d 450, 454 n.5 (Ky. 1964). Further, "a court, once having obtained jurisdiction of a cause of action, has, as an incidental to its constitutional grant of power, inherent power to do all things reasonably necessary to the administration of justice in the case before it." *Smothers v. Lewis*, 672 S.W.2d 62, 64 (Ky. 1984). But unlike the legislative and executive branches, the judiciary does not seek out issues to address or disputes to decide; its role in the constitutional order is a passive one. "The judiciary intervenes only when called upon by the litigants to settle a case in controversy. But when so called upon it is part of the exercise of this function to enforce constitutional restrictions on legislative power. The judiciary cannot abdicate its responsibility by deferring to the legislature." *Gillis v. Yount*, 748 S.W.2d 357, 360 (Ky. 1988). The scope of the judicial power, therefore, is determined by the scope of the issues brought to a court in the cases pending before it.

Ex parte Auditor of Public Accounts

Supreme Court of Kentucky (1980)
609 S.W.2d 682

OPINION AND ORDER:

A controversy exists between the Auditor of Public Accounts (hereinafter the Auditor) and the Kentucky Bar Association (hereinafter the Association). The question is whether the Auditor is legally entitled or required to audit the books and accounts of the Association. It comes before this court on a direct application by Hon. James B. Graham, the present Auditor, addressed to the Chief Justice, requesting that the controversy be resolved by the Supreme Court. This court does not render advisory opinions. It is generally authorized to exercise "appellate jurisdiction only, except it shall have the power to issue all writs necessary in aid of its appellate jurisdiction, or the complete determination of any cause, or as may be required to exercise control of the Court of Justice." Const. Sec. 110(2)(a). This is an actual controversy requiring an official decision, and because the Association is an arm of the court itself, and therefore cannot properly be sued in any of the other courts of the state, this court is only forum in which the controversy can be heard and officially resolved. *See Ex parte Farley*, Ky., 570 S.W.2d 617, 621 (1978).

Until 1934 the state bar association was a voluntary organization. Before 1918 lawyers were admitted, or "licensed," to practice upon local examination. *Cf.* Ch. 100, Acts of 1892; Ch. 17, Acts of 1902. The first Board of Bar Examiners was established by Ch. 131, Acts of 1918. There were no "license" fees except for original admission. By Ch. 3, Acts of 1934, the General Assembly integrated the bar by requiring all persons practicing law to be members of a state bar association. This Act directed the then Court of Appeals to adopt rules defining the practice of law, prescribing a code of professional ethics, establishing practice and procedure for the discipline, suspension and removal of attorneys, and organizing and governing a bar association "to act as an administrative agency of the Court of Appeals of Kentucky for the purpose of enforcing such rules and regulations as are prescribed, adopted and promulgated by the Court of Appeals under this Act, providing for the government of the State Bar as a part of the judicial department of the State government," etc. * * * The 1934 Act also authorized the court to fix a schedule of fees (not exceeding $2.00 per annum) for its administration.

Upon the recodification of the Kentucky Statutes in 1942 the provisions relating to the Board of Bar Examiners, admission to the practice of law, the organization and government of a bar association by the then Court of Appeals, and the regulation of law practice and practitioners, were placed in KRS Chapter 30. As of this time, application fees for admission to the bar ($10.00) were required to be paid to and held by the Clerk of the Court of Appeals subject to disbursement upon order of the court. KRS 30.060 (1942). Bar dues were limited to $3.00, and their collection and disbursement were made subject to regulation by the court. KRS 30.170 (1942).

KRS 30.060 was amended by Ch. 207, Acts of 1946, to require that all funds derived from application fees be remitted to the State Treasury. In 1962 KRS 30.170(1)(e) was amended by deletion of the limitation (then $10.00) upon the amount of bar dues to be fixed by the court on recommendation of the governing body of the bar association. Ch. 5, Acts of 1962. Thereafter, and until adoption of the Judicial Amendment in 1975, these statutes remained substantially unchanged.

Whatever authority the court had possessed theretofore by statute with regard to admission to practice and regulation of the legal profession was superseded by Const. Sec. 116 as amended in 1975, the concluding sentence of which reads as follows: "The Supreme Court shall, by rule, govern admission to the Bar and the discipline of members of the Bar."

There can be no doubt that this constitutional amendment completely removed the subject from any legislative authority and rendered obsolete and ineffective the statutes pertaining to it. Strangely, nevertheless, at its 1976 regular session the General Assembly reenacted provisions authorizing the Supreme Court to appoint a board of bar examiners and to organize and govern the bar, and again requiring that admission fees be remitted to the state treasury. Ch. 58, Acts of 1976; KRS 21A.130, 21A.150, 21A.160, 21A.140. These statutory provisions are void because they purport to erect powers and limitations that no longer fall within the legislative province.

The root source of all power validly exercised by any officer or agency of the state government is, of course, its Constitution. Placing first things first, ours begins with a Bill of Rights consisting of 26 Sections, the last of which declares in substance that these rights shall prevail over and above all else and are not subject to the general powers of government.

The next two sections of the Constitution, entitled "Distribution of the Powers of Government," divide all governmental authority among "three distinct departments, and each of them to be confined to a separate body of magistracy, to wit: Those which are legislative, to one; those which are executive, to another; and those which are judicial, to another." Const. Sec. 27. This distribution of authority concludes with an unusually forceful command: "No person or collection of persons, being of one of those departments, shall exercise any power properly belonging to either of the others, except in the instances hereinafter expressly directed or permitted." Const. Sec. 28.

Sections 29–62, incl., provide for the legislative branch of government and limit its powers. Sections 69–108, incl., provide for the executive branch of government and delegate certain specific and exclusive powers to its officers. Any further powers this branch of government may possess—that is, beyond those expressly delegated or necessarily implied by the Constitution itself—must be conferred upon it by the legislative branch, which has all governmental authority not delegated elsewhere and not prohibited by the Constitution.

Sections 109–124, incl., the Judicial Amendment of 1975, provide for the judicial branch of government and, as in the instance of the executive branch, delegate certain specific and exclusive powers to its officers and agencies. The hallmark of this particular subdivision appears in its first section, as follows: "The judicial power of the commonwealth shall be vested exclusively in one Court of Justice.... The court shall constitute a unified judicial system for operation and administration...." Const. Sec. 109. Further on, Sec. 110(5)(b) states, "The chief justice of the commonwealth shall be the executive head of the Court of Justice and he shall appoint such administrative assistants as he deems necessary.... The chief justice shall submit the budget for the Court of Justice and perform all other necessary administrative functions relating to the court."

These references to administration and administrative functions do not appear in the Judicial Amendment by accident. Their purpose is to make it unmistakably clear that the judicial branch of this state government has exclusive authority to manage its own affairs. Significantly, whereas the Governor's authority with regard to the presentation of a biennial budget to the General Assembly is purely statutory, *cf.* KRS 45.030–45.050, the authority of the Chief Justice to submit the budget for the Court of Justice comes directly and expressly from the Constitution itself. Const. Sec. 110(5)(b). Hence that function can be neither assumed by nor delegated to the executive branch.

The constitutional check-and-balance relationship between the executive and judicial branches of the government consists of the provisions for filling vacancies in judicial offices and for the appointment of temporary substitutes when two or more justices of the Supreme Court decline or are unable to participate in the disposition of a cause pending before that court. Const. Secs. 118, 110(3). Those relationships between the legislature and judicial branches exist by virtue of Const. Secs. 110(4), 111(1), 112(2) and (3) and 113(2) and (3), pertaining to judicial districts and number of judges and justices; Const. Secs. 111(2), 112(5) and 113(6), pertaining to jurisdiction; and Sec. 120, which provides that the compensation of all judges and justices shall be fixed by the General Assembly and that all compensation and necessary expenses of the Court of Justice shall be paid out of the state treasury.

The purpose and significance of the judicial budget is that it provides a means by which the legislative body may assess how much it must appropriate from the treasury for the operation of the judicial system. Once it has made that appropriation, the authority for and responsibility of determining the necessity for and the propriety of expenditures from that source rest exclusively with the judicial branch itself, and are not subject to executive[1] or legislative regulation. Nevertheless, to the extent that it has appropriated funds from the general revenues of the state to the judicial branch of government the legislative body has a legitimate and necessary right to know how those funds have been spent. In short, the legislative body may require that the accounts so financed be audited.

At this point it is appropriate to consider the nature of the Auditor's office and the source and extent of its authority. This office, as a constitutional agency, first appeared in Sec. 25 of the third Constitution of Kentucky (1850), which provided: "A Treasurer shall be elected ... and an Auditor of Public Accounts.... The duties and responsibilities of these officers shall be prescribed by law." The same provisions were carried into Secs. 91 and 93 of the fourth Constitution (1891) and continue in force today. As their powers are to be prescribed by law, and therefore must be conferred by the legislative body, these offices are subject to whatever limitations of authority apply to the legislative body itself. In other words, and in the context of the controversy with which we are here concerned, with respect to the judicial branch of government the Auditor cannot constitutionally be given any authority that the legislative body has no right to confer.

The authority upon which the Auditor relies in support of his right to audit the accounts of the Association is set forth in KRS Chapter 43. KRS 43.050(2)(a) directs him (or her) to audit the accounts "of all state agencies, all private and semi-private agencies receiving state aid or having responsibility for the handling of any state funds, the accounts, records and transactions of the budget units, and the general accounts of the state." KRS 43.010 defines a "budget unit" as any department or unit for which a separate appropriation or appropriations are made, and a "state agency" as any state officer, department, institution, person or functional group that is authorized to or does exercise any powers, duties or obligations of state government.

We find it unnecessary to determine * * * that the Association and the Board of Bar Examiners do not fall within these statutory definitions. That is irrelevant. The real question is the extent to which they may validly be applied to the Court of Justice as a constitutionally separate branch of government.

As we have indicated, we have no doubt that the General Assembly has the authority to require an accounting of funds it has appropriated from revenues it has caused to be raised. What we have in this case, however, are funds that have not been collected pursuant to any statute and have not been appropriated by the legislative body and are not subject to legislative appropriation. Both the Association and the Board of Bar Examiners exist solely by virtue of rules of this court expressly and exclusively authorized by Const. Sec. 116. There is no constitutional authority by which they can be made accountable to either of the other two branches of government except for

1. *See In the Matter of County of Oneida v. Berle*, 49 N.Y.2d 515, 427 N.Y.S.2d 407, 404 N.E.2d 133 (1980).

their stewardship of such funds or property as may come into their possession through these sources. Neither of those agencies has any such funds or property. Their funds and property are public funds and property because their official functions are entirely public in nature, but their accountability is to this court only, of which they are an integral part.

Another contention by the Auditor is that bar dues are essentially occupational license taxes, which ordinarily the legislature has the exclusive power to levy, and that regardless of whether Const. Sec. 116 grants direct authority in that respect to the Supreme Court or "merely delegates legislative discretion to determine the amount" of the dues, because of their very identity as license fees collected by governmental authority they are public funds and, like the statutory license fees collected by the Department of Fish and Wildlife Resources and the fees of various county officials collected pursuant to Const. Sec. 106, are subject to the authority granted by the Constitution to the Auditor. Again, however, this argument assumes authority in the Auditor that is not granted by the Constitution. That funds are raised by governmental authority and are therefore "public" does not necessarily subject their collection and disbursement to the activities of the Auditor. It would make just as much sense to say that because these funds are "public" they can be used and disbursed only as directed by legislative appropriation. Such a result would open the floodgates to legislative control of the judicial branch of government, and that is exactly what the 1975 Judicial Amendment was designed to prevent.

Fees collected by the Department of Fish and Wildlife Resources are authorized entirely by legislative enactment. *Cf.* KRS 150.170 *et seq.* Indeed the Department itself is a creature of statute. KRS 150.021 *et seq.* Const. Sec. 106 expressly subjects the fees collected by county officials to legislative regulation. Hence all of those funds are subject to whatever authority the General Assembly sees fit to confer upon the Auditor, but funds raised under authority conferred by this court pursuant to its constitutional power to govern admission to the bar and the discipline of its members are not.

The Auditor has submitted an admirable brief in support of the contention that he has authority to audit the accounts of the Association. Among other things, he argues that the exercise of such authority would not interfere with the judicial function. What this argument overlooks, however, is that the 1975 Judicial Amendment extended the judicial function to include the administration of the business affairs of the judicial branch of government, and even though a post or performance audit by the Auditor might not actually "interfere" with that administrative function, certainly it would constitute an intrusion upon it. This intrusion need not be suffered, because appropriated funds are not involved. Experience teaches that a boundary not guarded will in time be lost.

Raney v. Stovall, Ky., 361 S.W.2d 518 (1962), and *Arnett v. Meade*, Ky., 462 S.W.2d 940 (1971), are cited in support of the Auditor's position. Both were decided before the adoption of the Judicial Amendment, and to a large extent the instructive commentary contained in them is obsolete.

In *Raney* the court held simply that the State Treasurer had standing to contest the legality of a warrant issued by the Department of Finance. Although the opinion refers to "the implied obligations" of the office, we construe that expression as connoting merely that a public official having public funds in his custody necessarily has authority to protect them against illegal dissipation. The same result had been reached in *Norman v. Kentucky Bd. of Managers*, 93 Ky. 537, 20 S.W. 901 (1892), holding that the Auditor, who then had the authority to issue warrants against the state treasury, was entitled to question the validity of a legislative act under which he was ordered to issue a warrant.

We do not by any means accede to the proposition that *Raney* somehow lends force to the argument that by virtue of its title alone, referring to "Public" Accounts, the office of the Auditor is invested with rights and powers that pervade the entire spectrum of state government. As we have previously demonstrated, the duties and responsibilities of the Auditor are those and only those legally prescribed by the legislature. Consequently, he has no inherent powers. For example, prior to the effective date of the Governmental Reorganization Act of 1936, KS 4618-68 *et seq*., the Auditor served only as the bookkeeper for the state. KS 4618-137 *et seq.* He had no authority or duty to conduct post or performance audits. These were the function of the State Inspector and Examiner. KS 1992b-59. The effect of the reorganization act was to transfer the duties of Auditor to the Department of Finance, to transfer the duties of the State Inspector and Examiner to the Auditor, and to abolish the office of State Inspector and Examiner. A clearer history of subjugation to the legislature cannot be found.

The bottom line of *Arnett v. Meade*, Ky., 462 S.W.2d 940 (1971), was its holding that an ancient but unrepealed statute (KRS 421.140) imposing limits on the punishment for contempt of court had become a material interference with the judicial function and for that reason was invalid. The opinion devotes a great deal of the discussion to the overlapping of legislative and judicial functions. The sentence from which the Auditor's position in this case would draw nourishment is to the effect that "the legislature may put reasonable restrictions upon constitutional functions of the courts, provided that such restrictions do not defeat or materially impair the exercise of those functions." *Arnett, supra*, at 946. The correct principle, as we view it, is that the legislative function cannot be so exercised as to interfere unreasonably with the functioning of the courts, and that any unconstitutional intrusion is per se unreasonable, unless it be determined by the court that it can and should be tolerated in a spirit of comity. The converse also is true, and in *Lunsford v. Commonwealth*, Ky., 436 S.W.2d 512 (1969), this court recognized that its own rule authorizing imprisonment for failure to execute a peace bond was an unconstitutional infringement upon the legislative prerogative. And in *Raney, supra*, for the same reason, we declined the invitation to trespass upon the exclusive right of the Senate to determine the qualifications and disqualifications of its own members. Such an inquiry is, of course, of a judicial nature, but the Constitution excludes it from the judicial process.

Inevitably, there is and always will be a gray area in which a line between the legislative prerogatives of the General Assembly and the rule-making authority of the courts is not easy to draw. The policy of this court is not to contest the propriety of legislation in this area to which we can accede through a wholesome comity. There is, for example, the statute providing for the disqualification of judges, KRS 26A.015, as contrasted with SCR 4.300 Canon 3, C(1), in which the same subject-matter is included as a part of the Code of Judicial Conduct. There is also the matter of court costs and fees. *See* KRS 24A.270. Even the statutory creation of a small claims division within the structure of the constitutionally-established district court, KRS 24A.230, is not beyond the pale of an honest difference of opinion. But we hold the General Assembly in the highest respect, and much prefer cooperation over conflict. It has done great work in accommodating the statutes to the new and hitherto-untried requirements of the 1975 Judicial Amendment, and to the extent that we are able to accept its judgments without leaving seeds of future jeopardy to the integrity of the judicial system we shall continue to do so. The point we make here is that the commentary in *Arnett* regarding legislative restriction upon judicial functions is and must be confined fundamentally to the area of comity.

The Association has had its financial records regularly audited by certified public accountants for many years.[2] Its books and records, except for what must be held in confidence incident to disciplinary proceedings, are open for inspection by the news media and by any legitimately interested member of the public. For 45 years there was no effort or attempt by the Auditor's office to assume any authority or responsibility over them. Traditionally at least, the weight of history is against this new-found claim of right.

One remaining question might be asked—why not? In other words, why not comity in this instance? The answer is that there really is no necessity for it and there is good reason against it. Moreover, the legislature is not the real source of the pressure anyway. Without ascribing any questionable motive to the present incumbent or any particular one or more of his predecessors, we think it is appropriate to consider that the office of the Auditor is essentially political in nature and has not always been altogether unaffected by partisan political currents. In keeping with the letter and spirit of the 1975 Judicial Amendment it is the policy of this court, insofar as possible, to isolate the judicial system from the political arena.

At the present time we have 120 circuit clerks who collect some $3,000,000 per month for the general fund of the state. They are not regularly audited because the Auditor does not have a sufficient appropriation to make it possible. So, except for "spot" audits of selected offices the Auditor is not in a position to audit this, the greatest source of public revenue passing through the judicial system. We have some difficulty in comprehending how an audit of the Association, never before undertaken and not prompted by any source outside the Auditor's office itself, can be justified when the 120 clerks' offices cannot be served.

2. The legislature has recognized such action as an acceptable substitute for the services of the Auditor for counties. KRS 43.070(1)(b).

* * *

There seems to be a rather prevalent misapprehension regarding the nature and function of the Association. It does not exist for the private benefit of the legal community. The members of the bar are entrusted with a privilege that places their duty of public service above their personal requirements and ambitions. The mission of the Association is to see to it that this trust is performed with fidelity to the high principles of their calling. This requires that the Association maintain a proper discipline of the bar, that it initiate and supervise appropriate means to insure a high standard of professional competence, and that it bear a substantial responsibility for promoting the efficiency and improvement of the judicial system itself. Without an arm such as the Association this court could not carry out its own responsibilities in those respects. As it is, the functioning of the Association in disciplinary and educational matters results in constant communication with this court and the Chief Justice in their supervisory capacities, entailing a consumption of time and effort that seems not to be realized by those not directly involved in the process.

* * *

In conclusion, it is our opinion that the Auditor has no legal authority with respect to the Association, and it is so ordered.

Aker, Clayton, Lukowsky, Stephens, Stephenson and Sternberg, JJ., sitting.

All concur.

Entered November 26, 1980.

/s/ John S. Palmore

Chief Justice

Notes and Questions

1. The holding in *Ex parte Auditor* relied principally upon Section 109 (which vests the judicial power in a unified Court of Justice), Section 110(5)(b) (which makes the Chief Justice the executive head of the Court of Justice), and Section 116 (which provides that the Supreme Court shall govern the bar). How does the Court's decision based upon these Sections further insulate the judiciary from intrusions into its authority by the other branches of government?
2. Justice Robert F. Stephens (who served as Chief Justice from 1982 to 1998—the longest serving Chief Justice in Kentucky's history) referred to the holding of *Ex parte Auditor* as the "Judicial Bill of Rights." Why might this be? What does this tell you about the importance of the separation of powers to the judicial branch?
3. The Court in *Ex parte Auditor* mentioned at the beginning of the opinion a prior decision, *Ex parte Farley*, 570 S.W.2d 617 (Ky. 1978). The Court held in *Ex parte Farley* that it was not required by the Kentucky Open Records Act to disclose to the state's Public Advocate the statistical information compiled on death penalty cases by the Administrative Office of the Courts (AOC) under KRS 532.075. The Court deter-

Figure 5-1. Official portrait of Chief Justice Robert F. Stephens, Kentucky State Capitol. Portrait by John Michael Carter, reproduced with permission of the artist and the Supreme Court of Kentucky.

mined that the AOC was "inseparable from the office of the Chief Justice itself" under Ky. Const. §110(5). Though not necessarily decided on separation of powers grounds, the Court held that "the custody and control of the records generated by the courts in the course of their work are inseparable from the judicial function itself, and are not subject to statutory regulation." *Ex parte Farley*, 570 S.W.2d at 624.

4. As mentioned in *Ex parte Auditor*, the Court will sometimes grant comity to a statute that it finds infringes on the judicial power, so long as the statute does not defeat or materially impair the judicial function. As but a few examples, the Supreme Court has granted comity to statutes requiring "truth in sentencing" in felony cases, *Com-*

monwealth v. Reneer, 734 S.W.2d 794 (Ky. 1987); allowing the Chief Justice to disqualify a trial court judge who will not afford a party a fair trial, *Foster v. Overstreet*, 905 S.W.2d 504 (Ky. 1995); providing for post-conviction DNA testing in capital cases, *Taylor v. Commonwealth*, 175 S.W.3d 68 (Ky. 2005); precluding discovery of KASPER prescription records retained by the Cabinet for Health and Family Services, *Commonwealth, Cabinet for Health & Family Servs. v. Chauvin*, 316 S.W.3d 279 (Ky. 2010); and permitting the Supreme Court to prescribe the number of peremptory challenges allowed each party in a jury trial, *Glenn v. Commonwealth*, 436 S.W.3d 186 (Ky. 2013). The decision whether to extend comity to a statute otherwise unconstitutional is a matter of "institutional policy reserved for the Supreme Court only," *O'Bryan v. Hedgespeth*, 892 S.W.2d 571, 577 (Ky. 1995), so a lower court may not grant comity to any statute it finds to be unconstitutional.

Smothers v. Lewis

Supreme Court of Kentucky (1984)
672 S.W.2d 62

OPINION OF THE COURT BY CHIEF JUSTICE STEPHENS.

The sole issue in this case is the constitutionality of KRS 243.580(2) and (3), which, in effect, prohibits all courts from interfering with an order of revocation of an alcoholic beverage license during an appeal.

This question is before this Court on Movant's request for CR 65.09 relief from an Opinion and Order of the Court of Appeals which granted CR 65.07 relief to the current Respondents.

Movant, William Smothers, d/b/a Jane Todd Inn, (hereinafter described as "Smothers") holds a retail beer license for a premises known as Jane Todd Inn which operates in Lebanon, Marion County, Kentucky.

As the result of a prior hearing by the Alcoholic Beverage Control Board on July 15, 1982, the Board entered an order revoking Smothers' retail beer license.

Smothers appealed from the Board's order to the Franklin Circuit Court. That Court issued a temporary restraining order staying enforcement of the Board's order of revocation during the pendency of the appeal.

The Board moved for dissolution of the restraining order. Smothers responded with a motion for a temporary injunction. The Franklin Circuit Court granted Smothers' motion for a temporary injunction to stay enforcement of the Board's order of revocation pending a determination of the appeal by the Court.

The Board moved the Court of Appeals for CR 65.07 relief from the Franklin Circuit Court's temporary injunction, based on KRS 243.580(2), (3). The Court of Appeals entered an Order granting the CR 65.07 relief sought by the Board. The Court of Appeals, 663 S.W.2d 228, upheld the constitutionality of KRS 243.580.

We disagree, and we hold that KRS 243.580(2) and (3) are unconstitutional as being in violation of §109, §116, §27 and §28 of the Kentucky Constitution.

KRS 243.580(2) and (3) read as follows:

> (2) If a license is revoked or suspended by an order of the board, the licensee shall at once suspend all operations authorized under his license, except as provided by KRS 243.540, though he files an appeal in the Franklin Circuit Court from the order of revocation of suspension.
>
> (3) No court may enjoin the operation of an order of revocation or suspension pending an appeal. If upon appeal to the Franklin Circuit Court an order of suspension or revocation is upheld, or if an order refusing to suspend or revoke a license is reversed, and an appeal is taken to the Court of Appeals, no court may enjoin the operation of the judgment of the Franklin Circuit Court pending the appeal.

We hold that KRS 243.580(2) and (3) are unconstitutional because their prohibitions against injunctive relief pending appeal are legislative encroachments upon the powers of the judicial branch of our government.

It is well settled law in the state of Kentucky that one branch of Kentucky's tripartite government may not encroach upon the inherent powers granted to any other branch. *LRC v. Brown*, Ky., 664 S.W.2d 907 (1984). The Constitution of Kentucky, Section 109 states explicitly that "The judicial power of the commonwealth shall be vested exclusively in one Court of Justice...." Section 116 of the Constitution of Kentucky's "Judicial Article" which was approved by the voters in 1976 provides that:

> The Supreme Court shall have the power to prescribe rules governing its appellate jurisdiction....

Thus, the source of the Court's rule making power is firmly rooted within the Constitution.

In addition to the Court's Constitutional rule making power, the Court is also vested with certain "inherent" powers to do that which is reasonably necessary for the administration of justice within the scope of their jurisdiction. *Craft v. Commonwealth*, Ky., 343 S.W.2d 150 (1961). In *Craft*, we said while considering the rule making power and the judicial power to be one and the same that "... the grant of judicial power [rule making power] to the courts by the constitution carries with it, as a necessary incident, the right to make that power effective in the administration of justice." *Id.* at 151.

It is a result of this foregoing line of thinking that we now adopt the language framework of 28 Am.Jur.2d, Injunctions, Section 15, and once and for all make clear that a court, once having obtained jurisdiction of a cause of action, has, as an incidental to its constitutional grant of power, inherent power to do all things reasonably necessary to the administration of justice in the case before it. In the exercise of this power, a court, when necessary in order to protect or preserve the subject matter of the litigation, to protect its jurisdiction and to make its judgment effective, may grant or issue a temporary injunction in aid of or ancillary to the principal action.

The control over this inherent judicial power, in this particular instance the injunction, is exclusively within the constitutional realm of the courts. As such, it is not within the purview of the legislature to grant or deny the power nor is it within the purview of the legislature to shape or fashion circumstances under which this inherently judicial power may be or may not be granted or denied.

This Court has historically recognized constitutional limitations upon the power of the legislature to interfere with or to inhibit the performance of constitutionally granted and inherently provided judicial functions. In *Arnett v. Meade*, Ky., 462 S.W.2d 940 (1971) we held that a legislatively enacted limit on the extent of punishment which could be meted for contempt so interfered with the judicial power as to render those legislated limits unconstitutional.

In applying the foregoing law to the case at bar it becomes clear that KRS 243.580(3) is unconstitutional. The statutorily granted right to appeal under KRS 243.560 and 243.570 was Smothers' basis for this action in the Franklin Circuit Court. However, the fact that the legislature statutorily provided for this appeal does not give it the right to encroach upon the constitutionally granted powers of the judiciary. Once the administrative action has ended and the right to appeal arises the legislature is void of any right to control a subsequent appellate judicial proceeding. The judicial rules have come into play and have preempted the field.

We reiterate our previously adopted language, "... a court, once having obtained jurisdiction of a cause of action, has, as incidental to its general jurisdiction, inherent power to do all things reasonably necessary to the administration of justice in the case before it...." This includes the inherent power to issue injunctions.

The language of KRS 243.580(3) directly locks horns with the constitutionally inherent injunction power of the courts when it says, "No court may enjoin the operation of an order of revocation or suspension pending an appeal." Such language is a classic example of the very type of legislative encroachment onto the power of the judicial branch of our government which is constitutionally impermissible. Section 27, Section 28, Kentucky Constitution. *LRC v. Brown, supra.*

We also hold that (2) of KRS 243.580 is unconstitutional. Under the terms of that section a licensee whose license has been revoked or suspended must "... at once suspend all operations authorized under his license...." Under the statute this is so even though "... he files an appeal...." The practical effect of this language is to pay lip service to the statutory provisions that establish the right for a licensee to appeal while eradicating any practical reason for taking the appeal. This is a classic example of putting a licensee in the position of winning the battle but losing the war. A licensee whose license has been revoked or suspended immediately suffers the irreparable penalty of loss of business for which there is no practical compensation. This happens even if said licensee wins an appeal and a decision holding that the license was wrongfully revoked. The purpose and impetus for appealing; i.e., to prevent having an irrevocable and irreparable penalty imposed, is erased when the statute requires imposition of the penalty prior to and despite the outcome of the appeal. Succinctly put, the statute gives an appeal and then takes it away. The contradiction and conflict here are obvious. The practical effect is to render the appeal a meaningless and merely ritualistic process.

To deny that courts possess the power to forestall the infliction of injustice through injunctive relief as the legislature has attempted to do so in KRS 243.580(2) is not only internally conflicting within that provision of the statute but is also constitutionally impermissible under the same rationale this Court has used today to find that (3) of the same statute is unconstitutional under the mandate of our constitution requiring a separation of powers.

Once again we emphasize that the grant of judicial power to the courts carries with it the right to make that power effective. To allow the courts the ability to right a wrong by granting an appeal but by denying the courts the ability to defer imposition of the penalty appended to that wrong would be to deny the court its inherent right to make its constitutional grant of power effective. This we cannot allow.

This issue is in essence the "flip side" of the *Arnett v. Meade*, *supra*, issue. As we discussed earlier, in *Arnett*, the legislature tried to place limits upon the punishment a court could mete out for contempt. This Court held that the legislature could not set limits that interfered with the inherent judicial power to function. *Id.* at 948. In the case at bar the legislature has attempted to interfere with the judicial power in an inverse manner. Rather than attempting to limit the court's power to punish, it has attempted to limit the court's power to stay a possibly unjustly imposed punishment. In KRS 243.580(2) as in *Arnett* the legislative attempt so interferes with the judicial power as to render those legislated limits unconstitutional.

For the reasons stated above, the Department's motion for CR 65.07 relief is denied and the injunction entered by the Franklin Circuit Court on October 26, 1982 is reinstated. The opinion and order of the Court of Appeals in this matter is vacated and set aside.

All concur.

Notes and Questions

1. The Court held in *Smothers* that "KRS 243.580(2) and (3) are unconstitutional as being in violation of §109, §116, §27 and §28 of the Kentucky Constitution." How did each of these constitutional provisions factor into the Court's decision?
2. In *Smothers*, the Court held that "a court, when necessary in order to protect or preserve the subject matter of the litigation, to protect its jurisdiction and to make its judgment effective, may grant or issue a temporary injunction in aid of or ancillary to the principal action." Civil Rule 65.01, however, permits injunctive relief to be obtained only in a Circuit Court action, not in the District Court. *Smothers* is there-

fore in tension with the rule, at least as far as the District Court is concerned. Does the District Court have inherent power to issue any temporary injunctions? How does the District Court's status as a court of limited jurisdiction affect your answer?

Kuprion v. Fitzgerald

Supreme Court of Kentucky (1994)
888 S.W.2d 679

OPINION OF THE COURT BY JUSTICE WINTERSHEIMER.

This appeal is from a decision of the Court of Appeals which denied a writ of mandamus challenging the constitutionality of what is known as the Jefferson Family Court, seeking to have the "Family Court" declared unconstitutional and requiring the "Family Court Judge" to transfer the case to a division of the regular circuit court.

The issues presented are whether a district judge lacks subject matter jurisdiction to grant a decree of dissolution; whether the Chief Justice can grant district judges the power to hear dissolution cases; whether the Jefferson Family Court violates Sections 27 and 28 of the Kentucky Constitution; whether the appellant is denied equal protection of the law under the Federal and State Constitutions and whether the Court of Appeals erred in denying mandamus.

On April 29, 1993, Penny L. Kuprion filed a petition for dissolution of marriage with the clerk of the Jefferson Circuit Court. A decree of dissolution was entered on April 29, 1994. Pursuant to the computerized system used by the clerk, the matter was assigned to the Jefferson "Family Court" to be presided over by the Honorable Richard J. Fitzgerald, a Jefferson County District Judge. Claiming that the "Family Court" was unconstitutional, she moved the Family Court Judge to reassign the matter to Jefferson Circuit Court. Her motion was denied. She then sought a writ of mandamus to request that her case be reassigned to the Jefferson Circuit Court and that the Family Court project be declared unconstitutional. The Court of Appeals denied mandamus and this appeal followed.

Our task is to determine the nature of what has been established in Jefferson County and whether it passes constitutional muster. We cannot deem a legislative resolution or judicial order constitutional merely because it may seem in our view to be expedient, necessary or wise, or even if it enjoys strong popular support. The Kentucky Constitution is, in matters of state law, the supreme law of this Commonwealth to which all acts of the legislature, the judiciary and any government agent are subordinate. It is our responsibility to consider only whether the action meets or violates constitutional requirements.

The Kentucky General Assembly, on March 31, 1988, passed a concurrent resolution directing the Legislative Research Commission to appoint a Task Force to examine the need for and feasibility of establishing a Family Court or division of court. 1988 Ky. Acts Ch. 128, HCR 30.

It should be observed that members of the public and even the legal profession might easily be lulled into the colloquial concept of "Family Court." The better definition would be to label it as a "Family Court Project." It should be recalled that within district court there are already the titles of "traffic court" and "probate court," as well as "juvenile court" and "small claims court," which were created by statute. KRS 24A.110(1); KRS 24A.120(2); KRS 24A.130; KRS 24A.230.

The Task Force was directed to make findings and conclusions, including summaries of any legislation it might recommend. The 16-member Task Force included five members of the General Assembly and, after due consideration, recommended that rather than immediately create a Family Court in Kentucky, a pilot Family Court project be initiated; that the pilot project be implemented by the Court of Justice; that the Chief Justice select the district judges; and that the 1990 General Assembly fund the project, including implementation and evaluation.

The Task Force report in 1989 amplified the preamble to the concurrent resolution which established it by making ten findings, including the idea that fractionalization of family jurisdiction leads to a waste of time and delays, that it increases the time and expense involved in these cases and creates an inordinate delay between intake and final resolution.

The Task Force recommended to the Supreme Court and to the General Assembly that the Supreme Court establish by rule, a pilot project for the 1990–92 biennium with at least one urban and one rural location and that the General Assembly fund the project. The recommendations of the Task Force were first implemented in Jefferson County where, once a family dispute entered the system, all matters related to it were to remain with the one judge who was initially assigned to the case.

The procedure of using an experimental Family Court Project to study the feasibility prior to establishment by the legislature or constitutional amendment reflects the practice followed in Florida, New York and Virginia.

In 1991, the Chief Justice selected three circuit judges to be sworn in as special district judges and three district judges to be sworn in as special circuit judges. His order of March 20, 1991 contains the language "This appointment shall remain in effect until further order of this Court." The Supreme Court of Kentucky subsequently approved rules of practice for the Jefferson Family Court. Currently the Family Court project hears 75 percent of the actions for dissolution of marriage, and 25 percent are heard in the circuit court. In 1994, the General Assembly increased funding to permit the size of the project to increase from six to eight judges in July, 1994. It is expected that all new dissolution actions will be placed in the Family Court project rather than on the regular circuit court docket. The Family Court project continues to hear all adoptions, terminations of parental rights, dependency/neglect, paternity and juvenile matters.

The assignment of judges to the Family Court project is made on a voluntary basis. The district judge in this case, as well as all other district judges who have been appointed as special circuit judges, have the necessary constitutional qualifications to serve as circuit judge. Ky. Const. §122.

Penny L. Kuprion claims that a district judge lacks subject matter jurisdiction to grant a decree of dissolution of marriage. She cites Section 113(6) of the Kentucky Constitution and KRS 24A.110–130; KRS 406.021 and KRS 406.140. We must agree that a district judge in his capacity as district judge has no jurisdiction to hear a dissolution case. However, in this situation the district judges involved are properly sworn as special circuit judges pursuant to Section 110(5)(b) of the Kentucky Constitution in order to hear cases which fall within the exclusive jurisdiction of the circuit court. The district court cannot hear divorce cases; Only the circuit court has that power.

It is inherent in the nature of the judicial branch that in a multi-judge court, the actions of a single member including the Chief Justice acting in an administrative capacity are subject to review. The reviewing court can take notice of a presumption of regularity to be accorded to the actions under review which does not preclude a review of the substance and constitutionality of such actions. Here the actions and orders of appointment were not improper. Accordingly, we now consider the constitutional aspect of the actions.

We must reject her claim because Section 110(5)(b) in pertinent part states that the Chief Justice shall assign temporarily any justice or judge of the Commonwealth to sit in any court other than the Supreme Court when he deems such assignment necessary for the prompt disposition of causes.

She also argues that the Chief Justice may not use Section 110(5)(b) to appoint a district judge as a temporary special circuit judge in order to hear dissolution actions under the authority of the Jefferson Family Court project because KRS 26A.020 provides in part what is to take place when a judge is unavailable to perform judicial duties.

We disagree. The appellant can cite no authority for the proposition that unavailability of a sitting judge is the sole grounds on which the Chief Justice can make a temporary appointment for the prompt disposition of causes. This Court sustained the appointment of a retired circuit judge as a special judge to allow him to complete his caseload despite the fact that his successor had already taken office. *Regency Pheasant Run Ltd. v. Karem*, Ky., 860 S.W.2d 755 (1993).

The Chief Justice has also appointed a retired circuit judge as a special circuit judge to hear the voluminous asbestos litigation in Jefferson Circuit Court because it would otherwise clog the dockets of every division of that court. *Huntzinger v. McCrae*, Ky. App., 818 S.W.2d 613 (1991), permitted a chief regional circuit judge to appoint a special circuit judge from outside the region. Although it is unclear whether the regular circuit judge was unavailable to sit, that panel of the Court of Appeals found that the fact that the Chief Justice had not appointed the special judge was not a material departure from the statute and upheld the special judge's dismissal of a complaint.

It should be remembered that Section 109 of the Constitution established a trial court of general jurisdiction, known as a circuit court, and a trial court of limited jurisdiction, known as the district court, as the only trial courts in Kentucky. Those two courts, together with the Supreme Court and the Court of Appeals, are the only judicial entities into which the single Court of Justice shall be divided. Section 113 of the Constitution provides that the General Assembly shall determine jurisdictional limitations for the district court and Section 112 provides that appellate jurisdiction shall be assigned to the circuit court as provided by law. The circuit court also exercises all other original jurisdiction not vested in some other court. It is further recognized that the legislature has no power to create a court not provided by the Constitution. *Hoblitzel v. Jenkins*, 204 Ky. 122, 263 S.W. 764 (1924).

We must conclude that KRS 26A.020 does not limit the appointment power of the Chief Justice pursuant to Section 110, but only establishes a procedure by which it is to be exercised when a judge is actually unavailable to sit.

Section 110(5)(b) provides the necessary authority for the Chief Justice to assign a judge temporarily to any court other than the Supreme Court for the prompt disposition of causes. The discretion of the Chief Justice in making such an appointment is limited to that necessary for the prompt disposition of causes. In this case, such discretion was supported by the report of the Family Court Feasibility Task Force and the adoption of HCR 30.

The second prong of Penny Kuprion's argument against the validity of Judge Fitzgerald as a special circuit judge is that the order of the Chief Justice dated March 20, 1991 is not temporary because it did not give a date certain on which the appointment would expire. The order recites that the appointment shall continue "until further orders of the court."

Section 110(5)(b) of the Constitution does not confer unbridled, absolute or unlimited power on the Chief Justice in his capacity as Chief Executive of the court system. The Section refers only to temporary appointments of judges to provide for the prompt disposition of causes. It should be pointed out that the word "temporary" relates only to the appointment of the judge. In no way can a temporary court be created by an order of the Chief Justice. Such an extraordinary action must be rooted in fact and the reason for the temporary appointment should be noted in the order of appointment. Section 113(6) states that the grant of jurisdiction for a district judge comes from the General Assembly and not from any other entity. The appointment of special judges has a foundation in the language of Section 115.

The situation here is that the Family Court project is a concurrent session of the already existing district and circuit court divisions and is convened in response to HCR 30. The purpose of the project is to determine if domestic cases involving aspects of family relations can be adjudicated more effectively under the so-called "one judge, one family" approach. The project is based on the temporary assignment of district and circuit judges as special judges to serve in a temporary capacity. No new divisions of the court have been created.

Penny L. Kuprion maintains that a new court has been created. The concurrent resolution considered both the possibilities of the development of a court or a division of court, leaving open the possibility that the ultimate solution of the problem faced by the Task Force might be a constitutional amendment creating a truly new court. This argument might have been rendered moot if the Task Force and the orders of this Court used the word "division" as in the case of the creation of a Small Claims Division of district courts. *See Hibberd v. Neil Huffman Datsun, Inc.*, Ky. App., 791 S.W.2d 726 (1990). It is obvious that the use of the word "court" does not by itself make a court any more than the "four courts" mentioned in the Constitution are in addition to the Unified Court of Justice. The words might have been used more precisely, but they do not give rise to any constitutional infirmity.

A particularly telling aspect of the temporary nature of this situation can be seen in the necessity for legislative funding of this project in each biennium as part of the judicial budget. This funding could be suspended by any succeeding General Assembly. *Hayes v. State Property*, Ky., 731 S.W.2d 797 (1987). The cases which have considered the relationship between budget questions and statutes reflect the fact that budgeting can be in many ways the most dramatic means by which a legislature can express itself. *Cf. Commonwealth, ex rel Armstrong v. Collins*, Ky., 709 S.W.2d 437 (1986); *Smith v. Kentucky State Racing Com'n*, Ky. App., 697 S.W.2d 153 (1985). "Since the budget is the principal instrument of resource allocation and policy planning, it reflects state government's public policy priorities." *See* P. Miller, *Kentucky Politics and Government: Do We Stand United* (1994) at p. 227.

The introduction of Senate Bills 83 and 84 by the 1994 General Assembly and the adjournment of that body without having acted upon the legislation is of no consequence in our consideration. It is mere dicta to say that it would be helpful if the General Assembly had indicated a time frame in which to conduct the Family Court project and had required a report to be submitted to it within that time frame. However, it does not affect our consideration of the concept of a temporary appointment.

The word "temporary" means transient or passing but not permanent. *Cf. Rogers v. City of Louisville*, 296 Ky. 238, 176 S.W.2d 387 (1943). "Temporary" is a word of much elasticity and it has no fixed meaning in the sense that it designates any fixed period of time. *Kahn v. Lockhard*, Mo., 392 S.W.2d 30 (1965). Perhaps the most colorful definition of the word "temporary" is "for a brief period of time, transitory, or limited, or on the highway of time, a cul-de-sac, but not a limitless boulevard of eternity." *Simplex Precast Industries, Inc. v. Biehl*, 395 Pa. 105, 149 A.2d 121 (1959).

Here the appointment of a special judge is for an indefinite time, but the language of the order limits the appointment by stating "until further order of the Court" which recognizes that upon the occurrence of some event the appointment will cease to exist. The Chief Justice has not exceeded his constitutional authority.

* * *

We must pause to consider the status of the actions of the Chief Justice. We find them to be acts of discretion that are not an abuse of that discretion. By means of comparison, we frame our standard of review along the lines of a clear abuse of discretion by a trial court. The term is usually related to trial court activities, but can be applied to the use of judicial authority in any respect, particularly when the authority is conferred by the Constitution. "Abuse of discretion in relation to the exercise of judicial power implies arbitrary action or capricious disposition under the circumstances, at least an unreasonable and unfair decision." *Kentucky National Park Com'n v. Russell*, 301 Ky. 187, 191 S.W.2d 214 (1945) (referring to *Harvey Coal Corp. v. York*, 252 Ky. 605, 67 S.W.2d 977 (1934)). *See Also City of Louisville v. Allen*, Ky., 385 S.W.2d 179 (1964). The exercise of discretion must be legally sound. See 5 Am.Jur.2d §774 *Appeal and Error* P. 217 (1962).

* * *

The need to address the problem of what has come to be known as "Family Court Practice" was demonstrated by the Task Force in sufficient detail. The authority of the Chief Justice is established by Sections 110 and 116 of the Constitution. The Chief Justice was within his constitutional authority to accept the report of the Task Force and then to exercise his sound discretion as to how and where to implement the request of the Task Force.

The third argument is that the Jefferson Family Court project violates Sections 27 and 28 of the Kentucky Constitution and is therefore unconstitutional. The issue is whether the establishment of the Family Court project has usurped the legislative power to assign jurisdiction of subject matter to the circuit court as provided in Section 109 of the Constitution and detailed by KRS 23A.010.

It involves the question of whether the Family Court project is a separate judicially created court within the Court of Justice and consequently unconstitutional despite the legality of appointment pursuant to the Constitution.

It should be observed that the judicial amendment of 1975 and the constitutional sections created by it may have resulted in some overlap of authority. *See* D. McSwin, note, *Judicial v. Legislative Power in Kentucky: A Comity of Errors*, 71 Ky.L.J. 829 (1983). However, there has never been any question that the Supreme Court has authority to act upon its responsibilities pursuant to Section 110 of the Constitution. *Ex Parte Farley*, Ky., 570 S.W.2d 617 (1978); *Regency Pheasant Run, Ltd., supra.*

There is legislative authorization through which HCR 30 delegates authority to the Legislative Research Commission to appoint a Task Force to study the establishment of a court or division of court devoted to family law problems and the management and resolution of family law cases. The Task Force recommended that the Chief Justice supervise the project in his capacity as head of the Court of Justice pursuant to Section 110(5) of the Constitution. The pilot project was developed using the existing judicial resources in the only constitutional manner available. The Chief Justice cannot and did not create any new judges or any new courts.

The Family Court project does not establish a new or separate court pursuant to Section 109 of the Constitution. The project has resulted in a constitutionally authorized judicial unit known as Family Court which uses judicial resources already in existence. Thus it complies with Sections 27 and 28 of the Constitution in preserving the separation of powers. The use of temporarily assigned judges who are already a part of the Court of Justice complies with Section 109 of the Constitution. Consequently the Family Court project is constitutional.

Penny L. Kuprion has not been denied equal protection of the law guaranteed by the Federal and State Constitutions. She has not suffered any discrimination by virtue of having her case assigned to an elected district judge sitting as an approved special circuit judge in the Family Court project. Such a submission could have resulted regardless of whether the cases were assigned alphabetically or in any other manner. It must be remembered that the hearing judges who may have been elected as district judges are not serving in that capacity but rather as special circuit judges pursuant to a proper appointment by the Chief Justice. The district judges involved in this project hear divorce and custody cases in their capacity as special circuit judges only.

Although the question of alphabetical discrimination may be real in some circumstances, it is not prejudicial here and does not require any interference with the Family Court project. There is no palpable error or manifest injustice as required by CR 61.02. There is no basis for relief on such grounds.

The Court of Appeals did not commit reversible error in denying the petition for mandamus. The Court of Appeals properly determined that the Jefferson Family Court project is a temporary "joint research project" of the judiciary and General Assembly and is structured in a constitutionally permissible manner. The panel of the Court of Appeals held that Judge Fitzgerald was constitutionally vested in his capacity as a special circuit judge with appropriate subject matter jurisdiction to consider the divorce proceedings. Accordingly the Court of Appeals was correct in denying the petition for a writ of mandamus.

It is not for us to say that the implementation of the project could have been accomplished in a better fashion. Perhaps the assignment of cases should be on a random basis; perhaps participation by the litigants should be voluntary; perhaps the establishment of a Family Court should have been as a division of the circuit court with a definite time limitation imposed by the legislature. Our only task is to determine the nature of what has been established and its constitutional status.

* * *

It should be clear that the creation of any court is vested only in the legislature by virtue of Sections 112 and 113 of the Constitution, and new district or circuit courts can be established only upon a certification of necessity by the Supreme Court.

The final form, if any, of the Family Court will need to be detailed in legislation. That does not mean that one branch of government cannot assist another branch of government in analyzing the methods to make a system of government including the administration of judicial matters more effective. The funding of the pilot program by the General Assembly gives approval to the actions taken by the Chief Justice to implement the recommendations of the Task Force set up by the General Assembly itself. The concurrent resolution which created the pilot project requires funding periodically by the legislature. The duration of such funding and the duration of the project is clearly within the bounds of the legislature. Under the rules of comity, the judiciary has not invaded the province of the legislature. The Chief Justice cannot and has not created a court system. The General Assembly could require a termination of the project or, in effect, a report which could be used to determine the permanent status of a Family Court.

* * *

There remains a vexing concern about how long the temporary appointments can be used to implement the Family Court project. It is not appropriate for this Court to advise the legislature as to when such a pilot project should be completed. Such a decision is within their sound legislative judgment. Future litigation as to the length of the project is not necessarily foreclosed by our decision here.

We must conclude that Judge Fitzgerald is presiding over the dissolution action in a proper and constitutional manner pursuant to his appointment as a special circuit judge in conformity with Section 110(5)(b) of the Constitution. The Family Court project does not create a new and unconstitutional court in violation of Sections 27, 28 or 109 of the Constitution. Consequently, Penny L. Kuprion has not been denied equal protection of the law pursuant to either the United States or Kentucky Constitutions. The Court of Appeals correctly denied mandamus.

The decision of the Court of Appeals to deny the writ of mandamus is affirmed.

Lambert, Spain, and Stumbo, JJ., and Robert S. Miller, Special Justice, concur.

Reynolds, J., concurs in majority opinion in result only.

Robert S. Miller, Special Justice, also files a separate concurring opinion in which Spain and Stumbo, JJ., join.

David Tachau, Special Justice, files a separate dissenting opinion.

Stephens, C.J., and Leibson, J., did not sit.

* * *

Notes and Questions

1. As noted in the majority opinion, *Kuprion* was decided prior to the formal creation of Family Courts statewide in Kentucky; the Court notes that they were only a pilot project in Jefferson County at the time. In 2002, Kentucky voters approved a constitutional amendment that added subsection (6) to Section 112 of the Kentucky Constitution, which reads: "The Supreme Court may designate one or more divisions of Circuit Court within a judicial circuit as a family court division. A Circuit Court division so designated shall retain the general jurisdiction of the Circuit Court and shall have additional jurisdiction as may be provided by the General Assembly." The amendment passed in all 120 Kentucky counties with more than 75% of the vote. Most Kentucky counties now have a Family Court.

2. What is the scope of the Chief Justice's appointment power under Section 110(5)(b) of the Constitution?

3. "Section 110(5)(b) states unequivocally that the Chief Justice 'shall assign temporarily any justice or judge of the commonwealth, *active or retired*, to sit in any court other than the Supreme Court when he deems such assignment necessary for the prompt disposition of causes.' (Emphasis added.) The language of this section clearly authorizes the Chief Justice to appoint a retired judge to serve as a special judge, *pro tempore*." *Regency Pheasant Run Ltd. v. Karem*, 860 S.W.2d 755, 757 (Ky. 1993). Where the Chief Justice appoints an active or retired justice or judge to serve under Section 110(5)(b), a party has no right to have a judge preside over his trial who was either elected under Section 117 or appointed by the Governor under Section 118. *Harris v. Commonwealth*, 338 S.W.3d 222, 224–26 (Ky. 2011).

4. Section 109 of the Kentucky Constitution vests the judicial power of the Commonwealth "in one Court of Justice which shall be divided into a Supreme Court, a Court of Appeals, *a trial court of general jurisdiction known as the Circuit Court* and a trial court of limited jurisdiction known as the District Court." (Emphasis added.) The Court of Justice is "a unified judicial system," *id.*, and Section 109 makes clear that there is "a"—singular—trial court of general jurisdiction in the Commonwealth. "Constitutionally speaking, Kentucky has but one circuit court and all circuit judges are members of that court and enjoy equal capacity to act throughout the state." *Baze v. Commonwealth*, 276 S.W.3d 761, 767 (Ky. 2008). Geography "do[es] not undermine the judge's basic authority to adjudicate matters that fall within the subject matter jurisdiction of the Circuit Court." *Winstead v. Commonwealth*, 327 S.W.3d 386, 410 (Ky. 2010).

O'Bryan v. Hedgespeth

Supreme Court of Kentucky (1995)
892 S.W.2d 571

OPINION OF THE COURT BY JUSTICE LEIBSON.

At issue is the constitutionality of KRS 411.188, a statute enacted in 1988 legislating the practice and procedure to apply to all civil actions wherein the plaintiff has received "collateral source payments" related to the same expenses for which he seeks damages in a civil action. Subsection (2) of the statute provides for notice to parties who "hold subrogation rights to any award received by the plaintiff as a result of the action," and an opportunity "to assert subrogation rights by intervention," and Subsection (3) of the statute specifies that "[c]ollateral source payments ... shall be an admissible fact in any civil trial."

The statute does not specify how the jury, as trier of fact, is to apply this evidence in deciding the damages to which the plaintiff is entitled in the pending case. In this case the evidence was the medical bills incurred by the appellant, Richard O'Bryan, totaled $48,068.04, his out-of-pocket expenses were $18,390.08, and he had received some $30,000 in collateral source payments. The jury awarded $18,400 for the medical expenses he had incurred. Without question, the jury simply awarded the plaintiff the amount submitted as evidence of his out-of-pocket expenses. Whether those entities who made collateral source payments had intervened to assert subrogation rights and were thus entitled to reimbursement from "any final award received by the plaintiff as a result of the action" as provided for in KRS 411.188, is not clear; nor was this explained to the jury, or covered by the judgment. To the extent that subrogation rights are protected, the statute contemplates the subrogees rather than O'Bryan would have first claim on the award for medical expenses regardless of the jury's intention.

The essential facts are as follows. The complaint alleges personal injuries suffered by Richard A. O'Bryan in two separate motor vehicle collisions, the first occurring June 4, 1989, wherein the appellee, Catherine M. Hedgespeth, is the defendant, and a second on July 14, 1989, involving Rebecca C. Murphy. The complaint included a claim on behalf of the appellant, Nancy O'Bryan, as Richard's wife, for loss of consortium. Claims against Ms. Murphy were settled before trial, and dismissed. Immediately before trial appellants made a motion in limine to exclude evidence of collateral source payments, specifying as grounds "the statute is unconstitutional and will be ... finally adjudicated so," and objecting "to any mention of collateral source during the course of this trial." The trial court responded, "your objection is on the record and I'll overrule it for the record. We'll go by the statute."

The judge having ruled that evidence of collateral source payments would be admitted, the plaintiff prepared and introduced a chart labeled "Medical Bills of Richard O'Bryan," specifying in columns: "Provider, Amount, Collateral Source, (and) Paid by O'Bryan." Plaintiff's Exhibit 6. As previously stated, the jury awarded damages for the plaintiff's out-of-pocket medical expenses rather than some lesser figure which might suggest some question as to whether all of these bills constituted reasonable and necessary expenses.

The jury verdict also awarded Mr. O'Bryan $3,200 for mental and physical pain and suffering, $3,500 for loss of wages and income, zero for permanent impairment of earning power, and zero for future medical expenses. The total award for damages was $25,100. Pursuant to other instructions covering liability and apportionment, the jury apportioned fault 100% to Hedgespeth and zero to O'Bryan in the case at issue, the accident involving Catherine Hedgespeth, but then attributed 50% of plaintiff's total damages to the accident involving Rebecca Murphy which had been settled before trial. The jury awarded zero to the appellant, Nancy O'Bryan, on her claim for loss of consortium. Pursuant to the jury award of $25,100 in total damages, 50% attributable to each accident, the trial court entered final judgment against the appellee, Catherine M. Hedgespeth, for $12,550. After the plaintiffs' motion for a new trial was overruled, the plaintiffs pursued an appeal to the Court of Appeals, which affirmed the judgment.

The issues presented and rejected in the Court of Appeals were: (1) whether the collateral source statute, KRS 411.188, is unconstitutional, and therefore the trial court erred in allowing the jury to hear evidence introduced pursuant to the statute of collateral source payments made to the plaintiff; (2) whether, if the statute is constitutional, nevertheless the trial court should have excluded evidence regarding the portion of collateral source payments which constituted payment of no-fault benefits; and (3) whether the award of zero dollars for permanent impairment of earning power was inadequate as a matter of law. The Court of Appeals overruled the challenge to the constitutionality of KRS 411.188, citing its previous decision in *Edwards v. Land*, Ky. App., 851 S.W.2d 484 (1992); agreed with the appellants that "no-fault benefits or PIP payments are not a collateral source within the purview of KRS 411.188(3)," citing our Court's decision in *Ohio Casualty Insurance Co. v. Ruschell*, Ky., 834 S.W.2d 166 (1992), but then held that "this issue is not preserved for our review"; and rejected the claim for a new trial because no award was made for permanent impairment of earning power, on grounds that under the evidence "the jury had every right to believe that O'Bryan was not permanently impaired by the accident with Catherine Hedgespeth."

We granted discretionary review to consider whether, as appellants claim, KRS 411.188 is unconstitutional, an issue of institutional importance because the statute impacts the trial of a great many civil actions. If this statute were constitutional, we would agree with the Court of Appeals that the appellants should not prevail on the remaining issues. The objection on constitutional grounds to all evidence of collateral source payments did not raise the separate question of whether no-fault benefits classify as collateral source payments. Further, we would not second-guess the Court of Appeals' decision affirming the jury award of zero dollars for permanent impairment of earning power. We reverse the award and order a new trial on damages only in the context that all evidence of collateral source payment was constitutionally impermissible, and prejudicial to the jury's consideration of damages.

On the other hand, we reject the appellee's claim the appellants' motion in limine, when denied, failed to preserve their objection to evidence of collateral source payments. The appellants elected to go forward with the evidence of collateral source payments in the presentation of their case once their motion in limine was overruled, rather than to leave it to the defendant to present this evidence. The judge had ruled admissible evidence that some $30,000 in medical expenses O'Bryan had incurred had already been reimbursed from other sources. The evidence as presented through the plaintiffs' case obviously prejudiced the jury's award. Left for the defendant to present after the plaintiffs had apparently concealed it, such evidence would have been even more devastating, adding insult to injury. The appellee argues that we should not assume that if the plaintiffs had not gone forward with this evidence the defendant would have done so. If such was not the defendant's intention, the time to say so was when the motion to exclude the evidence was made, thus mooting the issue. The likelihood the defendant would not present this evidence after prevailing against the motion in limine borders on absurdity.

Further, the record shows the exhibit the plaintiffs prepared, listing medical bills and collateral source payments, after the motion in limine was overruled incorporated defense counsel's "suggestion," confirming intent to present such evidence. Finally, we note that in the trial court's order overruling the plaintiffs' motion for a new trial the court specifically rejects lack of preservation, stating as follows:

> The Defendant argued that it was the Plaintiff who presented the collateral source payments and that is true. However, the Defendant argued against the Plaintiff's motion in limine to exclude any evidence of collateral source payments. The Court must assume that if the Plaintiff had not introduced such evidence, then the Defendant would have.

* * *

Thus we confront the central issue in this case: the constitutionality of KRS 411.188. The statute provides, in its entirety:

> (1) This section shall apply to all actions for damages, whether in contract or tort, commenced after July 15, 1988.
>
> (2) At the commencement of an action seeking to recover damages, it shall be the duty of the plaintiff or his attorney to notify, by certified mail, those parties believed by him to hold subrogation rights to any award received by the plaintiff as a result of the action. The notification shall state that a failure to assert subrogation rights by intervention, pursuant to Kentucky Civil Rule 24, will result in a loss of those rights with respect to any final award received by the plaintiff as a result of the action.
>
> (3) Collateral source payments, except life insurance, the value of any premiums paid by or on behalf of the plaintiff for same, and known subrogation rights shall be an admissible fact in any civil trial.
>
> (4) A certified list of the parties notified pursuant to subsection (2) of this section shall also be filed with the clerk of the court at the commencement of the action.

The statute was enacted in 1988 as part of an omnibus bill styled "An Act relating to civil actions," Ky. Acts 1988, Ch. 224, consisting of twenty-six sections addressing at least twelve different subjects: apportionment, punitive damages, collateral source payments, a two-year statute of limitations for injury to personal property, a five-year statute of repose for home builders, contents of articles of incorporation, limited liability for corporate directors, limited liability for directors of non-profit corporations, limited liability and periodic payments of damages in cases against municipal government, peer review confidentiality, articles of incorporation for professional service corporations, and limited liability for a municipal utility board or commission.

Section 4, now KRS 411.188, as quoted *supra*, covers both listing and notifying entities holding subrogation rights to any portion of the award the plaintiff seeks to receive as a result of the action, so such entity may "assert subrogation rights by intervention," and mandates that "collateral source payments ... shall be an admissible fact in any civil trial." Presumably, the term "Collateral source payments" would include, along with first-party medical and disability benefits, coverage for collision damage, fire loss, and personal property insurance of all kinds, now injected into the trial of a civil action against the wrongdoer.

The arguments against the constitutionality of this statute, in the main, track similar arguments made and rejected by the Court of Appeals in *Edwards v. Land, supra*, which was cited and followed by the Court of Appeals in deciding the appeal in this case. However, the issue is one of first impression in this Court. We denied discretionary review in *Edwards v. Land*. Denying discretionary review neither adopts the Court of Appeals' decision nor rejects it. Simply stated, it leaves the issue undecided at this level, albeit precedent for trial courts until such time as we should decide differently.

* * *

Next we consider the separation of powers doctrine, an argument based on the Kentucky Constitution, Sections 27 and 28, and Section 116. Sections 27 and 28 divide "the powers of the government ... into three distinct departments, each ... a separate body of magistracy," and further specify that no "persons, being of one of those departments, shall exercise any power properly belonging to either of the others." Kentucky Constitution Section 116 vests exclusive jurisdiction in the Supreme Court to prescribe "rules of practice and procedure for the Court of Justice."

Responsibility for deciding when evidence is relevant to an issue of fact which must be judicially determined, such as the medical expenses incurred for treatment of personal injuries, falls squarely within the parameters of "practice and procedure" assigned to the judicial branch by the separation of powers doctrine and Section 116. Before KRS 411.188 was enacted, evidence of payments to the plaintiff from medical or disability insurers was excluded as irrelevant, recognizing that such payments have no bearing on the issue to be judicially decided, the amount of damages the plaintiff has incurred and is entitled to recover from the wrongdoer in the civil action, nor does it matter that the source of the collateral source benefits may be entitled to reimbursement from the recovery because of contractual or statutory subrogation rights. *See, e.g., Davidson v. Vogler*, Ky., 507 S.W.2d 160, 164 (1974), and, more recently, *Burke Enterprises, Inc. v. Mitchell*, Ky., 700 S.W.2d 789, 796 (1985), stating that "to depart from the collateral source rule would provide the tortfeasor a 'windfall' to the substantial detriment of the injured party." There is no legal reason why the tortfeasor or his liability insurance company should receive a "windfall" for benefits to which the plaintiff may be entitled by reason of his own foresight in paying the premium or as part of what he has earned in his employment, and benefits received are usually subject to subrogation so there is no "double recovery" by any stretch of the imagination.

KRE 401 states:

> "Relevant evidence" means evidence having any tendency to make the existence of any fact that is of consequence to the determination of the action more probable or less probable than it would be without the evidence.

The only such facts of consequence here are those bearing on the expenses incurred. Collateral source benefits may relate to the plaintiff's *need* to recover damages from the wrongdoer, but they have no bearing on the plaintiff's *right* to recover such damages. This statute encourages the jury to disregard the plaintiff's evidence as to the medical bills incurred and to temper their verdict with an irrelevant consideration.

At oral argument before the Supreme Court, the appellee's counsel stated that at trial he made no attempt to explain or argue to the jury why or how the collateral source evidence should be used by the jury in deciding the amount of damages to which the plaintiff was otherwise entitled in this case. The reason is there is no way to explain it. So the jury was left to guess how to apply the evidence, and responded by deducting the collateral source payments from the medical bills incurred, awarding approximately $30,000 less than the amount to which plaintiff would have been otherwise entitled by the verdict.

Edwards v. Land concluded that KRS 411.188 should be embraced in lieu of the collateral source rule under "principles of comity," just as the Supreme Court had elected to embrace a statute prescribing practice and procedure at the sentencing phase of a criminal trial in *Commonwealth v. Reneer*, Ky., 734 S.W.2d 794 (1987). *Edwards v. Land*, 851 S.W.2d at 488. The Court of Appeals reasoned that to do so would not "interfere unreasonably with the functioning of the courts." *Id.* But it did so in this case.

"Comity," by definition, means judicial adoption of a rule unconstitutionally enacted by the legislature "not as a matter of obligation, but out of deference and respect." *Black's Law Dictionary*, "Judicial Comity," 5th Ed., p. 242 (1979). The decision whether to give life through comity to a statute otherwise unconstitutional because it violates separation of powers doctrine is one of institutional policy reserved for the Supreme Court level. SCR 1.010; 1.020(1)(a). The responsibility of lower courts, including the Court of Appeals, is to follow the law, which includes constitutional separation of powers doctrine, and to correct error accordingly, even if to do so means declaring a legislative enactment unconstitutional. Once having determined the collateral source payment statute violated the separation of powers doctrine, the Court of Appeals should have ruled the statute unconstitutional.

Nor is this a statute to which this Court could properly apply the principle of comity. In *Commonwealth v. Reneer, supra*, we concluded the practice and procedure legislatively prescribed would enhance rather than impair the judicial function in deciding an appropriate sentence. But the present statute does nothing to enhance the jury's fact-finding function. It provides no framework for the jury to relate the information the jury is to receive to the decision the jury must make regarding the amount of damages the plaintiff has incurred as a result of the injury, and we can conceive of none. It serves only to confuse the issue the jury must decide with considerations regarding the plaintiff's lack of need to be reimbursed for out-of-pocket expenses. The plaintiff will still need a judgment against the defendant covering such expenses if obligated to repay them because of contractual or statutory subrogation.

As yet, nobody has explained how this statute is supposed to work. When evidence of collateral source payments totaling $30,000 is admitted at trial, and the verdict reduced accordingly because the jury assumes the plaintiff will get the sum awarded, who gets the award? If the plaintiff gets it, the entities who paid collateral source benefits are cut off from their subrogation rights contrary to the statute. On the other hand, if the subrogees now get the $18,000 awarded, does the plaintiff who is out-of-pocket $18,000 then recover nothing? In this scenario, even if the plaintiff gets nothing and the entities paying collateral source benefits get the $18,000 to which they are subrogated, these entities are still out-of-pocket $12,000, the difference between $30,000 and $18,000.

In *Akers v. Baldwin*, Ky., 736 S.W.2d 294 (1987), this Court held separation of powers doctrine required we strike legislation creating a presumption in broad form deed cases "that the intention of the parties to the instrument was that the coal be extracted only by the method or methods of commercial coal extraction commonly known to be in use in Kentucky in the area affected at the time the instrument was executed." *Id.* at 308. We held that the statute in question transgressed the fact-finding function which falls within the exclusive province of the judiciary. How such deeds should be construed was modified in *Akers*, and subsequently overruled in *Ward v. Harding*, Ky., 860 S.W.2d 280 (1993). Further, the people enacted a constitutional amendment to replace the invalidated statute. Nevertheless, *Ward v. Harding* reiterates the separation of powers principle. It acknowledges the portion of *Akers v. Baldwin* recognizing the legislature must not intrude by statute into the judicial prerogative, reminding us that "[c]ourts are the proper forums to determine the issues presented in the interpretation of *past* transactions...." *Ward v. Harding*, 860 S.W.2d at 283 (emphasis original, citation omitted).

Thus, as a rule of practice and procedure, the present statute is constitutionally defective under the separation of powers doctrine. On the other hand, if we were to assume this statute intends a substantive rule limiting the damages recoverable in a civil action, the statute is constitutionally defective under Section 54 of the Constitution. Section 54 provides:

> The General Assembly shall have no power to limit the amount to be recovered for injuries resulting in death, or for injuries to person or property.

The plaintiff's right to recover against the wrongdoer in a personal injury claim for the expenses incurred, i.e., the special damages including medical expenses and wage loss, is one of long-standing, predating the Constitution and constitutionally protected by the "jural rights" doctrine as elaborated in cases from *Kentucky State Journal Co. v. Workmen's C. Board*, 161 Ky. 562, 170 S.W. 1166 (1914) and *Ludwig v. Johnson*, 243 Ky. 533, 49 S.W.2d 347 (1932) to *Perkins v. Northeastern Log Homes*, Ky., 808 S.W.2d 809 (1991). The right of every individual in society to access a system of justice to redress wrongs is basic and fundamental to our common law heritage, protected by Sections 14, 54 and 241 of our Kentucky Constitution. A substantive law change denying damages for medical expenses and wage loss in a civil action to those plaintiffs who have access to collateral source benefits would violate Section 54. Those plaintiffs receiving collateral source payments cannot have their tort remedy denied as punishment for their prudence in obtaining insurance coverage to assist them in the event of a catastrophe, and their misfortune compounded by making them appear to seek damages for which they have no need.

This statute was not so written as to express a substantive limitation on damages. If it were so, it would transgress Section 54, which probably explains why it was not so written. But by the same token as a change in the rules of practice and procedure it transgresses the judicial prerogative, and thus the Kentucky Constitution, Sections 27 and 28, and Section 116.

* * *

Thus we conclude KRS 411.188 is unconstitutional, and *Edwards v. Land*, *supra*, should be overruled. The statute is a violation of Kentucky constitutional sections mandating and elaborating on separation of powers doctrine. The statute intrudes on responsibility assigned exclusively to the judicial branch of government. Because, as demonstrated by this case, it functions to confuse the jury regarding the factual issue rather than to assist the jury in deciding the damages incurred, we reject any notion that it should be absorbed as judicial doctrine as a matter of comity.

The decision of the Court of Appeals is reversed. The judgment of the trial court is vacated, and the case is remanded for a new trial on damages in conformity with this decision.

All concur.

Notes and Questions

1. The subject of the "jural rights doctrine" will be discussed later. But considering the Court decided *O'Bryan* on separation of powers grounds, do you think the discussion of Section 54 and the jural rights doctrine at the end of the opinion is merely dicta?

2. Section 116 of the Kentucky Constitution explicitly confers on the Supreme Court the power to prescribe rules of practice and procedure for the Court of Justice. But even before the voters approved the Judicial Article in 1975, the old Court of Appeals had held that the power to prescribe such rules was inherent in the separation of powers: "[C]ourts (even without express authority given by the constitution, statute, or rule of a supreme court of a state) have inherent power to prescribe rules to regulate their proceedings and to facilitate the administration of justice.... When we say that an express constitutional grant of rule-making power is unnecessary we do not mean that the rule-making power does not flow from that instrument. The fountain source of that power is in the act of division of powers among the three branches of the government and the grant of judicial power to the courts by the constitution carries with it, as a necessary incident, the right to make that power effective in the

administration of justice." *Craft v. Commonwealth*, 343 S.W.2d 150, 151 (Ky. 1961). Thus, Section 116 made explicit what previously had been inferred from Sections 27 and 28.

3. Are the Rules of Evidence substantive or procedural in nature, or both? *See Commonwealth, Cabinet for Health & Family Servs. v. Chauvin*, 316 S.W.3d 279, 284–89 (Ky. 2010) (discussing difference between evidence rules that regulate practice and procedure and those that are substantive). Does the answer to this question determine whether the Court's holding in *O'Bryan* was correct?

4. In *O'Bryan*, the plaintiff's medical expenses were approximately $48,000, of which the plaintiff paid $18,000. The plaintiff's insurer paid the remaining $30,000, and thus was subrogated to that amount. But all the plaintiff's medical expenses were actually paid to his healthcare providers *by someone*. In *Baptist Healthcare Systems, Inc. v. Miller*, 177 S.W.3d 676, 682–84 (Ky. 2005), the jury awarded the plaintiff $34,000 in medical expenses, which was reduced to $22,100 by a 35% apportionment of liability. The doctor billed the plaintiff $31,840, but he received only $3,356.38 from Medicare. The remaining amount billed by the doctor was classified as a Medicare adjustment or a Medicare write-off, and nobody was responsible for paying it. The Court, following *O'Bryan*, held the plaintiff could recover the entire $22,100 net jury award, not only the much lesser amount actually paid by Medicare. To the extent the plaintiff received a windfall, it was because she "paid her premiums and deserves all appropriate benefits"; the Court found it "absurd to suggest that the tortfeasor should receive a benefit from a contractual arrangement between Medicare and the health care provider." *Id.* at 683. Thus, the plaintiff was even allowed to recover "phantom damages" that were "charged" by the doctor but never paid by anybody—because the doctor's charges (even if not actually paid) were presumed to be the "reasonable" cost of the medical services provided. Though perhaps dated considering the federal mandate generally requiring all Americans to purchase health insurance providing "minimum essential coverage," *see* 26 U.S.C. §5000A(a)—ostensibly eliminating the need for any American ever to be responsible for the "full amount" charged by a doctor—the collateral source rule is still viable in Kentucky.

Abernathy v. Nicholson

Supreme Court of Kentucky (1995)

899 S.W.2d 85

Opinion of the Court by Justice Lambert.

Petitioner brought this claim for relief as an original action in the Supreme Court of Kentucky. The claim asserted seeks a declaration that an administrative order promulgated by or entered at the behest of respondent, a Judge of the Jefferson District Court, is invalid as being in violation of Section 14 of the Constitution of Kentucky and various rules of this Court. Petitioner seeks to invoke our jurisdiction pursuant to Section 110(2)(a) of the Constitution.

On September 17, 1993, respondent, sitting in Traffic Division 101 of the Jefferson District Court, entered an administrative order which prohibited persons with an outstanding arrest warrant or bench warrant from appearing before him until all previously ordered contempt fines had been paid, or if there were none, until an appearance bond in the sum of fifty dollars had been posted for each case, or until a judge ordered the case redocketed. The order was as follows:

> The Jefferson District Court Clerk's Office is hereby Ordered not to redocket any cases in TRAFFIC DIVISION 101 wherein the Defendant has an outstanding Arrest Warrant or Bench Warrant, unless, at the time the request for redocketing is made:
>
> 1. The Defendant shall pay in full all Contempt fines previously ordered; or,
> 2. If no Contempt Order was previously entered, the Defendant shall personally post an Appearance Bond in the sum of $50.00 for each case the Defendant seeks to redocket; or,
> 3. If a Judge of the Jefferson District Court orders, in writing, the redocketing of the case.
>
> The Clerk should instruct the Defendant, or counsel, that payment of Contempt fines, posting of an Appearance Bond or judicial redocketing does not recall or set aside any prior Orders. The redocketing of a case only allows the Defendant to have his/her case placed on the docket for further motions.
>
> The Order shall apply to Defendants and Attorneys seeking to redocket any case.
>
> This Order shall be effective immediately.

Despite the existence of twenty-two other district court divisions and two other traffic divisions in the Jefferson District Court system, the foregoing order applied only in Traffic Division 101.

On March 31, 1994, respondent sentenced petitioner to ninety days incarceration plus fines totaling $600 for operating a motor vehicle on a suspended license. Because petitioner was unable to pay the fines, a show cause date for payment of fines and costs was set. On May 12, 1994, home incarceration with work release was granted and the show cause hearing was continued until July 11, 1994, at 1:00 p.m. On the day petitioner was to appear in court, he was arrested on an unrelated charge and was not released until two days later. While petitioner was incarcerated, respondent proceeded in his absence with the show cause hearing, issued an arrest warrant for failure to appear, and converted the unpaid fines to thirty days in jail. A contempt penalty of fifty dollars per case was also imposed.

On July 16, 1994, petitioner's public defender attorney went to the office of the district court clerk and sought to redocket the cases and file motions to withdraw the arrest warrants and vacate the orders which had been entered on July 11, 1994. In obedience to the order at issue here, the deputy clerk refused to accept the motion to redocket without payment of a fifty dollar appearance bond for each case. Subsequently all fines and penalties imposed by respondent upon petitioner were converted to "time served" by the judge who succeeded respondent in Traffic Division 101. As such, the charges from which this action arose have come to an end and there is no longer any controversy between these parties.

Petitioner contends that the order in question amounts to a standing administrative order "that effectively require[s] litigants to buy their way into court" in violation of Section 14 of the Constitution of Kentucky, the open courts provision. Petitioner contends that inasmuch as this Court has the exclusive right to promulgate rules of practice and procedure for the Court of Justice under Section 116, a right of prior approval over local rules pursuant to SCR 1.040(3)(a), and the right to exercise control of the Court of Justice pursuant to Section 110(2)(a) of the Constitution, his remedy is by means of an original action here.

It is respondent's position that petitioner has improperly invoked the original jurisdiction of this Court. He asserts that petitioner's remedy would be by appeal or by application for extraordinary writ in the circuit court. Respondent challenges petitioner's interpretation of the order as amounting to an admission fee for access to the Court of Justice and asserts that the claim is moot. In any event, however, respondent maintains that the order is not unconstitutional and is within his "inherent power" to make rules and regulate the proceedings in the court over which he presides.

Prior to reaching the issue we believe to be decisive, it is appropriate to comment upon the administrative order here under review. Whatever its appellation, the "order" is a rule. It is not limited to a particular case, but applies to all cases which fall within its confines. It directs the district court clerk to refrain from redocketing cases in certain circumstances until the defendant has satisfied its terms. Finally, the order appears to have been of an indefinite duration and subject to modification only by the Jefferson District Court Judge sitting in Traffic Division 101. Inasmuch as the order has the characteristics of a rule, whether it be regarded as a rule of court or as a local rule, its promulgation appears to be contrary to the Constitution of Kentucky or the rules of this Court. If the order is treated as a rule of court, it would likely fail as amounting to a violation of Section 116 of the Constitution, and if it is regarded as a local rule, it would appear to be invalid for failure of this Court to have given approval as required by SCR 1.040(3)(a).

Under Section 116 of the Constitution, the power to prescribe rules of practice and procedure for the Court of Justice is vested exclusively in the Supreme Court and should not be undertaken by other courts. The authorization to enact local rules pursuant to SCR 1.040(3)(a) is subject to two conditions: first, that no local rule shall contradict any substantive rule of law or any rule of practice and procedure promulgated by this Court, and second, that it shall be effective only upon Supreme Court approval.

For generations it has been widely believed that local rules were a trap for the unwary and disadvantageous for practitioners unfamiliar with a particular venue. It is this Court's intention to standardize practice and procedure in the Court of Justice to the greatest extent possible and permit local rules only to the extent necessary to satisfy a peculiar circumstance of the locality. In general, the rules of court adopted pursuant to Section 116 of the Constitution are sufficient and need no adornment in the form of local rules. Kentucky attorneys are licensed to practice law in all courts of this Commonwealth and should be able to practice wherever they choose, east and west, rural and urban, without the burden of superfluous local rules, whatever the form in which they may appear.

Despite the foregoing, the issue we believe to be controlling is whether this Court should entertain this case as an original action, or whether petitioner should have proceeded in circuit court by means of a petition for an extraordinary writ or in a declaratory judgment action pursuant to KRS 418.040, *et seq.* Initially it should be conceded that this Court possesses the raw power to entertain any case which fits generally within the rubric of its constitutional grant of authority. As Section 110(2)(a) of the Constitution contains a provision which grants the Supreme Court supervisory control of the Court of Justice, virtually any matter within that context would be subject to its jurisdiction.

Whether the Supreme Court should exercise its jurisdiction is another matter. The constitutional language here under review grants this Court jurisdiction "as may be required to exercise control of the Court of Justice." Such language is of a decidedly discretionary tone. The Court is not thereby required to do anything under this provision, but may exercise control if its discretion so indicates. In view of the essential nature of appellate courts, only in well defined or compelling circumstances should an original action be entertained therein.

In *Ex Parte Farley*, Ky., 570 S.W.2d 617, 622 (1978), this Court held that it alone, save the limited right of review of the Supreme Court of the United States, had jurisdiction to hear and determine a cause which had as its ultimate objective a judgment declaring what this Court must or must not do. As authority for this, we quoted that portion of Section 110(2)(a) of the Constitution which provides that it shall have such jurisdiction as may be required to exercise control of the Court of Justice. *Id.* at 621. In *Francis v. Taylor*, Ky., 593 S.W.2d 514 (1980), the Court recognized that in addition to appellate jurisdiction and the power to issue all writs necessary in aid of its appellate jurisdiction, the Supreme Court possessed an independent jurisdiction to exercise control of the Court of Justice. *Id.* at 515. The Court held nevertheless that the Court of Appeals had jurisdiction to issue a writ of mandamus against a circuit judge and that such did not constitute an act of control of the Court of Justice. *Id.* at 516. In *Ex parte Auditor of Public Accounts*, Ky., 609 S.W.2d 682 (1980), the question was whether the auditor was entitled to audit the books and accounts of the Kentucky Bar Association. Relying on *Ex parte Farley*, we held that "because the Association is an arm of the court itself, and therefore cannot properly be sued in any of the other courts of the state, this court is [the] only forum in which the controversy can be heard and officially resolved." 609 S.W.2d at 683. From these authorities, the following principles emerge: First, the Supreme Court has a basis of original jurisdiction by virtue of that portion of Section 110(2)(a) here under review. Second, such original jurisdiction should be sparingly exercised and generally only in cases where no other court has power to proceed.

In the instant case, petitioner appears to have been denied access to the Court of Justice by means of an order which had the effect of a local rule which imposed an unauthorized fee. In such a circumstance, an action for a writ of prohibition would appear to have been appropriate. *See* SCR 1.040(6) and *Salyers v. Cornett*, Ky., 566 S.W.2d 418 (1978). Petitioner might have contended that the district court lacked jurisdiction to enact such a rule, relying on SCR 1.040(3)(a) which provides that no local rule shall be effective until it is approved by the Supreme Court, and that he had no adequate remedy by appeal. Petitioner might have contended also that even if the district court was within its jurisdiction, but about to act incorrectly, he had no adequate remedy by appeal and in the absence of extraordinary relief, would suffer great injustice and irreparable injury. *Shumaker v. Paxton*, Ky., 613 S.W.2d 130 (1981). Whether petitioner had made either or both of the foregoing claims, or undertaken a declaratory judgment action, the forum would have been the circuit court and the resulting judgment would have been subject to appeal just as are other final judgments of circuit courts. In view of the availability of the foregoing remedies, it would be unwise and inappropriate for this Court to reach the merits of this original action. As such, petitioner's claim will be dismissed on grounds that he should have sought relief in the trial court of general jurisdiction. *See* Ky. Const. §112(5).

In view of our disposition, we need not address respondent's contention that the claim asserted here is barred by the mootness doctrine. It may well be that in view of petitioner's having satisfied the Commonwealth's claims against him, and respondent's rotation from Traffic Division 101, and the subsequent vacation of the order by respondent's successor, that the claims asserted here are indeed moot. To so hold, however, would also require an analysis of whether promulgation of such an order was "capable of repetition yet evading review" which might constitute an exception to the mootness doctrine. *See Philpot v. Patton*, Ky., 837 S.W.2d 491 (1992). Prior to reaching any question as to mootness, we have determined that the action was brought in the wrong forum and we need not go beyond that point.

Accordingly, this action will be dismissed.

Lambert, Leibson, Reynolds, Spain and Wintersheimer, JJ., concur.

Stephens, C.J., dissents by separate opinion in which Stumbo, J., joins.

Chief Justice Stephens, dissenting.

Respectfully, I must dissent. The majority's interpretation of *Ex Parte Auditor of Public Accounts*, Ky., 609 S.W.2d 682 (1980), and *Ex Parte Farley*, Ky., 570 S.W.2d 617 (1978) is much too narrow. It limits the original jurisdiction of this Court to only those circumstances "where no other court has power to proceed." The majority takes this approach by suggesting this Court's exercise of jurisdiction in *Ex Parte Auditor of Public Accounts* was based solely upon the fact that "this court is [the] only forum in which the controversy [could] be heard and officially resolved." 609 S.W.2d at 683. The majority concluded this by stating that the decision in *Ex Parte Auditor of Public Accounts* relied upon *Ex Parte Farley*. Thus, when these two decisions are read together, a principle arises that the original jurisdiction of this Court can *only* be exercised where no other Court has power to proceed.

While both of these cases address the question of original jurisdiction, I find nothing in *Ex Parte Auditor of Public Accounts* that suggests its holding limits the exercise of original jurisdiction by this Court to only fact situations similar to those in that case *in which this Court can provide the only forum for relief.* The principles that arise in these cases are separate and distinct. "First, the Supreme Court has a basis of original jurisdiction by virtue of … Section 110(2)(a)." With this statement by the majority, I do agree. However, the second principle is that original jurisdiction *may* be exercised in cases where no other court has power to proceed.

This Court should not neglect to recognize other situations where original jurisdiction may be invoked by this Court, namely where it is necessary "to assure to the best of its ability the orderly and effective administration of justice in this jurisdiction." *Ex Parte Farley*, 570 S.W.2d 617, 621 (1978) (citing *In Re Appointment of Clerk of Court of Appeals*, Ky., 297 S.W.2d 764, 765 (1957)). This case involves an administrative action taken by a lower Court's judge. Because this is an administrative issue, this Court inherently has the authority to exercise jurisdiction to ensure the proper actions are being taken.

Stumbo, J., joins in this dissenting opinion.

Notes and Questions

1. Chief Justice Stephens chided the majority for the second part of its holding: "[The Supreme Court's] original jurisdiction should be *sparingly exercised* and *generally only* in cases where no other court has power to proceed." (Emphasis added.) The Chief Justice summarized the majority's opinion as holding that the Supreme Court should only exercise its original jurisdiction under Section 110(2)(a) "where no other court has power to proceed." Was this a fair criticism of the majority's holding?

2. It is rare for the Supreme Court to use its power under Section 110(2)(a) and *Abernathy* to issue a "supervisory writ" to "exercise control of the Court of Justice." This may be because such writs circumvent the ordinary rules of appellate practice. However, such supervisory writs, though rare, do exist. *See Commonwealth v. Carman*, 455 S.W.3d 916 (Ky. 2015) (granting supervisory writ "directing all judges of the Court of Justice to cease any ex parte communications regarding a criminal defendant's conditions of release after the initial fixing of bail"). The Supreme Court issued a supervisory writ in *Beshear v. Acree* that precluded the circuit courts in Boone and Scott counties from issuing any injunctions restraining the Governor's exercise of emergency powers during the COVID-19 pandemic, pending the Supreme Court's

ruling on the merits of any appeals in those cases. *See Acree*, 615 S.W.3d 780, 786 (Ky. 2020) ("In response to [the Boone Circuit Court entering a restraining order] with its imminent injunction hearing and at least one similar case [in the Scott Circuit Court], this Court entered an order on July 17, 2020, staying all injunctive orders directed at the Governor's COVID-19 response until those orders were properly before this Court, with full record, pursuant to the direction of the Court."); *see also Cameron v. Beshear*, 628 S.W.3d 61, 79 (Ky. 2021) (Hughes, J., concurring) ("Last summer prior to *Beshear v. Acree*, 615 S.W.3d 780 (Ky. 2020), we invoked Kentucky Constitution Section 110 and took unprecedented action to combine and expedite cases so we could address the multiple challenges to the Governor's COVID-19 response."). But the Court is not likely to issue such a writ to a party who has another avenue of seeking redress. *See Seadler v. Int'l Bhd. of Elec. Workers, Local 369*, 642 S.W.3d 712 (Ky. 2022) (denying supervisory writ under Section 110 of the Constitution because petitioner had an alternative remedy under the Supreme Court's rules to seek an ethics opinion from the Kentucky Bar Association's Ethics Committee and petition the Supreme Court for review of the ethics opinion).

3. How else might the Supreme Court exercise its power to "exercise control of the Court of Justice"?

Commonwealth, Cabinet for Health and Family Services, Department for Medicaid Services v. Sexton ex rel. Appalachian Regional Healthcare, Inc.

Supreme Court of Kentucky (2018)
566 S.W.3d 185

Opinion of the Court by Chief Justice Minton.

This case requires us to consider whether the courts of Kentucky can undertake a statutorily created judicial review of an administrative agency's final order when the person appealing that final order does not have a concrete injury. Our resolution requires us to apply the doctrine of constitutional standing, and, in doing so, we hold as a matter of first impression that the existence of a plaintiff's standing is a constitutional requirement to prosecute any action in the courts of this Commonwealth, adopting the United States Supreme Court's test for standing as espoused in *Lujan v. Defenders of Wildlife*.[1] Because this case reaches us via an interlocutory appeal from the circuit court's review of an agency ruling, we further hold that all of Kentucky's courts have the responsibility to ascertain, upon the court's own motion if the issue is not raised by a

---

1. 504 U.S. 555, 560–561, 112 S.Ct. 2130, 119 L.Ed.2d 351 (1992).

party opponent, whether a plaintiff has constitutional standing, an issue not waivable, to pursue the case in court. Under that test, we conclude that Medicaid beneficiary Lettie Sexton, the putative petitioner in the present case, does not have the requisite constitutional standing to pursue her case in the courts of the Commonwealth. So, we reverse the decision of the Court of Appeals, vacate the ruling of the circuit court, and remand this case to the circuit court with instructions to dismiss the case.

I. Background.

Lettie Sexton, a Medicaid beneficiary, was admitted to Appalachian Regional Healthcare ("ARH"), complaining of chest pain. ARH sent a request for preauthorization of medical services to Coventry Health and Life Insurance, d/b/a Coventry Cares, Inc. ("Coventry"), a managed-care organization that had contracted with the Kentucky Cabinet for Health and Human Services ("Cabinet") to provide reimbursement to hospitals for certain services provided to Medicaid beneficiaries. Coventry approved a 23-hour observation stay at ARH. Sexton, through ARH, her designated representative for any disputed claims, requested that the observation stay at ARH be extended 15 more hours for a cardiology consultation. Coventry denied reimbursement for this request. Sexton was eventually hospitalized at ARH for approximately 38 hours. ARH then requested an internal review by Coventry of its denial of reimbursement for the 15 hours of additional hospitalization. After review, Coventry upheld its denial. ARH, ostensibly acting for Sexton, then requested a Medicaid Fair Hearing to challenge Coventry's denial. A hearing officer for the administrative-services branch of the Cabinet conducted that hearing and ruled that Sexton lacked standing to pursue an appeal of Coventry's denial of reimbursement to ARH because Sexton herself had no stake in the outcome of the dispute between ARH and Coventry. The hearing officer's ruling was based upon the fact that because Medicaid had paid ARH for the services rendered to Sexton, she would owe nothing at all to ARH for the extended hospital stay.[2] In due course, the Cabinet Secretary adopted the hearing officer's recommendation as the Cabinet's final order. ARH, acting as Sexton's representative, then sought judicial review under Kentucky Revised Statute (KRS) 13B.140 of the Cabinet's final order by timely filing a petition for review in the Harlan Circuit Court. The Cabinet filed a motion to dismiss the petition, alleging that: (1) Sexton lacked standing; (2) ARH was not Sexton's authorized representative; (3) venue did not lie in Harlan County; and (4) that the petition was barred by the doctrine of sovereign immunity because it did not strictly comply with the requirements of KRS 13B.140. Coventry joined in the Cabinet's motion on the same grounds.

Following a hearing, the circuit court denied the motion to dismiss. On the issue of standing, the circuit court found that the individual ARH employees who had been authorized by Sexton to represent her interests were sufficiently identified in the exhibits to the petition to provide standing and to comply substantially with the requirements of KRS 13B.140. As for venue and subject-matter jurisdiction, the circuit court ruled

2. This argument is a reoccurring one used by several managed-care organizations that has resulted in numerous pending cases in the Court of Appeals.

that the addresses for Sexton's designated representatives were the address of the ARH hospital employees located in Harlan County, thus fixing venue there in accordance with KRS 13B.140. On the issue of sovereign immunity, the circuit court determined that this argument was based upon the proposition that a failure strictly to comply with KRS 13B.140 eliminated waiver of sovereign immunity. But since the circuit court found the petition to be otherwise sufficient, the limited waiver of immunity was not eliminated. So, the circuit court denied Coventry's and the Cabinet's motions to dismiss the petition.

Because the circuit court denied the Cabinet and Coventry's sovereign-immunity argument, they each filed an interlocutory appeal in the Court of Appeals. ARH initially sought a dismissal of the appeal, claiming that the circuit court's order was not final and appealable.

On ARH's motion to dismiss the appeal, the Court of Appeals found that the circuit court's rulings on sovereign immunity were immediately appealable, and therefore denied ARH's motion to dismiss the appeal. The Court of Appeals also found that there was no requirement that KRS 13B.140 be strictly followed for the waiver of sovereign immunity to apply. But the Court of Appeals also found that in Medicaid reimbursement cases like this one, sovereign immunity has been waived by the overwhelming implication of statutory language, including KRS 45A.235.[3] Additionally, the Court of Appeals found that the statutes governing the state Medicaid program, KRS 205.510–645, indicate that sovereign immunity had been waived.

Finally, the Court of Appeals found that venue, as provided in the Kentucky Model Procurement Code, specifically KRS 45A.245, mandated that an aggrieved person, firm, or corporation who has a valid written contract must bring an enforcement action in Franklin Circuit Court. Because the petition was filed in Harlan Circuit Court, the Court of Appeals held that the circuit court's ruling denying the motion to dismiss based on improper venue should be vacated and directed that the parties may make a motion to transfer the case to Franklin Circuit Court or file a new petition for review in Franklin Circuit Court.

Both parties then filed discretionary-review petitions, which we granted.

II. Analysis.

* * *

B. The principle of constitutional standing in Kentucky.

An elementary principle of the federal and state governmental structure is the division of power among three branches of government: the legislature, the executive, and the judiciary.[4] The United States Supreme Court has interpreted the United States Con-

3. All parties now agree that the Court of Appeals erred by applying KRS 45A.235 to this case.

4. *See* Ky. Const. §27 ("The powers of the government of the Commonwealth of Kentucky shall be divided into three distinct departments, and each of them be confined to a separate body of magistracy, to wit: Those which are legislative, to one; those which are executive, to another; and those which judicial, to another."); Ky. Const. §28 ("No person or collection of persons, being of one of

stitution as providing a "series of limits on the federal judicial power."[5] Identified as the "justiciability doctrines," these limits on the federal judicial power derive from Article III, Section 2, Clause 1 of the U.S. Constitution, which states, "The judicial Power shall extend to all *Cases* ... [and] *Controversies*. ..."[6] A federal court cannot adjudicate a case that does not meet the requirements of the justiciability doctrines.

The U.S. Supreme Court has identified five major justiciability doctrines: (1) the prohibition against advisory opinions, (2) standing, (3) ripeness, (4) mootness, and (5) the political-question doctrine.[7] The Court has also distinguished between justiciability requirements that are "constitutional," meaning that Congress by statute cannot override them, and "prudential," meaning that they are based on prudent judicial administration and can be overridden by Congress since they are not constitutional requirements.[8] Of most concern in this case is the standing requirement and the constitutional limitations, if any, the standing requirement imposes.

"In essence the question of standing is whether the litigant is entitled to have the court decide the merits of the dispute or of particular issues."[9] Federal constitutional standing has three requirements: the plaintiff must allege that 1) he or she has suffered or imminently will suffer an injury; 2) the injury is fairly traceable to the defendant's conduct; and 3) a favorable federal court decision is likely to redress the injury.[10] In addition to these federal constitutional requirements, two major federal prudential standing principles exist: (1) a party generally may assert only his or her own rights and cannot raise the claims of third parties not before the court, i.e. the prohibition against "third-party standing"; and (2) a plaintiff may not sue as a taxpayer who shares a grievance in common with all other taxpayers, i.e. the prohibition against "generalized grievances."[11]

To be clear, these standing requirements as outlined above are discussed in the context of application to the limit on *federal* judicial power, not *state* judicial power. Under principles of federalism, "[l]ong-established precedent holds that Article III standing requirements do not apply in state courts and courts of the territories."[12] So we now examine Kentucky's current standing doctrine.

---

those departments, shall exercise any power properly belonging to either of the others, except in the instances hereinafter expressly directed or permitted.").

5. Erwin Chemerinsky, *Constitutional Law*, 40 (Vicki Been et al. eds., 5th ed. 2013).
6. (emphasis added).
7. Chemerinsky, at 40.
8. *Id.*
9. *Warth v. Seldin*, 422 U.S. 490, 498, 95 S.Ct. 2197, 45 L.Ed.2d 343 (1975).
10. Chemerinsky, at 45.
11. *Id.*
12. John W. Curran, *Who's Standing in the District After Grayson v. AT&T Corp.? The Applicability of the Case-or-Controversy Requirement in D.C. Courts*, 62 Am. U. L. Rev. 739, 740 (2012) (citing *N.Y. State Club Ass'n v. City of New York*, 487 U.S. 1, 8 n.2, 108 S.Ct. 2225, 101 L.Ed.2d 1 (1988) ("[T]he special limitations that Article III of the Constitution imposes on the jurisdiction of the federal courts are not binding on the state courts.")).

A recently published law journal article[13] aptly summarizes Kentucky's standing doctrine:

> In Kentucky, standing is not a constitutional doctrine, but appears to be a self-imposed restraint based on a prohibition against generalized grievances as a "fundamental" principle of adjudication. Kentucky courts have offered limited explanation of their standing doctrine. The source of the doctrine appears to be a 1957 case challenging an alcohol board's decision to increase the number of licenses available.[14] There, [Kentucky's highest Court] held that "[i]t is fundamental that a person may attack a proceeding of this nature by independent suit only if he can show that his legal rights have been violated."[15] This was based on the principle that "[a] public wrong or neglect or breach of a public duty cannot be redressed in a suit in the name of an individual whose interest in the right asserted does not differ from that of the public generally, or who suffers injury only in common with the general public."[16]
>
> Under the modern Kentucky test, "[t]o have standing to sue, one must have a judicially cognizable interest in the subject matter of the suit" that is not "remote and speculative," but "a present and substantial interest in the subject matter."[17] Kentucky courts have not adopted the *Lujan* test, but have adopted elements of federal decisions on associational standing, which have seen substantially more elaboration than general standing doctrine in the Kentucky courts.[18]

Kentucky courts have seemingly created a judicially—as opposed to constitutionally—imposed standing requirement. At the federal level, where standing is partly grounded in Article III, Section 2, Clause 1 of the U.S. Constitution, while "[the legislature] may enact statutes creating legal rights, the invasion of which creates standing, even though no injury would exist without the statute,"[19] "[i]t is, of course, true that '[the legislature] may not confer jurisdiction on ... courts to render advisory opinions[.]'"[20] Federal law's constitutional standing requirement is a safeguard against the overreach

13. Wyatt Sassman, *A Survey of Constitutional Standing in State Courts*, 8 Ky. J. Equine, Agric. & Nat. Resources L. 349, 369–70 (2016).

14. *Lexington Retail Beverage Dealers Ass'n v. Dep't of Alcoholic Beverage Control Bd.*, 303 S.W.2d 268, 269–70 (Ky. 1957).

15. *Id.*

16. *Id.* (citing *Wegener v. Wehrman*, 312 Ky. 445, 227 S.W.2d 997, 998 (Ky. 1950)).

17. *Bailey v. Pres. Rural Roads of Madison Cnty., Inc.*, 394 S.W.3d 350, 355 (Ky. 2011).

18. *See Bailey*, 394 S.W.3d at 356; *see also Interactive Gaming*, 425 S.W.3d at 112–15. Kentucky does recognize taxpayer standing in specific circumstances. *See Price v. Commonwealth, Transp. Cabinet*, 945 S.W.2d 429, 432–33 (Ky. App. 1996) (citing *Rosenbalm v. Commercial Bank*, 838 S.W.2d 423 (Ky. App. 1992) (collecting cases where "Kentucky has consistently recognized taxpayer standing")).

19. *Linda R.S. v. Richard D.*, 410 U.S. 614, 617 n.3, 93 S.Ct. 1146, 35 L.Ed.2d 536 (1973) (citing *Trafficante v. Metropolitan Life Ins. Co.*, 409 U.S. 205, 212, 93 S.Ct. 364, 34 L.Ed.2d 415 (1972) (White, J., concurring); *Hardin v. Kentucky Utilities Co.*, 390 U.S. 1, 6, 88 S.Ct. 651, 19 L.Ed.2d 787 (1968)).

20. *Linda R.S.*, 410 U.S. at 617 n.3, 93 S.Ct. 1146 (quoting *Sierra Club v. Morton*, 405 U.S. 727, 732 n.3, 92 S.Ct. 1361, 31 L.Ed.2d 636 (1972)).

of judicial, legislative, and executive power. To ascertain what, if any, constitutional standing requirements exist in Kentucky, we turn to the Kentucky Constitution first and foremost.

Section 109 of the Kentucky Constitution states, "The judicial power of the Commonwealth shall be vested exclusively in one Court of Justice which shall be divided into a Supreme Court, a Court of Appeals, a trial court of general jurisdiction known as the Circuit Court and a trial court of limited jurisdiction known as the District Court." The Kentucky Constitution then goes on to outline the various levels of courts in Kentucky and their respective powers.

Most importantly, "The *Circuit Court* shall have *original jurisdiction* of all *justiciable causes* not vested in some other court. It shall have such appellate jurisdiction as may be provided by law."[21] "The *Court of Appeals* shall have *appellate jurisdiction only* ..." except in certain situations not relevant in this case.[22] "The *Supreme Court* shall have *appellate jurisdiction only* ..." except in certain situations not relevant to this case.[23] "The *district court* shall be a court of *limited jurisdiction* and shall exercise original jurisdiction as may be provided by the General Assembly."[24]

Notably, §109 of the Kentucky Constitution, describing the judicial power in Kentucky, does not contain the same *case or controversy* language contained in Article III, Section 2, Clause 1 of the U.S. Constitution, nor does any other provision of the Kentucky Constitution discussing judicial power in the various levels of courts. This case or controversy language in the U.S. Constitution is the lynchpin for all justiciability doctrines, including standing. Most notably, however, §112(5) of the Kentucky Constitution grants circuit courts original jurisdiction over all *justiciable causes* not vested in some other court.

The standing doctrine is said to have its origins in the U.S. Supreme Court case of *Fairchild v. Hughes*, a decision written by Justice Brandeis and rendered in 1922.[25] The U.S. Supreme Court later expounded on the doctrine: If a party does not have the requisite standing to bring suit, the case is said to be *nonjusticiable*; if a party does have the requisite standing to bring suit, the case is said to be *justiciable*.[26] The first appearance of the *justiciable causes* phrase in §112(5) appears in the 1974 Amendments to the Kentucky Constitution. By limiting the circuit court's jurisdiction to adjudicating

21. Ky. Const. §112(5) (emphasis added).

22. Ky. Const. §111(2) (emphasis added).

23. Ky. Const. §110(2)(a) (emphasis added).

24. Ky. Const. §113(6) (emphasis added).

25. 258 U.S. 126, 42 S.Ct. 274, 66 L.Ed. 499 (1922).

26. *See Flast v. Cohen*, 392 U.S. 83, 95, 88 S.Ct. 1942, 20 L.Ed.2d 947 (1968) ("[N]o *justiciable* controversy is presented when ... there is no standing to maintain the action.") (emphasis added) (citing *Tileston v. Ullman*, 318 U.S. 44, 63 S.Ct. 493, 87 L.Ed. 603 (1943); *Frothingham v. Mellon*, 262 U.S. 447, 43 S.Ct. 597, 67 L.Ed. 1078 (1923)); *Steel Co. v. Citizens for a Better Envt.*, 523 U.S. 83, 102, 118 S.Ct. 1003, 140 L.Ed.2d 210 (1998) ("Standing to sue is part of the common understanding of what it takes to make a *justiciable* case.") (emphasis added).

justiciable causes only, §112(5) appears to have adopted some notion of the *justiciability doctrines* articulated by the U.S. Supreme Court.

We have recognized the *justiciable causes* phrase as a constitutional limitation on Kentucky courts' judicial power before; "'Standing,' of course, in its most basic sense, refers to an integral component of the 'justiciable cause' requirement [in Ky. Const. §112(5)] underlying the trial court's jurisdiction."[27] *Lawson* also provided a potential constitutional test for Kentucky courts to examine standing: "To invoke the court's jurisdiction, the plaintiff must allege [1] an *injury* [2] *caused* by the defendant [3] of a sort the court is able to *redress*."[28] The emphasized words in the sentence quoted from *Lawson*—injury, causation, and redressability—are the three constitutional standing requirements as outlined by the U.S. Supreme Court in *Lujan*.[29] To provide clarity to Kentucky's standing doctrine, we formally adopt the *Lujan* test as the constitutional standing doctrine in Kentucky as a predicate for bringing suit in Kentucky's courts.

So, at bottom, for a party to sue in Kentucky, the initiating party must have the requisite constitutional standing to do so, defined by three requirements: (1) injury, (2) causation, and (3) redressability. In other words, "A plaintiff must allege personal injury fairly traceable to the defendant's allegedly unlawful conduct and likely to be redressed by the requested relief."[30] "[A] litigant must demonstrate that it has suffered a concrete and particularized injury that is either actual or imminent...."[31] "The injury must be... 'distinct and palpable,' and not 'abstract' or 'conjectural' or 'hypothetical.'"[32] "The injury must be 'fairly' traceable to the challenged action, and relief from the injury must be 'likely' to follow from a favorable decision."[33]

While the *justiciable causes* language only appears in §112(5), which specifically and only enumerates Kentucky circuit-court jurisdiction, the standing doctrine applies to cases brought before all Kentucky courts. Section 112(5) places *original jurisdiction* over a case in the circuit court; this means that all cases, not expressly designated by a rule of law to be heard by another court, must appear before the circuit court, the trial court of general jurisdiction. And recall that the circuit court "shall have original jurisdiction of all *justiciable causes*." If a case is not *justiciable*, specifically because the plaintiff does not have the requisite standing to sue, then the circuit court *cannot* hear the case. And because both this Court and the Court of Appeals "shall have *appellate jurisdiction only*," logically speaking, neither court can adjudicate a case on appeal that

27. *Lawson v. Office of Atty. Gen.*, 415 S.W.3d 59, 67 (Ky. 2013) (citing Ky. Const. §112) (emphasis added); *Rose v. Council for Better Education*, 790 S.W.2d 186 (Ky. 1989).

28. *Lawson*, 415 S.W.3d at 67 (emphasis added) (citing Ky. Const. §112; *Rose*, 790 S.W.2d at 186).

29. 504 U.S. at 560–61, 112 S.Ct. 2130.

30. *Allen v. Wright*, 468 U.S. 737, 751, 104 S.Ct. 3315, 82 L.Ed.2d 556 (1984) (overruled by *Lexmark Intern., Inc. v. Static Control Components, Inc.*, 572 U.S. 118, 134 S.Ct. 1377, 1386, 188 L.Ed.2d 392 (2014) on other grounds).

31. *Massachusetts v. EPA*, 549 U.S. 497, 517, 127 S.Ct. 1438, 167 L.Ed.2d 248 (2007) (citing *Lujan*, 504 U.S. at 578, 112 S.Ct. 2130).

32. *Allen*, 468 U.S. at 751, 104 S.Ct. 3315.

33. *Id.*

a circuit court cannot adjudicate because the exercise of appellate jurisdiction *necessarily assumes* that proper original jurisdiction has been established first at some point in the case.[34]

Therefore, if a circuit court cannot maintain proper original jurisdiction over a case to decide its merits because the case is *nonjusticiable* due to the plaintiff's failure to satisfy the constitutional standing requirement, the Court of Appeals and this Court are constitutionally precluded from exercising appellate jurisdiction over that case to decide its merits. This is so because the exercise of appellate jurisdiction to decide the merits of a case necessarily assumes that proper original jurisdiction in the circuit court first exists. Stated more simply, establishing the requisite ability to sue in circuit court is a necessary predicate for continuing that suit in appellate court. In this way, the *justiciable cause* requirement applies to cases at all levels of judicial relief.

Having outlined Kentucky's standing doctrine, we now turn to determining whether Lettie Sexton has the requisite standing to sue in this case.

C. Sexton lacks standing to sue.

Simply stated, Sexton, by and through her authorized representative, ARH, lacks the requisite standing to sue in this case. We emphasize the crucial determinative fact—because Sexton, not ARH, is the true plaintiff in this case, we must examine the standing requirement through the lens of Sexton's, not ARH's, purported satisfaction.

Sexton has not and will not suffer an "injury" in this case. Under Medicaid statutes and regulations, and as conceded by both parties, Sexton is not financially interested in any way whatsoever in the outcome of this dispute, which, at its core, is over whether ARH can pursue a reimbursement claim from Coventry through the Medicaid administrative process at the Cabinet.[35] Additionally, Sexton has not alleged that she did not receive all the proper medical care she needed. Nor has she alleged that she will be precluded from receiving medical care in the future.

At oral argument, a suggestion was made that in some broad sense Sexton and other Medicaid beneficiaries may have been or might be potentially harmed if ARH decided to withhold future medical care from Sexton because of Coventry's refusal to reimburse ARH for such care, absent administrative oversight of that decision. But the fear of ARH denying future medical care, a "conjectural" and "hypothetical" injury, cannot establish the requisite injury component to satisfy the standing doctrine. Additionally, "[plaintiffs] cannot manufacture standing merely ... based on their fears of hypothetical future harm that is not certainly impending."[36]

---

34. Black's Law Dictionary defines "Appellate Jurisdiction" as, "The power of a court to *review and revise a lower court's decision*." (10th ed. 2014). In contrast, Black's Law Dictionary defines "Original Jurisdiction" as, "A court's power to hear and decide a matter *before any other court can review the matter*."

35. *See* 42 C.F.R. §447.15.

36. *Clapper v. Amnesty Intern. USA*, 568 U.S. 398, 416, 133 S.Ct. 1138, 185 L.Ed.2d 264 (2013) ("We hold that respondents lack Article III standing because they cannot demonstrate that the future injury

Nor can Medicaid beneficiaries' purported interest in maintaining the integrity of the system satisfy the standing requirement. This is exactly the type of "abstract, conjectural, and hypothetical injury" that fails the injury-in-fact standing requirement: "[I]t would exceed [constitutional] limitations if, at the behest of [the legislature] and in the absence of any showing of concrete injury, we were to entertain citizen suits to vindicate the public's nonconcrete interest in the proper administration of the laws.... The party bringing suit must show that the action injures him in a concrete and personal way."[37]

Additionally, it has been argued that federal and state Medicaid statutes and regulations themselves create standing for Sexton to sue in court because they mandate a Medicaid State Fair Hearing be conducted to ascertain misconduct on the part of Coventry and that no such hearing was conducted. But, "deprivation of a procedural right without some concrete interest that is affected by the deprivation—a procedural right *in vacuo*—is insufficient to create ... standing. Only a 'person who has been accorded a procedural right to protect *his concrete interests* can assert that right without meeting all the normal standards for redressability and immediacy.'"[38]

If a court were to instruct the Cabinet to conduct an administrative hearing regarding Coventry's denial of reimbursement to ARH, nothing in Sexton's life would change. Regardless of the outcome of this administrative hearing, Sexton would be no better or worse off than before the hearing was conducted. Furthermore, "[i]t is settled that [the legislature] cannot erase [constitutional] standing requirements by statutorily granting the right to sue to a plaintiff who would not otherwise have standing."[39] * * *

Sexton's lack of standing becomes clearer when one looks at the root of what is being sought in this case. ARH is using Sexton as the front to redress its own potential loss. Coventry denied reimbursement to ARH in this case—ARH seeks to recover that reimbursement in some way circuitous or at least establish some process to appeal from the decisions of managed-care organizations not to reimburse providers for patient care. These are the true injuries in this case, having nothing to do with Sexton.

* * *

Our decision today is not that the Cabinet correctly decided that Sexton did not have the requisite standing to seek redress through an administrative agency hearing; rather, it is that Sexton does not have the requisite standing to seek redress for this alleged injury in a Kentucky court. Whether a party has the requisite standing to seek

---

they purportedly fear is certainly impending....") (citing *Pennsylvania v. New Jersey*, 426 U.S. 660, 664, 96 S.Ct. 2333, 49 L.Ed.2d 124 (1976)).

37. *Summers v. Earth Island Inst.*, 555 U.S. 488, 497, 129 S.Ct. 1142, 173 L.Ed.2d 1 (2009) (quoting *Lujan*, 504 U.S. at 580–81, 112 S.Ct. 2130 (Kennedy, J., concurring)) (emphasis in original).

38. *Summers*, 555 U.S. at 496, 129 S.Ct. 1142 (quoting *Lujan*, 504 U.S. at 572 n.7, 112 S.Ct. 2130) (emphasis in original).

39. *Spokeo, Inc. v. Robins*, ___ U.S. ___, 136 S.Ct. 1540, 1547–48, 194 L.Ed.2d 635 (2016) (quoting *Raines v. Byrd*, 521 U.S. 811, 820 n.3, 117 S.Ct. 2312, 138 L.Ed.2d 849 (1997)); *see also Gladstone, Realtors v. Village of Bellwood*, 441 U.S. 91, 100, 99 S.Ct. 1601, 60 L.Ed.2d 66 (1979) ("In no event ... may Congress abrogate the Art. III minima.").

redress through an administrative agency is an entirely different question than whether a party has the requisite standing to seek redress through a Kentucky court.[40]

* * *

III. Conclusion.

We hold that it is the constitutional responsibility of all Kentucky courts to consider, even upon their own motion, whether plaintiffs have the requisite standing, a constitutional predicate to a Kentucky court's adjudication of a case, to bring suit. We adopt the United States Supreme Court's test for standing as announced in *Lujan v. Defenders of Wildlife*.[41] Under that test, we hold that Sexton lacks the requisite standing to sue in this case. Therefore, we reverse the Court of Appeals, vacate the decision of the trial court, and remand this case to the trial court with instructions to dismiss Sexton's petition for judicial review.

All sitting. Minton, C.J., Cunningham, Hughes, Keller, VanMeter and Venters, JJ., concur. Wright, J., dissents by separate opinion.

* * *

Notes and Questions

1. How is the doctrine of "constitutional standing," as described in *Sexton*, related to "the judicial power" conferred on courts by Section 109 of the Constitution?
2. The case in *Sexton* originated in the Circuit Court, in which Section 112 required that the trial court hear only "justiciable causes." Even though Sections 110 and 111 do not include similar "justiciable causes" language, the Supreme Court found that the "appellate jurisdiction" language of those sections required any case pending before the Supreme Court or Court of Appeals also to be justiciable. The Court reasoned that, if the Circuit Court could not assume jurisdiction of nonjusticiable cases, then an appellate court's jurisdiction could not exceed that of the Circuit Court. Note, however, that Section 113 does not include an express "justiciable causes" limitation on the District Court's jurisdiction; rather, the District Court "shall exercise original jurisdiction as may be provided by the General Assembly." Ky. Const. §113(6). Would it be possible for the General Assembly to permit the District Court to have jurisdiction over nonjusticiable cases?

---

40. For a discussion of this distinction, *see* 13B Fed. Prac. & Proc. Juris. §3531.13 (3d ed.). We leave the issue of standing in an administrative agency adjudication for another day.

41. 504 U.S. at 560–561, 112 S.Ct. 2130.

B. The Right to a Jury Trial

> "The ancient mode of trial by jury shall be held sacred, and the right thereof remain inviolate, subject to such modifications as may be authorized by this Constitution." (Ky. Const. §7.)
>
> "A grand jury shall consist of twelve persons, nine of whom concurring, may find an indictment. In civil and misdemeanor cases, in courts inferior to the Circuit Courts, a jury shall consist of six persons. The General Assembly may provide that in any or all trials of civil actions in the Circuit Courts, three-fourths or more of the jurors concurring may return a verdict, which shall have the same force and effect as if rendered by the entire panel. But where a verdict is rendered by a less number than the whole jury, it shall be signed by all the jurors who agree to it." (Ky. Const. §248.)
>
> "It shall be the duty of the General Assembly to enact such laws as shall be necessary and proper to decide differences by arbitrators, the arbitrators to be appointed by the parties who may choose that summary mode of adjustment." (Ky. Const. §250.)

The right to a jury trial is the only right the Kentucky Constitution calls "sacred." Section 7 preserves the "ancient mode of trial by jury," and requires that the right remain "inviolate." There is an exception to the jury trial right, which is "subject to such modifications as may be authorized by this Constitution."

Section 248 prescribes the number of jury members on a grand jury (12), and states that, "in courts inferior to the Circuit Courts," *i.e.*, the District Court, a jury consists of six persons. However, neither Section 7 nor Section 248 prescribes the number of jurors who sit on a Circuit Court trial jury. This is because the Kentucky courts have long understood that the "ancient mode" of trial by jury required the jury to be composed of 12 persons, all of whom must agree upon a verdict. *Commonwealth v. Simmons*, 394 S.W.3d 903, 906 (Ky. 2013) (citing *Wendling v. Commonwealth*, 143 Ky. 587, 137 S.W. 205 (1911); *Wells v. Commonwealth*, 561 S.W.2d 85 (Ky. 1978); *Burnett v. Commonwealth*, 31 S.W.3d 878 (Ky. 2000)). Section 248 alters the number of jurors in District Court cases but leaves the common law unchanged regarding the number of Circuit Court jurors. The Constitution in Section 248 also alters the "ancient mode" of trial by jury in civil cases, by allowing the General Assembly to provide for a verdict to be rendered by three-fourths or more of the jurors, rather than requiring all verdicts to be unanimous. The General Assembly has done so in KRS 29A.280(3) (allowing verdicts to be rendered by 9 of 12 jurors in the Circuit Court, or 5 of 6 in the District Court). All verdicts in criminal cases still must be unanimous. *See id.*

Because of the command of Section 7 to hold "sacred" the right to a jury trial, Kentucky courts have at times gone to great lengths—even too far—to preserve the right. For example, the Supreme Court of the United States found that the Supreme Court of Kentucky had singled out arbitration agreements for disfavored treatment compared to other kinds of contracts, contrary to the Federal Arbitration Act, in *Kindred Nursing*

Centers L.P. v. Clark, 581 U.S. ___, 137 S.Ct. 1421 (2017). This anti-arbitration bias is remarkable, when the same Constitution that calls the jury trial right "sacred" in Section 7 also, in Section 250, requires the General Assembly to enact laws providing for arbitration of disputes between those "who may choose that summary mode of adjustment." For purposes of Section 7, it would seem that Section 250 provides a "modification[ ]" to the right to trial by jury.

Steelvest, Inc. v. Scansteel Service Center, Inc.

Supreme Court of Kentucky (1995)
908 S.W.2d 104

OPINION OF THE COURT BY JUSTICE REYNOLDS.

The denial of a trial by jury fosters this appeal. The background of the action appears in the opinion of *Steelvest, Inc. v. Scansteel Service Center, Inc.*, Ky., 807 S.W.2d 476 (1991). On remand, the trial court, despite timely demand, denied appellant a trial by jury.

The complaint and amended complaint both alleged a breach of fiduciary duties occasioned by appellee Scanlan. The allegations of the pleadings constituted tortious acts and sought damages, not equitable remedies.

At issue is whether the right to trial by jury, under the Kentucky Constitution, is contravened by Civil Rule 39.01(c), which permits a trial court to deny this right in an action at law for damages upon a determination that the case, because of the peculiar questions involved or because the action involves complicated accounts, or a great detail of facts, is impractical for a jury to intelligently try.

Following this Court's remand order to the trial court, appellees requested that the case be tried without a jury due to its complexity. The trial court, responding, stated that "everybody is going to have to agree to that because everybody is entitled to a jury trial" and the case was so docketed. After the passage of more than a year and on the morning of the scheduled trial, the court sustained appellees' most recent motion to conduct a bench trial pursuant to CR 39.01(c), after determining it impractical for a jury to intelligently try the case due to the great detail of facts and peculiar questions involved.

The Kentucky Constitution, in actions at law, gives the litigant an unqualified right to trial by jury. Section 7 of the Kentucky Bill of Rights provides: "The ancient mode of trial by jury shall be held sacred, and the right thereof remain inviolate, subject to such modifications as may be authorized by this Constitution." To emphasize the Bill of Rights, Section 26 of the Kentucky Constitution provides that "[t]o guard against transgression of the high powers which we have delegated, We Declare that everything in this Bill of Rights is excepted out of the general powers of government, and shall forever remain inviolate; and all laws contrary thereto, or contrary to this Constitution, shall be void." The broad right of preservation is again referenced in CR 38.01; i.e., "the right of trial jury as declared by the constitution of Kentucky or as given by the statute of Kentucky shall be preserved to the parties inviolate."

A deviation/problem arises with Civil Rule 39.01(c) as to whether it is violative of the right to a jury trial as guaranteed under the state constitution.

While the Seventh Amendment to the United States Constitution, along with Section 7 of the Kentucky Constitution, preserves the right to trial by jury as it existed in common law, Rule 39.01(c) is not, at this time, subject to federal constitutional review insofar as the Seventh Amendment right to a jury trial in civil cases has not yet been made applicable to the states through the Fourteenth Amendment. Both constitutions are deemed to guarantee the right of trial by jury as existed in 1791.

State constitutions may offer greater protections for their citizens than the federal constitution and the Kentucky courts are not bound by decisions of the United States Supreme Court when deciding whether a state statute, in this instance a procedural code provision, impermissibly infringes upon individual rights guaranteed by the state constitution, as long as the state constitutional protection does not fall below the federal floor. Because of the profoundly different approaches between the Seventh Amendment to the Constitution of the United States and the provisions of the Kentucky Constitution preserving the right to trial by jury, the federal decisions on this subject are of little utility in Kentucky practice. *See Kentucky Practice, Rules of Civil Procedure, Annotated*, Bertelsman & Philipps, Ky. Prac., 4th Ed., Vol. 7, Civil Rule 38.01. Appellees' resort to federal authorities to support their arguments to the contrary must fail.

The limitations upon trial by jury are pronounced in Civil Rule 39.01:

> When trial by jury has been demanded as provided in Rule 38, the action shall be designated upon the docket as a jury action. The trial of all issues so demanded shall be by jury, unless (a) the parties or their attorneys of record, by written stipulation filed with the court or by an oral stipulation made in open court and entered in the record, consent to trial by the court sitting without a jury, or (b) the court upon motion or of its own initiative finds that a right of trial by jury of some or all of those issues does not exist under the constitution or statutes of Kentucky, or (c) the court upon motion or of its own initiative finds that because of the peculiar questions involved, or because the action involves complicated accounts, or a great detail of facts, it is impracticable for a jury intelligently to try the case.

The constitutionality of Rule 39.01(c) is determinable from whether it was customary at common law in 1791 for a court, acting in its discretion, to deny a jury trial because the action involved peculiar questions, great detail of facts, or complicated accounts.

CR 39.01(c) is a remnant which was condensed from Section 10(4) of the now obsolete Civil Rules of Practice. The General Assembly by act of April 29, 1890, amended Section 10 of the Civil Code by the addition of subsection 4 which provided:

> The court may, in its discretion, on motion of either party, or without motion, order the transfer of an action from the ordinary to the equity docket, or from a court of purely common law to a court of purely equity jurisdiction, whenever the court, before which the action is pending, shall be of the opinion that

> such transfer is necessary because of the peculiar questions involved, or because the case involves accounts so complicated, or such great detail of facts, as to render it impracticable for a jury to intelligently try the case.

The older code section and the current rule mirror one another. Despite the strong constitutional language guaranteeing a trial by jury, some court decisions indiscriminately accepted the use of Civil Rule 39.01(c) and old Code Section 10(4). Several court opinions recited complicated issues as a basis for denial of a jury trial under the subsection of the rule. While neither rule makes reference to "complicated issues," CR 39.01(c) was applied in *McGuire v. Hammond*, Ky., 405 S.W.2d 191 (1966), wherein a jury trial was denied because of the long period of time anticipated necessary to hear the case and the many and complicated issues of fact involved. The reasoning was adopted erroneously on appeal.

Reusch v. Hemmer, 236 Ky. 546, 33 S.W.2d 618 (1930), admitted that a counterclaim for damages raised common law issues, but upheld a transfer of the entire action to equity because the issues "were so numerous and complicated" in view of the numerous items for which damages were claimed. Another example of where the court spoke of complicated issues as a basis for denial of a jury trial arose in *Coy v. King*, 199 Ky. 65, 250 S.W. 503 (1923). The denial of a jury trial occurred in *City of Shively v. Hyde*, Ky., 438 S.W.2d 512 (1969), and was upheld by brief reference to a detail of facts and complicated issues.

The constitutional term "inviolate" means that the right to trial by jury is unassailable. Henceforth, legislation and civil rules of practice shall be construed strictly and observed vigilantly in favor of the right and is not to be abrogated arbitrarily by the courts. The constitutional right to a jury trial cannot be annulled, obstructed, impaired, or restricted by legislative or judicial action. *Seymour v. Swart*, Okla., 695 P.2d 509, 511–512 (1985).

The jury trial provision of our state constitution has been held in similar light in *Commonwealth v. Jones*, 73 Ky. (10 Bush) 725, 756 (1874), wherein Judge Lindsay emphasized:

> That the rule of construction, whether applied to the constitution or to a statute, which will preserve unimpaired the ancient mode of trial by jury, is the rule which should always govern in interpreting laws involving the forfeiture of a civil or political right, seems to us to be apparent upon the mere statement of the proposition.

Further enunciated therein was that everything in the Bill of Rights "is declared to be excepted out of the general powers of government and to remain forever inviolate." *Id.* at 746–747.

O'Connor v. Henderson Bridge Co., 95 Ky. 633, 27 S.W. 251 (1894), set a standard applicable to Section 10(4):

> If the court was, at date of that statute, without authority to transfer an action from the ordinary to equity docket under circumstances and for causes there-

> in recited, it is still powerless in that respect, for the right of trial by jury can not be impaired or modified by legislative enactment. Therefore, whether this action was properly transferred depends not upon that statute, but proper interpretation and application of the language of the clause of the Constitution quoted.
>
> That clause never was intended to be so strictly construed or rigidly adhered to as to prevent, in any case, due and proper administration of justice.

The court's analysis does not reference or include factors of either great detail of fact or peculiar questions. The standard of *O'Connor*, *supra*, is a narrow one limiting the application of the principle embodied in both the predecessor and CR 39.01(c) to complicated cases of account. The zeal to enunciate broad applications of denying a trial by jury is apparent when a court admits that an action, issue, or claim is legal rather than equitable, but then goes on to apply CR 39.01(c) by denying a jury trial. *See Hoaglin v. Carr's Adm'x*, Ky., 294 S.W.2d 935 (1956).

This Court, in the case of *Johnson v. Holbrook*, Ky., 302 S.W.2d 608 (1957), stated clearly that in a reformation of a written instrument case, an equitable action, that the question was to be determined by the court without a jury. The separation remains between jury actions and nonjury causes, and what was, before the adoption of CR 39.01(c), an action at law is a jury action and what was a suit in equity is a nonjury action. Stated differently, causes of action historically legal are triable by jury and causes of action historically equitable are triable by the court—notwithstanding the rule. Thus, if both legal and equitable issues are joined in a single cause of action, the appropriate mode of trial must be followed as to each, and in that sequence which will promote efficient administration without curtailing the substantive rights of the respective parties.

Carder v. Weisengburgh, 95 Ky. 135, 23 S.W. 964 (1893), emphasized that there is a right to a jury trial in cases where a jury trial was customarily used at common law, but in cases of purely equitable cognizance, a trial by jury is not a matter of right, but is addressed to the discretion of the trial court. The right to a jury trial is secured by the state constitution and cannot be taken away or placed at the discretion of the trial judge by converting a legal right into an equitable one or by giving the trial judge an exclusive right to try legal issues because there is some equitable right that arises out of the establishment of the legal issues so as to infringe upon the right of a trial by jury.

CR 2 provides that there shall be one form of action to be known as a "civil action." The rule, while it provides for only one form of civil action, merged ordinary and equitable actions for procedural purposes only. This merger in no wise abolished the substantive distinction between the two actions and specifically with regard to the right to a jury trial. *Brock v. Farmer*, Ky., 291 S.W.2d 531 (1956); *Johnson*, *supra*.

It is the pleadings—not the proof—which are determinative of whether legal or equitable issues are involved. *Brandenburg v. Burns*, Ky., 451 S.W.2d 413 (1969); *Republic Coal Co. v. Ward*, 191 Ky. 368, 230 S.W. 295 (1921). The action now under consideration does not involve an equitable accounting and is one at law for damages wherein the pleadings do not assert any equitable cause or defense. Additionally, the fact that a number of items are involved does not convert a legal issue into an equitable one. *Shatz v. American Surety Company of New York*, Ky., 295 S.W.2d 809 (1955); *Brandenburg, supra.*

A civil cause of action for damages sustained "is the classical textbook paradigm of an action at law wherein '[t]he constitution guarantees a trial by jury in cases of this character.'" *Meyers v. Chapman Printing Co., Inc.*, Ky., 840 S.W.2d 814 (1992).

An argument which authorizes complexity as a basis for constitutionally removing a case from a jury enjoys no support. Complexity was not an equitable basis for a trial without a jury at the time of the adoption of Kentucky's Constitution and to deny a jury trial is to speculate on a jury's capabilities. A jury, historically, when used, has operated as a check against the arbitrary action of a trial court. A jury's capabilities are not to be ignored and at an early date Judge Hazelrigg observed in his opinion that:

> The jury are drawn from the various walks of life, and their combined knowledge and experience afford the very best opportunity for safe and wise conclusions. Judge Dillon is quoted as saying, "twelve good and lawful men are better judges of disputed facts than twelve learned judges."

Hudson v. Adams' Adm'r, Ky., 49 S.W. 192 (1899).

CR 39.01(c) violates the right to a trial by jury as guaranteed in Section 7 of the Kentucky Constitution in at least two respects. It has been used to deny a jury trial where there are raised issues of law and fact and it has broadened the range of application beyond cases of account. Civil Rule 39 shall, therefore, be redrafted as to be in conformity with Section 7 of the Kentucky Constitution.

* * *

The judgment of Jefferson Circuit Court is reversed as to Scanlan and Scansteel Service Center, Inc., and this case is remanded for a trial by jury as to these parties. * * *

Lambert, Leibson, Stumbo, and Wintersheimer, JJ., concur.

Stephens, C.J., concurs in result only.

Fuqua, J., not sitting.

Notes and Questions

1. One reason *Steelvest* is noteworthy is because the Court held that one of its own rules—Rule 39.01 of the Kentucky Rules of Civil Procedure, which was promulgated pursuant to the Supreme Court's authority under Section 116 of the Constitution—was unconstitutional. After the decision was rendered, the Supreme Court amended Rule 39.01 in 1996 by deleting subsection (c).
2. The case of *Steelvest, Inc. v. Scansteel Service Center, Inc.*, 807 S.W.2d 476 (Ky. 1991), cited near the beginning of this opinion, currently is regarded as the most authoritative case on the summary judgment standard used in Kentucky trial courts. In that case, the Supreme Court rejected the more liberal federal summary judgment stan-

dard enunciated by three 1986 cases—*Celotex Corp. v. Catrett*, 477 U.S. 317 (1986); *Anderson v. Liberty Lobby Inc.*, 477 U.S. 242 (1986); and *Matsushita Electric Industrial Co., Ltd. v. Zenith Radio Corp.*, 475 U.S. 574 (1986)—and held instead that summary judgment in Kentucky is proper only where the movant shows the adverse party cannot prevail under any circumstances. As noted in the opinion above, this was the second trip for the *Steelvest* case to the Supreme Court of Kentucky.

3. As the Court held in *Steelvest*, the right to a jury trial applies to any civil action, other than an action seeking an equitable remedy. The jury trial right attaches to any civil action where damages are sought, including causes of action created by statute, even if the statute does not specifically mention a right to a jury trial: "Once a cause of action for damages to be tried in the courts of this Commonwealth has been created by statute, a further provision providing the parties shall have a right to trial by jury is surplusage. To state otherwise would conflict with our Constitution.... But within the exercise of judicial power the right to jury trial is a jural right constitutionally protected, applying equally to those causes of action arising at law after as well as before the 1891 Constitution." *Meyers v. Chapman Printing Co.*, 840 S.W.2d 814, 819–20 (Ky. 1992) (holding jury trial right applies to claims under the Kentucky Civil Rights Act).

C. The Right to an Appeal

> "In all cases, civil and criminal, there shall be allowed as a matter of right at least one appeal to another court, except that the Commonwealth may not appeal from a judgment of acquittal in a criminal case, other than for the purpose of securing a certification of law, and the General Assembly may prescribe that there shall be no appeal from that portion of a judgment dissolving a marriage...." (Ky. Const. §115.)

There is no right to an appeal from an adverse trial court judgment under the federal constitution. The U.S. Constitution itself provides for no right to appeal, and the U.S. Supreme Court has held that such a right cannot be implied from the text: "There is, of course, no constitutional right to an appeal..." *Jones v. Barnes*, 463 U.S. 745, 751 (1983).

Prior to the 1976 amendments that created the unified Court of Justice, the Kentucky Constitution also contained no right to an appeal. *See Marlow v. Commonwealth*, 142 Ky. 106, 133 S.W. 1137, 1141 (1911) ("the right of appeal is purely a matter of legislative discretion"). But the Judicial Article amendments included in Section 115 a "right [to] at least one appeal," with only two exceptions: (1) the Commonwealth may not appeal from an acquittal in a criminal case (*cf.* Ky. Const. §13), except to obtain a certification of the law; and (2) the General Assembly may prohibit appeals from that portion of a judgment dissolving a marriage (which it has done in KRS 22A.020(3)). This section will consider what an appeal is, and how the right to an appeal is accessed.

Vessels v. Brown-Forman Distillers Corporation

Supreme Court of Kentucky (1990)
793 S.W.2d 795

Opinion of the Court by Justice Combs.

This novel workers' compensation case is one of first impression. It has spawned three separate proceedings in this Court. The first (89-SC-421-D) is a motion for discretionary review filed by James Vessels, as father and next friend of Lisa Ann Vessels, Mark Vessels, Christine Vessels and Timmy Vessels.

The second (89-SC-479-WC) is an appeal by the Vessels from an opinion of the Court of Appeals which reversed an award of the "new" Workers' Compensation Board rendered October 14, 1988, affirming the "old" Workers' Compensation Board award entered February 22, 1988.

The third (89-SC-480-WC) is a cross-appeal filed by Brown-Forman in this Court as a protective measure.

In addition to the issues presented by the parties, this Court has requested that they address the issue of whether this workers' compensation case is properly on appeal to this Court pursuant to CR 76.36(7) and Section 115 of the Kentucky Constitution, an appeal as a matter of right, or whether workers' compensation cases are restricted to discretionary review by this Court, pursuant to CR 76.25(12).

Procedurally, this action began when the "old" Board found the infant grandchildren to be partially dependent upon their grandmother and had awarded to them "the sum of the temporary total benefits heretofore paid to or on behalf of the deceased on or prior to her death on November 1, 1983 and shall further recover the sum of $51.47 per week on behalf of such partially dependent grandchildren beginning November 22, 1983, for the remainder of the deceased's life expectancy, or until each such grandchild has attained eighteen years of age, whichever shall first occur...." This decision was appealed by the employer to the "new" Workers' Compensation Board, pursuant to KRS 342.285, per *Jefferson County Board of Education v. Miller*, Ky. App., 744 S.W.2d 751 (1988).

In affirming the "old" Board, the "new" Board also found that the grandchildren were 25% partially dependent upon their grandmother at the time of the accident, and were properly awarded benefits pursuant to KRS 342.730(3)(d).

Brown-Forman then filed an appeal to the Court of Appeals, rather than to the circuit court, pursuant to KRS 342.290 and CR 76.25. The Court of Appeals reversed the "new" Board. In its appeal, Brown-Forman contended that the Board erred and that benefits should have terminated upon Ms. Vessels' death. Alternatively, Brown-Forman argued that if benefits did not terminate, the grandchildren were not her dependents and therefore not entitled to benefits. Brown-Forman further contended that, in any event, the award of benefits should be modified to provide for a reduction in the amount of the benefits as each grandchild is emancipated. The Court of Appeals found that the evidence before the Board compelled a finding that the grandchildren were not dependent upon Nellie Vessels, and reversed the award.

This brings us to the actions commenced in this Court. The Vessels filed a motion for discretionary review and a direct appeal as a matter of right. Brown-Forman filed a cross-appeal in which they ask us to:

(1) dismiss the appeal and cross-appeal but to review the issues via Vessels' motion for discretionary review and to accept their cross-appeal as a cross motion for discretionary review; and

(2) decline Vessels' motion for discretionary review or affirm the Court of Appeals' decision because:

a. Plaintiff failed to prove an essential element of his case—that Ms. Vessels' contributions to the family exceeded the value of the services she received from the family—and, therefore, there was no substantive evidence to support the Board's finding of dependency and award of continued benefits to the grandchildren; and/or

b. The proper time to test dependency under KRS 342.730(3) is at death, not injury, and the evidence precludes a finding that her grandchildren were dependent on Ms. Vessels in 1983 before her death.

Before addressing the merits of this case, we must initially address Brown-Forman's contention that there is no appeal as a matter of right to the Supreme Court from the Court of Appeals' review of a workers' compensation award. There are two routes through which a litigant may properly proceed to this Court from the ruling of a lower court. The first, and most often used route, is the one of discretionary review provided by CR 76.20. The second is a matter of right appeal provided by Section 115 of our constitution.

Being mindful of the legislature's 1987 amendment to the Workers' Compensation Act, KRS 342.290, and CR 76.20, CR 76.25(12), and Sections 109, 111(2) and 115 of Kentucky's Constitution, and out of an abundance of precaution, the Vessels proceeded to follow both routes to this Court. We have held their motion for discretionary review (89-SC-421-D) in abeyance, pending our determination of the threshold question. That question is what is the proper route to this Court in a workers' compensation case.

The Vessels, as appellants, contend that Section 115 of the constitution gives them a matter of right appeal to this Court since KRS 342.290 provides that a decision of the Board is judicially reviewed for the first time by the Court of Appeals, rather than by the circuit court. That is, appellants are entitled to two (2) judicial opportunities, at least one of which must be an appeal, as a matter of right, notwithstanding CR 76.25(12). Thus, the appeal to this Court becomes the first appeal to another court referred to in Section 115 of the Kentucky Constitution, and as such, is an appeal as a matter of right.

On the other hand, Brown-Forman contends that our constitution does not contemplate an appeal to the Supreme Court as a matter of right from the Court of Appeals in workers' compensation cases. In support of this contention it argues that Section

115 of our constitution does not mandate appeals in workers' compensation cases to this Court because "... the legislature and the Supreme Court have implemented the Constitution's Section 111(2) exception to the appellate jurisdiction of the Court of Appeals."

Brown-Forman further states that the exception created by Section 111(2) was first utilized in 1987 when the legislature amended the Kentucky Workers' Compensation Act to provide for a direct appeal from the newly constituted Workers' Compensation Board to the Kentucky Court of Appeals, as a matter of right. KRS 342.290. Pursuant to the legislature's request, this Court then implemented CR 76.25, a special rule for review of Workers' Compensation Board decisions effective January 15, 1988.

CR 76.25(12) provides, as a matter of right, an appeal by any party aggrieved by a decision of the Workers' Compensation Board to the Court of Appeals. In CR 76.25(12), the rule provides that further review may be sought in the Supreme Court of a final decision or final order of the Court of Appeals in a workers' compensation matter in accordance with the rules applicable to motions for discretionary review under CR 76.20.

We disagree and reject out of hand Brown-Forman's contention that Kentucky's Constitution does not mandate appeals in workers' compensation cases to this Court, and therefore hold that CR 76.25(12) is unconstitutional. We had thought this issue had been put to rest almost two centuries ago by the celebrated case of *Marbury v. Madison*, 5 U.S. (1 Cranch) 137, 2 L.Ed. 60 (1803). Congress, by the Judiciary Act of 1789, had sought to enlarge the Supreme Court's original jurisdiction by empowering it to issue writs of mandamus and other writs.

Article III, Section 2 had limited the Supreme Court's original jurisdiction "to all cases affecting ambassadors, other public ministers and consuls, and those in which a state shall be a party." Article VI, cl. 2 established that the United States Constitution, and "the laws of the United States which shall be made in pursuance thereof; and all treaties made, or which shall be made, under the authority of the United States, shall be the supreme law of the land...."

In the opinion by Justice Marshall, the Supreme Court held that inasmuch as the Judiciary Act conflicted with Article III, Section 2, and was not made pursuant to the United States Constitution as required by Article VI, that the writ issued by the court was void.

We are a constitutional government, and under Section 4 of the Kentucky Constitution, all power is retained by the people. Only the people by amendment or by convention have the power to amend or change the constitution.

The present KRS 342.290 in no way conflicts with Section 115 of the Kentucky Constitution. This statute simply eliminated the circuit court as the court authorized to review opinions, orders and awards of the Workers' Compensation Board. It gave the Court of Appeals the same power to review as had been originally given by statute to the circuit court—no more, and no less. Nor does Section 111(2) conflict with Section 115. Section 111(2) is as follows:

> The Court of Appeals shall have appellate jurisdiction only, except that it may be authorized by rules of the Supreme Court to review directly decisions of administrative agencies of the Commonwealth.... [Emphasis added.]

Section 115 of our constitution plainly and unequivocally provides:

> In all cases, civil and criminal, there shall be allowed as a matter of right at least one appeal to another court.... [Emphasis added.]

Had the intent been for Section 111(2) to modify or limit Section 115, the word "review" would not have been used. Section 111(2) is nothing more than an exception to the Court of Appeals' appellate jurisdiction. In this context, "review" and "appeal" are not synonymous. The original KRS 342.285 provided for reviews by "petition for review" to the circuit court. In fact, CR 76.25(12) also uses the word "review" rather than the word "appeal." We are aware that oftentimes the words "appeal" and "review" are used synonymously, but in Section 111(2) the word "review" must be treated in the context previously employed.

Brown-Forman contends that our rule, the statute, and Section 111(2) create an additional exception to Section 115. Had such an exception been intended, it could have been inserted in Section 115. Such has not been done, and we are powerless to do so.

Section 109 of the Kentucky Constitution created our Court of Justice and divided it into "a Supreme Court, a Court of Appeals, a trial court of general jurisdiction known as the Circuit Court, and the trial court of limited jurisdiction known as the District Court." Nothing in Section 109 contemplates an administrative agency, much less the Workers' Compensation Board, as the equivalent of a court. The phrase, "there shall be allowed as a matter of right at least one appeal to another court," of Section 115, is unambiguous. This presupposes that the tribunals of review and for appeal are courts within the constitutional meaning of the word. We have determined that KRS 342.290 is constitutional as it does not deprive the litigants before the Workers' Compensation Board of their right of review or right of appeal. We have also determined that Section 111(2) does not conflict with Section 115.

However, we now turn our attention to CR 76.25(12) adopted by this Court pursuant to Section 116 of the Kentucky Constitution. Section 116 gives the Supreme Court "... the power to *prescribe rules governing its appellate jurisdiction*, rule for the appointment of commissioners and other court personnel, and rules of practice and procedure for the Court of Justice." [Emphasis added.] This section did not empower this Court to ignore the plain and unambiguous mandate of Section 115, which guarantees to all litigants the right of one appeal to another court, nor did it empower us to amend the constitution. CR 76.25(12) purports to do just that and we, therefore, declare that rule to be unconstitutional.

By declaring CR 76.25(12) unconstitutional, workers' compensation claims that are first judicially reviewed in the Court of Appeals pursuant to KRS 342.290, and there ruled upon, may be appealed to the Kentucky Supreme Court as a matter of right pursuant to Section 115 of the Kentucky Constitution.

Having decided that the Vessels are properly before this Court by the matter of right appeal, we therefore deny their motion for discretionary review and turn to an examination of their matter of right appeal.

* * *

The motion for discretionary review is hereby denied, the cross-appeal is dismissed, and the case is reversed and remanded to the Board for enforcement of the award.

Lambert and Wintersheimer, JJ., concur.

Stephens, C.J., dissents by separate opinion.

Leibson, J., files a separate opinion, dissenting in part and concurring in part.

Vance, J., files a separate opinion, concurring in part and dissenting in part, in which Gant, J., joins.

CHIEF JUSTICE STEPHENS, DISSENTING.

Respectfully, I dissent.

A fair reading of Kentucky's constitution reveals that there is no matter of right appeal to this Court in workers' compensation cases.

Sections 111(2) and 115 of the state constitution must be read together. Section 115 affords litigants one direct appeal as a matter of right. The procedure established in Section 111(2) provides this direct appeal—to the Court of Appeals.

Requiring direct appeals of workers' compensation cases to this Court would also contravene the directive found in Section 115 that appeals be expeditious and inexpensive. What the majority is creating is an excess of procedure. A decision is made by an administrative law judge. This decision may be appealed as a matter of right to the Workers' Compensation Board, then to the Kentucky Court of Appeals, and now to the Supreme Court. This procedure will be neither inexpensive nor expeditious, as this Court becomes inundated with these appeals as a matter of right. The Judicial Article of the constitution makes it clear that the Supreme Court was intended to be a court of discretionary review, except for the most serious criminal cases. I fear that the spirit and intent of the Judicial Article will be negated as the Supreme Court's ability to perform its discretionary review function is impaired.

JUSTICE LEIBSON, DISSENTING IN PART AND CONCURRING IN PART.

I dissent because Kentucky Constitution §111(2) allows the Supreme Court to provide an alternative method of review in appeals from administrative agencies as an exception to the mandatory review in §115.

I have no doubt but the present procedure enacted by statute, as supplemented by the Supreme Court rule, is what the drafters of §111(2) had in mind when they stated that the Court of Appeals "may be authorized by rules of the Supreme Court to review directly decisions of administrative agencies of the Commonwealth."

The General Assembly's decision to modify the structure of the Workers' Compensation Act as was done was a long-time coming, but was an idea in being at the time the

Constitution was amended. The modification makes the Board the first appeal and the equal of a constitutional appeal under §115. The idea that §115 in these circumstances requires a second appeal exalts form over substance at the expense of the Constitution and the injured worker.

A workers' compensation case is decided by an administrative law judge, and reviewed by appeal to the Workers' Compensation Board. We have created a useless, unnecessary, counterproductive procedure by deciding that a second appellate review is necessary. Thus, I dissent.

* * *

JUSTICE VANCE, CONCURRING IN PART AND DISSENTING IN PART.

I fully agree with the majority opinion that a litigant in a workers' compensation case has a constitutional guarantee of a direct appeal to another court as a matter of right. Because, under our statutes, the first court to consider workers' compensation cases is the Court of Appeals, the matter of right appeal is to the Supreme Court.

* * *

Gant, J., joins in this opinion.

Notes and Questions

1. Only three of the seven Justices of the Supreme Court joined the *Vessels* opinion in full; Justices Vance and Gant agreed with the portion of the opinion concerning a matter-of-right appeal to the Supreme Court in worker's compensation cases. Chief Justice Stephens and Justice Leibson dissented on this point, both citing what they perceived as a conflict between Section 111(2) and Section 115 of the Constitution. Do you believe those two sections of the Constitution are in conflict? Was the majority's position or the dissenters' position more faithful to the text of the constitution?
2. Except for criminal convictions resulting in a sentence of death, life imprisonment, or 20 or more years (*see* Section 110(2)(b)), the Kentucky Constitution does not prescribe the court to which an appeal is to be taken. But Section 115 of the Kentucky Constitution provides, "Procedural rules shall provide for expeditious and inexpensive appeals." In part to implement that constitutional directive, the Supreme Court has adopted Rule 2(A)(1) of the Kentucky Rules of Appellate Procedure, which provides, "Appeals in civil proceedings shall be taken to the next higher court. Appeals in criminal proceedings shall be taken to the next higher court, except that an appeal from a judgment imposing a sentence of death, life imprisonment, or imprisonment for 20 years or more shall be taken directly to the Supreme Court. Appeals from family courts that are established pursuant to Ky. Const. §110(5)(b) or Ky. Const. §112(6) shall be taken to the Court of Appeals...."
3. Regarding appeals in criminal cases, the Supreme Court has construed Section 115 as precluding any appeal by the Commonwealth from a judgment of acquittal, whether the judgment was entered pursuant to a jury verdict or after the court entered a judgment n.o.v.: "We hold that Section 115 of the Kentucky Constitution bars

the Commonwealth from appealing a judgment of acquittal.... We also overrule any precedent [*e.g., Commonwealth v. Brindley*, 724 S.W.2d 214 (Ky. 1986)] stating that Section 115 derives itself from Section 13 of the Kentucky Constitution [regarding double jeopardy] and that the Commonwealth may appeal a judgment n.o.v." *Maupin v. Commonwealth*, 542 S.W.3d 926, 932 (Ky. 2018).

4. In an appeal from the decision of a county's fiscal court to the circuit court, the Supreme Court held that "a statutory 'appeal' to the circuit court from any agency or tribunal other than the district court is an original action and not an 'appeal.' *Cf.* KRS 23A.010(4). Though not effective until January 2, 1978, this statute reflects a proper construction of the term within the meaning of Const. Sec. 115(a) and the rules promulgated by this court." *Sarver v. Allen Cnty.*, 582 S.W.2d 40, 43 (Ky. 1979).

Six

The Executive Branch

A. The Executive Power

> "The supreme executive power of the Commonwealth shall be vested in a Chief Magistrate, who shall be styled the 'Governor of the Commonwealth of Kentucky.'" (Ky. Const. §69.)
>
> "[The Governor] shall take care that the laws be faithfully executed." (Ky. Const. §81.)
>
> "A Treasurer, Auditor of Public Accounts, Commissioner of Agriculture, Labor and Statistics, Secretary of State, and Attorney-General, shall be elected by the qualified voters of the State at the same time the Governor and Lieutenant Governor are elected, for the term of four years, each of whom shall be at least thirty years of age at the time of his election, and shall have been a resident citizen of the State at least two years next before his election. The duties of all these officers shall be such as may be prescribed by law...." (Ky. Const. §91.)
>
> "... The duties and responsibilities of [the Treasurer, Auditor of Public Accounts, Secretary of State, Commissioner of Agriculture, Labor and Statistics, and Attorney General] shall be prescribed by law...." (Ky. Const. §93.)

Section 69 of the Kentucky Constitution vests the "supreme executive power of the Commonwealth" in the Governor. But what is the scope of this "supreme" power? And what are the Governor's inherent constitutional powers, if any? The Constitution itself does not say.

Further, unlike the federal Constitution, which names only the President and Vice President as Executive Branch officers and leaves it to the Congress to create any other officials in the Executive Branch, the Kentucky Constitution names several other Executive Branch officers to be directly elected by the people: the Treasurer, Auditor of Public Accounts, Commissioner of Agriculture, Secretary of State, and Attorney General. How these officers relate to each other and what it means for the Governor to have the "supreme executive power" are important to an understanding of how the Executive Branch of the Kentucky government works.

Brown v. Barkley

Supreme Court of Kentucky (1982)
628 S.W.2d 616

Opinion of the Court by Chief Justice Palmore.

On January 14, 1981, the Governor of Kentucky issued an executive order (numbered 81–55) transferring various functions, personnel and funds from the Department of Agriculture (hereinafter called Agriculture) to another executive agency and, among other things, placing it and several other agencies within a newly-created Energy and Agriculture Cabinet. The Commissioner of Agriculture[1] thereupon brought suit challenging the validity of the order. The trial court adjudged it invalid on the ground that it was not authorized by KRS 12.025(1), the enabling statute pursuant to which it was issued. On appeal by the Governor the Court of Appeals held that the order did come within the literal authority of KRS 12.025(1) but was prohibited by a proviso added in 1980 to KRS 12.020, a related statute.

Our conclusion is that the trial court was correct in determining that KRS 12.025(1) does not authorize the transfer of functions, personnel and funds directed by the order. We have considered also whether the Governor nevertheless has constitutional power to effect such a reorganization regardless of the statute, and have determined that he does not.

* * *

The centerpiece of this litigation is KRS 12.025(1), which originated in 1960 as part of an act reorganizing the executive branch of the state government.[2] This statute provides that the Governor may:

> "(1) Establish, abolish or alter the organization of any agency or *statutory administrative department*, including changing the name of a department to explain more clearly the functions performed by it. Also included in this authority shall be permission to transfer functions, personnel, funds, equipment, facilities and records from one (1) department to another. Reorganization made under this section shall be set forth in an executive order, signed by the governor and filed in the office of the secretary of state, which shall explain the changes made and designate the functions, personnel, funds, equipment, facilities and records, as applicable, to be transferred. The governor shall recommend legislation to the next following session of the general assembly to confirm reorganizations effected under the provisions of this section." (Emphasis added.)

1. Properly speaking, "Commissioner of Agriculture, Labor and Statistics." Const. Sec. 95. In the constitutional debates much discussion was devoted to the particular wording of this title. See Debates, Constitutional Convention, pp. 1365 et seq., (Ky., 1890).

2. Ch. 68, Art. XV, Acts of 1960.

The term "statutory administrative department" used in KRS 12.025(1) related directly to KRS 12.020, by which, as amended in the same legislation, the various executive and administrative agencies of the state were classified as (1) "Constitutional Administrative Departments," (2) "Statutory Administrative Departments," and (3) "Independent Agencies." The Governor and the Departments of State, Law, Treasury, Agriculture, Education, and Military Affairs were enumerated as the "constitutional" administrative departments. As may be observed, this designation included all of the departments corresponding with the offices created by Const. Sec. 91 except for the Auditor of Public Accounts, whose office was classified among the "Independent Agencies," and the Register of the Land Office, which had been abolished pursuant to Const. Sec. 94; and it included one, the Department of Military Affairs, which does not relate to any of the offices named in Const. Sec. 91 but obviously falls under the military powers vested in the Governor by Const. Sec. 75.

Clearly, when it was enacted in 1960 KRS 12.025(1) would not have applied to those departments, including Agriculture, that were classified in KRS 12.020 as "constitutional" rather than "statutory." Today, however, though KRS 12.025 remains substantially unaltered, KRS 12.020 has been so amended that the term "statutory administrative department" has become an anachronism.

Whereas in 1960 the executive departments and agencies enumerated in KRS 12.020 were classified as "constitutional," "statutory," and "independent agencies," at the next regular session of the General Assembly[3] they were reclassified according to whether they were headed by elected officers or by appointed officers. In 1974 they were further reclassified as "Departments headed by elected officers," "Cabinet Departments headed by appointed officers," and "Other Departments headed by appointed officers,"[4] and through the amendments which have been enacted from that time until today this has remained the terminology by which KRS 12.020 classifies most of the administrative departments within the executive branch of government. The elected officers listed as such in KRS 12.020 are the Governor, Lieutenant Governor, Railroad Commissioner, and all of the officers named in Const. Sec. 91 except for the now-defunct Register of Lands.

In the massive reorganization statute enacted in 1974[5] the following sentence was added to KRS 12.020:

> "Every authority, board, bureau, interstate compact, commission, committee, conference, council, office or any other form of organization shall be included in or attached to the Department or program cabinet in which they are included or to which they are attached by statute or executive order."

3. Ch. 106, Art. I, Acts of 1962.

4. Ch. 74, Art. I, Sec. 6, Acts of 1974. Interestingly enough, here again, in KRS 11.060 (Governor's general cabinet), appear the terms "constitutional and statutory administrative departments." And so the statute remains today.

5. Ch. 74, Acts of 1974.

In 1980[6] the foregoing sentence was amended by addition of the following proviso, and this new language in KRS 12.020 is the basis on which the Court of Appeals held that the Governor cannot, under KRS 12.025, transfer functions, funds, personnel, etc., from Agriculture to another executive agency or department:

> "Provided, however, that where the attached department or administrative body is headed by a constitutionally elected officer such attachment shall be solely for the purpose of dissemination of information and coordination of activities and shall not include any authority over the functions, personnel, funds, equipment, facilities, or records of such department or administrative body."

It is argued by counsel for the Governor that Agriculture is in fact a statutory department, hence it is subject to the reorganizational authority specified by KRS 12.025. In that Const. Sec. 91 does no more than to create certain offices, by naming the officers to be elected to them, and does not expressly establish any department or organizational structure to be headed by those officers, we agree that the departments now headed by them are not truly "constitutional" departments.[7] In that sense, of course, all of the executive departments are statutory, but that does not answer the question in this case. The question is not whether Agriculture and the other departments categorized in the 1960 version of KRS 12.020 as "constitutional," but today as "headed by elected officers," are actually statutory departments, but whether that is what the General Assembly intended or intends for them to be considered; and whatever may be the correct definitions of "constitutional" and "statutory," it is an unavoidable conclusion that the word "statutory" as it appears in KRS 12.025 reflects the same legislative intent today as it did in 1960—that is, its purpose was to exclude those departments characterized in the 1960 act as "constitutional administrative departments" but renamed in the 1962 act and succeeding legislation as "departments headed by elected officers."

This distinction between purely statutory departments and agencies and those that have been established by the General Assembly under the supervision of the elective officers named in Const. Sec. 91 may very well suggest a lingering doubt on the part of the legislative body that it has the power to subject any of the constitutional officers, or the organizations it has placed under their supervision, to the superior authority of the Governor. Considering that the broad reorganization powers conferred upon the Governor under KRS 12.025 were enacted at a time or times when the General Assembly was generally regarded as more subservient to the wishes (or, in less polite terminology, the domination) of the Governor than it is today, we suspect that to be the case. On the other hand, it may be that the legislative body simply did not want the executive to have that much rein. In either event, the result is the same.

In discussing the extent of the Governor's power that is not dependent upon legislation it is necessary that we consider also the interrelation of constitutional powers

6. Ch. 295, Sec. 2, Acts of 1980.

7. Agriculture is established by KRS Ch. 246.

with respect both to the Governor, the General Assembly, and the officers named in Const. Sec. 91. This is so because (1) to the extent that the Governor has any implied or inherent powers in addition to those the Constitution expressly gives him, it seems clear that such unexpressed executive power is subservient to the overriding authority of the legislature, and (2) the officers named in Const. Sec. 91 have only such powers and duties as are assigned to them by legislative enactment or by executive order expressly authorized by statute.

The office of Governor is established by Const. Sec. 69, which provides: "The supreme executive power of the Commonwealth shall be vested in a Chief Magistrate, who shall be styled the 'Governor of the Commonwealth of Kentucky.'" The powers and duties expressly conferred upon him are, in substance:

1. He is the commander-in-chief of the military forces and affairs of the state. Const. Sec. 75.

2. He may fill vacancies in office except as otherwise provided by the Constitution. Const. Sec. 76.

3. He may remit fines and forfeitures and grant reprieves and pardons. Const. Sec. 77.

4. He may require written information from the officers of the Executive Department upon any subject relating to the duties of their respective offices. Const. Sec. 78.

5. He shall from time to time report the state of the Commonwealth to the General Assembly and recommend to it such measures as he deems expedient. Const. Sec. 79.

6. He may call the General Assembly into special session and may adjourn the General Assembly for a period not exceeding four months if its two Houses cannot agree upon an adjournment. Const. Sec. 80.

7. "He shall take care that the laws be faithfully executed." Const. Sec. 81.

The offices of Treasurer, Auditor of Public Accounts, Register of the Land Office, Commissioner of Agriculture, Labor and Statistics, Secretary of State, Attorney-General, and Superintendent of Public Instruction were established by Const. Sec. 91, which provides:

> "The duties of all these officers shall be such as may be prescribed by law, and the Secretary of State shall keep a fair register of and attest to all the official acts of the Governor, and shall, when required, lay the same and all papers … relative thereto before either House of the General Assembly."

The only other reference to powers, duties or functions of these officers is in Const. Sec. 93, as follows:

> "The duties and responsibilities of these officers shall be prescribed by law," etc.

It is interesting to observe that in dealing with the General Assembly and with the office of Governor the Constitution speaks in terms of "powers," but with regard to the Sec. 91 officers mentions only "duties" and "responsibilities."[8] Except for the Attorney-General, who has been held to possess by implication the powers inhering in the office as it existed at common law,[9] and except for the clerical duties placed on the Secretary of State by Const. Sec. 91 itself, the other officers named in Const. Sec. 91 have only such powers and responsibilities as are prescribed by statute. *Cf. Johnson v. Commonwealth*, 291 Ky. 829, 165 S.W.2d 820, 826 (1942); *Ferguson v. Chandler*, 266 Ky. 694, 99 S.W.2d 732, 736 (1936); *Ex Parte Auditor of Public Accounts*, Ky., 609 S.W.2d 682, 687 (1980). Whatever, therefore, the Commissioner of Agriculture may have in the way of functions, authority, funds or personnel can be removed to another agency at the will of the General Assembly.[10]

If the officers named in Const. Sec. 91 came into the world so naked of authority, one might well ask why they were not made appointive or, indeed, not mentioned at all. The answer, we think, though it may not have been articulated by the framers of the Constitution in their debates, is that these independent executive offices provide convenient receptacles for the diffusion of executive power. As the Governor is the "supreme executive power," it is not possible for the General Assembly to create another executive officer or officers who will not be subject to that supremacy, but it definitely has the prerogative of withholding executive powers from him by assigning them to these constitutional officers who are not amenable to his supervision and control.

Whether the Governor, in the exercise of his authority as the "supreme executive power of the Commonwealth" (Const. Sec. 69), can do the same thing in the absence of legislative authority is another matter. Though we are satisfied that the transfer of an existing, legislatively-created function from one executive agency or department to another is essentially an executive action, like the reassignment of troops or battle missions from one military command to another, and is not an exercise of legislative power by the chief executive, we do not believe that the chief executive has the power to do it without legislative sanction unless it is necessary in order for him to carry out a law or laws that the legislature has created without prescribing in sufficient detail how they are to be executed.

The powers given to the Governor by our Constitution closely resemble, for obvious historical reasons, those given to the President by the United States Constitution.[11]

8. *Cf.* Secs. 29, 39, 49, 52, 54, 69, 76, 77, 91 and 93.

9. Subject, however, to the overriding authority of the General Assembly.

10. The statement in *Covington Bridge Commission of the City of Covington*, 257 Ky. 813, 79 S.W.2d 216, 220 (1935) that the legislature "may not divest an office created by or named in the Constitution of its original and inherent functions" apparently assumed the presence of powers that do not exist. For the same reason, the admonition in *Johnson v. Commonwealth* that the legislature "cannot abolish the office ... indirectly by depriving the incumbent of all his substantial prerogatives or by practically preventing him from discharging the substantial things appertaining to the office" overlooks the fact that the legislature is under no compulsion to give such prerogatives or "substantial things" to the office in the first place.

11. That Article 2, Sec. 1, says "The executive power shall be vested in a president," whereas Sec. 69 of our Constitution vests the "supreme executive power" in the Governor probably reflects the fact that under our Constitution there are other constitutional officers in whom executive powers may be

See Article 2, Secs. 2 and 3, Constitution of the United States. What has been said by respectable authority on the question of whether and to what extent the President has powers beyond those specifically set forth in the Constitution has instructive value in the proper interpretation of our own Constitution with respect to the powers of the chief executive.

Ever since the time of Washington and Hamilton there has been an unresolved difference of opinion whether the President has any power beyond that which is specified in Article 2 of the Constitution. Schwartz, Constitutional Law, 176–184 (2d ed. 1979). "A century and a half of partisan debate and scholarly speculation yields no net result but only supplies more or less apt quotations from respected sources on each side of any question. They largely cancel each other. And court decisions are indecisive because of the judicial practice of dealing with the largest questions in the most narrow way."[12]

It is axiomatic that under our Constitution the General Assembly has all powers not denied to it or vested elsewhere by the Constitution. We do not doubt that if the General Assembly should pass a law that requires implementation, and appropriate funds for that purpose but omit specifying the manner in which it is to be carried out, the chief executive would be required to carry it out and have the right to choose the means by which to do it. That would not be so because of any implied or inherent power, however, but because it would be within the scope of authority and duty expressly conferred upon him by Const. Sec. 81.

In any event, whether the problem be largely semantic or otherwise, if it be postulated that the chief executive does possess implied or "inherent" powers, they would be subordinate to statute, as the inherent prerogatives of the Attorney-General were so held in *Johnson v. Commonwealth*, 291 Ky. 829, 165 S.W.2d 820 (1942). This means, we think, that when the General Assembly has placed a function, power or duty in one place there is no authority in the Governor to move it elsewhere unless the General Assembly gives him that authority. And in this case, as we have indicated already, KRS 12.025 does not give him that authority.

It is interesting as well as instructive to consider the constitutional contrast between the executive and judicial branches in their respective relationships to the legislative branch. Whereas the judicial branch must be and is largely independent of intrusion by the legislative branch, the executive branch exists principally to do its bidding. The real power of the executive branch springs directly from the long periods between legislative sessions, during which interims the legislature customarily has left broad discretionary powers to the chief executive. It is ironic, but a historic fact of life, that

---

vested by the legislative body. Sec. 69 makes it clear that these officers are inferior to the Governor and that no other executive office can be created which will not also be inferior to that of the Governor.

12. Jackson, J., concurring opinion in the Steel Seizure case, *Youngstown Co. v. Sawyer*, 343 U.S. 579 at p. 634, 72 S.Ct. 863 at p. 869, 96 L.Ed.2d 1153 (1952). No student of the subject should miss reading this as well as the extremely perceptive opinions filed by other members of the United States Supreme Court in this celebrated case.

in the past most chief executives have used this very power, given to them by the legislature, to influence the actions of individual legislators and thus exercise control over the legislative process itself. To put it mildly, it was not meant to be that way. It has been that way, however, for the simple reason that the legislature, either by choice or necessity, has conferred upon the executive branch more authority than was consistent with its own independence. Practically speaking, except for those conferred upon him specifically by the Constitution, his powers, like those of the executive officers created by Const. Sec. 91, are only what the General Assembly chooses to give him.

To round out this analysis of the respective powers and duties of the Governor, the General Assembly, and the officers established by Const. Sec. 91, we need to consider the relationship between the Governor and the Const. Sec. 91 officers. That the Const. Sec. 91 officers are to be elected by the people suggests that, whatever their duties, they are not answerable to the supervision of anyone else.[13] This inference finds support in that provision of our Constitution (Sec. 78) which empowers the Governor to require information in writing from the officers of the executive branch upon any subject relating to the duties of their offices. Had the framers of the Constitution intended the Governor to have any further authority over these officers, Sec. 78 would have been unnecessary and, indeed, an anomaly.

That the General Assembly itself recognizes this degree of independence on the part of the Const. Sec. 91 officers appears to be the basis for the 1980 amendment[14] which adds to KRS 12.020 the proviso to the effect that when a department headed by a constitutionally elected officer is attached to another department or program cabinet it is only for informational and liaison purposes. That approach consists also with our view that the powers of transfer given to the Governor by KRS 12.025 do not affect the departments listed in KRS 12.020 as being headed by elected officers.

Before proceeding to one last point, we shall follow some advice from the late Dr. Karl Llewellyn and "tidy up" this opinion by summarizing the conclusions we have reached, as follows:

1. Agriculture is not a "statutory administrative department" within the meaning of KRS 12.025. Hence that statute is no authority for the transfer of any functions, funds, property or personnel from Agriculture by Executive Order 81-55.

2. The Governor has no constitutional or statutory power to transfer powers, duties, personnel, funds or property that have been assigned by the General Assembly to a department headed by an officer named in Const. Sec. 91.

---

13. We recognize that this may not be true with respect to all elective officers. The clerk of a court, for example, necessarily is subject to the supervision of the court. The office of county tax assessor, though elective, may be abolished by the General Assembly. Const. Sec. 104. The power to abolish, we think, includes the power to subject the office to the supervision of the Department of Revenue. *Cf. Allphin v. Butler*, Ky., 619 S.W.2d 483, 484 (1981).

14. Ch. 295, Sec. 2, Acts of 1980.

3. The officers named in Const. Sec. 91 have no powers or duties not assigned to them by statute, except for the clerical duties placed on the Secretary of State by the Constitution and the common law prerogatives of the Attorney-General that have not been removed or diminished by statute.

4. Whatever powers, duties, personnel, funds or property are given to a Sec. 91 officer by statute may be removed by statute and may be transferred by executive order if, but only if, such a transfer is authorized by statute.

5. Except for the informational duty specified in Const. Sec. 78, the officers named in Const. Sec. 91 are not and cannot be placed under the control or supervision of the Governor.

The last major point that needs to be addressed in this case is raised by the Governor's contention that some of the functions transferred out of Agriculture by Executive Order 81-55 had been placed there initially by previous executive orders of the same type, hence if 81-55 is invalid so were the similar orders placing these functions with Agriculture in the first place. What this argument overlooks, however, is that these orders have been specifically ratified by the General Assembly, No. 76-664 by Ch. 155, Sec. 166, Acts of 1978, No. 79-1040 by Ch. 295, Sec. 93, Acts of 1980, and No. 79-834 by statutory amendment of KRS 246.030 in Ch. 295, Sec. 84, Acts of 1980.

KRS 12.025(1) requires that when the Governor has ordered any reorganizational adjustments under this statute he "shall recommend legislation to the next following session of the general assembly to confirm reorganizations effected under the provisions of this section."

Our conclusion is that these confirming statutes render moot the question of whether the orders were valid in the first instance, just as a similar statute, if enacted in the 1982 session of the General Assembly, would serve to ratify and validate Executive Order 81-55.

It is argued further that the proviso added to KRS 12.020 in 1980 necessarily connotes that a department headed by a constitutional officer can be attached to a cabinet by executive order. We do not agree. KRS 12.020 expressly refers to attachment by statute or by executive order. Agriculture has been statutorily attached to the Cabinet for Development since 1974. See Ch. 74, Art. VII, Sec. 4, Acts of 1974, which is reflected by the current listing of Agriculture in KRS 12.020 under both "Departments headed by elected officers" and "Cabinet departments headed by appointed officers."[15]

The judgment of the Franklin Circuit Court is affirmed.

Palmore, C.J., and Aker, Clayton, Stephens, Stephenson and Sternberg, JJ., sitting.

All concur.

---

15. This statute confirmed Executive Orders 72-1167 and 73-485, which had created the Development Cabinet and designated the chief officer of Agriculture as a member.

Notes and Questions

1. Does the "supreme executive power" vested in the Governor imply that the office has some inherent power? Or does the office of Governor have no inherent powers, aside from the seven powers *Brown v. Barkley* says are expressly conferred upon him or her by the Constitution itself or those conferred by statute?
2. If the General Assembly may take power away from the Governor and grant it to one of the other Constitutional Officers at its discretion, in what way is the Governor's executive power "supreme"?
3. Is there room for a "unitary executive" in Kentucky's constitutional order?

Fletcher v. Commonwealth, Office of the Attorney General ex rel. Stumbo

Supreme Court of Kentucky (2005)
163 S.W.3d 852

Opinion of the Court by Justice Cooper.

The issue presented by this appeal is whether the Governor of the Commonwealth of Kentucky may order money drawn from the state treasury to fund the operations of the executive department of government if the General Assembly fails to appropriate funds for that purpose. The issue arose when the General Assembly adjourned *sine die* on April 14, 2004, without adopting an executive department budget bill for the 2004–06 biennium.

Unlike some state constitutions, *e.g.*, Cal. Const. art. IV, §12(c), the Constitution of Kentucky does not require a state "budget." It does, however, require that any such budget be balanced. That constitutional requirement derives from Sections 49, 50, and 171, which together authorize and require the General Assembly to raise revenues sufficient to pay the debts and expenses of government. *See generally Dalton v. State Prop. & Bldg. Comm'n*, 304 S.W.2d 342, 347–51 (Ky. 1957); *State Budget Comm'n v. Lebus*, 244 Ky. 700, 51 S.W.2d 965 (1932). The first statutory provisions describing a budgeting process were enacted in 1918 and compiled at KS §1992, *et seq.* 1918 Ky. Acts, ch. 12. The present version, KRS Chapter 48, is a comprehensive scheme that describes the process for preparing and enacting a "budget bill" by which the revenues of the Commonwealth are appropriated for the operation of the three departments of government during the ensuing biennium. KRS 48.300(1). All provisions of a budget bill expire at the conclusion of the second fiscal year of the biennium. KRS 48.310(1). If a budget bill is enacted at an extraordinary session, Ky. Const. §80, its provisions expire on "July 1 of the year in which the next even-numbered year regular session takes place." KRS 48.310(1).

Prior to 2001, the General Assembly met in regular legislative session only for sixty legislative days in even-numbered years. Ky. Const. §§36 (unamended), 42 (unamended). Necessarily, the budget bill for the next biennium was enacted during those sessions. Sections 36 and 42 were amended in 2000 to add an additional regular session of thirty legislative days in odd-numbered years. *Id.* (as amended). However, because all existing budget bills expire on July 1 of even-numbered years, the General Assembly has continued to address budget issues during the sixty-day even-numbered-year sessions. On three occasions within a ten-year period, the General Assembly adjourned its sixty-day regular session without enacting an executive department budget bill for the next biennium. On the first occasion, 1994, Governor Jones reconvened the General Assembly into an extraordinary session, during which the members resolved their differences and enacted a budget bill for the 1994–96 biennium.

At the 2002 regular session, the Republican-controlled Senate and the Democratic-controlled House of Representatives deadlocked on whether to appropriate funds for the election campaign fund created by the Public Financing Campaign Act, KRS 121A.020, and adjourned *sine die* on April 15, 2002, without enacting a budget bill for either the executive or judicial departments for the 2002–04 biennium. On April 17, Governor Patton reconvened the General Assembly into an extraordinary session for the sole purpose of negotiating a budget bill. Recalcitrance prevailed, however, and the General Assembly adjourned the special session on May 1, 2002, without enacting a budget bill for either of the other two departments of government.

On June 26, Governor Patton promulgated an "Executive Spending Plan" and authorized the Secretary of the Finance and Administration Cabinet to issue warrants against the treasury to implement that plan "and to assist the Court of Justice as may be necessary to implement lawful expenditures for its operation." Exec. Order No. 2002-727, para. 6, at 4.[1] In essence, the Governor adopted his own executive department budget and ordered appropriations from the state treasury to fund it. The Treasurer filed a petition in the Franklin Circuit Court for a declaration of rights, KRS 418.040, to determine the constitutionality of the Executive Spending Plan. *Ky. Dept. of the Treasury ex rel. Miller v. Ky. Fin. and Admin. Cabinet*, No. 02-CI-00855 (Franklin Circuit Court, filed June 26, 2002). However, the legislative deadlock dissolved when all potential gubernatorial candidates announced their intentions to reject public financing of the 2003 election. During its 2003 regular thirty-day session, the General Assembly enacted a budget bill for the 2002–04 biennium that did not fund the election campaign fund and ratified the Governor's expenditures under the Executive Spending Plan, *nunc pro tunc*. The Franklin Circuit Court dismissed the declaration of rights action as moot. *See generally* Paul E. Salamanca, *The Constitutionality of an Executive Spending Plan*, 92 Ky. L.J. 149, 152–58 (2003–04).

---

1. On June 27, 2002, the Chief Justice promulgated an order implementing a spending plan to cover the expenses of the judicial department from and after July 1, 2002, and issued warrants against the treasury to fund that plan. The constitutional efficacy of this order is not before us. *But see* Ky. Const. §120, discussed *infra*.

At the 2004 regular session of the General Assembly, the Republican-controlled Senate and the Democratic-controlled House of Representatives again deadlocked, this time on whether the 2004 executive department budget bill should include new taxation measures proposed by Republican Governor Fletcher. On March 9, 2004 (day 44 of the 60-day session), the House passed a budget bill that substantially amended the budget recommendation submitted by the Governor pursuant to KRS 48.100(1) and 48.110(6). On March 10, the House's version of the budget bill officially arrived at the Senate. On March 11, the Governor unveiled his proposed new taxation measures. On March 29 (day 58), the Senate passed its version of the budget bill, restoring many of the Governor's original recommendations and adding the Governor's tax proposals. Conference committee negotiations failed and, on April 14, 2004 (day 60), the General Assembly adjourned *sine die* without enacting an executive department budget bill for the 2004–06 biennium.

Unlike Governors Jones and Patton before him, Governor Fletcher did not reconvene the General Assembly into extraordinary session for the purpose of further budget negotiations. When asked during oral argument whether the Governor should have called an extraordinary session so that the General Assembly could attempt to resolve its differences, the attorney for the President of the Senate responded that an extraordinary session would have been "futile." Instead, the Governor announced that he, like Governor Patton before him, would formulate his own executive department spending plan, i.e., his own budget.

On May 27, 2004, the Attorney General filed this action in the Franklin Circuit Court against the Governor, the Treasurer, and the Secretary of the Finance and Administration Cabinet seeking to preclude the anticipated suspension of 153 existing statutes in the Governor's executive spending plan. Other parties, including the President of the Senate, the Speaker of the House of Representatives, individual legislators, representatives of state employees, and the Board of Trustees of the Kentucky Employees Retirement System, intervened to assert limitations on the Governor's power to suspend statutes or to spend unappropriated funds. Common Cause of Kentucky, an unincorporated self-styled "non-profit, non-partisan organization which advocates ethics and constitutional law in Kentucky," intervened on the relation of its chairman, a self-described "Kentucky taxpayer," seeking an injunction against the Governor to preclude him "from implementing any spending plan which would draw money from the State Treasury without appropriations made by the Legislature" in contravention of Section 230 of the Constitution of Kentucky.

On June 28, 2004, Governor Fletcher promulgated Executive Order 2004-650, adopting an executive department budget which he denominated a "Public Services Continuation Plan." The Order noted that:

> Through its adoption of House Bill 396, the General Assembly has made appropriations for the use of the Judicial Branch totaling $234,648,400, and in House Bill 397 for the Legislative Branch totaling $40,731,400, leaving $20,739,752,600 in previously estimated revenues identified for use by the Executive Branch, as

> modified by the Consensus Forecasting Group estimates of June 8, 2004, for the operation and function of the Executive Branch of government.

The Public Services Continuation Plan proposed to appropriate exactly $20,739,752,600 to the executive department for its operations during fiscal year 2004–05 and authorized the Secretary of the Finance and Administration Cabinet to issue warrants against the state treasury to obtain those appropriations as needed.

On October 4, 2004, the Governor issued a proclamation convening the General Assembly into extraordinary session, but only to consider "the compensation, health insurance benefits and retirement benefits of active and retired public employees, and making an appropriation therefor." The General Assembly resolved those issues but Section 80 of the Constitution precluded it from considering any other unresolved budget issues.

On December 15, 2004, the Franklin Circuit Court declared the Public Services Continuation Plan unconstitutional but authorized its continuation until June 30, 2005,[2] after which, "absent legislative action, no public funds shall be expended from the State Treasury . . . , with the exception of those funds demonstrated to be for limited and specific essential services previously approved in *Quertermous* [*Miller v. Quertermous*, 304 Ky. 733, 202 S.W.2d 389 (1947)]." On January 13, 2005, the Governor and the Secretary of the Finance and Administration Cabinet appealed. We granted transfer, CR 74.02, ordered an expedited briefing schedule, and set oral arguments for March 9, 2005. * * *

III. Separation of Powers.

Section 27 of the Constitution of Kentucky provides:

> The powers of the government of the Commonwealth of Kentucky shall be divided into three distinct departments, and each of them be confined to a separate body of magistracy, to wit: Those which are legislative, to one; those which are executive, to another; and those which are judicial, to another.

Section 28 provides:

> No person or collection of persons being of one of those departments, shall exercise any power properly belonging to either of the others, except in the instances hereinafter expressly directed or permitted.

Section 28's "unusually forceful command," *Ex Parte Auditor of Public Accounts*, 609 S.W.2d 682, 684 (Ky. 1980), has no counterpart in the United States Constitution. It is reputed to have been penned by Thomas Jefferson.[3]

---

2. No doubt, the circuit court permitted the temporary continuation of the executive spending plan for reasons of expediency. However, as will be noted later in this opinion, expediency does not justify the judicial sanction of an unconstitutional act. The better course would have been to stay the judgment pending appeal.

3. Judge Du Relle cited to no authority for the following account of Jefferson's role. Later authorities cite only to Judge Du Relle's dissents in *George* and *Purnell*, *infra*.

> When Mr. Jefferson returned from France, the federal constitution had been adopted; and, having been appointed secretary of state, he obtained permission to go to Monticello for some months. John Breckinridge and George Nicholas paid him a visit there, and informed him that Kentucky was about to frame a constitution for herself, and that Virginia was about to permit Kentucky to become a separate and independent state. He told them that there was danger in the federal constitution, because the clause defining the powers of the departments of government was not sufficiently guarded, and that the first thing to be provided for by the Kentucky constitution should be to confine the judiciary to its powers, and the legislative and executive to theirs. Mr. Jefferson drew the form of the provision, and gave it to Nicholas and Breckinridge; and it was taken by Nicholas to the convention which met at Danville, and there presented,—Breckinridge not being present at the convention. There was much discussion and dissent when the article was offered, but, when its author was made known, the respect of Kentucky for the great name of Jefferson carried it through, and it was at once adopted.

Comm'rs of Sinking Fund v. George, 104 Ky. 260, 47 S.W. 779, 785 (1898) (Du Relle, J., dissenting). *See also Rouse v. Johnson*, 234 Ky. 473, 28 S.W.2d 745, 752 (1930) (Willis, J., dissenting); *Sibert v. Garrett*, 197 Ky. 17, 246 S.W. 455, 457 (1922); *Purnell v. Mann*, 105 Ky. 87, 48 S.W. 407, 50 S.W. 264, 264 (1899) (Du Relle, J., dissenting); Sheryl G. Snyder & Robert M. Ireland, *The Separation of Governmental Powers Under the Constitution of Kentucky: A Legal and Historical Analysis of L.R.C. v. Brown*, 73 Ky. L.J. 165, 206 (1984–85).

Though the separation of powers is not as forcefully enunciated in the United States Constitution, the principal drafter of that document clearly intended that there would be a strict separation. "If there is a principle in our Constitution, indeed in any free Constitution more sacred than another, it is that which separates the legislative, executive and judicial powers." James Madison, Speech on the Floor of the House of Representatives, June 22, 1789, in 1 Annals of Congress 581. The United States Supreme Court has consistently allayed Jefferson's purported fears. *E.g., Plaut v. Spendthrift Farm, Inc.*, 514 U.S. 211, 239, 115 S.Ct. 1447, 1463, 131 L.Ed.2d 328 (1995) ("[T]he doctrine of separation of powers is a structural safeguard ... a prophylactic device, establishing high walls and clear distinctions because low walls and vague distinctions will not be judicially defensible in the heat of interbranch conflict."); *Immigration and Naturalization Serv. v. Chadha*, 462 U.S. 919, 951, 103 S.Ct. 2764, 2784, 77 L.Ed.2d 317 (1983) ("The Constitution sought to divide the delegated powers of the new federal government into three defined categories, legislative, executive and judicial, to assure, as nearly as possible, that each Branch of government would confine itself to its assigned responsibility. The hydraulic pressure inherent within each of the separate Branches to exceed the outer limits of its power, even to accomplish desirable objectives, must be resisted."); *Nixon v. Fitzgerald*, 457 U.S. 731, 760–761, 102 S.Ct. 2690, 2707, 73 L.Ed.2d 349 (1982) ("The essential purpose of the separation of powers is to allow for independent functioning of each coequal branch of government within its assigned sphere of responsibility, free from risk of control, interference, or intimidation by other branches."); *Youngstown Sheet & Tube Co. v. Sawyer*, 343 U.S. 579, 588–89, 72 S.Ct. 863, 867, 96 L.Ed. 1153 (1952) (only Congress has authority to authorize seizure of private property for public use; consequently, the President exceeded his executive powers by seizing steel mills to avert a nationwide shut-down by labor union strike).

Likewise, we and our predecessor court have interpreted Sections 27 and 28 to mandate a strict separation of powers. Rejecting an argument that the provisions should be liberally construed in the modern era to permit some legislative encroachment on executive powers, Snyder & Ireland, *supra*, at 206–07, we noted in *Legislative Research Com'n ex rel. Prather v. Brown* ["*L.R.C. v. Brown* "], 664 S.W.2d 907 (Ky. 1984), that:

> Our present constitution contains explicit provisions which, on the one hand, mandate separation among the three branches of government, and on the other hand, specifically prohibit incursion of one branch of government into the powers and functions of the others.
>
> ...
>
> [I]t has been our view, in interpreting Sections 27 and 28, that the separation of powers doctrine is fundamental to Kentucky's tri-partite system of government and must be "strictly construed."
>
> ...
>
> The precedents established by this court have been uniform in retaining the goals set out by the framers. The separation of powers doctrine is set in the concrete of history and legal precedent.

Id. at 912, 914. *See also Diemer v. Commonwealth*, 786 S.W.2d 861, 864 (Ky. 1990) ("Kentucky is a strict adherent to the separation of powers doctrine."); *Sibert*, 246 S.W. at 458 ("The purpose was to have each of them to so operate in their respective spheres as to create checks to the operations of the others and to prevent the formation by one department of an oligarchy through the absorption of powers belonging to the others.").

As anticipated by the "except" clause in Section 28, the Constitution does articulate some exceptions to the strict separation of powers. For example, the Governor's veto power, Ky. Const. §88, is a legislative function. *Arnett v. Meredith*, 275 Ky. 223, 121 S.W.2d 36, 37 (1938). The power of the Senate to try impeachments, Ky. Const. §67, is a judicial function. And the Chief Justice's administrative powers, Ky. Const. §110(5)(b), are executive functions. Further, while the General Assembly cannot delegate its power to make law, it can make a law that delegates the power to determine some fact or state of things upon which the law makes its own action depend—so long as the law establishes policies and standards governing the exercise of that delegation. *L.R.C. v. Brown*, 664 S.W.2d at 915; *Bloemer v. Turner*, 281 Ky. 832, 137 S.W.2d 387, 391 (1939). *See Bd. of Trustees v. Attorney Gen.*, 132 S.W.3d 770, 781–85 (Ky. 2003), for a detailed discussion of the "nondelegation doctrine." The authority of the General Assembly to make a limited delegation to the executive department has, on occasion, been extended to expenditures of excess or emergency funds. *Hopkins v. Ford*, 534 S.W.2d 792, 795–96 (Ky. 1976); *Commonwealth ex rel. Meredith v. Johnson*, 292 Ky. 288, 166 S.W.2d 409, 412 (1942). In fact, KRS 48.150 anticipates that the budget will appropriate funds to each department of government to meet unexpected contingencies or emergencies. However, in the absence of a proper delegation of authority by one department to another, or a specific exception articulated by the Constitution, itself, Section 28 has erected a "high wall," *Plaut*, 514 U.S. at 239, 115 S.Ct. at 1463, which precludes the exercise by one department of a power vested solely in either of the others.

> The doctrine of the separation of powers was adopted ... not to promote efficiency but to preclude the exercise of arbitrary power. The purpose was not to avoid friction, but, by means of the inevitable friction incident to the distribution of the governmental powers among three departments, to save the people from autocracy.

Myers v. United States, 272 U.S. 52, 293, 47 S.Ct. 21, 85, 71 L.Ed. 160 (1926) (Brandeis, J., dissenting).

IV. Appropriations Power.

> I simply believe that "Congress shall make no law" means Congress shall make no law.

Hugo Black, *A Constitutional Faith* 45 (1969), referring, of course, to the First Amendment of the United States Constitution. That simple textual interpretation mirrors the primary rule of constitutional construction: "There is no room for construction of a Constitution outside of the words themselves, if they are unambiguous...." *Button v. Drake*, 302 Ky. 517, 195 S.W.2d 66, 68 (1946).

> When the framers of the Constitution use language that is in no sense ambiguous, it is not a function of this court to construe that language as meaning something that the framers of the Constitution did not say, or to hold that while the Constitution says something definitely and unequivocally, no special importance is to be attached to its language.

Harrod v. Hatcher, 281 Ky. 712, 137 S.W.2d 405, 407 (1940). *See also Pardue v. Miller*, 306 Ky. 110, 206 S.W.2d 75, 78 (1947) ("The basic rule ... is to interpret a constitutional provision according to what was said and not what might have been said...."). That rule applies to the unambiguous words of Section 230 of the Constitution of Kentucky, viz:

> No money shall be drawn from the State Treasury, except in pursuance of appropriations made by law....

We have consistently held that this provision means exactly what it says. *Commonwealth ex rel. Armstrong v. Collins*, 709 S.W.2d 437, 441 (Ky. 1986) ("It is clear that the power of the dollar—the raising and expenditure of the money necessary to operate state government—is one which is within the authority of the legislative branch of government. The Constitution of the Commonwealth so states and we have so stated."); *L.R.C. v. Brown*, 664 S.W.2d at 925 ("The budget, which provides the revenue for the Commonwealth and which determines how that revenue shall be spent, is fundamentally a legislative matter."); *Ferguson v. Oates*, 314 S.W.2d 518, 521 (Ky. 1958) ("[T]he purpose of [Section 230] was to prevent the expenditure of the State's money without the consent of the Legislature.") (internal citation and quotation omitted).

* * *

> It is an axiom of American government that the legislature holds the purse strings. The federal and most state constitutions, for example, require that the budget originate in the House of Representatives, the arm of government most representative of the populace. This is traditionally viewed as the means by which the representatives of the people hold their most powerful check and balance upon the executive branch.

Snyder & Ireland, *supra*, at 225.

The Governor asserts that Section 230 applies only if the General Assembly has enacted a budget bill. As noted at the outset of this opinion, there is no provision in the Constitution of Kentucky requiring the General Assembly to enact a budget bill. Such is purely a statutory requirement. Since Section 230 preexisted that statutory scheme, the Framers could not have intended for the Section to apply only when the General Assembly enacts a budget bill. Accordingly, we hold that, in the absence of a specific appropriation, or a statutory, constitutional, or federal mandate as discussed below, the unambiguous language of Section 230 prohibits the withdrawal of funds from the state treasury.

V. Statutory, Constitutional and Federal Mandates.

KRS 41.110 provides:

> No public money shall be withdrawn from the Treasury for any purpose other than that for which its withdrawal is proposed, nor unless it has been appropriated by the General Assembly or is a part of a revolving fund, and has been allotted as provided in KRS 48.010 to 48.800, and then only on the warrant of the Finance and Administration Cabinet. The provisions of this section do not apply to withdrawals of funds from state depository banks for immediate redeposit in other state depository banks or to funds held in trust for the security of bond holders.

Where the General Assembly has mandated that specific expenditures be made on a continuing basis, or has authorized a bonded indebtedness which must be paid, such is, in fact, an appropriation. Otherwise, the General Assembly has not delegated its constitutional power of appropriation to the executive department. It has even forbidden the expenditure of surplus monies in the general and road funds. KRS 48.700(8); KRS 48.710(8).

There are statutes that mandate appropriations even in the absence of a budget bill. * * * In those instances, the General Assembly has already made the necessary appropriations. *White v. Davis*, 108 Cal.App.4th 197, 133 Cal.Rptr.2d 691, 699–700 (2002), *reversed in part on other grounds by White v. Davis*, 30 Cal.4th 528, 133 Cal.Rptr.2d 648, 68 P.3d 74 (2003).

However, the mere existence of a statute that can be implemented only if funded does not mandate an appropriation. "[T]he General Assembly is permitted through the reduction or elimination of an appropriation, to effectively eliminate the efficacy of existing statutes...." *Commonwealth ex rel. Armstrong v. Collins*, 709 S.W.2d at 441. In fact, the State Senate's 2002 refusal to fund the election campaign fund established in KRS 121A.020 was the immediate cause of the collapse of that session's budget negotiations. Obviously, the mere existence of KRS 121A.020 was not a mandate to fund it.

A similar crisis occurred in the federal government in 1980 when it became apparent that Congress would not pass a federal budget or a budget continuation plan before October 1, the beginning of the next fiscal year. Former United States Attorney General Benjamin R. Civiletti opined, when interpreting 31 U.S.C. §1341, the "Anti-Deficiency Act," which precludes any officer or employee of the government from making or authorizing the expenditure of unappropriated funds, that:

> [S]tatutory authority to incur obligations in advance of appropriations ... may not ordinarily be inferred, in the absence of appropriations, from the kind of broad, categorical authority, standing alone, that often appears, for example, in the organic statutes of governmental agencies.

5 Op. Off. Legal Counsel 1, 2 (1980) (quoted in 43 Op. Atty. Gen. 293, 297 (1981)). We agree. Only those statutes specifically mandating that payments or contributions be made can be interpreted as self-executing appropriations. A mandated appropriation cannot be inferred from the mere existence of an unfunded statute.

In contrast, "constitutional provisions are mandatory and never directory." *Arnett v. Sullivan*, 279 Ky. 720, 132 S.W.2d 76, 78 (1939). Certain provisions of our Constitution mandate payments for services rendered, viz:

> Section 42 ("The members of the General Assembly shall severally receive from the State Treasury compensation for their services....");
> Section 74 ("The Governor and Lieutenant Governor shall at stated times receive for the performance of the duties of their respective offices compensation to be fixed by law.");
>
> Section 86 ("The President of the Senate shall receive for his services the same compensation which shall, for the same period, be allowed to the Speaker of the House of Representatives, and during the time he administers the government as Governor, he shall receive the same compensation which the Governor would have received had he been employed in the duties of his office.");
>
> Section 96 ("All officers mentioned in Section 95 shall be paid for their services by salary, and not otherwise.");
>
> Section 98 ("The compensation of the Commonwealth's Attorney shall be by salary and such percentage of fines and forfeitures as may be fixed by law, and such salary shall be uniform in so far as the same shall be paid out of the State Treasury, and not to exceed the sum of five hundred dollars per annum....");

Section 106 ("In counties or cities having a population of seventy-five thousand or more, the Clerks of the respective Courts thereof (except the Clerk of the City Court), the Marshals, the Sheriffs and the Jailers, shall be paid out of the State Treasury, by salary to be fixed by law, the salaries of said officers and of their deputies and necessary office expenses not to exceed seventy-five per centum of the fees collected by said officers, respectively, and paid into the Treasury.");

Section 120 ("All justices and judges shall be paid adequate compensation which shall be fixed by the General Assembly. All compensation and necessary expenses of the Court of Justice shall be paid out of the State Treasury. The compensation of a justice or judge shall not be reduced during his term."); and

Section 235 ("The salaries of public officers shall not be changed during the terms for which they were elected....").

There are other constitutional mandates that can only be implemented by the expenditure of funds from the treasury. These are:

Section 40 ("Each House of the General Assembly shall keep and publish daily a journal of its proceedings....");

Section 53 ("The General Assembly shall provide by law for monthly investigations into the accounts of the Treasurer and Auditor of Public Accounts....");

Section 147 ("The General Assembly shall provide by law for the registration of all persons entitled to vote in cities and towns having a population of five thousand or more....");

Section 151 ("The General Assembly shall provide suitable means for depriving of office any person who, to procure his nomination or election, has ... been guilty of any unlawful use of money, or other thing of value, or has been guilty of fraud, intimidation, bribery, or any other corrupt practice....");

Section 183 ("The General Assembly shall, by appropriate legislation, provide for an efficient system of common schools throughout the State.");

Section 220 ("The General Assembly shall provide for maintaining an organized militia....");

Section 221 ("The organization, equipment and discipline of the militia shall conform as nearly as practicable to the regulations for the government of the armies of the United States.");

Section 223 ("The General Assembly shall provide for the safekeeping of the public arms, military records, relics and banners of the Commonwealth of Kentucky.");

Section 244a ("The General Assembly shall prescribe such laws as may be necessary for the granting and paying of old persons an annuity or pension.");

Section 252 ("It shall be the duty of the General Assembly to provide by law ... for the establishment and maintenance of an institution or institutions for the

> detention, correction, instruction and reformation of all persons under the age of eighteen years, convicted of such felonies and such misdemeanors as may be designated by law. Said institution shall be known as the 'House of Reform.'"); and
>
> Section 254 ("The Commonwealth shall maintain control of the discipline, and provide for all supplies, and for the sanitary conditions of the convicts. . . .").

Unlike unfunded statutes, which are creatures of the General Assembly who may choose to fund them or not, these constitutional mandates must be implemented. "The Kentucky Constitution is, in matters of state law, the supreme law of this Commonwealth to which all acts of the legislature, the judiciary and any government agent are subordinate." *Kuprion v. Fitzgerald*, 888 S.W.2d 679, 681 (Ky. 1994). The General Assembly cannot prevent the implementation of constitutional mandates by simply withholding its appropriations power. In the absence of appropriations by the General Assembly, the Treasurer must fund these constitutional mandates at no more than existing levels until the General Assembly provides otherwise.

* * *

However, absent a statutory, constitutional, or valid federal mandate, Section 230 precludes the withdrawal of funds from the state treasury except pursuant to a specific appropriation by the General Assembly.

* * *

VII. Governor's Constitutional Powers.

The Governor asserts that when the General Assembly fails to exercise its appropriations power to fund the operations of the executive department, he (the Governor) possesses the inherent power to order the appropriations necessary to prevent the imminent collapse of governmental services. He cites Sections 69 and 81 of the Constitution as the source of that power.

Section 69 provides: "The supreme executive power of the Commonwealth shall be vested in a Chief Magistrate, who shall be styled the 'Governor of the Commonwealth of Kentucky.'" That provision only vests the Governor with executive powers, just as Section 29 vests the General Assembly with legislative powers and Section 109 vests the Court of Justice with judicial powers. Manifestly, Section 69 does not vest the Governor with legislative powers, which are specifically reserved by Sections 28 and 29 solely to the legislative department. Section 81 provides: "He shall take care that the laws be faithfully executed." The Governor asserts that he cannot faithfully execute the laws enacted by the General Assembly without the funds necessary to do so. However, as noted earlier in this opinion, the mere existence of a law does not mean that it must be implemented if doing so requires the expenditure of unappropriated funds. *Commonwealth ex rel. Armstrong v. Collins*, 709 S.W.2d at 441.

The same Constitutional powers and duties described in Sections 69 and 81 are granted to the President of the United States by Article II, Sections 1 and 3 of the United States Constitution. As Justice Black wrote in the lead opinion in the *Youngstown* case:

> In the framework of our Constitution, the President's power to see that the laws are faithfully executed refutes the idea that he is to be a lawmaker. The Constitution limits his functions in the lawmaking process to the recommending of laws he thinks wise and the vetoing of laws he thinks bad. And the Constitution is neither silent nor equivocal about who shall make laws which the President is to execute. The first section of the first article says that "All legislative Powers herein granted shall be vested in a Congress of the United States."

Youngstown, 343 U.S. at 587–88, 72 S.Ct. at 867. *See also Myers v. United States*, 272 U.S. at 295, 47 S.Ct. at 85 (Holmes, J., dissenting) ("The duty of the President to see that the laws be executed is a duty that does not go beyond the laws or require him to achieve more than Congress sees fit to leave within his power."). The Governor has no constitutional authority to exercise legislative powers even when the General Assembly has failed to do so.

VIII. Alleged Emergency Powers.

The Governor also cites the opinions of our predecessor court in *Miller v. Quertermous*, 304 Ky. 733, 202 S.W.2d 389 (1947), and *Rhea v. Newman*, 153 Ky. 604, 156 S.W. 154 (1913), for the proposition that he may expend unappropriated funds to provide essential services during emergencies. We easily distinguish *Rhea* because the funds in that case had, in fact, been appropriated by the General Assembly. There simply was insufficient money in the treasury to pay the warrant when it was submitted. A statute, 1910 Ky. Acts, ch. 72, §3, provided that, in such a circumstance, the Treasurer should endorse the warrant as bearing five percent interest from the date of its presentation. The issue was whether, considering the extent of other state indebtedness, that endorsement would violate Section 49 of the Constitution, which authorizes the General Assembly to contract debts to meet casual deficits but requires that such debts not exceed a maximum of $500,000. *Rhea*, 156 S.W. at 155. The case had nothing to do with Section 230.

Quertermous did have to do with Section 230, but has been regarded as an anomaly, at best. There, the General Assembly made what it believed to be sufficient appropriations for the maintenance of state prisons, correctional institutions for children, and mental institutions. Unfortunately, with the elimination of the price control system in effect during World War II, the cost of living rose unexpectedly and the appropriated funds proved insufficient to pay the necessary, ordinary and recurring expenses of those institutions. The Commissioner of Welfare sued the State Treasurer and the Commissioner of Finance for funds necessary to continue the operation of the institutions. Noting that the appropriated funds would expire on May 15, 1947 (the opinion was rendered on May 16, 1947), and that there was a substantial surplus in the treasury, *Quertermous*, 202 S.W.2d at 390, the court ordered the Treasurer to pay the funds necessary to operate the institutions. *Id.* at 392.

> We are justified in assuming that the Legislature was fully cognizant of its obligation to make such appropriation for the care of these institutions and

> inmates. The intention so to care for them is evidenced by the appropriation made. The fact that an unanticipated rising cost of living later shows the estimate to be erroneous, in no way operates to destroy that proper intention, nor could it in any way be justifiable grounds for criticism. A great untouched surplus of public funds, collected for public purposes, is on hand. An unexpected and unanticipated emergency requiring more than emotional gestures confronts us.

Id. at 391–92. Thus, the court inferred an intent on the part of the General Assembly to provide the additional funds for the operation of the institutions from the fact that it had already appropriated what it believed to be sufficient funds for their operation, and from the fact that a surplus of funds was on hand in the treasury sufficient to pay for their continued operation. The opinion can be partially justified by the constitutional mandates of Sections 252 and 254 and partially explained by expediency (though there is no explanation why the Commissioner of Welfare did not ask the Governor to call an extraordinary session of the General Assembly to obtain a proper legislative appropriation of the necessary funds, a process that would have required less time than it took to litigate the issue through the trial and appellate courts).

Nine years later, the Attorney General sued the Commissioner of Finance for funds needed to operate his office in excess of those appropriated by the General Assembly, citing *Quertermous*. *Ferguson v. Oates*, 314 S.W.2d at 519–20. Recognizing the fundamental impropriety of a court order directing payment of unappropriated funds to provide to the executive department additional funds that the legislature had deemed unnecessary, the court in *Ferguson* expressly limited *Quertermous* to its facts. "[T]he court's action was 'brought about by an inexorable necessity coupled with an inescapable responsibility,' and the case should not be considered as precedent except under comparable conditions." *Ferguson*, 314 S.W.2d at 520. In fact, despite the *Quertermous* court's obvious good intentions when faced with seemingly insoluble facts, the decision was *prima facie* an unconstitutional encroachment by the executive and judicial departments on the powers of the legislative department. Good intentions do not justify unconstitutional acts. *Dishman v. Coleman*, 244 Ky. 239, 50 S.W.2d 504, 508 (1932) (State Treasurer held personally liable for expenditure of unappropriated funds "even though the officer thought he was doing what was best for the commonwealth, and had the concurrence of the Attorney General at the time."[4]).

We reject the proposition that a Governor can unilaterally declare an emergency and spend unappropriated funds to resolve it. As Justice Jackson said in his famous concurring opinion in the *Youngstown* case:

> The Solicitor General lastly grounds support of the seizure upon nebulous, inherent powers never expressly granted but said to have accrued to the office

4. *Dishman* noted that the General Assembly had the power to appropriate funds to pay the judgment against the Treasurer, *id.* at 508, a solution similar to the General Assembly's ultimate ratifications of the executive spending plans promulgated by Governors Patton and Fletcher, respectively.

> from the customs and claims of preceding administrations. The plea is for a resulting power to deal with a crisis or an emergency according to the necessities of the case, the unarticulated assumption being that necessity knows no law.
>
> ...
>
> The appeal, however, that we declare the existence of inherent powers ex necessitate to meet an emergency asks us to do what many think would be wise, although it is something the forefathers omitted. They knew what emergencies were, knew the pressures they engender for authoritative action, knew, too, how they afford a ready pretext for usurpation. We may also suspect that they suspected that emergency powers would tend to kindle emergencies.
>
> ...
>
> [E]mergency powers are consistent with free government only when their control is lodged elsewhere than in the Executive who exercises them.
>
> ...
>
> With all its defects, delays and inconveniences, men have discovered no technique for long preserving free government except that the Executive be under the law, and that the law be made by parliamentary deliberations.

Youngstown, 343 U.S. at 646, 649–50, 652, 655, 72 S.Ct. at 875–76, 877, 878, 880 (Jackson, J., concurring).

The Governor possesses no "emergency" or "inherent" powers to appropriate money from the state treasury that the General Assembly, for whatever reason, has not appropriated. *Cf. Brown v. Barkley*, 628 S.W.2d 616, 623 (Ky. 1982) ("Practically speaking, except for those conferred upon him specifically by the Constitution, [the Governor's] powers, like those of the executive officers created by Const. Sec. 91, are only what the General Assembly chooses to give him."). Nor does the Court of Justice have the power to confer such authority. *Miller v. Quertermous* is overruled to the extent it holds or can be interpreted otherwise.

IX. Suspension of Statutes.

As earlier noted, the Attorney General initiated this action to prevent the Governor's anticipated suspension of 153 statutes. Among the statutes that the parties to this appeal claim were actually suspended in the Public Services Continuation Plan were KRS 18A.010(2) (number of state employees limited to 33,000); KRS 18A.355(1) (automatic 5% annual pay increases for all state employees); KRS 42.4585 (allocation of Local Government Economic Assistance Funds); KRS 61.565(2) (delegation of authority to Kentucky Retirement Systems Board of Trustees to determine employer contribution rates necessary to adequately fund the Kentucky Employees Retirement System).

Section 15 of our Constitution provides: "No power to suspend laws shall be exercised unless by the General Assembly or its authority." Since this provision is a part of the Bill of Rights, the Governor could not suspend statutes even if he possessed "emergency" or "inherent" powers under Sections 69 and 81. Ky. Const. §26 ("To guard

against transgression of the high powers which we have delegated, We Declare that everything in this Bill of Rights is excepted out of the general powers of government....").
The suspension of statutes by a Governor is also antithetical to the constitutional duty to "take care that the laws be faithfully executed." Ky. Const. §81. *A fortiori*, the suspension of any statutes by the Governor's Public Services Continuation Plan was unconstitutional and invalid *ab initio*.

However, neither the parties representing state employees[5] nor the Board of Trustees of the Kentucky Employees Retirement System presently seek remedial relief from the suspensions of KRS 18A.355(1) and KRS 61.565(2), admitting that those issues were resolved during the 2004 extraordinary session of the General Assembly.

X. CONCLUSION.

> Some truths are so basic that, like the air around us, they are easily overlooked. Much of the Constitution is concerned with setting forth the form of our government, and the courts have traditionally invalidated measures deviating from that form. The result may appear "formalistic" in a given case to partisans of the measure at issue, because such measures are typically the product of the era's perceived necessity. But the Constitution protects us from our own best intentions: It divides power ... among branches of government precisely so that we may resist the temptation to concentrate power in one location as an expedient solution to the crisis of the day.

New York v. United States, 505 U.S. at 187, 112 S.Ct. at 2434.

There is no constitutional mandate that the General Assembly enact a budget bill, and there is no statute providing for an alternative when it fails to do so. Despite much hand-wringing and doomsday forecasting by some of the parties to this action at the prospect that we would hold that Section 230 means what it unambiguously says, it is not our prerogative to amend the Constitution or enact statutes. When the General Assembly declines to exercise its appropriations power, that power does not flow over the "high wall" erected by Section 28 to another department of government.

> The separation of the powers of government did not make each branch completely autonomous. It left each in some measure, dependent on the others.... Obviously, the President cannot secure full execution of the laws, if Congress denies to him adequate means of doing so. Full execution may be defeated because Congress ... declines to make the indispensable appropriation.... If ... adequate means are denied to the President, the fault will lie with Congress. The President performs his full constitutional duty, if, with the means and instruments provided by Congress and within the limitations prescribed by it, he uses his best endeavors to secure the faithful execution of the laws enacted.

5. Those parties were permitted to withdraw from this litigation prior to oral argument.

Myers, 272 U.S. at 291–92, 47 S.Ct. at 84 (Brandeis, J., dissenting). If the legislative department fails to appropriate funds deemed sufficient to operate the executive department at a desired level of services, the executive department must serve the citizenry as best it can with what it is given. If the citizenry deems those services insufficient, it will exercise its own constitutional power—the ballot. Ky. Const. §§31, 70.

Accordingly, we affirm that portion of the Franklin Circuit Court's judgment that declares the Public Services Continuation Plan unconstitutional insofar as it requires expenditure from the treasury of unappropriated funds other than pursuant to statutory, constitutional, and federal mandates; and reverse that portion of the Franklin Circuit Court's judgment that authorizes unappropriated expenditures for other "limited and specific services previously approved in *Quertermous*."

Graves, Johnstone, and Wintersheimer, JJ., concur.

Lambert, C.J., concurs in part and dissents in part by separate opinion.

Keller, J., concurs in part and dissents in part by separate opinion, with Scott, J., joining that opinion.

* * *

Notes and Questions

1. Several years before the Court decided *Fletcher*, a law review article assessed whether the Governor had the constitutional power to order an executive spending plan upon the failure of the General Assembly to pass a budget bill. *See* Paul E. Salamanca, *The Constitutionality of an Executive Spending Plan*, 92 Ky. L.J. 149 (2003). The article anticipated the Court's discussion of Section 230, analyzed the exception to Section 230 represented by *Quertermous* (overruled in *Fletcher*), and discussed the self-executing nature of several constitutional provisions and the Governor's inherent powers regarding spending from the treasury. *Id.* at 163–80. The Court cited the article and agreed with its conclusions as to these issues, and so the article provides helpful background and analysis for understanding the *Fletcher* case. The article also discusses several matters not directly raised in *Fletcher*, such as opinions from federal courts and the courts of other states, standing, and justiciability.
2. The *Fletcher* Court observed that certain constitutional provisions require the expenditure of state funds, even absent an appropriation by the General Assembly under Section 230. Does the text of those constitutional provisions support that construction?
3. The Supreme Court held that the Governor could not unilaterally declare an emergency, and then use that emergency as a basis for spending unappropriated funds or suspending statutes. How might this principle apply in the context of other constitutional provisions?

Beshear v. Acree

Supreme Court of Kentucky (2020)
615 S.W.3d 780

Opinion of the Court by Justice Hughes.

Introduction

On March 6, 2020, as the COVID-19 global pandemic reached Kentucky, Governor Andy Beshear declared a state of emergency pursuant to Executive Order 2020-215. In the ensuing days and weeks, he issued additional executive orders and emergency regulations to address the public health and safety issues created by this highly contagious disease. In late June, three Northern Kentucky business owners filed suit in the Boone Circuit Court challenging various orders affecting the reopening of their respective businesses as well as the Governor's authority generally in emergencies. Attorney General Daniel Cameron intervened as a plaintiff, and the parties proceeded to obtain a restraining order that prohibited enforcement of certain of the emergency orders.

In response to that action with its imminent injunction hearing and at least one similar case elsewhere in the Commonwealth, this Court entered an order on July 17, 2020, staying all injunctive orders directed at the Governor's COVID-19 response until those orders were properly before this Court, with full record, pursuant to the direction of the Court. Having received briefs and heard oral argument, this Court addresses five primary questions. We begin by summarizing our answers to those questions.

I. Did the Governor Properly Declare a State of Emergency and Validly Invoke the Emergency Powers Granted to Him in Kentucky Revised Statute (KRS) Chapter 39A?

Yes. KRS 39A.100 authorizes the Governor to declare a state of emergency in the event of the occurrence of any of the situations or events contemplated by KRS 39A.010, which includes biological and etiological hazards such as the COVID-19 pandemic. Although the governing statutes do not require resort to the definition of "emergency" in KRS 39A.020(12), if that definition were applicable it would not inhibit the Governor's authority. The local emergency management agencies referenced in KRS 39A.020(12) "shall, for all purposes, be under the direction ... of the Governor when [he] deems that action necessary." KRS 39B.010(5). Thus, the Governor was authorized to act without deference to any determination by a local authority or emergency management agency. On March 30, 2020, the General Assembly acknowledged the state of emergency declared by the Governor and "the efforts of the Executive Branch to address ... the outbreak of COVID-19 virus, a public health emergency." 2020 S.B. 150.

II. Is KRS Chapter 39A With Its Provisions Regarding the Governor's Powers in the Event of an Emergency an Unconstitutional Delegation of Legislative Authority in Violation of the Separation of Powers Provisions of Sections 27 and 28 of the Kentucky Constitution?

No. The Kentucky Constitution does not directly address the exercise of authority in the event of an emergency except as to those events requiring the military, the Governor being the "commander-in-chief of the army and navy of this Commonwealth and of the militia thereof." Ky. Const. §75. However, our Constitution, which provides for a part-time legislature incapable of convening itself, tilts toward emergency powers in the executive branch. Section 80 provides the Governor "**may**, on extraordinary occasions, convene the General Assembly" and may do so at a different place if Frankfort has "become dangerous from an enemy or from contagious diseases." (Emphasis added.) The language is permissive, not mandatory. So emergency powers appear to reside primarily in the Governor in the first instance, but to the extent they are perceived as legislative, KRS Chapter 39A is a lawful delegation of that power with sufficient standards and procedural safeguards to pass constitutional muster. Kentucky has recognized the lawful delegation of legislative powers for decades, and we decline to overrule that precedent, especially in circumstances that would leave the Commonwealth without day-to-day leadership in the face of a pandemic affecting all parts of the state. Notably, the General Assembly, in 2020 Senate Bill 150, recognized the Governor's use of the KRS Chapter 39A emergency powers, directed him to declare in writing when the COVID-19 emergency "has ceased" and further provided: "In the event no such declaration is made by the Governor on or before the first day of the next regular session ... the General Assembly may make the determination."

* * *

IV. Do the Challenged Orders or Regulations Violate Sections 1 or 2 of the Kentucky Constitution Because They Represent the Exercise of "Absolute and Arbitrary Power Over the Lives, Liberty and Property" of Kentuckians?

Only one subpart of one order, no longer in effect, was violative of Section 2. Property rights are enumerated in the Kentucky Constitution and are entitled to great respect, but they are not fundamental rights in the sense that all governmental impingements on them are subject to strict scrutiny, particularly in the area of public health. As with all branches of government, the Governor is most definitely subject to constitutional constraints even when acting to address a declared emergency. In this case, however, the challenged orders and regulations have not been established to be arbitrary, i.e., lacking a rational basis, except for one subpart of one order regarding social distancing at entertainment venues that initially made no exception for families or individuals living in the same household. Executive orders in emergency circumstances, especially where public health and safety is threatened, are entitled to considerable deference by the judiciary. During the course of this litigation, several of the orders and regulations at issue were superseded or changed, rendering some of the challenges moot.

* * *

Before turning to the facts of this case, we note that if Plaintiffs and the Attorney General were successful on any one of the first three issues of law—proper invocation of emergency powers, separation of powers among the three branches of government or applicability of KRS Chapter 13A—it would be the proverbial "knock-out punch" because it would undermine all of the Governor's COVID-19 response.[1] Because the law does not support them on those issues, their remaining argument that the Governor has acted arbitrarily in violation of Sections 1 and 2 of the Kentucky Constitution requires consideration of certain challenged individual executive orders and regulations. We do that below. * * * With those clarifications, we turn to what is before this Court.

Facts and Procedural History

COVID-19 is a respiratory disease caused by a virus that transmits easily from person-to-person and can result in serious illness or death. According to the Centers for Disease Control and Prevention (CDC), the virus is primarily spread through respiratory droplets from infected individuals coughing, sneezing, or talking while in close proximity (within six feet) to other people.[2] On January 31, 2020, the United States Department of Health and Human Services declared a national public health emergency, effective January 27, 2020, based on the rising number of confirmed COVID-19 cases in the United States.[3] The CDC identified the potential public health threat posed by COVID-19 nationally and world-wide as "high."[4]

On March 6, 2020, Governor Andy Beshear, under the authority vested in him pursuant to KRS Chapter 39A, declared a state of emergency in Kentucky. Executive Order 2020-215. Subsequently, all 120 counties in Kentucky declared a state of emergency.[5] After the statewide declaration, Kentucky's Cabinet for Health and Family Services (the Cabinet) began issuing orders designed to reduce and slow the spread of COVID-19 and thereby promote public health and safety. Those orders included directives such as prohibiting on-site consumption of food and drink at restaurants, closing businesses that encourage congregation, and prohibiting mass gatherings. As knowledge regarding the heretofore unknown novel coronavirus (COVID-19) grew, the Governor and the Cabinet modified their orders accordingly.[6]

On March 17, 2020, the Cabinet issued an order requiring all public-facing businesses that encourage public congregation to close, including gyms, entertainment

1. The actual declaration of emergency would only be undermined if the first or second argument was successful.

2. In addition, a person possibly can contract COVID-19 by touching a surface or object that has the virus on it and then touching their own nose, mouth or eyes. CDC, *How COVID-19 Spreads* * * *.

3. U.S. Department of Health and Human Services, *Determination that a Public Health Emergency Exists* (Jan. 31, 2020) * * *.

4. *See* Anne Schuchat, *Public Health Response to the Initiation and Spread of Pandemic COVID-19 in the United States, February 24–April 21, 2020* (May 8, 2020) * * *; CDC, *Global COVID-19* * * * (last updated Nov. 5, 2020). *See also* World Health Org., *Novel Coronavirus (2019-nCoV): Situation Report-13* (Feb. 2, 2020) * * *.

5. Kentucky Association of Counties, *COVID-19 County Emergency Declarations* (Mar. 23, 2020) * * *.

6. We note at the outset that some of the challenged orders in this case were issued by the Cabinet, and others were issued by the Governor. Therefore, references to the challenged orders will include orders issued by both the Governor and the Cabinet, unless otherwise noted.

and recreational facilities, and theaters.[7] These emergency measures worked to reduce COVID-19 cases by limiting gatherings where the virus could be transmitted. The Governor announced on April 21, 2020, the "Healthy at Work" initiative, a phased reopening plan based on criteria set by public health and industry experts to help Kentucky businesses reopen safely. On May 11, 2020, the Commonwealth began reopening its economy and the Cabinet issued minimum requirements that all public and private entities were required to follow, such as maintaining social distance between persons, requiring employees to wash hands regularly, and routinely cleaning and sanitizing commonly touched surfaces.

On May 22, 2020, restaurants were permitted to reopen for in-person dining, subject to 33% maximum capacity for indoor dining. Pertinent to the underlying case, the Cabinet issued an order on June 3, 2020, allowing automobile racing tracks to reopen with specific requirements, such as only allowing authorized employees and essential drivers on the premises, utilizing social distancing, implementing cleaning and disinfecting procedures, and requiring the use of personal protective equipment (PPE) in certain instances.[8]

Florence Speedway, Inc., an automobile racing track in Walton, Kentucky, filed a complaint in the Boone Circuit Court on June 16, 2020, against the Northern Kentucky Independent Health District (NKIHD), the organization charged with enforcing public health orders in Northern Kentucky. The complaint requested judicial review of a series of orders issued by the Governor and the Cabinet, alleging violations of multiple provisions of the Kentucky Constitution. Florence Speedway sought declaratory and injunctive relief deeming the orders unconstitutional and enjoining NKIHD from enforcing them.

Shortly thereafter, Florence Speedway filed an amended verified class action complaint that included Ridgeway Properties, LLC, d/b/a Beans Cafe & Bakery (Beans Cafe), located in Dry Ridge, Kentucky, and Little Links Learning, LLC (Little Links), a childcare center in Fort Wright, Kentucky, as Plaintiffs (collectively referred to as Plaintiffs).[9] In addition to NKIHD, the June 22, 2020 amended complaint included Dr. Lynne Sadler (District Director of the NKIHD), Governor Beshear, the Cabinet, Eric Friedlander (Secretary of the Cabinet), and Dr. Steven Stack (Commissioner of Public Health) as Defendants. Plaintiffs assert that the challenged orders (1) violate Section 1

7. Other public-facing businesses required to close included salons and concert venues. Certain essential businesses were permitted to stay open, such as businesses providing food, banks, post offices, hardware stores, and health care facilities. These businesses were subject to minimum requirements, such as maintaining social distance between persons and regularly cleaning commonly touched surfaces.

8. Personal protective equipment refers to equipment worn for protection from COVID-19 and includes equipment such as face coverings, eye protection, gowns, and gloves. * * * In its June 1, 2020 requirements for automobile racing tracks, the Cabinet required that employees, racing crews, and emergency medical crews use appropriate face coverings and other PPE (last updated July 16, 2020).

9. Theodore J. Roberts was included as a Plaintiff in the amended complaint. * * * It is unclear whether he was dismissed by the trial court, but in any event, he is not named as a party in this appeal.

of the Kentucky Constitution, which protects the rights of life, liberty, pursuit of safety and happiness, and acquiring and protecting property; (2) are arbitrary, in violation of Section 2 of the Kentucky Constitution; (3) violate the separation of powers provisions in Sections 27 and 28 of the Kentucky Constitution; (4) exceed the Governor's statutory authority to act pursuant to KRS 39A.100; and (5) are illegal because they violate the procedures outlined in KRS Chapter 13A for the adoption of regulations.

The amended complaint alleges specific issues with particular orders as they pertain to each business. Florence Speedway alleges that only allowing authorized employees and essential drivers and crews on the speedway premises is arbitrary and discriminatory because outdoor gatherings are safer than indoor gatherings, such as those in restaurants and bowling alleys, which are allowed at 33% capacity. With outdoor grandstands for spectators, Florence Speedway maintains it could operate at 33% capacity and use social distancing measures and contrasts its restrictions to the requirements for outdoor auctions which have no attendance limitations. Additionally, Florence Speedway challenges limiting its food service to "carry-out only" as arbitrary and discriminatory given that restaurants are permitted to operate at 33% capacity indoors. Finally, Florence Speedway claims that requiring PPE with no exceptions is arbitrary and prevents it from complying with the Americans with Disabilities Act.[10]

Beans Cafe raises issues with the requirement that employees must wear PPE (unless it would jeopardize their health) whenever they are near other employees or customers. The cafe alleges there are no requirements for employees working in the hot kitchen to wear masks, yet face masks are required for other employees.[11] According to allegations in the amended complaint, little scientific basis exists for requiring face masks because cloth face masks do not protect the wearer, rendering the requirement arbitrary. The amended complaint also alleges that it is arbitrary and capricious to limit restaurants to 33% indoor capacity and require six feet of distance between customers because these requirements make it difficult, if not impossible, for restaurants to make a profit.

Little Links's allegations pertain to childcare facility restrictions. Center-based childcare programs, like Little Links, were closed on March 20, 2020, but Limited Duration Centers (LDCs) were permitted to open. LDCs are childcare programs that provide

---

10. 42 U.S.C. §§12101–12213 (2009).

11. The requirements for restaurants state that "Restaurants should ensure employees wear face masks for any interactions with customers, co-workers, or while in common travel areas of the business (e.g., aisles, hallways, loading docks, breakrooms, bathrooms, entries and exits). Restaurant employees are not required to wear face masks while alone in personal offices, while more than six (6) feet from any other individual, or if doing so would pose a serious threat to their health or safety." It is unclear why Beans Cafe states that employees working in the kitchen do not have to wear face masks—whether, due to the hot temperatures, it would pose risks to their health to cover their faces, or whether they are spaced further than six feet apart. As written, the regulation makes no distinction between employees in the kitchen and those working elsewhere in a restaurant.

temporary emergency childcare for employees of health care entities, first responders, corrections officers and Department for Community Based Services's workers.[12]

All childcare programs were permitted to reopen on June 15, 2020, subject to several requirements, including the following: (1) all childcare programs must utilize a maximum group size of ten children per group; (2) children must remain in the same group of ten children all day without being combined with another classroom; (3) childcare programs may not provide access to visitors or students conducting classroom observations; (4) adults must wear a face mask while inside a childcare program unless doing so would represent a serious risk to their health or safety or they are more than six feet away from any other individual; and (5) children five years of age and younger should not wear masks due to increased risks of suffocation and strangulation. Childcare programs were authorized to recommend to the parents of children over five years of age that their child wear a mask.

Conversely, LDCs were not subject to the ten children group size limitation and were instead subject to a premises requirement of thirty square feet per child. Presumably, if an LDC was particularly large, it could exceed the ten children per group requirement that was imposed on center-based childcare facilities.

Little Links alleges that the ten children per group requirement constitutes a significant limitation on the operation of a childcare facility and forces many providers to operate their businesses at a loss. Additionally, requiring that children remain in the same group all day poses issues for end-of-the-day operations because childcare centers are not permitted to combine children from the same household in the same room, a customary practice in the childcare industry. Little Links alleges that the fact that these children will be in the same car and household together makes this requirement arbitrary. The prohibition on visitors, according to Little Links in its amendment to the motion for temporary injunction, arbitrarily prevents tours for prospective clients. Lastly, the adult mask requirement presents significant issues in a childcare setting because it is difficult for adults in masks to comfort upset children or assist children in the learning process because non-verbal communication is typically used.

Several of the challenged orders and regulations changed after the filing of the amended complaint, some following the conclusion of injunction proceedings in the circuit court. As of September 1, 2020, center-based childcare programs and LDCs became subject to the same requirements with the promulgation of 922 Kentucky Administrative Regulation (KAR) 2:405E. The regulation permits both center-based childcare programs and LDCs to maintain a maximum group size of fifteen children[13]

---

12. On May 8, 2020, Inspector General Adam Mather issued supplemental guidance for verification of employment for childcare within an LDC. Comparing it to the March 19 guidance, it expands those able to use the LDCs. It provides that "Employees of a health care entity, First Responders (Law Enforcement, EMS, Fire Departments), Corrections Officers, Military, Activated National Guard, Domestic Violence Shelter Workers, Essential Governmental Workers, large structured physical plants employing 1000 staff or more, and Grocery Workers will be required to submit verification of employment...." * * *

13. The group size applies to children age twenty-four months and older.

but maintains the requirement that children remain in the same group throughout the day without combining with another group. In addition, the regulation allows tours to potential clients after regular operating hours if no children are in the facility during the tour and the provider ensures all affected areas are cleaned after the conclusion of the tour. The regulation also provides that childcare providers shall not divide classroom space using a temporary wall in a manner that results in less than thirty-five (35) square feet of space per child. 922 KAR 2:405E.[14] Further, as of September 1, 2020, the stated purpose for LDCs is "to provide temporary emergency childcare for nontraditional instruction during traditional school hours to meet instructional needs."[15]

On June 22, 2020, the requirements for restaurants were amended, allowing an increase from 33% to 50% indoor dining capacity. On June 29, 2020, the public-facing businesses order was amended to allow venues and event spaces, including Florence Speedway, to reopen to the public. The amendment allows 50% of the maximum capacity permitted at a venue, assuming all individuals can maintain six feet of space between them with that level of occupancy. Additionally, if the venues operate any form of dining service, those services must comply with the requirements for restaurants and bars.

On June 24, 2020, Plaintiffs filed in the Boone Circuit Court case an emergency motion for a restraining order pursuant to Kentucky Rule of Civil Procedure (CR) 65.03 and a temporary injunction pursuant to CR 65.04. Alleging irreparable damage to their respective businesses, Plaintiffs requested the circuit court enjoin all further enforcement of the challenged orders.

Meanwhile, in a similar case challenging the constitutionality of the COVID-19 emergency orders, Ryan Quarles, the Commissioner of Agriculture, and Evans Orchard and Cider Mill, LLC (Evans Orchard), filed a complaint in Scott Circuit Court on June 29, 2020. The Attorney General intervened in that action. As the Commissioner of Agriculture, Quarles is charged with promoting agritourism in Kentucky and assisting with sustaining the industry's viability and growth, including the 548 agritourism businesses currently operating in the Commonwealth. Evans Orchard is a family-owned business that operates "agritourism attractions," like pick-your-own fruits, a retail market that sells food products, a cafe and bakery, and an event barn for weddings and other events. Evans Orchard alleged that it would be unable to operate profitably certain aspects of its business while the COVID-19 emergency orders remain in effect. Generally, the complaint alleges that the orders are unconstitutional for the same reasons raised in the Boone County litigation.

---

14. *See also* Cabinet for Health and Family Services—Office of the Inspector General, *Novel Coronavirus (COVID-19) Limited Duration Centers Frequently Asked Questions* (Sept. 1, 2020) * * * (indicating that each LDC location should account for thirty-five square feet per child).

15. Cabinet for Health and Family Services—Office of the Inspector General, *supra* * * *; *compare with* Cabinet for Health and Family Services—Office of the Inspector General, *Novel Coronavirus (COVID-19) Limited Duration Centers Frequently Asked Questions* (Mar. 2020) * * * (identifying LDC to be a center approved to provide temporary emergency childcare to health care employees, first responders, corrections officers and DCBS workers). *See* 922 KAR 2:405E.

On June 30, 2020, the Governor responded in opposition to the Plaintiffs' restraining order/injunction motion, emphasizing the public health measures he and other public officials have taken to slow the escalation of COVID-19. Citing the injunction standard, Governor Beshear argued that Plaintiffs failed to demonstrate a substantial question on the merits of the case because they have no absolute right to operate free from health and safety regulations; failed to establish immediate, irreparable injury; and did not have the equities in their favor given the potential harm to public health and safety if the injunction issued. Additionally, he argued the orders are a valid use of the Commonwealth's police power and the Governor's statutory authority to respond to emergencies. The Governor also noted that since the complaint was filed, the orders were amended to allow restaurants to increase their indoor seating capacity from 33% to 50% and that venues, like the Florence Speedway, could now host 50% of their normal maximum capacity.

Attorney General Daniel Cameron filed a motion to intervene in the Boone Circuit Court action and simultaneously filed an intervening complaint on June 30, 2020.[16] The Attorney General's intervening complaint mirrored several of Florence Speedway's, Beans Café's, and Little Links's arguments, and sought the following declarations: KRS Chapter 39A is an unconstitutional delegation of lawmaking authority; the Governor's orders are arbitrary and invalid because they exceed his statutory authority; the Governor's orders must be promulgated under the provisions of KRS Chapter 13A; and the Governor's orders violate various sections of the Kentucky Constitution. He also filed a motion for a restraining order on July 1, 2020. The motion asserted that the Governor did not comply with KRS Chapter 39A in declaring an emergency and raised several allegations regarding the legality of the chapter, specifically noting the lack of any time limitations on the Governor's executive orders and suspension of laws.

Additionally, the Attorney General argued that Governor Beshear lacked authority to declare a state of emergency pursuant to KRS 39A.100(1) because KRS 39A.020(12) defines "emergency" as "any incident or situation which poses a major threat to public safety so as to cause, or threaten to cause, loss of life, serious injury, significant damage to property, or major harm to public health or the environment *and which a local emergency response agency determines is beyond its capabilities*." (Emphasis added.) The Attorney General argued that Governor Beshear failed to establish that any local emergency response agency had determined that the situation caused by COVID-19 was "beyond its capabilities." According to the Attorney General, this clause of the statute demonstrates the public policy of the legislature that disaster and emergency response

16. According to the Attorney General, the motion to intervene was filed pursuant to CR 24.01 and CR 24.02 to protect the rights of Kentucky citizens. The Commonwealth has a statutory right to intervene under KRS 15.020, which states that the Attorney General shall "enter his appearance in all cases, hearings, and proceedings in and before all other courts, tribunals, or commissions in or out of the state ... in which the Commonwealth has an interest." Attorney General Cameron also asserted that the trial court should grant permissive intervention pursuant to CR 24.02 because the Commonwealth sought to assert claims against the same group of state officials as the original complaint for violating the constitutional rights of Kentucky citizens.

be addressed first as a local matter, so that those closest to the scene of an "emergency" are entrusted with coordinating the response.

The Boone Circuit Court conducted a hearing on the motion for a restraining order on July 1, 2020. No witnesses were called, but the Plaintiffs provided the trial court with copies of the Healthy At Work Requirements for Automobile Racing Tracks, effective June 1, 2020; the Healthy At Work Requirements for Venue and Event Spaces, effective June 29, 2020; and the Attorney General opinion OAG 19-021.[17] The next day, the trial court granted Plaintiffs' motion for an emergency restraining order and enjoined the Governor and the Cabinet from enforcing the June 1, 2020 requirements for automobile racing tracks, specifically holding that automobile racing tracks can operate at 50% capacity so long as all individuals could maintain six feet of distance between households. The trial court also enjoined the Governor and the Cabinet from enforcing the June 8, 2020 requirements that limit group sizes in childcare facilities to ten children and require children to remain in the same group all day. The restraining order specifically states that childcare programs shall be permitted to maintain a maximum group size of twenty-eight children.

In its July 2 order, the trial court determined that two of the Plaintiffs were entitled to injunctive relief. The trial court was satisfied that the impending loss of business, including the goodwill built up through years of serving customers, constituted irreparable harm and that the equities favored Florence Speedway and Little Links. Additionally, the trial court determined that Florence Speedway and Little Links sufficiently established that a substantial question exists on the merits of their claim because "it is unclear what criteria is being used to establish which businesses may survive versus those that must shutter." The trial court specifically identified the fact that attendance at movie theaters is allowed, and the Governor has permitted horse races, yet attending automobile races is not allowed. The trial court scheduled a hearing for July 16, 2020 to hear the Attorney General's motion for a restraining order and Plaintiffs' motion for a temporary injunction.

In response, on July 6, 2020, the Governor filed a petition for a writ of mandamus in the Court of Appeals, along with a motion for intermediate relief pursuant to CR 76.36(4). The petition sought a writ to (1) mandate that the Boone Circuit Court dissolve the July 2, 2020 restraining order; (2) prohibit the Boone Circuit Court from hearing the Attorney General's motion for a restraining order and the temporary injunction motion of the remaining Plaintiffs; and (3) grant intermediate relief staying enforcement of the July 2, 2020 restraining order during the pendency of the writ action. The Governor argued that a writ was necessary because the restraining order negated the statewide public health response to the spread of COVID-19. Further, not only was the restraining order contrary to law but it dangerously eliminated re-

17. The Attorney General's opinion discussed whether a county judge or county executive could invoke the emergency powers of KRS Chapters 39A–39F to fill the position of County Road Supervisor in the absence of action by the Fiscal Court. The Attorney General opined that this type of vacancy does not constitute an "emergency" as contemplated by KRS Chapters 39A–39F.

strictions put in place based on the guidance of public health officials. The Governor insisted that the trial court's decision would inevitably lead to more COVID-19 cases, illnesses, and deaths.

Meanwhile the Scott Circuit Court entered an order on July 9, 2020, enjoining the Governor, and others, from enforcing an executive order against Evans Orchard or any other agritourism business in Kentucky. In addition, the order also stated that prior to issuing any other executive order pursuant to KRS Chapter 39A, the Governor must "specifically state the emergency that requires the order, the location of the emergency, and the name of the local emergency management agency that has determined that the emergency is beyond its capabilities." The Governor also filed a petition for a writ of mandamus with respect to the Scott Circuit Court action, seeking relief similar to that sought in the Boone Circuit Court action.

In the interest of judicial economy, Court of Appeals Judge Glenn Acree issued a consolidated order addressing both the Boone County and Scott County cases and denied intermediate relief in both on July 13, 2020. Judge Acree determined that CR 65, which allows a party to move to dissolve a restraining order, provided the Governor with a swift and adequate remedy, rendering a writ inappropriate. Additionally, he determined that any injury resulting from the Boone Circuit Court order could be rectified at the scheduled July 16, 2020 hearing. The Court of Appeals' order reflects that a three-judge panel would promptly consider the merits of the Governor's petitions for a writ of mandamus.

That same day, Plaintiffs filed an amendment to their motion for a temporary injunction to address new and supplemental orders and regulations issued by the Governor and the Cabinet. Plaintiffs argued that the revised orders were arbitrary and capricious, specifically identifying the six-foot distance requirement and the group size requirements for childcare centers. Plaintiffs noted that LDCs were not subject to the Cabinet's orders. Little Links asserted that the prohibition against visitors poses a significant problem because it prevents Little Links from conducting tours for new families seeking childcare services. Florence Speedway and Beans Cafe also argued that the statewide mask regulation, 902 KAR 2:190E, which states that businesses in continuing violation of the regulation can be immediately shut down, is not authorized by law.

On July 14, 2020, the Governor petitioned for a writ of mandamus in this Court and sought intermediate relief pursuant to CR 76.36(4) and CR 81, specifically requesting that this Court dissolve the Boone Circuit Court's restraining order. The Governor argued that Judge Acree erred in concluding that the Governor has an adequate remedy by appeal because a delayed judicial holding vindicating the Governor's actions offers no protection to the Kentuckians who may become ill, spread the disease to others, or die due to COVID-19 in the interim. The petition also criticized the failure of both lower courts to consider the presumption of constitutionality of the orders since the orders only implicate economic rights, not fundamental rights, requiring only a rational basis review of these emergency measures.

Plaintiffs responded on July 16, 2020, arguing that a writ is not an appropriate remedy because the parties were currently in the midst of an evidentiary hearing on their requested injunctive relief in the Boone Circuit Court, evidence which would be beneficial for this Court to review. They argued the Governor had a remedy by appeal once the trial court issued a ruling based on the hearing. Plaintiffs claimed that Supreme Court intervention at that stage in the proceedings would result in businesses failing, including Florence Speedway and childcare centers across the state. Additionally, Plaintiffs reiterated their arguments regarding the unconstitutionality and illegality of the various orders issued by the Governor and the Cabinet. The Attorney General filed a similar response arguing that the Governor did not satisfy the requirements for issuance of a writ.

The Boone Circuit Court conducted a twelve-and-one-half hour hearing on July 16, 2020. The trial court heard testimony from Plaintiff Christine Fairfield, owner of Little Links; Jennifer Washburn, childcare facility owner; Bradley Stevenson, Executive Director of the Childcare Council of Kentucky, a nonprofit agency located in Lexington, Kentucky, which provides support services to childcare providers; Greg Lee, small business owner; Larry Roberts, Kentucky Secretary of Labor; Josh King, promoter for Plaintiff Florence Speedway; Richard Hayhoe, owner of Plaintiff Beans Cafe and Bakery; John Ellison, general manager and part owner of the Hofbrauhaus, a brew pub, in Newport, Kentucky, as well as board member and past chair of the Kentucky Restaurant Association; Dr. John Garren, University of Kentucky economics professor; Dr. Sarah Vanover, Director of Kentucky's Division of Childcare; and Dr. Steven Stack, Commissioner of the Kentucky Department for Public Health.

Following the close of evidence, Plaintiffs sought a temporary injunction to require the Governor to increase the group sizes in childcare programs to fifteen children, to allow the combination of groups and to allow tours after hours. They also sought to allow customers at restaurants to sit back-to-back with three and one-half feet of spacing and to remove the "shut down" penalty for a business's continuing violation of the mask mandate.

On July 17, 2020 and pursuant to Section 110 of the Kentucky Constitution, this Court entered an order staying all orders of injunctive relief issued by lower courts of the Commonwealth in COVID-19 litigation pending further action of the Court. Noting the need for a clear and consistent statewide public health policy, the Court recognized that the Kentucky legislature has expressly given the Governor broad executive powers in a public health emergency. The stay continues in effect until the full record of proceedings below, including any evidence and pleadings considered by the lower courts, is reviewed by this Court and a final order is issued. The order expressly authorized the Scott and Boone Circuit Courts to proceed with matters pending before them and issue all findings of fact and conclusions of law they deem appropriate, but no order, however characterized, would be effective.

On July 20, 2020, the Boone Circuit Court issued an order that would have granted the temporary injunction against enforcement of the Governor's orders but for this

Court's July 17 stay order. The trial court determined that Florence Speedway and Little Links will suffer irreparable harm in the form of permanent closure or loss of goodwill under the challenged orders and believed the café's claim depends on whether "the executive" has authority to impose the orders.[18] However, the trial court concluded that the Attorney General's claim of injury depended on whether "the people's" rights are being violated and concluded that they were. According to the Boone Circuit Court, because the government cannot take inalienable rights, such as the right to acquire and protect property and assemble, and certainly cannot punish a person for exercising a protected constitutional right, the Attorney General established irreparable harm.

In balancing the equities, the trial court noted that the Constitution and Bill of Rights are pitted against "the projections of certain medical professionals" which are "still developing and not all in agreement," citing several studies introduced by Plaintiffs that purportedly contradicted the challenged orders. The court further noted the Attorney General's argument that the government can have no legitimate interest in violating the constitutional rights of its citizens. The trial court observed "a decreasing trend in deaths attributed to COVID-19 since mid-April 2020," and that in the period of weeks ending on January 4 and June 27, 2020, 508 persons in Kentucky died from COVID-19, making up only 0.011% of Kentucky's deaths from all causes during that time period.[19] The trial court disagreed with the Governor's insistence that equity supports the challenged executive orders, finding that the orders were neither constitutionally enacted nor narrowly tailored. Therefore, in the Boone Circuit Court's view, "the scale of equity tips decidedly to the Constitution and the Bill of Rights."

As to the third requirement that Plaintiffs present a substantial question on the merits, the trial court found no evidence that any local emergency response agency determined that the pandemic emergency was beyond its capabilities pursuant to KRS 39A.020(12). In questioning the scope of the Governor's authority in emergency situations, the trial court concluded that the power is not broad enough "to extinguish the separation of powers, and the inherent rights of Kentuckians, including the right to attend church, to pursue a livelihood, to peaceably assemble, and to seek the health care that they may deem to be essential." Ultimately, the trial court held that the Governor's reliance on KRS Chapter 39A is ineffectual because the Plaintiffs are likely to succeed on the merits of their claims that the emergency powers granted by that chapter violate Sections 1, 2, 15, 27, 28 and 29 of the Kentucky Constitution.

Shortly after the trial court's ruling, on July 22, 2020, the requirements for venues and event spaces, including Florence Speedway, were again revised and now state that

18. The owner of Beans Cafe testified that although the amended orders allow 50% indoor dining capacity, the six-foot distancing requirement limits his available seating to 30%. The orders limit his ability to function because Beans Cafe closes at 2:00 p.m. He suggested that if the distance requirement was reduced to three feet, and capacity increased to two-thirds, he would at least be able to break even.

19. Slightly over four months later the death toll has more than tripled with the total COVID-19 deaths in Kentucky standing at 1,534 on November 5, 2020. The non-partisan Kaiser Family Foundation has concluded that through October 15, 2020, COVID-19 now ranks third in the leading causes of death in the United States, behind only heart disease and cancer. * * *

"[a]ll individuals in the venue or event space must be able to maintain six (6) feet of space from everyone who is not a member of their household." This amendment alleviated one of Florence Speedway's primary issues with the challenged orders.

On August 7, 2020, this Court determined that, with entry of the trial court's July 20 order, the claims in the Boone Circuit Court case were ripe for review. The order also noted that no further action had occurred in the Scott Circuit Court case since it entered the restraining order on July 9, 2020. Although the Court of Appeals consolidated the Boone and Scott Circuit Court cases for purposes of judicial economy, this Court found that the cases are no longer similarly situated since only the Boone Circuit Court matter proceeded to an injunction hearing. Accordingly, the Court deconsolidated the two actions.[20] Oral argument on September 17, 2020, focused on the legal issues Plaintiffs and the Attorney General raised in the Boone Circuit Court challenging the Governor's COVID-19 executive orders and regulations.

Analysis

Before turning to the specific issues presented, we briefly address the history of emergency powers legislation, which has existed in Kentucky since 1952.[21] On March 5, 1952, the General Assembly enacted Chapter 39 of the Kentucky Revised Statutes, relating to civil defense. 1952 Ky. Acts ch. 58. While the stated purpose of the Act included minimizing the destructiveness caused by "fire, flood or other causes," preparing the state for emergencies and protecting the public, much of the Act specifically related to Kentucky's defense mechanisms for an enemy attack. *Id.* at §1. The Act authorized the Governor to make necessary orders and regulations to carry out the provisions of the Act and to prepare a comprehensive plan for civil defense. *Id.* at §9. In 1974, the Act was amended to create a state agency, the Department of Disaster and Emergency Services, in lieu of a state civil defense agency in order to focus on emergency response generally rather than civil defense matters only. Legis. Rec. Final Exec. Action—April 23, 1974, Reg. Sess. at 23 (Ky. 1974). In addition, the amendment redefined and expanded the scope of emergencies covered under the Chapter.[22] 1974 Ky. Acts ch. 114,

20. The order states that the Scott Circuit Court may proceed with matters before it and issue all findings of fact and conclusions of law it finds appropriate. The Court stated that any orders issued in the case should, after entry, be immediately transmitted to the Clerk of the Supreme Court.

21. In 1949, the Soviet Union successfully tested its first nuclear weapon. U.S. Department of Homeland Security National Preparedness Task Force, *Civil Defense and Homeland Security: A Short History of National Preparedness Efforts* (Sept. 2006) * * *. Fearing an imminent attack, local officials began demanding that the federal government create a plan for handling crisis situations. *Id.* While President Truman agreed that the United States should outline its civil defense functions, he believed that civil defense responsibilities should fall primarily on state and local governments. *Id.* On January 12, 1951, the Federal Civil Defense Act of 1950 was signed into law, which was the first comprehensive legislation pertaining to disaster relief. 64 Stat. 1245 (1951). The Act states: "It is further declared to be the policy and intent of Congress that this responsibility for civil defense shall be vested primarily in the several States and their political subdivisions." *Id.*

22. For example, instead of focusing on civil defense, the 1974 version of the statute specifically added a definition for "disaster and emergency response," which includes "preparation for and the carrying out of all emergency functions, other than functions for which military forces are primarily

§1. Additionally, KRS 39.401, the definitions portion of the Chapter, added the definition of "disaster," which was defined as "any incident or situation declared as such by executive order of the Governor pursuant to the provisions of this Act." *Id.* at §2.

Recognizing that the Commonwealth is always subject to both contained and widespread threatening occurrences, in 1998 the General Assembly replaced KRS Chapter 39 with KRS Chapter 39A, which establishes a statewide comprehensive emergency management system.[23] In enacting the Chapter, the General Assembly expressly noted that "response to these occurrences is a fundamental responsibility of elected government in the Commonwealth." KRS 39A.010. KRS Chapter 39A further expanded the scope of disasters and emergencies which necessitate the Governor's response and, notably, added biological and etiological hazards to the list of threats to public safety. The General Assembly recognized that the purpose of Kentucky's emergency management response had evolved from responding only to security and defense needs to responding to all types of natural and man-made hazards in order to address the contemporary needs of Kentucky citizens. KRS 39A.030. * * * KRS Chapter 39A powers have been invoked by every Governor who has served since the law's adoption in 1998. The emergencies have ranged from widespread events such as destructive storms to more localized concerns such as bridges and water supply. Since 1996, an emergency of some magnitude has been declared on approximately 115 occasions, leaving aside the accompanying orders in the face of those occurrences which prohibit price gouging or allow pharmacists to address prescription needs. As we address the issues in this case, we are cognizant of the Commonwealth's history and experience with emergency response.

I. The Governor Properly Invoked His Emergency Powers Pursuant to KRS 39A.100 by Declaring a State of Emergency Based on the "Occurrence" of One of the "Situations or Events" Contemplated by KRS 39A.010.

KRS 39A.100(1) recognizes the Governor's authority to declare a state of emergency and exercise emergency powers. The first sentence states: "In the event of the occurrence or threatened or impending occurrence of any of the situations or events contemplated by KRS 39A.010, 39A.020 or 39A.030, the Governor may declare, in writing, that a state of emergency exists." KRS 39A.100(1). KRS 39A.010, relevant here, is a statement of "Legislative intent—Necessity" and, although lengthy, justifies extensive quotation:

> The General Assembly realizes the Commonwealth is subject at all times to disaster or emergency occurrences which can range from crises affecting limited areas to widespread catastrophic events, and that response to these occurrences is a fundamental responsibility of elected government in the Commonwealth. It is the intent of the General Assembly to establish and to support a

---

responsible." The amendment also included "natural or man caused disasters," explosions, and transportation emergencies, among others, in the list of disasters and emergencies.

23. *Omnibus Revision of Disaster and Emergency Services Laws: Hearing on H.B. 453*, H. State Gov't Comm., 1998 Reg. Leg. Sess. 23 (Feb. 24, 1998) (statement of Rep. Charles Geveden, Chairman).

> statewide comprehensive emergency management program for the Commonwealth, and through it an integrated emergency management system, in order to provide for adequate assessment and mitigation of, preparation for, response to, and recovery from, the threats to public safety and the harmful effects or destruction resulting from all major hazards, including but not limited to: flood, flash flood, tornado, blizzard, ice storm, snow storm, wind storm, hail storm, or other severe storms; drought, extremes of temperature, earthquake, landslides, or other natural hazards; fire, forest fire, or other conflagration; enemy attack, threats to public safety and health involving nuclear, chemical, or biological agents or weapons; sabotage, riot, civil disorder or acts of terrorism, and other domestic or national security emergencies; explosion, power failure or energy shortages, major utility system failure, dam failure, building collapse, other infrastructure failures; transportation-related emergencies on, over, or through the highways, railways, air, land, and waters in the Commonwealth; emergencies caused by spill or release of hazardous materials or substances; mass-casualty or mass-fatality emergencies; other technological, biological, etiological, radiological, environmental, industrial, or agricultural hazards; or other disaster or emergency occurrences; or catastrophe; or other causes; and the potential, threatened, or impending occurrence of any of these events; and in order to protect life and property of the people of the Commonwealth, and to protect public peace, health, safety, and welfare, and the environment; and in order to ensure the continuity and effectiveness of government in time of emergency, disaster, or catastrophe in the Commonwealth,....

* * *

Preliminarily, we note the obvious, namely that our General Assembly has identified dozens of potential disasters, catastrophes, hazards, threats and emergencies which the Commonwealth may encounter—and in many instances has encountered—and has wisely provided for the exercise of emergency powers in those extraordinary circumstances. Our first responsibility is to determine what the legislature intended by examining carefully the laws enacted. When construing statutes we examine the language used to determine legislative intent, *Stephenson v. Woodward*, 182 S.W.3d 162, 169–70 (Ky. 2005), and if that language is clear and unambiguous, we look no further. *Richardson v. Louisville/Jefferson Cty. Metro Gov't*, 260 S.W.3d 777, 779 (Ky. 2008).

Here KRS 39A.100, in clear and unambiguous language, authorizes the Governor to declare a state of emergency "in the event of the occurrence or threatened or impending occurrence" of any of the events or situations listed in KRS 39A.010, which expressly include "biological ... or etiological ... hazards."[24] In short, the COVID-19 pandemic is the occurrence of both a biological hazard, generally, and an etiological

---

24. "Etiological" is defined as "causing or contributing to the development of a disease or condition." * * * The COVID-19 pandemic is properly deemed both an etiological hazard as well as a biological hazard, the genesis of the pandemic being a novel coronavirus.

hazard, more specifically, justifying the Governor's March 6, 2020 declaration of emergency. Our statutory analysis in this case is essentially a straight line from the first sentence of KRS 39A.100 to the contents of KRS 39A.010. With the "plain language" of these controlling statutes clear, "our inquiry ends." *Univ. of Louisville v. Rothstein*, 532 S.W.3d 644, 648 (Ky. 2017).

* * *

In sum, the Governor properly declared a state of emergency pursuant to KRS 39A.100 because the COVID-19 pandemic constitutes the "occurrence" of a biological and etiological hazard as delineated in KRS 39A.010. * * *

II. During the Emergency, the Governor Has Exercised Executive Powers But to the Extent, If Any, KRS Chapter 39A Grants Him Legislative Authority, No Violation of the Separation of Powers Provisions of the Kentucky Constitution Has Occurred, the General Assembly Having Properly Delegated that Authority.

The Kentucky Constitution directs the separation of powers among the legislative, executive and judicial branches, §27, and prohibits any one branch from exercising "any power properly belonging to either of the others, except in the instances hereinafter expressly directed or permitted," §28. The Governor maintains that in responding to the COVID-19 pandemic he has exercised executive powers derived from the Kentucky Constitution and that KRS Chapter 39A simply "recognizes, defines, and constrains" executive authority to direct an emergency response. To the extent any of his actions could be characterized as legislative, he notes that he is exercising authority lawfully delegated to him by the General Assembly in KRS Chapter 39A.

The Attorney General seemingly acknowledges some role for the Governor in the event of an emergency such as COVID-19 but generally insists that the Governor's response these last months via executive orders and emergency regulations is an unconstitutional encroachment on legislative authority. In advocating the striking of those portions of KRS Chapter 39A that permit the Governor to exercise legislative authority, particularly KRS 39A.100(1)(j) and KRS 39A.180(2), the Attorney General asks us to "use this case to restore the original meaning of the Constitution's separation of powers."[25] To the extent we decline that invitation, he argues that the legislative authority in KRS Chapter 39A has been improperly delegated to the Governor. As we consider this argument, we do so guided by the presumption that the challenged statutes were enacted by the legislature in accordance with constitutional requirements. *Cornelison v. Commonwealth*, 52 S.W.3d 570, 572 (Ky. 2001). "A constitutional infringement must be 'clear, complete and unmistakable' in order to render the statute unconstitutional." *Caneyville Volunteer Fire Dep't v. Green's Motorcycle Salvage, Inc.*, 286 S.W.3d 790, 806 (Ky. 2009) (citing *Kentucky Indus. Util. Customers, Inc. v. Kentucky Utils. Co.*, 983

25. Citing, *inter alia*, Blackstone's *Commentaries on the Laws of England*, John Locke, and *The Federalist Papers*, the Attorney General emphasizes the historical and philosophical underpinnings of the separation of powers principle. While these sources provide context, this Court's North Star is our own Kentucky Constitution, the language used and the tripod structure erected for Kentucky government.

S.W.2d 493, 499 (Ky. 1998)). Ultimately, we conclude that the Governor is largely exercising emergency executive power but to the extent legislative authority is involved it has been validly delegated by the General Assembly consistent with decades of Kentucky precedent, which we will not overturn.

The current Kentucky Constitution, emanating primarily from the 1890 Constitutional Convention,[26] does not address emergency occurrences or events[27] directly except as to military matters which are firmly assigned to the Governor as the "commander-in-chief" of military affairs. §75. Generally, Section 69 vests the Governor with the "supreme executive power of the Commonwealth" and Section 81 mandates the Governor "take care that the laws be faithfully executed." Also instructive for the present case, Section 80 provides that the Governor "may, on extraordinary occasions, convene the General Assembly at the seat of government, or at a different place, if that should have become dangerous from an enemy or from contagious diseases.... When he shall convene the General Assembly it shall be by proclamation, stating the subjects to be considered, and no other shall be considered."[28]

Although "extraordinary occasions" has been construed customarily to allow special legislative sessions for reasons of immediate import relating to funding and other matters,[29] it plainly extends to those events or occurrences that qualify as a natural or man-made emergency, underscored by the "clue" regarding the convening of the legislature somewhere other than Frankfort in the event of an enemy or contagious diseases. Notably, Section 80 contains the permissive "may ... convene" as opposed to the mandatory "shall ... convene." Even in times when the Commonwealth is confronted with something extraordinary, to include enemies and contagious diseases, the decision to convene the General Assembly in a special session is solely the Governor's.

The implied tilt of the Kentucky Constitution toward executive powers in times of emergency is not surprising, given our government's tripartite structure with a legislature that is not in continuous session. At least two commentators have opined that "[t]he sixty-day limit on biennial sessions was the most significant restriction placed

26. *See generally Official Report of the Proceedings and Debates in the Convention Assembled at Frankfort, on the Eighth Day of September 1890, to Adopt, Amend or Change the Constitution of the State of Kentucky* (1890).

27. "Emergency" only appears twice in the Kentucky Constitution. Section 55 provides that an act containing an emergency clause becomes effective upon the Governor's approval, rather than ninety days after adjournment of the session in which passed. Section 158 allows cities, counties and taxing districts to exceed their debt limit to cope with emergencies. "Extraordinary occasion" appears in the Constitution only in Section 80, which provides the Governor "may, on extraordinary occasions, convene the General Assembly."

28. A similar provision has appeared in all four Kentucky Constitutions. *See* Ky. Const. of 1891, §83; Ky. Const. of 1850, art. 3, §13; Ky. Const. of 1799, art. 3, §14; Ky. Const. of 1792, art. 2, §3.

29. *See, e.g.*, 2007 First Extraordinary Session (alternative energy policies, appropriation of funds for capital projects and road construction, taxation of military pay, pretrial diversion for substance abusers, and public employee insurance plans); 1997 First Extraordinary Session (postsecondary education and budget modifications); 1983 Extraordinary Session (flat rate tax on individual income, standard deduction increase on personal income, and state-federal tax uniformity). * * *

on the General Assembly by the [1890] Constitutional Convention." Sheryl G. Snyder & Robert M. Ireland, *The Separation of Governmental Powers under the Kentucky Constitution: A Legal and Historical Analysis of L.R.C. v. Brown*, 73 Ky. L.J. 165, 181 (1984). Under the 1792 and 1799 Kentucky Constitutions the General Assembly met annually with no restrictions on length of session, but under the 1850 Constitution that changed to biannual sixty-day sessions with power in the body to extend the session on a two-thirds vote in each house, which they often did. *Id.* So, before the 1890 Convention "the legislature had the power to hold continuous sessions," but "the framers of the present Constitution took that power away ... and, for the first time in the history of Kentucky, put an absolute limit on the number of days the legislature could sit." *Id.*

When the present Constitution was adopted in 1891, the Kentucky General Assembly could only meet for sixty days every other year, Ky. Const. §42, and the only power to call the legislature into an extraordinary session resided in the Governor, Ky. Const. §80. Even now after the 2000 constitutional amendments with the legislature convening annually, sessions are limited to thirty legislative days in odd-numbered years, Ky. Const. §36, and sixty legislative days in even-numbered years, Ky. Const. §42.[30] 2000 Ky. Acts ch. 407, §1, ratified November 2000. Moreover, the odd-numbered year sessions cannot extend beyond March 30 and the even-numbered year sessions cannot extend beyond April 15. Ky. Const. §42. And the power to convene in extraordinary session remains solely with the Governor. Ky. Const. §80.

Having a citizen legislature that meets part-time as opposed to a full-time legislative body that meets year-round, as some states have,[31] generally leaves our General Assembly without the ability to legislate quickly in the event of emergency unless the emergency arises during a regular legislative session. The COVID-19 pandemic arose during the latter part of the 2020 legislative session, after the deadline for introducing a new bill, resulting in fourteen proposed COVID-19 related amendments to existing bills, five of which eventually passed. * * * Most notably, Senate Bill 150, "AN ACT relating to the state of emergency in response to COVID-19 and declaring an emergency," acknowledged the Governor's declared emergency and provided:

---

30. In 1966, 1969 and 1972 constitutional amendments were proposed that would have amended the Constitution "to enable [the General Assembly] once again to become 'a continuous body,' but each proposed amendment was defeated by the people." Snyder & Ireland, 73 Ky. L.J. at 182.

31. Two states that have recently dealt with challenges to the authority of their Governor/executive branch officials during the COVID-19 pandemic, Michigan and Wisconsin, are examples. Pursuant to Michigan Constitution Article IV, Section 13, the Michigan legislature begins its session in January each year and remains in session year-round, with both the House and the Senate meeting an average of eight days per month in 2020. The Michigan legislature was thus readily available to address concerns presented by the pandemic. * * * The Wisconsin legislature meets annually, Wis. Stat. Ann. §13.02, and was in session this year from January 14, 2020 until May 13, 2020. Article V, Section 4 of the Wisconsin Constitution authorizes the governor "to convene the legislature on extraordinary occasions." Additionally, Article IV, Section 11 provides that "[t]he legislature shall meet at the seat of government at such time as shall be provided by law," a provision which has been construed to allow the legislature to convene itself in an extraordinary session. * * * Thus, the Wisconsin legislature also had the means to address immediately any needed COVID-19 response.

> Notwithstanding any state law to the contrary, the Governor shall declare, in writing, the date upon which the state of emergency in response to COVID-19, declared on March 6, 2020, by Executive Order 2020-215, has ceased. In the event no such declaration is made by the Governor on or before the first day of the next regular session of the General Assembly, the General Assembly may make the determination.

2020 S.B. 150, §3. The legislature thereby signaled its awareness of the emergency and that the Governor was undertaking to exercise the emergency powers under KRS Chapter 39A. Thus, even within the confines of limited legislative sessions, the timing of this particular emergency was such that the legislature had a few weeks to pass bills related to the COVID-19 pandemic and did so.

The Attorney General invites the Court to adopt a strict separation of powers stance by identifying the Governor's issuance of any rules, regulations or orders in an emergency as exercises of non-delegable legislative power (excepting only the Governor's initial declaration of an emergency perhaps) and then holding those emergency responses constitutionally invalid under Sections 27 and 28. We decline. First, our reading of the Kentucky Constitution leaves us with no evidence that the powers at issue must be deemed legislative. The "extraordinary occasion," §80, of a global pandemic gives rise to an obvious emergency and, as noted, the Constitution impliedly tilts to authority in the full-time executive branch to act in such circumstances. Indeed, the Governor's "commander-in-chief" status under Section 75 reinforces the concept. Second, the structure of Kentucky government as discussed renders it impractical, if not impossible, for the legislature, in session for only a limited period each year, to have the primary role in steering the Commonwealth through an emergency.

On this latter point, the Attorney General argues that Section 80 allows the Governor to call an extraordinary session and thus "envisions that the Governor will not go it alone during a crisis, but instead will work hand in hand with the People's representatives." Again, the language of the section is permissive not mandatory, leaving it to the Governor—also duly elected by the People—whether the General Assembly should be convened. Moreover, the view advocated by the Attorney General creates an obvious dilemma: if the Governor is not empowered to adopt emergency measures because that constitutes "legislation," the Commonwealth is left with no means for an immediate, comprehensive response because either the General Assembly is not in session and cannot convene itself or even if in session it will have limited time to deal with the matter under constitutionally mandated constraints on the length of the session.[32] So, our examination of the Kentucky Constitution causes us to conclude the emergency powers the Governor has exercised are executive in nature, never raising a separation of powers issue in the first instance.

---

32. This is particularly true in the case of an emergency that goes from an acute stage to chronic, as is the case with a pandemic. Unlike an ice storm, wildfires or other natural events which sweep across all or part of the state, leaving destruction, but ending in a relatively short time, a biological/etiological hazard can hover for weeks and even months.

Fortunately, the need to definitively label the powers necessary to steer the Commonwealth through an emergency as either solely executive or solely legislative is largely obviated by KRS Chapter 39A, "Statewide Emergency Management Programs," which reflects a cooperative approach between the two branches. Plaintiffs and the Attorney General insist that the statute is in large part unconstitutional, however, because it grants the Governor legislative authority in violation of the nondelegation doctrine. We disagree.

We acknowledge, of course, that making laws for the Commonwealth is the prerogative of the legislature. Addressing a statute that authorizes the Governor to reorganize governmental bodies during the period between annual legislative sessions, we recently observed, "[t]he legislative power we understand to be the authority under the constitution to make the laws, and to alter and repeal them." *Beshear v. Bevin*, 575 S.W.3d 673, 682 (Ky. 2019) (quoting *Purnell v. Mann*, 105 Ky. 87, 50 S.W. 264, 266 (1899)). "The nondelegation doctrine recognizes that the Constitution vests the powers of government in three separate branches and, under the doctrine of separation of powers, each branch must exercise its own power rather than delegating it to another branch." *Id.* at 681 (citing *TECO Mech. Contractor, Inc. v. Commonwealth*, 366 S.W.3d 386, 397 (Ky. 2012)). Nevertheless, we found KRS 12.028, at issue in that case, to be a valid delegation of legislative power, recognizing that legislative power can be delegated "if the law delegating that authority provides 'safeguards, procedural and otherwise, which prevent an abuse of discretion'" thereby "'protecting against unnecessary and uncontrolled discretionary power.'" *Id.* at 683 (citations omitted). Our holding was but one in a series of Kentucky cases over several decades addressing the proper delegation of legislative power.[33]

The United States Supreme Court in *J.W. Hampton, Jr., & Co. v. United States*, 276 U.S. 394, 409, 48 S.Ct. 348, 72 L.Ed. 624 (1928) held that "[i]f Congress shall lay down by legislative act an *intelligible principle* to which the person or body authorized to [act] ... is directed to conform, such legislative action is not a forbidden delegation of legislative power." (Emphasis added.) Recognition of the delegation of legislative powers in Kentucky largely began with *Commonwealth v. Associated Industries of Kentucky*, 370 S.W.2d 584, 586 (Ky. 1963): "We find nothing in our State Constitution that declares explicitly: 'Legislative power may not be delegated.'" Noting the seminal role of John Locke in the articulation of democratic principles and his insistence that the power to make laws remain always in the hands of the legislature, the Court continued:

33. In the seminal case, *Legislative Research Commission v. Brown*, 664 S.W.2d 907, 930 (Ky. 1984), this Court addressed the Governor's statutorily granted power to reorganize state government between legislative sessions and concluded once the General Assembly "determines that that power is in the hands of the Governor, such interim action is purely an executive function." However, in *Beshear v. Bevin*, 575 S.W.3d at 681–83, addressing the same statute but perceiving a factual distinction, a majority of this Court concluded that the statute was a "grant of legislative authority to the executive" and that the Governor was exercising legislative power. *But see id.* at 685 (VanMeter, J., concurring in result only) ("In my view, [the Governor] is exercising his 'executive power' as authorized by the legislature and the Kentucky Constitution.").

> Locke believed that all human ideas, even the most complex and abstract, ultimately depended upon 'experience' to dedicate their truth.... So, if Locke was the fountainhead of the thesis that power could not be delegated, we feel sure that the experience of the last several centuries would have caused him to repudiate this idea. Experience has demonstrated some of the power must be invested in other bodies so that the government may function in a world that progressively is becoming more complex. There is nothing wrong with this so long as the delegating authority retains the right to revoke the power.

Id. at 588.[34] More recently, in *Board of Trustees of Judicial Form Retirement System v. Attorney General,* 132 S.W.3d 770, 781 (Ky. 2003), we recognized "given the realities of modern rule-making" a legislative body "has neither the time nor the expertise to do it all; it must have help." (Citing *Mistretta v. United States,* 488 U.S. 361, 372, 109 S.Ct. 647, 102 L.Ed.2d 714 (1989)). Examining the nondelegation doctrine generally and finding the "intelligible-principle rule" instructive if somewhat "toothless" in application by the federal courts, *id.* at 782–83, the Court reviewed several Kentucky cases wherein a delegation of legislative authority was deemed unlawful because the "powers were granted without 'legislative criteria,'" *Miller v. Covington Dev. Auth.*, 539 S.W.2d 1, 4–5 (Ky. 1976), or the delegation lacked "standards controlling the exercise of administrative discretion," *Legislative Research Comm'n v. Brown*, 664 S.W.2d 907, 915 (Ky. 1984). The "unintelligible" legislative pension statute at issue in *Judicial Form Retirement* failed for those reasons—lack of "an intelligible principle" and the absence of any "standards controlling the exercise of administrative discretion." 132 S.W.3d at 785.

In the case before us, the intelligible principle enunciated by the General Assembly and the legislative criteria pertinent to the use of emergency powers are set forth in KRS 39A.010 quoted above. In the event of any of those multitude of threats, the Governor (and the Division of Emergency Management and local emergency agencies) are authorized to take action "to protect life and property of the people of the Commonwealth, and to protect public peace, health, safety and welfare ... and in order to ensure the continuity and effectiveness of government in time of emergency, disaster or catastrophe...." In KRS 39A.100(1), the Governor is granted twelve enumerated "emergency powers" including in subsection (j) the following: "Except as prohibited by this section or other law, to perform and exercise other functions, powers, and duties deemed necessary to promote and secure the safety and protection of the civilian population." Given the wide variance of occurrences that can constitute an emergency,

34. Even before *Associated Industries of Kentucky,* Kentucky courts recognized the right of the legislature "to delegate to executive officers the power to determine some fact upon which the act of the Legislature made or intended to make its own action to depend." *Comm. ex rel. Meredith v. Johnson,* 292 Ky. 288, 166 S.W.2d 409, 415 (1942) (upholding statute that conferred upon the Governor the power to determine whether an emergency exists and then upon such determination make expenditures from a fund appropriated for that purpose). *See also Ashland Transfer Co. v. State Tax Comm.*, 247 Ky. 144, 56 S.W.2d 691, 697 (1932) (upholding statute allowing highway commission and county judges to reduce load and speed limits for trucks or prohibit them altogether when necessary to prevent damage to roads "in order to protect the public safety and convenience").

disaster or catastrophe, the criteria are necessarily broad and result-oriented, "protect life and property ... and ... public ... health," KRS 39A.010, allowing the Governor working with the executive branch and emergency management agencies to determine what is necessary for the specific crisis at hand. Floods, tornadoes and ice storms require different responses than threats from nuclear, chemical or biological agents or biological, etiological, or radiological hazards but the emergency powers are always limited by the legislative criteria, i.e., they must be exercised in the context of a declared state of emergency, KRS 39A.100(1); designed to protect life, property, health and safety and to secure the continuity and effectiveness of government, KRS 39A.010; and exercised "to promote and secure the safety and protection of the civilian population." KRS 39A.100(1)(j).

In addition, KRS Chapter 39A contains procedural safeguards to prevent abuses. All written orders and administrative regulations promulgated by the Governor "shall have the full force of law" upon the filing of a copy with the Legislative Research Commission. KRS 39A.180(2).[35] This provides the requisite public notice. The duration of the state of emergency, at least the one at issue in this case, is also limited by the aforementioned 2020 Senate Bill 150, Section 3, which requires the Governor to state when the emergency has ceased but, in any event, allows the General Assembly to make the determination itself if the Governor has not declared an end to the emergency "before the first day of the next regular session of the General Assembly." The enunciation of criteria for use of the emergency powers, the timely, public notice provided for all orders and regulations promulgated by the Governor and the time limit on the duration of the emergency and accompanying powers all combine to render KRS Chapter 39A constitutional to the extent legislative powers are delegated.

* * * [Our] Governor does not have emergency powers of indefinite duration, 2020 S.B. 150, §3, and our legislature is not continuously in session, ready to accept the hand-off of responsibility for providing the government's response to an emergency such as the current global pandemic. * * * Moreover, with the breadth of potential emergencies identified in KRS 39A.010, the standards of protection of life, property, peace, health, safety and welfare (along with the "necessary" qualifier in KRS 39A.100(j)) are sufficiently specific to guide discretion while appropriately flexible to address a myriad of

35. Plaintiffs and the Attorney General object that the Governor has suspended laws in violation of Section 15 of the Kentucky Constitution: "No power to suspend laws shall be exercised unless by the General Assembly or its authority." They insist that suspensions are by their nature temporary and if an emergency continues at length, as in the present COVID-19 pandemic, the prolonged suspension of laws is invalid. However, the Governor is not suspending laws. His declaration of a state of emergency triggers his authority under KRS 39A.090 to "make, amend, and rescind any executive orders as deemed necessary" to carry out his responsibilities. The legislature has in KRS 39A.180(2) provided that all "existing laws, ordinances, and administrative regulations" that are inconsistent with KRS Chapters 39A to 39F or with the orders or administrative regulations issued under the authority of those KRS chapters "shall be suspended during the period of time and to the extent that the conflict exists." Thus, the General Assembly, not the Governor, has suspended the laws. The statute has no time limitations on the length of the suspension and we will not read in one that prohibits "prolonged" emergencies.

real-world events. While the authority exercised by the Governor in accordance with KRS Chapter 39A is necessarily broad, the checks on that authority are * * * judicial challenges to the existence of an emergency or to the content of a particular order or regulation; legislative amendment or revocation of the emergency powers granted the Governor; and finally the "ultimate check" of citizens holding the Governor accountable at the ballot box. * * *

Whatever import the principle of properly delegated legislative authority has in the ordinary workings of government, its import increases dramatically in the event of a statewide emergency in our Commonwealth. A legislature that is not in continuous session and without constitutional authority to convene itself cannot realistically manage a crisis on a day-to-day basis by the adoption and amendment of laws.[36] In any event, we decline to abandon approximately sixty years of precedent that appropriately channels and limits the delegation of legislative power in Kentucky. Applying that delegation precedent, KRS Chapter 39A passes muster as a constitutional delegation of power to the extent any of the powers accorded to and exercised by the Governor are in fact legislative.

In sum, the powers exercised by a Kentucky Governor in an emergency are likely executive powers in the first instance given provisions of our Kentucky Constitution, but to the extent those powers are seen as impinging on the legislative domain, our General Assembly has wisely addressed the situation in KRS Chapter 39A. That vital and often-used statutory scheme validly delegates any legislative authority at issue to the Governor with safeguards and criteria sufficient to pass constitutional muster.

* * *

IV. The Specifically Challenged Orders and Regulations Are Not Arbitrary Under Sections 1 and 2 of the Kentucky Constitution with One Limited Exception No Longer Applicable.

Plaintiffs and the Attorney General both contend that the Governor's challenged orders and two emergency regulations violate Sections 1 and 2 of the Kentucky Constitution. Section 1 provides that "[a]ll men are, by nature, free and equal, and have certain inherent and inalienable rights" including "[t]he right of acquiring and protecting property." Section 2 states: "Absolute and arbitrary power over the lives, liberty and property of freemen exists nowhere in a republic, not even in the largest majority." "Section 2 is broad enough to embrace the traditional concepts of both due process of law and equal protection of the law." *Kentucky Milk Mktg. & Antimonopoly Comm'n v. Kroger Co.*, 691 S.W.2d 893, 899 (Ky. 1985) (citing *Pritchett v. Marshall*, 375 S.W.2d 253, 258 (Ky. 1963)). Unlike the previously discussed legal arguments which are comprehensive attacks on all of the executive orders and regulations, this constitutional

36. The *amicus curiae* President of the Senate appears not to have advocated the same strict separation of powers, nondelegation position that the Attorney General advances. The *amicus curiae* brief defines the sole issue presented by this case as: "Did the Governor exceed the scope of the authority that the General Assembly provided to him in KRS Chapter 39A by issuing his executive orders declaring an emergency as a result of the novel coronavirus pandemic (COVID-19)?" * * *

argument requires consideration of each order or regulation on an individual basis. The first consideration is the appropriate standard of review.

Strict scrutiny applies to a statute challenged on equal protection grounds if the classification used adversely impacts a fundamental right or liberty explicitly or implicitly protected by the Constitution or discriminates based upon a suspect class such as race, national origin, or alienage. *Steven Lee Enters. v. Varney*, 36 S.W.3d 391, 394 (Ky. 2000); *Clark v. Jeter*, 486 U.S. 456, 461, 108 S.Ct. 1910, 100 L.Ed.2d 465 (1988); *San Antonio Indep. Sch. Dist. v. Rodriguez*, 411 U.S. 1, 17, 93 S.Ct. 1278, 36 L.Ed.2d 16 (1973). To survive strict scrutiny, the government must prove that the challenged action furthers a compelling governmental interest and is narrowly tailored to that interest. *D.F. v. Codell*, 127 S.W.3d 571, 575 (Ky. 2003) (citing *Varney*, 36 S.W.3d at 394); *Adarand Constructors, Inc. v. Pena*, 515 U.S. 200, 227, 115 S.Ct. 2097, 132 L.Ed.2d 158 (1995). Intermediate scrutiny, seldomly used, is generally used for discrimination based on gender or illegitimacy. *Codell*, 127 S.W.3d at 575–76; *Varney*, 36 S.W.3d at 394. Under this standard, the government must prove its action is substantially related to a legitimate state interest. *Id.* (citing *City of Cleburne v. Cleburne Living Center, Inc.*, 473 U.S. 432, 441, 105 S.Ct. 3249, 87 L.Ed.2d 313 (1985)). Rational basis scrutiny is used for laws not subject to strict or intermediate scrutiny. Under this deferential standard, the challenger has the burden of proving that the law is not rationally related to a legitimate government purpose. *Hunter v. Commonwealth*, 587 S.W.3d 298, 304 (Ky. 2019). Pertinent to this case, "[w]hen economic and business rights are involved, rather than fundamental rights, substantive due process requires that a statute be rationally related to a legitimate state objective." *Stephens v. State Farm Mut. Auto. Ins. Co.*, 894 S.W.2d 624, 627 (Ky. 1995).

* * *

With no precedent for applying strict scrutiny, Plaintiffs and the Attorney General advocate intermediate scrutiny, but again Kentucky law does not support that heightened level of constitutional review. Addressing the case law they believe supportive of their position, we begin with *City of Louisville v. Kuhn*, 284 Ky. 684, 145 S.W.2d 851 (1940), a case examining an ordinance that dictated the hours barbershops could be open for business. The Court began by noting the breadth of the police power exercised for the "public weal and for its betterment," which "if conditions demand it, would approve complete prohibitive legislation of some activities, or in certain areas if based upon sufficient reasons." *Id.* at 853. Further, "whatever direction or phase that the legislation may take—whether of a prohibitory or regulatory character—it must not exceed or go beyond the limits of reasonability, or be rested upon assumed grounds for which there is no foundation in fact, nor may the legislation as enacted be more destructive of the interest of the public at large than beneficial." *Id.* In striking the barbershop ordinance, the Court concluded the restrictions were "unreasonable." *Id.* at 856. In short, while health reasons justified licensing barbers and certain restrictions, the hours of operation were not reasonably related to any legitimate governmental purpose.

Similarly, in *Adams, Inc. v. Louisville & Jefferson County Board of Health*, 439 S.W.2d 586 (Ky. 1969), apartment complex owners challenged an ordinance applicable to their private swimming pools. The Court succinctly observed: "There is perhaps no broader field of police power than that of public health. The fact that its exercise impinges upon private interests does not restrict reasonable regulation." *Id.* at 589–90.

> Under these conceptions of general subordination of private rights to public rights, we have no doubt that the city may enact laws to preserve and promote the health, morals, security, and general welfare of the citizens as a unit, and has a broad discretion in determining for itself what is harmful and inimical. It is sufficient if the municipal legislation has a real, substantial relation to the object to be accomplished, and its operation tends in some degree to prevent or suppress an offense, condition, or evil detrimental to a public good or reasonably necessary to secure public safety and welfare.
>
> The community is to be considered as a whole in the matter of preservation of the health of all inhabitants, for a failure by a few to conform to sanitary measures may inflict ill health and death upon many.

Id. at 590 (quoting *Nourse*, 78 S.W.2d at 765).

The Court observed "while all swimming pools may present some common health hazards which would reasonably require the same regulatory safeguards, in certain areas the dissimilarity in prevailing conditions would make the application of a single standard inappropriate, unrealistic and unreasonable." *Id.* at 592. Given the nature of apartment complex swimming pools, the Court found the requirement of a lifeguard and pool attendant at all times, as well as shower facilities and separate gender-based entrances to be unreasonable. The Court struck part of the regulation but importantly for our purposes it stated, "insofar as public health is concerned, private property may become of public interest and the constitutional limitations upon the exercise of the power of regulation come down to a question of 'reasonability.'" *Id.* at 590 (citing *Kuhn*, 145 S.W.2d 851).

The other cases relied on by Plaintiffs and the Attorney General to insist intermediate scrutiny applies are similarly unavailing. In *Kentucky Milk Marketing*, 691 S.W.2d at 893, the Court found that the challenged statute was a minimum retail mark-up law applicable to milk and milk products, rather than an anti-monopoly law, and struck it as "inimical to the public interest … an invasion of the right of merchants to sell competitively, and of the public to buy competitively in the open market." *Id.* at 900. The Court began its Section 2 discussion by noting in part, "[t]he question of reasonableness is one of degree and must be based on the facts of a particular case." *Id.* at 899. *Kentucky Milk Marketing* involved no health and safety regulations, nor did it employ intermediate scrutiny.

* * *

A comprehensive review of Kentucky case law leaves no doubt that under Section 2 of our Constitution, laws and regulations directed to public health and safety are judged by their reasonableness. In *Graybeal v. McNevin*, 439 S.W.2d 323, 325–26 (Ky. 1969), a case involving fluoridation of a city's water supply, this Court stated:

> Among the police powers of government, the power to promote and safeguard the public health ranks at the top. If the right of an individual runs afoul of the exercise of this power, the right of the individual must yield.
>
> On the issue of arbitrariness, the burden was on the plaintiff to show that the regulation had **no reasonable basis in fact or had no reasonable relation to the protection of the public health.**

(Emphasis added.) In upholding the city's resolution to fluoridate its water pursuant to a state regulation, the *Graybeal* Court examined the credentials and testimony of both sides' witnesses at the bench trial and "the studies, tests, experiences, and recommendations of practically all the people and organizations into whose care the health of this nation has been entrusted" before concluding the plaintiff had "failed in his burden to prove the resolution was arbitrary." *Id.* at 331. The Court prefaced its holding that arbitrary exercises of public health powers are subject to judicial restraint but they "would have to be palpably so to justify a court in interfering with so salutary a power and one so necessary to the public health." *Id.* at 326. That principle has been reflected in our Kentucky case law for decades. *See, e.g., Lexington-Fayette Cty. Food & Bev. Ass'n v. Lexington-Fayette Urban Cty. Gov't*, 131 S.W.3d 745 (Ky. 2004) (upholding smoking ban as reasonable health regulation and noting public health interest is preferred over property interests).

* * *

Fully satisfied that the individual orders and regulations at issue in this case are only deficient under Sections 1 and 2 of the Kentucky Constitution if they are unreasonable—that is lack a rational basis[37]—we address only those individual orders and regulations that have been specifically challenged. Preliminarily, we note that by the time the Boone Circuit Court conducted an evidentiary hearing, some of the challenged restrictions had changed. Also, the trial court did not address the specific allegations of arbitrariness individually, but dealt with the claims as a whole stating, "[B]ased upon the disproportionate treatment meted out to different businesses versus that allowed for substantially similar activities,[[38]] the Court also finds Plaintiffs and Intervening Plaintiffs have made sufficient showing that the challenged orders violate Section 2 of the Kentucky Constitution as an attempt to exert '[a]bsolute and arbitrary power over the lives, liberty and property' of Kentucky citizens." Our analysis is focused, as it must be, on individual orders and regulations. And, we examine the record to determine whether Plaintiffs and the Attorney General have met their burden of showing the

37. The Attorney General argues intermediate or heightened scrutiny is particularly appropriate here because the orders are the result of the Governor's judgment alone, rather than the legislature's after a bicameral process. He points to no authority for this proposition and we find none that dictates a more stringent standard than reasonableness/rational basis in these circumstances.

38. The trial court Order states: "Plaintiffs insist that Defendants have presented no rational basis for the harshly disproportionate restrictions placed upon racetracks, daycares and cafes as compared to similarly situated activities such as baseball, auctions, and LDC's." It is not clear which standard of scrutiny the trial court used; the trial court also stated that "[I]t appears at this stage of the proceedings, that the challenged orders were neither constitutionally enacted nor narrowly tailored."

challenged orders and regulations lack a rational basis and thus are unconstitutional. *Johnson v. Comm. ex rel. Meredith*, 291 Ky. 829, 165 S.W.2d 820, 823 (1942) ("So, always the burden is upon one who questions the validity of an Act to sustain his contentions."); *Hunter*, 587 S.W.3d at 304.

A. Little Links's Allegations

Little Links's declaratory and injunctive action stems from the June 15, 2020 Healthy at Work: Requirements for Childcare.[39] Center-based childcare programs, like Little Links, were closed on March 20, 2020. To fill the childcare void for health care workers and first responders LDCs were permitted to open. When center-based childcare programs were permitted to reopen on June 15, 2020, some regulations differed from the LDCs which were continuing to operate but were scheduled to be phased out by the end of August. Thus, the center-based childcare programs and the LDCs' remaining operation period overlapped for about two and one-half months.

Little Links alleges three particular rules arbitrarily impose demands that are detrimental to survival of its business. Little Links complains that in contrast to LDCs, all other childcare programs must utilize a maximum group size of ten children per group, a significant limitation on the business's ability to be profitable. Rather than being limited to a specific maximum group size, the LDCs have capacity limitation of one child per thirty square feet.[40] Second, LDCs do not have the restriction that children must remain in the same group of ten children all day without being combined with another classroom. Little Links views this rule as arbitrary, interpreting it to not allow children of the same household to be grouped in the evening despite the children leaving the center in the same vehicle. Lastly, because programs may not provide access to visitors after hours Little Links cannot conduct tours for prospective clients. Plaintiffs' witnesses testified about these disparities and the negative impact on a childcare facility's business viability.

* * *

Plaintiffs point to the differences between LDCs and the reopened childcare program requirements, both of which are meant to keep children and staff safe, and argue that if the lesser requirements serve that function, more stringent requirements are arbitrary. However, the record reflects the two programs were developed under different circumstances with different foundations of evolving knowledge. The LDCs were

39. The Governor's June 15, 2020 order incorporated the Healthy at Work requirements. The Healthy at Work: Requirements for Childcare Programs addressed the requirements for in-home childcare programs, which opened June 8, and center-based childcare programs, which opened June 15.

40. Pursuant to 922 KAR 2:120, for Kentucky childcare center premises typically, "[e]xclusive of the kitchen, bathroom, hallway, and storage area, there shall be a minimum of thirty-five (35) square feet of space per child." When emphasizing the difference in the capacity limits for LDCs vis-a-vis regular childcare programs, the Attorney General misapplies the building restriction, noting one witness had a 43,500 square foot playground, allowing 4,000 square feet per child "a limit untethered to science or reality" and hypothesizing that if it were an LDC it could serve well over 1,000 children. The childcare square footage limitation applies to buildings, not playgrounds.

literally emergency childcare for healthcare workers and first responders in the very early days of the pandemic with regulations based on successful emergency childcare centers in other states. LDCs were limited to children of essential workers at a time when society was generally closed down, continued providing care when it was unclear that sufficient childcare would be available without them and now have evolved to provide temporary emergency childcare for nontraditional instruction during traditional school hours. When regular Kentucky childcare facilities generally reopened in June 2020, the group sizes and the tour restrictions for these centers were based on articulated public health reasons, i.e., efforts to limit the spread of disease as society in general was reopening. These facilities reopened serving the general population at a time when the potential for disease spread had increased. Thus, Plaintiffs failed to meet their burden of establishing that either of these challenged childcare restrictions lack a reasonable basis, standing alone or in comparison with LDC regulations. On the contrary, the record amply reflects a rational basis for both of them. As for the grouping of siblings, as noted above, the regulation does not prevent siblings being grouped together at the end of the day.

B. Florence Speedway's Allegations

Next, Florence Speedway complains that the June 1, 2020 Healthy at Work: Requirements for Automobile Racing Tracks[41] contains arbitrary provisions, those being: (1) only allowing authorized employees and essential drivers and crews on the premises when indoor facilities like restaurants and bowling alleys are allowed 33% capacity; (2) limiting its food service to "carry-out only" when restaurants are permitted to operate at 33% capacity indoors; and (3) requiring PPE with no exceptions, which prevents it from complying with the Americans with Disabilities Act.[42] Because this was at a time when it was not permitted to have fans, Florence Speedway indicated that it was willing to space spectators six feet from people of a different household. By the time the Boone Circuit Court conducted an evidentiary hearing for the injunction request and issued its order, however, the requirements directly challenged had all changed. When Florence Speedway amended its motion for a temporary injunction, it did not challenge the capacity requirement in effect but, as a business reliant on family attendance, objected to the social distancing requirement which did not allow household members to sit within six feet of one another. Florence Speedway argued the six-foot social distancing requirement was arbitrary as household members maintain close proximity to each other throughout everyday life.

As noted above, on June 22, 2020, the requirements for restaurants were amended, allowing an increase from 33% to 50% indoor dining capacity. On June 29, 2020, the public-facing businesses order was amended to allow venues and event spaces, includ-

41. The Governor's June 3, 2020 order, incorporating the Healthy at Work requirements, made them effective June 1, 2020.

42. The order actually provided: "Racetracks should ensure employees and racing crews wear appropriate face coverings at all times practicable...." The requirements state that for employees who are isolated with more than six feet of social distancing, face coverings are not necessary at all times.

ing Florence Speedway, to reopen to the public.[43] The amendment allows 50% of the maximum capacity permitted at a venue, assuming all individuals can maintain six feet of space between them with that level of occupancy. Additionally, if the venues operate any form of dining service, those services must comply with the requirements for restaurants and bars. On July 10, 2020, the emergency mask regulation provided a number of exemptions for the wearing of face coverings, one exemption being for "[a]ny person with disability, or a physical or mental impairment, that prevents them from safely wearing a face covering."

Except for the claim related to the inability of household members to sit within six feet of one another, which we discuss further below, the succeeding orders made Florence Speedway's initial claims of arbitrariness moot by the time the trial court entered its July 20 order. Of course, one exception to the mootness doctrine is the "capable of repetition, yet evading review" exception. *Philpot v. Patton*, 837 S.W.2d 491, 493 (Ky. 1992). Under this exception, Kentucky courts consider "whether (1) the 'challenged action is too short in duration to be fully litigated prior to its cessation or expiration and (2) there is a reasonable expectation that the same complaining party would be subject to the same action again.'" *Id.* (quoting *In re Commerce Oil Co.*, 847 F.2d 291, 293 (6th Cir. 1988)). However, the Florence Speedway's claims of arbitrariness as to the June 1, 2020 Healthy at Work: Requirements for Automobile Racing Tracks do not meet the criteria for the "capable of repetition, yet evading review" exception. The nature of this case, a public health pandemic, is extraordinary and evolving knowledge of the virus results in evolving responses. Consequently, this is not the usual case of a challenged action being too short in duration to be fully litigated prior to its cessation or expiration. And given the advancement of knowledge of COVID-19 and the ongoing attempts to balance that knowledge with keeping the economy open, no reasonable expectation exists that Florence Speedway will again be subject to the initially challenged business restrictions. In terms of Florence Speedway's challenge against the social distancing requirement which did not allow family members to sit within six feet of one another, we conclude that requirement was arbitrary.

During the July 16 hearing, Dr. Stack testified about the public health concerns related to sporting events. He said sporting events are particularly concerning because

---

43. The Healthy at Work: Requirements for Venues and Event Spaces applied to, among other businesses, "professional and amateur sporting/athletic stadiums and arenas."

During the July 1, 2020 hearing of Plaintiffs' motion for a temporary restraining order, Governor's counsel explained that Florence Speedway's capacity complaint was moot because the June 29 Healthy at Work order allowed it to open at 50% capacity. In response to Florence Speedway's concern that a footnote in the order suggested differently, Governor's counsel clarified that Florence Speedway was able to open at 50% capacity and offered to amend the order to address Florence Speedway's concern. A revised order was issued, effective July 10, 2020. The July 10 order maintained the six-foot social distancing requirement for individuals. Florence Speedway, its business relying on family attendance, testified at the July 16 injunction hearing about the negative business impact of not being allowed to have family members sit within six feet of each other. Effective July 22, 2020, the social distancing requirement for venues and event spaces was amended to "[a]ll individuals in the venue or event space must be able to maintain six (6) feet of space from everyone who is not a member of their household."

people are often shouting and cheering, which leads to an increased spread of the respiratory droplets that transmit the virus. This enhanced risk exists even outdoors due to the shouting and cheering. Also, eating and drinking increase saliva and spread respiratory droplets and consuming food and drink is not compatible with mask wearing. However, he agreed no medical or public health reason would prohibit household members sitting together at an event space and acknowledged that household seating had been permitted in other activities. Effective July 22, 2020, the social distancing requirement for venues and event spaces was amended to "[a]ll individuals in the venue or event space must be able to maintain six (6) feet of space from everyone who is not a member of their household." Based on Dr. Stack's testimony, we must conclude that there was not a rational basis for the social distancing requirement initially imposed on Florence Speedway. Given that the social distancing requirement was amended six days after the injunction hearing, Florence Speedway has now received the relief which it sought.

C. Beans Cafe's Allegations

Beans Cafe originally sought a declaration that certain provisions of the May 22, 2020 Healthy at Work: Requirements for Restaurants[44] are arbitrary. It complained that the requirement that employees wear PPE whenever they are near other employees or customers (so long as such use does not jeopardize the employee's health or safety) is not uniformly applied. Beans Cafe also alleged little scientific basis exists for requiring cloth facemasks, rendering the requirement arbitrary. The cafe challenged as arbitrary and capricious the order limiting restaurants to 33% indoor capacity and requiring six feet of distance between customers, noting these requirements make it difficult, if not impossible, for restaurants to make a profit. Beans Cafe also contends that it is arbitrary not to allow customers to sit back-to-back at tables with a three-and-one-half foot distance between the customers.

As indicated above, effective June 29, 2020, in the Healthy at Work: Requirements for Restaurants and Bars, the social distancing requirements for restaurants changed to a 50% capacity limit or the greatest number that permits individuals not from the same household to maintain six feet of space between each other with that level of occupancy. The PPE mask provisions stayed the same. However, the emergency mask regulation went into effect July 10, 2020. Based on the changes in regulations, the only issues remaining are whether a rational basis exists for requiring the six-foot social distancing and face coverings. Beans Cafe seeks an amendment in the six-foot social distancing requirement because that requirement, despite being allowed 50% capacity, reduces the business's seating capacity to about 30%.

Although the July 10, 2020 emergency mask regulation is more detailed than the May 22, 2020 face mask provision, the requirement that employees must wear face masks when they are near other employees or customers (so long as such use does not jeopardize the employee's health or safety) is reflected in 902 KAR 2:190E * * * Section

44. The Governor's May 22, 2020 order incorporated the Healthy at Work requirements.

(2), subsections (2)(a) and (4)(b), which requires any person in a restaurant (when not seated and consuming food or beverage) to wear a face covering when within six feet of another, unless that individual is of his household; the face covering provision does not apply when a person has a disability that prevents them from safely wearing a face covering. As identified in 902 KAR 2:190E, KRS 214.020, the Cabinet for Health and Family Services's broad police powers for dealing with contagious diseases,[45] KRS 211.025,[46] and KRS 211.180(1)[47] provide a rational basis for the face covering and the social distancing measure which Beans Cafe challenges. In addition, Dr. Stack testified during the evidentiary hearing regarding the scientific basis for the six-foot social distancing requirement and wearing face coverings to prevent the spread of COVID-19, a highly contagious respiratory disease. Beans Cafe's citation to a study questioning the efficacy of cloth masks does not in any way negate the established rational basis for these public health measures.[48]

In regard to Beans Cafe's allegation that it was arbitrary not to allow customers to sit back-to-back at tables with a three and one-half foot distance between them, Dr. Stack testified to the reasoning behind measures used in restaurants to mitigate spread of the virus. He first noted that eating and drinking increases saliva and spreads respiratory droplets because people do not wear masks while consuming food and drink. In terms of the six-foot spacing requirement for restaurant and bars, there is an exception for booth seating when there is a plexiglass barrier, as long as the barrier effectively separates the opposite side. The physical barrier is of added value and in theory prevents virus spreading easily back and forth. Dr. Stack contrasted that to the very different situation when people are sitting back-to-back with three-foot distance between them in the middle of an open restaurant, when people generally turn and move around, an

45. KRS 214.020 states:

> When the Cabinet for Health and Family Services believes that there is a probability that any infectious or contagious disease will invade this state, it shall take such action and adopt and enforce such rules and regulations as it deems efficient in preventing the introduction or spread of such infectious or contagious disease or diseases within this state, and to accomplish these objects shall establish and strictly maintain quarantine and isolation at such places as it deems proper.

46. KRS 211.025 states:

> Except as otherwise provided by law, the cabinet shall administer all provisions of law relating to public health; shall enforce all public health laws and all regulations of the secretary; shall supervise and assist all local boards of health and departments; shall do all other things reasonably necessary to protect and improve the health of the people; and may cooperate with federal and other health agencies and organizations in matters relating to public health.

47. KRS 211.180(1) states:

> The cabinet shall enforce the administrative regulations promulgated by the secretary of the Cabinet for Health and Family Services for the regulation and control of the matters set out below ... including but not limited to the following matters: (a) Detection, prevention, and control of communicable diseases,....

48. The Boone Circuit Court cited to the study but declined to rely on it as not being subject to judicial notice. The title of the study indicates it compared cloth masks to medical masks in healthcare workers.

environment where the virus can easily spread. On this restriction, Beans Cafe essentially had nothing more than an allegation of arbitrariness while Dr. Stack's testimony establishes a rational basis for this public health measure.

* * *

In summary, KRS 214.020 reflects the Cabinet's broad police powers (and the Governor's in conjunction with the Cabinet in the event of an emergency) to adopt measures that will prevent the introduction and spread of infectious diseases in this state. While a global pandemic is unprecedented for all but those who were alive during the 1918 influenza epidemic, * * * the measures employed to deal with the spread of COVID-19, including business closure, are not unprecedented in our Commonwealth. *See Allison v. Cash*, 143 Ky. 679, 137 S.W. 245 (1911) (smallpox epidemic in Lyon County grounds for closing millinery shop). Courts have long recognized the broad health care powers of the government will frequently affect and impinge on business and individual interests. * * *

Here, except for the initial social distancing requirement at Florence Speedway which violates Section 2, the challenged public health measures do not violate Sections 1 and 2 of the Kentucky Constitution. A rational basis exists for the other orders and regulations, all of which are reasonably designed to contain the spread of a highly contagious and potentially deadly disease. As to Florence Speedway, its social distancing complaint regarding household seating has been remedied with a subsequent executive order that became effective six days after the July 16 injunction hearing.

* * *

Conclusion

Upon finality of this Opinion, the stay entered July 17, 2020 shall be lifted as to any affected cases challenging the Governor's COVID-19 response and those cases may proceed consistent with this Opinion. As to the Boone Circuit Court litigation, the July 20, 2020 Order that has been held in abeyance is reversed and this matter is remanded to that Court for further proceedings, if any, consistent with this Opinion.

All sitting. All concur.

Notes and Questions

1. After *Beshear v. Acree* was remanded to the Boone Circuit Court, the plaintiffs amended their complaint to challenge the Governor's executive orders in light of subsequent legislation enacted by the General Assembly and proceeded to final judgment. On appeal, the Supreme Court held the plaintiffs had no injury, actual or imminent, caused by the defendants. *Beshear v. Ridgeway Props., LLC*, 647 S.W.3d 170, (Ky. 2022), *reh'g denied*.

2. In *Brown v. Barkley*, 628 S.W.2d 616 (Ky. 1982), the Court observed that, "to the extent that the Governor has any implied or inherent powers in addition to those the Constitution expressly gives him, it seems clear that such unexpressed executive power is subservient to the overriding authority of the legislature." This observation

may be viewed as a repudiation of any claim by the Governor to "inherent" executive powers under the Kentucky Constitution. After all, if the Governor has "inherent" powers, then they cannot be overriden by the legislative branch. However, in *Beshear v. Acree*, the Court held that "the powers exercised by a Kentucky Governor in an emergency are likely executive powers," rather than powers delegated to him by the General Assembly in KRS Chapter 39A. Is this statement from *Beshear v. Acree* correct? Absent a legislative enactment, from whence in the Constitution does the Governor's power come to issue the executive orders at issue in the case (*e.g.*, limiting the hours businesses could be open, imposing maximum capacity limits on businesses, and requiring individuals to wear face masks and stay at least six feet apart from others)?

3. In the alternative, if not issued pursuant to his executive powers, the Court holds in *Beshear v. Acree* that the Governor's executive orders issued in response to the COVID-19 pandemic are authorized by KRS Chapter 39A, which it says "validly delegates any legislative authority at issue to the Governor." Is any such delegation of legislative power consistent with Section 28 of the Kentucky Constitution ("No person or collection of persons, being of one of those departments, shall exercise any power properly belonging to either of the others, except in the instances hereinafter expressly directed or permitted.")?

4. In *Commonwealth ex rel. Beshear v. Bevin*, 575 S.W.3d 673 (Ky. 2019), the Supreme Court disapproved of (albeit in *dicta*) a hypothetical statute stating in its entirety, "The Governor shall have the power to change all laws of this Commonwealth between sessions of the General Assembly." The reason the Court gave in that case was that such a law would violate the separation of powers by allowing the Governor to make law, as opposed to merely executing a duly enacted statute. Then, when the Court decided *Beshear v. Acree* two years later, KRS 39A.180(2) provided in relevant part that, in an emergency declared by the Governor under KRS Chapter 39A, all "existing laws, ordinances, and administrative regulations" that conflict with the Governor's executive orders "shall be suspended during the period of time and to the extent that the conflict exists." Even though the Governor had the power to declare an emergency under KRS 39A.100(1) on almost any basis he deemed fit, at any time, for any duration, and could suspend any statute that conflicts with his executive orders during such an emergency, the Court was not troubled by the breadth of this grant of power to the Governor. Can the Court's holding in *Beshear v. Acree* be squared with its earlier statement in *Beshear v. Bevin*?

Cameron v. Beshear

Supreme Court of Kentucky (2021)
628 S.W.3d 61

Opinion of the Court by Justice VanMeter.

On transfer from the Court of Appeals, we are presented with Movant Attorney General Daniel Cameron's request for relief from a temporary injunction issued by the Franklin Circuit Court against implementation of House Bill (H.B.) 1,[1] Senate Bill (S.B.) 1,[2] S.B. 2,[3] and House Joint Resolution (H.J.R.) 77[4] which the General Assembly enacted during the 2021 regular session[5] and which amend the Governor's power to respond to emergencies as granted in KRS[6] Chapter 39A. We find that this matter presents a justiciable case or controversy but that the Franklin Circuit Court abused its discretion in issuing the temporary injunction. Accordingly, we remand this case to the trial court with instructions to dissolve the injunction.

I. Facts and Procedural Background

On March 6, 2020, in response to the COVID-19 pandemic, Respondent Governor Andy Beshear declared a state of emergency "by virtue of the authority vested in [him] by [KRS] Chapter 39A," *i.e.*, the "Statewide Emergency Management Programs" (KRS §§39A.010–990).[7] Business owners subsequently challenged the Governor's authority to issue executive orders and emergency regulations in response to the COVID-19 pandemic, and in November 2020, this Court held that the executive orders were valid since the legislature had given the Governor the power to issue them under the Statewide Emergency Management Programs regime in KRS Chapter 39A. *Beshear v. Acree*, 615 S.W.3d 780, 802 (Ky. 2020). Further, at the onset of the pandemic, the legislature had approved the Governor's emergency declaration. Act of Mar. 30, 2020, ch. 73, 2020 Ky. Acts 310 (2020 S.B. 150). However, in *Acree*, we clarified that going forward, the General Assembly could limit the Governor's statutorily-derived emergency powers should it wish to. *Id.* at 812–13 (noting that "[w]hile the authority exercised by the Governor in accordance with KRS Chapter 39A is necessarily broad," many "checks [exist] on that authority," including "legislative amendment or revocation of the emergency powers granted the Governor[ ]").

During the 2021 regular session, the General Assembly responded to *Acree* by passing H.B. 1, S.B. 1, and S.B. 2 which restrict the Governor's ability to take unilateral action during declared emergencies. The Governor vetoed those bills and the General Assembly overrode his vetoes. The bills became effective on February 2, 2021.

1. Act of Feb. 2, 2021, ch. 3, 2021 Ky. Acts 14.
2. Act of Feb. 2, 2021, ch. 6, 2021 Ky. Acts 17.
3. Act of Feb. 2, 2021, ch. 7, 2021 Ky. Acts 26.
4. Res. of Mar. 30, 2021, ch. 168, 2021 Ky. Acts 1059.
5. We refer to these four pieces of legislation collectively as "2021 legislation."
6. Kentucky Revised Statutes.
7. *See* Exec. Order 2020-215 (Ky. Mar. 6, 2020).

Thereafter, the Governor and Eric Friedlander, in his official capacity as Secretary of the Cabinet for Health and Family Services ("CHFS"),[8] filed this declaratory action in Franklin Circuit Court seeking a declaration that the recently-passed legislation unconstitutionally infringes upon his executive powers under Sections 2, 27, 28, 36, 42, 55, 59, 60, 69, 75, 80 and 81 of the Kentucky Constitution. The Governor sought injunctive relief preventing enforcement of the legislation pending adjudication of its constitutionality, arguing that the legislation undermines state government's ability to respond to the ongoing COVID-19 pandemic and creates a public health crisis that will result in increased disease and death. The Governor sued Speaker of the House David Osborne, Senate President Robert Stivers, the Legislative Research Commission ("LRC"), and Attorney General Daniel Cameron. The legislative defendants (Osborne, Stivers, and LRC) filed motions to dismiss based on legislative immunity, which the Franklin Circuit Court denied.[9]

Following an evidentiary hearing, the Franklin Circuit Court temporarily enjoined implementation of the challenged legislation, finding that the Governor had presented substantial legal questions concerning the validity of the legislation, the Governor and the public would suffer immediate and irreparable harm in the absence of injunctive relief, and the public interest and the balance of the equities required the granting of injunctive relief. The Attorney General filed for CR[10] 65.07[11] relief with the Court of Appeals to vacate the temporary injunction, arguing that the Franklin Circuit Court lacked jurisdiction to issue the temporary injunction since the Complaint does not present a justiciable issue and the Governor lacks standing.

Not long after the trial court granted injunctive relief, the General Assembly passed H.J.R. 77 ratifying and extending many of the Governor's executive orders and regulations for periods of time ranging from 30 to 90 days, but terminating all other COVID-related orders and regulations. The Governor vetoed that resolution, and the General Assembly overrode his veto. Most significantly, the General Assembly explicitly included Executive Order 2020-215, the Governor's original emergency declaration, as one of the executive actions which would expire in ninety days, or by June 28, 2021. The Governor then sought modification of the temporary injunction to cover HJR 77, to which the Attorney General objected. The Franklin Circuit Court granted the Governor's request and put a hold on the implementation of HJR 77 as well. The Attorney General immediately filed for CR 65.07 relief with the Court of Appeals to vacate the modified injunction. The Court of Appeals recommended transfer of the case to this

8. Respondents-Plaintiffs are collectively referred to as "the Governor" herein for ease of reference.

9. The trial court's denial of the legislative defendants' motion to dismiss is not at issue in this appeal.

10. Kentucky Rules of Civil Procedure.

11. A party may move for interlocutory relief pursuant to CR 65.07 when a circuit court "by interlocutory order has granted, denied, modified, or dissolved a temporary injunction[.]" CR 65.07(1). An appellate court may grant emergency relief if the movant demonstrates that the irreparable injury will occur before the motion for interlocutory relief may be considered by a three-judge panel. CR 65.07(6).

Court, which we accepted on an expedited basis due to these issues being of great and immediate statewide importance.

II. Analysis

Two questions are presented for our review: (1) whether this lawsuit presents a justiciable case or controversy and (2) if justiciable, whether a temporary injunction was warranted.

A. Justiciability

* * * Whether the Governor's emergency power in this situation is statutorily or constitutionally derived is at the heart of the Governor's Complaint and thus presents a justiciable case or controversy. * * *

B. Temporary Injunction Not Warranted

To justify the grant of a temporary injunction, a plaintiff must satisfy the following, well-recognized requirements:

> First, the trial court should determine whether plaintiff has complied with CR 65.04 by showing irreparable injury. This is a mandatory prerequisite to the issuance of any injunction. Secondly, the trial court should weigh the various equities involved. Although not an exclusive list, the court should consider such things as possible detriment to the public interest, harm to the defendant, and whether the injunction will merely preserve the status quo. Finally, the complaint should be evaluated to see whether a substantial question has been presented. If the party requesting relief has shown a probability of irreparable injury, presented a substantial question as to the merits, and the equities are in favor of issuance, the temporary injunction should be awarded. However, the actual overall merits of the case are not to be addressed in CR 65.04 motions.

Maupin v. Stansbury, 575 S.W.2d 695, 699 (Ky. App. 1978).

* * * Notably, "[a] motion for a temporary injunction does not call for, or justify, an adjudication of the ultimate rights of the parties ... [and] should issue only where it is clearly shown that one's rights will suffer immediate and irreparable injury pending trial." *Id.* at 161 (internal quotations and citations omitted). On appellate review, however, the appellate court may properly determine that findings are clearly erroneous if they are ... occasioned by an erroneous application of the law. *Rogers v. Lexington-Fayette Urb. Cnty. Gov't*, 175 S.W.3d 569, 571 (Ky. 2005). In this instance, we find that the trial court's issuance of injunctive relief was unsupported by sound legal principles occasioned by an erroneous application of the law.

To obtain an injunction, the Governor was required to show a probability of irreparable injury, present a substantial question as to the merits of his Complaint, and persuade the court that the equities balanced in favor of issuance.

1. Irreparable Injury.

Regarding irreparable injury, the Governor's argument essentially centers on the harm to his ability to protect the public during a global pandemic, and the claimed harm to the constitutional power and authority of his office. We emphasize that in our following discussion and analysis we do not question the Governor's good faith in taking steps he believes are necessary in dealing with the pandemic.[12] That noted, underlying consideration of all our COVID decisions, as aptly stated by Justice William O. Douglas, "no doubt that the emergency which caused the [executive to take action] was one that bore heavily on the country. But the emergency did not create power; it merely marked an occasion when power should be exercised." *Youngstown Sheet & Tube Co. v. Sawyer*, 343 U.S. 579, 629, 72 S.Ct. 863, 96 L.Ed. 1153 (1952) (Douglas, J., concurring). Over the last forty years, this Court has been explicit that the Governor's powers, except in a limited number of instances expressly set forth in the Constitution, derive from statutes passed by the General Assembly. *See, e.g., Commonwealth ex rel. Beshear v. Commonwealth ex rel. Bevin*, 498 S.W.3d 355, 369 (Ky. 2016) (stating "the Governor ... is bound by the law[ ]"); *Fletcher v. Commonwealth ex rel. Stumbo*, 163 S.W.3d 852, (Ky. 2005) (rejecting Governor's claim of implied authority to expend unappropriated funds to provide essential services in an emergency); *Brown v. Barkley*, 628 S.W.2d 616, 621 (Ky. 1982) (detailing the seven sections of our Commonwealth's constitution expressly conferring powers and duties on the Governor).[13] In fact, in *Brown*, we held that "to the extent that the Governor has any implied or inherent powers in addition to those the Constitution expressly gives him, it seems clear that such unexpressed executive power is subservient to the overriding authority of the legislature[.]" 628 S.W.2d at 621.

In *Fletcher*, we approvingly quoted the following,

> The appeal, however, that we declare the existence of inherent powers ex necessitate to meet an emergency asks us to do what many think would be wise, although it is something the forefathers omitted. They knew what emergencies were, knew the pressures they engender for authoritative action, knew, too, how they afford a ready pretext for usurpation. We may also suspect that they suspected that emergency powers would tend to kindle emergencies.
>
> ...
>
> [E]mergency powers are consistent with free government only when their control is lodged elsewhere than in the Executive who exercises them.
>
> ...

12. We similarly do not question the good faith of the General Assembly in enacting the 2021 legislation.

13. In brief, these powers and duties are to serve as commander-in-chief of military forces and affairs of the state, Ky. Const. §75; fill vacancies in office, except as otherwise provided by the Constitution, Ky. Const. §76; exercise pardon power, Ky. Const. §77; require written information from Executive branch officers, Ky. Const. §78; report on the state of the Commonwealth and recommend measures to the General Assembly, Ky. Const. §79; call the General Assembly into special session, Ky. Const. §80; and "take care that the laws be faithfully executed[.]" Ky. Const. §81.

> With all its defects, delays and inconveniences, men have discovered no technique for long preserving free government except that the Executive be under the law, and that the law be made by parliamentary deliberations.

Fletcher, 163 S.W.3d at 871 (quoting *Youngstown*, 343 U.S. at 646, 649–50, 652, 655, 72 S.Ct. 863 (Jackson, J., concurring)).

Another rule of interpretation is that we "'presum[e] that the challenged statutes were enacted by the legislature in accordance with constitutional requirements.'" *Acree*, 615 S.W.3d at 805 (quoting *Cornelison v. Commonwealth*, 52 S.W.3d 570, 572 (Ky. 2001)). "A constitutional infringement must be 'clear, complete and unmistakable' in order to render the statute unconstitutional." *Caneyville Volunteer Fire Dep't v. Green's Motorcycle Salvage, Inc.*, 286 S.W.3d 790, 806 (Ky. 2009) (quoting *Ky. Indus. Util. Customers, Inc. v. Ky. Utils. Co.*, 983 S.W.2d 493, 499 (Ky. 1998)). Considering that the General Assembly is the policy-making body for the Commonwealth, not the Governor or the courts, equitable considerations support enforcing a legislative body's policy choices. In fact, non-enforcement of a duly-enacted statute constitutes irreparable harm to the public and the government. *See Boone Creek Props., LLC v. Lexington-Fayette Urb. Cnty. Bd. of Adjustment*, 442 S.W.3d 36, 40 (Ky. 2014) (holding that the statute's enactment constitutes an implied finding by the legislature that the public interest required it). Whether the Governor has shown an irreparable injury is tied to his constitutional claims and the likelihood of success.

2. Substantial Questions on the Merits.

As to the potential for success on the merits of the Governor's Complaint, the extent of the Governor's exercise of emergency authority during the COVID-19 pandemic is confined to the statutory authority given to him by the legislature under KRS Chapter 39A. *Acree*, 615 S.W.3d at 812–13. Indeed, in *Brown v. Barkley*, this Court clarified:

> [T]o the extent that the Governor has any implied or inherent powers in addition to those the Constitution expressly gives him, it seems clear that such unexpressed executive power is subservient to the overriding authority of the legislature, and ... the officers named in Const. Sec. 91 have only such powers and duties as are assigned to them by legislative enactment or by executive order expressly authorized by statute.

628 S.W.2d at 621 (holding that the Governor did not have constitutional power to issue an executive order to reorganize agencies when not authorized by the enabling statute and a related statute pursuant to which the order was issued). Further,

> Whereas the judicial branch must be and is largely independent of intrusion by the legislative branch, the executive branch exists principally to do its bidding. The real power of the executive branch springs directly from the long periods between legislative sessions, during which interims the legislature customarily has left broad discretionary power to the chief executive.

Id. at 623.

"Practically speaking, except for those conferred upon him specifically by the Constitution, [the Governor's] powers, like those of the executive officers created by Const. Sec. 91, are only what the General Assembly chooses to give him." *Id.* Thus, the Governor has no implied or inherent emergency powers beyond that given him by the legislature, who, as elected officials, serve at the behest of the Commonwealth.[14]

a. Separation of Powers.

The trial court found serious separation of powers issues under Sections 27 and 28, the constitutional provisions that mandate that strict separation of powers under our tripartite government, citing *Legislative Research Commission ex rel. Prather v. Brown*, 664 S.W.2d 907 (Ky. 1984). The trial court stated,

> The legislature has every right, and even the duty, to adopt standards and rules to govern the Governor's exercise of emergency executive authority. But when the legislative role shifts from oversight and policymaking to micromanagement of administrative rules and orders there is a clash that implicates the separation of powers provisions of sections 27 and 28 of the Kentucky Constitution. *See Legislative Research Commission v. Brown*, 664 S.W.2d 907 (Ky. 1984). The challenged legislation here—HB1, SB 1 and SB 2—all raise serious separation of powers issues.

Order Granting Temporary Injunction Under CR 65.04, No, 21-CI-00089 (Franklin Circ. Ct. Mar. 3, 2021). This reliance on *L.R.C. v. Brown* is misplaced.

The precise issue in *Brown* was occasioned by the then statutory provisions that purported to give the General Assembly authority, through the L.R.C., to review and void executive branch administrative regulations. We held this review process was unconstitutional either as a legislative veto or as an impermissible extension of the legislative session.

By contrast, the current legislative review of administrative regulations is set forth in KRS Chapter 13A. Specifically, legislative committees may review new, emergency or existing regulations and, among other decisions, make determinations that the regulations are deficient. KRS 13A.030. Prior to S.B. 2, the statute referred to "nonbinding determinations." The trial court commented on the change to the statutory language in S.B. 2 that deleted the word "nonbinding" from the statute. S.B. 2 §2(2). As a rule of construction, courts generally presume that statutory amendment is made with a view to change the law. *Jefferson Cnty. Bd. of Educ. v. Fell*, 391 S.W.3d 713, 724 (Ky. 2012). In *Fell*, however, we also noted the overarching consideration is to discern legislative intent:

> As important as it is for a court to scrutinize the particular statute *in toto*, our statutory construction principles also mandate considering the statute in con-

14. Any claim of the Governor regarding his authority as commander-in-chief, under Section 75, is similarly unavailing. "That military powers of the Commander-in-Chief were not to supersede representative government of internal affairs seems obvious from the Constitution and from elementary American history." *Youngstown*, 343 U.S. at 644, 72 S.Ct. 863 (Jackson, J., concurring).

> text with other statutes surrounding it. *Petitioner F.* [*v. Brown*], 306 S.W.3d [80] 85–86 [(Ky. 2010)] (statutory enactment to be read as a whole and also in context with other parts of statute). This comes as no surprise because given that the cardinal rule of statutory construction is discerning legislative intent, it is entirely logical for the judiciary to see what else our General Assembly has said on the particular topic underlying the controversy.

Id. at 721–22. Notwithstanding the deletion of the word "nonbinding," our review of KRS Chapter 13A reveals that even though a legislative committee may find that a regulation is "deficient," the regulation at issue remains in the purview of the executive branch as to what is to become of the "deficient" regulation. *See* KRS 13A.330 (vesting Governor with final authority as to whether a "deficient" administrative regulation shall be withdrawn, amended, or become effective notwithstanding deficiency). Section 17 of S.B. 2 amends KRS 13A.330 principally to include reference to emergency administrative regulations. The Governor's final say over the disposition of any "deficient" emergency regulations remains intact.

Because the executive branch retains final say as to administrative regulations, the 2021 legislation does not violate Sections 27 and 28, or this court's holding in *L.R.C. v. Brown.* If the trial court's conclusion was based on what it termed the General Assembly's "micromanagement" of state government, the simple answer, of course, is that it did so during its constitutionally authorized annual session, and not during an out-of-session committee hearing. As we have noted time and again, so many times that we need not provide citation, the General Assembly establishes the public policy of the Commonwealth.

b. Power to Call Special Sessions.

The Governor argues that the legislation at issue requires him to call the legislature into session every thirty days in order for him to continue to exercise his emergency powers. S.B. 1 §2(2)(a). In other words, the Governor claims the General Assembly infringes on his exclusive authority to call it into special session. Ky. Const. §80.

Since 1942, special sessions have been called 52 times. * * * No doubt each involved some matter that the then-Governor believed could not wait for the regular session of the General Assembly. In a word, an emergency not theretofore addressed by the statutes. Typically, the remedy, as for all governors over the past 130 years of the 1891 Constitution, is to do the hard work of consulting with the General Assembly and agreeing on statutory amendment in advance of a special call. The General Assembly, as well as the Governor, are trustees of the Commonwealth's welfare. *See Youngstown*, 343 U.S. at 629, 72 S.Ct. 863 (Douglas, J., concurring) (stating "[t]he Congress, as well as the President, is trustee of the national welfare[ ]"). Recent experience demonstrates the futility of calling a special session without that advance work.[15] Furthermore, the assertion that the Governor would be forced to call a special session every 30 days is

---

15. In 2018, Governor Bevin called a special session to address the pension crisis that lasted two days and without any legislation passed.

not credible. H.J.R. 77 extended emergency measures anywhere from 30 to 90 days. In the future, depending on the circumstances, nothing prohibits the Governor and General Assembly from agreeing on emergency powers in excess of 30 days.

These items noted, we do not believe this issue has been adequately addressed by the parties and therefore make no definitive pronouncement concerning the constitutionality of thirty-day limitation contained within the 2021 legislation.

c. Power to Suspend Statutes

The Governor argues that S.B. 1 §4 infringes on his supreme executive authority by placing his authority to suspend statutes under the veto power of the Attorney General. Ky. Const. §69; *Barkley*, 628 S.W.2d at 624. Again, we disagree.

The power to suspend statutes does not belong to the Governor. It belongs to the General Assembly. Ky. Const. §15. This section is especially succinct and clear: "[n]o power to suspend laws shall be exercised unless by the General Assembly or its authority." In fact, the drafters of our Constitution deemed this provision so important, they placed it in the Bill of Rights:

> Since this provision is a part of the Bill of Rights, the Governor could not suspend statutes even if he possessed "emergency" or "inherent" powers under Sections 69 and 81. Ky. Const. §26 ("To guard against transgression of the high powers which we have delegated, We Declare that everything in this Bill of Rights is excepted out of the general powers of government...."). The suspension of statutes by a Governor is also antithetical to the constitutional duty to "take care that the laws be faithfully executed." Ky. Const. §81.

Fletcher, 163 S.W.3d at 872. From this, we conclude that the power to suspend statutes ought to be exercised judiciously, soberly and upon due consideration.

Barkley is instructive in this regard, but not as the Governor argues. Under Section 15, the General Assembly might grant the Governor the power to suspend statutes. Or, it properly might grant that power to the Attorney General. *See Barkley*, 628 S.W.2d at 621 (stating "the officers named in [Section] 91 have only such powers and duties as are assigned to them by legislative enactment or by executive order expressly authorized by statute[ ]"). In *Barkley*, we recognized the Constitution framers created these independent, statewide-elected officers to "provide convenient receptacles for the diffusion of executive power." *Id.* at 622. Given the importance of the power to suspend laws, we see no valid reason why the General Assembly might not properly grant the power to two independently-elected constitutional officers.

The Governor argues that the immediately following sentence in *Barkley* supports his argument that by doing so, the General Assembly has impermissibly "create[d] another executive officer or officers who will not be subject to [the Governor's] supremacy[.]" *Id.* The complete quotation is

> As the Governor is the "supreme executive power," it is not possible for the General Assembly to create another executive officer or officers who will not be subject to that supremacy, but **it definitely has the prerogative of withhold-**

> **ing executive powers from him by assigning them to these constitutional officers who are not amenable to his supervision and control.**

Id. (emphasis added).[16] S.B. 1 §4 constitutes a valid exercise of the General Assembly's authority to suspend statutes.

d. Arbitrary Legislation

The trial court expressed that the 2021 legislation "presents questions as to whether the thirty-day limitation period for Executive Orders and [emergency regulations] are arbitrary under Section 2." The Governor expands this concept by arguing the bills are arbitrary, vague and unenforceable, asserting the public's due process rights. In our view, the Governor has no standing to assert the public's due process rights. *See World-wide Equip., Inc. v. Mullins*, 11 S.W.3d 50, 60–61 (Ky. App. 1999) (holding that motor vehicle seller had no standing to claim certain regulations and statutes were arbitrary, void as vague, and violative of due process since it was not charged with violation of that regulation/statute, and no party then in the action had been so charged).[17]

e. Special Legislation

The Governor argues that the 2021 legislation is special legislation in violation of Sections 59 and 60. His argument is that these bills grant businesses, schools, local governments and others the authority or power to exercise discretion as to what health care guidance to follow, citing *Young v. Willis*, 305 Ky. 201, 204–05, 203 S.W. 2d 5, 7 (1947). Any argument that the 2021 legislation constitutes special legislation in violation of Kentucky Constitution §59 is easily disposed of by our decision in *Calloway County Sheriff's Department v. Woodall*, 607 S.W.3d 557 (Ky. 2020). The legislature did not identify or single out any particular person, business, school, locality or entity to which the 2021 legislation would apply. *Id.* at 573. Instead, the legislation applies statewide.

We similarly reject the Governor's argument that Section 60,[18] and our predecessor court's decision in *Young*, compels a finding of unconstitutionality. The claim is that the

---

16. The Governor also cites *L.R.C. v Brown* in support of this argument. This case did not address suspension of statutes, but the authority of the General Assembly, through the L.R.C., to disapprove administrative regulations while it, the General Assembly, was not in session. We therefore fail to perceive the applicability of this case, unless it is for the proposition as to the executive powers and responsibilities lying within the province of the Governor. 664 S.W.2d at 919. We hold that *Fletcher* and our analysis of Sections 15 and 91 are more directly on point.

17. In *Commonwealth ex rel. Beshear v. Commonwealth ex rel. Bevin*, 498 S.W.3d 355, 360–66 (Ky. 2016), we recognized that the Attorney General has standing as the chief legal officer of the state to vindicate public rights. In the same case, we held that three individual legislators did not have that same standing because they were not the chief legal officer(s) for the public. *Id.* at 367. We similarly conclude as to the Governor's lack of standing in this case as to these claims.

18. In pertinent part, Section 60 provides,

> No law, except such as relates to ... public buildings or improvements, ... matters pertaining to common schools, ... and the regulation by counties, cities, towns or other municipalities of their local affairs, shall be enacted to take effect upon the approval of any other authority than the General Assembly, unless otherwise expressly provided in this Constitution.

2021 legislation permits localities or any number of other entities to establish their own pandemic guidance. We again disagree. Our statutes are replete with many instances of localities, schools, businesses being permitted to make choices that conform to local conditions or individual choice. We see this legislation as no different.

3. Balancing Equities

The trial court made extensive findings concerning the COVID-19 pandemic, its ongoing nature, and the good occasioned by the Governor's emergency measures.[19] In balancing the equities, the trial court considered these facts, as well as its interpretation of the injury to the Governor's constitutional powers, juxtaposed with the 2021 legislation and the more localized approach to the pandemic that implementation of that legislation would entail. Our expression, however, in *Acree* that a global pandemic justified a statewide response, 615 S.W.3d at 808, in no way expressed or implied it was the sole method in dealing with the pandemic. In fact, we expressly held that the General Assembly could limit the Governor's statutorily-derived emergency powers should it wish to. *Id.* at 812–13. That noted, as we have discussed, the Governor's emergency powers derive from the statutes enacted by the General Assembly, not from our Constitution and not from his "inherent" powers. The trial court's findings substituted its view of the public interest for that expressed by the General Assembly. The fact that a statute is enacted "constitutes [the legislature's] implied finding" that the public will be harmed if the statute is not enforced. *Boone Creek Props.*, 442 S.W.3d at 40. Thus, the public interest strongly favors adherence to the 2021 legislation.

III. Conclusion

The trial court emphasized that "[t]he Governor has alleged irreparable injury to his constitutional powers and made preliminary showing that the bills impair the exercise of his constitutional duty." As discussed, these findings are largely unsupported by sound legal principles because they are occasioned by erroneous interpretations of the constitutional authority of the Governor and law. As a result, we find that the trial court's issuance of injunctive relief was improper.

In sum, considering that the challenged legislation was lawfully passed, the Governor's Complaint does not present a substantial legal question that would necessitate staying the effectiveness of the legislation. And as the equities clearly favor implementation of the legislation pending an adjudication of its constitutionality, we conclude that the Franklin Circuit Court abused its discretion in finding otherwise. Thus, we remand this case to the Franklin Circuit Court with instructions to dissolve the injunction. This case is reversed and remanded to the Franklin Circuit Court for further proceedings consistent with this Opinion. In the event certain sections of the 2021 legislation may be ultimately found invalid, the likely remedy may be severability. KRS 446.090.

All sitting. All concur.

---

19. Additionally, we can take judicial notice that the Delta variant, and perhaps others, are raising positivity rates throughout the nation and Kentucky.

Justice Hughes, concurring, joined by Chief Justice Minton:

I concur with the lead opinion's conclusion that a blanket injunction essentially precluding enforcement of any of the 2021 legislation should not have issued in this matter. The Attorney General insists this case presents no justiciable controversy and, in my view, his point has legal merit despite the obvious serious disagreements among the parties regarding emergency powers. Moreover, with the passage of time, the expiration of executive orders and the absence of any enforcement measures that collide with the limitations in the 2021 legislation, we have (at least on the record before us) currently no specific real-world dispute about the application of any portion of H.B. 1, S.B. 1, S.B. 2 or H.J.R. 77. That said, the Governor has alleged unconstitutional encroachment on his emergency powers, and the seemingly relentless nature of the COVID-19 pandemic ensures that the issues he raises will continually resurface, leading to constant litigation and conflicting results from circuit courts across the Commonwealth. Last summer prior to *Beshear v. Acree*, 615 S.W.3d 780 (Ky. 2020), we invoked Kentucky Constitution Section 110 and took unprecedented action to combine and expedite cases so we could address the multiple challenges to the Governor's COVID-19 response. Recognizing all that has transpired, I am persuaded that in these unusual circumstances the lead opinion properly proceeds to the merits of the trial court's injunction. Simply put, the maelstrom will continue absent some direction from this Court. As I read the lead opinion, we address the Governor's substantive constitutional challenges in the context of this appeal of a temporary injunction to determine whether substantial questions on the merits have been raised, not to rule definitively on all issues presented. This point bears emphasis because the Attorney General has not briefed in this Court, or in the trial court for that matter, the merits of the various constitutional challenges but has stood on his position that the case presents no justiciable controversy.

As we recognized in *Acree*, the Kentucky General Assembly granted specific emergency powers and authority to the Governor in KRS Chapter 39A and the legislature has the authority to restrict and expand those statutory powers. *Id.* Many of the challenged provisions of the 2021 legislation are within the legislature's domain, are entitled to the presumption of constitutionality, and should not be enjoined wholesale. For example, as the lead opinion aptly notes Section 15 of the Kentucky Constitution allows for the suspension of statutes "by the General Assembly or its authority." Consequently, the legislature can amend KRS 39A.180 to alter the manner in which statutes are suspended in an emergency. Similarly, the legislature may, as it did in H.B. 1, provide that businesses can operate in any emergency pertaining to a "virus or disease" under plans consistent with either the directives of the executive branch or applicable guidance from the Center for Disease Control. The Governor—and others for that matter—may question the efficacy and wisdom of that patchwork approach but that is a policy decision that our legislature can make by duly-passed statute and neither the executive nor the judiciary can reject it outright on "best practices" grounds. In sum, passing generally applicable laws that provide the framework for governmental action in the Commonwealth is the legislature's prerogative. Thus, I do not believe a substantial question on the merits was presented as to those parts of the 2021 legislation that were within the legislature's law-making authority.

That said, in *Acree* this Court did not conclude that all emergency powers are lodged solely in the legislature. Emergency powers are not expressly mentioned in our state Constitution but we discerned "[t]he implied tilt of the Kentucky Constitution toward executive powers in time of emergency ... given our government's tripartite structure with a legislature that is not in continuous session." *Id.* at 806. We noted that the Kentucky Constitution provides the framework for the three branches and the exercise and separation of their respective powers. *Id.* at 805. The executive branch is charged with the "supreme executive power of the Commonwealth," Kentucky Constitution Section 69, and authorized to administer state government year-round, just as the judicial branch is in session year-round to perform the judicial function of interpreting and applying the law. The legislature is not in year-round session but, to the contrary, has carefully circumscribed legislative sessions. Kentucky Constitution Sections 36 and 42 limit the legislature to sixty-day sessions ending no later than April 15 in even numbered years and to thirty-day sessions ending no later than March 30 in odd-numbered years. The legislature has no power to call itself into session at any other time but the Governor may exercise his discretion to do so under Section 80 on "extraordinary occasions." This constitutional structure led to our observations and conclusion about the power and necessity of the executive branch to act in managing an emergency. We concluded that "[f]ortunately, the need to definitively label the powers necessary to steer the Commonwealth through an emergency as either solely executive or solely legislative is largely obviated by KRS Chapter 39A ... which reflects a cooperative approach between the two branches." *Id.* at 809. Regrettably, recent events have strained that cooperative approach.

Historically, the Governor and various agencies of the executive branch including the Cabinet for Health and Family Services and the Division of Emergency Management have managed emergencies on a day-to-day, evolving basis, relying on the statutory guidelines provided by the legislature and executive branch administrative expertise. The executive branch has acted through the Governor's issuance of executive orders and various emergency administrative regulations. The legislature's emergency management involvement has been confined to the exercise of its traditional law-making function. Thus, during the 2020 and 2021 legislative sessions the General Assembly passed laws addressing various COVID-19 emergency issues, approving and supplementing some of the Governor's directives while limiting and discontinuing others. The 2021 legislation extends the legislature's reach and control beyond the laws passed in the constitutionally-mandated sessions, curtailing the Governor's powers through a thirty-day limit on the exercise of his emergency authority. The thirty-day limit operates as a "kill switch" that essentially transfers the day-to-day management of emergencies to the legislature by rendering the executive branch powerless to act after thirty days, forcing the call of a special legislative session. This type of special legislative session trigger has no antecedent in Kentucky law to my knowledge and requires careful constitutional analysis. Is it consistent with our current constitutional framework? Can the legislature pass a law that *de facto* nullifies the Governor's constitutionally-granted discretion regarding the calling and content of special legislative sessions and forces their recall, perhaps repeatedly as an emergency evolves over many months?[20]

This concept of time-limited executive emergency authority that relies on the recall of the legislature into special session appears throughout the 2021 legislation, raising serious constitutional questions that require further focused examination. The Attorney General, maintaining that no justiciable controversy exists, has not engaged on this or any other merits issues; the trial court needs the benefit of legal analysis from both sides. The lead opinion wisely recognizes that on remand the circuit court should address this issue and I wholeheartedly agree.

In closing, 7,477 Kentuckians have lost their lives to COVID-19 as of August 19, 2021. That number is considerably higher than the entire population of my Western Kentucky hometown and the cities where many Kentuckians live and work. The death toll does not even account for the hundreds of thousands of citizens whose lives have been irrevocably changed by the impact of the disease on their own lives, their families and their communities. And still the COVID-19 scourge continues with coronavirus cases and hospitalizations increasing these past few weeks. Whatever disagreements citizens may have about how best to address the seemingly limitless thorny issues raised by the pandemic, they are undoubtedly united in their desire to see our Commonwealth travel as safely and quickly as possible to the other side, to find some semblance of normal again. As a Justice, and more pertinently as a lifelong Kentuckian, I implore all parties to this matter to lay down their swords and work together cooperatively to finish this immensely important task for the benefit of the people they serve.

Notes and Questions

1. Though the Supreme Court in *Beshear v. Acree* was content to allow the Governor some latitude to deal with the public health emergency caused by the COVID-19 pandemic, the Governor's policies eventually fell out of favor with voters. At the November 2020 general election, the party opposite the Governor—campaigning on a promise to check the Governor's emergency powers—won enough House and Senate seats to capture supermajorities in both chambers. At the session that began in January 2021, the General Assembly enacted the statutes that were at issue in *Cameron v. Beshear.*

2. Did the Court in *Cameron* retreat from its earlier pronouncement in *Acree* that there was an "implied tilt [in] the Kentucky Constitution toward executive powers in time of emergency"? Justice Hughes in her concurrence, joined by Chief Justice Minton,

20. The 2021 Session passed H.B. 4 which will place on the 2022 general election ballot a proposed amendment to the Kentucky Constitution allowing the President of the Senate and the Speaker of the House to convene the legislature by Joint Proclamation "for no more than twelve legislative days annually." If Kentucky voters approve, this amendment would put the imprimatur of our Constitution on the convening of the General Assembly beyond the current constitutionally-authorized annual sessions and the "extraordinary circumstances" special sessions called at the discretion of the Governor under Section 80.

seems to think not. The *Cameron* Court reiterated the holding of *Brown v. Barkley* that the Governor has no "inherent" powers. From where does any "implied tilt" remaining after *Cameron* come?

3. *Brown v. Barkley* held that executive powers could be taken from the Governor and assigned instead to the other executive officers referred to in Section 91 of the Constitution. In *Cameron*, the Court held that the General Assembly also could require the Governor and a Section 91 officer, in this case the Attorney General, to act jointly. Does it matter that the power at issue in *Cameron* was the power to suspend laws, to which Section 15 speaks directly? Or, may the General Assembly require the Governor to share other executive powers with a Section 91 officer, consistent with Section 69? For example, may the General Assembly require that the Governor and a Section 91 officer jointly exercise the power to appoint members to a board or commission? Does it matter whether the Governor is allowed to make the majority of appointments to that board or commission?
4. *Cameron* was an interlocutory appeal from a trial court order issuing a temporary injunction. In this posture, the majority opinion stated, "the equities clearly favor implementation of the legislation pending an adjudication of its constitutionality," thus disclaiming any final adjudication of the constitutional issues. Other than the Section 80 issue, which both the majority and concurrence agreed was not fully developed and briefed, what of the other constitutional issues remained to be decided in the case?

B. The Constitutional and Common Law Role of the Attorney General

The Attorney General holds a unique position in the Executive Branch under the Kentucky Constitution. Of all Executive Branch officials specifically mentioned in the Constitution, the Attorney General alone possesses any inherent powers under the common law. Courts therefore have frequently had to grapple with the scope of the Attorney General's powers and responsibilities, but there is no single, comprehensive listing of those powers and responsibilities.

Constitutional Role

The office of Attorney General—like the offices of Treasurer, Auditor of Public Accounts, Commissioner of Agriculture, and Secretary of State—is established in Section 91 of the Kentucky Constitution. The Attorney General is elected in November of odd-numbered years, at the same time as the Governor and Lieutenant Governor,[1]

1. Ky. Const. §95; *see also id.* §91 (Attorney General and other Section 91 officers "shall be elected by the qualified voters of the State at the same time the Governor and Lieutenant Governor are elected").

for a four-year term that begins the following January.[2] Like all Section 91 officers, the Attorney General must be at least 30 years old and have been a Kentucky resident for the two years preceding his election,[3] and may serve no more than two consecutive terms.[4] In addition, the Attorney General also must have been "a practicing lawyer" for eight years before his election.[5]

The Attorney General is to be paid by salary, "and not otherwise."[6] His salary shall not be changed during the term for which he is elected.[7]

Under Section 91, the "duties" of the Attorney General "shall be such as may be prescribed by law."[8] Section 93 reiterates this requirement in slightly different language: "The duties and responsibilities" of the Attorney General "shall be prescribed by law."[9]

The Kentucky Constitution prescribes two additional roles for the Attorney General. First, the Attorney General has a role to play in gubernatorial succession. He may petition the Supreme Court to have the Governor declared disabled if, due to physical or mental incapacitation, the Governor is unable to discharge the duties of his office.[10] The Attorney General is third in line to succeed the Governor, following the Lieutenant Governor and President of the Senate.[11] Finally, the Attorney General also is charged with enforcing the Constitution's non-discrimination provisions applicable to railroads.[12]

Statutory Codification of the Attorney General's Common Law Authority

The entire scope of the Attorney General's statutory responsibilities is beyond the scope of this essay. The principal statute outlining the Attorney General's authority is KRS 15.020. That statute provides that "[t]he Attorney General is the chief law officer of the Commonwealth of Kentucky," and in that role, he is "the legal adviser of all state officers, departments, commissions, and agencies."[13]

Kentucky law requires the Attorney General to "appear for the Commonwealth in all cases in the Supreme Court or Court of Appeals wherein the Commonwealth is

2. Ky. Const. §91.
3. *Id.*
4. Ky. Const. §93.
5. Ky. Const. §92.
6. Ky. Const. §96.
7. Ky. Const. §235.
8. Ky. Const. §91.
9. Ky. Const. §93.
10. Ky. Const. §84.
11. Ky. Const. §87; *see also id.* §84 (Lieutenant Governor to act as Governor if the Governor is impeached and removed from office, dies, refuses to qualify, resigns, or is unable to discharge the duties of the office), *id.* §85 (President of the Senate to act as Governor during a vacancy if the Lieutenant Governor is impeached and removed from office, refuses to qualify, resigns, or dies).
12. Ky. Const. §217.
13. KRS 15.020(1).

interested,"[14] and to that end, the General Assembly has given him authority to appoint a Solicitor General and set his salary.[15] The Attorney General "shall also commence all actions or enter an appearance in all cases, hearings, and proceedings in and before all other courts, tribunals, or commissions in or out of the state, and attend to all litigation and legal business in or out of the state required of the office by law, or in which the Commonwealth has an interest, and any litigation or legal business that any state officer, department, commission, or agency may have in connection with, or growing out of, his, her, or its official duties, except where it is made the duty of the Commonwealth's attorney or county attorney to represent the Commonwealth."[16]

The Commonwealth's Attorneys, by statute, are given the primary responsibility for representing the Commonwealth in criminal cases in the Circuit Court,[17] while County Attorneys have the primary responsibility for representing the Commonwealth in criminal cases in the District Court.[18] But where the Attorney General's "participation in a given case is desirable to effect the administration of justice and the proper enforcement of the laws of the Commonwealth," the Governor, the President of the Senate, the Speaker of the House of Representatives, any court or grand jury in the Commonwealth, and certain local officials may request that "the Attorney General ... intervene, participate in, or direct any investigation or criminal action, or portions thereof, within the Commonwealth of Kentucky necessary to enforce the laws of the Commonwealth."[19] In such a case, the Attorney General may appear in the case himself,[20] or may, at his discretion, direct a Commonwealth's Attorney or County Attorney from a different judicial circuit or judicial district to participate in the case as a special prosecutor for the Commonwealth.[21]

KRS 15.020 also codifies certain powers that the office of Attorney General has under the common law. It provides that the Attorney General "shall exercise all common law duties and authority pertaining to the office of the Attorney General under the common law, except when modified by statutory enactment."[22] The statute does not attempt to delineate the Attorney General's common law duties and authority. Rather, it merely recognizes that these common law duties and authority exist, but that they are subservient to the overriding power of the General Assembly to modify the common law.

The question then becomes, what are the "common law duties and authority pertaining to the office of the Attorney General"?

---

14. KRS 15.020(3).
15. KRS 15.100(1).
16. KRS 15.020(3).
17. KRS 15.725(1).
18. KRS 15.725(2).
19. KRS 15.200(1).
20. *Id.*; *see also* KRS 15.210; *Hancock v. Schroering*, 481 S.W.2d 57, 61 (Ky. 1972) (when the Attorney General intervenes in a criminal case under KRS 15.200, he thereafter has "the right to exclusively control the investigation and any resultant prosecutions").
21. KRS 15.205.
22. KRS 15.020(1).

Defining the Attorney General's Common Law Duties and Authority

Unlike the office of Governor, which has no inherent or implied powers not expressly provided in the Constitution, the Supreme Court noted in *Brown v. Barkley* that the Attorney General "has been held to possess by implication the powers inhering in the office as it existed at common law."[23] The common law duties and authority of the Attorney General may be traced to English law predating the American Revolution:

> The office of Attorney General existed in England from an early date. Most of the American colonies established an office of the same name, and it was carried into the succeeding state governments. Legal historians are not in accord as to just what were the powers and prerogatives of the Attorney General in the mother country, but they are agreed that he was the chief law officer of the Crown, managing all the king's legal affairs, attending to all suits, civil and criminal, in which he was interested, and exercising other high duties and prerogatives, some of which were quite foreign to the legal. To what extent those undefined powers attached to the same office in this country is likewise the subject of different views. However, it is certain that the Attorney General has been the chief law officer of the federal or the state governments with the duty of representing the sovereign, national or state in such capacity.[24]

But the Attorney General's common law powers are subject to regulation by the General Assembly: "[I]t must be presumed that, when the office [of Attorney General] was created in Kentucky, it was contemplated that the officer should have all the powers then recognized as belonging to it, except so far as these powers were limited by statute."[25] "This, however, is subject to the limitation that the office may not be stripped of all duties and rights so as to leave it an empty shell, for, obviously, as the legislature cannot abolish the office directly, it cannot do so indirectly by depriving the incumbent of all his substantial prerogatives or by practically preventing him from discharging the substantial things appertaining to the office."[26]

At common law, the Attorney General has the power to bring any action which he thinks necessary to protect the public interest.[27] This is "a broad grant of authority,"[28] and includes "the power to institute, conduct and maintain suits and proceedings for

---

23. *Brown v. Barkley*, 628 S.W.2d 616, 621 (Ky. 1982); *see also Johnson v. Commonwealth ex rel. Meredith*, 291 Ky. 829, 165 S.W.2d 820, 827 (1942) ("It cannot be presumed that, in creating the state government and in creating the law department, [the Kentucky Constitution] contemplated that the head of the law department should not have such authority as was exercised by the Attorney General at common law.").

24. *Johnson*, 165 S.W.2d at 826.

25. *Respass v. Commonwealth*, 131 Ky. 807, 115 S.W. 1131, 1132 (1909); *see also Brown v. Barkley*, 628 S.W.2d at 622 n.10 (the Attorney General's common law powers are "[s]ubject ... to the overriding authority of the General Assembly").

26. *Johnson*, 165 S.W.2d at 829.

27. *Commonwealth ex rel. Conway v. Thompson*, 300 S.W.3d 152, 173 (Ky. 2009).

28. *Id.*

the enforcement of the laws of the state, the preservation of order, and the protection of public rights."[29] "[I]n the exercise of his common-law powers, an attorney general may not only control and manage all litigation in behalf of the state, but he may also intervene in all suits or proceedings which are of concern to the general public."[30]

In addition to initiating, maintaining, and controlling litigation on behalf of the Commonwealth, it is also within the Attorney General's power to determine not to bring an action: "As a constitutionally elected officer, the Attorney General is entrusted with broad discretion in the performance of his duties, which includes evaluating the evidence and other facts to determine whether a particular claim should be brought."[31]

The Attorney General has discretion to determine "what matters may, or may not, be of interest to the people generally."[32] The Attorney General serves as lawyer for the people of the Commonwealth. Because in this Commonwealth, "the people are king, ... the Attorney General's duties are to that sovereign rather than to the machinery of government."[33] Thus, the Attorney General's fealty is to the people of the Commonwealth of Kentucky. As such, the Attorney General has an obligation to defend the people from unconstitutional government action. "[I]f the Constitution is threatened by an item of legislation [or act of the Executive], the Attorney General may rise to the defense of the Constitution by bringing a suit, and is not required to wait until someone else sues."[34] Likewise, the Attorney General must defend duly adopted statutory enactments that are not unconstitutional.[35]

Even though the Attorney General is the primary legal advisor to the Commonwealth and its officers and agencies under KRS 15.020, the General Assembly has allowed agencies the option to retain their own counsel.[36] The Supreme Court has recognized that the General Assembly may "divest some of the powers of the Attorney General (*i.e.*, serving as legal counsel to a given state entity) and invest them in another (*i.e.*, private counsel of the entity's choosing)."[37] However, the Court has rejected the further argument that "when a state agency hires, or can hire, its own attorneys pursuant to statutory authority, the Attorney General no longer has authority to unilaterally

29. *Commonwealth ex rel. Hancock v. Paxton*, 516 S.W.2d 865, 867 (Ky. 1974).

30. *Hancock v. Terry Elkhorn Mining Co.*, 503 S.W.2d 710, 715 (Ky. 1973) (internal citation omitted).

31. *Overstreet v. Mayberry*, 603 S.W.3d 244, 265 (Ky. 2020).

32. *Commonwealth ex rel. Beshear v. Commonwealth, Office of the Governor ex rel. Bevin*, 498 S.W.3d 355, 366 (Ky. 2016) (internal citation omitted).

33. *Paxton*, 516 S.W.2d at 867; *accord, Thompson*, 300 S.W.3d at 173.

34. *Beshear*, 498 S.W.3d at 364 (quoting *Paxton*, 516 S.W.2d at 868).

35. *Id.*

36. *See* KRS 12.210.

37. *Beshear*, 498 S.W.3d at 364 (citing *Johnson*, 165 S.W.2d at 829); *see also Kentucky State Bd. of Dental Examiners v. Payne*, 213 Ky. 382, 281 S.W. 188, 189 (1926) ("There is nothing in our Constitution limiting or circumscribing the power or authority of the Legislature to prescribe by whom such actions when maintainable at all may be prosecuted" on behalf of the Commonwealth or a state agency).

decide to act for that agency."[38] Rather, the Court held, the delegation of "day-to-day operational powers," including to a state agency's private counsel, "does not preclude a need for the Attorney General to protect the interest of all the people when ... unlawful conduct is claimed ... toward" that state agency.[39]

Finally, the Attorney General also has authority at common law to investigate, which may be somewhat broader than his power to prosecute, violations of the law. The Supreme Court has recognized that the Attorney General's office is "an investigatory body."[40] The Attorney General's power to institute actions includes the power to inspect and review documents and information necessary for him to determine whether a good faith belief exists to bring a legal action.[41] This common law investigatory power reflects "the common sense concept of investigating before filing a suit."[42] The Attorney General's "investigative authority is not plenary and must comport with relevant criminal and civil statutory directives. In other words, although such investigative power may no longer be in full Elizabethan plume, it is still a feather in the Attorney General's cap."[43]

So long as the Attorney General believes the investigation might yield evidence upon which a civil or criminal action within his authority to litigate could be based, he may proceed with the investigation. A later determination that the evidence does not support an action within the Attorney General's authority does not necessarily imply that the investigation was beyond his investigative power in the first instance.

---

38. *Id.*

39. *Id.*

40. *Stilger v. Flint*, 391 S.W.3d 751, 754 (Ky. 2013); *see also Commonwealth ex rel. Ferguson v. Gardner*, 327 S.W.2d 947, 948–49 (Ky. 1959) (noting that the Attorney General's authority to supervise the administration of certain trusts necessarily implies some authority to investigate).

41. *Strong v. Chandler*, 70 S.W.3d 405, 409 (Ky. 2002) (*citing Folks v. Barren Cnty.*, 313 Ky. 515, 232 S.W.2d 1010 (1950)).

42. *Id.* at 410.

43. *Commonwealth v. Johnson*, 423 S.W.3d 718, 725 (Ky. 2014).

C. The Pardon Power

> "He shall have power to remit fines and forfeitures, commute sentences, grant reprieves and pardons, except in case of impeachment, and he shall file with each application therefor a statement of the reasons for his decision thereon, which application and statement shall always be open to public inspection. In cases of treason, he shall have power to grant reprieves until the end of the next session of the General Assembly, in which the power of pardoning shall be vested; but he shall have no power to remit the fees of the Clerk, Sheriff or Commonwealth's Attorney in penal or criminal cases." (Ky. Const. §77.)

> "... [T]he following persons ... shall not have the right to vote.... Persons convicted in any court of competent jurisdiction of treason, or felony, or bribery in an election, or of such high misdemeanor as the General Assembly may declare shall operate as an exclusion from the right of suffrage, but persons hereby excluded may be restored to their civil rights by executive pardon...." (Ky. Const. §145.)

> "... All persons shall be excluded from office who have been, or shall hereafter be, convicted of a felony, or of such high misdemeanor as may be prescribed by law, but such disability may be removed by pardon of the Governor...." (Ky. Const. §150.)

> "The Governor shall have power, after five years from the time of the offense, to pardon any person who shall have participated in a duel as principal, second or otherwise, and to restore him to all the rights, privileges and immunities to which he was entitled before such participation...." (Ky. Const. §240.)

The Governor, like the President of the United States (*cf.* U.S. Const. Art. II §2), enjoys a broad power to remit fines and forfeitures and grant reprieves and pardons. Though it is the duty and function of the Judicial Branch to ensure that *justice* is done in a criminal case, the pardon power allows the Chief Executive to show *mercy* to persons convicted of crimes or facing criminal prosecution.

In addition to allowing for commutation of a sentence and for a full pardon, the Kentucky Constitution also permits the Governor to provide lesser included relief from the consequences of a criminal conviction, usually referred to as a "restoration of civil rights." In this way, Kentucky's Governor has the power to exercise the discretion to restore less than all the rights taken from a person upon a felony conviction. Under Sections 145 and 150, a felony conviction forever bars a person from ever being able to vote or hold public office again. But those same provisions also permit the Governor remove those disabilities. By statute, the General Assembly has recognized that, in restoring the civil rights of a convicted felon, the Governor will usually restore the rights to vote, serve on a jury, obtain a professional or vocational license, and hold elective office, but not the right to keep and bear arms. *See* KRS 196.045.

Section 239 prohibits any person who gives, accepts, or knowingly carries a challenge to a duel from ever holding public office in the Commonwealth again. The oath of office required by Section 228, which is prescribed for both pubic officials and attorneys at law, also requires a person taking the oath to swear or affirm that they have never fought in a duel, sent or accepted a challenge to a duel, or acted as a second in carrying a challenge to a duel. Section 240 allows the Governor to relieve a person of the disability imposed by Section 239, but only after five years have passed since the offense.

Fletcher v. Graham

Supreme Court of Kentucky (2006)
192 S.W.3d 350

Opinion of the Court by Justice Johnstone.

In an original action before the Court of Appeals, Appellant, Governor Ernie Fletcher, in his official capacity as Governor of the Commonwealth of Kentucky, sought a writ of mandamus directing the Franklin Circuit Court to issue supplemental instructions to a special grand jury. This special grand jury had been summoned by the Attorney General to investigate allegations of criminal violations of the state's merit system hiring scheme. While the grand jury was in the process of investigating these allegations, and after several indictments had been issued against executive branch employees, Governor Fletcher issued an executive order pardoning all criminal conduct that was under investigation by that special grand jury. Following the issuance of the pardon, Governor Fletcher moved the Franklin Circuit Court to instruct the grand jury concerning the effect of the pardon—to wit, that the grand jury had no authority to issue further indictments for pardoned conduct. The Franklin Circuit Court declined to issue the supplemental instructions, prompting Governor Fletcher to seek a writ of mandamus in the Court of Appeals. The Court of Appeals denied the petition, determining that the pardon, though valid, did not compel the circuit court to issue supplemental instructions to the grand jury investigating the pardoned offenses. Governor Fletcher appealed to this Court as a matter of right. For the reasons set forth herein, we affirm in part and reverse in part.

Background

The investigation began in May 2005, when an employee of the Kentucky Transportation Cabinet contacted the Attorney General and presented evidence of alleged criminal violations of the state merit employee hiring system.[1] On May 25, 2005, upon motion of the Attorney General, the Franklin Circuit Court summoned a special grand jury. For several months, the grand jury proceeded to investigate the matter and eventually issued several indictments against executive branch employees alleging both misdemeanor violations of the merit system laws and felony violations concerning evidence and witness tampering. Some three months into the investigation, on August 29, 2005, Governor Fletcher issued Executive Order 2005-924, whereby he sought to pardon nine individuals indicted by the grand jury as well as "any and all persons who

1. *See* KRS Chapter 18A.

have committed, or may be accused of committing, any offense up to and including the date hereof, relating in any way to the current merit system investigation."[2]

Notwithstanding the pardon, the grand jury continued its work and issued indictments for pardoned offenses. In response, Governor Fletcher moved the Franklin Circuit Court to supplement its instructions to the grand jury. Specifically, Governor Fletcher sought an instruction advising the grand jury that "pardoned conduct that preceded the pardon is no longer an indictable offense and therefore cannot constitutionally form the basis for an indictment." Governor Fletcher further asked that the grand jury be instructed that pardoned persons may not be indicted "solely for the purposes of naming them in a report." The Franklin Circuit Court denied the Governor's motion, instead telling the grand jurors that the Governor's pardon had no bearing on their work whatsoever. While recognizing the Governor's constitutional authority to issue pardons, the trial court concluded that the requested instructions would impermissibly infringe upon the grand jury's independence. Rather, the trial court determined that the grand jury could continue issuing indictments, even against pardoned persons, though such indictments would immediately be dismissed.

Governor Fletcher then petitioned the Court of Appeals for a writ of mandamus directing the Franklin Circuit Court to deliver the requested instructions. The Court of Appeals denied the petition, ultimately concluding that the Governor's pardon, though valid, did not oblige the circuit court to instruct the grand jury concerning the effect of the pardon. Governor Fletcher now appeals to this Court as a matter of right.

Standard of Review

We first address our standard of review of a request for a writ of mandamus. A writ of mandamus is essentially a command from a higher court to "stop some action which is threatened by or is being proceeded with by an inferior court."[3] It has long been characterized as an "extraordinary remedy"[4] that is granted conservatively and only in "exceptional situations."[5] Accordingly, a writ of this nature is granted for only two purposes: (1) when the lower court is acting beyond its jurisdiction, and (2) when the lower court is acting or is about to act erroneously, and there exists no adequate remedy by appeal or otherwise and great injustice and irreparable injury will result if the petition is not granted.[6] In reviewing the grant or denial of a writ of mandamus, the standard of our review depends on the nature of the writ and the circumstances of the case.[7] Generally speaking, however, the basic standard of review of the grant or denial of a writ is abuse of discretion, while questions of law are reviewed de novo.[8]

---

2. Reference to any persons indicted during the pendency of this appeal are inappropriate, as such matters have not been made a part of the record before us.

3. *Stafford v. Bailey*, 301 Ky. 155, 191 S.W.2d 218, 219 (1945).

4. *Clark v. Jones*, 258 S.W.2d 902 (Ky. 1953).

5. *Haight v. Williamson*, 833 S.W.2d 821, 823 (Ky. 1992).

6. *Newell Enterprises, Inc. v. Bowling*, 158 S.W.3d 750, 754 (Ky. 2005).

7. *Grange Mutual Insurance Co. v. Trude*, 151 S.W.3d 803, 810 (Ky. 2004). ("Thus, it is apparent that the proper standard [of appellate review] actually depends on the class, or category, of writ case.")

8. *Newell*, 158 S.W.3d at 754.

Here, the Governor sought a writ of mandamus of the second category, and the Court of Appeals determined that the petition was properly before the court. Noting that Governor Fletcher sought to completely prohibit indictments for pardoned offenses rather than simply prevent erroneous indictments, the Court of Appeals agreed that no adequate remedy by appeal existed. The Court of Appeals further found that the potential "insult" to the Governor's pardoning power fulfilled the "great and irreparable injury" requirement. The Attorney General now argues that the Court of Appeals erred in its holding that great and irreparable injury would potentially result from the denial of the requested writ.

We agree with the Court of Appeals' determination that the prerequisites for a writ of mandamus—*i.e.*, no adequate remedy by appeal, and great and irreparable harm—were met in this instance. Because the Governor specifically seeks to prevent the indictment of any pardoned person, it would not be an adequate remedy to simply dismiss any indictments as they were issued. As the Court of Appeals noted, "a post-indictment remedy ... would not protect the interests the Governor asserts." We also concur with the Court of Appeals' holding that, if his arguments are correct, the Governor faces great and irreparable injury. The Governor alleges a violation of the separation of powers, as well as misconstruction of his constitutional power to pardon; correction of this possible error is certainly "necessary and appropriate in the interest of orderly judicial administration."[9] Accordingly, the Court of Appeals did not abuse its discretion in concluding that the procedural prerequisites for a writ of mandamus were satisfied in this case.

Supplemental Instructions to the Grand Jury

Turning to the merits of the case, we must first determine the validity of the August 29 pardon, as the circuit court would be under no obligation to instruct the grand jury concerning a legally ineffectual document. The pardon, contained in Executive Order 2005-924 read, in pertinent part:

> [B]y virtue of the authority vested in me by Section 77 and related provisions in the Constitution of the Commonwealth of Kentucky, I ERNIE FLETCHER, Governor of the Commonwealth of Kentucky, do hereby grant a full, complete, and unconditional pardon to James L. Adams, Darrell D. Brock, Jr., Danny G. Druen, Tim Hazlette, Charles W. Nighbert, Cory W. Meadows, Richard L. Murgatroyd, Basil W. Turbyfill, Robert W. Wilson, Jr., and any and all persons who have committed, or may be accused of committing, any offense up to and including the date hereof, relating in any way to the current merit system investigation being conducted by the special grand jury presently sitting in Franklin County, Kentucky and the Office of the Attorney General.... The provisions of this Order shall not apply to Ernie Fletcher, Governor of the Commonwealth of Kentucky.

9. *Grange*, 151 S.W.3d at 808.

The Attorney General challenges the scope of the Governor's pardon on three grounds: (1) that Section 77 does not authorize general, or blanket, pardons; (2) that pardons may not be granted prior to indictment; and (3) that formal acts of acceptance are essential to a valid pardon. We first address the issue of the so-called "blanket" pardon.

The Attorney General maintains that the language of Section 77 does not expressly authorize blanket pardons, which are pardons issued to classes of persons rather than specified individuals. Here, though the Governor does pardon nine identified individuals, the pardon also included a class of persons: "any and all persons who have committed, or may be accused of committing, any offense up to and including the date hereof." The Governor argues that nothing in the language of Section 77 prohibits this type of general or blanket pardon, and that the governor's power to issue general pardons has long been recognized. We agree.

Section 77 provides: "[The Governor] shall have power to remit fines and forfeitures, commute sentences, grant reprieves and pardons, except in case of impeachment, and he shall file with each application therefor a statement of the reasons for this decision thereon, which application and statement shall always be open to public inspection." When interpreting constitutional provisions, our focus rests on the express language of the provision, and words must be given their plain and usual meaning.[10] This Court is "not at liberty to construe ... plain and definite language of the Constitution in such a manner as to thwart the deliberate purpose and intent of the framers of that instrument."[11] In fact, our predecessor Court recognized as a "cardinal rule" of constitutional interpretation the principle that rules of construction may not be employed where the language of the provision is clear and unambiguous.[12] "It is to be presumed that in framing the constitution great care was exercised in the language used to convey its meaning and as little as possible left to implication...."[13]

The language of Section 77 is clear, and its meaning unambiguous. The Governor is given authority to grant pardons. Aside from cases of impeachment, absolutely no restriction is placed on this delegation of authority. Nothing in the language of Section 77 infers that general pardons are prohibited, nor is there any indication that a governor may not pardon a class of persons. We are not at liberty to insert meaning where the language of the provision is clear. Instead, the language of Section 77 leads to only one reasonable interpretation: that the framers intended to give the Governor broad and unrestricted discretion to issue pardons to whomever.

Though not necessary because the language of Section 77 is clear, we note that our conclusion gives effect to the intent of the framers of Kentucky's constitution. A review of the debates of the constitutional convention of 1890 confirms that the delegates considered general pardons. Included in these debates is frequent reference to Governor Bramlette who, following the end of the Civil War, asked the General Assembly

10. *City of Louisville Mun. Hous. Comm'n v. Pub. Hous. Admin.*, 261 S.W.2d 286, 287 (Ky. 1953).

11. *Harrod v. Hatcher*, 281 Ky. 712, 137 S.W.2d 405, 408 (1940).

12. *Grantz v. Grauman*, 302 S.W.2d 364, 366 (Ky. 1957).

13. *City of Louisville v. German*, 286 Ky. 477, 150 S.W.2d 931, 935 (1940).

to pardon all Confederate soldiers.[14] The delegates also discussed the similarity of the provision to the corresponding federal provision, noting that Presidents Lincoln and Grant had wisely exercised the authority under the federal Constitution to pardon scores of former Confederate soldiers.[15] At least two delegates referenced King James II, who suspended conviction for any religious offenses in an effort to permit his fellow Catholics to practice their faith openly in Protestant England.[16] This delegate warned that an unrestricted pardoning power would permit a future governor to believe, as James II had, that "if he could pardon one individual before trial, he could pardon all individuals before trial...."[17] Without doubt, the framers of our constitution were cognizant that the pardoning power could potentially be used to issue general pardons to persons falling within a specified class, yet declined to expressly prohibit such discretion. In light of these debates, this Court can only conclude that, if the framers sought to prohibit general pardons, they would have so stated in the language of the provision.[18]

For largely similar reasons, we likewise agree with the Governor and the Court of Appeals that he is not prevented from issuing pardons prior to formal indictment for the pardoned offenses.[19] Foremost, the language of Section 77 does not restrict the pardoning power to those offenses for which an indictment has been issued. Indeed, there is no language whatsoever in Section 77 identifying a particular stage in the criminal proceedings after which a pardon is permissible. For this reason, there is simply no support in the language of the section itself for the Attorney General's proposition that pardons may only be issued for indicted offenses. And, though bearing little precedential value to our decision herein, we note that Governor Fletcher is not the first Kentucky governor attempting to issue a pardon prior to indictment, contrary to the representations of the Attorney General.[20]

---

14. Debates, Ky. Constitutional Convention of 1890, Vol. I, p. 1116.

15. *Id.* at 1105.

16. *Id.* at 1271.

17. *Id.* at 1272.

18. *Pardue v. Miller*, 306 Ky. 110, 206 S.W.2d 75, 78 (1947) (declining to interpret the phrase "public officer" as to include employees of state universities or other state employees, the Court noted that if the framers had sought to include such employees, "nothing would have been simpler than to so phrase the section as to exclude implication or speculation") (internal citations omitted).

19. We reject the Attorney General's assertion that the pardon, by its own terms, only applies to indicted individuals. The class specified in the pardon is "any and all persons who have committed, or may be accused of committing, any offense up to and including the date hereof, relating in any way to the current merit system investigation." We find no indication that the pardon was intended only for indicted, or "accused," persons. The Governor's use of the word "or" clearly intends to establish two subsets of the class of pardoned persons: those who have committed an offense, and those who may be accused of committing an offense. "[A] pardon is to be taken most beneficially for the recipient and most strongly against the authority by which it is granted, wherever its meaning is in doubt." *Ex parte Paquette*, 112 Vt. 441, 27 A.2d 129, 131 (1942).

20. *Adkins v. Commonwealth*, 232 Ky. 312, 23 S.W.2d 277 (1929). ("Before an indictment was returned against him, on December 12, 1927, the day before his term of office expired, Governor William J. Fields issued an unconditional pardon to Adkins for this crime.")

The Attorney General refers extensively to the constitutional debates in urging a prohibition on pre-indictment pardons, indicating that the delegates did not specifically address such a pardon. In his dissenting opinion, Justice Cooper likewise includes numerous references to the debates in support of his proposition that the framers neither intended a pre-indictment pardon, nor even contemplated it as a real possibility. While both are correct that the pre-indictment pardon was not particularly debated at length, it is simply disingenuous to report that the framers did not consider such a pardon.

One of the most contentious and lengthy debates concerning the gubernatorial pardon focused on the issue of a pre-conviction pardon.[21] As enumerated at length in Justice Cooper's dissenting opinion, numerous amendments were proposed that would have allowed a pardon only "after conviction" or "after judgment."[22] Those seeking to restrict the pardon to post-conviction offenses relied primarily on the principle that a pardon implies that there is guilt, and should only follow a democratic society's formal indication of guilt—conviction. Such a delegation of power, it was argued, would derogate the autonomy of the judicial branch, as adequate safeguards existed within the judicial system to protect against false conviction and to protect the rights of the innocent, who need no pardon.[23] According to some, a pardon prior to conviction eroded the rights of the pardonee's victim and the public, by denying "the right to come in and have a fair investigation ... and to let the facts be submitted to a candid world."[24] Conversely, those delegates urging a broad, unrestricted pardon power argued that no distinction existed between a pre-conviction and postconviction pardon, as the ultimate purpose of the pardon was to grant mercy in exceptional circumstances, rendering a formal conviction irrelevant: "It is not the time when the pardon is granted that is material ... [it is] that he may relieve the defendant from the penalty of the law."[25] These delegates also indicated that circumstances often necessitate an expedient pardon, one rhetorically asking whether there was a "man in this House who regrets the exercise of the Executive clemency by Governor Bramlette *before indictment*, judgment or conviction?"[26]

Through these extensive discussions wherein the delegates speculated as to the potential abuses of the gubernatorial pardon, it is evident that the framers considered a pre-indictment pardon as a valid possibility under a broadly drafted provision. This conclusion does not rest upon isolated statements of certain delegates, or upon proposed amendments that were ultimately rejected by the delegates. Rather, a genuine and comprehensive review of the entire debates makes clear that, with respect to the timing of a pardon, the primary interest of the delegates was whether a formal finding of guilt should precede a pardon. Naturally, little distinction would be drawn between a

21. *See* Debates, Vol. I, pp. 1096–1123, 1251–72.
22. *Id.* at 1123.
23. *Id.* at 1113.
24. *Id.* at 1120–21.
25. *Id.* at 1099.
26. *Id.* at 1099 (emphasis added).

pardon prior to indictment versus a pardon prior to conviction, as both precede a legal determination of guilt. In fact, even beyond repeated reference to Governor Bramlette's pre-indictment pardons, it was acknowledged that if pre-conviction pardons were allowed, a future governor might exercise his authority even prior to indictment. One delegate in favor of a pre-conviction pardon expressly advocated pardons prior to indictment, first reminding his colleagues that grand jury proceedings are ex parte and therefore inconsequential to a determination of guilt: "[Delegates] question the wisdom of allowing the power to pardon before conviction, and yet are willing to give the power to pardon after conviction. [They] say he shall not have the power to pardon a man from what? From a *charge* of crime. That is what he is pardoned from...."[27] The delegates fully considered limiting pardons to post-conviction offenses, and as noted by Justice Cooper, several amendments to this effect were offered. Notwithstanding Justice Cooper's faulty analysis and summary of these debates, and the above-referenced statements of Delegate Whitaker, our conclusion remains the same: regardless of whether the delegates intended that a pre-indictment pardon would actually occur, there is simply no doubt that they recognized such a pardon as a possibility. Ultimately, the delegates of the Constitutional Convention ultimately declined to adopt any limitation as to when pardons could be issued. It is contrary to logic to recognize that the framers considered and rejected multiple amendments limiting the pardon power, but conclude that the framers intended that such limitations be implied nonetheless. Where no express language in Section 77 supports the proposition that preindictment pardons are prohibited, and the debates indicate that none was intended, this Court is without authority to interpret the provision otherwise.[28]

Lastly, the Attorney General claims that formal acts of acceptance are essential to the effectiveness of a gubernatorial pardon, and that the Governor lacks authority to assert a pardon that has not yet been formally accepted. No Kentucky court has squarely answered this question, although the Attorney General is correct that our predecessor court has acknowledged the widely accepted, general principle that delivery and acceptance are required for a valid pardon.[29] What satisfies this acceptance requirement, however, has not been specifically defined in Kentucky.

Other jurisdictions have addressed the acceptance requirement, and there seems to be general agreement that a pardon may be rejected or, in other words, not accepted. Where a person wishes to refuse to testify before a grand jury, claiming his Fifth Amendment privilege against self-incrimination, he may refuse to accept a presidential pardon, which would have had the unwanted effect of negating the privilege and compelling testimony.[30] Recognizing that the consequences flowing from the offense itself might sometimes be less harsh than those of a pardon, the Second Circuit has observed that the acceptance requirement is "a principle designed to protect the individual from

---

27. *Id.* at 1104 (emphasis added).
28. *Harrod*, 137 S.W.2d at 408.
29. *Adkins*, 23 S.W.2d at 280–81.
30. *Burdick v. United States*, 236 U.S. 79, 35 S.Ct. 267, 59 L.Ed. 476 (1915).

unwanted consequences of a forced grant of ... a pardon."[31] This point becomes particularly salient in the case of a conditional pardon, where the pardonee may view the conditions of pardon more loathsome than punishment for the actual offense. Thus, a pardon may not be thrust upon an unwilling recipient; it may be refused, and therefore acceptance must be a logical prerequisite to a fully effectual pardon.

However, acknowledging that a pardon may be refused does not answer the question of what constitutes acceptance, particularly in the case of a general pardon such as here, where the pardon potentially applies to numerous, unidentified individuals. Courts have determined that delivery of the pardon to the pardonee's attorney suffices,[32] or other person acting on the pardonee's behalf.[33] These courts consider the concept of delivery and acceptance of a pardon analogous to that of a deed, so that delivery is complete when the grantor has parted with control of the document with the intention that it passes to the grantee.[34] Contrary to Justice Cooper's assertion, other courts have extended this reasoning to conclude that acceptance of a pardon is assumed, once brought to the court's attention, absent proof indicating otherwise. Over a century ago, the Supreme Court of Arkansas considered whether the testimony of a witness who had previously been pardoned should be admitted at another defendant's criminal trial; the validity of the pardon was challenged.[35] Relying upon Alabama and Texas jurisprudence, the Arkansas court specifically held that "acceptance of [the pardon], we think, in the absence of any proof to the contrary, must be presumed."[36]

Upon thorough review of these cases, we agree that acceptance of a pardon need not be formal, but may be inferred by the circumstances. This position embodies the notion that a pardon may be rejected, but also the common-sense assumption that such rejection will be the rare exception. Where the circumstances of the case evidence the clear intent of the governor to issue the pardon, and there is no evidence or circumstances from which to infer that it was rejected, acceptance must be assumed. Here, the intent of the Governor to pardon any and all offenses falling within the grand jury's investigation cannot be questioned. Moreover, there is no indication that any person within its ambit has rejected the pardon. We therefore conclude that the pardon has been validly accepted.

Having determined that Governor Fletcher's pardon is valid, we now turn to the effect such pardon has on the grand jury proceedings in the Franklin Circuit Court. Governor Fletcher contends that a pardoned person cannot be validly indicted for a

31. *Marino v. INS*, 537 F.2d 686, 693 (2nd Cir. 1976).

32. *Ex parte Williams*, 149 N.C. 436, 63 S.E. 108 (1908).

33. *Ex parte Crump*, 10 Okla. Crim. 133, 135 P. 428, 431 (1913).

34. *Williams*, 63 S.E. at 109.

35. *Redd v. State*, 65 Ark. 475, 47 S.W. 119 (Ar. 1898).

36. *Id.*, 47 S.W. at 122. *See also Territory v. Richardson*, 9 Okla. 579, 60 P. 244, 247 (1900); *Hannicutt v. State*, 18 Tex. App. 489 (Tex. Ct. App. 1885) ("We are of opinion that *the circumstances* show a delivery by the Governor and such assent on the part of the witness as amounts to a delivery and acceptance of law.") (emphasis added). Even upon consideration of Justice Cooper's discussion of this authority, we still firmly adhere to our interpretation of these cases and our holding herein.

pardoned offense, and therefore the Franklin Circuit Court has a duty to inform the grand jury of the pardon. The Attorney General argues that, even if valid, the pardon cannot operate to halt the grand jury proceedings.

The parties agree that a pardon serves to relieve the pardonee of criminal prosecution. "A 'pardon' is '[t]he act or an instance of officially nullifying punishment or other legal consequences of a crime.'"[37] It operates to eviscerate prosecution of the pardoned offense, because the pardonee is regarded as innocent: "The pardoned man is relieved from all the consequences which the law has annexed to the commission of the public offense of which he has been pardoned, and attains new credit and capacity, as if he had never committed that public offense."[38] However, the Governor and Attorney General disagree as to the full scope of the pardon or, more specifically, whether the pardon precludes an indictment for the pardoned offense.

The Attorney General argues that the pardon may bar punishment for the pardoned offenses, but it does not erase the fact that an offense occurred, so that the grand jury may continue to investigate and return indictments. Indeed, this Court has recognized limitations on the scope of a pardon. A pardon does not prevent any and all consequences of the pardoned offense: collateral consequences of the offense may still follow. For example, an attorney who has been pardoned for the offense of forgery may not be punished for that crime, but may be disbarred as a result of that offense.[39] Our predecessor court also recognized that a gubernatorial pardon does not restore the character of the witness/pardonee, so that he or she could still be impeached as a felon.[40] Thus, while a pardon will foreclose punishment of the offense itself, it does not erase the fact that the offense occurred, and that fact may later be used to the pardonee's detriment.

However, the Attorney General's reliance on the theoretical underpinnings of these cases is misplaced, as they address the collateral consequences of the pardoned offense. There are no legal or semantic gymnastics by which an indictment may be characterized as a collateral consequence of an offense. It is axiomatic that grand jury investigations and indictments are stages in the criminal prosecution of the offense itself. The law is clear and well-established: "the pardon is itself an absolute exemption from any further legal proceedings...."[41] There is no room for equivocation on this point. When a pardon has been issued, the court is without jurisdiction or constitutional authority to continue legal proceedings against the pardonee: "[w]hen a pardon ... is brought to the attention of the court, it is the duty of the court to discharge the defendant and dismiss the proceedings against him...."[42]

37. *Anderson v. Commonwealth*, 107 S.W.3d 193, 196 (Ky. 2003) (quoting *Black's Law Dictionary*, 7th ed. 1999).

38. *Nelson v. Commonwealth*, 128 Ky. 779, 109 S.W. 337, 338 (1908).

39. *Id.*

40. *Parson v. Commonwealth*, 112 S.W. 617 (Ky. 1908).

41. *Jackson v. Rose*, 3 S.W.2d 641, 643 (Ky. 1928). *See also Nelson*, 109 S.W. at 339. ("[T]he pardon obliterates the offense against the public ... [and] relieves the offender from the punishment affixed to it by that law....")

42. *Id.*

We now turn to the Franklin Circuit Court's responsibility with respect to the grand jury. The grand jury has competing, but balanced, functions: on the one hand, its purpose is to investigate allegations of criminal conduct and determine if there is probable cause to believe that a crime has been committed; on the other, the grand jury serves to protect the public against unfounded criminal prosecutions where probable cause is lacking.[43] The grand jury is unique in our criminal justice system, because it operates independent of the court and the prosecutor: "[t]he hallmark of the grand jury is its independence from outside influence."[44] The Attorney General relies on the inherent independence of the grand jury to assert that the Franklin Circuit Court is without authority to instruct the jury concerning the Governor's pardon and its effect.

This position overstates the independence of the grand jury. A grand jury's authority to investigate is not without limits; for example, a grand jury may not compel a person to appear before it and testify against himself for the purpose of bringing an indictment against that person.[45] Furthermore, there are instances where judicial supervision of the grand jury's action is necessary and proper: "[a] Grand Jury is a part of the court, and under judicial control."[46] This Court has previously granted a writ of mandamus directing the circuit court to strike portions of a grand jury report that were improperly included.[47] And, more directly related to the present matter, the court is under a duty to instruct the grand jury concerning "any other matter affecting their rights and duties as grand jurors which the court believes will assist them in the conduct of their business."[48]

We can think of no matter that would more affect the duties of a grand jury, or would more assist it in the conduct of its business, than an instruction informing it that the very offenses which it is investigating have been pardoned, and could never be criminally prosecuted. The court must instruct a grand jury accurately of the relevant and material legal issues. An instruction informing the grand jury of the pardon's effect would in no way be encroaching on the grand jury's prerogative, simply because the grand jury no longer holds any legal prerogative to indict pardoned persons. Moreover, any person falling within the class specified by the Governor's pardon now holds a right, by virtue of the constitutional force of the pardon, to be free of any further legal proceedings. "In their proceedings the grand jurors cannot deprive a citizen of any substantial right assured by the constitution."[49] Finally, we cannot ignore certain practical concerns of the grand jurors themselves, who have sacrificed significant amounts of time in service to the public. Common sense and courtesy dictate that, where the subjects of a grand jury investigation have been pardoned and no criminal prosecution of the alleged offenses could ever result, the jurors should be so informed.

---

43. *Bowling v. Sinnette*, 666 S.W.2d 743, 745 (Ky. 1984).
44. *Democratic Party of Ky. v. Graham*, 976 S.W.2d 423, 426 (Ky. 1998).
45. *Taylor v. Commonwealth*, 274 Ky. 51, 118 S.W.2d 140, 143 (1938).
46. *Bowling*, 666 S.W.2d at 745.
47. *Id. See also Matthews v. Pound*, 403 S.W.2d 7 (Ky. 1966).
48. RCr 5.02.
49. *Taylor*, 118 S.W.2d at 143.

Accordingly, the Franklin Circuit Court must inform the grand jury of the legal effects of a gubernatorial pardon, and the effects it necessarily has on the present grand jury investigation. For the reasons explained herein, the grand jury must be advised that it has no authority to issue indictments against persons named in the pardon or persons falling within the class specified in the pardon. Because the Governor has conceded at oral argument that it is the prerogative of the grand jury to issue a general report of its investigation, so long as pardoned or unindicted individuals are not specifically identified, we need not address the issue. Furthermore, we note that neither this opinion, nor Governor Fletcher's pardon, has any affect whatsoever on the grand jury's investigation of post-pardon allegations of criminal conduct or an investigation of the Governor himself, who specifically and expressly excluded himself from the pardon.

* * *

For the reasons set forth herein, we hold that the Franklin Circuit Court abused its discretion in declining to issue supplemental instructions to the grand jury. By virtue of the broad discretion afforded by Section 77 of the Kentucky Constitution, the Governor may extend general, preindictment pardons, and he validly did so by Executive Order 2005-924. A gubernatorial pardon operates to cease any further legal proceeding concerning the pardoned conduct, including indictments. When a grand jury is investigating alleged criminal conduct that is subsequently pardoned, it is the duty of the supervising court to instruct the grand jury of the legal effect of that pardon, as such information is relevant and material to the business of the grand jury. Accordingly, the opinion of the Court of Appeals is affirmed in part and reversed in part. Further, this matter is remanded to the Court of Appeals for entry of a writ of prohibition in conformity with this opinion.

* * *

Notes and Questions

1. In *Fletcher v. Graham*, the Court recognized that the Governor has the power to issue pardons to people even before they are indicted. Does this holding comport with the text of Section 77?
2. Both the President of the United States and the Governor of Kentucky may exercise their pardon power before indictment. (Recall that President Ford pardoned President Nixon before Nixon could be indicted for his role in the Watergate scandal.) Both also may issue pardons in the nature of a general amnesty, *i.e.*, in which entire classes of persons receive the benefit of the pardon without having been singled out by name. (For example, President Carter pardoned the Vietnam-era "draft dodgers," without naming specific persons in the pardon.) Is the breadth of the pardon power, as expressed in *Fletcher v. Graham*, consistent with the constitutional text?
3. Under Section 77, as interpreted by Fletcher v. Graham, may the Governor pardon a person for a crime that may occur in the future?

D. The Appointment Power

> "He shall have the power, except as otherwise provided in this Constitution, to fill vacancies by granting commissions, which shall expire when such vacancies shall have been filled according to the provisions of this Constitution." (Ky. Const. §76.)
>
> "… Inferior State officers and members of boards and commissions, not specifically provided for in this Constitution, may be appointed or elected, in such manner as may be prescribed by law, which may include a requirement of consent by the Senate, for a term not exceeding four years, and until their successors are appointed or elected and qualified." (Ky. Const. §93.)
>
> "Except as otherwise provided in this Constitution, vacancies in all elective offices shall be filled by election or appointment, as follows: If the unexpired term will end at the next succeeding annual election at which either city, town, county, district or State officers are to be elected, the office shall be filled by appointment for the remainder of the term. If the unexpired term will not end at the next succeeding annual election at which either city, town, county, district or State officers are to be elected, and if three months intervene before said succeeding annual election at which either city, town, county, district or State officers are to be elected, the office shall be filled by appointment until said election, and then said vacancy shall be filled by election for the remainder of the term. If three months do not intervene between the happening of said vacancy and the next succeeding election at which city, town, county, district or State officers are to be elected, the office shall be filled by appointment until the second succeeding annual election at which city, town, county, district or State officers are to be elected; and then, if any part of the term remains unexpired, the office shall be filled by election until the regular time for the election of officers to fill said offices. Vacancies in all offices for the State at large, or for districts larger than a county, shall be filled by appointment of the Governor; all other appointments shall be made as may be prescribed by law. No person shall ever be appointed a member of the General Assembly, but vacancies therein may be filled at a special election, in such manner as may be provided by law." (Ky. Const. §152.)

Under Section 76, the Governor has power to make appointments, "except as otherwise provided in this Constitution." Section 93 allows inferior state officers, including members of boards and commissions, to be "appointed or elected, in such manner as may be prescribed by law." Putting these two provisions together, Section 76 does not apply to any "inferior" officers, and instead, applies only to officers whose offices are created by the Constitution itself. *See Rouse v. Johnson*, 234 Ky. 473, 28 S.W.2d 745, 751 (1930) (when Sections 76 and 93 are read together, "it would confine the vacancies mentioned in section 76 to such officers as are created by the Constitution, and not to the filling of vacancies in those created by the Legislature under the provisions of … section 93").

The appointment power vested in the Governor by the Kentucky Constitution permits only temporary appointments. Under Section 76, the power to fill vacancies is temporally limited, as the Governor's appointments expire when otherwise filled according to the dictates of the Constitution. This is in contradistinction to the appointment power of the President, which allows lifetime appointments to judicial offices. Section 152 provides an additional temporal limitation on the Governor's power to fill vacancies in elective offices. Depending on when the next general election will be held and when the vacancy occurs, the Governor's appointment expires at the next general election or the second general election after the vacancy occurs, and the balance of the term remaining after the expiration of the appointment is to be filled by the voters in a special election.

The terms of office for those inferior offices created under Section 93 may be no more than four years long, and the laws providing for gubernatorial appointments to those offices "may include a requirement of consent by the Senate." The default rule under Section 93, therefore, is that the consent of the Senate is only necessary as to those offices where the authorizing statute specifically requires it. Under Article II of the U.S. Constitution, the default rule is that presidential appointments may be made only "by and with the advice and consent of the Senate," but Congress "may by law vest the appointment of such inferior officers, as they think proper, in the President alone, in the courts of law, or in the heads of departments" (U.S. Const. art. II, §2), thus allowing the elimination of the Senate's role of advice and consent where specifically provided by statute.

Sibert v. Garrett

Court of Appeals of Kentucky (1922)
197 Ky. 17, 246 S.W. 455

Opinion of the Court by Judge Thomas.

This action involves the constitutionality of an act attempted to be passed at the 1922 session of the General Assembly of Kentucky, commonly known as the "Simmons Road Bill[.]" * * * It is entitled "An act to amend an act relating to roads and bridges," etc., and it repeals in part and amends chapter 17 of the Acts of 1920, p. 76. The latter act created a commission composed of four members to be known as the "state highway commission," and it, by the terms of the act, was authorized to administer and perform all the duties belonging to the department of public roads in and for the commonwealth. The members of the commission in that act were appointed by the Governor, and its duties and the tenure of office of the members are set out in the act, and which are not necessary to repeat here. The 1922 act involved in this litigation amended in various respects the 1920 act, two of which were that the first members of the commission were selected by the act itself, and thereafter it was provided that the members should be elected by the Legislature, and salaries were attached to the position, whereas there were none in the 1920 act.

The constitutionality of the 1922 act is assailed on a number of urged grounds, but only three of which do we consider of sufficient materiality to deserve our consideration, and they are: (1) That the Legislature possessed no constitutional right to name in the bill the first members of the commission, or to elect their successors thereafter; (2) because the act carried with it an appropriation of money for the payment of the designated salaries of the members of the commission, and it received but 19 votes in the Senate, whereas an appropriation bill, under the provisions of section 46 of the Constitution, must receive a majority of all the members elected to each house, and the 19 votes which the act received in the Senate was not a majority of that body; and (3) that the Lieutenant Governor did not sign or affix his signature to the enrolled bill within the contemplation of section 56 of the Constitution. This action to test the validity of the act was filed by some of the designated members in it against others who declined to join as plaintiffs, and against the members of the commission under the 1920 act. Defendants set up in their answer the various grounds relied on as rendering the act unconstitutional, to which a demurrer was filed, which was overruled, and, plaintiffs declining to plead further, the act was adjudged unconstitutional, and the petition was dismissed, whereupon plaintiffs prosecute this appeal.

Ground (1) urged against the validity of the statute, it is claimed by defendants, finds support in the provisions of sections 27 and 28 of our Constitution, the first of which says:

> "The powers of the government of the commonwealth of Kentucky shall be divided into three distinct departments, and each of them be confined to a separate body of magistracy, to wit: Those which are legislative, to one; those which are executive, to another; and those which are judicial, to another."

While the language of the next one is:

> "no person, or collection of persons, being of one of those departments, shall exercise any power properly belonging to either of the others, except in the instances hereinafter expressly directed or permitted."

It is insisted that the filling of an office or the selection or designation of the person clothed with official functions is essentially an executive duty and properly belongs to the executive department, and that by the terms of the above sections of the Constitution the Legislature is forbidden to exercise it, but, if not strictly so, that the officer should be appointed by that department with which his duties are allied and closely connected, and that in either event it was incompetent for the Legislature to name in the act, or to subsequently elect, the members of the state highway commission created thereby, whose duties are strictly and essentially executive or administrative, the latter of which is a part of, and belongs to, the executive department.

Able briefs are filed by counsel for both sides exhibiting a most exhaustive research of the decisions involving the question and of the statements by law-writers upon the subject, many of which are cited and relied on by respective counsel as supporting their divergent views; and in some instances counsel rely upon the same case or cases or upon the same text-book authority, because of different constructions each of them places thereon. Counsel for appellants include the following as supporting their contention, *viz.*: * * * *McArthur v. Nelson*, 81 Ky. 67; *Sinking Fund Commissioners v. George*, 104 Ky. 260, 47 S. W. 779, 20 Ky. Law Rep. 938, 84 Am. St. Rep. 454; and the three closely following cases of *Purnell v. Mann*, 105 Ky. 87, 48 S. W. 407, 49 S. W. 346, 50 S. W. 264, 20 Ky. Law Rep. 1146, 1396, 21 Ky. Law Rep. 1129; *Poyntz v. Shackelford*, 107 Ky. 546, 54 S. W. 855, 21 Ky. Law Rep. 1323; and *Sweeney v. Coulter*, 109 Ky. 295, 58 S. W. 784, 22 Ky. Law Rep. 885. While appellees' counsel rely upon the cases of * * * *Taylor v. Commonwealth*, 3 J. J. Marsh. 401, and *Pratt v. Breckinridge*, 112 Ky. 1, 65 S. W. 136, 66 S. W. 405, 23 Ky. Law Rep. 1356, 1858.

To notice in detail all of the cases relied on by both sides, or to discuss the grounds upon which the court in each of them rested its opinion, and to point out the distinguishing features between many of them, would expand this opinion to the dimensions of an ordinary size law book, which we do not regard as necessary to a statement of our position and the reasons therefor, even if the crowded time of this court did not warn against it.

Perhaps no state forming a part of the national government of the United States has a Constitution whose language more emphatically separates and perpetuates what might be termed the American tripod form of government than does our Constitution, which history tells us came from the pen of the great declaimer of American independence, Thomas Jefferson, when delegates from Kentucky, just after it was admitted to the Union, waited upon him, and he penned for them the substance of what is now section 28, *supra*, of our Constitution, containing an affirmative prohibition against one department exercising powers properly belonging to the others, and which without it contained only the negative prohibition found in section 27 of that instrument, and which was the extent of the separation of the powers found in the federal Constitution and in those of a number of the states composing the confederated Union at that time. Following the adoption of our first Constitution, other incoming states, either in their first Constitutions or in subsequent ones, copied, either literally or in substance, the two sections of our Constitution, and the courts of some of them have announced divergent views as to the proper construction of the two sections, and in nearly every instance the opinion was made to turn upon the existence of some fact or facts extraneous to their language, notably among which were other provisions of the Constitution containing them, and which were made to apply to the particular facts under consideration, and thereby furnished the reason for the particular conclusion reached; while another instance was that the appointment to the particular office involved, in the manner then being tested, had been exercised in that manner under a prior Constitution containing the same clauses as the subsequent one, and it was held that such contemporaneous construction of the prior Constitution was adopted as part of the subsequently framed one. In addition to those reasons for the apparent conflicts in the opinions there must also be mentioned the ever-existing one of different courts arriving at different conclusions under the exact or similar states of fact, which condition of the law is familiar to all practitioners. It would be but little trouble to point out instances since the formation of the United States wherein the court of only one state took a position diametrically opposed to all the others upon the same state of facts and later that position was adopted by a majority of the courts, a notable illustration of which is when this court held in the case of *Paducah Lumber Co. v. Paducah Water Supply Co.*, 89 Ky. 340, 12 S. W. 554, 13 S. W. 249, 11 Ky. Law Rep. 738, 7 L. R. A. 77, 25 Am. St. Rep. 536, that a citizen might sue a local public utilities company to recover special damages for the violation of its local franchise contract made with the municipality in which it was operated. At that time every court in all the states of the Union, as well as in Canada and England, denied any such right to the citizen and taxpayer; but that opinion was followed shortly by one of the North Carolina Supreme Court, and now a substantial number of the courts of last resort have adopted the principle.

It is insisted by counsel for appellants that the Legislature under the Constitutions of the respective states, unlike Congress under the federal Constitution, has all the power not withheld from it by the Constitution of the state, which as a general proposition is true, as will be seen from 12 Corpus Juris, 745, and which contains but a repetition of what all other writers on the subject as well as the courts say. But a deeper probing into and investigation of the subject will reveal the truth that the rule so generally stated means, not that the Legislature has "all powers" not withheld by the Constitution, but that it "may pass any acts that are not expressly or by necessary implication inhibited by their own Constitutions or by the federal Constitution." In other words, the Legislature may perform all legislative acts not expressly or by necessary implication withheld from it, but it may not perform or undertake to perform executive or judicial acts, except in such instances as may be expressly or by necessary implication directed or permitted by the Constitution of the particular state. To adopt the latitudinous construction that the Legislature may do anything not expressly or impliedly prohibited by the Constitution would to our minds at once destroy the separation of the powers of government into the three great departments.

In an early day this court, in an opinion written by one of the greatest lawyers who ever occupied a seat on the Court of Appeals (Chief Justice Robertson), in the case of *Taylor v. Commonwealth*, 3 J. J. Marsh. 401, said that "appointment to office is intrinsically 'executive,'" but that, even so, it might be performed by a judicial officer when the duties of the office appertain strictly to the court, which was a clerk in that case. To the same effect are * * * the text in 22 R. C. L. 424, wherein it is said:

> "The appointment of officers is intrinsically an administrative or executive act, but this does not imply that no appointment can be made by any department of government other than the executive, for all the authorities agree that the courts and the Legislature may appoint those public officers which are *necessary* to the exercise of *their own functions*" (our italics).

Some of the cases cited and relied on by learned counsel for appellants contain statements indicating a contrary view, but a critical examination of them will show that the peculiar facts of those cases, some of which we have hereinbefore recited, entered into the shaping of the courts' opinions. But, however that may be, we do not regard an exact, or correct classification of the act of appointment to office as essential to the decision of the question in this case for reasons hereinafter to be noticed.

It cannot fail to be observed that the reasons underlying the separation of our republican form of government into the three branches was to prevent one of the departments from absorbing and appropriating unto itself the functions of either of the others. The purpose was to have each of them to so operate in their respective spheres as to create checks to the operations of the others and to prevent the formation by one department of an oligarchy through the absorption of powers belonging to the others. The evil effects from such concentration of power were outstanding in the pages of past history, the instances of which we need not stop to enumerate. It was to prevent such evil effects and a possible eventual revolution, and to preserve and forever perpetuate, if possible, the constitutional form of government, that sections 27 and 28 and similar ones were adopted, and we conceive it to be the duty of the courts to adopt the construction most conducive to such perpetuation rather than one which would open a possible door for the destruction of the edifice as contemplated, and especially so, when the language involved and to be construed is plainly susceptible to such a construction.

In doing so we are aware of the universally applied and often reiterated admonition that it is the duty of the courts to declare an act constitutional and within the power of the Legislature to enact rather than otherwise; but such admonition does not destroy the power of the courts to pronounce an act unconstitutional when its enactment is either expressly or by necessary implication inhibited and subversive of the purposes and intention of the makers of the particular constitution under consideration. In the light of these observations we will now approach a determination of the question under consideration.

To begin with, the latest utterance of this court in the *Pratt-Breckinridge* Case, *supra*, holds that under no provisions of our present Constitution is it competent for the Legislature to itself elect, designate, or appoint officers whose duties are of the nature and character attempted to be conferred on appellants in this case. But it is said that the opinion in that case was what might be termed a political one, and which in a sense may be accepted as true, and that its reasoning should not be followed on that account, but rather should the doctrine of *Sinking Fund Commissioners v. George*, *supra*, and the other named cases immediately following it, be applied in this case. Answering that contention, it might be conceded that there would be much force in it if the *George* opinion and those following it were supported by reasoning as sound or sounder than is found in the *Pratt-Breckinridge* opinion, which, however, we are not prepared to admit. Without incorporating excerpts from the latter opinion, we are convinced, beyond doubt, that its reasoning is far more convincing than that contained in its short-lived predecessors, and, according to our view, is practically unanswerable. Besides, the doctrine of *stare decisis* has not lost its place in the law, and, as said, in substance, in the case of *Kentland Coal & Coke Co. v. Keen*, 168 Ky. 836, 183 S. W. 247, L. R. A.

1916D, 924, it is entitled to great weight and is adhered to by most courts, unless the principle established by the prior decisions is clearly erroneous. "But the rule should not be departed from except on the fullest conviction that such an error has been committed." As intimated, we are by no means convinced that such an error was committed in the rendition of the *Pratt-Breckinridge* opinion, which has stood unchallenged for more than 20 years, and for that reason, plus its sound and, as we conceive it, almost unanswerable reasoning we would hesitate to overrule it at this late day unless we were more thoroughly convinced of its unsoundness.

At the time the *George* opinion was rendered the penitentiaries were under the management of a board elected by the Legislature as provided by chapter 4, Session Acts 1898, and the opinion in that case upheld the validity of that act. The *Pratt-Breckinridge* opinion was rendered on November 20, 1901, at a time when the penitentiary commissioners elected by the Legislature under the 1898 act were still in office, and they were, without testing the question, continued to be so elected until 1906, when the Legislature enacted chapter 18 of the published Session Acts for that year, which repealed the 1898 act and provided for the appointment of the members of the board of control by the Governor. From that time forward the doctrine of the *Pratt-Breckinridge* Case has been scrupulously followed by the Legislature in not assuming to elect officers, except those whose duties pertain to its own sessions, and, except that of librarian, the grounds for which are fully set out in the *Pratt-Breckenridge* opinion * * *.

Primarily the power of selecting public officers rests with the people they serve, but they may confide it in the Constitution they adopt, either expressly or by necessary implication, to whatever department of the government they see proper, and the question at last becomes one of the correct interpretation of the particular Constitution involved. Without naming them, and for the sake of brevity, it is sufficient to say that our Constitution creates certain named state officers, and certain designated district and county officers, and provides how they shall be filled by election, or by appointment in case of a vacancy, and in the latter part of section 93 relating to legislatively created state officers it is said:

> "Inferior state officers, not specifically provided for in this Constitution, may be appointed or elected, in such a manner as may be prescribed by law, for a term not exceeding four years, and until their successors are appointed or elected and qualified."

Section 107 of the same instrument provides that—

> "The General Assembly may provide for the election or appointment, for a term not exceeding four years, of such other county or district ministerial and executive officers as may, from time to time, be necessary."

So far as we have been able to ascertain, those sections are the only ones in the Constitution relating to the authority of the Legislature with reference to the election or appointment of persons to fill office, except section 249, which relates exclusively to officers whose duties are immediately connected with and entirely appertain to the enactment of laws, and whose terms are only coextensive with that of the members of the Legislature. It is therefore insisted by counsel for appellants, as it must be in order to maintain their position, that under the language of sections 93 and 107 of the Constitution, which is in substance the same in each of them, power is delegated to the Legislature to itself select, either by election, or by appointment in the creating act itself, the officer or officers whose duties are to execute it; while it is contended by appellees' counsel that those sections by necessary implication limit the authority of the Legislature to provide in the statute the prescribed method or means by which the officers created to execute it shall be appointed or elected, but that the Legislature is given therein no authority to itself exercise the electing or appointing power. In other words, it is contended by appellees that the authority to prescribe a manner or mode by which an office may be filled is a distinct and separate power or authority from that of filling the office, and that contention is fortified, not only by the *Pratt-Breckinridge* Case, but also by the case of *Clarke v. Rogers*, 81 Ky. 44, which arose under our former Constitution, which our present one succeeded, and in which (section 10 of article 6) practically the same language is found as in sections 93 and 107 of our present Constitution. * * *

Mr. Cooley, in his excellent work on Constitutional Limitations (7th Ed.) p. 127, states the rule to be that—

> "Every positive direction (in the Constitution) contains an implication against anything contrary to it or which would frustrate or disappoint the purpose of that provision."

And on page 99 of the same work he says:

> "When the Constitution defines the circumstances under which a right may be exercised, ... the specification is an implied prohibition against legislative interference to add to the condition."

Those principles applicable to interpretation of Constitutions are everywhere recognized, and when sections 93 and 107 conferred the power upon the Legislature to provide for the "filling of inferior state officers in such manner as may be prescribed by law," or to "provide for the election or appointment" of created county or district officers, the conclusion is inevitable, from the language employed and in the light of the purpose of the constitutional requirement segregating and separating the functions of government, that the authority of the Legislature is limited to making such provisions by exercising its authority to pass an act containing them and directing upon whom or with whom the power to appoint or elect was lodged, which electing and appointing agency should, perhaps, be selected from the department to which the duties of the office necessarily appertain.

It may be true that numerically a greater number of courts take a contrary view, though it is untrue that only two state courts adopt the conclusions herein expressed * * *. But, whatever the number, we are convinced that they by doing so are inviting the destruction of the constitutional barriers separating the departments of government, and that our interpretation is much the sounder one and is essential to the future preservation of our constitutional form of government as originally intended by the forefathers who conceived it. Moreover, foreign opinions are no precedents to be followed by this court and are looked to only for their persuasive effect, and, if they fail to "persuade" by the use of sound and logical reasoning, they should not be followed, howsoever great their number, since false reasoning may not be looked to for the establishment of truth, whatever its quantity, and its dangerous tendencies are increased in proportions to the extent it is employed.

Besides the cited cases supporting the contention of appellees as to the limitations of the authority of the Legislature under sections 93 and 107 of the Constitution, were we to adopt the opposite construction, insisted on by appellants, it would lead to a virtual overthrow of its sections 27 and 28, separating the functions of the state government into three grand departments. It will be observed that only in section 107 is the power of the Legislature to "prescribe" and "provide" limited to any one of the three departments. It is broad enough in section 93 to confer the power on the Legislature, if appellants' contention be true, to appoint all inferior state officers, and under section 107 to appoint all district and county ministerial and executive officers not provided for in the Constitution, whether their functions be strictly legislative, executive, or judicial. The logical result of the contention, if adopted and followed, would empower the Legislature to appoint or elect the private secretary to the Governor; the Commissioner, sergeant at arms, tipstaff, and bailiff of the Court of Appeals; all the officers connected with the insurance department; the enforcement officers of the Blue Sky Law; the officers in the geological department; the state tax commission; the state board department, as in this case; the members of the state board of health, as well as those of the various counties; the county school superintendents of all the counties as well as their tax commissioners; and numerous other state, county, and district officers now in existence and untold positions which may hereafter be created. If such power would not tend or serve to destroy the purpose and intention sought to be accomplished by separating the powers of government in the Constitution, it would be difficult to conceive of one that would. To thus throw open the doors would offer an incentive for the assembling of strong and corrupt lobbies at each recurring session of the Legislature to procure the passage of laws, not so much for the benefit of the public, but to enable the lobbyists or some political friend of his or of members of the Legislature to obtain a salaried berth for either past or future favors, and the partial check or curb which the Constitution intended to provide against such contaminating activities would be wholly destroyed. Furthermore, such power on the part of the Legislature, if a full exercise of it should be persisted in, would enable it to gradually absorb to itself the patronage and control of the greater part of the functioning agencies of the state and county governments, and, thus endowed, it would be little short of a legislative oligarchy. We do not in the least intimate that any such motives influenced the 1922 session of the Legislature or any of the appellants in the passage of the act now under consideration, nor do we attribute any such designs to any of the members of that Legislature, but our suggestions apply only to probabilities which it was the intention of the people in framing and adopting the Constitution to prevent as far as possible.

* * *

Because * * * of the conclusions expressed with reference to the legislative appointment of the commissioners created by the act, about which we have no doubt, but which was reluctantly reached, we are forced to hold the act unconstitutional, and the judgment of the trial court in doing so is affirmed.

* * *

Notes and Questions

1. *Sibert*, though dating from 1922, is still often cited for its strong language in support of the separation of powers and our "tripod" form of government.

2. To whom the appointment power belongs has not always been clear under the Kentucky Constitution. In *Commissioners of Sinking Fund v. George*, 104 Ky. 260, 47 S.W. 779 (1898), which was rendered shortly after the current Constitution entered into force, the Court of Appeals observed that, "[u]nder [S]ection 93 of the Constitution, the legislature could not only provide for inferior state officers, but could designate how they should be appointed or elected." 47 S.W. at 781. The Court held "the election of the commissioners [to the board of penitentiary commissioners] was not essentially an executive function, and that the legislature had the right to elect them." *Id.* at 782.

   The Court's holding in *George* was short-lived. In *Pratt v. Breckenridge*, 112 Ky. 1, 65 S.W. 136 (1901), the Court had to decide the constitutionality of the so-called "Goebel Election Law" in the context of an 1899 election contest for the office of Attorney General. The Goebel Election Law created a three-person state election commission with power to resolve election disputes and to appoint the members of every local election commission in the state. The members of the State Election Commission were to be appointed by the General Assembly. The Court, in a decision that was controversial at the time, held that the appointment, by the General Assembly, of members of the Election Commission violated the separation of powers. Specifically, the Court held, "The creation of an office is accomplished by the exercise of legislative power. It is done by the enactment of a law. The filling of it, when not exercised by the people, or in some manner directed or permitted by the constitution, is executive, and must be performed by an executive officer." *Pratt*, 65 S.W. at 137.

   Sewell v. Bennett, 220 S.W. 517 (Ky. 1920), can be read as a slight, temporary retreat from *Pratt*. There, in considering appointments to the Workmen's Compensation Board, the Court stated that "the Workmen's Compensation Act is purely a legislative creation and in providing for the appointment of members of the board the Legislature had the undoubted power to make these appointments itself or give them to the Governor, or indeed any other person or body that it might designate." *Sewell*, 220 S.W. at 519. The *Sewell* Court cited *George* approvingly and did not cite or mention *Pratt* at all. *Id.*

   But the Court of Appeals then decided *Sibert*, which remains the seminal Kentucky case on the appointment power. *Sibert* relied on *Pratt*, referring to its reasoning as "unanswerable," thereby overruling *George*, *Sewell*, and similar cases. Under Section 93, as interpreted by *Pratt* and *Sibert*, creating an inferior office, and deciding who may fill it, are legislative functions. But appointing someone to that legislatively created office is an executive function and must be done by an executive branch official. *Pratt* and *Sibert* remain good law today. *See Legislative Research Comm'n ex rel. Prather v. Brown*, 664 S.W.2d 907, 920–24 (Ky. 1984).

3. Does the appointment power being an "executive" function mean that it must be exercised by the Governor? *See* Sheryl G. Snyder & Robert M. Ireland, *The Separation of Powers Under the Constitution of Kentucky: A Legal and Historical Analysis of L.R.C. v. Brown*, 73 Ky. L.J. 165, 216 n.262 (1984) ("Under *Rouse v. Johnson*, *Brown v. Barkley* and *Ex parte Auditor of Public Accounts*, the executive power of appointment can be conferred on other elected constitutional Executive Officers. At what point would that infringe upon the Governor's 'supreme executive power' under §69?").

4. In *Craig v. O'Rear*, 199 Ky. 553, 251 S.W. 828 (1923), the Court of Appeals stated, "While the purpose of the language employed was to call attention to the exception to the rule, and cannot be regarded as controlling, practically all of the courts hold that mere temporary agents appointed to perform a particular task, who serve without term and without pay, and whose functions cease when the purpose is accomplished, may be appointed by the Legislature itself, or in any manner that it may provide, and we have no doubt of the correctness of this view." The statute at issue in the case established a commission that was "empowered to establish two new normal schools for the training of white elementary teachers, one to be located in the western part of the state and one to be located in the eastern part of the state," and allowed the Speaker of the House of Representatives and the President of the Senate to appoint the members of the commission. The Court upheld the statute. (The schools established by the commission were Morehead State Normal School and Murray State Normal School, now known as Morehead State University and Murray State University, respectively.) Why does the distinction between "temporary agents" and "officers" have any constitutional significance with respect to the appointment power?

5. One of the more colorful cases concerning the appointment power is *Commonwealth ex rel. Cowan v. Wilkinson*, 828 S.W.2d 610 (Ky. 1992). In that case, the Supreme Court held that Governor Wallace Wilkinson could appoint himself to serve on the board of trustees of the University of Kentucky. The Court reasoned that the Kentucky Constitution empowers the Governor to fill vacancies. *Id.* at 613. Because the statute prescribing the qualifications of university trustees did not prohibit the Governor from appointing himself, the Court declined to read that requirement into the statute or the Constitution: "There is no express or implied restriction on the Governor from appointing himself to the Board of Trustees in either the statutes or the Constitution. The courts cannot legitimately usurp the province of the executive by applying some theory of common law public policy. Judicially created common law must always yield to the superior policy of legislative enactment and the Constitution." *Id.* at 614. The Court noted that several constitutional provisions (Sections 44,

160, 165, and 237) prohibit certain officeholders from filling other, incompatible offices, but none of those provisions applied to the university's board of trustees. *Id.*

Fox v. Grayson

Supreme Court of Kentucky (2010)
317 S.W.3d 1

OPINION OF THE COURT BY CHIEF JUSTICE MINTON.

I. *INTRODUCTION.*

In 1992, the voters approved amendments to §93 of Kentucky's Constitution. The narrow question now before this Court is whether §93, as amended in 1992, vests in the Kentucky State Senate alone the right to confirm appointees to so-called inferior state offices and nominees to boards and commissions. After careful consideration, we hold that §93 of the Constitution, as amended, gives the Senate the sole right of confirmation.

II. *FACTUAL AND PROCEDURAL HISTORY.*

In July 2007, Governor Ernie Fletcher appointed Virginia Fox to the Council on Postsecondary Education (CPE) for a term expiring December 31, 2012. Fox took her seat on the CPE immediately because the General Assembly was not in session at the time.[1] Before the next session of the General Assembly convened in January 2008, Steven L. Beshear replaced Fletcher as Governor of Kentucky.

During the 2008 regular session of the General Assembly, the Senate voted to confirm Fox's appointment to the CPE; but the House of Representatives failed to act on Fox's appointment before it adjourned *sine die*.[2] Because Fox was not confirmed timely by both legislative bodies as KRS 164.011(1) purports to require,[3] Governor Beshear's general counsel informed Fox that her seat on the CPE "has become vacant by oper-

---

1. *See* Kentucky Revised Statutes (KRS) 11.160(2)(h) ("During periods when the General Assembly is not in session, the Governor's or other appointing authority's power of appointment shall not be diminished, and nominees may assume the responsibilities of the position pending confirmation. During that period, they shall be considered for all purposes to have been appointed and to be lawful occupants of the post to which they have been nominated, except that they shall be subject to the confirmation process when the General Assembly is next in regular session or special session called for the purpose of confirming the nominees.").

2. The Senate's vote to confirm Fox is, at least on its face, curious because KRS 11.160(2)(f) says, "[t]he confirmation shall originate in the House of Representatives. If the House of Representatives does not confirm an appointment, the Senate shall not consider the appointment." We take no position on whether the Senate's vote to confirm Fox was valid. That issue is not properly before us because it was not fully developed in the circuit court.

3. KRS 164.011(1) states, in relevant part, that "[t]he citizen members [of the CPE] shall be confirmed by the Senate and the House of Representatives under KRS 11.160...."

ation of law." A few weeks later, Governor Beshear appointed Pam Miller to replace Fox on the CPE. Because the General Assembly was not in session at the time of her appointment, Miller took her seat on the CPE immediately.

Fox filed a declaratory judgment action in the Franklin Circuit Court against Miller; Governor Beshear, in his official capacity; and Trey Grayson, in his official capacity as Secretary of State of the Commonwealth of Kentucky. The heart of Fox's complaint was her contention that §93 of the Kentucky Constitution vests the Senate with the sole power to confirm appointees such as she. For that reason, Fox argued, Miller's appointment was legally ineffective because Fox had already been duly confirmed by the Senate.

Secretary Grayson filed an answer in which he, essentially, took no position regarding the merits of Fox's complaint. Instead, Secretary Grayson asked to be relieved of any responsibility to file further responsive pleadings and to be designated as a nominal party. Governor Beshear, joined by Miller, however, took an active position against Fox's contentions, choosing—in lieu of an answer— to file a motion to dismiss under Kentucky Rules of Civil Procedure (CR) 12.02, arguing Fox's failure to state a claim upon which relief may be granted.[4] After briefing was completed, the trial court granted the Governor's motion to dismiss.

Fox appealed that dismissal to the Kentucky Court of Appeals.[5] Because her appeal involves issues of great and immediate public importance, we granted Fox's unopposed motion to transfer her appeal to this Court. Now, having fully considered the well-presented arguments of the parties, as well as the applicable law, we conclude that Fox's assertion that §93 of the Kentucky Constitution provides the Senate with the sole power to confirm gubernatorial appointments is correct. We reverse the trial court's order of dismissal and remand this case to Franklin Circuit Court for all necessary further proceedings.

III. *Analysis.*

A. *Section 93 and its Constitutional Predecessors.*

In order to understand fully the current version of §93, we must first examine its historical underpinnings. As the Governor notes, our first two state constitutions each indisputably conferred upon the Senate the exclusive authority to confirm gubernatorial appointments.[6] Our third constitution, adopted in 1850, however, did not so clearly

4. Miller joined Governor Beshear's CR 12.02 motion in the circuit court and has filed a brief with us simply stating that she agrees with the arguments contained in Governor Beshear's brief. So we shall simply use the shortened term "Governor" when referring to arguments advanced by both Governor Beshear and Miller.

5. Apparently, in March 2009, before we granted transfer of Fox's appeal from the Court of Appeals, both the Senate and the House voted to confirm Miller as a member of the CPE.

6. Article II, §8, of the 1792 Kentucky Constitution provided, in relevant part, that the Governor "shall nominate, and by and with the advice and consent of the Senate, appoint all officers, whose offices are established by this Constitution, or shall be established by law, and whose appointments are not herein otherwise provided for. . . ." * * *

provide the manner of appointment and confirmation of inferior state officers. Instead, Article III, §25, of the 1850 Constitution merely provided that "inferior State officers, not specially provided for in this Constitution, may be appointed or elected in such manner as shall be prescribed by law...." * * *

Our current Kentucky Constitution, our Commonwealth's fourth, was adopted in 1891. As originally adopted, §93 of our current Constitution provided, in relevant part, that "[i]nferior State officers, not specifically provided for in this Constitution, may be appointed or elected, in such manner as may be prescribed by law...." So, as originally adopted, §93 was quite similar to its predecessor in the 1850 Constitution.

Section 93 remained unchanged for about a century, during which time the voters of the Commonwealth rejected three proposed amendments to it.[7] Then, in 1992, the General Assembly enacted SB 226,[8] which again placed—among other things—proposed amendments to §93 before the voters of the Commonwealth for their rejection or ratification.[9] Undoubtedly, the most well-known part of SB 226 was a clause permitting many statewide constitutional officers, most notably the Governor, to serve two consecutive terms. This case focuses upon a less heralded part of that bill that gives the Senate the express right to confirm nominees.

The voters approved the proposed constitutional amendments contained in SB 226.[10] So, after the amendments of 1992, §93 reads as follows:[11]

> The Treasurer, Auditor of Public Accounts, Secretary of State, Commissioner of Agriculture, Labor and Statistics, *and* Attorney General, ~~Superintendent of Public Instruction and Register of the Land Office~~ shall be ineligible to re-election for the succeeding four years after the expiration of ~~the~~ *any second consecutive* term for which they shall have been elected. The duties and responsibilities of these officers shall be prescribed by law, and all fees collected by any of said officers shall be covered into the treasury. Inferior State officers *and members of boards and commissions*, not specifically provided for in this Constitu-

7. The voters of the Commonwealth rejected proposed amendments to §93 in 1972, 1980, and 1986. * * *

8. *See* 1992 Ky. Acts, Ch. 168 (S.B. 226), §12.

9. *See* Ky. Const. §256 ("Amendments to this Constitution may be proposed in either House of the General Assembly at a regular session, and if such amendment or amendments shall be agreed to by three-fifths of all the members elected to each House, such proposed amendment or amendments, with the yeas and nays of the members of each House taken thereon, shall be entered in full in their respective journals. Then such proposed amendment or amendments shall be submitted to the voters of the State for their ratification or rejection....").

10. Interestingly, although they approved the amendment at issue in the case at hand, the voters also rejected another proposed amendment to §93 in 1992. * * * The amendment rejected by the voters in 1992 would have, among other things, changed the offices of State Treasurer, Secretary of State, and Commissioner of Agriculture from elective to appointive offices. *See* 1992 Ky. Acts, Ch. 112, §2 (S.B. 262). That defeated amendment also would have contained language providing that inferior state officers and members of boards and commissions could be appointed or elected in the manner prescribed by law, "which may include a requirement of consent by the Senate...." *Id.*

11. Additions to §93 occasioned by the 1992 amendments are referenced in italics and deletions of the former language of §93 occasioned by the 1992 amendments are referenced by strikethrough.

> tion, may be appointed or elected, in such manner as may be prescribed by law, *which may include a requirement of consent by the Senate*, for a term not exceeding four years, and until their successors are appointed or elected and qualified.[12]

B. *Related Statutes.*

Although the wording of §93 is paramount in our analysis, we must also consider related statutes that have a direct bearing on this case.

We have already cited KRS 11.160(2)(h), which permitted Fox to take her seat on the CPE in the interim pending a confirmation vote. But we must also consider KRS 164.011(1), which describes the nomination procedure for members of the CPE. As originally enacted in 1992, that statutory subsection provided as follows:

There shall be a Council on Higher Education in Kentucky, appointed for a term set by law pursuant to Section 23 of the Constitution of Kentucky. The council shall be composed of the chief state school officer, and seventeen (17) lay members appointed by the Governor: one (1) from each Supreme Court district, ten (10) at large members which shall include a student member.[13]

In 1994, KRS 164.011 was amended in a manner not germane to this case. In 1997, however, KRS 164.011 was substantively amended to require members to be confirmed by both chambers of the General Assembly.[14] After the 1997 amendments, KRS 164.011(1) provides as follows:[15]

> There is hereby created and established a Council on Postsecondary Education in Kentucky as an agency, instrumentality, and political subdivision of the Commonwealth and a public body corporate and politic having all powers, duties, and responsibilities as are provided to it by law, appointed for a term set by law pursuant to Section 23 of the Constitution of Kentucky. The council shall be composed of the commissioner of education, a faculty member, a student member, and thirteen (13) citizen members appointed by the Governor. The citizen members shall be confirmed by the Senate and the House of Representatives under KRS 11.160, and the commissioner of education shall serve as a nonvoting ex officio member. Citizen council members shall be selected from a list of nominees provided to the Governor under the nominating process set forth in KRS 164.005. If the General Assembly is not in session at the time of the appointment, persons appointed shall serve prior to confirmation, but the Governor shall seek the consent of the General Assembly at the next regular session or at an intervening extraordinary session if the matter is included in the call of the General Assembly.

(Emphasis added.)

12. *See* 1992 Ky. Acts, Ch. 168 (S.B. 226), §12.
13. *See* 1992 Ky. Acts, Ch. 10 (H.B. 149), §7.
14. *See* 1997 Ky. Acts, 1st Extra Sess., Ch. 1 (H.B. 1), §73.
15. There have been no amendments to KRS 164.011 since 1997.

C. *The Main Issue and the Standard of Review.*

KRS 164.011(1) clearly purports to require Fox to be confirmed by both chambers of the General Assembly. This bicameral confirmation requirement goes to the heart of Fox's complaint. Essentially, Fox argues that the bicameral confirmation requirement for members of the CPE contained in KRS 164.011(1) violates §93 of the Kentucky Constitution. In Fox's view, §93 permits only the Senate to confirm appointees. By contrast, the Governor contends the phrase in §93 regarding confirmation by the Senate is merely illustrative of how appointees such as Fox could be confirmed; but the phrase was not meant to preclude confirmation by both chambers of the General Assembly. We agree with Fox.

Although the parties, oddly, do not focus upon it, the procedural stance of this appeal does not require us to determine as a matter of law whether Fox should prevail in her quest to regain her seat on the CPE. We see the question properly before us as far narrower: did the trial court err by granting the Governor's CR 12.02 motion to dismiss Fox's complaint for failure to state a claim upon which relief may be granted? In other words, our conclusion that §93 prohibits bicameral confirmation does not end this case because little or no proof was adduced at the trial court level before the Governor filed his motion to dismiss; and Fox never filed a dispositive motion before the trial court. The Governor has not even filed an answer to Fox's complaint. On remand, the Governor and Miller may raise whatever other defenses or legal reasons they believe preclude Fox from regaining her seat on the CPE; and Fox may present whatever evidence or legal arguments she deems necessary to convince the trial court to order her CPE seat to be restored to her.

* * * Since a motion to dismiss for failure to state a claim upon which relief may be granted is a pure question of law, a reviewing court owes no deference to a trial court's determination; instead, an appellate court reviews the issue de novo.[16] Of course, in determining de novo whether Fox's complaint stated a claim upon which relief may be given, "we must give words [in the Kentucky Constitution] their plain and ordinary meanings."[17]

D. *Plain Meaning of §93.*

The plain and ordinary meaning of "which may include a requirement of consent by the Senate" appears to be straightforward at first blush: the General Assembly may, in its discretion, choose to make inferior state officers and members of the various applicable state boards and commissions subject to a confirmation in the Senate. In other words, all the plain language of the pertinent part of §93 seems to do is grant the

---

16. *Morgan*, 289 S.W.3d at 226 ("It is well established that a court should not dismiss an action for failure to state a claim unless the pleading party appears not to be entitled to relief under any set of facts which could be proven in support of his claim. In ruling on a motion to dismiss, the pleadings should be liberally construed in the light most favorable to the plaintiff, all allegations being taken as true. Therefore, the question is purely a matter of law. Accordingly, the trial court's decision will be reviewed de novo.") (citations and internal quotation marks omitted). * * *

17. *Freeman v. St. Andrew Orthodox Church, Inc.*, 294 S.W.3d 425, 428 (Ky. 2009).

Senate a right to confirm nominees. Conversely, there is nothing in the plain language of §93 that permits the House to have any role in the confirmation vote. Undeniably, the House is not even mentioned in §93. We cannot dismiss the notable omission of language specifically referencing the House as a mere accidental oversight. It is well settled law that a court may not add language to the written law to achieve a desired result.[18] And the conspicuous absence of any mention of the House having a role in the confirmation process could, therefore, be construed as a definite signal that there was no intent for that chamber to participate in the confirmation process.

An argument could be made that the plain language of §93 evidences that nominees may only be subjected to confirmation by the Senate. Such a conclusion would be in accordance with the logic expressed by our country's most famous jurist, Chief Justice John Marshall, in his most famous opinion: "[a]ffirmative words are often, in their operation, negative of other objects than those affirmed...."[19] Likewise, another Chief Justice of the United States, William Howard Taft, used similar logic in interpreting a treaty: "[t]here certainly are no express words granting such [a construction]. Why should it be implied? If it was intended by the parties why should it not have been expressed?"[20]

Following that line of thought, one could ask: since there is no language even mentioning the House in §93, how can a reviewing court imply that it exists? In other words, for the Governor's arguments to succeed, the clause of §93 at issue should logically read, "which may include a requirement of consent by the Senate or House of Representatives."

When the Governor's arguments and citations to authority are fully considered, however, the superficial clarity of §93 appreciably dims. In truth, close examination of the relevant language appears to reveal a latent ambiguity. So we must consider all of the relevant accompanying facts, circumstances, and laws, including the time-honored canons of construction, in order to interpret §93 properly.

E. *Ambiguity and the Maxim of Interpretation Expressio Unius.*

"It is a familiar and general rule of statutory construction that the mention of one thing implies the exclusion of another...."[21] This basic tenet of statutory construction

---

18. *Cf. Beckham v. Board of Educ. of Jefferson County*, 873 S.W.2d 575, 577 (Ky. 1994) ("We are not at liberty to add or subtract from the legislative enactment nor discover meaning not reasonably ascertainable from the language used."); *Mills v. City of Barbourville*, 273 Ky. 490, 117 S.W.2d 187, 188 (1938) ("The cardinal rule in construing statutes is, if possible, to ascertain the meaning of the Legislature from the language used, and if that be plain, clear, and unambiguous, resort to collateral rules of construction is unnecessary.").

19. *Marbury v. Madison*, 5 U.S. 137, 174, 1 Cranch 137, 2 L.Ed. 60 (1803).

20. *Ford v. United States*, 273 U.S. 593, 611, 47 S.Ct. 531, 71 L.Ed. 793 (1927).

21. *Jefferson County v. Gray*, 198 Ky. 600, 249 S.W. 771, 772 (1923). The maxim may also be used to interpret or construe constitutional provisions. *See* 2A NORMAN J. SINGER & J.D. SHAMBIE SINGER, SUTHERLAND STATUTES AND STATUTORY CONSTRUCTION §47:24 (7th ed. 2009) ("The maxim has been employed in the interpretation of constitutions....").

is usually referred to by the Latin phrase *expressio unius est exclusio alterius.*[22] Often that maxim is shortened to *expressio unius*. Of course, like all canons of construction, *expressio unius* is not useful in every case. And we do not resort to canons of interpretation if the meaning of the law is clear.[23]

As explained, however, the relevant portion of §93 is ambiguous, at least as applied to situations like the one at hand. So we will use *expressio unius*, but "only as an aid in arriving at [legislative] intention, and not to defeat it."[24] Because the *expressio unius* maxim is only a rule of construction, and not substantive law, we must use it only "'when ... that which is expressed is so set over by way of strong contrast to that which is omitted that the contrast enforces the affirmative inference that that which is omitted must be intended to have opposite and contrary treatment.'"[25] In other words, *expressio unius* is most helpful when there is a strong, unmistakable contrast between what is expressed and what is omitted.

Use of the *expressio unius* maxim is particularly appropriate in this case because, even under an expansive reading of §93, a very small number of possibilities exists—three, to be exact—regarding how the General Assembly may determine how appointees such as Fox may be confirmed.[26] First, §93 could be construed to provide that the General Assembly may pass legislation providing that the Senate alone is vested with the power to confirm a particular type of appointee.[27] Second, §93 could be interpreted to provide that the General Assembly could pass legislation providing that the House alone could be vested with the power to confirm a particular type of appointee.[28] Third, §93 could be interpreted to provide that the General Assembly could pass legislation requiring both the Senate and the House each to confirm a particular type of appointee.

An unmistakable difference appears among those three possibilities. Use of one approach necessarily precludes use of one of the remaining two because a statute cannot, for example, provide in one section that an appointee should be confirmed by the

22. *See, e.g., Jefferson County*, 249 S.W. at 772 (using Latin phrase).

23. *See, e.g., King Drugs, Inc. v. Commonwealth*, 250 S.W.3d 643, 645 (Ky. 2008) ("Only if the statute is ambiguous, however, or otherwise frustrates a plain reading, do we resort to the canons or rules of construction...."); 16 C.J.S. *Constitutional Law* §62 (2009) ("Neither rules of construction nor rules of interpretation may be used to defeat the clear and certain meaning of a constitutional provision.... There is no occasion for construction where the language is plain and definite....").

24. *Jefferson County*, 249 S.W. at 772.

25. *Union Light, Heat & Power Co. v. Louisville & N.R. Co.*, 257 Ky. 761, 79 S.W.2d 199, 202 (1935), *quoting Ford*, 273 U.S. at 611, 47 S.Ct. 531.

26. Of course, since not all appointed state employees must undergo the confirmation process, the three choices presuppose that the General Assembly has enacted legislation requiring the appointee in question to be confirmed to the position to which appointed.

27. There are several statutes that use this approach. Among those statutes are KRS 342.230(3) (workers' compensation administrative law judges); KRS 121.110(1) (members of Kentucky Registry of Election Finance); and KRS 131.315(1) (members of Kentucky Board of Tax Appeals).

28. We are aware of no statute employing this approach. But we agree with Fox's contention that the General Assembly would have the power to use that approach if we accepted the Governor's position.

Senate alone while stating somewhere else that that same appointee is subject to both House and Senate confirmation. The limited number of possible constructions of §93 and the exclusivity and vast difference among the other possible constructions makes this case an ideal situation to apply the *expressio unius* maxim.

We recognize, as the Governor argues, the United States Supreme Court has held that phrases such as "may include" are not well-suited to interpretation by use of *expressio unius* because the phrase "may include" is "expansive...."[29] But the differences between what was expressed and what was not were not as clear in the authorities relied upon by the Governor. The Supreme Court itself recognized that *expressio unius* was inapplicable in *Chevron USA, Inc.*, because, among other reasons, the range of possibilities if *expressio unius* were used was vast. In fact, the Court held that "that there is no apparent stopping point" if it applied *expressio unius* to the statute under construction.[30]

Likewise, our decision in *Cornelison v. Commonwealth*,[31] greatly relied upon by the Governor, is similarly distinguishable. In *Cornelison*, a defendant argued that error occurred when a police officer was permitted to testify during a sentencing hearing about the effect good-time credit would have on a potential sentence.[32] On appeal, Cornelison argued the officer's good-time-credit testimony was improper because KRS 532.055 listed several items of evidence that the Commonwealth could offer relevant to sentencing; but that statute did not mention good-time credit.

We rejected Cornelison's argument that the *expressio unius* maxim should apply, holding that "the list [in KRS 532.055] is illustrative rather than exhaustive."[33] But, as with *Chevron USA, Inc.*, our decision in *Cornelison* seems to have been at least partly based upon the potentially vast array of evidence that could properly be relevant to a sentencing determination. We held that good-time-credit-related evidence was "no less relevant nor more speculative than" another type of evidence listed in the statute.[34] In other words, the inclusion of types of evidence expressly deemed admissible by the statute did not lead to the logical conclusion that all other types of evidence were inadmissible, especially in light of the fact that one of the purposes of KRS 532.055 was to ensure a well-informed jury. In the case at hand, however, the list of potential,

29. *Chevron USA, Inc. v. Echazabal*, 536 U.S. 73, 80, 122 S.Ct. 2045, 153 L.Ed.2d 82 (2002) ("Far from supporting Echazabal's position, the expansive phrasing of 'may include' points directly away from the sort of exclusive specification he claims.").

30. *Id.* at 83–84, 122 S.Ct. 2045 ("There is even a third strike against applying the expression-exclusion rule here. It is simply that there is no apparent stopping point to the argument that by specifying a threat-to-others defense Congress intended a negative implication about those whose safety could be considered. When Congress specified threats to others in the workplace, for example, could it possibly have meant that an employer could not defend a refusal to hire when a worker's disability would threaten others outside the workplace? If Typhoid Mary had come under the ADA, would a meat packer have been defenseless if Mary had sued after being turned away?").

31. 990 S.W.2d 609 (Ky. 1999).

32. *Id.* at 610.

33. *Id.*

34. *Id.* at 611.

rational interpretations of §93 is very short; and, accordingly, the inclusion of language permitting the Senate to confirm nominees leads to a strong presumption that the House was intentionally excluded from the confirmation process.

Also, *Chevron USA, Inc.*, relied upon by the Governor, is distinguishable because the Supreme Court found in that case that "language suggesting exclusiveness is missing" from the statute being construed (part of the Americans with Disabilities Act).[35] In the case at hand, since there are only, at most, three rational interpretations of the pertinent language of §93, the express language setting forth one of those three possibilities gives rise to a strong presumption that the other two possibilities were intentionally excluded.

In short, the fact that there are only three rational, yet completely discrete, ways of interpreting the relevant language of §93 means that the expression of one of those choices (confirmation by the Senate) carries great weight in implying that the other choices (confirmation by the House, either alone or acting along with the Senate) were intentionally excluded.

As one esteemed treatise on statutory construction notes, "[t]here is generally an inference that omissions are intentional. This rule is based on logic and common sense. It expresses the concept that when people say one thing they do not mean something else."[36] Another leading treatise agrees, stating, "the enumeration of certain specified things in a constitutional provision will usually be construed to exclude all things not enumerated."[37] We conclude, therefore, that the application of the *expressio unius* interpretive maxim works logically in this case and that the application of that maxim leads to a reasonable conclusion that the Senate alone has the constitutional confirmation power under §93. We may not properly infer from utter silence a concomitant power for the House.

This conclusion does not end our inquiry because the Governor raises several arguments that he contends do, nevertheless, afford the House a role in the confirmation process even though that body is not expressly mentioned in §93.

F. *Historical Analysis of Confirmation Process.*

According to the Governor, the historical arc of the constitutional treatment of confirmation of state officers shows that the 1992 amendments were meant to depart from a Senate-only confirmation process. We disagree.

The Governor correctly points out that the framers of our 1891 Constitution rejected a proposed section that would have required all non-constitutionally mandated state officers to have been confirmed by the Senate. More specifically, the framers deleted a proposed section that would have provided, in relevant part, that the Governor "shall appoint, with the advice and consent of the Senate, all state officers who are not required by this Constitution, or the laws made thereunder, to be elected by the

35. 536 U.S. at 81, 122 S.Ct. 2045.

36. 2A SINGER & SINGER, *supra*, §47:25 (footnote omitted).

37. 16 C.J.S. *CONSTITUTIONAL LAW* §64 (2009).

people."[38] The Governor argues that this deletion shows that "the framers of Kentucky's most recent constitutions have departed from a framework in which exclusive Senate confirmation is constitutionally required of all inferior state officers."

We are not convinced. The Governor is correct when he notes that the delegates to the 1890 Constitutional Convention did vote to delete a proposed constitutional section that would plainly have required senatorial confirmation of gubernatorial appointments.[39] But the Governor has pointed to nothing concrete that shows that deletion was aimed at allowing the House to have confirmation powers. Rather, as we have recognized in an earlier case, the section requiring senatorial confirmation was deleted only in order to permit the General Assembly to "determine[ ] by legislative enactment [which inferior state officers] should be subject to such senate consent."[40]

As Delegate Charles J. Bronston of Fayette County pointed out to his fellow delegates in 1890, the section requiring senatorial confirmation of all appointees, which was later deleted, was originally intended only to permit the Governor to appoint the state Librarian.[41] The delegates instead wanted to retain the more general language of what ultimately became §93 in order to allow the General Assembly to have flexibility in determining whether inferior state officers should be elected or appointed. As Delegate Bronston argued, requiring legislative confirmation of all appointees "would disturb that settled principle which, we believe, has been approved by the people, that as to all these subordinates, it should be left to the power of the General Assembly to say whether they should be elected or appointed...."[42] So we disagree with the Governor's argument that the delegates to the 1890 Constitutional Convention clearly wanted to take the confirmation power from the Senate alone; instead, the official records of that Convention show that the delegates voted to delete the section requiring senatorial confirmation only to give the General Assembly flexibility in determining which inferior state officers must be subjected to confirmation at all.

We also do not agree with the Governor that the current version of §93, as amended, reflects a conscious desire to move away from a Senate-only confirmation process. The language of §93 belies such a construction.

Although when it was originally adopted, §93 did not contain a clause directly pertaining to senatorial confirmation, the 1992 amendments to §93 added the Senate-only confirmation language to our current constitution. So even if we assumed, solely for purposes of argument, that §93, as originally adopted, did not vest the Senate with the

38. *See IV OFFICIAL REPORT OF THE PROCEEDINGS AND DEBATES IN THE CONVENTION*, 5728 (1890).

39. *Id.*

40. *Kraus v. Kentucky State Senate*, 872 S.W.2d 433, 437 (Ky. 1994).

41. *IV OFFICIAL REPORT OF THE PROCEEDINGS AND DEBATES IN THE CONVENTION* at 5728 ("We, of the Committee, were fully aware that at the time section 76 [requiring senatorial confirmation of all state officers] was adopted, it was thought important to allow the Governor to appoint the Librarian. It was not understood at that time that the appointing power should be extended to any other official save that.").

42. *Id.*

exclusive right to confirm gubernatorial appointees, the 1992 amendments to §93 were an unmistakable about-face from any purported retreat from Senate-only confirmation power. Since Fox convincingly argues that Kentucky has never in its constitutional history afforded the House confirmation powers, it logically follows that the framers of §93 would have used clear language specifically permitting the House to have a role in the confirmation process if the framers had intended to enact such a sweeping change.

Perhaps the clearest indication that there was no intent for §93, as originally enacted, to afford the House a role in the confirmation process is the General Assembly's enactment of legislation (since repealed) in 1893—hard on the heels of the adoption of the present Constitution—that provided, in relevant part, that "[u]nless otherwise provided, all persons appointed to an office by the Governor, whether to fill a vacancy, or as an original appointment, shall hold office, subject to the advice and consent of the Senate, which body shall take appropriate action upon such appointments at its first session held thereafter."[43] Nothing in that statute afforded the House the right to confirm nominees. In reality, the opposite is true because the statute clearly contemplated confirmation only by the Senate.

G. *The Word May.*

This desire to preserve the General Assembly's flexibility to determine which state officers must be subjected to the confirmation process also explains the use of the much-discussed word *may* in the 1992 amendments to §93.[44] The Governor contends that since the word *may* is permissive and nonexclusive, the provision in §93 providing that appointees *may* be subject to confirmation by the Senate is properly construed as being illustrative of how confirmation can occur. Although we agree with the Governor that *may* is generally a permissive term, we disagree that the use of that word in §93 means that the House has the right to confirm appointees.

Of course, as the Governor correctly points out, the word *may* generally signifies something as being permissive in nature in contrast to the word *shall*, which generally signifies something being mandatory.[45] It is also evident from the Constitutional Debates of 1890 that a proposed section of the Constitution requiring senatorial confirmation of all inferior state officers was deleted in favor of the more general language in §93 (as originally enacted) in order to provide the General Assembly with as much leeway as possible to determine which state officers would be subject to senatorial

---

43. *Sewell v. Bennett*, 187 Ky. 626, 220 S.W. 517, 519 (1920) (quoting former §3750 of the Kentucky Statutes and noting that statute was passed in 1893).

44. As previously quoted, §93 provides that inferior state officers and members of boards and commissions "may be appointed or elected, in such manner as may be prescribed by law, which may include a requirement of consent by the Senate…."

45. *See, e.g., Alexander v. S & M Motors, Inc.*, 28 S.W.3d 303, 305 (Ky. 2000) ("Not only have Kentucky courts long construed 'may' to be a permissive word, rather than a mandatory word, but our legislature has given guidance in this regard. When considering the construction of statutes, KRS 446.010(20) provides that 'may' is permissive, and 'shall' is mandatory.").

confirmation.[46] The most logical conclusion, therefore, is that the term *may* in §93 signifies only that the General Assembly has the permissive discretion to choose which gubernatorial appointees must be subjected to a confirmation.

In other words, absent some constitutional prohibition against doing so, appointees, like Fox, may be subject to confirmation if the General Assembly so directs, or appointees may be permitted to serve without ever having to be confirmed, if the General Assembly has not directed to the contrary. Either way is generally permissible under §93. But we have not been shown evidence that the use of the term may in §93 is evidence that the House has the constitutionally authorized ability to confirm nominees.

Indeed, the relative silence of our present Constitution, as originally enacted, regarding how (or if) appointees such as Fox would be confirmed led to *Kraus v. Kentucky State Senate*[47]—the court case that likely was the impetus for the 1992 amendments to §93.

H. *Kraus v. Kentucky State Senate.*

As stated, §93 of our current Constitution, as originally enacted, was silent on whether the Senate or even the House had the power to confirm inferior state officers. This constitutional silence resulted in a landmark decision from this Court.

In 1990, David Kraus was appointed to be an administrative law judge (ALJ) in the Kentucky Workers' Compensation system.[48] The Senate, however, rejected Kraus's nomination.[49] Kraus then filed an action challenging the constitutionality of the statute that granted the Senate the right to confirm nominees such as he. In 1991, the circuit court ruled that the statute was constitutional. Kraus appealed to the Court of Appeals.[50] Ultimately, late in 1992, the Court of Appeals affirmed the circuit court's decision. This Court granted discretionary review and eventually affirmed the Court of Appeals.

Kraus had argued on appeal, as the Governor argues in this case, that "the Senate does not have the authority to advise and consent because the [1890] constitutional convention amended and deleted mandatory 'advice and consent' language from Section 76 of the Constitution."[51] We ultimately rejected Kraus's argument, just as we now reject the Governor's argument in the case at hand, because the proposed mandatory

---

46. *See IV OFFICIAL REPORT OF THE PROCEEDINGS AND DEBATES IN THE CONVENTION* at 5728 (Delegate Bronston stating that the section requiring the Senate to confirm all gubernatorially appointed state officers should be deleted, among other reasons, because that mandatory confirmation section "would disturb that settled principle which, we believe, has been approved by the people, that as to all these subordinates, it should be left to the power of the General Assembly to say whether they should be elected or appointed....").

47. 872 S.W.2d 433.

48. Consistent with the law at the time, the appointment was made by the Workers' Compensation Board, not the governor. *Id.* at 435. Current law gives the governor the power to appoint Workers' Compensation ALJs, subject to the Senate's consent. *See* KRS 342.230(3).

49. *Kraus*, 872 S.W.2d at 435.

50. These timelines are available for public viewing * * *.

51. 872 S.W.2d at 437.

confirmation language "had to be changed into the general terms which permitted Senate consent to any inferior state official that the General Assembly determined by legislative enactment should be subject to such [S]enate consent."[52] In other words, as stated before, the proposed mandatory confirmation language was deleted in 1890 in order for the General Assembly to preserve its discretion to determine precisely which inferior state officers— instead of all state officers—it wanted to be subjected to a confirmation vote.

This Court took definite note in *Kraus* of the fact that numerous statutes provide for executive appointment of state officers "subject to Senate and/or House approval."[53] And we relied in *Kraus* upon the fact that this Court or its predecessor had issued many decisions "acknowledg[ing] that the Senate has the power to consent to the appointment of inferior state officers."[54] So this Court rejected Kraus's arguments and affirmed the lower courts because we had reached a "conclusion that the Senate has the inherent power to advise and consent on executive branch appointments of inferior state officers."[55]

But during the length of the 1992 General Assembly's regular session, the separation of powers questions raised by Kraus awaited a final answer in the appellate courts. And it requires no blind leap of faith to infer that securing the Senate's role in the confirmation process was the context from which some relevant part of SB 226 arose. This logical inference did not escape the Governor's notice in the case at hand: he mentions it in his brief.[56] So we agree with the Governor's conclusion that the relevant amendment to §93 "was offered to prospectively settle ... [*Kraus*'s] separation-of-powers question" and to "remove[ ] all doubt that the 'manner' of appointing inferior officers to be 'prescribed by law' 'may include a requirement of consent by the Senate.'"[57]

Acceptance of this premise, however, actually undermines the Governor's position in the case. If we accept the premise that the framers of the revisions to §93 were motivated to amend the constitution to thwart Kraus's constitutional challenges, then the framers should only have logically been concerned with the Senate's power to confirm nominees because Kraus's lawsuit did not present any issue involving the House in the confirmation process because Kraus was not subject to confirmation in the House. In other words, the deliberate words chosen by the General Assembly in SB 226, which became the proposed amendments to §93, reflected concern about senatorial con-

52. *Id.* at 437.

53. *Id.*

54. *Id.*

55. *Id.* at 438.

56. The Governor correctly notes that "[i]n 1992, during the litigation of the *Kraus* case discussed above, the General Assembly drafted, passed, and proposed an amendment to Section 93 of the Kentucky Constitution."

57. The wisdom of adding failsafe language to §93 to preserve the Senate's right to confirm nominees is proven by the fact that this Court's decision upholding the Senate's inherent right to confirm nominees such as Kraus was not a unanimous decision. *See* 872 S.W.2d at 440–41 (dissenting opinion of Justice Lambert, joined by Justice Combs).

firmation rights because that was all that was at issue in *Kraus*. So the Governor's argument is unpersuasive to the extent that it relies upon the then-unresolved *Kraus* appeal to prove that the General Assembly intended the amendments to §93 to permit the House constitutionally a role in confirming executive appointments.

Kraus is important to the case at hand for reasons beyond supplying the historical context for SB 226 and the 1992 amendments to §93. First, as previously discussed, our decision in *Kraus* provides compelling precedent for us to reject the Governor's argument that the constitutional convention's decision to delete proposed language requiring mandatory confirmation by the Senate for all appointees means that the House is constitutionally authorized to have a role in the confirmation process. Second, analysis of our decision in *Kraus* affords us the opportunity to correct some unfortunately imprecise language in that opinion. Specifically, we stated in a clause the Governor relies upon that "for more than the last one hundred years, the independent branches of government have recognized that *the General Assembly* has authority to confirm nominations from other branches of government."[58] To be accurate, what we should have said was that history shows that the Senate's right to confirm nominees has long been recognized.

Toward the beginning of our opinion, we noted that "the House is not involved in the confirmation process" for Kraus.[59] It is clear that the issue in *Kraus* involved only whether the Senate had the inherent authority to confirm (or reject) certain executive appointments. The question of whether the House was constitutionally permitted to play any role in confirming nominees such as Kraus was not at issue. Even the first sentence of our opinion in Kraus says that "David L. Kraus challenges the authority *of the Kentucky State Senate* to grant to itself the power to consent to the employment ... of an Administrative Law Judge...."[60]

It is obvious, therefore, that we painted with too broad a brush in *Kraus* when we referred to a purported historical recognition of the General Assembly's authority to confirm nominees. To the contrary, Fox has ably and conclusively shown in this case that Kentucky's history provided for confirmation by the Senate alone.[61] So, in *Kraus*, we did not need to discuss what role the House could, or could not, play in confirming nominees.

Close scrutiny of our opinion in *Kraus* reveals that we did not intend to confer confirmation rights upon the House, our unfortunately broad language notwithstanding. Instead, when our opinion is examined carefully, it appears evident that we mentioned the House in *Kraus* in passing only to point out, without comment, that some

58. *Id.* at 437 (emphasis added).

59. *Id.* at 435.

60. *Id.* at 434 (emphasis added).

61. We have already quoted our former state constitutions that unequivocally authorized the Senate alone to confirm nominees, and we will not belabor this opinion with all the additional citations provided by Fox for this proposition. But suffice it to say that we generally agree with her assertion that Kentucky has a largely "unbroken practice ... of almost 200 years ... of authorizing only the Senate to exercise a power of confirmation."

statutes then-existing provided "for executive appointments subject to Senate and/or House approval."[62] We used imprecise language when we stated that other branches of Government have historically recognized *the General Assembly's* right to confirm nominees. To our knowledge, Fox's action is the first challenge to the recently enacted statutes purporting to give the House a role concomitant with the Senate's role in the confirmation process. The question of what role, if any, the House may permissibly take in the confirmation process was not before us in *Kraus*; and nothing in that opinion should be interpreted to stand for a ruling by us that the House is constitutionally entitled to play a role in the confirmation process.

I. *Contemporary Construction, Statutes Permitting the House to Perform a Role in the Confirmation Process, and the Ballot Question Prepared by the Secretary of State.*

As noted in our discussion of *Kraus*, there are several recent statutes that clearly afford the House a role equal to the Senate in the confirmation process. The Governor relies heavily upon those statutes to buttress his argument that §93 was intended to—and actually does—afford the House a role in the confirmation process.

KRS 11.160, which provides the general framework for the confirmation of gubernatorial appointments, was first enacted in 1990. As originally enacted, it did not mention confirmation by the House.[63] In 1992, however, the General Assembly amended KRS 11.160 to specify the manner of confirmation of appointees who were statutorily required to be confirmed by both the House and the Senate.[64] The addition in 1992 of language pertaining to the House having a defined role in the confirmation of appointees was done in the same legislative session in which the General Assembly passed, and thereby presented to the electorate, SB 226 and the amendments to §93 at hand.

The Governor argues that this contemporaneous recognition of bicameral confirmation requirements in KRS 11.160 is entitled to great weight in interpreting the 1992 amendments to §93. We agree, of course, that contemporaneous legislative explanation or clarification of a constitutional provision should ordinarily be given deference by a reviewing court.[65] But we disagree with the Governor's ultimate assertion that the enactment of statutes purporting to specify the manner of bicameral confirmation of appointees nullifies clear constitutional language to the contrary. Obviously, because "the constitution controls any legislative act repugnant to it[,]"[66] no statute can validly direct or authorize the performance of an unconstitutional act.[67]

It appears that there were at least two statutes requiring bicameral confirmation of gubernatorial nominees existing before the 1992 amendments to §93. In 1990, for

62. *Id.* at 437.

63. 1990 Ky. Acts, Ch. 505 (S.B. 176).

64. 1990 Ky. Acts, Ch. 415 (S.B. 107), §1(2).

65. *See, e.g., Coleman v. Mulligan*, 234 Ky. 691, 28 S.W.2d 980, 981 (1930).

66. *Marbury*, 5 U.S. at 177.

67. *See, e.g., Commonwealth v. Barroso*, 122 S.W.3d 554, 558 (Ky. 2003) ("As a general proposition, constitutional rights prevail over conflicting statutes and rules.").

example, the General Assembly created the State Board for Elementary and Secondary Education.[68] The act creating that Board, currently codified at KRS 156.029, requires the eleven Board members to be appointed by the Governor and confirmed by both the Senate and the House.[69] Also, in 1990, as part of the same act that created this State Board for Elementary and Educational Education, the General Assembly also created the Council for Education Technology.[70] The nine members of that Board were also required to be appointed by the Governor and confirmed by both the Senate and the House.[71] But in 1992, the General Assembly repealed the section of the KRS covering the Council for Education Technology.[72] In its place, the General Assembly created a new Council for Education Technology.[73] But that new Technology Council consisted of several ex officio members and eight members appointed by the Governor.[74] Notably, however, that bill did not require those eight appointed members to be confirmed by either the House or the Senate.

It is important to note that when those statutes providing for bicameral confirmation were enacted in 1990, the Constitution had not been amended to preclude the House from having a role in the confirmation process. Nor had the amendment to §93 specifically giving the Senate alone the right to confirm nominees been ratified by the people when, in 1992, the General Assembly amended KRS 11.160(2) to specify the bicameral confirmation procedures.[75]

It is apparent that the General Assembly, the body that originally drafted the amendments to §93 at issue, had already shown its ability and willingness to put specific language in legislation requiring appointees to be confirmed by both the Senate and the House. Tellingly, however, the General Assembly chose not to put specific language in the relevant amendments to §93 that would have required, or at least authorized, the House to confirm appointees.

We are unwilling to assume that the General Assembly omitted reference to the House in §93 by oversight. Instead, we agree with Fox that the absence of language mentioning the House in §93 should rationally be interpreted as a conscious decision by the General Assembly not to include the House in confirming nominees.

Although not memorialized in a statute, there are, in fact, some indicators that the contemporaneous construction of the 1992 amendments to §93 envisioned only senatorial confirmation. First, the May 4, 1992, *Legislative Record*, a newspaper-style summary of Kentucky legislative activities edited and published by the Legislative Research Commission (LRC) (an entity charged with assisting the General Assembly), contains

68. Ky. Acts 1990, Ch. 476, Pt. II, §35.
69. *Id.* KRS 156.029(1) still requires bicameral confirmation of Board members.
70. Ky. Acts 1990, Ch. 476, Pt. I, §21.
71. *Id.*
72. Ky. Acts 1992, Ch. 195, §15.
73. *Id.* at §8.
74. *Id.*
75. Ky. Acts 1992, Ch. 415, §1(2).

the steps that SB 226 took along the path to being enacted by both legislative chambers. That *Legislative Record* also contains a summary of SB 226. That summary states that one aspect of SB 226 was to "authorize appointment of members of boards and commissions with the consent of the Senate...."[76] The bill log for the House Committee on Elections and Constitutional Amendments likewise summarizes SB 226, in pertinent part, as a proposal "to amend Section 93 to ... authorize appointment of members of boards and commissions with consent of the Senate...." * * * These are, therefore, at least two contemporaneous indications that the General Assembly contemplated only the Senate having the ability to confirm (or reject) appointments such as Fox's. * * *

Of course, the General Assembly has the ability to propose amendments to our Constitution; but those amendments must be ratified by the electorate. As our predecessor-Court memorably held, "[i]n the ultimate sense, the legislature does nothing unless and until the people ratify and choose to give the revised constitution life by their own direct action."[77] Indeed, §256 of our Kentucky Constitution provides that after appropriate passage of a proposed amendment by the General Assembly, "such proposed amendment or amendments shall be submitted to the voters of the State for their ratification or rejection...." Obviously, therefore, the will of the people regarding constitutional amendments is paramount. Because the electorate has an inviolable right to be informed of all proposed constitutional amendments upon which it will pass judgment, §257 of our Kentucky Constitution provides, in relevant part, that "[b]efore an amendment shall be submitted to a vote, the Secretary of State shall cause such proposed amendment, and the time that the same is to be voted upon, to be published at least ninety days before the vote is to be taken thereon...."

Of great assistance to our determination of this matter is the actual question the Secretary of State directed the county clerks to place on the ballot in 1992. Since proposals to our Kentucky Constitution are "nothing" until a majority of the electorate gives the amendment "force and effect[,]"[78] what could be more critical to our decision than reading the actual question presented to the voters of Kentucky? So we granted Fox's request to supplement the record with a copy of the Secretary of State's official certification of the ballot question at hand.

In pertinent part, the ballot question presented to the voters * * * asked them whether they were in favor of "permitting the General Assembly to require *the Senate's consent* to the selection of inferior state officers and members of boards and commissions...." (Emphasis added.) Unlike previous proposed amendments that have spawned lawsuits challenging the form of the ballot question,[79] we have been cited to no actions, nor are

---

76. *Legislative Record*, May 4, 1992 (Vol. 20, No. 102, Regular Session), p. 37.

77. *Gatewood v. Matthews*, 403 S.W.2d 716, 720 (Ky. 1966).

78. *Gatewood*, 403 S.W.2d at 721.

79. *See, e.g., Ferguson v. Redding*, 304 S.W.2d 927 (Ky. 1957) (action challenging ballot question regarding proposed amendments to, among others, §93); *Smith v. Hatcher*, 311 Ky. 386, 223 S.W.2d 182 (1949) (action challenging ballot question for proposed amendments to §246); *Funk v. Fielder*, 243 S.W.2d 474 (1951) (action challenging ballot question for proposed amendment to §256).

we independently aware of any, that were filed to contest the sufficiency or accuracy of the ballot question in this case.

The question proposed to the voters plainly asked them whether they favored giving the Senate the express authority to consent to appointments. No reasonable voter could have construed that ballot question to mean that the House had any right whatsoever to confirm nominees. And, of course, since any constitutional provision "does not derive its force from the convention which framed it, but from the people who ratified it, the intent to be arrived at is that of the people, and it is not to be supposed that they have looked for any ... abstruse meaning in the words employed...."[80] Instead, we must accept that the people, who, after all, were responsible for giving life to the constitutional provision, "accepted ... [its terms] in the sense most obvious to the common understanding, and ratified the instrument in the belief that was the sense designed to be conveyed. Accordingly, in construing a constitution, it is presumed that the language has been employed with sufficient precision to convey the intention...."[81]

Yet the Governor's construction of §93 would logically authorize the House to have a role, either alone or in conjunction with the Senate, to confirm appointments such as Fox's even though there is no mention of any role for the House in either §93 itself or in the ballot question prepared by the Secretary of State. No voter reading the ballot question for the 1992 amendments to §93 reasonably could have foreseen such a result.

We are aware that mainly since the 1992 amendments to §93 were ratified, the General Assembly has enacted new statutes, or has amended existing statutes, to require certain nominees to be confirmed by both the House and the Senate.[82] But, as stated before, the intent of the people who ratified the constitutional provision must be considered the paramount consideration in constitutional interpretation.[83] And it has been conclusively shown that no reasonable voter would have believed that voter was authorizing bicameral confirmation (or confirmation by the House alone) by voting to approve the 1992 amendments to §93. So the General Assembly's later attempts to require bicameral confirmation of certain appointees contravenes the will of the people, as unmistakably expressed by their approval of the amendments to §93.

J. *Remand for Further Proceedings is Necessary.*

For the reasons we have discussed at some length in this opinion, we agree with Fox that §93 permits only the Senate to confirm nominees. So the bicameral confirmation requirement set forth in KRS 164.011(1) is invalid, even taking into account the pre-

80. 16 C.J.S. *CONSTITUTIONAL LAW* §59 (2009).

81. *Id.*

82. *See, e.g.*, KRS 248.707(2)(b) (Agricultural Development Board); KRS 351.1041(2) (Mine Safety Review Commission); KRS 161.028(2)(b) (Education Professional Standards Board); KRS 164.005(1) (Governor's Postsecondary Education Nominating Committee); KRS 7B.030(1)(b)(2) (Kentucky Long-Term Policy Research Center).

83. 16 C.J.S. *CONSTITUTIONAL LAW* §59 (2009).

sumption of constitutionality generally afforded to statutes.[84] This conclusion does not necessarily mean, however, that Fox is entitled to return to her seat on the CPE.

As stated before, this case was early in the pleading stage when the trial court granted the Governor's motion to dismiss for failure to state a legally cognizable claim. Our conclusion that bicameral confirmation requirements in statutes such as KRS 164.011(1) are constitutionally infirm, however, leads to the inevitable conclusion that the trial court erred by dismissing Fox's complaint based upon its contrary interpretation of §93. The ultimate merits of Fox's complaint, however, are an entirely separate matter, which the parties have not yet had a full opportunity to either prove or defend.

The only proper question before us is whether the trial court erred by dismissing Fox's complaint for failure to state a claim because of the purported bicameral confirmation requirement for members of the CPE. We have determined that the attempted bicameral confirmation requirement is contrary to §93 of the Constitution of Kentucky. The merits of Fox's demand that she be restored to a place on the CPE were not fully presented to the trial court and, consequently, are not properly before this Court on appeal. Remand is necessary so that the parties may present their proof to advance or defend the ultimate merits of Fox's demand.

IV. *Conclusion.*

We reverse the circuit court's order dismissing Virginia Fox's complaint for the reasons discussed in this opinion, and we remand the matter to the trial court for all necessary further proceedings.

All sitting. Noble, Scott, and Venters, JJ., concur.

Abramson, J., concurs in result only by separate opinion.

Cunningham, J., dissents by separate opinion in which Schroder, J., joins.

Schroder, J., dissents by separate opinion in which Cunningham, J., joins.

Justice Abramson, concurring in result only.

I concur in result only and write separately to state a point of fundamental disagreement with the well-reasoned majority opinion. Specifically, I disagree with the following observation by the majority regarding how it came to pass that the confirmation provision in §93, as amended in 1992, was confined to the Senate:

> We are unwilling to assume that the General Assembly omitted reference to the House in §93 by oversight. Instead, we agree with Fox that the absence of language referencing the House in §93 should rationally be interpreted as a conscious decision by the General Assembly not to include the House in confirming nominees.

84. *See, e.g., Commonwealth v. Harrelson*, 14 S.W.3d 541, 547 (Ky. 2000) ("It is uncontroverted that a statute is presumed to be constitutional unless it clearly offends the limitations and prohibitions of the Constitution.").

Before, during and after the 1992 legislative session, the Kentucky General Assembly has passed legislation, which provides for bicameral confirmation of appointments to at least eight different boards and commissions. In my view, these laws reflect a clear, good faith belief on the part of the majority of both houses of the General Assembly that bicameral confirmation is constitutionally permissible. Unfortunately, given the plain wording of §93, it is not. I firmly believe that the wording of §93 was chosen to address the separation of powers issue raised, and eventually addressed by this Court, in *Kraus v. Kentucky State Senate*, 872 S.W.2d 433 (Ky. 1994). In a classic case of focusing on the tree and forgetting to see the forest, SB 226 produced a constitutional amendment which specifically recognized the Senate confirmation provision at issue in Kraus but inadvertently undermined the bicameral confirmation provisions which had been deliberately included in prior legislation and which would continue to be included in laws relating to various boards and commissions in the years that followed.

The majority is correct that this Court must construe what it has before it and in §93 we have language that does not admit a construction that is most likely what the General Assembly actually intended if their prior, contemporaneous and subsequent acts are considered. As for the idea that their intent has been rendered of secondary import, or even irrelevant, by the vote of the people, I cannot fully subscribe to that view. Notably, we have entrusted to the legislature the significant responsibility of initiating the constitutional amendment process. Ky. Const. §256. As representatives of the people, their intent in proposing a constitutional amendment is vital and, therefore, it is equally vital that that intent be fully and painstakingly stated in any ballot question. If the overarching concept of the confirmation process, which in some instances is confined to the Senate but which in other instances has been shared by both houses of the Kentucky General Assembly, had been carefully considered in drafting the proposed amendment, I truly believe that we would not have been left with the "tree" that is now before us. We have been, however, and the language used in §93 is so unambiguous that I can find no defensible basis for looking beyond that clear language. Consequently, I must reluctantly concur in result.

Justice Cunningham, dissenting.

With due respect, I dissent.

We are bound by law to adhere to a strong presumption of the constitutionality of statutes. Analysis begins with the presumption that legislative acts are constitutional. *Cain v. Lodestar Energy, Inc.*, 302 S.W.3d 39, 43 (Ky. 2009) (footnote omitted). In my opinion, this presumption has been ignored in our holding that the "bicameral confirmation requirement" of KRS 164.011(1) is "constitutionally infirm."

* * *

I take major issue with the statement of the majority that "there is nothing in the plain language of §93 that permits the House to have any role in the confirmation vote." That provision clearly authorizes both houses of the General Assembly to "prescribe by law" the method of Appellant's appointment to the Council on Postsecondary Education.

This section of the Kentucky Constitution plainly states that the office in question is to be appointed by the Governor "in such manner as may be prescribed by law." There is no ambiguity in those words. The provision simply broadens the representative involvement of the law-making body into the appointment process. There is ambiguity in the words "which may include a requirement of consent by the Senate." In fact, the majority spends page after page explaining what it means. In short, the majority gives minimal thrift to the precise and direct language of the constitutional provision and reverses this case on the ambiguous wording.

Our Court today gives hefty consideration to the fact that the voters of Kentucky approved this constitutional amendment and, therefore, must have endorsed Senate only confirmation. Says the Court, "No reasonable voter could have construed that ballot question to mean the House had any right whatsoever to confirm nominees." This requires a complete whiteout on the ballots throughout this state of the words "in such manner as may be prescribed by law." Of course, that was not the case.

In truth, when §93 was on the ballot, it was all about the heart of the issue—authorizing the reelection of constitutional officers for one additional term. It is pure fantasy to think that the voters fully understood the last sentence we deal with here today when it has taken over a year of much consideration and discussion, and our Kentucky State Supreme Court almost forty pages, to tell us what it means.

In keeping with strong presumption of the constitutionality of statutes passed by our legislature, representing the citizenship of this state, I would affirm the decision below. Therefore, with deep appreciation for the five minds that differ, I respectfully dissent.

Schroder, J., joins.

Justice Schroder, dissenting.

The bicameral confirmation requirement for members of the CPE contained in KRS 164.011(1) does not violate Section 93 of the Kentucky Constitution. The phrase in Section 93 regarding confirmation by the Senate is merely illustrative of how appointees could be confirmed. The phrase does not preclude a statute that requires confirmation by both chambers of the General Assembly. The language is clear; it says what it says.

Cunningham, J., joins.

Notes and Questions

1. After *Fox v. Grayson* was decided by the Court, the General Assembly amended KRS 164.011 to provide for confirmation of Council of Postsecondary Education members by the Senate only.

2. Even after *Fox v. Grayson*, the General Assembly has yet to amend KRS 11.160, subsection (2) of which still provides the procedures for joint House and Senate confirmation of executive appointments. In addition, the Kentucky Revised Statutes still include several provisions purporting to require joint Senate and House of Representatives confirmation of appointments to certain boards and commissions. *E.g.*, KRS

7B.030 (Kentucky Long-Term Policy Research Center); KRS 164.005 (Governor's Postsecondary Education Nominating Committee); KRS 247.090 (State Fair Board); KRS 247.944 (Kentucky Agricultural Finance Corporation); KRS 248.707 (Agricultural Development Board); KRS 351.1041 (Mine Safety Review Commission). These statutes presumably are unconstitutional under *Fox v. Grayson*.

3. Justice Cunningham dissented in *Fox v. Grayson* because he found the "prescribed by law" language in Section 93 to permit the General Assembly to require bicameral confirmation of gubernatorial appointees. Justice Schroder agreed with him, finding the "consent of the Senate" language in Section 93 to be merely "illustrative of how appointees could be confirmed." Neither dissenting opinion addressed the *expressio unius* analysis employed by the majority. Does the *expressio unius* canon of construction apply with respect to Section 93? Did the majority correctly apply it?

Seven

The Jural Rights Doctrine: Separation of Powers or Individual Right?

> "All courts shall be open, and every person for an injury done him in his lands, goods, person or reputation, shall have remedy by due course of law, and right and justice administered without sale, denial or delay." (Ky. Const. §14.)
>
> "The General Assembly shall have no power to limit the amount to be recovered for injuries resulting in death, or for injuries to person or property." (Ky. Const. §54.)
>
> "Whenever the death of a person shall result from an injury inflicted by negligence or wrongful act, then, in every such case, damages may be recovered for such death, from the corporations and persons so causing the same. Until otherwise provided by law, the action to recover such damages shall in all cases be prosecuted by the personal representative of the deceased person. The General Assembly may provide how the recovery shall go and to whom belong; and until such provision is made, the same shall form part of the personal estate of the deceased person." (Ky. Const. §241.)

The "jural rights doctrine" is a unique creation of the Kentucky courts. As described in the cases that follow, the doctrine stands for the proposition that the common law rules governing redress for injuries sustained to persons or property, as those rules existed at the time Kentucky's current Constitution was adopted, may not be abrogated by the Kentucky General Assembly.

In his seminal article on the jural rights doctrine, University of Kentucky Professor Thomas P. Lewis argued that Sections 14, 54, and 241, on their face, do not support so wide-ranging a rule. *See* Thomas P. Lewis, *Jural Rights under Kentucky's Constitution: Realities Grounded in Myth*, 80 Ky. L.J. 953 (1992). For example, Section 14 requires that a person "shall have remedy by due course of law" for "an injury done him," but it does not necessarily define what the "due course of law" is in a particular fact scenario, or what a legally cognizable "injury" is. Section 54 prohibits the General Assembly from placing a cap on "the amount to be recovered for injuries," but like Section 14, it also does not define "injury." Nor does it say whether the General Assembly may limit damages recoverable other than "for injuries," such as punitive damages, which are designed not to compensate for injury but to deter and punish. And on its face, Section 54 speaks only to the amount of damages that may be recovered for a past wrong; it says nothing about the General Assembly's power to modify the substantive common law on a prospective basis, such as changing the elements required to prove a tort claim or abolishing a cause of action altogether. Finally, Section 241 overturned the prior common law that held that there could be no recovery for wrongful death. But it does not define what conduct constitutes a "negligen[t] or wrongful act," or state whether wrongfulness should be defined as the term would have been understood in 1891 or should change or evolve over time. Professor Lewis's article continues to be cited in dissenting opinions of Supreme Court justices in jural rights cases, and it continues to inform the debate concerning the meaning of Sections 14, 54, and 241. *See, e.g.*, Chief Justice Minton's discussion of Professor Lewis's article in *Commonwealth, Cabinet for Health and Family Services ex rel. Meier v. Claycomb ex rel. Claycomb*, 566 S.W.3d 202 (Ky. 2018).

It should be noted that the jural rights doctrine is in tension with another constitutional provision. Section 233 states: "All laws which, on the first day of June, one thousand seven hundred and ninety-two [the date Kentucky was admitted as a state into the Union, 1 Stat. 189], were in force in the State of Virginia, and which are of a general nature and not local to that State, and not repugnant to this Constitution, nor to the laws which have been enacted by the General Assembly of this Commonwealth, shall be in force within this State *until they shall be altered or repealed by the General Assembly*." Ky. Const. §233 (emphasis added). Each of Kentucky's four constitutions has included a substantially similar provision. *Aetna Ins. Co. v. Commonwealth*, 106 Ky. 864, 51 S.W. 624, 628 (1899). Thus, the General Assembly has always had the power to change the common law. Yet the jural rights doctrine seems to hold that the legislature may alter the common law as it existed on June 1, 1792 (under Section 233) but cannot also alter the common law that developed later (under Sections 14, 54, and 241). This tension echoes throughout the cases that follow.

Ludwig v. Johnson

Court of Appeals of Kentucky (1932)

243 Ky. 533, 49 S.W.2d 347

OPINION OF THE COURT BY JUDGE REES.

This is an action for damages for personal injuries resulting from the alleged negligent operation of an automobile by the appellee Darwin Johnson. Appellant, who was the plaintiff below, was riding in the automobile as the guest of Darwin Johnson at the time of the accident in which he received his alleged injuries. The appellee Thomas J. Johnson was made a defendant on the theory that he was liable under the "family purpose" doctrine.

* * *

Darwin Johnson's demurrer to the petition was overruled, and he filed an answer which was in two paragraphs. The first paragraph was a traverse, and in the second paragraph the defendant alleged that upon the occasion referred to in the petition the plaintiff was being transported in the automobile operated by defendant as the defendant's guest without payment for such transportation. The plaintiff filed a demurrer to the second paragraph of the answer, the demurrer was overruled, he declined to plead further, and a judgment was entered dismissing his petition.

The second paragraph of the answer stated facts constituting a defense to the cause of action set up in the petition if the act of the General Assembly of 1930, commonly known as the "guest statute," is valid. Chapter 85, Acts 1930; Baldwin's 1931 Supplement to Carroll's Kentucky Statutes, §12-7. That act, including the title, reads: "An Act releasing owners of motor vehicles from responsibility for injuries to passengers therein.... No person transported by the owner or operator of a motor vehicle, as his guest, without payment for such transportation shall have a cause of action for damages against such owner or operator for any injuries received, death, or any loss sustained, in case of accident, unless such accident shall have resulted from an intentional act on the part of said owner or operator."

It is appellant's contention that this act violates sections 14, 54, and 241 of our Constitution, and is void. We are met at the outset, of course, with the universally applied principle that every presumption is in favor of the validity of an act of the Legislature, and that every doubt as to the constitutionality of a law must be resolved in favor of its validity. *Campbell v. Commonwealth*, 229 Ky. 264, 17 S.W.(2d) 227, 63 A.L.R. 932; *Harbison v. George*, 228 Ky. 168, 14 S.W.(2d) 405. Such principle, however, has no application when the enactment of the particular statute under consideration is either expressly or by necessary implication inhibited or is subversive of the purposes and intentions of the makers of the Constitution. It then becomes the duty of the courts to pronounce the statute unconstitutional.

Prior to the enactment of the "guest statute," the rule was well settled in this state that the driver of an automobile owed an invited guest the duty of exercising ordinary care in its operation. *Beard v. Klusmeier*, 158 Ky. 153, 164 S.W. 319, 50 L.R.A. (N. S.) 1100, Ann. Cas. 1915D, 342; *Chambers v. Hawkins*, 233 Ky. 211, 25 S.W.(2d) 363. Section 241 of the Constitution reads in part: "Whenever the death of a person shall result from an injury inflicted by negligence or wrongful act, then, in every such case, damages may be recovered for such death, from the corporations and persons so causing the same." Under the common law an action could not be maintained for the wrongful death of another. *Smith's Adm'r v. National Coal & Iron Company*, 135 Ky. 671, 117 S.W. 280; *Eden v. Lexington & Frankfort Railroad Company*, 14 B. Mon. 204. An action to recover for the wrongful death of a person can only be maintained in this state by virtue of section 241 of the Constitution and section 6, Kentucky Statutes, enacted pursuant thereto. It was clearly the purpose of this provision of the Constitution to do away with the common-law principle that a civil action could not be maintained to recover damages for the wrongful death of a person and thus to cure the then existing inequalities in rights and liabilities flowing from negligent or wrongful conduct.

Under the present Constitution, actions for death are governed by the same principles as actions for injuries where death does not result. The "guest statute" under consideration undertakes to take away the right to recover for death resulting from negligence, or wrongful act amounting to anything less than an intentional act, and to that extent it clearly contravenes section 241 of the Constitution. In *Howard's Adm'r v. Hunter*, 126 Ky. 685, 104 S.W. 723, 724, 31 Ky. Law Rep. 1092, the court, speaking of this section of the Constitution, said: "It was the manifest intention of the constitutional provision quoted to allow an action to be maintained whenever the death of a person was caused by the negligent or wrongful act of another and it is not within the power of the Legislature to deny this right of action. The section is as comprehensive as language can make it. The words 'negligence' and 'wrongful act' are sufficiently broad to embrace every degree of tort that can be committed against the person."

It is argued that, if this concededly invalid provision of the statute is eliminated by eliminating the word "death," the remaining provisions of the statute, which apply only to a gratuitous passenger in an automobile who receives nonfatal injuries, do not contravene section 241 of the Constitution, and are therefore valid, and should be sustained on the ground that the invalid part of the act is not vital to the whole and can be separated from the valid part.

On the other hand, the appellant argues that, if the act should be given such a construction, it would be repugnant to the equal protection clause of Amendment 14 of the Constitution of the United States, since, if the law applies to nonfatal injuries and not to fatal injuries, an unreasonable classification is created. It is unnecessary to pursue that avenue of inquiry, however, as we have concluded that the act as a whole is repugnant to other provisions of our own Constitution, and is therefore void.

Section 54 of the Constitution reads: "The general assembly shall have no power to limit the amount to be recovered for injuries resulting in death, or for injuries to person or property." It is insisted that this section of the Constitution does not guarantee the continuation of the right of action theretofore existent, but merely applies to such causes of action as continue to exist, and prohibits the Legislature from limiting the amount of damages to be recovered for injuries resulting in death or for injuries to person or property so long as a right of action exists for such injuries, but does not prohibit it from abolishing the right of action.

In *Kentucky State Journal Co. v. Workmen's Compensation Board*, 161 Ky. 562, 170 S.W. 437, 1166, 1168, L.R.A. 1916A, 389, Ann. Cas. 1916B, 1273, the Workmen's Compensation Act was declared invalid because it violated section 54 of the Constitution. In the course of the opinion it was said:

> "We will go a little further and examine the provisions of section 32 of this act. Suppose the employee, desiring to rely upon the causes of action given him by

> the Constitution and laws of this state, does not accept the so-called benefits of this act, then in that event, under section 32 of this act, the employee, prior to receiving an injury, is compelled to give notice to his employer and to the board that he will not accept the provisions of this act. This notice must be served as provided by the Civil Code for serving notices.
>
> So if, after this notice has been served, the employee should be injured or killed while in the service of the employer, he or his personal representative may sue his employer to recover damages; then his right to recover is barred by the provisions of this act, if his injury was caused or contributed to by the negligence of any other employee of said employer, or if the injury was due to any of the ordinary hazards or risks of the employment, or if due to any defect in the tools, machinery, appliances, instrumentality, or place of work, if the defect was known or could have been discovered by the injured employee by the exercise of ordinary care on his part, or was not known or could not have been discovered by the employer by the exercise of ordinary care in time to have prevented the injury, nor in any event if the negligence of the injured employee contributed to such injuries.
>
> Now when his right to recover is restricted by such qualifications and conditions as these, we think these qualifications and conditions constitute, within the meaning of section 54 of the Constitution, not only a limitation upon the amount to be recovered, but practically destroy his right to recovery."

In the *Kentucky State Journal Company* Case the court, by implication, if not expressly, held that section 54 of the Constitution inhibited the Legislature from taking away from an employee, without affording him the right of election to work under the act, his right to recover damages for injuries resulting from the negligence of his employer. It might be argued that the court was not required to go that far in that case in order to hold invalid the act there under consideration, but we think the interpretation there given to section 54 of the Constitution is sound. When that section is read in connection with other sections of the same instrument, such as sections 14 and 241, the conclusion is inescapable that the intention of the framers of the Constitution was to inhibit the Legislature from abolishing rights of action for damages for death or injuries caused by negligence.

Section 14 of the Constitution provides that: "All courts shall be open and every person, for an injury done him in his lands, goods, person or reputation, shall have remedy by due course of law, and right and justice administered without sale, denial or delay." No exception is made to the provision that every person for an injury done him in his person shall have remedy by due course of law.

* * *

In *Stewart v. Houk*, 127 Or. 589, 271 P. 998, 999, 272 P. 893, 61 A. L. R. 1236, a guest statute similar to the one under consideration was declared to be in conflict with article 1, § 10, of the Oregon Constitution, which provides: "... And every man shall have remedy by due course of law for injury done him in his person, property, or reputation." The court said: "The purpose of this provision is to save from legislative abolishment those jural rights which had become well established prior to the enactment of our Constitution." And further: "The proponents of this act doubtlessly felt it was unjust, that one who gratuitously conveys another in his automobile should be subjected to a claim for damages if an injury should befall the latter. But, if the buttress erected by this constitutional provision for the safeguarding of long-established rights can be pierced by this piece of legislation, an entry will be effected through which may come other legislation in substitution for the safeguarded common-law rights. It is clear we possess no power to sanction the entry and the substitution."

* * *

In *Johnson v. Higgins*, 3 Metc. 566, and also in *Barkley v. Glover*, 4 Metc. 44, it is said in effect that section 14 of our Constitution is a restriction on the judicial, and not on the legislative, branch of government, but this observation was unnecessary in the decision of those cases, and is clearly unsound in view of section 26 of our Constitution, which is the concluding section of the Bill of Rights, and which reads: "To guard against transgression of the high powers which we have delegated, We Declare that everything in this Bill of Rights is excepted out of the general powers of government, and shall forever remain inviolate; and all laws contrary thereto, or contrary to this constitution, shall be void."

In the much later case of *Williams v. Wedding*, 165 Ky. 361, 176 S.W. 1176, a legislative act was held to be in violation of section 14.

The statute under consideration violates the spirit of our Constitution as well as its letter as found in sections 14, 54, and 241. It was the manifest purpose of the framers of that instrument to preserve and perpetuate the common-law right of a citizen injured by the negligent act of another to sue to recover damages for his injury. The imperative mandate of section 14 is that every person, for an injury done him in his person, shall have remedy by due course of law. If the allegations of appellant's petition are true, he has suffered serious injuries occasioned by the negligent acts of the appellee Darwin Johnson. The Constitution guarantees to him his right to a day in court for the purpose of establishing the alleged wrong perpetrated on him and recovery of his resultant damages. We conclude that chapter 85 of the Acts of the General Assembly of 1930 is unconstitutional and void.

The judgment is * * * reversed as to Darwin Johnson, with directions to sustain the demurrer to paragraph 2 of the answer and for further proceedings consistent herewith.

The whole court sitting.

Dietzman, C. J., and Thomas, J., dissent from so much of the opinion as holds the act in contravention of sections 14 and 54 of the Constitution.

Notes and Questions

1. *Ludwig v. Johnson* is regarded as the first Kentucky case to espouse the "jural rights doctrine," which holds that the General Assembly is without power to eliminate common law tort causes of action. The *Ludwig* Court found the conclusion "inescapable" that "the intention of the framers of the Constitution was to inhibit the Legislature from abolishing rights of action for damages for death or injuries caused by negligence."

2. Consider, however, that the cause of action for negligence involves the breach of a legal duty owed by the defendant to the plaintiff, and consequent injury to the plaintiff. A statute like the automobile guest statute at issue in *Ludwig* essentially modifies the duty element of the cause of action. If no duty is owed to a guest passenger, then there can be no breach, and thus, no negligence. The cause of action for negligence still exists, but the statute constricts the legal duties owed. As espoused by *Ludwig*, the jural rights doctrine precludes legislative *constriction* of the scope of the legal duties owed.

3. *Ludwig* relied, in part, on the Oregon case of *Stewart v. Houk*, 271 P. 998 (Or. 1928), for its holding that Sections 14, 54, and 241 of the Kentucky Constitution barred Kentucky's automobile guest statute. But the Supreme Court of Oregon abrogated its decision in *Stewart* seven years later (and three years after *Ludwig* was decided) in *Perozzi v. Ganiere*, 40 P.2d 1009 (Or. 1935). After observing that "[t]he common law is not a fixed and changeless code for the government of human conduct," *id.* at 1015, the court held that "[t]here was and is no constitutional inhibition against the enactment of our guest statute," *id.* at 1016. For a detailed history of the cases decided under the "remedy clause" of Oregon's constitution, which is analogous to Section 14 of the Kentucky Constitution, see *Horton v. Oregon Health & Science University*, 376 P.3d 998 (Or. 2016).

4. Note that the Kentucky jural rights doctrine does not preclude the General Assembly from *expanding* the scope of legal duties that are owed. The entire tort doctrine of negligence *per se* is premised upon the notion that the legislative branch may create a legal standard of care that did not already exist, thus altering the common law.

Perkins v. Northeastern Log Homes

Supreme Court of Kentucky (1991)
808 S.W.2d 809

OPINION OF THE COURT BY JUSTICE LEIBSON.

The U.S. District Court for the Western District of Kentucky has certified to the Kentucky Supreme Court the following *Questions of Law* at issue in the above-styled case:

> "(1) whether KRS 413.135 violates Kentucky Constitution §§14, 54, 59, and/or 241; and
>
> (2) whether KRS 413.135 applies to latent disease cases and, if so, whether the statute of limitations commences from the date the plaintiff knows or should have discovered the injury or disease."

For reasons that we will address, our answer to the first question is that the statute in question violates the Kentucky Constitution, and our answer to the second question is that KRS 413.135 does not nullify the "discovery rule" which applies "to tort actions for injury from latent disease caused by exposure to a harmful substance." *Louisville Trust Co. v. Johns-Manville Products*, Ky., 580 S.W.2d 497, 501 (1979).

The Certification from the U.S. District Court states the following facts:

> "Plaintiffs Eloise and Dennis Perkins (the Perkins) filed their product liability action against defendants Northeastern Log Homes, Inc. (Northeastern), Roberts Consolidated Industries, Inc. (Roberts), and DAP, Inc. (DAP), on June 16, 1989. Defendants removed the case [from Jefferson Circuit Court to federal court] on July 10, 1989.
>
> Plaintiffs purchased a log home kit from Northeastern on June 24, 1977. Northeastern manufactured the construction components of the log home. Roberts and DAP designed and manufactured "Woodlife," a product used to preserve the log home. The Perkins finished constructing their home in November 1978 and they lived in it until June 1989.
>
> Eloise Perkins discovered she had non-Hodgkin's lymphoma around March 31, 1986. She alleges that her illness developed from continued exposure to Pentachlorophenol, which "Woodlife" contained."

Appellants' Complaint is an exhibit to the Brief filed by Roberts and DAP (hereinafter "Roberts"). It identifies Northeastern's product as a "Log Home Kit" which the appellants purchased and then assembled and constructed into a log home which they located in Floyds Knob, Indiana. It alleges: "[b]eginning with the construction period in approximately August, 1977 through June 9, 1989, Plaintiffs were exposed in their log home, built from the Northeastern kit, to toxic concentrations of the chemical, technical-grade Pentachlorophenol, which was an active ingredient in the 'Woodlife' ..."; the "log home is unfit for human habitation ... as a result of said toxic contamination"; and a cause of action for strict liability "by reason of defects in the product ... rendering the product unreasonably dangerous," and, separately, for "negligent failure to design, negligent failure to properly manufacture and assemble the product . . . , failure to adequately warn and instruct concerning the use and failure to adequately test and inspect the product."

Appellants have supplemented their Brief with affidavits from a medical expert and their attorney, stating in substance that Eloise Perkins suffers from a non-Hodgkins' lymphoma, a cancer caused by exposure to Pentachlorophenol, with the "appearance of symptoms . . . in March of 1986," that her first notice of any possible connection between her cancer and the log home kit in question occurred in February 1989, the first medical confirmation occurred in March 1989, and the suit was filed on June 16, 1989. We accept these claims along with the facts stated in the Certification as a factual premise in addressing the underlying legal issues.

I. Does KRS 413.135 Violate Kentucky Constitution §§14, 54, 59 and/or 241

KRS 413.135 is the latest edition of a statute first enacted in 1964 and 1966,[1] to protect builders and others engaged in the "design, planning, supervision, inspection, or construction of any improvement to real property" from suit for damages, personal injury or wrongful death, five years after the substantial completion of such improvement. The statute was referred to as the builders, architects and engineers "no action" statute and is mislabeled "an act relating to limitations of actions," because its purpose is not to signal the end of the period for filing a cause of action that has already accrued, but to cut off the period of exposure to liability for a construction defect where no cause of action has yet accrued because the damage, injury or death caused by the deficiency first occurred more than five years after substantial completion of construction. It is not a statute of limitations but a statute of repose because it extinguishes the claim before it exists. For that reason, the 1964/66 edition of the statute of repose for persons in the construction industry has been challenged as unconstitutional in previous cases before this Court. Its legal history can be summarized as follows:

1) In *Saylor v. Hall*, Ky., 497 S.W.2d 218 (1973), the statute was held unconstitutional as a violation of our Kentucky Constitution, §§14, 54 and 241.

Kentucky Constitution §14 is part of the Bill of Rights in our first constitution of 1792. It is the "open courts" provision and states as follows:

> "All courts shall be open, and every person for an injury done him in his lands, goods, person or reputation, shall have remedy by due course of law, and right and justice administered without sale, denial or delay."

Kentucky Constitution §§54 and 241 were added as new provisions in our Fourth (and last) Constitution of 1891. These were enacted along with many other provisions to limit the power of the General Assembly, which was then widely perceived as abusing its power with the grant of privileges and immunities to railroads and other powerful corporate interests. *See* Debates, Constitutional Convention of 1890, 4 Vol.

1. Two statutes were later combined into one.

> "Most of the delegates to the Constitutional Convention felt that the real root of Kentucky's governmental problems was the almost unlimited power of the General Assembly. One of them even said that '... the principal, if not the sole purpose of the constitution which we are here to frame, is to restrain its [the Legislature's] will and restrict its authority....'
>
> They distrusted the General Assembly, so they wrote many details of law into the Constitution." p. 161, Research Report No. 137, Legislative Research Commission, Jan. 1987.

Kentucky Constitution §54 prohibits the General Assembly from enacting any "restriction on recovery for injury or death." It provides:

> "The General Assembly shall have no power to limit the amount to be recovered for injuries resulting in death, or for injuries to person or property."

Section 241 was enacted to protect the right of "recovery for wrongful death" against legislative interference. It provides in pertinent part:

> "Whenever the death of a person shall result from an injury inflicted by negligence or wrongful act, then, in every such case, damages may be recovered for such death, from the corporations and persons so causing the same."

The essence of *Saylor v. Hall* is found in the following quote:

> ""It is not within the power of the legislature, under the guise of a limitation provision, to cut off an existing remedy entirely, since this would amount to a denial of justice, and, manifestly, an existing right of action cannot be taken away by legislation which shortens the period of limitation to a time that is already run.' [Citation omitted.] Surely then, the application of purported limitation statutes in such manner as to destroy a cause of action before it legally exists cannot be permissible if it accomplishes destruction of a constitutionally protected right of action." *Id.* at 225.

2) *Carney v. Moody*, Ky., 646 S.W.2d 40, 41 (1983), did not overrule *Saylor v. Hall*, but it reached the opposite result. The Court stated the "problem with the *Saylor* opinion" was it "did not discuss or decide the question of whether the facts would have given rise to a legal cause of action not only when the statutes of limitation were enacted in 1964 and 1966, but also when the Constitution was adopted in 1891." Of course, this was not so because *Saylor v. Hall* specifically held the constitutional defect in the statute was it:

> "[D]estroys, pro tanto, a common-law right of action for negligence that proximately causes personal injury or death, which existed at the time the *statutes were enacted.* [Emphasis added.] The statutory expressions as they relate to actions based on negligence perform an abortion on the right of action, not in the first trimester, but before conception." 497 S.W.2d at 224.

3) *In re Beverly Hills Fire Litigation*, Ky., 672 S.W.2d 922 (1984), we again addressed the constitutionality of KRS 413.135, now restored by *Carney v. Moody*, but it did not directly answer the question. The subject matter of the controversy was allegedly defective aluminum circuit wiring installed at the Beverly Hills Supper Club which burned

to the ground. We held this material was beyond the reach of the statute's application, stating:

> "(1) Properly construed this statute has no application here to what is essentially a products liability case.
>
> (2) Otherwise construed, this statute would be 'special' legislation in violation of the Kentucky Constitution, §59." 672 S.W.2d at 923.

4) *Tabler v. Wallace*, Ky., 704 S.W.2d 179 (1986), again addressed the statute in terms of the Kentucky Constitution, §59. This time we declared the 1964/66 statute was unconstitutional as lacking "a rational justification for creating a special class and conferring special privileges and immunity on that class at the time the statute in question was enacted." *Id.* at 187.

One aspect of the Opinion discussed the irrationality of creating immunity for the builder or designer in circumstances where the materialman or supplier would still be liable. Before the ink was dry on *Tabler v. Wallace*, the General Assembly reenacted KRS 413.135 in present form which extends the subject matter of the statute to "construction components," and which extends the statutory protection to "any person," so long as the gravamen on the action is a deficiency in real estate. The new statute also changed the period before which the right of action would be cut off, extending it from five to seven years.

* * *

Next, we consider the impact of §§14, 54 and 241 of our Constitution, quoted earlier in this Opinion. In *Tabler v. Wallace*, having decided KRS 413.135 was unconstitutional as special legislation, we elected not to "write Chapter Three to *Saylor v. Hall* and *Carney v. Moody*." *Id.* at 187. This was misconstrued as an opening to revise the statute to meet certain language in the *Tabler v. Wallace* opinion. This time we will address whether the statute is unconstitutional under §§14, 54 and 241 in order to fully answer the question certified and to avoid, if possible, yet another round of statutory revision and opinion.

The holding in *Saylor v. Hall*, was:

> "The legislature's *power to enact statutes of limitation* governing the time in which a cause of action must be asserted by suit *is*, of course, *unquestioned*. In this state, however, it is *equally well settled* that the legislature *may not abolish an existing common-law right of action for personal injuries or wrongful death caused by negligence*.... [T]he application of these statutory expressions to the claims here asserted *destroys*, pro tanto, *a common-law right of action* for negligence that proximately causes personal injury or death, *which existed at the times the statutes were enacted*. The statutory expressions as they relate to actions based on negligence perform an abortion on the right of action, not in the first trimester, but before conception.
>
> The right of action for negligence proximately causing injury or death, which is constitutionally protected in this state, requires more than mere conduct before recovery can be attempted. Recovery is not possible until a cause of

> action exists. *A cause of action does not exist until the conduct causes injury that produces loss or damage....*
>
> '[M]anifestly, an existing right of action cannot be taken away by legislation which shortens the period of limitation to a time that has already run.' [Citation omitted.] Surely then, the application of purported limitation statutes in such manner as to destroy a cause of action before it legally exists cannot be permissible if it accomplishes destruction of a constitutionally protected right of action.
>
> ....
>
> In our judgment [this statute] cannot be applied to bar the plaintiffs' claims in this action. Such application is constitutionally impermissible in this state because it would violate the spirit and language of Sections 14, 54, and 241 of the Constitution of Kentucky when read together." [Emphasis added.] 497 S.W.2d at 224–25.

We subscribe to the law as stated in *Saylor v. Hall. Carney v. Moody* reaches a different result without overruling *Saylor v. Hall*, by limiting the application of these constitutional provisions to whether "the law as it prevailed in 1891 would have afforded the injured parties a remedy against the negligent builder or builders." 646 S.W.2d at 41. We believe that in *Carney v. Moody* the controlling constitutional sections have been applied more narrowly than the constitution permits so as to cause an arbitrary result, and that the cases cited in the *Carney v. Moody* opinion to justify the decision, *Happy v. Erwin*, Ky., 330 S.W.2d 412 (1959), *Ludwig v. Johnson*, 243 Ky. 533, 49 S.W.2d 347 (1932), and *Ky. Utilities Co. v. Jackson-County Rural Electric Coop. Assoc.*, Ky., 438 S.W.2d 788 (1969), do not support its conclusions. Each of these cases involved statutes held unconstitutional as infringing constitutionally protected jural rights. In each it is very questionable whether the specific fact situation involved "would have given rise to a legal cause of action ... when the Constitution was adopted in 1891." *Carney v. Moody* as quoted *supra*. For example, the first definitive case on the subject is *Ludwig v. Johnson, supra*, holding the automobile "guest statute" unconstitutional in violation of §§14, 54 and 241 of our Constitution. The statute barred a cause of action for damages by a guest passenger in an automobile against an owner or operator for "any injuries received, death, or any loss sustained, in case of accident, unless such accident shall have resulted from an intentional act on the part of said owner or operator." 49 S.W.2d at 348. Surely there were no cases in Kentucky establishing a cause of action, as such, for a guest passenger in an automobile against the host driver in 1890 when Kentucky Constitution §§54 and 241 were written. Speaking to the principle of statutory construction affording presumptive validity to statutes, our Court said:

> "Such principle, however, has no application when the enactment of the particular statute under consideration is either expressly or by necessary implication inhibited or is subversive of the purposes and intentions of the makers of the Constitution. It then becomes the duty of the courts to pronounce the statute unconstitutional.

> Prior to the enactment of the 'guest statute,' the rule was well settled in this state that the driver of an automobile owed an invited guest the duty of exercising ordinary care in its operation." *Id.* at 348–49.

The opinion reviews the three sections of the Constitution at issue, §§14, 54 and 241, with appropriate comments on each. It then addresses one of the arguments presented by the appellees in the present case, that the "guest statute" had been upheld in most of our sister states where its constitutionality had been considered, stating:

> "The Constitution of each of these states contains a provision similar to the provisions of section 14 of our Constitution, but there is no provision in either of the Constitutions similar to the provisions of sections 54 and 241 of our Constitution." *Id.* at 350.

The court then quotes from an Oregon case the phrase that became the principal bone of contention in *Carney v. Moody*, "[t]he purpose of this provision is to save from legislative abolishment those jural rights which had become well established prior to the enactment of our Constitution." *Ludwig*, 49 S.W.2d at 350. But the concept of jural rights must be understood in the broader context in which it was used in *Ludwig*, where it was applied to a fact situation nonexistent at the time of the 1890 Constitution. This is clear from the concluding paragraph in the *Ludwig* opinion:

> "The statute under consideration violates the spirit of our Constitution as well as its letter as found in sections 14, 54, and 241. It was the manifest purpose of the framers of that instrument to *preserve and perpetuate the common-law right of a citizen injured by the negligent act of another* to sue to recover damages for his injury." [Emphasis added.] *Id.* at 351.

The jural right to sue for personal injury or death caused by negligence or other wrongful acts was well recognized in 1891 when our Constitution was adopted. The right had been fenced in, depending on circumstances, by artificial barriers such as privity, which *Saylor v. Hall* describes as "the erroneous interpretation of the 1842 English case of *Winterbottom v. Wright*, 152 Eng.Rep. 402, that generated the steadily eroded 'general rule' that there was no liability of a contracting party to one with whom he was not in 'privity.'" *Saylor v. Hall, supra*, 497 S.W.2d at 223. In the present case Mrs. Perkins was in privity of contract with Northeastern Log Homes if she was a co-purchaser, or indeed, even if not under the concept of privity codified in KRS 355.2-318, in 1958, which includes "any natural person who is in the family or household of [the] buyer ... if it is reasonable to expect that such person may use, consume or be affected by the goods."

The point is that the critical cases on this subject, which we have cited above, afford protection of "jural rights" in a broad context as our Kentucky Constitution intended, and not in the narrow context utilized in *Carney v. Moody*. As stated in *Tabler v. Wallace*, the concept of negligence expresses "a generalized standard of care," and one that "preexisted the Kentucky Constitution." 704 S.W.2d at 187. In drafting our constitutional protections in §§14, 54 and 241, our founding fathers were protecting the jural rights of the individual citizens of Kentucky against the power of the government to abridge such rights, speaking to their rights as they would be commonly understood by those citizens in any year, not just in 1891. The protection afforded to jural rights is not limited definitively to fact situations existing in the year 1891. *Carney v. Moody* opines that not "every enlargement in the field of liability" is beyond the reach of the policy of the General Assembly, 646 S.W.2d at 41. We agree. But we do not agree that anything as fundamental as the cause of action for personal injury or wrongful death based on negligence, or, indeed, at this point in time, as the cause of action against a manufacturer based on liability in tort for a defective product, can be abolished at will by the General Assembly. Liability in tort for a defective product is not "liability without fault," as mistakenly stated in *Fireman's Fund Ins. v. Gov't. Employees Ins., Co.*, Ky., 635 S.W.2d 475, 477 (1982). It is simply liability for negligent conduct as that concept has evolved over the last forty years. *Nichols v. Union Underwear*, Ky., 602 S.W.2d 429 (1980), the landmark case on the subject, explains that "[t]he strict liability standard is no different from that of negligence, they say, except that the seller is presumed to have knowledge of the actual condition of the product when it leaves his hands." *Id.* at 433. Product liability law is nothing more than the continuing historic evolution of the ancient cause of action for trespass on the case as that principle now applies in products liability cases. The plaintiffs in this case have asserted a cause of action in tort for both negligence as such and for a defective product. Both theories are based on a finding of fault and there is no reason to deny the protection of §§14, 54 and 241 to one or the other.

The appellants stated at oral argument that every time since 1973 that our Court has held the "no action" statute unconstitutional, it has done so for one basic reason, the statute is fundamentally unfair. The appellees responded that "fairness is not the issue ... it may be unfair, but it is not unconstitutional." Fundamental fairness is part and parcel of the concept underlying the rights guaranteed to us by our constitution; and, conversely, the various sections in it protecting individual rights from legislative interference cannot be understood or applied without reference to fundamental fairness.

The statute of repose stratagem has spread. There is hardly a commercial segment in our society that does not now approach the General Assembly with the argument that it confers some significant benefit on "the state's economy" (to use the reason stated in the prefatory clause to the present act), which deserves some special privilege or immunity. Statutes of repose have been enacted in some states for products liability cases, and those in the health care industry have also enjoyed success elsewhere in this regard. The most recent case in point in Kentucky is *McCollum v. Sisters of Charity*, Ky., 799 S.W.2d 15 (1990), holding unconstitutional under Kentucky Constitution §§14, 54 and 241, a recently enacted statute cutting off any cause of action "against a physician, surgeon, dentist or hospital ... for negligence or medical malpractice" not "commence[d] within five years from the date on which the alleged negligent act or omission is said to have occurred," regardless of whether the cause of action had yet accrued. The object of this statute was, of course, to avoid the "discovery rule" of *Tomlinson v. Siehl*, Ky., 459 S.W.2d 166 (1970) and *Hackworth v. Hart*, Ky., 474 S.W.2d 377 (1971). The evolution of judicial doctrine to include the discovery rule within the ambit of jural rights is as much of recent origin as the fall of the citadel of privity. The

McCollum case refers to the fact that in some instances, narrowly circumscribed, there was a cause of action in tort against a physician preexisting the 1891 Constitution, but the fundamental concept involved in *McCollum* is the same as present circumstances, i.e., the Kentucky Constitution must be applied to fundamental jural rights as presently accepted in society, not frozen in time to the year 1891. * * *

In *McCollum v. Sisters of Charity*, we state:

> "McCollum could not recover until a cause of action existed. Proof of damage is an essential part of his medical malpractice cause of action. Such proof was not available to him until 1985, when he first discovered his injury. Yet the legislature, through the five-year cap in KRS 413.140(2), would require McCollum to do the impossible—sue before he had any reason to know he should sue. This is antithetical to the purpose of the open courts provisions in the Kentucky Constitution. Movant need not board this bus to Topsy-Turvy Land."[2] *Id.* 799 S.W.2d at 19.

Thus, we conclude the 1986 version of KRS 413.135 is still constitutionally defective as special legislation and further attempts to amend it to overcome the constitutional defects fatally impale upon Kentucky Constitution §§14, 54 and 241. If the statute were amended, or a new statute written, to impose a statute of repose for every conceivable cause of action in tort, thus avoiding §59, such would be a clear violation of §§14, 54 and 241.

Thus, to the extent that the decisions of this Court in *Carney v. Moody*, *supra* and in *Fireman's Fund Ins. v. Government Emp. Ins.*, Ky., 635 S.W.2d 475 (1982), are in conflict with our decision in this case, they are overruled. Further, the Briefs in this case have been supplemented by a recent decision in the Kentucky Court of Appeals in *Brown v. Neel*, Ky. App., 798 S.W.2d 690 (1990), which is in conflict with the decision in this case, and which is also overruled.

* * *

Recognizing that a majority of the states have upheld the construction industry's statute of repose against attack on constitutional grounds, our obligation is to comply with the letter and spirit of the Kentucky Constitution. If that places us in a statistical minority, we can only commiserate with the citizens of other states who do not enjoy similar protection.

* * *

The answers as stated in this Opinion are so certified.

Stephens, C.J., and Combs, Lambert, Leibson, Spain and Wintersheimer, JJ., concur.

Reynolds, J., concurs in results only.

---

2. "Topsy-Turvy Land," a place described by Judge Jerome Frank in *Dincher v. Marlin Firearms Co.*, 198 F.2d 821, 823 (2d Cir. 1952), where you "die before you are conceived, or be divorced before ever you marry, or harvest a crop never planted, or burn down a house never built, or miss a train running on a non-existent railroad."

Figure 7-1. Official portrait of Justice Charles M. Leibson, Kentucky State Capitol. Portrait by John Michael Carter, reproduced with permission of the artist and the Supreme Court of Kentucky.

Notes and Questions

1. In *Perkins*, Justice Leibson's opinion for the Court stated that "the Kentucky Constitution must be applied to fundamental jural rights as presently accepted in society, not frozen in time to the year 1891." Thus, *Perkins* seems to hold that the General Assembly cannot turn back the clock once the common law evolves under the Supreme Court's decisions. But who is the better judge of what is "presently accepted in society"—the democratically elected members of the General Assembly, who are elected by the people every two or four years, or the justices and judges of the Court of Justice?

2. Even though strict liability for tort product liability claims did not exist in 1891, because it exists in Kentucky's common law of torts now, is the General Assembly without power to turn back the clock? Put another way, does the holding in *Perkins* act as a one-way ratchet on the evolution of tort law in Kentucky? Or, could the General Assembly enact a law, as in other states, stating, "There shall be no strict liability in tort in product liability actions."? (*See* N.C. Gen. Stat. §99B-1.1.)

Williams v. Wilson

Supreme Court of Kentucky (1998)
972 S.W.2d 260

OPINION OF THE COURT BY JUSTICE LAMBERT.

This Court granted discretionary review (CR 76.20) to consider whether KRS 411.184 violates one or more provisions of the Constitution of Kentucky, thereby rendering the statute invalid and unenforceable. To resolve this question of constitutional law, it is necessary to first determine whether, in material respects, the statute impairs the common law of this Commonwealth as it existed prior to adoption of our present Constitution, thereby implicating the doctrine of jural rights. In the event we determine that the statute does change well settled common law with respect to recovery of punitive damages, we will proceed to re-examine the doctrine of jural rights as it has been attacked in this forum as erroneous and unsound.

In 1988 the Kentucky General Assembly considered broad tort reform legislation embodied in HB 551. From among the proposals, the Legislature enacted a statute codified at KRS 411.184 intended to modify Kentucky law with respect to punitive damages. Sparks, *A Survey of Kentucky Tort Reform*, 17 Northern Ky. L. Rev. 473 (1989). In general, the intent of the Legislature was to redefine the circumstances in which punitive damages were recoverable, and toward that end a new legal standard was established. Departing from the traditional common law standard which permitted a jury to impose punitive damages upon a finding of gross negligence as measured by an objective standard, the new statutory standard, here under review, requires a determination that the defendant acted with "flagrant indifference to the rights of the plaintiff and with a subjective awareness that such conduct will result in human death or bodily harm." It also requires proof by clear and convincing evidence. The Fayette Circuit Court and the Court of Appeals decided the constitutional question and invalidated the statute on the view that it offends Sections 14, 54 and 241 of the Constitution of Kentucky.[1] Both courts below held that the statute effectively destroyed the common

1. In addition to its principal holding, the Court of Appeals found reversible error in the trial court's decision to instruct the jury upon common law principles after the case had been practiced in reliance on the statutory standard. As a result, the Court of Appeals vacated the punitive damages

law right of action for punitive damages and that such was precluded by the doctrine of jural rights.

The facts which give rise to this litigation are unremarkable but not unimportant. On May 18, 1990, at 7:00 a.m., appellee, Patricia Lynn Herald Wilson, was en route to the place of her employment as a school teacher. As she approached the intersection of Man-O-War and Palumbo in Lexington, she was struck by the vehicle being driven by appellant, a person who was intoxicated. At the scene, appellant was arrested and charged with DUI. She subsequently pled guilty to DUI in the Fayette District Court.

Appellee commenced litigation in the Fayette Circuit Court claiming compensatory and punitive damages. Appellant did not personally participate in the litigation although she was before the court and was represented by counsel. Appellee was unable to take appellant's deposition and appellant did not appear at trial or make an in-person defense.

At trial and after the close of all the evidence, appellant objected to the giving of an instruction on punitive damages. She asserted that the evidence did not support such an instruction due to the absence of evidence of her subjective awareness that her conduct would result in death or bodily harm. In response to this contention the trial court agreed with appellant, and for appellee's failure to present proof required by KRS 411.184, refused to give a punitive damages instruction. Appellee then modified her position asserting that the punitive damages statute was unconstitutional and sought a punitive damages instruction based on common law gross negligence. Upon review of the evidence the trial court held that such an instruction was warranted and submitted the case to the jury for a determination of punitive damages upon an instruction from *Horton v. Union Light, Heat & Power Co.*, Ky., 690 S.W.2d 382, 388 (1985), which requires proof of "wanton or reckless disregard for the lives, safety or property of others."[2]

In its findings of fact and conclusions of law rendered in support of its judgment holding KRS 411.184 unconstitutional, the trial court analyzed the statutory requirements and the common law requirements to determine whether the statute actually changed the common law. While the trial court believed the fact of appellant's intoxication would authorize a finding that she acted with flagrant indifference, the court found no evidence of appellant's subjective awareness that her conduct would result in death or bodily harm. On the other hand, the court found the evidence sufficient to satisfy the gross negligence standard of "wanton or reckless indifference to the rights of others." *Id.* Unmistakably, the trial court believed the statutory standard went far beyond the common law gross negligence standard, particularly with respect to knowledge of the inevitability of harm.

---

judgment and directed retrial of the issue. From this adverse decision, appellee did not seek further review by means of a cross-motion for discretionary review. CR 76.21. As such, the Court of Appeals' reversal for a new trial on punitive damages is not before this Court.

2. It should be noted that the trial court withheld entry of judgment until the Attorney General had been notified of the constitutional challenge and until after briefing and a determination that the statute was unconstitutional.

> [T]he Court found that the evidence did not support a jury finding of "malice" as defined in the statutes sufficient to warrant a jury instruction on the issue. No evidence was introduced at trial that the Defendant specifically intended to cause tangible or intangible injury to the Plaintiff. In addition, although this Court believes the evidence of the Defendant's intoxication at the time of the accident was sufficient to support a jury finding that the Defendant acted with flagrant indifference to the rights of the Plaintiff, no evidence was introduced regarding the Defendant's "*subjective awareness* * * * that such conduct [would] result in human death or bodily harm." Therefore, the evidence did not support an instruction to the jury on punitive damages under KRS 411.184.

Slip op. at 3. The Court of Appeals agreed with the trial court. It observed that in the pre-1891 cases in which gross negligence was defined, that neither intentional wrong nor the implication of bad faith belonged in the definition.

Despite its view that the pre-1891 cases represented "[d]ivergent lines of authority," Judge Johnstone, writing for the Court of Appeals' majority, stated:

> [W]hen Kentucky's highest court allowed the plaintiff to recover punitive damages for gross negligence using an objective, "reasonable person" standard, it fixed that recovery avenue as a "jural right." Consequently, by denying the plaintiff a common law gross negligence instruction and further imposing a subjective awareness standard in the definition of "malice," we find the legislature has limited punitive damage recovery in circumstances otherwise allowing these damages prior to the adoption of our Constitution.

Slip op. at 13.

The Statute Versus Common Law

Appellant contends that KRS 411.184 is not a departure from the common law standard as there was no "well-established" standard prior to adoption of our Constitution. She argues that the statute merely clarified the confusion existing in common law and codified an existing standard which would be applicable to all claims for punitive damages. Appellant also argues that pre-1891 case law and decisions in this century reveal that malice, as expressed in various forms, is no different than subjective awareness under the statute; that malice necessarily presumes actual awareness. Appellee responds that the right to recover punitive damages for gross negligence was well established prior to 1891 and that the statutory requirement of subjective awareness of death or bodily harm represents the effective abolishment of negligence-based recovery of punitive damages and substitution of a requirement of knowledge or intent.

The decisions of this Court which bear upon the legal question under consideration have been rendered over the course of a century and a half. While the numbers of such decisions are not vast, neither are they insubstantial. In the process of this analysis we will focus on a few of the leading cases trusting that they sufficiently express the major concepts and the development of the law.

Going first to the pre-1891 cases, one encounters *Chiles v. Drake*, 59 Ky. (2 Met.) 146 (1859), in which the right to recover vindictive damages was allowed on the basis of recklessness although the killing was "not intentional." In *Louisville & Nashville R.R. v. McCoy*, 81 Ky. 403 (1883), gross neglect was the basis for recovery of punitive damages, and the court held that the definition of gross negligence required no proof of a defendant's intention to cause harm or show bad faith. This definition was upheld in *Louisville & Nashville R.R. Co. v. Sheets*, 11 Ky. L. Rptr. 781, 13 S.W. 248 (1890). Other cases from this period are not inconsistent. *Fleet and Sample v. Hollenkemp*, 52 Ky. 219, 227, 56 Am.Rep. 563 (1852) (punitive damages were allowed for inexcusable gross negligence "whether ignorantly or by design, whether with or without knowledge of the defendants."); *Kountz v. Brown*, 55 Ky. (16 B. Mon.) 577, 586 (1856) (allowed recovery of exemplary damages for injuries "recklessly committed"); and *Hawkins Co. v. Riley*, 56 Ky. (17 B. Mon.) 101, 110 (1856) (punitive damages were allowed where a collision was caused by the defendant's "wantonness, recklessness, or gross negligence."). It is true that some cases from this period define gross negligence or wantonness or malice to include elements which approach knowing or intentional conduct. *See e.g., Louisville & Nashville R.R. Co. v. Robinson*, 4 Ky. 509 (1868), and *Louisville & Nashville R.R. Co. v. Chism*, 47 S.W. 251 (1898). Nevertheless, from our review of the cases, there is little doubt that prior to 1891, Kentucky law was well established that punitive damages could be recovered for negligent conduct which exceeded ordinary negligence whether such conduct was expressed as gross negligence, recklessness, wantonness, or some other such term.

In the period immediately after adoption of the Constitution, this Court decided *Louisville & Nashville R.R. v. Kelly's Adm'x*, 38 S.W. 852 (1897), and *Illinois Central R. Co. v. Stewart*, 63 S.W. 596 (1900). Not only are these cases well-reasoned and comprehensive, but due to the time of their rendition, they provide timely insight as to the state of Kentucky law when our 1891 Constitution was adopted. A powerful passage from *Kelly's Adm'x* is directly on point and worthy of repetition:

> It is well settled in this state that, for injuries not resulting in death, exemplary damages could be recovered where the negligence causing the injury was gross. "The civil law affirms the existence of three degrees of negligence,—slight, ordinary, and gross. The distinction between these degrees of negligence has been repeatedly recognized in the courts of common law; ... the term 'negligence' including all its grades." "This is a common-law proceeding to recover damages for a personal injury not resulting in death, and punitive damages were recoverable if the proof showed that the company failed to use such diligence in keeping its railroad bridge in repair as careless and inattentive persons usually exercise in the prosecution of business of like character. The absence of slight care in the management of a railroad train is gross negligence."

Id. at 854 (citations omitted).

Just four years after rendition of *Louisville & Nashville R.R. v. Kelly's Adm'x, supra*, this Court decided *Illinois Central R. Co. v. Stewart, supra*, and reaffirmed our reliance on the definition of gross negligence approved a generation earlier in *Louisville & Nashville R.R. Co. v. McCoy, supra*. The Court stated that "where gross negligence was shown, punitive damages might be allowed. This rule has been so often followed and approved by this court in subsequent cases that it is not an open question." *Stewart*, 63 S.W. at 599. Recent case law reaffirms the continued viability of these venerable decisions.

> Older cases, a number of which pre-date our constitution recognize and approve the award of punitive damages in addition to compensatory damages against corporations and other employers based on gross negligence of their employees.

Horton v. Union Light, Heat & Power Co., Ky., 690 S.W.2d 382, 388 (1985) (citations omitted). *Horton* also contains insightful discussion of the theory underlying punitive damages, the circumstances in which such damages may be awarded, and re-states the prevailing rule in this jurisdiction:

> In order to justify punitive damages there must be first a finding of failure to exercise reasonable care, and then an additional finding that this negligence was accompanied by a "wanton or reckless disregard for the lives, safety or property of others." This bears an element not distinguishable from malice implied from the facts.

Id. at 389–90.

Appellant asserts that "the Court will find no 'definitive statement,' 'point of recognition' or 'well established' rule regarding liability for punitive damages at common law." We disagree. As shown by the decisions discussed hereinabove, the well established common law standard for awarding punitive damages was gross negligence. While the concept was not expressed in the same language in every opinion rendered prior to adoption of our Constitution, and while the language has not remained perfectly constant in this century, there is no doubt that unintentional conduct amounting to gross negligence, as that concept is well defined in *Horton*, was sufficient to authorize recovery of punitive damages. As the new statute requires proof of a subjective awareness that harm will result, it amounts to a vastly elevated standard for the recovery of punitive damages and a clear departure from the common law. The facts of this case well illustrate the fundamental change brought about by the statute.

By the literal language of the statute proof of "subjective awareness that such conduct will result in human death or bodily harm" is required. Ordinarily, such proof could only be obtained from the party who inflicted the harm, but in the instant case the defendant did not participate and her testimony could not be taken. As such, there was no way to prove essential elements of the statute. From this a new litigation strategy might well emerge. In cases of gross negligence, but where compensatory damages for wrongful death or personal injury would otherwise be modest, a defendant might elect to forego any participation, relying on the court to prevent an excessive award of compensatory damages, safe in the knowledge that despite his gross negligence, no award of punitive damages could be made.

Relying on *Maysville & Lexington Turnpike Co. v. G.C. Kniffen*, 4 Ky. Op. 92 (1870), and other cases which predicate exemplary damages on malicious conduct, appellant argues that "'[n]egligence so gross as to raise a presumption of malice' is qualitatively no different than 'a subjective awareness that such conduct will result in human death or bodily injury.'" With this we vehemently disagree. Gross negligence, however it may be qualified, is conduct lacking intent or actual knowledge of the result. Moreover, and while recognizing that at some point along the continuum between negligent conduct and intentional conduct there may be a convergence of the concepts, this Court must remain mindful that where statutes are applicable, trial courts must instruct in statutory language. "It is fundamental that an instruction based on a statute should encompass the wording of the statute so far as possible." *Sorg v. Purvis*, Ky., 487 S.W.2d 943, 945 (1972). "Where the statute speaks in no uncertain terms, it hardly can be said that the use in an instruction of other terms not meaning substantially the same thing is not prejudicial error." *McCullouch's Adm'r v. Abell's Adm'r*, Ky., 272 Ky. 756, 115 S.W.2d 386, 390 (1938).

Under these authorities, whatever theoretical merger of gross negligence and subjective awareness of harm might be perceived by the court and counsel, the jury would be informed only of the legal standard contained in the statute and by any reasonable reckoning, the statutory standard far exceeds gross negligence. We are unimpressed by the argument that the statute could be "loosely interpreted" so as to avoid limiting or destroying the common law right to recovery of punitive damages. It would be the height of duplicity to at once uphold the constitutionality of a statute and declare that it not be literally observed.

Contrary to appellant's assertion, it is unnecessary that we discover a precise, infallible common law rule prior to application of the doctrine of jural rights. *Ludwig v. Johnson*, 243 Ky. 533, 49 S.W.2d 347 (1932), uses phrases such as "well-established prior to the enactment of our constitution," "long established rights" and "safeguarded common law rights." We believe these are sufficiently flexible standards to support the conclusion that recovery of punitive damages for grossly negligent conduct was a recognized common law right which predated the 1891 Constitution.

Jural Rights

Appellant makes a multi-faceted attack upon the jural rights doctrine relying extensively on Lewis, *Jural Rights under Kentucky's Constitution: Realities Grounded in Myth*, ___ Ky. L. Rev. 953 (1991–92). She contends that constitutional text does not support any such doctrine of law; that the Debates of the Constitutional Convention provide no support, and she effectively agrees with Professor Lewis' view that jural rights is illegitimate and "evolve[d] from the pen of the judiciary." *Id.* at 973.[3] Predictably, appellee relies on this Court's decision in *Ludwig v. Johnson*, *supra*, and the virtually unbroken line of decisions following and applying it for more than sixty years. She also relies on

3. Illustrative of his strongly held view, Professor Lewis has written "no court is *that infallible* in its development of the common law. Under the jural rights doctrine, however, the Kentucky Supreme Court is infallible. *Any* legislative abolition or restriction of a common law right of recovery within the scope of the jural rights doctrine is invalid."

the history and tradition in this Commonwealth of protecting the right of recovery of injured persons. With the conflict thus joined, we will weigh in.

The doctrine of jural rights was first articulated as such in this Court's 1932 decision in *Ludwig v. Johnson, supra.* However, language in *Kelly's Adm'x, supra,* an 1897 case, suggests that the idea of placing certain rights of recovery of damages for death or personal injury off-limits to legislative abolishment had been recognized much earlier.

> In other words, we are of opinion that the convention intended to extend the common-law right of action to recover both compensatory and exemplary damages for injuries not resulting in death to cases in which death ensued; and a very forcible argument in favor of this construction is found in section 54 of the constitution, where it is provided that "the general assembly shall have no power to limit the amount to be recovered for injuries resulting in death or for injuries to person or property." It seems evident that this denial of power to the legislature to limit the amount of recovery would hardly have been inserted if the intent of section 241 was to place a limit upon the amount of recovery.

Kelly's Adm'x, 38 S.W. at 854.

Ludwig v. Johnson, supra, concerned the constitutionality of an automobile guest statute whereby a non-paying passenger in an automobile was prohibited from bringing a civil action for recovery of damages for injuries negligently inflicted by the host. Appellant asserted that by virtue of Sections 14, 54 and 241 of the Constitution of Kentucky, the statute was void. After duly noting the strong presumption in favor of the constitutionality of acts of the General Assembly, the Court meticulously considered the constitutional provisions at issue. For its central holding, the Court concluded that when Section 54 was read in conjunction with Sections 14 and 241, "the conclusion is inescapable that the intention of the framers of the Constitution was to inhibit the Legislature from abolishing rights of action for damages for death or injuries caused by negligence." *Id.* 49 S.W.2d at 350. Analyzing similar statutes and decisions from other jurisdictions, the Court quoted with approval from a decision of the high court of Oregon, *Stewart v. Houk*, 127 Or. 589, 271 P. 998, 272 P. 893, 61 A.L.R. 1236, analyzing a constitutional provision similar to the one found in Section 14. "The purpose of this provision is to save from legislative abolishment those jural rights which had become well established prior to the enactment of our Constitution." *Ludwig*, 49 S.W.2d 347 at 350 (quoting *Stewart*, 271 P. at 999).

The final substantive paragraph of *Ludwig v. Johnson* states the philosophical principles so often repeated by which this Court has protected from legislative infringement the rights of citizens for recovery of damages for personal injuries and death:

> The statute [guest statute] under consideration violates the spirit of our constitution as well as its letter as found in sections 14, 54, and 241. It was the manifest purpose of the framers of that instrument to preserve and perpetuate the common-law right of a citizen injured by the negligent act of another to sue to recover damages for his injury. The imperative mandate of section 14 is that every person, for an injury done him in his person, shall have remedy by

> due course of law. If the allegations of appellant's petition are true, he has suffered serious injuries occasioned by the negligent acts of the appellee Darwin Johnson. The constitution guarantees to him his right to a day in court for the purpose of establishing the alleged wrong perpetrated on him and recovery of his resultant damages.

Ludwig, 49 S.W.2d 347 at 351.

Since its rendition, *Ludwig v. Johnson* has been followed many times. One of the more significant cases adhering to its principles is *Happy v. Erwin*, Ky., 330 S.W.2d 412 (1959), which invalidated a statute by which city employees were exempted from liability. The Court held that Sections 14 and 54 as interpreted in *Ludwig* protected the common law right of citizens to bring suit for recovery of damages from municipal employees. Expressing a view appropriate to the instant case, the Court said that if the Legislature could immunize certain classes of public officers, it could exempt all public officers and employees from liability, and if logically extended, could immunize private groups the Legislature determined to be entitled to immunity. The Court concluded by saying, "[t]hat is exactly what the constitutional provisions above quoted were designed to prevent." *Happy v. Erwin*, 330 S.W.2d at 414.

In *Kentucky Utilities Co. v. Jackson County Rural Electric Cooperative*, Ky., 438 S.W.2d 788 (1968), this Court held the right of indemnity to be a jural right which existed prior to adoption of the Constitution and thus a right protected from elimination by the General Assembly. In *Saylor v. Hall*, Ky., 497 S.W.2d 218 (1973), we invalidated a statute which required actions against home builders to be brought within five years after substantial completion of the home. As grounds for our decision we stated that the statute "destroys, pro tanto, a common-law right of action for negligence that proximately causes personal injury or death, which existed at the times the statutes were enacted." *Id.* at 224. Other cases in this line and relying on *Ludwig v. Johnson* are *Carney v. Moody*, Ky., 646 S.W.2d 40 (1982), *Gould v. O'Bannon*, Ky., 770 S.W.2d 220 (1989), *McCollum v. Sisters of Charity*, Ky., 799 S.W.2d 15 (1990), and *Perkins v. Northeastern Log Homes*, Ky., 808 S.W.2d 809 (1991).

The doctrine of jural rights has also been examined and found to be inapplicable where the statute did not eliminate or restrict claims recognized at common law. *Kirschner v. Louisville Gas & Electric Co.*, Ky., 743 S.W.2d 840 (1988). *Fireman's Fund Ins. v. Government*, Ky., 635 S.W.2d 475 (1982), expressed the principle as follows:

> There is still another ground upon which Const. Secs. 14 and 54 cannot be applicable. Aside from the mention of defamation in Sec. 14, these constitutional provisions expressly apply only to actions for death, personal injuries, and property damage. *Cf. Kentucky Hotel v. Cinotti*, 298 Ky. 88, 182 S.W.2d 27, 29 (1944), and *Zurich Fire Ins. Co. of New York v. Weil*, Ky., 259 S.W.2d 54, 57 (1953), in both of which it is recognized that Sec. 54 refers to actions in tort. In a subrogation suit, of course, the plaintiff asserts the rights of his subrogor, but in an action for indemnity he sues in his own right, and upon a basis even more tenuous than an implied contract.

Id. at 477–478. In *Fireman's Fund,* Chief Justice Palmore, being ever a scholar, corrected an overly broad phrase in *Happy v. Erwin, supra,* which had been attributed to *Ludwig v. Johnson.* He restated the actual holding in *Ludwig* as follows: "The actual holding of *Ludwig* is that the intention of the Constitution was 'to inhibit the Legislature from abolishing rights of action for damages *for death or injuries caused by negligence.*'" (Emphasis added.) 49 S.W.2d at 350. *Fireman's Fund,* 635 S.W.2d at n. 7.

By virtue of its long duration and frequent repetition, the jural rights doctrine has become virtually axiomatic. Moreover, by dictum in *Wittmer v. Jones,* Ky., 864 S.W.2d 885 (1993), the statute here under review has been broadly circumscribed.

> Throughout this litigation State Farm has presented various arguments against submitting the issue of punitive damages to the jury based on its interpretation of statutory language found in the new punitive damages statute enacted in 1988, now codified as KRS 411.184. It suffices to say that this Court could not interpret KRS 411.184 to destroy a cause of action for punitive damages otherwise appropriate without fatally impaling upon jural rights guaranteed by the Kentucky Constitution, Sections 14, 54, and 241. *Perkins v. Northeastern Log Homes,* Ky., 808 S.W.2d 809, 817 (1991). As we stated when addressing a similar problem in *In Re: Beverly Hills Fire Litigation,* Ky., 672 S.W.2d 922, 926 (1984): "We shall not so interpret it."

Id. at 890.

As the foregoing authorities demonstrate, to the exclusion of any reasonable opinion to the contrary, the doctrine of jural rights is deeply ingrained in Kentucky law and to abandon it now would amount to an extraordinary change. Principles of predictability counsel against such major shifts in the law. Of course, constitutional doctrine is not immune from reconsideration (*Harmelin v. Michigan,* 501 U.S. 957, 111 S.Ct. 2680, 115 L.Ed.2d 836 (1991)) and indeed this Court has declared that we will refrain from "sanctification of ancient fallacy." *Hilen v. Hays,* Ky., 673 S.W.2d 713, 717 (1984). Therefore, we will reconsider the central premise of the jural rights doctrine to determine whether it is fallacious.

Sections 14, 54 and 241 have been interpreted to work in tandem and to establish a limitation upon the power of the General Assembly to limit common law rights to recover for personal injury or death. The fact that these provisions might not have been "conceived as some sort of package" (Lewis, *Jural Rights* at 972) does not prevent them from being construed together to arrive at a separate principle. Section 14, which provides that "every person for an injury done him in his lands, goods, person or reputation, shall have remedy by due course of law," has been held to prevent abolishment of those jural rights which were well established prior to adoption of the Constitution. One may disagree with such a construction, but the language used does not exclude it. Some discern no substantive law component in Section 14 and depend on *Johnson v. Higgins,* 60 Ky. (3 Met.) 566 (1861), and its construction of the predecessor of Section 14 which contained identical language, to safeguard only procedural due process. Notwithstanding the view expressed in *Johnson v. Higgins,* the prevailing political climate at the time of adoption of the 1891 Constitution and the language used permits an inference that the Constitutional Convention desired to impose limitations upon legislative authority and cases decided contemporaneously or close in time would appear to be persuasive of Delegates' intent. *See Perkins v. Northeastern Log Homes*, 808 S.W.2d at 812. *Kentucky State Board for Elementary and Secondary Education v. Rudasill*, Ky., 589 S.W.2d 877 (1979), observed that:

> [T]hese delegates [to the 1890 Constitutional Convention] examined the guarantees afforded the citizens of sister states by their constitutions along with the traditional protections given to and expected by the citizens of Kentucky. Then guided by their own consciences, they drafted a comprehensive bill of rights for the new constitution. It is generally recognized that the convention of 1890 was comprised of competent and educated delegates who were sincerely concerned with individual liberties.

Id. at 880. This Court has endorsed the principle of contemporaneous construction as providing special insight to the Delegates' intent: "The judges recognizing that tradition in their opinions wrote with a direct, firsthand knowledge of the mind set of the constitutional fathers,...." *Commonwealth v. Wasson*, Ky., 842 S.W.2d 487, 492 (1992). Accordingly, our decisions in *Louisville & Nashville R.R. v. Kelly's Adm'x*, *supra*, and *Illinois Central R. Co. v. Stewart*, *supra*, are entitled to greater weight in our constitutional analysis.

Section 54 is more explicit. It provides that the General Assembly "shall have no power to limit the amount to be recovered for injuries resulting in death, or for injuries to person or property." Despite this forthright, compelling language, it has been contended that while the General Assembly would have no power to impose limitations on the amount recoverable in an action for injuries to person or property, it could abolish an action for such injuries. Such is at odds with the tenor of Section 54. With their extraordinary distrust of powerful economic interests, particularly corporations and railroads (Lewis, *Jural Rights*, at 968), it is inconceivable that the Delegates would have forbidden imposition of damage limitations but allowed abolishment of the underlying cause of action, thereby facilitating the ultimate limitation on damages. Sections 14 and 54 have been read together to prohibit the Legislature from limiting the amount of recovery by destroying the right.

> In holding such act unconstitutional, it was pointed out that the objective of section 14 was to preserve those jural rights which had become well established prior to the adoption of the Constitution. It was also decided that section 54 prohibited the legislature from limiting the amount of recovery by destroying the right.

Happy v. Erwin, 330 S.W.2d at 414.

While Section 241 does not apply expressly to injury cases, it is a component of the constitutional limitation on the power of the General Assembly to limit or destroy actions for recovery of damages arising from negligence and serves to prevent legislative encroachment in proper cases.

Appellant contends that our previous jural rights cases, *Ludwig v. Johnson, supra*, and its progeny, fails to take account of Section 233 of the Constitution of Kentucky. This section declares that on the day of Kentucky's statehood, June 1, 1792, all laws

> in force in the State of Virginia, and which are of a general nature and not local to that State, and not repugnant to this Constitution, nor to the laws which have been enacted by the General Assembly of this Commonwealth, shall be in force within this State until they shall be altered or repealed by the General Assembly.

Appellant interprets this section to give the General Assembly plenary power to abrogate or modify the common law. The fallacy of her argument is apparent. This Court has held that Sections 14, 54 and 241 of our Constitution render certain common law rights impervious to legislative dilution or destruction. Such rights are therefore subject to the same restrictions with respect to modification by the General Assembly as are constitutional provisions.

With respect to the contention that punitive damages fall outside the scope of rights protected by Sections 14 and 54 of the Constitution of Kentucky on the view that such damages do not compensate for injuries, *Chiles v. Drake, supra, Louisville & Nashville R.R. Co. v. Kelly's Adm'x, supra*, and *Horton v. Union Light, Heat & Power, supra*, are dispositive.

Perhaps the most controversial aspect of our jural rights decisions has been the "constitutionalization" of newly discovered rights. This heavily criticized concept is best exemplified in *Perkins v. Northeastern Log Homes, supra*, as follows:

> In drafting our constitutional protections in §§14, 54 and 241, our founding fathers were protecting the jural rights of the individual citizens of Kentucky against the power of the government to abridge such rights, speaking to their rights as they would be commonly understood by those citizens in any year, not just in 1891.

Id. at 816. On the foregoing theory, *Carney v. Moody, supra*, and *Fireman's Fund Ins. v. Government, supra*, which had taken a more restrictive view of the scope of jural rights, were overruled.

Whatever the wisdom of the extension of the jural rights doctrine from its point of origin, i.e., preservation of well established rights to recover damages for negligently inflicted injury or death as recognized in 1891, the outcome in this case does not depend on the validity of any such extension. The rights at issue here were well established in 1891 and the courts below have properly applied the jural rights doctrine to prevent legislative erosion or abolishment.

This Court's decision in *Kentucky State Board for Elementary and Secondary Education v. Rudasill, supra*, provides a proper methodology for constitutional analysis. It requires that text be the beginning point and then shifts to the Debates of the 1890 Constitutional Convention. Thereafter, the focus becomes decisions of the high court and our history and traditions. When the foregoing factors are applied to the jural rights doctrine, no abolishment is required. Such flaws as may have crept into the theory arise from improper application and not from fundamental misconception.

Conclusion

Both the trial court and the Court of Appeals held KRS 411.184(1)(c) to be in violation of the jural rights doctrine and unconstitutional. As stated hereinabove, we agree and therefore affirm the courts below. The trial court and the Court of Appeals differed on whether KRS 411.184(2) was properly before the court, with the Court of Appeals having determined that it was not. We affirm the Court of Appeals in its conclusion and express no opinion herein as to the constitutionality of KRS 411.184(2).

This cause is hereby remanded to the Fayette Circuit Court for further proceedings not inconsistent herewith.

Graves, Lambert, Stumbo and Wintersheimer, JJ., and Ronald P. Hillerich, Special Justice, concur.

Stephens, C.J., concurs by separate opinion.

Cooper, J., dissents by separate opinion.

Chief Justice Stephens, concurring.

I reluctantly concur with the majority opinion.

However, for some time, I have begun to doubt the validity of the doctrine of the jural rights which "popped" into our law in 1932. *Ludwig v. Johnson*, 243 Ky. 533, 49 S.W.2d 347 (1932).

As the dissent points out, and as the Law Journal Article by Professor Thomas Lewis emphasizes, there is very little, if any, basis for this now routinely accepted doctrine in the Kentucky Constitution or in the Constitutional Debates. *Jural Rights Under Kentucky's Constitution: Realities Grounded in Myth*, 80 K.L.J. 953 (1991–92).

Perhaps even more importantly, and recent in years, this Court has moved the jural rights doctrine far beyond its original aegis, so as to restrict even the General Assembly and this Court from changing its precedents, even though created after the adoption of the present constitution.

Although, I believe this Court should carefully consider the powerful arguments set forth in Justice Cooper's dissent, reliance on precedent is a strong tenet of our common law. Precedent should not lightly be overruled.

The doctrine of stare decisis is a judicial policy implemented to maintain stability and continuity in our jurisprudence. It is based upon the belief that similar cases should be decided in a similar manner. When a court of institutional review announces a principle of law to apply to a general set of facts, the doctrine of stare decisis requires the court, in the absence of "sound legal reasons to the contrary" to adhere to that same principle in future cases where there is a similar factual pattern. *Hilen v. Hays*, Ky., 673 S.W.2d 713, 717 (1984). "Stare decisis is ordinarily a wise rule of action. But it is not a universal, inexorable command." *Washington v. W.C. Dawson & Co.*, 264 U.S. 219, 238, 44 S.Ct. 302, 309, 68 L.Ed. 646 (1924) (Brandeis, J., dissenting).

The principle of stare decisis does not require us to adhere blindly to previous decisions when we determine those decisions were in error. *D&W Auto Supply v. Department of Revenue*, Ky., 602 S.W.2d 420, 424 (1980) (citing *Daniel's Adm'r v. Hoofnel*, 287 Ky. 834, 155 S.W.2d 469, 471 (1941)). I only concur because I believe there should be extensive debate before this Court changes such an established rule of law. I hope that the logic of the dissent will be the beginning of such a process.

Justice Cooper, dissenting.

This case arrives in this Court in a peculiar procedural posture. Under a factual scenario clearly entitling the plaintiff/Appellee to an instruction on punitive damages, the trial court ruled first that the language of KRS 411.184(1)(c) precluded such an instruction, then that KRS 411.184 was unconstitutional because it abolished the common law right to punitive damages. Having thus discarded KRS 411.184, the trial court instructed the jury in accordance with the common law standard established in *Horton v. Union Light, Heat & Power Co.*, Ky., 690 S.W.2d 382, 389–90 (1985), *viz*: conduct exhibiting a wanton or reckless disregard for the lives and safety of other persons, or a willful or malicious act. From this set of circumstances has arisen the great and unnecessary debate as to (1) whether KRS 411.184 is unconstitutional as violative of the so-called "jural rights" doctrine, and (2) whether the "jural rights" doctrine has any valid constitutional basis.

I.

There was no need to address the "jural rights" doctrine in this case, for KRS 411.184 does not abolish the common law right to punitive damages. Faced with an argument similar to that accepted by the trial court in this case, we specifically so held in *Wittmer v. Jones*, Ky., 864 S.W.2d 885 (1993). Justice Leibson wrote in that case:

> Throughout this litigation State Farm has presented various arguments against submitting the issue of punitive damages to the jury based on its interpretation of statutory language found in the new punitive damages statute enacted in 1988, now codified as KRS 411.184. It suffices to say that this Court could not interpret KRS 411.184 to destroy a cause of action for punitive damages otherwise appropriate without fatally impaling upon jural rights guaranteed by the Kentucky Constitution, Sections 14, 54, and 241.... "We shall not so interpret it."

Id. at 890 (citations omitted).

KRS 411.184 and .186 did not destroy the cause of action for punitive damages, but merely established standards to guide the jury in its determination of whether such damages are appropriate and the amount to be awarded. Never before have we questioned the authority of the General Assembly to enact statutes establishing the degree of culpability necessary to entitle a litigant to recover punitive damages. * * *

The only possible argument for the proposition that KRS 411.184 "abolished" the right to punitive damages is the one rejected in *Wittmer v. Jones*, *supra*, but accepted by the trial court in this case, *i.e.*, that the element of "subjective awareness" set forth in the definition of malice, KRS 411.184(1)(c), can be proven only by the direct testimony of the person against whom punitive damages are sought. Since the defendant/Appellant was unavailable to testify, the trial court reasoned that Appellee could not prove Appellant's "subjective awareness," thus was not entitled to an instruction on punitive damages. However, as Justice Leibson also wrote in *Fowler v. Mantooth*, Ky., 683 S.W.2d 250 (1984), a case addressing the requirement of proof of malice as a condition precedent to an award of punitive damages, "Malice may be implied from outrageous conduct, and need not be express so long as the conduct is sufficient to evidence conscious wrongdoing." *Id.* at 252. * * *

It is no longer arguable in this day and age that proof of the act of driving while intoxicated creates an inference of "subjective awareness" on the part of the actor of the potential consequences of the act. If that inference would satisfy the "beyond a reasonable doubt" standard of proof in a criminal case, it is sufficient to satisfy the "clear and convincing evidence" standard set forth in KRS 411.184(2).

The majority opinion also takes umbrage with the statute's use of the "clear and convincing evidence" standard as a "vastly elevated standard for the recovery of punitive damages and a clear departure from the common law." (Op., p. 264.) Even if that were true, such would not implicate the "jural rights" doctrine, since the establishment of a heightened standard of proof would not "abolish" the right to collect punitive damages, but only establish the standard of proof to be applied by the jury in determining whether to award them. In fact, both malice and fraud have always required proof by clear and convincing evidence. *E.g., Hardin v. Savageau*, Ky., 906 S.W.2d 356 (1995); *Warford v. Lexington Herald-Leader Co.*, Ky., 789 S.W.2d 758 (1990), *cert. denied*, 498 U.S. 1047, 111 S.Ct. 754, 112 L.Ed.2d 774 (1991). The standard recognizes the quasi-criminal nature of punitive damages by taking the middle ground between the standard ordinarily used in civil cases of proof by a "preponderance of the evidence," and the criminal law standard of proof "beyond a reasonable doubt." * * * The "clear and convincing evidence" standard for punitive damages has been adopted by legislative enactment or judicial decision in twenty-nine other states and the District of Columbia,[1] and has been

1. 1 ALA. CODE §6-11-20 (1993); ALASKA STAT. §09-17-020 (1994); CAL. CIV. CODE §3294(a) (West 1970 & Supp. 1995); GA. CODE ANN. §51-12-5.1 (Supp. 1995); ILL. REV. STAT. ch. 735, para. 5/2-1115.05(b) (1995); IOWA CODE ANN. §668A.1 (West 1987); KAN. STAT. ANN. §60-3701(c) (1994); MINN. STAT. ANN. §549.20 (West 1988 & Supp. 1995); MISS. CODE ANN. §11-1-65(1)(a) (Supp. 1995); MONT. CODE ANN. §27-1-221(5) (1995); NEV. REV. STAT. ANN. §42.005(1) (1991); N.J. STAT. ANN. §2A:15-5.12 (1995); N.C. GEN STAT. §1D-15(b) (1996); N.D. CENT. CODE §32-03.2-11 (Supp. 1995); OHIO REV. CODE ANN. §2307.80(A) (Anderson 1991); OKLA. STAT. ANN. tit. 23, §9.1 (West Supp. 1995); OR. REV. STAT. §18.537 (1995); S.C. CODE ANN. §15-33-135 (Law. Co-op. Supp. 1995); S.D. CODIFIED LAWS ANN. §21-1-4.1 (1987); TEX. CIV. PRAC. & REM. CODE ANN. §41.003 (West 1997); UTAH CODE ANN. §78-18-1 (1992); *Linthicum v. Nationwide Life Ins. Co.*, 150 Ariz. 326, 723 P.2d 675 (1986); *Jonathan Woodner, Co. v. Breeden*, 665 A.2d 929 (D.C. 1995), *cert. denied*, 519 U.S. 1148, 117 S.Ct. 1080, 137 L.Ed.2d 215 (1997); *Masaki v. General Motors Corp.*, 71 Haw. 1, 780 P.2d 566 (1989); *Travelers Indem. Co. v. Armstrong*, 442 N.E.2d 349 (Ind. 1982); *Tuttle v. Raymond*, 494 A.2d 1353 (Me. 1985); *Owens-Illinois v. Zenobia*, 325 Md. 420, 601 A.2d 633 (1992); *Hodges v. S.C. Toof & Co.*, 833 S.W.2d 896 (Tenn. 1992); *Wangen v. Ford Motor Co.*, 97 Wis.2d 260, 294 N.W.2d 437 (1980); *Rodriguez v. Suzuki Motor Corp.*, 936 S.W.2d 104 (Mo. 1996) (en banc).

recommended by each of the principal academic groups to analyze the law of punitive damages since 1979, *i.e.*, the American Bar Association,[2] the American College of Trial Lawyers,[3] the American Law Institute,[4] and the National Conference of Commissioners on Uniform State Laws.[5]

The jury in this case should have been instructed on punitive damages in accordance with KRS 411.184 and .186 as initially requested by the plaintiff/Appellee. If the trial court had done so, there would have been no need to address whether the "jural rights" doctrine has any basis in our Constitution.

II.

In his well reasoned and well documented article, *Jural Rights Under Kentucky's Constitution: Realities Grounded in Myth*, 80 Ky. L.J. 953 (1991–92), Professor Thomas P. Lewis, a preeminent scholar of Kentucky constitutional law, makes a compelling case for the proposition that the "jural rights" doctrine is nothing more nor less than a judicial usurpation of a traditional legislative prerogative. *Id.* at 964 and 976. As first enunciated in the case of *Ludwig v. Johnson*, 243 Ky. 533, 49 S.W.2d 347 (1932), the doctrine appears to have been intended to perpetually tether the jurisprudence of this Commonwealth to nineteenth century tort principles, *i.e.*, any common law right of action existing prior to the adoption of the 1891 Constitution is sacrosanct and cannot be abolished. *Id.*, 49 S.W.2d at 351; *cf. Carney v. Moody*, Ky., 646 S.W.2d 40 (1983). In arriving at that conclusion and in coining the phrase "jural rights," the *Ludwig* court relied principally upon the Oregon case of *Stewart v. Houk*, 127 Or. 589, 271 P. 998, 999 (1928). *Ludwig v. Johnson, supra*, 49 S.W.2d at 350. Oregon subsequently abandoned the "jural rights" concept. *Josephs v. Burns*, 260 Or. 493, 491 P.2d 203, 207 (1971). We, on the other hand, have expanded it to include any common law right of action, whether or not that right existed prior to the adoption of the 1891 Constitution. *Perkins v. Northeastern Log Homes*, Ky., 808 S.W.2d 809, 815–18 (1991), *overruling, Carney v. Moody, supra. Ergo*, any act of the legislature abolishing any right created by judicial decision violates the "jural rights" doctrine and is, therefore, unconstitutional. (!) As if that were not expansive enough, the majority of this Court today declares that any act of the legislature which "impairs," though does not "abolish," a common law right, is also unconstitutional. * * * As Professor Lewis foresaw, this Court has now assumed for itself the sole power to make any meaningful changes in the area of tort law. Lewis, *supra*, at 980.

If that had been the intent of the framers of the 1891 Constitution, one can only wonder why they included Section 233 and the First paragraph of the Schedule accom-

---

One state, Colorado, requires proof beyond a reasonable doubt in punitive damages cases. *See* COLO. REV. STAT. §13-25-127(2) (1987).

2. American Bar Association, Special Committee on Punitive Damages of the American Bar Association, Section on Litigation, *Punitive Damages: A Constructive Analysis* 19 (1986).

3. American College of Trial Lawyers, *Report on punitive Damages of the Committee on Special Problems in the Administration of Justice: Approved by the Board of Regents*. 15–16 (1989).

4. American Law Institute, 1 *Enterprise Responsibility for Personal Injury: Reporters' Study* 248–49 (1991).

5. *MODEL PUNITIVE DAMAGES ACT* §5 (1996).

panying the Constitution, both of which vest in the legislature the power to alter or repeal any laws in force and effect at the time of the adoption of the Constitution. *Aetna Ins. Co. v. Commonwealth*, 106 Ky. 864, 51 S.W. 624 (1899). In *Fireman's Fund Ins. Co. v. Government Employees Ins. Co.*, Ky., 635 S.W.2d 475 (1982), we reiterated that Section 233 and the First paragraph of the Schedule explicitly recognize that the common law is subject to repeal or alteration by the legislature. *Id.* at 476; *see also Ruby Lumber Co. v. K.V. Johnson Co.*, 299 Ky. 811, 187 S.W.2d 449, 453 (1945). And as recently as *Commonwealth, ex rel. Cowan v. Wilkinson*, Ky., 828 S.W.2d 610 (1992), we held that "Judicially created common law must always yield to the superior policy of legislative enactment and the Constitution." *Id.* at 614. There is not one word in the 6,023 typewritten pages (double columns, elite type) of the reported *Proceedings and Debates of the Constitutional Convention of 1890* (hereinafter "*Debates*") which supports a contrary conclusion. As Professor Lewis points out, there is no factual basis for a belief that the framers ever entertained the notion that the common law is immune from repeal or alteration. Lewis, *supra*, at 983. Certainly, no such intent can be discerned in the three constitutional provisions relied upon in *Ludwig, supra*, and in the majority opinion in this case.

Section 14 is as follows:

> All courts shall be open and every person for an injury done him in his lands, goods, person or reputation, shall have remedy by due course of law, and right and justice administered without sale, denial or delay.

This provision was first adopted as Article XII, Section 13, of our 1792 Constitution. It was readopted verbatim as Article X, Section 13, of the Constitution of 1799 and as Article XII, Section 15, of the Constitution of 1850. As Professor Lewis explains, it has its roots in Chapter XXIX of Magna Charta, a fact recognized by delegate Robert Rodes of Warren County, chairman of the Committee on Preamble and Bill of Rights, during his report of this provision to the other delegates at the 1890 Convention. Lewis, *supra*, at 965; 1 *Debates*, *supra*, at 444. More than ten years after the adoption of the Constitution of 1850 and thirty years prior to the adoption of the Constitution of 1891, our predecessor Court was called upon in the case of *Johnson v. Higgins*, 3 Metc. 566, 60 Ky. 566 (1861) to interpret the meaning of this provision.

> This provision is found in the bill of rights. It prescribes certain general duties for the courts of the State, and also lays down general rules for the manner of conducting their business, the effect of which may be thus stated: 1. They are to be held in an open and public manner, and their proceedings are not to be secret or concealed from public view. 2. They are to administer justice without sale—that is, they are not to accept compensation from litigants; and 3. They are not to deny any one a fair trial, nor to delay the same, except upon sufficient legal grounds for continuance.
>
> The terms and import of this provision show that it relates altogether to the judicial department of the government, which is to administer justice "by due course of law," and not to the legislative department, by which such "due course" may be prescribed.

> Any other construction would make it inconsistent with other clauses of the constitution, and, in fact, render it practically absurd.

Id., 60 Ky. at 570–71. This interpretation was reaffirmed in *Barkley v. Glover*, 4 Metc. 44, 61 Ky. 44 (1862).

In rendering his report to the 1890 convention, delegate Rodes first read the language of what is now Section 14, then reported: "That is unobjected to, and is the equivalent of section 15 of the present Constitution." 1 *Debates, supra*, at 439. In re-adopting this provision verbatim and without debate, *Id.* at 1001, the delegates are presumed to have also adopted the construction given to it in *Johnson v. Higgins* and *Barkley v. Glover. Hodgkin v. Kentucky Chamber of Commerce*, Ky., 246 S.W.2d 1014, 1016–17 (1952); *cf. Butler v. Groce*, Ky., 880 S.W.2d 547 (1994); *Cawood v. Coleman*, 294 Ky. 858, 172 S.W.2d 548 (1943); *Ray v. Spiers*, 281 Ky. 549, 136 S.W.2d 750 (1940) (same presumption applies to statutes reenacted after judicial construction). The holdings in *Johnson v. Higgins* and *Barkley v. Glover* having thus been ingrafted into Section 14 at the time of its adoption, the subsequent characterization of those holdings in *Ludwig v. Johnson, supra*, at 351, as "clearly unsound" is legally irrelevant.

Section 54 is as follows:

> The General Assembly shall have no power to limit the amount to be recovered for injuries resulting in death, or for injuries to person or property.

On its face, the purpose of this Section is to prevent the legislature from placing dollar limits on awards of damages "for injuries." It has nothing to do with punitive damages, which are not awarded as compensation "for injuries," but to punish and deter wrongdoing. *Hensley v. Paul Miller Ford, Inc.*, Ky., 508 S.W.2d 759, 762–63 (1974); *Ashland Dry Goods Co. v. Wages*, 302 Ky. 577, 195 S.W.2d 312, 315 (1946). In reporting what became Section 54 to the 1890 convention, delegate Ignatius A. Spalding of Union County, chairman of the Committee on Legislative Department, explained it as follows:

> Section thirty-nine [of the committee report] is a new section, forbidding the General Assembly from limiting amount recovered for damage to person or property. The Legislature has, perhaps, in some cases, put a limit upon the amount to be recovered for damages by railroad accidents to persons resulting in death or in injury to person or property. This section forbids the General Assembly from putting any limit upon the amount of damages to be recovered, leaving it to the jury.

3 *Debates, supra*, at 3793. Following the rejection of an amendment to strike this provision, it was adopted without further debate. *Id.* at 3916.

If the words contained in a constitutional provision are ambiguous, the debates of the constitutional convention which adopted it may be resorted to in ascertaining the purpose sought to be accomplished or the mischief designed to be remedied by that provision. *Barker v. Stearns Coal & Lumber Co.*, 287 Ky. 340, 152 S.W.2d 953, 956 (1941); *Commonwealth v. Kentucky Jockey Club*, 238 Ky. 739, 38 S.W.2d 987, 993 (1931); *Higgins v. Prater*, 91 Ky. 6, 14 S.W. 910, 912 (1890) (interpreting a provision of the Constitution of 1850). In fact, there is nothing ambiguous about Section 54. If there were, the explanation by delegate Spalding clarifies that its purpose was to preclude legislation placing dollar limits on awards of damages for injuries to persons or property. Nothing in its language or history suggests an intent to strip the legislature of its historical prerogative reiterated in Section 233 and the First paragraph of the Schedule to enact legislation in derogation of the common law.

Section 241 is as follows:

> Whenever the death of a person shall result from an injury, inflicted by negligence or wrongful act, then, in every death case, damages may be recovered for such death, from corporations and persons so causing the same. Until otherwise provided by law, the action to recover such damages shall in all cases be prosecuted by the personal representative of the deceased person. The General Assembly may provide how the recovery shall go and to whom belong; and until such provision is made, the same shall form part of the personal estate of the deceased person.

It would be incongruous to suggest that this section was designed to protect and preserve a common law right of action; for there is not and never has been a common law right of action for wrongful death. *Smith's Adm'r v. National Coal & Iron Co.*, 135 Ky. 671, 117 S.W. 280 (1909); *Eden v. Lexington & Frankfort R.R. Co.*, 53 Ky. (14 B. Mon.) 165 (1853). "The maxim, 'Actio personalis moritur cum persona,' was the uniform rule of the common law, and prevails in Kentucky to-day (sic), except where it has been modified by the express language of the Constitution and statute." *Gregory v. Illinois Cent. R. Co.*, Ky., 80 S.W. 795 (1904). There were wrongful death statutes in existence at the time of the 1890 convention, but there was substantial uncertainty not only as to whom the cause of action belonged, but when the action might be maintained, if at all. *Howard's Adm'r v. Hunter*, 126 Ky. 685, 104 S.W. 723, 725 (1907); *see Henderson's Adm'r v. Kentucky C. Ry. Co.*, 86 Ky. 389, 5 S.W. 875 (1887). Just prior to the convention, a judge of the Jefferson Circuit Court had declared a section of the wrongful death act unconstitutional because it purportedly discriminated against railroads.[6] *Debates, supra*, at 4687. The delegates obviously were concerned about the future viability of tort recovery for wrongful death and trusted neither the legislature nor the courts to protect that statutory cause of action. Just as obviously, the adoption of Section 241 had nothing to do with protecting common law rights.

If, as posited in *Ludwig v. Johnson* and *Perkins v. Northeastern Log Homes*, common law causes of action in tort are cloaked with constitutional protection, that protection is not limited to acts of the legislature, but must apply also to acts of the judiciary. Surely, the majority of this Court does not believe that the Constitution applies only to the legislature and not to us.[7] We would be forced to conclude under the logic perpetuated

6. The Jefferson Circuit Court's ruling was reversed on appeal, *Louisville Safety-Vault & Trust Co. v. Louisville & N.R. Co.*, 92 Ky. 233, 17 S.W. 567 (1891), but not until after the convention had concluded its work.

7. *But see Giuliani v. Guiler*, Ky., 951 S.W.2d 318, 326 (1997) (dissenting opinion).

by the majority opinion in this case that this Court, itself, acted unconstitutionally when we abolished the common law tort of alienation of affections by unanimous vote in *Hoye v. Hoye*, Ky., 824 S.W.2d 422 (1992).

This Court has recently reiterated the maxim that public policy is within the constitutional domain of the legislature.

> [T]he establishment of public policy is not within the authority of the courts. Section 27 of the Kentucky Constitution provides that the powers of government be divided into three distinct units: Executive, Legislative and Judicial. The establishment of public policy is granted to the legislature alone....

Commonwealth, ex rel. Cowan v. Wilkinson, *supra*, at 614.

Courts are well suited to adjudicate individual disputes concerning discrete issues and parties. The Founding Fathers recognized this when they drafted the United States Constitution to give the judiciary jurisdiction to decide "cases and controversies." U.S. Const. art. III §2 cl. 1; *Flast v. Cohen*, 392 U.S. 83, 94, 88 S.Ct. 1942, 1949, 20 L.Ed.2d 947 (1968); *Associated Industries of Kentucky v. Commonwealth*, Ky., 912 S.W.2d 947, 951 (1995). On the other hand, the judicial process is not well suited to the formulation of public policy. As Professor Lewis notes, individuals, lobbies, or other collectives cannot talk to a court.

> Briefs *amicus curiae* may be filed, but the virtue of the judicial system is that its primary focus must be on the trial record and parties before it; judges are not generally equipped or expected to make textually generalized, interrelated rule-type decisions based on "legislative facts." The common law decisions of a court are law, and no better system has been devised than this technique, by which general principles of law emerge from small bits of real life experience. But the technique has worked so well not because judges have a monopoly on wisdom but because the people have always reserved the power to modify principles that in the light of mounting experience have failed to work to their satisfaction.

Lewis, *supra*, at 983.

On the other hand, legislatures are uniquely well equipped to reach fully informed decisions about the need for broad public policy changes in the law. They have more complete access to information, including the ability to receive comments from persons representing a multiplicity of perspectives and to use the legislative process to obtain new information. If a point needs further elaboration, a witness can be recalled. The rationale for legislative preeminence in formulating broad public policy is reflective of these inherent strengths in the legislative process.

Section 28 of the Constitution provides as follows:

> No person or collection of persons, being of one of those departments [legislative, executive or judicial] shall exercise any power properly belonging to either of the others, except in the instances hereinafter *expressly* directed or permitted. (Emphasis added.)

There is nothing in Section 14, 54 or 241 which *expressly* transfers the power to formulate public policy in the area of tort law from the legislative department to the judicial department. In the absence of such an *express* provision, *Ludwig v. Johnson* and its progeny have simply ignored Section 28 and discerned *implied* support for this transfer of power in a combined interpretation of Sections 14, 54 and 241. Of course, premising the "jural rights" doctrine upon mere implication is itself a direct violation of Section 28. Nevertheless, the historical analysis of the origins and purposes of Sections 14, 54 and 241, as set forth in Professor Lewis's article and in this dissenting opinion, reveals not even an implication that those sections are interrelated or that the framers intended for any or all of them, read separately or together, to transfer power over public policy with respect to tort law from the legislature to the judiciary. We, like Bonaparte, have placed that crown upon our own head.

Nor do I subscribe to the proposition that sixty-six years of error must be perpetuated for the sake of "predictability." * * * After all, although *Ludwig v. Johnson* has been on the books for sixty-six years, it purported to overrule over seventy years of precedent represented by *Johnson v. Higgins* and *Barkley v. Glover*, *supra*; and it and its progeny have effectively reversed 800 years of settled Anglo-Saxon jurisprudence. Lewis, *supra*, at 964. I agree with Justice Leibson that "[t]he doctrine of stare decisis does not commit us to the sanctification of ancient fallacy." *Hilen v. Hays*, Ky., 673 S.W.2d 713, 717 (1984). As for "predictability," who could have predicted that after sixty-six years of applying the "jural rights" doctrine to legislative enactments which "abolish" common law rights of action, this Court would now extend its scope to enactments which merely "impair" those rights?

* * *

I would reverse the Court of Appeals and the Fayette Circuit Court and remand this case for a new trial on the issue of punitive damages with directions to instruct the jury in accordance with KRS 411.184 and .186.

Notes and Questions

1. Does the *Williams* Court's extension of the jural rights doctrine to punitive damages comport with the text of Section 54? In his dissent, Justice Cooper took issue with the application of the doctrine to punitive damages because punitive damages are not, in the words of Section 54, awarded "for injuries," but to punish and deter wrongdoing. In other words, Justice Cooper would not have held that Section 54 had any application to punitive damages at all.
2. Consider also that there is no substantive *cause of action* for punitive damages. Rather, punitive damages are a *remedy* that an injured plaintiff may recover, over and above compensatory damages. Consequently, the *Williams* decision may be read as an expansion of the jural rights doctrine; not only does it preclude the abolition of certain causes of action, but also prevents legislative curtailment of the remedies that may be had by a prevailing party in a tort action.

3. Recall that, in *O'Bryan v. Hedgespeth*, 892 S.W.2d 571 (Ky. 1995), near the end of its opinion the Supreme Court also observed in dicta that a statute altering the admissibility of evidence, if it also worked as a substantive limitation on the amount of damages recoverable, would violate the jural rights doctrine, especially Section 54.

Gilbert v. Barkes

Supreme Court of Kentucky (1999)
987 S.W.2d 772

OPINION OF THE COURT BY JUSTICE STEPHENS.

The issue we decide on this appeal is whether the claim of breach of promise to marry is still a viable legal cause of action in Kentucky. Recently, the Jefferson Circuit Court granted summary judgment to appellant dismissing a claim brought under this cause of action. Thereafter, the Kentucky Court of Appeals overruled the circuit court and reinstated the claim.

In reversing the Jefferson Circuit Court, the appellate panel expressed its disagreement with our previous decisions on this issue. However, the Court of Appeals correctly noted that under SCR 1.030(8)(a) and *Special Fund v. Francis*, Ky., 708 S.W.2d 641, 642 (1986), it lacked the authority to overrule a precedent established by this Court.

The facts which give rise to this action are as follows. Ms. Suzanne Barkes, appellee, and Dr. Alvin Gilbert, appellant, entered into a relationship beginning in January of 1989 which continued until June of 1994. Ms. Barkes claims that in September of 1990, Dr. Gilbert proposed marriage to her and that in December of 1990, she accepted. Ms. Barkes submits that she received an engagement ring from Dr. Gilbert. In reliance upon her impending marriage and at Dr. Gilbert's insistence, Ms. Barkes claims that she took early retirement in 1992. Subsequently, Ms. Barkes sold her home in January of 1993 and moved into Dr. Gilbert's home.

Sometime in 1994, the parties' relationship began to deteriorate and Ms. Barkes left Dr. Gilbert's home. In June of 1994 Ms. Barkes filed an action for Breach of Promise to Marry (BPM). Following Ms. Barkes' deposition, Dr. Gilbert filed a motion for summary judgment, which the trial court granted. Ms. Barkes appealed the decision of the trial court. As noted, the Kentucky Court of Appeals reversed the trial court and remanded the case for trial. Upon proper motion, we granted discretionary review. We now reverse the Court of Appeals.

I. History of Action for Breach of Promise to Marry.

The right of an individual to sue for Breach of Promise to Marry is a common law hybrid of tort and contract. Homer H. Clark, Jr., *The Law of Domestic Relations in the United States*, 1 (2d ed. 1987). Its origin, however, goes back to canon law, which only enforced such a breach through specific performance of the promise. W.J. Brockelbank,

The Nature of the Promise to Marry, 41 Ill. L. Rev. 1, 3 (1946); Harter F. Wright, *The Action for Breach of the Marriage Promise,* 10 Va. L. Rev. 361, 364 (1924). Through time such harsh measures were no longer enforced. The common law has since adopted the action.

In the fifteenth century, English courts embraced the action, primarily because the basis of marriage was largely viewed as a property transaction. Clark, *supra*, at 2; G.M. Tevelyan, *English Social History* 313 (1942); W. Goodsell, *A History of Marriage and the Family* 328–31 (1934). However, in those early times, the aggrieved party was only able to recover monies expended on a deceitful promise to marry. Clark, *supra*, at 1. In the seventeenth century, the need to prove deceit was eliminated from the cause of action. Clark, *supra*, at 1; Brockelbank, *supra*, at 3–4.

Following the lead of England, the American colonies adopted the action. Wright, *supra*, at 366. The action found a receptive audience in this country eventually becoming more popular in America than in England. Michael Grossberg, *Governing the Hearth: Law and Family in Nineteenth-Century America*, 37 (1985). However, by the end of the last century commentators became highly critical of the BPM action and favored restricting or eliminating it. McCormick, *Handbook on the Law of Damages*, 403–04 & n. 56 (1935); Wright, *supra*, at 371–75.

Today, the concept of marriage is generally no longer perceived as an economic transaction. Rather is regarded as a union of two persons borne out of love and affection, rather than a device by which property is exchanged. Clark, *supra*, at 3; Jeffrey Kobar, Note, *Heartbalm Statutes and Deceit Actions*, 83 Mich. L. Rev. 1770, 1778 (1985).

The elements of the BPM action are predicated upon contract principles with the exception of damages, which has its roots in tort. *Scharringhaus v. Hazen*, 269 Ky. 425, 107 S.W.2d 329, 336 (1937). Case authority with respect to the elements is quite old. First, there must be mutual promises to marry one another. *Burnham v. Cornwell*, 55 Ky. (16 B. Mon.) 284, 286, 63 Am. Dec. 529 (1855). Furthermore, an offer and acceptance of the promise must be proven for an action to lie. *Burks v. Shain*, 5 Ky. (2 Bibb) 341, 342, 5 Am. Dec. 616 (1811). The offer, however, need not be formal. "Any expression … of readiness to be married is sufficient." *Elmore v. Haddix*, Ky., 254 Ky. 292, 71 S.W.2d 620, 622 (1934) (citing 9 C.J. 336). In addition, the contract to marry must be free from fraud based on the presumptions of innocence and purity of each promising party when entering into the agreement. *Barrett v. Vander-Meulen*, Ky., 264 Ky. 441, 94 S.W.2d 983, 985 (1936).

When the contract to marry has been breached, the injured party must suffer some form of damages. Because the issue of damages stems from tort principles, the amount is not limited to what is recoverable in the typical contract action for a breach of promise. *Scharringhaus v. Hazen*, Ky., 269 Ky. 425, 107 S.W.2d 329, 336 (1937). Three general classes of damages have emerged from this action: compensatory damages relating to the loss of the marriage, aggravated damages for seduction under promise of marriage, and punitive damages for malicious conduct. *Stanard v. Bolin*, 88 Wash.2d 614,

617–19, 565 P.2d 94, 96 (1977). *See also Annotation: Measure and Elements for Breach of Contract to Marry*, 73 A.L.R.2d 553 (1960). In Kentucky, this Court laid down an exhaustive list of factors to consider when estimating damages:

> [I]t is proper to consider anxiety of mind produced by the breach; loss of time and expenses incurred in preparation for the marriage; advantages which might have accrued to plaintiff from the marriage; the loss of a permanent home and advantageous establishment; plaintiff's loss of employment in consequence of the engagement or loss of health in consequence of the breach; the length of the engagement; the depth of plaintiff's devotion to defendant; defendant's conduct and treatment of plaintiff in his whole intercourse with her; injury to plaintiff's reputation or future prospects of marriage; plaintiff's loss of other opportunities of marriage by reason of her engagement to defendant; plaintiff's lack of independent means; her altered social condition in relation to her home and family, due to defendant's conduct; and the fact that she was living unhappily at the time of the alleged promise.

Scharringhaus at 336 citing, 9 C.J. 372.

The last case in which this Court issued a ruling on the breach of promise to marry action was in the 1937 *Scharringhaus* case.

II. Should the Cause of Action for Breach of Promise to Marry Be Abolished from Kentucky Common Law?

In deciding whether to modify the common law, this Court must weigh the benefits versus the burdens of the proposed change. We shall examine the rationale for removing the BPM action from the common law and then we shall discuss the reasons why it should be retained.

The primary argument in favor of abolition of the BPM action is that society's view of marriage and women have changed dramatically since this cause of action was adopted. While technically either a man or a woman could bring the cause of action in question, this Court is unaware of a man ever asserting such claim before the courts of the Commonwealth. The cases which interpret this cause of action make clear the party who is sought to be protected:

> A promise to marry is not infrequently one of the base and wicked tricks of the wily seducer to accomplish his purposes by overcoming that resistance which female virtue makes to his unholy designs.

Scharringhaus v. Hazen, 269 Ky. 425, 107 S.W.2d 329, 336 (1937) (citing *Goodall v. Thurman*, 38 Tenn. 209, 1 Head 209 (Tenn. Dec. Term 1858). This language reflects the sexism and paternalism that pervade this cause of action. While one could certainly debate whether equality has been achieved between women and men in our society, it is certainly beyond issue that women today possess far more economic, legal and political rights than did their predecessors. Accordingly, we must examine the utility of the BPM action in the context of the present day, not in the era in which it was created.

Our review of the actions taken by other jurisdictions indicates that twenty-eight states have legislatively or judicially abolished the Breach of Promise to Marry action.[1] The work of various commentators on this issue demonstrates criticism starting late in the last century and continuing up to the present.[2]

"Although marriages are still contracted for material advantages, it is now popularly believed that the choice of a spouse should be the result of that complex experience called love." Clark, *supra*, at 3. The public policy of the Commonwealth undoubtedly calls for this Court to uphold marriage vows; however, "we see no benefit in discouraging or penalizing persons who realize, *before* making these vows, that for whatever reason, they are unprepared to take such an important step." *Jackson v. Brown*, 904 P.2d 685, 687 (Utah 1995) (emphasis in original).

Given these arguments in favor of abolition as well as the support offered by other jurisdictions and commentators, we now turn to the arguments in favor of its retention. There are two primary arguments in favor of retaining the BPM action. The first is that the General Assembly has implicitly adopted it by placing a statute of limitations upon the period in which such an action can be brought. KRS 413.140(1)(c). The second is that the doctrine of stare decisis compels this Court to retain the action since it is a long-standing remedy and there is no sound reason to eliminate it because it still serves the useful purpose of remedying injury to those who are left standing at the altar.

We find no merit in the first argument that the General Assembly affirms a common law cause of action, such as BPM, by placing a statute of limitations upon it. No legislative approval or disapproval of this court-created claim is indicated by such proceedings. Rather, KRS 413.140(1)(c) merely restricts the time span in which such a claim

---

1. Alabama (Ala. Code §6-5-330 (1975)); California (Cal. Civ. Code §43.5 (Deering 1998)); Colorado (Colo. Rev. Stat. §13-20-202 (1997)); Connecticut (Conn. Gen. Stat. Ann. §52-572b (West 1991)); Delaware (Del. Code Ann. tit. 10 §3924 (1996)); District of Columbia (D.C. Code Ann. §16-923 (1998)); Florida (Fla. Stat. Ann. §771.01 (West 1991)); Indiana (Ind. Code Ann. §34-12-2-1 (Michie 1998)); Maine (Me. Rev. Stat. Ann. tit. 14, §854 (West 1980)); Maryland (Md. Code Ann., Cts. & Jud. Proc. §5-801(1997)) and (Md. Code Ann., Fam. Law §3-102 (1997)); Massachusetts (Mass. Gen. Laws Ann. Ch. 207, §47A (West 1987)); Michigan (Mich. Comp. Laws Ann. §600.2901 (West 1998)); Minnesota (Minn. Stat. Ann. §553.03 (West 1998)); Montana (Mont. Code Ann. §27-1-602 (1997)); Nevada (Nev. Rev. Stat. §41.380 (1995)); New Hampshire (N.H. Rev. Stat. Ann §508:11 (1997)); New Jersey (N.J. Stat. Ann. §2A:23-1 (West 1987)); New York (N.Y. Civ. Rights Law §80-a (McKinney 1992)); North Dakota (N.D. Cent. Code §14-02-06 (1997)); Ohio (Ohio Rev. Code Ann. §2305.29 (Anderson 1997)); Pennsylvania (23 Pa. Cons. Stat. Ann. §1902 (West 1998)); Utah (Jackson v. Brown, 904 P.2d 685 (Utah 1995)); Vermont (Vt. Stat. Ann. tit. 15, §1001 (1997)); Virginia (Va. Code Ann. §8.01-220 (Michie 1997)); West Virginia (W. Va. Code §56-3-2a (1997)); Wisconsin (Wis. Stat. Ann. §768.01 (West 1993)); Wyoming (Wyo. Stat. Ann. §1-23-101 (Michie 1977)).

2. Note, *Domestic Relations: Avoid of Anti-Heartbalm Legislation by the Action of Fraud*, 8 Hasting L.J. 210 (1957); Comment, *California Reopens the 'Heartbalm' Action*, 9 Stan. L. Rev. 406 (1957); *Recent Cases, Breach of Promise—Statute Outlawing Breach-of-Promise Suits Does not Bar Action Based on Fraudulent Promise to Marry*; 70 Harv. L. Rev. 1098, 1099 (1957); W.J. Brockelbank, *The Nature of the Promise to Marry—A Study in Comparative Law*, 41 Ill. L. Rev. 1, 199 (1946); Feinsinger, *Legislative Attack on Heart Balm*, 33 Mich. L. Rev. 983 (1935); Brown, *Breach of Promise Suits*, 77 U. Pa. L. Rev. 474 (1929); Wright, *The Action for Breach of Promise of Marriage*, 10 Va. L. Rev. 361 (1924); White, *Breach of Promise of Marriage*, 10 L.Q. Rev. 135 (1894).

can be brought before the Court of Justice. It is well established that the legislature has the power to limit the time in which a common law action can be brought. *Saylor v. Hall*, Ky., 497 S.W.2d 218, 223 (1973). At the same time, however, this Court is entitled to find that a common law cause of action should no longer be maintained. *D&W Auto Supply v. Department of Revenue*, Ky., 602 S.W.2d 420, 424 (1980). Accordingly, the fact that the legislature has limited the time in which a BPM action must be brought is of no significance and has no relevance to this case.

The second argument is equally as unpersuasive. Stare decisis is a doctrine which has real meaning to this Court. "When a court of institutional review announces a principle of law to apply to a general set of facts, the doctrine of stare decisis requires the court, in the absence of 'sound reasons to the contrary' to adhere to that same principle in future cases where there is a similar factual pattern." *Williams v. Wilson*, Ky., 972 S.W.2d 260, 269 (1998) (Stephens, C.J., concurring) (*quoting Hilen v. Hays*, Ky., 673 S.W.2d 713, 717 (1984)). However, when this Court finds a common law cause of action to be anomalous, unworkable or contrary to public policy, it will abolish the action. *D&W Auto Supply v. Department of Revenue*, Ky., 602 S.W.2d 420, 424 (1980).

We believe the cause of action for breach of promise to marry has become an anachronism that has out-lived its usefulness and should be removed from the common law of the Commonwealth. "It is a barbarous remedy, outgrown by advancing civilization and, like other outgrown relics of a barbarous age, it must go." Wright, *supra*, at 382. As when this Court abolished the action for intentional interference with the marital relation in *Hoye v. Hoye*, Ky., 824 S.W.2d 422, 425 (1992), we "have the power as an appellate court to resolve the question of whether to abolish" the action for BPM. *Craft v. Commonwealth*, Ky., 343 S.W.2d 150 (1961). Accordingly, the action for Breach of Promise to Marry is no longer a valid cause of action before the courts of the Commonwealth.

This Court wishes to make clear that it in no way prohibits other remedies, such as claims for breach of contract and intentional infliction of emotional distress, should a party be able to make such a case. As the Supreme Court of Utah noted in *Jackson v. Brown*, 904 P.2d 685, 687 (1995), any direct "economic losses suffered because of ... [the defendant's] promise to marry [the plaintiff] (such as normal expenses attendant to a wedding) may be recoverable under a theory of ... breach of contract.... [I]f a proper case is made out, emotional damages resulting from [the defendant's] actions may be remedied by an action for intentional infliction of emotional distress. Accordingly, no fundamental remedy is lost to this or any other plaintiff by our decision that a breach of promise to marry no longer has any legal significance." *Id.*

While we are removing a cause of action from the common law, we are not eradicating the ability of a party to seek a remedy for such a wrong, but rather we are modifying the form that remedy may take. Accordingly, our jural rights doctrine, enunciated in *Ludwig v. Johnson*, 243 Ky. 533, 49 S.W.2d 347 (1932), is not implicated in this matter. *Williams v. Wilson*, Ky., 972 S.W.2d 260, 271 (1998) (Cooper, J., dissenting) (stating that modification of a jural right is permissible as long as the right itself is not abolished).

Since we have merely modified the means by which certain wrongs may be remedied, we have no need to address the jural rights doctrine in this case as our action here today does not abolish a common law right existing at the adoption of the 1891 Kentucky Constitution.[3]

* * *

Conclusion

The ideas which predominated in the era that begat the cause of action for Breach of Promise to Marry no longer command the allegiance of the Citizens of the Commonwealth. Accordingly, this Court must act to keep the Common Law of Kentucky in step with its citizens. For the reasons stated above we no longer believe that this cause of action should be a part of our common law. When we find our common law to be anomalous, unworkable or contrary to public policy, we are bound to modify it. *D&W Auto Supply v. Department of Revenue*, Ky., 602 S.W.2d 420, 424 (1980). That is what we have done in this matter. We wish to stress that no fundamental right had been impaired by this Court. Rather we have simply modified the methods by which relief for violation of those rights may be recovered by the injured parties. We reverse the Kentucky Court of Appeals and reinstate the trial court's order dismissing this claim.

Lambert, C.J., Johnstone and Stumbo, JJ., concur.

Cooper, J., dissents in a separate dissenting opinion.

Graves and Wintersheimer, JJ., join this dissenting opinion.

Justice Cooper, dissenting.

Having successfully purged the common law of the tort of alienation of affections in *Hoye v. Hoye*, Ky., 824 S.W.2d 422 (1992), the majority of this Court now consigns to oblivion yet another ancient tort, the breach of promise to marry. While I claim no affection for either of these musty causes of action, I do defend this Court's obligation to apply the law with some degree of consistency, including the application of constitutional principles to ourselves the same as we apply them to the General Assembly. In *Williams v. Wilson*, Ky., 972 S.W.2d 260 (1998), a majority of this Court reiterated the constitutional myth that common law causes of action which existed prior to the adoption of the present Constitution are "jural rights" which cannot be abolished. Like the cause of action for alienation of affections, the cause of action for breach of promise to marry falls into that category. *Burnham v. Cornwell*, 55 Ky. 284, (16 B. Mon. 284) (1855); *Burks v. Shain*, 5 Ky. (2 Bibb) 341 (1811). Far be it from me to defend the jural rights doctrine. *Williams v. Wilson*, *supra*, at 269–76 (dissenting opinion). However, if

3. We wish to distinguish this case from *Williams v. Wilson*, Ky., 972 S.W.2d 260 (1998), in which this Court struck down part of KRS 411.184. We struck that law because it did not simply modify an existing jural right, but rather it impaired the right by changing the common law standard of proof. Under KRS 411.184, recovery was made substantially harder by raising the standard of proof. Accordingly, KRS 411.184 impaired a fundamental right in an impermissible fashion. Our action today does not impair any right, but simply modifies the means by which those rights may be accessed.

a pre-1891 cause of action is cloaked with constitutional protection, it is protected as well from an act of this Court as it is from an act of the legislature. *Id.* at 274.

I am aware that some advocates of the jural rights doctrine now assert that it applies only to "rights of action for damages for death or injuries caused by negligence." *See Fireman's Fund Ins. Co. v. Government Employees Ins. Co.*, Ky., 635 S.W.2d 475, 478, n. 7 (1982), *overruled on other grounds, Perkins v. Northeastern Log Homes*, Ky., 808 S.W.2d 809 (1991), narrowing the scope previously established in *Happy v. Erwin*, Ky., 330 S.W.2d 412, 413 (1959). However, the jural right protected in *Williams v. Wilson, supra*, was the right to punitive damages, which are awarded not as damages to compensate for death or injuries, but to punish and deter wrongdoing. *Id.* at 273 (dissenting opinion), citing *Hensley v. Paul Miller Ford, Inc.*, Ky., 508 S.W.2d 759, 762–63 (1974) and *Ashland Dry Goods Co. v. Wages*, 302 Ky. 577, 195 S.W.2d 312, 315 (1946). *See also Kentucky Utilities Co. v. Jackson County R.E.C.C.*, Ky., 438 S.W.2d 788, 790 (1968), deeming a cause of action for indemnity to be a jural right, and *Meyers v. Chapman Printing Co.*, Ky., 840 S.W.2d 814, 820 (1992), declaring that the protections contained in the Civil Rights Act are jural rights.

The majority opinion asserts that today's decision does not implicate the jural rights doctrine at all, because "we are not eradicating the ability of a party to seek a remedy for such a wrong, but rather we are modifying the form that remedy may take." * * * In *Williams v. Wilson, supra*, the jural rights doctrine was extended past protection against the abolition of a common law right of action to protection against any impairment thereof. (The statute at issue in *Williams* did not abolish punitive damages, but only set standards to guide the jury in determining whether to award such damages and how much to award.) Regardless, the majority opinion states that "the action for Breach of Promise to Marry is no longer a valid cause of action before the courts of the Commonwealth." * * * That language can lead to but one conclusion: the cause of action for breach of promise to marry has thereby been abolished.

Graves and Wintersheimer, JJ., join this dissent.

Notes and Questions

1. In *Hoye v. Hoye*, 824 S.W.2d 422 (Ky. 1992), referenced in the *Gilbert* opinion, the Supreme Court of Kentucky abolished the tort of intentional interference with the marital relation. The Court held, "We conclude that the tort of intentional interference with the marital relation should be abolished because foundation of this action is based on the misperception that spousal affection is capable of theft by a third party. This concept, abandoned by the majority of the states, has its origin in the antiquated premise that a wife is her husband's chattel." *Id.* at 423. *Hoye* was decided by a unanimous Court, and the opinion did not mention the jural rights doctrine or the Kentucky Constitution at all.
2. Quite often, more than one common law cause of action could apply to a given situation. For example, in the classic law school case of *Hawkins v. McGee*, 84 N.H. 114, 146 A. 641 (1929), the plaintiff was allowed to sue on a breach of warranty theory

when his surgeon promised him "a hundred per cent perfect hand or a hundred per cent good hand" after a skin graft operation, but as it turned out, his hand was not perfect after the procedure. Today, courts would probably recognize a medical malpractice or negligence claim under that fact scenario, and a similarly situated plaintiff could sue for damages in either contract or tort. Similarly, quite often a plaintiff may assert both intentional tort and negligence claims as alternative theories of recovery in the same case. Under *Gilbert*, do you think the Supreme Court of Kentucky would countenance the General Assembly abolishing one of these causes of action, so long as the plaintiff still had another means of accessing those rights and obtaining a recovery?

3. Justice Cooper's dissenting opinion in *Gilbert* charges the majority with treating the General Assembly differently than it treats itself when one or the other seeks to modify the common law. Do you think his criticism is well taken?

4. In short, *Gilbert* holds that the Supreme Court can abolish common law causes of action. Of course, the jural rights doctrine asserts that the General Assembly cannot. Kentucky courts like to say the jural rights doctrine protects the individual right to access the courts to redress tort injuries. But if the jural rights doctrine truly was intended to preserve an individual right—after all, Section 14, one of the three constitutional provisions involved, is a part of the Kentucky Bill of Rights—it would preclude both legislative and judicial impairments of the personal right. *See Commonwealth, Cabinet for Health and Family Services ex rel. Meier v. Claycomb ex rel. Claycomb*, 566 S.W.3d 202, 210 (Ky. 2018) ("[W]e hold that Section 14 acts as a restraint on the power of all departments of state government.... Section 14 is a right 'of the people,' and the people deserve to be protected against all departments of government infringing on their right to seek immediate redress for common-law personal-injury claims."). Though usually articulated by the courts as a protection of individual constitutional rights under Sections 14, 54, and 241, the jural rights doctrine, in practice, looks more like a separation of powers doctrine, in which the courts claim superiority over the General Assembly in the field of tort law.

Caneyville Volunteer Fire Department. v. Green's Motorcycle Salvage, Inc.

Supreme Court of Kentucky (2009)
286 S.W.3d 790

Opinion of the Court by Justice Scott.

The present appeal comes to this Court by way of discretionary review from an action asserting negligence brought by Appellees, Orville Green, Catherine Green and Green's Motorcycle Salvage, Inc., against Appellants, Caneyville Volunteer Fire Department (hereinafter CVFD), the City of Caneyville and CVFD Fire Chief, Anthony Clark.

At the outset, we note that the City of Caneyville was entitled to dismissal. CVFD is an agent of the Commonwealth, having been recognized as such by the General Assembly by KRS 75.070 and declared immune from suit in tort. Because fire departments are thus immune from suit in tort, and are agents of the Commonwealth, albeit operating on a local basis, there can be no attendant municipality liability for CVFD's firefighting actions. Therefore, it is not within our authority to impose civil liability on an arm of the government carrying out such a government function. This is also consistent with KRS 95.830(2) in this instance.

Additionally, Chief Clark is immune in his official capacity as Fire Chief of CVFD. In his individual capacity, Chief Clark is entitled to qualified official immunity for his discretionary acts. Accordingly, we reverse the decision of the Court of Appeals to the extent that it conflicts with these holdings and the rationale articulated herein.

I. Introduction

Unquestionably, the prudent path between sovereign immunity and jural rights is a formidable legal quagmire to traverse. As a number of my esteemed colleagues on the bench have observed through the years, immunity is an area fraught with complexities which have divided the courts and confounded jurists. However, the complexity in immunity analysis has much to do with the courts' genuine attempt, over time, to eliminate the guesswork from determining when immunity has been properly and constitutionally recognized. Naturally, striking the appropriate balance has been no small task.

At times during this endeavor, proponents and recipients of immunity have bumped against Kentucky's jural rights or open courts doctrine. While the doctrine is not without its critics, it is a deep-rooted aspect of the Commonwealth's legal canon. And, although some would liken it to legal fiction, we are disinclined to reach such a conclusion. Indeed, thirty-nine (39) other states contain similar such provisions in their state constitutions. Jonathan M. Hoffman, *By the Course of Law: The Origins of the Open Courts Clause of State Constitutions*, 74 Or. L. Rev. 1279 (1995). In fact, the doctrine traces its genesis back to the Magna Carta and was espoused by no less venerated a jurist than Sir Edward Coke who, in his historically significant Second Institute, envisioned it as a vehicle to "ensure the integrity of the judicial process by stating that justice was not for sale," and to avoid undue interference with the judiciary in the courts of law by outside forces.[1] *Id.* at 1281, 1317. Over a century after Coke penned his Second Institute, the doctrine rang true with the American Colonies who feared that the British Crown was meddling in the colonial courts. *Id.* at 1288. Thus, the doctrine found its way into early state constitutions.

Nonetheless, we have been called upon, here, to examine the General Assembly's recognition of immunity in this state's fire departments, which inherently dredges up considerations of sovereign immunity and jural rights. Thus, the matter is one of constitutional interpretation and common law application. As such, this Court is bound, as it has oft been in the past, to articulate a plausible and constitutionally sound solution to an immunity problem while respecting the doctrine of jural rights. That this area of the law is complex in undeniable; however, this does not mean, as the minority suggests, that the remedy is to wipe the slate clean with regards to the evolution and history of the common law in this arena.

As always, the doctrine of stare decisis remains an ever-present guidepost in our undertaking. Stare Decisis compels us to decide every case with deference to precedent. "Thus, it is with anything but a cavalier attitude that we broach the subject of changing the ebb and flow of settled law [and while], we do not feel that the doctrine compels us to unquestioningly follow prior decisions when this Court finds itself otherwise compelled," we recognize that "'stare decisis [is] the means by which we ensure that the law will not merely change erratically, but will develop in a principled and intelligible fashion.'" *Chestnut v. Commonwealth*, 250 S.W.3d 288, 295 (Ky. 2008) (quoting *Vasquez v. Hillery*, 474 U.S. 254, 265–265, 106 S.Ct. 617, 88 L.Ed.2d 598, (1986)).

The open courts provision appears in our constitution, Ky. Const. §14, which was ratified in 1891, and was linked with §§54 and 241 and ascribed the moniker of jural rights doctrine in 1932 in *Ludwig v. Johnson*, 243 Ky. 533, 49 S.W.2d 347 (1932). This is a longstanding common law principle of nearly fourscore years, to which this Court should defer—unless we are strongly compelled otherwise, which we are not.

II. Background

The Greens own a motorcycle salvage business in Grayson County outside the city of Caneyville. Their business caught fire on December 3, 2003, and CVFD responded to the call to extinguish the fire. CVFD is a volunteer fire department which provides fire protection services to Caneyville and the surrounding areas. Despite the fire de-

---

1. "[T]he clause was apparently taken from Sir Edward Coke's restatement of Magna Carta Chapter 40. It was first incorporated into the Delaware Declaration of Rights while the Revolutionary War was still being fought, well before the United States Constitution established the federal judiciary as an independent branch of government. There is little indication that it was the subject of debate when newer states copied it into their own constitutions. A few states, such as Kentucky and Montana, appear to have made certain assumptions about the meaning of the open courts clause when adopting or revising their constitutions, but they are the exception. In most instances, states simply adopted the open courts clause wholesale and without discussion." *Id.* at 1284–1285 (internal notations omitted).

partment's attempt to contain the fire, the business along with much of its inventory was destroyed. Appellees subsequently brought suit alleging that CVFD, its Chief, and thus the City of Caneyville were negligent in failing to timely extinguish the fire and that, as a result of this alleged negligence, they suffered more severe property damage than they otherwise would have if additional measures had been taken to extinguish the fire.[2] Appellees also argued that KRS 75.070 and KRS 95.830(2) were unconstitutional.

KRS 75.070, which purports to provide fire departments and firefighters with immunity from civil liability, states as follows:

> (1) A municipal fire department, fire protection district fire department, and volunteer fire department and the personnel of each, answering any fire alarms, performing fire prevention services, or other duly authorized emergency services inside and outside of the corporate limits of its municipality, fire protection district, or area normally served by a volunteer fire department, *shall be considered an agent of the Commonwealth of Kentucky, and acting solely and alone in a governmental capacity*, and such municipality, fire protection district, or area normally served by a volunteer fire department, *shall not be liable in damages for any omission or act of commission or negligence while answering an alarm, performing fire prevention services, or other duly authorized emergency services.*
>
> (2) No municipal fire department, fire protection district fire department or volunteer fire department answering any fire alarms, performing fire prevention services or volunteer fire department services inside the corporate limits of the district shall be liable in damages for any omission or act of commission or negligence while answering or returning from any fire or reported fire, or doing or performing any fire prevention work under and by virtue of this chapter and said fire departments shall be considered agents of the Commonwealth of Kentucky, and acting solely and alone in a governmental capacity.

(Emphasis added.) KRS 95.830(2) is a companion statute dealing with use of fire apparatus, which purports to mandate that "[t]he city shall not be liable in any manner on account of the use of the apparatus at any point outside of the corporate limits of the city. The apparatus shall be deemed to be employed in the exercise of a governmental function of the city."

The Grayson Circuit Court found KRS 75.070 constitutional and dismissed the case with prejudice. On appeal, however, the Court of Appeals reversed the trial court, finding both KRS 75.070 and KRS 95.830(2) unconstitutional for reasons that they violated Ky. Const. §§14, 54, commonly known as the jural rights or open courts doctrine.[3] In

2. Specifically, Appellees assert CVFD and Chief Clark should have recognized the need for further assistance in combating the fire earlier and called for additional help from surrounding fire departments.

3. In addition to sections 14 and 54, the jural rights doctrine also encompasses section 241 of the Kentucky Constitution. Section 14 provides, "[a]ll courts shall be open, and every person for an injury

its reasoning, the Court of Appeals found that KRS 75.070's attempt to confer sovereign immunity on fire departments and firefighters was an impermissible extension of immunity by the General Assembly akin to the type previously struck down by our predecessor Court in *Happy v. Erwin*, 330 S.W.2d 412 (Ky. 1959) and *Haney v. City of Lexington*, 386 S.W.2d 738 (Ky. 1964). The Court of Appeals held KRS 95.830(2) was unconstitutional because *Haney* had previously determined cities could only enjoy immunity for real or quasi-legislative or judicial functions.

As to the Fire Chief, the Court of Appeals found he was entitled to qualified official immunity, but the record was insufficient to determine whether his acts were discretionary or ministerial in nature, and thus remanded the matter back to the trial court for further proceedings. This Court granted discretionary review.

The impetus of the foregoing is that once again this Court is faced with the prospect of defining the permissible boundaries of sovereign immunity within this Commonwealth and the lengths to which such immunity may extend without improperly impinging upon the citizenry's constitutional right to have access to its courts and to obtain redress therein. Specifically, the task before this Court is to determine whether the Caneyville Volunteer Fire Department is, or should be, afforded governmental immunity from tort liability either by virtue of its status as a governmental or quasigovernmental agency, or pursuant to KRS 75.070, which attempts to confer such immunity, and whether that statute is constitutional.

III. Analysis

The Interplay of Sovereign Immunity and Jural Rights

The present matter requires this Court to examine an apparent tension between two doctrines implied in the Kentucky Constitution: sovereign immunity and jural rights. The issue is whether the General Assembly has the right, through the enactment of legislation, to confer immunity on fire departments and volunteer fire departments, or whether jural rights preclude this grant of immunity as unconstitutional.

Firefighting has always been inherently intertwined with American civil governance. Dating back to the establishment of Jamestown in 1607, which was subsequently ravaged by fire a year later, the threat of fire and the need to curtail that threat became a pressing concern for the fledgling American colonies. Firefighting in Colonial America * * *. As early as 1648, the Governor of New Amsterdam, in what is present-day New York, appointed four fire wardens to enforce fire safety rules. *Id.* Volunteer firefighting can likewise trace its roots to colonial America as the vast majority of these early organizations were staffed by volunteer citizen-firefighters. During this

done him in his lands, goods, person or reputation, shall have remedy by due course of law, and right and justice administered without sale, denial or delay." Ky. Const. §14. Section 54 states, "[t]he General Assembly shall have no power to limit the amount to be recovered for injuries resulting in death, or for injuries to person or property." Ky. Const. §54. And, section 241 mandates, in part, "[w]henever the death of a person shall result from an injury inflicted by negligence or wrongful act, then, in every such case, damages may be recovered for such death, from the corporations and persons so causing the same." Ky. Const. §241.

same period in New Amsterdam, city burghers appointed citizens to a "Rattle Watch," who volunteered to patrol the city streets at night to alert citizens if they saw a fire and organize a bucket brigade to extinguish it. *Id.* Boston, too, took steps to secure itself from the danger of fire as early as 1631 and already had a remedial fire engine when the city was consumed by fire in 1676. *Id.* When the engine proved ineffective for thwarting the fire, the city subsequently purchased a state of the art machine from England whose tank was filled by bucket brigade. *Id.* This engine brought about the need for the first organized fire department in the colonies, beginning service on January 27, 1678, requiring the General Court to seek out twelve men and a captain to man the engine and fight fires. *Id.*

As with so many things in the emerging Union, Benjamin Franklin played a pivotal role in the development of the modern-day volunteer fire department.[4] Upon a visit to Boston, Franklin observed that the city had a far better established infrastructure for fighting fire than did his hometown of Philadelphia. *See* The Electric Ben Franklin, Franklin's Philadelphia: A Journey Through Franklin's Philadelphia * * *. In 1735, in an effort to drum up support and raise public awareness about the need for organized firefighting, Franklin wrote to his own newspaper, the *Pennsylvania Gazette*, under the alias of "old citizen" as to the threat of fire:

> In the first Place, as an Ounce of Prevention is worth a Pound of Cure, I would advise 'em to take care how they suffer living Coals in a full Shovel, to be carried out of one Room into another, or up or down Stairs, unless in a Warming-pan shut; for Scraps of Fire may fall into Chinks and make no Appearance until Midnight; when your Stairs being in Flames, you may be forced, (as I once was) to leap out of your Windows, and hazard your Necks to avoid being oven-roasted.

Id. Soon thereafter, on December 7, 1736, Franklin established the Union Fire Company, which served as the model for volunteer firefighter organization in the rest of the colonies. *Id.* By the time of the Civil War, volunteer fire departments were widespread and were emerging as an entrenched aspect of state and local government.

The evolution of firefighting in Kentucky mirrored that of much of the rest of the colonies and, ultimately, the newly formed country. For instance, organized firefighting was first commenced in Winchester in 1792, consisting largely of organized bucket brigades. * * * These remedial tactics soon gave way to engine pumps, filled by buckets and pumped by hand. * * * In 1838, in an effort to modernize the firefighting force, the city levied a tax to purchase a modern fire engine dubbed the old "Rough and Ready." * * * In 1848, the General Assembly, eager to advance the organization and discipline of the profession, legislated the charter of the Rough and Ready Fire Company, so named after the city's beloved engine, mandating the "duty of each member of said company, when alarms of fire are given, to meet promptly, with their engine, buckets,

4. Interestingly, George Washington served as a volunteer fireman in Alexandria, Virginia in 1774 and Thomas Jefferson also served on a volunteer brigade. * * *

and other apparatus, the same; and shall, in all cases, render obedience to the officers of said company." * * * Like other cities in the state, modernization in technologies and population increases soon begat more advanced firefighting techniques and closer governmental regulation. Around 1886, Winchester obtained its first horse-drawn steam engine, capable of dispensing with 400 gallons per minute, and by 1909 the fire department had a Webb hose truck, which was apparently one of the first motorized engines in Kentucky. * * *

Likewise, the capitol city, Frankfort, has had tax supported fire service since at least the early 1820s and additionally had regulations in effect during that period empowering fire engineers to require the assistance of lay citizens in answering fire alarms and mandating that households own one leather bucket for every three fireplaces found in the home for purposes of fighting house fires. * * * In 1895, the Common Council passed an ordinance to establish and maintain a fire company and set forth the manner in which it would be governed. * * *

The thrust of the aforementioned historical perspective is to note that the development of fire departments in Kentucky has arisen out of the common need of public service and grown alongside government legislation, regulation, and financial support of these entities. Fire departments, however, are particularly unique in their evolution in that, of necessity, they have been forced to maintain roots confined to the locality in which they serve. Because the nature of firefighting involves the need for expeditious and virtually instantaneous response to the scene of a fire, fire departments are maintained and operated in local areas, despite the fact that the authority from whence their existence arises stems from the central state legislature. *See* KRS 75.010; *see generally* §§KRS 95.010–.015

It is incontrovertible that fire departments perform a paradigmatic function of the government in keeping the populous and its property safe from fire. Indeed, one would be hard-pressed to think of a more representative government function. Notably, Kentucky has a longstanding tradition of treating firefighting as a governmental function and thereby cloaking it in immunity. * * *

The doctrine of sovereign immunity, as embodied in Ky. Const. §231, purports to prohibit claims against the government treasury absent the consent of the sovereign.[5] Sovereign immunity is a bedrock component of the American governmental ideal, and is a holdover from the earliest days of the Commonwealth, having been brought over from the English common law. The doctrine has been included in all four of the Com-

5. "As noted in *Reyes v. Hardin Memorial Hospital*, [55 S.W.3d 337 (Ky. 2001)] the words 'sovereign immunity' are not found in the Constitution of Kentucky. Rather, sovereign immunity is a common law concept recognized as an inherent attribute of the state. Thus, contrary to assertions sometimes found in our case law, Sections 230 and 231 of our Constitution are not the source of sovereign immunity in Kentucky, but are provisions that permit the General Assembly to waive the Commonwealth's inherent immunity either by direct appropriation of money from the state treasury (Section 230) and/or by specifying where and in what manner the Commonwealth may be sued (Section 231)." *Yanero v. Davis*, 65 S.W.3d 510, 523–524 (Ky. 2001) (internal citations omitted).

monwealth's constitutions and predates each. *Kentucky Center for the Arts Corporation v. Berns*, 801 S.W.2d 327, 329 (Ky. 1990).

In recent years this Court has examined the history of sovereign immunity in Kentucky in *Yanero* and in *Berns*, noting that the doctrine made its way into the Commonwealth's jurisprudence at least as early as 1828. *See Yanero*, 65 S.W.3d at 517–518 *citing Divine v. Harvie*, 23 Ky. (7 T.B. Mon) 439 (1828). Thus, by the time our second Constitution was in effect, our courts had recognized that the applicable constitutional provision in force at that time—which manifested authority in the General Assembly to determine the manner in which the Commonwealth could be sued—was but a voluntary grant of ability to sue the state, and that the state was otherwise immune from suit in its own courts. *See Divine*, 23 Ky. (7 T.B. Mon.) 439 at *2–3.

On the other hand, what has come to be known as the jural rights doctrine exists as the constitutional counterbalance to sovereign immunity. Under Kentucky jurisprudence, three provisions of the Kentucky Constitution have been read in conjunction to assert a canon of jural rights whose purpose is to ensure that citizens are afforded an opportunity to have their causes heard in open court and to prevent the legislature from unnecessarily inhibiting that right. In *Ludwig v. Johnson*, which was the first case to recognize these three sections together as implementing the doctrine, the Court found that the statute under review in that instance

> violates the spirit of our Constitution as well as its letter as found in sections 14, 54, and 241. It was the manifest purpose of the framers of that instrument to preserve and perpetuate the common-law right of a citizen injured by the negligent act of another to sue to recover damages for his injury. The imperative mandate of section 14 is that every person, for an injury done him in his person, shall have remedy by due course of law.

Ludwig v. Johnson, 243 Ky. 533, 49 S.W.2d 347, 351 (1932).

Happy is typically regarded as extending the reasoning in *Ludwig* and giving rise to the line of cases proffering jural rights as sovereign immunity's counterargument, although nowhere does the case mention sovereign or official immunity. "The line of cases originating from *Happy* provides that the application of official immunity should be limited, that an individual's right to suit should be protected, and that the Kentucky Constitution sections 14, 54, and 241 serve to prohibit the abolition or diminution of legal remedies for personal injuries." G. Thomas Barker, *Official Immunity in Kentucky: The New Standard under Yanero v. Davis*, 90 Ky. L.J. 635, 646–647 (2002) (internal citations omitted).

In *Happy*, a fire truck operator, responding to a call to fight a fire in a neighboring city, was involved in an accident which injured the appellant-bystander. 330 S.W.2d at 413. Therein, the appellant argued that an earlier version of KRS 95.830(2), which purported to grant absolute immunity to firefighters and municipalities engaged in the use of a fire apparatus outside of the city, was unconstitutional because it prevented the appellant from bringing suit against the alleged firefighter tortfeasor. Our predecessor Court agreed, holding unconstitutional the version of KRS 95.830(2) in effect at the time on the grounds that the statute was an impermissible restraint on a person's right to bring suit for damages done to person or property. *See Happy*, 330 S.W.2d at 414. (finding that the statute ran afoul of Ky. Const. §§14, 54).

Accordingly, since the *Happy* decision, this reasoning has typically been asserted by those injured by a government agent for the proposition that sovereign immunity should be limited in scope. *See* G. Thomas Barker, *Official Immunity in Kentucky: The New Standard under Yanero v. Davis*, 90 Ky. L.J. 635, 648 (2002). At first blush, it would appear, then, that the two seminal cases for sovereign immunity and jural rights, *Yanero* and *Happy* respectively, are at odds with one another. Admittedly, these cases and their progeny, espouse two distinct theories based on common law principles. *Yanero* seeks to clarify the sovereign immunity defense to which qualified government agents are entitled under the common law, while "*Happy*, and the jural rights doctrine protect against the overextension of immunity by the legislature." G. Thomas Barker, *Official Immunity in Kentucky: The New Standard under Yanero v. Davis*, 90 Ky. L.J. 635, 654 (2002) (citing *Happy*, 330 S.W.2d at 412; *Ludwig v. Johnson*, 49 S.W.2d at 351). However, these two lines of cases and competing common law principles need not represent mutually exclusive objectives. Indeed, we believe they may be read together and harmonized to produce compatible ends. Namely, *Yanero* may be construed as providing the proper framework for analyzing liability of a government agent, while *Happy* may be construed to limit the reach of *Yanero* in determining when a statute has extended immunity beyond constitutional constraints. Here, we believe the General Assembly's recognition of firefighters and fire departments' immunity was constitutional and, therefore, not repugnant to jural rights.

Organizational Framework of Immunity Analysis

* * *

This Court has long struggled with where the permissible limits of sovereign immunity extend. "The decision when the sovereign immunity defense applies to an entity created by an act of the General Assembly has been historically troublesome to our Court, resulting in diverse decisions difficult to reconcile." *Berns*, 801 S.W.2d at 328. To be sure,

> [t]he only positive conclusion one can draw from the various cases is that the appropriate line separating persons and entities entitled to claim inclusion in the Commonwealth's sovereign immunity is not a line which the General Assembly may draw in its discretion, but a problem of constitutional law which our Court must address on a case by case basis.

Id. at 329. The reigning authority on the matter holds that sovereign immunity (as embodied in Ky. Const. §231) will trump jural rights (Ky. Const. §§14, 54, 241) because it is a specific provision of the Constitution, rather than a general provision. *See id.* However, this only holds true in instances wherein it is the Commonwealth who is being sued. Thus, the crucial determination in sovereign immunity analysis boils down to: whether the entity being sued is the sovereign, its agency, or one who goes about the business of conducting the sovereign's work. Therefore, if CVFD was an agent of the Commonwealth, engaged in the Commonwealth's work, KRS 75.070 is constitutional.

Determining Agency

Whether an entity is a government agent is a threshold consideration in governmental immunity analysis. However, as *Berns* alludes to, the determination of which entities are to be deemed agents of the state government has, historically, not been a conclusion easily forthcoming and is one which has proven troublesome for our courts in the past, leading to various tests with sometime conflicting results.

One such test for determining whether an entity is an agent of the state is whether, "when viewed as a whole, the entity is carrying out a function integral to state government." *Berns*, 801 S.W.2d at 332; *see also Schwindel v. Meade County*, 113 S.W.3d 159, 168 (Ky. 2003). This holistic view of the entity necessarily requires several underlying, subsidiary considerations in making the "integral government function" determination.

In *Berns*, we recognized that *Gnau v. Louisville & Jefferson Co. Metropolitan Sewer Dist.*, 346 S.W.2d 754 (Ky. 1961) established a two-pronged test for determining whether an entity was an agent of the state government within the meaning of the waiver provision of the Board of Claims Act, KRS 44.070, with the first prong "consisting of the direction and control of the central state government/and the second addressing the extent to which the entity was 'supported by monies which are disbursed by authority of the Commissioner of Finance out of the State Treasury.'" *Berns*, 801 S.W.2d at 331. However, this "test" may be more accurately characterized as a factorial analysis, whose showing will lend weight to deciding if an entity should be considered a state agency. *See Yanero*,[6] 65 S.W.3d at 520 ("These [*Berns*] factors are primarily relevant to determining whether an entity is properly classified as a state agency."); *see also Withers v. University of Kentucky*, 939 S.W.2d 340, 342–343 (Ky. 1997). The real thrust of the "test" is the third factor that *Berns* adds to the *Gnau* factors, which is whether the entity carries out an integral governmental function.

Thus, building off of *Berns* and *Gnau*, in *Autry v. Western Kentucky University*, 219 S.W.3d 713, 717 (Ky. 2007), we tried once more to articulate a workable test, stating

> [g]overnmental immunity extends to state agencies that perform governmental functions (i.e., act as an arm of the central state government) and are supported by money from the state treasury. However, unless created to perform a governmental function, a state agency is not entitled to governmental immunity. An analysis of what an agency actually does is required to determine its immunity status.

---

6. *Yanero*, which is presently the seminal Kentucky immunity case, did not expressly address the issue of how to determine whether an entity is an agent, instead limiting its focus on distinguishing what properly constitutes governmental versus sovereign immunity.

(Internal citations omitted.) We believe that *Autry* provides a good reference point for this analysis in recognizing that there must be a subsidiary inquiry into what an entity "actually does" to determine if it should be entitled to government immunity. * * *

Certainly, fire departments and volunteer fire departments are government agents engaged in governmental, as opposed to, proprietary functions. * * * Significantly, KRS 75.070 characterizes fire departments and volunteer fire departments as "an agent of the Commonwealth" that acts "solely and alone in a governmental capacity." *See also* KRS 95A.010(1) ("This chapter shall apply to the personnel of all fire departments in the state whether paid or unpaid, or both.").

Fire departments of all kinds receive funding from taxes and government backing.[7] They do not sell goods nor conduct their business with an eye toward making a profit. To be sure, the very term "volunteer fire department" attests to their task: that is to provide a gratuitous service to the population whereby volunteer citizens risk life and limb to provide a public service.

Looking to the factors previously employed by this Court and those considered by the federal courts, they weigh overwhelmingly in favor of acknowledging that fire departments and volunteer fire departments are government agents who engage in a governmental (not proprietary) function. *Autry*, 219 S.W.3d at 717. Thus, "these facts compel the conclusion that our constitutional fathers would ... view this activity as qualifying for sovereign immunity." *Berns*, 801 S.W.2d at 331.

The General Assembly's Recognition of Immunity

The Court of Appeals found KRS 75.070 to be unconstitutional insofar as it purported to impart personal immunity upon firefighters for negligent conduct and because fire departments were not agents of state or county government.[8] We disagree.

Fire departments are agents of the Commonwealth who engage in an essential governmental function in providing for the safety and well-being of its citizens—and because there is likely no more epitomizing symbol of government function—reason dictates they must be considered an agent of the sovereign. As such, they are cloaked in immunity from suit in tort. When an entity is entitled to government immunity, the General Assembly may draft legislation recognizing that immunity. "Where sovereign immunity exists by reason of the constitution, the General Assembly may extend or limit waiver as it sees fit, but where no constitutionally protected sovereign immunity exists the General Assembly cannot by statute create it." *Berns*, 801 S.W.2d at 329. Thus, as in *Yanero* where we found that the KHSAA, as an agent of the Kentucky

7. That they receive some contributions from the citizenry is no different than the tolls which states often charge in building parkways.

8. It would seem only logical that fire departments are an agent of one or the other. Here, the General Assembly was clearly within its constitutional authority to acknowledge the immunity to the Commonwealth's fire departments because these entities are agents of the sovereign who engage locally in necessary government functions.

Board of Education, was entitled to immunity, so too should the CVFD be afforded immunity as an agent of the Commonwealth of Kentucky. *See Yanero*, 65 S.W.3d at 530.

* * *

In its Opinion below, the Court of Appeals cited to *Haney* and *Happy* for the proposition that KRS 75.070's extension of immunity to municipal fire departments was unconstitutional. *Haney*, however, is inapplicable because KRS 75.070 is not premised on a grant of municipal immunity. Nor does it offend *Happy* as it does not attempt to grant absolute immunity, but rather recognizes and extends waiver of immunity for acts carried out only in a government capacity.

Moreover, considering the present statute, the General Assembly has articulated a clear public policy determination—as manifested by the passage of such legislation—that it intends for all fire departments, volunteer fire departments, and firefighters to be immune from tort liability for their governmental or official acts. We would be remiss to ignore a directive which is so clearly within the purview of this Commonwealth's legislature.

* * *

Shaping public policy is the exclusive domain of the General Assembly. We have held that "[t]he establishment of public policy is granted to the legislature alone. It is beyond the power of a court to vitiate an act of the legislature on the grounds that public policy promulgated therein is contrary to what the court considers to be in the public interest." *Commonwealth ex rel. Cowan v. Wilkinson*, 828 S.W.2d 610, 614 (Ky. 1992). Through its enactment of KRS 75.070, the General Assembly has articulated the public policy that firefighters and fire departments within the Commonwealth should not be liable for negligent acts committed in good faith in emergency situations while engaged in fighting a fire or responding to a call.

Stated otherwise, the statute in question confers governmental immunity to fire departments and qualified official immunity to firefighters engaged in discretionary functions. Thus, the statute fully comports with constitutional law. Unless the General Assembly is prohibited by the Kentucky or Federal Constitutions from enacting such legislation, it must be free to do so. *See Boone County v. Town of Verona*, 190 Ky. 430, 432, 227 S.W. 804, 805 (1921). Here, it is not so prohibited. And, as noted in *Berns*, in the present matter, independent constitutional justification for immunity exists, as KRS 75.070 does not conflict with Ky. Const §231. *See Berns*, 801 S.W.2d at 329.

Accordingly, we hold KRS 75.070 is constitutional and confers governmental immunity upon municipal fire departments, fire protection district fire departments and volunteer fire departments. CVFD is therefore entitled to governmental immunity.

* * *

KRS 95.830(2)

Moving now to the constitutionality of KRS 95.830(2), the Court of Appeals recognized that the trial court did not rely upon the statute in rendering its decision, nor was the statute principally addressed on appeal. Yet, it employed the rationale of *Happy* (which struck down an earlier statute bearing the same numeration) in determining that the present version of KRS 95.830(2) was unconstitutional. We disagree for reasons that the statute does not offend jural rights.

The former version of KRS 95.830(2) stated:

> Neither the city nor its officers or employees shall be liable in any manner on account of the use of the apparatus at any point outside of the corporate limits of the city. The apparatus shall be deemed to be employed in the exercise of a governmental function of the city.

The present version of KRS 95.830(2) states:

> The city shall not be liable in any manner on account of the use of the apparatus at any point outside of the corporate limits of the city. The apparatus shall be deemed to be employed in the exercise of a governmental function of the city.

The primary distinction between the statutes is the grant of immunity to city officers and employees in the former statute, whereas, the present statute limits immunity to the city only.

In *Happy*, the principal justification for rendering the former version of KRS 95.830(2) unconstitutional was that it attempted to confer immunity to city officers and employees in their personal capacity. *See Happy*, 330 S.W.2d at 414. At the time of the decision cities still enjoyed municipal immunity. Thus, as the Court of Appeals correctly noted, municipal firefighters would have been immune to the extent they were sued in their official capacity. Therefore, though *Happy* does not expressly indicate as much, it must be presumed that our predecessor Court was troubled about extending immunity to firefighters in their personal capacity for ministerial actions, i.e. actions that involve merely following through on the orders of others or executing a duty under preexisting facts, and accordingly struck down the statute for that reason. *Cf. Sloas*, 201 S.W.3d at 478; *Yanero*, 65 S.W.3d at 522.

However, the Court in *Happy* also premised its finding, in part, on the conclusion that the provision violated jural rights. It does not. Ky. Const. §54 states, "the General Assembly shall have no power to limit the amount to be recovered for injuries resulting in death, or for injuries to person or property." This section has since come to be interpreted as meaning that the legislature may not take away a cause of action which existed as of the inclusion of this section into Kentucky's constitution, which was ratified in 1891.

In 1877, in *Greenwood*, 76 Ky. (13 Bush) 226 at *2, our courts recognized that a city could not be liable for the negligence of its firefighters. Thus, no cause of action existed against the city for the negligent acts of firefighters at that time. As such, KRS 95.830(2), in its present or former manifestation, does not take away a right to suit enjoyed by the citizenry in 1891 and does not offend Ky. Const. §54. Thus, to the extent that it says otherwise, *Happy* is incorrect.

Nor does *Haney* compel a different conclusion, as *Haney* departed only from previous common law decisions of this Court. *See Haney*, 386 S.W.2d at 741 ("We must make a choice as to whether the change in such a rule [concerning municipal immunity] should be made by the legislature or by us. The majority of the court [in *V.T.C. Lines, Inc. v. City of Harlan*, 313 S.W.2d 573, (Ky. 1957)] believe[d] that the change addresse[d] itself to legislative discretion and that we must content ourselves only with criticism of the rule *which we have created*. We think we were incorrect in [previously] taking such a position. The very foundation upon which such an attitude is based is not a solid one. We have no reason to believe that the members of the legislature approve all existing common law rules concerning tort actions; in fact, many members of that body, when acting in individual capacities as lawyers, have rather forceably [sic] indicated in briefs and petitions for rehearing that they do not. It seems to us that an equally reasonable assumption is that the legislature might expect the courts themselves to correct an unjust rule *which was judicially created*" (internal quotations omitted)). Haney did not attempt to assert any constitutional right of this Court to override the legislature's prerogative, i.e., that of the legislative power. Ky. Const. §29.

IV. Conclusion

In sum, we hold KRS 75.070 constitutional as a permissible recognition, by the General Assembly, of governmental immunity of fire departments and volunteer fire departments; official immunity to firefighters sued in their representative capacity; and, consequently, qualified official immunity to firefighters sued in their personal capacity but engaged in good faith discretionary functions.

As a matter of observation, it cannot be overlooked that were we to hold otherwise, the very survival of a vital profession, which predates the Commonwealth itself, would be significantly called into question. One must but momentarily pause to consider the substantial ramifications of assessing financial liability on volunteer firefighters and fire departments that fall short in their efforts of lending aid to the public. Truly, it is entirely plausible that many such persons would no longer continue to volunteer their services in this endeavor and that these institutions as a whole would be unable to survive, monetarily, the effects of litigation. Extrapolate this conjecture further and one must but pause to see the very real danger this poses to the public in both actual and financial terms.

Further, we also find KRS 95.830(2) to be constitutional. For these reasons, we hereby reverse the decision of the Court of Appeals and affirm the decision of the Grayson Circuit Court, albeit, in some instances, for different reasons.

All sitting. Venters, J., concurs by separate opinion.

Minton, C.J., concurs in result only by separate opinion, in which Cunningham and Schroder, JJ., join.

Abramson, J., concurs in result only by separate opinion.

Noble, J., concurs in result only.

Justice Venters, concurring:

I concur with Justice Scott's opinion. At the risk of extending an already lengthy series of opinions, I submit that regardless of the immunity issue the Appellee's complaint does not state a claim for which relief may be granted. Its only basis for asserting liability is the claim that Appellants negligently "failed to expeditiously extinguish the fire" at Appellee's business. We are informed by Appellee's counsel at oral argument that the only act or omission of the Caneyville VFD deemed negligent by Appellees was that it lacked sufficient manpower and equipment to defeat the blaze. The same could be said of any fire department at any fire where property is damaged. There is no allegation that members of the Caneyville VFD caused any injury or damage to Appellee, beyond that damage caused by the fire. A fire department does not insure property owners from fire losses, and it has no duty to a property owner to save his property. The record before us consists of nothing more than the complaint, the motion to dismiss, the trial court's ruling, and the appellate pleadings. No answer was even filed. We should not scrap the jural rights doctrine or undertake a major reevaluation of governmental immunity on what I perceive is an insufficient claim and an exceedingly sparse record. A fire department is not liable for failing, due to its lack of equipment and manpower, to "expeditiously extinguish the fire."

Chief Justice Minton, concurring in result only:

I concur with the majority's conclusion that the CVFD enjoys immunity because it is performing a governmental function and not a proprietary function. *Yanero v. Davis*, 65 S.W.3d 510, 520–21 (Ky. 2001). I also agree with the result reached by the majority in which neither Chief Clark nor the City of Caneyville will be liable in this action, but I do not agree with the majority's methodology or reasoning.

Immunity, sovereign and otherwise, has been made into a difficult area of the law, full of rules with subsets. Before delving into the details of this case, I feel compelled to say that we should endeavor to drain this judge-made swamp. Said simply, my view of immunity is this: the Commonwealth enjoys inherent immunity by virtue of its status as a sovereign state. As such, the Commonwealth may choose to lend its immunity to its arms and agents, whether those arms and agents are organizations like the CVFD or individuals like Chief Clark. And I would eliminate, or at least reduce, the arbitrary differentiations that have grown up in this Court around the concept of immunity and its various subsets (*e.g.*, sovereign, official, qualified official, etc.) and the various tests that we have formulated in this area over the years (*e.g.*, premising qualified official immunity of a state actor based upon whether the acts in question were ministerial or discretionary in nature).

The Commonwealth, speaking through the General Assembly, is forbidden by Section 2 of our Constitution from acting arbitrarily in lending its immunity (*i.e.*, the Commonwealth may not lend its immunity to non-state actors). But absent some specific constitutional prohibition, I believe the General Assembly is free to declare if, when, or how the Commonwealth lends its immunity to its arms and agents. With those general principles in mind, I turn to the facts of this case.

Under our current precedent, a governmental employee receives qualified official immunity for his or her discretionary acts but receives no immunity for the performance of ministerial acts. *Id.* at 522. So it is possible for the employee of an arm of the Commonwealth to have personal liability for actions taken in the scope of, and in furtherance of, the employee's job performance. Unlike the majority, I believe the General Assembly has the power to grant immunity to state actors in their individual capacity. In fact, I believe the General Assembly did just that in KRS 75.070(1).

KRS 75.070(1) provides, in relevant part, that a "volunteer fire department and [its] ... personnel ..., answering any fire alarms ... shall be considered an agent of the Commonwealth of Kentucky, and acting solely and alone in a governmental capacity, and ... shall not be liable in damages for *any* omission or act of commission or negligence while answering an alarm...." (Emphasis added.) The statute is straightforward and uses language broad enough to demonstrate the General Assembly's intent to provide as much immunity and protection as possible, both to fire departments and to their employees answering fire alarms. But the majority construes the statute to limit immunity to Chief Clark and similarly situated firefighters in their official capacities and holds that the firefighters' individual-capacity liability depends upon whether the acts in question were discretionary or ministerial. The artificial distinction between discretionary and ministerial functions appears nowhere in the wording of KRS 75.070(1). So I believe the majority has judicially amended the statute effectively to provide that fire departments and the personnel of fire departments are not liable in damages for "any omission or act of commission or negligence while answering an alarm *provided that the omission or act of commission or negligence is a discretionary, not ministerial act*." I refuse to graft such a restriction on an otherwise clear statute. *Beckham v. Board of Education of Jefferson County*, 873 S.W.2d 575, 577 (Ky. 1994) ("[We are] not at liberty to add or subtract from legislative enactment or to discover meaning not reasonably ascertainable from language used.").

My reading of KRS 75.070(1) causes me to conclude that the General Assembly intended to grant immunity to fire department employees to the same extent enjoyed by fire departments themselves. So I would hold that Chief Clark enjoys immunity in both his official and individual capacity. And although overruled by *Yanero*, our precedent once followed that precise line of reasoning. *Franklin County, Kentucky v. Malone*, 957 S.W.2d 195, 202 (Ky. 1997) ("As long as the police officer acts within the scope of the authority of office, the actions are those of the government and the officer is entitled to the same immunity....").

My conclusion runs contrary to our precedent. More particularly, my conclusion regarding Chief Clark's liability runs headlong into the often-cited jural rights theory, under which Sections 14,* * * 54,* * * and 241* * * of our Kentucky Constitution are jointly interpreted to mean that "any common law right of action existing prior to the adoption of the 1891 Constitution is sacrosanct and cannot be abolished." *Williams v. Wilson*, 972 S.W.2d 260, 272 (Ky. 1998) (Cooper, J., dissenting). But I consider the jural rights theory to be a judicially created legal fiction to which we should no longer cling. Rather, as Professor Thomas Lewis convincingly declared, "the formal jural rights doctrine is founded on a misconception of Kentucky's 1891 [C]onstitution. It should be abandoned." Thomas P. Lewis, *Jural Rights Under Kentucky's Constitution: Realities Grounded in Myth*, 80 Ky. L.J. 953, 985 (1991–92).

The jural rights theory first appeared in Kentucky in 1932. *Ludwig v. Johnson*, 243 Ky. 533, 49 S.W.2d 347 (1932). But the case that has the most direct bearing on the one at hand dates to 1959. That 1959 case involved the potential immunity of an employee of a municipal fire department. *Happy v. Erwin*, 330 S.W.2d 412 (Ky. 1959). Although it did not expressly use the term "jural rights," a majority of our predecessor court concluded in *Happy* that the General Assembly lacked the constitutional power to enact a statute that provided that a city employee could not be liable for operating a fire apparatus outside the city limits. *Id.* at 413–14. Specifically, our predecessor court opined that "[c]learly the statute violates sections 14 and 54 of the Kentucky Constitution (and would violate section 241 if death were involved.)" *Id.* at 413. Following the logic in *Happy* would lead to the conclusion reached by the majority in this case—*i.e.*, that the General Assembly could not constitutionally enact a statute that provided that Chief Clark and all similarly situated firefighters are immune in their individual capacities for both discretionary and ministerial acts. But because I place no stock in the jural rights theory, I conclude that *Happy* was erroneously decided and should be overruled.

The Commonwealth enjoys immunity simply by virtue of its existence as a sovereign state; and the General Assembly is the governmental body constitutionally authorized to determine if, when, and how that immunity will be waived. *Yanero*, 65 S.W.3d at 523–24. By specifically stating in KRS 75.070 that firefighters are not liable for "any" acts that occur during the course of their firefighting duties, I conclude that the General Assembly has expressed its intention completely to immunize Chief Clark and all similarly situated firefighters. But the majority in *Happy*, proceeding under the jural rights theory, essentially held that the General Assembly lacked the authority to refuse to waive the immunity of state actors. Actually, the *Happy* court went so far as to hold that the elected representatives of the people of this Commonwealth—the General Assembly—lacked the power to declare, as a matter of public policy, that public servants are immune from suit.

Specifically, the *Happy* court opined as follows: "It is argued that the liability of public servants is a matter of public policy for the legislature to determine. However, the public policy of the legislature cannot supersede the public policy of the people of this Commonwealth expressed in their Constitution." 330 S.W.2d at 414. But as Professor Lewis has convincingly argued, "the formal jural rights doctrine is founded on a misconception of Kentucky's 1891 constitution." Lewis, 80 Ky. L.J. at 985. Although I will not belabor this opinion by recapping the results of his scholarly and convincing research, Professor Lewis traces the history of the adoption of Sections 14, 54, and 241 of the Kentucky Constitution and arrives at the conclusion that the framers of our Constitution did not intend for all tort laws extant in 1891 to be inviolable. In other words, history caused Professor Lewis to declare that the jural rights theory was nonsense, an opinion shared by former Justice William Cooper.[9] Tellingly, we have been cited to nothing that disputes Professor Lewis's scholastic research. Why, then, do we cling to a legal theory that has no basis in history or the law? Accordingly, I have concluded that *Happy*, along with all the jural rights cases that preceded and succeed it, are unsupportable.

Referring to Professor Lewis's article, former Justice Cooper memorably opined that jural rights "is nothing more nor less than a judicial usurpation of a traditional legislative prerogative." *Williams*, 972 S.W.2d at 272 (Cooper, J., dissenting). I agree. We should disabuse ourselves of the jural rights theory and return the power to "formulate public policy in the area of tort law" to the General Assembly. *Williams*, 972 S.W.2d at 275 (Cooper, J., dissenting). In short, we should abdicate the public policy crown that "[w]e, like Bonaparte, have placed ... upon our own head." *Id.* And if we abdicate our self-imposed position of control in this area of tort law, we will recognize that the General Assembly may choose when, if, and how it will waive immunity for state actors. Because there is nothing in the words of KRS 75.070(1) that evidences an intent to waive any immunity for Chief Clark—the opposite, in fact, appears—then the removal of the fallacious jural rights theory leaves no impediment to Chief Clark's enjoying immunity in his individual capacity, regardless of whether the acts in question underlying the Greens' complaint are deemed ministerial or discretionary.

I recognize that abolishing the jural rights theory will logically result in the General Assembly having the discretion to "exempt all public officers and employees from any type of liability." *Happy*, 330 S.W.2d at 414. But the General Assembly had that power all along. We have simply refused to recognize that power, instead preferring to cling to the fictitious jural rights theory.

I also see that recognizing the General Assembly's wide-reaching power in this area creates a potential for abuse and may well result in unwise public policy decisions. But the formulation of public policy, whether wise or unwise, is the sole province of the General Assembly, not the judicial branch. *See Williams*, 972 S.W.2d at 275 (Cooper, J., dissenting).

Application of my conclusions regarding the jural rights theory leads to the inevitable conclusion that under KRS 75.070(1), Chief Clark has immunity for actions performed within the scope of his employment, regardless of whether those actions are ministerial or discretionary. Although I do not agree with its reasoning, I do agree with the majority's ultimate conclusion that Chief Clark is not liable in either his official or individual capacity.

---

9. *See Williams*, 972 S.W.2d at 275 (Cooper, J., dissenting) ("[T]he historical analysis of the origins and purposes of Sections 14, 54 and 241 [of the Kentucky Constitution], as set forth in Professor Lewis's article ... reveals not even an implication that those sections are interrelated or that the framers intended for any or all of them, read separately or together, to transform power over public policy with respect to tort law from the legislature to the judiciary.").

Finally, under my approach, the City of Caneyville's liability would be extinguished because neither the CVFD nor Chief Clark would have any potential liability. The majority also concludes that the City of Caneyville should not be liable. * * *

For the reasons discussed, I concur with the majority's ultimate result, but respectfully disagree with its reasoning.

Cunningham and Schroder, JJ., join.

Justice Abramson, concurring in result only:

I respectfully concur in result only.

While Justice Venters correctly notes that the record before us is "exceedingly sparse," the Caneyville Volunteer Fire Department's representation to this Court regarding its legal status has been unchallenged. The CVFD notes that "contrary to the Appellees' assertion that [CVFD] is the agent of the city, volunteer fire districts are created through special taxing districts set up by *the County* under KRS 75.010 and KRS 65.182. Thus, these agencies are more appropriately characterized as agents of the county and protected by sovereign immunity." (Emphasis in the original.) Indeed, it is fair to say that the City of Caneyville has no legal role in this controversy whatsoever and thus discussions of municipal immunity, jural rights and, indeed, the constitutionality of KRS 95.830 are beyond the scope of the controversy before this Court. In my view, the CVFD is a county authorized taxing district and whether viewed in that light or through the "agent of the Commonwealth" status accorded it in KRS 75.070 it has sovereign immunity. The majority is correct that Chief Clark in his official capacity is entitled to the same immunity as the CVFD. Discussions of individual capacity claims and the qualified official immunity doctrine, again in my view, are beyond the scope of this controversy because the Appellees did not state any individual capacity claims against Chief Clark. In sum, I believe that the majority is correct that the trial court properly dismissed the case but I disagree with its rationale.

Notes and Questions

1. Only two of seven Justices, Scott and Venters, fully joined the opinion of the Court in *Caneyville*. Chief Justice Minton's opinion concurring in the result was joined by two others, Justices Cunningham and Schroder. Justices Abramson and Noble also concurred in result only but did not join either Justice Scott's or the Chief Justice's opinions. The three-justice plurality represented by the Chief Justice's opinion is the closest the Supreme Court has come to overruling the jural rights doctrine since it was first recognized in *Ludwig* in 1932. (Note also that three justices joined in Justice Cooper's dissent in *Gilbert v. Barkes*.)

2. In his *Caneyville* concurrence, Chief Justice Minton argued that the historical research found in Professor Lewis's law review article on the jural rights doctrine—probably the most-cited law review article by Kentucky's courts—could not be disputed. But in his opinion for the Court in *Commonwealth, Cabinet for Health and Family Services ex rel. Meier v. Claycomb ex rel. Claycomb*, 566 S.W.3d 202 (Ky.

2018), the Chief Justice disagreed somewhat with Professor Lewis's historical analysis of Section 14 of the Kentucky Constitution. Can the Chief Justice's positions in these cases be reconciled?

3. One federal court judge has cited Chief Justice Minton's *Caneyville* concurrence as having "abrogated" the jural rights doctrine. *See Tonsetic v. Rafferty's Inc.*, No. 1:14-cv-00170-GNS-HBB, 2016 WL 4083455, *2 (W.D. Ky. Aug. 1, 2016) (Stivers, J.) ("Thus, it appears that the jural rights doctrine is no longer viable."). This may be a bit of hyperbole. But Judge Stivers certainly was familiar with the *Caneyville* case because, prior to taking the bench in 2014, he represented the appellant before the Supreme Court in that case. He also co-authored an article in which he opined that Chief Justice Minton's *Caneyville* concurrence signaled that "[t]he days of the jural rights doctrine appear to be numbered." Greg N. Stivers & Scott D. Laufenberg, *The Impending End of the Jural Rights Doctrine in Kentucky Jurisprudence*, 99 Ky. L.J. Online 63, 82 (2010–11). If the days of the jural rights doctrine are in fact numbered, it has proven to be a large number indeed.

Eight

Individual Rights under the Kentucky Constitution

A. The Bill of Rights

> "That the great and essential principles of liberty and free government may be recognized and established, we declare that ..." (Ky. Const. Bill of Rights, pmbl.)
>
> "To guard against transgression of the high powers which we have delegated, We Declare that every thing in this Bill of Rights is excepted out of the general powers of government, and shall forever remain inviolate; and all laws contrary thereto, or contrary to this Constitution, shall be void." (Ky. Const. §26.)

"The root source of all power validly exercised by any officer or agency of the state government is, of course, its Constitution. Placing first things first, Kentucky's begins with a Bill of Rights consisting of 26 Sections, the last of which declares in substance that these rights shall prevail over and above all else and are not subject to the general powers of government." *Ex parte Auditor of Public Accounts*, 609 S.W.2d 682, 684 (Ky. 1980). "The Bill of Rights has always been recognized as the supreme law of the Commonwealth. That fact is emphasized by section 26 of the Constitution, which is carried over from the past constitutions." *Gatewood v. Matthews*, 403 S.W.2d 716, 718 (Ky. 1966).

Much of the Bill of Rights in Kentucky's Constitution initially was borrowed from the Pennsylvania Constitution of 1790, and the text has remained fairly consistent through each of Kentucky's four constitutions. Note that, as was typical of early state constitutions, more than one subject is often covered by a single section of the Bill of Rights.

The last section of the Bill of Rights, Section 26, states that those matters governed by the Bill of Rights are "excepted out of the general powers of government, and shall forever remain inviolate." Conceptually, therefore, no branch of the government has power to interfere with or violate any provision in the Bill of Rights; the rights thus secured are declared to be outside, or "excepted" from, the power of lawful government.

The purpose of the Bill of Rights is stated in its preamble: to "recognize[ ] and establish[ ]" the "great and essential principles of liberty and free government." Thus, under one view, each section of the Bill of Rights may be classified as having been included either to preserve liberty or to promote free government. The "liberty" sections can be subdivided between those that protect individual liberty and those that are "mixed," or promote more than one purpose. The "free government" sections either establish free government principles, provide explicit instructions to the government, or are "mixed." This categorization of the Bill of Rights provisions is reflected as in the following chart.

Liberty		Free Government		
Individual Rights	Mixed Rights or Principles	Principles	Mixed	Explicit Instructions
1	4	2	3	6
21	7	26	5	12
	8		20	13
	9		22	15
	10			16
	11			17
	14			18
				19(1)
				23
				24
				25

Consider whether you agree with this classification of each section of the Bill of Rights. Consider also whether some of the sections could be classified as both a "liberty" and a "free government" protection.

Ely v. Thompson

Court of Appeals of Kentucky (1820)

10 Ky. 70

Opinion of the Court by Judge Mills.

This is an action of trespass, assault, battery and imprisonment, brought by a free person of color, against a justice of the peace and constable, in their individual characters. The justice pleaded his office, and the fact, that the plaintiff had lifted his hand in opposition to a white man, who had proved the fact before him, and that he had issued his warrant to apprehend the plaintiff, who was accordingly brought before him, and that he gave sentence that for the offence the plaintiff should receive thirty lashes on his bare back, according to an act of assembly in such cases provided, and avers this to be the same trespass in the declaration mentioned. The constable likewise justifies by alleging his office, and the execution of the warrant, and the infliction of the stripes, pursuant to the sentence of the justice.

To these pleas of the defendants, the plaintiff replied in avoidance, that he was a free person of color. To this replication the defendants demurred. The court below sustained the demurrer, and gave judgment for the defendants. To reverse this judgment, this writ of error is prosecuted.

The section of the statute relied on in these pleas, will be found in 2d Littell, 116, and reads as follows: "If any negro or mulatto, or Indian, bond or free, shall, at any time, lift his or her hand in opposition to any person not being a negro, mulatto or Indian, he or she, so offending, shall, for every such offence, proved by the oath of the party, before a justice of the peace of the county where such offence shall be committed, receive thirty lashes on his or her bare back, well laid on by order of such justice."

It is contended for the plaintiff in error, that this section of this statute is repealed by the act to suppress riots, routs, unlawful assemblies of the people, and breaches of the peace, which repeals all laws within its purview. And if it is not repealed, that it is contrary to the constitution of this state, and therefore void; and that in either case the justice or constable could not justify under it.

On the contrary it is contended, that this section is not repealed; and if it is not, that it is consistent with, and does not contravene any of, the provisions of the constitution, and that the legislature might adopt this punishment, notwithstanding its cruelty, with regard to white persons. But it is further contended, that although this section may contravene the provisions of the constitution, yet free persons of color are no parties to our political compact, and of course are not entitled to its privileges or shielded by its provisions, and that they are subject to any regulation which the legislature may adopt, although such regulations are contrary to the constitution in their terms. And, finally, it is insisted, that if all these points are against the defendants in error, yet the one being a judicial officer, can not be responsible for this error in judgment; and the other, being a ministerial officer, and not entitled to judge of the matter, but bound to execute process without enquiring into its validity, neither can be responsible.

The act to suppress riots, routs and unlawful assemblies of the people, which is passed as a substitute for another of the same nature, previously adopted, does repeal all acts coming within its purview. The fair construction of this repealing clause is, that it repeals all statutes which provide punishments for the same offences; the punishment of which is fixed by that act. * * * We are then of the opinion, that the statute relied on by the defendants, was repealed as to all affrays, assaults and batteries, committed by free persons of color, and that their case comes under the latter act.

We have before said, that the act relied on by the defendants, included within it affrays, assaults and batteries by free persons of color. But it in fact includes far more, and affrays, assaults and batteries are not the only offences which come within its letter, and therefore as to these other offences it is not repealed. Its expression, "lift his or her hand in opposition to any person," includes many acts which will not be either an affray or assault or battery. It is not necessary, according to the letter of the act, that this lifting of "hand in opposition," should be so directly against the person as to commit either. It is not necessary that it should be done in an angry or threatening manner. It may be done in self defence, or in warding off injury, or in repelling attempts on the virtue of the female of color, by an intended ravisher. Another remarkable feature exists in the act. The proof is pointed out. The oath of the party complaining is conclusive, and the justice must inflict the punishment, although the proof may be untrue, and he disbelieves it. This extensive nature of the act imposes upon us the disagreeable necessity of deciding upon its constitutionality, so far as it operates on free persons of color.

In deciding this question, we shall not long descant upon the severity of the act, and its want of those mild features which characterize the rest of our code; nor can they have much influence in deciding this question. For however severe, cruel and rigorous its features may be, if it does not contravene the constitution, it must be executed, till the legislative power of the government shall see cause to change it. It would, however, be difficult to exempt this section from the imputation of cruelty, within the meaning of the 15th section of the 10th article of the constitution, so far as the act subjects a free person of color to thirty lashes for lifting his hand in oppression to a white person who was attempting wantonly to violate his or her person, contrary to the peace and good order of society. That section provides, "That excessive bail shall not be required, nor excessive fines imposed, nor cruel punishments inflicted." If a justice of the peace, or any other tribunal, should, under this act, inflict the stripes against a free person of color, who lifted his hand to save him or herself from death or severe bodily harm, all men must pronounce the punishment cruel indeed. Several clauses of the constitution have been quoted, as repugnant to this statute. We shall, however, content ourselves with one more, and that is the 10th section of the 10th article, which provides, "That in all criminal prosecutions, the accused hath a right to be heard by himself and counsel; to demand the nature and cause of the accusation against him; to meet the witnesses face to face; to have compulsory process for obtaining witnesses in his favor; and in prosecutions by indictment or information, a speedy public trial by an impartial jury of the vicinage; that he can not be compelled to give evidence against himself, nor can he be deprived of his life, liberty, or property, unless by the judgment of his peers, or the law of the land." It is evident that this section contemplates more kinds of public or criminal prosecutions, than those which are carried on by indictment or information. In all, it secures the right of being heard; of obtaining the nature and cause of the accusation; of confronting the witnesses, and disproving their evidence: In those by indictment or information, a trial by jury is secured. Determining what is the meaning of, and included in, the words "criminal prosecutions," in this section, measurably controls he whole section. They evidently mean, any prosecution carried on in the name of the commonwealth, for any offence or crime against society. The word "criminal" is used as opposed to civil suits or actions. The one includes all suits of the government, the end and design of which is the punishment of the accused; the other embraces all actions for individual redress. If this be not the meaning of the words, and they are designed to embrace the quality of those offences only of deeper dye and greater magnitude, usually denominated crimes, the section then absurdly makes a distinction between the whole class and those prosecuted by indictment or information. For all those greater crimes are so prosecuted, and the convention must be convicted of the absurdity of first providing for all, and then for a particular class, which included all. The act then in question, as it subjects the free person of color to punishment, on the oath of the party, without trial, and without the possibility of contradicting and disproving his statements, is against both the letter and spirit of the constitution, and, of course, so far as it is not repealed, it has no force, and could furnish no defence or justification to the defendants in error.

But we are still met by the argument, that free persons of color are not parties to the political compact. This we can not admit, to the extent contended for. They are certainly, in some measure, parties. Although they have not every benefit or privilege which the constitution secures, yet they have many secured by it. We need not take the trouble of inquiring how far they are, or are not, parties. For, suppose the premises are admitted, the conclusion would not follow that the legislature had a right to do with them as it chose, and that their acts on that subject could never be brought to a constitutional test. Although they are not parties to the compact, yet they are entitled to repose under its shadow, and thus secure themselves from the heated vengeance of the organs of government. Aliens, who sojourn here, and belong to another, and claim nothing of our government, but the right of passage, could not be taken up and hung by a justice of the peace, without a hearing, without an opportunity of proving themselves innocent, and without a jury, even if the legislature, by a solemn act, should direct it to be done. The tenth section of the constitution, which we have quoted, restricts the powers of the legislature and every department of government. The powers which they are therein forbidden to exercise, they do not possess, and can not exercise over any man or class of men, be they aliens, free persons of color, or citizens. This is demonstrable from the last section of that article, which declares, "that every thing, in this article, is excepted out of the general powers of government, and shall forever remain inviolate; and that all laws contrary thereto, on contrary to this constitution, shall be void." But it is still insisted, that notwithstanding all this, the judicial act of one of the defendants, and executive character of the other, ought to secure them from this action.

It is very true, that a judicial officer can not be punished for errors in judgment, on subjects within the scope of his authority, and over which he has jurisdiction. But this does not hold good when he attempts to exercise authority when he has none, and assumes jurisdiction without any power. Hence it was decided in the case of *Kennedy v. Terrill and Duley*, Hard. 490, that a justice of the peace was liable for issuing a warrant unknown to the provisions of the law. If this doctrine be correct, in the case of an illegal warrant, how much more so ought it to be in a case where the constitution is violated? It is an instrument that every officer of government is bound to know and preserve, at his peril, whether his office be judicial or ministerial; and he can not justify an act against its provisions, even with the authority of the legislature to aid him, however much that may mitigate his case.

The judgment of the court below must, therefore, be reversed with costs, and the cause remanded, with directions to overrule the demurrer, and for new proceedings to be had consistent with this opinion.

Notes and Questions

1. *Ely* was decided in 1820, while the second of Kentucky's four constitutions was in effect. The opinion quotes several provisions of the second constitution, which closely mirror sections of the Kentucky Constitution of 1891. *Cf.* Ky. Const. §§11, 17, 26.
2. Decided prior to the Civil War, and while slavery was still legal in Kentucky, *Ely* is remarkable in that it declares that the civil rights of free persons of color were equivalent to those of white citizens: "[T]hey are entitled to repose under [the constitution's] shadow, and thus secure themselves from the heated vengeance of the organs of government." Note that, rather than viewing the applicable sections of the Bill of Rights as conferring individual rights, the *Ely* Court conceived of those sections as a restraint on, or denial of, the powers of the government. ("The powers which [the government in the Bill of Rights is] forbidden to exercise, they do not possess, and can not exercise over any man or class of men, be they aliens, free persons of color, or citizens.") Would the outcome of the case have been the same if the Court construes those sections as conferring individual rights to citizens?

Short v. Commonwealth

Court of Appeals of Kentucky (1975)
519 S.W.2d 828

Opinion of the Court by Commissioner Catinna.

Carter Mitchell Short appeals from a judgment entered after a trial before the Fayette Circuit Court, without the intervention of a jury, by which he was found guilty of housebreaking and robbery and his punishment fixed at two years' imprisonment on each count. Short asserts that reversible error was committed in that (1) upon his plea of not guilty he could not waive his right to a jury trial because this would violate Section 7 of the Constitution of the Commonwealth; (2) he was not competent to knowingly and intelligently waive a jury trial; (3) the trial court should not have admitted a confession that had been procured without a prior waiver of his Miranda rights; (4) the confession had been procured under circumstances that made it totally untrustworthy; and (5) he should have been found not guilty by reason of diminished capacity.

On December 2, 1973, Short, along with three companions, went to the home of Mrs. Willie Lawson intending to take her Mustang automobile. When they determined that Mrs. Lawson was not there, they broke in and ransacked the house. When Mrs. Lawson returned, the intruders overpowered her and bound her with a rope. Money was removed from her purse and a watch and ring were taken. The four men then took the Lawson car and drove it to northern Kentucky. Mrs. Lawson recognized Short as one of the intruders. When Short returned to Lexington, he was arrested. While in custody, Short signed a written confession that had been prepared by Lt. Arnett of the Lexington Metropolitan Police Department.

Short entered a plea of not guilty and prior to trial filed a motion requesting an order allowing him to waive his right to trial by jury. In open court Short and his attorney again requested the trial court to try the case without a jury; the Commonwealth also agreed to trial without a jury. By agreement of all parties concerned, the court tried Short without the intervention of a jury and found him guilty of house-breaking and robbery. Short asserts that the right to a jury trial guaranteed by Section 7 of the Kentucky Constitution is inviolate and cannot be waived; therefore, the trial court erred in granting his motion for a trial without a jury. Following this argument to its logical conclusion would establish the rule that under no circumstances could the accused waive a jury trial in a criminal proceeding, whether he be charged with a felony or misdemeanor, for such was the common law of England prior to March 24, 1967. *Cf.* Kentucky Constitution, Section 233; *Aetna Insurance Company v. Commonwealth*, 106 Ky. 864, 51 S.W. 624 (1899).

Section 7 of the Kentucky Constitution provides:

> 'The ancient mode of trial by jury shall be held sacred, and the right thereof remain inviolate, subject to such modifications as may be authorized by this constitution.'

The only modification of this right to be found in the Constitution is the provision of Section 248 which authorizes a six-man jury in all civil and misdemeanor cases in courts inferior to the circuit courts.

In *Wendling v. Commonwealth*, 143 Ky. 587, 137 S.W. 205, (1911), we said:

> '... when we wish to ascertain what is meant by the right of a trial by a jury as expressed in the Constitution, we turn for information to the common law, where the right originated and from whence it came to us. In looking to this source for information, we find it laid down in 3 Blackstone's Commentaries, p. 350 et seq., and in 1 Hale's Pleas of the Crown, p. 33, that the essential features of a trial by a jury were the right of an accused in a criminal or penal case to demand, when put upon his trial in a court of justice presided over by a judge, that he be tried by a jury of 12 men, and that all of them should agree upon the verdict. These were the fundamental principles intended to be, and that have been, preserved inviolate.'

Although we have held that the constitutional right to a jury trial cannot be waived in felony cases, an aura of uncertainty pervades the soundness of our reasoning. In fact, we have never been required to meet 'head on' the claim that an accused in a felony case may waive his right to a jury trial and have the question of his guilt or innocence submitted to the court. A majority of our cases that have been cited as authority for the proposition that an accused may not waive a jury trial concern not the jury in its entirety but other facets of a jury trial. We have held that an accused may not agree to a trial by a jury composed of less than the constitutionally required 12 members. *Branham v. Commonwealth*, 209 Ky. 734, 273 S.W. 489 (1925), seven jurors; *Jackson v. Commonwealth*, 221 Ky. 823, 299 S.W. 983 (1927), eleven jurors; *Allison v. Gray*, Ky., 296 S.W.2d 735 (1956).

In *McPerkin v. Commonwealth*, 236 Ky. 528, 33 S.W.2d 622 (1931), and *Hayes v. Commonwealth*, Ky., 470 S.W.2d 601 (1971), we examined the 'other side of the coin' and held that there was nothing in the Kentucky Constitution which granted an accused the unqualified right to be tried by a judge without the intervention of a jury. Two of our more recent cases say that the constitutional right to a jury trial cannot be waived in a felony case; however, in neither case was the right to waive an issue before the court.

The only issue on appeal in *Tackett v. Commonwealth*, Ky., 320 S.W.2d 299 (1959), concerned the sufficiency of the evidence. The record disclosed that Tackett had waived trial by jury. However, the constitutionality of this waiver was not put in issue by the parties. The court, having concluded that this question required consideration, held that the right to a jury trial as guaranteed by Kentucky Constitution Section 7 could not be waived in a felony case.

Meyer v. Commonwealth, Ky., 472 S.W.2d 479 (1971), questioned, among other grounds, the manner of selecting a jury to try a capital offense. No effort was made to waive a jury trial or agree to a trial by a jury of less than 12 members. In discussing the rights of an accused in a murder trial, the opinion stated:

> 'Of course, the Commonwealth may waive its right to demand the death penalty. The defendant may not waive jury trial when he enters a plea of not guilty.'

The common-law doctrine that an accused could not waive a jury trial arose in those days when the accused could not testify in his own behalf, was not allowed counsel, and was punished, if convicted, by the death penalty or some other grievous punishment out of all proportion to the gravity of his crime. Our present system of criminal justice has, to a great extent, eliminated the harshness of the common-law system. Constitutional protection of the rights of an accused is now so extensive that the prohibition against waiver is no longer essential.

The rationale of the doctrine that an accused could waive nothing is one of the primary concepts of our Bill of Rights. However, as our present system of criminal jurisprudence has evolved, the strict prohibition against any type of waiver has been modified to the extent that an accused may by his own act waive the protective aspects of an otherwise guaranteed constitutional right. We have recognized the right of an accused to waive a jury by pleading guilty. *Lee v. Buchanan*, Ky., 264 S.W.2d 661 (1954); *Allison v. Gray*, Ky., 296 S.W.2d 735 (1956). In is well established that a jury trial may be waived in a misdemeanor case. *Ashton v. Commonwealth*, Ky., 405 S.W.2d 562 (1966). An accused may also waive his right to freedom from self-incrimination, Kentucky Constitution Section 11, *Jasper v. Commonwealth*, Ky., 471 S.W.2d 7 (1971); his right against unreasonable search and seizure, Kentucky Constitution Section 10, *Fugate v. Commonwealth*, 294 Ky. 410, 171 S.W.2d 1020 (1943), *Hall v. Commonwealth*, Ky., 261 S.W.2d 677 (1953); his right to counsel, Kentucky Constitution Section 11, *Carson v. Commonwealth*, Ky., 382 S.W.2d 85 (1964); and in misdemeanor cases, the right to a unanimous verdict by the jury, *Ashton v. Commonwealth*, Ky., 405 S.W.2d 562 (1966).

An examination of the rule in those jurisdictions having a constitutionally guaranteed right to a jury trial similar to that of the Kentucky Constitution discloses that a majority of them now allow an accused to waive a jury trial on the question of guilt or innocence. * * * We have concluded that current constitutional safeguards are so comprehensive that there remains no further necessity for the rule that an accused may not waive a jury trial. We have long held that an accused in a misdemeanor case could waive a jury trial; agree to a trial by a jury composed of less than the 12-member common-law jury required by the Constitution; and agree that the jury verdict need not be unanimous. In *Ashton v. Commonwealth*, Ky., 405 S.W.2d 562 (1966), we held that an agreement allowing other than a unanimous verdict in a misdemeanor case did not encroach upon the constitutional rights of the accused. In so holding, we reasoned:

> 'We think the time has come to abandon the romantic aspects of the ancient mode of trial by jury and consider the matter pragmatically. No one questions the right of a defendant in a criminal case to invoke the protection of any or all of his constitutional rights. On the other hand, we can find no sound reason to deny him the right of waiving procedural requirements which exist principally for his benefit. We have recognized that he can waive a jury completely by pleading guilty. He can waive the right to counsel, the right to freedom from self-incrimination, the right to have excluded evidence obtained by unreasonable search or seizure, and at least in misdemeanor cases, the right to a 12-man jury.

On what logical basis is unanimity a more sacred right?

> 'It is true this Court has heretofore adhered to the theory that in a felony case the defendant cannot waive a 12-man jury. *Branham v. Commonwealth*, 209 Ky. 734, 274 S.W. 489; *Tackett v. Commonwealth*, Ky., 320 S.W.2d 299. A serious question may be raised as to whether a valid distinction can be made between the waiver of defendant's rights in felony cases on the one hand and misdemeanors on the other. *See Patton v. United States*, 281 U.S. 276, 50 S.Ct. 253, 74 L.Ed. 854; Waiver of Trial Jury in Felony Cases in Kentucky, 48 Ky.L.Journal 457. We do not have that question here and will not re-examine it.
>
> 'It is our conviction that at least in misdemeanor cases the defendant may waive not only a 12-man jury but unanimity of the jurors in reaching their verdict, provided always that such waiver agreement is entered into understandingly and voluntarily, and provided of course the Commonwealth agrees and the trial court approves. Since no suggestion is made that the defendant in this case did not understandingly and voluntarily enter into the agreement to accept a majority verdict (and our solicitude for the rights of the defendant

> can be maintained by careful scrutiny of these two conditions), he was bound by his agreement. We find no error here.'

There is no reason for the continued distinction between the rights of the accused charged with a misdemeanor and the accused charged with a felony. Both of them enjoy equal constitutional protection under Section 7 of our Constitution. The Supreme Court said in *Patton v. United States*, 281 U.S. 276, 309, 50 S.Ct. 253, 262, 74 L.Ed. 854 (1930):

> '... We are unable to find in the decisions any convincing ground for holding that a waiver is effective in misdemeanor cases, but not effective in the case of felonies....'

This court is of the opinion that there is nothing in the Kentucky Constitution which denies an accused the right to waive a jury trial. The reasoning and guidelines of *Ashton v. Commonwealth, supra*, shall hereafter govern the waiver of a jury trial in felony cases. The prerequisites of a valid waiver, as set out in *Patton v. United States, supra*, at page 312, 50 S.Ct. at page 263, are:

> 'In affirming the power of the defendant in any criminal case to waive a trial by a constitutional jury and submit to trial by a jury of less than twelve persons, or by the court, we do not mean to hold that the waiver must be put into effect at all events. That perhaps sufficiently appears already. Trial by jury is the normal and, with occasional exceptions, the preferable mode of disposing of issues of fact in criminal cases above the grade of petty offenses. In such cases the value and appropriateness of jury trial have been established by long experience, and are not now to be denied. Not only must the right of the accused to a trial by a constitutional jury be jealously preserved, but the maintenance of the jury as a fact finding body in criminal cases is of such importance and has such a place in our traditions, that, before any waiver can become effective, the consent of government counsel and the sanction of the court must be had, in addition to the express and intelligent consent of the defendant. And the duty of the trial court in that regard is not to be discharged as a mere matter of rote, but with sound and advised discretion, with an eye to avoid unreasonable or undue departures from that mode of trial or from any of the essential elements thereof, and with a caution increasing in degree as the offenses dealt with increase in gravity.'

Branham v. Commonwealth, 209 Ky. 734, 273 S.W. 489 (1925); *Jackson v. Commonwealth*, 221 Ky. 823, 299 S.W. 983 (1927); *Allison v. Gray*, Ky., 296 S.W.2d 735 (1956); *Tackett v. Commonwealth*, Ky., 320 S.W.2d 299 (1959); *Meyer v. Commonwealth*, Ky., 472 S.W.2d 479 (1971); and all other cases holding that an accused may not waive a jury trial in felony cases or agree to a trial by a jury of less than 12 members are hereby overruled.

In determining whether a waiver of a jury trial is made understandingly, intelligently, competently, and voluntarily, the court must apply the same standards that are required on the acceptance of a guilty plea. The record made at the hearing preceding the acceptance of a waiver by the court must affirmatively set out facts which will permit an independent determination of its validity. *Cf. Boykin v. Alabama*, 395 U.S. 238, 89 S.Ct. 1709, 23 L.Ed.2d 274 (1969); *Raymer v. Commonwealth*, Ky., 489 S.W.2d 831 (1973); *Lucas v. Commonwealth*, Ky., 465 S.W.2d 267 (1971); *Patton v. United States*, 281 U.S. 276, 50 S.Ct. 253, 74 L.Ed. 854 (1930).

The totality of the evidence before the trial court discloses that Short was competent to stand trial and participate in his defense. This being so, it would be anomalous to say he could not waive a jury trial or his *Miranda* rights. (*Miranda v. Arizona*, 384 U.S. 436, 86 S.Ct. 1602, 16 L.Ed.2d 694.) Finally, there is no merit in the other errors asserted by Short.

The judgment is affirmed.

All concur.

Notes and Questions

1. The Supreme Court of Kentucky observed in *Commonwealth v. Green*, 194 S.W.3d 277, 283–84 (Ky. 2006), "In *Short v. Commonwealth*, 519 S.W.2d 828 (Ky. 1975), our predecessor court held that a felony defendant was entitled to waive his right to a jury trial, although that opinion included an important caveat: 'the maintenance of the jury as a fact finding body in criminal cases is of such importance and has such a place in our traditions, that, before any waiver can become effective, the consent of government counsel and the sanction of the court must be had, in addition to the express and intelligent consent of the defendant.' *Id.* at 833. After *Short*, therefore, criminal defendants in Kentucky, whether charged with a misdemeanor or felony, were permitted to waive their right to trial by jury, provided that such waiver was approved by both the Commonwealth and the trial court. In 1981, we adopted the current [Kentucky Rule of Criminal Procedure (RCr)] 9.26 'which essentially codifies the holding in *Short*....' *Jackson* [*v. Commonwealth*], 113 S.W.3d [128,] 131–32 [(Ky. 2003)]." RCr 9.26(1) now provides, "Cases required to be tried by jury shall be so tried unless the defendant waives a jury trial in writing with the approval of the court and the consent of the Commonwealth."
2. Under *Short* and similar cases, the rights protected by the Bill of Rights are waivable. These cases have as a starting point the position that these rights belong to the individual, so that it is the individual who decides whether to assert them, or not. However, taking another view (as mentioned at the beginning of this chapter), some of the provisions of the Bill of Rights could be understood as "free government" provisions that provide explicit instructions to the government regarding how it operates or how it engages with its citizens. Is that an appropriate understanding of these provisions?
3. After outlining several individual rights of the accused in a criminal case, Section 11 then says the accused "shall have a speedy public trial by an impartial jury of the vicinage." Notwithstanding the holding of *Short*, is this portion of Section 11 a command to the government, as opposed to a right held by the individual? If so, can the protections afforded by those provisions be waived by the individual?

Malone v. Commonwealth

Supreme Court of Kentucky (2000)

30 S.W.3d 180

OPINION OF THE COURT BY JUSTICE GRAVES.

I. Facts

Based on a plea of guilty, Appellant, Gilbert Dewayne Malone, was convicted of three felonies in the Jefferson Circuit Court. Malone appealed the convictions on the ground that he was prosecuted by information rather than by indictment. On its own motion, the Court of Appeals requested transfer of the matter to this Court. The only issue before us is whether a circuit court has authority to adjudicate felony charges if the defendant waives his right to be prosecuted by indictment. That is, whether the constitutional requirement of an indictment by a grand jury in a prosecution for a felony preempts a court rule which permits a prosecution upon information if the accused so elects.

II. Kentucky Constitution

The preamble to the Kentucky Constitution states the reasons for and purposes of the document. Our Kentucky preamble is brief and simple:

> We, the people of the Commonwealth of Kentucky, grateful to Almighty God for the civil, political and religious liberties we enjoy, and invoking the continuance of these blessings, do ordain and establish this Constitution.

The bill of rights is contained in Sections 1 through 26 of Kentucky's Constitution.

The guarantees of the Kentucky Bill of Rights are derived from the centuries-old struggle of Englishmen to gain personal freedom. The purpose of a bill of rights is to protect individuals from the arbitrary actions of government decision-makers. Among the rights specifically protected in Kentucky's Constitution is not only the right to have a grand jury indictment as a prerequisite to a felony prosecution, but also the right to a jury trial.

Section 12 of the Kentucky Constitution serves as a check on arbitrary government prosecution by providing that:

> No person, for an indictable offense, shall be proceeded against criminally by information, except in cases arising in the land or naval forces, or in the militia, when in actual service, in time of war or public danger, or by leave of court for oppression or misdemeanor in office.

III. The Grand Jury

A review of typical Kentucky grand jury procedure is helpful. The prosecutor initiates a grand jury investigation upon evidence of wrongdoing, no matter how slight. The grand jury subsequently must assess whether probable cause exists to believe that a crime has been committed. The prosecutor assists the grand jury investigation and in determining which witnesses the grand jury will subpoena, selecting the documents or evidence presented and criminal charges pursued, as well as explaining the law and instructing the grand jury on burden of proof. The grand jury is unable to conduct independent investigations inside the grand jury room. If sufficient evidence of commission of a crime is found, a grand jury may return an indictment but is not constitutionally required to do so. If no indictment is returned, constituting a "no true bill," the prosecutor may resubmit the case to another grand jury. Double jeopardy or collateral estoppel defenses do not apply to multiple grand jury proceedings. Grand jury proceedings are conducted in secret, with only the jurors, prosecutor, witnesses, stenographer, recording device operator or interpreter present.

The indictment is the formal written accusation of a crime, made by a grand jury, and presented to the court for prosecution against the accused person. An indictment issued by a grand jury is merely a charge of commission of a crime and is not any evidence of guilt. Before an individual may be convicted, the charge must be proved beyond a reasonable doubt. The purpose for an indictment is merely to inform an accused individual of the essential facts of the charge against him so he will be able to prepare a defense.

The Waiver of Grand Jury Indictment which Malone signed reads, in part, as follows:

> I understand that by agreeing to the filing of an information in the Circuit Court I am waiving and giving up my right to have the case presented to the Jefferson County Grand Jury and my right to have any felony charges against me in Jefferson County by indictment only. I understand that the Commonwealth may not proceed against me by information without this waiver. After consultation with my attorney I elect to give up my Kentucky constitutional right [Section 12 of the Kentucky Constitution] to have these charges initiated by the indictment and hereby give the written notice to the circuit court of my intention to allow this prosecution by information as provided in RCr 6.02.

IV. Circuit Court Jurisdiction

Jurisdiction is a court's power to decide a case. As a prerequisite for presiding over the case, a court must have jurisdiction of the subject matter of an offense and of the person of the defendant. That is, two jurisdictional requirements must be satisfied before a court has authority to hear and determine a particular cause of action. Kentucky Constitution Sec. 112(5) and KRS 23A.010(1) gives the circuit court jurisdiction of felony offenses.

A criminal prosecution requires the existence of an accusation charging the commission of an offense. Such an accusation either in the form of an indictment or an information, is an essential requisite of jurisdiction. In Kentucky, subject matter jurisdiction over a felony offense may be invoked either by a grand jury indictment or by information in cases where the individual consents. Information is an agreement between the state and the individual to proceed without the formalities of a grand jury indictment.

V. Notice of Accusation of a Crime

Substantive due process requires that a defendant be informed of the acts alleged as criminal and the crime with which he is charged. The right to waive a particular form, mode, or kind of accusation in a particular instance is an individual right of the accused. It is a personal privilege that may be waived. Every accused person still enjoys an absolute procedural due process right to be prosecuted by indictment. However, he can be prosecuted by information if he knowingly waives that right.

The purpose of proceeding by information rather than by indictment is to expedite matters for the benefit of alleged offenders who desire such expedition. Although it is designed primarily for the benefit of persons who have no defense, and who wish to plead guilty and begin service of their sentence without awaiting indictment by a grand jury, it is not confined to such persons, and an individual may waive indictment though he or she intends to plead not guilty. The rules governing prosecution by information are identical to those relating to prosecution by indictment.

VI. Kentucky Rules of Criminal Procedure

RCr 6.02 of the 1981 amendments to the Kentucky Rules of Criminal Procedure enable the defendant to waive indictment and consent instead to be proceeded against by information. The provision that no person shall be proceeded against by information for an indictable offense is part of the Bill of Rights and not mentioned in the judicial article. It is reasonably clear that this provision is not jurisdictional, rather it is for the protection of the accused and hence subject to waiver.

VII. Use of Informations in Other Jurisdictions

Federal courts have held that a similar provision in the Fifth Amendment is a personal right which may be waived. * * * The constitutionality of the waiver provision is thoroughly settled. This is quite analogous to other situations in which a defendant is allowed to waive procedural protections provided for his or her benefit. * * *

Provisions to the effect that no person shall be held or required to answer, or held for or put upon trial, for a criminal offense, or for a specified kind or grade of offense, except by or upon indictment have been construed, in most jurisdictions as not being mandatory or jurisdictional in character but merely conferring a personal privilege which may be waived. * * *

VIII. Waiver of Procedural Due Process Right

Section 12 of the Kentucky Constitution providing for accusation of felony offenses by indictment is itself a matter of substantive due process, but the manner of waiving that right and of consenting to be prosecuted instead by information is a matter of procedural due process. Substantive due process is satisfied by giving the accused written notice of the elements of the offense with which he is charged. Consequently, there is no constitutional barrier to such waiver being authorized by court rule.

Waiving the formalities of a grand jury indictment is analogous to waiving the right of trial by jury in criminal cases. Both are personal rights which may be waived. *Short v. Commonwealth*, Ky., 519 S.W.2d 828 (1975).

In *Patton v. United States,* 281 U.S. 276, 50 S.Ct. 253, 258, 74 L.Ed. 854 (1930), the United States Supreme Court held that the right to trial by jury "is not jurisdictional, but was meant to confer a right upon the accused which he may forego at his election. To deny his power to do so is to convert a privilege into an imperative requirement."

Inasmuch as an accused can plead guilty to a crime and waive the right to a trial by jury, we perceive no constitutional violation or prejudice to an accused by allowing an individual to state that he neither needs nor desires the protection of formal action by the grand jury in a particular proceeding. By pleading guilty and giving up a jury trial, the accused waives a greater right than accusation by formal indictment.

The judgment of the Jefferson Circuit Court is hereby affirmed.

Cooper, Graves, Johnstone, Keller, and Wintersheimer, J.J., concur.

Stumbo, J., dissents in a separate opinion in which Lambert, C.J., joins.

Justice Stumbo, dissenting.

Section 12 of the Kentucky constitution provides as follows:

> No person, for an indictable offense, shall be proceeded against criminally by information, except in cases arising in the land or naval forces, or in the militia, when in the actual service in time of war or public danger, by leave of court for oppression or misdemeanor in office.

An indictable offense is defined as one that carries an infamous punishment which includes offenses punishable by imprisonment in the state penitentiary. *Lakes v. Goodloe,* Ky. 195 Ky. 240, 242 S.W. 632 (1922). An indictment is of fundamental importance in the criminal process because it determines both the subject matter jurisdiction of the trial court and the status of the accused. *Commonwealth v. Adams,* Ky., 17 S.W. 276 (1891); *King v. City of Pineville,* Ky., 222 Ky. 73, 299 S.W. 1082 (1927); *Singleton v. Commonwealth,* Ky., 306 Ky. 454, 208 S.W.2d 325 (1948).

The jurisdiction conferred by an indictment extends only to the offense charged and any lesser included offense. *Cody v. Commonwealth,* Ky., 449 S.W.2d 749, 751 (1970). The indictment has been held not to be subject to waiver. *Commonwealth v. Adams,* Ky., 17 S.W. 276, 277 (1891). To quote *Commonwealth v. Adams*:

> The law creates courts and defines their powers. Consent [by the accused] can not authorize a judge to do what the law has not given him the power to do.... It is the sole province of the grand jury, under our law, to find an indictment. It, and not the court, must say upon what charge the party shall be arraigned.

Id., 17 S.W. at 277.

RCr 6.02(1) permits the waiver of an indictment by the defendant, requiring only that same be in writing. The rule itself specifically refers to Section 12, noting that the Constitution requires that certain offenses be prosecuted by indictment. That rule was promulgated by the authority given to us in Section 116, which gives to the Supreme Court the power to prescribe the rules of practice and procedure for the Court of Justice. To my mind, practice and procedure simply do not rise to the level of a guaranteed constitutional right to face only those charges with an infamous punishment that have passed through the Grand Jury process. Practice and procedure tell you how to prosecute a charge, not which court has the authority to pass judgment on it. The power granted to this Court by Section 116 does not, in my view, additionally give us the power to determine that a separate section of the same Constitution need not be preserved and followed. I would hold that RCr 6.02(1) is unconstitutional and, therefore, the judgment appealed from is void as it has no constitutionally valid basis.

Lambert, C.J., concurs.

Notes and Questions

1. Kentucky Rule of Criminal Procedure (RCr) 6.02, to which both the *Malone* majority and the dissent refer, states:

   (1) All offenses required to be prosecuted by indictment pursuant to Section 12 of the Kentucky Constitution shall be prosecuted by indictment unless the defendant waives indictment by notice in writing to the circuit court, in which event the offense may be prosecuted forthwith by information.

   (2) All other offenses shall be prosecuted by indictment, information, complaint, post-arrest complaint, or, in the case of traffic offenses or fish and wildlife offenses, may be prosecuted by uniform citation.

2. Justice Graves's opinion for the 5–2 *Malone* majority held that Section 12's requirement of a grand jury indictment as a prerequisite to a felony prosecution may be waived by a criminal defendant who chooses to allow the prosecution to proceed by information. Justice Stumbo argued in dissent that RCr 6.02 is unconstitutional in that it permits the defendant to waive Section 12's protections, thus signaling a belief that Section 12 represents a constitutional directive to the government rather than an individual right. Which view do you believe to be correct, and why?

Crutcher v. Commonwealth

Supreme Court of Kentucky (2016)

500 S.W.3d 811

Opinion of the Court by Chief Justice Minton.

A Circuit Court jury convicted Anthony Wayne Crutcher of first-degree robbery and of being a first-degree persistent felony offender (PFO I). The jury recommended a sentence of 15 years' imprisonment for the robbery conviction, enhanced to 35 years for the PFO I conviction. Crutcher appeals as a matter of right, arguing the trial court violated his right to a public trial when it removed all spectators during the victim's testimony and when it denied Crutcher's motion to suppress a photo identification. Having reviewed the record and the arguments of the parties, we affirm the judgment of the trial court.

I. Background.

Ricky Goldsmith testified that three men—later identified as Jamaur Yocum, Crutcher, and a man known only by the nickname "SD"—approached him in an apartment breezeway and asked him to sell them marijuana. Goldsmith went into the apartment he shared with his girlfriend, got a "dime bag," and returned to the breezeway. Crutcher pulled out a handgun and pointed it at Goldsmith. Yocum and Crutcher went through Goldsmith's pockets, taking $100, the marijuana, and other items. Yocum then ran and Crutcher told Goldsmith to turn around and run. * * * Goldsmith did so and, when he was about two steps away, Crutcher shot him in the shoulder. Goldsmith then ran to a nearby apartment building, and a neighbor called the police and EMS. Emergency personnel transported Goldsmith to a hospital where he was treated for his wound and released. SD did not participate in the robbery.

In an interview with police that night, Goldsmith stated that someone named "Yocum," whom he had seen around the neighborhood, had participated in the robbery. Goldsmith could not identify either Crutcher or SD. Shortly thereafter, Goldsmith, who said he was too afraid to stay in town, moved * * * away.

Months later, another police officer, Kyle Toms, tracked down Goldsmith and asked him to come to the department to try to identify "Yocum." Officer Toms put together a six-picture photo lineup from which Goldsmith identified Yocum as one of the men who robbed him.

While talking to Officer Toms, Goldsmith stated that a relative told him that someone named "Little Anthony" had been the shooter. Officer Toms found Crutcher's photo by using that nickname to search the department's database. Officer Toms then used the department's database to put together a photo lineup that included Crutcher's photo. Goldsmith picked Crutcher's photo from the lineup and identified him as the shooter.

Yocum and Crutcher were arrested and charged with the robbery. Yocum pled guilty, but Crutcher, who insisted that he was not present during the robbery, went to trial. After hearing testimony from Yocum, the two police officers, Goldsmith's emergency room physician, and Goldsmith, a jury convicted Crutcher of first-degree robbery and of being a PFO. We set forth additional facts as necessary below.

* * *

III. Analysis.

A. Denial of Public Trial.

When the Commonwealth called Goldsmith as a witness, the trial court's bailiff and counsel approached the bench. The bailiff stated that an officer who was outside the courtroom advised him that Goldsmith was reluctant to testify because a person in the courtroom had threatened Goldsmith. The bailiff stated that he did not know who had allegedly made the threat and that he was reluctant to investigate Goldsmith's statement without some direction from the trial court. The Commonwealth's attorney stated that: someone had threatened Goldsmith and "his family," Goldsmith was "terrified," and "[they] had a hard time getting him down here." The trial court then suggested clearing the courtroom while Goldsmith testified. The bailiff asked if people would be re-admitted after Goldsmith testified, and the trial court responded affirmatively. Crutcher's attorney stood silent while this conversation took place. The bailiff then cleared visitors from the courtroom and Goldsmith testified. Crutcher now argues that this violated his right to a public trial as guaranteed by the U.S. and Kentucky Constitutions. The Commonwealth argues that, by failing to object, Crutcher waived this argument for appeal and, in the alternative, that any error was not palpable. And we agree.

The Sixth Amendment to the United States Constitution guarantees all criminal defendants the ability to "enjoy the right to a speedy and public trial." A similar protection is included in Section 11 of the Kentucky Constitution, boldly declaring that "in all prosecutions by indictment or information, he [the accused] shall have a speedy public trial by an impartial jury of the vicinage." The right to public trial is, of course, primarily for the benefit of the accused, allowing the public to see that he is "fairly dealt with and not unjustly condemned, and that the presence of interested spectators may keep his triers keenly alive to a sense of their responsibility and to the importance of their functions." *Waller v. Georgia*, 467 U.S. 39, 46, 104 S.Ct. 2210, 81 L.Ed.2d 31 (1984). And we agree that public trials are foundational prerequisites to any American notion of due process of law, guaranteeing defendants a serious and fair tribunal, and disincentivizing courts of law from devolving into dystopian kangaroo courts. But we simply hold that this right may be waived through a defendant's failure to object.

In *Waller v. Georgia*, the United States Supreme Court articulated its four-part test for trial courts to administer when considering whether to close the courtroom *over a defendant's objection*. In other words, the Supreme Court held that if the courtroom is closed over the accused's objection, and the *Waller* test is not satisfied, the constitutionally enshrined right to public trial is violated. Under *Waller*, a court, when considering whether to close a trial or a portion of a trial to the public must consider three factors: (1) whether the party seeking to close the proceedings has "an overriding interest that is likely to be prejudiced;" (2) what the narrowest method of protecting that interest is; and (3) whether there are "reasonable alternatives to closing the proceedings." *Id.* at 48, 104 S.Ct. 2210. Once the court makes the determination to close the proceedings or a portion of the proceedings, "it must make findings adequate to support the closure." *Id.*

In this case, the trial court clearly did not engage in a *Waller* colloquy and did not address the prerequisite factors before ordering the courtroom briefly closed for Goldsmith's testimony. But unlike *Waller*, Crutcher failed to object to the closure. *Waller* is noticeably silent about instances where the defendant fails to object to the closure at all.

Despite *Waller*'s silence, Crutcher argues that waiver is unavailable in this situation, but he fails to present any federal or state case law in support of that proposition. And he ignores the plain reading of the Sixth Circuit's opinion in *Johnson v. Sherry*, authority we find highly persuasive, holding that a defendant may waive his right to public trial absent any express objection or compliance with the *Waller* test. 586 F.3d 439, 444 (6th Cir. 2009). In *Johnson*, not only did defense counsel fail to object, he actually consented to closing the courtroom. The panel-majority accordingly held that, "While we agree that the right to a public trial is an important structural right, it is also one that can be waived *when a defendant fails to object to the closure of the courtroom* ..." *Id.* (emphasis added). Obviously, Crutcher's attorney did not consent to closure. But this difference in form does not undermine the substance behind the *Johnson* Court's central holding that a defendant may waive his right to public trial through failure to preserve the issue for review.

* * *

Crutcher's understanding of waiver not only misreads *Johnson*, but it also undermines the Supreme Court's holding in *Waller*. If we are to accept his view that this right cannot be waived absent a knowing, voluntary, and intelligent waiver personally executed by the defendant, the *Waller* test itself may be unconstitutional. Assuming this right belongs in the company of others that require express waiver—right to counsel, *Miranda* warnings, etc.—the trial court is powerless to close the courtroom under any circumstances, *particularly* over a defendant's objection. Unless Crutcher also contends that the express-waiver characterization is also the improper measurement for public-trial rights, his understanding of the Sixth Amendment would preclude any type of deprivation of the right, without regard to whether the defendant chooses to object to the closure or not.

* * *

We understand that denial of a defendant's right to a public trial is considered a structural error. *See McCleery v. Commonwealth*, 410 S.W.3d 597, 604 (Ky. 2013). Structural errors, to be sure, undermine the overall integrity of the proceeding, and such mistakes warrant automatic reversal. *Id.* But the Sixth Circuit recognized that while *denial* of a defendant's right to public trial is quite clearly structural and worthy of automatic reversal, that standard has no bearing on whether that right may be waived, either through agreeing to the closure or by failing to raise an objection in the record. The structural-error analysis is only relevant once a defendant's right is denied; there is no denial of right when the defendant is complicit in its abrogation.

In effect, Crutcher's characterization of this right subtly undermines the validity of *Waller* in Kentucky law. The only way we can imagine reconciling this position with Kentucky law is essentially to declare that, in Kentucky, an accused's right to public trial is more robust than its federal counterpart. And that is something we are free to decide as a matter of state constitutional law, if we can conclude that our constitution includes a more expansive liberty than the baseline the Sixth Amendment requires. We are often receptive and interested in such arguments, but one was not presented to us today.

As the matter stands today, we see no reason for this issue to depart from our time-honored paradigm requiring parties who feel aggrieved by some action taken at the trial court to expend the minimal energy required to preserve that issue in the record. Excluding spectators from the courtroom is not an action of judicial legerdemain that can catch even an attentive attorney off balance. Rather, it is unmistakable; any attorney not asleep in his chair would understand the change in scenery and face the conscious decision of whether to state an objection to the trial court's decision. Defense counsel obviously chose not to object here, and we see no reason why it is our duty to do his job for him.

There is understandably extreme caution when it comes to waiving constitutional rights, and we express no hostility toward those rights already requiring express waiver. But there is nothing in today's case, in light of federal Sixth Amendment precedent, suggesting a defendant's right to public trial may not be waived by failure to object.

* * *

IV. Conclusion.

For the foregoing reasons, we affirm the trial court's judgment below on both issues.

All sitting. Minton, C.J., Cunningham, Hughes and Noble, JJ., concur. Venters, J., concurs by separate opinion in which Keller, and Wright, JJ., join.

Justice Venters, concurring:

I fully concur with the Majority opinion including the conclusion that Crutcher is entitled to no relief with respect to his belated discovery that the right to a public trial was somewhat abridged. I also agree that this is not the case to parse the difference between the public trial right protected by the Sixth Amendment of the United States Constitution and the corresponding right set forth in Section 11 of the Kentucky Constitution, but I write separately to highlight an important but subtle difference between the two.

Section 11 may not be "more robust than its federal counterpart," but it is different in a way that is worth noting. I suggest that under the Kentucky Constitution, the right to a public trial belongs to the people, the general citizenry; it does not belong exclusively to the defendant, and so the right to a public trial is not his to waive. A criminal defendant cannot waive the right to a public trial, although he may waive his right to complain on appeal about the denial of a public trial.

The Sixth Amendment provides in pertinent part, "In all criminal prosecutions, the accused shall enjoy the right to a … public trial." That language presents a clear manifestation of a right that is the defendant's to enjoy. In contrast, Section 11 of the Kentucky Constitution provides that "in all prosecutions … [the accused] shall have a speedy public trial." I take that language to mean the trial shall be public whether the defendant wants it that way or not. Section 11 makes it imperative that criminal trials are to be open to the public. It creates a right that belongs to the people, anyone of the general citizenry, to assure that no criminal adjudications take place behind closed doors regardless of the defendant's preference on the subject.

I do not diminish the usual interest of the accused to have a public trial. But in my view, the greater menace averted by Section 11 is the secret disposition of criminal cases without the public's knowledge. Section 11 protects the greater good of assuring that the public business of administering justice is done in the open for all to see. To that extent, I submit that Crutcher had no ability to waive the right to a public trial, but he certainly could, and he certainly did waive his right to complain about it.

Keller, and Wright, JJ., join.

Notes and Questions

1. Consider the following passage from *Lexington Herald Leader Co. v. Tackett*, 601 S.W.2d 905, 907 (Ky. 1980): "Courtrooms are kept open not so that members of the public can expose wrongdoings; rather, they are open to allow the citizens to see for themselves how their laws are impartially applied. It is to the benefit of a free society that judicial proceedings be publicly conducted. Not only are all citizens to be treated equally under the law they must be able to see that they are equally treated in their courts." Is this statement of the law—which was made by the Court in a case involving media access to a courtroom to watch a criminal trial—in tension with the holding in *Crutcher*?
2. The three concurring Justices found that the public trial right guaranteed by Section 11 is held by the "general citizenry," and not to an individual criminal defendant. They distinguish between a waiver of the right and a waiver of the right to complain about it on appeal. Do you find their reasoning persuasive? Is the individual-right view or publicly-held right view more consistent with the text of the Constitution?

B. Criminal Procedure

> "The people shall be secure in their persons, houses, papers and possessions, from unreasonable search and seizure; and no warrant shall issue to search any place, or seize any person or thing, without describing them as nearly as may be, nor without probable cause supported by oath or affirmation." (Ky. Const. §10.)
>
> "In all criminal prosecutions the accused has the right to be heard by himself and counsel; to demand the nature and cause of the accusation against him; to meet the witnesses face to face, and to have compulsory process for obtaining witnesses in his favor. He cannot be compelled to give evidence against himself, nor can he be deprived of his life, liberty or property, unless by the judgment of his peers or the law of the land; and in prosecutions by indictment or information, he shall have a speedy public trial by an impartial jury of the vicinage; but the General Assembly may provide by a general law for a change of venue in such prosecutions for both the defendant and the Commonwealth, the change to be made to the most convenient county in which a fair trial can be obtained." (Ky. Const. §11.)

> "No person, for an indictable offense, shall be proceeded against criminally by information, except in cases arising in the land or naval forces, or in the militia, when in actual service, in time of war or public danger, or by leave of court for oppression or misdemeanor in office." (Ky. Const. §12.)
>
> "No person shall, for the same offense, be twice put in jeopardy of his life or limb, nor shall any man's property be taken or applied to public use without the consent of his representatives, and without just compensation being previously made to him." (Ky. Const. §13.)

Sections 10 to 13 of the Kentucky Constitution bear a striking resemblance to the Fourth, Fifth, and Sixth Amendments to the U.S. Constitution. The coverage of the state provisions is similar to that of their federal counterparts. There are some differences between the state and federal constitutional texts, which sometimes lead the Kentucky courts to apply heightened protections for individual rights. But the cases below illustrate a general uneasiness on the part of the Supreme Court of Kentucky with interpreting the state constitution's protections of the accused in criminal cases differently than the U.S. Supreme Court interprets comparable provisions of the U.S. Constitution.

Section 10

Holbrook v. Knopf

Supreme Court of Kentucky (1992)
847 S.W.2d 52

Opinion of the Court by Justice Leibson.

Holbrook and Petty are codefendants under indictment in Jefferson Circuit Court for sex offenses arising out of a single criminal episode. The Commonwealth filed a motion asking the trial court to order both appellants to submit to the taking of "blood, head hair, body hair, saliva, and pubic hair specimen ... for testing and comparison with evidence gathered during the investigation into the rape, sodomy and sexual abuse charges placed against" them. The motion was supported by the affidavit of the Assistant Commonwealth's Attorney assigned to prosecute the case, representing that "unidentified semen and other trace evidence" had been gathered during the investigation of the case and that "physical specimens from [appellants] are imperative to the further investigation" of the case.

The trial court sustained the Commonwealth's motion, and the appellant, Holbrook, then filed an original action with the Kentucky Court of Appeals seeking an order prohibiting the trial judge from enforcing his order. Petty was joined as a real party in interest, and pursuant to subsequent motion has been designated as an additional appellant. The Court of Appeals denied the writ of prohibition, and this appeal followed, as a matter of right, to our Court. For reasons that follow we affirm the Court of Appeals' order denying the writ of prohibition.

The issue in this case is whether the Commonwealth, in a case of this nature, upon motion and affidavit supporting the potential relevancy of the evidence sought, may obtain an order requiring the defendant to submit to the involuntary taking of physical specimens from his person.

The appellants' argument is built on four interdependent premises, and fails if any one of the four is unreasonable:

1) That, unlike the Federal Constitution, Kentucky Constitution Section Ten (our search and seizure clause) applies only to searching places and not to searching persons.

2) That Kentucky Constitutional protection against searching persons (rather than places) depends on Section One analysis rather than Section Ten analysis.

3) That the Kentucky Constitution provides a "right of personal security" which is subject to reasonable regulation, but exclusively by act of the General Assembly.

4) That, therefore, absent a statute authorizing the procedure the judiciary lacks power to order a search procedure involving the person of the accused, however reasonable and safeguarded the procedure may be in terms of search and seizure analysis.

The Court of Appeals order does not explain its reason for denying the writ. Thus we are left to speculate whether the writ was denied on procedural grounds, because the trial court was acting within its jurisdiction and there was an adequate remedy by appeal (*See Green Valley Envtl. Corp. v. Clay*, Ky., 798 S.W.2d 141, 144 (1990)), or on substantive grounds because the Court of Appeals found no merit to the appellants' claim for relief.

The essence of the appellants' claim is that there is a state constitutional law "right of personal security" found in Section 1(1) of the Kentucky Constitution, which would be infringed by the taking of blood and body samples as part of a criminal investigation, a right which has "no analogue" in the Federal Constitution, and a right which can only be redressed by preventing the procedure rather than by suppressing the evidence thus obtained.

Section 1 of our Kentucky Constitution states:

> "All men are, by nature, free and equal, and have certain inherent and inalienable rights, among which may be reckoned:
>
> First: The right of enjoying and defending their lives and liberties."

Addressing first the procedural grounds, if our Court were in agreement that the taking of blood and body samples from the person of the appellants as ordered by the trial court in this case constituted a constitutionally impermissible intrusion into a constitutionally guaranteed right of personal security, we might well agree that suppressing evidence thus obtained would be an inadequate remedy. Since, however, we reject the merits of the appellants' arguments, we need not decide whether an extraordinary writ might be justified if the situation were otherwise.

Insofar as the taking of body samples may be viewed as an issue involving rights of the criminally accused protected by the Federal Constitution, the issue presented here was laid to rest in *Schmerber v. California*, 384 U.S. 757, 86 S.Ct. 1826, 16 L.Ed.2d 908 (1966). *Schmerber* upheld a state statute permitting a police officer to obtain a blood sample in connection with a drunken driving investigation, without a search warrant and despite the defendant's refusal to consent. The United States Supreme Court held the Fifth Amendment privilege against self-incrimination is testimonial and thus not implicated, and that the taking of blood is reasonably non-intrusive testing, a constitutionally permissible search within the Fourth Amendment test of reasonableness, stating "[s]uch testing procedures plainly constitute searches of 'persons,' and depend antecedently upon seizures of 'persons,' within the meaning of [the Fourth] Amendment." *Id.* at 918.

Schmerber was, of course, a warrantless search justified on the basis of "exigent circumstances," whereas the present testing takes on a different look because it is a post-indictment procedure searching for evidence pursuant to court order. But if taking a blood sample is a search without a warrant justified on exigent circumstances that passes the constitutional test of reasonableness, surely the fact of indictment, coupled with the prosecutor's motion and affidavit, and the decision of a judicial officer that the scope of the examination is reasonable and should be so ordered, taken together are the equivalent of a legally obtained search warrant procedure.

The appellants argue that under Kentucky law this is not a search and seizure case, because the search and seizure provision found in Section 10 of our Kentucky Constitution is worded differently from the Fourth Amendment in the United States Constitution, and thus calls for a different conclusion. Section 10 provides:

> "The people shall be secure in their persons, houses, papers and possessions, from unreasonable search and seizure; and no warrant shall issue *to search any place*, or seize any person or thing, without describing them as nearly as may be, nor without probable cause supported by oath or affirmation." [Emphasis added.]

The appellants' argument is that Section 10 "authorized search warrants [only] for places"; that it authorizes warrants to seize persons, but it does not allow warrants to search persons in order to look for evidence of crime. But insofar as the taking of body samples is concerned, we see no significant difference between the language of the state and federal constitutions and no substantial reasons calling for a different result. The Federal Constitution provides in pertinent part:

> "... and no Warrants shall issue, but upon probable cause, supported by Oath or affirmation, and particularly describing the *place to be searched*, and the persons or things to be seized." [Emphasis added.]

The legal formula is the same, albeit the words are somewhat differently arranged. We recognize that *Wagner v. Commonwealth*, Ky., 581 S.W.2d 352 (1979), interpreted state constitutional guarantees of the rights of the criminally accused against unreasonable search and seizure as granting broader protection than the Federal counterpart, but our more recent decision overruled *Wagner*, *Estep v. Commonwealth*, Ky., 663 S.W.2d 213, 216 (1984), and held state protection should be interpreted coextensively with federal guarantees. And in our most recent decision addressing whether our own Section 10 should be interpreted to provide greater protection against search and seizure, *Crayton v. Commonwealth*, Ky., 846 S.W.2d 684 (1992), we stated:

> "An examination of Section 10 of the Constitution of Kentucky and the Fourth Amendment to the Constitution of the United States reveals little textual difference. The language used is virtually the same and only the arrangement of the words is different. The absence of material difference between these constitutional provisions was recognized in *Benge v. Commonwealth*, Ky., 321 S.W.2d 247 (1959)."

In *Crayton*, in answering "yes" to the question whether the so-called "good faith" exception to the "exclusionary rule," as enunciated in *United States v. Leon*, 468 U.S. 897, 104 S.Ct. 3405, 82 L.Ed.2d 677 (1984) should be applied in Kentucky, we interpreted Kentucky Constitution Section 10 consonant with the Fourth Amendment.

To our knowledge, the judicial procedure utilized here, ordering the search for evidence after indictment by obtaining body samples from the accused by a reasonably non-intrusive means, has been routinely followed for a number of years with no legal challenge made on constitutional grounds to the procedure. Appellants' Brief has cited neither case law from elsewhere nor learned commentary supporting their theory that such procedure violates constitutional protection of personal security. While we have decided several recent cases protecting individual rights on state constitutional law grounds (*See, e.g., Rose v. Council for Better Educ., Inc.*, Ky., 790 S.W.2d 186 (1989); *Commonwealth v. Wasson*, Ky., 842 S.W.2d 487 (1992) (rendered September 24, 1992)), our stated purpose is to do so only where the dictates of our Kentucky Constitution, tradition, and other relevant precedents call for such action. We have no intention that such cases should encourage lawsuits espousing novel theories to revise well-established legal practice and principles.

The only authority remotely relevant to which we have been cited is *Tabor v. Scobee*, Ky., 254 S.W.2d 474 (1952), a civil case having nothing whatsoever to do with the rights of the criminally accused, which are covered with specificity in our Kentucky Constitution, Sections 10–13. As with any subject of statutory or constitutional construction, when dealing with the rights of those accused of crimes by the state the specific takes precedence over the general. *Commonwealth v. Schindler*, Ky., 685 S.W.2d 544 (1984). *See also* Sutherland, *Statutory Construction*, Volume 2B, Sec. 51.05, stating that if there is any "conflict" between a provision dealing with a subject in general terms and another dealing with a part of the same subject in a more detailed way, if the two cannot be harmonized, "the latter will prevail." Here the specific provisions in Section Ten protect the accused against "unreasonable search and seizure," and against a search of any nature except where ordered by an appropriate judicial authority after sufficient grounds providing "probable cause supported by oath or affirmation." It is these provisions rather than the general provisions in Section One that control the present decision.

* * *

The appellants' arguments are long on ingenuity and short on substance. Rather than extending this opinion by further discussion, it suffices to say that before attacking established practice and procedure on constitutional grounds, it is important that counsel, however well-meaning, consider carefully whether there is genuine legal underpinning so substantial as to merit the expenditure of judicial resources triggered by pursuing such a case. The cause of individual rights must not drown in a sea of sterile cases.

The decision of the Court of Appeals denying the Writ of Prohibition is affirmed.

All concur.

Notes and Questions

1. *Holbrook* observes that, under *Crayton v. Commonwealth*, 846 S.W.2d 864 (Ky. 1992), Section 10 of the Kentucky Constitution is to be interpreted "consonant with the Fourth Amendment." *See also LaFollette v. Commonwealth*, 915 S.W.2d 747, 458 (Ky. 1996), *overruled on other grounds by Hunter v. Commonwealth*, 587 S.W.3d 298 (Ky. 2019) ("Section 10 of the Kentucky Constitution provides no greater protection than does the federal Fourth Amendment." (citing *Estep v. Commonwealth*, 663 S.W.2d 213 (Ky. 1983))); *but see Commonwealth v. Reed*, 647 S.W.3d 237, 256–58, (Ky. 2022) (Minton, C.J., concurring) ("We should take the opportunity today to reexamine the defective legal foundation on which *LaFollette* relies. The practical result of this Court's statement in *LaFollette* is that Kentucky courts have been stifled in their interpretation and application of Section 10 and the protections it affords. We should decide today to abandon further unreflexive adoption.... Insofar as *LaFollette* stands for the proposition that Section 10 and the Fourth Amendment are co-extensive in every application, we should overrule it."). Is the Court's current interpretation of Section 10 consistent with its text?
2. The Supreme Court unanimously held in *Holbrook* that there is no "right of personal security" under Section 1(1) of the Kentucky Constitution. Later, in *Commonwealth, Cabinet for Health and Family Services ex rel. Meier v. Claycomb ex rel. Claycomb*, 566 S.W.3d 202, 212 (Ky. 2018), Chief Justice Minton's opinion for the Court acknowledged that Blackstone had identified "personal security"—which includes "the right to life and limb, and ... to body (freedom from assault), health, and reputation"—as one of the three "absolute rights" protected by "open courts" provisions such as Section 14. Is *Claycomb* in tension with *Holbrook* on the issue of whether the Kentucky Constitution protects a "right of personal security" at all?

Parker v. Commonwealth

Supreme Court of Kentucky (2014)
440 S.W.3d 381

Opinion of the Court by Justice Cunningham.

On January 12, 2009, Louisville Metro Police Officer Brian Reccius observed a vehicle driven by Appellant, Robert Mason Parker, cross the center line of the road after leaving a bar. After stopping the vehicle, Officer Reccius discovered that Parker's driver's license had been suspended. Reccius asked Parker to step out of the car. Parker complied and walked to the rear of the vehicle where he was questioned by Officer Reccius. After another officer arrived on the scene, Reccius asked Parker if there was anything illegal in his car to which Parker responded in the negative. Parker stood at the rear of the car with the other officer while Officer Reccius searched the vehicle. Parker was not handcuffed at the time. As a result of the search, the officer discovered a loaded handgun and some marijuana. Parker was then taken into custody.

Parker was subsequently indicted by a Jefferson County grand jury for possession of a hand gun by a convicted felon; illegal possession of a controlled substance, schedule I hallucinogen, marijuana; and operating a motor vehicle while license is revoked or suspended for driving under the influence, first offense. Parker filed a motion to suppress the evidence recovered from his vehicle, which was granted by the trial court. The Commonwealth filed a motion, pursuant to CR 59.05, to alter, amend, or vacate the order suppressing, or in the alternative, to enter findings of fact and conclusions of law. In an opinion and order entered on May 27, 2010, the trial court issued additional findings and denied the CR 59.05 motion.

A Court of Appeals panel unanimously reversed the circuit court's order suppressing the evidence. The court found that the Commonwealth's appeal was timely filed because "the running of the time to file an appeal of any judgment is tolled by a timely filed CR 59.05 motion." See CR 73.02. Regarding the suppression of the evidence, the Court of Appeals found that while the search was unlawful, the exclusionary rule did not require suppression because the police officer searching Parker's car followed existing precedent.

* * *

Suppression of the Evidence

In support of his argument, Parker offers a very thorough and intriguing analysis of the evolution of Kentucky's search and seizure jurisprudence. However, our decision in the present case turns on what the law was on the date of the search and whether the police officer conducting the search was objectively reasonable in his reliance on the law at that time.

The search at issue occurred on January 12, 2009. As of that date, the U.S. Supreme Court's ruling in *New York v. Belton* was the law of the land. 453 U.S. 454, 101 S.Ct. 2860, 69 L.Ed.2d 768 (1981). *Belton* permitted law enforcement officers to search a vehicle incident to the arrest of the occupant, without probable cause and even if the occupant could not gain access to the vehicle at the time of search. *Id.*; *see also Henry v. Commonwealth*, 275 S.W.3d 194 (Ky. 2008) (holding that a search of defendant's vehicle was a valid search incident to defendant's arrest, even though defendant was secured in the back of a police cruiser at the time of the search). Thus, at the time it was conducted, the search in the present case was lawful under *Belton* and *Henry*.

Although *Henry* became final only four days prior to the search in the present case, *Belton* had been in effect since 1981. However, in *Clark v. Commonwealth*, the Court of Appeals held that *Belton* did not apply where the arrest was for a traffic violation and the arrestee was secured in the police cruiser prior to the search. 868 S.W.2d 101 (Ky. App. 1993). Yet, *Clark* was an outlier and did not comport with binding decisions from this Court that were in effect at the time of the search in the present case. *See Penman v. Commonwealth*, 194 S.W.3d 237 (Ky. 2006); *Rainey v. Commonwealth*, 197 S.W.3d 89 (Ky. 2006). To the extent that there was any conflict based on Kentucky Constitutional provisions, it arose from *Clark*. Nevertheless, *Clark* was disavowed prior to *Henry* and does not instruct our decision in the present case.

On April, 21, 2009, the U.S. Supreme Court decided *Arizona v. Gant*, 556 U.S. 332, 129 S.Ct. 1710, 173 L.Ed.2d 485 (2009). In overruling *Belton*, *Gant* held that a vehicle search, incident to arrest, is only authorized "when the arrestee is unsecured and within reaching distance of the passenger compartment at the time of the search" or "when it is reasonable to believe evidence relevant to the crime of arrest might be found in the vehicle." *Id.* at 343, 129 S.Ct. 1710 (citation omitted). *Gant* is the current U.S. Supreme Court precedent applicable to automobile searches and was officially recognized in *Rose v. Commonwealth*, 322 S.W.3d 76 (Ky. 2010). The Commonwealth concedes that the search in the present case was unconstitutional under *Gant* and thus, *Rose*.

Also, the Commonwealth does not contest that *Gant* applies retroactively pursuant to the U.S. Supreme Court's decision in *Griffith v. Kentucky*, 479 U.S. 314, 328, 107 S.Ct. 708, 93 L.Ed.2d 649 (1987). However, the Commonwealth argues that the evidence recovered by the contested search should not be suppressed because of the police officer's reasonable and good-faith reliance on *Belton* at the time of Parker's arrest. In support, the Commonwealth leans heavily on *Davis v. United States*, which held that the good-faith exception to the exclusionary rule allows for the admission of evidence obtained as a result of an objectively reasonable reliance on "binding appellate precedent." ___ U.S. ___, 131 S.Ct. 2419, 180 L.Ed.2d 285 (2011). The dissonance between *Gant*, *Griffith*, and *Davis*, paints the law in shades of gray where blackletter is desperately needed. To provide clarity, it is first necessary to present a brief foundation.

The Exclusionary Rule and its Exceptions

Both our state and federal constitutions provide a bill of rights, yet offer no bill of remedies when those rights are abridged. See Kentucky Const. §10; U.S. Const. Amendment IV. In order to resolve this textual divide, courts have long since held that unlawfully obtained evidence and the fruits resulting therefrom are inadmissible in criminal proceedings. This axiomatic principle is known as the exclusionary rule.

The U.S. Supreme Court established this rule in *Weeks v. United States*, 232 U.S. 383, 34 S.Ct. 341, 58 L.Ed. 652 (1914) and extended it to state court proceedings in *Mapp v. Ohio*, 367 U.S. 643, 81 S.Ct. 1684, 6 L.Ed.2d 1081 (1961). However, Kentucky was a pioneer, applying the exclusionary rule long before it was mandated by our nation's highest court. *See Youman v. Commonwealth*, 189 Ky. 152, 224 S.W. 860 (1920) (applying the exclusionary rule for the first time in Kentucky). Yet, since its inception, the exclusionary rule has been tempered with exceptions.

In *United States v. Leon*, the U.S. Supreme Court first adopted a good-faith exception to the exclusionary rule, holding that the rule does not apply when law enforcement officers conduct a search in "objectively reasonable reliance" on a warrant later held invalid. 468 U.S. 897, 922, 104 S.Ct. 3405, 82 L.Ed.2d 677 (1984). Since *Leon*, the U.S. Supreme Court has recognized additional exceptions. *See Illinois v. Krull*, 480 U.S. 340, 349, 107 S.Ct. 1160, 94 L.Ed.2d 364 (1987) (holding that "evidence obtained by an officer acting in objectively reasonable reliance on a statute" need not be suppressed when statute is later determined to be unconstitutional); *Arizona v. Evans*, 514 U.S. 1, 16–17, 115 S.Ct. 1185, 131 L.Ed.2d 34 (1995); *Herring v. United States*, 555 U.S. 135, 146, 129 S.Ct. 695, 172 L.Ed.2d 496 (2009). Most germane to the present case is the recent expansion of the good-faith exception to the exclusionary rule announced in *Davis*.

Davis involved a vehicle search, incident to arrest, which produced a revolver. *Davis*, 131 S.Ct. at 2425. As a result of the search, the defendant, Davis, was indicted on one count of possession of a firearm by a convicted felon. *Id.* at 2425–26. The search in that case complied with *Belton*, which was the law at that time. *Id.* at 2426. Accordingly, the District Court refused to suppress the revolver as evidence and Davis was convicted on the firearm charge. *Id.* While Davis' case was on appeal, the U.S. Supreme Court decided *Gant*. Relying on *Gant*, the U.S. Court of Appeals for the Eleventh Circuit held that the search violated Davis' rights but did not require suppression of the evidence. *Davis*, 131 S.Ct. at 2426.

On appeal to the U.S. Supreme Court, the Court affirmed the judgment of the Eleventh Circuit and held that, "when the police conduct a search in objectively reasonable reliance on binding appellate precedent, the exclusionary rule does not apply." *Id.* at 2434. In so holding, the Court noted that the searching officers "acted in strict compliance with binding precedent," which, at that time, was *Belton*. *Davis*, 131 S.Ct. at 2428. The Court concluded that exclusion of the evidence in that instance would only serve to deter "conscientious police work." *Id.* at 2429.

Applying Davis in Kentucky

This Court is charged with protecting the rights afforded by the Fourth Amendment to the U.S. Constitution and the U.S. Supreme Court's ever-evolving interpretation thereof. However, states are not required to apply the numerous exceptions to the exclusionary rule. Accordingly, some recognize a good-faith exception, but not in every instance adopted by the U.S. Supreme Court. *People v. Krueger*, 175 Ill.2d 60, 221 Ill. Dec. 409, 675 N.E.2d 604 (1996). Other states reject the good-faith exception entirely. *E.g., State v. Gutierrez*, 116 N.M. 431, 863 P.2d 1052, 1053 (1993); *State v. Oakes*, 157

Vt. 171, 598 A.2d 119 (1991); *Commonwealth v. Edmunds*, 526 Pa. 374, 586 A.2d 887 (1991).

In Kentucky, we have consistently interpreted Section 10 of our state Constitution in congruence with the Fourth Amendment regarding the application of both rights and remedies. The present case provides no imperative for departure. *See, e.g., Dunn v. Commonwealth*, 360 S.W.3d 751, 758 (Ky. 2012) ("this Court has consistently held that the protections of Section 10 of the Kentucky Constitution are no greater than those of the federal Fourth Amendment."); *Williams v. Commonwealth*, 364 S.W.3d 65, 68 (Ky. 2011). Therefore, although we recognize that *Davis* controls in this instance, we narrowly define and apply its holding as follows: when law enforcement officers conduct a search in objectively reasonable reliance on clearly established precedent from this Court or the United States Supreme Court, the exclusionary rule does not apply to exclude the admission of evidence obtained as a result of the search.

By narrowly defining the holding in *Davis*, we seek to avoid confusion regarding what law controls and, thus, when courts should apply the exclusionary rule. Moreover, our decision adequately preserves the protections provided by our state and federal constitutions while not penalizing police officers for performing their duties conscientiously and in good-faith.

Law enforcement officers are the vanguard of our legal system. They operate in real time without the benefit of judicial hindsight and must rely on their training and experience. Here, Officer Reccius testified that the search of Parker's vehicle complied with the training he received prior to the search and that this type of search was common practice in his police department at that time. Reccius further testified that since the contested search in this case, he was informed by the Louisville Metro Police Department's legal division and his superiors that automobile searches must now comply with Gant. This is exactly the type of diligence and prudent instruction that should be encouraged.

However, our decision here does not condone erroneous policies and procedures or compel judicial enforcement of an officer's mistake of law. *See, e.g., Commonwealth v. Miller*, 78 Mass. App. Ct. 860, 944 N.E.2d 179, 183 (2011) (requiring suppression of evidence obtained as a result of a vehicle search conducted where "the trooper based his stop on the entirely erroneous belief that the stripe on the defendant's license plate violated [state law] ..."); *Commonwealth v. Rivas*, 77 Mass. App. Ct. 210, 929 N.E.2d 328, 333 n. 6 (2010) (vehicle stops premised on police officer's mistake of law, even a reasonable, good-faith mistake, are generally held to be unconstitutional); *United States v. Chanthasouxat*, 342 F.3d 1271, 1280 (11th Cir. 2003); *United States v. McDonald*, 453 F.3d 958, 961–62 (7th Cir. 2006).

Furthermore, Parker devotes a significant segment of his brief seeking to revive an argument previously rejected by this Court in *Henry*—that there exists "an independent Kentucky tradition of excluding tainted evidence not simply to deter police misconduct but more broadly to ensure that courts do not become implicated in constitutional violations." *Henry*, 275 S.W.3d at 199 (overruled) (citing *Youman*, 224 S.W. at 866). Parker's reliance on *Youman* is misguided.

In *Youman*, the Court held that police officers' warrantless search of the defendant's home was deliberate and flagrant, thus requiring suppression of the illegally obtained evidence. *Id.* As such, the result in *Youman* remains sound under its clearly distinguishable facts, and indeed, is enduring evidence that the purpose of the exclusionary rule is to deter police misconduct. *See also Crayton v. Commonwealth*, 846 S.W.2d 684, 688 (Ky. 1992) ("deterrence of police misconduct is the primary, if not the only, legitimate objective of evidentiary suppression."); *Davis*, 131 S.Ct. at 2426 ("The rule's sole purpose, we have repeatedly held, is to deter future Fourth Amendment violations.") (citations omitted). Thus, *Youman* is incongruous with our modern search and seizure jurisprudence to the extent that it is interpreted as establishing a broad Kentucky tradition of applying the exclusionary rule for purposes other than police deterrence.

Lastly, we stress that when interpreting our own Kentucky Constitution, this Court is not tethered to the decisions of the U.S. Supreme Court or the reasoning upon which those decisions are founded. Although the weight of our modern search and seizure precedent comports with federal law, we are not beholden to interpreting every provision of the Kentucky Constitution as identical to its analogous federal counterpart.

We hold the search in the present case was conducted by Officer Reccius in an objectively reasonable reliance on clearly established precedent provided under *New York v. Belton*, 453 U.S. 454, 101 S.Ct. 2860, 69 L.Ed.2d 768 (1981) and *Henry v. Commonwealth*, 275 S.W.3d 194 (Ky. 2008). Accordingly, the exclusionary rule does not apply to exclude the contraband discovered in Parker's vehicle.

Conclusion

For the foregoing reasons, we hereby affirm the Court of Appeals' decision vacating the Jefferson Circuit Court's order suppressing the evidence discovered in Parker's vehicle.

All sitting. Minton, C.J.; Keller, Noble, Scott, and Venters, JJ., concur. Abramson, J., concurs in result only.

Notes and Questions

1. Note that *Youman v. Commonwealth*, 189 Ky. 152, 224 S.W. 860 (1920), discussed in the *Parker* opinion, applied the exclusionary rule in Kentucky long before the U.S. Supreme Court extended the rule to the States in *Mapp v. Ohio*, 367 U.S. 643 (1961).
2. Not all States have adopted the "good faith" exception to the exclusionary rule. However, the Court noted in *Parker* that Kentucky has "consistently interpreted Section 10 of our state Constitution in congruence with the Fourth Amendment regarding the application of both rights and remedies."

Cobb v. Commonwealth

Supreme Court of Kentucky (2017)

509 S.W.3d 705

Opinion of the Court by Justice Wright.

Clarence Cobb entered a conditional guilty plea in Graves Circuit Court to possessing a handgun as a convicted felon, possessing marijuana, and operating a motor vehicle on a suspended license. The trial court sentenced Cobb to five years' imprisonment; however, the plea agreement allowed Cobb to appeal the trial court's order denying his motion to suppress evidence found in the vehicle he drove at the time of his arrest. Cobb appealed the trial court's order, and the Court of Appeals affirmed. Cobb moved this Court for discretionary review, and we granted his motion. On appeal, Cobb argues the Court of Appeals erred by affirming the trial court's order denying his motion to suppress evidence because police illegally seized and searched his vehicle. We disagree. Therefore, we affirm the judgment of the Court of Appeals.

I. Background

While on routine patrol, Mayfield Police Officer Rodney Smith believed he recognized a driver whom he previously arrested for driving on a suspended license. Officer Smith followed the car until it pulled into a driveway and the occupant exited the vehicle. The driver identified himself as Keith Burton when questioned by Officer Smith. Believing he confused the driver of this car with the previous arrestee, Officer Smith returned to his cruiser. Officer Smith watched as the driver entered a different residence from the driveway in which he parked. At that point, Officer Smith accessed the jail's website and retrieved a photo of Keith Burton. He realized the driver of the car had given him a false name, and he went to the house the driver entered. Once confronted with a photo of Keith Burton, the driver admitted he was Clarence Cobb—the man Officer Smith previously arrested for driving on a suspended license. After verifying that Cobb's license remained suspended, Officer Smith placed Cobb under arrest.

Having seen the police make an arrest, a vigilant neighbor came outside and informed Officer Smith she was the caretaker of the elderly man in whose driveway Cobb parked. The neighbor told police that Cobb did not live in that home, that Cobb's car did not belong in the driveway where he parked it, and Cobb did not have permission to park there.

At that point, Officer Smith seized the vehicle, called a tow truck, and conducted an inventory search pursuant to department policy. Another officer arrived on the scene to assist in the inventory search. During that search, police opened the center console of the vehicle and found marijuana, rolling papers, and a loaded handgun. The seizure of Cobb's vehicle and its subsequent search are the focus of this appeal.

II. Analysis

* * *

Now, we review de novo the application of the law to these facts. * * *

B. Warrantless Searches Are Per Se Unreasonable, Subject Only to a Few Well-Established Exceptions

1. A Search Incident to Arrest is But One Exception to the Warrant Requirement

Cobb contends that police illegally seized and searched his car, thus requiring this Court to reverse the judgment of the Court of Appeals. As we said in *Robbins v. Commonwealth*, 336 S.W.3d 60, 63 (Ky. 2011), "[w]arrantless searches are 'per se unreasonable under the Fourth Amendment—subject only to a few specifically established and well-delineated exceptions.'" (Quoting *Katz v. United States*, 389 U.S. 347, 357, 88 S.Ct. 507, 19 L.Ed.2d 576 (1967)). Therefore, in order to determine whether police illegally seized and searched Cobb's car, we must analyze whether the search and seizure fits into one of the exceptions to the Fourth Amendment's general warrant requirement.

In this case, Cobb conflates two wholly-separate exceptions to the warrant requirement: 1) a search incident to arrest, and 2) an inventory search after seizure. Cobb argues that police conducted a thinly-veiled search incident to arrest that does not comport with the dictates of the Supreme Court of the United States opinion in *Arizona v. Gant*, 556 U.S. 332, 338, 129 S.Ct. 1710, 173 L.Ed.2d 485 (2009). *Gant* significantly narrowed the circumstances under which police may search an automobile incident to arrest. The Supreme Court of the United States set out two permissible scenarios when the passenger compartment of a car may be searched, after an arrest, without a warrant. First, "[p]olice may search a vehicle incident to a recent occupant's arrest only if the arrestee is within reaching distance of the passenger compartment at the time of the search...." *Gant*, 556 U.S. at 351, 129 S.Ct. 1710. Secondly, police may search a vehicle incident to a recent occupant's arrest if "it is reasonable to believe the vehicle contains evidence of the offense of arrest." *Id.* Importantly, however, the *Gant* Court clarified that "[w]hen these justifications are absent, a search of an arrestee's vehicle will be unreasonable *unless* police obtain a warrant *or show that another exception to the warrant requirement applies.*" *Id.* (emphasis added). Despite Cobb's argument to the contrary, the holding in *Gant* limiting searches incident to arrest does not apply here. *Gant* exempted from its holding searches covered by other exceptions to the warrant requirement. The Commonwealth never argued that it met the *Gant* exceptions. As such, our analysis turns upon whether another exception to the warrant requirement applies to the instant case.

2. Inventory Searches are a Well-Defined Exception to the Warrant Requirement of the Fourth Amendment

The Supreme Court of the United States recognized in *Colorado v. Bertine*, 479 U.S. 367, 371, 107 S.Ct. 738, 93 L.Ed.2d 739 (1987), that inventory searches are a well-defined exception to the Fourth Amendment's warrant requirement. After *Bertine*, courts across the country have recognized that "[v]ehicle inventories are an exception to the general warrant requirement." *Hunnicutt-Carter v. State*, 308 P.3d 847, 851 (Wyo. 2013); *Accord United States v. Hockenberry*, 730 F.3d 645, 658 (6th Cir. 2013); *State v.*

Gauster, 752 N.W.2d 496, 502 (Minn. 2008); *Commonwealth v. Lagenella*, 623 Pa. 434, 83 A.3d 94, 102 (2013).

An inventory search is a well-defined exception to the general warrant requirement; therefore, we analyze the lawfulness of the seizure of Cobb's vehicle and its subsequent search within the confines of that exception.

a. A Lawful Inventory Search Requires a Reasonable Seizure

Since the need for an inventory search arises only after police seize a vehicle without a warrant, the lawfulness of that inventory search turns first upon the reasonableness of the seizure. *Commonwealth v. Campbell*, 475 Mass. 611, 59 N.E.3d 394, 398 (2016) ("Reasonableness" is the "touchstone" when determining the propriety of a warrantless seizure.); *Gauster*, 752 N.W.2d at 502. Noting that the Fourth Amendment only prohibits unreasonable searches and seizures, the Supreme Court of the United States stated that when determining the lawfulness of a seizure, "[t]he relevant test is … the reasonableness of the seizure under all of the circumstances. The test of reasonableness cannot be fixed by Per se Rules; each case must be decided on its own facts." *South Dakota v. Opperman*, 428 U.S. 364, 373, 96 S.Ct. 3092, 49 L.Ed.2d 1000 (1976) (citing *Coolidge v. New Hampshire*, 403 U.S. 443, 509–510, 91 S.Ct. 2022, 29 L.Ed.2d 564 (1971); *see also Cooper v. California*, 386 U.S. 58, 59, 87 S.Ct. 788, 17 L.Ed.2d 730 (1967) ("Whether a search and seizure is unreasonable within the meaning of the Fourth Amendment depends upon the facts and circumstances of each case…."). Therefore, we must look to the facts of this case concerning what information Officer Smith knew when he seized Cobb's vehicle.

At the time of the seizure, Officer Smith: 1) observed Cobb operating a vehicle on a public roadway after previously arresting him for driving on a suspended license; 2) attempted to confirm his identity by asking for his name; 3) observed Cobb park his vehicle in a different driveway from the residence he entered; 4) verified that Cobb lied by providing a false name; 5) confirmed that Cobb's license remained suspended; 6) was told by the caretaker of the elderly man who owned the property that Cobb parked his vehicle on private property without permission; and 7) arrested Cobb for operating a vehicle on a suspended license.

In *Opperman*, 428 U.S. at 373, 96 S.Ct. 3092, the Supreme Court upheld an inventory search after police seized and impounded a vehicle with multiple parking violations that was unlawfully parked in a parking spot on the side of a public street. Here, according to the record on appeal, courts in Fulton and Graves County entered a combined total of six guilty judgments against Cobb for driving on a suspended license, while a seventh charge remained pending at the time of this incident. We are unclear whether Officer Smith knew of all seven times police charged Cobb with driving on a suspended license. However, per Officer Smith's testimony at the suppression hearing, he knew of at least one instance: he assisted in a prior arrest of Cobb for driving on a suspended license.

In *United States v. Petty*, 367 F.3d 1009, 1012 (8th Cir. 2004), the United States Court of Appeals for the Eighth Circuit stated that "[p]olice may take protective custody of a vehicle when they have arrested its occupants, even if it is lawfully parked and poses no public safety hazard." (Internal citations and quotation marks omitted.) And in *United States v. Evans*, 781 F.3d 433, 437 (8th Cir. 2015), the Eighth Circuit upheld the warrantless seizure and inventory search of Evans' vehicle after police arrested him for driving without a valid license and after parking his vehicle on private property without permission. As in *Evans*, Cobb drove without a valid license and parked his vehicle on private property without permission. Not only did Cobb commit an offense against the Commonwealth and violate a court order by driving on a suspended license, Cobb also trespassed upon the private property of an elderly man. And once police arrested Cobb, his vehicle would have been left illegally blocking the elderly man's driveway had it not been impounded.

Once Officer Smith diligently ascertained the totality of the situation, he arrested Cobb and seized Cobb's car. Officer Smith followed his Department's policy by conducting an inventory search before towing Cobb's vehicle. We see no indication that Officer Smith arrested Cobb and then seized his vehicle in order to search it for evidence of an additional crime without obtaining a warrant. Likewise, we see no difference between seizing the vehicle of one who received multiple parking violations, as in *Opperman*, and seizing the vehicle driven by Cobb who habitually violated the law by operating a vehicle on a suspended license. Nor do we see a distinction between the rationale validating the seizure of a vehicle unlawfully parked in a parking spot on the side of a public street, as in *Opperman*, and seizing a vehicle used to trespass unlawfully upon private property. In sum, we hold that under these circumstances, police acted reasonably in seizing Cobb's vehicle and performing the subsequent inventory search of its contents.

b. The Scope of the Inventory Search Was Reasonable

Cobb contends that the seizure and search in question violate principles outlined in *Bertine*, 479 U.S. 367, 107 S.Ct. 738, and *Florida v. Wells*, 495 U.S. 1, 110 S.Ct. 1632, 109 L.Ed.2d 1 (1990). In *Bertine*, when conducting the inventory search of the impounded vehicle, "[t]he officer opened a closed backpack in which he found controlled substances, cocaine paraphernalia, and a large amount of cash." *Bertine*, 479 U.S. at 369, 107 S.Ct. 738. The Supreme Court's analysis primarily focused on the standardized criteria necessary in the conduct of the inventory search, specifically whether the Officer improperly opened and searched the backpack. The Court upheld the search of the backpack and went on to uphold the discretion given to the officer in deciding to impound rather than lock and park the vehicle.

In *Wells*, the Supreme Court invalidated part of an inventory search in which the Florida Highway Patrol opened a locked suitcase found in the trunk of an impounded car. The locked suitcase contained a large quantity of marijuana. Because the Florida Highway Patrol lacked a policy with respect to opening closed containers in the course of an inventory search, the Court affirmed the suppression of the evidence of the marijuana found in the suitcase.

Contrary to Cobb's assertion, these two cases concern the necessity that police abide by standard criteria while conducting an inventory search. In fact, the Supreme Court's holding in *Bertine* specifically references inventory procedures, "[w]e conclude that here, as in [*Illinois v.*] *Lafayette*, [462 U.S. 640, 648, 103 S.Ct. 2605, 77 L.Ed.2d 65 (1983),] reasonable police regulations *relating to inventory procedures* administered in good faith satisfy the Fourth Amendment, even though courts might as a matter of hindsight be able to devise equally reasonable rules requiring a different procedure." *Bertine*, 479 U.S. at 374, 107 S.Ct. 738 (emphasis added).

In *Wells*, 495 U.S. at 4, 110 S.Ct. 1632, the Supreme Court stated, "[o]ur view that standardized criteria, *or established routine*, must *regulate the opening of containers found during inventory searches* is based on the principle that an inventory search must not be a ruse for a general rummaging in order to discover incriminating evidence" (internal citations and quotation marks omitted) (emphasis added). The Court reasoned, that "[t]he policy *or practice governing inventory searches* should be designed to produce an inventory. The individual police officer must not be allowed so much latitude that inventory searches are turned into a purposeful and general means of discovering evidence of crime[.]" *Id.* (emphasis added).

Here, when police found the loaded handgun during the inventory search, they merely opened the center console—a factory installed component of the vehicle—a routine practice when inventorying the contents of a vehicle. In fact, it would be impossible for police to complete an inventory search of the vehicle without opening a compartment in the center of the car. Therefore, we conclude that police acted reasonably in conducting the inventory search.

C. Section 10 of the Kentucky Constitution Provides No Greater Protection than the Federal Fourth Amendment in the Context of Warrantless Searches

Cobb argued to the Court of Appeals—and argues now—that Section 10 of the Kentucky Constitution provides greater protection than the Fourth Amendment of the federal Constitution. Cobb contends that this Court's holding limiting the circumstances in which a vehicle may be impounded outlined in *Wagner v. Commonwealth*, 581 S.W.2d 352, 356 (Ky. 1979), *overruled by Estep v. Commonwealth*, 663 S.W.2d 213 (Ky. 1983), governs the outcome of this case. However, in *LaFollette v. Commonwealth*, 915 S.W.2d 747, 748 (Ky. 1996), after noting the similarities in language between the state and federal provisions in the context of warrantless searches, we held that "Section 10 of the Kentucky Constitution provides no greater protection than does the federal Fourth Amendment." For more than two decades, this Court has rendered opinions affirming this principle of Kentucky constitutional law, and we see no reason to address Cobb's argument further.

To the extent not previously made clear over twenty years of our case law from *LaFollette* to *Chavies*, 354 S.W.3d at 107, to our recent holding in *Commonwealth v. Cox*, 491 S.W.3d 167, 170, fn. 2 (Ky. 2015) ("The Kentucky Constitution on this subject mirrors its federal counterpart and is considered co-extensive to the Fourth Amendment."), we expressly overrule the holding in *Wagner*, 581 S.W.2d at 356, that within the context of warrantless searches, Section 10 of the Constitution of this Commonwealth provides greater protection than the Fourth Amendment of the Constitution of the United States.

III. Conclusion

For the foregoing reasons, we affirm the judgment of the Court of Appeals.

All sitting. All concur.

Notes and Questions

1. *Cobb* holds that Section 10 of the Kentucky Constitution affords no greater protection to the accused regarding warrantless searches than does the Fourth Amendment. Does the Court faithfully construe the text of Section 10?

2. In *Wagner v. Commonwealth*, 581 S.W.2d 352 (Ky. 1979), which *Cobb* expressly overrules, the Supreme Court of Kentucky had interpreted Section 10 to provide greater protection from unreasonable searches and seizures than the Fourth Amendment. Over two dissents, *Wagner* had permitted the police to impound an automobile and to search or inventory its contents in *only* four situations: (1) the owner or permissive user consents; (2) the vehicle, if not removed, constitutes a danger to other persons or property or the public safety; (3) the police have probable cause to believe that the vehicle constitutes an instrumentality or fruit of a crime; or (4) the police have probable cause to believe both that the vehicle contains evidence of a crime. *Wagner*, 581 S.W.2d at 356. The Court specifically rejected the U.S. Supreme Court's holding in *South Dakota v. Opperman*, 428 U.S. 364 (1976), that under the Fourth Amendment, the police could conduct an inventory search of an automobile impounded for violations of municipal parking ordinances.

Section 11

Commonwealth v. Cooper

Supreme Court of Kentucky (1995)

899 S.W.2d 75

Opinion of the Court by Justice Lambert.

The question before the Court is whether Section Eleven of the Constitution of Kentucky or a viable doctrine of the common law requires suppression of a confession coerced or improperly obtained by private parties. Prevailing decisional law answers firmly in the negative (*Peek v. Commonwealth*, Ky., 415 S.W.2d 854 (1967)), and is in accord with controlling precedent interpreting the Constitution of the United States. *Colorado v. Connelly*, 479 U.S. 157, 107 S.Ct. 515, 93 L.Ed.2d 473 (1986).[1] Despite the

1. Our "involuntary confession" jurisprudence is entirely consistent with the settled law requiring some sort of "state action" to support a claim of violation of the Due Process Clause of the Fourteenth Amendment.

foregoing, the trial court held that Section Eleven of the Constitution of Kentucky was without any requirement of state action, thereby subjecting incriminating statements made to purely private persons to a "compelled ... evidence" analysis. The Court of Appeals disclaimed reliance on either federal or state constitutional law, but relied on "an ancient doctrine conceived in the common law. ..." that confessions obtained by coercive techniques, whether by state or private actors, were involuntary and inadmissible in criminal prosecutions. We granted discretionary review and now reverse the courts below.

The facts, as found by the trial court and relied upon by the Court of Appeals, are substantially as follows. While employed by United Parcel Service in Louisville, appellee Robert Edward Cooper was observed standing over two parcels, one of which was open. On questioning by his supervisor, appellee soon confessed to having opened the parcel. On further questioning, he admitted having committed other UPS thefts and provided tangible evidence which confirmed his oral and written confessions. However, in the course of the interrogation, UPS personnel assumed the role of authority figures and asserted control over appellee. He felt significantly intimidated by virtue of being questioned for something over one hour in a windowless room which had a motion detector and closed, possibly locked, doors. Moreover, UPS personnel expressly or impliedly promised appellee that in exchange for his cooperation, he would not be prosecuted.

On the other hand, there was no evidence of violence or threat of violence against appellee. He was not physically prevented from leaving the scene and was urged only to tell the truth. The only police officer present was appellee, a military policeman with the Kentucky National Guard, and he testified to being familiar with police procedures.

Upon the foregoing evidence, the trial court ordered suppression of appellee's statements and on the Commonwealth's interlocutory appeal, pursuant to KRS 22A.010, the Court of Appeals affirmed. Both courts below acknowledged the absence of grounds for suppression pursuant to the Constitution of the United States, but interpreted Kentucky law more broadly than corresponding federal constitutional rights. Holding that state action is not required to trigger a right to seek suppression under state law, the Court of Appeals stated:

> It matters not whether undesired results, like involuntary confessions, emanate from the badge of authority or from an ordinary citizen cloaked with

---

....

> The most outrageous behavior by a private party seeking to secure evidence against a defendant does not make that evidence inadmissible under the Due Process Clause.
>
> ....
>
> We hold that coercive police activity is a necessary predicate to the finding that a confession is not "voluntary" within the meaning of the Due Process Clause of the Fourteenth Amendment....

Colorado v. Connelly, 479 U.S. at 165–167, 107 S.Ct. at 520–522.

> actual or perceived superiority. In the eyes of the law of this Commonwealth, the consequence is no less odious. (Slip op., p. 5.)

Contrary to the view of the courts below, the decisions of this Court are virtually unanimous that "state action" is required before any claim of suppression on grounds of compelled testimony will be entertained. Such was the direct holding in *Peek v. Commonwealth, supra*, in which a bail bondsman refused to file a bond until a defendant in custody made what amounted to a confession. Despite the existence of circumstances which might have suggested state action, the Court said:

> The State is not, and should not be, charged with any undue influence, pressure, sweating, or inducement exercised by a private citizen, acting on his own, not in concert with the officers of the State.

Id. at 856. Similarly, in *Hood v. Commonwealth*, Ky., 448 S.W.2d 388 (1969), in which the appellant contended that he should have been given all the warnings and admonitions set forth in *Miranda v. Arizona*, 384 U.S. 436, 86 S.Ct. 1602, 16 L.Ed.2d 694 (1966), the Court held that *Miranda* rights do not apply to a citizen arrest.

> The thrust of *Miranda* relates to actions of law enforcement agencies, and not to the actions of private citizens. We have no hesitancy in holding that *Miranda* does not apply in the instant case.

Hood, at 391. Likewise *Jaggers v. Commonwealth*, Ky., 439 S.W.2d 580 (1969), held that statements made to a person other than a "law enforcement official" were not subject to *Miranda* protection.

> These statements were not made to any law enforcement officer, nor were they made when appellant was under arrest.

Id. at 584.

It should be observed that *Hood* and *Jaggers* and a great many other Kentucky decisions addressing the right against self-incrimination were rendered in the era shortly after *Miranda v. Arizona*. In Kentucky and throughout this nation, *Miranda* represented a change in the law of seismic proportions and the rights it acknowledged went far beyond those which were recognized under the Constitution of Kentucky. Thus the phrase "*Miranda* rights" became virtually synonymous with the most conceivably far-reaching rights against self-incrimination. Disdainfully, the Court knuckled under in *Meyer v. Commonwealth*, Ky., 472 S.W.2d 479 (1971) (overruled on other grounds by *Short v. Commonwealth*, Ky., 519 S.W.2d 828 (1975)), as follows:

> The word "compelled" contemplates the use of "sweating" or other means of coercing a citizen to incriminate himself. Nowhere in any constitution, either Federal or state, is a requirement that officers charged with the investigation of a crime must enlighten the suspect of his rights against self-incrimination. But *Miranda* does just that, and until it is overruled we must try to live with it.

While the foregoing decisions did not directly address Kentucky constitutional law, it appears to have been implicit that there were no greater protections than federal constitutional protections or that state constitutional rights were no more than coextensive with federal rights. In fact, the Court said just that in *Newman v. Stinson*, Ky., 489 S.W.2d 826 (1972):

> The Fifth Amendment right against self-incrimination and the right given by Section Eleven of the Kentucky Constitution both arise from a common historical desire to prohibit the employment of legal process to extract from a person's own lips an admission of guilt which would thus take the place of other evidence. 8 Wigmore, *Evidence* (McNaughton Revision 1961), Section 2263. That the guarantees against self-incrimination of both the Federal and State Constitutions should have the same interpretation as far as possible despite some variance of wording is supported by Wigmore, 8 Wigmore, *Evidence*, Sections 2252 and 2263, and is affirmed by *Schmerber v. California, supra*. We conclude therefore that the protection against self-incrimination given by the Fifth Amendment to the United States Constitution is identical with that afforded by Section Eleven of the Kentucky Constitution.

Id. at 829.

We recognize that *Newman v. Stinson* did not deal with testimonial confessions, but such was clearly within the Court's contemplation as shown by its discussion of the historical parallel between the Fifth Amendment to the Constitution of the United States and Section Eleven of the Constitution of Kentucky. Moreover, an interpretation that Section Eleven requires "state action" is strengthened by analogy to other rights of persons accused of criminal conduct. In *Stone v. Commonwealth*, Ky., 418 S.W.2d 646 (1967), the Court held that evidence obtained by private persons was not subject to exclusion under Section 10. Quoting from *Chapman v. Commonwealth*, 206 Ky. 439, 267 S.W. 181 (1924), the Court said:

> It [Section 10] has never been held, however, to embrace or be applicable to a private individual who, through a process of spying or other form of trespass, discloses evidence against another.

Stone v. Commonwealth at 650. Similarly, in *Wilson v. Commonwealth*, Ky., 695 S.W.2d 854, 857 (1985), the Court held, though it failed to specify whether it was interpreting federal or state constitutional law, that

> in order to establish that a pre-trial confrontation was unduly suggestive, the defendant must first show that the government's agents arranged the confrontation or took some action during the confrontation which singled out the defendant.

From time to time in recent years this Court has interpreted the Constitution of Kentucky in a manner which differs from the interpretation of parallel federal constitutional rights by the Supreme Court of the United States. However, when we have differed from the Supreme Court, it has been because of Kentucky constitutional text, the Debates of the Constitutional Convention, history, tradition, and relevant precedent. We have admonished against "novel theories to revise well-established legal practice and principle" and stated the prevailing rule as follows:

> While we have decided several recent cases protecting individual rights on state constitutional law grounds, our stated purpose is to do so only where the dictates of our Kentucky Constitution, tradition, and other relevant precedents call for such action. (Citations omitted.)

Holbrook v. Knopf, Ky., 847 S.W.2d 52, 55 (1992).

Newman v. Stinson, *supra*, and our prior decisions are clear and we reiterate that Section Eleven of the Constitution of Kentucky and the Fifth Amendment to the Constitution of the United States are coextensive and provide identical protections against self-incrimination. State action is indispensable.

For the conclusion that appellee's statements should be suppressed, the courts below relied to a great extent upon four cases rendered between 1872 and 1924. The trial court extravagantly described these cases as exemplifying the "expansionist interpretation of the right against self-incrimination" thus eliminating the requirement of state action under Section Eleven. The Court of Appeals interpretation differed somewhat as it saw in these decisions an

> ancient doctrine conceived in the common law of this Commonwealth that a confession induced by coercive techniques, including the use of promises or of undue influence, while under the authority of civil as well as police personnel during an interrogation is, indeed, involuntary and inadmissible in a criminal prosecution. (Slip op., p. 4.)

The first of these cases is *Young v. Commonwealth*, 71 Ky. (8 Bush) 366 (1872), in which the defendant sought suppression of a statement made by him to the sheriff after having been arrested. The defendant contended, however, that the statement was made at the urging of one working in cooperation with the state and that but for assurances given by the other that he would be better off to make the statement, he would not have done so. In response to the contention that the statements were not voluntary but were made under the influence of hopes and fears held out to him, the Court said:

> The general doctrine is indisputable, that confessions which are "forced from the mind by the flattery of hope or the torture of fear" are considered as made under mental duress, and therefore incompetent as evidence; but whether they are so extorted must depend on the character of the authority, power, or influence by which they are induced; and it will not be presumed that a person having no control over a prisoner, or the charge against him, or authority to make good a promise or execute a threat, could without physical force, or duress at least, so far inspire either hope or fear in his mind as to induce a false confession of his guilt. While therefore it is clear that confessions induced by promises, threats, or advice of the prosecutor or officer having the prisoner in charge, or of anyone having authority over him, or the prosecution itself, or of "a private person in the presence of one in authority," whose acquiescence may be presumed, will not be deemed voluntary, and will be rejected, the rule is generally the reverse in relation to confessions superin-

> duced by indifferent persons, acting officiously, without any kind of authority; and confessions made under such circumstances will be admitted in evidence. (Citations omitted.)

Discerning no error in the trial court's admission of the statement in evidence, the Court concluded:

> Whatever may have been the peril of the appellant, and the effect on his mind of the circumstances which surround him, we can see no sufficient reason for treating the advice of Denson otherwise than as the counsel of a private friend of the defendant, which did not render his subsequent admissions incompetent as evidence, although it may have induced him to make the admissions.

The second of the cases so heavily relied upon is *Rector v. Commonwealth*, 80 Ky. 468 (1883), in which a theft was committed by two persons. After the thieves were arrested and were being returned to the county where the crime had been committed, the victim stated to them that if they would tell him where the stolen property was located, things would go better for them and the victim would not prosecute them "hard." In response to this state of affairs, the Court held:

> It is a general rule that confessions which are induced by hopes or fears raised by the promise or threats of the prosecutor, or of any person having authority over the prisoner at the time, are not considered voluntary, having been made under mental duress, and therefore not competent.

Due to the paucity of facts, it is difficult to say with certainty whether the evidence in *Rector* was excluded on the basis of representations of the victim, a private person, or whether the fact of appellants' custody and a presumed cooperation between the victim and the authorities was decisive.

The next case is *Renaker v. Commonwealth*, 172 Ky. 714, 189 S.W. 928 (1916), where state action was clearly present. In response to appellant's motion to suppress, the Court said:

> To render evidence of such confession incompetent, it must have been influenced by promises, threats, or advice of the prosecutor or officer having the prisoner in charge, or of any one having him in duress or having authority over him.

Id. at 932.

Finally is *Baughman v. Commonwealth*, 206 Ky. 441, 267 S.W. 231 (1924), wherein the sixteen-year-old defendant was brutalized by "one of the deputy sheriffs during the course of interrogating him about the crime." *Id.* at 232. The trial judge excluded the defendant's confession as constitutionally infirm but admitted evidence of collateral facts obtained as a result of the confession. On appeal from the conviction, the appellant challenged the admission of this evidence and the court was led to write at length on the admissibility of confessions. It noted that in English history, torture had been administered to extract confessions by duly constituted officers and by ecclesiastical and other voluntary inquisitors. As a result, the Court wrote, a modern rule emerged excluding confessions obtained by duress, coercion, threat, promise of reward or other unlawful means. The theory was that because of the unlawful means, the confession might be false. Such confessions were also to be excluded as a means of judicial condemnation of inhumane methods.

While there was state action in *Baughman*, dictum in the opinion is broad enough to permit the conclusion that state action was not always required; that a confession obtained by private actors engaged in barbarous practices should also be excluded. Of the cases discussed hereinabove, the oldest and most lucid is *Young v. Commonwealth*, and it quite clearly requires state action in ordinary circumstances. However, there is language in *Young* ("or of anyone having authority over him") which is capable of broad construction, but the context generally requires the conclusion that the authority be under color of law. In fact, the Court said that confessions made to "indifferent persons, acting officiously, without any kind of authority" would be admitted in evidence. Nevertheless, all of the cases acknowledge that the use of physical force or some other means which would shock the conscience is intolerable and that statements obtained thereby should be excluded. Moreover, it is doubtful that statements obtained in such a manner would meet the test of relevancy set forth in KRE 401 or survive a motion to exclude pursuant to KRE 403.

Exclusion of statements or confessions by virtue of our common law tradition which condemns confessions obtained by severe duress or physical force is limited and statements or confessions should be excluded on such grounds only in compelling circumstances. In most cases, one aggrieved by the admission of a statement or confession believed by him to have been unfairly obtained by a private person will be limited to the rights assured in *Crane v. Kentucky*, 476 U.S. 683, 106 S.Ct. 2142, 90 L.Ed.2d 636 (1986).

> [Evidence of] the physical and psychological environment that yielded the confession can also be of substantial relevance to the ultimate factual issue of the defendant's guilt or innocence. Confessions, even those that have been found to be voluntary, are not conclusive of guilt.... Accordingly, regardless of whether the defendant marshaled the same evidence earlier in support of an unsuccessful motion to suppress, and entirely independent of any question of voluntariness, a defendant's case may stand or fall on his ability to convince the jury that the manner in which the confession was obtained casts doubt on its credibility.

Id., 476 U.S. at 689, 106 S.Ct. at 2146.

The central findings of the trial court, the findings on which it and the Court of Appeals determined that appellant's confession should be suppressed, were that during the questioning, appellee felt intimidated and coerced and that he was led to believe that in exchange for his cooperation, he would not be prosecuted. These findings are woefully insufficient to justify application of the common law rule discussed hereinabove. In the circumstances which prevailed here, our decision in *Peek v. Commonwealth*, *supra*, is dispositive.

* * *

The opinion of the Court of Appeals is reversed and this cause remanded to the Jefferson Circuit Court for further proceedings consistent herewith.

Reynolds, Spain and Wintersheimer, JJ., concur.

Leibson, J., dissents by separate opinion in which Stephens, C.J., and Stumbo, J., join.

JUSTICE LEIBSON, DISSENTING.

Respectfully, I dissent.

This Court has relied on *Colorado v. Connelly*, 479 U.S. 157, 107 S.Ct. 515, 93 L.Ed.2d 473 (1986), which is not and should not be considered dispositive of the issues in this case. *Colorado v. Connelly* is factually inapposite in critical particulars. Further, as I will document, it turns on different constitutional principles than those that should control our decision here. If the only value our forbearers intended to constitutionalize by the privilege against compulsory self-incrimination was to deter oppressive police activity, it would be proper to confine the privilege to the activities of public officials, and to confine our discussion to standards that would be appropriate in deciding when police activity is so oppressive self-incriminating statements should be suppressed. But once we recognize that the *primary* purpose of this inalienable right was not to deter police activity but to establish standards of decency and respect for human dignity that must not be transgressed in a free society, we must conclude the purpose of this constitutional clause is to deny the use of coerced confessions from whatever source, whether public or private: whether the sheriff, the church inquisitor, the local lynch mob, or rampaging vigilantes. The problem with the Majority Opinion is that we have failed to recognize that the privilege is there, whether the coercion is public or private, but *different limitations* apply to what activities can be tolerated from the police before evidence should be suppressed than apply where private persons are involved.

When Thomas Jefferson articulated in *The Declaration of Independence* that we "are endowed by [our] Creator with certain unalienable rights," and that "to secure these rights governments are instituted among men," when, speaking for all of us, he proclaimed, "I have sworn upon the altar of God eternal hostility against every form of tyranny of the minds of man,"[1] the scope of this vision was not limited to deterring oppressive police activity.

In *Colorado v. Connelly*, Connelly, on his own volition, approached a police officer on the streets of downtown Denver and stated that he had committed a murder and wanted to talk about it. He was given *Miranda* warnings (*Miranda v. Arizona*, 384 U.S. 436, 86 S.Ct. 1602, 16 L.Ed.2d 694 (1966)) and he then provided the details, which were later confirmed. The compulsion involved, if it should be viewed as such, was the power of his own conscience, and compulsion from a "third party" was involved only in the sense Connelly believed that he was following the "voice of God." He confessed because he believed "God's voice had told him either to confess or to commit suicide."

1. Letter to Dr. Benjamin Rush dated September 23, 1800.

He questioned the right to use the confession because he had had psychiatric problems which, he claimed, interfered with the exercise of his own free will. It takes no stretch of the imagination to conclude that this is not the situation our constitutional forbearers, state and federal (and I perceive no difference in this respect), had in mind when they constitutionalized the privilege against compulsory self-incrimination. In *Colorado v. Connelly* it would have been enough to hold that one's own psyche cannot unconstitutionally compel his confession. But Chief Justice Rehnquist's opinion in *Colorado v. Connelly* goes further to generalize that "coercive police activity is a necessary predicate to the finding that a confession is not 'voluntary' within the meaning of the Due Process Clause of the Fourteenth Amendment." 479 U.S. at 165, 107 S.Ct. at 522, 93 L.Ed.2d at 483. He states:

> The most outrageous behavior by a private party seeking to secure evidence against a defendant does not make that evidence inadmissible under the Due Process Clause. 479 U.S. at 166, 107 S.Ct. at 521, 93 L.Ed.2d at 483.

This has been misperceived as authority that the citizen's right to constitutional protection against compulsory self-incrimination does not extend to "outrageous behavior by a private party." Actually the opinion simply restates the longstanding principle that rights guaranteed by the Federal Constitution only apply in state prosecutions through the Fourteenth Amendment, which requires that "state action" be involved in the violation of such rights. All that *Colorado v. Connelly* really holds is that unless there is state action there is no federal question. Other language in the opinion that has been read to suggest that the scope of constitutional protection against the use of coerced confessions is limited to the activities of governmental officials, and suggesting there is historical precedent for refusing to apply it to the coercive activities of private parties, however outrageous, is simply a failed constitutional analysis.

Far more persuasive than Chief Justice Rehnquist's brief and undocumented generalizations in *Colorado v. Connelly* about the background of the Fifth Amendment's self-incrimination clause are the numerous opinions of sister states with constitutional clauses similar to our own applying protection to confessions coerced by private persons. *See* cases cited in the Appellee's Brief, pp. 17–19. A few in particular that I would urge my colleagues to consider are *Fisher v. State*, 145 Miss. 116, 110 So. 361 (1926); *Lawton v. State*, 152 Fl. 821, 13 So.2d 211 (1943); and *State v. Bowe*, 77 Hawai'i 51, 881 P.2d 538 (1994).

Recognizing there must be some reasonable limits on the length of this dissent, I will limit my discussion to just a few of the historical resources refuting this failed constitutional analysis of the self-incrimination privilege. An excellent discussion is found in Pittman, *The Colonial and Constitutional History of the Privilege Against Self-Incrimination in America*, 21 Va. L. Rev. 763 (1935), which includes this quote from English History found in the "Case of the Army ['Cromwell's Army'] Truly Stated" (1647):

> That it be declared that *no person* or court shall have power or be permitted to enforce any person to ... answer to any Interrogatories against himself in any criminal cause. *Id.* at 773. (Emphasis added.)

Another excellent source is a lengthy article found in the Harvard Law Review, *Developments in the Law—Confessions*, 79 Harv. L. Rev. 935–1120, *see* "Voluntariness", pp. 954–84, which, *inter alia*, discusses the appropriate rule where pressure to confess comes from the employer as a "person in authority" (our present problem), and then concludes:

> A confession obtained by threats and beatings is, of course, inadmissible without reference to the 'authority' of the assailant. *Id.* at 958.

To quote from a recent publication in the Harvard Law Review, *Right Against Self-Incrimination—Involuntary Confessions*, 101 Harv. L. Rev. 179 (1987), citing supporting cases and authorities:

> The privilege against self-incrimination ... is founded on perhaps the most basic constitutional value, "the respect a government—state or federal—must accord to the dignity and integrity of its citizens." However, any person who coerces a confession necessarily violates a suspect's dignity by overriding his free will, and the state participates in that violation by allowing coerced statements to be used as evidence. Therefore, admitting coerced confessions, no matter who coerced them, is fundamentally unfair.
>
> Admitting confessions coerced by third parties is also contrary to precedent. Both state and federal courts have ruled that confessions coerced by private parties or foreign policemen are inadmissible, and the Supreme Court itself excluded a confession coerced by a foreign policeman in *Bram v. United States* [168 U.S. 532, 18 S.Ct. 183, 42 L.Ed. 568 (1897)]. *Id.* [168 U.S. at 540–45, 18 S.Ct.] at 186–87. (Citations omitted.)
>
> As stated by Justice Brennan in his dissenting opinion in *Colorado v. Connelly*:
>
> This Court's assertion that we would be required "to establish a brand new constitutional right" to recognize the respondent's claim, [citation omitted], ignores 200 years of constitutional jurisprudence. 479 U.S. at 176, 107 S.Ct. at 526–27, 93 L.Ed.2d at 490.

Justice Brennan cites, *inter alia*, "W. Hawkins, Pleas of the Crown (6th ed 1787): '[a] confession, therefore, whether made upon an official examination or *in discourse with private persons*, which is obtained from a defendant ... is not admissible evidence; for the law will not suffer a prisoner to be made the deluded instrument of his own conviction.'" *Id.*

Our state constitutional clause protecting against compulsory self-incrimination is drawn from a common law heritage and the text of other state constitutions, not the federal Bill of Rights. *See* Gormley and Hartman, *The Kentucky Bill of Rights: A Bicentennial Celebration*, 80 Ky. L. J. 1 (1990–91). But textual differences between the federal and state constitutions is not the issue here. There is no less reason why in a federal prosecution the confession should not be suppressed if coerced by private persons by physical abuse or intimidation than in a state prosecution. I fully agree that *Miranda* should not apply to cases involving the activities of private persons, and that cases involving only persuasion or inducement to confess by private persons, even if there is an element of deception, do not fall within the privilege. But historical precedent for federal as well as state constitutional law calls for suppression when truly the accused has been coerced into confessing.

Our Majority Opinion quotes from *Newman v. Stinson*, Ky., 489 S.W.2d 826 (1972). The case holds parallel interpretation of the state and federal clauses was appropriate for the issue presented. But the quote is out of context. *Newman v. Stinson* holds, quite simply, that requiring a breathalyzer and using evidence of refusal is non-testimonial in nature, and that this is not covered by either the Fifth Amendment or Section Eleven. The decision in *Newman v. Stinson* is beside the point.

It is important to understand why the United States Supreme Court has held that state action is required before Fifth Amendment protection applies in state cases. It is because the Fifth Amendment applies to state prosecution only because of the Fourteenth Amendment. *Malloy v. Hogan*, 378 U.S. 1, 84 S.Ct. 1489, 12 L.Ed.2d 653 (1964). It is the Fourteenth Amendment that requires state actors, not the Fifth Amendment. However, the question before us is not what the United States Supreme Court would say if asked to decide whether Cooper was protected by the Federal Constitution against the use of his statements. It is whether the law of our state, Kentucky, as expressed in the constitutional mandate in Section Eleven of the Kentucky Constitution and our cases interpreting Kentucky's self-incrimination privilege, is limited to official misconduct or extends to intolerable behavior used by private persons to extract a confession.

Clearly, it does. Given evidence a confession is coerced, our Kentucky Constitution, Section Eleven, since 1792 and independent of the Federal Constitution, requires it should be suppressed,[2] and this principle is not limited: it extends to voluntary inquisitions in which no state action is implicated in appropriate circumstances. The four seminal cases in Kentucky cited in the Majority Opinion are more than enough to compel this conclusion: *Young v. Commonwealth*, 71 Ky. (8 Bush.) 366 (1872); *Rector v. Commonwealth*, 80 Ky. 468 (1882); *Renaker v. Commonwealth*, 172 Ky. 714, 189 S.W. 928 (1916); and *Baughman v. Commonwealth*, 206 Ky. 441, 267 S.W. 231 (1924). The Majority Opinion states that in *Baughman v. Commonwealth* our Court

> ... noted that in English history, torture had been administered to extract confessions by duly constituted officers *and by ecclesiastical and other voluntary inquisitors*. As a result, the [*Baughman*] Court wrote, a modern rule emerged excluding confessions obtained by duress, coercion, threat, promise of award or other unlawful means. The theory was that because of the unlawful means, the confession might be false. Such confessions were also to be excluded as a means of judicial condemnation of inhumane methods. (Majority Op., p. 79, emphasis added.)

2. "He ['the accused'] cannot be compelled to give evidence against himself, ..." Ky. Const., Section 11.

Yet the Majority Opinion has concluded that Section Eleven does not apply unless official misconduct is involved. This decision is refuted by the cases it cites.

No doubt recognizing the enormity of denying protection against the coercive activities of private persons in all circumstances, no matter how coercive, the Majority softens the denial of the constitutional privilege by advising the accused to look for help to other rules of evidence, specifically KRE 401 and 403. Majority Op., p. 79. Rule 401 and 403 address excluding evidence because it is either irrelevant or is not sufficiently probative of the issues presented. But a coerced confession is both highly relevant and extremely probative of the guilt of the accused, and the method by which it is obtained makes it no less so. Had the evidence here been that the appellee was brutally beaten by his UPS supervisors to force him to give evidence against himself, the evidence would have been no less relevant and probative. And while such methods sometimes raise questions of credibility, credibility is not grounds for exclusion, but an issue for the jury who hears the confession, and the use of force will not affect credibility where there are corroborating circumstances. KRE 401 and 403 are not viable alternatives for the constitutional right to be protected here, the privilege against the use of coerced self-incrimination whether the confession is extracted by public officials or voluntary inquisitors. It only confuses the law of evidence to suggest otherwise.

A trial is a search of the truth. The rules of evidence are an attempt to construct neutral principles to arrive at the truth. Rare indeed is there a reason strong enough to override this principle. But suppressing self-incriminating evidence coerced from an accused is one of those rare instances developed in our law where suppressing the means used for obtaining the evidence is more important than the search for the truth. That is why, as illustrated by *Jackson v. Denno*, 378 U.S. 368, 84 S.Ct. 1774, 12 L.Ed.2d 908 (1964), when the proof is clear that the evidence has been coerced, truth is not to be considered.

> The aim of the requirement of due process [in suppressing coerced confessions] is not to exclude presumptively false evidence, but to prevent fundamental unfairness in the use of evidence, whether true or false. *Lisenba v. California*, 314 U.S. 219, 236, 62 S.Ct. 280, 289–90, 86 L.Ed. 166 (1941).

The arena where it matters whether the confession has been extracted through misconduct of public officials or the activities of private actors is where it comes to deciding what set of circumstances call for applying the constitutional principle. It is here that, quite properly, over time we have evolved higher and different standards in judging whether to suppress for police activity than the standards that are suitable in judging the inducements used by private persons to extract self-incriminating statements. For instance, promises not to prosecute made by private persons who cannot speak for the government ordinarily do not constitute circumstances that require constitutional protection. Nor does the threat to withhold helping the accused make bond (*Peek v. Commonwealth*, Ky., 415 S.W.2d 854 (1967)). What has that to do with cases involving pressure from those in authority with power to command compliance, whether public or private, or lynch mobs applying force or duress, or private persons who confine and mistreat the accused until he confesses? The constitutional principle applies to the action of these volunteers as clearly as it does to those involved in state action. How can we think otherwise?

The real problem with this case is not whether there is no self-incrimination privilege. It is whether or not the circumstances involved here are such that the privilege should apply, and the evidence should be suppressed. In resolving this problem, how the United States Supreme Court might decide to interpret the Fifth Amendment, or to apply it in state prosecutions covered by the Due Process Clause, is useful in interpreting our own Kentucky constitutional protection only where the federal case is persuasive. And *Colorado v. Connelly* is certainly not persuasive where confessions coerced by private persons are concerned. There is no reason to abandon or discard our Kentucky constitutional protection and the language of our own precedents because the United States Supreme Court might hold differently. Further, there is really no good reason why the United States Supreme Court would interpret Fifth Amendment protection inapplicable to a federal prosecution in circumstances, unlike *Colorado v. Connelly*, where there is proof of intimidation used by private persons to compel a confession. Comparing the language applied to the situation presented in *Brown v. Mississippi*, 297 U.S. 278, 56 S.Ct. 461, 80 L.Ed. 682 (1936), one would conclude otherwise.

* * *

When in the future a law professor will need a case to illustrate how "hard cases made bad law," he can cite this case. The issue should be *whether* the constitutional principle should apply to the *methods* used here by UPS personnel to induce Cooper to confess, not whether we have a clause in our Kentucky Constitution protecting our citizens against compulsory self-incrimination, whether from public officials or private oppressors.

The privilege against compulsory self-incrimination extends to voluntary inquisitions in which no state action is implicated when the coercive interrogation is conducted by persons reasonably appearing to the accused as "having him in duress or having authority over him." *Renaker v. Commonwealth*, 172 Ky. 714, 189 S.W. 928, 932 (1916). The historical understanding of how Kentucky interprets our protection against self-incrimination is thus stated in *Young v. Commonwealth*, 71 Ky. (8 Bush) 366, 370 (1872):

> The general doctrine is indisputable, that confessions which are 'forced from the mind by the flattery of hope or the torture of fear' are considered as made under mental duress, and therefore incompetent as evidence; but *whether they are so extorted must depend on the character of the authority, power or influence by which they are induced. Id.* Emphasis added.

To deny Section Eleven protection unless there is misconduct by public officials is to lose sight of its historical underpinnings, to lose sight of the reasons why we have this self-incrimination clause in our Kentucky Constitution. Further, to relegate protection of the accused in these circumstances to rulings the trial court might consider under KRE 401 or KRE 403 is an error of monumental proportions.

Therefore, I dissent.

Stephens, C.J., and Stumbo, J., join.

Notes and Questions

1. The 4–3 *Cooper* majority held Section 11 of the Kentucky Constitution is "coextensive" with the Fifth Amendment and provides "identical protections against self-incrimination," notwithstanding language in *Young v. Commonwealth*, 71 Ky. 366 (1872), to the effect that the state constitution applies not only to state actors but also to "anyone having authority over" the accused. The *Cooper* Court did hold open the possibility, however, that a statement could still be suppressed if coerced by a private person who used "physical force or some other means which would shock the conscience."

2. Section 11 provides that a defendant in a criminal case cannot be compelled to "*give evidence* against himself," whereas the Fifth Amendment provides that the defendant cannot be compelled to "*be a witness* against himself." Did the Cooper Court correctly hold that these provisions are "coextensive" with each other?

Commonwealth v. Ayers

Supreme Court of Kentucky (2013)
435 S.W.3d 625

Opinion of the Court by Justice Cunningham.

Appellee, William Ayers, was an attorney licensed in Kentucky with extensive experience in the practice of criminal law. However, such knowledge appears remiss from his professional and personal choices. On April 10, 2008, a Jefferson County grand jury indicted Ayers on five counts of failure to file Kentucky tax returns for the years 2002–2006.

For the nearly two-year period between indictment and trial, Ayers appeared on his own behalf without expressing a desire for counsel until the day before a previously continued jury trial was scheduled to begin. Only at this delinquent date did Ayers request yet another continuance for the stated purpose of possibly retaining private counsel, which was overruled by the trial judge. Prior to any proof being presented at trial, the court noted the difference between typical pro se proceedings and this case, in which the defendant is an experienced criminal trial attorney and well-versed in evidence and court rules. However, no formal *Faretta* hearing was ever conducted at any stage of the trial court proceedings. *See Faretta v. California*, 422 U.S. 806, 95 S.Ct. 2525, 45 L.Ed.2d 562 (1975). At trial, evidence was presented that Ayers used his fiduciary status to launder money through clients' bank accounts. Most damning, he perpetuated his scheme through the misuse of his status as power of attorney for his client Robert Miller, a homeless man.

A Jefferson Circuit Court jury found Ayers guilty of five counts of failing to file a state tax return and recommended a sentence of three years on each count, to run concurrently. The trial court then sentenced Ayers in accord with the jury's recommendation. The Court of Appeals reversed the conviction and we granted discretionary review. The sole issue on appeal is whether the trial court's failure to conduct a *Faretta* hearing requires us to set aside Ayers' conviction and order a new trial. After reviewing the record and the law, we reverse the decision of the Court of Appeals and reinstate Ayers' conviction.

Faretta *Hearing*

At the time of his conviction, Ayers had practiced criminal defense law in the Commonwealth for over fifteen years. It is undisputed that Ayers was a well-known criminal defense attorney who regularly practiced in the very court in which he was tried and convicted. In fact, over two-hundred pages of records from the Administrative Office of the Courts detailing Ayers' appearances as counsel in criminal cases were admitted into evidence. Taken in this context, we refuse to sustain Ayers' rigid interpretation of our prior decisions requiring a *Faretta* hearing. Any result to the contrary would have us sanction a legal formalism over reality. "Common sense," as spoken so eloquently by former Chief Justice John Palmore, "must not be a stranger in the house of the law." *Cantrell v. Kentucky Unemployment Ins. Comm'n*, 450 S.W.2d 235, 237 (Ky. 1970). Under the unique facts of this case, we hold that Ayers was not entitled to a *Faretta* hearing.

"The Sixth Amendment to the United States Constitution and Section Eleven of the Kentucky Constitution guarantee criminal defendants the right to counsel[.]" *King v. Commonwealth*, 374 S.W.3d 281, 290 (Ky. 2012). Additionally, a defendant has a constitutional right to proceed without counsel when the defendant knowingly and intelligently elects to do so. *Faretta*, 422 U.S. at 835, 95 S.Ct. 2525. This directive is well-established in the Commonwealth. *See, e.g., Depp v. Commonwealth*, 278 S.W.3d 615, 619 (Ky. 2009); *Grady v. Commonwealth*, 325 S.W.3d 333, 342 (Ky. 2010). Although our prior decisions prove instructive, a closer look at the purpose of *Faretta* is dispositive of our decision in the present case.

The right of a criminal defendant to proceed without counsel is not a textual directive of the Sixth Amendment, but is rather a judicial interpretation. In so holding, *Faretta* has created a Janus-faced quandary for trial judges. They must look in two directions at once. They must avoid erroneously denying the defendant the right to proceed without counsel. And at the same time, they must avoid erroneously concluding that the defendant has effectively waived his right to counsel. *See Martinez v. Court of Appeal of California*, 528 U.S. 152, 164, 120 S.Ct. 684, 145 L.Ed.2d 597 (2000) ("[J]udges closer to the firing line have sometimes expressed dismay about the practical consequences of [*Faretta*].") (Breyer, J., concurring); *see also United States v. Farhad*, 190 F.3d 1097, 1107 (9th Cir. 1999). Such difficulty in navigating the Sixth Amendment's dueling rights has often forced courts, including this one, to walk a fine line. Appearing to recognize this conflict, the Supreme Court has offered only tepid support for *Faretta* in its more recent opinions. For example, in *Martinez*, the Court held that there is no constitutional right to proceed without counsel on appeal. In arriving at this conclusion, the wisdom of *Faretta* was called into question. *Martinez*, 528 U.S. 152 at 161, 120 S.Ct. 684 ("No one ... attempts to argue that as a rule *pro se* representation is wise, desirable, or efficient."). The majority specifically cast doubt on *Faretta*'s strong reliance on the colonial and pre-colonial English legal traditions as sufficient justification. *Id.* at 156–57, 120 S.Ct. 684.

No matter the historical underpinnings upon which this seminal case was decided, "*Faretta* applies only where a defendant ... foregoes the benefits associated with the right to counsel." *United States v. Leggett*, 81 F.3d 220, 224 (D.C. Cir. 1996). A *Faretta* hearing was unnecessary in the present case because Ayers was not exercising his right to proceed without a lawyer. As an attorney, Ayers never forewent the benefits of counsel. There was a lawyer and a defendant who, in this case, were uniquely one and the same. The analogy of "hybrid representation" proves instructive.

Kentucky is within the minority of jurisdictions that recognize a criminal defendant's right to make a limited waiver of counsel and accept representation in certain matters. *Wake v. Barker*, 514 S.W.2d 692 (Ky. 1974) (citing Ky. Const. §11) ("[T]here is no valid basis for interpreting ['by himself and counsel'] as meaning that the only right guaranteed is to appear with counsel."). This limited waiver is sometimes known as "hybrid representation" and requires trial courts to conduct a *Faretta* hearing to determine whether the waiver is made knowingly, voluntarily, and intelligently. *Hill v. Commonwealth*, 125 S.W.3d 221, 226 (Ky. 2004) (overruled on other grounds by *Grady v. Commonwealth*, 325 S.W.3d 333 (Ky. 2010)). In contrast, the majority of federal and state courts hold that there is no constitutional right to hybrid representation. *See, e.g., McKaskle v. Wiggins*, 465 U.S. 168, 183, 104 S.Ct. 944, 79 L.Ed.2d 122 (1984); *United States v. Mosely*, 810 F.2d 93, 97–98 (6th Cir. 1987). Accordingly, most trial courts permit hybrid representation only as a "matter of grace." *State v. Melson*, 638 S.W.2d 342, 359 (Tenn. 1982). Since our predecessor Court has recognized the right to hybrid representation, primarily under our own Kentucky Constitution, we may construe such matters, either directly or by analogy, with greater constitutional latitude than if we were strictly beholden to a federal directive. *Peters v. Commonwealth* is one such example. No. 97-SC-000316-MR (Ky., Feb. 19, 1998) (unpublished).

In *Peters*, we held that *Faretta* warnings were unnecessary because the defendant received hybrid representation and therefore was never without the assistance of counsel. *Peters, id.* After an appeal from a habeas corpus petition, the United States Court of Appeals for the Sixth Circuit agreed, noting that no Supreme Court precedent clearly requires *Faretta* warnings in these circumstances. *Peters v. Chandler*, 292 Fed. Appx. 453, 457–58 (6th Cir. 2008) (unpublished).

Similarly, in *Metcalf v. State*, a case in which hybrid representation had been granted, the Supreme Court of Mississippi stated that since the defendant "was never without the advice and expertise of his attorney ... there was no need for a waiver instruction." 629 So.2d 558, 566 (Miss. 1993). The Court held that waiver was not even an issue, "[r]egardless of how we label the representation [the defendant] received[.]" *Id.*

Further, in *People v. Lindsey*, the Illinois appellate court held that the defendant had not waived counsel in a manner required by the Illinois rule of procedure. 17 Ill. App.3d 137, 308 N.E.2d 111, 115 (1974). Instead, the court found that the trial judge had utilized his discretion in granting the defendant "the best of both worlds: freedom to conduct his own defense and benefit from the assistance of counsel." *Id.* Other jurisdictions have arrived at a similar conclusion. *See, e.g., United States v. Cromer*, 389 F.3d 662, 680 (6th Cir. 2004); *Phillips v. State*, 604 S.W.2d 904, 908 (Tex. Crim. App. 1979). Most notably, the above-cited hybrid representation cases all involve non-lawyer defendants. Yet, these courts still held that, under the circumstances, *Faretta* did not apply. Therefore, this logic applies to the present case with even greater force because Ayers was himself an attorney. Thus, from indictment through sentencing, Ayers was never without the benefit of counsel—an experienced criminal counsel no less.

Moreover, requiring the trial court to obtain a waiver of counsel in this case would have been a vain and idle endeavor. *Faretta* protections were intended to educate people who are not aware of the benefits of counsel. Clearly, this is not the case here. *See Depp*, 278 S.W.3d at 619 ("[t]o the extent [Kentucky case law] purports to require a rigid, formulaic review of waiver of counsel, it is modified to comport with common sense.").

We fully recognize that our holding here today is somewhat conflicting with other jurisdictions. Some apply *Faretta* in cases involving defendants who are attorneys, as well as defendants with enhanced legal knowledge. *See, e.g., Butler v. State*, 767 So.2d 534 (Fla. Dist. Ct. App. 2000); *U.S. v. Maldonado-Rivera*, 922 F.2d 934 (2nd Cir. 1990); *Neal v. State of Texas*, 870 F.2d 312 (5th Cir. 1989); *U.S. v. Campbell*, 874 F.2d 838 (1st Cir. 1989). While these courts purport to apply *Faretta* (most likely out of an abundance of caution), they apply a bare minimum standard based on the defendants' superior legal acumen. *See Iowa v. Tovar*, 541 U.S. 77, 88, 124 S.Ct. 1379, 158 L.Ed.2d 209 (2004) (recognizing a pragmatic approach to *Faretta* inquiries based on "case specific factors, including the defendant's education or sophistication, the complex or easily grasped nature of the charge, and the stage of the proceeding").

Unlike other jurisdictions, we dispense with the charade of combing the record for some shred of evidence that *Faretta* was satisfied. Instead of reducing the standard for a *Faretta* inquiry to an unrecognizable level, we expand this reasoning to its logical and more appropriate end.

Lastly, *Faretta* does not address the quality of counsel. Its requirements are not invoked when a defendant is represented by a callow and inexperienced lawyer fresh from the bar exam. It would seem to be a glaring incongruity to invoke its requirements when a capable and experienced criminal lawyer is representing himself. Allowing Ayers to avail himself of *Faretta* protections would offend the very purpose and integrity of *Faretta* and its progeny.

Therefore, we hold that criminal defendants who are experienced criminal trial attorneys are not entitled to a *Faretta* hearing or inquiry prior to representing themselves. This holding is not intended to disturb our prior decisions relating to various forms of hybrid representation as applied to non-attorneys.

Conclusion

For the foregoing reasons, we reverse the Court of Appeals and reinstate the Jefferson Circuit Court's judgment.

All sitting. All concur.

Notes and Questions

1. As explained in *Ayers*, a state constitutional right to "hybrid counsel" places Kentucky in the minority among the States.
2. Note that Section 11 of the Kentucky Constitution protects the right of a defendant "to be heard by himself and counsel," whereas the Sixth Amendment provides that the defendant has the right to "Assistance of Counsel for his defence." In what ways is the right protected by the Kentucky Constitution different (or broader) than the federal right?

Section 12

Bowling v. Sinnette

Supreme Court of Kentucky (1984)

666 S.W.2d 743

Opinion of the Court by Justice Vance.

The September, 1982 Grand Jury of Boyd County, Kentucky conducted an investigation and heard evidence relating to certain actions of four former sheriffs of the county. The investigation was not completed, and the matter was referred to the next Grand Jury.

The investigation was continued by the January, 1983 Grand Jury which did not return any indictment as a result of the investigation and did not refer the matter to any subsequent Grand Jury. The final report of the January, 1983 Grand Jury contained the following language:

> "We, the Grand Jury, upon investigating the matter of delinquent tax dismursements (sic) to former sheriffs of this county, have concluded there is evidence of some practices that do not reasonable (sic) confirm (sic) to the applicable statutes and regulations of this state.
>
> "However, we could not unanimously conclude that there was criminal intent or forethought of wrongdoing.
>
> "We cannot reach a decision due to material evidence not being available for our consideration.
>
> "The purpose of this investigation was a legitimate exercise of our duties and responsibilities to the citizens of this county. We are proud that all connected

> with this investigation have acted properly with the best of intentions. The magnitude of this type of investigation naturally draws more public attention than routine investigative matters. However, as instructed by circuit Judge Charles Sinette, as an inquisitorial body we are prevented from drawing conclusions or inferences as to individuals, outside any indictment, nor revealing the substance or proceedings before us.
>
> "The extended term provided was partially due to the complexity of this and other investigations, exclusive of the routine workload.
>
> "The Commonwealth's Attorney's Office, charged with the difficult task of helping twelve lay people through criminal investigatory procedures, and in spite of any undue criticism, have acted admirably and without any attempt to take advantage of our inexperience. Therefore, we wish to express our thanks to the office and staff of the Commonwealth's Attorney's office, having well upheld the ethical duties and high professional standards of their office.
>
> "We hope the citizens of this county recognize the difficult task presented to any grand jury and that this jury and the others preceeding us, have attempted to uphold the history and integrity of our position."

The four former sheriffs filed an ex parte motion styled "In Re: Grand Jury Report filed January 28, 1983" in which they requested that the portions of the Grand Jury report quoted above be stricken. The court sustained the motion upon the ground that the material stricken was surplusage and outside the scope of the Grand Jury and its duties.

There was no appeal from the order. However, an original petition was filed in the Kentucky Court of Appeals against the appellee, Judge of the Boyd Circuit Court, which sought to compel him to vacate the order striking portions of the Grand Jury report.

The Court of Appeals denied the mandamus, and an appeal was taken to this court as a matter of right. We affirm the decision of the Court of Appeals, but for a reason different from the reason stated in the order of the Court of Appeals.

The Court of Appeals dismissed the petition for mandamus for the reason that appellants appeared to have an adequate remedy by appeal. Appellants contend they had no remedy by appeal because the order of circuit court was granted as a result of an ex parte motion in which they were not made parties. They contend there was no civil action as defined by our rules of practice. Consequently, appellants contend there were no parties who could be designated as appellants or appellees in a notice of appeal and a statement of appeal. Their only relief, they contend, lay in a petition for mandamus.

We conclude that the petition for mandamus should not have been dismissed on the ground that appellants had an adequate remedy by appeal. It does not follow, however, that the decision of the Court of Appeals is erroneous if the petition should have been denied for another reason.

A Grand Jury is a part of the court, and under judicial control, so there can be no doubt that a session of the Grand Jury is a proceeding in a circuit court. *Greenwell v. Commonwealth*, Ky., 317 S.W.2d 859, 861 (1958). A Grand Jury is required to inquire into every offense for which any person has been held to answer and for which an indictment or information has not been filed, or other offenses which come to their attention or of which any of them has knowledge. RCr 5.02.

Indictments must be returned to the circuit judge by the foreman of the Grand Jury in the presence of the Grand Jury in open court. RCr 5.20. The Grand Jury must report to the court in writing if there is an insufficient number of votes to indict a person held to answer and must report to the court in writing any case in which the investigation of charges against a defendant are referred to the next Grand Jury.

We are not advised in briefs submitted by the parties to this appeal of any other reports to the court which are required of Grand Juries.

In *Matthews v. Pound*, Ky., 403 S.W.2d 7 (1966), we stated:

> "Again referring to the serious duties and responsibilities of such an inquisitorial and accusing body, it has been held that in the absence of statute a grand jury has no right to file a report reflecting on the character of conduct of public officers or citizens unless it is followed by an indictment. *Coons v. State*, 191 Ind. 580, 134 N.E. 194, 20 A.L.R. 900; *Bennett v. Kalamazoo Circuit Judge*, 183 Mich. 200, 150 N.W. 141, Ann.Cas. 1916E, 223. When the report does not amount to an indictment or presentment, it has been held that such report is not privileged and may be the basis for a libel action. *Poston v. Washington, A. & Mt. V. R. Co.*, 36 App.D.C. 359, 32 L.R.A., N.S., 785. Thus, it is in the interest of the grand jurors to see that all matter which is believed to be a proper basis for future investigation and prosecution should be included in the report. Accusations with substance lacking are baseless."

Matthews v. Pound, *supra*, at page 10. *See also* 38 Am.Jur.2d, *Grand Jury*, §30 and 38 C.J.S., *Grand Juries*, §34.

We align ourselves with those jurisdictions which hold that a Grand Jury has no right to file a report which reflects on the character of a citizen or public officer when no indictment is returned against the citizen or officer. The Grand Jury is an important body under our constitution designed in large part to protect citizens from the necessity of defending themselves against baseless charges. It should not be permitted to cast aspersions on citizens when the evidence before it is insufficient to persuade the members of the Jury that probable cause exists that an offense was committed.

Because the report of a Grand Jury is a judicial proceeding under judicial control, the circuit court has jurisdiction to expunge from a report matters which cannot be properly included therein. Any question of abuse of discretion by the trial court can be resolved by an original action in the Court of Appeals.

The report of the Grand Jury herein indicates that the four former sheriffs engaged in some practices contrary to statute; that the Jury was unable to reach a decision because material evidence was not available for consideration by the Jury, yet the matter was not referred to the next Grand Jury; and no indictment was returned. It was entirely proper for the trial judge to strike these portions of the Grand Jury report.

The decision of the Court of Appeals is affirmed.

All concur.

Notes and Questions

1. The Court also discussed the function and importance of grand juries in our constitutional system in *Fletcher v. Graham*, 192 S.W.3d 350 (Ky. 2006).
2. In *Bowling*, the Court states that the grand jury is "designed in large part to protect citizens from the necessity of defending themselves against baseless charges." How does this view of the role of the grand jury differ from the commonly held view that the grand jury is a tool of the prosecution to investigate and prosecute crime? Or may these views be harmonized?
3. Note that the Fifth Amendment right to indictment by grand jury "is not part of the due process of law guaranteed to state criminal defendants by the Fourteenth Amendment." *Branzburg v. Hayes*, 408 U.S. 665, 688 n.25 (1972) (citing *Hurtado v. California*, 110 U.S. 516 (1884)). Some states permit prosecutors to charge any crime, even felony offenses, by information.
4. Section 12 of the Kentucky Constitution states that "No person, for an indictable offense, shall be proceeded against criminally by information," but it does not itself state which crimes are "indictable offense[s]." The Kentucky courts have said the term refers to "common-law offenses or to statutory offenses the punishments for which are 'infamous.'" *Lakes v. Goodloe*, 195 Ky. 240, 242 S.W. 632, 639 (1922), *abrogated on other grounds by Calloway Cnty. Sheriff's Dep't v. Woodall*, 607 S.W.3d 557 (Ky. 2020). The courts define "infamous" punishment to mean "death or imprisonment in the penitentiary of the state, following a conviction of a felony." *Id.* Therefore, misdemeanors are not "indictable offense[s]." *Id.*

C. Privacy, Sanctity of the Home, and Free Association

"All men are, by nature, free and equal, and have certain inherent and inalienable rights, among which may be reckoned:

First: The right of enjoying and defending their lives and liberties.

...

Third: The right of seeking and pursuing their safety and happiness...." (Ky. Const. §1.)

"Absolute and arbitrary power over the lives, liberty and property of freemen exists nowhere in a republic, not even in the largest majority." (Ky. Const. §2.)

"All men, when they form a social compact, are equal..." (Ky. Const. §3.)

The Supreme Court of Kentucky has noted that "[t]he Commonwealth has a long judicial tradition of leaving its citizens alone." *Yeoman v. Commonwealth, Health Policy Bd.*, 983 S.W.2d 459, 473 (Ky. 1998). As will be demonstrated by the cases that follow, "the privacy rights guaranteed by the Kentucky Constitution exceed those granted by the United States Constitution." *Id.* at 474.

In 1927, the highest Court in the Commonwealth recognized a general right of privacy, based in part on the *Harvard Law Review* article co-authored by Louisville native (and later U.S. Supreme Court Justice) Louis D. Brandeis in December 1890. The Court observed that the right to privacy "has not been concretely defined, and probably is not subject to a concrete definition, but it is generally recognized as the right to be let alone, that is, the right of a person to be free from unwarranted publicity, or the right to live without unwarranted interference by the public about matters with which the public is not necessarily concerned." *Brents v. Morgan*, 221 Ky. 765, 299 S.W. 967, 969–70 (1927).

Though many of the privacy cases decided under the Constitution involve activities conducted within the home, a person's right to privacy is not without limit while there—a person has no right "to do as he pleases on his own property." *Lynch v. Commonwealth*, 902 S.W.2d 813, 815 (Ky. 1995). Thus, for example, the General Assembly may prohibit the operation of a motor vehicle while under the influence of alcohol anywhere in the Commonwealth, even on the driver's own property. *Id.*

The cases that follow will consider the source and scope of the right to privacy in Kentucky. In addition, a similar right of more recent vintage—the right of free association—also will be considered.

Commonwealth v. Campbell

Court of Appeals of Kentucky (1909)
133 Ky. 50, 117 S.W. 383

Opinion of the Court by Judge Barker.

The appellee, Peter Campbell, was arraigned before the police court of Nicholasville (a city of the fourth class) under the following warrant: "Nicholasville Police Court. The Commonwealth of Kentucky, to the Chief of Police of Nicholasville, or to Any Sheriff, Coroner, Jailer, Marshal or Policeman in This State: You are commanded to arrest Pete Campbell and bring him before the Nicholasville police court to answer to the charge of said commonwealth (which sues for the use and benefit of the board of councilmen of the city of Nicholasville) of a breach of the ordinances of said city, to wit: Bringing into the town of Nicholasville spirituous, vinous or malt liquors upon his person or as his personal baggage exceeding a quart in quantity, committed by him in said city on or before the 19th day of February, 1908. Given under my hand as judge of said court, this 19th day of February, 1908. John Traynor, J. N. P. C." He was tried and found guilty in the police court, and a fine of $100 assessed against him. Upon appeal to the Jessamine circuit court, the judgment of the police court was reversed, and the warrant dismissed. From this judgment the commonwealth has appealed.

The ordinance, by virtue of which the warrant was issued, is as follows:

"An ordinance to regulate the carrying, moving, delivering, transferring or distributing intoxicating liquors in the town of Nicholasville.

"Be it ordained by the board of councilmen of the town of Nicholasville:

"(1) It shall be unlawful for any person or persons, individuals or corporations, public or private carrier to bring into, transfer to any other person or persons, corporations, carrier or agent, or servant, deliver or distribute in the town of Nicholasville, Kentucky, any spirituous, vinous, malt or other intoxicating liquor, regardless of the name by which it may be called; either in broken or unbroken packages, provided individuals may bring into said town, upon their person or as their personal baggage, and for their own private use, such liquors in quantity not exceeding one quart.

"(2) Each package of such spirituous, vinous, malt or other intoxicating liquor, regardless of the name by which it may be called, whether broken or unbroken packages, brought into and transferred to other person or persons, corporations, carrier or agents, or servants, delivered or distributed in said town shall constitute a separate offense.

"(3) Any person or persons, individual or corporation, public or private carrier violating the provisions of this ordinance shall be fined not less than $50 nor more than $100 for each offense.

"(4) Provided the provisions of this ordinance do not apply to interstate commerce carriers when engaged in interstate commerce transportation.

"(5) This ordinance shall take effect and be in force from and after its passage and publication.

"Approved this 7th day of February, 1908.

"W. L. Steele, Mayor."

The following subsections of section 3490, Ky. St. (charter of cities of the fourth class), are referred to in the briefs of counsel as having a bearing upon the question in hand:

"The board of council shall have power ... within the city—

"(1) To pass ordinances not in conflict with the Constitution or laws of this state or of the United States, and to impose and collect license fees and taxes on stock used for breeding purposes, and on all franchises, trades, occupations and professions."

"(7) To prevent and remove nuisances at the cost of the owners or occupants, or of the parties upon whose ground they exist, and define and declare by ordinance what shall be a nuisance within the limits of the city, and to punish by fine any person for causing or permitting a nuisance."

"(27) The council shall have power, by ordinance, to license, permit, regulate or restrain the sale of all kinds of vinous, spirituous or malt liquors within the limits of the city, or to restrain or prohibit the sale thereof within one mile of

> the limits thereof, provided nothing herein shall be construed as granting the power or right to one town or city to license, permit, regulate, restrain or prohibit the sale of vinous, spirituous or malt liquors in any other town or city, and may fix the penalty or fine for violation of an ordinance under this section at any sum not exceeding one hundred dollars; provided, that no license to sell such liquors, to be drunk on the premises where sold, granted under this section, shall be for a less amount than two hundred and fifty dollars nor for a greater amount than one thousand dollars. For license to sell same by retail, for medical purposes, they may charge not less than fifty dollars nor more than five hundred dollars. For license to sell same by retail in quantities not less than a quart they may charge not less than one hundred dollars nor more than five hundred dollars. The board of council shall, at any time, have the power and authority to refuse to grant any license, and to suspend or revoke any license granted under or by virtue of the authority conferred by this section, when the board shall deem it necessary so to do in order to preserve the peace or good morals of said towns, and said board of council shall be the exclusive judges of the necessity."
>
> "33. Said city council shall have legislative power to make by-laws and ordinances for the carrying into effect of all the powers herein granted for the government of the city, and to do all things properly belonging to the police of incorporated cities. Said board of council may change the boundary line of any ward or wards of any city now divided into wards, or hereafter divided into wards, under the provisions of this act, not less than sixty days previous to any November election."

It will be observed that the warrant issued against the defendant charges him with bringing into the town of Nicholasville spirituous, vinous, or malt liquors, upon his person or as his personal baggage, exceeding a quart in quantity. So far as the warrant is concerned therefore there is nothing to negative the idea but what the defendant had the liquor for his own use, and for no other purpose. We presume it will not be controverted that, if the council of Nicholasville could limit the quantity of liquor which a person might have in his possession for his own use to a quart, it could prohibit his having in his possession any quantity whatever. We are confronted therefore with the proposition as to whether or not, in this state, it is competent under the police power for any legislative body to prohibit the possession or use of liquor by one for his own necessity or comfort. Broadly stated, the question before us is whether or not it is competent for the Legislature to prohibit a citizen from having in his own possession spirituous liquor for his own use. It will not require any elucidation to show that, if the citizen may be prohibited from having liquor in his possession, he can be prohibited from drinking it, because, of necessity, no one can drink that which he has not in his possession. So that if it is competent for the legislative body of any given city or district, or even the Legislature of the state, to prohibit the citizen from having liquor in his own possession, then a new and more complete way has been discovered for the establishment of total prohibition, not only in any precinct, town, or county, but throughout the state, because, if it is competent to prohibit the citizen from having liquor in his possession, it necessarily follows that he can neither sell nor use it, as it is a physical impossibility to do either without first having had the possession of the interdicted liquor.

When the constitutional convention was in session, it was confronted with the question of how the use of spirituous liquor should be regulated. There were two forces brought strongly to bear upon the convention: First, there were the Prohibitionists, who desired to facilitate and advance in every way the means of banishing liquor from the state; and, on the other hand, there were those who were engaged in the business of manufacturing and selling liquor, who strongly advocated the utmost freedom of the citizen with reference to its use. The convention gave patient and full hearing to both parties to this controversy, and, as a result, formulated a system by which the sale of vinous, spirituous, or malt liquors throughout the state was to be regulated by general laws. By subsection 27 of section 59 of the Constitution, it is provided that the General Assembly shall not pass local or special acts to provide a means of taking the sense of the people of any city, town, district, precinct, or county, whether they wish to authorize, regulate, or prohibit therein the sale of vinous, spirituous, or malt liquors or alter the liquor laws. And by section 61 it is provided that the General Assembly shall, "by general law, provide a means whereby the sense of the people of any county, city, town, district or precinct may be taken, as to whether or not spirituous, vinous or malt liquors shall be sold, bartered or loaned therein, or the sale thereof regulated. But nothing herein shall be construed to interfere with or to repeal any law in force relating to the sale or gift of such liquors. All elections on this question may be held on a day other than the regular election days." Section 154 is as follows: "The General Assembly shall prescribe such laws as may be necessary for the restriction or prohibition of the sale or gift of spirituous, vinous or malt liquors on election days." It will thus be seen that the Constitution prescribes fully the power of the Legislature with reference to the regulation of liquor. The General Assembly is given ample power by general laws to submit to the people the question of whether or not any given district shall have prohibition, and by section 154 they are authorized to prohibit either the sale or gift of liquor on election days.

Now, can it be contended with any show of reason that the framers of the Constitution intended to leave the question of the retailing of liquor in a given district to a vote of the majority of the qualified voters in the district, and yet leave it in the power of the Legislature upon its own motion to prohibit the possession of liquor by the citizen? Before the present Constitution, it was competent for the Legislature to prohibit the sale of liquor by retail in any county, town, or district without any vote being taken by the citizens, or without giving them any voice in the matter; but no one doubts that, under the present Constitution, it is not competent for the Legislature, without a vote of the citizens, to declare the retailing of liquor in any part of the state unlawful. How vain it would be, then, for the framers of the Constitution to thus take from the Legislature the power to regulate the retailing of liquor and place that question within the competency of the qualified voters, and yet leave within the competency of the Legislature the greater power of prohibiting the citizen either from possessing liquor or using it for his own benefit or comfort. It is self-evident that, if the Legislature may pass a general law prohibiting any citizen from possessing or using liquor in any quantity, this would in itself be the most perfect prohibition law possible, because no man could retail liquor without first having possession of it. We cannot believe that the framers of the Constitution intended to thus carefully take from the Legislature the power to regulate the sale of liquor, and at the same time leave with that department of the state government the greater power of prohibiting the possession or ownership of liquor.

The fact that the Constitution, by section 154, leaves with the General Assembly the power of restricting or prohibiting the sale or gift of liquor on election days, clearly shows that the convention had it in mind that but for this special power the Legislature could not even regulate the sale of liquor on election days. The history of our state from its beginning shows that there was never even the claim of a right on the part of the Legislature to interfere with the citizen using liquor for his own comfort, provided that in so doing he committed no offense against public decency by being intoxicated; and we are of opinion that it never has been within the competency of the Legislature to so restrict the liberty of the citizen, and certainly not since the adoption of the present Constitution. The Bill of Rights, which declares that among the inalienable rights possessed by the citizens is that of seeking and pursuing their safety and happiness, and that the absolute and arbitrary power over the lives, liberty, and property of freeman exists nowhere in a republic, not even in the largest majority, would be but an empty sound if the Legislature could prohibit the citizen the right of owning or drinking liquor, when in so doing he did not offend the laws of decency by being intoxicated in public. Man in his natural state has a right to do whatever he chooses and has the power to do. When he becomes a member of organized society, under governmental regulation, he surrenders, of necessity, all of his natural right the exercise of which is, or may be, injurious to his fellow citizens. This is the price that he pays for governmental protection, but it is not within the competency of a free government to invade the sanctity of the absolute rights of the citizen any further than the direct protection of society requires. Therefore the question of what a man will drink, or eat, or own, provided the rights of others are not invaded, is one which addresses itself alone to the will of the citizen. It is not within the competency of government to invade the privacy of a citizen's life and to regulate his conduct in matters in which he alone is concerned, or to prohibit him any liberty the exercise of which will not directly injure society.

The difference between the absolute and relative rights of man, and the power of the government with reference thereto, is thus set forth by Blackstone in his Commentaries on the Laws of England: "The rights of persons considered in their natural capacities are also of two sorts, absolute and relative: Absolute, which are such as appertain and belong to particular men, merely as individuals or single persons; relative, which are incident to them as members of society, and standing in various relations to each other. The first—that is, absolute rights—will be the subject of the present chapter. By the absolute rights of individuals, we mean those which are so in their primary and strictest sense; such as would belong to their persons merely in a state of nature, and which every man is entitled to enjoy, whether out of society or in it. But with regard to the absolute duties, which man is bound to perform considered as a mere individual, it is not to be expected that any human municipal law should at all explain or enforce them. For the end and intent of such laws being only to regulate the behavior of mankind, as they are members of society, and stand in various relations to each other, they have consequently no concern with any other but social or relative duties. Let a man therefore be ever so abandoned in his principles, or vicious in his practice, provided he keeps his wickedness to himself, and does not offend against the rules of public decency, he is out of the reach of human laws. But if he makes his vices public, though they be such as seem principally to affect himself (as drunkenness, or the like), they then become, by the bad example they set, of pernicious effects to society; and therefore it is then the business of human laws to correct them. Here the circumstances of publication is what alters the nature of the case. Public sobriety is a relative duty, and therefore enjoined by our laws; private sobriety is an absolute duty, which, whether it be performed or not, human tribunals can never know; and therefore they can never enforce it by any civil sanction." Book 1, pp. 123, 124.

Cooley, in his work on Constitutional Limitations, thus states the rule with reference to sumptuary laws, and the right of the Legislature to enact them: "In former times sumptuary laws were sometimes passed, and they were even deemed essential in republics to restrain the luxury so fatal to that species of government. But the ideas which suggested such laws are now exploded utterly, and no one would seriously attempt to justify them in the present age. The right of every man to do what he will with his own, not interfering with the reciprocal right of others, is accepted among the fundamentals of our law." Pages 549, 550.

John Stuart Mill, in his great work on Liberty, says: "The object of this essay is to assert one very simple principle, as entitled to govern absolutely the dealings of society with the individual in the way of compulsion and control, whether the means used be physical force in the form of legal penalties, or the moral coercion of public opinion. That principle is that the sole end for which mankind are warranted, individually or collectively, in interfering with the liberty of action of any of their numbers is self-protection. That the only purpose for which power can be rightfully exercised over any member of a civilized community, against his will, is to prevent harm to others. His own good, either physical or moral, is not a sufficient warrant. He cannot rightfully be compelled to do or forbear because it will be better for him to do so, because it will make him happier, because, in the opinions of others, to do so would be wise, or even right. These are good reasons for demonstrating with him, or reasoning with him, or persuading him, or entreating him, but not for compelling him, or visiting him with any evil, in case he do otherwise. To justify that, the conduct from which it is desired to deter him must be calculated to produce evil to some one else. The only part of the conduct of any one, for which he is amenable to society, is that which concerns others. In the part which merely concerns himself, his independence is, of right, absolute. Over himself, over his own body and mind, the individual is sovereign." Pages 22, 23. And again: "Secondly, the principle requires liberty of tastes and pursuits; of framing the plan of our life to suit our own character; of doing as we like, subject to such consequences as may follow; without impediment from our fellow creatures, so long as what we do does not harm them, even though they should think our conduct foolish, perverse, or wrong." Page 28.

In discussing the limits of the authority of society over the individual, our author says: "Though society is not founded on a contract, and though no good purpose is answered by inventing a contract in order to deduce social obligations from it, every one who receives the protection of society owes a return for the benefit, and the fact of living in society renders it indispensable that each should be bound to observe a certain line of conduct towards the rest. This conduct consists: First, in not injuring the interests of one another, or rather certain interests, which either by express legal provision or by tacit understanding, ought to be considered as rights; and, secondly, in each person's bearing his share (to be fixed on some equitable principle) of the labors and sacrifices incurred for defending the society or its members from injury and molestation. These conditions society is justified in enforcing, at all costs to those who endeavor to withhold fulfillment. Nor is this all that society may do. The acts of an individual may be hurtful to others, or wanting in due consideration for their welfare, without going the length of violating any of their constituted rights. The offender may then be justly punished by opinion, though not by law. As soon as any part of a person's conduct affects prejudicially the interests of others, society has jurisdiction over it, and the question whether the general welfare will or will not be promoted by interfering with it becomes open to discussion. But there is no room for entertaining any such question when a person's conduct affects the interests of no persons besides himself, or needs not affect them unless they like (all the persons concerned being of full age, and the ordinary amount of understanding). In all such cases there should be perfect freedom, legal and social, to do the action and stand the consequences." Pages 144, 145 and 146. Again: "In like manner, when a person disables himself, by conduct purely self regarding, from the performance of some definite duty incumbent on him to the public, he is guilty of a social offense. No person ought to be punished simply for being drunk, but a soldier or a policeman should be punished for being drunk on duty. Whenever, in short, there is a definite damage, or a definite risk of damage, either to an individual or to the public, the case is taken out of the province of liberty, and placed in that of morality or law." Pages 157, 158.

Black, in his work on Intoxicating Liquors (page 50, §38), says: "But it is justly held that a provision in such a law that no person, without a state license, shall 'keep in his possession, for another, spirituous liquors,' is unconstitutional and void. 'The keeping of liquors in his possession by a person, whether for himself or for another, unless he does so for the illegal sale of it, or for some other improper purpose, can by no possibility injure or affect the health, morals, or safety of the public, and therefore the statute prohibiting such keeping in possession is not a legitimate exertion of the police power. It is an abridgment of the privileges and immunities of the citizen without any legal justification, and therefore void.'"

* * *

In discussing the question before us, we have assumed that the general council of the city of Nicholasville has been clothed with all the authority to enforce what is called the police power which the General Assembly possesses, and also that the city of Nicholasville has by regular proceedings prohibited the sale of liquor within its boundary; but with these assumptions we have not been able to uphold the warrant in this case. It will be observed that the defendant is not charged with having the liquor in his possession for the purpose of selling it, or even giving it to another. The sole charge against him is that he had it in his possession, and therefore we must presume that he had it there for a lawful purpose if he could so hold it. Nothing that we have said herein is in derogation of the power of the state under the Constitution to regulate the sale of liquor, or any other use of it which in itself is inimical to the public health, morals, or safety; but as spirituous liquor is a legitimate subject of property, its ownership and possession cannot be denied when that ownership and possession is not in itself injurious to the public. The right to use liquor for one's own comfort, if the use is without direct injury to the public, is one of the citizen's natural and inalienable rights, guaranteed to him by the Constitution, and cannot be abridged as long as the absolute power of a majority is limited by our present Constitution. The theory of our government is to allow the largest liberty to the individual commensurate with the public safety, or, as it has been otherwise expressed, that government is best which governs the least. Under our institutions there is no room for that inquisitorial and protective spirit which seeks to regulate the conduct of men in matters in themselves indifferent, and to make them conform to a standard, not of their own choosing, but the choosing of the lawgiver; that inquisitorial and protective spirit which seeks to prescribe what a man shall eat and wear, or drink or think, thus crushing out individuality and insuring Chinese inertia by the enforcement of the use of the Chinese shoe in the matter of the private conduct of mankind. We hold that the police power—vague and wide and undefined as it is—has limits, and in matters such as that we have in hand its utmost frontier is marked by the maxim: "Sic utere tuo ut alienum non lædas."

The judgment of the circuit court, quashing the warrant in this case, is affirmed.

Notes and Questions

1. The Latin phrase in the penultimate line of the opinion may be translated as "Use your own property in such a way that it does not harm others."
2. The final paragraph also refers to a Chinese proverb. The "enforcement of the use of the Chinese shoe" could refer to someone who, in the proverb, "reshapes one's own foot to try to fit into a new shoe." The reference likely connotes changing the individual to suit the strictures of the government, rather than fashioning a government that suits the people. How does this proverb assist in understanding the relationship between the government and the governed?
3. The philosophy of John Stuart Mill (1806–1873) looms large over the Court's analysis in *Campbell*. Mill was perhaps the most influential English-speaking philosopher of

the 19th century. He conceived of liberty as justifying the freedom of the individual in opposition to unlimited state and social control. He was a proponent of the ethical theory of "utilitarianism," which prescribed actions that maximize happiness and well-being for all affected individuals. (The "utility" to be maximized in utilitarian thought may be defined as whatever tends to produce benefit, advantage, pleasure, good, or happiness, or prevent the happening of mischief, pain, evil, or unhappiness.) Mill's most famous work, On Liberty (quoted at length in *Campbell*), is most famous for espousing the "harm principle": "[T]he only purpose for which power can be rightfully exercised over any member of a civilised community, against his will, is to prevent harm to others." By 21st century standards, this is an exceptionally libertarian point of view.

4. *Campbell* essentially imports Mill's "harm principle" into Sections 1(3) and 2 of the Kentucky Constitution, holding that a person does no harm to another by enjoying liquor "for his own comfort" while at home, so long as he does not appear intoxicated in public.

Hershberg v. City of Barbourville

Court of Appeals of Kentucky (1911)
142 Ky. 60, 133 S.W. 985

Opinion of the Court by Chief Justice Hobson.

Barbourville is a city of the fifth class. The board of council of the city enacted the following ordinance: "That if any person shall smoke a cigarette or cigarettes within the corporate limits of the city of Barbourville after such person shall have had actual notice of the passage of this ordinance, he shall be deemed guilty of a misdemeanor and upon conviction shall be fined not less than one dollar nor more than fifteen dollars, for each offense." The police judge issued a warrant against Henry M. Hershberg, in which he was charged with having violated the ordinance by smoking cigarettes in the city. He was arrested by the Marshall under the warrant and taken before the police judge for trial. Upon a trial of the case he was found guilty and fined. He failed to pay the fine and was committed to jail upon its nonpayment. Thereupon he brought this suit against the city alleging that the ordinance was illegal and void, and that he was unlawfully arrested and imprisoned by reason thereof to his damage in the sum of $5,000, for which he prayed judgment. The circuit court sustained a general demurrer to his petition, and, he declining to plead further, dismissed it. He appeals.

The circuit court in a written opinion held the ordinance void as an unreasonable invasion of the citizen's right of personal liberty. We concur in the conclusion that it is not a reasonable ordinance, and that the circuit court properly so held. *Commonwealth v. Campbell*, 133 Ky. 50, 117 S.W. 383, 24 L.R.A. (N.S.) 172. The ordinance is so broad as to prohibit one from smoking a cigarette in his own home or on any private premises in the city. To prohibit the smoking of cigarettes in the citizen's own home or on other private premises is an invasion of his right to control his own personal indulgences. The city council is authorized by statute to enact and enforce all such local, police, sanitary, and other regulations as do not conflict with general laws. Ky. St. §3637, subd. 7 (Russell's St. §1643, subd. 6). But under this power it may not unreasonably interfere with the right of the citizen to determine for himself such personal matters. If the council may prohibit cigarette smoking in the city, it may prohibit pipe smoking or cigar smoking, or any other use of tobacco. The Legislature did not contemplate conferring such power upon the council. If the ordinance had provided a penalty for smoking cigarettes on the streets of the city, a different question would be presented; but whether such an ordinance would be valid is a question not now presented or decided.

* * *

Judgment affirmed.

Notes and Questions

1. *Hershberg*, relying upon *Campbell*, affirmed a lower court ruling that the ordinance at issue invaded the individual's "right of personal liberty." The opinion emphasizes the sanctity of the home under the Kentucky Constitution, declaring the city's ordinance invalid because it prevented a citizen from smoking cigarettes in his own home. The Court held this was "an invasion of his right to control his own personal indulgences."
2. Note that the Court in *Hershberg* left open the possibility that the city could have prohibited smoking "on the streets of the city," thereby emphasizing that it was not so much the conduct itself—smoking cigarettes—that was dispositive of the constitutional issue in the case, but rather, the location where that conduct occurred. A local ordinance that prohibited indoor tobacco use in all public buildings was upheld as constitutional in *Lexington Fayette County Food & Beverage Association v. Lexington-Fayette Urban County Government*, 131 S.W.3d 745 (Ky. 2004).
3. Historically, the distilling and tobacco industries have been significant players in Kentucky's economy. Perhaps cynically, one could explain the holdings of *Campbell* and *Hershberg* as the Court showing favor to two of the state's leading industries. Do you agree? Or is there a deeper principle involved?

Commonwealth v. Wasson

Supreme Court of Kentucky (1992)
842 S.W.2d 487

Opinion of the Court by Justice Leibson.

Appellee, Jeffrey Wasson, is charged with having solicited an undercover Lexington policeman to engage in deviate sexual intercourse. KRS 510.100 punishes "deviate sexual intercourse with another person of the same sex" as a criminal offense, and specifies "consent of the other person shall not be a defense." Nor does it matter that the act is private and involves a caring relationship rather than a commercial one. It is classified as a Class A misdemeanor.

The appellee is actually charged under KRS 506.030, which covers "solicitation" to commit any criminal offense. If the offense solicited is a Class A misdemeanor, solicitation of the offense is punished as a Class B misdemeanor. KRS 506.030(2)(d). The issue here is whether KRS 510.100, which defines the underlying criminal offense, is constitutional.

The charges were brought in the Fayette District Court where appellee moved to dismiss the charge on grounds that a statute criminalizing deviate sexual intercourse between consenting adults of the same sex, even if the act is committed in the privacy of a home, violates the Kentucky Constitution as: (1) an invasion of a constitutionally protected right of privacy; and (2) invidious discrimination in violation of constitutionally protected rights to equal treatment.

The Fayette District Judge held the statute violated appellee's right of privacy, and dismissed the charge. The Commonwealth appealed to Fayette Circuit Court which affirmed, and further held this statute infringed upon equal protection guarantees found in the Kentucky Constitution. Once more the Commonwealth appealed, and, because of the constitutional issues involved, this Court granted transfer.

Both courts below decided the issues solely on state constitutional law grounds, and our decision today, affirming the judgments of the lower courts, is likewise so limited. Federal constitutional protection under the Equal Protection Clause was not an issue reached in the lower courts and we need not address it. *Bowers v. Hardwick*, 478 U.S. 186, 106 S.Ct. 2841, 92 L.Ed.2d 140 (1986) held federal constitutional protection of the right of privacy was not implicated in laws penalizing homosexual sodomy. We discuss *Bowers* in particular, and federal cases in general, not in the process of construing the United States Constitution or federal law, but only where their reasoning is relevant to discussing questions of state law.

A third issue presented at the trial level was whether KRS 510.100 violated state and federal constitutional protections against cruel punishment. This issue was decided against Wasson in District Court, but not addressed in the Circuit Court judgment. The issue is not preserved, and we decline to discuss it.

The brief statement of facts upon which the District Court rendered judgment is as follows:

Lexington police were conducting a downtown undercover operation. Their modus operandi was to drive to a certain parking area, in plain clothes with microphones on their persons, and try to engage in conversation with persons passing by to see whether they would be solicited for sexual contact. The taped conversation between the undercover officer and Wasson covered approximately 20–25 minutes, toward the end of which Wasson invited the officer to "come home" to his residence. The officer then prodded Wasson for details, and Wasson suggested sexual activities which violated KRS 510.100. There was no suggestion that sexual activity would occur anyplace other than in the privacy of Wasson's home. The sexual activity was intended to have been between consenting adults. No money was offered or solicited.

Seven expert witnesses testified in support of Wasson's case: (1) a cultural anthropologist testified about the presence of homosexuals in every recorded human culture, including societies where they were rejected and those where they have been tolerated or even welcomed; (2) a Presbyterian minister discussed Biblical references, providing a modern interpretation that these references were not an indictment of homosexuals as such, but rather statements against aggression, inhospitality and uncaring relationships; (3) a social historian testified about the presence of homosexuals throughout the history of the United States, despite what was at times exceptionally strict punishment for homosexual acts; (4) a sociologist and sex researcher (a co-author of the Kinsey Report on homosexual behavior) testified that studies indicated "'homosexuality' is just as deep-rooted as 'heterosexuality,'" that it is not a choice and there is no "cure" for it, and that sexual acts prohibited to homosexuals by KRS 510.100, oral and anal sex, are practiced widely by heterosexuals; (5) a psychologist testified that homosexuality is no longer classified as a personality disorder by either the American Psychological Association or the American Psychiatric Association, and further, rather than being in and of themselves either harmful or pathological, the sexual acts outlawed by KRS 510.100 are a necessary adjunct to their sex life; (6) a therapist from a comprehensive care treatment center in Lexington, with fourteen years' experience counseling homosexual clients, testified that the statute criminalizing their sexual activities has an adverse impact on homosexuals and interferes with efforts to provide therapy to those who may need it; and (7) the Professor of Medicine at the University of Louisville, Chief of the Infectious Diseases section, testified at length about the origins and spread of AIDS, expressing the opinion that the statute in question offers no benefit in preventing the spread of the disease and can be a barrier to getting accurate medical histories, thus having an adverse effect on public health efforts.

The testimony from Wasson's expert witnesses is further substantiated by extensive citations to medical and social science literature and treatises supplied in Amicus Curiae Briefs filed by national and state associations of psychologists and clinical social workers, various national and state public health associations, and organizations covering a broad spectrum of religious denominations.[1]

---

1. Specifically, the associations and organizations represented on these Amici Curiae Briefs are: American Psychological Association, Kentucky Psychological Association, Kentucky Psychiatric As-

The Commonwealth, on the other hand, presented no witnesses and offers no scientific evidence or social science data. Succinctly stated, its position is that the majority, speaking through the General Assembly, has the right to criminalize sexual activity it deems immoral, without regard to whether the activity is conducted in private between consenting adults and is not, in and of itself, harmful to the participants or to others; that, if not in all instances, at least where there is a Biblical and historical tradition supporting it, there are no limitations in the Kentucky Constitution on the power of the General Assembly to criminalize sexual activity these elected representatives deem immoral.

The Commonwealth maintains that the United States Supreme Court's decision in *Bowers v. Hardwick, supra*, is dispositive of the right to privacy issue; that the "Kentucky Constitution did not intend to confer any greater right to privacy than was afforded by the U.S. Constitution." Turning to the equal protection argument raised by a statute which criminalizes oral or anal intercourse between persons of the same sex, but not between persons of different sexes, which was not addressed in the *Bowers* case, the Commonwealth argues there is "a rational basis for making such a distinction." To support this argument the Commonwealth takes bits and pieces from the testimony of Wasson's expert witnesses out of context and disregards their overwhelming evidence to the contrary. The thrust of the argument advanced by the Commonwealth as a rational basis for criminalizing consensual intercourse between persons of the same sex, when the same acts between persons of the opposite sex are not punished, is that the level of moral indignation felt by the majority of society against the sexual preference of homosexuals justifies having their legislative representatives criminalize these sexual activities. The Commonwealth believes that homosexual intercourse is immoral, and that what is beyond the pale of majoritarian morality is beyond the limits of constitutional protection.

At the outset the subject is made difficult by a confusion of terms. KRS 510.100 is styled a "sodomy" statute, but its reach is not limited to the Biblical or traditional common law definition of the term. It punishes "deviate sexual intercourse with another of the same sex." "Deviate sexual intercourse" is defined in KRS 510.010(1) as including "any act of sexual gratification involving the sex organs of one (1) person and the mouth or anus of another[.]"

sociation, Kentucky Chapter of the National Association of Social Workers, and Kentucky Society for Clinical Social Workers; American Public Health Association, Community Health Trust, Inc., Heart To Heart, Inc., St. Jude Guild, Inc., and AIDS Education Coalition, Inc.; American Friends Service Committee, American Jewish Committee, Central Presbyterian Church, Louisville, First Unitarian Church of Louisville, Honesty, Louisville, Lexington Friends Meeting, Religious Society of Friends (Quakers), The United Church of Christ, Telos, Louisville, The Temple, Union of American Hebrew Congregations, Unitarian Universalist Association and Universalist Church of Lexington, Central Kentucky Council for Peace and Justice, Fellowship of Reconciliation, Central Kentucky and Louisville Chapters, Presbyterian Church [U.S.A.] and the United Methodist Church.

A significant part of the Commonwealth's argument rests on the proposition that homosexual sodomy was punished as an offense at common law, that it has been punished by statute in Kentucky since 1860, predating our Kentucky Constitution. Indeed, in *Bowers v. Hardwick, supra*, 478 U.S. at 193, n. 6, 106 S.Ct. at 2846, n. 6, the United States Supreme Court takes note of the original Kentucky statute codifying the common law found at 1 Ky. Rev. Stat., Ch. 28, Art. IV, Sec. 11 (1860). This, of course, would lend credence to the historical and traditional basis for punishing acts of sodomy, but for the fact that "sodomy" as defined at common law and in this 1860 statute is an offense significantly different from KRS 510.100, limited to anal intercourse between men. Unlike the present statute our common law tradition punished neither oral copulation nor any form of deviate sexual activity between women. The definitive Kentucky case on the subject is *Commonwealth v. Poindexter*, 133 Ky. 720, 118 S.W. 943 (1909), summarizing the common law and statutory background, and holding:

> "A penetration of the mouth is not sodomy."

In *Poindexter* two men were charged with sodomy "committed by the insertion of the private part of the one into the mouth of the other." The trial court dismissed the indictment as failing to state an offense, and our Court affirmed. In *United States v. Milby*, 400 F.2d 702, 704 (6th Cir. 1968), applying the *Poindexter* holding, the Court states:

> "Concededly, by virtue of *Commonwealth v. Poindexter*, 133 Ky. 720, 118 S.W. 943 (1909), in order for the act of sodomy to be committed by one person on another, under Kentucky law, it is necessary that there be anal penetration."

The Commentary to the Penal Code enacted in 1974 points out:

> "Under former Kentucky law penetration of the mouth was not sufficient....
>
> Sodomy in the fourth degree ... broadens former Kentucky law by including oral copulation." Commentary, KRS 510.070.

Thus the statute in question here punishes conduct which has been historically and traditionally viewed as immoral, but much of which has never been punished as criminal.

The grounds stated by the District Court for striking down the statute as unconstitutional are:

> "KRS 510.100 clearly seeks to regulate the most profoundly private conduct and in so doing impermissibly invades the privacy of the citizens of this state.
>
> Having so found, the Court need not address the other issues raised by the parties."

The Order expressing the judgment of the Fayette Circuit Court "agree[d] with that conclusion," and further held the statute "unjustifiably discriminates, and thus is unconstitutional under Sections 2 and 3 of our Kentucky Constitution." These Sections are:

> "§2. Absolute and arbitrary power over the lives, liberty and property of freemen exists nowhere in a republic, not even in the largest majority.
>
> §3. All men, when they form a social compact, are equal...."

These Sections, together with Sections 59 and 60 of our Kentucky Constitution which prohibit "local or special" legislation, express the guarantee of equal treatment provided by the law in our Kentucky Constitution. The lower courts' judgments limit their finding of unconstitutionality to state constitutional grounds. *Bowers v. Hardwick, supra*, speaks neither to rights of privacy under the state constitution nor to equal protection rights under either federal or state constitutions. *Bowers* addressed the constitutionality of a Georgia statute prohibiting acts of consensual sodomy between persons of the same sex or the opposite sex. Because the Georgia statute embraced both heterosexual and homosexual conduct, the *Bowers* opinion did not involve the Equal Protection Clause of the Fourteenth Amendment.

For reasons that follow, we hold the guarantees of individual liberty provided in our 1891 Kentucky Constitution offer greater protection of the right of privacy than provided by the Federal Constitution as interpreted by the United States Supreme Court, and that the statute in question is a violation of such rights; and, further, we hold that the statute in question violates rights of equal protection as guaranteed by our Kentucky Constitution.

I. Rights of Privacy

No language specifying "rights of privacy," as such, appears in either the Federal or State Constitution. The Commonwealth recognizes such rights exist, but takes the position that, since they are implicit rather than explicit, our Court should march in lock step with the United States Supreme Court in declaring when such rights exist. Such is not the formulation of federalism. On the contrary, under our system of dual sovereignty, it is our responsibility to interpret and apply our state constitution independently. We are not bound by decisions of the United States Supreme Court when deciding whether a state statute impermissibly infringes upon individual rights guaranteed in the State Constitution so long as state constitutional protection does not fall below the federal floor, meaning the minimum guarantee of individual rights under the United States Constitution as interpreted by the United States Supreme Court. *Oregon v. Hass*, 420 U.S. 714, 719, 95 S.Ct. 1215, 1219, 43 L.Ed.2d 570, 575 (1975). The holding in *Oregon v. Hass* is:

> "[A] State is free *as a matter of its own law* to impose greater restrictions on police activity than those this [United States Supreme] Court holds to be necessary upon federal constitutional standards." [Emphasis original.]

Contrary to popular belief, the Bill of Rights in the United States Constitution represents neither the primary source nor the maximum guarantee of state constitutional liberty. Our own constitutional guarantees against the intrusive power of the state do not derive from the Federal Constitution. The adoption of the Federal Constitution in 1791 was preceded by state constitutions developed over the preceding 15 years, and, while there is, of course, overlap between state and federal constitutional guarantees of individual rights, they are by no means identical. State constitutional law documents and the writings on liberty were more the source of federal law than the child of federal law. *See* Vol. 1:1988, "Emerging Issues in State Constitutional Law," A.E. Dick Howard,

The Renaissance of State Constitutional Law. The Virginia Bill of Rights, which had great impact, preceded not only the Bill of Rights in the United States Constitution, but by one month the Declaration of Independence. In an article in the Kentucky Law Journal, Vol. 80: 1991–92, No. 1, *The Kentucky Bill of Rights: A Bicentennial Celebration*, by Gormley and Hartman, the authors attribute the source of much of our original Kentucky Bill of Rights to the then recently enacted Pennsylvania counterpart:

> "A comparison of the Kentucky Bill of Rights of 1792 and a number of earlier, now defunct constitutions of the leading colonies, demonstrates unequivocally that the original Kentucky Bill of Rights was borrowed almost verbatim from the Pennsylvania Constitution of 1790."

The evidence supporting this proposition is carefully documented in the article. Thus, while we respect the decisions of the United States Supreme Court on protection of individual liberty, and on occasion we have deferred to its reasoning, certainly we are not bound to do so, and we should not do so when valid reasons lead to a different conclusion.

We are persuaded that we should not do so here for several significant reasons. First, there are both textual and structural differences between the United States Bill of Rights and our own, which suggest a different conclusion from that reached by the United States Supreme Court is more appropriate. More significantly, Kentucky has a rich and compelling tradition of recognizing and protecting individual rights from state intrusion in cases similar in nature, found in the Debates of the Kentucky Constitutional Convention of 1890 and cases from the same era when that Constitution was adopted. The judges recognizing that tradition in their opinions wrote with a direct, firsthand knowledge of the mind set of the constitutional fathers, upholding the right of privacy against the intrusive police power of the state. This tradition is formulated in ringing terms in the opinion of this Court in *Commonwealth v. Campbell*, 133 Ky. 50, 117 S.W. 383 (1909), but it is also the common thread found in *Commonwealth v. Smith*, 163 Ky. 227, 173 S.W. 340 (1915), *Hershberg v. City of Barbourville*, 142 Ky. 60, 133 S.W. 985 (1911), *Adams Express Co. v. Commonwealth*, 154 Ky. 462, 157 S.W. 908 (1913), and *Lewis v. Commonwealth*, 197 Ky. 449, 247 S.W. 749 (1923). Leading tort cases grounded on that same right of privacy include *Foster-Milburn Co. v. Chinn*, 134 Ky. 424, 120 S.W. 364 (1909), *Douglas v. Stokes*, 149 Ky. 506, 149 S.W. 849 (1912), and *Brents v. Morgan*, 221 Ky. 765, 299 S.W. 967 (1927).

Kentucky cases recognized a legally protected right of privacy based on our own constitution and common law tradition long before the United States Supreme Court first took notice of whether there were any rights of privacy inherent in the Federal Bill of Rights. The first mention of a federal guarantee of the right of privacy is in the Dissenting Opinion of Justice Louis Brandeis in *Olmstead v. United States*, 277 U.S. 438, 478, 48 S.Ct. 564, 572, 72 L.Ed. 944 (1928), in which he defined it as "the right to be let alone—the most comprehensive of rights and the right most valued by civilized men." Actual recognition by the majority as a working premise came much later in *Griswold v. Connecticut*, 381 U.S. 479, 85 S.Ct. 1678, 14 L.Ed.2d 510 (1965).

The list of individual rights guaranteed by the Federal Bill of Rights is patently incomplete; ergo the Ninth Amendment stating:

> "The enumeration in the Constitution, of certain rights, shall not be construed to deny or disparage others retained by the people."

Federal constitutional analysis has proceeded from so-called "emanations" and "penumbras" of the First, Third, Fourth and Fifth Amendments in the Bill of Rights. These amendments elaborate some of the "blessings of liberty" referred to in the Preamble to the United States Constitution, but by no means all of them. It is because the United States Supreme Court has recognized that the list is not exclusive, not even for purposes of federal constitutional protection, that it has undertaken, using the Due Process Clauses in the Fifth and Fourteenth Amendments, to create a so-called zone of privacy constitutionally beyond the reach of governmental intrusion. But the United States Supreme Court is extremely reticent in extending the reach of the Due Process Clauses in substantive matters, albeit this is the jurisprudence of this century and not before, following President Franklin D. Roosevelt's court packing efforts in the 1930's.

Bowers v. Hardwick, *supra*, expresses this reticence. The United States Supreme Court, defining the reach of the zone of privacy in terms of federal due process analysis, limits rights of privacy to "liberties that are 'deeply rooted in this Nation's history and tradition.'" 478 U.S. at 192, 106 S.Ct. at 2844. Sodomy is not one of them. *Bowers v. Hardwick* decides that rights protected by the Due Process Clauses in the Fifth and Fourteenth Amendments to the United States Constitution do not "extend a fundamental right to homosexuals to engage in acts of consensual sodomy." *See* 478 U.S. at 192, 106 S.Ct. at 2844.

Bowers decides nothing beyond this. But state constitutional jurisprudence in this area is not limited by the constraints inherent in federal due process analysis. Deviate sexual intercourse conducted in private by consenting adults is not beyond the protections of the guarantees of individual liberty in our Kentucky Constitution simply because "proscriptions against that conduct have ancient roots." 478 U.S. at 192. Kentucky constitutional guarantees against government intrusion address substantive rights. The only reference to individual liberties in the Federal Constitution is the statement in the Preamble that one of the purposes in writing in the Constitution is to "secure the Blessings of Liberty to ourselves and our Posterity." Similarly, the Kentucky Constitution has a Preamble:

> "We, the people of the Commonwealth of Kentucky, grateful to Almighty God for the civil, political and religious liberties we enjoy, and invoking the continuance of these blessings, do ordain and establish this Constitution."

But the Kentucky Constitution of 1891 does not limit the broadly stated guarantee of individual liberty to a statement in the Preamble. It amplifies the meaning of this statement of gratitude and purpose with a Bill of Rights in 26 sections, the first of which states:

> "§1. All men are, by nature, free and equal, and have certain inherent and inalienable rights, among which may be reckoned:

> First: The right of enjoying and defending their lives and liberties.
>
> ....
>
> Third: The right of seeking and pursuing their safety and happiness.
>
> ....
>
> §2. Absolute and arbitrary power over the lives, liberty and property of freemen exists nowhere in a republic, not even in the largest majority."

While addressing *some* of the same considerations as those expressed in the Preamble to the Federal Constitution, none of this textual material appears in the Federal Constitution. Both the record of the 1890–91 debates and the opinions of Justices of this Court who were the contemporaries of our founding fathers express protection of individual liberties significantly greater than the selective list of rights addressed by the Federal Bill of Rights. There was no mention of a right of privacy in these debates only because the concept was not verbalized as such until after the article by Warren and Brandeis, *The Right of Privacy*, 4 Harv. L. Rev. 193, December 15, 1890, had been publicly disseminated. The ideas Brandeis and Warren expressed in that article as the "right of privacy" were neither unique to the authors nor confined to the Harvard Law School. They were an expression of contemporary thought.

The Commonwealth has stressed that there was no discussion of the right of privacy at the 1890 Kentucky Constitutional Convention, but that is only partly true. The meaning of Sections One and Two as they apply to personal liberty is found in the remarks of J. Proctor Knott of Marion County (see Official Report of the Proceedings and Debates in the 1890 Convention, E. Polk Johnson, Vol. 1, p. 718):

> "[T]hose who exercise that power in organized society with any claim of justice, derive it from the people themselves. That with the whole of such power residing in the people, the people as a body rest under the highest of all moral obligations to protect each individual in the rights of life, liberty, and the pursuit of happiness, *provided that he shall in no wise injure his neighbor in so doing.*" [Emphasis added.]

See also Comments of Delegate J.A. Brents from Clinton County. Debates, Vol. 1, p. 614–18, concluding "majorities cannot and ought not exercise arbitrary power over the minority."

The leading case on this subject is *Commonwealth v. Campbell, supra*. At issue was an ordinance that criminalized possession of intoxicating liquor, even for "private use." Our Court held that the Bill of Rights in the 1891 Constitution prohibited state action thus intruding upon the "inalienable rights possessed by the citizens" of Kentucky. *Id.* 117 S.W. at 385.

Our Court interpreted the Kentucky Bill of Rights as defining a right of privacy, even though the constitution did not say so in that terminology:

> "Man in his natural state has the right to do whatever he chooses and has the power to do. When he becomes a member of organized society, under governmental regulation, he surrenders, of necessity, all of his natural right the exer-

> cise of which is, or may be, injurious to his fellow citizens. This is the price that he pays for governmental protection, but it is not within the competency of a free government to invade the sanctity of the absolute rights of the citizen any further than the direct protection of society requires.... It is *not within the competency of government to invade the privacy of a citizen's life and to regulate his conduct in matters in which he alone is concerned,* or to prohibit him any liberty the exercise of which will not directly injure society. *Id.* [Emphasis added.]
>
> ....
>
> ... let a man therefore be ever so abandoned in his principles, or vicious in his practice, provided he keeps his wickedness to himself, and does not offend against the rules of public decency, he is out of the reach of human laws." *Id.* at 386.

The Court concludes, at p. 387:

> "The theory of our government is to allow the largest liberty to the individual commensurate with the public safety, or, as it has been otherwise expressed, that government is best which governs least. Under our institutions there is no room for that inquisitorial and protective spirit which seeks to regulate the conduct of men in matters in themselves indifferent, and to make them conform to a standard, not of their own choosing, but the choosing of the lawgiver...."

The right of privacy has been recognized as an integral part of the guarantee of liberty in our 1891 Kentucky Constitution since its inception. The *Campbell* case is overwhelming affirmation of this proposition:

> "[W]e are of the opinion that it never has been within the competency of the Legislature to so restrict the liberty of this citizen, and certainly not since the adoption of the present [1891] Constitution. The Bill of Rights, which declares that among the inalienable rights possessed by the citizens is that of seeking and pursuing their safety and happiness, and that the absolute and arbitrary power over the lives, liberty, and property of freeman exists nowhere in a republic, not even in the largest majority, would be but an empty sound if the Legislature could prohibit the citizen the right of owning or drinking liquor, when in so doing he did not offend the laws of decency by being intoxicated in public...." *Id.* at 385.
>
> * * *

At the time *Campbell* was decided, the use of alcohol was as much an incendiary moral issue as deviate sexual behavior in private between consenting adults is today. Prohibition was the great moral issue of its time. It was addressed both in the 1891 Constitution and in the Nineteenth Amendment of the United States Constitution. In 1907, in *Board of Trustees of Town of New Castle v. Scott*, 125 Ky. 545, 101 S.W. 944 (1907), Chief Justice O'Rear passionately attacked the evil of alcohol in a pro-prohibition ruling interpreting Section 61 of the Kentucky Constitution, which provides for local option elections. He stated:

> "There is yet another view of the subject which we must assume was in the mind of the Convention. The liquor traffic had then [in 1891] come to be regarded as one of the most serious evils of the age, if not the most sinister menace to society that was known.
>
> ....
>
> No other subject had been more clearly settled upon as being within the legitimate exercise of the police power of the state than the regulation of the sale and use of intoxicating liquors." *Id.* 101 S.W. at 948.

Notwithstanding their strong views that drinking was immoral, this same Court with these same judges, including Judge O'Rear, in the *Campbell* case recognized that private possession and consumption of intoxicating liquor was a liberty interest beyond the reach of the state.

Nor is the *Campbell* case an aberration. Subsequent cases cited and followed *Campbell.* In *Commonwealth v. Smith*, 163 Ky. 227, 173 S.W. 340 (1915), citing *Campbell*, the Court declared a statute unconstitutional that had led to Smith being arrested for drinking beer in the backroom of an office:

> "The power of the state to regulate and control the conduct of a private individual is confined to those cases where his conduct injuriously affects others. With his faults or weaknesses, which he keeps to himself, and which do not operate to the detriment of others, the state as such has no concern." *Id.*, 173 S.W. at 343.

The holding in *Smith* is that "the police power may be called into play [only] when it is reasonably necessary to protect the *public* health, or *public* morals, or *public* safety." [Emphasis added.]

The clear implication is that immorality in private which does "not operate to the detriment of others," is placed beyond the reach of state action by the guarantees of liberty in the Kentucky Constitution.

In *Hershberg v. City of Barbourville*, 142 Ky. 60, 133 S.W. 985 (1911), also citing *Campbell*, the Court declared an ordinance which purported to regulate cigarette smoking in such broad terms that it could be applied to persons who smoked in the privacy of their own home "unreasonably interfere[ed] with the right of the citizen to determine for himself such personal matters." 133 S.W. at 986.

In the area of civil law, Kentucky has been in the forefront in recognizing the right of privacy. In 1909, our Court stepped outside traditional libel law and recognized invasion of privacy as a tort in *Foster-Milburn Co. v. Chinn*, *supra*. Then in 1927, in *Brents v. Morgan*, *supra*, our Court defined this emerging right as "the right to be left alone, that is, the right of a person to be free from unwarranted publicity, or the right to live without unwarranted interference by the public about matters with which the public is not necessarily concerned."

> "The right of privacy is incident to the person and not to property.... It is considered as a natural and an absolute or pure right springing from the instincts of nature. It is of that class of rights which every human being has in his natural state and which he did not surrender by becoming a member of organized society. The fundamental rights of personal security and personal liberty, include the right of privacy, the right to be left alone.... The right to enjoy life [Ky. Const., §1, first subpart] in the way most agreeable and pleasant, and the right of privacy is nothing more than a right to live in a particular way." *Id.* at 971, quoting 21 RCL parg. 3, p. 1197.

See also Grigsby and Wife v. R.J. Breckinridge, 65 Ky. (2 Bush) 480 (1867) and *Douglas v. Stokes*, 149 Ky. 506, 149 S.W. 849 (1912), for further confirmation that the right of privacy has long been considered an inalienable right legally protected in this state.

In the *Campbell* case our Court quoted at length from the "great work" *On Liberty* of the 19th century English philosopher and economist, John Stuart Mill. We repeat the quote in part:

> "The only part of the conduct of anyone, for which he is amenable to society, is that which concerns others. In the part which merely concerns himself, his independence is, of right, absolute.... The principle requires liberty of taste and pursuits; of framing the plan of our life to suit our own character; of doing as we like, subject to such consequences as may follow; without impediment from our fellow creatures, so long as what we do does not harm them, even though they should think our conduct foolish, perverse, or wrong." 117 S.W. at 386.

Mill's premise is that "physical force in the form of legal penalties," i.e., criminal sanctions, should not be used as a means to improve the citizen. *Id.* The majority has no moral right to dictate how everyone else should live. Public indignation, while given due weight, should be subject to the overriding test of rational and critical analysis, drawing the line at harmful consequences to others. Modern legal philosophers who follow Mill temper this test with an enlightened paternalism, permitting the law to intervene to stop self-inflicted harm such as the result of drug taking, or failure to use seat belts or crash helmets, not to enforce majoritarian or conventional morality, but because the victim of such self-inflicted harm becomes a burden on society. *See Introduction to Jurisprudence*, 4th ed, p. 59 (1979) by Lord Lloyd of Hampstead.

Based on the *Campbell* opinion, and on the Comments of the 1891 Convention Delegates, there is little doubt but that the views of John Stuart Mill, which were then held in high esteem, provided the philosophical underpinnings for the reworking and broadening of protection of individual rights that occurs throughout the 1891 Constitution.

We have recognized protection of individual rights greater than the federal floor in a number of cases, most recently: *Ingram v. Commonwealth*, Ky., 801 S.W.2d 321 (1990), involving protection against double jeopardy and *Dean v. Commonwealth*, Ky., 777 S.W.2d 900 (1989), involving the right of confrontation. Perhaps the most dramatic recent example of protection of individual rights under the state Constitution where the United States Supreme Court had refused to afford protection under the Federal Constitution, is *Rose v. Council for Better Educ., Inc.*, Ky., 790 S.W.2d 186 (1989). In *Rose*, our Court recognized our Kentucky Constitution afforded individual school children from property poor districts a fundamental right to an adequate education such as provided in wealthier school districts, even though 16 years earlier the United States Supreme Court held the Federal Constitution provided no such protection in *San Antonio Independent School District v. Rodriguez*, 411 U.S. 1, 93 S.Ct. 1278, 36 L.Ed.2d 16 (1973). The United States Supreme Court found there was no constitutional, or fundamental, right to a particular quality of education which justified invoking the Equal Protection Clause of the Fourteenth Amendment. Our Court found a duty in the Kentucky constitutional requirement that the General Assembly "provide an efficient system of common schools." Ky. Const. Sec. 183. In so doing we stated:

> "We have decided this case solely on the basis of our Kentucky Constitution, Sec. 183. We find it unnecessary to inject any issues raised under the United States Constitution or the United States Bill of Rights in this matter." *Rose* at 215.

In *Fannin v. Williams*, Ky., 655 S.W.2d 480 (1983), we held unconstitutional a statute that would permit the state librarian to supply textbooks to children in the state's non-public schools, even though in *Bd. of Education v. Allen*, 392 U.S. 236, 88 S.Ct. 1923, 20 L.Ed.2d 1060 (1968), the United States Supreme Court had held a statute accomplishing a similar purpose did not violate the "establishment of religion" clause in the United States Constitution. We stated:

> "The problem in this case is not whether the challenged statute passes muster under the federal constitution as interpreted by the United States Supreme Court, but whether it satisfies the much more detailed and explicit proscriptions of the Kentucky Constitution. It does not." 655 S.W.2d at 483.

We view the United States Supreme Court decision in *Bowers v. Hardwick*, *supra*, as a misdirected application of the theory of original intent. To illustrate: as a theory of majoritarian morality, miscegenation was an offense with ancient roots. It is highly unlikely that protecting the rights of persons of different races to copulate was one of the considerations behind the Fourteenth Amendment. Nevertheless, in *Loving v. Virginia*, 388 U.S. 1, 87 S.Ct. 1817, 18 L.Ed.2d 1010 (1967), the United States Supreme Court recognized that a contemporary, enlightened interpretation of the liberty interest involved in the sexual act made its punishment constitutionally impermissible.

* * *

II. Equal Protection

As stated earlier, in *Bowers v. Hardwick*, *supra*, the Equal Protection Clause was not implicated because the Georgia statute criminalized both heterosexual and homosexual sodomy. Unlike the Due Process Clause analysis provided in *Bowers v. Hardwick*, equal protection analysis does not turn on whether the law (KRS 510.100), transgresses "liberties that are 'deeply rooted in this Nation's history and tradition.'" 478 U.S. at 191–92, 106 S.Ct. at 2844–45.

* * *

Certainly, the practice of deviate sexual intercourse violates traditional morality. But so does the same act between heterosexuals, which activity is decriminalized. Going one step further, all sexual activity between consenting adults outside of marriage violates our traditional morality. The issue here is not whether sexual activity traditionally viewed as immoral can be punished by society, but whether it can be punished solely on the basis of sexual preference.

* * *

All are entitled to equal treatment, unless there is a substantial governmental interest, a rational basis, for different treatment. The statute before us is in violation of Kentucky constitutional protection in Section Three that "all men (persons), when they form a social compact, are equal," and in Section Two that "absolute and arbitrary power over the lives, liberty and property of free men (persons) exist nowhere in a republic, not even in the largest majority." We have concluded that it is "arbitrary" for the majority to criminalize sexual activity solely on the basis of majoritarian sexual preference, and that it denied "equal" treatment under the law when there is no rational basis, as this term is used and applied in our Kentucky cases.

* * *

In the final analysis we can attribute no legislative purpose to this statute except to single out homosexuals for different treatment for indulging their sexual preference by engaging in the same activity heterosexuals are now at liberty to perform. By 1974 there had already been a sea change in societal values insofar as attaching criminal penalties to extramarital sex. The question is whether a society that no longer criminalizes adultery, fornication, or deviate sexual intercourse between heterosexuals, has a rational basis to single out homosexual acts for different treatment. Is there a rational basis for declaring this one type of sexual immorality so destructive of family values as to merit criminal punishment whereas other acts of sexual immorality which were likewise forbidden by the same religious and traditional heritage of Western civilization are now decriminalized? If there is a rational basis for different treatment it has yet to be demonstrated in this case. We need not sympathize, agree with, or even understand the sexual preference of homosexuals in order to recognize their right to equal treatment before the bar of criminal justice.

To be treated equally by the law is a broader constitutional value than due process of law as discussed in the *Bowers* case. We recognize it as such under the Kentucky Constitution, without regard to whether the United States Supreme Court continues to do so in federal constitutional jurisprudence. "Equal Justice Under Law" inscribed above the entrance to the United States Supreme Court, expresses the unique goal to which all humanity aspires. In Kentucky it is more than a mere aspiration. It is part of the "inherent and inalienable" rights protected by our Kentucky Constitution. Our protection against exercise of "arbitrary power over the … liberty … of freemen" by the General Assembly (Section Two) and our guarantee that all persons are entitled to "equal" treatment (in Section Three) forbid a special act punishing the sexual preference of homosexuals. It matters not that the same act committed by persons of the same sex is more offensive to the majority because Section Two states such "power ... exists nowhere in a republic, not even in the largest majority."

The purpose of the present statute is not to protect the marital relationship against sexual activity outside of marriage, but only to punish one aspect of it while other activities similarly destructive of the marital relationship, if not more so, go unpunished. Sexual preference, and not the act committed, determines criminality, and is being punished. Simply because the majority, speaking through the General Assembly, finds one type of extramarital intercourse more offensive than another, does not provide a rational basis for criminalizing the sexual preference of homosexuals.

For the reasons stated, we affirm the decision of the Fayette Circuit Court, and the judgment on appeal from the Fayette District Court.

Stephens, C.J., and Combs, Leibson and Spain, JJ., concur.

Combs, J., concurs by separate opinion in which Stephens, C.J., joins.

Lambert, J., dissents by separate opinion in which Reynolds, J., joins.

Wintersheimer, J., dissents by separate opinion in which Reynolds, J., concurs in results only.

JUSTICE COMBS, CONCURRING.

I concur in the majority opinion unreservedly. By writing separately, I intend to detract nothing from this historic monument to freedom, liberty, and equality—the birthright of every citizen of Kentucky. In form and substance, the majority opinion is of a stature entirely commensurate with its noble purpose.

Of necessity, we choose today between competing principles of political, jurisprudential, and (some would say) moral philosophy. Sworn to uphold and protect the Constitution of Kentucky, we seven aspire to perform that high duty, each to the best of his ability, each confessing to finite wisdom.

It is essential to understand what the Constitution is, and what it is not. It is the instrument by which the people created a government and invested it with certain powers, directed to a specific end. The Constitution does not create any rights of, or grant any rights to, the people. It merely recognizes their primordial rights, and constructs a government as a means of protecting and preserving them. In the Bill of Rights, purposed to recognize and establish "the great and essential principles of liberty and free government," the very first section of the Constitution acknowledges that, by virtue of their species and nothing more, all persons are free and equal, and possess certain natural, inherent, inalienable rights. These include, but are not limited to, the enjoyment of life and liberty, the pursuit of happiness, and freedom of expression. In Section 5, freedom of conscience is recognized as another of these ascendant principles.

The purpose of the government born of the Constitution is to protect these individual liberties, not to take them away. The first sentence of the Constitution, the Preamble, declares its object to secure civil, political, and religious liberties. The Constitution does not establish an omnipotent government which may, condescending, dispense selected rights to the citizen. The legislative power vested in the General Assembly through Section 29 is not absolute power, but a power of government (Section 27), a government instituted to ensure the "peace, safety, and happiness" of the people, in whom all power inheres (Section 4). Ordained as the jealous guardian of individual freedom, government wields legitimate power only in execution of that function. Its authority to interfere with one's liberty derives solely from its duty to preserve the liberty of another. Where one seeks happiness in private, removed from others (indeed unknown to others, absent prying), and where the conduct is not relational to the rights of another, state interference is per se overweening, arbitrary, and unconstitutional.

It may be asked whether a majority, believing its own happiness will be enhanced by another's conformity, may not enforce its moral code upon all. The answer is that, first, morality is an individual, personal—one might say, private—matter of conscience, and dwells inviolate within the fortress of Section 5: "No human authority shall, in any case whatever, control or interfere with rights of conscience." Second, the Constitution promotes no particular morality, however popular. Indeed, the New World having been sought out by those fleeing state and/or majoritarian persecution, our systems of government are predicated upon such imperatives as that recognized in Kentucky Constitution Section 2: "Absolute and arbitrary power over the lives, liberty and property of freemen exists nowhere in a republic, not even in the largest majority." Third, morality is a matter of values. Insofar as it comprises a moral code, the Constitution embraces—yea, embodies—the immutable values of individual freedom, liberty, and equality.

Those who decry today's result are quick to note the absence of the word "privacy" from the Constitution. To them I say, first, that Section 1, in enumerating certain inherent rights, does not purport to be exclusive. Its words are that those may be reckoned *among* every person's inalienable rights. The Constitution also omits mention of one's right to play checkers, to smile or frown, to rise or rest, to eat or fast, to look at a king. I have no doubt, as a citizen or as a jurist, that these rights exist. (Likely, neither is this list exhaustive.) Second, the right to privacy is a necessary concomitant to general natural freedom and freedom of conscience, as well as to the rights to enjoy life and liberty and to seek and pursue happiness. Third, given the nature, the purpose, the promise of our Constitution, and its institution of a government charged as the conservator of individual freedom, I suggest that the appropriate question is not "Whence comes the right to privacy?" but rather, "Whence comes the right to deny it?"

Stephens, C.J., joins in this concurring opinion.

JUSTICE LAMBERT, DISSENTING.

The issue here is not whether private homosexual conduct should be allowed or prohibited. The only question properly before this Court is whether the Constitution of Kentucky denies the legislative branch a right to prohibit such conduct. Nothing in the majority opinion demonstrates such a limitation on legislative prerogative.

To justify its view that private homosexual conduct is protected by the Constitution of Kentucky, the majority has found it necessary to disregard virtually all of recorded history, the teachings of the religions most influential on Western Civilization,[1] the debates of the delegates to the Constitutional Convention, and the text of the Constitution itself. Rather than amounting to a decision based upon precedent as is suggested, this decision reflects the value judgment of the majority and its view that public law has no right to prohibit the conduct at issue here.

The majority concedes that "'proscriptions against that conduct [sodomy] have ancient roots.' 478 U.S. at 192 [106 S.Ct. at 2844]." It fails, however, to describe the depth of such roots as was done in *Bowers v. Hardwick*, 478 U.S. 186, 106 S.Ct. 2841, 92 L.Ed.2d 140 (1986):

> "Sodomy was a criminal offense at common law which was forbidden by the laws of the original 13 States when they ratified the Bill of Rights." 478 U.S. at 192, 106 S.Ct. at 2844.

* * *

The history and traditions of this Commonwealth are fully in accord with the Biblical, historical and common law view. Since at least 1860, sodomy has been a criminal offense in Kentucky and this fact was well known to the delegates at the time of the 1890 Constitutional Convention.

* * *

The majority also concedes that the debates of the Kentucky Constitutional Convention of 1890 contain no mention of a right of privacy or a right to engage in homosexual sodomy. It rationalizes this fact by indicating that the concept was not articulated until publication of an article by Warren and Brandeis in the Harvard Law Review on December 15, 1890. According to the majority, the delegates to the Constitutional Convention intended to create such a right but lacked the verbal skills to devise a phrase so complicated as "right of privacy."[2] For whatever reason, the debates contain only the most limited and inexplicit reference to any concept which could be translated into privacy.

Perhaps the greatest mischief to be found in the majority opinion is in its discovery of a constitutional right which lacks any textual support. The majority has referred generally to the twenty-six sections in the Bill of Rights of the Kentucky Constitution and quoted §1 First and Third and §2. None of the sections cited or quoted contain an inkling of reference to rights of privacy or sexual freedom of any kind. **This is conceded by the majority as follows: "No language specifying 'rights of privacy,' *as such*, ap-**

1. Leviticus 20:13; Romans 1:26–27.

2. The view of the majority is particularly curious since this Court said in *Kentucky State Board, Etc. v. Rudasill*, Ky., 589 S.W.2d 877, 880 (1979), that "[i]t is generally recognized that the convention of 1890 was comprised of competent and educated delegates who were sincerely concerned with individual liberties."

pears in either the Federal or State Constitution." The majority opinion is a departure from the accepted methodology of constitutional analysis which requires that text be the beginning point. *Kentucky State Board, Etc. v. Rudasill*, Ky., 589 S.W.2d 877 (1979). The majority reasons that differences between the text of the Kentucky Constitution and the United States Constitution free this Court from federal influence, but it fails to explain its discovery of the rights announced here in the absence of any textual basis. This is a dangerous practice. When judges free themselves of constitutional text, their values and notions of morality are given free rein and they, not the Constitution, become the supreme law. * * *

As has been demonstrated, a right of privacy protecting homosexual sodomy between or among consenting adults has no basis in the history and traditions of Western culture or in this nation or state. Likewise, the constitutional debates contain only the most oblique references to any right of privacy and Kentucky constitutional text is totally silent. As such, the majority must and does rest its entire case on a line of decisions rendered by this Court in the early twentieth century in which a right of privacy was held to exist with respect to the consumption of alcoholic beverages and the use of tobacco products. The leading decision of this genre is *Commonwealth v. Campbell*, 133 Ky. 50, 117 S.W. 383 (1909), in which a statute which criminalized the possession of intoxicating liquor for private use was held unconstitutional and which, with rhetorical flourish declared the broadest possible right of privacy.

* * *

The fact that this Court broadly declared a right of privacy prior to World War I in cases which one suspects were influenced by local economic forces does not mean that such a doctrine should be applied in the extreme nearly a century later to a moral question not remotely considered by the *Campbell* court.

The major premise in the majority opinion is that the Constitution forbids any legal restriction upon the private conduct of adults unless it can be shown that such conduct is harmful to another. This view represents the essence of the philosophy of John Stuart Mill in his essay *On Liberty*. While espousing such a view, however, Mill recognized the difficulty of distinguishing that part of a person's life which affected only himself from that which affected others. He recognized that one who by deleterious vices harmed himself indirectly harmed others and that society suffered indirect harm by the mere knowledge of immoral conduct. Nevertheless, Mill clung to his philosophy by insisting that society was without power to punish gambling or drunkenness. He made a ringing defense of the right of persons so disposed to practice polygamy.

While the philosophy of John Stuart Mill as adopted by this Court in *Campbell v. Commonwealth*, *supra*, exalts individuality in the extreme, it has, nevertheless, a superficial appeal. It rejects majoritarian morality as a basis for law and imposes legal limits on the conduct of man only insofar as it may harm others. Unfortunately for the purposes of the majority, the philosophy of Mill and the views contained in the *Campbell* case, if logically applied, would necessarily result in the eradication of numerous other criminal statutes. For example, if majoritarian morality is without a role in the formulation of criminal law and the only standard is harm to another, all laws proscribing the possession and use of dangerous or narcotic drugs would fall. Likewise, incest statutes which proscribe sexual intercourse between persons of close kinship regardless of age or consent would be rendered invalid. Laws prohibiting cruelty to animals, the abuse of dead human bodies, suicide and polygamy would be held unconstitutional. Despite the majority's disingenuous departure from Mill based on "an enlightened paternalism" to prevent self-inflicted harm, many prevailing criminal statutes would nevertheless fail the "harm to another" test. * * *

The majority has characterized Kentucky's highest Court of the early twentieth century as being "in the forefront in recognizing the right of privacy." It has quoted laudable phrases such as "'[t]he fundamental rights of personal security and personal liberty, include the right of privacy, the right to be left alone.... The right to enjoy life in the way most agreeable and pleasant....'" It has created an impression that this Court of that era was filled with enlightened jurists who sought to elevate mankind. Unfortunately, there is a darker side to this Court's past as evidenced by a decision rendered just three years prior to the *Campbell* case. In *Berea College v. Commonwealth*, 123 Ky. 209, 94 S.W. 623 (1906), Judge O'Rear, writing for this Court, enthusiastically upheld the constitutionality of a statute which prohibited "white and colored persons from attending the same school." * * *

A cursory reading of *Berea College v. Commonwealth* will convincingly dispel any notion of social enlightenment on the part of this Court's justices during the first decade of the twentieth century.

* * *

In final analysis, the question is whether a rational distinction may be drawn between acts of sodomy committed by heterosexuals and homosexuals. As cases such as *Griswold v. Connecticut, supra*, *Eisenstadt v. Baird, supra*, *Loving v. Virginia, supra*, and *Roe v. Wade, supra*, demonstrate, there is a heightened protection of the right of persons with respect to conduct in the context of marriage, procreation, contraception, family relationships, and child rearing and education. As such considerations are without any application as to acts of homosexual sodomy, the distinction is manifest.

* * *

I conclude with the view that this Court has strayed from its role of interpreting the Constitution and undertaken to make social policy. This decision is a vast extension of judicial power by which four Justices of this Court have overridden the will of the Legislative and Executive branches of Kentucky State Government and denied the people any say in this important social issue. No decision cited by the majority has ever gone so far and certainly none comes to mind. Where this slippery slope may lead is anybody's guess, but the ramifications of this decision will surely be profound.

For these reasons, I dissent.

Reynolds, J., joins in this dissenting opinion.

JUSTICE WINTERSHEIMER, DISSENTING.

I strongly dissent from the majority opinion because it totally misstates the case and proceeds to attack a statute that is not the direct subject of the criminal charge originally made in this case.

The majority opinion asserts that this is a case about privacy and yet it completely ignores that the criminal act for which the defendant was charged was a proposition made to a total stranger on a public street in downtown Lexington, Kentucky. Under such circumstances, there is no reasonable expectation of privacy.

* * *

The majority opinion seizes upon the *Campbell* decision and ecstatically embraces the philosophy of John Stewart Mill, an English philosopher of the mid-19th Century. Absolute adoption of the philosophy of Mill is not required by the Kentucky Constitution in any respect. Mill and his disciples express a kind of "anything goes" or laissez faire attitude towards what they construe as individual liberty.

Some scholars have observed that the emerging law of privacy has been based on the proposition that society may properly regulate the behavior of competent adults only if that behavior demonstrably threatens the rights, safety or interest of others. John Stuart Mill declared a maxim that "that the individual is not accountable to society for his actions, insofar as these concern the interest of no person but himself." A Michigan court has used this Mill philosophy as the basis of a decision invalidating a statute requiring motorcyclists to wear helmets. The Michigan court found that the law was related only to the safety of the motorcyclist and therefore was invalid. Their decisions are based on outdated philosophical premises. If the Mill concept was ever valid, it has been totally overcome by the development of the interconnection of modern society. If Mill's philosophy that "a man's conduct affects himself alone" was ever true it was not so today. The English-Irish poet, John Dunne, expressed it marvelously when he wrote:

> No man is an island. Ask not for whom the bell tolls, it tolls for you.

* * *

The judgment of the Fayette Circuit Court should be reversed with directions that the case be remanded to the Fayette District Court for trial on the merits.

Reynolds, J., concurs in the result reached by this dissent.

Notes and Questions

1. One commenter referred to *Wasson* as "a pinnacle of state constitutional jurisprudence." Jennifer DiGiovanni, *Justice Charles M. Leibson and the Revival of State Constitutional Law: A Microcosm of a Movement*, 89 Ky. L.J. 1009, 1040 (1998). Further, "[i]t would be difficult indeed to put forth an argument that *Wasson* did not provide the citizens and courts of Kentucky with a rich piece of state constitutional material that will prove valuable to litigants and courts." *Id.* at 1049. Do you agree?

2. *Wasson* disagreed with the outcome of U.S. Supreme Court case, *Bowers v. Hardwick*, 478 U.S. 186 (1986), which was decided under the Equal Protection Clause of the Fourteenth Amendment, calling it a "misdirected application of the theory of original intent." When *Bowers* was later overruled in *Lawrence v. Texas*, 539 U.S. 558 (2003), the U.S. Supreme Court cited *Wasson* and the decisions of four other state courts that "have declined to follow [*Bowers*] in interpreting provisions in their own state constitutions parallel to the Due Process Clause of the Fourteenth Amendment." *Id.* at 576.
3. Note that *Wasson* builds on *Campbell* and *Hershberg*, finding in Sections 1 and 2 of the Kentucky Constitution "greater protection of the right of privacy than provided by the Federal Constitution." It refers to *Campbell* as the "leading case on this subject," and it found in John Stuart Mill's On Liberty "the philosophical underpinnings for the reworking and broadening of protection of individual rights that occurs throughout the 1891 Constitution." In his dissent, Justice Lambert refers to Mill's philosophy as "exalt[ing] individuality in the extreme," and dismisses *Campbell* and *Hershberg* as "cases which one suspects were influenced by local economic forces" (*i.e.*, bourbon and tobacco).
4. *Wasson* stated that the Kentucky Constitution "offer[s] greater protection of the right of privacy than provided by the Federal Constitution as interpreted by the United States Supreme Court." *Commonwealth v. Wasson*, 842 S.W.2d 487, 491 (Ky. 1992). However, the Supreme Court of Kentucky "has never extended this greater privacy protection to searches and seizures," which are protected instead under the Fourth Amendment of the U.S. Constitution and Section 10 of the Kentucky Constitution. *Petitioner F v. Brown*, 306 S.W.3d 80, 91–92 (Ky. 2010); *see Colbert v. Commonwealth*, 43 S.W.3d 777, 780 (Ky. 2001) (same). Thus, the right to privacy did not preclude a statute providing for DNA sampling from convicted sex offenders. *Id.*
5. "A question could be raised as to whether the majority in *Wasson* has commingled the constitutional right of privacy with the tort of invasion of privacy. Future scholars and judges will have to unravel any such problem." Justice Donald C. Wintersheimer, *State Constitutional Law*, 20 N. Ky. L. Rev. 591, 604 (1993).
6. At the federal level, the right to privacy recognized in cases such as *Griswold v. Connecticut*, 381 U.S. 479 (1965), gave rise to the constitutionalizing of the right of a woman to obtain an abortion in *Roe v. Wade*, 410 U.S. 113 (1973). Pre-*Roe*, Kentucky's highest court had held the Commonwealth's abortion laws did not violate the Equal Protection and Due Process Clauses of the Fourteenth Amendment. *Sasaki v. Commonwealth*, 485 S.W.2d 897 (Ky. 1972), *vacated sub nom. Sasaki v. Kentucky*, 410 U.S. 951 (1973) (vacated and remanded for reconsideration in light of *Roe*), *judgment rev'd sub nom. Sasaki v. Commonwealth*, 497 S.W.2d 713 (Ky. 1973). But Justice Wintersheimer's law review article also notes, "In the emotionally charged area of abortion, there is no specific case involving privacy in Kentucky." Wintersheimer, *supra*, 20 N. Ky. L. Rev. at 604.

   Kentucky courts have grappled with the issue of when a legally cognizable life begins in a few criminal cases. In *Hollis v. Commonwealth*, 652 S.W.2d 61 (Ky. 1983), Justice

Figure 8-1. Official portrait of Justice Donald C. Wintersheimer, Kentucky State Capitol. Portrait by John Michael Carter, reproduced with permission of the artist and the Supreme Court of Kentucky.

Leibson, writing for a three-justice plurality, found that the killing of a viable, unborn child could not support an indictment for murder because, until the child was born alive and had a separate existence from its mother, it was not to be considered a "person" within the meaning of the criminal homicide statutes. *Hollis*, 652 S.W.2d at 62. Later, in *Jones v. Commonwealth*, 830 S.W.2d 877 (Ky. 1992), Justice Leibson wrote for a four-justice majority and distinguished *Hollis*, holding that where the injury occurred before the child was born, but the child was born alive and died 14 hours thereafter, the defendant could be convicted of manslaughter. *Jones*, 830 S.W.2d at 879. Three justices concurred in the result but would have gone further and overruled *Hollis*. Later, in *Commonwealth v. Morris*, the Supreme Court did overrule *Hollis*: "[W]e overrule *Hollis* and hold that a viable fetus is a 'human being' for purposes of KRS 500.080(12) and the KRS Chapter 507 homicide statutes." 142 S.W.3d 654, 660 (Ky. 2004). For purposes of the criminal homicide laws of the state, life begins at viability. *But see* KRS Chapter 507A (enacted in 2004 and creating the crimes of fetal homicide in the first, second, third, and fourth degrees; defining "unborn child" victims of those crimes to be "member[s] of the species homo sapiens in utero from conception onward, without regard to age, health, or condition of dependency").

A related civil case is *Grubbs ex rel. Grubbs v. Barbourville Family Health Center, P.S.C.*, 120 S.W.3d 682 (Ky. 2003). *Grubbs* arose out of two similar tort cases, in which physicians had performed early diagnostic procedures to detect potential birth defects in unborn children. The physicians failed to accurately interpret or report the results of the tests to the parents, who claimed that, had they been aware of their children's birth defects, they would have opted to terminate the pregnancies. After their suits had been dismissed by the trial court, the plaintiffs asked the Supreme Court on appeal "to consider whether Kentucky law recognizes so-called 'birth-related torts,' *i.e.*, wrongful conception or pregnancy, wrongful birth, and wrongful life." *Grubbs*, 120 S.W.3d at 686. The Supreme Court held the plaintiffs could not prove a legally cognizable tort injury: "[W]e are unwilling to equate the loss of an abortion opportunity resulting in a genetically or congenitally impaired human life, even severely impaired, with a cognizable legal injury." *Id.* at 689.

The U.S. Supreme Court overruled *Roe* and its federalization of the abortion issue in *Dobbs v. Jackson Women's Health Org.*, 597 U.S. ___, 142 S.Ct. 2228 (2022). There is no Kentucky appellate decision addressing whether there is a right to obtain an abortion under the Kentucky Constitution. The General Assembly proposed an amendment to the Kentucky Constitution, 2021 Ky. Acts ch. 174 §1, which would have added a new section to the Constitution stating, "To protect human life, nothing in this Constitution shall be construed to secure or protect a right to abortion or require the funding of abortion." The voters rejected the amendment at the polls in November 2022.

Commonwealth v. Harrelson

Supreme Court of Kentucky (2000)
14 S.W.3d 541

Opinion of the Court by Justice Wintersheimer.

This appeal is from a decision of the Court of Appeals vacating the judgment of the Lee Circuit Court which affirmed a ruling by the Lee District Court finding that the definition of marijuana in KRS 218A.010(12) is unconstitutionally overbroad. The Court of Appeals remanded the case to the circuit court with directions to dismiss the appeal on the ground that it was taken from a nonfinal order.

The major issue is whether the decision of the Lee District Court which held that KRS 218A.010(12) was unconstitutional is correct. Other questions presented are whether the circuit court erred in affirming the judgment of the Lee District Court; whether the circuit court erred in affirming a finding that a viable economic benefit could be derived from the nonhallucinogenic parts of the marijuana; whether the entire matter should be dismissed for territorial procedural defects and whether the appeal was taken from a nonfinal order of the district court.

The facts of this matter are not in dispute. On June 1, 1996, Woodrow Harrelson planted four hemp seeds on a tract of land in rural Lee County. He was cited and arrested for a violation of KRS 218A.1423(3), cultivation of marijuana, five or fewer plants, a Class A misdemeanor. The charge was later amended to possession of marijuana, KRS 218A.1422, also a Class A misdemeanor. He pled not guilty and moved to dismiss the charge contending that the hemp seeds did not come within a proper statutory definition of marijuana, or, if they did, that the statute was unconstitutionally overbroad and vague.

Harrelson specifically challenged the constitutionality of the 1992 amendment to KRS 218A.010(12), now subsection (14). After a hearing on the question of constitutionality, the district judge rejected the argument by Harrelson that the statute was void for vagueness but agreed that the statute is unconstitutionally overbroad by including the nonhallucinogenic parts of marijuana. The district court concluded that the statute violated Section Two of the Kentucky Constitution as an arbitrary exercise of state authority. He also found that an issue of fact remained concerning whether the seeds planted by Harrelson were capable of germination or producing plants that contain the hallucinogenic properties of marijuana. The matter was set for trial on that question. The Commonwealth filed an interlocutory appeal from the ruling of the district judge; the circuit court affirmed, and the Court of Appeals dismissed the appeal reasoning that it was taken from a nonfinal order. This Court granted discretionary review.

By agreement of the parties, a hearing on the motion to dismiss was held in Owsley County where both the Commonwealth and the defendant presented three witnesses each. The first witness for the Commonwealth was Sgt. James Tipton, a 24 year member of the Kentucky State Police who currently works for Special Operations as a Special Project Coordinator and member of the Governor's Marijuana Strike Force. It was not challenged that Sgt. Tipton had been involved in approximately one thousand drug investigations and that he had investigated all types of drug crimes, including marijuana. The witness held an undergraduate degree in police administration and was a graduate of the F.B.I. National Academy and the Southern Police Institute. He taught at the National Interagency Drug Institute in California as well as classes on drugs and crime at Eastern Kentucky University. He testified in hundreds of cases and had been permitted to give an expert opinion in both federal and state courts on marijuana and cocaine. He testified that his experience with countries in which hemp was legalized indicated that they were already having difficulties in the prosecution of marijuana cases because violators use hemp as a defense arguing that they thought they were growing lower-grade marijuana. He concluded that decriminalization of hemp would make it easy for the violators and difficult for law enforcement.

Next, the Commonwealth called an extension professor for the University of Kentucky who had been employed for 25 years, who had a B.S., M.S. and Ph.D. from Purdue University in plant breeding and genetics. He testified about a plant called kenaf, which is free of THC and which can be used for anything that wood is used for, including making paper. The witness testified that kenaf produced higher quality products than hemp because of its shorter fiber.

Finally, the prosecution called a professor and chairman of the Department of Agronomy at the University of Kentucky. This witness had received a bachelor and masters degree in biology and soil science from Cornell University and a Ph.D. in soil microbiology from Michigan State University. He had also authored a large portion of the report of the Governor's Task Force on Hemp and Alternative Fiber Products. His testimony indicated that the opportunities for hemp as a crop in Kentucky were limited. He stated that at one time hemp was a major cash crop in central Kentucky but that its uses went by the wayside so it failed economically for market reasons.

The defendant, a television and motion picture actor, testified that he owned a company in California that produced textile products in clothing derived from hemp. He testified that the seeds planted were "French seeds" and that these were less than one percent THC. He stated that his company had sales of $1.5 million in the United States but that the hemp for their products had to be imported from Hungary and China and that the price of hemp would be lower if it could be grown domestically.

On cross-examination, Harrelson admitted that he knew he was breaking the law when he planted the seeds but that he was concerned about the cutting and replacement of trees as well as the sale of hemp. Harrelson, who presented no academic credentials, acknowledged that he had no experience in law enforcement and that the police sergeant would be better qualified to determine if law enforcement would be impeded from enforcing marijuana laws if hemp were legalized.

Another defense witness was a professor of biology who testified about the economic uses of hemp at the present time and the differences in appearance of hemp and marijuana to the naked eye. He stated that if legalized, it would greatly reduce the cutting of trees and be a tremendous asset to the agricultural base of Kentucky. He admitted on cross-examination that he did not have any training in agricultural economics. The defense also presented a professor of pharmacology and toxicology at the University of Louisville who testified that hemp was less potent than marijuana in its THC level.

Upon the conclusion of the hearing and the filing of briefs by both parties, the trial judge determined that the statute was constitutionally defective because of its overbroad application by including nonhallucinogenic plant parts. The trial judge further determined that the amendment to KRS 218A.010(9) had no rational basis for including the nonhallucinogenic parts of the marijuana plants in the definition. The trial judge determined that the statute violated Section Two of the Kentucky Constitution and that the defendant had established a viable economic benefit of nonhallucinogenic parts of marijuana. He further held that the statute was an intrusion into the economic benefit of the product without a rational basis by the government. The Court severed the statute in question as it related to the issue of including nonhallucinogenic plant parts of marijuana as a controlled substance.

* * *

II. Circuit Court Error

The circuit court erred in affirming the decision of the district court which held that KRS 218A.010(12) was unconstitutional in part because the presumption of constitutionality which applies to every statute was ignored by the trial court and the circuit court. Harrelson did not overcome this presumption.

Originally, Harrelson challenged the constitutionality of the statute for vagueness and overbreadth. At the Court of Appeals, based on the facts developed in this case, Harrelson conceded that the statute is not vague as applied to him. He continues to argue that the statute is too broad and that it is so arbitrary as to be unconstitutional in violation of Section Two of the Kentucky Constitution.

In 1992, the General Assembly amended KRS 218A.010(12) so as to eliminate the following language from the definition of marijuana:

> It does not include mature stalks of the plant, fiber produced from the stalks, oil or cake made from the seeds of the plant, any other compound, manufacture, salt, derivative, mixture or preparation of the mature stalks (except the resin extracted therefrom), fiber, oil or cake, or the sterilized seed of the plant which is incapable of germination.

The remaining language of the statute provides a definition of marijuana in what is now (14), as follows:

> "Marijuana" means all parts of the plant cannabis sp., whether growing or not; the seeds thereof; the resin extracted from any part of the plant; and every compound, manufacture, salt, derivative, mixture, or preparation of the plant, its seeds or resin or any compound, mixture, or preparation which contains any quantity of these substances.

The legislature was well within its authority to designate and define *all parts* of the plant cannabis sp. as a controlled substance.

It is obvious that the legislative intent was to eliminate the previous exemptions. The literal language of the statute is both plain and unambiguous and must be given effect as written. The words used in the statute are to be given their ordinary meaning. *Cf. Lynch v. Commonwealth*, Ky., 902 S.W.2d 813 (1995), which cited *Griffin v. City of Bowling Green*, Ky., 458 S.W.2d 456 (1970).

The 1992 amendment is a specific response to a serious and growing concern of the public and the legislature regarding illegal drug activities in Kentucky. The section was amended to assist law enforcement authorities in the investigation and prosecution of illegal drugs at all levels. It cannot be seriously contended that the elimination of illegal drug trade is not a beneficial or worthwhile goal of the law.

Harrelson complains that the action of the General Assembly in amending the statute does not have a reasonable basis.

It is uncontroverted that a statute is presumed to be constitutional unless it clearly offends the limitations and prohibitions of the Constitution. "The one who questions the validity of an act bears the burden to sustain such a contention." *Stephens v. State Farm Mutual Auto Ins. Co.*, Ky., 894 S.W.2d 624 (1995).

The valid public interest in controlling marijuana is a public issue involving health, safety and criminal activity. *Kentucky Milk Marketing & Anti-monopoly Comn. v. Kroger Co.*, Ky., 691 S.W.2d 893 (1985) and *Commonwealth v. Foley*, Ky., 798 S.W.2d 947 (1990), state as follows:

> Whatever is contrary to democratic ideals, customs, and maxims is arbitrary. Likewise, whatever is essentially unjust and unequal or exceeds the reasonable and legitimate interests of the people is arbitrary. No board or officer vested with governmental authority may exercise it arbitrarily. If the action taken rests upon reasons so unsubstantial, or the consequences are so unjust as to work a hardship, judicial power may be interposed to protect the rights of persons adversely affected.

It cannot reasonably be argued that the inclusion of nonhallucinogenic plant parts in the definition of marijuana is in any way "essentially unjust and unequal," nor does it "exceed the reasonable and legitimate interests of the people."

Here, there is sufficient testimony from law enforcement that there would be serious difficulties for law enforcement in controlling marijuana trafficking if hemp were legalized. There is no evidence of any kind in the record that the commercial business interest of Harrelson has been compromised simply by the necessity of having to import hemp from other countries. Harrelson admitted under oath that he was not qualified to contradict the testimony of the police expert. This statute does not "clearly offend" the limitations and prohibitions of the Constitution as outlined in *Stephens, supra.*

Reliance by Harrelson on his reference to great moral issues of the current times is unpersuasive. The alleged moral concerns expressed in *Commonwealth v. Wasson*, Ky., 842 S.W.2d 487 (1992) and *Commonwealth v. Campbell*, 133 Ky. 50, 117 S.W. 383 (1909), are not evident here in view of the fact that the statute applies to the health, safety and well-being of the citizens of Kentucky without reference to so-called "moral" issues.

* * *

III. Clearly Erroneous

The circuit court erred in affirming the judgment of the district court because the district court made a clearly erroneous finding that the Commonwealth had failed to show a rational basis by the government for including hemp in the definition of marijuana.

* * * Notwithstanding the testimony of the police official, the district court found and the circuit court affirmed that no rational basis had been shown for the legislature to include hemp in the definition of marijuana. We disagree.

The test of the constitutionality of any statute is whether it is unreasonable or arbitrary. *Moore v. Ward*, Ky., 377 S.W.2d 881 (1964). A statute is constitutional if a reasonable and legitimate public purpose for it exists. The rational basis argument can be paraphrased as "Is there a good reason to adopt a law?" The answer is a stunningly simple "Yes." The legislature has broad discretion to determine what is harmful to the public health and welfare. *See Walters v. Bindner*, Ky., 435 S.W.2d 464 (1968). As noted in *Buford v. Commonwealth*, Ky. App., 942 S.W.2d 909 (1997) a succinct analysis of the problems with the illegal drug culture can be found in *People v. Shephard*, 169 Cal. App.2d 283, 337 P.2d 214 (1959), which stated:

> Anything which gives sustenance, solace, comfort or encouragement in the selling of narcotics or in the agreeing to sell narcotics, can be condemned and properly so, by the legislature. It is clear that the statute in question was aimed at discouraging any traffic in narcotics and is therefore within the police power of the state.

* * *

Consequently, upon our review of the testimonial evidence presented in this case, we must conclude that the district court was clearly erroneous when it determined that there was no rational basis for the action of the General Assembly in including hemp in the definition of marijuana.

An examination of the testimony of the police officer and the defense witnesses does not amount to the resolution of a conflict. This is not a case where there was sufficiently credible evidence on both sides of the issue. The findings of the district court were not supported by substantial evidence.

* * *

The arguments of the defendant regarding the legalization of hemp are matters more properly for the General Assembly and not the judicial branch of government.

The decisions of the Court of Appeals, the circuit court and the district court are reversed and this matter is remanded to the district court for trial or other appropriate action.

Lambert, C.J., Graves, Johnstone and Wintersheimer, JJ., concur.

Cooper, J., concurs by separate opinion in which Stumbo, J., joins.

Keller, J., concurs by separate opinion.

* * *

Notes and Questions

1. The Supreme Court declined actor Woody Harrelson's invitation to read *Campbell* and *Wasson* more broadly than as right-to-privacy cases. Harrelson apparently read those cases to stand for the proposition that the General Assembly could not "legislate morality." (See the Court's statement that the Kentucky marijuana statute did not "refer[ ] to so-called 'moral' issues.")
2. Unlike *Campbell* and *Hershberg*, which involved the private use of alcohol and tobacco by a person in his own home, and *Wasson*, which involved an invitation to engage in consensual, private conduct in the inviter's home, *Harrelson* involved a very public demonstration of planting marijuana seeds outdoors. Though not discussed in the *Harrelson* opinion, it would make sense to tether the "right to privacy" to conduct occurring in private.
3. The *Harrelson* case considered the statutory definition of marijuana in the context of a person who wished to cultivate hemp for economic purposes. In *Seum v. Bevin*, 584 S.W.3d 771 (Ky. App. 2019), the Court of Appeals again considered a challenge to Kentucky's marijuana laws. The *Seum* plaintiffs raised a constitutional challenge to the state prohibition on use of marijuana for medicinal purposes. However, the *Seum* court, relying upon *Harrelson*, found the marijuana statutes constitutional, and said any change to those laws would not come from the courts, but must come from the legislature. The fact that the proposed medicinal use of marijuana would have occurred in private was not dispositive.

Blue Movies, Inc. v. Louisville/Jefferson County Metro Government

Supreme Court of Kentucky (2010)
317 S.W.3d 23

Opinion of the Court by Justice Schroder.

This Court granted discretionary review of a Court of Appeals opinion adjudging that the Louisville/Jefferson County Metro Government's 2004 amendments to its code of ordinances, which placed numerous restrictions on adult entertainment businesses in the Metro area, were constitutional. Having considered the record and arguments of counsel, we adjudge that all of the restrictions, except for the blanket "no touch" provision, are constitutional. Accordingly, we affirm in part, reverse in part, and remand for further proceedings consistent with this opinion.

Facts

Appellants represent two types of adult entertainment businesses which operate in the Louisville Metro area: live entertainment establishments that sell alcohol (with the exception of one business); and retail businesses that do not sell alcohol. On March 1, 2004, Appellee, the Louisville/Jefferson County Metro Government ("Metro"), enacted Ordinance 21, Series 2004, which amended Chapter 111 of its Code of Ordinances. The amendments pertained to adult entertainment businesses in the Louisville Metro area, and the stated purpose of the amendments was to combat the adverse secondary effects of sexually oriented adult entertainment businesses. Appellants objected to the following provisions in the amendments: the licensing scheme (owner/officer disclosure, licensing fees, criminal disability provision); the anti-nudity provisions; restrictions on the hours of operation; no direct tipping provision; prohibition on sales of alcohol; buffer zones between patrons and dancers; and a "no touch" provision.

Appellants filed suit in Jefferson Circuit Court on March 5, 2004, challenging the amendments to Chapter 111 on numerous state constitutional grounds. Thereafter, Metro removed the case to federal court and Appellants filed a motion to remand. The federal court granted Appellants' motion, deciding that it lacked jurisdiction under 28 U.S.C. §1441 because Appellants did not make any claims under the federal Constitution.

The Jefferson Circuit Court granted summary judgment for Metro as to all the challenged provisions in the amendments except the requirement of disclosure of principal owners and the "no touch" provision, granting Appellants' motion for temporary injunction only as to enforcement of those two provisions. An appeal and a cross-appeal to the Court of Appeals followed.

On October 5, 2007, the Court of Appeals rendered its opinion wherein it upheld all of the challenged provisions, affirming the circuit court as to all the rulings adverse to Appellants and reversing on cross-appeal as to the two provisions construed in Appellants' favor. The case is now before us on Appellants' motion for discretionary review.

Because this case involves the construction and constitutionality of the ordinance at issue, our review of the case will be de novo. *Commonwealth v. Jameson*, 215 S.W.3d 9, 15 (Ky. 2006), *cert. denied*, 552 U.S. 825, 128 S.Ct. 190, 169 L.Ed.2d 36 (2007). At the outset, we note that many of the issues in this case are controlled by *Jameson*, and *Restaurant Ventures LLC v. Lexington-Fayette Urban County Government*, 60 S.W.3d 572 (Ky. App. 2001), two cases reviewing the constitutionality of local government ordinances regulating sexually oriented adult entertainment businesses.

In *Jameson*, this Court provided a thorough analysis of the United States Supreme Court decisions in the area of regulating nude dancing and sexually oriented businesses, some of which were plurality opinions, up through the Court's decision in *City of Los Angeles v. Alameda Books, Inc.*, 535 U.S. 425, 122 S.Ct. 1728, 152 L.Ed.2d 670 (2002). We have nothing to add to this analysis and are not inclined to depart from any of the reasoning or conclusions reached in *Jameson*. While state courts are free to expand individual rights beyond the federal floor, *see Commonwealth v. Wasson*, 842

S.W.2d 487, 492 (Ky. 1992), we adjudge that on the issue of regulating sexually oriented businesses, the Kentucky Constitution does not grant broader protections than the federal Constitution, except for the blanket ban on touching as discussed below. Thus, we reject Appellants' urging that we adopt the Pennsylvania courts' expansive view on erotic expression in interpreting §1 and §8 of the Kentucky Constitution.

The amendments to Metro's ordinance herein implicate at least two protected categories of speech. First, there is the sexually explicit, but not obscene, speech associated with the retail businesses, such as adult books and videos. Secondly, there is the "symbolic speech" associated with the nude or semi-nude dancing at the live entertainment establishments. *See Barnes v. Glen Theatre, Inc.*, 501 U.S. 560, 566, 111 S.Ct. 2456, 115 L.Ed.2d 504 (1991) (wherein a plurality held that nude dancing was "expressive conduct within the outer perimeters of the First Amendment"). "[R]egulations enacted for the purpose of restraining speech on the basis of its content presumptively violate the First Amendment." *City of Renton v. Playtime Theatres, Inc.*, 475 U.S. 41, 46–47, 106 S.Ct. 925, 89 L.Ed.2d 29 (1986). However, "content-neutral" time, place, and manner regulations which restrain speech will be upheld as constitutional if they are designed to serve a substantial governmental interest and do not unreasonably limit alternative avenues of communication. *Id.* at 47, 106 S.Ct. 925. If the regulations are content-based, they are subject to strict scrutiny. *City of Erie v. Pap's A.M.*, 529 U.S. 277, 289, 120 S.Ct. 1382, 146 L.Ed.2d 265 (2000). If the regulations governing a sexually oriented business are unrelated to the suppression of expression, they are content-neutral and thus subject to the intermediate standard of scrutiny set forth in *United States v. O'Brien*, 391 U.S. 367, 88 S.Ct. 1673, 20 L.Ed.2d 672 (1968). In *O'Brien*, the Court articulated the following four-part test for evaluating regulations affecting sexually oriented businesses:

> [A] government regulation is sufficiently justified if it is within the constitutional power of the Government; if it furthers an important or substantial governmental interest; if the governmental interest is unrelated to the suppression of free expression; and if the incidental restriction on alleged First Amendment freedoms is no greater than is essential to the furtherance of that interest.

Id. at 377, 88 S.Ct. 1673.

In *Jameson*, this Court found that the restrictions (no nudity, no physical contact, and limited hours) on sexually oriented businesses were content-neutral because they were enacted to prevent the negative secondary effects of such businesses—increased crime, lowered property values, and sexually transmitted diseases. 215 S.W.3d at 28. In the present case, Metro enacted the amendments to the ordinance regulating sexually oriented businesses to combat the following secondary effects: adverse effects on nearby parks, houses, and schools; urban blight; crime (including organized crime); prostitution; spread of sexually transmitted diseases; unsanitary conditions; public indecency; lewdness; loitering; illicit drug use and trafficking; negative impacts on property values; pornographic litter; sexual assault and exploitation; public indecency; obscenity; and noise. In addition, Metro cited to numerous reports and judicial opinions that have recognized or documented the adverse secondary effects of sexually oriented businesses.

Provisions Governed by Jameson or Restaurant Ventures

The anti-nudity, six-foot buffer zone, 18-inch stage height, and limited hours of operation provisions in the ordinance are all provisions that were addressed and upheld in *Jameson* and/or *Restaurant Ventures*. The buffer zone and stage height provisions are identical to those in *Restaurant Ventures*, and the restrictions on hours of operation in Metro's ordinance (cannot operate from 1:00 am–9:00 am) are more generous than those upheld in *Restaurant Ventures* (cannot be open from 1:00 a.m.–3:00 p.m.). 60 S.W.3d at 579–80. We decline to afford these restrictions any greater protection under the Kentucky Constitution than in *Jameson* and *Restaurant Ventures*.

"No Touch" Provision

Metro's "no touch" restriction provides: "It shall be a violation of this chapter for any employee, who regularly appears semi-nude in an adult entertainment establishment, to knowingly or intentionally touch a customer or the clothing of a customer." The trial court found that the restriction was unconstitutionally overbroad because it could be read to prohibit touching between an employee and a customer off the premises of the adult entertainment business and "otherwise legal and expressive touching such as a handshake between a patron and a dancer who is fully clothed and not performing at the time." The Court of Appeals upheld the restriction, rejecting the trial court's conclusion that the restriction could be read to apply to contact off the premises of the adult entertainment business. As for prohibiting otherwise legal and expressive touching in the establishment, the Court of Appeals held that such a ban is not constitutionally infirm because "touching between a performer and a customer is not protected expression." *See Hang On, Inc. v. City of Arlington*, 65 F.3d 1248, 1253–55 (5th Cir. 1995).

In *Jameson* and *Restaurant Ventures*, provisions prohibiting physical contact between adult entertainment employees and customers were upheld. However, the language in the "no touch" provisions in those cases was limited to when the employee was performing. *Jameson*, 215 S.W.3d at 11; *Restaurant Ventures*, 60 S.W.3d at 580. In the present case, the prohibition on touching between an employee and patron has no such limitation. Clearly, Metro's "no touch" provision would be valid if it applied to employees only while they were performing or while still in a state of nudity. *See Hang On, Inc.*, 65 F.3d at 1251. "By placing a reasonable distance between the patrons and the performers, there is a decreased opportunity to solicit sex, contract social disease, and renders the no touch rule easier." *Restaurant Ventures*, 60 S.W.3d at 580 (addressing the buffer zone, stage requirement and no touch provisions as they relate to the distance between the patrons and performers while they are performing).

However, the question in this case is whether Metro's "no touch" provision is overbroad because it would prohibit any intentional touching between an employee and patron, even if the performer is not performing or is fully clothed, and would prohibit even lawful touching of a nonsexual nature, such as a handshake. The Court of Appeals in *Restaurant Ventures* even questioned whether non-erotic touching could be prohibited:

> Appellants' argument that otherwise legal and expressive conduct, such as shaking hands or other non-erotic touching between people, could be prohibited under the ordinance is folly. The ordinance does not prohibit such social niceties (unless done while nude). The line between prohibited conduct and permitted conduct is clearly drawn by the ordinance.

Id. at 579. As recognized by the court in *Threesome Entertainment v. Strittmather*, wherein the court struck down a "no touch" provision:

> Thus, a semi-nude dancer could not even shake hands with a patron. A semi-nude dancer also could not accept a glass of water from a co-employee if their hands touched in the exchange. And, ironically, under this Ordinance, a semi-nude dancer could not even push a customer away to rebuff an advance without subjecting herself to criminal charges.

4 F.Supp.2d 710, 722 n. 6 (N.D. Ohio 1998) (finding "no touch" provision overbroad because it did not contain a mens rea requirement). While the "no touch" provision in the present case does contain a mens rea, it would still prohibit benign, non-sexual, consensual, otherwise lawful touching between an employee and a customer, even when the employee is not performing or in a state of nudity.

We do not agree with the Court of Appeals conclusion that all touching between a performer and a customer is not constitutionally protected. As noted above, touching during an erotic performance or while in a state of nudity is not protected expression. We would also agree that sexual touching would not be protected expression. However, we believe that nonsexual, consensual touching, such as a handshake or a pat on the back, as a greeting or show of fellowship, is a social custom and an integral part of our culture. This sort of touching is not based on any right of artistic expression, but on one's right to free association. Thus, it is afforded protection under §1 and §2 of the Kentucky Constitution as part of an individual's right to personal liberty. As this Court recognized in *Wasson*:

> The meaning of Sections One and Two as they apply to personal liberty is found in the remarks of J. Proctor Knott of Marion County (see Official Report of the Proceedings and Debates in the 1890 Convention, E. Polk Johnson, Vol. 1, p. 718):
>
> "[T]hose who exercise that power in organized society with any claim of justice, derive it from the people themselves. That with the whole of such power residing in the people, the people as a body rest under the highest of all moral obligations to protect each individual in the rights of life, liberty, and the pursuit of happiness, provided that he shall in no wise injure his neighbor in so doing."

842 S.W.2d at 494–95. The *Wasson* court goes on to quote from *Commonwealth v. Campbell*, 133 Ky. 50, 117 S.W. 383 (1909):

> Man in his natural state has the right to do whatever he chooses and has the power to do. When he becomes a member of organized society, under governmental regulation, he surrenders, of necessity, all of his natural right the exercise of which is, or may be, injurious to his fellow citizens. This is the price that he pays for governmental protection, but it is not within the competency of a free government to invade the sanctity of the absolute rights of the citizen any further than the direct protection of society requires.... It is not within the competency of government to invade the privacy of a citizen's life and to regulate his conduct in matters in which he alone is concerned, or to prohibit him any liberty the exercise of which will not directly injure society.

Wasson, 842 S.W.2d at 494–95 (quoting *Campbell*, 117 S.W. at 385).

We recognize that our nation's highest Court has rejected the notion of any right of "free association," unless it is the context of free speech or an intimate human relationship. *See City of Dallas v. Stanglin*, 490 U.S. 19, 23–25, 109 S.Ct. 1591, 104 L.Ed.2d 18 (1989); *Roberts v. United States Jaycees*, 468 U.S. 609, 617–18, 104 S.Ct. 3244, 82 L.Ed.2d 462 (1984). Nevertheless, we deem such a right exists in the Commonwealth under our state Constitution. However, we acknowledge this right is not absolute. Hence, we must apply the test of *O'Brien* to assess whether Metro's blanket "no touch" provision is sufficiently justified to combat the secondary effects of sexually oriented businesses.

There is no question that the first three parts of the *O'Brien* test have been met. As with the other restrictions we have upheld herein, Metro had the authority to enact the ordinance, there existed a substantial governmental interest in regulating sexually oriented businesses, and the provision was aimed at curbing the secondary effects of sexually oriented businesses, not the suppression of speech.

As for the fourth part of the test—whether the "no touch" provision would incidentally burden the protected conduct more than is necessary to further the governmental interest—we believe that the wording of the provision goes overboard in forbidding lawful, nonsexual, consensual touching. In regulating speech, an ordinance

> must be narrowly tailored to serve the government's legitimate, content-neutral interests but that it need not be the least restrictive or least intrusive means of doing so. Rather, the requirement of narrow tailoring is satisfied so long as the regulation promotes a substantial government interest that would be achieved less effectively absent the regulation. To be sure, this standard does not mean that a time, place, or manner regulation may burden substantially more speech than is necessary to further the government's legitimate interests. Government may not regulate expression in such a manner that a substantial portion of the burden on speech does not serve to advance its goals. So long as the means chosen are not substantially broader than necessary to achieve the government's interest, however, the regulation will not be invalid simply because a court concludes that the government's interest could be adequately served by some less-speech-restrictive alternative.

DLS, Inc. v. City of Chattanooga, 107 F.3d 403, 412 (6th Cir. 1997) (quoting *Ward v. Rock Against Racism*, 491 U.S. 781, 798–99, 109 S.Ct. 2746, 105 L.Ed.2d 661 (1989)) (internal citations and quotation omitted). Metro maintains that the "no touch" provision is necessary to combat prostitution and sexually transmitted disease. Although Metro has a valid interest in trying to stifle these negative secondary effects, we believe that prohibiting all touching, including benign, nonsexual touching, is substantially broader than necessary to achieve Metro's interest. The nonsexual touching that is common in our culture as a means of social greeting or as an expression of platonic affection does not always lead to sexual behavior, and we will not cynically presume otherwise. An ordinance could easily be more narrowly tailored to prohibit sexual touching, as in the ban on touching during a performance or while in a state of nudity. Further, there exist laws in the Commonwealth which criminalize unwanted sexual contact. *See* KRS 510.130. Accordingly, we adjudge that the "no touch" provision in this case is unconstitutionally overbroad.

* * *

Conclusion

For the reasons stated above, the judgment of the Jefferson Circuit Court is affirmed in part, reversed in part and remanded for proceedings consistent with this opinion.

All sitting. All concur.

Venters, J., concurs by separate opinion in which Abramson and Cunningham, JJ., join.

Justice Venters, concurring:

While I am in full agreement with the conclusions reached by the well-reasoned majority opinion, I write separately to more fully address the provision exclusively relied upon by Appellants in support of their constitutional claims, Section 1(4) of the Kentucky Constitution. Appellants make no federal First Amendment claims, and seek only to have their arguments addressed on state constitutional grounds. * * * Indeed, the Federal District Court, following removal by Metro, dismissed this very litigation from its docket for lack of jurisdiction on the basis that Appellants raised no federal constitutional claims.

Despite Appellants' disclaimer of their federally-protected constitutional rights, the majority bases its analysis of Section 1(4) of the Kentucky Constitution on federal cases decided under the United States Constitution or on other Kentucky decisions, such as *Commonwealth v. Jameson*, 215 S.W.3d 9 (Ky. 2006) and *Restaurant Ventures, LLC v. Lexington-Fayette Urban County Government*, 60 S.W.3d 572 (Ky. App. 2001) which rest on federal authority because, unlike the case now before us, First Amendment rights, as well as Section 1(4) rights were involved. Usually, those appearing in state courts asserting claims of fundamental constitutional liberties invoke the applicable sections of both federal and state constitutions, taking advantage of whichever proves to be more advantageous. Here, our analysis need not be tethered to a contemporaneous assertion of federal rights.

I appreciate the recognition of this point by the Court of Appeals in its lengthy opinion in this matter, and its attempt to ascertain the scope and breadth of Section 1(4) from Kentucky's own jurisprudential experience. That attempt was not especially fruitful, because as the Court of Appeals found, Kentucky's highest courts have rarely undertaken such analysis. Instead, we have rather consistently chosen to tie our interpretation of the Kentucky Constitution to the ebb and flow of federal constitutional analysis. I see no reason why our interpretation of the Kentucky Constitution is dependent to any degree whatsoever on the federal courts' analysis of the federal constitution. We may, of course, be persuasively informed by their view of analogous provisions, just as we are routinely informed by the decisions of the courts of our sister states, but we should not accept the federal interpretation of federal law as controlling in our interpretation of state law. Indeed, the United States Supreme Court has so held, stating in *Minnesota v. National Tea Co.*, 309 U.S. 551, 557, 60 S.Ct. 676, 84 L.Ed. 920 (1940):

> It is fundamental that state courts be left free and unfettered by us in interpreting their state constitutions.... [S]tate courts will not be the final arbiters of important issues under the federal constitution; and that we will not encroach on the constitutional jurisdiction of the states. This is not a mere technical rule nor a rule for our convenience. It touches the division of authority between state courts and this Court and is of equal importance to each. Only by such explicitness can the highest courts of the states and this Court keep within the bounds of their respective jurisdictions.

This Court is the final arbiter of the Kentucky Constitution, and our interpretation of its terms is not constrained by the words of used in the federal Constitution any more than it is by the Pennsylvania Constitution. Of course we recognize the United States Constitution as the supreme law of the land. We respectfully yield to the authority of the federal courts to interpret the federal Constitution, as we retain exclusive authority to interpret our own.

It has been suggested in this matter that while we are free to interpret state constitutional provisions more broadly than similar provisions of the federal Constitution, we may not conclude that our state constitution offers a lesser degree of protection than the federal. This Court itself has so stated, erroneously as dicta I believe, in *Commonwealth v. Wasson*, 842 S.W.2d 487, 492 (Ky. 1992) (stating "We are not bound by decisions of the United States Supreme Court when deciding whether a state statute impermissibly infringes upon individual rights guaranteed in the State Constitution so long as state constitutional protection does not fall below the federal floor, meaning the minimum guarantee of individual rights under the United States Constitution as interpreted by the United States Supreme Court.") *See also Elk Horn Coal Corp. v. Cheyenne Resources, Inc.*, 163 S.W.3d 408, 418 (Ky. 2005). The statement is, however, a misreading of the opinion of the United States Supreme Court decision in *Oregon v. Hass*, 420 U.S. 714, 719, 95 S.Ct. 1215, 43 L.Ed.2d 570 (1975). In *Hass*, the Oregon courts addressed search and seizure issues predicated on the Fourth Amendment of the federal Constitution, not the Oregon Constitution, and the United States Supreme Court simply stated the obvious, that a "state may not impose such greater restrictions *as a matter of federal constitutional law* when this Court specifically refrains from imposing them." *Id.* (emphasis added). The *Hass* decision says nothing that fetters the authority of a state's highest court to interpret *state constitutional rights* either more restrictively or less restrictively than the federal constitutional counterpart.

Therefore, addressing the issues presented without regard to the First Amendment interpretations relied upon by the majority, I conclude that the constitutional protections contained in Section 1(4) of our constitution do not extend to nude dancing, and thus the Metro ordinances proscribing this conduct do not violate its provisions. I would accordingly uphold the Metro ordinances at issue as constitutional under Section 1(4), with the exception of the no-touch provision, which I likewise conclude is overbroad under our state constitutional jurisprudence.

* * *

Accordingly, I concur with the majority in upholding the Metro ordinances, excepting the no touching provision, as constitutional under our state constitution for the reasons stated above.

Abramson and Cunningham, JJ., join.

Notes and Questions

1. The *Blue Movies* Court finds a right of "free association" in the Kentucky Constitution, exceeding any such right under the U.S. Constitution. Here, the Court finds the right applies to engage in "nonsexual, consensual touching, such as a handshake or a pat on the back, as a greeting or show of fellowship." No subsequent Kentucky cases discuss the scope of this right of free association. How far might this right extend?
2. Justice Venters's three-justice concurrence raises an interesting issue of state constitutional law. Kentucky courts often cite *Oregon v. Hass*, 420 U.S. 714 (1975), for the proposition that state courts may not construe the state constitution to provide constitutional protection that falls below the federal "floor." (Justice Venters cited *Wasson* as one such case.) There is no doubt that the Kentucky courts must follow the U.S. Supreme Court's interpretations of federal law, including the *federal* Constitution. But are the Kentucky courts obligated to import federal precedent into its interpretation of the Kentucky Constitution? Justice Venters said no: "The *Hass* decision says nothing that fetters the authority of a state's highest court to interpret *state constitutional rights* either more restrictively or less restrictively than the federal constitutional counterpart." How might the answer to this question affect the decisions a plaintiff might make before filing a lawsuit?

Figure 8-2. Official portrait of Justice Daniel J. Venters, Kentucky State Capitol. Portrait by Stephen Sawyer, reproduced with permission of the artist and the Supreme Court of Kentucky.

D. Right to Bear Arms

"All men are, by nature, free and equal, and have certain inherent and inalienable rights, among which may be reckoned: ... Seventh: The right to bear arms in defense of themselves and of the State, subject to the power of the General Assembly to enact laws to prevent persons from carrying concealed weapons." (Ky. Const. §1.)

> "The citizens of Kentucky have the personal right to hunt, fish, and harvest wildlife, using traditional methods, subject only to statutes enacted by the Legislature, and to administrative regulations adopted by the designated state agency to promote wildlife conservation and management and to preserve the future of hunting and fishing. Public hunting and fishing shall be a preferred means of managing and controlling wildlife. This section shall not be construed to modify any provision of law relating to trespass, property rights, or the regulation of commercial activities." (Ky. Const. §255A.)

Among the "inherent and inalienable rights" protected by the Bill of Rights is the right of "[a]ll men" to "bear arms in defense of themselves and of the State." Thus, the Kentucky Constitution clearly guarantees both the personal right of self-defense and a corporate right to defend the Commonwealth, as in the militia. The text is markedly different from the Second Amendment to the U.S. Constitution, which states, "A well regulated Militia, being necessary to the security of a free State, the right of the people to keep and bear Arms, shall not be infringed." Until the U.S. Supreme Court decided *District of Columbia v. Heller*, 554 U.S. 570 (2008), there was some debate concerning whether the Second Amendment even protected a personal right, or only some collective right to keep and bear arms as part of a "well regulated Militia." In *Heller*, the Supreme Court determined that the Second Amendment "guarantee[s] the individual right to possess and carry weapons in case of confrontation." *Id.* at 592. But Section 1(7) has always protected both the individual right and the collective right to self-defense.

The right is not absolute. On its face, Section 1(7) makes the right to "bear arms" subject to "the power of the General Assembly to enact laws to prevent persons from carrying concealed weapons." Thus, the carrying of concealed weapons—but not the open carrying of firearms—is properly the subject of regulation by the General Assembly. The cases that follow will further consider the power of the General Assembly to regulate firearms, and the extent to which the right to bear arms is "inherent" or "inalienable."

In addition to protecting the right to bear arms for self-defense and in defense of the Commonwealth, Section 255A of the Kentucky Constitution also protects the right to "hunt, fish, and harvest wildlife, using traditional methods," which includes but is not limited to the use of firearms for such purposes. The voters approved adding Section 255A to the Kentucky Constitution in 2012, but no reported decisions of Kentucky courts have yet construed it.

From the founding of the Nation to the mid-1990s, Vermont was the only State in the Union to constitutionalize the right to hunt and fish, a right included in its first constitution in 1777 and included in each subsequent constitution of the state. (*See* Vt. Const. ch. II, §67.) Twenty-three states, including Kentucky, now have a right to hunt and fish codified in their constitutions. Other states with such constitutional rights include Alabama (Ala. Const. art. I, §36.02, adopted 1996), Arkansas (Ark. Const. amend. 88, §1, adopted 2010), Georgia (Ga. Const. art. I, §1, ¶XXVIII, adopted 2006),

Idaho (Idaho Const. art. I, §23, adopted 2012), Indiana (Ind. Const. art. 1, §39, adopted 2016), Kansas (Kan. Const. Bill of Rights §21, adopted 2016), Louisiana (La. Const. art. I, §27, adopted 2004), Minnesota (Minn. Const. art. XIII, §12, adopted 1998), Mississippi (Miss. Const. art. 3, §12A, adopted 2014), Montana (Mont. Const. art. IX, §7, adopted 2004), Nebraska (Neb. Const. art. XV, §25, adopted 2012), North Carolina (N.C. Const. art. I, §38, adopted 2018), North Dakota (N.D. Const. art. XI, §27, adopted 2000), Oklahoma (Okla. Const. art. II, §36, adopted 2008), South Carolina (S.C. Const. art. I, §25, adopted 2010), Tennessee (Tenn. Const. art. XI, §13, adopted 2010), Texas (Tex. Const. art. I, §34, adopted 2015), Utah (Utah Const. art. I, §30, adopted 2020), Virginia (Va. Const. art. XI, §4, adopted 2000), Wisconsin (Wisc. Const. art. I, §26, adopted 2003), and Wyoming (Wyo. Const. art. 1, §39, adopted 2012). Two other states, California and Rhode Island, expressly protect the right to fish in their constitutions, but not the right to hunt. (*See* Cal. Const. art. I, §25; R.I. Const. art. I, §17.) Supporters of these right to hunt and fish provisions have argued they preserve a rich sporting tradition in the United States and are intended to preemptively guard against efforts by environmental protection, animal rights, and gun-control advocacy groups to outlaw the hunting of certain species or using certain traditional methods such as firearms. Few cases have construed the right to hunt and fish provisions in these states' constitutions.

Bliss v. Commonwealth

Court of Appeals of Kentucky (1822)

12 Ky. 90

Per Curiam.

This was an indictment founded on the act of the legislature of this state, "to prevent persons in this commonwealth from wearing concealed arms."

The act provides, that any person in this commonwealth, who shall hereafter wear a pocket pistol, dirk, large knife, or sword in a cane, concealed as a weapon, unless when travelling on a journey, shall be fined in any sum not less than one hundred dollars; which may be recovered in any court having jurisdiction of like sums, by action of debt, or on presentment of a grand jury.

The indictment, in the words of the act, charges Bliss with having worn concealed as a weapon, a sword in a cane.

Bliss was found guilty of the charge, and a fine of one hundred dollars assessed by the jury, and judgment was thereon rendered by the court. To reverse that judgment, Bliss appealed to this court.

In argument the judgment was assailed by the counsel of Bliss, exclusively on the ground of the act, on which the indictment is founded, being in conflict with the twenty-third section of the tenth article of the constitution of this state.

That section provides, "that the right of the citizens to bear arms in defense of themselves and the state, shall not be questioned."

The provision contained in this section, perhaps, is as well calculated to secure to the citizens the right to bear arms in defense of themselves and the state, as any that could have been adopted by the makers of the constitution. If the right be assailed, immaterial through what medium, whether by an act of the legislature or in any other form, it is equally opposed to the comprehensive import of the section. The legislature is nowhere expressly mentioned in the section; but the language employed is general, without containing any expression restricting its import to any particular department of government; and in the twenty-eighth section of the same article of the constitution, it is expressly declared, "that every thing in that article is excepted out of the general powers of government, and shall forever remain inviolate; and that all laws contrary thereto, or contrary to the constitution, shall be void."

The right of the citizens to bear arms in defence of themselves and the state, must be preserved entire.

It was not, however, contended by the attorney for the commonwealth, that it would be competent for the legislature, by the enactment of any law, to prevent the citizens from bearing arms either in defense of themselves or the state; but a distinction was taken between a law prohibiting the exercise of the right, and a law merely regulating the manner of exercising that right; and whilst the former was admitted to be incompatible with the constitution, it was insisted, that the latter is not so, and under that distinction, and by assigning the act in question a place in the latter description of laws, its consistency with the constitution was attempted to be maintained.

That the provisions of the act in question do not import an entire destruction of the right of the citizens to bear arms in defense of themselves and the state, will not be controverted by the court; for though the citizens are forbid wearing weapons concealed in the manner described in the act, they may, nevertheless, bear arms in any other admissible form. But to be in conflict with the constitution, it is not essential that the act should contain a prohibition against bearing arms in every possible form—it is the right to bear arms in defense of the citizens and the state, that is secured by the constitution, and whatever restrains the full and complete exercise of that right, though not an entire destruction of it, is forbidden by the explicit language of the constitution.

Not merely all legislative acts, which purport to take it away; but all which diminish or impair it as it existed when the constitution was formed, are void.

If, therefore, the act in question imposes any restraint on the right, immaterial what appellation may be given to the act, whether it be an act regulating the manner of bearing arms or any other, the consequence, in reference to the constitution, is precisely the same, and its collision with that instrument equally obvious.

And can there be entertained a reasonable doubt but the provisions of the act import a restraint on the right of the citizens to bear arms? The court apprehends not. The right existed at the adoption of the constitution; it had then no limits short of the moral power of the citizens to exercise it, and it in fact consisted in nothing else but in the liberty of the citizens to bear arms. Diminish that liberty, therefore, and you necessarily restrain the right; and such is the diminution and restraint, which the act in question most indisputably imports, by prohibiting the citizens wearing weapons in a manner which was lawful to wear them when the constitution was adopted. In truth, the right of the citizens to bear arms, has been as directly assailed by the provisions of the act, as though they were forbid carrying guns on their shoulders, swords in scabbards, or when in conflict with an enemy, were not allowed the use of bayonets; and if the act be consistent with the constitution, it can not be incompatible with that instrument for the legislature, by successive enactments, to entirely cut off the exercise of the right of the citizens to bear arms. For, in principle, there is no difference between a law prohibiting the wearing concealed arms, and a law forbidding the wearing such as are exposed; and if the former be unconstitutional, the latter must be so likewise.

We may possibly be told, that though a law of either description may be enacted consistently with the constitution, it would be incompatible with that instrument to enact laws of both descriptions. But if either, when alone, be consistent with the constitution, which, it may be asked, would be incompatible with that instrument, if both were enacted?

The law first enacted would not be; for, as the argument supposes either may be enacted consistent with the constitution, that which is first enacted must, at the time of enactment, be consistent with the constitution; and if then consistent, it can not become otherwise, by any subsequent act of the legislature. It must, therefore, be the latter act, which the argument infers would be incompatible with the constitution.

But suppose the order of enactment were reversed, and instead of being the first, that which was first, had been the last; the argument, to be consistent, should, nevertheless, insist on the last enactment being in conflict with the constitution. So, that the absurd consequence would thence follow, of making the same act of the legislature, either consistent with the constitution, or not so, according as it may precede or follow some other enactment of a different import. Besides, by insisting on the previous act producing any effect on the latter, the argument implies that the previous one operates as a partial restraint on the right of the citizens to bear arms, and proceeds on the notion, not by prohibiting the exercise of the residue of right, not affected by the first act, the latter act come in collision with the constitution. But it should not be forgotten, that it is not only a part of the right that is secured by the constitution; it is the right entire and complete, as it existed at the adoption of the constitution; and if any portion of that right be impaired, immaterial how small the part may be, and immaterial the order of time at which it be done, it is equally forbidden by the constitution.

Hence, we infer, that the act upon which the indictment against Bliss is founded, is in conflict with the constitution; and if so, the result is obvious—the result is what the constitution has declared it shall be, that the act is void.

The act to prevent persons from wearing concealed arms, is unconstitutional and void.

And if to be incompatible with the constitution makes void the act, we must have been correct, throughout the examination of this case, in treating the question of compatibility, as one proper to be decided by the court. For it is emphatically the duty of the court to decide what the law is; and how is the law to be decided, unless it be known? and how can it be known without ascertaining, from a comparison with the constitution, whether there exists such an incompatibility between the acts of the legislature and the constitution, as to make void the acts?

A blind enforcement of every act of the legislature, might relieve the court from the trouble and responsibility of deciding on the consistency of the legislative acts with the constitution; but the court would not be thereby released from its obligations to obey the mandates of the constitution, and maintain the paramount authority of that instrument; and those obligations must cease to be acknowledged, or the court become insensible to the impressions of moral sentiment, before the provisions of any act of the legislature, which in the opinion of the court, conflict with the constitution, can be enforced.

Whether or not an act of the legislature conflicts with the constitution, is, at all times, a question of great delicacy, and deserves the most mature and deliberate consideration of the court. But though a question of delicacy, yet as it is a judicial one, the court would be unworthy its station, were it to shrink from deciding it, whenever in the course of judicial examination, a decision becomes material to the right in contest. The court should never, on slight implication or vague conjecture, pronounce the legislature to have transcended its authority in the enactment of law; but when a clear and strong conviction is entertained, that an act of the legislature is incompatible with the constitution, there is no alternative for the court to pursue, but to declare that conviction, and pronounce the act inoperative and void. And such is the conviction entertained by a majority of the court, (Judge Mills dissenting,) in relation to the act in question.

The judgment must consequently be reversed.

Notes and Questions

1. The Court in *Bliss* strikes an absolutist position on the right to bear arms: "any restraint on the right" is held to be unconstitutional. Note also that not only a legislative act that takes away the right, but also an act that may "diminish or impair" the right, is void. Thus, the Court did not apply any balancing test in which it considered the fit between the nature of the governmental interest and the means of advancing that interest. The U.S. Supreme Court has adopted a similar test for cases arising under the Second Amendment: "When the Second Amendment's plain text covers an individual's conduct, the Constitution presumptively protects that conduct. The government must then justify its regulation by demonstrating that it is consistent with the Nation's historical tradition of firearm regulation. Only then may a court conclude that the individual's conduct falls outside the Second Amendment's unqualified command." *N.Y. State Rifle & Pistol Ass'n, Inc. v. Bruen*, 597 U.S. ___, 142 S. Ct. 2111, 2129–30 (2022) (quotation omitted).
2. *Bliss* was decided in 1822 under Kentucky's second constitution. The constitutional provision at the time *Bliss* was decided stated that "the right of the citizens to bear

arms in defense of themselves and the state, *shall not be questioned*" (emphasis added). Note that the last clause in Section 1(7) now states that the right to bear arms is "subject to the power of the General Assembly to enact laws to prevent persons from carrying concealed weapons"; otherwise, the operative text is the same today as it was in 1822.

3. The Ninth Circuit had occasion in a Second Amendment case to discuss some of the subsequent history that followed in the wake of *Bliss*:

> The court's decision in *Bliss* was soon attacked, and was overruled over a decade before the Civil War. In 1837, Governor James Clark, deeply concerned about the "bloodshed and violence" caused by concealed weapons in the wake of *Bliss,* called on the Kentucky legislature to pass a new statute banning the practice. The Kentucky legislative committee that received the Governor's message criticized the court for reading the state constitution too literally. *See* Robert M. Ireland, *The Problem of Concealed Weapons in Nineteenth-Century Kentucky*, 91 Reg. Ky. Hist. Soc'y 370, 373 (1993). In 1849, a Kentucky constitutional convention adopted without debate a provision authorizing the legislature to "pass laws to prevent persons from carrying concealed arms." Ky. Const. art. XIII, §25. Then, in 1854, the Kentucky legislature passed a new statute prohibiting the concealed carry of "any deadly weapons other than an ordinary pocket knife." *An Act to prohibit the carrying of concealed weapons*, Mar. 10, 1853, Ky. Acts, Chap. 1020 (1854).
>
> The Supreme Court stated in *Heller* that "*the majority* of the 19th-century courts to consider the question held that prohibitions on carrying concealed weapons were lawful under the Second Amendment or state analogues" 554 U.S. at 626, 128 S.Ct. 2783 (emphasis added). The Court substantially understated the matter. As just noted, with the exception of *Bliss*, those pre-Civil War state courts that considered the question *all* upheld prohibitions against concealed weapons. Four of the six courts upholding prohibitions specifically discussed, and disagreed with, *Bliss*. * * * Moreover, the two-to-one *Bliss* decision did not last. *Bliss* was decided in 1822; a state constitutional amendment was adopted in 1849 to overturn *Bliss*; the legislature then passed a statute in 1854 outlawing concealed weapons.

Peruta v. Cnty. of San Diego, 824 F.3d 919, 935–36 (9th Cir. 2016) (en banc).

Holland v. Commonwealth

Court of Appeals of Kentucky (1956)
294 S.W.2d 83

OPINION OF THE COURT BY JUDGE MOREMEN.

Appellant, Morton Holland, was convicted of carrying concealed a deadly weapon, and was sentenced to confinement in the penitentiary for a period of two years.

Appellant was appointed deputy sheriff of Breathitt County on August 26, 1955. Sometime prior to September 21, 1955, a justice of peace of Perry County delivered to Holland two warrants; one for the arrest of Bill Krintz, and the other for the arrest of Willie Strong. Holland had received information that Strong had moved to Perry County and was seen frequently in beer taverns there.

On the night of September 21, Holland entered Perry County with the intention to locate Strong and then to inform the sheriff of Perry County so that an arrest might be made pursuant to the warrant. He arrived at a tavern on Duane Mountain in Perry County about dark and commenced to drink beer in the company of Miss Jackie Steel. He testified that he carried a loaded 45 automatic in his front pocket and wore a sport shirt outside his trousers. When he entered a booth he took the gun from the pocket of his tight trousers and placed it on the seat of the booth.

Later three deputy sheriffs of Perry County, in discharge of their duty to check roadhouses, stopped at the tavern and two of the deputies, Jack Fields and Cephus Begley, went inside. They noticed the appellant drinking with a woman. There was no disorder so they returned to their car. Before they left, someone came from within the tavern and reported that the appellant was making trouble inside and was flourishing a gun. The three deputies reentered the building and when Fields started toward him, Holland arose and pointed the automatic pistol at Fields. The deputies testified that he drew the gun from under his shirt. Holland stated he picked it up from the seat of the booth, but, in any event, he pointed the weapon at Fields and told the deputies to back out of the tavern. They did. A warrant for carrying concealed a deadly weapon was obtained and later Holland was arrested in Perry County at his own establishment, which was also a beer tavern, situated a few miles from where the incident just related occurred. Appellant justified his action by stating that he had seen deputy sheriff Fields beat up people and he did not want to be beaten up himself.

Appellant was punished in the quarterly court for his action in flourishing the gun by being fined the sum of $50, so we are concerned here only with the remaining charge. Appellant contends that he was entitled to a peremptory instruction of acquittal because he was a duly appointed peace officer.

Section 1, subd. 7 of the Bill of Rights, which is concerned with inherent and inalienable rights, grants to all citizens:

> 'The right to bear arms in defense of themselves and of the State, subject to the power of the General Assembly to enact laws to prevent persons from carrying concealed weapons.'

The foregoing section is an exemplification of the broadest expression of the right to bear arms. Some states give the legislature the right to regulate the carrying of firearms; at least one state prohibits even the possession of firearms. See cases collected in the annotation of *Pierce v. State of Oklahoma*, 42 Okl.Cr. 272, 275 P. 393, 73 A.L.R. 833.

In our state the legislature is empowered only to deny to citizens the right to carry concealed weapons. The constitutional provision is an affirmation of the faith that all men have the inherent right to arm themselves for the defense of themselves and of the state. The only limitation concerns the mode of carrying such instruments. We observe, via obiter dicta, that although a person is granted the right to carry a weapon openly, a severe penalty is imposed for carrying it concealed. If the gun is worn outside the jacket or shirt in full view, no one may question the wearer's right so to do; but, if it is carried under the jacket or shirt, the violator is subject to imprisonment for not less than two nor more than five years. The heavy emphasis, we suppose, is upon the undue advantage given to a person who is able suddenly to expose and use a weapon, although the gun itself is the vicious instrument. Nevertheless the meaning of the constitutional provision is plain and the legislature has exercised the power granted it by enacting KRS 435.230, which reads:

> '(1) Any person, not expressly authorized by law, who carries concealed a deadly weapon, other than an ordinary pocket knife, on or about his person, or any person who sells a deadly weapon, other than an ordinary pocket knife, to a minor, shall be confined in the penitentiary for not less than two nor more than five years.
>
> '(2) Sheriffs, constables, marshals, policemen and other ministerial officers, when necessary for their protection in the discharge of their official duties; United States mail carriers, when actually engaged in their duties; and agents and messengers of express companies, when necessary for their protection in the discharge of their official duties, may carry concealed deadly weapons on or about their persons.'

It was sufficiently proved that appellant was a duly constituted deputy sheriff of Breathitt County and was permitted under subsection (2) above quoted to conceal a pistol when actually engaged in his duties.

We have had several cases in this state which deal generally with the problem here presented. In *Johnson v. Commonwealth*, 212 Ky. 372, 279 S.W. 341, 342, the court indicated that usually the question was one for the jury and that the accused was entitled to a concrete instruction under the statute as to whether under the facts proven, it was necessary for the officer to carry a concealed weapon in the discharge of his official duties, and it was pointed out:

> 'In some localities there is seldom if ever an occasion for the exercise of such authority. In such communities perhaps it would be unnecessary for an officer to carry arms for his protection except in the discharge of an actual duty, as above indicated. On the other hand, in congested districts and lawless com-

> munities an emergency may arise at any time, and an unarmed officer be powerless to protect himself or to exercise his authority, and, under the statute, it would seem that the necessity of an officer arming himself for the exercise of these general duties is a question to be determined by the facts and circumstances arising in the case.'

In *Voils v. Commonwealth*, 228 Ky. 149, 14 S.W.2d 381, a similar ruling was had. It was indicated in the opinion that an officer has the general duty to maintain peace in his community, that he may reasonably prepare for his own protection in the exercise of his general duty, and that the statute was not intended to limit the right to carry a concealed weapon for a specific errand only. This case also held that a special instruction under the statute should have been given.

The facts presented in *Wallace v. Commonwealth*, 197 Ky. 233, 246 S.W. 466, 467, parallel, to some extent, those presented here. There the defendant was a game warden who went from Irvine through Richmond to Boonesboro for the purpose of making an arrest. On his way back home he stopped in Richmond, went to a dance hall and upon leaving it was arrested for being drunk. A search disclosed that he had a concealed weapon upon his person. It was said:

> 'He had, as any other police officer, the right to have a deadly weapon concealed on his person at the time of making the arrest, and obviously in going to and returning from the performance of such duties, if it was reasonably necessary for his protection. Ministerial officers required to be on the lookout for criminals and make arrests must be afforded protection, and, when such officer is in the discharge of such duties and has a warrant for the arrest of such person, he comes clearly within the class of persons mentioned in section 1313, Kentucky Statutes, as exempt from prosecution for carrying concealed deadly weapons.'

While the foregoing case does not deal specifically with the question of a peace officer who is carrying a concealed weapon outside the jurisdiction of the authority which has appointed him, it recognizes that ministerial officers are charged with the duty to be continuously alert in the detection of criminal acts and criminals and to make arrests when the opportunity is afforded. We would be other than realistic if we failed to recognize the general practice among law enforcing agencies of going beyond the territorial limits of the appointing power to detect and apprehend criminals who have fled from the vicinity in which the crime was committed. The primary interest of locating such men lies in the ministerial officers where the prosecution will take place and even if it is necessary or, at least, appropriate to call in local officers to make the physical arrest, still the duty is upon the foreign officer to locate the accused.

We also must recognize that peace officers, who at the present time work definite shifts, are still charged with the duty under their office to act in times of emergency in behalf of the people generally even if off duty. We believe the statute did not intend that in every interlude between an actual arrest or other direct duty an officer must disarm himself, or expose his weapon.

In the case at bar appellant was certainly acting under his broad duties but, in addition to that, the undisputed proof showed that he was upon a specific journey to locate an alleged offender for the purpose of arrest. We think, therefore, a peremptory instruction should have been given.

We have in the consideration of this case set aside consideration of the personal reprehensible actions of appellant in flourishing his gun in an unlawful manner. This is something we believe addresses itself to the punitive power of the agency which appointed him. It would be inappropriate to handicap the vast majority of conscientious police officers in the fulfillment of their duties in order to punish one man who had not fulfilled the obligation of his office.

The judgment is therefore reversed with instructions that the indictment be dismissed.

Notes and Questions

1. Note that the Court describes Section 1(7) as "an exemplification of the broadest expression of the right to bear arms." It further observes that the protection of the right to bear arms afforded by Section 1(7) is nearly absolute: "In our state the legislature is empowered *only* to deny to citizens the right to carry *concealed* weapons" (emphasis added). Due in part to the absolute nature of the right described in *Holland*, it was long thought that the General Assembly had no power even to prohibit the possession of firearms by convicted felons.
2. However, the Court held in *Holland* that the deputy sheriff was exempted from the prohibition on carrying concealed weapons because subsection (2) of the statute applied to him, even while he was off duty. The Court did not find the statute unconstitutional. Is it reasonable to conclude that *Holland*'s statements about the breadth of the constitutional right are merely dicta?

Posey v. Commonwealth

Supreme Court of Kentucky (2006)
185 S.W.3d 170

Opinion of the Court by Justice Graves.

Appellant entered conditional guilty pleas to Trafficking in Marijuana (subsequent offense), Possession of a Firearm by a Convicted Felon, Misdemeanor Possession of a Controlled Substance, and Possession of Drug Paraphernalia in Jefferson Circuit Court. For these crimes, Appellant was sentenced to four years of probation with six months work release. Pursuant to his conditional pleas, Appellant took a direct appeal to the Court of Appeals. RCr 8.09. In an unpublished opinion, the Court of Appeals affirmed his convictions in all respects. * * * Appellant filed a petition for discretionary review in this Court, which we granted. CR 76.20. For the reasons set forth herein, we now affirm Appellant's convictions, but for reasons not stated in the Court of Appeals' opinion.

On January 6, 2002, two Louisville police officers attempted to serve an outstanding arrest warrant on an individual named James Powell. Powell's last known address was 1565 South Ninth Street. When the officers arrived at that address and knocked on the door, Appellant, Ricky L. Posey, appeared at the door. Appellant, who was standing immediately inside the threshold of the home, opened the door and began to talk with one of the officers. The other officer soon joined their conversation and as they were conversing with Appellant on the porch, they observed shotgun shells and individually wrapped packets of marijuana inside the home. They also smelled an odor of marijuana emanating from the home.

From these observations, the officers decided to step inside Appellant's home (through the open door) and arrest him for possession of a controlled substance. They immediately seized the marijuana and the shotgun shells in plain view and then proceeded to search the rest of the home. They found a gun lying on the floor in an adjoining room in plain view. In addition, they found a set of electronic scales and a bottle of codeine cough syrup.

Appellant was indicted for Trafficking in Marijuana (less than eight ounces) while in Possession of a Firearm (subsequent offense[1]), Possession of a Firearm by a Convicted Felon, Misdemeanor Possession of a Controlled Substance, and Possession of Drug Paraphernalia. Appellant filed a pretrial motion to suppress all of the evidence seized during the search of his home. Appellant also filed a motion to dismiss the firearm possession charge, arguing that KRS 527.040 (barring convicted felons from possessing handguns) was unconstitutional. The trial court denied both of Appellant's motions. Appellant subsequently entered conditional pleas of guilty for all charges, reserving for appeal the suppression issue and the constitutionality of KRS 527.040.

The Court of Appeals affirmed the trial court's rulings, holding that the officers' entry into the home for the purposes of arresting Appellant and seizing contraband in plain view did not violate the Fourth Amendment. The Court of Appeals further ruled KRS 527.040 constitutional, relying on this Court's decision in *Eary v. Commonwealth*, 659 S.W.2d 198 (Ky. 1983). We accepted discretionary review and now affirm on both issues.

* * *

Under KRS 527.040, it is a felony for convicted felons to possess, manufacture, or transport a firearm in the Commonwealth of Kentucky. Appellant contends that this law violates Section 1(7) of the Kentucky Constitution which states:

> All men are, by nature, free and equal, and have certain inherent and inalienable rights, among which may be reckoned: ... The right to bear arms in de-

1. This charge was subsequently amended to Trafficking in Marijuana (less than eight ounces) (subsequent offense).

> fense of themselves and of the State, subject to the power of the General Assembly to enact laws to prevent persons from carrying concealed weapons.

When considering the constitutionality of a statute, this Court draws all fair and reasonable inferences in favor of the statute's validity. *Kentucky Industrial Utility Customers, Inc. v. Kentucky Utilities Company*, 983 S.W.2d 493, 499 (Ky. 1998). "[T]he violation of the Constitution must be clear, complete and unmistakable in order to find the law unconstitutional." *Id.*; *see also Walters v. Bindner*, 435 S.W.2d 464, 467 (Ky. 1968) ("It is the rule that all presumptions and intendments are in favor of the constitutionality of statutes and, even in cases of reasonable doubt of their constitutionality, they should be upheld and the doubt resolved in favor of the voice of the people as expressed through their legislative department of government.")

Appellant concedes that KRS 527.040 would be a legitimate exercise of the General Assembly's broad police powers[2] if Section 1(7) were not enacted as a provision of the Kentucky Constitution. *See Walters, supra*, at *Id.* ("Our Legislature has a broad discretion to determine for itself what is harmful to health and morals or what is inimical to public welfare...."). Indeed, the legislature's power to pass laws, especially laws in the interest of public safety and welfare, is an essential attribute of government. *Manning v. Sims*, 308 Ky. 587, 213 S.W.2d 577, 592 (Ky. 1948) ("when the power of the Legislature to enact a law is called in question, the court should proceed with the greatest possible caution and should never declare an act invalid until after every doubt has been resolved in its favor") (quotation and citation omitted). Thus, we must always accord great deference to the legislature's exercise of these so-called "police powers," unless to do so would "clearly offend[ ] the limitations and prohibitions of the constitution." *Id., see also, Medtronic, Inc. v. Lohr*, 518 U.S. 470, 475, 116 S.Ct. 2240, 135 L.Ed.2d 700 (1996) ("States traditionally have had great latitude under their police powers to legislate as to the protection of the lives, limbs, health, comfort, and quiet of all persons.") (quoting *Metropolitan Life Ins. Co. v. Massachusetts*, 471 U.S. 724, 756, 105 S.Ct. 2380, 2398, 85 L.Ed.2d 728 (1985)).

However, Appellant contends that the mandates of Section 1(7) are clear and that its existence affirmatively operates to exempt the area of firearms possession from regulation by the General Assembly. Pursuant to Section 26 of our constitution, Appellant argues that KRS 527.040 is essentially nullified by Section 1(7) and should be declared invalid as an impermissible infringement upon the people's right to bear arms. For the reasons set forth herein, we disagree.

We begin by emphasizing that rights preserved to the people pursuant to Sections 1 through 26 of our constitution cannot be usurped by legislative fiat.[3] Ky. Const. §26, *see also Steelvest, Inc. v. Scansteel Service Center, Inc.*, 908 S.W.2d 104, 106 (Ky. 1995);

2. The General Assembly's broad power to enact laws for the purpose of protecting the public welfare is derived from Section 29 of the Kentucky Constitution. This Section vests all legislative power with that body. *See, e.g., Mullins v. Commonwealth*, 956 S.W.2d 222, 223 (Ky. App. 1997) ("[T]he legislature has the power to designate what is a crime and the sentences for violations thereof.").

3. Sections 1 through 26 are known collectively as "Kentucky's Bill of Rights."

Union Trust, Inc. v. Brown, 757 S.W.2d 218, 219 (Ky. App. 1988). The Kentucky Bill of Rights has always been, and continues to be, recognized as the supreme law of this Commonwealth. *Gatewood v. Matthews*, 403 S.W.2d 716, 718 (Ky. 1966). Accordingly, we consider carefully and fully any possible infringements upon these rights by a governmental power.

KRS 527.040 prohibits a specific class of individuals, namely convicted felons, from possessing firearms in the Commonwealth of Kentucky. Decades of decisions have taught us that a statute prohibiting a class of individuals from doing anything must, at a minimum, be based on some rational basis in order to satisfy constitutional standards. *See, e.g., Commonwealth Natural Resources & Env. Protection Cabinet v. Kentec Coal Co., Inc.*, 177 S.W.3d 718, 724–25 (Ky. 2005). In this case, neither party disputes that regulation of firearms among convicted felons is supported by substantial and rational concerns. *See Eary v. Commonwealth*, 659 S.W.2d 198, 200 (Ky. 1983) ("It is our opinion that a statute limiting the possession of firearms by persons who, by their past commission of serious felonies, have demonstrated a dangerous disregard for the law and thereby present a threat of further criminal activity is reasonable legislation in the interest of public welfare and safety...."); *see also*, Philip J. Cook and Jens Ludwig, *Principles for Effective Gun Policy*, 73 Fordham L. Rev. 589 (2004) (stating that gun misuse is concentrated among people with arrest records and arguing that effective gun policy should be designed to increase the "legal liability" to those who misuse guns); Matthew S. Miner, *Hearing the Danger of an Armed Felon—Allowing for a Detention Hearing under the Bail Reform Act for those who Unlawfully Possess Firearms*, 37 U. Mich. J.L. Reform 705 (2004) (arguing that unlawful firearms possession by felons is a serious threat to public safety), Judge Amy Karan and Helen Stampalia, *Domestic Violence and Firearms: A Deadly Combination*, 79 Fla. B.J. 79 (October 2005) (reporting that domestic abusers are more likely to seriously harm or kill somebody if they have access to firearms).

Rather, Appellant contends that the constitution expressly protects the convicted felon's right to bear arms in spite of these substantial risks to public welfare and safety. He points to the plain language of Section 1(7), and argues that when it is read in comparison to another right endowed by the constitution, there can be no doubt as to the meaning of the language. We disagree, finding nothing in the constitution, either express or implied, which support Appellant's positions.

First, Appellant argues that the language of Section 1(7) is plain and clear. It declares that all "men" have the right to bear arms in defense of themselves and of the Commonwealth subject only to "the power of the General Assembly to enact laws to prevent persons from carrying concealed weapons." Ky. Const. §1(7). He argues that use of the word "men" in the modern constitution rather than "citizens" (the word used in previous versions)[4] implies that the right is meant to encompass all persons and not

4. The previous version of the constitution read, in pertinent part: "That the right of the *citizens* to bear arms in defense of themselves and the State shall not be questioned." Ky. Const. §25 (1850) (emphasis added). In 1891, the language we see today was ratified: "All *men* are, by nature, free and

just those who were endowed with the rights and privileges which were commonly conferred on citizens.[5]

While we agree that it may be reasonable to infer from this language change that the 1890 constitutional convention desired to expand the lot of persons entitled to possess firearms, we disagree that this expansion reasonably or necessarily included convicted felons.[6] It is generally accepted that certain classes of persons are thought to lack the ability or the natural attributes to possess many of the rights which are recognized under our constitution. For example, none of the parties dispute the premise that children and insane or incompetent persons are likely not endowed with the natural right to bear arms. *See United States v. Emerson*, 270 F.3d 203, 227 n. 21 (5th Cir. 2001) (citing numerous authorities which document the fact that "violent criminals, children, and

---

equal, and have certain inherent and inalienable rights, among which may be reckoned: the right to bear arms in defense of themselves and of the State...." Ky. Const. §1(7) (emphasis added).

5. In the 1822 case of *Amy v. Smith*, 11 Ky. (1 Litt.) 326, our predecessor Court wrote:

> Before we can determine whether she was a citizen, or not, of either of those states, it is necessary to ascertain what it is that constitutes a citizen. In England, birth in the country was alone sufficient to make any one a subject. Even a villain or a slave, born within the king's allegiance is, according to the principles of the common law, a subject; but it never can be admitted that he is a citizen. One may, no doubt, be a citizen by birth, as well as a subject; but subject and citizen are evidently words of different import, and it indisputably requires something more to make a citizen, than it does to make a subject. It is, in fact, not the place of a man's birth, but the rights and privileges he may be entitled to enjoy, which make him a citizen. The term, citizen, is derived from the Latin word, *civis*, and in its primary sense signifies one who is vested with the freedom and privileges of a city. At an early period after the subversion of the Roman empire, when civilization had again begun to progress, the cities in every part of Europe, either by usurpation or concession from their sovereigns, obtained extraordinary privileges, in addition to those which were common to the other subjects of their respective countries; and one who was invested with these extraordinary privileges, whether he was an inhabitant of the city or not, or whether he was born in it or not, was deemed a citizen. In England, a citizen is not only entitled to all the local privileges of the city to which he belongs but he has also the right of electing and being elected to parliament, which is itself rather an extraordinary privilege, since it does not belong to every class of subjects.
>
> If we go back to Rome, whence the term, citizen, has its origin, we shall find, in the illustrious period of her republic, that citizens were the highest class of subjects to whom the *jus civitatis* belonged, and that the *jus civitatis* conferred upon those who were in possession of it, all rights and privileges, civil, political and religious.
>
> When the term came to be applied to the inhabitants of a state, it necessarily carried with it the same signification, with reference to the privileges of the state, which had been implied by it with reference to the privileges of a city, when it was applied to the inhabitants of the city; and it is in this sense, that the term, citizen, is believed to be generally, if not universally understood in the United States.

Id. at 334.

6. The meaning of the word "citizen" as it was construed during the latter half of the nineteenth century reveals a more probable purpose for expanding the language in Section 1(7) from "citizens" to "men." In order to be considered a citizen during that time, individuals were required to meet a slew of eligibility requirements, including but not limited to: being male, Caucasian, of appropriate age, and a property owner. Use of the word "men" operated to relax some of these onerous requirements. *See Amy v. Smith*, *supra*.

those of unsound mind" were never intended to be conferred with the right to bear arms). Historically, convicted felons were similarly accorded diminished status when it came to being endowed with certain natural rights.

Indeed, the view prevailing at the time our modern constitution was formulated was that felons were not endowed with the natural right to possess firearms. *See Emerson, supra*, at *Id.*; *State v. Hirsch*, 177 Or. App. 441, 34 P.3d 1209, 1212 (2001) ("Felons simply did not fall within the benefits of the common law right to possess arms. That law punished felons with automatic forfeiture of all goods, usually accompanied by death.") (quoting Don B. Kates, Jr., *Handgun Prohibition and the Original Meaning of the Second Amendment*, 82 Mich. L. Rev. 204, 266 (1983)); *see also* Glenn Harlan Reynolds, *A Critical Guide to the Second Amendment*, 62 Tenn. L. Rev. 461, 480 (1995) (reporting that felons did not historically possess a right to possess arms). Thus, without further evidence to suggest that convicted felons were somehow accorded more status by the 1890 constitutional convention than was historically attributed to them, we cannot say that the use of the word "men" within our modern constitution was intended to necessarily encompass those men who were convicted felons.

Appellant similarly argues that the framers' intent to include convicted felons within the scope of Section 1(7) of the Kentucky Constitution is illustrated by comparison to Section 145 of the constitution. Section 145 describes, in detailed form, the types of "persons" who are entitled to vote in the Commonwealth of Kentucky. It states that these "persons" must be (1) at least eighteen years of age; and (2) be a citizen of the United States of America. It excludes, with specificity, the following "persons": (1) convicted felons; (2) people who are incarcerated at the time of election; and (3) idiots and insane persons. Ky Const. §145.

Appellant contends that since Section 145 excludes convicted felons with specificity, but Section 1(7) does not, then it must be inferred that Section 1(7) meant to include convicted felons among the class of persons who were entitled to possess firearms. This argument is also flawed. First, it is notable that the right of suffrage is not contained within the sections entitled "Kentucky's Bill of Rights." Rather, it is located within its own section entitled "Suffrage and Elections."[7] Thus, Appellant's "consistency in form" argument is weak since the specimen provisions are found in two completely different sections of the constitution.

Moreover, the reason that voting rights exist within a completely different section of the constitution is because voting was not thought to be a natural, inalienable and inherent right of the people (like the right to bear arms) at the time that our modern constitution was drafted. *See* Ky Const. §1; Volume 1 *Proceedings and Debates of the Constitutional Convention of 1890*, 534 [hereinafter "Debates"] (Delegate Bronston, C.J.) (listing the absolute rights of man); *Yick Wo v. Hopkins*, 118 U.S. 356, 370, 6 S.Ct. 1064, 30 L.Ed. 220 (1886) (right to vote is "not regarded strictly as a natural right,

7. It is also interesting to note that prior to the establishment of one's eligibility and right to vote, the constitution establishes the following: (1) The Bill of Rights (the rights reserved to the people) and (2) the three branches of government—legislative, executive, and judicial.

but as a privilege merely conceded by society"). Rather, voting was a privilege which was conferred to the people through the prudence and consent of the legislature. It is self-evident that a grant of power requires some specificity so as to prevent such power from being swallowed within those powers which have otherwise been limited or reserved. *See Varney v. Justice*, 86 Ky. 596, 6 S.W. 457, 459 (1888). Such specificity is not particularly necessary or desired, however, when it comes to reserving (or perhaps, preserving) the people's natural and inherent rights. *See* Ky Const. §§1, 4, 26; 16 Am. Jur.2d *Constitutional Law* §40 (discussing constitutions as grants or limitations of power); *Cf. The Federalist* No. 45, at 236 (James Madison) ("The powers delegated by the proposed Constitution to the Federal Government, are few and defined. Those which are to remain in the State Governments are numerous and indefinite."). Accordingly, we also cannot infer a clear intent to endow convicted felons with the right to possess firearms by reference to language utilized in a different section of the constitution for a different purpose.

Finally, we find nothing to support Appellant's suggestion that the limiting language concerning "concealed weapons" utilized in Section 1(7) (in conjunction with Section 26) of the constitution somehow divests the legislature of power to reasonably regulate the area of firearms possession. The people's right to bear arms in defense of themselves and of the Commonwealth was first recognized and preserved by our constitution in 1792. Ky. Const. of 1792, art. 12, §23 ("The rights of the citizens to bear arms in defense of themselves and the State shall not be questioned."). The language as we know it today was ratified in 1891. A review of the debates which accompany the modern formulation of Section 1(7) indicate no intent on the part of the drafters to deem the right to bear arms in Kentucky absolute. See Debates, pg. 534 ("and hence arose civil liberty, which is but natural liberty, restrained by the necessities of the public good") (Bronston, C.J.); pg. 557 ("the right to bear arms in defense of themselves and the State, that means on all proper occasions") (Askew, J.F.); pg. 764 ("We are not freemen because we are licensed to do as we please, we are freemen because we are licensed to do what is right according to the law.") (Rodes, Robert); pg. 776 ("I know the object of this is to give every man the right to bear arms in defense of himself, his family, and country.") (Rodes, Robert); pg. 816–17 ("A man, of course, has a right to defend his life and liberty. His right to do it is inherent and inalienable, and he can enjoy that privilege without interfering with anybody else.") (Montgomery, J.F.).

In fact, the concept of an individual right to bear arms sprung from classical republican ideology which required the individual holding that right to maintain a certain degree of civic virtue. *Hirsch, supra*, at 1211 (quoting Don B. Kates, Jr., *The Second Amendment: A Dialogue*, 49 Law & Contemp Probs 143, 146 (Winter 1986) (footnote omitted)); *see also* Saul Cornell and Nathan DeDino, *The Second Amendment and the Future of Gun Regulation: Historical, Legal, Policy, and Cultural Perspectives*, 73 Fordham L. Rev. 487, 492 (2004) ("Historians have long recognized that the Second Amendment [of the U.S. Constitution] was strongly connected to the republican ideologies of the Founding Era, particularly the notion of civic virtue."). "One implication of this emphasis on the virtuous citizen is that the right to arms does not preclude laws disarming the unvirtuous citizens (i.e. criminals) or those, who, like children or the mentally unbalanced, are deemed incapable of virtue." *Hirsch*, *supra*, at 1212, *see also* Debates, pg. 764 ("We are not freemen because we are licensed to do as we please, we are freemen because we are licensed to do what is right according to the law.") (Rodes, Robert). This concept of civic virtue is similarly reflected in other provisions contained in Section 1 of our Constitution, such as the rights of all persons to life, liberty, and the pursuit of happiness. Yet, neither party would claim that these rights are absolute or somehow immune from reasonable limitations in the interest of public safety and welfare. *See* Robert M. Ireland, *The Kentucky State Constitution, A Reference Guide* 25 (1999) (commenting that Section 1 "is by no means an unlimited repository of rights against government regulation or judicial mandate" and citing to several decisions which uphold reasonable limitations on the rights contained within Section 1).

Moreover, the text in Section 1(7) does not support the notion that a person's right to bear arms is absolute since it plainly states that one may bear arms for the purpose of self-defense and defense of the State. Such language indicates that the right is conditioned on certain self-evident premises—that it be enjoyed lawfully and without undue interference with the rights of others. *See* Debates, pg. 816–17 ("A man, of course, has a right to defend his life and liberty. His right to do it is inherent and inalienable, and he can enjoy that privilege without interfering with anybody else.") (Montgomery, J.F.). Thus, we reject Appellant's contention that our constitution somehow confers on all persons an absolute right to bear arms or that the area of firearms possession is completely exempt from legislative regulation.[8]

In essence, Appellant's arguments boil down to mere presumptions or suggestions that could conceivably be inferred by the language present in our modern constitution.[9] However, the mere possibility that language could be interpreted in a particular way is insufficient to invalidate the plain language of a statute. Walters, *supra*, at 467

---

8. Numerous jurisdictions interpreting the right to arms provisions of their state constitutions have held likewise. * * *

9. Appellant's arguments merely highlight the inherent ambiguity contained within Section 1 and within constitutions in general. As an instrument, constitutions are intended to be written with a broad stroke, so as to encompass the general principles and philosophies of societies and the rights of individuals as they are contained therein. *See* 16 C.J.S. *Constitutional Law* §18 (2005). The rights enumerated in such instruments are not intended to be all-encompassing or absolute, but rather they are understood to be subject to certain wellrecognized exceptions, so as to preserve and balance the rights of the collective with the rights of the individual. *See, e.g., Robertson v. Baldwin*, 165 U.S. 275, 17 S.Ct. 326, 329, 41 L.Ed. 715 (1897) (interpreting the U.S. Bill of Rights) ("Thus, the freedom of speech and of the press (article 1) does not permit the publication of libels, blasphemous or indecent articles, or other publications injurious to public morals or private reputation; the right of the people to keep and bear arms (article 2) is not infringed by laws prohibiting the carrying of concealed weapons; the provision that no person shall be twice put in jeopardy (article 5) does not prevent a second trial, if upon the first trial the jury failed to agree, or if the verdict was set aside upon the defendant's motion; nor does the provision of the same article that no one shall be a witness against himself impair his obligation to testify, if a prosecution against him be barred by the lapse of time, a pardon, or by statutory enactment. Nor does the provision that an accused person shall be confronted with the witnesses against him prevent the admission of dying declarations, or the depositions of witnesses who have died since the former trial.") (citations omitted).

(ambiguities are to be resolved in favor of the legislative interpretation). In balance, we defer to the reasonable interpretation of our legislature, finding that the constitution permits some reasonable regulation of the people's right to bear arms, but only to the extent that such regulation is enacted to ensure the liberties of all persons by maintaining the proper and responsible exercise of the general right contained in Section 1(7). *See, e.g.*, KRS 237.060 (prohibition against armor-piercing ammunition); KRS 237.090 (providing for the disposition of forfeited firearms or ammunition); KRS 527.020 (making it unlawful to possess firearms or other weapons on school property); KRS 527.100 (prohibiting the possession of handguns by minors). Under no circumstances may regulation by the legislature be enacted for an arbitrary or irrational purpose, nor may it unduly infringe upon the general exercise of this right as it was envisioned and preserved pursuant to Section 1(7) of the Kentucky Constitution.

With this standard in mind, and considering that the vast majority of persons living in this Commonwealth are law-abiding and responsible individuals, we ultimately determine that the regulation contained within KRS 527.040 is not arbitrary or irrational and does not unduly infringe upon the right to bear arms which was reserved to the people through Section 1(7) of our constitution. As previously stated by this Court, KRS 527.040 is "reasonable legislation in the interest of public safety." *Eary*, *supra*, at 200. Since nothing in the constitution, either express or implied, undermines or prohibits such legislation, we find KRS 527.040 to be constitutional.

The decision of the Court of Appeals is affirmed.

Lambert, C.J., Cooper, Graves and Wintersheimer, JJ., concur.

Roach, J. concurs in a separate opinion in which Johnstone, J., joins.

Scott, J., concurs in part and dissents in part by a separate opinion.

Justice Roach, concurring.

I concur in the result reached by the majority opinion. However, I write separately to address the constitutionality of KRS 527.040. Ultimately, I think a proper historical understanding of the rights described in Section 1 of the Kentucky Constitution, particularly as they related to criminals, provides the sole ground necessary for the statute to withstand a constitutional challenge.

At first blush, Appellant's semantic argument seems compelling based on the facts that the rights contained in Section 1 of the Kentucky Constitution are for "all men," and, more specifically, that the subsection on the right to bear arms reserves to the General Assembly only the power to regulate the carrying of concealed weapons. But Appellant's argument fails when these rights are understood in the context of the common law when the Constitution was adopted in 1891.

At the Constitutional Convention of 1890, Robert Rodes served as the Chairman of the Committee on Preamble and Bill of Rights. Rodes described the seven subsections of Section 1 of the Constitution of Kentucky as a "general statement of our rights." 2 *Official Report of the Proceedings and Debates in the Convention Assembled at Frankfort, on the Eighth Day of September, 1890, to Adopt, Amend or Change the Constitution of the State of Kentucky*, at 435 (1890). He then described these rights, which he also claimed belong to "free men," as "certain inalienable and indefeasible rights." *Id.* at 436. In particular, Rodes traced these rights to the Magna Charta and the English Bill of Rights. *Id.* at 444–46; *see also* Ken Gormley & Rhonda G. Hartman, *The Kentucky Bill of Rights: A Bicentennial Celebration*, 80 Ky. L.J. 1, 5 (1990–91) ("Specifically, an examination of the Kentucky Bill of Rights of 1792 shows that it may be traced ultimately to the Magna Charta and the English Bill of Rights."). Thus, Section 1 concerns a group of rights that were commonly called the rights or liberties of Englishmen, *see* 1 William Blackstone, *Commentaries on the Laws of England* *144 (describing "the rights, or, as they are frequently termed, the liberties of Englishmen...."), which included the specific right to bear arms. *See id.* at *143–44 ("The fifth and last auxiliary right of the subject... is that of having arms for their defence....").

As pointed out by the majority opinion, felons did not have the right to possess firearms at common law. *See also* Robert Dowlut, *The Right to Arms: Does the Constitution or the Predilection of Judges Reign?*, 36 Okla. L. Rev. 65, 96 (1983) ("Colonial and English societies of the eighteenth century, as well as their modern counterparts, have excluded infants, idiots, lunatics, and felons [from possessing firearms]."). In fact, felons were stripped of all rights of station under the common law. Vernon M. Winters, Note, *Criminal RICO Forfeitures and the Eight Amendment: 'Rough' Justice Is Not Enough*, 14 Hastings Const. L.Q. 451, 457 (1987) ("A felon who had broken the social contract no longer had any right to social advantages, including transfer of property, and people believed that punishing the felon as well as his ancestors and heirs would serve as a more effective deterrent than would personal punishment alone" (footnote omitted)). In essence, a felon "could not own any property himself, nor could any heir born before or after the felony claim through him." 3 William S. Holdsworth, *A History of English Law* 69 (3d ed. 1927) (footnote omitted). This harsh treatment of felons was due to the legal effect of the felon's "blood [being] corrupted or attainted." *Id.* Blackstone explained the reason behind the treatment as follows:

> The true reason and only substantial ground of any forfeiture for crimes consist in this; that all property is derived from society, being one of those civil rights which are conferred upon individuals, in exchange for that degree of natural freedom, which every man must sacrifice when he enters into social communities. If, therefore, a member of any national community violates the fundamental contract of his association, by transgressing the municipal law, he forfeits his right to such privileges he claims by that contract; and the state may very justly resume that portion of property, or any part of it, which the law assigned him.

1 William Blackstone, *Commentaries on the Laws of England* *299–300.

The severe concept of attainder, or corruption of blood, was not carried over into the law of the United States, *see* U.S. Const. art. III, §3 ("[N]o Attainder of Treason shall work Corruption of Blood, or Forfeiture except during the Life of the Person Attainted."), or that of the individual states, including Kentucky. *See* Ky. Const. §20

("No person shall be attainted of treason or felony by the General Assembly, and no attainder shall work corruption of blood, nor, except during the life of the offender, forfeiture of estate to the Commonwealth."). Despite the exclusion of this harsh doctrine, the law in the United States still allowed for significant limitations on the rights of felons. Thus, while the law could allow for forfeiture of the felons' property, it simply could not affect their heirs.

The American colonists and early American citizens also understood that this deprivation of rights extended to the right to bear arms. Consider the following example: Part of the fight over ratification of the United States Constitution was the anti-Federalists' concern that it did not contain a bill of rights. Several days after the Pennsylvania Convention voted 46 to 23 to ratify the Constitution, twenty-one of the Convention's minority members issued a dissenting address calling for a Bill of Rights. Included in their proposed list of rights was a right to bear arms that stated in part: "[N]o law shall be passed for disarming the people or any of them, *unless for crimes committed,* or real danger of public injury from individuals...." The Address and Reasons of Dissent of the Minority of the Convention of Pennsylvania to their Constituents, 1787 (emphasis added), *excerpts reprinted in* Bernard Schwartz, *The Bill of Rights: A Documentary History* 665 (1971). There is little doubt that the citizens of the early United States were sensitive to the possible deprivation of their rights and liberties at the hands of the newly-formed federal government. It is equally clear, however, that their concern did not extend to the rights and liberties of criminals.

Further, this approach makes sense, especially when one considers the simple fact that felons are no longer "free men" under the criminal law. The very nature of the criminal law requires limitations on the rights of those convicted, either through limitations on liberty (imprisonment) or property (fines), as punishment. Limitations on the right to bear arms are part and parcel of that deprivation of rights. Since felons at common law were stripped of their privileges and rights, they are not entitled to the right to bear arms under Section 1(7) of the Constitution of Kentucky. Therefore, I concur in the majority opinion's conclusion that KRS 527.040 is constitutional.

Johnstone, J., joins this concurring opinion.

Justice Scott, concurring in part and dissenting in part.

I concur in the majority's opinion regarding the Fourth Amendment issue, but I dissent on the constitutional rights of "self-defense" and to "bear arms."

It is simply wrong to arrest, charge and convict Kentuckians of "felony crimes" for keeping a weapon in their own home—without any evidence the weapon was intended to be used for unlawful purposes. Such a practice violates all of our rights to "bear arms in defense of [ourselves and others]" and our rights of self-defense. See Ky. Const. § 1(1, 7). Thus, I write separately to remind Kentuckians of what our forefathers left us in the Bill of Rights under our Kentucky Constitution.

While writing this dissent, I noticed in the Appalachian News-Express of December 21, 2005, that Peggy Ligon, 27, pled guilty in the McCracken Circuit Court to *the felony of reckless homicide* in connection with the death of a five year-old boy, who was hit while crossing a street under her care.

Moments before he was hit, she told the child and four other children that it was okay to cross the street. She and the children had just started to cross when the child left her side and was struck by a pickup truck driven by a young man from Paducah. The young man was not charged. However, the child's mother said after the hearing that she had asked that the charge against Ligon be dropped. "We never blamed her for the accident," she said. However, the charge was not dropped and Peggy Ligon is now a "convicted felon." *Woman Pleads Guilty to Reckless Homicide in Child's Death*, Appalachian News-Express, December 21, 2005, at 11A.

Peggy Ligon, now a "convicted felon," has no further right under the laws of Kentucky to keep a firearm in her home to defend herself, or her children, irrespective of how dangerous a neighborhood she might live in. Nor, as the majority should concede, does she have a right to live in a house with *any other person who possesses a firearm*, since that would constitute her "constructive possession" of the weapon, rendering her liable again for unlawful possession of a weapon by a "convicted felon."

In this case, Mr. Posey was arrested in his own home.[1] When asked, after his arrest, if he had any weapons, he told the officers there was a pistol in the back room. From his record, it appears Mr. Posey is an addict. Thus, he was sentenced to four years in the penitentiary, probated, however, on the condition that he serve six-months in the Jefferson County Jail with work release and otherwise comply with other conditions established by the court to keep him clean from drugs and law abiding. Background information indicated he had served his country well in the military, receiving an honorable discharge. He was a high school graduate and had had steady employment throughout the years. Yet, because he had a weapon in his house—though in another room—he was charged with another felony crime.

Several premises underlie all arguments supporting disarmament of various segments of American society. One is that criminals *will abide* by our gun laws. The second and most subtle is that the police forces of society *can adequately protect us at all times anyway*—whether in our homes, workplaces, or places of enjoyment.

While these thoughts are comforting, each daily read of one's newspaper proves otherwise—not to mention the multitude of violent crimes we deal with in our courts each year, most of which are not reported in the papers. All of this, while many states have enacted statutes designed to keep guns out of the hands of violent criminals. Yet, the continuing violent crime just proves the point, that *once you outlaw guns, only outlaws will have them.*

My experience in life leads me to believe that the only successful way to keep "hardened criminals" away from weapons and "hurting people"—is to put them in prison

1. The amount of marijuana in his and his friend's possession was less than 1/2 ounce.

where they can't hurt anybody else. *We don't need to take away someone else's right to defend themselves, or their family, to do that.*

I believe we must continue to punish, *or even increase punishment*, for those who misuse weapons in an unlawful manner. *See* KRS 218A.992 (enhancement of offense if in actual[2] possession of a firearm during drug trafficking), KRS 532.045(2)(d) (use of a deadly weapon against a minor during an offense), KRS 533.060(1) (enhanced sentencing for use of a firearm during an offense), KRS 533.065 (wearing body armor and carrying deadly weapons during offense), and KRS 635.020(4) (use of firearm by child during a felony). However, I do not believe it is constitutionally valid to disarm, or imprison, those who would keep weapons for a purpose they hope will never occur—the defense of themselves and their families.

As of the 2000 census, Kentucky had a population of 4,041,769 people in an area of 40,395 square miles. Yet today, there are only 943 Kentucky State troopers available for patrol and response, and even they are divided into several work shifts per day. * * * Other areas, such as cities and counties, have supplemental police forces, but they too are limited in numbers and response time. And I might add—finance.

The point is that violence is most often quick, unpredictable and unexpected. Thus, it is up to each of us to defend ourselves and our families, if we can, until help (the police) can arrive. Because of *this need*, our forefathers made sure in 1891 that the "right of self-defense" and the "right to bear arms" were engraved deeply in our Constitution, Section 1(1–7), as well as our statutes. *See* KRS 503.070.

KRS 527.040, however, seeks to disarm all "convicted felons" by rendering their possession of firearms a further felony crime—as in this case. *The question then becomes (1) are "convicted felons" truly a class we need to deprive of firearms? and (2) if so, is it constitutional to do so under our State Constitutional Bill of Rights? See Ky. Const., §1(1 & 7), 26.*

* * *

Thus, as there is no "federal question" involved in this case, we must consider whether Kentucky's statute, KRS 527.040, prohibiting possession of a weapon by a "convicted felon," is valid under the Constitution of Kentucky, which has a Bill of Rights specifically guaranteeing the "right to bear arms," Ky. Const. §1(7), as well as the "right of self-defense." Ky. Const. §1(1). KRS 527.040 was first enacted in 1974. *It is the first, and only, statute in the history of Kentucky making possession of a firearm, other than a concealed weapon, a crime.* It provides, in part:

> (1) A person is guilty of possession of a firearm by a convicted felon when he possess, … a firearm when he has been convicted of a felony, … and has not: (a) been granted a full pardon.…

2. *Commonwealth v. Montaque*, 23 S.W.3d 629, 632 (Ky. 2000) ("The statute requires a nexus between the crime committed and the possession of a firearm.").

(2) Possession of a firearm by a convicted felon is a Class D felony unless the firearm possessed is a handgun in which case it is a Class C felony.

A pistol is a handgun. KRS 527.010(5).

The "police power," upon which the validity of KRS 527.040 rests, arises under Section 29 of the Kentucky Constitution. Section 29 provides: "The legislative powers shall be vested in a House of Representatives and a Senate, which, together, shall be styled the 'General Assembly of the Commonwealth of Kentucky.'" "The words 'the legislative power,' as here employed, are a comprehensive phrase, meaning all powers that appertain to, or are usually exercised by, a legislative body." *Booth's Ex'r v. Commonwealth*, 130 Ky. 88, 113 S.W. 61, 62 (Ky. 1908). "We hold that [KRS 527.040] is ... a valid exercise of the police power of the Commonwealth of Kentucky." *Eary v. Commonwealth*, 659 S.W.2d 198, 200 (Ky. 1983). Thus, the police power "[i]s a legislative power, and when the people, by their Constitution, create a department of government upon which they confer the power to make laws, the power ... is conferred as part of the *more general power*." *Booth's Ex'r*, 113 S.W. at 62, 63 (emphasis added).

To fully consider the conflict between KRS 527.040 and our "Bill of Rights," * * * we must fully understand the meaning and impact of our Bill of Rights, Section 1(1, 7) and 26.

To do this, we must review the "history of the times," the "First Amendment and its contextual relationship within the Kentucky Constitution" and the "historic comments of our forefathers" (who drafted our Constitution) from the recorded Constitutional Debates of 1849 and 1890, so that we might understand what they meant and intended by selection of the language they used. And we must look at our "older decisions" (our precedents), so we can better understand what the court felt about these rights at a time much closer to the time they were created.

* * *

The Bill of Rights and the Constitutions of Kentucky

The Bill of Rights to the Kentucky Constitution is contained in Sections 1 through 26. * * * Now let's look at its history. Although the first (and foremost) right to today, the "right of self-defense," Section 1(1), did not appear in the first Constitution of Kentucky in 1792, the "right to bear arms," Section 1(7), did, (as Section 23 of Article XII), which at the time read, "[t]he rights of the citizens to bear arms in defense of themselves and the State shall not be questioned." The "high powers clause" also appeared in the first Constitution (as Section 28 of Article XII thereof), standing guard against invasion of the liberties protected by the Bill of Rights. In fact, the language we see in the "high powers clause" today is the same language that appeared in 1792, 1799 and 1850.

The "right to bear arms" also appeared in the Second Constitution of Kentucky in 1799. It was the same language and the same section numbers, albeit under Article X. Section 1(1), the "right of self defense," as we know it today, *was still absent*.

It is noteworthy that several years after the adoption of the second Kentucky Constitution in 1799, the Kentucky legislature passed an act "to prevent persons in this

Commonwealth from wearing concealed arms." *Bliss v. Commonwealth*, 2 Litt. 90, 12 Ky. 90 (Ky. 1822). The Act provided "that any person in this commonwealth, who shall hereafter wear a pocket pistol, dirk, large knife, or sword in a cane, concealed as a weapon, unless when traveling on a journey, shall be fined in any sum not less than one hundred dollars." *Id.* The indictment in *Bliss* charged him with having worn a sword in a cane, concealed as a weapon.

Commenting in 1822 on the right of the citizens to bear arms in defense of themselves, our predecessor court *held the act unconstitutional* in violation of Section 1(7), the constitutional "right to bear arms," as well as the "high powers clause," * * *

Twenty-eight years later in 1850, Kentucky adopted its third Constitution. Section 1(1), the "right of self-defense," *was still absent*, but the "right to bear arms" and the "high powers clause" remained in Article XIII. Yet, several notable changes occurred. Dueling was outlawed. Ky. Const. art. VIII, §20 (1850). Also, the right to bear arms, then Section 25 of Article XIII, was amended to authorize laws prohibiting persons from carrying concealed arms, thereby abrogating the ruling in *Bliss*.

Thus, language was added and the "right to bear arms" in the 1850 Constitution thereafter read "[t]hat the rights of the citizens to bear arms in defense of themselves and their State shall not be questioned; but the General Assembly may pass laws to prevent persons from carrying concealed arms." Ky. Const. art. XIII, §25 (1850).

Our fourth and current Constitution was adopted and ratified on August 3, 1891. *For the first time, we see the Bill of Rights, Sections 1 through 26 moved to the forefront of the Constitution.* We see a new preamble. And we see (for the first time) grouped together, the seven "inherent and inalienable" rights of the new First Section of our Bill of Rights, * * *

For the first time we have an explicit "right of self-defense" in the First subsection of Section 1, "the right of enjoying and defending their lives and liberties." The "high powers clause," Section 26, remained unchanged, *declaring that the Bill of Rights "shall forever remain inviolate: and all laws contrary thereto or contrary to this Constitution, shall be void."*

Though we have had many constitutional amendments since then there have been no revisions or amendments to *these sections.*

* * *

Section One and Its Contextual Relationship in the Kentucky Constitution

We are assured by the logic of the majority opinion that the word "citizen" as used in the Kentucky Constitutions of 1792, 1799, and 1850, conceptually excluded "felons" as "citizens"—*even though the word used in Section 1 by the founders of our 1891 Constitution is "men."* We are cited to the case of *Amy v. Smith*, 1 Litt. 326, 11 Ky. 326 (Ky. 1822) for the language:

> Before we can determine whether she was a citizen, or not, of either of those states, it is necessary to ascertain what it is that constitutes a citizen. In England, birth in the country was alone sufficient to make any one a subject. Even

> a villain or a slave, born within the king's allegiance is, according to the principles of common law, a subject; but it can never be admitted that he is a citizen.

First, let me say, *Amy* dealt only with the question of whether a slave in 1822 could sue for her freedom, claiming the "privileges and immunities" of citizens under the Constitution of the United States. Let me also say, that since the comment regarding "villain" was made within the context of "a villain or a slave, *born within the king's allegiance*," the proper spelling of the word "villain" was, "villein." "A villein was a person attached to a manor, who was substantially in the condition of a slave, who performed the base and servile work upon the manor for the lord and was, in most respects, a subject of property belonging to him." *Black's Law Dictionary*, Rev. 4th Ed. at 1741. "A freeman was an allodial proprietor; the opposite of a vassal or feudal tenant; a free tenant or freeholder as distinguished from a *villein*." *Case of Fry*, 71 Pa. 302, 21 P.F. Smith 302, 306, 1872 WL 11181 (Pa. 1872) (emphasis added).

Secondly, it is suggested that to be a "citizen" of the times, individuals were required to meet a slew of eligibility requirements, including that of being a property owner. Thus, the word "men," rather than "citizen," operated to relax some of these onerous requirements. In response to this, let me point out that Kentucky *never required the ownership of property as a basis for the right to vote*. Kentucky was a Jacksonian western frontier State at the time of its inception, and that attitude during the frontier times never changed.

In clarifying the use of the word "men" in Section 1 of the Constitution, as well as clarifying the intent of the framers of our Constitution in regards to the "right to bear arms," and in illuminating the different opinions between Kentucky in *Bliss* and Tennessee in *Amy*, one needs to look to the debates in the Constitutional Convention between Mr. J.L. Phelps, a delegate from Louisville, and Mr. Robert Rodes, the chairmen of the standing committee for the Constitutional Preamble and Bill of Rights, which committee formulated the language used: * * * Thus, all arguments to the contrary—our founders constructed the Bill of Rights using the word "men" in a generic sense, to mean, for want of a better word, humanity. The reason it was used was to exclude corporations.

Moreover, the rights set out in Section 1 were defined as "inherent and inalienable" rights. "Inherent" is an "authority possessed without it being derived from another." *Black's Law Dictionary*, 921 (4th ed. 1968). "Inalienable" means "not subject to alienation ... e.g. liberty." *Id.* at 903.

Not only did the Constitutions of Kentucky not limit the word "citizen" as suggested by those who would have it exclude "convicted felons"—of the twenty-five rights granted under the Bill of Rights, *eleven (Section 7, 9, 10, 11, 12, 13, 16, 17, 18, 20, 25) deal specifically with crime and criminals*. Given this context, it is simply unacceptable to assert that the founders of our Constitution—people who chose words with a precision unknown today—ever intended for the "right to bear arms," or the "right of self-defense," to be limited only to those who had never committed a crime, without saying it!

* * *

I hope, by now, one understands that in Kentucky's earlier Constitutions the term "citizen" did not exclude "convicted felons" *by any implicit definition adopted from a country from which we seceded in war*. Nor did the word "men," in the first section of the Bill of Rights, limit the enjoyment of those Rights to males, as some might suggest. * * *

Precedents

Looking to prior decisions of our predecessor court to shed light on the subject, the first case I found on the "right to bear arms" is the decision of *Bliss v. Commonwealth*, 2 Litt. 90, 12 Ky. 90, 1822 WL 1085 (Ky. 1822). *One would assume that the issue presented was new to the Commonwealth* from the fact that this lengthy decision *contains no citations to any previous authority*. *Bliss* dealt with the constitutionality of the *then new* Kentucky statute that provided "that any person ... who shall hereafter wear a pocket pistol, dirk, large knife, or sword in a cane, concealed as a weapon, ... shall be fined in any sum not less than one hundred dollars." *Id.* In the words of the indictment presented, Bliss was charged with having carried a sword in a cane, concealed as a weapon. He was found guilty of the charge and fined one hundred dollars.

Our predecessor, the then Court of Appeals, reversed the conviction on grounds that the statute was unconstitutional as an infringement of Bliss's "right to bear arms" under the then twenty-third section of the tenth article of the 1799 Kentucky Constitution, which again, provided "the rights of the citizens to bear arms in defense of themselves and the state, shall not be questioned." In rendering the decision, the court noted:

> [I]t is the right to bear arms in defense of the citizens ... that is secured by the Constitution, and whatever restrains the full and complete exercise of that right, though not an entire destruction of it, is forbidden by the explicit language of the Constitution. Not merely all legislative acts, which purport to take it away; but all which diminish or impair it as it existed when the Constitution was formed, are void.

Id. at 91.

The next case I found was *Ogles v. Commonwealth*, 11 Ky. L. Rptr. 289, 11 S.W. 816 (Ky. 1889), decided the year before the 1890 Constitutional Convention. * * * *Ogles* recognized that a constitutional right may not be exercised to threaten, impede, or injure others in an unlawful manner; when it interferes with the lawful rights of others, it has no constitutional protection.

The next case I found is *Holland v. Commonwealth*, 294 S.W.2d 83, 85 (Ky. 1956). In *Holland*, the court stated:

> The foregoing [Section 1(7) of the Kentucky Constitution] is an exemplification of the broadest expression of the right to bear arms. Some states give the legislature the right to regulate the carrying of firearms; at least one state prohibits even the possession of firearms.
>
> In our state the legislature is empowered only to deny to citizens the right to carry concealed weapons. *The constitutional provision is an affirmation of the faith that all men have the inherent right to arm themselves for the defense of*

> *themselves and of the state. The only limitation concerns the mode of carrying such instruments.*

Id. at 85 (emphasis added).

Again, in 1971, the Criminal Law Revision Advisory Committee acknowledged the *Holland* opinion as binding authority. This committee *drafted* the law forbidding concealed weapons in the chapter of the penal code dealing with "firearms offenses." The commentary they wrote then reflected the belief of the time.

> Section 1(7) of the Kentucky Constitution gives all persons "[t]he right to bear arms in defense of themselves and the state, subject to the power of the General Assembly to enact laws to prevent persons from carrying concealed weapons." *No other legislative limitation to the Constitutional right to carry weapons is valid.*

Kentucky Penal Code, Final Draft, §2805, Commentary, 284 (1971) (citing *Holland v. Commonwealth*, 294 S.W.2d 83 (Ky. 1956) (emphasis added)).

However, in 1983, this court (in a new age) considered the "right to bear arms" under Section 1(7) of the Kentucky Constitution and, *as prophesized by the delegates at the 1890 Constitutional Convention*, reversed its position as previously set out in *Holland* and *Bliss* on the breadth of the "right to bear arms," stating,

> "[i]t is our opinion that a statute limiting the possession of firearms by persons *who, by their past commission of serious felonies*, have demonstrated a dangerous disregard for the law and thereby present a threat of further criminal activity is reasonable legislation in the interest of public welfare and safety and that such regulation is constitutionally permissible as a reasonable and legitimate exercise of the police power."

Eary v. Commonwealth, 659 S.W.2d 198, 200 (Ky. 1983).

Eary, upon which the majority now relies, does not, however, support their own position. A Class D felony based only on possession of marijuana is not normally regarded as a "*serious felony*." "*Eary* had been previously convicted of four felonies, viz, first-degree burglary ... storehouse breaking and possession of burglary tools." *Id.* at 199. *See also, Boulder v. Commonwealth*, 610 S.W.2d 615, 617 (Ky. 1980) (overruled on other grounds) (preceding conviction was First-Degree Assault).

Until the *Eary* opinion in 1983, *no one had ever suggested* that the "right to bear arms" under the Kentucky Constitution could be subjected to the "general" police power. Indeed, *being a general power, rather than a specific power*, such interference, as was approved in *Eary*, is in direct violation of Section 26 of the Kentucky Constitution: "We Declare that everything in this Bill of Rights *is excepted out of the general powers of government*, and shall forever remain inviolate; and all laws contrary thereto, or contrary to this Constitution shall be void." (Emphasis added.)

Constitutional conflicts between the Bill of Rights and specific powers are not reconciled by Section 26, but conflicts between the Bill of Rights and general powers are—with the Bill of Rights being held inviolate in such instances. * * * A general power may not intrude within any protected sphere of the Bill of Rights—"We Declare that every thing in this Bill of Rights is excepted out of the *general powers* of government..." Ky. Const. §26.

But as was shown by the excellent briefs in this case, the *Eary* court was not advised of the wealth of authority concerning the "right to bear arms," which has now been presented to us. But regardless of the reason for the decision in *Eary*, it completely misstates the Constitutional Law in Kentucky, as does the majority opinion in this case, which upholds *Eary*.

* * *

Conventional wisdom supports the idea of a police power that gives the legislature authority to enact all laws necessary for the good of society. If put to a plebiscite, through a constitutional amendment, doubtless some version supporting a statute similar to KRS 527.040 would be adopted by a majority. *I suggest, however, that there would be much more discussion about whether such a statute should apply to all "convicted felons," or just to those who have committed serious crimes that ordinarily portend a future pattern of violence involving weapons as was noted in Eary.* ("It is our opinion that the state limiting the possession of firearms by a person who, by their past commission of serious felonies.") *Eary*, 659 S.W.2d at 200.

Nobody wants this type of stereotypical convicted felon to have access to firearms, and his prior illegal use of such firearms would support such an objective, even under a "strict scrutiny" review. * * * *Ogles* would support such a view. "To this we cannot assent. It is equivalent to saying that a man may so exercise his Constitutional rights as to violate the law...." *Ogles*, 11 S.W. at 818.

* * *

However, we are not at this time construing a statute which is so limited. The state before us deprives all "convicted felons" in Kentucky of the right to bear arms, including people like Peggy Ligon.

The police power theory, relied on in *Eary* (unleashed now from its limitations to "serious" felonies), undermines constitutional precepts. If the court agrees that the police power allows regulation of possession, despite the plain language of our Kentucky Constitution, then no right is safe. In fact, when inquired of during oral arguments in this case, the Commonwealth asserted that, if the legislature so desired, it could use its "general police power" to limit possession of weapons only to those over the age of 25 years. *Power once acquired, knows no boundaries, except those stringently maintained by others.* This is our job, but we remain silent.

* * *

The language of our forefathers therein, being plain, understandable and forthright, Section 1(1, 7) and Section 26 say what they mean and mean what they say. Therefore, I must dissent from a majority opinion, which says otherwise.

Notes and Questions

1. The majority opinion in *Posey* states that, at the time the current Kentucky Constitution was adopted, "felons were not endowed with the natural right to possess firearms," that "all men" in Section 1 does not refer to felons as far as the right to bear arms is concerned, and that the right to bear arms in Kentucky is not "absolute." Further, the Court finds it "self-evident" that the right to bear arms cannot be absolute because it must be exercised "lawfully and without undue interference with the rights of others." Is the majority's analysis consistent with *Bliss* and *Holland*? Is it consistent with Section 1, which counts the right to bear arms among the "inherent and inalienable rights" of "[a]ll men"?
2. Justice Roach, joined by Justice Johnstone, did not join the majority opinion but concurred in result only. The concurrence notes that felons did not have a right to possess firearms at common law, and that they were "stripped of all rights of station under the common law" and were "no longer 'free men' under the criminal law." Justice Roach concludes that, "[s]ince felons at common law were stripped of their privileges and rights, they are not entitled to the right to bear arms." While undertaking this historical analysis of the right to bear arms at common law, the concurrence did not agree with the textual analysis by the majority, in fact agreeing with the dissent that "Appellant's semantic argument" concerning the use of "all men" in Section 1 "seems compelling."
3. In his dissent, Justice Scott cites both *Bliss* and *Holland* as authority. Is his use of those precedents persuasive?

E. Religious Liberty

"All men are, by nature, free and equal, and have certain inherent and inalienable rights, among which may be reckoned: ... Second: The right of worshipping Almighty God according to the dictates of their consciences...." (Ky. Const. §1.)

"No preference shall ever be given by law to any religious sect, society or denomination; nor to any particular creed, mode of worship or system of ecclesiastical polity; nor shall any person be compelled to attend any place of worship, to contribute to the erection or maintenance of any such place, or to the salary or support of any minister of religion; nor shall any man be compelled to send his child to any school to which he may be conscientiously opposed; and the civil rights, privileges or capacities of no person shall be taken away, or in anywise diminished or enlarged, on account of his belief or disbelief of any religious tenet, dogma or teaching. No human authority shall, in any case whatever, control or interfere with the rights of conscience." (Ky. Const. §5.)

Figure 8-3. Official portrait of Justice Will T. Scott, Kentucky State Capitol. Portrait by John Michael Carter, reproduced with permission of the artist and the Supreme Court of Kentucky.

"No portion of any fund or tax now existing, or that may hereafter be raised or levied for educational purposes, shall be appropriated to, or used by, or in aid of, any church, sectarian or denominational school." (Ky. Const. §189.)

The U.S. Constitution protects religious liberty in two places. First, Article VI of the U.S. Constitution declares that "no religious test shall ever be required as a qualification to any office or public trust under the United States." Second, the First Amendment provides that "Congress shall make no law respecting an establishment of religion, or prohibiting the free exercise thereof." Under the incorporation doctrine, the Establishment Clause and Free Exercise Clause have been applied to the States under the Fourteenth Amendment.

Unlike the U.S. Constitution, which makes just these brief references to religion, the Kentucky Constitution devotes much more space to the subject of religious liberty and covers the subject in much more detail.

Section 1(2) protects what might be called the "freedom of worship." Note that it refers specifically to "worshipping Almighty God," whereas the Free Exercise Clause refers to "the free exercise" of religion.

Section 5 includes both "free exercise" and "anti-establishment" protections. Most notably, the protection for the "rights of conscience" encompass both the right of a person to worship as they see fit (or not) and the right to live out the tenets of their faith, outside the context of worship services. Section 5, in part, also bears a resemblance to the Virginia Statute for Religious Freedom (1786), which was drafted by Thomas Jefferson and states:

> [N]o man shall be compelled to frequent or support any religious worship, place, or ministry whatsoever, nor shall be enforced, restrained, molested, or burthened in his body or goods, nor shall otherwise suffer, on account of his religious opinions or belief; but that all men shall be free to profess, and by argument to maintain, their opinions in matters of religion, and that the same shall in no wise diminish, enlarge, or affect their civil capacities.

The right of a person not to be "compelled to send his child to any school to which he may be conscientiously opposed" did not appear in prior Kentucky Constitutions and predates compulsory school attendance laws in the Commonwealth. It was added by the 1890 convention to what is now Section 5, to protect the right of parents to send their children to religious or parochial schools in the event the General Assembly enacted a compulsory education law. *See Ky. State Bd. for Elementary & Secondary Educ. v. Rudasill*, 589 S.W.2d 877, 881 (Ky. 1979). That provision also has been held to preclude legislation requiring private school teachers to be certified, and textbooks used in private schools to be approved, by the state. *Id.* at 883–84.

In a case predating the current Constitution, provisions of the 1850 Constitution similar to Sections 1(2) and 5 were held to prevent the government from precluding a person from testifying at a criminal trial on the grounds that he was an atheist: "We think that this provision of the constitution not only permits persons to testify without regard to religious belief or disbelief, but that it was intended to prevent any inquiry into that belief for the purpose of affecting credibility. It places the Atheist, in this regard, on the same footing as any other witness, and leaves the question as to credibility to be inquired into in the same way." *Bush v. Commonwealth*, 80 Ky. 244, 251 (1882).

The Court affirmed that the rationale of *Bush* still applied under Section 1(2) and Section 5 of the current Constitution in *Louisville & Nashville R.R. Co. v. Mayes*, 80 S.W. 1096, 1097 (Ky. 1904).

Section 189 prohibits any use of public funds earmarked for education to be used for the benefit of "any church, sectarian or denominational school." This provision has been interpreted to create a greater separation of church and state than exists under the Establishment Clause. For example, in *Fannin v. Williams*, 655 S.W.2d 480, 483–84 (Ky. 1983), the Court held unconstitutional under Section 189 a statute that provided for the purchase of textbooks for children in nonpublic schools, even though a similar statute had been upheld by the U.S. Supreme Court under the Establishment Clause in *Board of Education of Central School District No. 1 v. Allen*, 392 U.S. 236 (1968). The Court also found a county fiscal court violated Sections 5 and 189 when it appropriated county funds directly to private schools, which had been designated as transportation subsidies. *Fiscal Ct. of Jefferson Cnty. v. Brady*, 885 S.W.2d 681, 686–87 (Ky. 1994). It found that "[t]hese Kentucky constitutional provisions appear to restrict direct aid from state or local government to sectarian schools much more specifically and significantly than the" First Amendment's Establishment Clause. *Id.* at 686.

Free Exercise of Religion and Rights of Conscience

Lawson v. Commonwealth

Court of Appeals of Kentucky (1942)

291 Ky. 437, 164 S.W.2d 972

Opinion of the Court by Judge Tilford.

The appellants were jointly indicted convicted, and fined for violating Chapter 60 of the Acts of the 1940 General Assembly, Kentucky Statute, §1267a-1 which is as follows:

> "No person shall display, handle, or use any kind of snake or reptile in connection with any religious service or gathering.
>
> "(a) Any person violating the provisions of this Act shall be guilty of a misdemeanor and punished by a fine of not less than $50.00 nor more than $100.00."

The constitutionality of the Act is challenged as well as the interpretation placed upon it by the Trial Court. That interpretation is reflected in the Court's refusal to permit proof of the absence of coercion or disturbance during the religious meetings at which snakes were displayed and handled by appellants, and its refusal to permit appellants to read to the jury the scriptural passages upon which they base their beliefs and practices. Since neither breach of the peace nor the intent of the violator is an element of the offense denounced, it is obvious that the interpretation placed upon the Statute by the Court was correct, and that the only actual question necessary to be considered on this motion for an appeal is the Statute's constitutionality.

Many snakes are poisonous, and only the zoologist, herpetologist, or experienced woodsman is able to distinguish those which are not. Hence the suggestion that the enactment of the Statute was not a legitimate exercise of the State's police power because certain species of snakes are harmless and their handling and exhibition unattended by danger, is ineffectual. Legislation enacted by a state in the exercise of its police power may not be invalidated because included among the prohibited articles or acts are some, which, perchance, may be harmless, where only experts can distinguish between them and the public, for whose protection the legislation is enacted, is unable to do so. Notoriously, religious services or gatherings are not conducted by herpetologists, and rather than entrust the selection of the types of snakes to be displayed and handled at such meetings to the inexpert and thus imperil the lives of the participants, the Legislature had the right, unless forbidden by the State or Federal Constitution from so doing, to prohibit the practice altogether. Moreover, there is not pretense that the snakes handled or exhibited by the appellants were nonpoisonous, since the very purpose sought to be accomplished by their handling was to demonstrate appellants' immunity, through faith, to the fatal consequences which would ensue to those who possessed it not.

Appellants' main contention is that since they believe that the handling of snakes is a test of their faith, and it is part of their religious belief and practice, the Statute which would penalize the practice is violative of the freedom of religion guarantees contained in the Federal and State Constitutions. Thus it becomes necessary to examine the language of the constitutional guarantees and the circumstances which led to their enactment.

* * *

That the preservation of their religious freedom for which they had long struggled was of vital concern to the Colonists is evidenced by the fact that prior to the adoption of the First Amendment to the Federal Constitution, New York, Pennsylvania, New Hampshire, Virginia, and North Carolina had proposed amendments to the original document with that end in view. That it was thought that they had accomplished their object, so far as the Federal Government was concerned, is evidenced by the fact that the treaty with Tripoli, signed by President Washington and approved by the Senate in 1797, 8 Stat. 154, contains the statement:

> "The government of the United States of America is not in any sense founded on the Christian religion." Art. 11.

To protect themselves from local interference with their religious freedom, they incorporated variously worded provisions in their state constitutions. That these were not designed to prevent the states from prohibiting practices inimicable to the safety and rights of others, but were intended solely to insure their own right to believe as their consciences dictated is patent from the decisions construing them. As Colonists, with the exception of those who resided in Maryland, Rhode Island, and Pennsylvania, they had been subjected to punishment for nonconformance with the established religions, the punishments ranging from fines, whippings, and the pillory, to torture, exile and the gallows. As an example we quote the following, probably the first of the Blue Laws, enacted in 1610 at the behest of the Church of England for the governance of the Colony of Virginia:

> "Every man and woman shall repair in the morning to the divine service and sermons preached upon the Sabbath Day, and in the afternoon to divine service and catechizing, upon pain for the first fault to lose their provision and the allowance for the whole week following; for the second, to lose the said allowance and also to be whipped; and for the third to suffer death."

Almost every deviation from the established practice or faith constituted a crime. In Maryland and Pennsylvania it was only toleration that was guaranteed, and that only "to persons professing to believe in Jesus Christ". From these abuses they sought relief, not the right, under the guise of religious freedom, to jeopardize the safety, health, or welfare of their fellowman. * * *

Obviously, any recitation of the constitutional provisions and their interpretations would be impossible in an opinion of reasonable length. Their object, however, is clearly discernible from the enacting clause of "An Act for Establishing Religious Freedom" written by Thomas Jefferson, the leading exponent of the cause, adopted by the Virginia House of Assembly on December 26, 1785:

> "Be it therefore enacted by the General Assembly that no man shall be compelled to frequent or support any religious worship, place, or ministry whatsoever, nor shall be enforced, restrained, molested, or burthened in his body or goods, nor shall otherwise suffer on account of his religious opinions or belief; but that all men shall be free to profess, and by argument to maintain, their opinions in matters of religion, and that the same shall in nowise diminish, enlarge, or affect their civil capacities". Blakely's American State Papers, pp. 23 to 26.

The writings of Jefferson are too voluminous to permit of detailed scrutiny, but his views on the particular subject of inquiry have been thus accurately summarized by Chief Justice Gibson of the Supreme Court of Pennsylvania in the case of *Commonwealth v. Lesher*, 17 Serg. & R. 155, at page 161:

> "He denies the right of society to interfere, only where society is not a party in interest, the question, with its consequences, being between the man and his Creator; but as far as the interests of society are involved, its right to interfere, on principles of self-preservation, is not disputed. And this right is insolvable into the most absolute necessity; for, were the laws dispensed with, wherever they happen to be in collision with some supposed religious obligation, government would be perpetually falling short of the exigence."

The provision guaranteeing religious freedom incorporated in Kentucky's first Constitution, adopted April 19, 1792, is in the following language:

> "That the general, great, and essential principles of liberty and free government may be recognized and unalterably established, we declare ...

> "3. That all men have a natural and indefeasible right to worship Almighty God according to the dictates of their own consciences; that no man of right can be compelled to attend, erect, or support any place of worship, or to maintain any ministry against his consent; that no human authority can in any case whatever control or interfere with the rights of conscience; and that no preference shall ever be given by law to any religious societies or modes of worship" Art. 12, §§1, 3.

The same language appears in the second Constitution adopted August 17, 1799, art. 10, §3, and in the third Constitution adopted June 11, 1850, art. 13, §5. The language of the present Constitution is as follows:

> "No preference shall ever be given by law to any religious sect, society or denomination; nor to any particular creed, mode of worship or system of ecclesiastical polity; nor shall any person be compelled to attend any place of worship, to contribute to the erection or maintenance of any such place, or to the salary or support of any minister of religion; nor shall any man be compelled to send his child to any school to which he may be conscientiously opposed; and the civil rights, privileges or capacities of no person shall be taken away, or in any wise diminished or enlarged, on account of his belief or disbelief of any religious tenet, dogma or teaching. No human authority shall, in any case whatever, control or interfere with the rights of conscience." §5.

In the light of the historical background which we have attempted to sketch, it is apparent that the framers of these Constitutions were imbued with the ideals of Thomas Jefferson and had no thought of depriving the legislature of its inherent power to legislate for the welfare and safety of its citizens.

This Court has not been previously called upon to discuss at length the meaning of these constitutional provisions, but in the case of *Delk v. Commonwealth*, 166 Ky. 39, 178 S.W. 1129, 1132, L.R.A.1916B, 1117, Ann.Cas.1917C, 884, which was an appeal by a minister from a fine imposed upon him for using in his sermon to a large audience suggestive language calculated to disturb the public peace, we said:

> "The appellant's excuse that he was merely rebuking the sin of impurity, that he did not intend to disturb or embarrass any one, but made the statement as a warning and rebuke to sin, is wholly without justification. It does not avail appellant for him to say he has a right to propagate his religious views. That right is not denied; but one will not be permitted to commit a breach of the peace, under the guise of preaching the gospel. If one be licensed to use the pulpit for such disgraceful performances as the appellant admits he was guilty of in this case, then women and children are to be insulted with impunity by the use of the most obscene vulgarity in places where they go to worship."

If the State may punish a preacher for using language calculated to insult and offend the sensibilities of a congregation and thus breach the peace, preachers and members of his congregation may be prohibited by penal statutes from committing acts which are calculated to endanger the safety and lives of themselves and others. * * *

Other cases of similar import may be found in the footnotes to Sections 206a and 206b, "Constitutional Law" 16 Corpus Juris Secundum, pages 599 to 603, from which we quote the following excerpt:

> "Laws enacted for the purpose of restraining and punishing acts which have a tendency to disturb the public peace or to corrupt the public morals are not repugnant to the constitutional guaranties of religious liberty and freedom of conscience, although such acts may have been done pursuant to, and in conformity with, what was believed at the time to be a religious duty. Without violating the constitutional guaranties, the state, under the police power, may enact laws in order to promote the general welfare, public health, public safety and order, public morals, and to prevent fraud."

The appeal is granted and the judgment affirmed.

Whole Court sitting.

Notes and Questions

1. The 1940 statute at issue in *Lawson* was recodified in 1942 as KRS 437.060, and now reads as follows: "Any person who displays, handles or uses any kind of reptile in connection with any religious service or gathering shall be fined not less than fifty dollars ($50) nor more than one hundred dollars ($100)."
2. In *Seevers v. City of Somerset*, the Court, relying upon the U.S. Supreme Court's precedent in *Murdock v. Pennsylvania*, 319 U.S. 105 (1943), held that the City could not prohibit the distribution of religious literature without a license: "[O]ne distributing this ... character of literature was engaged in religious and not commercial activity and the ordinance forbidding commercial peddling had no application; that if it were applicable, it ran afoul both the State and the Federal Constitutions guaranteeing freedom of religion and was unconstitutional." 295 Ky. 595, 175 S.W.2d 18, 19 (1943). Unlike *Lawson*, in which the Court found the state had an interest in preventing "acts which are calculated to endanger the safety and lives of themselves and others," *Seevers* held that the government did not have an interest in preventing the free exercise of religion where there was no comparable public interest.

Gingerich v. Commonwealth

Supreme Court of Kentucky (2012)
382 S.W.3d 835

OPINION OF THE COURT BY JUSTICE NOBLE.

The Appellants in these two cases, Zook et al. and Gingerich et al.,[1] have argued to this Court that KRS 189.820 unconstitutionally interferes with their freedom to practice their religion as required by their beliefs. The Commonwealth argues that the statute regulates safety on the public highways by requiring slow-moving vehicles to display a particular brightly colored emblem to warn of the vehicles' slow speed. The Appellants, all members of the Old Order Swartzentruber Amish, claim that the bright orange-yellow of the requisite emblem and its triangular shape are at odds with their religious beliefs, and that forcing them to use the emblem interferes with their requirement to be plain and brightly displays the trinity, a symbol not adopted by the Amish.

Because we find that KRS 189.820 is a statute designed to protect the public and is not specifically targeted at preventing any religious practice, it is a statute of general applicability. The government need only establish a rational basis for the statute in order to pass constitutional muster.

Here, the lower courts found that common sense established that the bright color, reflective edge, and distinct shape of the slow-moving vehicle emblem required by the statute increased the visibility of the intended warning, both night and day, and was superior to the gray reflective tape proposed instead by Appellants, which only provides a protective warning at night. The lower courts, having established the requisite rational basis for the statute, were affirmed by the Court of Appeals, which is in turn affirmed.

I. Background

Before 2012,[2] Kentucky required that slow-moving vehicles whether "sold, leased, or rented" or "for use" on the public highways of Kentucky have a slow-moving vehicle emblem as standard equipment that was to be displayed both day and night when in operation. KRS 189.820. A slow-moving vehicle emblem (SMV emblem) "[c]onsists of a fluorescent yellow-orange triangle with a dark red reflective border as specified in American Society of Agriculture Engineers R276 or Society of Automotive Engineers J943 standards, or consisting of reasonably similar reflective qualities as specified in said standards." KRS 189.810(2). Failure to display the emblem on a slow-moving vehicle was a misdemeanor, punishable only by a fine for $20 to $35. KRS 189.993(5).

Appellants, members of the Old Order Swartzentruber sect of the Amish religion, operated horse-and-buggy vehicles on Kentucky roadways during daylight hours without displaying the SMV emblem. They were stopped and ticketed for being in violation

1. Though these are technically separate cases, they have identical legal issues and thus are being resolved in a single opinion.

2. These statutes were amended in 2012 to change the requirements for slow-moving vehicles. *See* 2012 Ky. Acts ch. 53, §§1–3.

of the statute, and thereby ostensibly creating a road hazard. Nine different persons were stopped and ticketed, one on four different occasions.

Three of the defendants below—Jacob Gingerich, Emanuel Yoder, and Levi Zook—proceeded with a joint bench trial in Graves District Court. The remaining six, Menno Zook, David Zook, Eli Zook, Mose Yoder, Levi Hostetler, Jacob Gingerich and Danny Byler were tried jointly by a jury in Graves District Court.

The bench-trial defendants claimed that KRS 189.820 violated their constitutional rights to the free exercise of their religion under Sections 1 and 5 of the Kentucky Constitution.[3] They were found guilty of violating the statute and fined the minimum amount, \$20.00, by the trial court, which took into account that the defendants were conflicted between the law and their religious beliefs. The trial court also imposed court costs of \$128, resulting in a total fine and costs of \$148.00 each.

The trial court analyzed the conflict between the defendants' stated religious beliefs and compliance with the statute's requirement of displaying a SMV emblem based on there being a "compelling state interest" in promoting highway safety, which it held overcame the defendants' free exercise of religion claims. The trial court found that since the violations occurred in the daytime, the bright color required by the statute for the SMV emblem served as an adequate warning to other drivers, and that since the gray reflective tape did not adequately fluoresce in daylight, the SMV emblem was the least restrictive alternative to provide for public safety. At least in terminology, the trial court applied the "strict scrutiny" standard of review to the statute.

The jury-trial defendants also argued that the statute violated their constitutional right under Sections 1 and 5 of the Kentucky Constitution in a pretrial motion to dismiss, which was denied. The case then went to trial before a jury. The defendants claimed in their defense that complying with the statute violated their religious beliefs, that they would be shunned by their religious community if they obeyed the statute, and that the silver reflective tape they were willing to use was the equivalent of the SMV emblem, a defense they claimed was supported by the language in the statute referencing materials of "reasonably similar reflecting qualities." They offered no testimony about how this would compare in daylight. The jury rejected these defenses, and found the defendants guilty on all counts, and recommended a \$25.00 fine. The trial court imposed the fine and costs.

Both the bench-trial defendants and the jury-trial defendants appealed to Graves Circuit Court.

As to the bench-trial defendants, the circuit court rejected "strict scrutiny" as the proper standard of review for the constitutionality of the statute, holding that the Kentucky Constitution was not more protective of the free exercise of religion than the United States Constitution was and thus offered no greater protection for the free exercise of religion than the federal courts allowed. The circuit court further noted that KRS 189.820 was not specifically enacted to prohibit the Old Order Swartzentruber

3. None of the defendants raised a claim based on the federal constitution.

Amish from practicing their religion, but rather was enacted as a law generally applicable to all slow-moving vehicles to promote public safety on the highways. The Graves District Court was affirmed, because its decision was appropriate under the "rational basis" standard of review.

As to the jury-trial defendants, the Graves Circuit Court recognized that the issues were the same as those in the appeal from the bench trial, and incorporated by reference its opinion in that case, affirming the Graves District Court jury verdict.

All the defendants filed motions for discretionary review with the Kentucky Court of Appeals, which were granted. That court rendered a unanimous opinion on June 3, 2011, resolving all the cases and affirming the Graves Circuit Court. The Court of Appeals agreed that the Kentucky Constitution does not offer more protection for religious freedom than the United States Constitution does, and found that the rational basis standard of review applied by the federal courts is the appropriate standard of review for Kentucky cases on laws of general applicability. Under that analysis, the Court of Appeals held that KRS 189.820 is a neutral law of general applicability enacted for the public welfare and does not impermissibly restrict religious practice. But that court did go further and analyzed the case under strict scrutiny and found that the statute passed that standard of review as well, which was more analysis than the cases called for, and could inevitably lead to confusion.

This Court granted discretionary review in order to clearly establish the standard of review for laws of general applicability, enacted for the common good, which only incidentally affect the practice of one's religion.

II. Analysis

These cases present an opportunity for this Court to clarify what the Kentucky Constitution requires when a claim is made that a statute violates religious freedom by interfering with the practice of a religion. While we have recognized that the Kentucky Constitution may afford greater protection of individual rights than those prescribed by the United States Supreme Court,[4] this Court has often stated regarding particular sections of the Kentucky Constitution that our state constitution offers no more protection than the same or similar section of the federal constitution. *See, e.g., LaFollette v. Commonwealth*, 915 S.W.2d 747, 748 (Ky. 1996) ("Section 10 of the Kentucky Con-

4. In *Commonwealth v. Wasson*, 842 S.W.2d 487 (Ky. 1992), this Court held that it is "not bound by decision of the United States Supreme Court when deciding whether a state statute impermissibly infringes upon individual rights guaranteed in the State Constitution so long as state constitutional protection does not fall below the federal *floor*, meaning the minimum guarantee of individual rights under the United States Constitution as interpreted by the United States Supreme Court." *Id.* at 492 (citing *Oregon v. Hass*, 420 U.S. 714, 719, 95 S.Ct. 1215, 43 L.Ed.2d 570 (1975)). In fact, *Wasson* read the Kentucky Constitution as providing greater equal protection rights than the federal courts had, at that time, read in the United States Constitution. *Id.* at 492–93. Other decisions have read portions of the Kentucky Constitution more broadly than the federal constitution has been read. *See, e.g., Baucom v. Commonwealth*, 134 S.W.3d 591, 592 (Ky. 2004) (recognizing that Section 11 of the Kentucky Constitution affords greater protection than the federal constitution because it guarantees "hybrid representation" for an accused).

stitution provides no greater protection than does the federal Fourth Amendment."); *McCall v. Courier-Journal and Louisville Times Co.*, 623 S.W.2d 882, 894–95 (Ky. 1981) ("Each of our four constitutions have qualified freedom of speech and press by responsibility for abuse of these liberties. Clearly these provisions were not intended to grant greater protection than the First Amendment to the federal constitution which antedated our first constitution adopted in 1792 by four months."). We now state that this principle is also true of the free-exercise-of-religion protections in Section 1 and Section 5 of the Kentucky Constitution.[5]

It has been argued in these cases that the last sentence of Section 5 of the Kentucky Constitution, "No human authority shall, in any case whatever, control or interfere with the rights of conscience," grants *more* protection to religious practice than the First Amendment of the United States Constitution. Certainly, the language in the Kentucky Constitution is more specific. But it is linguistically impossible for language to be more inclusive than that in the First Amendment: "Congress shall make *no law* respecting an establishment of religion, or prohibiting the free exercise thereof…" U.S. Const. amend. I (emphasis added). "Free exercise" of religion arguably requires a government to not place restrictions on the religious practice.

But governments are required to do many other things as well, some of which may conflict with a particular religious practice. In fact, Section 5 of the Kentucky Constitution, in its entirety, sets forth some of these things. Our state government may not give preference to any religious sect, society, denomination, creed, mode of worship or system of ecclesiastical polity. Our state government cannot compel religious attendance nor the participation in building or maintaining churches or paying ministers. Parents may not be compelled to send their children to schools which they conscientiously oppose. And no one can have his or her civil rights, privileges, or capacities taken away or enlarged because of religious belief.

But at times, varied religious beliefs come into conflict with one another. And the government is also charged with acting for the common good. As this Court's predecessor previously stated in *Lawson v. Commonwealth*, 291 Ky. 437, 164 S.W.2d 972, 976 (1942):

5. Section 1 states, in relevant part: "All men are, by nature, free and equal, and have certain inherent and inalienable rights, among which may be reckoned … [t]he right of worshipping Almighty God according to the dictates of their consciences."

Section 5 states:

> No preference shall ever be given by law to any religious sect, society or denomination; nor to any particular creed, mode of worship or system of ecclesiastical polity; nor shall any person be compelled to attend any place of worship, to contribute to the erection or maintenance of any such place, or to the salary or support of any minister of religion; nor shall any man be compelled to send his child to any school to which he may be conscientiously opposed; and the civil rights, privileges or capacities of no person shall be taken away, or in anywise diminished or enlarged, on account of his belief or disbelief of any religious tenet, dogma or teaching. No human authority shall, in any case whatever, control or interfere with the rights of conscience.

> Laws enacted for the purpose of restraining and punishing acts which have a tendency to disturb the public peace or to corrupt the public morals are not repugnant to the constitutional guaranties of religious liberty and freedom of conscience, although such acts may have been done pursuant to, and in conformity with, what was believed at the time to be religious duty. Without violating the constitutional guaranties, the state, under the police power, may enact laws in order to promote the general welfare, public health, public safety and order, public morals, and to prevent fraud.

In other words, the government is likely to be confronted with situations where the common good comes into conflict with the free exercise of a particular religion. But how does the government function when there are conflicting constitutional mandates?

Relying on precedent of the United States Supreme Court, this Court's predecessor held that religious freedom has two components: freedom to believe and freedom to act. *Mosier v. Barren County Board of Health*, 308 Ky. 829, 833, 215 S.W.2d 967, 969 (1948) (citing *United States v. Ballard*, 322 U.S. 78, 64 S.Ct. 882, 88 L.Ed. 1148 (1944), and *Cantwell v. Connecticut*, 310 U.S. 296, 60 S.Ct. 900, 84 L.Ed. 1213 (1940)); *Lawson*, 164 S.W.2d at 973 (citing the same cases). What one chooses to believe is an absolute freedom, which no power on earth can in reality arbitrate. *Mosier*, 215 S.W.2d at 969. But, "in the nature of things," freedom to act cannot be absolute in human society where beliefs and practices vary, and where a given practice, absolutely freely enacted, can inflict harm on others. *Id.* Thus religious conduct must remain subject to regulation for the protection of society. *Id.* Or stated another way, "the constitutional guarantee of religious freedom does not permit the practice of religious rites dangerous or detrimental to the lives, safety or health of the participants or to the public." *Id.* (citing *Lawson*, 164 S.W.2d at 976).

As both our state and federal law have long held, then, government can act to restrict the free exercise of religion when that exercise is detrimental to the common good. But given the certain terms of the Kentucky and federal constitutions regarding interference with religious practice, there must be a burden the government meets before it can do so. Whether the governmental regulation is subject to a heightened level of review or whether it must merely meet a rational governmental purpose is determined by the action the government takes, why it is taking it, and how much the act restricts religious practice.

The federal courts have made a clear distinction. Those courts have determined that governmental acts done for the health, safety and welfare of the public, which are applied generally to everyone, need only have a rational basis even when they incidentally affect religious practice. *See Employment Division, Department of Human Resources of Oregon v. Smith*, 494 U.S. 872, 110 S.Ct. 1595, 108 L.Ed.2d 876 (1990).

In *Smith*, the respondents were fired from their jobs at a private drug rehabilitation facility for ingesting peyote, a hallucinogenic drug prohibited by Oregon statute, as part of a religious ritual of the Native American Church, of which both were members.

When they applied for unemployment compensation, their applications were denied on the grounds that they were fired for violating the law. They challenged the law on the grounds that it violated the Free Exercise Clause of the First Amendment of the United States Constitution. The United States Supreme Court held that "the First Amendment has not been offended" because "prohibiting the exercise of religion ... is not the object of the [statute] but merely the incidental effect of a generally applicable and otherwise valid provision." *Id.* at 878, 110 S.Ct. 1595. Moreover, the Court held that government actions that substantially burden a religious practice need not be justified by a "compelling governmental interest," so long as they are generally applicable. *Id.* at 884, 110 S.Ct. 1595.[6]

Subsequent United States Supreme Court cases that have cited Smith approvingly have stated that it stands for the proposition that "a law that is neutral and of general applicability need not be justified by a compelling governmental interest even if the law has the incidental effect of burdening a particular religious practice." *Church of the Lukumi Babalu Aye, Inc. v. City of Hialeah*, 508 U.S. 520, 531, 113 S.Ct. 2217, 124 L.Ed.2d 472 (1993). Though the Supreme Court has not expressly said so, the test for such statutes is the rational-basis test, *e.g., Combs v. Homer-Center School Dist.*, 540 F.3d 231, 242–43 (3d Cir. 2008), under which the statute is presumed to be constitutional and which provides that "'[t]he burden is on the one attacking the legislative arrangement to negative every conceivable basis which might support it,' whether or not the basis has a foundation in the record." *Heller v. Doe by Doe*, 509 U.S. 312, 320–21, 113 S.Ct. 2637, 125 L.Ed.2d 257 (1993) (quoting *Lehnhausen v. Lake Shore Auto Parts Co.*, 410 U.S. 356, 364, 93 S.Ct. 1001, 35 L.Ed.2d 351 (1973)).

But on the other hand, the U.S. Supreme Court has held that governmental acts that are directed specifically at restricting a given religious practice, and are thus not generally applicable, are subject to strict scrutiny. *Church of Lukumi*, 508 U.S. at 531, 113 S.Ct. 2217. *When* a statute must pass the strict scrutiny standard of review, the government must establish a "compelling state interest" requiring the enactment, and that the method it applies in the statute is "narrowly tailored to advance that interest" (often referred to as the least restrictive alternative) before the statute can restrict the religious practice. *Id.* at 531–32, 113 S.Ct. 2217.

In *Church of the Lukumi*, the United States Supreme Court held that a city ordinance prohibiting animal sacrifice was an unconstitutional violation of the Free Exercise

---

6. Congress enacted the Religious Freedom Restoration Act (RFRA) in 1993 as a response to the Court's holding in *Smith*. The RFRA, enacted pursuant to Congress' power under Section 5 of the Fourteenth Amendment, responded to *Smith* by expressly requiring the government to demonstrate that a statute burdening a religion is "(1) in furtherance of a compelling governmental interest; and (2) is the least restrictive means of furthering that compelling governmental interest." 42 U.S.C. §2000bb-1(c) (1993). In *City of Boerne v. Flores*, 521 U.S. 507, 117 S.Ct. 2157, 138 L.Ed.2d 624 (1997), the Supreme Court declared RFRA unconstitutional as applied to the states. However, the RFRA, as subsequently amended, has been upheld as valid as applied to the federal government. *See Gonzales v. O Centro Espirita Beneficente Uniao do Vegetal*, 546 U.S. 418, 126 S.Ct. 1211, 163 L.Ed.2d 1017 (2006). Therefore, the Court's holding in *Smith* remains good law with respect to the states.

Clause because the ordinance was targeted at practitioners of the Santeria religion, and was therefore neither generally applicable nor neutral. The Court made clear that "[f]acial neutrality is not determinative" and that "[o]fficial action that targets religious conduct for distinctive treatment cannot be shielded by mere compliance with the requirement of facial neutrality. The Free Exercise Clause protects against governmental hostility which is masked, as well as overt." *Id.* at 535, 113 S.Ct. 2217. Thus, the city council had the burden of proving that it had a "compelling government interest" and that the ordinance was "narrowly tailored to achieving that interest," burdens that the city council did not meet.

The distinction between the different levels of review has not been as clear in the decisions of this Court and its predecessor. The Kentucky courts have often found it difficult not to blend these levels of review, as *Lawson* and *Mosier* illustrate. Both cases are commonly viewed as using a strict scrutiny standard, but the cases blend some of the analysis.[7] Thus, the question of the proper standard of review under the Kentucky Constitution remains open.

In *Lawson*, this Court reviewed a statute that specifically prohibited the use of snakes in a religious service. 164 S.W.2d at 972. Thus, the actual practice of religion was targeted by the statute. As noted above, when a statute is aimed at a particular religious practice, federal law requires that strict scrutiny be applied to the purpose of the statute, and the government is required to have a compelling interest to support the enactment, and the statute must be narrowly tailored to achieve the interest. *See Church of the Lukumi*, 508 U.S. at 546, 113 S.Ct. 2217. In *Lawson*, the Court focused primarily on public safety through prohibiting exposing citizens to venomous snake bites, clearly a compelling governmental interest, and because of the potential for death, there really was no other alternative to the governmental regulation. *Id.* at 976. Though *Lawson* does not use the words, this meant the law was narrowly tailored. Thus

7. It is important to note that this Court is not suggesting that *Lawson* and *Mosier* were incorrect applications of federal precedent. Placing the cases in their historical contexts demonstrates that the highest court in Kentucky would have had no reason to pay mind to whether the cases required strict scrutiny or rational basis review because those notions were not clearly established or quantified in the 1940s. The notion of a heightened standard of review was not introduced until 1938 in the infamous Footnote 4 of *United States v. Carolene Products*, 304 U.S. 144, 152 n. 4, 58 S.Ct. 778, 82 L.Ed. 1234 (1938), a mere four years before *Lawson*. Importantly, Footnote 4 did not elucidate what the heightened standard was; it merely introduced the notion that statutes burdening certain fundamental rights require more scrutiny than other statutes. It was not until 1944, two years *after Lawson* and only four years before *Mosier*, that the Supreme Court first acknowledged the specific standard of "strict scrutiny" in *Korematsu v. United States*, 323 U.S. 214, 65 S.Ct. 193, 89 L.Ed. 194 (1944). In that case, Justice Black wrote, "It should be noted, to begin with, that all legal restrictions which curtail the civil rights of a single racial group are immediately suspect. That is not to say that all such restrictions are unconstitutional. It is to say that courts must subject them to the most rigid scrutiny. Pressing public necessity may sometimes justify the existence of such restrictions; racial antagonism never can." *Id.* at 216, 65 S.Ct. 193. This historical context demonstrates that today's opinion is neither a criticism nor a departure from prior jurisprudence; rather, it is a long-needed clarification of the question of which standard of review should apply to these situations.

Lawson is perceived as a strict scrutiny case, and since the statute actually prohibited a particular religious practice, that is the appropriate standard of review.

On the other hand, though also viewed as a case applying strict scrutiny, *Mosier* did not require it. The Board of Health had issued a regulation requiring all children to be vaccinated for smallpox, and any child who was not vaccinated was to be excluded from the city schools. 215 S.W.2d at 968. The evidence supported the public health concerns behind the regulations, and the regulations applied to all children. *Id.* Two fathers, Mosier and a man named Stuart stated several reasons why their children should not be vaccinated. Stuart specifically claimed that "his religious and conscientious belief prevented him from subjecting his children to vaccination by injecting foreign substances into the veins," and that requiring him to have the children vaccinated thus violated Section 1 of the Kentucky Constitution. *Id.* at 969.

The Court cited *Lawson* as authority, but the facts establish a distinct difference. The regulation was not directed at a specific religious practice, but rather applied generally to all children, and any impact on religious practice was purely incidental. The regulation stood because there was a rational basis for enactment, which the Court specifically found: to stop the spread of a dangerous disease. Glasgow was located on a central travel artery with many soldiers coming home from Europe (World War II), and the traffic could spread the very contagious disease; vaccination was a sure preventive of the disease; and it was too late to vaccinate when an epidemic occurred. *Id.* at 968. The Court did not discuss whether this was the least restrictive alternative, and did not need to because the regulation had general applicability and was not aimed at a specific religious practice. Rather, the Court simply concluded that while religious beliefs could not be regulated, conduct could, and thus Stuart could "not endanger the health of the community by refusing to have his daughter vaccinated." *Id.* at 969.

This Court now finds that statutes, regulations, or other governmental enactments which provide for the public health, safety and welfare, *and* which are statutes of general applicability that only incidentally affect the practice of religion, are properly reviewed for a rational basis under the Kentucky Constitution, as they are under the federal constitution. Enactments that directly prohibit or restrain a religious practice are subject to a strict scrutiny standard of review. As discussed above, providing this clearer standard brings Kentucky's jurisprudence in line with United States Supreme Court precedent.

Given the facts of this case, then which standard of review applies? Are KRS 189.820(1) and (2) constitutional?

KRS 189.820 is on its face most directly aimed at farm vehicles, rather than the Amish conveyance buggies, but clearly applies to *all* slow-moving vehicles on the public highways. The emblem standards specified refer to agriculture and *motor* vehicles. The statute is clearly a statute of general applicability, aimed at protecting public safety on the highways by requiring a brightly colored, reflective, universally shaped warning emblem. It does not prohibit any religious practice, and only incidentally impacts the Amish way of life because the Amish believe that they should generally travel in horse-drawn buggies. In fact, the record indicates some exceptions are made for vehicles driven by non-Amish persons. We need not debate whether this is a lifestyle choice or an actual religious choice. In either event, the statute is not aimed at slow-moving vehicles because they are a choice (or a religious practice), but rather because they are dangerous, in comparison to posted legal speeds on the highway. And, if a slow-moving vehicle is dark in color or is in deep shade, it is difficult to see whether it is an Amish buggy or a dusty combine.

The slow-moving buggies of the Appellants that did not display the SMV emblem, *or any other warning mechanism*, presented the potential harm the statute was enacted to counter, and the vehicles are regulated on the public highways because they are slow, not because they are a religious choice. Since the Kentucky Constitution provides no greater protection to religious practice than the federal Constitution does, this Court will follow federal precedent, and thus the statute is presumed constitutional unless there is *no* rational basis for it. But there is ample rational basis for such a statute: it is aimed at public general safety, and works toward that goal in several ways (e.g., by using a universal symbol, increasing visibility over vehicles without the emblem). Thus, this Court finds that KRS 189.820 meets the rational basis standard of review and is thus not unconstitutional. Appellant's convictions and penalties must stand.

III. Conclusion

The opinion of the Court of Appeals is affirmed.

All sitting. Minton, C.J.; Cunningham and Schroder, JJ., concur. Venters, J., concurs in result only by separate opinion. Scott, J., dissents by separate opinion in which Abramson, J., joins.

Justice Venters, concurring:

I concur with the Majority's conclusion: the enforcement of KRS 189.820 against Appellants does not violate their religious liberty under either the Kentucky Constitution or the United States Constitution. However, I write separately to register my disagreement with the proposition that the protection of liberty provided by the Kentucky Constitution simply mirrors the comparable protections afforded by the federal Constitution.

The words used in each document are somewhat different and each document should be interpreted in light of the words used within it. To the extent that the different words used may describe the same concept, some of the protections afforded by one document may overlap with the other. However, to the extent that different words denote different meanings, each Constitution must be respected in its own right.

This Court is the final arbiter of the meaning of the Kentucky Constitution, and our interpretation of its terms should not be constrained by the opinions of federal courts interpreting the United States Constitution. Those opinions may be instructive and influential in our review of our state Constitution, but they do not control the meaning of the Kentucky Constitution; nor do they define the protections of liberty contained therein. We should no longer tether the meaning of the Kentucky Constitution to the pendulum of the federal court interpretations of the federal Constitution.

JUSTICE SCOTT, DISSENTING:

I respectfully dissent. In my opinion, the Kentucky Constitution unquestionably affords greater protection to the free exercise of religion than does the Federal Constitution. Accordingly, any law interfering with an individual's free exercise of religion must pass strict scrutiny or else be declared unconstitutional. Given that KRS 189.820 cannot pass strict scrutiny, Appellants' convictions cannot stand. Thus, I would reverse the Court of Appeals' judgment.

I. Kentucky's Constitution

I begin by rejecting the majority's conclusion that Kentucky's Constitution does not afford greater protection to the free exercise of religion than its federal counterpart. First, the majority contends that "it is linguistically impossible for language to be more inclusive than that in the First Amendment: 'Congress shall make *no law* respecting an establishment of religion, or prohibiting the free exercise thereof....'" *Ante*, op. at 840 (*quoting* U.S. Const. amend. I). Not only is it linguistically *possible* to be more inclusive than the First Amendment, Section 5 of Kentucky's Constitution is linguistically *more inclusive*. Presumably, the framers of Kentucky's Constitution used more inclusive language with the intent it would offer *greater* protection than the Federal Constitution.

When Kentucky's current Constitution was adopted in 1891, the Federal Constitution had been in effect for nearly a century. If, as the majority suggests, the framers of Kentucky's Constitution intended its provisions to be co-extensive with the Federal Constitution, it *could have* (and, one would expect, *would have*) used the same language. *See Ky. State Bd. for Elementary and Secondary Ed. v. Rudasill*, 589 S.W.2d 877, 880 and n. 2 (Ky. 1979). Instead, the framers went beyond the mandates of the Federal Constitution and proscribed *more* activity than does the First Amendment.

For example, the First Amendment provides, in relevant part, that: (1) *Congress*, shall make (2) no *law* (3) *prohibiting* the free exercise of religion. *See* U.S. Const. amend. I. In contrast, Kentucky's Constitution provides, in relevant part, that: (1) *no human authority* shall (2) *in any case whatever* (3) *control or interfere* with the rights of conscience. *See* Ky. Const. §5. Obviously, "no human authority" is broader than "Congress"; "any case whatever" is broader than "law"; and "control or interfere with" proscribes more activity than an outright "prohibiti[on]." Thus, it is clear to me that the framers of Kentucky's Constitution *intended* to afford greater protection under Section 5 than does the First Amendment.

This conclusion is reinforced by the rest of Section 5:

> No preference shall ever be given by law to any religious sect, society or denomination; nor to any particular creed, mode of worship or system of ecclesiastical polity; nor shall any person be compelled to attend any place of worship, to contribute to the erection or maintenance of any such place, or to the salary or support of any minister of religion; nor shall any man be compelled to send his child to any school to which he may be conscientiously opposed; and the civil rights, privileges or capacities of no person shall be taken away, or in anywise diminished or enlarged, on account of his belief or disbelief of any religious tenet, dogma or teaching.

This goes far beyond proscribing a legislative body from making a law prohibiting the free exercise of religion. It makes clear the framers' intent that religious liberty should be zealously protected.

Additionally, Section 26 of Kentucky's Constitution protects Sections 1 through 25:

> To guard against transgression of the high powers which we have delegated, We Declare that everything in this Bill of Rights is excepted out of the general powers of government, and shall forever remain inviolate; and all laws contrary thereto, or contrary to this Constitution, shall be void.

Because KRS 189.820, as applied to the Swartzentruber Amish, is contrary to Sections 1[8] and 5 of the Bill of Rights, I would hold that it is void *unless* it passes strict scrutiny—any weaker standard does little to "guard against transgressions of the high powers which [the framers] have delegated." Ky. Const. §26. Stated differently, "[a] court cannot deprive a person of a 'core value' constitutional right with a 'rational basis' test." *Posey v. Commonwealth*, 185 S.W.3d 170, 204 (Ky. 2006) (Scott, J., concurring in part and dissenting in part) (*citing Republican Party of Minn. v. White*, 536 U.S. 765, 774, 122 S.Ct. 2528, 153 L.Ed.2d 694 (2002)).

Finally, other jurisdictions have analyzed identical issues as the one before us under strict scrutiny and held the SMV emblem requirement violated a state constitutional provision. *See, e.g., Wisconsin v. Miller*, 202 Wis.2d 56, 549 N.W.2d 235, 239–40 (1996). In Miller, the Supreme Court of Wisconsin recognized that the U.S. Supreme Court held in *Employment Division, Department of Human Resources v. Smith*, 494 U.S. 872, 110 S.Ct. 1595, 108 L.Ed.2d 876 (1990) that a rational basis standard of review would be employed for federal constitutional challenges to laws of general applicability. *Id.* at 240. However, it concluded "that the guarantees of [Wisconsin's] state constitution will best be furthered through continued use of the compelling interest/least restrictive alternative analysis of free conscience claims and see no need to depart from this time-tested standard." *Id.* at 241. I agree with the Supreme Court of Wisconsin.

Employing a rational basis standard renders inconsequential Kentucky's free exercise guarantee in that virtually any asserted governmental interest could justify laws of general applicability that have the effect of substantially burdening individuals' religious liberty. Such a deferential view of government action cannot adequately protect members of non-mainstream faiths from governmental encroachment upon their religious liberty and should be rejected because "construction [of a constitutional provision that is] so loose as to virtually nullify the section, which is mandatory in its terms, should not be adopted." *Bd. of Penitentiary Comm'rs v. Spencer*, 159 Ky. 255, 166 S.W. 1017, 1018 (1914).

---

8. Section 1 states, in relevant part: "All men are, by nature, free and equal, and have certain inherent and inalienable rights, among which may be reckoned ... [t]he right of worshipping Almighty God *according to the dictates of their consciences*." (Emphasis added.) Obviously, requiring the Swartzentruber Amish to comply with a law that violates the dictates of their consciences would be unconstitutional.

II. Strict Scrutiny

This Court's strict scrutiny review involves a three-step inquiry: "First, does a statute pose a significant burden on a constitutional right? Secondly, does the statute further [a] compell[ing] state interest? Thirdly, if so, does the statute further that interest too broadly, or in the alternative is the statute narrowly tailored to protect that interest?" *Associated Indus. of Ky. v. Commonwealth*, 912 S.W.2d 947, 953 (Ky. 1995) (*citing Buckley v. Valeo*, 424 U.S. 1, 96 S.Ct. 612, 46 L.Ed.2d 659 (1976)).

A. Significant Burden on a Constitutional Right

Under the first prong of this inquiry, we ask whether KRS 189.820 significantly burdens Appellants' constitutional rights. As a threshold matter, when the free exercise of religion is at issue, courts generally require a showing that the statute's challengers have a "sincerely held religious belief." *See, e.g., Wisconsin v. Yoder*, 406 U.S. 205, 209, 92 S.Ct. 1526, 32 L.Ed.2d 15 (1972) ("The State stipulated that respondents' religious beliefs were sincere"); *Murphy v. Mo. Dep't of Corr.*, 372 F.3d 979, 983 (8th Cir. 2004) ("In analyzing [whether a state law infringes on the Appellant's free-exercise right], we consider first the threshold issue of whether the challenged governmental action 'infringes upon a sincerely held religious belief....'") (citation omitted); *DeHart v. Horn*, 227 F.3d 47, 52 (3d Cir. 2000) ("[I]f a prisoner's request for a particular diet is *not* the result of sincerely held religious beliefs, the First Amendment imposes no obligation on the prison to honor that request...."). "Thus, for a burden on religion to be substantial, the government regulation must compel action or inaction with respect to the sincerely held belief; mere inconvenience to the religious institution or adherent is insufficient." *Lyster v. Woodford Cnty. Bd. of Adjustment Members*, No. 2005-CA-001336-MR, 2007 WL 542719, *4 (Ky. App. Feb. 23, 2007) (*citing Jolly v. Coughlin*, 76 F.3d 468, 477 (2d Cir. 1996)).

Whether a religious belief is sincerely held is a factual determination. As such, the trial court is in the best position to determine whether a belief is, in fact, sincerely held, and we should accept the trial court's determination unless it is clearly erroneous. *Gen. Motors Corp. v. Herald*, 833 S.W.2d 804, 806 (Ky. 1992) ("This Court in its appellate capacity is bound by the trial court's finding of fact unless there is clear error...."). *See also Murphy*, 372 F.3d at 983 ("Whether or not group worship is a sincerely held religious belief is a factual determination....").

The trial court in Appellants Gingerich, Yoder, and Zook's cases affirmatively found that they "do hold genuine and sincere religious beliefs, and based on their indoctrination and up-bringing, have a genuine fear of shunning or banishment from their Church and immediate communities if they obey the law of the state and violate the rule of the church."[9] Although it is unclear whether any affirmative finding of fact was entered with respect to the Appellants in the second case, I will assume that they have

9. Although the trial court included this finding in its "Conclusions of Law" section, whether one has a sincerely held religious belief is obviously a factual determination. I assume the trial court included this finding in its "Conclusions of Law" because the sincerity of the belief is inextricably connected to whether compliance of the law at issue would impose a substantial burden upon the exercise of those beliefs, which is a matter of law.

an identical sincerely held religious belief as the Appellants in the first case. Indeed, one of the Appellants from the first case was also a defendant in the second case.

The finding that Appellants have a sincerely held religious belief is not clearly erroneous. The record establishes the following: that the Swartzentruber Amish shun the display of worldly symbols due to the Bible's admonition to "be not conformed to this world"; to them, the SMV emblem is a worldly symbol irrespective of the purpose for which it was created; they are prohibited by their religious code of conduct from displaying the orange-red triangle on their horse-drawn buggies because of its worldly garish colors and its function as a secular symbol; and failure to comply with this religious mandate will result in their (and their families) being shunned from the religious community. Accordingly, I conclude that Appellants have established their burden of showing a sincerely held religious belief.

Second, based on the same evidence, I conclude that compliance with KRS 189.820 significantly burdens Appellants' sincerely held religious beliefs. Accordingly, Appellants have satisfied the first prong of the test by showing KRS 189.820 imposes a significant burden on their fundamental constitutional right to the free exercise of religion. The statute is therefore presumptively unconstitutional. *See Harris v. McRae*, 448 U.S. 297, 312, 100 S.Ct. 2671, 65 L.Ed.2d 784 (1980) (citation and internal quotation marks omitted) ("It is well settled that ... if a law impinges upon a fundamental right explicitly or implicitly secured by the Constitution [it] is presumptively unconstitutional.").

B. Compelling State Interest

Because Appellants satisfied the first prong of the test, the burden shifts to the Commonwealth to prove that KRS 189.820 furthers a compelling state interest. The trial court found a compelling interest "in promoting highway safety for all." The Commonwealth echoes this interest and asserts an additional, more specific interest "in placing highly-visible materials on the rear ends of buggies to prevent daytime accidents."

In support of its argument, the Commonwealth cites two studies. Both studies demonstrate that there is a serious, life-threatening problem of slow-moving vehicle crashes. *See* P.M. Garvey, *Motorist Comprehension of the Slow-Moving Vehicle (SMV) Emblem*, 9(2) J. Agric. Safety & Health 159 (2003); Cory Alexander Anderson, *Causative Factors of Crashes between a Motor Vehicle and the Amish and Old Order Mennonite Horse and Buggy* (2008) (unpublished Master's thesis in Urban and Regional Planning at Virginia Commonwealth University).

The Garvey study illustrates generally the problem with slow-moving vehicles. For example, "when a vehicle travelling at 55 mph is 500 ft behind a vehicle travelling at 45 mph, the time to contact between the two vehicles is 34 sec[onds]. However, if the lead vehicle is travelling at 25 mph, [time to contact] reduces to 11.2 sec[onds], and if the lead vehicle's speed is 5 mph, as with horsedrawn vehicles, [time to contact] falls to 6.8 seconds." Garvey, *supra*, at 159.

The Anderson study focused on the seventy-six motor-vehicle-to-buggy crashes in Pennsylvania in 2006. *See* Anderson, *supra*, at 1. However, it cited other studies, one of which found that in 43% of reported crashes the buggies "sustained extensive damage or were destroyed, and about 10% … involved a fatality." *Id.* at 2. Another study cited by Anderson found that "buggy crashes with motor vehicles constituted the second highest reason for Amish admissions to the hospital." *Id.* at 2–3. Citing an Ohio Department of Transportation study of 575 buggy crashes over a seven-year period, "the top causative factor to crashes was motor vehicles 'following too close,' … that rear end crashes were the most common, and that a majority of crashes occurred during daylight hours." *Id.* at 4.

I believe the Commonwealth has satisfied its burden of proving it has a compelling interest in promoting highway safety for all, and specifically in ensuring the visibility of slow-moving vehicles. I would therefore conclude that the Commonwealth satisfied the second prong of the test.

C. Narrowly Tailored/Least Restrictive Alternative

Having established a compelling state interest, the Commonwealth must finally show that use of this particular SMV emblem is narrowly tailored to achieving that interest. *See Associated Indus. of Ky.*, 912 S.W.2d at 953 (*citing Buckley*, 424 U.S. 1, 96 S.Ct. 612 (1976)). Although not necessarily identical to the notion of "narrow tailoring," the United States Supreme Court, analyzing a similar state-law infringement on the free exercise of religion, defined this third prong of the test as requiring the state to show that its means are "*the least restrictive* means of achieving" its compelling interest. *Thomas v. Review Bd. of Ind. Emp't Sec. Div.*, 450 U.S. 707, 718, 101 S.Ct. 1425, 67 L.Ed.2d 624 (1981) (emphasis added); *see also Emp't Div., Dep't of Human Res. v. Smith*, 494 U.S. 872, 899, 110 S.Ct. 1595, 108 L.Ed.2d 876 (1990), *superseded by statute*. Indeed, this is the test that is specifically defined in the federal Religious Freedom Restoration Act, 42 U.S.C. §2000bb-1 (2012), and appears to be the test that most states employ for free exercise issues challenged on state law grounds.[10] As this "least restrictive alternative" test is a less nebulous and arbitrary determination—and the test the Commonwealth, Appellants, the courts below, the federal courts and most states use for free exercise issues—I would require the Commonwealth to prove the *absence* of a less restrictive alternative (notwithstanding our *Associated Industries*, 912 S.W.2d at 953, formulation).

The Commonwealth contends that the fluorescent-colored triangle is the least restrictive means of ensuring driver safety. However, twenty-three states and the District of Columbia do not require animal-drawn vehicles to display the SMV triangle mandated by KRS 189.820.[11] In these other jurisdictions, various uses of white and red

10. *See, e.g., Humphrey v. Lane*, 89 Ohio St.3d 62, 728 N.E.2d 1039, 1040 (2000); *Munns v. Martin*, 131 Wash.2d 192, 930 P.2d 318, 321 (1997) (en banc); *Miller*, 549 N.W.2d at 241.

11. *See* Ariz. Rev. Stat. Ann. §28-937 (Arizona); Ark. Code Ann. §27-36-219 (Arkansas); Conn. Gen. Stat. Ann. §14-96n (Connecticut); 21 Del. Code Ann. tit. 21, §4345 (Delaware); D.C. Mun. Regs. tit. 18, §739 (SMV emblem requirement applies only to motor vehicles), D.C. Code §8-2006 (animal-drawn vehicles in the "horse-drawn carriage trade" required to display SMV emblem) (District of Columbia); Iowa Admin. Code §761-452.3(321) (Iowa); Me. Rev. Stat. Ann. tit. 29, §1925 (Maine); Mich. Comp. Laws Ann. §257.688 (Michigan) (although §257.688(g) would require the SMV emblem,

lanterns on back and/or front of animal-drawn vehicles is required. *See, e.g.*, Ariz. Rev. Stat. Ann. §28-937; Ark. Code Ann. §27-36-219. Other jurisdictions mandate the additional requirement of red reflectors. *See, e.g.*, Conn. Gen. Stat. Ann. §14-96n. Still others permit those with objection to the SMV triangle to use a certain amount of reflective tape. *See, e.g.*, Iowa Admin. Code §761-452.3(321) (permitting the use of at least seventy-two inches of black, gray, silver, or white reflective material as alternative to emblem).

Clearly, at least some of these alternatives to the SMV emblem required by KRS 189.820 are less restrictive on Appellants' freedom to exercise religion according to the dictates of their consciences. Whether the SMV emblem is *more effective* than these alternatives is irrelevant so long as the alternatives are *viable*. Of course, "[t]o be a 'less restrictive alternative,' [the alternative] must be both less restrictive in the sense that it inhibits [the free exercise of religion] to a lesser degree and it must be a viable alternative in that it allows the Government to achieve the ends that are its compelling interest." *Playboy Entm't Grp., Inc. v. United States*, 30 F.Supp.2d 702, 717 (D. Del. 1998). I believe that there are viable, less restrictive alternatives to the SMV emblem.

For example, Appellants testified that they were using a plausible alternative to the SMV emblem in the form of over one hundred square inches of gray reflective tape, plus lanterns at nighttime. The Appellants' expert witness, a highway safety expert with specific expertise in Amish buggy safety, testified that the reflective tape/lantern combination used by Appellants is a viable alternative to the SMV emblem and one that is used in several other jurisdictions. Additionally, the alternative slowmoving vehicle requirements in other states all appear to be both viable and less restrictive than the SMV emblem required by KRS 189.820. *See supra* note 4.

In fact, since Appellants' convictions, Kentucky has joined these states in finding an effective way to advance roadway safety with respect to slow moving vehicles in a manner that does not interfere with the Swartzentruber Amish's beliefs. Effective April 11, 2012, the General Assembly modified KRS 189.820 to add subsection (4) which allows use of reflective tape instead of the SMV triangle.[12] Thus, Kentucky's own legislature has found an acceptable, less restrictive alternative to address its roadway

---

Appellants brief indicates that after *Michigan v. Swartzentruber*, 170 Mich. App. 682, 429 N.W.2d 225 (1988), horse-drawn buggies driven by Amish may display reflector tape and red lanterns); *State v. Hershberger*, 462 N.W.2d 393 (Minn. 1990) (Minnesota); Miss. Code Ann. §63-7-91 (Mississippi); N.J. Stat. Ann. §39:4-25 (New Jersey); N.M. Stat. Ann. §66-3-887 (New Mexico); N.Y. Comp. Codes R. & Regs. tit. 15, §68.8(c) (New York); (no applicable law) (North Carolina); N.D. Cent. Code Ann. §§39-21-50 and 39-21-16 (North Dakota); Ohio Rev. Code Ann. §4513.11, Ohio Admin. Code 4501-39-03 (Ohio); R.I. Gen. Laws Ann. §§31-23-47 and 31-24-35 (Rhode Island); S.C. Code Ann. §56-5-4650 (South Carolina); Tenn. Code Ann. §55-9-401 (Tennessee); Vt. Stat. Ann. tit. 23, §1361 (Vermont); W. Va. Code Ann. §§17C-15-16, 17C-15-2 (West Virginia); Wis. Stat. Ann. §347.245 held unconstitutional as applied to Old Order Amish by *State v. Miller*, 196 Wis.2d 238, 538 N.W.2d 573 (Wis. App. 1995); according to Appellants' brief, the use of white reflective tape and a lantern may be used as an alternative safety measure (Wisconsin); Wyo. Stat. Ann. §31-5-921 (Wyoming).

12. KRS 189.820(4) provides:

> As an alternative to the slow-moving vehicle emblem, one (l)-inch-wide white or silver reflective tape may be used on motorless slow-moving vehicles as follows:

safety concerns. Accordingly, I believe that the Commonwealth failed to satisfy its burden of proving that the SMV emblem is the least restrictive alternative to achieving its compelling interest.

III. Conclusion

In light of the foregoing, I would hold that strict scrutiny applies to laws infringing upon the free exercise of religion under Sections 1 and 5 of Kentucky's Constitution. Applying strict scrutiny, I would hold that: (1) Appellants have satisfied their requirement of establishing a sincerely-held religious belief, and that KRS 189.820 significantly burdens their constitutional rights; (2) the Commonwealth has a compelling interest in highway safety for all, and specifically in ensuring the visibility of slow-moving vehicles; and (3) the Commonwealth failed to prove that requiring the display of the SMV emblem is the least restrictive alternative to achieving that interest. I would therefore hold KRS 189.820 unconstitutional as applied to the Swartzentruber Amish, and reverse the judgment of the Court of Appeals.

Abramson, J., joins.

Notes and Questions

1. Just as Congress responded to *Employment Division, Department of Human Resources of Oregon v. Smith*, 494 U.S. 872 (1990), by enacting the Religious Freedom Restoration Act (RFRA), the General Assembly responded to *Gingerich* in 2013 by enacting a state-level RFRA, which is now codified at KRS 446.350. That statute provides: "Government shall not substantially burden a person's freedom of religion. The right to act or refuse to act in a manner motivated by a sincerely held religious belief may not be substantially burdened unless the government proves by clear and convincing evidence that it has a compelling governmental interest in infringing the specific act or refusal to act and has used the least restrictive means to further that interest. A 'burden' shall include indirect burdens such as withholding benefits, assessing penalties, or an exclusion from programs or access to facilities."
2. In explaining the scope of Section 5's protection of "rights of conscience," the author of one law review article has explained the difference between belief and exercise in terms of three concentric circles: inner personal conscientious belief being within the innermost circle; worship, being the outward manifestation of belief in a religious setting, lies within the second circle; and exercise, which the author defines as "the right to act in all of life in accordance with conscience," lies within the outermost circle. *See* Samuel Weaver, *Protecting Unbelief: Restoring Section Five of Kentucky's*

(a) The rear of the vehicle shall be covered with a minimum of one hundred (100) square inches of the reflective tape;

(b) The reflective tape on the rear of the vehicle shall, at a minimum, outline the entire rear of the vehicle;

(c) Each side of the vehicle shall be covered with a minimum of thirty-six (36) square inches of reflective tape; and

(d) The highest point of the left front of the vehicle shall be covered with a minimum of twenty-four (24) square inches of reflective tape.

Constitution, 110 Ky. L.J. 173, 180 (2022). The article argues that "rights of conscience" is "broader at the core" than purely religious belief; therefore, "Kentucky's provision establishes a much broader base of protection [than the First Amendment], which then extends outward to protect exercise based thereon." *Id.* at 180–81. Because "the phrase 'rights of conscience' by its nature protects religious and non-religious belief *and exercise*," *id.* at 184 (emphasis in original), the author argued that *Gingerich* was wrongly decided. Did the Court correctly construe Section 5's guarantee that "[n]o human authority shall, in any case whatever, control or interfere with the rights of conscience"? Is the scope of "rights of conscience" under Section 5 no greater than the scope of the Free Exercise Clause?

3. Justice Venters's concurrence in *Gingerich* echoed his concurrence in *Blue Movies, Inc. v. Louisville/Jefferson County Metro Government*, 317 S.W.3d 23 (Ky. 2010), decided two years earlier, in which he argued that the Supreme Court of Kentucky should not tether its interpretation of individual provisions of the Kentucky Constitution to the U.S. Supreme Court's interpretation of comparable provisions of the U.S. Constitution.

4. Related to the free exercise of religion is the concept of state non-interference in the internal affairs of religious organizations. The U.S. Supreme Court has long recognized the freedom of religious organizations "from secular control or manipulation, in short, power to decide for themselves, free from state interference, matters of church government as well as those of faith and doctrine." *Kedroff v. St. Nicholas Cathedral of Russian Orthodox Church in N. Am.*, 344 U.S. 94, 116 (1952). More recently, in *Hosanna-Tabor Evangelical Lutheran Church & School v. EEOC*, 565 U.S. 171 (2012), the U.S. Supreme Court recognized for the first time the "ministerial exception" to the Civil Rights Act of 1964 and other civil rights laws, which "precludes application of such legislation to claims concerning the employment relationship between a religious institution and its ministers." *Id.* at 188. The Court found the ministerial exception was derived from both Free Exercise and Establishment Clause principles: "The members of a religious group put their faith in the hands of their ministers. Requiring a church to accept or retain an unwanted minister, or punishing a church for failing to do so, intrudes upon more than a mere employment decision. Such action interferes with the internal governance of the church, depriving the church of control over the selection of those who will personify its beliefs. By imposing an unwanted minister, the state infringes the Free Exercise Clause, which protects a religious group's right to shape its own faith and mission through its appointments. According the state the power to determine which individuals will minister to the faithful also violates the Establishment Clause, which prohibits government involvement in such ecclesiastical decisions." *Id.* at 188–89. Thus, the church in *Hosanna-Tabor* was free to dismiss a ministerial employee who did not comply with its religious beliefs.

   Religious organizations' independence in "matters of church government," the Court observed in *Our Lady of Guadalupe School v. Morrissey-Berru*, 591 U.S. ___, 140 S.Ct. 2049 (2020), "protect their autonomy with respect to internal management decisions that are essential to the institution's central mission. And a component of this autonomy is the selection of the individuals who play certain key roles." *Id.* at 2060. The Court in *Our Lady of Guadalupe* extended the ministerial exception to apply to parochial school teachers because "educating young people in their faith, inculcating its teachings, and training them to live their faith are responsibilities that lie at the very core of the mission of a private religious school," and "[w]hat matters, at bottom, is what an employee does." *Id.* at 2064.

The Supreme Court of Kentucky has adopted the ministerial exception in Kentucky, but not as a matter of state constitutional law. In *Kirby v. Lexington Theological Seminary*, 426 S.W.3d 597 (Ky. 2014), the Court "explicitly adopt[ed] the ministerial exception as applicable to employment claims—especially discrimination claims—asserted against a religious institutional employer by an employee who is directly involved in promulgating and espousing the tenets of the employer's faith." *Id.* at 601. The Court understood the ministerial exception as "a narrow, more focused subsidiary of the ecclesiastical abstention doctrine." *Id.* at 604. In *Kirby*, the ministerial exception barred a seminary professor's civil rights claims because he qualified as a minister. But in another case decided the same day as *Kirby*, the Court held that the claims of another professor at the same seminary, who did not qualify as a minister, were not barred by the ministerial exception. *Kant v. Lexington Theological Seminary*, 426 S.W.3d 587 (Ky. 2014).

The ministerial exception must be raised as an affirmative defense to litigation, and it is therefore analogous to a government official's defense of qualified immunity. *Kirby*, 426 S.W.3d at 608.

The related ecclesiastical abstention doctrine holds that, "[i]n such matters relating to the faith and practice of the church and its members, the decision of the church court is not only supreme, but is wholly without the sphere of legal or secular judicial inquiry." *Kirby*, 426 S.W.3d at 618 (quoting *Marsh v. Johnson*, 259 Ky. 305, 82 S.W.2d 345, 346 (1935)). Under the doctrine, "the secular courts have no jurisdiction over ecclesiastical controversies and will not interfere with religious judicature or with any decision of a church tribunal relating to its internal affairs, as in matters of discipline or excision, or of purely ecclesiastical cognizance. Secular courts may, however, have jurisdiction over a case involving a church if neutral principles of law can be applied in reaching the resolution." *Id.* (cleaned up). The test is whether the plaintiff's claim "can be decided without wading into doctrinal waters." *Id.* at 620. Thus, the ecclesiastical abstention doctrine did not bar a seminary professor's breach of contract claim that did not involve any matter of ecclesiastical concern.

The ecclesiastical abstention doctrine does not divest a court of subject matter jurisdiction, but only jurisdiction over specific cases "pervaded by religious issues." *St. Joseph Catholic Orphan Soc'y v. Edwards*, 449 S.W.3d 727, 736–37 (Ky. 2014). It is therefore an affirmative defense that must be pleaded and proved by a litigation defendant. *Id.* at 737.

Religious Establishments and State Support of Religion

Rawlings v. Butler

Court of Appeals of Kentucky (1956)
290 S.W.2d 801

Opinion of the Court by Judge Sims.

This appeal is from a judgment of the Franklin Circuit Court denying an injunction and dismissing the complaint. J. C. Rawlings, as a citizen and taxpayer of Marion County, brought this class action against Wendell P. Butler, Superintendent of Public Instruction in Kentucky, and the Boards of Education of Casey, Marion, Washington, Nelson, Meade and Grayson Counties, in which he questioned on constitutional grounds the right of the State Superintendent and of the respective Boards of Education to expend public tax money in the payment of the salaries of nuns of the Roman Catholic Church teaching in the public schools of these counties when dressed in religious garb and wearing symbols of their religion; as well as the payment of rent to the Catholic Church for buildings in which public schools are taught; and the cost of transporting Catholic children to parochial schools. An injunction was asked against appellees to prevent them from this averred illegal expenditure of public funds raised by taxation, and of school funds.

The case was tried before the court upon a stipulation which showed these facts. The Sisters are all members of orders or religious communities within the Roman Catholic Church and each recognizes the Pontiff of that church as her spiritual superior. She lives and teaches under her religious name, and regularly turns over her compensation as a teacher, after deducting living expenses, to her order or religious community. 'She has assumed the religious relationship peculiar to her order, and has taken a vow of chastity, poverty, and obedience as hereafter defined. She owes obedience to the superiors of her order in spiritual matters; the reference to 'poverty' means that each sister delegates to some other person the right to control and manage any property which she might own.'

It is further stipulated, 'These Sisters, at all times during their teaching services, wear clothing similar to the following: 'The Dominican Sisters' Habit comprises a tunic and scapular of white wool. The tunic is girded with a leather belt to which is attached a rosary. The head is covered with a veil, a guimpe and a white linen headband. A mantle of black wool is worn when traveling.'

The stipulation shows that the various County School Boards involved have the following number of Sisters teaching in their public, tax-supported schools: 'Casey County, 2 Sisters; Marion County, 43 Sisters; Washington County, 9 Sisters; Nelson County, 13 Sisters; Meade County, 14 Sisters; Grayson County, 3 Sisters.'

It is stipulated the school boards of these counties conduct public schools in properties owned by the Catholic Church and rented to the boards at the following prices: 'Casey County—1 building— rent free; Washington County—1 building—rent free; Marion County—various rooms—$75 per room per year; Nelson County—1 building—$900 per year; Meade County—1 building—$32 per year and 1 building—$200 per year; Grayson County—1 building—$2400 per year.'

That part of the stipulation relating to the transportation cost of children shows the Nelson County Board of Education expended for transportation of pupils during the school year 1953–1954 a total of $66,198.13, including a depreciation of 10% on school buses, amounting to $7,372.94; that parochial pupils are 19.1 per cent and public school pupils are 80.9 per cent of the total number of pupils transported; that the Nelson County Fiscal Court for that school year appropriated $10,000 to the County School Board under KRS 158.115 for the transportation of elementary pupils of parochial schools; that the school buses travel a total of 1,731.5 miles per day in picking up all students in Nelson County, with a total of 1,568 stops made per day, of which 222 stops are for parochial students only; that the total mileage occasioned by picking up parochial students only is 23.1 miles.

At the outset of his brief appellant explains he does not question the scholastic standards or the moral qualifications of the Sisters to teach in public schools; and he does not question the right of the 'ordinary Roman Catholic citizen to teach in our free public schools.' Nor does appellant contend the Sisters teach the tenets of the Catholic Church. His sole objection to their teaching is based upon the fact they wear their religious garb and emblems in the classrooms and donate their compensation to their respective religious orders after the payment of their living expenses.

The framers of the Federal Constitution, as well as the authors of the Constitutions of the various States, were careful 'to preserve and perpetuate religious liberty, and to guard against the slightest ... inequality in the civil and political rights of citizens, which shall have for its basis only their differences of religious belief.... The general voice has been, that persons of every religious persuasion should be made equal before the law, and that questions of religious belief and religious worship should be questions between each individual man and his Maker.' 2 Cooley's Const. Lim. 8 Ed. p. 960.

Judge Cooley further wrote, 'Those things which are not lawful under any of the American Constitutions may be stated thus: ... Compulsory support, by taxation or otherwise of religious instruction. Not only is no one denomination to be favored at the expense of the rest, but all support of religious instruction must be entirely voluntary. It is not within the sphere of government to coerce it.' 2 Cooley's Const. Lim. 8 Ed. pp. 966, 967.

Article 6 and the First Amendment of the Federal Constitution and §§1 and 5 of the Kentucky Constitution guarantee religious freedom to the citizens of this Commonwealth; while §§171 and 189 of our Constitution forbid the use of money raised by taxation for public purposes, or for educational purposes, to be used in the aid of any church, sectarian or denominational school.

While the dress and emblems worn by these Sisters proclaim them to be members of certain organizations of the Roman Catholic Church and that they have taken certain religious vows, these facts do not deprive them of their right to teach in public schools, so long as they do not inject religion or the dogma of their church. The garb does not teach. It is the woman within who teaches. The dress of the Sisters denotes modesty, unworldliness and an unselfish life. No mere significance or insignificance of garb could conceal a teacher's character. Her daily life would either exalt or make obnoxious the sectarian belief of a teacher.

Our General Assembly has not yet prescribed what dress a woman teaching in the public schools must wear, or whether she may adorn herself with a ring, button, or any other emblem signifying she is a member of a sorority. These Sisters are not teaching religion in the public schools or attempting to force their religious views on the pupils under their charge. The religious views of these Sisters and their mode of dress are entirely personal to them. If they were prevented from teaching in the public schools because of their religious beliefs, then they would be denied equal protection of the law in violation of the Fourteenth Amendment of the Federal Constitution. *Cantwell v. State of Connecticut*, 310 U.S. 296, 60 S.Ct. 900, 84 L.Ed. 1213.

* * *

We reach a more difficult question under §189 of our Constitution: 'No portion of any fund or tax now existing, or that may hereafter be raised or levied for educational purposes, shall be appropriated to, or used by, or in aid of, any church, sectarian or denominational school.'

The United States Supreme Court in the *Slaughter-House Cases*, 16 Wall. 36, 127, 83 U.S. 36, 127, 21 L.Ed. 394, 425, wrote that labor is property and one has the right to dispose of property according to the will of the owner. The salaries paid these Sisters are theirs and they may do therewith as they choose. One employed by the state or any of its subdivisions is not forbidden under §189 from contributing any part, or all, of the salary earned to a religious body of which he or she is a member. To deny such right of contribution would be a denial of religious liberty. *Hysong v. Gallitzin Borough School District*, 164 Pa. 629, 30 A. 482, 26 L.R.A. 203, 44 Am.St.Rep. 632; *Gerhardt v. Heid*, 66 N.D. 444, 267 N.W. 127, 135; *State ex rel. Johnson v. Boyd*, 217 Ind. 348, 28 N.E.2d 256.

From the stipulation in the record it appears the Sisters are paid like other teachers, and after providing for their living expenses, they contribute the balance of their compensation to the orders to which they belong. Their vow of poverty is not controlling from a legal angle. Many people are poverty stricken without taking such vows. The vow of obedience to ecclesiastical and secular authorities is not uncommon in the lives of people. No one can object to the vow of chastity. In *Zellers v. Huff*, 55 N.M. 501, 236 P.2d 949, at page 962, it was held there was no violation of the New Mexico Constitution, forbidding public funds to be used for the support of a church, when the Sisters turned over to the Catholic Church their compensation received as teachers after deducting actual living expenses. However, we would have a different question if these Sisters were but the conduits through which public school funds are channeled into the coffers of the Catholic Church. Then §189 could be violated. But where the Sisters are paid separately and endorse their own checks, then they may dispose of their earnings as they desire.

We can see no constitutional objection to the various county school boards concerned in this litigation renting buildings from the Catholic Church in which to conduct schools, since the church in no manner attempts to influence or control the way the schools are conducted or operated or how they are taught. This question was disposed of contrary to appellant's contention in *Crain v. Walker*, 222 Ky. 828, 2 S.W.2d 654, at page 659. It was there written it was not the intention of §189 to withhold the right to teach school in buildings rented from any particular religious denomination where that denomination did not attempt to influence or exercise any control over the school or how it was taught. From what is said in the *Crain* opinion on page 659 of *Williams v. Board of Trustees*, 173 Ky. 708, 191 S.W. 507, L.R.A.1917D, 453, it is evident that the facts in the *Williams* case distinguish it from the one at bar. In *Kentucky Building Commission v. Effron*, 310 Ky. 355, 220 S.W.2d 836, at page 838, we said §5 of our Constitution was not violated when funds were given to a hospital carrying the name of a religious denomination and governed by a board whose members were of a particular faith, in the event the hospital received patients regardless of faith or creed.

Here, the fact that two of the buildings were furnished free of rent by the Catholic Church and another was rented to the School Board for the nominal sum of $32 per year, does not affect the constitutional question so long as the church does not attempt to exercise any dominion or control over the school or classes taught therein and the Board has full and complete control of the buildings throughout the school year.

The stipulation does not show the buildings rented to the school boards by the church were under the same roof as the church or church school, or were immediately adjoining the church or the priest house, or that the nuns resided in the buildings rented to the county school boards, or that these buildings had religious emblems on them. The facts in the *Berghorn* case, 364 Mo. 121, 260 S.W.2d 573, 576, show such conditions did exist in Missouri. And it seems that practically the same conditions existed in New Mexico as in Missouri, because in the *Zellers* opinion, 55 N.M. 501, 236 P.2d 949, it is written on page 954, 'In short, New Mexico had a Roman Catholic school system supported by public funds within its public school system.' The record before us does not show the Catholic Church attempted in any way to influence the teaching in the schools conducted in the buildings and rooms rented from it, or attempted to exercise any dominion over these schools. So far as this record shows, they were conducted in the same manner as other public schools in the respective counties.

We find no provisions of the Federal Constitution or of the Kentucky Constitution which are violated by the Sisters teaching while wearing religious garb and emblems, or in donating to their religious orders the lion's share of their salaries, or in the various school boards renting buildings from the Roman Catholic Church in which public schools are conducted. As the circuit court so held, this part of its judgment is affirmed.

* * *

The judgment is affirmed in part and reversed in part.

Hogg, J., dissents.

Judge Hogg, dissenting.

In good conscience I cannot agree with the majority opinion. While I have no sectarian prejudice and no sense of religious intolerance, and while I profoundly respect the religious faith of the membership of the Catholic Church, as I do the creeds of all church denominations, at the same time I deeply respect and strongly adhere to the fundamental principle established by the wisdom of the founding fathers of the absolute and unequivocal separation of church and state.

It is the determined policy and purpose of the American people that our public school system, supported by taxation of all alike—Catholic, Protestant, Jew, believer and infidel—shall not be used directly or indirectly for religious instruction. Above all, that no school shall be made an instrumentality of proselyting influence in favor of any religious organization, sect, creed or belief. *Knowlton v. Baumhover*, 182 Iowa 691, 166 N.W. 202, 207, 5 A.L.R. 841. And, as said in that opinion: 'To constitute a sectarian school or sectarian instruction which may not lawfully be maintained at public expense, it is not necessary to show that the school is wholly devoted to religious or sectarian teaching.' What is generally regarded as sectarianism, or the special tenets of any branch of any church, whether it be Christian or Jew or Moslem, must not be directly or indirectly or subtly taught or inculcated in our system of public schools.

* * *

The distinctive garbs, so exclusively peculiar to the Roman Catholic Church, create a religious atmosphere in the school-room. They have a subtle influence upon the tender minds being taught and trained by the nuns. In and of themselves they proclaim the Catholic Church and the representative character of the teachers in the schoolroom. They silently promulgate sectarianism.

Indeed, these good women are the Catholic Church in action in the most fertile field—the impressionable minds of the children. * * *

It is well known that the Catholic Church maintains its own parochial schools and forbids its children attending the public schools—as it has the perfect right to do. * * * The children who attend the public schools and their parents are, with rare exceptions, Protestants. But by the majority opinion these children and their parents are deprived of their constitutional right to be free from sectarian influence and indirect teachings of the Catholic Church at public expense. It is of significance that the nuns pursue their vocations of nursing and teaching and charitable service in Catholic institutions excepting only when opportunity is afforded to teach in public schools; and Catholic children do not attend public schools except where teachers are nuns.

* * *

The garbs of the Catholic Sisters are not merely an odd mode or style of dress nor mere badges of office or tokens of sisterhood. The habit is strictly and prominently religious. Its purpose proclaims identity and doctrinal religious service.

If some of the many school-teachers who are members of the Baptist or Methodist or any other Protestant Church should withdraw from outside activities except those of their Church and reside in a community home apart from all other people and become subservient to ecclesiastical authority and wear some distinctive garb or uniform setting them apart from others of their profession and wear conspicuous badges prominently declaiming, 'I am a Baptist,' or Methodist, or the like, with insignia that they are devoting their complete lives in the service of their denominational churches; or if clergymen should go into the schoolroom as teachers wearing their canonical robes, with prayer books suspended from their necks, I would be the first to condemn the practice and to declare that this was the injection of the particular denominational religion into the schoolhouse and teaching of the children.

By no stretch of the imagination would I deny the Sisters the right to teach in our public schools. Let these Sisters when in the schoolrooms exchange their religious raiment and insignia for a dress or garment that is without distinctive suggestion and which does not itself proclaim sectarianism in action, and I shall be the first to approve.

Upon reason and authority, I respectfully dissent from the majority opinion to the extent indicated.

Notes and Questions

1. In *Rawlings*, the majority found that the nuns who taught in the public schools, absent a dress code that applied to all teachers, had a right under Sections 1 and 5 to wear their habits while teaching. The dissent, on the other hand, believed that the nuns' distinctive apparel "silently promulgate[d] sectarianism." Which opinion made the better argument? Would the Court have reached the same result if the teachers instead wore t-shirts with a religious message on them?
2. The nuns received paychecks, which they then signed over to their religious orders. The Court said this did not violate Section 189 because the local school boards were not making direct payments to the church. However, it distinguished a hypothetical direct payment to the church, which it said would present "a different question." Is the distinction the Court made one with a difference?
3. The Court also held that the payment of rent to the Catholic Church for the use of its buildings for educational purposes was constitutional under Section 189. Though not discussed in the opinion, would these rent payments also be consistent with Section 3 of the Constitution?

University of the Cumberlands v. Pennybacker

Supreme Court of Kentucky (2010)
308 S.W.3d 668

OPINION OF THE COURT BY JUSTICE ABRAMSON.

In the 2006 Budget Bill, the Kentucky General Assembly appropriated $10 million for the construction of a pharmacy school building on the campus of the University of the Cumberlands, a Baptist college located in Whitley County. The legislature also appropriated $1 million for a Pharmacy Scholarship Program to benefit pharmacy students "at a private four (4) year institution of higher education with a main campus located in an Appalachian Regional Commission county...." KRS 164.7901(1). In a declaratory judgment action challenging both appropriations, the Franklin Circuit Court held that the Pharmacy School appropriation violated Sections 5 and 189 of the Kentucky Constitution and the Pharmacy Scholarship Program violated Section 51. This Court granted transfer of the case from the Court of Appeals pursuant to Kentucky Rule of Civil Procedure 74.02. Following review of the record and applicable law, we affirm the circuit court's holding that the Pharmacy School appropriation violates Section 189, which prohibits public funding of "any church, sectarian or denominational school," and further find the Pharmacy Scholarship Program violates Section 59, which prohibits special legislation.

Relevant Facts

The University of the Cumberlands, Inc. (UC), formerly Cumberland College, is a private university founded by Baptists in 1887 and located in Williamsburg, Whitley County, Kentucky. UC is accredited by the Commission on Colleges of the Southern Association of Colleges and Schools and is affiliated with both the Southern Baptist Convention and the Kentucky Baptist Convention. According to UC, it currently provides approximately 1700 students from "diverse religious backgrounds, a liberal arts education enriched with Christian values." Under a 1986 Covenant Agreement between UC and the Kentucky Baptist Convention, as well as the 2005 Restated Articles of Incorporation for UC, if the corporate entity ever dissolves all assets are to be distributed to the Kentucky Baptist Convention.

On April 11, 2006, in its biennial budget bill, the General Assembly approved $10 million in public bond financing for the construction of a pharmacy school on the UC campus. HB 380, 2006 Ky. Acts 252. The bonds are to be sold by the Kentucky Infrastructure Authority to private investors with the principal on the bonds paid from coal severance taxes levied pursuant to KRS 143.020 and the interest paid from the General Fund.

HB 380 also included a $1 million allocation from the General Fund to a Pharmacy Scholarship Program. That provision, codified at KRS 164.7901 provides in subsection (1):

> It is the intent of the General Assembly to establish a scholarship program to provide eligible Kentucky students the opportunity to attend an accredited

> school of pharmacy at a private four (4) year institution of higher education with a main campus located in an Appalachian Regional Commission county in the Commonwealth and become certified pharmacists in the Commonwealth.

Subsection 3 provides that scholarship recipients must be Kentucky residents enrolled full-time in a Kentucky pharmacy school and must provide one year of service as a pharmacist in Kentucky for each year the scholarship is awarded. The scholarship amount is set forth in subsection (4) which provides:

> The amount of the scholarship awarded to an eligible student by the authority shall be equal to the difference between:
>
> (a) The amount charged for in-state tuition at the University of Kentucky College of Pharmacy; and
>
> (b) The prevailing amount charged for tuition at the institution in which the student is enrolled.

After the initial funding, the "special trust fund" necessary to sustain the Scholarship Program is to be generated from coal severance tax revenues levied under KRS 143.020. KRS 164.7901(11) provides that up to 4% of the coal severance tax revenues collected annually "shall be transferred to the special trust fund ... in an amount that permits each Kentucky resident eligible" under the statute to receive a scholarship award as provided in subsection (4), i.e., the difference between UK Pharmacy School tuition and the institution's tuition.

After Governor Ernie L. Fletcher declined to veto the aforementioned appropriations, Appellee Christina Gilgor filed a declaratory judgment action against the Governor on April 25, 2006 challenging both the Pharmacy School and the Pharmacy Scholarship Program appropriations as violating specific provisions of the Kentucky Constitution. Subsequently, through amended complaints, the Kentucky Fairness Alliance, the Jefferson County Teachers Association and two taxpayers, Rev. Albert M. Pennybacker and Rev. Dr. Paul D. Simmons, also became plaintiffs. The Franklin Circuit Court later allowed UC and a group of thirteen members of the General Assembly to intervene as defendants in support of the challenged legislation. For clarity, those challenging the legislation are hereafter referred to as "Plaintiffs" and those defending it are collectively referred to as "Defendants".

Twenty months after HB 380 passed, on December 10, 2007, UC and the Governor's Office for Local Development entered into a Memorandum of Understanding (MOU) designed to address some of the issues raised in the declaratory judgment action. UC committed in the MOU *inter alia* that no portion of the funds would be "used for any church, sectarian or denominational purpose" and that if the building ever ceased to be used as a pharmacy school it would revert to Whitley County.

Meanwhile, UC had moved for summary judgment in October, 2007 and Plaintiffs had filed a response and counter-motion for summary judgment in November. Following additional briefing and oral arguments, the circuit court entered its Judgment and Order on March 6, 2008 granting Plaintiffs' cross-motion for summary judgment and declaring both appropriations unconstitutional. UC and the intervening legislators filed timely appeals and this Court granted transfer of those appeals from the Court of Appeals pursuant to CR 74.02.

Analysis

I. The Pharmacy School Appropriation for UC Violates Section 189 of the Kentucky Constitution.

Kentucky's fourth and present Constitution, adopted in 1891, includes in Section 5 a "Right of religious freedom." In pertinent part, the provision states that "no preference shall ever be given by law to any religious sect, society or denomination; ..."[1] In the sections of the Constitution pertaining to "Education" the drafters addressed religious schools in Section 189 which states: "No portion of any fund or tax now existing, or that may hereafter be raised or levied for educational purposes, shall be appropriated to, or used by, or in aid of, any church, sectarian or denominational school." These two specific provisions along with Section 171, which provides in relevant part that "taxes shall be levied and collected for public purposes only," form the basis of Plaintiffs' challenge to the Pharmacy School appropriation. Because we find the appropriation violative of Section 189, we need not address the other constitutional infirmities they allege.[2]

A. Section 189 Prohibits Appropriations of Public Funds to Religious Schools.

Beginning with the language of Section 189, and more specifically the closing phrase of the provision, it is apparent that UC is a "church, sectarian or denominational school." From its founding by the Mt. Zion Association of Baptists in September 1887 through its present day Covenant Agreement with the Kentucky Baptist Convention (KBC), UC has been supported by members and churches of the Baptist faith. According to the Covenant Agreement, KBC's primary purpose in supporting UC is "to advance the Kingdom of God in the area of Christian higher education. Such purpose should at all times be recognizable within the ministry of Cumberland College [now UC]." Although UC agreed in the December 2007 Memorandum of Understanding not to use any of the pharmacy building funds for "church, sectarian or denominational" purposes, this MOU cannot change the character of the institution itself. It is precisely the type of school referenced in Section 189, and clearly state funds have been

1. "No preference shall ever be given by law to any religious sect, society or denomination; nor to any particular creed, mode of worship or system of ecclesiastical polity; nor shall any person be compelled to attend any place of worship, to contribute to the erection or maintenance of any such place, or to the salary or support to any minister of religion; nor shall any man be compelled to send his child to any school to which he may be conscientiously opposed; and the civil rights, privileges or capacities of no person shall be taken away, or in anywise diminished or enlarged, on account of his belief or disbelief of any religious tenet, dogma or teaching. No human authority shall, in any case whatever, control or interfere with the rights of conscience."

2. Plaintiffs also alleged the Pharmacy School appropriation violated Sections 2, 3 and 184 of the Kentucky Constitution.

"appropriated to, or [will be] used by, or in aid of" the school. Thus, our focus turns to the opening phrases of the section.

Section 189 begins with the following language: "[n]o portion of any fund or tax now existing, or that may hereafter be raised or levied for educational purposes...." The phrase "for educational purposes" plainly modifies "raised or levied" so the section literally focuses on the purpose for which the funds or taxes were collected. However, given Kentucky jurisprudence, Defendants have couched their primary defense of the pharmacy school in terms of whether the appropriation itself was for an educational purpose. Because this construction of the section has some basis in precedent, it is necessary to consider both the purpose for which the funds were appropriated and the purpose for which the funds were "raised or levied" in the first instance. We begin with the former construction that focuses on the purpose for which the funds will be used.

Relying on *Kentucky Building Comm. v. Effron*, 310 Ky. 355, 220 S.W.2d 836 (1949), Defendants insist the funds to construct the Pharmacy School building were appropriated for a "health and welfare purpose" rather than "educational purposes." Specifically, they maintain that the shortage of pharmacists in Kentucky generally and in the Appalachian area particularly prompted the legislature to act.[3] Assuming this legislative intent, this argument begs the question—how can an appropriation to construct a pharmacy school not entail an educational purpose? What could the construction of a building possibly accomplish in addressing the alleged shortage of pharmacists in the Commonwealth unless faculty are retained and students are then recruited and educated in a manner that will enable them to pass the requisite professional licensing examinations? The $10 million appropriation is for bricks and mortar but its ultimate purpose is to provide a venue for the education of pharmacy students.

Education was not an issue in *Effron*, *supra*, the case Defendants primarily rely upon. To take advantage of federal funding for the construction of public and nonprofit hospitals, the Kentucky General Assembly appropriated funds to hospitals associated with the Episcopal Church and the Roman Catholic Church. The hospitals served the health care needs of Kentuckians and, significantly, had no educational mission. This Court's predecessor found the appropriations constitutional noting "[t]he hospitals are open to the public of all creeds and faiths—and even to those who profess no certain religious belief. Religion is not taught in these hospitals nor is any one sect given preference over another." 220 S.W.2d at 838. The *Effron* Court contrasted the case before it with prior cases involving appropriations for parochial school students noting specifically that "[section] 189 of our Constitution forbids the use of any taxes levied for educational purposes from being appropriated in aid of any private, sectarian or denominational schools." *Id.*

3. Plaintiffs argue that the record is void of any legislative or executive branch consideration of a shortage of pharmacists or pharmacy schools in Kentucky generally or the Appalachian region specifically prior to the passage of HB 380. While there may be merit to this point, it has no bearing on our disposition of the constitutional issues before this Court.

By contrast, education was at issue in *Fannin v. Williams*, 655 S.W.2d 480 (Ky. 1983), a case in which this Court invalidated a statute that supplied textbooks to children attending nonpublic schools. In *Fannin*, this Court concluded that the funds were not being spent for "public purposes", as required by Section 171 of the Kentucky Constitution, and that because it was impossible to classify the textbooks "as anything but educational" the appropriation violated Section 189. 655 S.W.2d at 482–84. As to Section 171, the Court noted that "nonpublic schools are open to selected people in the state, as contrasted with public schools which are open to 'all people in the state'". *Id.* at 482. The *Fannin* Court addressed the intersection of public purpose and education, acknowledging that education is definitely a public purpose but concluding that the Kentucky Constitution is unyielding as to where public funds can be used for educational purposes.

> In sum, the Kentucky Constitution contemplates that public funds shall be expended for public education. The Commonwealth is obliged to furnish every child in this state an education in the public schools, but it is constitutionally proscribed from providing aid to furnish a private education. *Pollitt v. Lewis*, 269 Ky. 680, 108 S.W.2d 671 (1937). We cannot sell the people of Kentucky a mule and call it a horse, even if we believe the public needs a mule.
>
> Unlike the statute extending transportation to children in nonpublic schools, it is impossible to classify textbooks as anything but educational. As such the statute must meet the constitutional limitations of those sections of the Constitution covering "Education."
>
> One can argue, quite reasonably, that this statute (and any statute) furthering education is of public benefit, whether selective or not. Unfortunately, this approach begs the question, because the Constitution establishes a public school system and limits spending money for education to spending it in public schools.

655 S.W.2d at 484. Just as the textbooks in *Fannin* were unquestionably educational, a pharmacy school is unquestionably educational. As the trial court concluded, *Fannin*, not *Effron*, is the controlling precedent and the Pharmacy School appropriation is patently "for educational purposes."

Defendants also direct this Court's attention to an earlier case involving appropriations to nonpublic schools as indicative of the propriety of allowing public funds to private schools if a public purpose is evident. In *Butler v. United Cerebral Palsy of N. Ky., Inc.*, 352 S.W.2d 203 (Ky. 1961), with then-Judge, later Chief Justice, Palmore writing, the predecessor to this Court upheld a statute authorizing the payment of public funds to private institutions for the education of "exceptional children." The institutions involved in that case were schools operated by "nonsectarian charities", but the statute's use of the term "private schools" raised the spectre of violation of Section 189.

> We come lastly to the question of whether the act permits public funds to be used by sectarian or denominational schools in violation of Const. §189. It so happens that the schools involved in this lawsuit are nonsectarian charities, but the term 'private schools,' of course, admits of no such limitation. Literally

> it would appear to mean any school outside the common school system. However, we may properly indulge the presumption that the legislature did not intend to include schools to which the payments could not legally be made. It is not unreasonable to presume, for example, that the term was not meant to include schools not within the state, and it is equally reasonable to infer that it does not include schools that give sectarian instruction or have any denominational requirements with respect to their teachers or pupils.

352 S.W.2d at 208–09. Thus, *Butler* does not support Defendants' contention but quite squarely rejects it: appropriations to private schools can be constitutional but not if the school is a "church, sectarian or denominational school."

Defendants fare no better if we focus on the purpose for which the funds were raised. *Butler* merits closer examination because it identifies Kentucky precedent wherein the emphasis, at least in the "common school"[4] context, shifted from the purpose for which state funds were raised to the purpose for which the funds were appropriated or used. In fact, *Butler, supra*, confronted the closely related issue of the reference in Section 184 of the Kentucky Constitution to monies "raised or collected for education." That Court noted that in *Pollitt v. Lewis*, 269 Ky. 680, 108 S.W.2d 671, 672 (1937), the Court held that the restriction was on the "legislative power to expend money for education other than in the common schools" and not whether the funds were expressly raised for education. 352 S.W.2d at 207 (emphasis in original). Similarly, in *Talbott v. Ky. State Bd. of Education*, 244 Ky. 826, 52 S.W.2d 727 (1932), Kentucky's High Court held that "any funds raised by taxation become a part of the school fund as soon as they are appropriated for school purposes." 352 S.W.2d at 207. As *Butler* notes, however, there is dictum in at least one case to the contrary. *Hodgkin v. Bd. for Louisville & Jefferson Co. Children's Home*, 242 S.W.2d 1008 (Ky. 1951) (common school funds cannot be spent outside common school system but other state funds can be so spent.) The *Butler* Court did not have to resolve this issue because the nonsectarian schools in that case were not prohibited recipients of public funds. By contrast, we must address the comparable language in Section 189 regarding funds "raised or levied for educational purposes." Kentucky constitutional history supports the conclusion that Section 189 was specifically directed at postsecondary or higher education and, further, that the intent was to prohibit all public funding of sectarian or religious colleges.

Section 189 was adopted on March 11, 1890, during the 1890 Constitutional Convention, with virtually no discussion immediately preceding the vote. *Official Report of the Proceedings and Debates in the Convention Assembled at Frankfort on the Eighth Day of September, 1890, to Adopt, Amend or Change the Constitution of the State of Kentucky* [hereafter "*Official Report of the 1890 Convention*"] at 4606–07. However, the delegates had debated for two full days the contents of the "Education" portion of the Kentucky Constitution set forth in Sections 183–189. *Id.* at 4452–4606. There was much debate about what "common schools" encompassed and what, if any, role the

4. A "common school" is now defined in KRS 158.030 as "an elementary or secondary school of the state supported in whole or in part by public taxation."

state should play in providing higher education. Some delegates opposed any public support of schools with curricula that went beyond the rudiments of reading, writing and arithmetic, advocating that all higher education be left to sectarian schools or other private institutions.[5] Several delegates supported compulsory education for younger children but mandatory attendance at common schools did not find its way into the Kentucky Constitution. The wide-ranging debates addressed *inter alia* teacher education, parity among schools across the Commonwealth, the education of black schoolchildren, the length of the school year, nepotism in school hiring, and state financing of education at all levels.

To gain insight into the meaning of Section 189, it is necessary to understand Section 184, the provision establishing the "common school" fund which also was adopted on March 11, 1890. *Official Report of the 1890 Convention* at 4598–99. Section 184 identified the then existing bonds and stocks which would comprise the "common school" fund along with interest and dividends therefrom as well as "any sum which may be produced by taxation or otherwise for purposes of common school education." The section ends as follows:

> No sum shall be raised or collected for education other than in common schools until the question of taxation is submitted to the legal voters, and the majority of the votes cast at said election shall be in favor of such taxation: Provided, The tax now imposed for educational purposes, and for the endowment and maintenance of the Agricultural and Mechanical College, shall remain until changed by law.

The Agricultural and Mechanical College referred to in the closing sentence, now the University of Kentucky, was at the center of the fierce debate about state support of higher education. Several delegates, but most notably Judge William M. Beckner of Winchester in Clark County, the primary author of Section 189, urged continued state support of this fledgling institution for which the federal government had made an initial grant of 330,000 acres of land. Kentucky had sold off much of the land grant to private purchasers and had done little beyond enacting a meager tax to support the A & M College.[6] Judge Beckner noted that sectarian influences were seeking to under-

5. Delegate L.W. Lassing of Boone County passionately decried state involvement in higher education noting that the farmers in agrarian Kentucky did not "need to be philosophers to carry out their mission in life." *Official Report of the 1890 Convention* at 4506. He also advocated a "rudimental common school education" and threatened to "immediately emigrate" from Kentucky if compulsory education were ever adopted. *Id.* at 4507.

6. "In 1880 the General Assembly, realizing that the State had done practically nothing for the institution, that it had wasted its endowment in making such a hasty sale of its lands, that the people were interested in having a school directly under State control, non-sectarian in character, admitting to its halls both males and females, and encouraging the young of the humbler walks of life to seek for higher education on more practical lines than they could in the ordinary college, voted for its use an annual tax of one-half of one per cent on each $100 of value of the property in the State liable to taxation for State revenue. This produces an additional income of about $24,000 per year, and, added to the interest received on the fund arising from the sale of lands, makes a foundation for an institution worthy of Kentucky." *Official Report of the 1890 Convention* at 4473. (Remarks of Judge William H. Beckner).

mine continued support by eliminating the A & M College tax, leaving the future of higher education in the Commonwealth to those institutions founded or controlled by churches and religious groups.[7] Judge Beckner was successful in turning back those who wished to remove the Commonwealth from the business of higher education. In lengthy remarks regarding his respect for religiously-affiliated colleges (which he and his children had attended), he noted bluntly: "The location and endowment of these institutions is a matter that concerns the church." *Official Report of the 1890 Convention* at 4543. In the end, Section 184 of the Kentucky Constitution preserved both the integrity of the common school fund and the taxes[8] used to support it as well as the separate tax for the A & M College.

Thus when the delegates to the 1890 Constitutional Convention adopted Section 189 the reference to "educational purposes" included not only primary and secondary education but most assuredly postsecondary education. Indeed, the ban on appropriations to "church, sectarian and denominational schools" was most particularly directed at those then-existing colleges and universities operated by various religious organizations. In fact, all of the references by constitutional convention delegates to specific sectarian or denominational schools arose in the context of the debate over higher education, not primary and secondary schools.[9] Equally significant, the "fund[s] or tax[es]" that were not to be appropriated to religious schools were all of the monies then being raised or levied for educational purposes.

The Commonwealth's commitment to public institutions of higher learning has grown dramatically over the ensuing 120 years[10] but there are no longer specific taxes "raised or levied" for the University of Kentucky or its sister state universities. In fact, KRS 47.010 provides, with a few exceptions regarding primarily taxes directed to the state road fund, "all state revenue shall be credited to the general fund." In KRS 48.010(13)(a) for "Budget" purposes, the "General Fund" is "all moneys, not otherwise restricted, available for the general operations of state government." KRS 48.010(13)(f) defines a "Restricted Fund" as "budget unit receipts restricted as to purpose by statute." Presently, postsecondary education in Kentucky is funded primarily by the General Fund and the institutions' own receipts such as fees and tuition, i.e., Restricted Funds. In the 2008–2009 Operating Budget, for example, Postsecondary Education received a total of $5,239,769,000 consisting of some monies from Federal Funds and a special General Fund created by the Tobacco Settlement but primarily appropriations (approximately $4.5 billion) from the aforementioned General Fund and Restricted Funds. *See* Michie's *Kentucky Revised Statutes*, 2008 Cumulative Supp. at Appendix A, State/Executive Branch Budget ("2008 State/Executive Branch Budget") at p. 88.

7. *See* Judge Beckner's remarks *infra* at p. 682.

8. One of Judge Beckner's allies, Delegate H.H. Smith of Hardin County, noted at one point that by 1890 "the school tax is equal to one-half of the amount of taxes collected by the Commonwealth." *Official Report of the 1890 Convention* at 4513.

9. Centre College figured prominently in the debates but there were also references to Georgetown College, the Wesleyan College at Winchester and other religiously affiliated colleges.

10. *See generally* KRS Chapter 164.

None of these funds (or for that matter any of the approximately $3.85 billion in General Fund appropriations allocated to the Department of Education for primary and secondary education) were taxes specifically "raised or levied" for educational purposes. 2008 State/Executive Branch Budget at p. 54. Education is now a firmly entrenched part of the "general operations of state government" and public educational institutions rely on revenues from the General Fund. Notably, the debt service for bonds issued for Eastern Kentucky University, Kentucky State University, the Universities of Louisville and Kentucky, Murray State University, Western Kentucky University, and all other Kentucky public universities is provided by General Fund monies. *Id.* at pp. 84–87. Thus, Kentucky public universities rely on the same source of debt service for their bonds, i.e., the General Fund, as UC would rely on for the Pharmacy School bonds. In short, while the tax structure in late nineteenth century Kentucky may have involved taxes levied or funds specifically raised for the A & M College, twenty-first century Kentucky tax law does not draw such distinctions. Instead, all revenue raised or taxes levied by the Commonwealth may fairly be said to have been collected for state government purposes and one leading purpose is indisputably public education at the primary, secondary and postsecondary levels. Under these circumstances, Section 189 is properly read to prohibit appropriation of any public funds to religious schools.

Just as General Fund monies cannot be appropriated to pay the interest on the Pharmacy School bonds without running afoul of Section 189 of the Kentucky Constitution, the same conclusion must be reached as to the coal severance tax revenues used to repay the principal on those bonds. KRS 143.020 imposes the so-called coal severance tax on the "privilege of severing and processing coal." Pursuant to KRS 143.090, a portion of the tax revenues is designated for the road fund and a portion for the Office of Energy Policy (OEP). All receipts in excess of the amounts statutorily required for the road fund and OEP are required to be deposited "to the credit of the general fund." KRS 143.090(4). Thus, the coal severance tax surplus monies that would be used to repay the principal on the bonds for the Pharmacy School (and to create the Pharmacy Scholarship Program as discussed infra) are in fact General Fund monies or, at the very least, monies that were required to be deposited to the General Fund for state government purposes. Simply put, designating the coal severance tax as the primary source of the bond funding does not avoid the Pharmacy School appropriation's conflict with Section 189. It is all public money which cannot be constitutionally directed to UC.

In sum, the Pharmacy School appropriation clearly violates Section 189 of the Kentucky Constitution because it is an allocation of public funds for educational purposes to a "church, sectarian or denominational school." Whether the focus is on the purpose for which the funds were appropriated (pharmacy education) or the purpose for which the funds were "raised or levied" (the General Fund which supports the operations of state government including public education), the result is the same. The Pharmacy School appropriation is unconstitutional and that portion of HB 380 cannot be implemented.

B. Section 189 Does Not Offend the First Amendment of the U.S. Constitution.

Taking a different tack, Defendants also challenge any construction of Section 189 that would prohibit funding of the Pharmacy School on the grounds that such construction would violate the First Amendment of the United States Constitution. Specifically, they contend that it would violate the Free Exercise Clause of that amendment as well as the Free Speech Clause. In fact, Section 189, as construed today and over the past 120 years, does not violate the First Amendment of our nation's Constitution in any discernible way.

The First Amendment provides: "Congress shall make no law respecting an establishment of religion, or prohibiting the free exercise thereof."[11] As the United States Supreme Court noted in *Locke v. Davey*, 540 U.S. 712, 718, 124 S.Ct. 1307, 158 L.Ed.2d 1 (2004), the two clauses in that amendment, the Establishment Clause and the Free Exercise Clause, "are frequently in tension." *Locke* involved a challenge by a college student, Davey, who was not allowed to use a state-funded scholarship if he pursued a degree in devotional theology. Relevant language in Article I, section 11 of the Washington Constitution included the following: "No public money or property shall be appropriated for or applied to any religious worship, exercise or instruction, or the support of any religious establishment." In *Locke*, the U.S. Supreme Court held the Free Exercise Clause did not prohibit the State of Washington denying scholarship funds to theology degree students on state constitutional grounds. Noting the right of the states to erect a stronger wall between church and state than even that required by the U.S. Constitution, Justice Rehnquist wrote:

> Even though the differently worded Washington Constitution draws a more stringent line than that drawn by the United States Constitution, the interest it seeks to further is scarcely novel. In fact, we can think of few areas in which a State's antiestablishment interests come more into play. Since the founding of our country, there have been popular uprisings against procuring taxpayer funds to support church leaders, which was one of the hallmarks of an "established" religion.
>
> ...
>
> Most States that sought to avoid an establishment of religion around the time of the founding placed in their constitutions formal prohibitions against using tax funds to support the ministry.

540 U.S. at 722–23, 124 S.Ct. 1307 (citations and footnotes omitted). (One of the state constitutions cited was the 1792 Kentucky Constitution which contained such a provision in Art. XII, Section 3.) In upholding application of the prohibited spending language in the Washington Constitution, the Court specifically noted "Washington

11. The same restrictions have been held to apply to state legislatures by virtue of the Fourteenth Amendment to the United States Constitution. *Cantwell v. State of Connecticut*, 310 U.S. 296, 60 S.Ct. 900, 84 L.Ed. 1213 (1940).

has been solicitous in ensuring that its constitution is not hostile toward religion." *Id.* at 724, n. 8, 124 S.Ct. 1307.

Just as there are strong state "antiestablishment interests" in formal prohibitions on using tax funds to support the ministry there are strong state antiestablishment interests in prohibitions on the support of religious establishments such as the "church, sectarian or denominational schools" referenced in Section 189 of our Constitution. *Locke v. Davey* firmly supports our conclusion that the Kentucky Constitution does not contravene the Free Exercise Clause when it prohibits appropriations of public tax monies to religious schools. Moreover, it bears noting that Kentucky constitutional law, like Washington's, has not been hostile toward religion. Indeed, *Effron, supra*, reflects the Commonwealth's recognition of the constitutionality of funding religiously-affiliated hospitals where those institutions will provide needed public health services to all, regardless of their religious beliefs or lack thereof, and will not engage in any form of education. The drafters of the Kentucky Constitution drew the line, however, at funds which support religious schools, an inevitable consequence of the Pharmacy School appropriation which would add a $10 million building to UC's campus and allow it to expand its student body. As in *Locke v. Davey*, any tension between the Establishment Clause and the Free Exercise Clause in this case must be resolved in favor of the state's legitimate and fully constitutional antiestablishment concerns.

Appellants also maintain that construing Section 189 as prohibiting the Pharmacy School appropriation constitutes "viewpoint discrimination" in violation of the Free Speech Clause of the First Amendment. This same argument was roundly rejected in *Locke v. Davey*:

> Davey contends that the Promise Scholarship Program is an unconstitutional viewpoint restriction on speech. But the Promise Scholarship Program is not a forum for speech. The purpose of the Promise Scholarship Program is to assist students from low- and middle-income families with the cost of postsecondary education, not to "'encourage a diversity of views from private speakers.'" Our cases dealing with speech forums are simply inapplicable.

540 U.S. at 720 n. 3, 124 S.Ct. 1307 (citations omitted). Similarly, there is no speech forum at issue in this case where Defendants allege discrimination in the expenditure of public funds for education. More recently, in *Pleasant Grove City, Utah v. Summum*, 555 U.S. 460, 129 S.Ct. 1125, 1137, 172 L.Ed.2d 853 (2009), a case involving the erection of monuments with religious messages in a city-owned park, the court noted "[t]he forum doctrine has been applied in situations in which government-owned property or a government program was capable of accommodating a large number of *public speakers* without defeating the essential function of the land or the program" (emphasis supplied). Citing *United States v. American Library Association, Inc.*, 539 U.S. 194, 205, 123 S.Ct. 2297, 156 L.Ed.2d 221 (2003), a case holding that internet access from computers in public libraries was not a public forum, the Court in *Pleasant Grove* said succinctly "public forum principles ... are out of place in the context of this case." 129 S.Ct. at 1137. The same can be said here, *albeit* for different reasons. There is no

unconstitutional viewpoint restriction on speech simply because a state constitution prohibits appropriations of public funds to religious schools.

C. Section 189 is Not an Anti-Catholic Blaine Amendment and Does Not Violate the Equal Protection Clause or the Free Exercise Clause.

Finally, Section 189 is assailed as Kentucky's own "Blaine Amendment" borne of the rampant anti-Catholicism that affected the country in the latter-half of the 19th century. Based on this premise, Defendants and amicus curiae, The Becket Fund for Religious Liberty, contend Section 189 violates the Equal Protection Clause and Free Exercise Clause of the U.S. Constitution. We reject their premise and thus the conclusion.

As noted in *Mitchell v. Helms*, 530 U.S. 793, 828, 120 S.Ct. 2530, 147 L.Ed.2d 660 (2000), the U.S. Congress considered, and nearly passed in the 1870's, the Blaine Amendment, a proposed amendment to the United States Constitution which would have expressly banned any aid to sectarian institutions. The amendment "arose at a time of pervasive hostility to the Catholic church and to Catholics in general...." *Id.* While Kentucky, regrettably, was not immune to this virulent sentiment, as evidenced most notably by the Bloody Monday riots in Louisville on August 6, 1855,[12] there is no basis for labeling Section 189 a Blaine Amendment in light of the Official Report of the 1890 Convention. None of the allegedly telling statements cited, including a quote from Andrew Carnegie and a reference to Martin Luther's support of public schools, is supportive of this argument.[13] By contrast the only reference to the Catholic faith came from Judge Beckner, the author of Section 189, which was an amendment to the initial report rendered by the Committee on Education. Recognizing the importance of religious colleges but insisting on the Commonwealth's obligation to provide non-denominational higher education, he stated:

> The denominational colleges have done great work, and have turned out great men. That will not be denied. They are usually patronized by those who entertain the peculiar views they represent. A Presbyterian prefers to have his boy go to a Presbyterian College. The Methodist prefers to have his go to a Meth-

12. As noted in *The Kentucky Encyclopedia* published by the University Press of Kentucky, the Know-Nothing party, founded in the mid-1800s, rose to power in Kentucky on a strong anti-Irish and anti-German immigrant platform which included obvious anti-Catholic hostility. August 6, 1855 was an Election Day that resulted in the deaths of twenty-two people in Louisville, mostly Irish or German Catholic immigrants, who were the victims of a vicious mob. The city was "chastened" by the violence and although the Know-Nothing slate swept Louisville and Jefferson County that day, the party rapidly fell by the wayside. By 1857, the Know-Nothing party headquarters on Jefferson Street had been turned into a German theatre. The Civil War washed "the last vestiges of the Know-Nothing phenomenon from Louisville and Jefferson County." * * *

13. The "offending" statement from Martin Luther followed a quote wherein Luther stated that education was "not only the duty of the parents, but also of the State." Judge Beckner then said "The apostle of an open Bible was the first prophet of a State school." *Official Report of the 1890 Convention* at 4460. Shortly thereafter Becker quoted Andrew Carnegie as follows: "The public school ... is the mill into whose hopper may be poured Germans, Irishmen, Italians, Englishmen, Scandinavians, or the representatives of any other race, and yet may be relied on to turn out Americans, patriotic in purpose and intelligent in their devotion to our institutions." *Id.* at 4461.

> odist College, and the Catholic prefers to have his boy go to a Catholic College. That is a matter of preference, and the denominational colleges are founded for the benefit of those who hold to these respective views; but there is a large class who prefer not to have their boys educated at a denominational college. Then there are many of those who prefer not to have their children brought up at the particular place where the college may be located, or to subject them to the particular views maintained in other respects by those in charge of that college. They may not hold to something that the college represents, and they do not choose to send their children to it, but whether that be so or not, it is the duty of the State to furnish to its children facilities for high education.... What I have criticized was not the education received at the [sectarian] colleges, nor the fact that church people maintain these colleges ... what I do object to is, that any of these officers should come here and attempt to destroy another seat of learning in the State ... to destroy competition....

Official Report of the 1890 Convention at 4544–4545. Immediately prior, Judge Beckner had noted that he himself had attended a denominational college, had sent his children to such schools and had supported the religious colleges of his own Presbyterian denomination and other denominations but, again, as he bluntly put it, "The location and endowment of these institutions is a matter that concerns the church." Having reviewed the 1890 Constitutional Debates, we conclude that Section 189 was clearly borne of the framers desire to avoid state support of *all* religious institutions' schools not of any animosity toward Catholics or any other specific religion.

In summary, the UC Pharmacy School appropriation violates Section 189 of the Kentucky Constitution. If Kentucky needs to expand the opportunities for pharmacy school education within the Commonwealth, the Kentucky General Assembly may most certainly address that pressing public need but not by appropriating public funds to an educational institution that is religiously affiliated.

* * *

Conclusion

The Pharmacy School appropriation violates Section 189 of the Kentucky Constitution and the Pharmacy Scholarship Program violates Section 59. On those grounds, we affirm the trial court's judgment in favor of Plaintiffs.

Minton, C.J.; Cunningham, Noble, and Schroder, JJ., concur.

Cunningham, J., concurs by separate opinion in which Scott, J., joins.

Scott, J., concurs in part and dissents in part by separate opinion in which Venters, J., joins.

Justice Cunningham, concurring.

I write to concur with the excellent work of Justice Abramson, mindful that my writing can neither add to nor improve upon her well-written opinion.

Our majority opinion today deals primarily with the spending provision of Section 189 of our state constitution. But that provision is seeded in a religious context. That is why the trial court also based its findings on the guarantee of religious freedom in Section 5 of the Kentucky Constitution. The overarching principle guiding our enforcement of these constitutional directives is that of separation of church and state.

Therefore, I deem it needful for me to write in an attempt to dispel any abiding notion that courts, such as this one, in marking clearly the divide between church and state, are taking a legalistic swipe at religion.

Nothing could be further from the truth. Decisions like that endorsed by our majority here today have paved the way for religion to grow and prosper in this land of the free.

* * *

This wholesome and blessed balance between church and state can only be maintained through our courts. These grand constitutional commandments speak not only to the genius and wisdom of our forefathers, but also to their astounding reverence for the soul.

Our humble decision here today is one small ripple enveloped in the marching billows of the ages.

Scott, J., joins.

JUSTICE SCOTT, CONCURRING IN PART AND DISSENTING IN PART.

Although I concur with the majority opinion and join Justice Cunningham's concurring opinion as to why, historically, an appropriation to one particular college affiliated with one particular denomination—among the many in America—violates Section 189 of the Kentucky Constitution, I must respectfully dissent from the majority's opinion that the Pharmacy Scholarship Program is special legislation and therefore in contravention of Section 59 of the Kentucky Constitution. * * *

Venters, J., joins.

Notes and Questions

1. In 2015, the Montana legislature enacted a scholarship program for students attending private schools. The legislation gave a tax credit to any taxpayer who donated to a participating "student scholarship organization," which then would use the donations to award scholarships to children for tuition at private schools. Shortly after the legislation was enacted, the Montana Department of Revenue promulgated an administrative regulation that prohibited families from using the scholarships at religious schools. The Department explained that the regulation was required to comply with the "no-aid" provision of Montana's constitution, which provides: "The legislature, counties, cities, towns, school districts, and public corporations shall not make any direct or indirect appropriation or payment from any public fund or monies, or any grant of lands or other property *for any sectarian purpose or to aid any* church, *school*, academy, seminary, *college*, *university*, or other literary or scientific institution, *controlled in whole or in part by any church, sect, or denomination*." Mont. Const. art. X, §6(1) (emphasis added). The Montana Supreme Court upheld the regulation,

finding that the scholarship program violated the Montana Constitution's "no-aid" provision by using tax credits to subsidize tuition payments at private schools that are religiously affiliated or controlled in whole or in part by churches. *See Espinoza v. Montana Dep't of Revenue*, 435 P.3d 603, 612–13 (Mont. 2018).

The U.S. Supreme Court reversed. It held, under *Trinity Lutheran Church of Columbia, Inc. v. Comer*, 582 U.S. ___, 137 S.Ct. 2012 (2017), that strict scrutiny applied to a state constitutional provision that disqualifies otherwise eligible recipients from a public benefit "solely because of their religious character." *Espinoza v. Montana Dep't of Revenue*, 591 U.S. ___, 140 S.Ct. 2246, 2257 (2020). The Court distinguished *Locke v. Davey*, 540 U.S. 712 (2004), which the Supreme Court of Kentucky relied on in *Pennybacker*, as a case that upheld a state's prohibition on using public funds for "the 'essentially religious endeavor' of training a minister to lead a congregation." *Espinoza*, 140 S.Ct. at 2257 (quoting *Locke*, 540 U.S. at 721). Rather than prohibiting the use of public funds based upon a particular field of study (*i.e.*, theology), the Montana Constitution prohibited a public benefit based upon the religious identity of the recipient (*i.e.*, a school controlled by any "church, sect, or denomination"). The Court found that Montana's "no-aid" provision penalizes the decision of parents sending their children to religious schools "by cutting families off from otherwise available benefits if they choose a religious private school rather than a secular one, and for no other reason." *Id.* at 2261. It held that "[a] State need not subsidize private education. But once a State decides to do so, it cannot disqualify some private schools solely because they are religious." *Id.*

More recently, the U.S. Supreme Court reaffirmed the principles it had announced in *Trinity Lutheran* and *Espinoza* in *Carson v. Makin*, 596 U.S. ___, 142 S.Ct. 1987 (2022).

2. Does Section 189 of the Kentucky Constitution differ in any meaningful respect from the Montana constitutional provision at issue in *Espinoza*? Does the Supreme Court of Kentucky's holding in *Pennybacker* survive *Espinoza*?
3. In *Trinity Lutheran*, the U.S. Supreme Court held that "denying a generally available benefit solely on account of religious identity imposes a penalty on the free exercise of religion that can be justified," if at all, "only by a state interest of the highest order." 137 S.Ct. at 2019 (internal quotation omitted). Was the pharmacy school appropriation at issue in *Pennybacker* a "generally available benefit"?

Table of Cases

References are to pages. Cases reproduced in this text are in SMALL CAPS, while cases merely mentioned in the essays and notes are in Roman type.

Index

R

S

T